RULES

DISCARDED

1. — **Permanent Residents.** The library books are free to all permanent residents of Bar Harbor.
2. — **Non-residents and summer visitors.** $20.00 deposit, refundable; 3 books may be borrowed at one time.
3. — Books may be kept two weeks and, with the exception of new books, may be renewed twice for the same period.
4. — Ten cents a day is charged for each book kept overtime.
5. — Each borrower is held responsible for all books drawn on his card.
6. — All losses or injury to books shall be paid for.
7. — Mailing service is not available except under inter-library loan.

Monty

BY THE SAME AUTHOR

Royal Greenwich (*with Olive Hamilton*)
The Brothers Mann
Monty: The Making of a General 1887–1942
Monty: Master of the Battlefield 1942–1944

MONTY
Final Years of the Field-Marshal, 1944–1976

NIGEL HAMILTON

McGRAW-HILL BOOK COMPANY

New York St. Louis San Francisco
Hamburg Mexico

First published in Great Britain in 1986 by Hamish Hamilton Ltd.,
Garden House, 57-59 Long Acre, London WC2E 9Jz
First U.S. publication in 1986 by the McGraw-Hill Book Company.

1 2 3 4 5 6 7 8 9 D O C D O C 8 7 6

ISBN 0-07-025807-4

LIBRARY OF CONGRESS CATALOGING-IN-PUBLICATION DATA

Hamilton, Nigel.
Monty—field marshal.
1. Montgomery of Alamein, Bernard Law Montgomery, Viscount, 1887–1976. 2. Generals—Great Britain—Biography. 3. Great Britain. Army—Biography.
I. Title.
DA69.3.M56H345 1987 941.082′092′4 [B] 86-10369
ISBN 0-07-025807-4

Contents

List of Illustrations

Between pages 36 and 37

Between pages 164 and 165

Between pages 420 and 421

Between pages 548 and 549

Between pages 676 and 677

Between pages 804 and 805

Between pages 932 and 933

List of Maps

Author's Note

To hosts of petty truths man much prefers
A single edifying lie

wrote Pushkin. It saddens me that Monty's supremely eventful life is sometimes reduced to a superficial caricature. For Monty's sheer professionalism surely repays investigation; and in the story of the untalented, unwanted child who nevertheless willed himself to greatness there is to be found a case history of enormous biographical as well as historical interest.

How Monty applied the lessons of a lifetime to the field of battle was the subject of the second volume of this study.[1] His response to the pressures of greatness is the underlying theme of this, the final volume. Against the backcloth of great events—the battles of Arnhem and the Ardennes, the crossing of the Rhine, the Allied failure to take Berlin, the German surrender at Lüneburg, the governing of occupied Germany, command of the British Army, the creation of Western European defence at Western Union and then NATO—we can see clearly Monty's strengths; and his failings.

A previous biographer has excoriated Montgomery as an affront to the 'courtesy, modesty and commitment to civilised values' bred by the British Army. Monty himself was quite clear that he would be denigrated after his death—'the rats will get at me', he would say—and certainly he never claimed that he was a ' "nice" chap'.

Monty's inconsiderateness could, it must be admitted, be breathtaking, as was his monumental ego. It was, however, the ego of a victorious soldier, and largely forgiven by those who admired his battlefield prowess. Even Eisenhower acknowledged privately that, without Monty, the D-Day landings would not have been successful, and extolled Monty's generalship in the field—until, with the publication of Monty's *Memoirs*, Eisenhower's patience snapped and he declared of Monty: 'He's just a little man, he's just as little inside as he is outside'.[2]

The quality of meanness and inconsiderateness—so spectacularly shown by Monty's failure to attend his own mother's funeral—ran

[1] *Monty: Master of the Battlefield 1942–1944*, London 1983.
[2] P. Lyon, *Eisenhower: Portrait of the Hero*, Boston 1974.

however in the strangest tandem with his curiosity and concern for others younger than himself, concern which never dimmed. His platonic love of children was extraordinary in one so exalted, but it was patently sincere and unaffected. I suppose that, widowed and having pulled down the curtains on his inner life, he could only feel totally free of his great 'burdens of state' in the companionship of those younger than himself, children whose innocence delighted him, who were impressionable and upon whom he could exercise his didactic skill and profound Christian urge to help. His affection, once bestowed, was for life; but it never blinded him. When one of his protégés, John Ackroyd, son of the Lord Mayor of London, reminded Monty of his promise to make him an ADC in France for the final six months of his military service before going up to Oxford, Monty wrote *instanter*:

> My dear John
>
> . . . You must finish your military service in the Middle East, which is one of the storm centres of today. I am not convinced that if you moved further West it would have any effect on your studies for Oxford!! My advice would be to get down to work in your spare time *in the Canal Zone* about which I can see no difficulty. In fact I can see no difficulty about any work anywhere.
>
> It is entirely a matter as to whether the spirit is willing or whether the flesh is weak.
>
> So you must 'do your stuff' in these troublesome days, and finish your National Service in the places where the Nation sends you.

Ackroyd remained in the Canal Zone. Nevertheless, after Oxford, Monty attended Ackroyd's wedding, kept up the friendship and in later years welcomed Ackroyd's children to his mill at Isington.

Even in his eighty-sixth year he could, with a chuckle, recite the precise address of my own digs in Cambridge to which he had so often written when I was a student in the 1960s—and laugh despairingly at the mixed-up youth he had sought to guide. 'I forgot to say that Nigel began by trying to sell me a ping-pong table! He finished by smashing my car on the way to the station! That boy will do well,' he once wrote to my parents. His last words written to me were: 'I am here to help you and to comfort you if you need comfort. My love to you. Ever your friend, Montgomery of Alamein.'

I can see him now, his eyes piercing and kind at once; I can feel his hand on my own as we negotiated steps; I can hear his voice, clipped and warm. Of his generalship I am not qualified to form an opinion; as a man I felt for him admiration and a great affection. I am glad I knew him; he added a glowing strand to my life, and anyone attacking him in my presence is in for an unpleasant surprise. May the earth lie lightly on a soldier's bones.

Thus wrote Bernard Levin in 1976, the year of Monty's death.[1] If these three volumes have dwelled at inordinate length on the life of one man, I can only assert that no work, however long, can ever really unravel the enigma that was Monty—nor do justice to the magnitude of Monty's achievement, and the debt owed to him by the free world—warts and all.

In writing this final volume I have, as with its predecessors, been blessed by the loving help of my father, Sir Denis Hamilton. Without his unflagging assistance—despite often debilitating illness—I could not have completed the task. I only hope that it has fulfilled, in small measure, the hopes he invested in me almost ten years ago.

Similarly, I am deeply grateful to Monty's son David, Viscount Montgomery of Alamein, who has supported me from the start with remarkable good will and objectivity, never seeking to influence or alter my judgment of his father.

To Monty's sister Winsome, Lady Michelmore, to Monty's brother, Lt-Colonel Brian Montgomery, to Monty's stepsons, Lt-Colonel John and Colonel Richard Carver, and their wives Jocelyn and Audrey, I extend also my grateful thanks.

To General Sir Charles Richardson and Brigadier Sir Edgar Williams, who have read each section and commented upon it 'in the making', I must record not only the indebtedness of an amateur military historian, but admiration and affection too, for their guiding spirits of truthfulness and balance have given me courage in many an hour.

To the following people who have helped with interviews, correspondence or the loan of documents I wish also to record my gratitude: Sir John Ackroyd, Professor Stephen Ambrose, Lord Annan, Professor Henri Bernard, Brigadier R. H. S. ('Ginger') Bidwell, Lt-Colonel Tom Bigland, Air Chief Marshal Sir Harry Broadhurst, Ian Calvocoressi, Field-Marshal Lord Carver, Warwick Charlton, Mrs Henriette Claessens-Heuten, General J. L. Collins, Sir John Colville, Major Terry Coverdale, I. R. Crossthwaite, The duchesse de Dangu, Lt-Colonel C. P. ('Kit') Dawnay, Mrs Frances Denby, Lt-Colonel Carlo D'Este, Professor David Dilks, Colonel Peter Earle, General Sir David Fraser, General James L. Gavin,

[1] *The Times*, 31.3.76.

Frank Gillard, General Sir John Hackett, Field-Marshal Lord Harding, J. R. ('Johnny') Henderson, Lord Hunter of Newington, Major-General J. D. Lunt, Brigadier Charles Mackenzie, Carol Mather, Drew Middleton, Sir Richard O'Brien, Paul Odgers, General Sir Nigel Poett, Lord Porritt, Robert Priestley, the late Tom Reynolds, Major-General G. P. B. Roberts, Lt-Colonel L. G. S. Sanderson, General Sir Frank Simpson, Major-General Eric Sixsmith, Lady Soames, M. Brook Taylor, General Maxwell Taylor, Lady Templer, Sir Peter Tennant, Dr Lucien Trueb, Major-General R. E. Urquhart, General Sir Dudley Ward, Brigadier A. D. R. G. Wilson, Mark Wathen and Philip Ziegler.

To the staffs of the following institutions I owe my gratitude: Dr Alan Borg, Director, Mr Robert Crawford, Deputy Director, Mr Roderick Suddaby, Keeper of Documents, Jane Carmichael, Keeper of Photographs; Rose Gerrard, Jim Lucas and the unfailingly helpful staff of the Imperial War Museum, London; Marshal of the RAF Lord Cameron, Principal of King's College, Miss Patricia Methven, Archivist and the staff of the Liddell Hart Centre for Military Archives, London; the staff of the Public Record Office, Kew; Dr J. Wickman and the staff of the Eisenhower Library; John Slonaker, Dr R. Sommers and the staff of the Military History Institute, Carlisle, Pennsylvania; Anne Sutton, Archivist of The Mercers' Company, Mercers' Hall, London; Mr R. Reid and the staff of the National Army Museum, Chelsea; Miss J. Langton, Registrar, and the staff of The Royal Archives, Windsor; the RAF Museum, Hendon; Churchill College Archives. I am also indebted for assistance over photographs to David Chipp, Editor-in-Chief, and Paddy (F. S.) Hicks, Picture Editor, Press Association; Michael Cranmer, Picture Editor, *Sunday Times*; W. R. Blackmore, Managing Director, Paul Popper Ltd. Also to Joan Thomas, PA to the Editor of the *Sunday Times*, who provided copies of all Monty's articles in the *Sunday Times*, and to Christopher Glass, son of the photographer Douglas Glass. I am also grateful to Her Majesty the Queen for gracious permission to quote copyright material.

To the team at Hamish Hamilton in London and McGraw-Hill in New York I owe the very existence of this book and its predecessors: in particular to Christopher Sinclair-Stevenson, Leslie Meredith and Gladys Carr. Bruce Hunter and Claire Smith have faithfully acted on my behalf as my literary agents; Miss Winifred Marshall has been my loyal and accurate typist since the inception of this trilogy, and she and my father's secretary, Joan Crockford, have given unstinting help which has been a godsend. Once again Robin Dodd has been responsible for the maps and picture layouts, and Ken White for the index. To them all, my gratitude for contributions which are as important to an undertaking of this kind as the text itself.

Finally, after ten years of marriage, there remains my wife Outi to thank. As a result of her understanding and unfailing support, with four children to look after, I have enjoyed every hour of this extended, investigatory tribute to a revered and, let me confess it, deeply loved friend and shepherd.

NIGEL HAMILTON
London 1985

PART ONE

Gateway to Germany

CHAPTER ONE

A Chance to End the War Quickly

COULD THE WAR against Nazi Germany have been ended in 1944?

Though General Eisenhower, the Supreme Allied Commander, sought later to veil the issue in chronicling Allied post-Normandy strategy, Monty was quite certain that the war could and should have been won after the Normandy break-out. Even Eisenhower's own planners assumed in August 1944 that the end of Germany was imminent; indeed the Allied Control Commission 'was called upon to make itself ready to operate in Berlin by 1st November [1944]', the British Official Historian later chronicled.[1] Churchill was equally confident, as his Private Secretary noted in his diary: 'Our Armies are racing to the Belgian frontier, faster by far than went the Panzers in 1940. There is a feeling of elation, of expectancy and almost bewilderment, and it may well be that the end is now very close.'[2]

Equally, most senior German generals in the West assumed that the war was lost in August 1944. 'All the [German] generals to whom I talked were of the opinion that the Allied Supreme Command had missed a great opportunity of ending the war in the autumn of 1944,' wrote the military historian Basil Liddell Hart after the war. 'They agreed with Montgomery's view that this could best have been achieved by concentrating all possible resources in a thrust in the north, towards Berlin.'[3]

The Chief of Staff to the then German C-in-C West, Field-Marshal von Rundstedt, later considered

> the best course of the Allies would have been to concentrate a really strong striking force with which to break through past Aachen to the Ruhr area. Strategically and politically, Berlin was the target. Germany's strength is in the north. He who holds northern Germany holds Germany. Such a break-through, coupled with

[1] F. S. V. Donnison, *Civil Affairs and Military Government North-West Europe 1944–1946*, London 1961.

[2] Entry of 1.9.44, J. Colville, *The Fringes of Power*, London 1985.

[3] B. H. Liddell Hart, *The Other Side of the Hill*, first published London 1948, revised edition 1951.

> air domination, would have torn in pieces the weak German front and ended the war. Berlin and Prague would have been occupied ahead of the Russians. There were no German forces behind the Rhine, and at the end of August our front was wide open.[1]

Monty had argued, as has been seen,[2] for such a concentration of Allied strength ever since 17 August 1944 while the battle of Falaise still raged. 'After crossing SEINE, 12 and 21 Army Groups should keep together as a solid mass of some 40 Divisions which would be so strong it need fear nothing,' he had urged.[3] The CIGS, Field-Marshal Sir Alan Brooke, had agreed. Even Patton had briefly suggested an 'end-run' with his Third US Army around the German forces on the lower Seine on 23 August, keeping the four Allied armies together.[4] But General Eisenhower was determined to take field command by the end of August, as well as retaining the title of Supreme Allied Commander—and had not the heart to close down the promising American thrust towards Metz and the Saar. Day after day in the final fortnight of August 1944, Monty attempted to persuade Eisenhower to concentrate upon an all-out Allied drive to the Ruhr: but each day's delay encouraged the American field commanders to exploit eastwards. 'I couldn't get him to budge,' de Guingand recorded of Eisenhower's intransigent belief in driving eastwards rather than northwards;[5] and Monty fared little better. 'I do not see what there is to oppose us,' Monty wrote on 21 August concerning an Allied invasion of the Ruhr by way of Aachen and Cologne. 'Provided I can persuade the Americans to put everything into this movement, then it would end the war—and quickly. But many political cross-currents are now likely to arise; and if these are allowed to influence what we

[1] General Blumentritt, in *The Other Side of the Hill*, op. cit. Blumentritt reiterated his view on publication of Monty's *Memoirs* in 1958, as did General Kurt von Manteuffel, who commanded the Fifth Panzer Army in the Battle of the Bulge: 'I am in full agreement with Montgomery. I believe General Eisenhower's insistence on spreading the Allied forces out for a broader advance was wrong. The acceptance of Montgomery's plan would have shortened the war considerably. Above all, tens of thousands of lives—on both sides—would have been saved': *Daily Mail*, 16.10.58. Even Bradley's 12th US Army Group staff came to believe Eisenhower made a fatal mistake by dividing his forces in August 1944—Bradley's Deputy Chief of Deception considering that 'if Eisenhower had not been so "wishy washy" and had backed either Montgomery *or* Bradley in the fall of 1944, the war would have been over by Christmas. Instead he [Eisenhower] hesitated, then backed Montgomery when it was too late': R. Hoopes, *Ralph Ingersoll: A Biography*, New York 1985.

[2] 'A Fateful Week', 'A Lost Cause' and 'Triumph and Tragedy', chapters 15–17, Part Six of author's *Monty: Master of the Battlefield, 1942–1944*, London 1983.

[3] Ibid.

[4] Ibid.

[5] Ibid.

do, then the quick end of the German war may be endangered.'[1]

It was. With Churchill in southern France, the CIGS, Field-Marshal Brooke, in Italy, the Secretary of State for War, P. J. Grigg, away and the Director of Military Operations at the War Office on leave, Monty was left to argue the case for strategic concentration alone. Meeting Eisenhower on 23 August Monty had asked for a minimum of twelve American divisions to participate in the Ruhr thrust. Eisenhower, stunned, pointed out that 'if this were done then 12 [US] Army Group would have only one Army in it [on the Metz front], and public opinion in the States would object.'[2] Monty offered to serve *under* Bradley—but to no avail. Eisenhower was adamant that 'he must now separate the two Army Groups, take command himself of the ground forces and send the two Army Groups in such different directions that there could be no question of the American Army Group being under the operational control of a British General. This is really the guts of the matter,' Monty wrote in disgust to Brooke's deputy, General Nye on 26 August.[3]

Monty was not exaggerating. 'I get along with Monty fine enough,' Bradley had stated at his headquarters the day before. 'But we've got to make it clear to the American public that we are no longer under control of Monty's.'[4]

The great Allied triumph thus turned to tragedy. Within days, as he watched Eisenhower's disastrous separation of thrusts, Hitler began to plan a German counter-offensive that would slice open the British and American Army Groups once they had run out of steam. Brooke, returning from Italy on 28 August, noted with resignation in his diary: 'Eisenhower's plan is likely to add another three to six months to the war. Eisenhower straight away wants to split his force, sending an American contingent towards Nancy, whilst the British Army Group moves along the coast.'[5]

Nevertheless Monty's protests had at least caused Eisenhower to review his strategy. To the chagrin of the American field commanders, Eisenhower had in fact directed Bradley on 24 August to send enough temporary forces into Belgium to enable Monty to carry out his coastal mission before resuming the American 'advance eastward from the Paris area'.[6] 'I cannot tell you how anxious I am to get the forces accumulated for starting the thrust eastward from

[1] Ibid.
[2] Ibid.
[3] Ibid.
[4] Ibid.
[5] Ibid.
[6] Letter to Monty, 24.8.44, in *The Papers of Dwight David Eisenhower*, ed. Alfred D. Chandler, *The War Years* Vol. III, Baltimore 1970.

Paris,' he excused himself in a signal to his American 'boss', General Marshall in Washington[1]—knowing the mounting American excitement at reports of Patton's army streaking eastwards across France after the months of constriction in Normandy.

By 29 August when he had to fly back to England to meet Churchill, however, Eisenhower had yet again altered his plans. The signs 'are not wanting that he [the enemy] is nearing collapse,' Eisenhower considered. Following the Allied landings in the south of France, the Seventh US Army was 'rapidly advancing on Dijon from the South'.[2] Instead of only temporarily assisting Montgomery in the north, Bradley was now directed to split his Army Group of the Centre into two. Hodges' First US Army would support Monty's 21st Army Group thrust to the north, while all incoming American divisions and units would continue to be sent east of Paris to help Patton's 3rd US Army in its drive towards the Saar—a drive that would in time be reinforced by Seventh US Army from Dijon. 'The August battles have done it and the enemy in the West has had it. Two and a half months of bitter fighting have brought the end of the war in Europe within sight, almost within reach,' Eisenhower's Intelligence staff had already announced.[3] In an interview with over a hundred Allied war correspondents in London on 31 August, Eisenhower frankly admitted that he had split the Allied advance: 'General Montgomery's forces were expected to beat the Germans on the north; General Bradley's to defeat them in the centre, and the Mediterranean forces, under General Devers, to press from the south.'[4]

At this Press conference Eisenhower loyally defended Montgomery from the ignorant jibes of those commentators who saw the slowness of the British forces at Caen in marked contrast to American mobility under Patton. 'The Germans had thrown in every Panzer division available to hold that region,' Eisenhower explained. 'Every piece of dust on the Caen front was more than a diamond to them.' By holding the German armour at Caen, the Americans had been permitted to 'break through westward from Saint-Lô and start the

[1] Letter of 24.8.44. Ibid.

[2] Message to Commanders, 29.8.44. Ibid.

[3] SHAEF GI Intelligence Summary, 23.8.44, quoted in Stephen Ambrose, *Eisenhower 1890–1952*, New York 1983.

[4] H. C. Butcher, *Three Years with Eisenhower*, New York 1948. As Eisenhower explained a few weeks later to General Marshall, his plan was to 'hustle all our forces up against the Rhine, including Devers' forces, build up our maintenance facilities and our reserves as rapidly as possible and then put on one sustained and unremitting advance against the heart of the enemy country': letter of 14.9.44 in *The Papers of Dwight David Eisenhower*, op. cit.

end run which eventually dislodged the Germans west of the Seine'. As his naval ADC and PR executive noted in his diary, Eisenhower 'praised Monty and said that anyone who misinterpreted the transition of command as a demotion for General Montgomery simply did not look facts in the face. He said Montgomery is one of the great soldiers of this or any other war and he would now have the job of handling the battles on his side of the front. It would be most unfortunate if this plan of campagn, which had developed as it was conceived from the start, should be interpreted as a demotion or a slap at anybody. . . . He made clear that when the initial beachhead was established, it was very restricted, and since there was only one tactical battle to be conducted, he had put General Montgomery in tactical control of the American land force. Montgomery's control was to exist until we could break out of the base of the Cherbourg Peninsula. The time had come when they *had* broken out, and General Bradley was taking over part of the job and reporting directly to SHAEF [Supreme Headquarters Allied Expeditionary Force]. Ike described Monty as a "great and personal friend" and emphasized that he had a great admiration for him.'[1]

Eisenhower's Press conference was admirably conceived and conducted. It certainly did much to dispel inter-Allied rivalry. 'As signs of victory appear in the air,' Eisenhower wrote sadly to Marshall after the conference, 'I note little instances that seem to indicate that the Allies cannot hang so effectively in prosperity as they can in adversity.'[2]

At a military level, however, Eisenhower's performance was nothing less than disastrous in Monty's eyes. By separating the Allied thrusts, Eisenhower was committing the cardinal military sin. Since mid-August Eisenhower had seen Monty only twice. 'His ignorance as to how to run a war is absolute and complete; he has all the popular cries, but nothing else,' Monty had written after Eisenhower's visit on 13 August.[3] Thereafter, despite all Monty's pleas, Eisenhower had refused to keep the Allied Armies together. As the spearheads of the northern thrust now raced across the Somme towards the Belgian border, and Patton's Third US Army crossed the Meuse around Verdun only thirty miles from Metz, Eisenhower remained convinced he had chosen the right course, Monty that he was frittering away the spoils of Normandy.

[1] Ibid.
[2] *The Papers of Dwight David Eisenhower*, op. cit.
[3] *Monty: Master of the Battlefield, 1942–1944*, op. cit.

CHAPTER TWO

Field-Marshal Montgomery

ON 1 SEPTEMBER 1944 Tac Headquarters 21st Army Group, having crossed the Seine, established itself in the grounds of the Château de Dangu. As the duchesse de Dangu later recalled:

> One early morning an army vehicle appeared in the courtyard with a few red cap officers aboard. My husband the Duc de Dangu was told that a general was planning to establish a headquarters in the Park. . . .
>
> A couple of days later after many wires had been laid in the midst of a vast armada [of vehicles] a caravan was parked at the foot of the castle.
>
> My eldest son in the morning noticed a private with khaki sweater and black beret walking in one of the alleys; later a cousin of ours came across the same private. After discussion they agreed this could only be Montgomery.[1]

The figure *was* Montgomery; and in the same grey sweater, corduroy trousers and black beret Monty now sat for the portrait which James Gunn had been painting each day for the past fortnight, despite the five moves. Gunn's canvas depicted Monty seated on a simple mahogany armchair, beneath the camouflaged awning of one of his famous caravans—much as a medieval English King might have sat after Crécy or Agincourt.

Congratulations had begun to pour in—for on 1 September it was announced that General Montgomery had been promoted to the rank of Field-Marshal 'in circumstances that are certainly unique in the history of such things', as the King's Private Secretary wrote. 'There could be no more appropriate recognition of what you and 21 Army Group have done for the world.' 'Congratulations on this latest acknowledgment of the magnificent fighting service you have rendered the Allied cause,' General Marshall, Chairman of the Combined Chiefs of Staff in Washington, cabled to Monty.[2] 'Done on the Field of Battle at the moment of your greatest triumph

[1] Letter to the author, 1981.

[2] FWD 14549, teleprinted via Eisenhower, Montgomery Papers.

enhances its value a hundred-fold,' wrote Sir John Dill, British Military Representative to the Combined Chiefs of Staff.[1] King George VI had already congratulated Monty on the magnitude of the Allied victory: 'Ever since you explained to me your masterly plan for your part in the campaign in western France, I have followed with admiration its day to day development. I congratulate you most heartily on its overwhelming success.' Perhaps the most moving message had been that sent by General O'Connor:

> I feel I must write and congratulate you on what seems likely to be one of the most decisive battles in the world's history,

O'Connor wrote.

> It has in every way justified your strategy and tactics, which I well remember you expounding long before we left England. How we were to bear the brunt of the battle for the first few weeks by constantly attacking the enemy, never giving him any rest, and never letting him have the chance of regaining the initiative. All this to take the pressure off the Americans so that they might achieve, what in fact they did achieve, and are achieving.
>
> But apart from that side of it, your own courage and confidence has done such a tremendous lot to keep up the morale of the officers and men serving under you. It has been worth many Army Corps.
>
> I have never before served under anyone whose judgment I trusted in everything. It is a very pleasant change.[2]

From the commander of 8 Corps, which had done so much in its 'Goodwood' operation to help ensure the retention of German armour on the eastern flank so that the eventual American break-out might prosper in the west, this was indeed a tribute.

With the true extent of Monty's victory becoming apparent, moreover, the world's Press now joined in the jubilation. The *News Chronicle* prefaced its front-page headline on 1 September 1944: 'Eisenhower gives the facts of victory: 400,000 German casualties, including 47 divisions destroyed, mauled or trapped; in material the enemy has lost 1,300 tanks, 2,000 guns, and 3,500 planes.'

These, however, were statistics. It was the headline itself which, after three months of battle since D-Day, affixed the seal to Allied victory in France:

[1] Letter of 1.9.44 (misfiled in 'Letters 1945–6' file), Montgomery Papers.
[2] Letter of 24.8.44 (misfiled in 'Germany: 1945 onwards' file), Montgomery Papers.

> *ALLIES CROSS THE MEUSE AND SOMME*
> The British are over the Somme; the Americans are over the Meuse and driving on Sedan and Charleville.
>
> The German front, it was stated in despatches from the war fronts last night, is completely broken and the battle of France is rapidly drawing to a close.
>
> Robert Reuben, Reuter's special correspondent with the First American Army, cabling last night, said: The German front has completely broken, and the battle has turned into a rout. The Germans are fleeing so fast that it is becoming most difficult for the American forces to maintain contact. 'It has turned into a pursuit instead of a battle,' said a military official. . . .

Recording that General O'Connor's armoured troops had driven '60 miles in 48 hours to seize Amiens',

> it was clear that the British left flank was advancing as fast or faster than Patton. Amiens is ours. Last night we had three bridges over the Somme.
>
> It now seems impossible for the enemy to hold on to a line anywhere, and it looks as though it may not be long before the Channel coast with the flying bomb sites will fall to us.[1]

In the adjacent column, carrying a photograph of Monty in beret, battle-dress and flying jacket, there ran the simple headline: 'FIELD-MARSHAL MONTGOMERY.'[2]

The duc de Dangu, anxious lest his own sympathies as a Frenchman be considered suspect—his château had been occupied by the German Luftwaffe since 1940—attempted to assemble as many members of the local *résistance* as possible for inspection. But Monty, sitting for his portrait, refused to see them. His gnarled hands were clenched. His steel-blue eyes stared; and to his Military Assistant he dictated a letter addressed to his Chief of Staff—not the letter of a newly promoted field-marshal, but tart and vexed: for it was on 1 September 1944 that the Supreme Commander, General Eisenhower, had insisted on taking from him the mantle of C-in-C Allied Ground Forces: a day that would mark, in Monty's later estimation, the end of the Allies' dearly won victory in the West.

[1] British Newspaper Library, Colindale.
[2] Ibid.

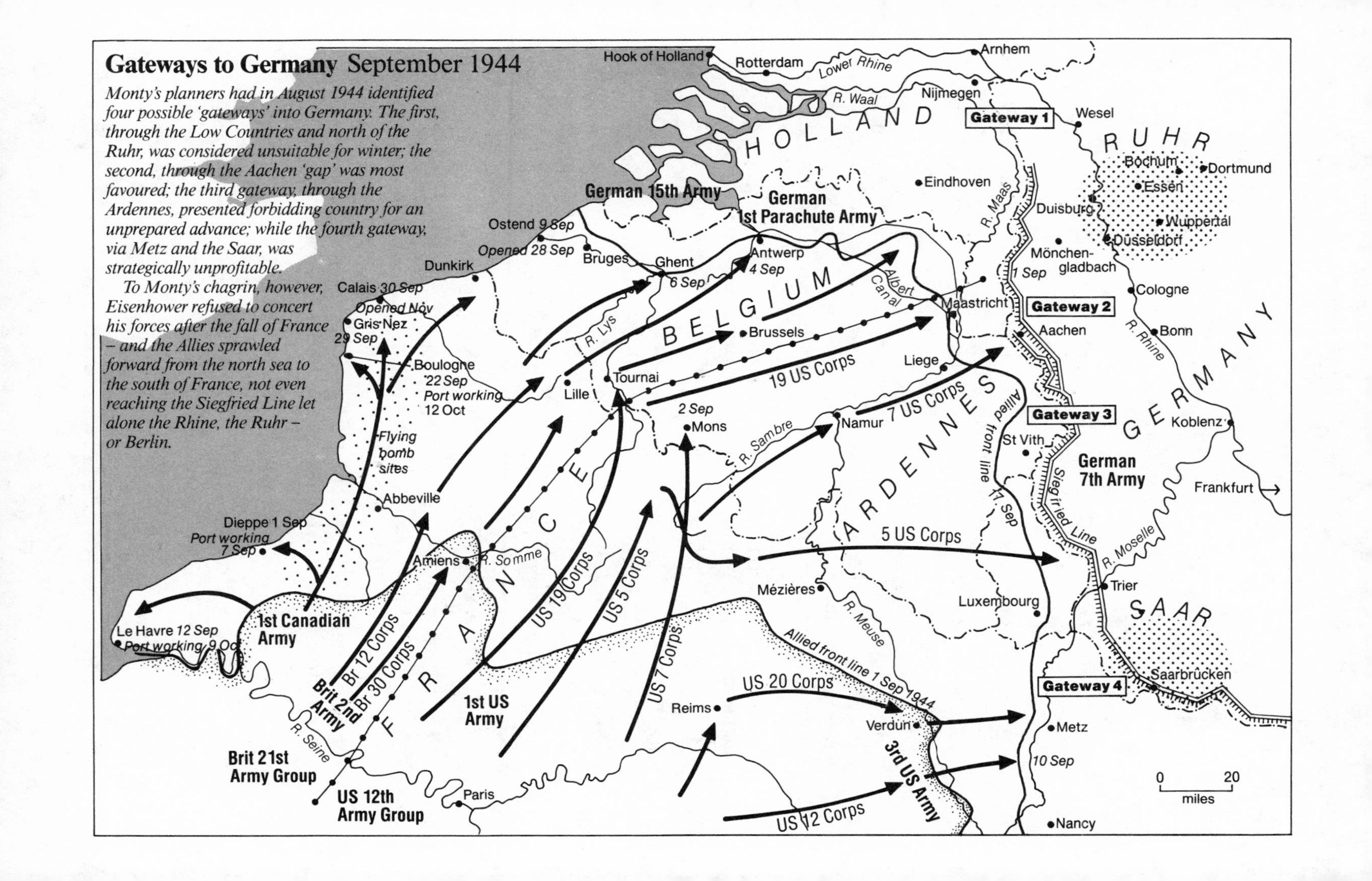

Gateways to Germany September 1944
Monty's planners had in August 1944 identified four possible 'gateways' into Germany. The first, through the Low Countries and north of the Ruhr, was considered unsuitable for winter; the second, through the Aachen 'gap' was most favoured; the third gateway, through the Ardennes, presented forbidding country for an unprepared advance; while the fourth gateway, via Metz and the Saar, was strategically unprofitable.
To Monty's chagrin, however, Eisenhower refused to concert his forces after the fall of France – and the Allies sprawled forward from the north sea to the south of France, not even reaching the Siegfried Line let alone the Rhine, the Ruhr – or Berlin.
Hook of Holland
Rotterdam
Lower Rhine
Arnhem
R. Waal
Nijmegen
HOLLAND
Gateway 1
Wesel
RUHR
Bochum
Dortmund
Essen
Wuppertal
Duisburg
Düsseldorf
Eindhoven
R. Maas
Mönchen-gladbach
1 Sep
Cologne
Gateway 2
Aachen
Bonn
R. Rhine
GERMANY
German 15th Army
German 1st Parachute Army
Ostend 9 Sep
Opened 28 Sep
Bruges
Ghent
6 Sep
Antwerp
4 Sep
Albert Canal
Maastricht
BELGIUM
Brussels
Dunkirk
Calais 30 Sep
Opened Nov
Gris Nez
29 Sep
Boulogne
22 Sep
Port working
12 Oct
R. Lys
Lille
Tournai
19 US Corps
Liege
2 Sep
Mons
Namur
7 US Corps
R. Sambre
ARDENNES
Allied front line 17 Sep
Gateway 3
St Vith
German 7th Army
Koblenz
Frankfurt
Siegfried Line
R. Moselle
Flying bomb sites
Abbeville
Dieppe 1 Sep
Port working
7 Sep
Amiens
R. Somme
FRANCE
US 19 Corps
US 5 Corps
5 US Corps
Mézières
Trier
SAAR
Luxembourg
R. Meuse
Le Havre 12 Sep
Port working 9 Oct
1st Canadian Army
Br 12 Corps
Br 30 Corps
Brit 2nd Army
1st US Army
US 7 Corps
Allied front line 1 Sep 1944
US 20 Corps
Reims
Verdun
Gateway 4
Saarbrücken
Metz
10 Sep
R. Seine
Brit 21st Army Group
US 12th Army Group
Paris
3rd US Army
US 12 Corps
Nancy
0 20
miles

CHAPTER THREE

Helping Bradley to Aachen

THE WEEKS OF disagreement with Eisenhower had undoubtedly taken their toll. However enthralled the world's Press might be by the sprawling onrush of the Allied armies from the coast of France to the 'iron and steel centres of Lorraine at the southern end of the line', Monty was not.

By failing to impose a clear strategic plan upon the battlefield, weighed down by the civil, political and military responsibilities of a Supreme Commander, Eisenhower had in Monty's view squandered a great and decisive Allied victory. How Eisenhower proposed to exercise field command of the Allied armies from his new SHAEF headquarters at Granville, on the Atlantic side of the Cherbourg Peninsula, many hundreds of miles from the front lines, Monty was at a loss to understand. As he put it later to the historian Chester Wilmot, Eisenhower would have been in better and closer touch with his field commanders had he stayed in London. Thus, when Monty's Chief of Staff, Maj-General de Guingand, wrote on 1 September that Eisenhower 'was trying to get you on the 'phone in order to congratulate you [on being promoted Field-Marshal]', but had 'not been successful so far',[1] Monty replied testily, 'I do not suppose that IKE or anyone else will be able to telephone me for months.'[2]

De Guingand's enquiries about Operation 'Talisman', the Supreme Headquarters' plan for the Allied take-over of Germany in the event of sudden German collapse, seemed to Monty fatuous—as did the War Office's enquiry about the possibility of furnishing an Army Headquarters Staff from 21st Army Group to go to Burma:

> I have never heard of Talisman. In any case it is quite impossible for me to give up an Army Headquarters for BURMA or anywhere else at present,

he snapped.[3] As for the question of detaching Belgian troops so that they might enter Brussels first, as Leclerc had done with his 2ème

[1] 21st Army Group War Diaries (WO 205/5B), PRO.
[2] Ibid.
[3] Ibid.

Division Blindée in Paris, Monty was caustic. He had already given orders, he wrote,

> to Canadian Army to transfer the Belgian detachment to Second Army at once. They will be the first troops to enter BRUSSELS. They will all get tight in BRUSSELS, and I hope that is the last we shall see of them.
>
> The Dutch contingent I am leaving with the Canadian Army as there is a bit of HOLLAND just beyond BRUGES and they can frig about in that.[1]

Such unbridled sarcasm betrayed the very frustration Monty felt.

With Dempsey's Second British Army and Hodges' First US Army steaming across the Belgian border, Monty felt the Allies must set their open sights on the Aachen gap—in the view of Monty's planning staff 'the most satisfactory approach to the Ruhr and being on high ground is likely to be best in Autumn and Winter'.[2]

What irked Monty was that, having compromised to the extent of sending Hodges' First US Army towards Antwerp and Aachen, on Monty's right flank, Eisenhower had balked at putting a single commander in charge of the operation, despite Monty's offer to serve under Bradley. 'The operation between the ARDENNES and the sea will most profitably take the form of a powerful drive . . . with right hooks to envelop the enemy and destroy him against the sea, coupled with frontal pressure along the coastal belt. The two wings of this operation—the MAUBEUGE [—AACHEN] thrust and the coastal thrust will require the closest co-ordination and form part of one operation,' Monty's Chief Planner had suggested in an 'Appreciation' drawn up at Monty's request.'[3]

But who would exercise this closest co-ordination? Eisenhower had already confessed to his superior, General Marshall, that, based back at Granville, he would not 'even have minimum communications at my headquarters'[4] by 1 September, the date he himself had set for his take-over. Moreover, having so recently insisted on splitting Monty's 21st Army Group and Bradley's 12th US Army Group into the 'Army Group of the North' and the 'Army Group of the Center'[5], Eisenhower had effectively bound his own hands in terms of tactical flexibility.

[1] Ibid.
[2] 'Appreciation' of 22.8.44, 21st Army Group War Diaries (WO 205/8), PRO.
[3] Ibid.
[4] Letter to General Marshall, 24.8.44, loc. cit.
[5] SCAF 67, Report to Combined Chiefs of Staff, 22.8.44, in *The Papers of Dwight David Eisenhower*, op. cit.

Meanwhile, from his Liaison Officer to Bradley's headquarters at Chartres, Monty was fully aware how hard Patton was tugging Bradley eastwards towards the Saar. With the Argonne area seemingly denuded of German troops, Patton was, as in Sicily, lured by territory, irrespective of its strategic value, and was making a 'national' issue of the divergence of opinion whether to go north to the Ruhr or east to the Saar.

It was for this reason that Monty, convinced to his very bones that the Ruhr ought to be the prime target of the Allied offensive after Normandy, did all within his power to help Bradley's Aachen thrust to prosper. The existing 21st Army Group plan to drop an airborne corps in the Pas de Calais was cancelled; instead General Browning was now told to drop with three Allied airborne divisions at Tournai on Hodges' First US Army left flank. In this way Dempsey's Second Army would be able to take over a front some seventy kilometres east of Antwerp, thus freeing all First US Army divisions to head straight for Aachen instead of Antwerp.

The Tournai airborne drop (Operation 'Linnet Two') had been fixed for 3 September; but by midday on 2 September Dempsey was noting in his diary that the operation 'looks unlikely . . . owing to the weather'.[1] After days of glorious summer sunshine, the skies lowered and heavy rain had begun to fall, making airborne operations impossible. By the afternoon of 2 September de Guingand was signalling:

> In view of delay and uncertain weather feel we should dispense with LINNET if possible and prepare similar operation to suit your future plans. Please signal your decision most immediate.[2]

First Allied Airborne Army had been expecting this and had meanwhile been planning a new operation to give Bradley more impetus in breaching the Aachen gap into Germany—as Monty's Chief Planner signalled at 10.25 that evening.

> Allied AIRBORNE Army have planned and prepared following op which could be launched within 36 hours. Land same forces as before astride R. MAAS and seize all br[idges] between incl MAASTRICHT and LIEGE. Forces standing by on airfield at readiness. Will obtain further details but meanwhile request your views on value of op.[3]

With 21st Army Group's armoured spearheads already ap-

[1] Diary of General Sir Miles Dempsey (WO 285/10), PRO.
[2] 21st Army Group War Diaries (WO 205/5B), PRO.
[3] Ibid.

proaching Brussels and Antwerp—the immediate objectives laid down in Eisenhower's directive—and Hodges' troops halted at Mons on Bradley's orders, Monty cancelled the airborne landings at Tournai.[1] It was vital, Monty felt, to make a new plan. Eisenhower was out of touch in Granville. In the circumstances Monty did the only thing he could: he asked the Commander of the Army Group of the Centre, General Bradley, for an urgent meeting.

[1] 'The airborne operation in the TOURNAI area is cancelled owing to bad weather': M145, Montgomery Papers.

CHAPTER FOUR

A Fatal Conference

BRADLEY'S 12TH US Army Group headquarters were near Chartres; nevertheless, when summoned by Monty, he responded immediately. 'Hodges and I will come Bimbo's [Dempsey's] headquarters as requested,' Bradley signalled on the afternoon of 2 September,[1] and on the morning of 3 September flew to Lailly, near Amiens, for a conference which was as important for the final course of World War II as Monty's conference with Eisenhower on 22 August.

In rejecting Monty's forty-divisional thrust, Eisenhower had been willing to consider an advance by Monty's Army Group of the North only as far as Brussels and Antwerp for the present. But with Brussels now about to fall to the armoured spearhead of 21st Army Group, and the capture of Antwerp seemingly imminent, the question at the conference was: Where next? Did Bradley intend to go on to the Rhine via Aachen, and if so, would he need First Allied Airborne Army?

No minutes exist of the conference, but from the diaries of the participants and their aides, the gist can be gleaned.

Why was General Eisenhower, the new Land Forces C-in-C of the Allied Armies, not there? The previous day, 2 September, Eisenhower had flown from his HQ at Granville to Bradley's headquarters at Chartres, seeing Bradley, Hodges and Patton. Patton, determined to reach Metz and the Saar, was dismayed by Eisenhower's caution which made him, as well as Bradley and Hodges, he claimed, 'quite ill'.[2]

Eisenhower's 'caution' consisted of an unwillingness to push Patton east to the Saar until the Channel ports at least had been secured. Meanwhile, Hodges was to 'curl up both VII and XIX Corps short of Tournai and Mons respectively', with the possibility that they would have to move northwards into Ghent and Antwerp if Monty's 'Linnet' operation at Tournai met serious resistance. Alternatively, if Brussels and Antwerp fell to Monty without difficulty, 5 US Corps would be diverted across the tail of 7 US Corps

[1] C-in-C's Operational Messages file, Montgomery Papers.
[2] *The Patton Papers*, ed. M. Blumenson, Boston 1974.

and race east to the Rhine to guard the left flank of Patton's own thrust to the Rhine. 'There have been so many changes in the First Army direction that indeed there seems at times as if those on top did not have an altogether clear and consistent conception of the direction from which they wish to cross the German frontier,' Hodges' aide noted with feeling.[1]

Meanwhile, Bradley, unaware of the bridging problems holding up the advance of the Canadian Army, had since 23 August 'vigorously' disputed Eisenhower's decision 'to give Montgomery all three Corps of 1st Army. One, I insisted, would have been enough.'[2] Bradley's eyes, like Patton's, were on the Saar. On 1 September he had told his ADC Major Hansen that he was 'going to sell Ike on the possibility of turnhing [sic] his effort to the East and head for the German border, break through the Siegfried Line while the enemy is disorganized and before he can plug it, make for the Rhine and drop paratroops to protect the Bridge crossings'.[3] He had told Eisenhower on the occasion of the Supreme Commander's last visit 'that Monty didn't need anything to help him in his effort that what he had was plenty and that he wouldn't find any opposition going up there—that we should turn east, through [throw] everything we've got into Germany and now by Krist we can . . . Give me 8,000 tons east of Paris and we'll get going. I'll stop effort over on [21st Army Group] flank almost altogether and turn everything toward Germany. We can start nine divisions almost immediately. Six should certainly get to the Rhine and very quickly.' According to Hansen, 'General [Bradley] expects to be on the Rhine a week on Sunday [i.e. 10 September] if Ike will give him the go ahead sign on the movement he wants to make. Had we been able to go [before], perhaps we should have been there today.'[4]

From Hansen's diary it is clear that Bradley, with his headquarters at Chartres, was still sold on an eastward thrust to the Rhine and into Germany *south* of the Ardennes—and shortly after Eisenhower left his headquarters, Bradley issued Patton with instructions that Third US Army was 'to prepare to seize river crossings of the Rhine

[1] Diary of William Sylvan, Military History Institute (MHI), Carlisle, Pennsylvania.
[2] O. N. Bradley, *A Soldier's Story*, London 1951. 'Not long afterwards, however, I was forced to concede that Eisenhower was probably right in his allotment of these two additional Corps, for I had underestimated the resistance that confronted Monty': ibid. In fact, by swinging Collins' 7 US Corps north to Mons in one of the 'right hooks to envelop the enemy' which Monty's Chief Planner had recommended, Hodges was able to capture some 25,000 German troops of Seventh German Army in three days alone, 2–5.9.44.
[3] Diary of Chester B. Hansen, MHI, Carlisle, Pennsylvania.
[4] Ibid.

river from Mannheim to Coblenz'—an offensive that would take place as soon as Eisenhower's first priority, the seizure of the Channel ports, was enacted. Hodges' 5 US Corps was meanwhile ordered to reassemble on Patton's left flank, in readiness.

Meeting Monty near Amiens on 3 September, then, Bradley professed no real interest in his own northern thrust by First US Army through the Aachen gap—the very axis which Monty's planners considered the best route into Germany of all. The First Allied Airborne Army idea of an operation to seize the main bridges over the Maas to accelerate such a thrust through the Aachen gap[1] Bradley rejected. As Monty signalled to de Guingand after the conference broke up:

> Have consulted Bradley and he does NOT require airborne drop on LIEGE line. We both consider that all available aircraft should go on to transport work so that we can maintain momentum of advance.[2]

But what was to be the direction of this advance?

> I had a meeting today with Bradley and it is quite clear to me that the Americans are planning to make their main effort via METZ and NANCY directed on FRANKFURT and the First US Army on my flank will be depleted accordingly,

Monty informed Brooke that evening. With Eisenhower absent and Bradley insisting upon making his main effort south of the Ardennes, Monty was left to make his own plans to seize the Ruhr:

> I have not seen Eisenhower since 26 August and have had no orders from him, so I am making my own plans for advancing against the RUHR and am getting Bradley to lend a hand.

Bradley afterwards was to deny this:

> On September 3rd, I visited Marshal Montgomery at Lailly (6 miles southwest of Amiens) to discuss our coordinated effort along our Army Group Boundary,

he stated in 1958. The boundary ran 'slightly north of east from just south of Brussels', and Monty 'further agreed upon our sticking close together along this line so as to avoid exposure of more flanks than absolutely necessary'.[3]

Bradley thus claimed to be astonished when, a few days after the conference, he heard of Monty's plan to seize Arnhem:

[1] Ibid.
[2] M148, Montgomery Papers.
[3] Bradley Papers, MHI, Carlisle, Pennsylvania.

Imagine my surprise a few days late[r] to hear of 'Operation Market', an airborne operation into Holland. The 101st US Airborne Division at Nijmegen, and the 1st British Airborne Division at Arnhem. These areas were designated to form a path for a quick rush to a bridgehead across the Rhine. Each of the three divisions were to seize certain bridgeheads and clear areas for a quick advance by armoured and motorized units. This route to Arnhem was off to an oblique from the advance upon which Marshal Montgomery and I had agreed on September 3rd. It left my north flank exposed and created a salient into the German position for the British with two exposed flanks.[1]

But Bradley was telescoping the Arnhem story—for the tragedy of 3 September 1944 was that Eisenhower, the new C-in-C Land Forces, was not present, and each commander seemed only to be concerned with his own thrust-line. In his diary General Dempsey recorded:

C-in-C [21st Army Group], General Bradley and General Hodges came to my headquarters. We discussed future plans and agreed the inter-Army Group boundary, which will be the boundary between Second Army and First American Army. It will run just SOUTH of a line BRUSSELS–DUSSELDORF, which gives the whole of the RHUR [sic] to me. We will, if possible, by-pass the RHUR to the NORTH and come in behind it near HAMM.[2]

Such a plan, giving the 'whole of the Rhur' to Dempsey's Second British Army, made nonsense of Monty's original notion of a forty-divisional Allied thrust 'so strong that it need fear nothing'. With the Canadian Army still stuck on the Seine and the Somme, *hundreds* of miles behind Second Army, it was inconceivable that Dempsey would have enough British troops to secure the Antwerp approaches *and* turn north-east to attack the Ruhr from the north without American help. Yet this is what appears to have been agreed. General Crerar failed to attend the meeting at all, and General Hodges returned to his headquarters relieved that he would not have to carry out the tasks alluded to by Eisenhower the day before:

He returned at four o'clock with news that we are to push on East as settled previously and not drive north to Antwerp or Ghent as was presented as a possibility,

Hodges' ADC noted.

[1] Ibid.
[2] Diary of General Sir Miles Dempsey, loc. cit.

> V and VII Corps will cross columns, V Corps to be on the right and to drive straight to Germany, through Luxembourg [i.e. south of the Ardennes].

What made the decision doubly fateful was the absence of the Canadian Army commander, General Crerar, who had failed to turn up for the conference despite repeated signals ordering him to attend. Instead, Crerar insisted on taking a memorial parade in Dieppe in honour of the men of 2nd Canadian Division killed in the abortive raid of August 1942. On top of a '48-hour halt quite essential in order it [2nd Canadian Division] can absorb approx. 1000 reinforcements', this was in Monty's eyes 'obstructionism' by Lt-General Crerar—who was suffering acute dysentery, high blood pressure and had become very emotional about honouring the Canadian dead of 1942. The Canadian Official Historian and subsequent Canadian writers later excused Crerar's failure to attend the vital conference at Dempsey's headquarters by claiming that there were no new operational tasks to be assigned to 1st Canadian Army. This was not, however, the point. In the absence of a clear strategic directive by the Supreme Commander, the front-line commanders were being compelled to initiate their own strategy. Crerar's failure, by his absence, to present the Canadian case for caution in assigning bold missions for the Allied armies without first ensuring priority to the seizure of the Channel ports and Antwerp, as well as the capture of the 150,000 Germans reckoned to be retreating along the coast, was to be of profound significance.

With Crerar unable to point out the difficulties in seizing quickly the Channel ports upon which to base a full-blooded Allied advance into Germany, the other Army commanders were duly authorized to mount their own offensive thrusts into Germany, each virtually independent of the other—Dempsey north of the Ruhr, Hodges south of the Ruhr on each side of the Ardennes, and Patton via the Saar.

Bradley himself seems to have been divided. His ADC, Major Hansen, recorded that

> Gen's original plan called for supply shedule [sic] that would assign supply to Third Army, hold First in place until Third got on the Rhine. Now [4 September] it is planned to shoot both armies on to the Rhine in force and for that reason it has been necessary to hold them up for supply. When both are up to the Rhine, the force of the effort will go to the First Army which will then gain a bridgehead and together with the British Army plan to cut off an[d] isolate the Rhur [sic] from the rest of Germany, the British

> fr. the north and we from the south. If possible, we shall extend a bridgehead on the far side of the Rhine as a base for future operations in the Third Army sector.[1]

No senior general should be hoisted on the petard of his young ADC's diary, but Bradley does appear to have succumbed to a fatal division of priorities at this time. Forced to concede that the Ruhr was the most important strategic target for the Allied armies entering Germany, Bradley reluctantly assigned to Hodges the task of a thrust south of the Ruhr to Aachen with two Corps, but refused to halt or switch troops from Patton's Third Army until Patton had got a bridgehead across the Rhine. To state later that the British thrust to Arnhem 'exposed' his north flank was to argue backwards—for on 3 September the talk was of spearhead thrusts, irrespective of flanks. On Monty's map accompanying his M523 plan that night, Dempsey's Second Army was to mount only a feint attack towards the face of the Ruhr, on Hodges' left (marked 'THREAT').[2] The British 'MAIN ATTACK' was to go *north* of the Ruhr, crossing the Rhine between Wesel and Arnhem, as Hansen clearly noted in his diary at Bradley's headquarters.[3]

Meanwhile Bradley assigned half of all 12th Army Group supplies to Patton, and even assigned a further four additional divisions to Patton's Third Army. Antwerp and the coastal belt were, to all intents and purposes, ignored.

> I had a meeting today with Bradley and it is quite clear to me that the Americans are planning to make their main effort via METZ and FRANKFURT and the first US Army on my flank will be depleted accordingly. The present system of command in the northern thrust is far from satisfactory and I have powers only of coordination and not of operational direction,

Monty lamented to Brooke.[4]

It was in this atmosphere, in the absence of Eisenhower, that Monty now addressed himself to the detail of his plan to seize the Ruhr from the north, during the afternoon of 3 September. As Bradley and Hodges departed from Dempsey's headquarters that afternoon, with Bradley having turned down the proposal for an airborne operation on the Aachen front, Monty began to consider using the British airborne division of First Allied Airborne Army to help his armoured spearheads across the Rhine—without American help.

[1] Diary of Chester B. Hansen, loc. cit.
[2] Alanbrooke Papers, LHCMA, King's College, London.
[3] Diary of Chester B. Hansen, loc. cit.
[4] M156, Montgomery Papers.

CHAPTER FIVE

The Choice of Arnhem

At 4 p.m. on 3 September Monty signalled to his Chief of Staff:

> Second Army will advance from line BRUSSELS–ANTWERP on 6 Sep directed on WESEL and ARNHEM and passing round North side of the RUHR. Require airborne operation of one British Division and Poles on evening 6 Sep or morning 7 Sep to secure bridges over RHINE between WESEL and ARNHEM.[1]

This was the true origin of one of the most fateful and epic battles of World War II—a full week before the date which most historians use as their starting reference. The choice of Arnhem thus had nothing to do with the cutting-off of Holland, nor was it conceived originally as a task for First Airborne Army. The line of Dempsey's intended advance was quite clearly marked as running from Antwerp directly north-east through Eindhoven, Goch, Cleves, Emmerich, Bocholt and swinging around the north face of the Ruhr short of Osnabrück. Arnhem was *not* the objective of this route: it was merely the left parameter of the thrust across the Rhine, with Wesel on the right.

What though were the 'bridges over Rhine between WESEL and ARNHEM'? As Monty began to study the maps of Holland and western Germany, it was evident that the river Meuse (or Maas) presented a considerable obstacle, with only one tiny crossing between Venlo and Grave; similarly, between Wesel and Arnhem there was only one bridge across the Rhine, at Emmerich. With 21st Army Group's bridging material and engineers already employed from the Seine to the Somme, the capture of existing bridges was vital. By 8 p.m. on 3 September Monty was signalling to de Guingand:

> Consider we may want considerable airborne drop to make certain of getting over MEUSE and RHINE. Order BROWNING to come to see me tomorrow and you come too.[2]

Thus began the inexorable chain of events leading to the disaster at Arnhem—for neither de Guingand's 21st Army Group head-

[1] M148, Montgomery Papers.

[2] M149, Montgomery Papers.

quarters nor First Allied Airborne Army had yet planned for such an eventuality. Brigadier Richardson's planning staff had for weeks rejected a lowland entry into Germany during the autumn months, and had backed the idea of an all-out thrust through the Aachen gap. De Guingand had even written to Monty in the course of 3 September, confirming that Brereton's First Allied Airborne Army was prepared to carry out a major airborne drop in support of the Aachen-gap thrust:

> *LIEGE–MAASTRICHT air operation*
> As you already know, they [Airborne Army] are prepared to carry out this operation tomorrow. Provided events don't outrun the project, it has certain merits in that we should secure the important bridges over the MAAS, and in view of Bill WILLIAMS'S [Intelligence] news this morning, we should get behind the remnants of the enemy's armour that he is concentrating in the areas to the West of the dropping zones.[1]

Bradley's veto had already damned the project, however, even as de Guingand's letter was typed. Monty's new plan came as a shock to the staff at Main 21st Army Group headquarters. Though Antwerp had been taken virtually intact that morning, the port would not be operable until the approaches were captured and the Scheldt estuary cleared of mines—perhaps a further month away. Moreover there was a considerable enemy army bottled up on the coast—as Monty revealed to the CIGS in his next nightly telegram: 'it is estimated that there are some 150,000 Germans north of the general line ANTWERP LILLE BETHUNE HESDIN but the bottle is now corked and they will not be able to get out. A great many prisoners are being taken every day by every unit and one Corps today took 10,000.' But the lure of the Ruhr was nevertheless too great to give priority to the Scheldt approaches and the mopping-up of a seemingly surrounded enemy army. 'You will have got my M523 giving my plans for future action,' Monty remarked. 'The only addition to that is that I am planning a big airborne drop to secure the bridges over the RHINE and MEUSE ahead of my thrust.'[2]

With the remnants of the German coastal armies and 15th Army Group 'bottled' up along the coast, it is in retrospect incredible that Monty should have allowed himself to be enticed by the idea of a unilateral British drive into Germany to the exclusion of the vital need to secure quickly the Channel ports, open Antwerp and ensure the capture of the German forces corseted between Second Army

[1] Letter of 3.9.44, loc. cit.
[2] M161, Montgomery Papers.

and the sea. Yet, apart from planning to detach 'one division, or if necessary a Corps, to turn northwards towards ROTTERDAM and AMSTERDAM',[1] Monty was unwilling to give extra support to his coastal responsibility.

The breach between Monty's Tactical and his Main headquarters now became a chasm. With his armour racing almost unopposed through Belgium and now into Holland, Monty claimed that Main headquarters was out of touch with the operational picture. The Antwerp approaches and the Channel ports would in any case take weeks to open, even when captured. Time was running out. If the Germans—who were well known to Monty for their astonishing ability to organize defensive lines—were to be defeated and the Ruhr seized there was no time to lose. Browning was thus told to set up an airborne operation using 1st British Airborne Division and the Polish Parachute Brigade; meanwhile, anxious lest the last chance of quick success be prejudiced by lack of supplies, Monty signalled to the absent Supreme Commander:

> I consider we have now reached a stage where one really powerful and full blooded thrust toward BERLIN is likely to get there and thus end the German war.
>
> We have not enough maintenance resources for two full blooded thrusts.
>
> The selected thrust must have all the maintenance resources it needs without any qualification and any other operation must do the best it can with what is left over.
>
> There are only two possible thrusts, one via the RUHR and the other via METZ and the SAAR.
>
> In my opinion the thrust likely to give the best and quickest results is the northern one via the RUHR.
>
> Time is vital and the decision regarding the selected thrust must be made at once . . . if we attempt a compromise solution and split our maintenance resources so that neither thrust is full blooded we will prolong the war,

Monty prophesied.[2] What he did not explain was that there were now not two but *three* thrusts competing for priority in resources—with the new British thrust routed on a lowland axis which, although it promised to by-pass the Siegfried Line (which ended at Wesel), had been rejected as unsuitable by Monty's own planners: a route bisected by 'numerous rivers' and beset by a 'maze of inundatable areas'.

[1] M523 (21st Army Group General Operational Situational Directive of 3.9.44), Montgomery Papers.

[2] M160, Montgomery Papers.

In the context of the lightning advance into Holland, however, such autumnal considerations were irrelevant in Monty's mind. He wanted a lightning decision from Eisenhower—and suggested they meet the next day, 5 September:

> The matter is of such vital importance that I feel sure you will agree that a decision on the above lines is required at once. If you are coming this way perhaps you would look in and discuss it. If so delighted to see you lunch tomorrow. Do not feel I can leave this battle just at present.[1]

The phrasing of this suggestion—as if Eisenhower were wont to fly about a thousand-mile front and could 'look in' for lunch—is utterly remarkable, the more so since Monty had not seen Eisenhower since 26 August, *ten days* before.

Eisenhower was certainly at fault in having insisted on taking over field command of the Allied Land Forces on 1 September—for it is evident from his papers that, at this critical juncture of the war, he was being bombarded by civil and political, as well as world-military, problems that would have tested all his resources as Supreme Commander, even without land armies to command. Worse still, returning from Bradley's headquarters on 2 September, he had wrenched his knee—his aeroplane had been forced by high winds to land on a beach near Julloville and Eisenhower had tried to help the crew pull the aircraft to a sheltered spot lest it be blown over. He had then to make a broadcast to the 'peoples of Northwest Europe', consider the next way in which the Italian campaign could assist the 'Overlord' forces, and hold a conference with General Devers to discuss operational control of the Franco-American forces coming up through southern France. He also had to consider a request that 100 transport planes be sent to the Mediterranean theatre for an operation in Greece.

It was in the midst of such discussions that Monty's urgent cable arrived. As Major-General Strong, Eisenhower's Chief of Intelligence, reported in London several days afterwards, Eisenhower was as torn now over what to do as was his staff. When Monty's telegram 'was received by Eisenhower, it was read out by Bedell Smith to a small meeting consisting of Freddy Morgan, Humphrey Gale (P), Strong (I), Jock Whiteley (O). Each in turn was asked to comment on it. Strong voted strongly for one army to go with 21 Army Group to make a strong thrust through Belgium to the Rhine. Following this he had an hour with Ike in which Ike showed him a telegram from Stimson [US Secretary of State for War] urging him to take control.

[1] Ibid.

"What can you do in the face of this?" he said. Ike has to weigh the political aspects. He wants both armies to strike Germany together [i.e. simultaneously but on separate axes]. His changing of the name of the US and 21 Army Groups to Army Group of the North, Army Group of the Centre, Army Group of the South is designed principally to do away with the words British and American. . . .'[1]

Bedell Smith, Eisenhower's Chief of Staff, was thus ordered to draft a reply on 5 September. This began by saying that although Eisenhower agreed to Monty's conception of a 'powerful and full-blooded thrust towards Berlin', he did *not* agree that it should be initiated at this moment 'to the exclusion of all other maneuver'.[2] Eisenhower's official SHAEF policy had been formally set out in a directive the day before.[3] The Ruhr *and* the Saar were considered the chief targets of the Allied advance—but until Le Havre and Antwerp harbours were operating there was no question of a thrust to Berlin, Bedell Smith emphasized. Meanwhile, priority had always been given to the *Ruhr* thrust, he went on—not only was the entire First Allied Airborne Army instructed to operate in support of Monty's Northern Group of Armies, but 'locomotives and rolling stock are today being allocated on the basis of this priority to maintain the momentum of the advance of your forces, and those of Bradley northwest of the Ardennes'.[4]

Although this sounded unequivocal, it masked three tragic misunderstandings. First, as Monty discovered when he eventually received Eisenhower's official SHAEF policy instruction, there was no *specific* order regarding the priority which the Ruhr thrust should be accorded; secondly, Eisenhower was loth to halt Patton in his thrust towards the Saar; and thirdly, Eisenhower seemed to be under the mistaken impression that Monty's northern thrust to the Ruhr would be part of a co-ordinated Allied effort via the Aachen gap.

It is this last misunderstanding which is perhaps the most surprising. Had Eisenhower only attended the fateful conference on 3 September, or even flown to meet Monty on 5 September as suggested, the misconception might have been avoided. Yet even this is unlikely;

[1] Diary kept by Military Assistant to CIGS, then Major P. Earle, entry of 7.9.44, recording meeting with General Strong, communicated to author by Colonel Earle, 1985.

[2] Cable in desk diary of C-in-C, Diary of Harry C. Butcher, Eisenhower Library, Abilene, Kansas.

[3] Cable FWD 13765 to Montgomery, Bradley, Ramsay (Naval C-in-C), Leigh-Mallory (Air C-in-C), Brereton (Allied Airborne Army C-in-C), Spaatz (American Air Forces C-in-C) and Harris (RAF Bomber Command C-in-C), 4.9.44.

[4] Montgomery Papers.

Eisenhower hung back not simply because of a wrenched knee and the vital 'affairs of state' he must consider as Supreme Commander, but because he feared, at heart, a shoot-out between his field commanders. It is in this respect that Eisenhower cannot be considered a great field commander, despite the aspirations of his entourage. As Brooke and others were aware, Eisenhower was at bottom frightened of Monty's military expertise—and it is inconceivable that, even if he had met Monty at this time, he would have insisted that the Allied thrust to the Ruhr be concentrated through the Aachen gap. Dispersal of thrusts had characterized his strategic and tactical thinking ever since 'Torch' in November 1942. In an office memorandum on 5 September Eisenhower now noted that 'from the beginning of this campaign I have always visualized that as soon as substantial destruction of the enemy forces in France could be accomplished, we should advance rapidly on the Rhine by pushing through the Aachen gap in the north *and* the Metz gap in the south.[1] The virtue of this movement is that it takes advantage of all existing lines of communication in the advance towards Germany and brings the southern force on the Rhine at Coblenz, practically on the flank of the forces that would advance straight eastward through Aachen.' Far from agreeing with Monty about a single thrust, Eisenhower 'deem[ed] it important, while supporting the advance on Eastward through Belgium, to get Patton moving once again so that we may be fully prepared to carry out the original conception for the final stages of the campaign'[2]—the seizure of Berlin.

Eisenhower thus continued to believe in two thrusts, two days after the fateful Lailly conference between Monty and Bradley—and, incarcerated in his ironically named 'Villa Montgomery' by the Atlantic near Granville, failed to perceive that the Allied offensive was now being dissipated into *three* thrusts—apart from numerous subsidiary attacks, on Brest, on Amsterdam, on the Channel ports, and with Devers's army striking northwards up the Rhône Valley. Administratively such dispersion of efforts was bound to result in failure. Bradley's 8 US Corps investing Brest, for instance had alone been issued with almost a million gallons of petrol in the first days of September—while Patton's recce columns were starved, and Monty was grounding whole divisions in both Second British and First Canadian Armies for lack of fuel.[3]

[1] Author's italics.

[2] Diary of Harry C. Butcher, loc. cit.

[3] See Diary of General Gay, COS, Third US Army, MHI, Carlisle, Pennsylvania. Monty's 8 British Corps was grounded and its transport used for supply. 1 British Corps (in Canadian Army) was also grounded once Le Havre was captured.

While Eisenhower sought to clarify his own muddled strategic thinking in his office memorandum, Monty was chafing at his tactical headquarters 400 miles further forward. Without airborne help he could not hope to reach and cross the Rhine north of the Ruhr, since he had been told there was no possibility of bringing up sufficient bridging material before mid-September at the earliest. Unless the airborne troops could seize existing bridges by a *coup de main*, Monty would be unable to exploit the current disorganization of German resistance. But RAF reaction to the Rhine crossing was, as Monty later told Chester Wilmot, considerably influenced by the density of anti-aircraft fire in the vicinity of the Ruhr. If Second Army chose to try and seize a crossing at Wesel, the unarmed troop-carrying planes would be easy prey to the Ruhr batteries (Wesel was a bare fifteen miles from Essen). Browning therefore argued that it would be best to follow the main road network via Grave, Nijmegen and Arnhem itself, taking the operation out of reach of the Ruhr anti-aircraft fire and putting it within supporting distance of fighters and fighter-bombers based in England. Monty thus decided on Arnhem as the airborne target:

> I chose Arnhem and not Wesel, because the air forces could not tackle the Wesel operation from Bases in England, and anyway they were concerned about the fiercer enemy reaction which would have to be faced in that area.[1]

Far from warning Monty that Arnhem might be a 'bridge too far',[2] Browning considered at this juncture that a *single* British airborne division, together with the Polish Parachute Brigade, could by night seize *all* the bridges—at Arnhem, Nijmegen and Grave. To the CIGS therefore Monty signalled on the night of 5 September:

> The advance of Second Army northeastwards towards the Rhine will begin on 7 September from LOUVAIN and ANTWERP in

[1] Notes on conversation with Monty (of) 18.5.46, in Wilmot Papers, LHCMA, King's College, London.

[2] Neither the Commander of the 1st Airborne Division, Major-General Urquhart, nor Brigadier Hackett, the Commander of 4th Parachute Brigade, ever heard Browning use the phrase; indeed Hackett considered Browning's overambitiousness in encouraging Monty to undertake the 'Comet' operation to be a mark of Browning's 'boy scout' attitude to warfare against professional soldiers like the Germans, an attitude that was also distrusted by the Polish Commander, Maj-General Sosabowski—interviews with Maj-General R. E. Urquhart, 13.10.83 and General Sir John Hackett, 15.12.85.

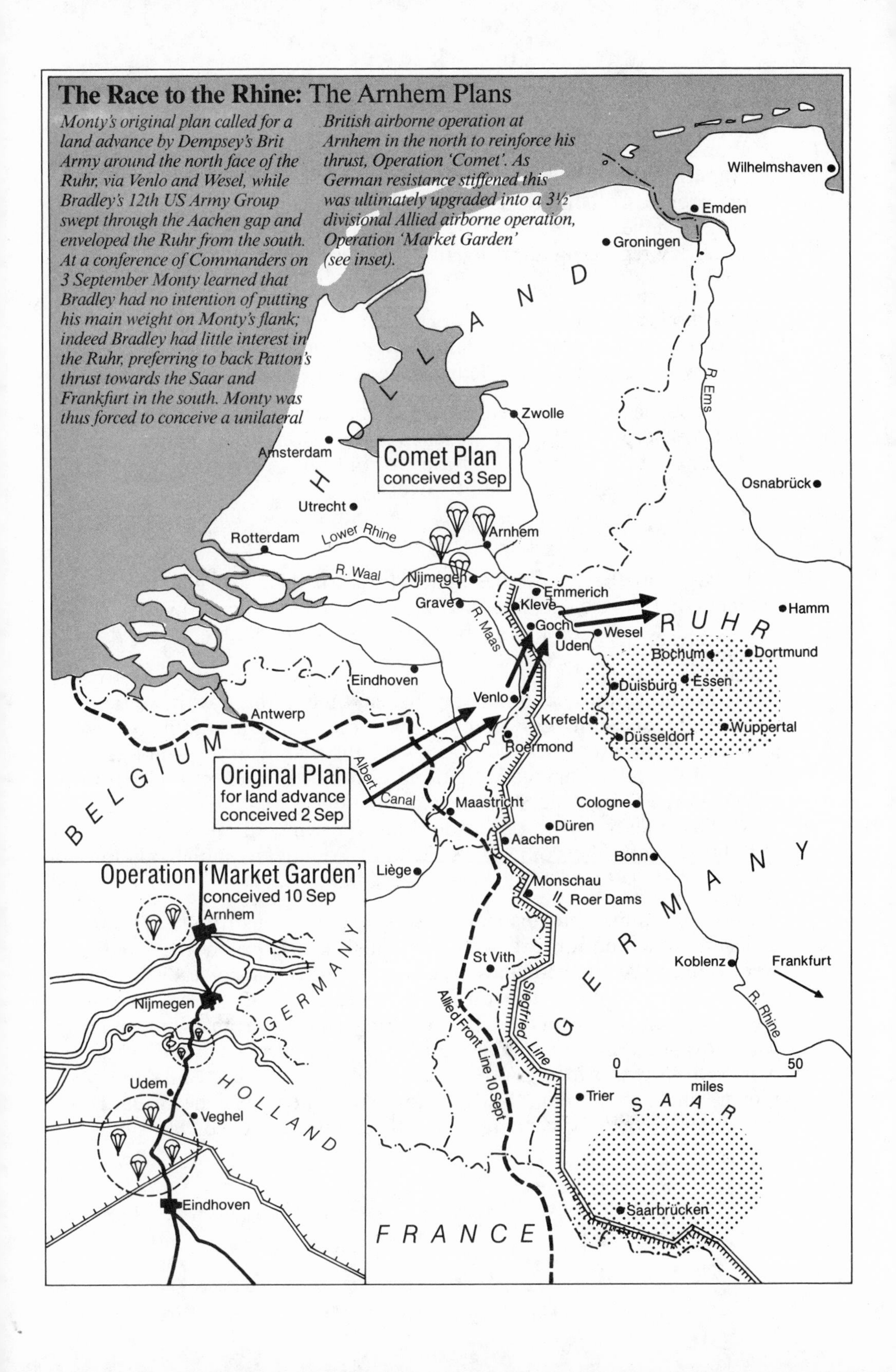

The Race to the Rhine: The Arnhem Plans
Monty's original plan called for a land advance by Dempsey's Brit Army around the north face of the Ruhr, via Venlo and Wesel, while Bradley's 12th US Army Group swept through the Aachen gap and enveloped the Ruhr from the south. At a conference of Commanders on 3 September Monty learned that Bradley had no intention of putting his main weight on Monty's flank; indeed Bradley had little interest in the Ruhr, preferring to back Patton's thrust towards the Saar and Frankfurt in the south. Monty was thus forced to conceive a unilateral British airborne operation at Arnhem in the north to reinforce his thrust, Operation 'Comet'. As German resistance stiffened this was ultimately upgraded into a 3½ divisional Allied airborne operation, Operation 'Market Garden' (see inset).
Wilhelmshaven
Emden
Groningen
HOLLAND
R. Ems
Zwolle
Amsterdam
Comet Plan
conceived 3 Sep
Osnabrück
Utrecht
Arnhem
Rotterdam
Lower Rhine
R. Waal
Nijmegen
Emmerich
Grave
Kleve
R. Maas
Goch
Uden
Wesel
RUHR
Hamm
Bochum
Dortmund
Eindhoven
Duisburg
Essen
Venlo
Antwerp
Krefeld
Wuppertal
Düsseldorf
Roermond
BELGIUM
Original Plan
for land advance
conceived 2 Sep
Albert Canal
Maastricht
Cologne
Düren
Aachen
Bonn
Liège
Monschau
Roer Dams
GERMANY
St Vith
Koblenz
Frankfurt
R. Rhine
Siegfried Line
Allied Front Line 10 Sept
0
50
miles
Trier
SAAR
Saarbrücken
FRANCE
Operation 'Market Garden'
conceived 10 Sep
Arnhem
Nijmegen
GERMANY
Udem
Veghel
HOLLAND
Eindhoven

> cooperation with airborne forces which will be dropped that evening to secure the RHINE bridges. A very limiting factor in the progress of this thrust is going to be maintenance and transport. I have as yet no reply from Eisenhower to my telegram yesterday regarding allotting all available resources to one selected thrust.[1]

Eisenhower's silence was worrying. To Maj-General 'Simbo' Simpson, the Director of Military Operations at the War Office, Monty wrote the same day, fearing the worst:

> The historic march of events continues, and we are now in Brussels and Antwerp. . . . We have reached a vital moment in the war and if we now take the right decision we could be in Berlin in 3 weeks and the German war would be over. . . .
>
> I fear very much we shall have a compromise, and so prolong the war.[2]

It was vital that the Allies concentrate all their energies on one target rather than dispersing their effort in three separate thrusts. To the King, Monty had already written in identical vein the day before:

> We are now approaching a very critical time in the war; if we take the right decision *now* we could win the German war in a few weeks; if we take the wrong decision the war will be prolonged. Our great Allies are very 'nationally minded', and it is election year in the States; the Supreme Commander is an American; I fear we may take the wrong decision. I am throwing all my weight and influence into the contest; but fear of American public opinion may cause us to take the wrong decision.[3]

Monty's certainty that dispersed thrusts would constitute a 'wrong decision' was undoubtedly based on his experience in the Mediterranean in 1943—particularly the chaotic Allied bid to reach Rome in 1943; but it rested too on his Liaison Officers' reports of increasing enemy resistance. The headlong pursuit from Normandy was now petering out; although 11th Armoured Division had captured Antwerp intact, all bridges across the Albert Canal were blown, and the small bridgehead established by the Guards Armoured Division was being resolutely counter-attacked. The sands

[1] M167, Montgomery Papers.
[2] Copy in Montgomery Papers.
[3] Letter to Sir Alan Lascelles (the King's Private Secretary) of 4.9.44, Royal Archives, Windsor.

of victory were running out and when Monty finished breakfast on the morning of 7 September 1944, he was handed the decrypt of enough of Eisenhower's garbled SHAEF telegram of 5 September to recognize the fingerprint of failure.

CHAPTER SIX

'I Cannot Capture the Ruhr'

So much historical attention has been focused on the battle of Arnhem that, in tracing its origins, Monty's state of mind must needs be assessed. That he himself had misgivings about the chances of success is evidenced by his letters of 4 and 5 September to the King and to the DMO, Maj-General Simpson. Perhaps, in his heart of hearts, Monty knew it was wrong. Certainly he put off the operation—currently code-named 'Comet'—from day to day: from 6 September to 7 September, and then from 7 September to 10 September. The lives of his men were at stake—lives he had refused to sacrifice unnecessarily a few months earlier at Caen, on the eastern flank of his Normandy bridgehead, merely to fill headlines.

> If I had attacked Caen early in June [1944]

he explained privately to Chester Wilmot after the war,

> I might have wrecked the whole plan. We were short of ammunition, we were short of troops, the enemy had brought in two very strong divisions to hold them. At best it would have been touch and go whether we could take it or not. If we had failed, we would have been forced on the defensive. We might have had such losses that we could not even hold the ground we had, and we certainly could not have attacked again for some time. That would have given the Germans the opportunity to switch their armoured divisions to the American sector. You must remember that the British Army was a wasting asset. The War Office told me before D-Day that it would guarantee replacements only for the first months.[1] After that I would have to break up divisions or ancillary

[1] Recording a message from General Marshall on 30 May 1944, Field-Marshal Brooke's MA had noted in his diary: 'It occurred to us that the U.S. Chiefs might be getting cold feet. There are certain factors which might induce this.' One was the move of German divisions into Normandy, another the growing number of German divisions in the West, available for the defence of France: some sixty-two against an Allied total, when landed over three months, of fifty divisions. 'They [the Americans] are used in the Pacific to the strategy of the "sledgehammer to crack the nut". This is a different matter.' Although Brooke remained sanguine, the anxiety at the War Office was primarily over reinforcements. 'Perhaps the biggest factor of doubt . . . is

> troops. Consequently there was no sense in incurring casualties to gain ground, when we were doing our job on this flank anyway. It would have been very easy for me to yield to the public criticism and the American pressure and to have made greater efforts to gain ground on this flank. It might have helped my immediate reputation but it would have crippled the British Army.[1]

Why then did Monty insist on risking the 'wasting asset' of the British Army in a unilateral British drive across the Rhine early in September 1944? Was it *folie de grandeur nationale*, as most American historians imply? Such *folie* certainly lay within his character—and was well illustrated by the painting of a new oil painting of himself in the field by James Gunn.

Gunn's second portrait was this time of Monty in field-marshal's uniform, with the baton of that rank—a sort of parade ground Lely. Monty was inordinately proud of Gunn's first portrait, displaying in a letter to his son David's guardians, the Reynolds, his by now characteristic boastfulness:

> The portrait is completely the cat's whiskers; it will without doubt be the great picture of the year at next year's Academy.[2]

Like his Flying Fortress in the spring of 1943, Gunn's portrait now became an almost obsessive 'bee in his bonnet'. Letter after letter now referred to the portrait—'the best picture he [Gunn] has ever painted; it is definitely superb and will create a sensation at next year's Academy—to which I have agreed it should go'.[3]

Such claims were excessive; but the fact that Monty was being painted in the field following the greatest Allied land victory of World War II was not in itself proof of undue arrogance. Even the self-effacing General Bradley was having his portrait painted at this time[4]—in fact even General Hodges, the far-from-famous commander of First US Army, was having one done.[5] A great and historic victory had been won; the victors can hardly be criticized for wanting themselves encapsulated in oils.

MANPOWER. In the second half of this year we will be approximately 90,000 men short in 21 Army Group and AA. . . . We are about to enter on this vast project with ONLY THREE WEEKS RESERVES. This is unheard of in the annals of history': Diary of Lt-Colonel Peter Earle, entry of 30.5.44, communicated to author, 1985.

[1] Wilmot Papers, loc. cit.

[2] Letter of 10.9.44, Montgomery Papers.

[3] Letter to Phyllis Reynolds of 20.9.44, Montgomery Papers.

[4] Cf. the Diary of Chester B. Hansen, loc. cit.

[5] Cf. the Diary of William C. Sylvan, loc. cit.

Where, however, was such a victory to lead? It is in this respect that Monty's egoism has, of necessity, to be more deeply examined. Was he caught up in the general euphoria that swept all headquarters at this time—the feeling that the war was, almost at a stroke, won, and that Berlin was now truly within Allied grasp? Bradley, looking at his wall maps of France and Germany on 5 September, remarked optimistically that his next headquarters 'would be in Metz, the one thereafter for an army of occupation in Weisbaden [sic]'.[1] Supreme Headquarters was despatching reams of planning papers on the military and civil government of Germany once resistance collapsed; and Eisenhower, far from recognizing the need for personal discussion with Monty (whom he had not seen now for twelve critical days), excitedly flew to Paris on 8 September for a grand parade down the Champs Elysées, climbing out of his sedan and standing on the running board despite his twisted knee to acknowledge the cheers of the crowds.

However boastful and vain, Monty at least had no interest in parading in Paris at this critical juncture of the war.[2] If he bombarded Eisenhower with signals daily more urgent in their appeal for a meeting, for a concentrated strategy, for priority to be given to one thrust and all resources to be thrown behind it, it was because he did *not* consider the war all but won. He had himself witnessed, in the autumn of 1918, how the German rout soon developed into an orderly retreat. That he was driven to the brink of despair in these first days of September is well illustrated by the story of his treatment of General Crerar, who had failed, in his eyes, to recognize the critical importance of exploiting the Allied victory and thus avoiding a long-drawn-out winter campaign. Crerar had arrived at Dempsey's headquarters too late for the conference of Allied Army and Army Group commanders on 3 September, and was driven to Monty's nearby Tactical Headquarters at Conty, near Amiens, for one of the most abrasive interviews Monty had ever conducted in the field. As Crerar noted in his diary, 'the Field Marshal addressed me abruptly, asking me why I had not turned up at the meeting, in accordance with his instructions.' When Crerar attempted to explain about the Dieppe memorial parade, Monty cut him short. 'The C-in-C intimated that he was not interested in my explanation—that the Canadian aspect of the Dieppe ceremonial was of no importance

[1] Diary of Chester B. Hansen, loc. cit.

[2] 'Grateful if you will excuse me from attending ceremony in Paris. Am planning advance against RHINE in cooperation with airborne operations beginning on seventh [September]. Operations now in vital stage and I cannot well leave the battle area': Montgomery signal to Eisenhower, M166 of 5.9.44 (WO 205/5E), PRO.

compared to getting on with the war.' Monty then accused Crerar of disobeying orders in the field, and by his self-opinionated, obstinate attitude prejudicing the winning of the war.

Crerar, stung by Monty's venom, defended himself by reiterating the importance of the Dieppe memorial service to Canadian honour, and his own position as head of Canadian forces in the field—protesting that 'I was neither self-opinionated, nor unreasonable, but that, also, I would never consent to be pushed about by anyone.'[1]

At first Monty's reaction was to state, icily, that Crerar's disobedience 'could only result in his decision that our ways must part';[2] but recognizing the difficulties involved in sacking the senior officer of an Allied combatant nation at such a critical moment, Monty thought better of it and, declaring the matter 'closed', proceeded to give Crerar an outline of the conference and the ramifications of his and Bradley's decisions.

Crerar, however, was beside himself with rage at the way Monty had spoken to him—as Monty's Canadian PA well recalled:

> Just before the battle of Arnhem, Montgomery called a conference of all the top guys to co-ordinate their plans, so that they'd all know what was going to happen. Now everybody came except Crerar, who was commanding the First Canadian Army. He didn't turn up. So Monty got on the phone, found out Crerar was taking a memorial parade at Dieppe. My guy just went through the roof. . . .
>
> I don't know what happened because I wasn't in on it in the caravan, but when Crerar came out, I've never seen a chap so mad. And he got into this car, going back to his little aeroplane, and he said, 'That guy is not getting away with that. He can't tick me off like that.' So I think the old man, he really chewed him out for not being there.[3]

In the car, travelling to the airfield, Crerar announced that he would take the matter up with the Canadian Minister of National Defence, Mr Ralston. When Monty's PA, Colonel Warren, reported back, Monty showed no alarm or remorse. 'I'm trying to fight a war,' he told Warren, 'and I can't help it.'

> I said, there's going to be a hell of a row, he's going to Ralston about it. He's not going to swallow. And I said, it's unfortunate, something like that happening. (The previous year there'd been a terrible row with McNaughton, head of the Canadian Army.)

[1] C. P. Stacey, *The Victory Campaign*, Ottawa 1960.
[2] Ibid.
[3] Lt-Colonel Trumbull Warren, interview of 9.11.81.

He said, 'I can't do anything about it.' And I said, yes, you can!

He said, 'What can I do?'

I said, 'You write him a letter of apology.'

And he said, 'Get out of here.'

I thought I was finished. I don't know why I said it, it just came out. I wasn't trying to be a big guy.

This was about five or six o'clock at night. And the next morning my buzzer went. I wasn't even dressed. I still had my pyjamas on. I beat it over, and he's standing in the doorway [of his caravan], with pyjama bottoms on and he's got shaving cream all over his face, and he's waving his shaving brush. He barked, 'Come in here. Now sit down there!'

I sat down at the desk.

And he said: 'Now read that letter!'

And I read the letter.

It was a tear-jerker. 'My dear Harry, I want to apologise for my behaviour—I'm sorry I behaved the way I did,' and so on.

And he said, 'That suit you?'

I said, Yes, sir.

And he said, 'All right, away you go.' And I got dressed and drove like a son of a bitch to Crerar's headquarters. . . .

Now that's a silly little thing, but jeez, it could have been hell, after all the business of McNaughton.[1]

Monty, by supreme effort of will, was trying to control himself and his frustration at the lack of decisive command from above, resulting in the potentially disastrous dispersal of Allied strength between the Channel coast and Patton's eastern corridor towards Germany via Metz. Eisenhower's refusal to concentrate his Allied forces left Monty deeply disturbed—as did Bradley's lack of interest in the Ruhr operation, evidenced by the American Army Group Commander's latest plan, relayed on 7 September by Major Bigland (Monty's Liaison Officer with 12th Army Group) to site his next headquarters at Metz, on the route to the Saar.[2] In a second letter to Crerar Monty again apologized for being 'a bit rude the other day, and somewhat outspoken. I was annoyed that no one [from First Canadian Army] came to a very important conference. But forget about it—and let us get on with the war.' Yet in reality Monty was filled with further foreboding.

[1] Ibid.

[2] Diary of Major T. S. Bigland, communicated to author by Lt-Colonel Bigland. In fact Bradley's Advanced Headquarters was set up in Verdun on 12 September 1944.

On 1 September 1944, as British tanks swept across the Seine towards Belgium and Germany (**3** *below*) Monty was promoted Field-Marshal in the field. At his mobile Tactical HQ he was painted (**1** *left*) by James Gunn; also more domestically in his typical flying jacket and corduroy trousers, lunching with his personal staff (**2** *above*).

To Monty's chagrin, General Eisenhower now insisted upon taking personal command of the Allied forces in the field from inadequate headquarters near Cherbourg – and the great Allied victory won in Normandy was dissipated in fragmented 'national' thrusts.

Keeping close touch with Generals Crerar and Dempsey, his Canadian and British Army Commanders (**6** *below left*), Monty himself crossed the Seine (**4** *above*) fêted in every town and village (**5** *left*) while German prisoners were marched to the rear in their thousands (**7** *above right*).

At Lailly on 3 September Monty requested a meeting with the American commanders on his right flank in order to coordinate plans, in the absence of Eisenhower, for crossing the Rhine (**8** *below right*). To Monty's disappointment Bradley showed no interest in seizing the Ruhr, preferring an easterly advance into Germany via Metz and Frankfurt: thereby giving rise to Monty's first plan for a unilateral British advance in the north, helped by airborne forces at Arnhem – Operation 'Comet'.

M239485

Eisenhower's failure to pursue a consistent co-ordinated Allied strategy drove Monty into greater and greater isolation as the Allied advance through Belgium prospered, and both Brussels and Antwerp fell to the British.

Monty was certain the Allies must concentrate their strength if they were to avoid the deadly stalemate and trench warfare of 1914–18. **9** *left* Monty visits the Canadian War Memorial at Vimy Ridge on 8 September with its harrowing associations of mass slaughter.

As the Allied vanguards began to run out of petrol, troops and ammunition, Monty upgraded his 'Comet' operation into an Allied Airborne Army assault on Arnhem,

designed to breach the German defences around the Ruhr before the Germans could react: Operation 'Market Garden'. Monty's mobile headquarters had moved to the Princesse de Mérode's Château d'Everberg (**10** *centre left*) where the Allied Naval C-in-C, Admiral Ramsay, urged Monty to turn more attention to the opening of the Scheldt approaches and Antwerp (**11** *below left*).

Eisenhower, aware of stiffening German opposition and growing Allied logistical problems, authorized Monty's Arnhem thrust, but refused to give Monty tactical command over American forces north of the Ardennes; nor did Supreme Headquarters fulfil Eisenhower's promises of priority in supplies.

Monty toured his 21 Army Group front (**14** *below*) and went over the Arnhem plans with his commanders (**13** *above right*). Privately however he had misgivings and railed against Eisenhower's dispersion of strength between the North Sea and Switzerland, with fading chances of seizing the Ruhr before winter – leading to a bitter exchange of signals (**12** *above left*) with the absentee Allied Land Forces C-in-C, General Eisenhower.

Arnhem

15 *above* Troop-carrying planes fly over the Belgian border towards Arnhem on Sunday 17 September 1944.

The Airborne Corps Commander Lt-General 'Boy' Browning (far left of photo **16** *left*) had concerted plans with the Deputy Supreme Commander, Air Marshal Tedder (centre in photo **16** *left*), and with Monty, but the days of swift advance, following the German downfall in Normandy, were over.

Though British armoured vehicles struck northwards across the low, polder countryside to link up the three airborne landings (**17** *below*), time and terrain were against them.

18 *above* Tanks cross Nijmegen Bridge, spanning the southern fork of the river Rhine or Waal, captured by troops of 82nd US Airborne Division. However the Germans were able to recapture the main bridge across the Lower Rhine at Arnhem from paratroops of 1st British Airborne Division on 21 September and to erase Monty's Rhine bridgehead at Oosterbeek.

On the night of 25 September Maj-General Urquhart (**19** *right*, photographed at his headquarters at Oosterbeek) withdrew the survivors of his 1st Airborne Division across the Lower Rhine to Driel, after the Polish Airborne Brigade had made gallant but vain attempts to reinforce it. **20** *below* Monty talking to Polish paratroopers after the battle, with Polish ATS canteen girls in attendance.

Winter Stalemate
After the failure at Arnhem, Monty turned to the opening of Antwerp, giving command of the operation to his Canadian protégé, Lt-General Guy Simonds (**24** *below*). Despite Churchill's opposition King George VI stayed with Monty in the field for a week in October (**21** *above and* **22** *above right*).

A second El Alamein anniversary dinner was given in Brussels (**23** *right*) but when Eisenhower visited Monty at his winter headquarters in Holland (**25** *below right*) Monty vainly warned against American weakness in the Ardennes and lack of reserves: 'a first class example of the futile doctrine of everybody attacking everywhere with no reserves anywhere.'

The tragedy is that the chief protagonists were now locked on a course which, in retrospect, was bound to fail. Churchill, Roosevelt, Marshall and Brooke were all travelling to a conference in Quebec, leaving Eisenhower alone to conduct the North-west Europe campaign. Eisenhower, torn between personalities and priorities, procrastinated. Had he unequivocally ordered Monty to secure, as first priority, the Channel ports and the surrender of the 150,000 estimated enemy soldiers ringed by the Canadian and Second British Armies, Monty would without doubt have obeyed. Instead, Eisenhower sent his cable of 5 September calling for seizure of the Ruhr *and* Saar *and* Brest *and* Le Havre *and* Antwerp (which arrived in two parts at Monty's headquarters on 7 and 9 September)—and then ignored the issue for a further five days!

Monty became daily more perplexed. He had agreed with Bradley that, given the current supply crisis, it would be better to use Allied troop-carrying air transport to maintain the momentum of advance. This advance was, however, already beginning to meet fierce resistance. Those Germans compressed against the coast were far from surrendering: 'it looks as if the Germans will hold on the line BRUGES–GHENT,' Monty reported to the CIGS in his nightly telegram on 7 September, adding that 'on Second Army front the enemy is offering very determined resistance in the northern outskirts of ANTWERP and along the general line of the ALBERT CANAL from ANTWERP to MAASTRICHT'. To Eisenhower he therefore appealed for increased supply-allocation: 'my maintenance is stretched to the limit . . . my transport is based on operating 150 miles from my ports and at present I am over 300 miles from BAYEUX. . . . It is clear therefore that based as I am at present I cannot capture the RUHR. . . . Would it be possible for you to come and see me.' [1]

Because of the Allied victory parade in Paris on 8 September, Eisenhower—like Crerar on 3 September—felt unable to oblige. Moreover the following day he travelled in the *opposite* direction, to 8 US Corps headquarters outside Brest, and subsequently stayed overnight with Bradley at the latter's Rear headquarters at Versailles.

In growing frustration Monty meanwhile postponed the British airborne drop at Arnhem—to the chagrin of Browning and the parachute troops. It was the seventeenth operation planned by 1st Airborne Division—and the tempers of the men were becoming distinctly frayed, as a divisional ditty, circulated at the time, well illustrates:

[1] M175, 7.9.44, Montgomery Papers.

Come stand to your glasses steady
Here's a toast to the men of the sky.
To the First (British) Airborne Division
Past masters at how to stand by.
(Their's not to reason for why!)

The number of bum operations
For which they've prepared since D-Day
Would require a mathematician
With Slide-rule, Slidex and maphy.
(A month of brain storms anyway!)

The LOs in Jeeps are returning
Having driven back hard through the night
The last Op but one has been cancelled
The next Op but one is in sight
(The Boy's off to France in full flight.)

Conclusion
And now that the whole thing is over,
Now that the party is cancelled once more,
Signal 'Finis' from Tarrant to Dover,
Then collapse in a heap on the floor,
(Cursing blindly the whole Airborne Corps.)[1]

Browning could not fail to be aware of this—and began to bombard 21st Army Group with worrying signals about morale, such as the following, sent on 3 September after Operation Linnet was cancelled:

> As thirteen Airborne operations have been cancelled since OVERLORD D-Day and as four of these reached immediate stage of readiness on airfields and as Corps HQ and 1 Airborne Div and 52 Div have NOT repeat NOT fought in France and as all seaborne TAILS already in France I have the following request for C-in-C. That Corps HQ and both Divs be landed on Continent by air or sea for active operations immediately.[2]

Admiral Ramsay had begun, simultaneously, to express his anxiety about the capture of the coastal approaches to Antwerp, either side

[1] Contained in personal scrapbook of Maj-General R. E. Urquhart, communicated to author.

[2] 21st Army Group War Diaries (WO 205/5F), PRO. General Sir John Hackett, Brigade Commander in 1st Airborne Division at Arnhem, later considered that, if the division had not been put into battle in September, be it from air, sea or land, after so many abortive operations, it would have lost battleworthiness and have required retraining to restore morale—interview of 15.12.85.

of the Scheldt estuary—without which the port was unusable. The Airborne staffs, however, ruled out the use of parachute troops in capturing either the approaches or the vital offshore island of Walcheren,[1] so that Monty could only secure the area by using ground forces from Second British or First Canadian Armies. He chose the latter, hoping that Walcheren would be captured by the Canadians as Dempsey advanced into Germany.

The prospect of a successful invasion of Germany became hourly less certain however. Had Monty retained command at least of all forces north of the Ardennes, he might well have acted differently, either cancelling Dempsey's unilateral drive on Osnabrück and concentrating on a thrust through the Aachen gap, or transferring sufficient weight from Hodges' First US Army front to ensure at least that Dempsey's strike be mounted in overwhelming strength.[2]

Instead, impotently, Monty was forced to watch while Bradley actually transferred further First US Army troops south for the Metz thrust, and even divided his supply 50–50 between his two American thrusts:

> On 4 September my LO with 12 Army Group told me that Bradley had given orders to split his maintenance—half to First Army and half to Third Army. The effort of First Army on my right was being scaled down accordingly; one of its divisions (79 Inf. Div.) was being sent away to reinforce Third Army,

Monty subsequently lamented.[3] For a moment, short of troops and with growing enemy resistance, Monty was tempted to abandon his

[1] Browning was first consulted about the possibility of using airborne troops around Antwerp on 2 September. Browning considered it was already 'too late'. Thereafter, each time the question of using airborne troops to help capture Walcheren and the Scheldt approaches to Antwerp was raised, it was vetoed by Brereton's First Allied Airborne Army staff.

[2] In a conversation with Chester Wilmot early in 1946 Monty alluded to this. 'After we crossed the Seine I wanted to keep going North with both 21 A Gp and 12 A Gp keeping west of the Ardennes . . . I'd have left the Canadians to mop up the coast. Third Army could have covered the flank—Paris to Aachen. Two strong armies could have got through to the Rhine.' Notes of conversation with Monty of 13.3.46, Wilmot Papers, loc. cit.

[3] Letter of 10.9.44 to Sir Alan Brooke, Montgomery Papers. Major Bigland's diary records how anxious Monty had become since early September about American plans and priorities. On 2 September he recorded: 'See Monty and give him the form here [re Bradley's plans]. For half an hour he went through all his future plans *and* the reasons behind them and what information he wanted. I am to report to him personally each day now.' On 4 September Bigland noted having visited Bradley's Main Headquarters at Versailles in the morning. 'On to New Tac [21 Army Group] site. See Monty late at night.' Loc. cit.

notion of a unilateral thrust to the Ruhr via Arnhem. On 9 September, not having seen Eisenhower now for fifteen days (and that 'only for 10 minutes'), Monty postponed his airborne drop on Arnhem yet again. 'Second Army are meeting with very determined resistance on the ALBERT CANAL line and rapid progress here cannot now be expected,' he cabled to the CIGS. 'The airborne drop in the ARNHEM area on the RHINE has now been postponed for the present.'[1] The port of Le Havre was still not in Canadian hands; Boulogne, Calais and Dunkirk were also uncaptured and would possibly 'require to be methodically reduced'; the surrounded Germans on the Bruges–Ghent coast were actually counter-attacking. It seemed—particularly as he had just heard that 'the left two corps of First US Army have very little opposition but they cannot get on as they are short of petrol'[2]—that Monty might cancel the Arnhem thrust altogether and concentrate upon the Belgian and Dutch coast, even transferring fuel supplies to Hodges' two gas-starved corps.

But instead of cancelling his thrust on 9 September, Monty now astonished his own operational and planning staff. Far from closing down the British Arnhem operation Monty suddenly insisted it be remounted—with the entire available strength of First Allied Airborne Army, including British, American and Polish troops. Why?

[1] M184, Montgomery Papers.
[2] Ibid.

CHAPTER SEVEN

Grave Concern

IT WAS ON the fateful day of 9 September 1944, in deteriorating operational conditions, that two important telegrams reached Monty—telegrams which, in the absence of his Chief of Staff who had returned to England for medical treatment, tipped the scales of Monty's otherwise profoundly professional and generally deeply realistic mind. The first was from Eisenhower, the Supreme Commander and now also Allied C-in-C Ground Forces:

> The bulk of the German Army that was in the west has now been destroyed. Must immediately exploit our success by promptly breaching the SIEGFRIED LINES crossing the RHINE on a wide front and seizing the SAAR and the RUHR. This will give us a stranglehold on two of Germany's main industrial areas and largely destroy her capacity to wage war whatever course events may take.

In fact this signal, received at 9.15 a.m. on 9 September, was dated 4 September—a lapse of five days before an intelligible decrypt could be obtained.[1] The decrypt of the second part of the cable (received on 7 September) suggested that Eisenhower was going to 'give priority to the RUHR repeat RUHR, and the northern route of advance', but the new decrypt of the first part made no reference to this—a fact which, in view of Eisenhower's simultaneous despatch of the directive to all senior Allied commanders, worried Monty greatly. That very day, 9 September, Eisenhower was signalling to the Combined Chiefs of Staff that his intention was 'to press on with all speed to destroy the German Armed Forces and occupy the heart of Germany . . . striking at the Ruhr and Saar. . . . The main effort will be on the left . . . Antwerp having been seized, the Northern Group of Armies and that part of the Central Group of Armies operating northwest of the Ardennes will breach the Siegfried Line covering the Ruhr and seize the Ruhr. The First Allied Airborne Army supports the Northern Group of Armies in the attainment of first objectives. An operation to seize the crossings over the Rhine and in the area Arnhem–Nijmegen has been twice postponed on account of weather and only awaits favourable weather conditions. . . .'

[1] Montgomery Papers.

For Monty now to cancel the British part of 'the main effort' of the Allies because of stiffening enemy resistance, even *had* he wished to do so, would thus have been tantamount to insubordination, leaving him open to charges of timidity at a moment when American forces were thrusting towards the German border. Moreover the Arnhem–Nijmegen axis had been Monty's own proposal, making it doubly hard to rescind.

Eisenhower's directive was not the only signal committing Monty to the continuation of his planned thrust via Arnhem on 9 September—for during the afternoon a 'Secret' cable arrived from the War Office, sent by the VCIGS, General Nye, in the absence of Field-Marshal Brooke:

> Two rockets so called V.2 landed in England yesterday. Believed to have been fired from areas near ROTTERDAM and AMSTERDAM.
>
> Will you please report most urgently by what approximate date you consider you can rope off the Coastal area contained by ANTWERP–UTRECHT–ROTTERDAM. When this area is in our hands the threat from this weapon will probably have disappeared.[1]

By striking north-east from Eindhoven to Arnhem, 21st Army Group would be in a position to 'rope off' the whole of Holland, including the 150,000 fleeing German troops *and* the V2 bomb sites. To Nye Monty thus signalled back:

> Your 75237 re V 2. As things stand at present it may take up to two weeks but very difficult to give accurate estimate. There are aspects of the present situation which cause me grave concern and these are first the present system of command of the land battle and secondly the admin situation. My letter being sent by DAWNAY will give you all the facts. These matters affect the time we will take to do what you want.

To Eisenhower Monty also signalled, recording his disquiet:

> Have studied your directive no. FWD 13765 carefully and cannot see it stated that the northern advance to the RUHR is to have priority over the eastern advance to the SAAR. Actually 19 US Corps is unable to advance properly for lack of petrol. Could you send a responsible staff officer to see me and so that I can explain things to him.[2]

[1] Telegram 75237, despatched 1310 hours, 9.9.44, Montgomery Papers.
[2] M181, Montgomery Papers.

Inexorably Monty was moving from possible cancellation of the Arnhem thrust towards a more substantial remounting of the operation.

My dear CIGS,

Monty meanwhile wrote to Field-Marshal Sir Alan Brooke:

> When you visited me on Tuesday 29 August you asked me if I was quite happy about the general war situation, and the future possibilities. I said that I had managed to reach a compromise solution with Eisenhower; an American Army of nine divisions was to move forward on my right flank, and I was to have the power of operational control and coordination of the whole northern thrust.

Such control had, however, never been given—and Monty listed, day by day, the disagreements that had arisen, and the signals sent between the protagonists. As in Italy in 1943 there had been no 'grip':

> It became clear during the advance northwards that a very tight grip was necessary over the general battle that was going on.
>
> There was no such grip.
>
> Bradley's HQ moved eastwards.
>
> My HQ moved northwards.
>
> Bradley's left Army (First US Army under Hodges) was moving on my right flank. But I had to effect coordination through Bradley, and had no communication with him except W/T.
>
> Eisenhower's HQ were at Granville, on the west coast of the Cherbourg peninsula.

At the Lailly conference between Monty and Bradley on 3 September Bradley had insisted that a third of Hodges' Army advance south of the Ardennes; Monty had therefore, if he wished to seize the Ruhr, to conceive his own 'plan for the advance to the Rhine'. This he had done—but even this seemed doomed to failure when SHAEF did not allot overall priority to the Ruhr thrust in terms of supplies, and Bradley decided to transfer troops from Hodges' army to Patton.

> Eisenhower has apparently decided to capture the RUHR *and* the SAAR, and then develop one or both thrusts to Berlin,

Monty summarized.

> He keeps saying that he has ordered that the northern thrust to the RUHR is to have priority; but he has NOT ordered this.

> The staff at SHAEF, and all the Americans generally, want to scale down the RUHR thrust and give more impetus to the SAAR thrust; and this they are doing whatever Eisenhower may say.
>
> My own maintenance situation is that under present conditions I can get Second Army positioned as follows:
>
> One Corps—ARNHEM area
> One Corps—BREDA–EINDHOVEN area
> One Corps—still back on the SEINE
> Canadian Army—ANTWERP–GHENT–CALAIS area
>
> On my right flank the two Corps of First US Army that are north of the ARDENNES (7 and 19 Corps) were stopped yesterday as they had no petrol; today they have been given enough to move one Bde. Group forward a few miles; there are very few enemy in front of them and *this is where we want to push on hard*,

he remarked with feeling, adding two further emphasis-strokes in the margin of the typewritten letter. For if Hodges could penetrate to the Ruhr via the Aachen gap, the success of the northern thrust seemed assured, since the Germans had not the troops currently to defend both the north and south faces of their industrial heartland.

> Meanwhile, away in the east,

Monty lamented,

> Third US Army under Patton is meeting heavy resistance and has been pushed back in some places.
>
> I am afraid we are now paying for changing the system of command.

Such a calamity brought Monty back to the man who was supposed to be commanding the Allied field armies, Eisenhower.

> Eisenhower has taken personal command of the land armies; he sits back at GRANVILLE and has no communication to his commanders except W/T, and this takes over 24 hours to reach him,

Monty remarked, with an exclamation mark added in the margin.

> He would be closer to the battle in flying distance if he was in London; and he would have better communications.
>
> He is completely out of touch with what is going on; he tries to win the war by issuing long telegraphic directives.
>
> Eisenhower himself does not really know anything about the business of fighting the Germans; he has not got the right sort of chaps on his staff for the job, and no one there understands the matter.

Such condemnation of his commanding officer in the field, written to the head of one of the two primary Allied armies, was of course reprehensible (though Eisenhower did much the same in his private letters and signals to Marshall, and in the memoranda he dictated to be included in Lt-Commander Butcher's desk diary at Granville). It certainly smacked of disloyalty—yet the force of Monty's logic was undeniable.

> Eisenhower does not come to see me and discuss the matter; I last saw him on 26 August, and then only for 10 minutes. . . . It is very clear that the northward thrust to capture the RUHR must be controlled and directed by one commander, who will grip the battle properly. The term 'co-ordination' means nothing.
>
> I very much fear that we shall NOT get either the RUHR or the SAAR quickly. In fact if things go drifting along much longer like this, then we shall not get them in time to finish this war off quickly.
>
> I am definitely convinced that if this show had been gripped tightly all the time, and a firm grip had been kept on the operational conduct of the war, we could have followed up our advantage.
>
> We could have thrust quickly and with great strength to the RUHR. We should have put everything we had into one terrific blow, and smashed right through.
>
> Just when a firm grip was needed, there was no grip.
>
> The 'command' factor has broken down,

he concluded. It marked the end of any hopes of the war ending before winter:

> In the Battle of Normandy, and up to the Seine, the operational command of the land war was vested in one commander. Now there is no C-in-C of the land armies; the Supreme Commander acts in this capacity, in addition to his other duties.
>
> I do not know what he does in actual fact, but he seems to have no time to spare for the land battle; this is not surprising, as it is a whole time job for one man.
>
> In fact unless something can be done about it pretty quickly, I do not see this war ending as soon as one had hoped. It may well now go on into the winter.
>
> I hope the above will put you fully into what is going on,

Monty ended—adding in pen: 'I do not know if you can do anything, but I thought you should know the facts.'[1]

[1] M524, drafted 9.9.44, typed 10.9.44, Montgomery Papers. In an accompanying

As viewed from Monty's Tactical Headquarters the facts looked bleak. What Monty could not see was that coalition warfare *necessitated* such compromises and lack of grip—since those leaders most suited to coalition command were of necessity conciliators, such as Eisenhower and Alexander. Monty knew how important, however, were Eisenhower's conciliatory talents. As Supreme Commander, Eisenhower possessed powers that Monty genuinely admired. But as Ground Forces C-in-C Eisenhower was as disastrous as Lord Gort had been in 1940—both men ignorant of current battle reality not only through personal inadequacy, but by their inability to dominate the battlefield by insisting on first-class mobile headquarters with first-class communications. That Eisenhower's headquarters at Granville were one of the most misplaced in the history of modern warfare, even Eisenhower's senior signals officer admitted:

> Chief trouble came in early September. It was felt that for psychological reasons Ike had to have a Hq in Europe. Had they known matters were going to proceed so fast they wouldn't have chosen Granville for a Hq, but was assumed that he would need Hq there since Brittany fight might take some time.[1]

That Eisenhower believed he could command armies in the field from such headquarters on the western seaboard of France, barely thirty miles from the Channel Islands, was to Monty the ultimate

---

handwritten letter to the VCIGS, General Nye, Monty wrote on 10 September: 'The situation is NOT good; the Bosch is firming up on the Albert Canal; Second Army will now have to bring 8 Corps up from the Seine; we shall change over from a petrol war to an ammunition war, involving more delay.

'I have no power of operational direction or control over the US Army on my right; the whole Northern thrust should really be under MY COMMAND. The U.S. Troops on my right have no resistance in front of them but they cannot get on because they have no petrol!! The whole show is lamentable . . .

'I shall go on hammering at it myself—until I go mad': Alanbrooke Papers (14/32), Liddell Hart Centre for Military Archives, King's College, London. That Nye was sympathetic is demonstrated by the entry in the private diary kept by Brooke's MA, Major Earle, in London: 'The most poignant thing today was a long letter to the CIGS from Monty . . . By and large it says that he is at the limit of his maintenance and no-one seems to be helping. He has no command over 1 US Army except through 12 Army Gp which is only just in W/T [radio] range. 1 US Army has nothing in front of it north of the Ardennes but has no petrol. Patton has got a bloody nose at Metz. Ike insists that he has the maintenance resources to push on to the Saar and Ruhr simultaneously. Monty says the results of this decision will be that we will take ages to get either and the length of the war will be prolonged into the winter': entry of 10.9.44, communicated to author by Colonel Peter Earle.

[1] Maj-General C. H. H. Vulliamy, interview with Forrest C. Pogue of 22.1.47, OCMH Collection, MHI, Carlisle, Pennsylvania.

example of Eisenhower's battlefield ignorance. But what could be done? Field-Marshal Brooke was still aboard the *Queen Mary* on his way, with Churchill, to Quebec. Passing on to Brooke a summary of Monty's letter, Nye remarked presciently: 'I suspect Eisenhower doesn't know what his maintenance resources will do and hopes he will be able to bring off both thrusts. If he fails to do so, the war may be prolonged into the Spring.'[1] But to Monty, meanwhile, Nye confessed in a cable his own impotence in Whitehall:

> I fully sympathize with you in these difficulties which must seem exasperating. Unfortunately we are *NOT* fully informed in the WAR OFFICE on the total maintenance resources available to SHAEF and how the remainder of resources are allocated as between the Army GROUPS yourself and BRADLEY. But even if we had full facts about this it would be difficult to intervene with Eisenhower at COS [Chiefs of Staff] level. Indeed it would probably do more harm than good. However much we would like to help therefore there does NOT seem much we can do from here.[2]

Brooke, when he received the gist of Monty's letter by special cypher at Quebec, returned to his maps of Belgium, Holland and Germany. The depth of his penetrating vision can be gauged in the signal he then sent to Monty via the War Office:

> Personal for Field Marshal Montgomery from CIGS
>
> Looking at operations from this distance it seems to me that early opening of Antwerp and clearance of river Scheldt is likely to be of great importance. Now that Operation COMET [the British airborne drop at Arnhem] is postponed have you considered possibility using your airborne forces or part of these in Walcheren area? This would have further advantage of cutting off further withdrawal 15 Army from their present bridgehead.[3]

Brooke's signal arrived, alas, early on the morning of 12 September 1944. By then the vacuum left by the postponement of 'Comet' and the increasing enemy resistance had been filled. For on the morning of 10 September Eisenhower had at last flown up to the battlefield to see Monty for the first time since assuming his mantle as Allied Ground Force Commander. His wrenched knee was still giving him such pain that he could not even climb down from the aircraft. Monty therefore mounted the steps at Brussels airfield to meet his C-in-C: a meeting that was to have historic repercussions in the days and months ahead.

[1] Letter of 10.9.44, received in Quebec 11.9.44, Alanbrooke Papers (14/32), Liddell Hart Centre of Military Archives.

[2] 21st Army Group War Diaries (WO 205/5E), PRO.

[3] Telegram 7584. Ibid.

CHAPTER EIGHT

Reviving Arnhem

EISENHOWER'S BIOGRAPHER LATER wrote that on 10 September Eisenhower summoned Monty to a conference at Granville, but that Monty 'said he had to meet Dempsey and could not do it'.[1] According to Ambrose, Eisenhower was thus forced to fly to meet Monty.

Neither the documents nor circumstances support such a version of events. Eisenhower well knew Monty's 'principle of war' about senior commanders going forward to confer with field commanders.[2] Monty had been asking Eisenhower to fly up for almost a week; Eisenhower had not in fact seen Monty for fifteen days and was now required to report to the Combined Chiefs of Staff. With hopeless communications and no liaison officers at Granville Eisenhower had only the sketchiest idea of current operations in the north. His visit to Monty, together with his Deputy, Air Marshal Tedder, and Chief Administrative Officer, General Gale, was made in order to determine exactly what was and was not logistically possible in the light of the Supreme Commander's recent directive, calling for the capture of the Ruhr, the Saar, the Channel ports, Antwerp, Le Havre and Brest. Only the venue of the proposed meeting was altered; owing to Monty's 9 a.m. conference with Dempsey, Monty asked Eisenhower to fly to Brussels rather than Amiens.[3] Again, Eisenhower's biographer claimed that Monty proposed on 10 September to 'make a single thrust through Arnhem to Berlin', and that Eisenhower refused to sanction this.[4] In fact by 10 September Monty had discarded any

[1] Stephen Ambrose, *Eisenhower 1890–1952*, New York 1983.

[2] See Eisenhower interview with S. L. A. Marshall, 3.6.46, OCMH Collection, loc. cit.

[3] '9 September 1944: Air C-in-C [Leigh-Mallory] spoke AVM from Forward SHAEF [at Granville] to state that Supreme Commander had been trying to get in touch with the C-in-C 21 Army Group without success. He therefore asked that Advanced Headquarters AEAF get in touch with 21 Army Group through 2 TAF [Tactical Air Force] to inform the C-in-C 21 Army Group that the Supreme Commander wished to meet C-in-C 21 Army Group at Amiens at 1200 hours on Sunday September 10th': Diary of AVM Strafford (Air 37/574), PRO.

[4] Stephen Ambrose, op. cit. In a letter to General Marshall four days after the Brussels meeting, Eisenhower reported that 'due to the decisiveness of our victory below the Seine I determined to go all out in effort and in risk to continue the

notion of getting to Berlin in the immediate future. As he said after the war to Chester Wilmot:

> I knew now [the time of Eisenhower's visit on 10 September 1944] that we could not hope to get much more than a bridgehead beyond the Rhine before the winter, and be nicely poised for breaking out in the New Year. By the time MARKET GARDEN was undertaken [the revised airdrop on Arnhem] its significance was more tactical than strategic.[1]

Monty's statement is supported by the evidence of Tedder himself, when interviewed just after the war by the American Official Historian, Dr Pogue:

> Monty had no idea of going on to Berlin from here [Arnhem]. By this time he was ready to settle for a position across the Rhine.[2]

In a signal to the British Chief of Air Staff (Air-Marshal Portal) immediately after the 10 September meeting, Tedder stated that

> the advance to Berlin was not discussed as a serious issue.[3]

What *was* the issue then? No minutes were kept of the meeting, and Monty refused to allow General Gale to sit in on the proceedings. To the end of his life Monty remained touchy about it. 'This obviously was a most important meeting, for as soon as I mentioned it and asked what took place and mentioned some points that had been discussed, he [Monty] said: "No one else was there—only Eisenhower and myself," ' Wilmot noted after a talk with Monty in 1946.[4]

Why should Monty have been so sensitive about the meeting?

It is quite untrue that the purpose of the meeting was to propose the airborne landings at Arnhem. As Monty put it to Wilmot, 'we discussed the big picture—the administrative problems . . . the broad strategy . . . not much about Arnhem. That was decided upon already.'

[Allied] drive beyond the German border, up to and including the Rhine before we began the process of regrouping and refitting. While this was going on Montgomery suddenly became obsessed with the idea that his Army Group could rush right on into Berlin provided we gave him all the maintenance that was in the theater. . . . Examination of this scheme exposes it as a fantastic idea': *The Papers of Dwight David Eisenhower*, op. cit. This was, to say the least, a most misleading version of Monty's attempts, since 17 August, to get all-out priority given to the thrust to the Ruhr and Berlin. To Monty's lasting indignation Eisenhower was to repeat the version in his book *Crusade in Europe*, London 1948, as will be seen.

[1] Notes on conversation with Monty of 13.3.46, Wilmot Papers, loc. cit.

[2] Interview of 13.2.47, OCMH Collection, loc. cit.

[3] Quoted in Tedder, *With Prejudice*, London 1966.

[4] Loc. cit. In fact Air-Marshal Tedder was also present.

Although this was true, it glossed over the 'stop-go' story of the Arnhem operation. Arnhem and the river crossings at Nijmegen and Grave had indeed been the target of an air drop for seven days already, under the codename 'Comet'. Each day the operation had been postponed owing to the inability of Second Army to penetrate beyond the Albert Canal. On 8 September Dempsey noted in his diary that the operations of his Armoured Corps over the canal 'are being strongly opposed by the enemy'.

> The time has clearly not yet come when we can drop 1 Airborne Div in the ARNHEM area, and I told Commander 30 Corps to postpone it until night 9/10 Sep at the earliest.

The next morning, 9 September, Dempsey noted:

> Saw Commander 30 Corps at his Headquarters at DIEST. His operations in the ALBERT Canal bridgehead continue to be strongly opposed and I told him to postpone the airborne landing until night 11/12 Sep at the earliest.

By the evening of 9 September Dempsey was having second thoughts about the whole operation, reflecting the same ominous foreboding that characterized the letter Monty was writing to Brooke that day.

> It is clear that enemy is bringing up all the reinforcements he can lay hands on for the defence of the ALBERT Canal,

Dempsey recorded,

> and that he appreciates the importance of the area ARNHEM–NIMEGEN. It looks as though he is going to do all he can to hold it. This being the case, any question of a rapid advance to the North-East seems unlikely.

This was prophetic—but still Dempsey declined, like Monty, to consider shifting Second Army's attention to the clearing of Antwerp, the capture of Fifteenth German Army currently escaping in ferries across the Scheldt, and the seizing of Rotterdam and the V2 bomb area. Instead his eyes were locked on the Ruhr, albeit the southern face:

> Owing to our maintenance situation, we will not be in a position to fight a real battle for perhaps ten days or a fortnight. Are we right to direct Second Army to ARNHEM,

he asked, posing one of the biggest questions of the entire campaign,

> or would it be better to hold a LEFT flank along the ALBERT

Canal, and strike due EAST, towards COLOGNE [south of the Ruhr] in conjunction with First Army?[1]

Did Dempsey put the question to Monty that night, 9 September? The sky was cloudless but cold—the weather in fact seemed to provide no drawback to the use of airborne forces. Whether or not Dempsey asked Monty by telephone, he drove next morning to Monty's Tactical Headquarters, arriving at 9 a.m. on 10 September. In Monty's map lorry both men agreed that 'in view of increasing strength in the ARNHEM–NIJMEGEN area the employment of one airborne division in this area will not be sufficient. I got from C-in-C his agreement to the use of three airborne divisions,' Dempsey recorded in his diary.[2]

Thus instead of re-directing his British forces towards Cologne, Monty authorized the revival of the airdrop on Arnhem; only now, rather than a 1½-divisional affair, the operation would employ all three Anglo-American parachute divisions currently ready for battle—1st British, 82nd US and 101st US Airborne Divisions, virtually the entire available forces of First Airborne Army. Dempsey left immediately to start planning—and less than two hours later was conferring with General Browning at Second Army Tactical Headquarters. 'Fixed with him the outline of the operation. He can be ready to carry this out on 16 Sep 44 at the earliest.'[3]

It is hard to avoid the inference that, aware that Eisenhower was due to land at noon that day at Brussels, Monty wished to present Eisenhower with a *fait accompli*—a major Allied airborne operation that would help *force* Eisenhower to stop procrastinating and allocate full priority in supplies to the thrust on the Ruhr.

At all events the mid-day meeting between Monty and Eisenhower began dramatically. Monty, waving Eisenhower's most recent directives, decried the lack of supplies and support for 21st Army Group, and referred scathingly to Eisenhower's dispersal of Allied effort—with Patton, Hodges and Dempsey all meeting serious opposition. 'Steady, Monty, you can't speak to me like that. I'm your boss,' Eisenhower warned, putting his hand on Monty's knee. Monty apologized.

Like Patton, Monty was in a sense overbidding his hand—by involving the entire Anglo-American airborne army he hoped to persuade Eisenhower to throw all his weight behind the Ruhr thrust. To be successful, Monty claimed, he would *have* to have operational control over Hodges' two American Corps currently pushing towards

[1] Diary of General Sir Miles Dempsey, loc. cit.
[2] Ibid.
[3] Ibid.

Cologne and the south face of the Ruhr, for the operations would have to be controlled by one man, he insisted.

Eisenhower, abashed by Monty's peremptory tone, authorized the use of First Airborne Army but refused to give Monty overall command in the north, or indeed priority of supplies over Patton's attempt to reach the Saar. Logistically Eisenhower now saw no hope of deep incursions into Germany until further Allied ports were opened; it was meanwhile important to get across the Rhine both in the Ruhr region *and* the Saar, he felt. 'We must fight with both hands at present, and the moment for the left hook had not come yet and could not come until Northern Army Group maintenance was based securely on the Channel ports,' Tedder recorded.[1]

It was Monty who thus felt defeated; he had only hours previously decided to involve the whole of First Allied Airborne Army in order to win Eisenhower over to priority for the Ruhr offensive—but, while agreeing to a massive Allied air drop at Arnhem, Eisenhower had refused to give logistical priority to the Ruhr offensive. 'Monty made great play over word 'priority' and insisted that his interpretation of the word implies absolute priority, if necessary to the exclusion of all other operations. Argument on such a basis futile,' Tedder commented sourly.[2] Eisenhower's PA, Kay Summersby, noted that 'Monty's suggestion is simple, "give him everything", which is mad'.[3]

General Gale, though excluded from the meeting, had obviously briefed Eisenhower in advance. Gale had clashed with Monty in the past. To Brooke Monty had written only the day before: 'I have recently come to the conclusion that GALE is a man of no character and is useless in his present job—and quite unfit for it. We knew his form very well in Italy; he was responsible for the bad administrative scandals we had there.'

As General Sir Frank ('Simbo') Simpson later remarked, Monty was being unjust to Gale, who was an administrative staff officer of considerable distinction. What Monty failed to take into account was, as Simpson explained, 'that Gale really did not control the administrative set-up. The British forces were controlled by the Quarter-Master General Staff at the War Office, and the American forces by their own set-up based in England.'[4] Nevertheless, there is no doubt that Gale was out to obstruct Monty. As Gale himself told Dr Pogue after the war: 'I advised Gen. Eisenhower as his subordinate against things Monty wanted. I told Gen E. that there was no way we could comply with Monty's view to stop everything on

[1] Tedder's signal to Air-Marshal Portal, in *With Prejudice*, op. cit.
[2] Ibid.
[3] Summersby diary, Eisenhower Library, Abilene, Kansas.
[4] Eugene Wason interview for Sir Denis Hamilton.

the right while he went to Berlin. We couldn't move the stuff to him in the first place. It was not sound to stop the [American] advance. . . . Besides Monty didn't see that the stuff wasn't his—it was American stuff.'[1]

Such a view infuriated Monty the soldier. The Allies had already cast away the possibility of reaching Berlin that year; now they were in danger of *not even reaching the Ruhr*—and thus allowing the Germans continued industrial war production all through the autumn and winter. To General Nye he signalled despondently:

> IKE came to see me today at BRUSSELS airport. He is lame and cannot walk and we talked in his plane. I said it was essential he should know my views and the action to be taken was then for him to decide. I gave him my opinion on the need to concentrate on one selected thrust vide my M160 of 4 Sep. He did NOT repeat NOT agree. I said that in para 4 of Part 4 of his 13889 of 5 Sep he stated he had always given and still did give priority to the RUHR and the northern route of advance. He then said that he did not mean priority as absolute priority and could not scale down the SAAR thrust in any way. He said he had not meant what was in the telegram as regards priority for the RUHR thrust,

Monty remarked with frustration bordering on contempt.

> Everything was very friendly and amicable,

he ridered, however, lest Nye become alarmed.

> But we have got no further. I foresee considerable delay before I can build up enough strength to develop operations northwards with Second Army towards ARNHEM and UTRECHT as I have not the transport to get forward any maintenance and bridging. A great deal of bridging will be required.[2]

No mention was made of the increased Anglo-American scale of the proposed air drop at Arnhem—in fact the whole operation, in the wake of Eisenhower's meeting with Monty, looked like being postponed for weeks. At an administrative conference called to discuss the revised operation on 11 September, Dempsey considered that it was 'clear that, with the existing administrative facilities, we will not be able to develop our operations to the NORTH before 23 Sep 44'.[3]

From Brooke's telegraphic response from Quebec, it is reasonable

[1] Pogue interview with General Sir Humphrey Gale, 27.1.47, OCMH Collection, loc. cit.

[2] M186, Montgomery Papers.

[3] Diary of General Sir Miles Dempsey, loc. cit.

to infer that, had he been Supreme Commander in North-west Europe, Brooke would now have cancelled immediate British offensive preparations towards the Ruhr in order to concentrate upon Antwerp and the Channel ports. Had Eisenhower so ordered, Monty would have had to comply. But Eisenhower was, as Monty later explained to Wilmot, constitutionally incapable of that form of decisive generalship:

> The trouble was that Eisenhower did not know what he should do. He had no experience and no philosophy of battle by which to judge the rival plans. His method was to talk to everyone and then try to work out a compromise solution which would please everyone. He had no plan of his own. He was a sociable chap who liked talking, and he used to go from one HQ to another finding out what his various subordinates thought, instead of going to them and saying—here is the plan, you will do this, and so and so will do that. Eisenhower held conferences to collect ideas; I held conferences to issue orders.[1]

This was the crux of the matter. Yet Monty's presentation of the situation had more impact on Eisenhower than Monty believed. As Tedder cabled to Portal:

> I feel the discussion cleared the air, though Montgomery will, of course, be dissatisfied in not getting a blank cheque. It will help ensure that the Ruhr thrust does get the proper priority which we all feel it should have.[2]

Tedder, though he had recommended Monty's removal in July, was now belatedly convinced that Monty's assault should have comparative, though not absolute, priority in supplies. No one seems to have dared raise Dempsey's question: should not Second Army support Hodges in a single Allied thrust via Aachen and Cologne? Such a proposition would once again entail discussion of who should command such a thrust, and this Eisenhower was loth to do. Bradley did not favour the Ruhr thrust; it was therefore better, Eisenhower felt, to keep the three Allied army groups separate as he had laid down in August than to risk personal confrontations over command.

Not knowing of Dempsey's decision to postpone the Arnhem operation for several weeks given the lack of supplies, Tedder reported Monty's revised Arnhem plan to a conference of Allied Air Commanders at Granville on 11 September. If there had been little sympathy for Monty's repeated calls for concentration of Allied

[1] Notes on conversation with Monty of 23.3.49, loc. cit.

[2] *With Prejudice*, op. cit.

effort since 17 August, there was now even less. General Gale confessed that up until then, Bradley had been receiving *two-thirds* of all Allied air-lifted supplies. If all air transport was withdrawn on 12 September in readiness for the new operation, Bradley's advance would be paralysed. Why could Montgomery not advance with the supplies he already had?

Bedell Smith, Eisenhower's Chief of Staff, was more worried by the implications relating to Antwerp—'restriction of air lift for freight would be very serious, and the airborne operation did not give them a new port, which was an urgent need. This was the fourth time that air lift had been diverted for an operation which so far had not materialised.' Tedder concurred, believing that the chance quickly to open the port of Antwerp might already have been 'thrown away'—and that there was much to be said for an airborne drop to seize the island of Walcheren, 'for which the Navy had been pressing'.

Only days previously the Allies had seemed within spitting distance of Berlin. Now, backwards and forwards, the ball was tossed. 'After further discussion, *it was agreed* that Operation 'COMET', if it succeeded in its objective of putting the Army across the Rhine [at Arnhem] and turning the Siegfried Line, would make the most valuable contribution at the present juncture.' [1]

The wild hopes engendered by the spectacular advance of the armies in the first days of September were now tempered by a realization that by trying to do too much, the Allies were failing in everything. As Monty later said to Wilmot of his meeting with Eisenhower on 10 September, 'I think he [Eisenhower] realised now that he'd made a grave mistake, but he was not immediately prepared to give absolute priority to the left.' [2] Military intelligence pointed to the increasing quality and number of German divisions facing Patton. The way to the Saar seemed well and truly blocked now.

It was in this doleful context that Monty's latest signal was received at Eisenhower's headquarters—postponing the revised airborne drop across the Rhine for another twelve days owing to lack of supplies. Instead of seeing in this a sign from the Almighty, Eisenhower however gave in. Despatching his Chief of Staff for only the second time in the entire campaign since D-Day to see Monty, he told Bedell Smith to give Monty all he asked—everything. The race to the Rhine was on.

[1] SHAEF War Diaries (Air 37/564), PRO. At a meeting of the Air commanders at SHAEF the following day, 12 September, it was considered 'obvious that the enemy must relinquish his position on the ALBERT CANAL to the SIEGFRIED LINE'—SHAEF War Diaries (AIR 37/1118) PRO.

[2] Loc. cit.

CHAPTER NINE

The Race to the Rhine

THE RACE TO the Rhine in mid-September 1944 was to be a race against reality. It was Monty's worst mistake of the war, defying all the principles of logistic back-up, of adequate reserves, and the relentless application of superior firepower that had characterized his march of victories from 1942 onwards. Nevertheless the operation has exercised a lasting fascination upon the minds of historians, for, in General Bradley's words, it was also 'one of the most imaginative [plans] of the war.'[1]

Monty's previous record in mounting such narrow offensive thrusts was not a good one. His attempt to break the German defences at Mareth on a single-brigade front, across the Wadi Zigzaou, had ended in March 1943 in disaster—and only the simultaneous inland hook by 2nd New Zealand and 1st Armoured Divisions saved the day. Similarly, in Sicily Eighth Army's attempt to seize Catania by a combination of airborne assault and narrow coastal drive proved abortive—leading Monty belatedly to beg Patton to outflank the German defences in front of him.

Why then did Monty imagine that a thrust across the Rhine at Arnhem would fare better?

The simple answer is that Monty was by nature far more adventurous than popular legend would allow. Self-discipline and a profound military realism ensured that this side to his nature was for the most part kept in check. At Arnhem it was not—with results this time far more disastrous than at Mareth or Catania. Not only were the lives of many brave men needlessly sacrificed, but the defeat at Arnhem marked the end of the initiative Monty had seized and relentlessly maintained from the day the Allied armies landed on the soil of France.

Monty certainly did not enter the race lightly. Like Bradley, who was having to fight both forwards and backwards (at Brest), Monty was aware of the importance of more ports. Thus on 9 September he had designated Canadian Army priorities as, first, the seizure of the port of Boulogne, then the capture of the port of Dunkirk, then the mopping up of the coastal area north of Ghent to Antwerp, and finally

[1] O. N. Bradley, *A Soldier's Story*, New York 1951.

'the reduction of the islands guarding the entrance to Antwerp'. But with growing German resistance and Eisenhower's revelation that Brest might never become operational as a port, Monty belatedly recognized that Antwerp would be of vital importance to the American effort. He had already asked General Brereton, the commander of First Allied Airborne Army, if airborne troops could take the island of Walcheren, and on 10 September received Brereton's negative reply.[1] Monty had therefore immediately ordered Canadian Army to prepare plans for an amphibious assault landing, codenamed 'Infatuate'. Only if Eisenhower had ordered Monty to switch his Second Army troops to the capture of the Scheldt approaches could Antwerp have been opened any sooner; but Eisenhower's decision to back the thrust to Arnhem precluded this. Ironically it was Eisenhower's new-found enthusiasm for the Ruhr thrust which resurrected a dying plan. Monty had himself given up hope of an early launch, signalling to the CIGS on 11 September:

> Second Army is in a very poor administrative condition with no reserves in the depots and it will not be possible to undertake large scale operations involving an advance northwards to the MEUSE and the RHINE between GRAVES and ARNHEM before about 23 September.[2]

Bedell Smith's visit on behalf of the Supreme Commander transformed the situation. As Monty informed Brooke on the evening of 12 September:

> Following my meeting with IKE . . . I sent him a telegram to confirm his decision that the RUHR thrust was to have no priority and pointing out what the repercussions of that decision must be as regards my operations. This produced ELECTRIC results.
>
> IKE has given way and he sent BEDELL to see me today.
>
> The SAAR thrust is to be stopped.
>
> Three American divisions are to be grounded and their transport used to give extra maintenance to 21 Army Group.

[1] 'Ref capture of Walcheren. Examination indicates such operation not feasible for following reasons: One. No airborne troops available. . . . Two. Intense heavy flak now on island and mobile flak being moved to island indicate excessive losses aircraft in the air. Three. Small size of island indicates excessive losses due to drowning of troops dropped in water. Four. Terrain on the island makes landing of gliders impracticable . . .': 21st Army Group War Diaries (WO 205/194), PRO.

[2] M194, Montgomery Papers. At 1955 hours 21 Army Group Main Headquarters signalled to SHAEF: 'Revised Op COMET can NOT repeat NOT take place before 23 September. Request continuance of present air lift of freight tomorrow and subsequently in view of postponement.'—21 Army Group War Diaries (WO 205/693). PRO.

> The whole of the maintenance of 12 Army Group is to be given to First US Army on my right and that army is to cooperate closely with me and I am to be allowed to deal directly with HODGES.
>
> Airborne Army H.Q. had refused my demand for airborne troops to help capture WALCHEREN as not being a suitable job for airborne troops and they are now going to be ordered by IKE to do what I ask.
>
> As a result of these changed conditions I have now fixed D day for operation MARKET previously known as COMET for next Sunday 17 Sept.
>
> So we have gained a great victory. I feel somewhat exhausted by it all but hope we shall now win the war reasonably quickly.[1]

Almost all these 'electric' results were illusory. The Saar thrust was *not* stopped; the three US divisions were *not* grounded to hand over their transport to 21 Army Group; the whole of Bradley's maintenance was *not* switched to Hodges; Monty was *not* able to deal directly with Hodges; Brereton's Airborne Army was *not* ordered by Eisenhower to help carry out Monty's Walcheren operation. Only the new D-day for Arnhem was adhered to. The 'great victory' was pyrrhic; the war, far from being won more quickly, would now be won more slowly, and with more loss of life.

Yet Monty's new optimism was infectious—and served to brush aside all scepticism. Bradley flew to meet Monty the next afternoon, 13 September—afterwards claiming that this was the first time he had heard of Monty's plan to go to Arnhem. In fact Bradley had known of the Arnhem thrust since 4 September under the code-name 'Comet'; what disturbed him was that the revised plan, employing almost the entire First Allied Airborne Army, would virtually halt the massive airlift of supplies he was receiving. 'Opposed to use of airborne effort on Monty's front since he feels it will accomplish little that the ground troops could not do,' his ADC noted that night, on his return.[2]

Such an attitude stemmed from the myriad airborne operations planned and then abandoned in the wake of Allied ground advance in France. In the very different circumstances of September 1944, with enemy resistance stiffening and German reinforcements from other theatres likely to arrive in October, Bradley's opposition was ill-founded. But Bradley's real objection was not so much to the use of the Allied Airborne Army for an operation Monty's ground forces

[1] M196, Montgomery Papers.
[2] Diary of Chester B. Hansen, loc. cit.

could equally well achieve, but the ramifications upon his own 12th Army Group operations. Whatever Eisenhower might agree with Monty, Bradley was still opposed to a concentrated attack on the Ruhr north of the Ardennes. As his ADC also noted after Bradley's 13 September meeting with Monty:

> Ike anxious that Brad put the main effort with the first army and push on to the north . . . concentrating the bulk of his effort on the left flank of the group. Brad is opposed to this, sensing the possibility of a breakthrough in the V corps sector [*south* of the Ardennes] where sharp penetrations have already been made, or in the area of the 3rd Army which may then pinch the Ruhr from the south and plunge through to the Rhine. Ike, however, has his heart set with Monty on main effort to the Rhine.

Bradley's response to Monty's northern thrust was thus far from enthusiastic—especially when Monty asked that, to help Dempsey strike faster overland to Arnhem, Hodges' left-hand boundary be moved thirty miles north. 'Had I known this gap was going to be created,' Bradley reported to Eisenhower, 'I would have left 79th Division [moved to Patton's Third Army in the first week of September] with Hodges.' This was unfair, since Monty had objected strongly to the removal of 79th Division at the time. The truth, as Bradley knew, was that Patton's appeals to be allowed to push on to the Rhine via Metz had been too seductive for him to reject. As Bradley explained in a letter to Eisenhower the day after meeting Monty: 'The situation in front of Patton looks very hopeful this morning [14 September]. I believe he has written off a lot of Boches during his fighting here in the last few days. The next forty-eight hours will give us some indication as to how fast he can go, but he has definitely crossed the [Moselle] river in strength, and a major defeat administered here may be of tremendous assistance all along the line later.'[1] Only if Patton was unsuccessful 'in the vicinity of Metz' would Bradley agree to halt his thrust and transfer his weight to Hodges' Ruhr thrust.

Did Monty realize that he was being deceived—that Bradley could not resist the temptation to put his weight behind Patton's southern thrust, and that Eisenhower could not resist the temptation to support Bradley, his senior American commander? On 14 September Eisenhower approved of Patton continuing his attack—'There is no reason why Patton should not keep acting offensively if the conditions for offensive action are right'—[2] and like a juggler at the circus,

[1] Bradley Papers, loc. cit.

[2] *The Papers of Dwight David Eisenhower*, op. cit.

the Supreme Commander strove to make each of his army group commanders believe he, Eisenhower, was behind his conception of advance.

Monty cannot but have been aware of this. Not only did his Liaison Officer, Major Bigland, report on American plans, order of battle and current fighting, but Bradley himself made no secret of the fact that he was not going to halt Patton in mid-battle; rather he assured Monty that he would begin to swing Patton's thrust northwards, once across the Moselle, to reinforce Hodges' assault on the Ruhr:

> As I told you yesterday, he [Patton] will either advance northeast from the vicinity of Metz or I will have him shift one Corps north of the Moselle River.[1]

Patton of course did neither. Nor would Bradley permit Monty to deal directly with Hodges—'I will not have the tail wagging the dog,' he retorted to Eisenhower's Chief of Operations, General Bull, who had come from SHAEF 'to discuss the effort of our armies in conjunction with the effort of Montgomery'.[2]

In such circumstances it was hardly surprising that Monty's Ruhr thrust became hour by hour a British rather than an Allied one. 'Goddamit Brad, you kept the [American] flag waving; I'm proud of you,' remarked Patton.[3]

Such Anglo-American discord was indeed a tragedy after the great victory in Normandy. But the senior American commanders had been too long under Monty's tutelage to countenance a return, now that they had won their freedom and were by far the predominant Allied force—something which Monty found hard to grasp, as his Chief of Intelligence, Brigadier Williams, later recalled. After first speaking to de Guingand, Williams had himself attempted to convince Monty that he could not continue to command the Allied Field armies:

> Freddie said, 'You might be able to say it to him—I can't. You represent "the enemy" [as Chief of Intelligence, concerned with German capabilities], and you're only a war chap—you can get out after the war'! That was roughly the atmosphere.
>
> I remember going and saying to Monty, 'If the Americans were to think you the best general in the world—and they don't—it would still be impossible for you to continue being the Land Forces Commander if more and more American forces are pouring over here, and we are cannibalizing divisions. It's not possible.'

[1] Bradley Papers, loc. cit.
[2] Diary of Chester B. Hansen, loc. cit.
[3] Ibid.

According to Williams, Monty was surprised—'a very surprising point of view which he would think about'. But the more Monty reflected upon it, in the days afterwards when Eisenhower assumed the role of Ground Forces Commander, the more Monty railed against the resultant dispersion of effort.

I think it was a reluctance to accept the 'hand-over'

Williams commented,

> and a feeling that nobody was gripping, because he wasn't gripping—and Ike wasn't; because Ike in fact was just letting things go really unstitched—to use Lloyd George's expression in the previous war—to the Rhine. I think as a good soldier he [Monty] couldn't bear it, and as a proud commander he found it intolerable. He was very naughty about it I think, but I think his reaction was that he couldn't bear the sort of *messiness* of it, and the fact that he was there, he could get the thing going properly, if only. . . .[1]

There can certainly be no doubt that Monty's 'honeymoon' with Bradley was now over. Bradley's ADC noted in his diary of 15 September:

> Brad represents Amerk viewpoint . . . Monty hopes to control all of effort. Ike apparently unable to say 'go to hell' for diplomatic reasons which are involved. Monty is the darling of the British public, irascible and difficult to work with. . . .
>
> Bull has difficult time trying to get Ike's plan across, everyone worries for fear Ike favors the Brit. too much . . . Brad and Patton agree neither will be too surprised if we [12th Army Group] are on the Rhine in a week.[2]

When Patton received news, during the Bull conference, that Nancy had fallen to Third US Army, he was cock-a-hoop. ' "Damn! How do you like that. Better congratulate me!" Pleased as punch with effort,' Hansen recorded.[3] As a result of this Bradley decided then and there to rescind his order that Patton must halt if by Thursday he was not across the Moselle—'Patton now across the Moselle in force and an earlier decision of the general [Bradley] to call off his effort by Thursday [14 September] evening if he did not force a crossing is now revoked.'[4]

Bradley plainly did not have the personal authority to stand up to

[1] Interview with Brigadier Sir Edgar Williams, 20.12.79.
[2] Diary of Chester B. Hansen, loc. cit.
[3] Ibid.
[4] Ibid.

Patton's bigoted American approach, nor his desire constantly to bull ahead, regardless of losses. Casualties in Third US Army were increasing—rising above 30,000 by mid-September. Indeed Bradley still called Patton 'Sir'—'a habit he has never broken since Sicily and Italy', as Hansen noted.[1]

Meanwhile, despite reports that Bradley was *not* closing down his Saar offensive, Monty was girding his loins for his northern thrust to the Ruhr, as well as seizure of the Antwerp approaches. 'Most grateful to you personally and to BEDELL for all you are doing for me,' Monty signalled to Eisenhower on 14 September, assuring him that the Arnhem air drop would take place on Sunday 17 September, and that, following the surrender of Le Havre, he was racing up 49th Division and 1 Corps HQ at once 'to develop as early as possible operations designed to enable the port of ANTWERP to be used'.[2]

Monty's gratitude to Eisenhower and Bedell Smith was, however, short lived. Bedell Smith's promise of a 1,000-ton-per-day airlift proved impossible to mount owing to the necessary air transport planes being readied for the parachute operation. Instead, a huge daily trucking-convoy was to be mounted, using American Air Force lorries. This also proved impossible to mount, at any rate for the moment. There was no grounding of three US divisions; and to Monty's chagrin Eisenhower's radio telegrams and letters began to make it all too clear that the Allied drive was *not* to be to the Ruhr as first priority—that in fact Eisenhower's erstwhile policy of driving towards the Ruhr *and* the Saar was still operative.

Eisenhower, aware that Monty would be disappointed, attempted to placate him by assurances that the Ruhr thrust would not suffer—'while he [Bradley] had issued a temporary directive on September 10 that on the surface did not conform clearly to this conception of making our principal drive with our left, the actual fact is that everything he is doing will work out exactly as you visualize it . . . Bradley's left is striking hard to support you; Third Army is pushing north to support Hodges; and Sixth Army Group is being pushed up to give right flank support to the whole.'[3]

On paper such assurances seemed sincere; but coming from a commander as inexperienced in battlefield command as Eisenhower they struck horror in Monty's heart. Eisenhower seemed certain that the battle would now be fought and won west of the Rhine; he also believed that he was 'concentrating for that purpose'—i.e. an all-out battle west of the Rhine. Eisenhower's notion of concentration was

[1] Ibid.
[2] M205, Montgomery Papers.
[3] Letter of 16.9.44, original in Montgomery Papers.

very different from Monty's, however—'by concentrating I include all troops and supplies that can be efficiently employed in battle', Eisenhower explained. It was a return to the 'bulling ahead on all fronts' with all available troops. Thus when Monty received not only this letter from Eisenhower on 16 September, but an accompanying Supreme Commander's directive airily reciting the possible thrusts to Berlin that would be mounted once the Allies were 'soon' in possession of 'the RUHR, the SAAR and the FRANKFURT areas', Monty saw red. 'Simply stated it is my desire to move on BERLIN by the most direct and expeditious route . . . there is no doubt whatsoever, in my mind, that we should concentrate all our energies and resources on a rapid thrust to Berlin,' Eisenhower stated[1]—contradicting, in Monty's view, Eisenhower's current scheme of separate army thrusts to the Ruhr, Frankfurt *and* the Saar.

As Brigadier Sir Edgar Williams later remarked, Monty's objection was not primarily logistical, however much he might talk of cutting down supplies to secondary fronts. What Monty was arguing against was the idea of separated, unco-ordinated thrusts, none of which could succeed against determined enemy resistance. There had to be, Monty felt, a *tactical* strategy that would force the Germans to react in a certain way—the 'break-in' at Alamein, the 'break-in' at Caen—all examples of the way in which the enemy was *compelled* to react, employing his best reserves and thus enabling the aggressor either to prolong the 'break-in' until the enemy cracked or, if possible, to outflank him while his main forces were engaged in meeting the major break-in.

The lessons of the desert and of Normandy seemed to Monty to be wilfully discarded now by Eisenhower, who appeared to have forgotten the relentless strategy the Allies had pursued in Normandy. Bowing to the pressure of Patton and Bradley, Eisenhower was once again dispersing the Allied effort—and Monty was profoundly disturbed. By attempting simultaneously to seize the Ruhr *and* Frankfurt *and* the Saar, the Allies risked failing to achieve any of these—thus surrendering the chance of a concentrated drive upon Berlin. Only by deciding upon which axis to 'break-in' could Eisenhower ever hope to cross the Rhine, let alone be in a position to drive on Berlin, Monty felt.

But before Monty could formulate his reply—for Eisenhower had, as was his wont, solicited the 'views' of the recipients of the letter—the first battle for Arnhem and the Ruhr had already begun.

[1] Formal letter of 15.9.44, Montgomery papers.

CHAPTER TEN

A Bridge Too Far?

ALL MAJOR OPERATIONS of war are 'organized chaos', the American Tactical Fighter Chief, General Pete Quesada, once remarked.[1] Because the Arnhem part of the Allied Ruhr thrust failed, a self-perpetuating literature has resulted, making Arnhem into one of the most controversial battles of World War II.

General Browning, Corps Commander of the three and a half divisions designated to participate in the carpet-drop on Zon, Vegel, Graves, Nijmegen and Arnhem, is supposed to have remarked to Monty that Arnhem might be a 'bridge too far'. This is inherently unlikely, since Browning saw Dempsey, not Monty, on the day the revised 'Comet' operation, re-named Operation 'Market Garden', was resurrected. For seven days Browning's airborne Corps had been preparing to seize all the bridges up to Arnhem with only a single British division and a Polish parachute brigade; to have protested that Arnhem was a 'bridge too far' when Dempsey now offered him no less than *three* airborne divisions plus the Polish brigade would have been inherently unlikely. Dempsey's decision to ask Monty for the inclusion of the two American airborne divisions—82nd and 101st, both of which had performed with distinction in Normandy—transformed an operation that looked increasingly impracticable into a much more serious operation of war with much greater chances of success. Besides, it was not in Browning's nature to speculate pessimistically. He had urged the immediate use of his airborne troops in any role, even as ground forces, lest morale suffer from the repeated cancellation of airborne operations. When he flew over from England to see Dempsey on 10 September, he was so anxious either to insist that 'Comet' be launched or, if not, that a new operation be mounted instantly in its stead, he left a simple list of code words with his staff which he would signal back from Dempsey's headquarters. Thus at 1300 hours on 10 September his cryptic message was broadcast: 'NEW'.[2]

[1] Oral History interview, MHI, Carlisle, Pennsylvania.

[2] 21st Army Group War Diaries (WO 205/692), PRO. Heads of Intelligence, Staff Duties, Air, Plans and Operations at 21 Army Group's Main Headquarters were ordered to assemble at 1830 hours on 10 September 'to discuss COMET II'. Ibid.

Even if Browning *had* felt the operation to be too ambitious, he was not a man to say so. As a Grenadier Guardsman, Browning had achieved an almost legendary reputation in the British army for discipline and decisiveness. He was not a man for discussion, and he detested the new commander of the First Allied Airborne Army, General Brereton, who had been promoted to command all Allied airborne troops without the remotest experience of airborne operations. Brereton was in Browning's view confused, weak-willed, and over-cautious. In August they had clashed to the point of Browning's actual resignation over the role and tactical employment of airborne troops, Brereton insisting that the primary responsibility of any air operation was that the first troops must secure landing zones for re-supply, while Browning favoured the immediate seizure of the targets while the enemy was stunned. Far more risky operations than 'Comet' had been proposed in the days and weeks after D-Day, and Browning had always been confident of his ability to carry them out—as his chief operations officer, Colonel Charles Mackenzie, later recalled when describing the almost suicidal projected airborne drop near Caen to help encircle the Panzer divisions locked there after D-Day:

> When the Caen project came up, 'Boy' Browning said to me, 'I want you to come with me to see General Dick O'Connor, the commander of 8 Corps.'
>
> We drove down in his MG and I remember quite clearly saying to him—for there were many snags—'General, how are you going to play this thing?'
>
> And he just sort of half-looked at me from the wheel and said, 'Charles—you just sit tight and hold your water; you'll see it'll turn out our way all right.'[1]

Browning prided himself on his Guardsman's stiff upper lip. He was always immaculately turned out, and it must be remembered that he was a frustrated man, not having, as yet, fought in North-west Europe—unlike Generals Ridgway, Gavin and Taylor, the American Airborne Corps and Divisional commanders.

Major-General Roy Urquhart, Commander of 1st British Airborne Division, had the highest admiration for Browning who, he felt, set the standard of all British airborne troops. Nor did Urquhart himself feel the operation was misguided. On the contrary, he later recollected the men were 'bored of training' and 'battle-hungry—longing to go'. He had established his own small Tactical Headquarters on Browning's doorstep at Moor Park so as to be able to plan operations the moment Browning gave orders, hand-in-glove with

[1] Interview with Brigadier Charles Mackenzie, 5.7.83.

Browning's staff. Far from sensing any concern about 'a bridge too far' there had been a concern that the war might end without the airborne forces being used at all.

> By the time we went on Market Garden we couldn't have cared less. I mean I really shouldn't admit that, but we really couldn't . . . we became callous. Every operation was planned to the best of our ability in every way. But we got so bored, and the troops were more bored than we were. . . . We had approached the state of mind when we weren't thinking as hard about the risks as we possibly had done earlier.
>
> What you've got to do is visualize the euphoria which existed across the Channel and in the Airborne Corps that the war was nearly over. It was regarded as nearly over and they felt that any new operations needed would be the final nudge to complete [German] defeat.[1]

Nevertheless, despite the euphoria, there were snags. The 'Comet' operation had been conceived originally as a night landing, with *coup de main* parties seizing the river crossings at Grave, Nijmegen and Arnhem. By the time Market Garden was to be launched, on 17 September, there was, however, no moon; moreover the American airmen, operating always by day, refused to contemplate a night assault. In any event, there were insufficient aircraft to drop all three divisions on the same night. It was thus agreed that Taylor's 101st Division—targeted on the canal crossings at Zon and Vegel—would be given full lift on D-Day, Gavin's 82nd Division—assaulting Grave and Nijmegen—half-lift, and Urquhart's 1st Division a third of its necessary lift. This was quite logical, since there would be little point in seizing the Arnhem crossing if Dempsey's ground forces were unable to get across the canals at Zon and Vegel, the Maas at Grave or the Waal at Nijmegen. 'It's no use my having all the aircraft and succeeding at Arnhem, if the Americans didn't get enough and failed down below—that would be writing off the whole operation, because they wouldn't get through and reach me,' Urquhart later explained. 'They had to make quite certain of achieving the target from south to north . . . So it stood to reason really that although my target was the most important of the lot it was no use being successful and the others failing.'[2]

Urquhart thus accepted the fewest aircraft and the need to drop in three lifts, over three days. It was a fateful decision he accepted in an Allied cause—just as Monty had accepted the need to drop two

[1] Interview with Maj-General R. E. Urquhart, 13.10.83.
[2] Ibid.

American airborne divisions on Bradley's First US Army flank for the Normandy landings—denying himself extra airborne help in seizing Caen, but guaranteeing a secure Allied bridgehead.

This decision was to have critical repercussions. Just as at Caen, the presence of German armour at Arnhem would thwart British ambitions. Yet whereas in Normandy Monty had been able to turn Rommel's concentration of armour on the British flank to Allied advantage, at Arnhem he would be impotent to exploit the fierce German resistance—for without control of the Allied armies he would not have sufficient forces to work his way around the German flank. Not only would Monty not have the tactical control over Hodges which Eisenhower promised; Patton's eastern thrust towards the Saar, encouraged by Eisenhower in a spirit of opportunism, had already over-extended the Allied front into a series of unco-ordinated Allied efforts, each liable to be contained by the enemy, each starved of reinforcements and re-supply.

The year before, as General Mark Clark's forces ground to a halt north of Naples, Monty had attempted a unilateral thrust across the Sangro, designed to break open the German Gustav Line and force the Germans to cede Rome. Such hopes had been dashed amid mud and rain and insurmountable German resistance. Though the Sangro was successfully crossed, the bridgehead proved difficult to expand and Eighth Army's isolated offensive had petered out in the snow and carnage of the hilltowns around Orsogna and Ortona.

Why then did Monty repeat this error at Arnhem?

Many books have been written about the 'epic' of Arnhem. Planning and operational mistakes have been—as in every failure—exhaustively analyzed and debated. Indeed one might say that few six-day battles in history have seen so much fighting after the event, between veterans, military critics and historians. If the presence of two refitting German armoured divisions had been properly taken into account in the planning, if radio communications had been better, if the landing grounds had been closer to Arnhem, if troops had been landed on both sides of the bridge, if close support by fighter-bombers from Belgium had been arranged, if the men of Horrocks' 30 Corps had only got up faster. . . .

Such speculations are the stuff of battle history. Many important historical lessons *were* learned—in fact Second Army and 21st Army Group were sponsoring reports on the lessons of the battle within days of its end: lessons which were soon assimilated and which affected the planning of all airborne operations conducted thereafter. As will be seen, Monty was himself among the first to hear 'from the horse's mouth' the course of the struggle at Arnhem. Yet the individual failings in the planning and execution of the battle ought not to blind us to the larger truth. For the revised carpet-air drop between Zon and Arnhem, as ordered on 10 September 1944, did not fail because of the unrecognized presence of German Panzer divisions, or poor radio communications, or bad operational planning, or lack of zeal among the ground formations. It failed because, as in the case of resistance on Patton's front at Metz and Hodges' front at Aachen, it was too late for a *unilateral* thrust to succeed on its own against stiffening German resistance. And with failure came the belated realization that, without the port of Brest, the Allies *must* open Antwerp before any further offensive could be undertaken—that it would have been better indeed not to have undertaken Arnhem at all.

PART TWO

Arnhem

CHAPTER ONE

The Darkening Operational Picture

HAD MONTY HAD the firmness to reassess the military situation in the final days before Arnhem; to recognize the consequences of growing German resistance, to cancel his ground force drive/airborne carpet and to insist on unified, co-ordinated field command before the Allies undertook further major operations into Germany, then the history of the Allied campaign in North-west Europe might have been very different—and Monty's place in the pantheon of great commanders more secure.

In this sense it may justly be said that Monty did not rise to the heights of military greatness he had shown in mounting the Normandy landings at a time when greatness was most needed. A part of him knew this, and the increasing succession of his signals 'hammering at it—until I go mad', urging Eisenhower to appoint a single Land Forces Commander who would 'grip the show' and ensure concentration of Allied endeavour based on cohesive tactical strategy, proves this. To his detractors, such signals demonstrate only Monty's vanity and insensitivity to the political reality of an Anglo-American coalition in which, increasingly, America was the dominant military partner; but to the biographer and historian they are the messages of a true soldier's despair—a soldier who in his heart of hearts sensed the coming misfortunes. Thus while Eisenhower, many hundreds of miles behind his fronts, began to send out wildly optimistic signals about the forthcoming 'rapid thrust to Berlin', Monty became more and more anxious. There was no possibility, he finally replied to Eisenhower's letter soliciting his views on the invasion of Germany and subsequent thrust to Berlin, of *all* the Allied armies moving forward into Germany; more than ever Eisenhower *must* decide on the axis of attack and subordinate all remaining forces to that attack. 'If you consider that . . . the proper axis of advance is by FRANKFURT and central Germany, then I suggest that 12 Army Group of three Armies would be used and would have all the maintenance. 21 Army Group would do the best it could with what was left over; or possibly the Second British Army would be wanted in a secondary role on the left flank of the movement,' he suggested on 18 September.[1]

[1] M526, Montgomery Papers.

To have formally offered Dempsey's Second British Army on the flank of an *American* thrust eastwards, south of the Moselle, is an illustration of Monty's sincere belief in the need for military concentration.

This letter, as Monty's previous signals and correspondence on the subject, was ignored by Eisenhower. It was, in any case, too late—for the previous morning two columns of aircraft the equivalent of three hundred and fifty miles long, protected by one thousand five hundred fighters, had made their way across the Channel and had swung northwards towards the Lower Rhine.

What made the Arnhem operation the more tragic was that Monty's own staff were largely against it. Monty's Chief of Operations, Brigadier Belchem, disliked the narrowness of the thrust to Arnhem, along the low, polder ground in which all advance was necessarily canalized by the Dutch waterways. Like Dempsey's own staff, Belchem would have preferred a thrust towards Wesel—if necessary without airborne forces if the airmen would not 'play'. Monty's Chief of Plans, Brigadier Richardson, did not even know of the revised Arnhem drop until several days *after* it had been agreed; his recommendation had *always* been for a concerted Allied drive through the Aachen gap, not through the lowlands of Holland, with their 'maze of inundatable areas' and 'numerous rivers'; Monty's Chief of Intelligence was disturbed by increasing indications that German Panzer divisions were refitting in the area—an area already known to have been put under the command of the German Parachute Army under General Student, conqueror of Crete. Colonel Poole, deputy Chief of Administration and Supplies, was worried by the lack of port capacity to nourish such a thrust. Finally, Monty's Chief of Staff, Freddie de Guingand, telephoned from his hospital bed in England to warn Monty that the combined effects of increasing enemy resistance and logistical dependence on the winning of more deep-water ports, made such a unilateral thrust a very doubtful proposition, even if it succeeded in reaching Arnhem.[1]

[1] De Guingand's views have often been misunderstood, e.g. in 'Eisenhower as Military Commander: Single Thrust Versus Broad Front', an essayistic summary drawn up for the final volume of *The Papers of Dwight David Eisenhower* by Stephen Ambrose in 1970. 'Even Montgomery's chief of staff disliked the single thrust,' Ambrose recorded. 'Francis de Guingand saw Eisenhower on a number of occasions in late August and early September, and made it clear that he did not think the plan would work.' This is untrue: de Guingand's doubts about the feasibility of a single thrust only began *after* Eisenhower failed to concert the Allied advance following the great battle in Normandy. With Eisenhower determined to link Patton's eastward drive with the Allied forces approaching Dijon, it was too late to mount a concentrated forty-divisional thrust to Berlin, and doubtful if a slimmed-down northern

Isolated at his forward Tactical Headquarters, however, Monty refused to listen to the exhortations of his Main headquarters staff. Even if Arnhem itself was not reached, the operation would help swing Second Army eastwards across the Rhine at Emmerich or even Wesel (as Second Army headquarters had originally intended), providing that sufficient bridging material could be got up. German reinforcements were bound to start arriving from Norway, Finland and Denmark unless the thrust could be mounted immediately; every day's delay gave the Germans more time to stabilize their defences.

Though with one hand Monty had consistently pointed to the need for an agreed Allied plan, a concentrated and overpowering Allied effort on a chosen axis, he had with his other arm silenced the doubters, overridden the objections of his Chief of Staff and invested the full resources both of his Second British Army and the Allied Airborne Army in a perilous undertaking which, though promising exceptional rewards if it succeeded, threatened to wreck the entire Allied offensive initiative if it failed.

Monty's slowness to appreciate the consequences of failure, indeed his slowness to recognize the failure itself, were extraordinary for such a professional general. Time and again since World War I Monty had laid down the cardinal responsibility of the field commander to put his troops into battle in such a way that they must succeed, irrespective of local reverses. In underestimating the difficulties facing Dempsey's Second Army Monty fell far below the standard he himself had set as a field general. His surviving signals and letters, moreover, testify to several days of a remarkable lack of realism which overtook him until his Chief of Staff returned from hospital at Aldershot. Thus on the night of Sunday, 17 September, he was confidently predicting to the CIGS that his forward ground troops would 'tomorrow get right through to Arnhem', once they had disposed of the crust of resistance around Valkensward, south of Eindhoven.[1] Moreover he himself intended to pitch camp hard upon the heels of his advancing spearhead—which, he hoped, might well be encircling the Ruhr by midweek:

---

thrust could succeed without absolute Allied priority in maintenance—itself impossible given Eisenhower's 'political' sensibilities: Sir Francis de Guingand, interview of 7.5.78. 'Personally I was never keen on this [Arnhem] operation as I considered that we had left it too late and would probably encounter bad weather and by the launching date the Germans would probably have reinforced this area,' de Guingand later recorded. 'Arnham' [sic], 9-page essay written in 1970s, Papers of Sir Denis Hamilton.

[1] M212, Montgomery Papers.

> I understand the King of GREECE wishes to come and visit me on Thursday [21 September] and stay the night. I regret that this will be quite impossible. The operation by that time will be very exciting and will require my whole attention and I have no idea where I shall be.[1]

The atmosphere at Monty's Tactical Headquarters was well reflected by Major Odgers, the officer in charge of the operations staff, in the brief chronicle he wrote shortly after the war:

> The speed of events ever since the crossing of the SEINE had given an almost unreal quality to life in which nothing now seemed impossible. This fantastic quality still persisted as the Dakotas and gliders roared ceaselessly overhead and reports came back of Eindhoven's capture and the great river bridges secured.[2]

On the night of 18 September, with news of the capture of Eindhoven, Monty still had no idea that his plan was in jeopardy—though a note of realism did begin to temper his signals:

> Guards Armoured Division have now joined up with the 101 Airborne Division who extend from EINDHOVEN as far north as VEGHEL. . . .
>
> This advance is being made on a single road and movement by wheeled and tracked vehicles off the road is extremely difficult owing to the low lying nature of the country which is intersected by ditches and dykes and which has been made very wet by the recent heavy rain.[3]

The rain in fact had sundered the planned second lift of troops and supplies to 1st Airborne and 82nd US Airborne Divisions. From the former there was, ominously no further news at all; from 82nd Airborne there was reassuring information that the crossing at Grave was in Allied hands, and the bridge at Nijmegen, though not yet captured, was intact. 'Operations are going well on the front of Second Army,' Monty over-confidently reported to Brooke—but given the fierce German resistance and the narrowness of the corridor Horrocks had achieved, it was too early to crow.

The following evening (19 September), as the Allied ground corridor penetrated as far as the Waal itself at Nijmegen and radio

[1] Ibid.
[2] 'A Tac Chronicle', communicated to author by Major Odgers.
[3] M213, Montgomery Papers.

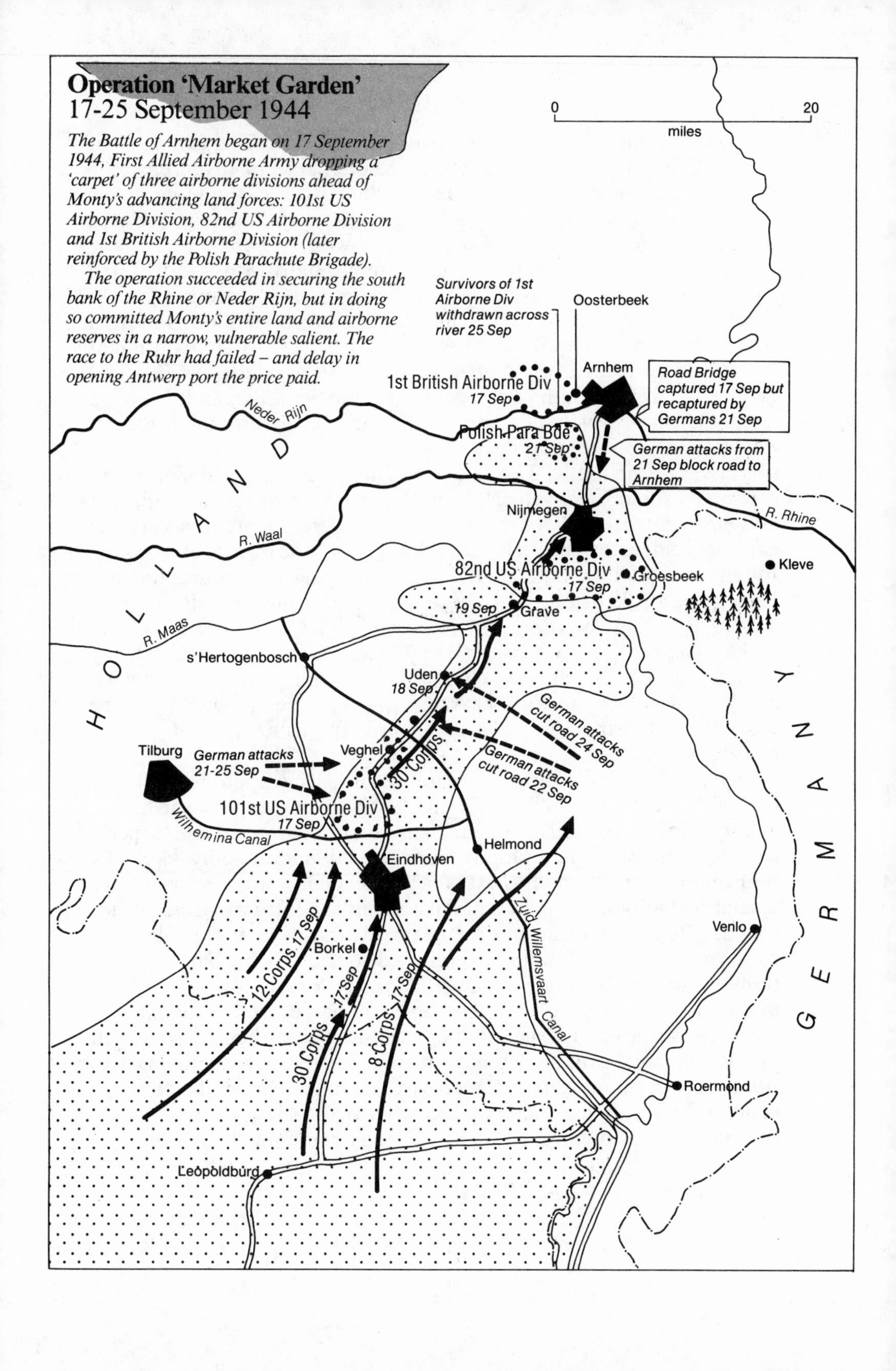

Operation 'Market Garden'
17-25 September 1944

The Battle of Arnhem began on 17 September 1944, First Allied Airborne Army dropping a 'carpet' of three airborne divisions ahead of Monty's advancing land forces: 101st US Airborne Division, 82nd US Airborne Division and 1st British Airborne Division (later reinforced by the Polish Parachute Brigade).

The operation succeeded in securing the south bank of the Rhine or Neder Rijn, but in doing so committed Monty's entire land and airborne reserves in a narrow, vulnerable salient. The race to the Ruhr had failed – and delay in opening Antwerp port the price paid.

contact was finally established with 1st Airborne Division west of Arnhem, Monty turned his attention to the flanks of his offensive—'Second Army is engaged in widening the corridor beginning at the south end and good progress is being made in this task by 8 Corps on the eastern flank and 12 Corps on the western flank.'[1]

Such progress was, however, increasingly hard-won—and by the fourth day of the offensive Monty's optimism regarding a break-through began to fade. True, his forces were across the southern fork of the Rhine, the Waal, after 82nd Airborne Division's brilliant capture of Nijmegen bridge; true, the Polish Parachute Brigade had dropped at Driel, south of the Neder Rijn at Arnhem, and it looked as though there was 'a good sporting chance of getting the bridge at ARNHEM'. But the bridges, however luring, were not the true objectives of the battle. The target remained the Ruhr; 30 Corps had assembled some 2,300 vehicles and some 9,000 engineers to transport and erect bridges if the airborne divisions were unable to secure the existing bridges intact. 'The corridor running northwards through Eindhoven is still a bit narrow and is not yet very secure and has been twice broken today by the enemy a few miles north of Eindhoven. But this situation will improve as 8 Corps and 12 Corps make progress northwards on the flanks of the corridor,' Monty assured the CIGS.[2] But would the two flanking corps make such progress? And if opposition at Arnhem was so great, would it not be wiser to start swinging eastwards towards the Ruhr without bothering about Arnhem?

Dempsey's diary at Second Army recorded his apparent satisfaction with the advance of his flanking Corps at this stage of the battle. Monty, writing to his son's guardians, again boasted of the 'superb' new portrait by James Gunn which would undoubtedly 'create a tremendous sensation at next year's Academy—to which I have agreed it shall go.' Despatching largesse in the form of Brussels lace for Mrs Reynolds, cigarettes for Major Reynolds, and chocolate for his own son David, Monty also referred to the way his 'latest operations' were 'developing very satisfactorily'. Yet at the back of his mind was the nagging fear that, even if he reached Arnhem, the resources sufficient to exploit the break-through into the promised thrust around the Ruhr would not materialize. 'My administrative situation is beginning to cause me some concern and the tonnage promised by rail has not so far been forthcoming,' he informed Brooke on 20 September.[3] He had already summoned Eisenhower's

[1] M216, Montgomery Papers.
[2] M219, Montgomery Papers.
[3] Ibid.

Chief Administrative Officer to come and see him; when Gale arrived on 21 September bearing Eisenhower's response to Monty's letter of 18 September, recommending that either the Saar *or* the Ruhr thrust be pursued, but not both, Monty's doubts became feverish. For Eisenhower was still referring to an Anglo-American drive to *Berlin*, to be mounted by Second British Army and First US Army, while insisting that Patton's Third US Army, reinforced by Simpson's Ninth US Army (from Brest), continue its Metz advance in order to *accompany* the Berlin drive. To Monty the soldier, this notion of a 250-mile-wide drive was anathema—and Eisenhower's attempt to reconcile such dispersal with Monty's calls for concentration seemed self-deluding.

> I cannot agree that our concepts are the same and I am sure you would wish me to be quite frank.

Monty signalled to the Supreme Commander's new headquarters at Versailles.

> I have always said stop the right and go on with the left but the right has been allowed to go on so far that it has outstripped its maintenance and we have lost flexibility. In your letter you still want to go on further with your right and you state in your para 6 that ALL of BRADLEY's Army Group will move forward sufficiently etc. I would say that the right flank of 12 Army Group should be given a very direct order to halt and if this order is not obeyed we shall get into further difficulties.

By 'further difficulties' Monty meant the rapidly darkening operational picture.

Far from enabling the Allies to drive on to Berlin, Monty warned, such dispersal would mean that the Allies would not now even get the Ruhr:

> The nett result in my opinion is that if you want to get the RUHR you will have to put every single thing into this left hook and stop everything else. It is my opinion that if this is NOT done then you will NOT get the RUHR,

Monty prophesied—although to soften the sting he signed himself 'Your very great friend MONTY.'[1]

To the signals officers encyphering and decyphering such messages after the great victory in Normandy, at a time when the Allies seemed poised to break through into Germany and end the war, such messages must have appeared very strange. Eisenhower's desk diarist

[1] M223, Montgomery Papers.

referred to the way 'messages still continue to pour in from Field-Marshal Montgomery', recording, sarcastically, Monty's 'latest prose effort'.[1]

Whatever idle tongues might impute, however, Monty was not arguing from vanity or megalomania, but from the alarming realization that not even the Ruhr would now be captured before winter—unless Eisenhower acted fast.

As it turned out, it was in any case already too late.

[1] Desk diary of C-in-C/Diary of Harry C. Butcher, entry of 21.9.44, loc. cit.

CHAPTER TWO

The Collapse of Monty's Ruhr Thrust

LEST THE WAR Office in London be in any doubt about the critical nature of the situation in North-west Europe, Monty had invited the Director of Military Operations to stay with him at his new Tactical Headquarters at the Château Everberg. Maj-General Simpson arrived there three days after the launching of operation 'Market Garden', and witnessed the tumultuous Dutch reception given to the British forces as they drove through Eindhoven.

But Monty, Simpson found, was far from happy about the future—and on Monty's behalf Simpson flew to Versailles. There he explained that, given the precarious development of such a unique ground-and-airborne operation towards Arnhem, there was no question of Monty's leaving the front to attend the SHAEF conference Eisenhower was convening for the afternoon of 22 September at Versailles; even if Monty managed to get away from his Tac HQ at Everberg, the deteriorating weather might prevent him returning to the front after the conference.

Eisenhower's Chief of Staff, Bedell Smith, appeared relieved to hear this.

> Bedell said: 'I am glad you have given me this message because we were feeling it very much that the Field-Marshal could not manage to come. Now we know the reasons. I will tell Ike at once what you have said,'

Simpson later recalled. Simpson then proceeded to explain Monty's views.

> I then went on to tell Bedell about how Monty viewed the operational situation.
>
> There were 150,000 Germans to the west of the British force and unlimited opportunity to the east, but that Monty would not be able to take full advantage of that opportunity unless all resources were put behind him.[1]

[1] 'We are up on the Rhine at NIJMEGEN now; but there is a lot to be done, and there are 100,000 Germans to the west of us who will have to be cleaned up': letter from Monty to the King's Private Secretary, 20.9.44, Royal Archives, Windsor.

> Bedell assured me that he quite understood and that Eisenhower understood also, and that they fully intended that all resources were to be put behind him. All that Eisenhower was concerned about was that Monty should not go straight off to Berlin on a narrow front.

Simpson was able to allay such fears instantly:

> I replied that while an advance to Berlin might come later, Monty's present intention was to capture the Ruhr. That was what Eisenhower had told him to do, and that is what SHAEF ought to give him the logistic resources for. Bedell repeated in a most emphatic way that Monty could rest quite assured that everything possible to support him in capturing the Ruhr would be done.

In fact Bedell Smith gave Simpson to understand that Eisenhower was now a changed man: that from that very afternoon (22 September) the Supreme Commander intended at last to assert himself as the Allied Ground Force Commander.

> He said quite openly that orders given to Bradley and Patton about conserving administrative resources had not been obeyed. In Bedell's words: 'The trouble is Ike, instead of giving direct and clear orders, dresses them up in polite language and that is why our senior American commanders take advantage. However Ike has given me full authority to make it quite clear to them today that they are to obey orders.'
>
> Bedell said that he had thought of asking me to the Army Commanders' Conference that afternoon, but again in his words, 'so much dirty linen is going to be washed there that it would be better if an outsider is not present'. The impression given was that Eisenhower intended to savage his senior commanders. Bedell assured me again that Eisenhower fully intended to support Monty's major thrust to the Ruhr and he, Bedell, was advising Eisenhower that the First US Army should be placed under command of Monty.

Such advice was later 'hushed' up. Yet, in Simpson's clear recollection, Bedell Smith was fully aware of the 'political' implications in giving Eisenhower such advice.

> He realised that that would not be palatable in the United States.
>
> Bedell then told me confidentially that when they were first discussing the command set-up a month previously, the President sent

the Secretary of State [Stimson] to see Ike and tell him that all Americans must be kept under Bradley's command. Bedell went on to say, 'I think Ike is quite prepared now to disobey this instruction and to put Hodges, of 1st American Army, under Monty. If it is the best way to get the Ruhr and thus win the war, the chips then fall as they will.'[1]

As Simpson understood Bedell Smith, both Eisenhower and his Chief of Staff were now prepared to risk dismissal if Roosevelt objected.

This momentous change of mind on the part of the Supreme Commander, as British and American forces battled their way across the Waal (a continuation of the Rhine) at Nijmegen, was as short-lived as it was sudden. Though Simpson sent word immediately to Monty about the 'grand' reversal of attitudes, Eisenhower balked at the task of actually transferring 1st US Army to Monty's command. 'I was adamant that U.S. troops be retained under U.S. command,' Bradley afterwards wrote;[2] and Eisenhower, in front of some twenty-two Allied generals and air-marshals on 22 September, could not bring himself to dictate a radical revision of policy that would humiliate Bradley and might appear as a bewildering change of mind on the part of the Supreme Commander.

The conference was nevertheless dominated by the eminence *in absentia* of Montgomery. Why had he not come himself, if a re-direction of the Allied effort was urgently required? Outside the conference room the ADCs had been betting whether Monty would arrive or not; no one seemed willing to wager he would. A dangerously vociferous inter-Allied rivalry was now in evidence, often fanned by unscrupulous staff officers and journalists with an inadequate understanding of either operational reality or high command. One such man was a 12th Army Group staff officer, Major Ralph Ingersoll, who was currently stalking the corridors of Versailles proclaiming to all that Monty was now attempting to do what he had done in Normandy, over the taking of Cherbourg—break out on the British flank while fobbing off the American forces with pointless subsidiary roles. As Bradley's ADC recorded:

Ritz Bar, Paris. Surprised to see great change in attitude among so many old Anglophiles. Ralph [Ingersoll] certain to do a book on it after the war, was enraged with the attitude of Brit. Told how Monty was referred to as 'The Master' and how the master prior

[1] General Sir Frank Simpson, Eugene Wason interview for Sir Denis Hamilton, loc. cit.

[2] O. N. Bradley, *A Soldier's Story*, New York 1951.

to our seizure of Cherbourg, had the thing cased, that they [the British] would smash through and destroy the German army at Caen but that Brad. would be obliged to take Cherbourg, simply as a matter of discipline. The latter beat me and Ralph scoffed deeply.[1]

That Hansen, who had been at Bradley's side all through the Normandy campaign, should have credited this travesty of the truth, was unfortunate; nevertheless, like the increasing German resistance now confronting the Allies all along the front, it was symptomatic of a profound and cruel change. The fact that Allies who had together inflicted the greatest military defeat of the entire war upon the Germans should now distrust and deride each other was an ill omen for the future of Europe after hostilities ceased. At Quebec the question of post-war military zones of occupation and the very future of the state of Germany were at issue; meanwhile at Versailles the senior Allied commanders tortured each other with their divergent views on the dénouement of those hostilities.

If Monty refused to leave his headquarters and attend the SHAEF meeting, it was undoubtedly because he could not abide Eisenhower's ineffectual conferences. Military operations should be pursued according to the relentless dictates of a decisive soldier, not the discordant voices of a twenty-two-man sanhedrin. In three days he, Monty, had heard out the views of the defeatist COSSAC planners in January 1944; whereupon he had given out his decision and set the Allied armies upon a fair course for victory in 'Overlord'. Eisenhower's endless conferences, thereafter, had only served to 'rock the boat', and to procrastinate for months upon 'Anvil'. Although Monty had the highest respect for Eisenhower's extraordinary balancing act as an impartial Supreme Allied Commander, his contempt for Eisenhower as a field commander was equally strong. Monty's refusal to attend was thus on the one hand a deliberate mark of disrespect; on the other it was an acknowledgement of his own failing as a 'committee-man'. Sentence by sentence he had written down what he wished to be said at the meeting; and had given the memorandum to de Guingand—who had only just returned from hospital—to deliver.

Meanwhile, after five days of deliberation, Bradley had himself answered Eisenhower's request for his views on the Allied thrust into Germany—and had accepted Monty's logic! The Ruhr, Bradley now agreed, *should* have priority as the Allies' primary target.

[1] Diary of Chester B. Hansen, loc. cit.

For a moment it looked as if, in agreeing to this *volte-face*, Bradley might accept the idea of a single ground commander for the Ruhr thrust. Lest Eisenhower imagine any such thing, however, Bradley introduced a new card into the pack. Instead of Second British Army and First US Army attacking the Ruhr in Monty's pincer movement, Bradley recommended to Eisenhower his own Ruhr scheme: a plan in which the portion of 12th Army Group currently battling towards the Saar would *also* swing northwards towards the Ruhr, via *Frankfurt*, thus doubling the Aachen pincer.

Bradley's turnabout was, from a strictly American standpoint, a master-stroke, concocted by his staff to take the wind out of Monty's sails; by recommending the involvement of three American armies (Simpson's imminent Ninth US Army, Patton's Third US Army as well as First US Army) in the thrust it would make it virtually impossible for Eisenhower to appoint Monty the overall commander.

Eisenhower was at first tempted to credit Bradley's new strategic reasoning, but Bedell Smith's clear and soldierly insight soon disillusioned him. Monty's call for concentration stemmed from the inescapable fact that there was insufficient logistical back-up for a drive into Germany on a 300-mile front between Arnhem and Frankfurt, even if it were to be directed in a treble-development of the Ruhr. Brest had finally fallen, but would not be usable probably before the end of the war; similarly, Antwerp, even when the Scheldt approaches had been captured, could not be opened overnight. If the Allies were to crack open the German defensive line before the Germans could 'dig in', they must do it instantly and with a concentration of all the resources and reserves at hand. Eisenhower therefore approved Monty's Ruhr proposals. First US Army Group was ordered to sidestep northwards and thus enable Dempsey's 8 Corps to start immediate offensive action eastwards from the Nijmegen corridor to the Rhine at Wesel. 'The task is to isolate and capture the RUHR,' Monty had summarized for de Guingand. 'The best way to do this is to take quick advantage of our favourable situation and deliver a strong left hook [around the Ruhr] with Second Army. First US Army should use its left wing in a holding role, so that Second Army can develop its full potential.' [1]

Although Monty's request that the Ruhr thrust be put under the command of one man was turned down in order to placate Bradley, de Guingand was delighted with the results of the conference. 'Excellent conference. IKE supported your plan one hundred per cent,'

[1] Montgomery Papers.

he signalled to Monty.[1] In his nightly telegram to the CIGS, Monty remarked: 'My communications with Eisenhower regarding the conduct of operations against the RUHR objective have borne good fruit and I think he is going to order what I have recommended.'[2] Eisenhower's orders were indeed given so as to stick this time: not only was Bradley given verbal orders at the conference, but Eisenhower followed them with a signalled directive to Bradley that could leave no shade of doubt that the Supreme Commander was now fully behind the northern thrust to the Ruhr.

> In order to implement the decisions taken at yesterday's conference I wish you immediately to arrange to meet Field Marshal Montgomery and agree on detail of operational plan, particularly for the First Army's part in the main effort in the present approved campaign against the RUHR. In accordance with the tactical plan agreed upon with the Field Marshal, you should direct Hodges to exert his main effort to meet the Field Marshal's developing requirements. . . .[3]

Eisenhower went on to say that, if the operational situation demanded, Monty was authorized to take 'any tactical action' with Hodges without consulting Bradley. Moreover Patton's operations at Metz were to be stopped: 'the remainder of 12th Army Group will take no more aggressive action than is permitted by the maintenance situation after the full requirements of the main effort have been met'.[4]

Bradley was crestfallen. All week he had refused to recant on the necessity for maintaining offensive effort in Patton's sector 'with possibility of an early breakthrough on the line'.[5] Eisenhower's new orders were a bitter pill—and Monty's reputation at Bradley's headquarters now plummeted further. '"The Master" is too big for the corduroy pants he wears,' was the way Bradley's ADC saw the position after the Versailles conference. After a night on the town, Hansen woke to find his own master despondent and exhausted. 'Found that Brad had not slept well and he is beginning to look tired. Disappointed with the results of the conf they had had.'[6]

[1] Ibid.
[2] M229. Ibid.
[3] FWD 15510, copy in Montgomery Papers.
[4] Ibid.
[5] Diary of Chester B. Hansen, loc. cit.
[6] Ibid.

Behind the humiliation of having to give way to the British field-marshal there was, however, a growing realization that the war, which had only days before seemed poised to enter its final chapter, would be unlikely now to end before 1945. 'It begins to look as though we may be faced with a winter campaign here on the line and this is precisely what we are trying to avoid.'[1] Until Antwerp was working there seemed no chance of an American drive into Germany—'this means necessary postponement of our plans to go busting into Germany'.[2] Indeed, not only was 12th US Army Group meeting increasingly stubborn enemy resistance, it was actually having to withdraw in places, owing to enemy counter-attacks. Without sufficient supplies coming up, Bradley had even had to agree to the transfer of an entire corps from Third US Army to the 6th Army Group of General Devers, who could maintain them from supplies coming through Marseilles.

From a purely American standpoint, therefore, it would have been wiser, in view of the logistical position, to do what Monty had done after the catastrophic gales that lashed the Normandy beach in the second week of the campaign: assume an aggressive-defensive posture while giving priority to the capture and opening of the port of Cherbourg—or in this instance the approaches to Antwerp. Had Bradley pressed for this, Eisenhower might well have listened; but with his field commanders all pressing for immediate exploitation into Germany, Eisenhower was too anxious to prove himself as the new Ground Forces C-in-C to play safe.

Eisenhower did certainly attempt to give the opening of Antwerp a high priority in Allied commitments. Yet he knew that if he insisted that Monty turn Second Army over to the task, in addition to the Canadian Army, any hopes of seizing the Ruhr in 1944 would be lost, since the Germans would thereby be given time to reinforce the Siegfried Line. Eisenhower's procrastination and preference for pragmatic advance on different fronts had wasted the fruits of Monty's Normandy victory and now, when it was too late, he was turning to Montgomery, hoping Monty might salvage the day. Bradley's more professional colleagues looked on with misgiving. 'We're putting a lot of money into an unprofitable stock on this movement,' Bradley's Chief of Staff, Lev Allen, was heard to say.[3]

Monty's victory, *in absentia*, was short-lived. In his personal letter to Monty recording the outcome of the conference, Eisenhower remarked that, given the logistical situation, Hodges' First US Army

[1] Ibid.
[2] Ibid.
[3] Ibid.

attack on the Ruhr from the south, via Aachen, might even 'have to be suspended, due to lack of strength, although its prosecution would fit in perfectly with your left hook'. In fact Eisenhower was aware that, in belatedly supporting Monty's Ruhr offensive, he was chancing his arm: 'Naturally you and I realise that our present bid for a big prize must be considered as rather bold when compared with our general maintenance situation. However, it is amply worth the risk.'[1]

But was it? Even as Eisenhower's conference dispersed, the race to the Ruhr was collapsing. To mount his promised Second Army hook across the Rhine at Wesel, Monty had intended to employ O'Connor's 8 Corps, currently holding the eastern flank of the Nijmegen 'corridor'. This sector was to be taken over in turn by Hodges' First US Army.[2] But already on 22 September the Germans had counter-attacked the corridor and cut the vital Vegel–Uden road upon which Horrocks' spearheading 30 Corps depended for supplies. Dempsey had thus been forced to send one of O'Connor's divisions to reinforce 101st US Airborne Division at Vegel—leaving 8 Corps with only two and a half divisions for the thrust to the Ruhr. By 23 September Monty was admitting to Brooke that 'on Second Army front things have been a little difficult during the last 24 hours as the enemy has been in occupation of certain parts of the road north of VEGHEL which has prevented supplies proceeding up to 30 Corps'.[3] Moreover he was aware of the perilous condition of 1st British Airborne Division, for Urquhart's Chief of Staff had managed to get over the Neder Rijn and had now reported the division's plight to Browning's staff in person. Although one brigade had been forced to surrender in Arnhem itself, the rest of the division held a bridgehead on the north bank of the Neder Rijn at Oosterbeck. To Brooke, therefore, Monty declared his aims as twofold: to cross the river with Horrocks' 30 Corps at Oosterbeck to reinforce Urquhart's bridgehead as if threatening to seize Arnhem; meanwhile to turn O'Connor's 8 Corps eastwards towards the Ruhr while the Germans dealt with Horrocks' Arnhem threat in the north.

By the time Bradley arrived at Monty's headquarters the next day (24 September), Monty was abandoning the plan to reinforce Urquhart's precarious bridgehead across the Neder Rijn. The Germans had again cut Horrocks' lines of communication at Vegel,

[1] Letter of 24.9.44. Handwritten original in Montgomery Papers.
[2] 'General Bradley to bring up two divisions as quickly as possible to take over the sector now held by 8th Corps': 'Minutes of meeting held in War Room at SHAEF FORWARD at 1430 hours, 22nd September 1944', Montgomery Papers.
[3] M229, Montgomery Papers.

and although a few hundred gallant Poles of the Polish Parachute Brigade had got across the river to reinforce Urquhart, the crossing was overlooked by German positions—'last night reinforcements from the Polish Para Bde were passed across the river but suffered considerable casualties in so doing as the river is swept by machine gun fire from both flanks', Monty sadly explained to Brooke. 'A further attempt is being made tonight to get an infantry brigade of 43 Div over the river but it is a very tricky business as we have not sufficient troops up there on a wide front. If we suffer heavy casualties tonight in trying to get across the Neder Rijn I shall probably give it up and withdraw 1 Airborne Div south of the river. This decision will be taken tomorrow morning. It may well be that we can attain our object equally well if not better by developing thrust lines eastwards and we shall have greater resources for these if we abandon the attempt to cross the NEDER RIJN west of ARNHEM.'[1]

Many writers on the subject of Arnhem have questioned why Monty, so strict in his insistence on remaining on the field of battle rather than attending SHAEF meetings way back in France, should have failed to visit General Horrocks during the epic battle for Arnhem, or to put personal 'ginger' into the forces struggling to relieve Urquhart. There can be no doubt that Monty *was* distracted by the plethora of messages and signals incurred by his dispute over strategy with Eisenhower; but the real reason why he did not personally go up to Nijmegen was straightforward. He sent his BGS (Plans) to visit the front personally and report back; for thirty-six hours Brigadier Richardson was cut off by the German counter-attack. Similarly, General Dempsey's Chief of Staff also flew up by air; his aircraft was shot down and he signalled to Dempsey on 22 September that Horrocks considered a bridgehead west of Arnhem 'will be difficult with present resources. . . . Was shot down today. Do NOT you fly tomorrow.'[2]

Given Horrocks' worrying signals all day on 22 September, Dempsey had had in fact no other recourse but to give O'Connor's 8 Corps the task of holding open Horrocks' L of C. Yet this was the very Corps intended to drive through to the Ruhr. Worse still, if Horrocks managed to cross the Neder Rijn and relieve 1st Airborne Division, he would need, as he signalled urgently on 23 September, a further infantry division 'for subsequent exploitation'—a division Dempsey simply did not have. The only reserve which could be fed

[1] M233 of 24.9.44, Montgomery Papers.

[2] 'Operations at Nijmegen, messages between 2nd Army and 30 Corps' file, the Papers of General Sir Miles Dempsey (WO 285/15), PRO.

in was 52nd Air-Landing Brigade—but Browning reported that Grave airfield could only take thirty-six aircraft per hour—and the division required some 2,000 lifts. At a moment when Browning needed vital air re-supply for his existing airborne forces, this was clearly impossible. Later that evening Browning found a clearing which could be made into an airfield. Dempsey approved—but the sands were running out. Strong enemy resistance on the west flank of the corridor was making the task of Dempsey's third Corps—Lt-General Ritchie's 12 Corps—as difficult as that of the other two. Whatever Monty might agree with Bradley about side-stepping Hodges' First US Army to relieve 8 Corps for a British thrust eastwards to the Ruhr, it was impossible for Dempsey to disengage O'Connor's divisions from the battle for such an offensive thrust until the corridor up to Nijmegen was secure. Bradley left after lunch—'we have arranged everything satisfactorily', Monty cabled to Brooke[1]—but by 5 p.m. Dempsey was again recording in his diary that the Nijmegen corridor had been cut between St Oedenrode and Vegel—an interdiction that this time was to last two critical days.

At 9 p.m. on 24 September, shortly after Bradley had returned to 12th US Army Group, Monty's Tac Headquarters received a despairing signal from Urquhart, still holding out in a small bridgehead north of the Neder Rijn. 'All ranks exhausted. Lack of rations, water, ammunition and weapons, with high officer casualty rate. . . .'[2] At 11 a.m. the next day therefore, when Dempsey met Monty at the headquarters of 50th Division, it was agreed that 1st Airborne Division would be withdrawn under cover of darkness that night.

To the CIGS Monty attempted to put on a brave face—'the fact that we shall not now have a crossing over the NEDER RIJN will not affect the operations eastwards against the RUHR. In fact by giving up that bridgehead we shall now be able to keep more within ourselves and be less stretched. I shall hold a very strong bridgehead across the RHINE at NIJMEGEN.'[3] But the real truth was that the so-called Rhine bridgehead had not only been achieved at the cost of almost an entire British airborne division; it had also provided 21st Army Group with a useless strip of low-lying land or island between the Waal and the Neder Rijn the seizing of which had used up the offensive capability of Second British Army. Though Monty would try to shift the overall blame for this onto Eisenhower in the months and years ahead, it was in truth his own doing. He had misjudged

[1] M233, Montgomery Papers.
[2] Copy communicated to author by Major Paul Odgers.
[3] M236, Montgomery Papers.

the enemy's powers of resistance. He, who had always taught the need for balanced dispositions in defence and attack, had mounted a major British thrust which so stretched the Allied line that not only did the thrust itself run out of steam, but the remainder of the Allied line also came near to breaking point.

Had this been all, it would have been a grave indictment of Monty's generalship. But there was worse still in the 'complaints book'. Had Monty managed to break through the German cordon and outflank the Ruhr by dint of the Allied airborne landings, his name would have gone down in history as a greater field commander than even Wellington. Such a victory might still have been possible early in September 1944, had Eisenhower backed such a thrust—for without the Ruhr it is doubtful if Germany could have prolonged the war into 1945. But in the much-altered situation in the second half of September 1944, Monty's bid for the Ruhr via Arnhem had proved nothing less than foolhardy. Like Patton's abortive attacks on Metz, it was an expensive squandering of men and matériel. Unlike Patton's vain offensive, however, Monty's Arnhem operation had always carried with it a penalty of incalculable significance to the Allied campaign in the west: Antwerp.

CHAPTER THREE

The Epic of Arnhem

THE ALLIES HAD clearly attempted to do too much, on too broad a front, in the wake of their historic victory in Normandy. Monty afterwards blamed Eisenhower—saying that Eisenhower's *volte-face* on 22 September had come 'too late. Enemy resistance had been given time to stiffen. We had lost administrative flexibility. The maintenance situation had got bad and we were now to pay the price.'[1] In reality it was Monty's own belated thrust to Arnhem which now sucked in the major offensive resources of the Allies—and thereby lost the Allies the initiative they had seized and so relentlessly wielded since D-Day. How near to victory Monty had come was proved by the German C-in-C's pessimistic message to Hitler on 24 September, requesting permission for a phased withdrawal of all German forces in Holland to the line of the Maas, Waal and subsequently the extended Siegfried Line. Von Rundstedt clearly appreciated that the Allies would now drive upon the north and south faces of the Ruhr, and recommended that all German Panzer reserves be withdrawn from the south to counter the threat.[2]

Hitler refused—ordering instead that von Rundstedt counter-attack and annihilate Montgomery's threat to the Ruhr via Nijmegen. To the astonishment of those who had been hurriedly making plans for the occupation of Germany and disarming of the German armed forces, there arose the spectacle of a beaten enemy rising up and assailing the victor.

If this was difficult for Allied military and civilian planners to believe, it was doubly so for the battlefield commanders who had mounted the great Allied offensive beginning on 17 September. The

[1] B. L. Montgomery, *Memoirs*, London 1958. For the tactical failure of 1st Airborne Division's landings at Arnhem Monty himself took the blame. As he wrote afterwards in a letter to the historian John North, 'It is quite clear that the Parachute Troops were dropped too far away from the bridge, and if say one Brigade had been dropped at the bridge itself, things might have been different. The Parachute people themselves wished it done that way, as they were frightened of ack-ack fire around the bridge itself. I ought not to have allowed it. As I was the Commander-in-Chief in that part of Europe, I must be responsible.' Letter of 3.10.58, copy in the papers of Sir Denis Hamilton.

[2] L. F. Ellis, *Victory in Normandy* Vol. II, London 1962.

decimation of 1st Airborne Division at Arnhem was still not appreciated as the turning of the Allied tide of victory. By containing the bulk of the 2nd Panzer Corps around Arnhem, Urquhart had enabled the Allies to seize Nijmegen, and although Monty's attention now shifted to an attack eastwards towards the Ruhr, General Horrocks was certain he could re-establish a bridgehead across the Neder Rijn west of Arnhem and mop up Holland by striking north towards Amsterdam and the Zuider Zee.

> After tonight's ops completed [retrieving the survivors of 1st Airborne Division from across the Neder Rijn]

Horrocks signalled to Dempsey at 7 p.m. on 25 September,

> great opportunties of developing vigorous offensive in NORTH and NORTH EAST direction when time is ripe. Gen axis of adv[ance] which is suitable in every way would be across NEDERRIJN–WAGENINGEN thence EDE and NORTH EAST to secure crossing over IJSSEL. Troops req[uire]d 43 DIV for crossing br[idge]h[ea]d, 52 DIV and GDS ARMD DIV for exploitation and subsequently one more DIV possibly 50 DIV to take over brhd and free 43 DIV. Have examined thrust to EAST crossing NEDERRIJN between ARNHEM and MILLINGHEN country and rds are so bad that this offers NO rpt NO prospect of success whatever. Hope to discuss future with you tomorrow afternoon if rd is open.[1]

Dempsey held this option open for several days; meanwhile on 25 September Monty was still so confident of soon being on German soil that he was writing to the Reynolds:

> The autumn weather is very wet and cold . . . I still live a caravan life in the fields but will very soon have to take to the villages in order to get the men under cover. I shall look forward to turning the German families out of the *best* houses—very quickly!!

Browning's attitude was similarly over-confident—and critical of the airborne troops' failure across the Neder Rijn. He sent in an adverse report on Sosabowski's performance commanding the Polish air drop at Driel, and when Urquhart, wet, cold and exhausted after nine continuous days of battle, was brought to his headquarters on the night of 26 September, Browning at first declined to see him, as Urquhart recalled:

> I got back to the river bank, over the river . . . and Browning's

[1] Papers of General Sir Miles Dempsey (WO 285/15), PRO.

> Military Assistant Harry Cator picked me up, and drove me back to Nijmegen. I was absolutely soaked, I mean, having . . . well, flogged too, because one hadn't appreciated till the next day how *mentally* flogged one was. I couldn't even think for a few days—it really was incredible how one couldn't even dictate a letter. One was absolutely mentally stymied.
>
> And so I got back to Browning's headquarters. Cator being a perfect aide said, 'Now, I'll get you a change of clothing and you can have a bath and lie down.'
>
> And I refused to, because I felt that I'd got to report to Browning—this was in the middle of the night, one or two o'clock in the morning. 'I must see Browning before I do anything,' I said. In any case I was rather keen that Browning could see me as I was, and not tidied up the next day! So I waited what seemed an age and finally Browning appeared, absolutely immaculate—he'd got up, quite obviously, dressed himself. And this I'd like to make quite clear because the film ['A Bridge Too Far'] was completely a misrepresentation. He appeared and I said to him, 'I don't think we did everything we should have done.'
>
> And I think Browning said, 'Well you did your best.' And after a bit he sent me off to bed.
>
> Now I repeat I've always had the greatest respect for Browning. I had the greatest respect then, I touched my hat in the proper way—and I still hold great respect for him. There was nothing acrimonious at all. And there was no question of him saying 'I think we went a bridge too far', as appears in the film. That was not said to me at any time, much less in the early hours of the morning.[1]

What was, in retrospect, surprising is that Browning asked Urquhart no questions, either as to the course of the battle or the current enemy strength. Nor did he ask Urquhart's views concerning Horrocks' idea of re-establishing a bridgehead and breaking out to the north and north-east of Arnhem. Instead, to Urquhart's amazement, he organized a dinner party at his Airborne Corps Headquarters mess for the following night, 26 September. Urquhart, exhausted and distressed by the bitter and bloody battle of Arnhem, found the subsequent evening shameful:

> Browning gave a dinner party in his mess, at which he invited Horrocks. And he produced a slap-up meal with chicken and also wine. And I remember hating the whole thing like hell, because one had got out of the way of eating. I didn't enjoy a minute of it. And I was very tired. . . .[2]

[1] Loc. cit.
[2] Ibid.

Browning's insensitivity to Urquhart's feelings as a defeated airborne commander mirrored the general insensitivity on the part of British commanders to the changed battlefield situation—that the days of great advances were over.

Urquhart's reception at Monty's Tactical Headquarters was very different on 27 September. Browning's lack of expressed interest in what had actually happened at Arnhem reflected the Grenadier Guardsman's notion of taciturn command on the one hand, social conventions on the other. But when Urquhart stepped out of his car at Eindhoven, where Monty had set up his new Tactical Headquarters, there was no icy reserve or immaculate turn-out to belittle the airborne commander. Instead he was greeted by Monty's twenty-three-year-old ADC, Captain Henderson, 'who was worried because two of Monty's pets—rabbits or squirrels or canaries—had escaped. At any rate I was well received and put in a caravan. And then I sat down outside Monty's caravan where there were a couple of chairs, and Monty came out and someone produced a map and I went through the battle with him.'[1]

If Monty was tactless in his badgering relationship with Eisenhower, and in his relations with American commanders in general, he was not so towards Urquhart. He wanted to know, from the horse's mouth, what had taken place from the moment the airborne division took off from England. He listened quietly and with that total attention that had once struck the Oxford don, Goronwy Rees, as the mark of a thinker:

> He always gave the impression that he had nothing in the world to do except the business which was in hand. There were never any papers on his desk, there were never any interruptions. . . . Most remarkable of all, to myself, was that he actually listened to what I said, gravely and politely . . . I began to think that the difference between him and other commanders I had known was that he actually *thought*, in the same sense as a scientist or a scholar thinks. . . .[2]

Monty asked Urquhart various questions—the questions of a fellow soldier, a father-confessor:

> Oh he was in a very good frame of mind, *sympathetic* frame of mind. There was no question of 'you bloody well failed', or anything of that kind. It was a sympathetic enquiry as to how I'd got on and roughly the sequence of events. It couldn't have been more

[1] Ibid.
[2] Goronwy Rees, *A Bundle of Sensations*, London 1960.

friendly—and he was keen to know as much detail as I could tell him. And he asked me a lot of questions.[1]

The meeting with Urquhart, who stayed the night with him, was salutary. The next morning, as Urquhart stretched his legs, Monty emerged from his caravan holding a piece of paper.

We had dinner in his mess. And I got up the next morning and was walking around, just sort of sniffing the air, recovering, when he came down the steps of his caravan with a bit of paper and said, 'I've written this. I wrote it in my own handwriting, and I've had it typed since. And I'm giving it to my Public Relations Officer to issue to the Press. I want you to have this.'[2]

Monty handed Urquhart the handwritten original of the statement. Urquhart 'put it into my pocket. I didn't read it at all, because I was leaving very shortly afterwards to go back to Brussels.'[3]

Later, on board the aircraft flying him back to England, Urquhart took out the statement. It was immensely moving:

TAC HEADQUARTERS
21 ARMY GROUP
28 September 1944

Major-Gen. R. E. Urquhart
Comd. 1 Airborne Division

1. I want to express to you personally, and to every officer and man in your Division, my appreciation of what you all did at ARNHEM for the Allied cause.
   I also want to express to you my own admiration, and the admiration of us all in 21 Army Group, for the magnificent fighting spirit that your Division displayed in battle against great odds on the north bank of the Lower Rhine in Holland.
2. There is no shadow of doubt that, had you failed, operations elsewhere would have been gravely compromised. You did not fail, and all is well elsewhere.
   I would like all Britain to know that in your final message from the ARNHEM area you said:
   'All will be ordered to break out rather than surrender. We have attempted our best, and we will continue to do our best as long as possible.'
   And all Britain will say to you:

[1] Interview with Maj-General R. E. Urquhart, loc. cit.
[2] Ibid.
[3] Ibid.

'You did your best; you all did your duty; and we are proud of you.'

3. In the annals of the British Army there are many glorious deeds. In our Army we have always drawn great strength and inspiration from past traditions, and endeavoured to live up to the high standards of those who have gone before.
   But there can be few episodes more glorious than the epic of ARNHEM, and those that follow after will find it hard to live up to the standards that you have set.
4. So long as we have in the armies of the British Empire officers and men who will do as you have done, then we can indeed look forward with complete confidence to the future. In years to come it will be a great thing for a man to be able to say:
   'I fought at ARNHEM.'
5. Please give my best wishes, and my grateful thanks, to every officer and man in your Division.

B. L. Montgomery
Field Marshal,
In The Field C.-in-C., 21 Army Group.

Cynics would say that here was evidence of Monty's mastery of public relations, but General Urquhart did not agree. Urquhart, veteran of El Alamein, of Tripoli, Medenine, Mareth, Wadi Akarit, of Sicily and Italy—where in an assault landing at Rizo he had encountered the most vicious fighting of the war and been subsequently decorated by Montgomery with a second DSO—knew the difference between bombast and sincerity. Browning had asked nothing; Monty had wanted to know all. That Monty should, after retiring after dinner, have written out a message which he, Urquhart, could show his 2000 survivors, a message the men could be proud of, was simply a manifestation of Monty's grasp of one of the many yet vital qualities of generalship—a quality that made Urquhart not only proud of what he had attempted at Arnhem, but, even forty years later, convinced that, even if he had known all that emerged later—such as the presence of German Panzer divisions—he would still have done the same.

I did not know about those armoured divisions at Arnhem, when I took off,

Urquhart insisted.

I also thank God I didn't!

My briefing from General Browning was that opposition might be a weak brigade group with some tanks—those were his very words, 'a few tanks'. There was no mention of any armour refitting in that area.

And if I had known? I don't know—at that late stage. . . . Everything was in train. This operation had been planned in a hectic way over six days. The machine was moving and unless you called the whole bloody thing off, you couldn't alter details at that stage. You either went in or you didn't. . . . Don't forget that our gliders with our guns and things like that are loaded four days, three or four days before we take off—rather like sending your luggage ahead!

There were no more anti-tank guns—we used every one there was—all we could have done was to warn our own people of this possibility [of enemy armour] so that they were forewarned. There was certainly no bad feeling about not knowing. To start with, everyone was keen to go, irrespective of the consequences, because they were so bored with popping in and out of aircraft and transit camps. They'd reached the state of mind—'we must go'—and they wouldn't have been put off easily.

And secondly in airborne forces you expect the unexpected the whole time—that's part of your make-up, I think.

And thirdly, I don't think, bar odd individuals, that may be, but on the whole a majority felt: we took a reasonable chance.[1]

Urquhart's loyalty and his trust in Monty's sincerity was not misplaced. Unknown to Urquhart, Monty had, after writing out his message to the division, written privately to Brooke:

My dear CIGS

I am sending home to England tomorrow Urquhart who commands the First Airborne Division. He has been staying with me since his withdrawal from ARNHEM, and has given me the whole story; I am sure you would be very interested to hear it. . . .

Of the senior officers in the Division, the only ones who have returned are the Divisional Commander (Urquhart), one brigadier (Hicks), and the CRA (Loder-Symonds). All the battalion commanders have been lost except one.

The following numbers of officers and men have been got back:

125 officers
400 glider pilots
About 1700 O[ther] R[ank]s

The Division has had a very hard time, and after talking with Urquhart I am quite certain that the men should not be employed in battle again for two or three months. They require some leave

[1] Ibid.

and then a good period of training so that they can recover from the great strain they have been through. . . . Urquhart himself is perfectly all right; he is a completely imperturbable person and has not suffered in the least from the very trying experience he has had.

Brigadier Hicks is aged 49. When I saw the Division in England I told Urquhart that I thought Hicks was too old for this sort of thing, but he wanted to keep him. . . . There is no doubt that Hicks did extremely well at Arnhem, but there is also no doubt that it has been too much for him and he is not now fit to fight again in battle in this war . . . He has done great work and I would ask that he should be considered for command of an area in England or overseas in the rank of Brigadier. He is a very good organiser and disciplinarian. He will definitely require a good rest in England first.

The personnel of the Division are all being returned to England in returning aircraft during the next two or three days. I think it is important that they should all be collected in some suitable centre where they can be 'caught hold of' again, checked over and generally looked after before they are sent on leave. I suggest that Urquhart himself, with Hicks to help him, should do all this. It would be a great thing for them if you yourself, or the Secretary of State, could go down there and see them all and give them a good pat on the back.

This was the side of Montgomery which those who did not like him utterly failed to acknowledge—the *paterfamilias* who looked upon all those who served under him as members of his family—members for whose welfare he felt responsible even after they were to leave him. This was as true of Monty in defeat as in victory, and in this respect, as in so many others, he had few equals. That an Army Group Commander, responsible for almost a million troops in battle, should have shown such genuine concern for his men, collectively and individually, is at bottom the key to an understanding of the unique loyalty Monty inspired, despite all the quirks of his vanity.

'A good many of the Division have been taken prisoner,' Monty continued his letter to Brooke—and begged that, as a special exception, 'a definite number of decorations are to be set aside for officers and men of the Division who are now prisoner.' If the Division had to be disbanded for lack of reinforcing officers and men, he asked that they be absorbed into the 6th Airborne Division—which could be renamed the '1/6th Airborne Division'.

> As regards Urquhart, I know him very well and he is quite first-class. He would command an infantry division excellently. He would also be very good for the job of Deputy Commander of the Airborne Army should Browning be required elsewhere.[1]

Browning himself could replace General Sir Richard O'Connor as commander of 8 Corps. Monty's affection and respect for O'Connor were profound, but the experience of capture and imprisonment in Italy from 1941 to 1943 had taken its toll, and O'Connor was often only a ghost of his former self. If 8 Corps was to spearhead the new thrust eastwards across the Rhine, it required a new commander who would galvanize the divisions to strike offensively. In the meantime, the fate of 1st Airborne Division and the bitter fighting still going on to widen the Nijmegen corridor had forced Monty to postpone such a thrust. 'There will have to be a pause to build up stocks before I can launch the next phase, and as far as I can see at present this pause will be for about ten days,'[2] he warned. As his MA confided to the King's Private Secretary, Monty 'regretted not having been able to put it [the Arnhem operation] on a fortnight earlier as he had originally intended, when the weather was much more favourable, and when he thinks he could have "bounced" the Germans right across the Rhine. He is now faced by what he calls a killing battle, which may last some time.'[3]

General Student, in a statement after the war, considered the 'Market Garden' operation to have 'proved to be a great success. At one stroke it brought the British 2nd Army into the possession of vital bridges and valuable territory. The conquest of the Nijmegen area meant the creation of a good jumping board for the offensive which contributed to the end of the war.' Student was expressing the professional admiration of an airborne commander—'those who had planned and inaugurated with complete success the first airborne operations of military history, had not now even thought of such a possible action by the enemy . . . the Allied Airborne action completely surprised us. The operation hit my army nearly in the centre and split it into two parts. . . . In spite of all precautions, all bridges fell intact into the hands of the Allied airborne forces—another proof of the paralysing effect of surprise by airborne forces!'[4]

[1] Letter of 28.9.44. Signed copy in 'Arnhem' file, Montgomery Papers.
[2] Ibid.
[3] Memo from Sir Alan Lascelles to King George VI, 30.9.44 (GVI/PS/7214), Royal Archives, Windsor.
[4] Kurt Student statement, supplied by Basil Liddell Hart in 1949, in 'Arnhem' file, Montgomery Papers.

Such praise, however, could not conceal the fact that, with the lucky discovery of the entire Allied plan of manoeuvre on the body of an American parachute officer, Student had been able, with his C-in-C Field Marshal Model, to mastermind one of the finest defensive battles of the war, containing the Allied bridgehead at Arnhem and subjecting the Allied lines of communication—the 'wasp's waist' as he called it—to a series of such virulent and often successful attacks that Monty's entire Second Army was sucked into the fighting, leaving nothing with which to mount the *real* offensive task behind the operation—namely the thrust towards the Ruhr. Even the less ambitious fruits of a break-through were rendered impossible by Student's amazing recovery. On 17 September, as the Allied airborne army flew across the Channel towards the dropping zones, Monty's Chief of Plans, Brigadier Richardson, had put up a plan to seize either Amsterdam or Rotterdam via Utrecht, which de Guingand discussed with Monty the next day—'I discussed this with C-in-C who has taken note but is not prepared to issue anything at present.'[1] Yet by 25 September, when Monty approved orders for the withdrawal of 1st Airborne Division from Arnhem, even this limited prospect looked doubtful.

Brigadier Williams, Monty's Chief of Intelligence, was quite certain from Ultra intercepts that tactical and even strategic surprise were now past; that the enemy had appreciated the importance of the northern pincer threat to the Ruhr and would do everything in his power to contain it: 'There is no doubt that Second Army is receiving and will receive this priority [in enemy reinforcements]. The threat to turn the Siegfried Line, to nullify the defensive value of the Rhine and thus eventually to outflank the Ruhr must be given first priority. You will know that two more divisions have come in already . . . and that Hitler has ordered the refitting S.S. Pz. Divs to come in as battlegroups to the same sector.'[2] From General Graham, the chief administrative officer, Williams understood there would have to be a pause at the end of the Arnhem battle. 'During this time the enemy will again form a crust, this time perhaps a stronger one, against us and we shall have a proper battle, preparations for which may even lengthen the administrative pause,' he recorded gloomily, 'unless we can alter this priority in the enemy's mind.'[3]

But how deceive the Germans? How 'take the enemy's eye off the northern ball'? Would a feint to make it appear that 21st Army Group was first going to clear up Holland succeed in weakening the

[1] 21st Army Group War Diaries (WO 205/693), PRO.
[2] Appreciation of 25.9.44, Montgomery Papers.
[3] Ibid.

Ruhr front enough for an attack there to break through? Or should the Americans start first with an offensive south of the Ruhr 'to draw off a proportion of the enemy strength'?[1]

With Horrocks urging another attack across the Lower Rhine, and Dempsey preparing a Ruhr thrust south-eastwards from the flank of 8 Corps, Monty held open his options, pending a build-up of supplies and reinforcements. Yet as Williams had forewarned, with every day's delay the enemy's crust grew harder, and the build-up required for a break-through consequently necessitated an even longer pause. By 30 September Williams was referring to the same enemy tactics as in the Normandy bocage: 'it is a return to the old game in Normandy: an attempt to extract the Panzers from their positional role to form a counter-attacking force.'[2] In Normandy Monty had succeeded in tying down the German armour on Dempsey's eastern flank so that Bradley's First US Army could seize Cherbourg and then thrust south to Brittany and subsequently eastwards to Paris. But without cohesive Allied command in Belgium and Holland, could the same successful Allied strategy be applied? 'The enemy will try an aggressive policy against the fist of our salient until 1 US Army's actual thrust to Köln-Bonn hurts him more than 2 Brit Army's potential threat,' Williams concluded.[3]

The Allied situation was, however, vastly different from that of Normandy. The troops were tiring, casualties had removed many of the best officers and men; the lines of transport and communication were much longer, the heavy air forces had been removed from Eisenhower's command. Eisenhower himself had taken over personal field command of ground forces; above all, the front was now 450 miles long from Arnhem to the Swiss border. Bradley had not originally favoured Monty's northern pincer around the Ruhr, and had resisted all blandishments relating to the appointment of a single Allied commander to conduct the Ruhr thrust.

Hour by hour, as Hitler now ordered up 2nd and 116th Panzer Divisions as well as more infantry to the Nijmegen bridgehead, Monty's room for manoeuvre decreased. Hour by hour, just as the 1st Airborne Division had been surrounded and threatened with annihilation, the candle Monty had lit by his bold thrust through Holland was extinguished by the blast of German artillery, mortars, machine-gun fire and even air attack. From fighting for a foothold on the Ruhr or even Amsterdam, Monty now found himself fighting for his life, as he sought to retain the very bridgehead up to Nijmegen

[1] Ibid.
[2] Appreciation of 30.9.44, Montgomery Papers.
[3] Ibid.

he had so dramatically established. Huffing and puffing he had, in his M527 21st Army Group directive, threatened to blow down Hitler's house by a converging Second British Army/First US Army attack upon the Ruhr. But with his own jumping-off area now under heavy German attack and with First US Army failing to make any headway in its southern pincer attack towards Aachen, the British threat began to ring very thin.

CHAPTER FOUR

Antwerp

WITH THE GERMANS reacting so violently to the Nijmegen bridgehead, Monty's attention now shifted to First US Army on his right. It was time, he felt, that advantage be taken of German preoccupation with Nijmegen; Nijmegen would now become the Caen of the battle for Germany. But, although two divisions had been transferred from Patton's Third US Army to Hodges' First US Army, Hodges' southern pincer attack failed to make progress. The American generals blamed logistics, and the need to open Antwerp if a real offensive was to be mounted; Monty blamed the command structure which made it impossible for the Allies to co-ordinate, concentrate and develop their operations. With an enemy as professional as the Germans, Monty felt, it was imperative that the Allies be even more professional. To the chagrin of the Americans and even his own British staff, Monty now revived his campaign for single command of the Ruhr thrust—a campaign that was to bring the whole military alliance between Britain and America in the field to the brink of collapse, incurring a quality of inter-Allied antagonism that still smoulders forty years on.

Monty's campaign was indeed impolitic, given the dwindling resources Britain could provide for the war in North-west Europe. Early in September Monty was asked to provide an Army HQ for Mountbatten's campaign in Burma; then to send two divisions to Burma; then to surrender his only airborne reserve, the 52nd Division; and finally to provide a Corps HQ for Burma. Monty had already had to disband the 59th Division towards the end of the Normandy battle; he would soon have to disband the 50th Division for lack of reinforcements. So threatened had the Nijmegen bridgehead become that instead of allowing the Canadian Army to devote its full effort to the capture of the Antwerp approaches, Monty laid down that its right-hand Corps was to reinforce the left flank of Dempsey's corridor, up to s'Hertogenbosch. In view of all this, it did appear to most Americans that the tail was indeed trying to wag the dog, and Monty's reputation as an arrogant, opinionated and self-serving 'Brit' rapidly began to outweigh the admiration he had inspired before and after D-Day.

No biographer can exonerate Monty in this respect. He was his own worst enemy, incapable of understanding that the days of Anglo-American quasi-equality were over—that Britain was now a junior partner in the military alliance in Europe, and that junior partners must know their place. It was in fact Monty's failure to 'know his place' throughout the autumn and winter of 1944 that upset Americans—and the great German counter-offensive that smashed through Bradley's 12th Army Group in December, though it proved Monty's point militarily, would only add insult to injury. To suffer a braggart was one thing; to see him proved right was doubly galling.

From a purely military point of view, Monty was quite justified in seeking the establishment of a single commander to be responsible for operations north of the Ardennes; but equally, from a military point of view, he refused to recognize that Eisenhower's 'broad-front' strategy of employing three army groups in line from Holland to Switzerland made the opening of Antwerp a matter of critical importance to the Americans. Time after time Monty had paid lip-service to the necessity of capturing the approaches to Antwerp, from early September; but in actuality he failed to provide the ground forces to effect this quickly—thereby allowing more than 60,000 troops of von Zangen's Fifteenth German Army to escape from encirclement across the Scheldt, as well as delaying the opening of the port. In his *Memoirs* Monty accepted the blame for not ensuring the quick opening of Antwerp—'I must admit a bad mistake on my part—I underestimated the difficulties of opening up the approaches to Antwerp . . . I reckoned the Canadian Army could do it *while* we were going for the Ruhr. I was wrong.'[1] Monty's Chief of Staff also later accepted part of the blame—'I suppose we did not realise what a difficult job it would turn out to be to clear the Scheldt, so probably I can take some blame for not pressing the issue more strongly';[2] but these 'confessions' were made long after the war. At the time, Monty brooked no criticism of his slowness in seizing the Scheldt approaches, and clung to his vision of co-ordinated field command of assault upon the Ruhr as obstinately as a dog to a trouser leg. The stage was rapidly being set for a confrontation between Eisenhower, the Allied Land Forces C-in-C and the C-in-C Army Group of the North.

Eisenhower, sensing that his strategy was now seriously awry, convened a new conference of commanders for 5 October at Versailles. This time Monty did not dare stay away, for Eisenhower's

[1] Op. cit.
[2] Maj-General Sir Francis de Guingand, answers to questionnaire from author, 1978.

request that he attend was accompanied by a piece of information Monty could not ignore: 'Chief of Imperial Staff will also be present.'[1]

Field-Marshal Sir Alan Brooke's presence made Monty's appearance mandatory—Brooke being perhaps the only man in his whole life whom Monty feared. But when Monty attended the conference, it bore out all his prejudices about such gatherings. Nothing new was decided. Each commander presented the situation as he saw it; and when Admiral Ramsay got up to give the naval point of view, Monty was forced to endure open criticism for not having yet cleared the approaches to Antwerp. As Admiral Sir Bertram Ramsay recorded in his diary:

> *5 October*
> Attended High Level C-in-C meeting at S[upreme] HQ. Ike, CIGS, Tedder, self, L-M [Leigh-Mallory], Bradley and Devers. Very interesting exposition of situation on Army Group fronts. Monty made startling announcement that we could take the Ruhr without Antwerp. This afforded me the cue I needed to lambast him for not having made the capture of Antwerp the immediate objective at highest priority and let fly with all my guns at the faulty strategy we had allowed. Our large forces were now practically grounded for lack of supply and had we now got Antwerp and the rest of the [Scheldt] Corridor we should be in a far better position for launching the knock-out blow . . . 1st Army have withdrawn six divisions ready to launch attack to the Rhine with British 2nd Army on 12 October. I got approving looks from Tedder and Bedell-Smith and both of them together with CIGS told me after the meeting that I had spoken their thoughts and it was high time that someone expressed them.[2]

Ramsay was quite correct about the CIGS, Sir Alan Brooke. In his own diary Brooke was equally forthright. Though about to fly to Moscow with Churchill, Brooke had deemed it imperative first to have a word with Eisenhower and Monty; he had stayed the night with Eisenhower in Versailles, and the conference of commanders at 11.30 a.m. the next day confirmed Brooke's growing pessimism about chances of ending the campaign that year:

> Ike ran the conference very well. It consisted first of all of statements by Army Group Commanders, followed by Air and Navy. Ike then explained his future strategy which consisted of the

[1] FWD 16749, Montgomery Papers.

[2] Extracts from diary of Naval C-in-C, Admiral Sir Bertram Ramsay (CAB 106/1124), PRO.

capture of Antwerp, an advance to the Rhine in the north and south, forcing the Rhine north and south of the Ruhr, followed by an advance to Berlin either from Ruhr or from Frankfurt, depending on which proved most promising. Meanwhile Devers in the south to threaten Munich as a cover plan. During the whole discussion one fact stood out clearly, that [access to] Antwerp must be captured with the least possible delay.

I feel that Monty's strategy for once is at fault. Instead of carrying out the advance on Arnhem he ought to have made certain of Antwerp in the first place. Ramsay brought this out well in the discussion and criticized Monty freely. Ike nobly took all blame on himself as he had approved Monty's suggestion to operate on Arnhem. The atmosphere was friendly.[1]

After lunch, Brooke flew back to England and Monty to Eindhoven. Brooke's and Ramsay's criticisms certainly bore fruit, for the next day (6 October) Monty drove to the Canadian Army's headquarters to check up in person the plans for securing Antwerp's approaches. These operations had already been given first priority for the Canadian Army—but only second priority, administratively, within 21st Army Group, after Second Army's planned thrust towards the Ruhr. Meeting General Simonds that morning (Monty had sent General Crerar back to England on 27 September for medical treatment)[2] Monty obstinately refused to alter this allocation of priority. Whatever rear-headquarters staff officers might say, whatever naval commanders might feel, he, Monty, was the Army Group Commander in the North, with unrivalled experience of large-scale operations in the field against the German armies. All his Intelligence and all his military intuition since the unfolding of his great Normandy design had pointed to the need for swift exploitation of German confusion and disorder. Latest Intelligence revealed that, in the past month, the Germans had moved no fewer than '17 [nominal] Infantry Divisions, 9 Panzer Brigades and 14 G.A.F. [Luftwaffe] Battlions' to western Germany—resulting in a 'total actual strength on the Western Front' of 'the equivalent of 17 Infantry Divisions and 7 Panzer Divisions, with perhaps 500 tanks'.[3] With 'rather more than 50 Divisions in the line', Allied superiority was still pronounced—but was decreasing each day. It was small

[1] Quoted in Arthur Bryant, *Triumph and Tragedy*, London 1959.

[2] 'Regret to inform you that CRERAR is not at all well and is suffering from some form of anaemia and internal troubles. I am sending him home tomorrow for thorough examination and treatment': M237 of 26.8.44, signal to CIGS, Montgomery Papers.

[3] Desk diary of C-in-C/Diary of Harry C. Butcher, loc. cit.

wonder that Allied attention was now nervously shifting to Antwerp—but Monty was loth to admit the Allies had failed. At the beginning of September it was estimated that German strength was a bare *third* of that which it might be able to employ, in the field, by late October. How *could* the Allies have thrown away such a God-sent opportunity—and how dared they blame him, when Antwerp could *never* have been operational before late October, even if he had directed his entire Army Group to the capture of the Scheldt estuary!

Patton, too, had raged at Eisenhower's failure to decide upon a single, concentrated thrust across the Rhine at the end of the battle of Normandy. In fact it was Patton who urged Bradley to resign rather than permit Eisenhower to place American armies once more under Monty's command. Yet when confronted by Eisenhower's decision to favour the Ruhr thrust, Patton had declined to obey, and the casualties suffered by Third US Army in its vain bid to capture Metz were, to all intents and purposes, criminal in their waste of brave American lives. 'Anyone else would probably be fired for such an attitude,' Bradley's ADC had noted in his diary when Monty failed to attend Eisenhower's conference at Versailles on 22 September;[1] but Patton's patent disregard of Eisenhower's and Bradley's orders in the ensuing days had resulted in casualties which—though never published then or since—actually exceeded those suffered in the abortive Allied thrust to Arnhem. An average of more than a *thousand* casualties *per day* were recorded in Third US Army—and Patton's thrust showed no sign of succeeding. Patton flew to Paris to protest against the transfer of one of his Corps to 6th Army Group for maintenance reasons, and battled on futilely against the old forts around Metz like an early medieval crusader, regardless of losses or even the physical and medical welfare of his men. By the end of September the number of troops reporting sick in Third US Army was almost the same as those killed or wounded in battle[2]—and still Patton refused to halt. Early in October he ordered his 20 US Corps to occupy Fort Driant 'if it took every man in the Corps'. Fort Driant was not taken.

Such mindless blood-letting sickened Monty. As he once later remarked, 'Patton could ruin your battle in an afternoon'[3]—though no field general was better in pursuit tactics. Having ordered Simonds on 6 October to continue his operations to capture the Scheldt ap-

[1] Diary of Chester B. Hansen, loc. cit.

[2] See casualty returns from Third US Army in the Diary of Chester B. Hansen, loc. cit. Casualties for September in Third US Army exceeded 30,000.

[3] To Sir Ian Jacob, later recounted by Lt-Gen Jacob to author.

proaches simultaneously with Second Army's preparations for a renewed Ruhr offensive, Monty returned to his caravan at Eindhoven. There he found discouraging news from Dempsey, who had been to see Hodges at First US Army HQ—'a dismal picture' as Monty signalled to Eisenhower at 7.45 p.m.:

> First US Army is apparently unable to develop its operations properly because it has not got the necessary ammunition. This does not promise well for the success of our plans. Hodges' own view is that if he had the ammunition and the troops he could go through to the RHINE easily. I considered I had better report this matter to you.

Eisenhower cabled back instantly. 'Thank you very much for your M260. Will put steam behind it at once.' Monty meanwhile summoned Bradley and Hodges—'very grateful if you and HODGES could come and see me tomorrow Sunday. Will stay in all day so that you can choose your own time'—on 7 October;[1] but already he was having doubts about the wisdom of the Ruhr offensive planned to begin on 12 October—for at 10.30 a.m. he had visited Dempsey's Tac Headquarters. Dempsey told him that he could not attack the Ruhr with O'Connor's 8 Corps until the ground on his right, between the corridor to Nijmegen and the Meuse, was clear; and that the 7th US Armoured Division could not do this alone. He had in fact ordered 8 Corps to take over from 7th US Armoured Division and to suspend its forthcoming assault to the Rhine. Monty had to agree. Thus at 7.40 p.m. on 7 October Monty signalled to Eisenhower that Second Army's attack was to be postponed. 'I had hoped that First US Army would clear the country west of the MEUSE but it appears to be too much for 7 US Armd Div. I must therefore do it myself.'[2]

It was in this context that Monty's frustration with the way operations were being managed began to erupt. There was no directing mind behind the Allied efforts to seize the Ruhr: the Allied advance was disjointed, the initiative was being squandered, and Army commanders were having to dance to the enemy's tune—as was the case with Dempsey and the west bank of the Meuse.

> The operations of Second Army and First US Army are very intimately related and it is my opinion that the present system of command is most unsatisfactory,

Monty unwisely added to his signal to Eisenhower. 'TEDDER is coming to see me tomorrow and I will explain the whole problem to him.'[3]

[1] M262, Montgomery Papers.
[2] M264, Montgomery Papers.
[3] Ibid.

Monty was returning to his old hobby-horse: command of the main Allied field armies. Thus when General Marshall, on a visit from the USA, appeared at his Tac Headquarters the next day, 8 October, Monty gave way to his exasperation with the Allied situation. 'Our operations had, in fact, become ragged and disjointed, and we had got ourselves into a real mess,' Monty explained to Marshall. 'Marshall listened,' Monty later recalled, 'but said little. It was clear that he entirely disagreed.'[1]

This was hardly surprising. General Marshall, who had spent the previous day with Patton and resented missing the opportunity of actually witnessing an American battle—the ill-advised Third US Army attack on Fort Driant—was not impressed by Monty's assessment of the situation, or Monty's solution, or Monty. To see so many American divisions in combat, from Switzerland to Holland, was profoundly inspiring to Marshall—and the idea that they or a portion of them should be commanded by a British general now that they had come of age did not impress him. As Monty scorned the lack of effective Allied command since Normandy, Marshall sensed only egoism in Monty's peroration: a junior ally who was far too self-important for Marshall's liking.

Aware of Marshall's hostility, Monty did in fact subsequently 'pipe down' about command—but his soldier's heart revolted at the cumbersome Allied methods. Nor was his foreboding mistaken; within days the Germans were able to transfer Panzer and SS forces from Arnhem to oppose Hodges' thrust. The Allied offensive was turning to ashes.

Meanwhile, to ginger up the Canadian attack on the Scheldt, Monty transferred 7th (British) Armoured Division to 1 Corps of the Canadian Army, and brought up 51st Highland Division to reinforce it on 7 October. By 8 October a fifth of Walcheren Island was under water after Allied bombing to cut the dykes, and on 9 and 10 October assault landings were mounted against the Breskens bridgehead. Monty also arranged that 52nd (British) Division should be landed through Ostend on 13 October and fed into the Canadian Army's attacks, as well as 104th US Infantry Division on 15 October. In a 21st Army Group directive on 9 October Monty laid down that '. . . the operations to open the port [of Antwerp] must have priority as regards troops, ammunition, and so on. . . . The opening of this port will take priority over all other offensive operations.'[2] When a signal arrived on the evening of 9 October from Eisenhower, chiding Monty for his slowness to take the Antwerp approaches ('we are now squarely up against the situation which has been anticipated for

[1] B. L. Montgomery, *Memoirs*, op. cit.

[2] M530, Montgomery Papers.

months . . . I emphasize that of all our operations on our entire front from Switzerland to the Channel I consider Antwerp of first importance . . . I believe that the operation to clear up the entrance requires your personal attention')[1] Monty was furious. 'Request you will ask Ramsay from me by what authority he makes wild statements to you concerning my operations about which he can know nothing,' Monty replied instantly. 'The facts are that Canadian Army attack began two days ago. . . . The operations *are* receiving my personal attention. . . . You can rely on me to do every single thing possible to get ANTWERP opened for shipping as soon as possible.'[2] Eisenhower apologized for misunderstanding; but his stock in Monty's book sank yet lower. As Lt-Colonel Dawnay, Monty's personal diarist, noted:

> It was quite clear from General Eisenhower's cables mentioned above that he was not in sufficiently close touch with the battle to be able to put forward a plan of any practical value, and that he did not know the situation of the Canadian Army or what operation it was in a position to undertake.[3]

In fact Eisenhower's headquarters had ruled out Monty's appeal for an airborne assault on Walcheren early in September, repeated on 10 September; they had also ruled out Monty's request for a series of heavy bomber attacks to inundate the German defences on 29 September[4]—and when Tedder informed Monty on 7 October that Leigh-Mallory was departing to South-East Asia and would not be replaced as Air C-in-C,[5] Monty had told Eisenhower of his 'considerable alarm'.[6] Indeed, the unholy squabbles that had already surfaced in the meetings of the air 'barons' bore out Monty's anxiety—for Allied air operations fragmented now into an incoherent, unco-ordinated series of attacks without any laid down plan or clear idea of priorities[7]—as if to mirror Eisenhower's very policy of dispersal and *laissez faire* on the ground.

[1] S61466, Montgomery Papers.
[2] M268, Montgomery Papers.
[3] 'Notes on the Campaign in Western Europe', Montgomery Papers.
[4] See 'Minutes of Air Commanders' meetings, SHAEF FORWARD' (AIR 37/1118), PRO.
[5] The post was offered to Tedder, but Tedder rejected it, considering that it would be a demotion after being Deputy Supreme Commander.
[6] M266, Montgomery Papers.
[7] See 'Minutes of Air Commanders' meetings' (Air 37/1118), PRO. John Terraine's *The Right of the Line: The Royal Air Force in the European War 1939–1945*, published in 1985, unfortunately presents a wilfully distorted view of the development of the campaign and the Allied command structure, despite attempts even by eminent veterans such as Field-Marshal Lord Carver to correct Terraine's account.

In growing resentment, Monty now launched his own V2 rocket at SHAEF. Hitherto Bedell Smith had shown the clearest grasp of the need for concentrated Allied effort and clear-cut, decisive field command. The Germans could shift forces from one sector to another, making fools of the numerically superior Allies who, thanks to their cumbersome system of command and nationally segregated fronts, were unable to do the same.

Monty's letter, though never subsequently published, resulted in uproar at SHAEF. On two sheets of foolscap paper Monty set out his 'Notes on Command in Western Europe' for Bedell Smith, beginning: 'The present organisation for command within the Allied forces in Western Europe is not satisfactory. . . .' He instanced the battle of Normandy as an example of what the Allies could achieve under a Supreme Commander and three C-in-Cs to run the land, sea and air battles under him. This system had now been abandoned. There was no Air C-in-C, and no effective Ground Forces commander. The Land Forces 'have been separated on a national basis and not on a geographical basis'. To Monty this was a recipe for disaster:

> There is no longer a question of one commander being responsible for certain definite operations,

he complained,

> and being given direct operational control of all the forces allotted to capture the objective laid down.
>
> Both British and American armies are involved in the capture of the RUHR, and it has been laid down that the main effort of the present phase of operations is to capture that area. But the job is not handed over to one commander; two commanders are involved, i.e. the commanders of the two Army Groups whose Armies are concerned.

Eisenhower's fudging of the issue flew in the face of all sound military practice:

> A formula is possibly very suitable in political life, when the answer to most problems is a compromise between conflicting interests. But in battle very direct and quick action is required; a compromise will never produce good results and may often produce very bad ones; delays are dangerous and may lead to the initiative passing to the enemy.

This was patently what was happening now. If the Ruhr thrust were to succeed, Monty contended, Eisenhower had two choices: to run the actual battle himself or to appoint a commander responsible for capturing the Ruhr. In this case there were only two alternatives. Either

> C-in-C 21 Army Group should be named as the Commander, and C-in-C 12 Army Group should be under his operational command. As was done in Normandy in fact, and with the very best results,

or

> C-in-C 12 Army Group should be named as the commander and C-in-C 21 Army Group should be under his operational command.[1]

Monty asked Bedell Smith to show Eisenhower this paper. But the result was the very opposite of the one Monty had intended. Monty had understood, after receiving 'Simbo' Simpson's letter in September, that Bedell Smith personally favoured the notion of Monty taking command of all Allied forces north of the Ardennes. But in the wake of General Marshall's visit, Bedell Smith's espousal appeared to have been but a momentary lapse. Eisenhower was angry—and, refusing to consider Bradley for the task, he killed the suggestion by stating in his reply to Monty that the Ruhr was no longer the 'real issue at hand. That issue is Antwerp.' According to Eisenhower, both Brooke and Marshall had considered giving the Supreme Commander 'a flat order' directing him to put the capture of Antwerp approaches above any other Allied operational commitment. Antwerp was more important than the matter of command. It had to be opened—pronto.

As regards command of the Ruhr thrust, Eisenhower pointed out that the thrust had, in fact, failed. Dempsey's Second Army was now incapable of mounting the primary thrust, and could only be expected to 'carry out strong flanking operations supporting the main attack upon the Ruhr'—which would be carried out by Bradley, once Antwerp was working. Bradley would thus, effectively, be the commander responsible for the Ruhr thrust. If Monty disagreed with this and found he must still class Allied operations as 'unsatisfactory', then 'indeed we have an issue that must be settled soon in the interests of future efficiency. I am quite well aware of the powers and limitations of an Allied Command, and if you, as the senior Commander in this theatre of one of the great Allies, feel that my conceptions and directives are such as to endanger the success of operations, it is our duty to refer the matter to higher authority for any action they may choose to take, however drastic.'

[1] 'Notes on Command in Western Europe, Holland', 10.10.44 (in 'North West Europe—Thrust Line and Command set-up' file), Montgomery Papers. Monty annotated the file on its cover in the 1960s: 'The file is of the greatest importance as representing my views on Command in the campaign in N-W Europe. M. of A.'

Eisenhower's reply, drafted together with Bedell Smith, was decisive. It was written on 13 October, but delivered by hand—taking three days. By then Monty had himself recognized the sterility of his argument over command—for Hodges' advance appeared well and truly halted, and Dempsey in no shape to mount a unilateral effort:

> All my information suggests that it will not be possible for First Army to reach the RHINE at present as it has not got the necessary reserves of ammunition for continuous and prolonged heavy fighting . . . The next important thing seems to me to be to pull Second Army in to help Canadian Army and so speed up the opening of ANTWERP . . . There seems no point in my going off alone towards the RUHR and to do so would not be good. When BRADLEY is ready in all respects for a dogfight battle for at least two weeks then we can all go together,

Monty cabled to Eisenhower at 7.15 p.m. on 14 October.[1] When Eisenhower's four-page letter arrived at breakfast time on 16 October, with its threat to place the matter of command before a 'higher' tribunal, Monty was dismayed. 'Dear Ike,' he cabled instantly, 'I have received your letter of 13 October. You will hear no more on the subject of command from me. I have given my views and you have given your answer. That ends the matter and I and all of us up here will weigh in one hundred per cent to do what you want and we will pull it through without a doubt. I have given ANTWERP top priority in all operations in 21 Army Group and all energies and efforts will be now devoted towards opening that place. Your very devoted and loyal subordinate MONTY.'[2]

Eisenhower was delighted. Monty had climbed down.

But in Hitler's headquarters, there was equal satisfaction. By dispersing their efforts, the Allies had played straight into German hands. Not only was the Allied advantage after the fall of France nullified; now, as if to show his contempt for Eisenhower, Hitler, dictator of a nation fighting in Russia, Eastern Europe, Italy, Scandinavia and on a line stretching from Switzerland to Holland, was able to pull out and build up a new Panzer Army reserve, designed to produce the very concentration of effort Monty had begged for—an offensive that would confound Eisenhower and finally *force* him to assign to Monty the command of all troops north of the Ardennes which Monty had urged since August of that year. The battle for Arnhem was over; the Battle of the Ardennes was yet to begin.

[1] M277, Montgomery Papers.
[2] M281, Montgomery Papers.

PART THREE

Prelude to the Ardennes

CHAPTER ONE

Filling the Mall

MONTY'S SIGNAL TO Eisenhower on 16 October marked the end, temporarily, of his campaign to get command of the Allied thrust to the Ruhr. As in Sicily when Mark Clark was given command of the main impending assault upon the Italian mainland, Monty turned to his canaries for solace. He had resigned himself to a long winter campaign and had sent Kit Dawnay to England to fetch his warm underwear, as he informed the Reynolds:

> I am sending by him some summer wear to be put away, vests, pants, shirts, etc.
>
> And I want him to bring out my winter wear:
>
> Jaeger dressing gown
> Woollen pyjamas
> Thick vests and short pants. There are some very nice white woollen ones I think.
>
> Four of each is enough.[1]

Now that the front had stabilized, it proved possible to receive King George VI in the field—a visit first suggested by the King in August as the true magnitude of Monty's Normandy victory became apparent. Air Marshal Sir Arthur Coningham, the New Zealand commander of all 21st Army Group's tactical support fighters and bombers, had by now developed an almost paranoid jealousy of Monty, having consistently sought, with Tedder, to cast doubt on Monty's Normandy strategy and having been proved spectacularly wrong when in August the German armies disintegrated. Coningham thus attempted to stop the King's visit by announcing that not only the flight to Eindhoven was unsafe, but road access too.[2] Monty was contemptuous. 'In my opinion this is complete and utter nonsense. Everyone who comes to see me uses the airfield at Eindhoven, without any (fighter) escort; no enemy aircraft have been over Eindhoven since I was here. . . . Motoring on the roads is perfectly safe.'[3] It was obvious to Monty that his supposed air colleague had never been further forward than

[1] Letter of 6.10.44, Montgomery Papers.
[2] Message from Air Marshal Coningham via Air Commodore Geddes in notes made by Sir Alan Lascelles, 4.10.44 (GVI/PS/7214), Royal Archives, Windsor.
[3] Letter of 6.10.44 (GVI/PS/7214) Royal Archives, Windsor.

Brussels—which is where Coningham advised Churchill to halt the King, at Coningham's own palatial headquarters.

The King, however, had no desire to sit in luxury on the edge of the Belgian capital. He had stayed in Monty's caravan in the field in North Africa and had visited Monty's Tac HQ within the sound of German artillery only ten days after the D-Day landings. The King 'would rather put the whole thing off if the only alternative was to go and sit in the outskirts of Brussels', Sir Alan Lascelles recorded.[1] Monty finally signalled to Churchill that he would take full responsibility for the King's safety, and the King thus stayed with Monty at Eindhoven in his own caravan for six days, from 11 to 16 October, visiting British troops in the field, the Canadian Army and Hodges' First US Army. 'We have all enjoyed the King's visit,' Monty wrote to the Reynolds. 'He stayed with me as an ordinary soldier guest, with no formality at all; it has been great fun. And today he attends our Service in the local church—after which he goes back to England by aeroplane.'[2]

Monty was approaching his fifty-eighth birthday; the October weather in Holland was cold and very wet—so bad in fact that the King had to return by boat via Ostend. Yet when, for a few days, Monty moved to his Main Headquarters in Brussels to be nearer the Canadian Army's operations to open Antwerp, he missed his caravan life:

> I have for a few days left my caravans and am spending a few days at my Main HQ—where I am living in a very palatial house, with beautiful furniture, bath rooms, etc. It is very comfortable but I do not care for it; I like the healthy open air life. Rommel is not too fit, and he is taking a very long time to get over his pneumonia,

he remarked of his spaniel; 'I doubt if he will be really fit again till the spring.'[3]

Meanwhile, ever since August he had been pondering and discussing the likely post-war problems the Allies would have to face—leading him to meddle in matters which went far beyond simple soldiering. This temptation had always been a feature of his character—and his image as the austere, non-smoking, teetotaller general devoted entirely to the conduct of war was exaggerated. Certainly his professionalism had by now become legendary, inspiring dread among the slack. But like so many great achievers, the key to his

[1] Memo from Lascelles to King George VI, 6.10.44 (GVI/PS/7214) Royal Archives, Windsor.

[2] Letter of 15.10.44, Montgomery Papers.

[3] Letter of 27.10.44, Montgomery Papers. Field-Marshal Erwin Rommel had commited enforced suicide on 14.10.44, after being implicated in the July plot to kill Hitler.

character was a superabundance of energy—a surfeit made all the more vigorous by his strict regime of simple food, no alcohol, no tobacco, and early nights. Not even for the King of England would he stay up after 9.30 p.m.—leaving his ADCs to amuse the royal guest. 'Genius comes of a good night's sleep,' Thomas Mann had once retorted to a critic who mocked his disciplined life—and Monty bore out Mann's dictum to a T. It was this abundance of energy that made it possible for him to go out each day visiting commanders, formations and units, inspiring all with whom he came in contact. His no-nonsense brusqueness, his simplicity of taste, his quick grasp of what was important and what was irrelevant, his driving curiosity and pride in the performance of 'his' troops—these were virtues that distinguished him from other senior commanders. But to say that such talents stopped there and that he knew his limitations would not be true. The same insistent gremlin that caused him so unwisely to lecture the Chief of US Army Staff on tactics and command was in evidence in far more spheres than the purely military. Thus, just as he could not forbear from tutoring General Marshall, so too he found it difficult to divorce himself from the political and social aspirations of his men after the war. To Anthony Eden, the British Foreign Minister, he had boasted in August 1944 that his troops would vote the way he told them to vote—a ridiculously brash claim. Yet such *folie de grandeur* was not simple egoism—it was his unabashed, over-energetic involvement in the welfare of the men who served him that was at the heart of such absurd statements—as Eden's Private Secretary wisely noted in his diary:

> The Gen. sat up like a little bird with his head on one side, sharp as a needle, and with very bright eyes. He was in a most genial mood and kept putting questions to A[nthony] E[den], such as 'What are the statesmen going to do when the soldiers have done?' 'Is there going to be an election?' 'What are you going to do with Germany?'. . . .
>
> He said the soldiers must be able to vote in the elections or there would be trouble. They must get more pay if they were to go on fighting the Japs. 'My soldiers will probably vote as I tell them.' 'They will vote *sensibly*. . . .' He said he was working on them through his padres but he thrust out two hands. One hand, he said, was what you wanted to do, the other was what it was your duty to do. It was necessary to bring the two together. 'It may be your duty to go to Japan!'
>
> A most striking little man with his bright eyes and long beaky nose. I daresay he is pretty ruthless with his generals,

Oliver Harvey surmised.

> Anthony Eden said to me afterwards he thought they had got on well and he had never seen M. so mellow. I told A.E. I was certain it was a most useful talk for them both to have, to know each other's mind. M[onty] would have great influence after the war and I felt A.E. could probably guide him. M. is evidently a bit *naïf* in political matters.[1]

Monty's concern with matters outside the immediate purview of a serving battlefield general was also well illustrated by his correspondence with Sir James Grigg, the Secretary of State for War, at this time. Two days before the great Allied air armada set off for Arnhem, Monty was writing about the vacant post of Chaplain-General:

> My dear P.J.
> You once spoke about the Chaplain-General. Hughes [F. L. Hughes, promoted Chief Padre of Eighth Army at Alamein and subsequent Chief Padre in 21st Army Group] is a Territorial; he would take the job if you decided he was the right man.
>
> I am quite certain that out of the comradeship of the great armies in this war can be born a new factor—the factor which will carry us through the difficult days that lie ahead. *It must be so born*; and it will NOT be, unless the chaplains, as a team, get on to it. The urgency of the matter is recognized here, and Hughes has the matter in hand—and successfully.
>
> But a much larger public is involved,

he warned.

> The problem must be tackled energetically in all the theatres of war, and in England. Inspiration and guidance must come from above, and at present nothing happens in that line as far as the Chaplain-General's Dept is concerned; I would say it is completely out of touch with the practical realities of the battlefronts. The new Chaplain-General should have been through the mill in this war.[2]

When Grigg replied to say the choice was to be between Padre Hughes and the Bishop of Maidstone, Monty wrote back with alacrity, even as the survivors of the epic battle at Arnhem were collected and reclothed south of the Lower Rhine and Monty himself moved his headquarters up into Holland:

[1] *The War Diaries of Oliver Harvey*, ed. John Harvey, London 1978.
[2] Churchill College Archives, Cambridge.

I have met Maidstone; as Chaplain-General he would be quite useless—at this period of our history. I sent Hughes over to see the Archbishop last week—on the invitation of His Grace.[1]

Monty's meddling *did* bear fruit; Hughes was appointed Chaplain-General of the British Army.[2]

Grigg smiled upon Monty's Christian politics—but took gross exception when it came to temporal politics. Monty had written to Grigg on 15 September that morale was still high in 21st Army Group; but with the failure of Arnhem and the gradual recognition that the war would drag on for another year, Monty began to consider the question of rest-camps and newspapers. Personally he favoured the notion of a new British newspaper to be run by his desert protégé Captain Warwick Charlton—a newspaper that might help vent and debate the questions of the post-war world uppermost in men's minds. A journalist, Tom Driberg, published a story in *Reynolds News* on 8 October, claiming that Monty had personally sponsored Charlton for the editorship. On 12 October another piece appeared in the *Daily Herald*, written by Hannan Swaffer:

> Should the British Forces on the Western Front have a weekly journal free from political censorship? General Montgomery thinks 'Yes'. Sir James Grigg and Lord Croft say 'No'. Who will win? . . . Although London dailies, flown to the front, supply his men with news, Monty wanted a weekly concerned with spreading a community spirit among his men. . . . But the appointment, and the policy, is barred by Grigg. . . .
> Monty has just sent Colonel Medlicott, M.P., his chief welfare officer, home to stress his views.

Grigg would not relent—and when he read Swaffer's piece on 12 October wrote a sneering letter to Monty beginning:

> I enclose two bits of stuff about your projected newspaper:
> *Driberg* is—Austrian
> Jew
> Anglo-Catholic
> Churchwarden
> Homosexual
> Communist

[1] Letter of 27.9.44, Ibid.

[2] Hughes later became Dean of Ripon, but was denied a bishopric after the war, much as Montgomery's grandfather Dean Farrar had been.

> *Hannen Swaffer* is—Jew
> Unwashed
> Near communist
> Toady of Beaverbrook
>
> If I am to judge Charlton by his friends then I am quite right to veto your employing him where he has anything to do with a newspaper on that account alone. Apart from that I got into endless hot water over his conduct of the 8th Army News after you left Italy. . . .[1]

Monty, unwilling to engage in a battle with a Secretary of State who had backed him consistently and loyally throughout the Normandy campaign, climbed down on 14 October, as soon as he received Grigg's letter—just as he would do over command with Eisenhower a day later. No longer was he the Moghul of the Eighth Army, thousands of miles from England, upon whom alone the very fortunes of the land war depended. His dictatorial methods, though giving rise to great umbrage, had been tolerated in England before D-Day because, again, the very success of the long awaited Second Front seemed personally to depend on him, with no time to waste. But now, in the autumn of 1944, with their own popularity dwindling as the war dragged on, such politicians increasingly resented Monty's supra-soldier's popularity. 'I will go into the matter, and will not have a paper at all—unless I am sure there is a real demand for it,' Monty responded gingerly. 'P.S. *Later* I have given orders that we will NOT have a paper, B.L.M.'[2]

Nor was Grigg the only politician to feel irritated by Monty's quasi-political standing. At a time when certain Americans were already grooming Eisenhower as a future President, Churchill gave expression to almost paranoid fears of Monty's fame. Churchill was in Moscow to discuss the Quebec agreements with Stalin, particularly regarding Poland and the Balkans, when he astonished the CIGS by an outburst about Monty, thousands of miles away in Holland:

> He suddenly looked up at me and asked, 'Why did not the King give Monty his baton when he visited him in France?'

Brooke had no idea, save perhaps that batons had to be specially made, and that the requisite one was not ready.

> 'No', replied Winston, 'that is not it. Monty wants to fill the Mall when he gets his baton! And he will not fill the Mall!'

[1] 'Correspondence with Secretary of State, 1944–5' file, Montgomery Papers.
[2] Ibid.

I assured him that there was no reason for Monty to fill the Mall on that occasion. But he continued, 'Yes, he will fill the Mall because he is Monty, and I will not have him filling the Mall!'

Apparently he went on turning this matter over in his mind, for on the journey home he suddenly turned to me and said: 'Monty will not fill the Mall when he gets his baton!' [1]

Was Churchill's anxiety entirely misplaced? It was certainly clear from Monty's signals that he intended to be military dictator of Germany—or at least the British-occupied zone of Germany—when the war was won. Even while the battle of Arnhem was in progress Monty had been writing to Grigg, rejecting the War Office's proposal for a tandem of Military Government and Wehrkreis Control Mission to oversee German disarmament.

> We are now approaching the frontiers of Germany and I have therefore been examining the proposals for the Military Government of that country, for which I understand I will be responsible,

he began.

> I am quite clear on the proposals for the Military Government of Germany, which in my opinion includes the control of all military affairs, including the tasks of the disarmament and disbandment of the armed forces of the enemy.
>
> I am, however, horrified to hear that in addition to the Military Government it is intended to create an entirely separate organization, to be called the Wehrkreis Control Mission, specially to be responsible for the disarmament and disbandment of the armed forces of the enemy. I have not yet received details of the functions of this Mission, but I am told that it will have a large staff including many Major-Generals, will be run by [Maj-General] West, and will be organized on the basis of the German Wehrkreis areas. . . .
>
> If this is correct, I consider that it is open to many grave objections. It will create a separate but parallel organization to that of the Military Government, which will involve the employment of an inflated number of officers, and especially of senior officers.
>
> But far more serious is the possibility that it will give the Germans loopholes for evasion, owing to the existence of duplicate organizations whose boundaries are not identical.

[1] Quoted in Arthur Bryant, op. cit.

As in war, so in projected peace Monty's dictum was to 'keep it simple'.

> I consider that the proper organization for the control of Germany would be for the control to be undertaken by the Army, through the normal chain of command. For this the Military Commanders and their staffs will require an adequate increment of specialists. One organization will thus be responsible for all matters of military government, and for the forces with which to implement it. Any other organization would to my mind be cumbersome and unsound.[1]

It is easy to see how the popular 'Cromwellian' aspect of Monty's leadership gave rise to the fears of Churchill and others. His clear soldierly mind cut through bureaucratic muddle as through military confusion. His own view of military government was simple, set out by his Chief of Plans, Brigadier Richardson, the day before the Arnhem operation:

> Military Government, as it will be practised in GERMANY (and perhaps DENMARK in a modified form) consists in the direct imposition, by force if needs be, of the will of the Commander-in-Chief, 21 Army Group, upon the civil population of the occupied territory. The Commander-in-Chief's powers will be limited only by international law and by such other policies as may arise out of the surrender.[2]

Yet even Monty's own staff bridled at 'Master's' proprietorial concern with post-war matters—as his Intelligence Chief, Brigadier Williams, later recalled:

> At Brussels, after addressing the Staff in some smokeless cinema or other, he went on to talk of the post-war world.
>
> Since half the Staff seemed to be waiting to be elected to the House of Commons for one political party or another, this part of his address was bitterly resented by some; and I was told by Freddie [de Guingand] that it wouldn't do any harm if I let Master know this in the course of a routine session on other matters. 'After all, you're a civilian,' Freddie said.
>
> Fortunately, 'Master' raised the matter himself. So I explained that whereas we would all follow him to the death till war ended—there wasn't much option anyway—nevertheless, we reserved the privacy of our own post-war. 'You'll remember Wellington's windows, sir,' I ventured.

[1] 'Correspondence with Secretary of State, 1944–5' file, Montgomery Papers.
[2] 21st Army Group War Diaries (WO 205/681), PRO.

No, he didn't.

'Well, sir, the fact that the Duke of Wellington won the Battle of Waterloo, just down the road, didn't stop his windows being stoned when he turned politician.'[1]

Stung, Monty went 'down the road' to inspect the field of Waterloo. 'I visited Waterloo yesterday and enclose some old bullets!!' he wrote to Phyllis Reynolds on 30 October; meanwhile, on 28 October he replied to the Editor of the *Sunday Chronicle*, who had requested a newspaper article:[2]

> I regret that I cannot contribute towards your series of articles. There are two main reasons:
>
> *FIRST*—I am a soldier on the active list of the Army and as such I cannot write articles in the Press.
>
> *SECOND*—It would not be possible to deal adequately with the subject you mention without expressing views about what we should all do when this war is over. That subject is nothing whatever to do with me,

Monty disclaimed,

> and if I were to write about such things it might convey the impression that I intended to seek a political career. I have seen articles in the press which have indicated that I am considering joining one of the political parties; *I have no intention whatsoever of doing anything of the sort*,

he assured the Editor,

> and it would be very foolish to get mixed up in matters about which I know nothing. I am a soldier and all my training has been in matters military; I must stick to things I know something about, and not get mixed up in things about which I know nothing.

The Editor, J. W. Drawbell, might well have felt the Field-Marshal 'protesteth too much' to be convincing; he cannot have realized that Monty's reply was directed as much to his own staff. Soon de Guingand was writing to 'Heads of all Branches, Main and Rear HQs, 21st Army Group:

[1] Draft article for *The Times* by Brig. Sir Edgar Williams, 1975, published in *Monty at Close Quarters*, ed, T. E. B. Howarth, London 1985.

[2] 'I remember so well our period of youthful post-war disillusionment after the last war, and I feel sure that this series of articles could do a great deal of good,' the Editor of the *Sunday Chronicle* had written on 20.10.44: 'Miscellaneous correspondence' file, Montgomery Papers.

> After the Commander in Chief's address the other day I was asked by several officers whether the Commander-in-Chief intended taking up a political career. The attached correspondence, I think, answers this question[1]—

and he enclosed copies of the newspaper's request and Monty's negative reply.

For the most part Monty's staff were impressed by Monty's retraction—'he sent a charming note to Freddie to let the Staff know that he was sorry to have given the impression of having trodden on their postwar corns,' Sir Edgar Williams recalled even thirty years after the event.[2]

With the defeat at Arnhem and the subsequent focus of Allied attention upon opening up Antwerp; the resentment of his staff at his 'political' harangue; the rejection of his projected 21st Army Group newspaper; Eisenhower's threat to refer to higher authority the command question; and the transfer of the main Ruhr thrust to Bradley's 12th US Army Group, Monty became strangely silent in the second half of October. 'After Arnhem Monty went back to Brussels and sulked,' one of his Liaison Officers put it.[3] He had been in battle continuously since D-Day; he himself began to feel the need of a brief rest. Finally, on 6 November 1944, he flew back to England.

He had promised Eisenhower that the Supreme Commander would 'hear no more' on the subject of command. But as the Canadian Army, under the energetic temporary command of Lt-General Guy Simonds, cleared the Scheldt approaches, Monty's attention started to shift back to the Allied assault upon Germany—preparations for which filled him with such gloom that, in all conscience, he found he could not remain silent. To his simple, soldierly mind the Allied campaign had degenerated into a shambles—and the fault he once again laid squarely at the door of his successor as Land Forces C-in-C, General Dwight D. Eisenhower.

[1] Letter of 28.10.44 in War Diaries, 21st Army Group (WO 205/5D), PRO.
[2] Draft article for *The Times*, loc. cit.
[3] Lt-Colonel T. S. Bigland, interview of 23.2.84.

CHAPTER TWO

Attacking All Along the Front

IN HIS DESPATCHES and his war memoirs, Eisenhower later gave the impression that he was the unrepentant champion of a 'broad-front' Allied policy, a policy to which he consistently stuck.

The truth was, however, very different—and it was Eisenhower's inconsistency as Supreme Commander and Land Forces C-in-C that most irked his subordinates at the time. By a policy of dispersed thrusts in different directions he had cast away the fruits of Monty's great Normandy victory and had produced the very stalemate the prospect of which had so frightened him in July 1944. Yet he seemed incapable of resolving a way out of this impasse, and his lack of leadership in the field became a mockery of high command—as even Admiral Ramsay, his Naval C-in-C, confessed in his diary. 'How shallow is the planning of SHAEF', he lamented[1]—for Eisenhower seemed incapable of saying no to any promising Allied thrust, with the result that all failed. It was Tunisia, the planning for Sicily, and the Italian campaign all over again—with the same alienation between Eisenhower's headquarters in the rear and his battlefield commanders.

Some historians would later blame the Allied troops for their failure to carry out the bolder ambitions of the generals, adducing that Monty's pride in the fighting abilities of his men was largely rhetorical.[2] But in reality Monty *was* proud of his men. His contempt was reserved for those generals who failed the men—who sat in palaces at Versailles, enjoying the fleshpots of Paris, and giving rise to the death, wounding or capture of tens of thousands of Allied soldiers in unnecessary scattering of effort, as in World War I. Monty flabbergasted Admiral Ramsay by claiming that he could, in September, fight his way to the Ruhr without Antwerp; but his was the claim of a fighting soldier based on the unique experience of campaigning from Alamein to Tunis, from Sicily to the Sangro, and

[1] Extracts from the diary of the Naval C-and-C, Admiral Sir Bertram Ramsay, loc. cit.

[2] Cf. Michael Howard, *Sunday Times*, 16.10.83, and M. Hastings, *Washington Post Book World*, 19.2.84.

from Normandy to Holland. In Monty's eyes the true reason for the relative collapse of Allied hostilities was in no measure the absence of a deep-water port other than Cherbourg or Marseilles. It was a combination of the administrative bungle whereby a shortage of artillery ammunition had arisen in the American zone; of the growing lack of infantry reinforcements; and of Eisenhower's failure to take a firm 'grip' on the campaign. These problems were exacerbated by the paucity of ports but the failure to get Antwerp working before November was *not* the primary reason why the Allied offensive against Germany had ground to a virtual halt,[1] since Antwerp could never have been operational before October, even if all 21st Army Group resources had been assigned to it.

Monty's aversion to such administrative and command incompetence has been characterized as ill-bred, even demented. Certainly, to those who did not appreciate Monty's professionalism, his unceasing campaign to get Allied command in North-west Europe on a sound footing seemed at best wearying, at worst egotistical, even megalomaniacal. Eisenhower became, in the eyes of many sympathetic historians, the 'long-suffering', forbearing Supreme Commander arbitrating between prima-donnas. Eisenhower's own view of his task, as spelled out in his 'put-down' of 13 October to Monty, was 'adjusting the larger boundaries to tasks commensurate to the several groups operating in these several areas, assigning additional support by air or reinforcements by ground and airborne troops, when [there is] a general pool, and shifting the emphasis in maintenance arrangements'.

If this was Eisenhower's conception of an Allied Land Forces C-and-C, the battlefield commander in a war against troops as mili-

[1] St Malo fell on 17 August, Brest on 18 September 1944; neither was used. Monty's own chief of administration, 21st Army Group, Maj-General Miles Graham later considered that 'at the period at which the advance would have taken place we were no longer based on the Normandy beaches. The port of Dieppe was opened on September 5 and by the end of the month was dealing with over 6,000 tons a day. Ostend was captured on September 9 and opened on the 28th of the same month. Boulogne and Calais were captured on September 22 and 30 respectively. Meanwhile the depôts on the Normandy beaches were being rapidly cleared by rail and road and the new Advance Base established in central and northern Belgium. An additional 17 General Transport companies with a lift of some 8,000 tons and preloaded with petrol and supplies were borrowed from the War Office and arrived in the latter half of September and early October.

'I personally have no doubt from a purely administrative point of view that, based as we were on the Channel ports, it would have been possible to carry out successfully the operation which Field-Marshal Montgomery desired:' Letter to *The Times*, 24.2.47.

taristically indoctrinated and well-trained as the Germans, then Monty felt every right to feel alarmed. But what could he do? In his diary (kept by Lt.-Colonel Dawnay on his behalf and written in the third person), he had recorded his soul-searching:

> It seemed clear to the Field-Marshal that General Eisenhower was bearing a very difficult burden, and was unhappy about the whole thing, and that we must all help him to the utmost of our power. He therefore decided to drop the whole matter of command, hoping that possibly some good might come out of what had been done.
>
> The great thing was to preserve the very friendly relations that existed between the Field-Marshal and the senior American generals; this was vital.
>
> The Field-Marshal therefore sent General Eisenhower a telegraphic letter, which ended with the words 'Your very devoted and loyal subordinate MONTY.'[1]

As the weeks went by, however, Monty's devotion became strained to the limit, and by the time he flew back to England in November 1944 his loyal subordination was wearing very thin. At a conference in Brussels on 18 October in the presence of Eisenhower, Bedell Smith, Bradley and de Guingand, Monty had himself proposed that Bradley be put in overall Allied command of the Ruhr thrust—'12 US Army Group to be in command of the operations to capture the Ruhr.' These operations could commence as soon as Hodges' First US Army reached Cologne, gained a bridgehead, and the territory west of the Rhine had been cleared. In Monty's eyes the operation would in fact be similar to the battle in Normandy:

> The Field-Marshal also stressed his opinion that the situation was very similar to that which existed before the Allies broke out of the Normandy bridgehead. It seemed possible that the decisive battle for Germany might be fought west of the RHINE, in the same way that the decisive battle for France was fought south of the SEINE.

The Germans would be forced to react to the threat to Cologne; General Simpson's Ninth US Army was being transferred to the left flank of Hodges' First US Army; as Hodges drove towards and across the Rhine at Cologne, Simpson would strike northwards and Dempsey south-eastwards, pincering the remaining German forces west of the river.

[1] 'Notes on the Campaign in North-Western Europe', loc. cit.

> The Allies would not win the battle easily. He [Monty] strongly emphasized his opinion that the Allies would have to put everything in to these thrusts towards the RHINE; they must be really full-blooded. 21 Army Group would see to it that its thrust towards KREFELD would be full-blooded. He asked that 12 US Army Group would also ensure that its thrust towards COLOGNE was in great strength; he was assured that this thrust would be made by ten divisions.

With Eisenhower and Bradley's agreement, Monty's plan had been adopted—but Bradley was not given overall Allied command. Hodges' target date for attack was settled as 5 November, Dempsey's 10 November. Everything possible was to be thrown into the attack, assuming the Scheldt approaches to Antwerp had by then been cleared.

To his chagrin, having relinquished command of the Ruhr thrust to Bradley, Monty then discovered that there had been a misunderstanding. A fierce pocket of enemy resistance around Venlo turned into a German counter-attack, pushing back the 7th US Armoured Division and Belgian Brigade, capturing Meijel and Liesel and threatening Deurne and Aslen. Monty instantly transferred two British divisions to the area, 'and by the 30th [October] the position on this flank had been stabilized'. Although stabilized, Monty became anxious lest a renewed German counter-attack hit him in the flank when once he launched his intended drive to Krefeld. If Bradley's Cologne thrust was mounted with sufficient strength, he need not worry, since 'it would force the enemy to concentrate substantial forces to hold it, and thus lessen the pressure on the British front'. But would Bradley deliver?

> In the new situation created by the enemy concentration in the MEUSE pocket [around Venlo], the Field-Marshal commenced to enquire into the plan of 12 US Army Group for the advance of its left wing to the RHINE. At the conference in BRUSSELS on the 18th October, General Bradley had stated that this attack would be made by ten divisions. The Field-Marshal now discovered, through the visit of a senior staff officer to the HQ of First and Ninth Armies, that the main American attack would be made by only four divisions. In view of the stiffening of enemy resistance he [Monty] considered that an attack of this size could achieve no decisive results; and it would certainly not draw off any enemy troops, and thus enable Second Army to attack without eliminating the MEUSE pocket.

Monty was aghast—as his diary recounted.

> It was clear that a weak American thrust of four divisions towards the RHINE would achieve no success. It appeared, therefore, to the Field-Marshal that the decisions reached in BRUSSELS on the 18th October were no longer practicable on the 30th October.[1]

What made Monty all the more angry was that Eisenhower had taken no fewer than *ten days* to issue, in writing, his C-in-C's directive following the meeting on 18 October.

> The directive issued by General Eisenhower on the 28th October would have to be amended,

Monty concluded—an almost comic situation were it not for the seriousness of the situation with so many lives at stake. If Monty gave way to renewed contempt for his Land Forces Commander, this was understandable—and not confined to Monty. De Guingand, normally so sympathetic to the problems faced by the Supreme Commander, some weeks later confessed the same to Admiral Ramsay—who agreed:

> Went to see Fred de Guingand, he was rather depressed at the state of the war in the west, saying that the SHAEF plan had achieved nothing beyond killing and capturing a lot of Germans and that we were no nearer to knocking out Germany. He said in fact that the higher direction of the war had been bad in the last 2 months, that Ike's policy was only skin deep and anyone could deflect it. . . . He said that the American leadership had been bad, the Generals being too inexperienced. They did not know how to combine artillery with infantry, put all divisions in line and had no supports to leap-frog and make headway, that they were everywhere too weak to break through and that they had utterly failed to reach their objectives—the Rhine. This was all very depressing but no surprise to me,

noted Ramsay, whose opinion was that Eisenhower's 'strategy is decidedly shallow'.[2]

Monty's own diary entry reveals the torment he suffered, attempting loyally to support his Commander-in-Chief, but painfully aware of the military farrago Eisenhower's assumption of command had produced:

> The basic reason underlying the necessity for this change of plan

[1] Ibid.

[2] Extracts from the diary of the Naval C-in-C, entry of 28.11.44 (CAB 106/1124), PRO.

was the unsatisfactory nature of the set-up for command of the land forces. General Eisenhower was exercising command of the land forces from PARIS, with his Tac HQ at RHEIMS; at both places he was remote from the battle, and was out of touch with the practical realities of the situation. His visits forward were infrequent, and he seldom had time to go in any detail into the military situation with the Army Group or Army Commanders. It may be noted that during September and October, General Eisenhower met the Field-Marshal on only three occasions —twice in BRUSSELS and once at his conference at VERSAILLES (10th September, 5th and 18th October). As a result, General Eisenhower's directives were frequently long delayed, and when issued, were already out of touch with the changing situation.

Owing to this lack of control from on top, the operations of the American Armies showed a serious lack of co-ordination. Furthermore, a close touch was not kept on the maintenance situation; this quickly got into difficulties, and these American maintenance difficulties were responsible for creating the urgency to open the port of ANTWERP.

The Field-Marshal had done all he could during the first part of October to get the 'command' set-up put on a proper basis. In this he had been unsuccessful, as General Eisenhower did not accept his views on command. The Field-Marshal could not continue to press his views without danger of damaging the good relations which existed between himself and the Supreme Commander.

To Monty's consternation, Eisenhower's belated directive of 28 October bore no relation to the decisions Monty believed Eisenhower to have made at the conference of 18 October. Monty had, at the conference, 'succeeded in getting capture of the RUHR allotted to General Bradley'. But according to Eisenhower's directive, Bradley was still to attack both the Ruhr *and* the Saar—with 21st Army Group striking to the north of the Ruhr and 6th Army Group, in the south, also penetrating the Siegfried Line and crossing the Rhine 'in strength'—all at the same time!

It will be seen that the land armies of the Allies were ordered to attack all along the front from Switzerland to Holland. The Supreme Commander had always agreed in conversation that the main effort must be made in the north to capture the RUHR, and this was in fact so stated in para 6 of the directive of the 28th October; but the directive then went on to order attacks all along the front. . . .

> The American administration was also in a thoroughly bad way. There was no proper system for ensuring that what was wanted in the front was sent up from behind; the Army Group Commander [Bradley] had no control over the L of C Commander [Gen. Lee], who was also a Commanding General; the Army Group had no 'Q' control, and the Commanding General of the L of C dealt direct with the Armies; the Corps had no 'Q' staff and Armies dealt direct with divisions.

To a professional fighting general like Montgomery, the American system was a recipe for disaster.

> The Field-Marshal's opinion was that despite a very good start and the very satisfactory position by the end of August, the Allies had by November got themselves in a most frightful muddle.

Monty had called a conference at Eindhoven on 31 October, attended by Bradley, Simpson and Dempsey. All Monty's worst fears were now confirmed; Bradley's attack upon Cologne was to be mounted in effect by four divisions, and 'he [Bradley] was not able on his 250 miles front to concentrate sufficient strength anywhere to deal a really hard blow. He [Bradley] also stated that he was launching Third US Army (General Patton) in an attack at the southern end of his front at the same time, i.e. towards the SAAR.' Monty had argued that, in his opinion, 'it was useless to launch towards the RHINE two weak attacks, each separated by about 50 miles'. Monty's suggestion had been that 'one decisive attack' should be launched, and that this attack 'should be made by 12 US Army Group'. For such an attack Monty would release all American divisions serving in 21st Army Group, take over a proportion of Bradley's defensive front, and support 'the left flank of 12 US Army Group'.

Bradley appeared to accept Monty's plan—and the Allied Forces C-in-C's directive of 28 October was thus discarded as irrelevant. On 4 November Monty signalled to Eisenhower that the Scheldt estuary was clear for minesweeping to commence, and on 6 November, as his armies re-grouped to support Bradley's Ruhr operations, Monty flew to England. He was exhausted, but determined that, if the Allies were to avoid further failures on the Western Front, with so much concomitant loss of life, they must find a Land Force Commander to deputise for Eisenhower—'someone to take very drastic action.' Either it should be 'a Foch', or it should at least be 'a commander who would take charge of the operations on land and do that and that only, and get them [the Allies] out of this dreadful situation'. In

Monty's opinion 'the Allies would win the war all right; but unless they pulled themselves together quickly the war would drag on all through the winter and well on into 1945—and quite possibly all through 1945, unless the Russians could get into Germany on the eastern front'.[1]

This was the message that Monty brought home from the front: that unless the western Allies 'pulled themselves together' Russia, not the western Allies, would win the war.

[1] 'Notes on the Campaign in North-Western Europe', loc. cit.

CHAPTER THREE

Warning the War Office

MONTY'S JOURNEY BACK to England marked a watershed in World War II. To his incredulity Sir Alan Brooke, returning from Moscow, found a telegram from General Marshall predicting that the war against Germany could still be won in 1944, and proposing that this be the substance of a new Combined Chiefs of Staff directive to Eisenhower. Brooke was amazed—and noted with undisguised contempt in his diary on 26 October: 'discussed with them [the planners] the wonderful telegram from Marshall in which he seems to consider that if we really set our hearts on it . . . we ought to be able to finish the war before the end of the year!'[1]

Marshall's obtuseness was all the more criminal because he had so recently visited Eisenhower and toured the Western Front. Years later he still felt no guilt or embarrassment, but only blamed Monty for daring to question Eisenhower's policy of dispersal at their meeting on 8 October. 'I came pretty near to blowing off out of turn,' he recalled in 1956, since 'it was very hard for me to restrain myself because I didn't think there was any logic in what he said but overwhelming egotism'.[2]

This misunderstanding of Monty's profound professionalism was tragic. Whatever ignorant misconceptions might be broadcast in Washington and in the American press, however, Monty was determined that his own superiors in London should know the truth, on behalf of men who were not living in comfort at home with their families and working in warm offices—men whose lives were being sacrificed to culpable American High Command. 'I am seriously considering the possibility of nipping over to England next week for a couple of days. I have a great many matters to discuss with the War Office,' he wrote to Phyllis Reynolds on 3 November. 'It is all rather vague at present and it depends a good deal on how things go. The trouble these days is the weather for flying; it is so uncertain and one might be stuck in England and be unable to get back,' he explained.

Despite nightly telegrams to the CIGS, as well as letters every few

[1] Quoted in Arthur Bryant, op. cit.

[2] Quoted in Forrest C. Pogue, *George C. Marshall: Organizer of Victory*, New York 1973.

days to Brooke, Simpson or the Secretary of State, Monty was adamant that both the Government and the War Office be personally briefed on the progress of the war in North-west Europe: namely that, far from being within sight of victory in 1944, the war was going to drag on until the summer of 1945—or even longer if the Russian offensive also petered out. From an administrative point of view this would require some very clear and drastic decisions: on reinforcements, ammunition, supplies, soldiers' leave. Marshall's wildly optimistic draft directive should be rejected. The Allies had lost their opportunity; what faced them now were blood, toil, sweat and many tears.

Churchill at first refused to listen; he saw Monty once only in the four days Monty remained in England, and then only for a brief interview before lunch on 7 November; he was obsessed still with the fear that Monty would 'fill the Mall' when receiving his field-marshal's baton from the King that afternoon, and paid no serious attention to Monty's dire warnings of a prolonged war against Germany unless the Allied Command system was revised and its forces concentrated. 'Both to the Prime Minister, and to the senior officers in the War Office, the Field-Marshal emphasized that in his opinion an early end to the war with GERMANY was now unlikely, and that future plans would have to take into account this possibility.'[1]

Churchill was now only months away from his own political defeat; as he would misjudge the tide of political aspiration in the country, so as Minister of Defence he now failed to heed the warnings either of the CIGS or of the C-in-C 21st Army Group. Monty's urgent appeal to Brooke was that the Combined Chiefs of Staff must understand it was impossible for Eisenhower successfully to marry the duties of a Supreme Commander with those of a Ground Forces C-in-C. But when Brooke attended the British Chiefs of Staff Committee on the morning of 7 November, it was to find that Churchill wished Alexander to become Supreme Commander in the Mediterranean as well as continuing as C-in-C of the Land Forces in Italy—a decision Churchill wished to incorporate in a telegram to be sent by 3 p.m. that day! Small wonder, then, that Monty's protestations about Allied command failure on the Western Front met Churchill's deaf ear at twelve noon when they met—and Brooke's diary, recording his lunch thereafter with Monty, was understandably despondent. For if the American Chiefs of Staff did not see the defects of the Allied High Command in North-west Europe and were supported in their ignorance by Churchill, who wished Eisenhower's

[1] 'Notes on the Campaign in North-Western Europe,' loc. cit.

example to be followed in the Mediterranean, there was little chance that Monty's pleas could be answered. Thus Brooke was reduced to perhaps the saddest expression of impotence of the entire Second World War. The British, he prefaced his recommendation to Monty, could say nothing. 'The set-up is bad, but it is not one which can be easily altered, as the Americans naturally consider that they should have a major say.'[1] The only answer was to let them court disaster. Only then might they perhaps see the error of their ways: 'Perhaps, after they see the results of dispersing their strength all along their front it may become easier to convince them that some drastic change is desirable. . . .'[2]

To Monty, charged with the lives of almost a million Canadian, British and American soldiers in 21st Army Group, this was distressing. In 1917, writing of the futile Canadian bravery shown at Passchendaele, he had remarked, 'They forget that the whole art of war is to gain your objective with as little loss as possible.'[3] Now, almost thirty years after the futile butchery of World War I, the CIGS was recommending that Monty keep silent while tens of thousands of brave and innocent soldiers were killed or maimed in the hope that from this the Americans might learn their lesson.

Upset and empty-handed, Monty thus returned to his Main Headquarters in Belgium, while Brooke and Churchill flew to the great junketings that had been arranged in Paris.

'My dear Phyllis,' Monty wrote the next day,

> I took off from London according to plan at 10 a.m. on Friday (yesterday) and got back to Brussels at 11.30 a.m. All is well here. Thank you for my very pleasant—though short—stay at home, and for all you did to give me a rest.

That his attempts in London had failed he did not say. Brooke had ordered him *not* to raise the subject of command with Eisenhower; he thus remained a silent spectator as Eisenhower's November offensive took its inevitable course. Second Army concentrated on clearing the Venlo pocket and taking over a portion of the American line in order to enable Bradley to concentrate his forces for the US thrust to the Ruhr. Monty's record of the American thrust, in his diary, makes baleful reading:

> Some progress was made initially, but from the start the attack met stiff German opposition. The Germans counter-attacked

[1] Quoted in Arthur Bryant, op. cit.
[2] Ibid.
[3] Quoted in Nigel Hamilton, *Monty: The Making of a General, 1887–1942*, London 1981.

> strongly, and Ninth US Army had considerable casualties. In spite of bad weather, which on most days made air support impossible, the Americans kept up their attacks. But owing to continuous fighting without relief, the American troops rapidly tired; man-management was bad, the infantry were very wet and tired, and some men did not have a hot meal for four days running. No reserves were available for either Ninth or First US Armies, they were advancing on a wide front, and the attack was nowhere sufficiently concentrated. As a result, the attack was everywhere halted west of the River ROER. . . .[1]

Monty had warned both Churchill and Brooke that this would happen: 'The Field-Marshal expressed to the Prime Minister and to the CIGS his definite opinion that the 12 US Army Group offensive in November east of AACHEN would not be sufficiently powerful to reach the RHINE, and that in fact the results of this offensive would not be very great. The thrust was not sufficiently concentrated, nor were there sufficient reserves of fresh troops or of ammunition to maintain the offensive until a break-through had been achieved.' As Lt.-Colonel Dawnay dolefully observed after Bradley's failure: 'The forecast made by the Field-Marshal regarding this attack had proved correct.'[2]

Generations of journalists and writers would blame Allied equipment, the weather, worst of all the fighting abilities of the troops. Monty had nothing but compassion for the men, however—largely citizen soldiery, in this case Americans serving in a European theatre thousands of miles from home. His heart, which in relation to his own kin could be so begrudging and even vindictive, went out as a soldier to these men. It was all so wrong: so foreseeable and unnecessary. It was not the men, nor the weather, but the generals who were at fault; and listening to stories of Eisenhower's life at Versailles and Rheims together with his driver/secretary, Kay Summersby, Monty may perhaps be forgiven that his heart hardened towards the Supreme Commander and he began to intrigue against him.

[1] 'Notes on the Campaign in North-Western Europe', loc. cit.
[2] Ibid.

CHAPTER FOUR

A New Plot

OMAR BRADLEY had launched his November offensive with high hopes. As his ADC noted, his public image had declined since taking command of 12th US Army Group—'Brad has slumped into greater obscurity than ever before as a result of his remote command in group.'[1]

Bradley's two-pronged November offensive, north and south of the Ardennes, was thus a matter of great personal importance to Bradley; on it he pinned the same hopes that he had invested in the American breakout in Normandy:

> The success of this effort can easily determine the length of the war. If we are able to drive through on the Rhine, perhaps seize an initial bridgehead, we will have destroyed the enemy's industrial potential, deprived him of the opportunity to replace the losses he is going to suffer. . . .
>
> Bradley banks heavily on this effort as he did on the St. Lo breakthrough. Pattern is quite similar, though apparently on a less intense scale. Heavy bombers will support the effort of the Third Army in their breakthrough and fighter bomber groups will give support to the First Army.
>
> Bradley has ordered bridgehead on the far side of the river even if we are unable to construct a bridge to supply the troops, will gladly gamble on supply by barge and boat to carry them across.[2]

Eisenhower was similarly deluded. A reporter, following Eisenhower's visit to some of the American divisions in the attack, extolled the Supreme Commander's 'captivating personality': 'There's something about the guy, the way he brushes along, the way he breaks out in a big grin, the way his voice, harsh and loud, cracks out, that disarms all within his vicinity. . . . That's the way he is, gay, loud, democratic, dynamic, thinking fast, acting fast, spreading confidence.' In Brussels, where there was a ceremony in the Belgian Chamber of Deputies, the reporter remarked: 'That day in Brussels will be memorable. General Eisenhower was never more

[1] Diary of Chester B. Hansen, loc. cit.

[2] Ibid.

personable than he was that day, never more sincere with himself and with his constituents, and surely never more American.'[1] On 3 November President Roosevelt had been re-elected; but the reporter following Eisenhower might well have been describing an American election trail.

There was of course nothing reprehensible in this; indeed, Eisenhower's contribution to American and Allied morale was a battle-winning factor of the first magnitude. If it is recorded here, it is in order that the Allied watershed of November 1944 may be properly understood. In the summer of 1944 the American armies in France had come of age; in November American predominance in men and matériel meant that less and less attention was paid to the British. Bradley seems to have either forgotten or to have subsumed Monty's appeals for a concentrated Allied thrust. By concentration Bradley understood, as did Eisenhower, the simultaneous effort of all possible forces; thus when Monty announced to Bradley that there would be no British pincer north of the Ruhr and suggested that Dempsey merely take over Bradley's left flank, Bradley was delighted. 'I told him [Monty] that I considered this a much better plan than the one that had been contemplated; that I had always thought more power could be secured by keeping the Second British Army parallel and alongside our forces.'[2] In Bradley's ADC's diary it in fact became Bradley's suggestion: 'Bradley effectively sold Monty on idea of discarding his effort to the north. . . . This represents a definite change in control where Monty is now tagging along on an effort rather than directing one. It is also indicative of the overwhelming American power now in France to continue the fight into Germany.'[3] Major Hansen had even pinned the badges of Bradley's original 2 US Corps, First US Army, and 12th Army Group on Bradley's helmet to 'duplicate' Monty's insignia. 'Little flashy, isn't it?' Bradley asked, demurring.[4]

In offering to use Second Army on Bradley's left flank, Monty had hoped to help Bradley concentrate his Ruhr offensive; to his chagrin Bradley had merely accepted the offer and continued with his preparations for a double offensive, to the Ruhr *and* the Saar. On 13 November Monty reported in his nightly telegram to the CIGS that he had visited General Simpson, Commander of the Ninth US Army at Maastricht and had had a 'long talk': 'That Army and the First Army on its right are due to launch the big attack tomor-

[1] Copy filed in the Diary of Chester B. Hansen, loc. cit., also in desk diary of C-in-C/Diary of Harry C. Butcher, Eisenhower Library, Abilene, Kansas.

[2] Memorandum for Record of 13.12.44, Bradley Papers, loc. cit.

[3] Diary of Chester B. Hansen, loc. cit.

[4] Ibid.

row. . . . I think the attacks will start well but in my opinion neither Army has the resources of reserve divisions and of ammunition to maintain a sustained offensive. In Ninth Army the ammunition allotment is 100 rounds per gun for the first two days and then dropping to 60 rounds per gun which is quite inadequate. I think the advance may reach the ROER river . . . but I do NOT think it will get any further. . . . Bradley's HQ are now at LUXEMBOURG which is a long way away from me. There is heavy snow on the ground in the ARDENNES and my L O with 12 US Army Group has great difficulty in getting back to me. I have asked Bradley to meet me at MAASTRICHT on Thursday.'[1]

Bradley's offensive, delayed by the appalling weather in the same way as the St Lô attack, soon failed. Unable to control his frustration, Monty had a 'heart-to-heart' with General 'Jock' Whiteley, Eisenhower's senior British operations officer. He had promised Brooke he would not resurrect the question of command—but the senseless waste of life was too much for him, as he wrote to Brooke on 17 November:

My dear C.I.G.S.

Whiteley came to see me from SHAEF yesterday. He is worried about the general conduct of operations in Western Europe; the complete lack of grip over the land operations; the complete lack of air command; and so on.

I am delighted that at last someone from SHAEF is beginning to see the red light. To be quite frank, there is no command at all; the whole affair is disjointed and ragged.

The days are slipping by; we are wasting a great deal of precious time.

A glance at the set-up will show you the situation.

a) Eisenhower is at a Forward HQ at REIMS. The directives he issues from there have no relation to the practical realities of the battle. It is quite impossible for me to carry out my present orders.
b) If Eisenhower is to command the land operations he must have the Air C-in-C with him.

   But there is no Air C-in-C.

   Tedder should do this; but he says he is Deputy Supreme Commander and will not discuss air matters.

   The air matters are handled by a staff section at SHAEF, under [Air Vice-Marshal] Robb.
c) As a result of the faulty air system, the great air power we possess is being wasted.

[1] M328, Montgomery Papers.

The November offensive was thus being mounted without the full benefit of Allied air superiority; worse still, the thrust itself was being split.

> d) Operations are going on north of the ARDENNES, and south of the ARDENNES.
>
> Bradley's Army Group is concerned on both sides of the ARDENNES; the main effort is supposed to be with his two armies on the north, but he himself has his HQ down south near Patton.
>
> I have moved my HQ right down to the inter-Army Group boundary so as to be near the Americans, but Bradley remains at LUXEMBOURG.
>
> It seems to me that if the main effort is to be made in the north, then Bradley and myself should have our HQ close together.
>
> And if Eisenhower will not give to one of us the power of operational control, then Eisenhower himself should be near us and should have the Air C-in-C with him.
>
> I think the issue is very clear.
>
> Eisenhower should himself take proper control of operations; or he should appoint someone else to do this. If we go drifting along as at present we are merely playing into the enemy hands, and the war will go on indefinitely.[1]

Monty had asked to meet Bradley at Simpson's Ninth US Army headquarters on 16 November. There, at noon, he had questioned Bradley. As Bradley recorded, 'Marshal Montgomery wanted my estimate as to how soon we could reach the Rhine and what our future plans were. I told him . . . I would hazard a guess that we would be on the Rhine in the vicinity of Cologne by December 15; that I hoped we would be on the Rhine in the vicinity of Frankfurt about the same time.'[2]

Such optimism might convince the Supreme Commander—who was so out of touch with operations that he had had to ask Mrs Summersby to telephone earlier in the week 'asking if the attack had gone off yet as we planned', as Major Hansen noted in his diary.[3] But Monty was unimpressed. To Brooke he recorded:

> I met Bradley at MAASTRICHT yesterday, 16 Nov. He explained to me the American strategy in Western Europe.
>
> They intend to line up on the Rhine from the Swiss frontier to DUSSELDORF . . . He said he reckoned to achieve all this by 1st January.

[1] M535, Montgomery Papers.
[2] Memorandum for record of 19.11.44, Bradley Papers, loc. cit.
[3] Diary of Chester B. Hansen, loc. cit.

There will then be a pause while they move their air force up, and re-group. They will then cross the Rhine on a broad front and advance into Germany, the right being directed on MUNICH and the left on BERLIN.

No priority had been laid down, there was no concentration for a selected thrust, no reserves to exploit a breakthrough. To Monty it was galling, and despite his promise to keep silent, he protested:

I said that if we went on pursuing this policy of 'stretch' we would be nowhere strong enough to bring such pressure to bear on the enemy that we smashed through towards the selected objective. Also, these tactics give the Germans exactly what they want, i.e. time.

The Germans are bound to bring divisions to the western front—from Norway, from the Russian front, and from elsewhere.

The only way to finish the business *quickly* is to concentrate great strength at some selected place and hit the Germans a colossal crack, and have ready the fresh divisions to exploit the success gained.

But all arguments on that line are quite useless,[1]

Monty bewailed. 'Advance on a wide front,' despite the crippling losses in World War One, was the official American policy—and it made Monty despair.

At present there are 17 American divisions south of the Ardennes, and 18 north of the Ardennes; and I failed to discover from Bradley any system or plan for switching strength across to the area where initial success offered promising prospects for exploitation.[2]

Bradley did not attempt to conceal this. As he remarked in his own Memorandum of their meeting:

Marshal Montgomery questioned our ability to keep the attack going toward Cologne and as to whether we had sufficient fresh divisions to keep it going. He also inquired as to whether or not we had any plans for shifting divisions from the Metz area to the Aachen area, or vice versa, if such shift was indicated. I informed him that I did not anticipate any such shift.[3]

'Our present strategy all seems so futile,' Monty summarized to

[1] M535, loc. cit.
[2] Ibid.
[3] Memorandum for record of 19.11.44, loc. cit.

Brooke. 'Of course the Russians may do great things and the situation inside Germany may deteriorate, and other things may happen; but if we rely on getting deep into Germany on what we do on the western front, I am afraid we may prove a broken reed,' he warned.[1] Indeed the situation would be comic were it not so heartbreaking. He had seen his Commanding General, the supposed Allied Land Forces C-in-C, four times in the past four months! He had not 'seen him, or spoken to him on the telephone for a month'—'since 18 October'.[2]

Unconvinced by Eisenhower's and Bradley's policy of dispersion, Monty had not promised Bradley any British offensive to coincide with Bradley's Rhine offensive beyond helping to shorten Bradley's front and give possible flank protection. In his Memorandum, Bradley put this down simply to British man-power problems; but the true reason was that Monty felt Bradley had not a 'hope in hell' of reaching the Rhine by the end of December, let alone the middle.[3] Until a policy of concentrated, overwhelming Allied punch, with absolute priority of air, maintenance and reinforcements, was adopted, he intended to concentrate solely on preparing the ground northwest of the Ruhr for an offensive in 1945.

But would a British attack upon the north side of the Ruhr succeed even in 1945 if Bradley continued to dissipate his forces, and the Allies ran out of steam? 'Bradley tells me that the American ammunition situation is going to get worse and his allotment is already being scaled down; the reason is that the Pacific theatre is now coming to the fore and ammunition has to be diverted there; the Americans have not enough ammunition to give adequate amounts to two theatres—both going at full blast. So the urgency to finish the German war quickly is very great,' Monty alerted Brooke.[4]

For Brooke these were grave warnings; the Germans were making herculean efforts to increase war production. The German ME262 jet fighter was already entering service; V2 rockets were being launched in their hundreds without hope of their mobile launching pads being located; and there was now fear among scientists that the Germans might actually be first to produce an atom bomb. Added to this there were increasing indications that a sizeable Panzer SS Army was being formed and equipped in reserve.

[1] M535, loc. cit.

[2] Ibid.

[3] 'Early lunch and to Tac [21st Army Group] by teatime. Monty sure that present [American] attack won't get anywhere & I am beginning to waver—he is always right': Diary of Major T. S. Bigland, entry of 25.11.44, loc. cit.

[4] M535, loc. cit.

I have always valued your wisdom and advice and I would be grateful for it now,

Monty wrote.

I feel we must not make a false step at this very critical moment.

When I saw you in London last week you agreed with me that I could do no more just at present, but should 'shove at the back of the scrum' as it were.

But since I have got back things do not look to me too good.

I do not believe myself that Eisenhower is a happy man these days. Whiteley says he is certain he is worried about something, but cannot find out what it is.

I think in his own heart he knows the show is not going well, and that the future does not look bright as regards an early end to the German war; and he does not know how to put the matter right.

He has never commanded anything before in his whole career; now, for the first time, he has elected to take direct command of very large scale operations, and he does not know how to do it.

Do you think I should approach Eisenhower again?

Or should I remain silent?[1]

Brooke, though burdened by problems on a world scale, took the matter very much to heart. Draft after draft exists still, among his papers, in his spidery green handwriting, as he attempted to formulate a reply. He asked Monty what command set-up he would favour; given the 'American preponderance in strength they will insist on any Land Commander being an American'; this being so, did Monty think Bradley was 'fit for the job? Will he be able to control Patton and Devers [commander of 6th Army Group]? Would he discuss plans with you sufficiently? Give me replies to the above.'[2]

Air-Marshal Portal, the Chief of Air Staff, personally brought Brooke's letter on a visit to Monty's Tac Headquarters; but meanwhile Monty had heard from Whiteley that Eisenhower was going to pull his socks up and make an attempt at generalship—'since I sent you M535 on 17 Nov some definite progress has been made. I used the tactics of the indirect approach and WHITELEY lined up to IKE . . . and put certain facts to him. . . . The main points were that he should not go whizzing about with no Air adviser and no staff officer so that no one knows what he is doing. If he wants to direct the land war he must organize a proper Tac HQ and sit there

[1] Ibid.

[2] Alanbrooke Papers, LHCMA, King's College, London.

with his Air C-in-C and consult his Army Group commanders and in fact command properly. To my delight I am informed today that Ike agreed that things were definitely bad and that something must be done about it and that he will do as suggested.'[1]

Such was Monty's cable on the night of 21 November; the next day Portal returned to London with a letter from Monty to Brooke, answering Brooke's questions. In Monty's view, Eisenhower should take proper command of the front, but in doing so should re-divide this front:

> I suggest the answer is this:
>
> Ike seems determined to show he is a great general in the field. Let him do so, and let us all lend a hand to pull him through.
>
> The theatre divides itself naturally into two 'fronts'—one north of the Ardennes, and one south.
>
> I should command north of the Ardennes, and Bradley south of the Ardennes.
>
> I do not believe we shall ever get a land commander. I have offered in writing to serve under Bradley, but it is no use; Ike is determined to do it himself!![2]

Brooke exploded at this suggestion. Monty was insisting that unless the Allies gave real priority to a single thrust, the German Siegfried Line could not be punctured for many months to come. From a strategic point of view priority ought to be given to the Ruhr thrust—and Monty was proposing himself as the commander! The Americans would never accept such an arrangement. Brooke's logic thus drove him to conclude that, instead, Bradley should be made Land Forces Commander, with Monty commanding the northern front under him, and Patton south of the Ardennes. 'Now Weeks [DCIGS] informs me of a new plot by which you are contemplating re-opening the matter with Ike,' Brooke wrote like an angry parent, and demanded 'a reply from you by return telling me exactly what you are doing'.[3]

In his diary Brooke confessed that 'it is one of the most difficult problems I have had to tackle'[4] and doubted whether the solution, however logical, could be brought off. Meanwhile Monty was undoubtedly shaken by the tone of Brooke's letters and begged to be allowed to speak to him in person. 'It was so difficult to make any progress by correspondence,' Monty's diarist recorded, 'and the

[1] M340, Montgomery Papers.
[2] Letter of 22.11.44, Montgomery Papers.
[3] Letter of 24.11.44, Montgomery Papers.
[4] Quoted in Arthur Bryant, op. cit.

matter was so serious, that the Field-Marshal decided to fly over to England and have a personal talk with the CIGS.'[1]

Matters were coming to a head—for Eisenhower had arranged to visit Monty at his new Zonhoven HQ[2] on Tuesday 28 November. 'Would much like a talk with you before IKE visits me,' Monty cabled to Brooke therefore. 'If I fly to HARTFORD BRIDGE FLATS tomorrow morning could you meet me for a talk in my aeroplane or in your house?'[3]

It was thus at the private country house of the CIGS, near Aldershot, that the next stage of the 'plot' against the American conduct of war on the Western Front took place.

27.11.44

My dear Phyllis

I was over in England yesterday: but only for two hours. I flew to the big airfield on Hartford Bridge Flats, and drove from there to the house of the C.I.G.S. in a nearby village; I had a talk with the C.I.G.S. for one hour and took off at 1230 hrs, flew over you all at Hindhead, had lunch in the air, and arrived back in Holland at 2 p.m.

I saw you all very well from the front of the plane—where I was standing by the pilot. It was a lovely day for flying and in the channel there was complete calm.

The calmness of the sea was in direct contrast to the turbulence now affecting the Allies. At Brooke's house Monty 'explained his views to the C.I.G.S.', Lt-Colonel Dawnay recorded. 'He said that two points must be very clearly realized by the Prime Minister and the Chiefs of Staff:

1. As Commander in charge of land operations, General Eisenhower was quite useless. There must be no mistake on this point; he was completely and utterly useless.
2. The American conception of making war on land, if allowed to continue, would mean that the war would go on all through 1945.

These two points had landed the Allies in the present very unsatisfactory situation; if no solution could be found, then the war would go on indefinitely.

If General Eisenhower had acted in September as advised by

[1] 'Notes on the Campaign in North-Western Europe', loc. cit.

[2] Monty's Tactical Headquarters moved to Zonhoven on 9.11.44 to be nearer to Bradley's left flank.

[3] M536, Montgomery Papers.

> the Field-Marshal, then the war might well have been won this year; he did not do so, and as a result the Allies had suffered a major strategic reverse and had no hope of gaining their strategical objective, namely the RUHR. A new plan was required. . . .[1]

Brooke had recommended that Eisenhower appoint Bradley the Allied Land Force Commander, with Monty and Patton commanding two Allied fronts north and south of the Ardennes; but as Monty pointed out to Brooke, it was Bradley's predilection for dispersed thrusts that was behind Eisenhower's refusal to concentrate his efforts! Unless Bradley could be persuaded or *ordered* to concentrate, such an alteration in the Allied High Command would not of itself achieve anything. In Monty's view there was only one sure way to get real Allied concentration now upon the Ruhr, and that was to ensure that Patton was brought into the Army Group *north of the Ardennes*:

> If it was considered that a land forces commander could be forced on General Eisenhower, then by all means let it be General Bradley. But in this case it was necessary to ensure that the present American plan of campaign did not continue, and this would not be easy as General Bradley considered it to be very good. In fact, the present plan was General Bradley's. The only way to ensure that adequate resources were allotted to the main thrust would be to include General Patton in that thrust; he carried great weight with the Americans, and had much influence in political circles.[2]

Brooke thus dropped his suggestion that Patton become the Army Group Commander south of the Ardennes, and authorized Monty to put a new concept to Eisenhower at his meeting the following Tuesday: Eisenhower to revert to being Supreme Commander; Bradley to be Land Commander; Monty to be Army Group Commander north of the Ardennes (with Patton's Third US Army transferred north within it); and Devers the Army Group Commander south of the Ardennes.

How Brooke can have persuaded himself that such a plan was feasible, and that Monty should be the one to break the news of the plan to Eisenhower, is a mystery. A week before, he had anticipated the 'greatest difficulty in getting the American Chiefs of Staff to agree to any change in the set-up' and had forbidden Monty to re-open the subject in the sternest of terms. Yet at his home in Hampshire on Sunday 26 November, Brooke agreed to let Eisen-

[1] 'Notes on the Campaign in North-Western Europe', loc. cit.
[2] Ibid.

hower's British subordinate criticize the Allied command structure and to suggest a remedy. Brooke promised, for his part, to put the plan to Churchill and to request General Marshall to 'come over and discuss the matter'.[1]

Serenely unaware that he would be further rocking the Allied boat, Monty returned to Zonhoven. Far from anticipating difficulties, he was full of optimism, as his letter to Phyllis Reynolds the next day shows, with plans even to get back to England for Christmas:

> I have a kind of dim plot to get away for a few days at Christmas and come home for the festival; but we must see if it will be possible, nearer the time. Don't say anything about it to David: anyhow just yet.[2]

He was greatly amused by the concert party he had attended the previous Friday in Brussels—

> an ENSA show put on by Noel Coward: who had a party of stars including Will Hay, Bobby Howes, Frances Day, and others. Frances Day sang some songs directed actually to individuals in the audience and finally came to rest in front of me and sang AT me. Then she handed me a small present, wrapped up in paper; I luckily did not open it THEN, as when I did so later I found it contained a miniature pair of ladies knickers with a small note, 'Please hang these up on the Siegfried Line.'!!

Still chuckling at the thought, Monty finished the letter and retired to bed. The next day would see whether he was to become Army Group Commander North of the Ardennes with Patton under him, and with Bradley as Allied Land Forces C-in-C.

[1] Arthur Bryant, op. cit.
[2] Letter of 27.11.44, Montgomery Papers.

CHAPTER FIVE

Completely Stuck, Completely Crazy

EISENHOWER'S VISIT ON 28 November was intended to be Eisenhower's first attempt at being a Land Commander. As he had written to Monty on 22 November, 'I have been very anxious for some time to pay a visit to the Second and First Canadian Army. If you have no objection I would like to do so next week if that would be convenient to everyone. I suggest, if their accommodation permits, I could spend one night at each of their Headquarters. This would give me an opportunity to see some of the Commanders and troops in each of the Armies. I will, of course, be guided by you on the whole question. As you will appreciate, I would not want my visit to take anyone's eye off the ball. Sincerely, Ike.'[1]

This was not the letter of an autocratic soldier, used to commanding men in battle. Its humble, almost servile tone was, in a war against a nation as militaristic as Nazi Germany, nothing short of disastrous.

Brooke's view was that Eisenhower's hand *must* be taken off the tiller if the Allied ship was to reach port. But Monty himself was divided. With his cruel military eye, Monty recognized Eisenhower's amateurishness as a battle commander; with his other, human eye he saw a warm, generous individual, transparently honest, wedded to the Allied cause, and almost boyishly willing to learn. There can be no doubt that, again and again, from the Mediterranean to North-west Europe, Monty fell under this personal spell of Eisenhower. As the 'election' reporter had described when Eisenhower visited Brussels on 9 November: 'Into this picture [of stiffness and formality] stepped a man from the farm lands of Kansas, his face shining and clean like a little boy dressed for his first time at Sunday School. There was a youthfulness in his eyes that belied the receded hairline. There was a wrinkle in his forehead that indicated he understood the seriousness of the situation.'[2]

Maj-General 'Simbo' Simpson had already noted Monty's susceptibility in this respect:

[1] Montgomery Papers.
[2] Loc. cit.

> We had begun to see that there was a certain pattern in his [Monty's] dealings with Supreme HQ. He would go and talk to Eisenhower, or at least get Eisenhower to talk to him, or perhaps even get de Guingand to talk to Bedell Smith; or sometimes I went over on a visit or was needed as an intermediary. As a result of these talks Monty always got a bit optimistic and thought that he had received agreement with Ike as to what he, Monty, wanted to do: namely concentration of resources behind one single thrust and some amelioration of the somewhat chaotic Command system.
>
> Then Ike used to go and talk to some of the American generals, and perhaps without even realising it go back on what he had agreed earlier with Monty. I think Ike was a bit inarticulate when in the presence of Monty. Monty used to make what he thought was an extremely clear statement—what most of us would call an extremely clear statement—and it seemed quite clear to Ike until he went away and thought about it and talked to somebody else; then he swivered and tried to please everybody . . . he felt he had to keep them all sweet. Then he had American public opinion. Bradley and Patton—especially Patton—were the great heroes who were able to get on and perhaps finish the war much earlier than the rather 'sticky' British in the north. . . . This swivering by Eisenhower used to make Monty more depressed again: what he thought was a complete agreement with his point of view became watered down, which meant that his own point of view could not be met properly.

Indeed it appeared to Simpson that the pattern followed a somewhat cyclical course:

> It seemed that the cycle of this sort of change around took place over a month: agreement, say, in the middle of October, which got watered down; Monty did not realise it until the end of October; he realised early in November that things seemed to be going very wrong from his point of view, and he was in a state of despair until all the forces to help him—the CIGS in London, sometimes even the Prime Minister, lesser people like his chief-of-staff and myself—had to be mobilised again to try to get another agreement, which in due course was got by the middle of November, and then the whole cycle used to start up again.[1]

Simpson's analysis was close to the mark. Brooke had already posed the Allied Command conundrum to a meeting of the Chiefs of

[1] Wason interviews, loc. cit.

Staff in Whitehall on 24 November; opinion was that Marshall ought to be informed or better still summoned—but Brooke himself was unsure about this. Marshall had been, according to General Simpson, 'somewhat insolent' when Brooke had questioned General Stilwell's command set-up in South-east Asia—'so rude', Simpson recalled, that Brooke was loth to tackle him now over Eisenhower's command set-up. 'Marshall was a wonderful administrator and a wonderful raiser of enormous armies, but he was not the sort of great Chief-of-Staff that the Allied forces needed at the time,' Simpson summarized feeling in the War Office; 'Brooke had realized two years before that Marshall had no great strategic outlook.' Nor had Marshall any notion how to fight a war other than by raising armies; not only would he be reluctant to acknowledge the failings in Allied battlefield strategy on the Western Front, but 'being a very close friend of Ike's, would have to be approached very carefully if he was not to take umbrage at any suggestion that Ike was not doing his job properly', Simpson recalled. Simpson had personally drafted a telegram on behalf of the British Chiefs of Staff, to air their dissatisfaction with the conduct of the European campaign; but reading it, Brooke decided not to despatch it, but rather to work on Churchill, who could then raise the problem with Roosevelt. Thus, the day that Monty was due to see Eisenhower, Brooke had arranged an interview with Churchill—'on the instructions, so to speak, of his brother chiefs-of-staff', Simpson afterwards related.[1]

Brooke did not mince his words. The Allies, he claimed in front of the Prime Minister, had suffered the 'first strategic reverse . . . since landing in France', owing to American strategy and American command. 'As regards strategy, the American conception of always attacking all along the front, irrespective of strength available, was sheer madness. In the present offensive we had attacked on six Army fronts without any reserves anywhere.'[2] On the matter of command, Brooke proposed that Eisenhower appoint Bradley the Land Commander, with Monty and Devers taking the Allied fronts north and south of the Ardennes.

Brooke's interview was at 12.30. Some hours later, in his caravan at Zonhoven, Monty put the same points to the Supreme Commander.

Churchill, in England, and Eisenhower in Zonhoven were both taken aback by such doom-laden pronouncements. Both knew that the Allied offensive on the Western Front had petered out, but neither had analyzed the reasons. Brooke's diary recorded: 'Winston

[1] Ibid.

[2] Copy in Montgomery Papers.

said that he also was worried. . . . He agreed with most of what I had said, but was doubtful as to the necessity of a Land Forces Commander. I think I succeeded in pointing out that we must take control out of Eisenhower's hands.'[1]

But how would Eisenhower feel about control being wrested from him? To help convince Churchill, Brooke used the analogy of Tunisia: 'The best plan was to repeat what we did in Tunisia when we brought in Alex as Deputy to Eisenhower to command the Land Forces for him.'[2]

Churchill, who had an undoubted blind spot with regard to Alexander, warmed to this proposal. Brooke had only intended it as an illustration—but the seed was sown in Churchill's mind that Alexander might be brought home from Supreme Command in the Mediterranean[3] and given Land Forces Command in North-west Europe. Yet even now Churchill procrastinated, asking for a few days' grace before sending such a signal to Marshall.

Meanwhile Eisenhower himself heard his sentence from Monty—his own subordinate. This was very hard for the Supreme Commander to swallow. Eisenhower had tried not to think about the command problem, hoping that it would 'go away' once Bradley's November offensive succeeded in reaching the Rhine. But with Bradley's failure and the interminable letters, cables and visits to England, Monty's own patience had worn paper-thin. As Monty wrote on 27 November to 'Simbo' Simpson, on the eve of Eisenhower's visit:

> The present situation is that we are completely stuck. You would think from the papers that the whole German army was cracking; in actual fact the Germans have the First and Ninth armies well held.
>
> We ourselves have suffered a major strategic reverse; there is no hope that we can get to our objective, i.e. the RUHR.
>
> A new plan is wanted.
>
> And we want it *soon*: there are all sorts of things dependent on it, e.g. priorities, bridging, ammunition, etc., etc. I fear we shall get no plan.
>
> The real trouble is this.
>
> The task ahead calls for the highest professional skill in the planning and conduct of this campaign.

[1] Quoted in Arthur Bryant, op. cit.

[2] Ibid.

[3] General Alexander had been appointed to succeed the Supreme Commander in the Mediterranean, General Maitland Wilson, when the latter was sent to Washington as British Military Representative to the US Chiefs of Staff upon the death of Field-Marshal Dill on 4 November 1944.

> But Eisenhower is useless.
>
> And there is no one at SHAEF who knows anything about it; even if a plan is produced, the staff at SHAEF is incapable of implementing it; they are the wrong sort of chaps.[1]

Monty had told all this to Brooke at Hartley Wintney. 'As a commander in charge of the land operations, Eisenhower is quite useless. There must be no misconception on this matter; he is completely and utterly useless.'[2] Rarely in the history of war can a senior field commander have so emphatically condemned his C-in-C in the field.

Yet it was Eisenhower's miserable performance as a field commander that reduced Monty to exasperation. In a matter of three months, as Land Forces Commander, Monty had landed two million Allied soldiers upon a hostile shore and inflicted upon the German armies in Normandy their greatest defeat in World War II. Since assuming overall field command Eisenhower had frittered away this advantage and adopted an American tactical strategy of bulling ahead with thrusts on all fronts simultaneously—a policy of 'stretch-out', as Eisenhower's ADC called it.[3] This policy had failed—and in condemning Eisenhower Monty was careful to emphasize the consequences of Eisenhower's policy:

> If the American conception of how to make war is allowed to continue, then you must not expect any good results in Western Europe and the war will go on all next year.[4]

It was to 'ensure that these points are negatived in some way'[5] that Monty tried with might and main to get the Allied command set-up and tactical strategy altered in 1944—an effort that has gone down in American history as self-serving, but which was undoubtedly motivated by professionalism aghast at the 'mess' which Eisenhower's conduct of field command had produced. Nor was this exasperation reserved for Eisenhower; he was, as his nightly signals to Brooke demonstrate, disappointed by the lack of professionalism in Simpson's Ninth US Army—particularly as it affected the poor American infantryman. Bradley had failed to make good his promise to move his headquarters north, nearer to Monty; Bradley was thus hundreds of miles from Simpson when the virgin Ninth US Army floundered in the November mud. On 21 November, while dining at

[1] Letter of 27.11.44, Montgomery Papers.
[2] Ibid.
[3] Diary of Harry C. Butcher, loc. cit.
[4] Letter of 27.11.44 to Maj-General Simpson, loc. cit.
[5] Ibid.

his headquarters with Marlene Dietrich, Bradley received a phone call from Simpson. As Bradley's ADC recorded, 'Simpson called to tell Brad the 29th Division had pushed out. He was undecided as to whether to keep it going or have it stop and button up for a possible counter-attack. Returning from the gaiety of the evening to the weight of the decision required of him, the general answered without a moment's hesitation,' Major Hansen proudly recorded. 'Keep it going as far and as fast as you can.'[1]

If Hansen thought this Patton-like brashness in itself constituted great generalship, he was to be rudely shaken. The days of American cavalry exploitation against nominal opposition were over, and when Bradley finally visited Simpson on 22 November Hansen recorded both his own lost wager and American puzzlement at the lack of progress.

> The resistance up north has been extremely heavy, perhaps heavier than we first realised. An original bet of mine that would put the First [US Army] on the Rhine by November 25 was certainly far off. The German is defending each village as though it were the gateway to Berlin. . . .
>
> Many people here are resigned to a static winter which is hard to understand after the encouraging progress we made during the summer.[2]

Bradley spent only one day visiting his two armies north of the Ardennes; thereafter, having celebrated Thanksgiving at Luxembourg, he set off to see Devers' 6th Army Group. Meanwhile Monty was deeply concerned at the way things were going north of the Ardennes, and for the second time visited Simpson, on 23 November. Bradley had been very satisfied by what he saw on 22 November—'I want to go up and tell them what a good job they are doing,' he had said before leaving; 'such excellent progress has been made in the attack' was his opinion when he congratulated 19 Corps headquarters.[3]

But to Monty, who had spent four years of his life on the Western Front in World War I, the picture looked very different, as he reported that night to Brooke:

> I visited Ninth US Army today. The general picture is one of tired, cold and wet troops operating over country which is a sea of mud. There are no proper plans for giving hot food to the forward

[1] Diary of Chester B. Hansen, loc. cit.
[2] Ibid.
[3] Ibid.

> troops and some men have not had a hot meal for four days. 84 US Div. tried to attack BEEK today and though the artillery fire came down to plan the wet and tired infantry did not even attempt to start. The enemy has been counter-attacking savagely and has pushed the American troops back in some places. There is the usual optimism at Army HQ but when you go down below and investigate it is obvious there are no grounds for optimism.

Monty's professional eye was ruthless:

> The army is struggling to maintain its advance but the troops are wet and tired and the man management is bad and there are no fresh reserves. The state of the forward troops is not realised at Army HQ and the handling of the battle on the Army and Corps level is I am afraid amateur. [On] 13 Nov I expressed the opinion that the attack of the American armies might reach the ROER river but would get no further. The attack was launched on 16 Nov and today 23 Nov I am prepared to reaffirm my previously expressed opinion. I consider that Ninth Army has very little chance of advancing beyond the ROER river except possibly with odd patrols unless it is given some fresh infantry divisions and a proper plan is made. So far as I can discover there is only one fresh infantry division in sight for Ninth Army due to arrive from UK by 1 Dec and that division has never fought before. The making of a proper plan is not understood,[1]

he lamented. Nor was the outlook for Hodges' First US Army any better.

> First army is struggling forward slowly but here again there are no reserves. . . . The whole business is a first class example of the futile doctrine of everybody attacking everywhere with no reserves anywhere,[2]

he concluded in what was perhaps his most pungent and deeply-felt criticism of American tactics in World War II.

Thus when Monty greeted Eisenhower at 4.30 p.m. on 28 November, he was far from diplomatic. Immediately after tea Monty took Eisenhower into his office trailer, and in front of the great wall-map of the Western Front he began by declaring that the Supreme Commander's directive of 28 October had not worked. Far from drawing the German armies into a decisive battle west of the Rhine, as had been done in Normandy west of the Seine, the Allies had

[1] M344 of 23.11.44, Montgomery Papers.
[2] Ibid.

bulled ahead on all fronts, dissipated their superiority, and allowed the Germans to collect such powerful Panzer reserves that no Allied thrust to the Rhine, let across it, could be mounted for months to come. Churchill had even had to abandon his proposed broadcast to the people of Germany, lest it seem 'a sign of weakness'[1] in the wake of Allied failure.

> The Allies had suffered a strategic reverse. It was therefore necessary to make a new plan, *which must not fail*, as the necessity for an early end of the war with Germany was vital. The new plan must get away from the doctrine of attacking in so many places that nowhere was the attack strong enough to achieve decisive results. Instead, it was essential to concentrate such great strength on the main selected thrust-line that success would be certain,

Monty's diarist recorded.

> As the theatre was divided naturally by the ARDENNES into two 'fronts', there should be one commander in full operational control north of the ARDENNES, and one south of the ARDENNES.[2]

Eisenhower appeared to agree with this prologue—at least Monty thought so—'to all of this General Eisenhower agreed generally'.[3]

Monty therefore produced his remedy, as agreed with Brooke, saying casually that 'it seemed a pity he did not have Bradley as Land Force Commander to take off him the work of running the operations on land'. Eisenhower however balked at this, and 'the Field-Marshal did not pursue the subject'.[4]

But if Eisenhower would not accept a Land Force Commander, who would command the group of Allied armies north of the Ardennes? As Brooke had warned, it was north of the Ardennes that the Allies intended to make their major effort; if Bradley was assigned the front south of the Ardennes, he would be relegated to a subsidiary front. Bradley *must*, therefore, continue to command Twelfth US Army Group, Eisenhower stipulated. Nevertheless, he agreed that the *whole* of Twelfth US Army Group *would* be moved north of the Ardennes and Monty be given overall command on that front, with Devers' 6th Army Group taking responsibility for the line south of the Ardennes, which would become a holding front—'he said he would be quite prepared to put a strong Army Group under

[1] Desk diary of C-in-C/Diary of Harry C. Butcher, loc. cit.
[2] 'Notes on the Campaign in North-Western Europe', loc. cit.
[3] Ibid.
[4] Ibid.

BRADLEY north of the ARDENNES and to put BRADLEY under my operational command north of the ARDENNES'.[1]

The talk lasted three hours. Next morning Eisenhower awoke 'worried and ill at ease', as Monty reported to Brooke.[2] Nevertheless Eisenhower confirmed that he wanted to shift Bradley's group north, and that, as in Normandy, it would be under Monty's operational control.

Monty was cock-a-hoop, and his signal to Brooke that morning was full of confidence and optimism.[3] Brooke was less convinced, particularly as Eisenhower was to remain Land Force Commander and was prey to being swayed by the last person to whom he talked. What would happen when Eisenhower put this new proposal to Marshall—and to Bradley? 'This may be all right, but I still have grave doubts, as Ike is incapable of running a land battle and it is all dependent on how well Monty can handle him,' Brooke noted in his own diary.[4]

Before leaving Monty, Eisenhower agreed that a conference between the two of them and Bradley should take place the following week at Maastricht. 'In order to clear my own mind I would like to confirm the main points that were agreed on during the conversations we had,' Monty meanwhile wrote to Eisenhower on Thursday 30 November—lest Eisenhower 'welch' on his agreement at the forthcoming conference. Indeed, it seemed so important to Monty that the Allies should concentrate their main armies north of the Ardennes that he left open the final decision as to who would have overall command in the north: 'one of us [i.e. Monty or Bradley] should have operational control north of the ARDENNES; and if you decide that I should do that work—that is O.K. by me'.[5]

Brooke held his breath when he received a copy of Monty's letter: 'if only all Monty thinks he has settled materializes we shall be all right, but I have fears of Ike going back when he has discussed with Bedell Smith, Tedder, etc.'[6]

Even before seeing Bedell Smith and Tedder, though, Eisenhower began to waver. On Friday 1 December he responded, from General Simpson's headquarters, with his own version of his discussion with Monty on 28/29 November. Maj-General Strong, his Chief of Intelligence at SHAEF, had for some weeks been claiming to all who

[1] M351 of 2230 hrs, 28.11.44, Montgomery Papers.
[2] M352 of 29.11.44, Montgomery Papers.
[3] 'He now definitely wants me to handle the main business but wants BRADLEY to be in on it and therefore he will put him under me'—M352 of 0935 hrs.
[4] Quoted in Arthur Bryant, op. cit.
[5] 'C-in-C's correspondence with Supreme Commander' file, Montgomery Papers.
[6] Quoted in Arthur Bryant, op. cit.

would listen that 'he would not be surprised to see them [the Germans] collapse during the next 90 days'.[1] He now furnished Eisenhower with a paper pointing out that, in a war of attrition, the German forces were being worn down at such a rate that by attrition alone the Allies must win soon, and that heavy attacks south of the Ardennes, in the region of the Saar, must continue.[2] As a consequence Eisenhower did not now agree that operations south of the Ardennes should be scaled down—'I have no intention of stopping Devers' and Patton's operations.' He was not even sure whether to make the new dividing line between his Allied fronts the line of the Ruhr, or the line of the Ardennes: 'There was some question in my mind whether the Ardennes or the Ruhr should be the dividing line, if such a plan should be adopted.'[3]

Monty had unwisely referred to the 'strategic reverse' suffered by the Allies, and had insisted that at the forthcoming conference, to take place at Simpson's HQ at Maastricht, the various Chiefs of Staff, although present, should not be permitted to speak. 'I will not by any means insult him [Bedell Smith] by telling him that he should remain mute at any conference he and I both attend,' Eisenhower retorted; nor did he like Monty rubbing salt in his wound by referring to a 'strategic reverse'; the situation, he claimed, was 'somewhat analogous' to that of Normandy, in the weeks before 'Bradley's brilliant break through.'[4]

Monty quickly pointed out that, in talking of strategic reverse, he was referring only to Eisenhower's directive of 28 October, which had planned to put the Allies on the Rhine—a feat that was now impossible before the spring or even summer of 1945.[5] But such protestations were becoming academic—for it was obvious that

[1] Diary of Lt-Colonel Peter Earle, entry of 4.11.44 (recording dinner conversation with Strong the previous night), communicated by Lt-Colonel Earle to author, 1985.

[2] Maj-General Strong estimated that between 8 and 26 November the Allies had inflicted 128,000 casualties upon the Germans, costing Hitler 'three quarters of a division per day' or some twenty divisions per month. Hitler could form only twelve per month, plus five divisions reformed in or near the front line. 'Exclusive of other fronts, therefore, we are, by our present offensive, imposing a severe strain on his man power resources. . . . I feel from an enemy viewpoint, we cannot do anything else at the moment, but continue the attack'—extract from Strong's appreciation of 29.11.44 in 'Eisenhower–Montgomery Correspondence' file, Eisenhower Library, Abilene, Kansas. Monty never forgave Strong for trying to influence Allied strategy and tactics—see *The Diaries of Sir Robert Bruce Lockhart 1939–1965*, ed. Kenneth Young, London 1980.

[3] Montgomery Papers.

[4] Ibid.

[5] Letter of 2.12.44, Montgomery Papers.

Eisenhower had, in the two days since leaving Monty, changed his tune. Monty had stated that capture of the Ruhr was 'the only really worth-while objective on the western front . . . and if this was cut off from Germany, her capacity to continue the war must gradually peter out'.[1] Eisenhower had appeared to agree—so much so that he had insisted Bradley be allowed a role in its capture rather than taking command of all land forces south of the Ardennes. Now however Eisenhower was claiming that the Ruhr was not in itself important as a strategic objective—it was the killing or capture of Germans that was crucial, wherever this might take place.

That Eisenhower's tactical view should have been so swayed by the report of an Intelligence staff officer was to Monty yet another example of Eisenhower's naïveté as Land Force Commander: for if the Germans were faced with manpower problems, so too were the Allies. Within weeks Eisenhower would be forced to cable urgently to America for more infantry reinforcements, as well as having to put supply and transport soldiers into the firing line.

Monty had been aware of this looming manpower crisis for some time—indeed it had been the ostensible reason for his first trip back to England in early November—'I have much to discuss with the C.I.G.S. about manpower,' he had written to Eisenhower when requesting permission, 'both for British and Canadian troops. I shall have to break up another infantry division unless I can get more reinforcements.'[2] By the end of November Monty had been forced to disband the famous 50th Division and send its skeletal remains to England as a training division for young recruits; he had also to tailor all operational commitments in 21st Army Group to ensure that he could keep up offensive operations to clear the west bank of the Meuse. Churchill had talked idly of two or three divisions being used to smash north out of the Nijmegen bridgehead and cut off Holland by throwing a cordon across to Amsterdam; but with the Germans flooding the Nijmegen 'island' between the Neder Rijn and the Waal, Monty crushed such expectations. Even his own plan to effect the final capture of Dunkirk he had abandoned on 21st November—just as he had given up the idea of seizing Shouwen Island. 'I do not think we should get a good dividend from the casualties this operation might involve,' he explained to Brooke; and the same was true of Dunkirk: 'Here again we might suffer considerable casualties, and I have decided to leave the place alone.'[3]

[1] 'Notes on the Campaign in North-Western Europe', loc. cit.
[2] Handwritten letter of 2.11.44 in 'Montgomery–Eisenhower Correspondence' file, Eisenhower Library, Abilene, Kansas.
[3] M341, Montgomery Papers.

When Churchill heard that 50th Division was being broken up and its elements dispersed into other fighting divisions, he attempted to stop Monty—'the breaking up process that impulsively started on December 6th will be suspended for a few days,' Churchill cabled Monty—'I am doing my utmost here to get a bigger intake for the army and in particular to save the 50th Division but it is very difficult to understand this cutting up of first rate units,' he remarked[1]—a full *month* after Monty's trip to England to warn of the consequences of a winter of American attritional tactics. 'Both I and my staff are grieved that you should think we do things impulsively and without due thought,' Monty replied. 'Perhaps you did not mean this,' he suggested. 'Every single thing we do is done with one object and only one object and that is to defeat the enemy in battle and to end the German war as soon as possible.'[2] To the Secretary of State for War and the CIGS Monty was less forgiving. 'All the men have been told. All the infantry drafts have gone off and been absorbed in other divisions . . . in fact the [50th] division does not now exist. . . . The plan as you know is that 50 Div shall be a training division in UK for the intensive training of infantry riflemen. The infantry reinforcement situation is bad and with this plan we shall just and only just pull through. If there is any delay or argument about it at this stage it will crash the whole business. It has gone so far now that to attempt to stop it would create a scene of intense military confusion and will have the most serious repercussions on my projected winter operations for which a major regrouping is now taking place. I have been out all day on urgent battle affairs and on my return after dark I was given this ghastly news. I most earnestly request that the stand fast order may be cancelled at once by telephone as every day we lose will affect adversely my plans. . . . Please reply urgently.'[3]

Churchill was forced to give way, but if Monty's frame of mind in the winter of 1944 is to be understood, then the lack of professional understanding by Eisenhower and Churchill of the consequences of a vague and formless tactical battle strategy must be taken into account.

Eisenhower's first 'swivering' letter had been written from General Simpson's HQ at Maastricht on 1 December; that evening Eisenhower drove on to Luxembourg to stay with Bradley. The next morning he set off for his main SHAEF headquarters for a talk with Bedell Smith.

All Brooke's fears were now realized. Monty's 'agreement' with

[1] 'Miscellaneous correspondence' file, Montgomery Papers.
[2] M371. Ibid.
[3] M373. Ibid.

Eisenhower was redundant. As Eisenhower's erstwhile British driver, now his PA, recorded in her diary:

> As soon as he arrives he has a long talk with Bedell re Monty. Monty is most anxious to have Bradley under his command, keeps on saying that there would be a lot of advantages, of course he is completely crazy to even think of such a thing.[1]

[1] Summersby Diary, Eisenhower Library, Abilene, Kansas.

CHAPTER SIX

Maastricht—the Fateful Conference

MEANWHILE BRADLEY HAD been unwell—he had been confined to his bed for a week with a cold at the end of November—and after Eisenhower's visit things did not improve. His doctor 'advised that the General take a rest for several days preferably in the Rivers [sic]'.[1]

Eisenhower had presented Bradley with a comfortable and armour-plated Cadillac to make his long journeys easier, but although delighted, it was clear to those who knew Bradley well that he was under considerable strain. 'Although the General displays little evidence of nervousness, he keeps it to himself and is obviously worried and greatly concerned over the progress of attacks on our front,' his ADC recorded on 5 December.[2] The same sinusitis that had afflicted him in Sicily, in command of 2 US Corps, and in Normandy in command of First US Army, had recurred. Eisenhower returned to Luxembourg again on 6 December, on the eve of the Maastricht Conference, and the tension mounted still further. 'Today General Ike came up with Air Marshal Tedder to consult with the General before going on to the Ninth Army tomorrow to meet Monty for a conference on our tactics for the next push which may end this stalemate and at least push through to the Rhine,' Hansen recorded. 'On this decision and the decisions that will follow this Bradley must stand pathetically alone. Billy [Col. Harris, head of Deception] claims it is his knowledge of the critical times facing him that has caused the nervousness now evident in him for the first time. He is not irritable but he is more brusque than usual, he looks tired and the slight physical irritations have combined to wear him down physically as well as mentally.'[3]

Accompanied by Eisenhower and Tedder, Bradley set off early on 7 December for Maastricht.

Monty, who had carefully drawn up his own master-plan for a fifty-divisional attack on the Ruhr north of the Ardennes, had been warned some days previously by the DMO, Maj-General 'Simbo'

[1] Diary of Chester B. Hansen, loc. cit.

[2] Ibid.

[3] Ibid.

Simpson, that the conference would not necessarily go Monty's way. Despite Eisenhower's 'swivering' letter of 1 December, Monty was at first disinclined to believe this; but 'after sleeping on this for the night and a short talk with me [Simpson] this morning, F.M. Montgomery stated that he was not sure that I wasn't right and that he was going to have trouble at the conference on Thursday. He attributed any change of mind to General Bradley's influence, Simpson informed Brooke on 3 December.[1]

Monty's attribution was confirmed when he received a letter from Bradley, dated 3 December, saying that, owing to his recent cold Bradley had not been able to see either of his two army commanders north of the Ardennes—armies which 'did not progress as rapidly as I had hoped due to more determined resistance than I had anticipated'. Nevertheless Bradley was loth to admit that he had in any way failed. Hodges' and Simpson's attacks had 'resulted in a very material improvement in our position as well as severe casualties for the enemy'. Meanwhile Bradley blamed the inadequacy of the Channel ports for his decision to use Patton's Third US Army in support of 6th Army Group instead of the north—an attack which had 'so far achieved very satisfactory results' in the hope of 'cleaning up Lorraine, and, if possible, the Saar'. 'I believe that between the Seventh Army [of 6th Army Group] and Third Army, this very important attack can be kept up', Bradley added ominously.[2]

It was clear from this letter that Bradley did *not* favour moving Patton north of the Ardennes, and concentrating Allied strength for an advance to the Ruhr—indeed no mention was made of any strategic object for the twenty-eight divisions of 12th Army Group other than to advance on all fronts and get 'as much use out of' his divisions 'as possible'.[3] It was only when the Maastricht Conference convened on 7 December therefore that Monty learned of the new SHAEF-American plan—a resurrection of Bradley's old plan to split the Allied offensive into Germany into two: one blow being struck at the Ruhr, the other at Frankfurt, north and south of the Ardennes.

Monty, despite Simpson's warning, could scarcely believe his ears. 'I personally regard the whole thing as dreadful,' he lamented in a letter to Brooke after the conference that evening. 'Eisenhower and Bradley have their eyes firmly on FRANKFURT and the route thence to KASSEL. We shall split our resources, and our strength, and we shall fail. . . . I fear this is a rather dismal letter. The whole

[1] Copy in 'Command set-up in Western Europe December 1944–January 1945' file, Montgomery Papers.
[2] Bradley Papers, loc. cit.
[3] Ibid.

thing is really rather a tragedy. I think now that if we want the war to end within any reasonable period you will have to get Eisenhower's hand taken off the land battle. I regret to say that in my opinion he just doesn't know what he is doing. And you will have to see that Bradley's influence is curbed; he is behind Eisenhower in the business. Tedder is in on it also.'[1]

Such remarks were excised from the letter when Monty published it in 1958; conversely Bradley would not permit publication of his own record of the Conference during his lifetime—a record which ended equally personally:

> Marshal Montgomery made a very poor impression in that after putting forth his views and hearing everyone else's views, he refused to admit that there was any merit in anybody else's views except his own. Personally I gained the impression that his views as to future operations were largely colored by his desire to command the whole show. Marshal Montgomery has continuously argued, even up to the present time, that he should be given command of all ground forces. This would involve duplication of General Eisenhower's staff and, in the opinion of many, it is too wide a front to be actively controlled by one man. In my opinion, General Eisenhower has no intention of giving Marshal Montgomery command of the whole battle front or of the Twelfth Army Group. I told General Eisenhower that, of course, if he put the Twelfth Army Group under Marshal Montgomery, he would of necessity have to relieve me of command, because it would be an indication that I had failed as a separate Army Group Commander.[2]

It is clear that, faced with Bradley's threat, Eisenhower had had no option but to give in to Bradley's strategy. Meanwhile to the Secretary of State, Sir James Grigg, Monty lamented: 'The American plan for winning the war is quite dreadful; it will not succeed, and the war will go on. If you want to end the war in any reasonable time you will have to remove Ike's hand from the control of the land battle; and Bradley's hand too. How you will do this I do not know,' Monty acknowledged; 'but unless you do so, the war will go on. I hope the American public will realise that, owing to the handling of the campaign in western Europe from 1 Sept onwards, the German war will now go on during 1945. And they should realise very clearly that the handling of the campaign is entirely in American hands.'[3]

[1] M537, Montgomery Papers.
[2] Memorandum for Record, 13.12.44, loc. cit.
[3] Letter of 7.12.44, Montgomery Papers.

For Monty, after his experience of Lord Gort's incompetence in France and Belgium in 1939/40 and the poor British performance thereafter until 1942, there was nothing *inherently* better in British command—it was simply a matter of learning the lessons of modern warfare. 'One must just keep plugging away at it,' he remarked of the command issue; 'possibly some miracle will happen. But the experience of war is that you pay dearly for mistakes; no one knows that better than we British.'[1]

It seemed to Monty a tragedy that so many lives would now have to be sacrificed in a further winter of fighting, 'and one would not mind if success came at the end of it. But success will not come,' he prophesied, judging by the casualties suffered by the Americans in their abortive November offensive.[2] Even Bradley had confessed to his ADC that he looked to the Russians now for a 'winter campaign that may possibly spell victory for the Allies'.[3]

What Monty could not understand was Bradley's reluctance, ever since the end of the battle of Normandy, to concentrate upon seizing the Ruhr. Although the Arnhem drop had failed in its attempt to put the Allies across the Rhine, it had provided nevertheless a valuable staging area behind the Meuse for the northern pincer of an Allied thrust to outflank the Ruhr. Yet to the Americans at Bradley's headquarters, the whole northern front was considered 'a virtually unimportant role' beside the 'giant steamroller' of 12th US Army Group—as Bradley's ADC recorded before the Maastricht Conference:

> It is certain that whatever the plan of the next attack we (Americans) shall certainly carry the burden of it. Ours is now the main effort any way you look at it. Monty has arrested himself in the abortive Holland push. He is spread over a large front where a good proportion of his limited forces must be used to contain the Germans opposite him. Almost eleven of his divisions are simply employed in a containing action – giving him only three or four to use in an offensive. Accordingly, his forces are now relegated to a very minor and virtually unimportant role in this campaign where they are used simply to protect the left flank of our giant steamroller. This picture, however, has been vastly distorted by the German or British newspapers.[4]

But the picture had not been distorted. The giant American

[1] Ibid.
[2] Ibid.
[3] Diary of Chester B. Hansen, loc. cit.
[4] Ibid.

At the fatal Maastricht Conference of commanders on 7 December 1944 Monty's appeal to concentrate the Allied armies and bring Patton north of the Ardennes was dismissed. 'Eisenhower and Bradley have their eyes firmly on FRANKFURT and the route thence to KASSEL. We shall split our resources, and our strength, and we shall fail.... The whole thing is a tragedy,' Monty wrote to the CIGS. **26** *right* Tedder, Bradley and Eisenhower emerge from the conference delighted, Monty scowls.

Nine days later three German armies smashed open the extended American front. Intending to spend Christmas in England, Monty recorded his carol service and message to his troops early, on 17 December (**27** *below*). As American command disintegrated Monty, in danger of being cut off like the BEF in 1940, cancelled his trip to England and began to make certain the Germans would never cross the Meuse.

The Battle of the Ardennes
For four long days Eisenhower refused to consult Monty as the German offensive in the Ardennes swept through the front of First US Army under General Hodges.

At last, at 10.30 a.m. on 20 December 1944, Eisenhower telephoned to ask Monty to take immediate command of both Ninth US and First US Armies, and to restore order out of chaos.

While Eisenhower and Bradley remained confined to their headquarters for fear of German assassination, Monty ordered his familiar Rolls-Royce and Military Police outriders to take him to Hodges's HQ, where Monty's cool grasp of the situation and his tactical measures to meet the German onslaught soon fortified Hodges's flagging morale (**28** *above left*). In particular, Monty's instant decision to form an American reserve Corps under General 'Lightning Joe' Collins (**29** *centre left*) helped transform the menacing outlook – an example of superlative leadership to which Americans in the field such as General Simpson's Ninth US Army HQ (**30** *below left*) responded with respect, gratitude and relief.

31 *Top* Monty surveys the ruins of Aachen on a visit to General Simpson's Ninth US Army front during the Ardennes battle after coordinating plans with Generals Dempsey, Hodges, Simpson and Crerar, his four subordinate army commanders (**32** *centre above*) – the largest Allied Army Group ever commanded by a Briton in the field. Bradley's 12 US Army Group had meanwhile been reduced to a single army (Patton's Third US Army) – a humiliation for which Bradley would subsequently make Monty pay dear.

33 *right* German prisoners taken during the bitter fighting.

By the end of the battle of the Ardennes Monty, aged fifty-seven, was tiring (**34** *left*). Fighting the Germans seemed comparatively straightforward when compared with his struggle to obtain from Eisenhower a consistent plan, with clear-cut priorities and command. To Monty's disappointment one of his two American armies (First US Army) was returned on 16 January 1945 to Bradley's 12 US Army Group and ordered to fight on in the Ardennes 'for the sole reason of keeping Bradley employed offensively.... One has to keep a sense of humour these days otherwise one would go mad,' Monty wrote.

On 1 February 1945, after fierce argument, Eisenhower finally closed down Bradley's offensive in the Ardennes. Monty was authorized to proceed with his pincer attack on the Rhineland, using three Allied Armies. The Anglo-Canadian left pincer began on 8 February, but German flooding of the Roer delayed the American pincer, while British and Canadian troops fought the German parachute army to a standstill. **35** *above centre* Monty visits a British assault group and gives orders to his Chief of Staff Maj-General Sir Francis de Guingand (**36** *below left*).

Eisenhower's decision to back Monty's Rhineland pincer attacks, Operations 'Veritable' and 'Grenade', caused great sourness at Bradley's 12 US Army Group headquarters – particularly when Eisenhower also ordered Bradley to move his headquarters further north in order to better coordinate operations on the flank of 21 Army Group.

Meanwhile Monty attempted to give heart to his battling troops in the battle of the Reichswald Forest (**37** *above*) distributing magazines to the troops (**38** *right*) and regularly visiting the 30 Corps Commander, General Horrocks (**39** *below*).

Monty was convinced that the more the Germans used their armour and élite infantry to counter Monty's northern pincer, the less the Germans would be able to withstand the southern pincer when finally the flood waters of the Roer subsided.

Mounted by Ninth US Army on 24 February, Operation 'Grenade' proved a triumphant success – as even Bradley had to admit when joining Eisenhower for a conference with Monty and his 21 Army Group commanders, Crerar, Simpson and Dempsey, at Eindhoven on 1 March 1945 (**40** *above left*).

Churchill, also visiting, was equally impressed (**41** *centre left*), witnessing for himself Ninth US Army's operations as 21 Army Group reached the Rhine (**42** *below*).

43 *above right* Monty explains to the CIGS, Field-Marshal Brooke, his successful pincer attack to the Rhine. Monty's Liaison Officer, John Poston, holds the map board.

With Ninth US Army still under command, Monty planned for an assault crossing of the Rhine with his army commanders Dempsey and Simpson, as well as the Airborne Corps Commander General Ridgway (**45** *below*). Wherever he toured the assault divisions Monty found himself mobbed by crowds (**44** *centre right*) as the last stage of the war against Germany neared.

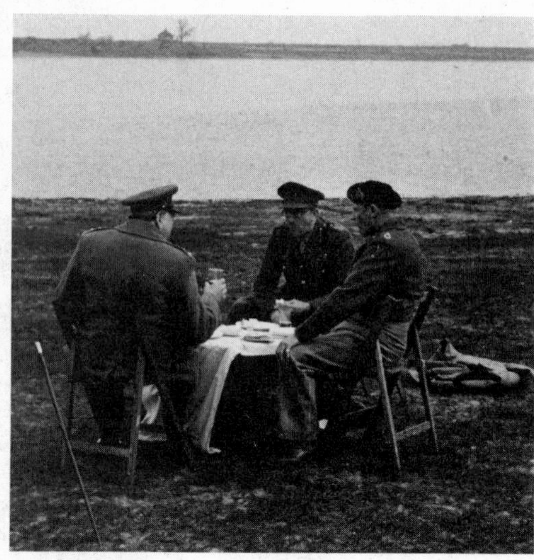

46 *above left* 5.5 artillery guns firing on the night of 23 March 1945 as 21 Army Group launched the largest Allied assault crossing since D-Day. Despite heavy airborne casualties from flak, the assault soon saw German resistance crumbling and the roads to Berlin beckoning.

47 *above right and* **48** *left* Churchill insisted upon witnessing the crossing of the Rhine from Monty's headquarters. 'I didn't want him but he was determined to come,' Monty wrote. 'It was difficult to get down to the battle properly till he had gone.'

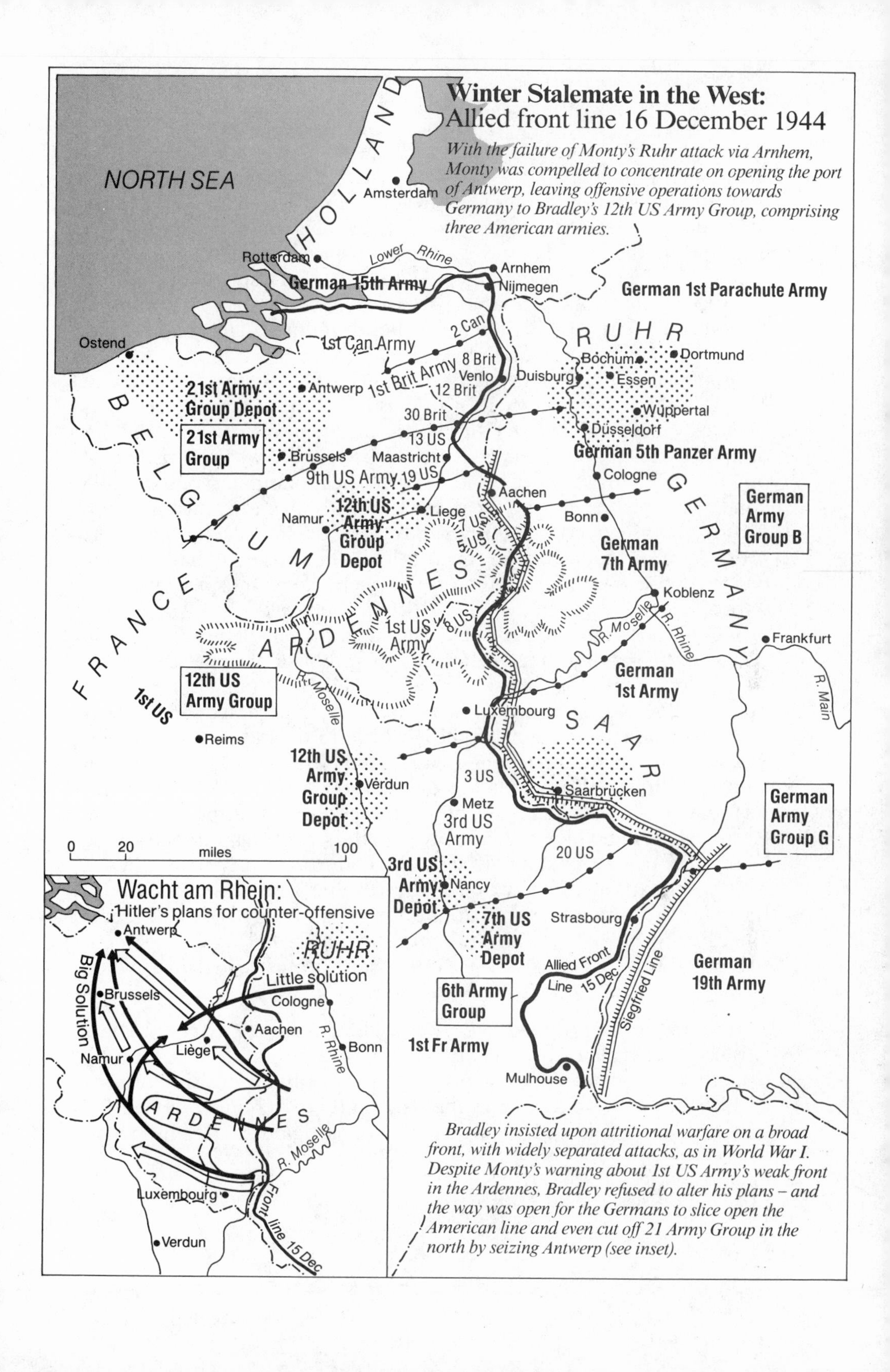

Winter Stalemate in the West:
Allied front line 16 December 1944
With the failure of Monty's Ruhr attack via Arnhem, Monty was compelled to concentrate on opening the port of Antwerp, leaving offensive operations towards Germany to Bradley's 12th US Army Group, comprising three American armies.
NORTH SEA
HOLLAND
Amsterdam
Rotterdam
Lower Rhine
Arnhem
Nijmegen
German 15th Army
German 1st Parachute Army
2 Can
1st Can Army
8 Brit
1st Brit Army
Venlo
12 Brit
Duisburg
RUHR
Bochum
Dortmund
Essen
Wuppertal
Düsseldorf
Ostend
21st Army Group Depot
Antwerp
21st Army Group
30 Brit
13 US
Brussels
Maastricht
German 5th Panzer Army
9th US Army
19 US
Cologne
Aachen
German Army Group B
12th US Army Group Depot
Namur
Liege
7 US
5 US
Bonn
German 7th Army
BELGIUM
GERMANY
ARDENNES
Koblenz
FRANCE
1st US Army
8 US
R. Moselle
R. Rhine
Frankfurt
R. Main
12th US Army Group
German 1st Army
1st US
Luxembourg
SAAR
Reims
12th US Army Group Depot
Verdun
3 US
Saarbrücken
Metz
3rd US Army
German Army Group G
0 20 miles 100
20 US
3rd US Army Depot
Nancy
7th US Army Depot
Strasbourg
Allied Front Line 15 Dec
Siegfried Line
German 19th Army
6th Army Group
1st Fr Army
Mulhouse
Wacht am Rhein:
Hitler's plans for counter-offensive
Antwerp
RUHR
Big Solution
Little solution
Brussels
Cologne
Aachen
R. Rhine
Bonn
Namur
Liège
ARDENNES
R. Moselle
Luxembourg
Front line 15 Dec
Verdun
Bradley insisted upon attritional warfare on a broad front, with widely separated attacks, as in World War I. Despite Monty's warning about 1st US Army's weak front in the Ardennes, Bradley refused to alter his plans – and the way was open for the Germans to slice open the American line and even cut off 21 Army Group in the north by seizing Antwerp (see inset).

steamroller was fatally ill-balanced; far from being constructed of heavy, crushing metal it was in parts rusted through and wafer-thin—and Bradley's refusal to move either his Third US Army or even his headquarters further north was to prove his undoing. No better example of the effectiveness of concentration would be given than the battle currently being planned by Hitler. Despite hopeless inferiority in the air and on land, Hitler managed to form an armoured reserve that was to slice open Bradley's vaunted 'steamroller' like the proverbial knife through butter.

While Monty lamented his misfortune—'The conference today at MAASTRICHT produced no good results. Eisenhower has obviously been 'got at' by the American generals; he reversed his opinion on all major points on which he had agreed when he visited me on 20 Nov' [1]—Bradley was elated. His ill-health and nervousness had gone. 'The general has bounced back quickly from his meeting with Monty,' Hansen recorded the next day. 'Their resolution in solving the problem of further advances toward the Ruhr appears to have lifted a burden from his mind and he is happier, gayer in spirit and less oppressed looking than he was earlier in the week. . . .' [2] The doctor pronounced that his sinusitis had cleared, and all in all he appeared 'in good health and high spirits'. Bradley's strategy of pragmatic advance on two main fronts, giving him the flexibility to pursue whichever break-out across the Rhine came first, had been accepted, and he was over the moon. 'He is now in the position to exploit a gain in either sector,' Hansen summarized—relating that Bradley in his heart still favoured a break-through on Patton's Third US Army front to Frankfurt and Berlin—'General Bradley believes the best approach to the German heartland may be made through the southern approach on the Frankfurt axis—a channel directly through to the city of Berlin . . . with a concurrent offensive on his north and south fronts, General Bradley puts himself in a position to throw his weight where he seems most like to break through the thin German wall.' [3]

It was this attitude that Monty had protested against when stating to Eisenhower, at the Maastricht Conference, that their ideas

> differed, not slightly, *but widely and on fundamental issues*. I said I was quite unable to agree with his plan. If we split our resources, neither thrust would be strong enough to obtain decisive results; this is what we had done in the past, and we were now paying for our mistake; I hoped we would not do it again. . . . I finished up

[1] M537, loc. cit.
[2] Diary of Chester B. Hansen, loc. cit.
[3] Ibid.

> with a strong plea for concentration of all available strength in the north, and for making the northern offensive so strong that success was certain. . . . Eisenhower did not agree with my views. He considered the way to win the war was to have two strong thrusts: a) one round the north of the RUHR. b) one on the axis FRANKFURT–KASSEL. In between these two thrusts the plan would be to threaten, and make feints. You will see that although the present plan has failed, we are still to continue to consider it has not failed and are to work on it. The only difference that I can see is that Eisenhower intends to hold back the left wing of the American armies when they get to the Bonn area (if ever!) and to put their main strength into the FRANKFURT project. . . . Bradley would obviously stay at Luxembourg in the south, for the FRANKFURT thrust. I had moved my Tac H.Q. to Zonhoven so as to be near Bradley; but he had never come north.[1]

More and more writers, since the war, have pinned the blame on Monty for this sequence of events—claiming that Monty's boastful personality drove both Eisenhower and Bradley to separate British and American forces. While Monty's cocksure personality certainly did not help his cause, there is however no evidence that Eisenhower or Bradley were responding negatively to Monty the man in making their decisions. In declining to give either Monty or Bradley command of the Allied front north of the Ardennes, Eisenhower was not simply shying from a decision that would involve serious politico-military ramifications; he was shunning an approach to war which, though it had brought the greatest Allied victory of the war in Normandy, was in fact wholly foreign to his own or to Bradley's military approach. As if to demonstrate that his decision was neither personally nor politically motivated, but rested on his genuine military belief in the new American army, Eisenhower offered Monty command of Simpson's Ninth US Army in the northern pincer attack on the Ruhr, as well as two American airborne divisions.

That Monty shunned this offer and repeated his conviction that the Allies were unbalanced was construed by Bradley and those Americans who heard of this, as ingratitude, even megalomania. Worse still, a few days after the Maastricht Conference, Monty withdrew his own 21st Army Group plan to undertake the clearing of the Heinsberg area (north of Maastricht) in preparation for the American thrust across the Roer—something which caused Bradley and his entourage further to 'write off' the British contribution to their supposedly invincible 'giant steamroller'.

[1] M537, Montgomery Papers.

Monty undoubtedly played into nationalistic American hands by his insistence on the need for Allied concentration, plus his decision not to carry out the Heinsberg operation (a decision largely determined by the appalling weather). But in the days after the Maastricht Conference, Monty felt disinclined to waste British lives and losses in an offensive he knew was doomed to fail. This was the lesson of his experience in World War I, and however irritating to American sensibilities, he was too profound a soldier to countenance unnecessary deaths merely to be seen as a loyal and obedient ally. It is easy, in retrospect, to blame him, as British and American authors have done, for being a bad mixer. But the loyalty and admiration, indeed the very willingness to fight, which Monty had inculcated in his men at Alamein and thereafter was built upon those men's faith in his generalship: the certainty that Monty would never ask them to undertake operations that were foolhardy or lacked a fair chance of success. No other Allied commander evinced this quality of trust among ordinary men—and if Monty put this loyalty before that of being a 'good co-operator', can one rightfully condemn him? Maj-General Silvester, the commander of the 7th US Armoured Division, was dismissed by Bradley after his poor showing; both O'Connor and Dempsey signed polite testimonials to the fact that General Silvester had 'co-operated whole-heartedly with Comd 8 Corps'. Monty had to forward the two reports to Bradley; he himself declined to write one, contenting himself with the pithy postscript: 'Maj-General Silvester was obviously a very good co-operator. As a Divisional Commander he was definitely below standard.'[1]

Allied co-operation was one thing; sound battle planning another. By the end of the Maastricht Conference Monty had realized that he himself was impotent to stop Eisenhower's policy of Allied dispersal of effort. Only Field-Marshal Brooke could help now—and once again it was to the CIGS that Monty turned.

Brooke had already spent a seeming lifetime arguing with Churchill about strategy. When he now received Monty's mournful letter about the Maastricht Conference on Friday 8 December, he nevertheless decided he must act. Monty's letter was so clearly set out that, with two amendments, Brooke proposed to present it to Churchill and, in view of the divergence of Allied thinking on the matter, use it as a lever to get General Marshall to come to England to discuss the controversy. However, knowing Churchill's propensity to fire off telegrams without Chiefs of Staff approval, Brooke decided not to show Monty's letter until the following Monday, 'to prevent the P.M. taking any unexpected action during the weekend. CIGS

[1] 'MS Appointments' file, Montgomery Papers.

then intended to advise the P.M. that he should wait for the President's reactions to the telegram requesting the attendance in England of the Chiefs of Staff,' the DMO, Maj-General 'Simbo' Simpson informed Monty.[1]

Eisenhower, however, was too quick for Brooke. Although the Maastricht Conference had not been intended to be more than a planning meeting to air and share views, Eisenhower was anxious to exploit his, Bradley's and Tedder's victory as soon as possible. Thus 'the night before last [8 December] the P.M. got a telegram from General Eisenhower saying that he hoped to make a short visit to London early this week accompanied by Tedder,' Simpson informed Monty. General Eisenhower added, 'If you and the British Chiefs of Staff might like to have a personal and very informal presentation of our situation and general plans, Tedder and I will be happy to come anywhere you might say.'[2]

Brooke was flabbergasted—not least because Eisenhower had seemingly deliberately gone 'over his head' in appealing to Churchill for an audience. Worse still Churchill had 'replied immediately, without consulting anyone, that he and the British Chiefs of Staff would be glad to meet General Eisenhower and Tedder for a conference on Tuesday afternoon [12 December]; Eisenhower and Tedder were invited to dinner at 10 Downing Street on Tuesday night.'[3]

Brooke's whole policy of quietly working upon Churchill and through him upon the President and American Chiefs of Staff was now in tatters. It was evident to Brooke, Nye and Simpson that Eisenhower would not have proposed a meeting with Churchill unless he was sure he had Marshall's backing. If Brooke now used Monty's letter to try and 'shake Ike's decision already taken', then 'it will produce a somewhat obstinate attitude on the path of both Ike and the American C.O.S.,' Simpson warned Monty.[4] Brooke's only hope of overruling Eisenhower had been to first convince Marshall of the need to shift Bradley's American forces north. This now seemed hopeless—it was too late. He would have to 'stick close' to Churchill and attempt to break up any collusion between Churchill and Eisenhower. Brooke 'fully realises the dangers, and views the whole project with dismay, but no other course is now possible,' Simpson bewailed.[5]

Eisenhower's political dexterity was awesome. According to

[1] Letter of 10.12.44 (DMO/104/M), Montgomery Papers.
[2] Ibid.
[3] Ibid.
[4] Ibid.
[5] Ibid.

Simpson, neither the Secretary of State for War, Sir James Grigg, nor the British Chiefs of Air and Army Staff, approved of Eisenhower's battlefield policy—yet in signalling direct to Churchill, Eisenhower had appealed above their heads to the one man in Whitehall who did not have the heart or professional military stature to say no.

Nor was this all. Tedder sent his Military Attaché to see 'Simbo' Simpson on 11 December to help 'sell' Eisenhower's plan to the CIGS before the 12 December meeting. When Simpson enquired what was Eisenhower's plan exactly, Colonel Milne said 'that Ike was considering appointing some sort of Super-Planning Staff to work out the plan', as Simpson recorded with incredulity in a new letter to Monty. 'This was going to consist of some high-level chaps from SHAEF, augmented by planners from each of the three Army Groups. The D[irector] Plans from the War Office was also going to be invited.'[1]

In the wake of Eisenhower's appeal direct to Churchill, this new bombshell reduced the War Office to virtual speechlessness. 'Ike, not knowing what to do, now apparently proposes to hand over the making of a plan to a sort of Committee. This, incidentally, is what is now going on at Mountbatten's Headquarters and we see the mess they have made of it there,' Simpson remarked.[2]

Eisenhower's biographer would later write that autumn was never Eisenhower's best time, but that he was forced by circumstances to become the Grant of his time, beating the Germans 'to the ground' in a great Allied battle of attrition. Certainly this was how, after the war, Eisenhower wished to be seen.[3] Unfortunately there is no shred of contemporary evidence to support such an image of Eisenhower as Land Force Commander, even after two long years of high command since November 1942—and his decision to hand over the plan of Allied attack upon Germany to a committee of staff officers from his own headquarters, Whitehall and the three Allied Army Groups was, after all his vacillation and changes of mind that autumn, a final admission of his inaptitude as Land Force Commander. Even Eisenhower's MA, Colonel Milne, confessed to Maj-General Simpson that the 'command set-up' was 'giving Ike much food for anxious thought'.[4]

On Tuesday 12 December Eisenhower now arrived in London with Tedder. Brooke managed to scotch the planned preliminary tête-à-

[1] Letter of 12.12.44 (DMO/105/M), Montgomery Papers.
[2] Ibid.
[3] Stephen Ambrose, *Eisenhower: Soldier, General of the Army, President-Elect 1890–1952*, New York 1983.
[4] Letter of 12.12.44, loc. cit.

tête between Churchill and Eisenhower; but how the full meeting, followed by dinner, would go, Maj-General Simpson was unable to guess—'I will not know until tomorrow how things went,' he informed Monty.[1]

Brooke, in his diary that night, was crestfallen; indeed he seriously considered resigning. 'I have just finished one of those days which should have been one of the keystones of the final days of the war.... I feel I have utterly failed to do what is required,' he grieved.[2] The critical situation in Greece (where Elas's forces had surrounded the British garrison in Athens) pre-occupied Churchill, who had thus failed to read Monty's Maastricht Conference letter, and refused to discuss it that morning. When at 6 p.m. the Chiefs of Staff, Eisenhower and Tedder all met with Churchill in the War Room, Brooke protested that Eisenhower's strategy violated the principle of concentration of superior strength, and had already resulted in the 'present failures. I criticized his future plans and pointed out impossibility of double invasion [of Germany, north and south of the Ardennes] with the limited forces he has got.'[3]

Churchill, however, would give Brooke no support. As he explained the following day, 'he had to support Ike last night as he was one American against five of us with only Tedder to support him. And also he was his guest.'[4] In fact Churchill had spent much of the time arguing about 'the possibility of floating mines down the Rhine!'[5] It was clear that, as regards battlefield strategy against the Germans, Churchill was as vague as the Land Force Commander.

Fortunately Brooke had gone to great pains to be ready armed for the confrontation—and his despairing diary entry did not do justice to his presentation that day. As General Simpson later recalled: 'The CIGS had been extremely worried before he went to his talk with the Prime Minister and Eisenhower. He rehearsed the whole argument with the VCIGS and myself again and again. He could not have briefed himself more thoroughly. The discussion, which was timed to open at 6 o'clock, was a bit late because the Prime Minister had been engaged at a Cabinet Meeting over Greece. At the conference itself . . . Eisenhower opened by expounding his plan at length. There was nothing new in what he said. Tedder said little, but showed that he agreed with Ike.'[6]

[1] Ibid.
[2] Arthur Bryant, op. cit.
[3] Ibid.
[4] Ibid.
[5] Ibid.
[6] Wason interviews, loc. cit.

It was at this point that Brooke stood up:

> CIGS then commented on Ike's plan very fully. He pointed out that the northern and southern offensives were being carried out with forces of approximately equal strength though the number of German divisions facing the northern thrust was very much greater than the number facing the southern. He said that this was not in accordance with the decision of the Combined Chiefs-of-Staff at the Octagon Conference. The main effort must be in the north, and he felt that Ike's plan for the spring was going to fail for the same reason: forces were not enough to sustain a double enveloping movement. What we must do was to make up our minds which of the thrusts was the important one, and give that all our attention, and all preliminary operations in the winter had to be in direct relation to the plan for the spring.
>
> The CIGS had learned his stuff thoroughly and he pointed out that on March 1 Eisenhower might hope to dispose of some eighty divisions. This had been news to Ike. Ike had to admit he did not really know how many divisions he would have.[1]

Brooke brushed aside Eisenhower's confession of ignorance, and continued relentlessly to take apart the Supreme Commander's plan:

> Purely defensive sectors might take five of these divisions in the north, five in the central sector, and up to eleven in the south. (It was admitted that those were probably high figures for defensive purposes but it also meant that tired divisions could be rested in that way and could be kept up for the offensive fronts.)
>
> So the CIGS had pointed out, after deducting five divisions for defensive purposes in 21st Army Group, Monty would have twelve remaining, to which could be added ten United States divisions, making twenty-two in all for the northern offensive thrust. Twelve United States divisions could fairly be allotted to the containing movement towards Bonn. That would leave 25 divisions for the Frankfurt thrust—which meant that in spite of all assertions to the contrary, it was going to be stronger than the northern thrust![2]

Though ignored by later writers and deprecated by Brooke himself, this was in fact one of Brooke's finest expositions as CIGS—and must cause the serious historian to reflect how different would have been the conduct of the Allied campaign had Brooke in fact been given Supreme Command, as Churchill had once promised him.

[1] Ibid.

[2] Ibid.

Eisenhower was stunned, as Simpson recorded:

> These calculations apparently shook Eisenhower considerably, and he eventually stated that he had in his mind the establishment of a General Reserve, something that incidentally he had never yet had. He was asked where he would locate it, or could locate it. He was clearly not sure about that,[1]

Simpson related, for Eisenhower had in truth given no thought to the idea. Brooke was insistent that, if formed, it *must* be built up behind the northern thrust in order to ensure its success.

Brooke had not exaggerated his despair in his diary—for in reporting the result of the conference to Monty on 14 December, Simpson remarked that 'the meeting eventually broke up at 2 a.m. and CIGS did not then feel that he had made much progress'.[2]

But Brooke was wrong. Though Tedder went about claiming—because of Churchill's attitude—that 'everyone had agreed with Eisenhower except the CIGS',[3] Brooke found Churchill the next day in a strangely anxious state, and intent upon convening a full War Cabinet meeting to face the issue, as Brooke recorded in his diary:

> I was very depressed last night and seriously thought of resigning, as Winston did not seem to attach any importance to my views. I found, however, today that the situation was far better than I thought. . . . What I had said last night had had far more effect on him than I had thought. He decided that the War Cabinet must assemble at 5.30 p.m. this evening and that I must put the whole strategic situation. In addition he wanted me to put in a paper on the whole matter.[4]

Churchill's new-found urgency was, however, too late. While Eisenhower had frittered away Monty's great victory in Normandy, and as Land Force Commander had spread out his divisions across a vast offensive front without any strategic reserve, Hitler had built up and equipped two entire Panzer Armies in reserve, as well as meeting the Allied attacks with positional infantry and artillery.

Brooke meanwhile cautioned Monty, via Simpson, not to approach Eisenhower or anyone at SHAEF regarding the issue—'CIGS also asked me to let you know that he thinks it would be advisable for you not to press your views on General Eisenhower, or indeed anyone at SHAEF, any further for the time being. He feels that they

[1] Ibid.
[2] Montgomery Papers.
[3] Ibid.
[4] Quoted in Arthur Bryant, op. cit.

are already fully in the picture as regards what you think and that anything further done by you now might well have harmful rather than good results. The matter must be handled at this end, and he will let you know when he wants you to do anything more.'[1]

Monty was thus to keep silent and await events. On behalf of the British Chiefs of Staff, Brooke and his colleagues began to draw up an official paper that might be presented to the Joint Mission in Washington and the American Chiefs of Staff, intending to have it ready for the next British Chiefs of Staff meeting on 18 December.

Monty fumed at the delay, but accepted 'Brookie's' orders. No communication passed between him and Eisenhower, and he concentrated on his plans for Operation 'Veritable', the Second Army attack to seize the necessary jumping off area for a spring assault towards and across the Rhine. Appalling December weather caused him to abandon his offer to clear the Heinsberg area up to the Wurm and Roer rivers, or to postpone 'Veritable'—'It will be for Ike to say which he wants me to do,' Monty wrote to Simpson on 12 December. 'I am planning to spend Christmas quietly at Hindhead with David. If all is well I would fly to London on Saturday 23 Dec. I could easily see the C.I.G.S. from Hindhead, and it might be better that way. I have no idea how long I would be able to stay; it would depend on a variety of factors: all at present unknown,' he remarked, referring to the current 'marking-time' while Eisenhower re-formulated his offensive plans. 'If we go on as we are at present for much longer it will be a very remarkable thing if I don't go mad!!'[2]

Simpson had warned Monty about Eisenhower's proposal to get planning staffs to put up the Allied plan—and when emissaries arrived from SHAEF to pursue this idea, Monty put his foot down. As he added to his letter to the DMO on 15 December,

> My Chief of Staff has been approached by SHAEF as to whether I will send my complete planning staff down to Versailles to help work out a plan for the campaign of 1945. The matter was referred to me and I have refused, *absolutely and definitely*, to do this.
>
> I have had it made clear to SHAEF that I will not on any account be drawn away from first principles; that it is for commanders to make plans and give decisions, and staffs then to work out the details *of those plans*; on no account will I have a plan forced on me by a planning staff; when the Supreme Commander has made his plan and issued his orders, the detailed planning for my part of that plan will be done at my HQ *and nowhere else*. I

[1] Letter of 14.12.44 (DMO/106/M), Montgomery Papers.
[2] Montgomery Papers.

will send a staff officer to SHAEF, at any time, to give the SHAEF planners any information they may want about my front, or situation, which will help them to decide on their own plan. I have told them that I will do all I can to help them; but I refuse to be involved in unsound procedure.[1]

Though Monty would be pilloried for such supposed 'obstructionism' he was reacting as a professional and experienced warrior—one who had, by personal leadership after a lifetime's preparation for High Command, raised his country's forces from the mire of bungling defeat. It was not anti-Americanism, as so many superficial commentators had assumed, that motivated Monty's passionate campaign to see the Allied offensive now mounted on sound lines: it was a profound professional conviction, based on years of clashes with his own British superiors over the decades of his apprenticeship.

In deteriorating weather Monty cancelled the Heinsberg operation. He had, in writing to 'Simbo' Simpson the day before the Maastricht Conference, emphasized the importance of keeping up offensive operations through the winter, according to a sound plan in preparation for a springtime crossing of the Rhine—'I am quite certain we cannot possibly lie fallow till March; it would be exactly what the Germans would like and would give them time to build up new divisions, and so on.

'We have got to keep wasting them away all the winter and draw in, and get mucked up, the only strategic reserve they have in Western Europe: Pz Army 6.

'But this winter battle must be equated with the master plan; everything done in the winter must lead up to the big plan, and be stages in its development.'[2]

In the hope that Brooke might still force a change of plan upon Eisenhower (as seemed possible now that Churchill had recognized the force of Brooke's argument[3]), Monty also postponed Operation 'Veritable' for a month in order to save casualties.

Monty's own master-plan, vainly proposed at Maastricht, was that the *whole* of Bradley's 12th Army Group should be moved north,

[1] Postscript of 15.12.44. Ibid.

[2] Letter to DMO, Maj-General Simpson, of 6.12.44, Montgomery Papers.

[3] 'CIGS again saw the Prime Minister yesterday and found that the PM very much agreed with him. CIGS is now preparing a paper on the subject which he will submit to the Prime Minister, who will then decide what action should next be taken. CIGS asked me to assure you that he fully agrees with your conception of the correct strategy to be adopted': Simpson letter to Montgomery of 14.12.44, loc. cit.

with its right flank 'on or in the ARDENNES', Simpson had told Brooke. 'F.M. Montgomery made it quite clear, in answer to a question of mine, that he did not envisage General Bradley having any part of his command south of the ARDENNES: the exact boundary, probably somewhere in the ARDENNES, would be determined when the plan is made.'[1] Eisenhower, Tedder and Bradley had, however, refused to countenance such a radical change in Allied strategy, command and dispositions. 'SAC [Supreme Allied Commander] unable to agree,' Tedder had recorded in his own notes on the Maastricht Conference.[2]

Nothing Monty, Brooke or even Churchill could say had yet been enough to change Eisenhower's mind. But Brooke's prophecy that events might well become the determining factor was about to come true—events that would within days *force* Eisenhower to switch the whole of 12th US Army Group into and north of the Ardennes, as Monty had for so long vainly requested.

First 25 November, then 10 December had been set as the target dates for Hitler's offensive. At last, at 3 p.m. on 15 December 1944 Hitler gave the go-ahead. Early the next morning, along a sixty-mile sector between Monschau and Echternach, the German counter-offensive began.

[1] Memo from DMO to CIGS (DMO/BM/577). Copy in Montgomery Papers.
[2] Notes of Meeting (DSC/TS/100/12), 8.12.44. Copy in Montgomery Papers.

PART FOUR

The Battle of the Ardennes

CHAPTER ONE

The Price of Drift

THE BATTLE OF the Ardennes was to be America's greatest defeat since Pearl Harbor—Kasserine writ large. Within five days Hitler's armies captured 25,000 American soldiers and destroyed over three hundred American tanks, as well as completely disrupting American offensive plans to reach the Rhine. Aimed first at the Meuse, in the rear of Hodges' First US Army, thence at Antwerp, it was a remarkable demonstration of the effectiveness of concentrated attack. Moreover it followed the outline of the battle of Alamein, with infantry attacks preceding and paving the way for an armoured second wave. Twenty-eight German divisions were assembled for the operation—whose main aim, Hitler had declared when planning began in October, was to destroy enemy forces and smash up the forthcoming Allied offensive directed at the Ruhr.

Despite Intelligence indications of a possible enemy attack, the Allied High Command persisted throughout November and early December in believing that Hitler's strategic reserve—the Sixth SS Panzer Army—would be used defensively in a fire-fighting role once the Allied offensive towards the Rhine was re-launched. Eisenhower continued to believe his Intelligence chief at SHAEF that current German losses were so great that the Germans could not withstand continued Allied attacks. Bradley's chief of deception, Colonel Harris, claimed on 6 December that 'we are now in the position to end the war in three or four weeks or drag it into another six months. He believes the German has reached a crisis in manpower and material. . . . Accordingly . . . an all out effort might compel him to realize the futility of his stand, cause him to collapse before he disintegrates.'[1]

Though Bradley did not necessarily believe such predictions, he underrated the German ability to launch a counter-attack on his 12th US Army Group front, dismissed Hitler as a spent force, and rejected Monty's qualms about the thinness of his American line, held by Hodges' First US Army, in the Ardennes. When a visiting congressman—a member of the House Military Affairs Committee—asked Bradley on 5 December if Hitler was ill, Bradley replied that

[1] Diary of Chester B. Hansen, Military History Institute, Carlisle, Pennsylvania.

he thought he was; or that, if not, he had given back field command of the armies in the west to the German General Staff, remarking with sarcasm, 'If he is ill—I wish he'd recover and take command again.'[1]

Bradley calculated that, opposing Hodges' First US Army, the Germans had twelve nominal divisions—or only 'eight actuals' in realistic terms. He and his staff were dismissive of the visiting congressmen (one of whom was drunk and had fallen asleep), Bradley confiding afterwards that 'he felt as though he was talking to an empty room when he addressed the committee'.[2]

Bradley would certainly come to rue his derisive remarks about Hitler, as well as his insistence that American losses in the abortive November offensive had been modest, and that by spreading his steamroller strength he could best break German resistance. When Bradley heard from Eisenhower, on the night of 2 December, that Monty had expressed a professional concern about the thinness of the American forces positioned in the Ardennes, he had immediately defended himself in a letter to Monty of 3 December—'the question of whether I should transfer some of Patton's divisions to the north was given careful consideration,' he emphasized, but the notion had been turned down in order to give Patton's Saar attacks 'greater strength'.[3]

Monty had, however, continued to show concern about Bradley's front—the more so because, in contrast to General Bradley's confidence, Monty did not think highly of either Hodges or Simpson, the First and Ninth US Army Commanders. If only Bradley would transfer Patton to the Ardennes or preferably to Ninth US Army's sector, then Monty was sure all would be well—'F.M. Montgomery entirely agreed with your point that it would be a great help to future operations if General Patton is transferred North of the ARDENNES,' Maj-General 'Simbo' Simpson had reported to Brooke on 3 December. 'He [Monty] said that he always intended that General Patton should come North as part of General Bradley's command . . . I told F.M. Montgomery that you had wondered what he thought of Generals Simpson and Hodges. He said that Simpson was a delightful man and extremely easy to work with, but he was not up to the standard of an Army Commander: he was "not really very much good." The latter remark applied also to General Hodges but I gathered that he was not quite so delightful a personality as Simpson.'[4]

[1] Ibid.
[2] Ibid.
[3] Bradley Papers, Military History Institute, Carlisle, Pennsylvania.
[4] Memo to CIGS. Copy in 'Command set-up' file, Montgomery Papers.

On 12 December Monty had written to the Reynolds with news of his latest plan to spend Christmas in England—his first since 1941. 'My present plans are to fly over to London on Sat 23 Dec. I should have to stay that night in London attending to one or two matters, and I would come down to Hindhead on Sunday 24 (Xmas Eve) and spend Christmas with you.' To make this possible his men had been busy rehearsing Christmas carols:

> On Xmas Eve the BBC is going to broadcast carol singing from my Tac HQ; it will last for about ½ hour, and in the middle my Xmas message to the troops will be broadcast. It should be rather effective. Two choirs of men are very busy practising. It will be done on 17 Dec and records made and the actual thing on Xmas Eve will be from the records. I said it must be like this in case I came home to you on Xmas Eve.
>
> All well here; dogs, canaries, goldfish, A.D.C.'s etc.
>
> Love to you all,
>
> Monty

By 12 December Monty was remarking about the weather: 'here it rains unceasingly, and the whole country is completely waterlogged. Many parts, as for instance in the area south of ARNHEM, are under water.' He proposed to get a wrist-watch for David's guardian, Major Tom Reynolds; for David a suit-case. But on 16 December such Christmas plans were made redundant; he flew to Eindhoven for a game of golf with Dai Rees, the professional golfer currently serving as Air Vice-Marshal Broadhurst's driver, and it was there, on the course, that he received the first reports of a German attack in the Ardennes sector of Hodges' First US Army. Monty flew straight back to his headquarters at Zonhoven. He had signalled in the evening of 15 December to Brooke that he did 'not propose to send any more evening situation reports until the war becomes more exciting';[1] he cannot have imagined that within a few hours of this telegram the war, seemingly bogged down in winter stalemate, could become so dramatically inflamed.

Eisenhower had meanwhile returned from his 'salesman's' trip to London, but had decided to stay at his more comfortable Main Headquarters in the Trianon Palace Hotel, Versailles, rather than his forward headquarters in Reims. He heard that day that the President was submitting his name to the Senate for nomination as 5-star General of the Armies. 'From Lt-Colonel to 5-star General of the Armies

[1] M379, Montgomery Papers.

in 3 years, 3 months and 16 days!' his diarist recorded proudly.[1] That afternoon General Bradley arrived to spend the night at Versailles. Eisenhower, Bradley, Bedell Smith and General Hughes sat down to play bridge; and it was at the bridge table in the Trianon Palace Hotel that the first news of German attack on Bradley's front came through.

Bradley's sang-froid in the face of the German counter-offensive in his sector is difficult to understand, save in terms of his recent 'victory' with Eisenhower at Maastricht. Having won agreement to divide the Allied offensive effort into two unrelated thrusts to the Ruhr and Frankfurt, and in the centre to feint only, Bradley was understandably unwilling to move troops away from Patton's new thrust against the Saar, designed to kick off on 19 December. Eisenhower's own biographer, Stephen Ambrose, blamed the Supreme Commander/Land Force Commander as 'the man responsible for the weakness of the line in the Ardennes, the one who had insisted on continuing the offensive north and south of the area. As a result of his policies there was no general SHAEF reserve available.'[2] But Ambrose was being harsh on Eisenhower. It was Bradley's plan which Eisenhower had accepted. Bradley was loth to call it off. The game of bridge, like Drake's bowls, thus went on.

General Hodges, upon whose front the main German blow had fallen, reacted very differently. From the very beginning it was clear that it was no small affair. An enemy order captured on the first day of the German attack spoke of a counter-offensive order 'signed by von Rundstedt' and on which 'the enemy is gambling his life. According to von Rundstedt the fate of the German nation depends upon the success or failure of this savage blow directed at the VIII Corps. According to PW's captured, who were more precise, the counter-offensive is a pincer-movement on AACHEN, and an attack is apparently about to begin in the Ninth Army area to join up with those troops who have attacked to the south,' Hodges' ADC noted already on the night of 16 December.[3]

Because the enemy began his assault with infantry, Hodges was initially inclined to underrate the seriousness of the attack—'at first it appeared that these counter attacks of the Boche were only what the General called "spoiling attacks", Captain Sylvan recorded,

> to take pressure off the important V Corps drive towards the ROER river dams. But by eleven o'clock [a.m. on 16 December] it

[1] Diary of Harry C. Butcher, Eisenhower Library, Abilene, Kansas.
[2] Stephen Ambrose, *Eisenhower1890–1952*, New York 1983.
[3] Diary of William C. Sylvan, Military History Institute, Carlisle, Pennsylvania.

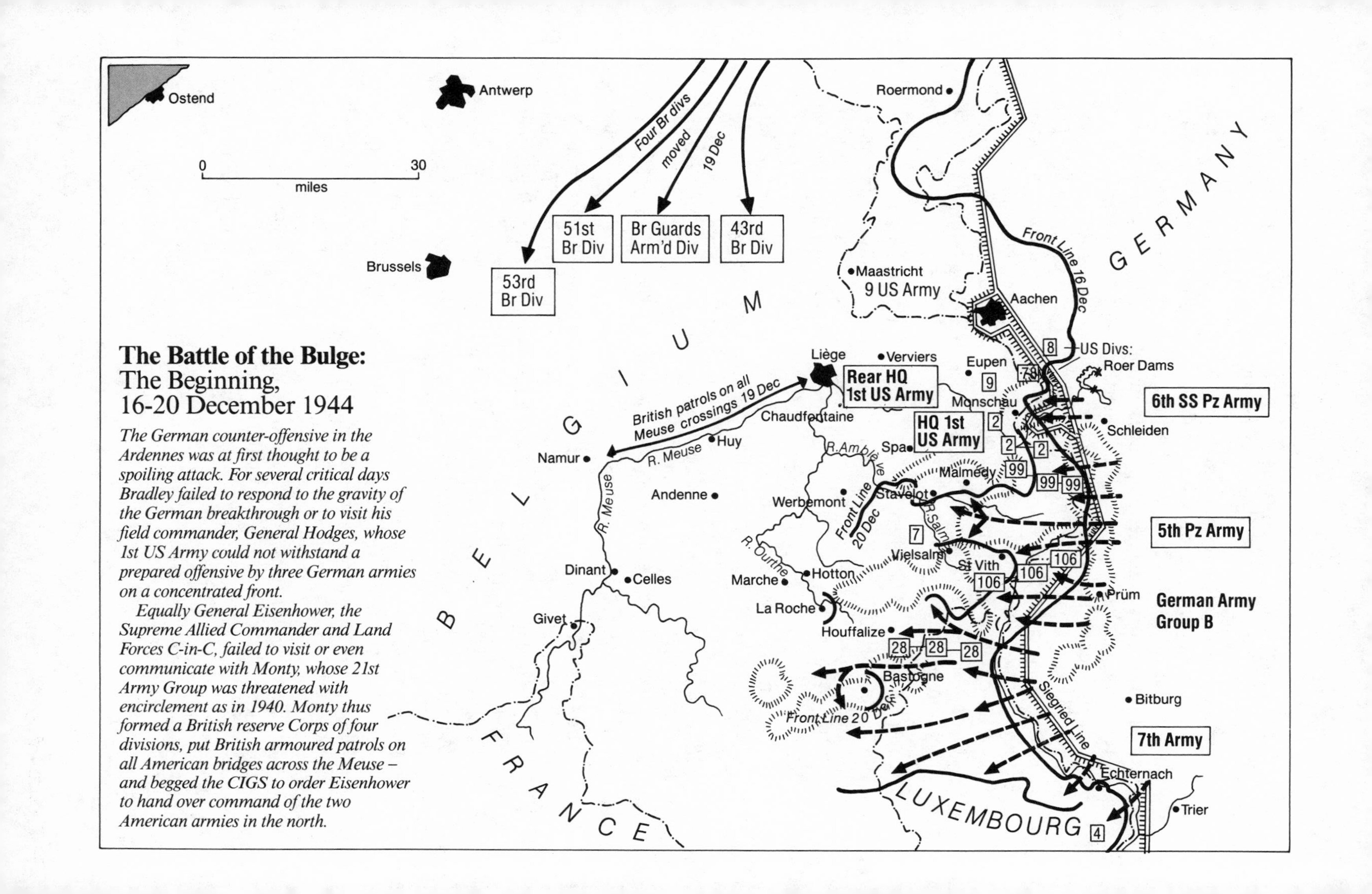

The Battle of the Bulge:
The Beginning, 16-20 December 1944

The German counter-offensive in the Ardennes was at first thought to be a spoiling attack. For several critical days Bradley failed to respond to the gravity of the German breakthrough or to visit his field commander, General Hodges, whose 1st US Army could not withstand a prepared offensive by three German armies on a concentrated front.

Equally General Eisenhower, the Supreme Allied Commander and Land Forces C-in-C, failed to visit or even communicate with Monty, whose 21st Army Group was threatened with encirclement as in 1940. Monty thus formed a British reserve Corps of four divisions, put British armoured patrols on all American bridges across the Meuse – and begged the CIGS to order Eisenhower to hand over command of the two American armies in the north.

> became more evident that the enemy was staking all on this drive and that he was putting his maximum strength against the 106th Div and in the general area bordering the boundary between V and VIII Corps. General Hodges immediately put the 1st Div, resting in AUBEL, on a six hour alert and not long afterward in a call to General Bradley he was given the 7th Armd Div of the Ninth Army and the 10th Armd Div of the 3rd Army. . . . The General was neither optimistic nor pessimistic during the day; knowing on the basis of the evidence thus far received, that this is an all-out enemy effort, he believes that we can not only handle them but that this is the quickest way to bring about the decimation of the Wehrmacht.[1]

But if Hodges believed he could crush the German counter-offensive with his existing forces and two extra American armoured divisions, he was remarkably optimistic. Bradley had been out of touch for much of the day, having left his Luxembourg headquarters at breakfast time by car, and lunching at the Ritz in Paris before driving on to join the Supreme Commander at Versailles. His aide left him there to discuss manpower shortages and play bridge, returning to a boozy afternoon and evening in the company of Ernest Hemingway, which ended at the Lido 'where we saw bare-breasted girls do the hootchy kootchie until it was late and we hurried home'.[2]

Early the following morning, 17 December, Bradley admitted to his ADC the first signs of anxiety:

> The General did not look worried but he was tired. Last night he and Ike cracked a bottle of champagne to mark Ike's fifth star. Hughes brought the champagne in from Paris with him. They then played five rubbers of bridge, got to bed about twelve.
>
> General Bradley admitted however that he had not slept well. He lay awake, thinking of the problem posed by the German attack. While it is threatening, it is not yet dangerous or critical. The main force is aimed towards Liege in an effort to cut off our supply line while the feint was aimed towards Luxembourg, both attacks being made in those sectors only lightly held by our troops while we massed the strength before the logical approaches to Germany.[3]

Bradley was still convinced that von Rundstedt was trying to 'spoil' the American offensive—particularly Patton's thrust towards the Saar. 'He is getting worried about the Third [US Army] which is

[1] Ibid.
[2] Diary of Chester B. Hansen, loc. cit.
[3] Ibid.

now up against the wall and threatening to break through,' Bradley told his ADC. 'Of course, if he can force us to pull our strength out of there to stop his counter attack, he will achieve his primary purpose.'[1]

Bradley thus assumed the Germans were reacting to Patton's threat—though neither then nor later was there evidence to show the Germans were in any way anxious about a 'break through' by Patton. Bradley's obstinate belief in this respect was to have dire effects on his handling of the battle in the next few days.

That the situation was dangerous and indeed critical must have been hourly more apparent to Bradley as he received reports of German progress. The commander of the 4th US Infantry Division called up Bradley's Chief of Staff on the morning of 17 December to say he had committed all his men to battle at Echternach, but could not halt the advance of the German Volksgrenadier divisions without American armour. The Germans were across the river, and could strike south into the city of Luxembourg unless reinforcements arrived soon. 'If you don't get the armor up here quickly, you had better get set to move,' he had warned, referring to Bradley's Army Group headquarters.[2]

Bradley finally arrived back at his HQ at mid-afternoon on 17 December—thirty-six hours after the attack had begun. Like Rommel at Alamein and in Normandy, he had been absent when the enemy's blow was struck—and as Monty had always argued, it is hard to recover from a faulty plan or dispositions. Bradley was so certain that von Rundstedt would use his Panzer Army reserve to stifle either the Ruhr thrust or Patton's Metz offensive that he had failed to echelon his forces in the Ardennes for defence in depth. 'Our lines have not been built in depth with the offensive mindedness of our command,' Bradley's ADC acknowledged that day. 'Our reserves existed in moderate strength but it is difficult to estimate how much of a drive they might be able to contain.'[3]

The American strategy of 'bulling ahead' on too many fronts was being embarrassingly exposed. Far from 'stretching out' the German forces to breaking point, it had enabled Hitler to regroup and form a striking reserve which left Bradley stunned. 'Pardon my French—but where in hell has this son of a bitch gotten all his strength?' he exclaimed when he surveyed his situation maps in Luxembourg.[4]

Bradley himself never lost his composure—indeed his stature as a

[1] Ibid.
[2] Ibid.
[3] Ibid.
[4] Ibid.

soldier is well illustrated by the remark he made to his ADC when asked if he would move back his headquarters from Luxembourg, in line with the American fighter squadrons that were retreating to safer airfields in the rear. 'I will never move backwards with a headquarters,' he said. 'There is too much prestige at stake.'[1]

Bradley's rock-like composure, however, was not reflected either at his own or in subordinate headquarters. The German parachute operation on 16 December, with troops dressed in American uniforms, as well as the report, on 17 December, that SS units had machine-gunned 200 American prisoners, helped create a sense of panic, intensifying as the rolling German advance destroyed American communications.

Monty kept in close touch with the situation by means of his famous team of young Liaison Officers, trained to report in person back to him without the use of telephones or signals equipment. Thus when Monty himself signalled his first nightly report to Brooke on the evening of 17 December, he was fully in the picture, despite having received no information whatever from Eisenhower or from Bradley, his neighbouring Army Group Commander. On 16 December, as the German attack began, Eisenhower had sent his Deputy Chief of Staff, Lt-General Whiteley, to ask Monty's views of the SHAEF staff's plan for future Allied operations:

> This was much on the same lines as IKE's plan. He asked me for my views and I left him in no doubt on that matter. I rubbed in to him the points that must form the main features of any plan. I also suggested the staff might well represent that commanders are supposed to make their own plans and said that unless IKE could make up his mind quickly as to what he wanted to do and would issue definite orders we were quite likely to drift into an unfavourable situation vis-à-vis the enemy.

Not even Monty can have realized, on the morning of 16 December, how prescient was this warning. Eisenhower had issued no directive as Land Force Commander since 28 October—almost *eight weeks* past. To Monty's professional mind this was culpably wrong—and the growing reports of German counter-offensive did not therefore surprise him, as he reported to Brooke on the night of 17 December:

> Meanwhile the Germans have put in a strong attack against the centre of 12 Army Group. The main enemy weight is north of PRUM and his thrust line there seems to be on the general axis

[1] Ibid.

HALLSCHLAG–BULLANGE–MALMEDY. Enemy troops had penetrated to within three miles of MALMEDY at 1600 hrs today. The area EUPEN–MALMEDY–SPA–LIEGE–VERVIERS is one huge administrative area full of petrol and workshops.

My LO has just returned from First US Army HQ at SPA. It seems clear that the enemy gained surprise. The Americans have practically all their troops in the front line from LINNICH to KARLSRUHE and have no reserves immediately available to hold the enemy penetration. Two divisions [sic] are being sent south from Ninth Army and one from the DUREN sector of First Army. One division has been sent north from Third Army. BRADLEY's HQ are at LUXEMBOURG. The Americans are definitely tactically unbalanced and First Army at 1700 hrs had no idea as to how they could deal with the problem.[1]

Monty appreciated the danger to his own 21st Army Group if the German forces sliced through Hodges' front and crossed the Meuse for the Canadians and British would be as effectively cut off as the Belgians and BEF had been in May 1940. Irrespective of Eisenhower he had therefore ordered certain units to start defending 21st Army Group's southern flank—'I am taking certain measures myself to ensure adequate security in my southern flank and shall get 43 Div and Gds Armd Div out of the area southeast of MAESEYCK tomorrow and move them west of the MEUSE. I am also moving 53 Div from the ROERMOND area to TURNHOUT.'[2]

As to the future, Monty was adamant that Bradley should, however belatedly, take the point that his Saar offensive was a mistake, and move Patton north, as Monty had pleaded at Maastricht:

It looks as if we may now have to pay the price for the policy of drift and lack of proper control of the operations which has been a marked feature of the last three months.

Also the present enemy offensive is likely to show up our faulty command set up,

he predicted.

The Americans have had to react at once and are now milking their northern flank to get troops to restore the situation.

I have represented to SHAEF that the proper answer to the enemy offensive is to launch operation VERITABLE [the preparatory stage for a crossing of the Rhine in the north] as early as

[1] Cable to CIGS, M380, of 2155 hrs, 17.12.44 in 'Command Set-up in Western Europe December 44–January 45' file, Montgomery Papers.

[2] Ibid.

possible. But to do this they must draw on their south flank for troops and if they draw on their north flank then VERITABLE will not be able to be launched. If this happens we shall have to admit that we have suffered a bad set-back.

Bradley disagreed – indeed he only agreed (in consultation with Eisenhower) to send up the 10th US Armoured Division from Patton's army with great misgivings, knowing that Patton would protest. Patton did—recording in his diary that Bradley was taking 'counsel of his fears' and was contemptibly 'timid'.[1] Far from wondering whether the American policy of dispersal was really correct, in view of the German counter-offensive, Patton blamed Hodges' troops in the Ardennes for not having been 'more aggressive'; 'one must never sit still,' he opined with typically obtuse bravado[2]—ignoring the fact that it was his own Metz-Saar thrust which had so weakened Bradley's front further north that Hodges, left on his own, was quite unable to stem the concentrated assault by three German armies.

The next day, 18 December, Bradley intended to fly north to see Hodges, but the German parachute drop behind American lines had made Hodges' staff jumpy, and Hodges' ADC rang Bradley to suggest the Army Group Commander fly to Liège and be escorted thence by car to First US Army HQ at Spa. The previous evening Bradley had obtained Eisenhower's consent to use SHAEF's only airborne reserve, the 82nd and 101st US Airborne Divisions, in a ground defence role at Bastogne and further north; but by the morning of 18 December it was evident that even the use of these two SHAEF reserve divisions would not be enough to save Hodges. Whether Monty's emphatic advice to General Whiteley was responsible or not, at 10.30 a.m. on 18 December Bradley finally gave in. He phoned Patton at Nancy, and told him to drive straight to Luxembourg with his senior Intelligence, operations and supply officers. 'What he was going to suggest would be unacceptable to me, but he wanted to see me,' Patton recorded.[3] Patton was to close down his Saar offensive and move north, as Monty had counselled for so long.

At Luxembourg Bradley asked how many units Patton could switch immediately north; Patton replied three, to be ready to move in twenty-four hours. Even as Patton drove back to Nancy, though, Bradley was phoning Patton's Chief of Staff to state that the situation was getting worse every hour, and to ask if one combat command could move already that night.

[1] *The Patton Papers*, ed. M. Blumenson, Boston 1982.
[2] Ibid.
[3] Ibid.

Although later writers would extol Eisenhower's prompt and confident performance in the 'Battle of the Bulge', the truth is that Eisenhower reacted with amazing slowness and indecision for a supposed Land Force Commander. It was to take him three entire days before he convened a meeting of his Army Group Commanders—and five days before he even spoke to Monty on the telephone. By then Eisenhower's headquarters was in a state of extreme apprehension, with the Supreme Commander locked up in his office for fear of assassination.

Bradley's earlier refusal to move his headquarters further north, nearer to First US Army's Ruhr thrust, now proved a grave handicap. As the chief SHAEF signals officer later acknowledged, Luxembourg was a dead end in terms of signals. By insisting on remaining in Luxembourg Bradley impressed his staff and the local population with his imperturbability—but as far as communications were concerned he thereby surrendered his ability to exercise command of the major part of his forces north of the German penetration.

Despite his conference with Patton, Bradley still hoped to contain the German offensive without taking too many forces from the Saar thrust—a thrust Bradley *still* believed, according to his ADC's diary on 18 December, was 'the logical one for us to take into Germany', and one which threatened the Germans with a 'crack through' that would justify Bradley's long-standing belief in the southern advance route into Germany. In fact Major Hansen assumed that the new conference convened by Eisenhower for 19 December 'will probably determine our ability to launch an all out offensive on the southern effort of Patton's, enable us to rush the Siegfried Line and hurry our way to the Rhine down in the sector of the Saar'—where 'the German according to Bradley, was desperately afraid of our strength there'.[1]

It was Bradley's obsession—it cannot be termed less—with this Saar thrust that was to be his and Eisenhower's undoing. In order to prepare for the conference on the 19 December, Bradley now dropped his plans to fly north to see Hodges—leaving Hodges to fight three German armies, two of them Panzer armies, on his own.

Bradley's confidence was inspiring to the staff around him, but of very little help to Hodges as the Sixth SS Panzer Army stormed that day into Stavelot, only a few miles south of Hodges' own headquarters at Spa. Bradley, having decided not to visit Hodges, went home for dinner and returned to his office 'after dinner in good spirits despite the situation—which he obviously did not view as seriously as most of the others,' Major Hansen recorded.[2]

[1] Diary of Chester B. Hansen, loc. cit.

[2] Ibid.

This was precisely what worried Hodges. 'The situation is rapidly deteriorating,' Hodges' ADC noted that night. 'It is not yet known whether Twelfth Army Group fully appreciates the seriousness of the situation though both General Hodges and General Kean [Chief of Staff] talked with General Bradley half a dozen times during the day.'[1] By 4 p.m., as German tanks were reported heading northwards towards Spa itself, Hodges turned out his whole headquarters staff to man a road-block; his Chief of Intelligence declared that General Hodges 'ought to be prepared to leave at once and that a Cub plane was waiting . . . to take him away'.[2] With over four million gallons of petrol at the Spa storage dump, the Germans were within an ace of getting the very fuel they required for a drive on Antwerp; but by 'one of the fortunes of war that can never be explained'[3] the Germans suddenly turned south-west instead of striking further north. Hodges, nevertheless, decided it was high time to move. His headquarters, in haste bordering on panic, began to burn secret files and retreat to First US Army's rear headquarters at Chaudfontaine. By 10 p.m. Hodges, his Chief of Staff and other senior officers had left—having omitted to inform anyone else of their departure.

Monty, hearing still nothing of the battlefield situation from Eisenhower or Bradley or Hodges, meanwhile sent out his entire Liaison Officer team to assemble what was to be the clearest picture of the German penetration in the Allied camp—even sending them to American Corps commanders when Hodges' headquarters proved unable to give an accurate report. 'A very confused situation exists in First Army area and the HQ of higher formations do not really know what is going in,' Monty signalled at 10 p.m. on 18 December to Brooke.

> I have had to send down to the HQ of Corps to ascertain the picture.
>
> The main enemy thrust has now penetrated some 20 miles and reached STAVELOT and the road centre at TROIS PONTS and VIELSAM. Indications point to a possible strong attack coming in north of MONSCHAU directed on EUPEN and VERVIERS.
>
> There is much confusion in the area of 5 and 8 [U.S.] Corps where hospitals and administrative echelons are being moved back and divisions are being moved in. Incoming divisions are being thrown at these two Corps, each of which has now seven divisions and neither Corps can handle so many.

[1] Diary of William C. Sylvan, loc. cit.
[2] Ibid.
[3] Ibid.

> The two American airborne divisions 82 and 101 have been sent up for use in a ground role.
>
> I think the Americans ought to be able to hold the enemy if they take a proper control at Army and Corps HQ level but a strong enemy thrust north of MONSCHAU if successful would be most awkward for them.
>
> I have been urging for two days that the whole southern front should close down and become defensive under PATCH [Commander, 7th US Army] and that Patton's *army* should be moved northward to put in a strong attack on the axis PRUM–BONN.
>
> I have heard tonight that IKE has now agreed to do this but we have had to enlist the help of the Germans to make him do so. Such a thrust would completely queer the German pitch. . . .
>
> I had hoped to come home and spend a quiet Xmas at HINDHEAD but unless the situation improves I shall not leave here.[1]

Monty's personal Liaison Officer to Bradley's headquarters had reported that afternoon that Bradley's headquarters were not overly worried by the situation; but as Monty's other Liaison Officers began to report in, it became obvious that the situation was, if anything, deteriorating—and that Monty would himself have to take a hand.

[1] M381, Montgomery Papers.

CHAPTER TWO

Cut Clean in Half

BRADLEY WAS so removed from the reality of Hodges' predicament on the evening of 18 December that, according to his ADC's diary, he still believed that Hodges' headquarters at Spa was 'not planning to move out'.[1] The following morning, after main telephone communication with Hodges had been cut, Bradley was even more ignorant of what was really happening. 'Bastogne is in enemy hands,' his ADC recorded. 'In the center area of the principal breakthrough the situation remains obscure,' Major Hansen confessed.[2] According to Captain Butcher, Eisenhower's naval ADC-cum-PR-executive, there was speculation 'that Bradley's tactical headquarters at Luxembourg might have to be moved, as the enemy was getting close',[3] but Bradley remained adamant the headquarters would remain in Luxembourg. 'Bradley was up early this morning but apparently unworried even though the situation continued to become more aggravated with the commitment of additional enemy reserves in the breakthrough near Bastogne,' Hansen recorded.[4]

At 9.30 a.m. on 19 December Bradley left Luxembourg for his Rear Headquarters at Verdun to attend the conference which Eisenhower had requested late the previous night. Eisenhower's SHAEF staff had, as Monty understood to be the case, prepared a directive to be issued 'after the meeting tomorrow'[5]—a directive which ordered Devers to close down all offensive operations in the south, and to relieve Patton's Third US Army so that this could be shifted north. Having restored the situation on Hodges' First US Army front, 12th US Army Group was then to mount the single northern offensive Monty had proposed at the Maastricht conference, em-

[1] Diary of Chester B. Hansen, loc. cit.
[2] Ibid.
[3] H. C. Butcher, *My Three Years with Eisenhower*, New York 1948.
[4] Ibid.
[5] Intended directive set out in cable S71400 to Bradley and Devers from Eisenhower, 18.12.44. *The Papers of Dwight David Eisenhower*, ed. Alfred D. Chandler, *The War Years* Vol. III, Baltimore 1970. Montgomery must have been informed by telephone by Whiteley, judging by the cable, M381, he sent Brooke at 10 p.m. on 18.12.44.

ploying all of its three American constituent armies—'to launch a counter-offensive North of the Moselle. Attacks comprising this counter-offensive will converge on the general area Bonn–Cologne.'[1]

How the Allies could alter their offensive plan overnight, and how they could mount such an offensive in the middle of an alarming German counter-offensive were matters that were presumably to be resolved at Verdun. But how serious was the German penetration in the Ardennes? At the 9 a.m. SHAEF Chiefs of Staff and Air Staff Conference at Versailles on 19 December, Bedell Smith announced that 'last night General Bradley was inclined to take a fairly optimistic view of the situation. The German armoured forces which had made the break-through were relatively small and the disorganisation of the U.S. divisions who had taken the force of this thrust was less than he had feared earlier.'[2]

That such a complacent view of events could have been presented, without dissent, at the senior Allied Chiefs of Staff conference some three days after the enemy offensive began is an illustration of the battlefield ignorance of SHAEF, as well as a grave indictment of Eisenhower's claim to be an effective Land Force Commander.

Meanwhile Eisenhower had himself departed to Verdun, taking with him his Chief of Intelligence, Maj-General Kenneth Strong—the Intelligence staff officer most responsible for Eisenhower's policy of splitting the Allied thrust into Ruhr and Frankfurt offensives. The atmosphere was tense, but still remote from practical reality. Eisenhower was tempted to take field command himself, but instead turned to Patton. 'Said he wanted me to get to Luxembourg and take command of the battle and make a strong counter attack with at least six divisions. The fact that three of these divisions [overrun by the German advance] exist only on paper did not enter his head,' Patton recorded with some savagery.[3] Patton offered to attack in three days' time, with three divisions. Patton's biographer and Official American Historian, Martin Blumenson, nevertheless considered that this was 'the sublime moment' of Patton's career, requiring him to 'reorient his entire army from an eastward direction to the north, a 90-degree turn. . . . Altogether, it was an operation that only a master could think of executing.'[4]

In fact Patton, like Monty, had been alerted the previous night about Eisenhower's intention to move Third US Army north of the

[1] Intended directive, cable S71400, loc. cit.

[2] Chiefs of Staff and Air Staff Conference, SHAEF War Diaries (AIR 37/1118), PRO.

[3] *The Patton Papers*, op. cit.

[4] Commentary in *The Patton Papers*, op. cit.

Moselle; but the fact that it had taken three entire days of battle for the Americans to accept the need to close down their Saar front and move Patton north testifies to the sheer obstinacy of Eisenhower, Bradley and their staffs. It is ironic that Patton's obsession with the Metz–Saar route into Germany had been responsible in large part for the American refusal to concentrate their forces upon the Ruhr thrust as Monty desired; yet as soon as Eisenhower offered Patton command of the American forces in the southern part of the Ardennes, Patton accepted and abandoned his planned Saar offensive with such alacrity that Eisenhower was bewildered. Patton immediately gave orders that his Third US Army headquarters was to move from Nancy to Luxembourg. Had Eisenhower ordered such a move in September, October, November or at the Maastricht conference on 7 December, Patton would have doubtless objected—but he would certainly have obeyed, as he now did on 19 December.

Patton's *volte-face* was all the more extraordinary, since a bare five days before he had been berating Monty in his diary for insisting that the Allies close down the Saar offensive and concentrate their forces—'I do not see how they stand such conversation,' Patton noted, certain that with God's help it was 'up to me to make a breakthrough [to the Saar], and I feel that, God helping, it will come about'.[1]

While Patton's army was belatedly switched north, however, the anxious cocoon in which Eisenhower, Bradley and the SHAEF staff were living was finally stripped—for, returning from Versailles, Maj-General Strong received reports which at last confounded his view that the Germans were engaged only in a spoiling attack, designed to force the Allies to react. From unrealistic optimism ('This situation might develop very favourably for the Allies,' Strong's deputy, Brigadier-General Betts had remarked at the 9 a.m. conference[2]) the staff at SHAEF suddenly began to panic—as Monty's Chief of Intelligence related to the American Official Historian after the war:

> Bedell [Smith] told a direct lie when he said there was no flap at SHAEF over the Ardennes. They kept calling us until we thought we would go crazy. Strong . . . got hysterical over the Ardennes. . . .[3]

To the same historian Maj-General Strong himself confessed (also in 1947), that it was not 'until on Tuesday [19 December] when he

[1] *The Patton Papers*, op. cit.

[2] Chiefs of Staff and Air Staff Conferences, SHAEF War Diaries, loc. cit.

[3] Brigadier E. T. Williams, Pogue interview of 30–31.5.1947, OCMH Collection, MHI, Carlisle, Pennsylvania.

came back from conference at Verdun and found evidence of parts of 10 [enemy] divs around Bastogne' that he became 'worried'.[1] Strong also admitted that although Eisenhower was 'completely right in insisting on Allied drive in north and south', he was in retrospect unsure 'that the administrative situation was in proper touch with strategy. Couldn't maintain two front attacks at the time,' he confided.[2] Such a confession he omitted, however, in his memoirs, in which he was at pains to assist the SHAEF 'cover-up'.

Monty, meanwhile, had still heard nothing direct from Eisenhower, his supposed C-in-C—as he reported in a telephone call to General Simpson at the War Office. 'Monty spoke to me on the telephone and asked me to tell the CIGS what he was doing about the situation,' the Director of Military Operations later recalled.[3]

> Not having had any communication whatever from Bradley or Eisenhower—he had found it impossible to get any information out of either of those HQs—he had gone on with his policy of sending out a great many Liaison Officers to cover the front of the First US Army, to find out exactly what was happening. . . .
>
> He had had a report, which he did not quite believe, that the Germans had got to Bastogne and were in that town, thirty-five miles north-east of Luxembourg, and they had also got to Larouche, which was thirty-six miles due south of Liège, but he did not believe that either. He hoped to have more information later and it might merely be found that they were reconnaissance elements.
>
> What he had found out was that neither General Hodges nor General Simpson had had any communication whatever from General Bradley, at 12th Army Group HQ, and he did not see how they could have had any communication, with Bradley positioned as far south as Luxembourg.
>
> Monty asked me to tell the CIGS that he was still watching the situation very carefully. He was uneasy about his southern flank, and he could make available at short notice a corps of four divisions to look after that flank and indeed help the Americans if they wanted it—the HQ of 30 Corps.[4]

Up until this point Monty had been confident that, despite the confusion and lack of up-to-date information, the Americans would be able to run their own battle in the Ardennes.[5] But during the

[1] Maj-General K. W. D. Strong, Pogue interview of 12.12.47, loc. cit.

[2] Ibid.

[3] Eugene Wason interview for Sir Denis Hamilton.

[4] Ibid.

[5] 'I think the Americans ought to be able to hold the enemy if they take proper control at Army and Corps HQ level': M381 of 18.12.44, loc. cit.

morning of 19 December he received alarming news. Two of his Liaison Officers had driven to Hodges' headquarters at Spa—and found the cupboard bare! As Major Tom Bigland recorded in his diary: 'Find HQ deserted & b'fast laid!' [1] In a letter to the American author Ralph Ingersoll after the war, Bigland described his arrival in greater detail:

> Another of the Field Marshal's Liaison Officers came with me so that he could report back to him while I went on to Eagle Tac [Bradley's headquarters in Luxembourg] with details of his [Monty's] plans. We found no Army M.Ps. in Spa and walked into the H.Q. to find literally not one single person there except a German woman. Breakfast was laid and the Christmas tree was decorated in the dining room, telephones were in all the offices, papers were all over the place but there was no one left to tell visitors where they had gone to. Germans in the town said that they had gone suddenly and quickly down the road at 3 a.m. I found them again at their rear H.Q. and here they had even less control of the battle than the day before.[2]

Bigland had been detailed to speak to Hodges, obtain an up-to-date situation report and send it back to Monty via Major Carol Mather while he, Bigland, continued to Bradley's headquarters at Luxembourg. The empty headquarters at Spa—'abandoned more or less intact' as Mather afterwards recalled—'was what set the panic off'.[3]

Hodges had not impressed Monty as an Army Commander. The news that he had abandoned his headquarters without informing anybody worried Monty—indeed raised the spectre of a complete breakdown of command in the American sector. Monty therefore telephoned Dempsey at 5 p.m. Irrespective of what the Americans might eventually do, Monty had decided to transfer Horrocks' 30 Corps HQ from the Canadian Army to Dempsey's Second British Army; it was to become Dempsey's reserve Corps on the west bank of the Meuse in case the Germans did break right through Hodges' Army. The Guards Armoured Division, which on 17 December he had ordered to be pulled out of the front line as a reserve, was now to be sent to the west bank of the Meuse; 51st Highland Division was also being transferred forthwith from the Canadian Army, so that from dawn the next morning Dempsey would have four full-blooded British divisions ready to halt any German attempt to cross the

[1] Diary of Lt-Colonel T. S. Bigland, communicated to author.
[2] Letter of August 1946, communicated to author.
[3] Letter from Major C. Mather to author, March 1984.

Meuse. Meanwhile, having heard from his LOs that there were no garrisons on the Meuse bridges in the First US Army sector, Monty gave Dempsey the 2nd Battalion of the Household Cavalry Regiment and ordered patrols along the river from Namur to Vige, ten miles north of Liège, as well as sending patrols southwards along the Meuse as far as Givet. To send such British patrols some twenty to fifty miles into the American sectors of the American First and Ninth Armies in the dark was perhaps foolhardy; but the British regiment was safely 'disposed on the river line shortly after first light' the next day, as Dempsey recorded in his diary.[1] The victor of the classic defensive battles of Alam Halfa and Medenine was taking no chances. His own diarist noted:

> As soon as the Field-Marshal saw what was happening, although he had received no orders or requests of any kind from General Eisenhower, he took certain precautionary measures to ensure that, if the Germans got to the MEUSE, they would certainly not get over that river. It was necessary for these steps to be carried out quickly, as otherwise the British area might be in grave danger, and a threat might develop to BRUSSELS and even to ANTWERP.
>
> To safeguard the British area therefore, and to be able if necessary to intervene in the battle, on the 19th December he ordered 30 Corps with three divisions under command to assemble in the general area LOUVAIN–ST. TROND–GEMBLOUX, and he also placed reconnaissance patrols on all bridges over the MEUSE between LIEGE and GIVET, although these were outside the British area.[2]

British patrols now covered every Meuse crossing between Maastricht in Simpson's Ninth US Army sector and Givet, forty miles west of Bastogne, in Hodges' First US Army sector. Horrocks was warned that, if the Germans swept on, he must be prepared to advance into the US sector and meet the enemy on the Meuse.

Monty was undoubtedly in his element. As he reported to the CIGS that night:

> I have myself had no orders or requests of any sort. But in order to safeguard the British area and also to be able to intervene in the battle if the Germans attempt to cross the MEUSE I am acting as follows. Officers and recce patrols are being established at all MEUSE bridges and crossing places between incl LIEGE and GIVET by dawn tomorrow to report by W/T direct to me.

[1] Diary of General Sir Miles Dempsey, PRO.

[2] 'Notes on the Campaign in North west Europe', Montgomery Papers.

> 30 Corps with under command 43 DIV 51 DIV 53 DIV Guards Armoured DIV and three independent armoured brigades is being assembled . . . I can add 4 C'dn Armd DIV to 30 Corps in 48 hrs time making it five divisions in all. I shall then direct 30 Corps under Second Army to operate to maintain intact the line of the MEUSE from LIEGE to NAMUR and DINANT.[1]

It was from this moment that the chances of an enemy break-through to Antwerp were sealed, whatever happened in the Ardennes. But the confusion that existed in the various American headquarters and the lack of unified and coherent Allied command was an affront to Monty's professional pride.

'My own opinion is that the general situation is ugly,' he commented to Brooke,

> as the American forces have been cut clean in half and the Germans can reach the MEUSE at NAMUR without any opposition. The command set up has always been very faulty and now is quite futile with BRADLEY at LUXEMBOURG and the front cut into two. I have told WHITELEY [at SHAEF] that IKE ought to place me in operational charge of all troops on the northern half of the front. I consider he should be given a direct order by someone to do so. This situation needs to be handled very firmly and with a tight grip.[2]

But who could *compel* Eisenhower to take such action, other than the Combined Chiefs of Staff? And what of the 'political' ramifications of a British general being given command of the main American front in the midst of the greatest American setback of World War II since Pearl Harbor?

At one level the notion seemed preposterous. But in the context of the battlefield it was far from being so. Monty was not exaggerating when he told 'Simbo' Simpson at the War Office that he had found it 'impossible to get any information' out of Eisenhower's or Bradley's

[1] M382 of 2315 hrs, 19.12.44, Montgomery Papers. At 1700 hrs General Crerar, the Commander of First Canadian Army, noted a telephone call from Monty, ordering Horrocks' 30 Corps to leave Canadian Army and 'move tonight to HASSELT, coming under command Second British Army'. Horrocks was to take 43rd, 53rd, and the Guards Armoured Division under immediate command, with 51st Highland Division being assembled in the Canadian Army sector ready to be moved. 'The enemy penetration of the front First US Army was deep and, potentially, serious. With that in mind, he [Monty] had decided to make immediate re-dispositions in 21 Army Group, in order to secure its right flank': Memorandum, 19.12.44, War Diary (CAB 106/1064), PRO.

[2] Ibid.

headquarters.[1] Thus, although the Combined Chiefs of Staff, Roosevelt and Churchill were supposed to obtain their battle-front information via SHAEF, both the War Office and Churchill now turned to Monty as the only Allied commander capable of giving a realistic picture of the battlefield. Indeed, as General Simpson informed Monty, the Prime Minister began to use Monty's nightly signals to Brooke in his Cabinet War Room to mark up the maps.[2]

Monty's signal on the night 19 December was the clearest Churchill was to receive that day:

> The situation in the American area is not good. The base of the German penetration is from UDENBRATH in the north to ECHTERNACH in the south. Enemy troops have penetrated westwards from this base for varying distances the deepest being in the north where German armour has reached HOTTON and LAROCHE and MARCHE.
>
> On the north flank of the penetration the Americans hold a fairly firm line from UDENBRATH westwards through WAIMES to about DURBUY. I can get no firm information as to the south flank between ECHTERNACH and BASTOGNE but it seems clear that the Americans hold BASTOGNE. On the west flank there are no American troops west of the line DURBUY—BASTOGNE and the Germans may well reach the NAMUR area tomorrow as there is nothing to stop them.
>
> In that part of First Army area north of the line UDENBRATH to DURBUY there is great confusion and all signs of a full-scale withdrawal.
>
> There is a definite lack of grip and control and no one has a clear picture as to the situation. First Army left SPA very hurriedly and my LO arrived there this morning to find a deserted HQ and stores and office equipment lying about. There is an atmosphere of great pessimism in First and Ninth Armies due I think to the fact that everyone knows something has gone wrong and no one knows what or why.[3]

[1] Eugene Wason interview for Sir Denis Hamilton. As Monty's LO to Bradley later remarked, 'even the local people [civilians] knew more than the staff at Luxembourg': Lt-Colonel Tom Bigland, interview of 23.2.84.

[2] 'Knowing that you sent to CIGS a telegram containing operational news most nights he [the Prime Minister] asked that a copy of this telegram should be sent to the Defence Office each day. They mark up his map there and also send him a copy for his personal perusal . . . They [SHAEF] seem disinclined to tell us anything: I think it is because they don't know much themselves': letter from General Simpson to Monty (DMO/113/M) of 23.12.44, Montgomery Papers.

[3] M382, loc. cit.

Not unnaturally American writers have avoided having to give an honest reconstruction of this débâcle; as Colonel J. O. Curtis, one of Eisenhower's senior operational Intelligence officers, later remarked to the American Official historian, 'Ardennes business much bigger than [at first] believed. Will never have all the story.'[1] Even Monty, when writing his memoirs some fourteen years after the event, declined to tell the full story lest it further upset American amour-propre and the Atlantic Alliance; his Ardennes signals have therefore remained unpublished for four decades.

'BRADLEY is still at LUXEMBOURG,' Monty's 19 December report continued,

> but I understand he is moving as his HQ are in danger. I have no information as to where he is moving.[2] I presume IKE is at REIMS but I have heard nothing from him or from BRADLEY.[3]

In fact Eisenhower was at Versailles, locked up in the Trianon Palace Hotel with the windows closed, curtains drawn and shutters latched, day and night, as Air Vice-Marshal Robb recorded.[4] Telephone communication did however exist between SHAEF and 21st Army Group.

> I have impressed on SHAEF the urgent need to establish definite defensive garrisons at all the MEUSE bridges between LIEGE and GIVET even if the garrison is only a workshop or RASC company or any administrative unit,

Monty informed the CIGS.[5] He had heard that Patton *was* to be moved north to help meet the German counter-offensive, but this would not be in time to stop the Panzer thrust towards NAMUR:

> Patton with five or six divisions is moving up from the south to the BASTOGNE area but this move will not be completed by Saturday. The present American tendency is to throw reserves in piecemeal as they arrive and I have suggested a warning against this.[6]

[1] Pogue interview of 16.5.1950, loc. cit.
[2] A part of Bradley's headquarters staff, belonging to the Intelligence section, was moved on 19.12.44, but operations and administration and supply staff in fact remained in Luxembourg.
[3] M382, loc. cit.
[4] Air Chief Marshal Sir James Robb, Pogue interview of 3.2. 47, loc. cit.
[5] M382, loc. cit.
[6] Ibid.

What was truly remarkable was that even after three nights and four days of fighting Monty, as 21st Army Group Commander, had received no single order or request: 'I have myself had no orders or requests of any sort,' Monty commented almost with disbelief—and urged Brooke to put pressure on Eisenhower either to take a grip of the battle or put Monty in command.[1]

Monty's signal went off at 11.15 p.m., on 19 December in cypher; but General Whiteley was still uneasy about suggesting to Eisenhower that Monty be given command. According to Maj-General Strong's memoirs, it was only at midnight that reports about the German offensive became so alarming that Strong decided they must act: 'By midnight the news from the front had become so bad that I felt it absolutely essential to inform Bedell Smith about my growing doubts whether the Allies were matching up to the situation. Some German units had penetrated well beyond Bastogne and were getting far too near the Meuse for my liking. So together with General Whiteley . . . I went to the Chief of Staff's quarters, next to his office and got him [Bedell Smith] out of bed.'[2]

Strong begged Smith to recommend to Eisenhower that Monty be given command at least of the Allied troops north of the penetration. 'General Whiteley added some operational details, saying that, to his sure knowledge, there had been no contact between General Bradley and the headquarters of his First Army in the north for two days. He had also received a report from an officer who had carried out an extensive personal reconnaissance in the rear of the American troops and found considerable confusion and disorganization.'[3]

Accounts differ about what happened next. Bradley recorded in 1948 that Bedell Smith had rung that night to ask if Bradley would object to Monty taking over the whole of his front north of Bastogne—and that he, Bradley, advanced no objection. Once again, however, Bradley's memory was telescoping events, for when Bedell Smith rang, Bradley in fact objected strongly to the proposal—so much so that Bedell Smith became ashamed at having suggested it, and rounded on the two hapless British officers with whom it had originated, calling them 'sons of bitches' and 'Limey bastards' in one of the fits of rough American temper for which he was well known. Strong, in the aftermath of World War II, declined to tell the American Official Historian the real story, pretending that there had been but a 'long discussion with Bedell. No serious argument.'[4] After

[1] Ibid.

[2] K. Strong, *Intelligence at the Top*, London 1968.

[3] Ibid.

[4] Pogue interview, loc. cit.

Bedell Smith's death, however, Strong felt free to chronicle the true sequence of events, including Bradley's continued lack of appreciation of the crisis faced by First US Army.

> Bedell Smith telephoned Bradley in our presence [on night of 19 December] and told him what we had said. Bradley replied that he doubted whether the situation was serious enough to warrant such a fundamental change of command, especially considering the effect it might have on opinion in America. . . . Bedell Smith himself then criticized our suggestions and said that whenever there was any real trouble the British did not appear to trust the Americans to handle it efficiently. Our proposal, he said, would be completely inacceptable to the Americans.[1]

In fact in his fury Bedell Smith announced that Strong and Whiteley were sacked: 'because of the view we had taken of the situation, neither Whiteley nor I could any longer be acceptable as staff officers to General Eisenhower. Next day instructions would be issued relieving us of our appointments and returning us to the United Kingdom.'[2]

Whether Whiteley telephoned Monty to inform him of this development—his own and Strong's dismissal for daring to advance the notion of Monty taking command—is unknown; but at 4.15 (Strong recalled that his meeting with Bedell Smith ended at 3 a.m.) on the morning of 20 December Maj-General Simpson was awakened at the United Services Club in London:

> It was a most unusual occurrence because somebody had to get the War Office to get onto the United Services Club (where I was staying) and then they had to wake me and take me down to the porter's lodge.
>
> I was awoken. I went down to the telephone to find Monty in a state of quite high excitement. He said he had just sent a telegram to the CIGS saying that really somebody must take charge of the whole northern flank at least, nobody was getting any orders, and there would be a major disaster if something was not done . . . He asked me to go down to the War Office immediately, to get hold of his telegram from the signals people, then to wake the CIGS and ask him to do something immediately. So I dressed at once and went to the War Office, and there was the telegram.[3]

[1] K. Strong, op, cit.
[2] Ibid.
[3] Wason interview, loc. cit.

Simpson read it very carefully, aware of the critical situation on the main Allied front—a crisis that affected the very future of the war.

'Well, the fact is I did nothing,' Simpson afterwards confided.

> It was no good waking up the CIGS; there was nothing he could do; there was nothing he could even get the other Chiefs-of-Staff to do. They would have to take the matter up with Washington, and the few hours remaining before the CIGS came to the office at nine o'clock meant that no time was really lost. So I went back and had breakfast. I then returned to carry on the day's work.
>
> I told the CIGS when he came in exactly what had happened. He said I was quite right. There was nothing I could do and nothing he was going to do now. He would tell the other Chiefs of Staff but they could not possibly give orders to Eisenhower, however dangerous the situation.[1]

The impotence and incoherence of a democratic Allied High Command in war against a dictatorship was perhaps never better illustrated than this scene in Brooke's office early on the morning of 20 December 1944, as the German Panzer armies swept on towards the Meuse. Even Monty's unilateral action in securing the Meuse bridges with British armoured patrols—translated into a SHAEF order early on 20 December—was mocked at Bradley's headquarters. Far from considering it necessary to place garrisons on the bridges, Bradley's headquarters were derisive. 'What the devil do they think we're doing?' Bradley's Chief of Staff discarded the idea, 'starting back for the beaches?'[2]

But Bradley's bravura in the face of Hitler's counter-offensive was growing less and less convincing to anyone save his own staff in Luxembourg. As Generals Strong and Whiteley prepared to pack their bags at Versailles, Eisenhower's Chief of Staff underwent a spectacular conversion.

[1] Ibid.
[2] Diary of Chester B. Hansen, loc. cit.

CHAPTER THREE

An Open and Shut Case

'I GAVE [MY LAST] briefing of the enemy situation', Maj-General Strong wrote nearly twenty-five years later. 'Bedell Smith, who presided, was glum and scarcely spoke. But as Whiteley and I started to walk across to Eisenhower's office after the briefing, he quietly joined us and took hold of my arm. He intended, he said, to put our proposals to General Eisenhower as his own; he would recommend giving Montgomery charge of the northern attack against the salient. Above all, he asked us to remain silent when he was speaking to Eisenhower since such a proposal would come much better from an American.'[1]

What was it that altered Bedell Smith's hot-tempered intransigence of the night before? At the 9 a.m. Chiefs of Staff meeting Colonel Lash of the Operations Staff reported that

> the two armoured thrusts that had pierced our front north of the Luxembourg frontier had made further progress and may now have joined up. . . . General Strong said that two further divisions of 6th Panzer Army were now committed, but two Panzer Grenadier Divisions were still unlocated. . . . It was appreciated that the Germans might be prepared to give ground on the Eastern Front and in ITALY in order to reinforce the counter offensive in the West, and there are rumours that two Panzer Corps that were last heard of in RUSSIA were now in the Black Forest area. General Spaatz asked whether the Germans had picked up much gasoline in the area which they had overrun. General Smith said that small local dumps might have been overrun, but orders had immediately been given that big dumps were to be evacuated or destroyed. General Spaatz said that American supplies of gasoline were so liberal that what was regarded as a Company supply for the U.S. Army could run a German division for several weeks.[2]

The picture, like the weather, looked bleak. Visibility was so poor, with fog, sub-zero temperatures and snow, that no Allied aircraft were able to operate. Worse still, German paratroopers in American

[1] K. Strong, op. cit.
[2] Chiefs of Staff and Air Conference, SHAEF War Diaries (AIR 37/1118), PRO.

uniforms and with American weapons were known to have been dropped behind the lines with the orders to assassinate the senior Allied commanders. As Eisenhower's PA noted in her diary, 'G2 reported that an attempt is to be made on E's life. 60 Germans are supposed to be on their way to Paris for this purpose, they will be in Allied uniforms and will stop at nothing. E. is urged by all his senior staff members to stay in the office and not go home at all.'[1]

This was how on 20 December Eisenhower became a prisoner in his own headquarters office, his staff alarmed for his life. With Eisenhower thus incarcerated and Bradley cut off from his First and Ninth US Armies at Luxembourg, could the Supreme Commander/Land Force Commander risk further delay in giving Monty charge of the American front? The Germans had by-passed Bastogne and were sweeping towards the Meuse virtually unchecked. *There were now no Allied reserves save those which Monty had amassed.* Patton might make a dent on the southern flank of the German counter-offensive—but it would be a pin-prick in relation to the relentless onslaught of up to thirty enemy divisions westwards. By failing to act swiftly, Eisenhower might prejudice his whole career.

For a few hours Bedell Smith had again considered the idea of Eisenhower himself taking battlefield command in the Ardennes—but Eisenhower's forward headquarters had been set up at Reims, south of the German penetration in the same way as Bradley's, and it was simply not possible to create overnight a mobile Tac Headquarters such as that which Monty possessed. Bedell Smith had sent a cypher message in the early hours of the morning belatedly to pick Monty's brains—'please let me have your personal appreciation of the situation on the northern flank of the penetration particularly with reference to the possibility of giving up, if necessary, some ground on the front of First Army and to the north thereof, in order to shorten our line and collect a strong reserve for the purpose of destroying the enemy in Belgium'.[2] But by the time Lash and Strong gave their morning briefing on the enemy's progress, and with the new danger to the Supreme Commander's life, Bedell Smith recognized Eisenhower could never handle the battle. 'What made me really mad was that I knew you were right,' he admitted to Strong afterwards. 'But my American feelings got the better of me because I also knew of the outcry there would be in the United States about your proposal, if it was put into effect.'[3]

[1] Diary of Mrs K. Summersby, Eisenhower Library, Abilene, Kansas.
[2] Montgomery Papers.
[3] K. Strong, op. cit.

Eisenhower was as surprised as Bradley when Bedell Smith mooted the change of command at the Supreme Commander's meeting at 10 a.m.[1] However, on Bedell Smith's recommendation the Supreme Commander concurred. According to Maj-General Strong's version in 1946, Eisenhower called Monty first, then Bradley. Air Vice-Marshal Robb, who was present and who kept a diary, gave no hint of dissent on Bradley's part—'Supreme Commander discussed this [the change in command] with General Bradley, who agreed. . . .'[2] But other accounts have suggested that Bradley at first objected, only to be overruled by Eisenhower, who said it was an order and put down the phone. 'A long conversation ensued of which we naturally could hear only one end, but General Bradley was obviously protesting strongly, for the conversation ended with Eisenhower saying, "Well, Brad, those are my orders."'[3]

Bradley certainly gave no hint of such protest in his 1948 version—but, as Bedell Smith confided to the American Official Historian, the order shattered Bradley:

> I thought Bradley could handle the armies, and so flared up when Strong and Whiteley came to me with the suggestion that Montgomery take over. . . . However, we traced our roads communications and noted directions the enemy was coming. I called Bradley's Headquarters and found he had not contacted First Army for 2–3 days. It was an open and shut case, so I agreed to recommend to Ike the change. He accepted it and called up Bradley and Montgomery. It hurt Bradley.[4]

Bradley later claimed that he had never lost communication with Hodges or Simpson, but the Chief SHAEF signals Officer, Maj-General Vulliamy, disagreed. Although Bradley was ordered to surrender command of First and Ninth US Armies to Monty, maintenance was to remain the responsibility of Bradley's headquarters. Bradley having lost telephone contact not only with Simpson and Hodges,

[1] 'Again pointed out danger of enemy coming through at Bastogne. Bedell, on basis of this, said he would recommend putting Monty in temporarily. Ike said "oh"': Maj-General Strong, Pogue interview, loc. cit. In his diary Admiral Ramsay, the Allied Naval C-in-C, noted: 'News of German offensive is less reassuring than before. It is evident that little opposition confronts the German Panzer forces who have broken through. I cannot understand why our Intelligence did not give warning of what was impending. It will take 2–3 days to make regrouping dispositions that will take effect. Meanwhile the situation gives rise to anxiety': entry of 20.12.44, extracts from the Diary of Admiral Sir Bertram Ramsay (CAB 106/1124), PRO.

[2] Robb Papers (AIR/1117), PRO.

[3] K. Strong, op. cit.

[4] Lt-General Walter Bedell Smith, Pogue interview of 8.5.47, OCMH Collection, MHI, Carlisle, Pennsylvania.

but with his air commanders too, it fell to Vulliamy to restore them as soon as possible, as Vulliamy related to the American Official Historian in 1947:

> One of great jobs of Signals was during the breakthrough in December. After Bradley gave up command of Northern units, he continued to maintain them. Was essential to replace his communications . . . SHAEF signals arranged for the restoration of his lines to Third Army and to the units in the north. Was done in a few days. Was made possible because of the speedy resuscitation of the French and Belgian communications system . . . under SHAEF coordination.[1]

Bradley's own ADC recorded how Bradley was not even aware that his telephone communications had been cut. When telephone lines were temporarily restored to 3 and 8 US Corps late that day (20 December), Bradley was surprised at the news. '"Were they cut?" he asked, smiling.'[2] Major Hansen was under the impression that Bastogne had been 'overrun' although there was still fighting going on.[3] 'The situation is confusing,' he acknowledged; but without air support, Bradley seemed stupefied—'shook his head in resignation when they told him again that there would be no air activity. Air would seem to be the pivotal center of our counter-attacking force.'[4] Bradley's communications with the air commanders were so poor, however, that Eisenhower not only decided to give Monty command of the land forces, but to give Monty's chief tactical air support commander, Air-Marshal Coningham, command of all American supporting air forces, irrespective of geographical sectors:

> is agreed that Coningham will take over the 9th and 29th Tactical Commands (Quesada and Nugent). They are reported as saying they are glad, because have had no word from Bradley for some time,

Air Marshal Robb recorded in his diary.[5] Because of the 'furore'

[1] Maj-General C. H. H. Vulliamy, Pogue interview of 22.1.47, loc. cit.

[2] Diary of Chester B. Hansen, loc. cit.

[3] Ibid.

[4] Ibid.

[5] Robb Papers, loc. cit. In fact Monty had already summoned his friend, Air Vice-Marshal Broadhurst, commander of 83rd British Tactical Fighter Group, on the morning of 20.12.44 and asked him to 'take charge of all air support on Hodges' and Simpson's fronts if, as Monty suspected, Eisenhower gave him command of 1st and 9th US Armies'. Broadhurst rang Coningham's Chief of Staff, who was unaware of any such impending command transfer. Broadhurst was at Monty's Tac Headquarters when Eisenhower's call came through. 'By the afternoon we had convoys moving forward to set up the cab-rank system using British air support

likely to rage in the press over Monty's assumption of command, Eisenhower favoured keeping both command appointments secret—and to this day virtually no mention has ever been made by historians of British air command during the battle of the Ardennes.[1]

Bradley, having had to give up command of two of his three armies, gave up all desk-work too. 'With his mind on tactical problems he has let the paper work go hang itself,' Major Hansen remarked that evening. 'Don't feel much like looking at it,' Hansen recorded him as saying.[2] More seriously, he now allowed himself, like Eisenhower, to become a victim of the American scare over possible assassination:

> The threat of enemy attack on the person of the General has grown more real. Reports indicate that an enemy sabotage b[attalio]n has now filtered between our lines. Paratroopers dressed in American uniforms, equipped with our weapons, driving our jeeps are supposed to be behind our lines: 40 of them are detailed to sabotage and assassin duties—directing their efforts particularly toward high ranking officers. . . .
>
> All this has led to increased security precautions in the headquarters. We have removed the plates from the General's jeep—he rides in nothing else, no more sedans.[3]

The Cadillac Eisenhower had given Bradley on the eve of the fateful Maastricht conference was now locked away in a garage. Not only did Bradley now ride in an open jeep without any markings in sub-zero temperatures, but he was persuaded to surrender his helmet with its three general's stars also—even his bedroom, as well as agreeing only to use the back entrance of the hotel, through the kitchen. Even these 'entrances and exits from the hotel' were henceforth to be 'hurried'. 'The general looks on all this with a mild skepticism. When we suggested he sleep in another room, he looked slightly askance at

---

teams and squadrons of rocket-firing Typhoons. These had very good effect, but were never subsequently publicized, the change of air command being kept secret. In fact the Americans had no rocket-firing aircraft there, and no cab-rank system to direct close air support': Air Chief Marshal Sir Harry Broadhurst, interview of 30.4.84.

[1] Viz J. Terraine, *The Right of the Line, The Royal Air Force in The European War 1939–1945*, London 1985, in which neither the transfer of command to Coningham nor RAF contribution to the battle is even mentioned—despite the fact that Allied air attacks probably did more to stop the German offensive and ensure eventual German withdrawal than any other factor.

[2] Diary of Chester B. Hansen, loc. cit.

[3] Ibid.

first, realized the feasibility of it afterwards, however, and has agreed to use another room.'[1]

For Bradley it was the nadir of his fortunes—fortunes which, after his success at the Maastricht Conference a fortnight before had seemed to place him on the threshold of greatness, with the prospect of almost sixty American divisions under his command.

For Monty it was the reverse. In the days after 1 September, when he had been forced to surrender tactical command of the American armies of 12th US Army Group, Monty had been considered by some to be verging on madness in his campaign for the unified command of a single thrust via the Ruhr into Germany. General Crerar, commander of the First Canadian Army, wrote to a colleague on 5 September: 'Monty . . . is very upset at the loss of operational command over the US Armies and his nomination to Field-Marshal's rank has accentuated rather than eased his mental disturbance. It is a pity he cannot see that his importance to Allied Governments, based essentially on the fact that he is a great field commander, tends to diminish as final victory comes ever more assured.'[2]

But victory was suddenly no longer assured—at least in the immediate future. At Bradley's headquarters Major Hansen recorded speculation that the end of the war had been put back six months, with all that this would entail in human life and in war matériel.[3]

If ever the Allies needed a great field commander, it was now, on 20 December 1944, with the victorious German armies poised, it seemed, to renew their great Panzer offensive into the very rear of the Allied lines, as they had done so spectacularly in 1940.

Whatever his 'mental disturbance', his cocksure ego, his irksome vanity, his tactlessness and lack of understanding of the larger issues beyond the battlefield, Monty was nothing if not a great field commander. After the misfortunes of the autumn—the loss of Land Force command and the failure of his Arnhem offensive—Monty now bounced back with a vengeance. As at Alamein in August 1942 he was determined to spread his gospel of certain victory—and all were infected.

[1] Ibid.
[2] Crerar Papers, Canadian National Archives, Ottawa.
[3] Diary of Chester B. Hansen, loc. cit.

CHAPTER FOUR

Monty Takes Over

> To achieve success, the tactical battle will require very tight control and very careful handling.
> I recommend that the Supreme Commander hands the job over to me, and gives me powers of operational control over First US Army.[1]

Monty's request, made in the above terms to Lt-General Bedell Smith, was dated 21 September 1944. It had taken some three months almost to the day for Bedell Smith and Eisenhower to accede to that request. But at 10.30 a.m. on 20 December, Eisenhower's call at last came through to Monty's Tactical Headquarters at Zonhoven. Monty's MA, Lt-Colonel 'Kit' Dawnay, was on duty; he would never forget the moment. The line was very poor, with considerable 'crackle'. It was clear that Eisenhower wished to talk to Monty about the situation; it was equally clear that Monty had no interest in discussing the battle with Eisenhower. Words were now redundant. Four long days had elapsed since the Germans began their offensive. During that time Eisenhower had never once telephoned Monty, but had left all liaison between SHAEF and Monty to Lt-General Whiteley. Monty had told 'Jock' Whiteley that only by handing over command of the American armies in and north of the Ardennes could the German thrust be stopped. Whiteley had asked Monty the previous night when, if Eisenhower so ordered, he could assume command. Monty had answered him, 'Tomorrow morning.'[2]

Now, some hours after Whiteley's and Strong's 'dismissal', a personal call had come from Eisenhower. Monty's sole interest was whether Eisenhower wished him to take command of First and Ninth US Armies. The moment Eisenhower said yes, Monty exaggerated the indistinctness of the line. He thanked the Supreme Commander, and after listening for a little to Eisenhower's high-pitched voice crackling in the receiver, he shouted, 'I can't hear you properly. I shall take command straight away'—and put the phone down. Then, turning to Dawnay, he said, 'Kit, I want the largest Union Jack that

[1] Montgomery Papers.
[2] Maj-General J. F. M. Whiteley, Pogue interview of 18.12.46, loc, cit.

will go on the bonnet of the car. Also eight motor-cycle outriders.'[1]

Eisenhower might remain a prisoner in his office, and Bradley allow himself and his vehicles to be stripped of all insignia, but Monty refused to hearken to the assassin story. What the American field commanders needed was a boost to their self-confidence after four days' fighting against a force of twenty-six enemy divisions, without once seeing their C-in-C; and he proposed to provide it. 'Monty was a showman,' Lt-Colonel Dawnay acknowledged—'but, my goodness, he understood the nature of morale.'[2]

In a letter written five days later Monty himself described the 'call':

> At 1030 hrs on 20 Dec Eisenhower got on to me by telephone from SHAEF.
>
> He was very excited and it was difficult to understand what he was talking about; he roared into the telephone, speaking very fast. The only point I really grasped was that 'it seems to me we now have two fronts' and that I was to assume command of the northern front. This was all I wanted to know. He then went on talking wildly about other things; I could not hear, and said so; at last the line cut out before he had finished.[3]

Monty had already summoned Dempsey and Crerar for a conference at Zonhoven at 11 a.m. Announcing that the Supreme Commander had given him command of First and Ninth US Armies, Monty outlined to them the situation as he saw it. German Panzers seemed to have reached Marche, less than thirty miles from Namur. Three American divisions appeared to have been overrun—the 7th, 28th and 106th. On the other hand, no German forces had reached the Meuse. Under his own personal command as C-in-C 21st Army Group, Monty had placed an *ad hoc* British armoured force consisting of 29th Armoured Brigade, 61st Recce Regiment, 8th Recce Brigade (Motor Battalion) and some additional armour to 'cover and hold the R. MEUSE crossings NAMUR–GIVET'. Anti-aircraft artillery was being moved up from Brussels to be used in an anti-tank ground role, similar to the German 88s. Dempsey was to assume responsibility for all Meuse crossings east of Namur; for the moment 30 British Corps, currently being assembled under General Horrocks, would remain under Monty's personal command to be prepared to take part in a northern counter-stroke; but if it had to be used for such a task, Operation 'Veritable', the essential preliminary to an

[1] Lt-Colonel 'Kit' Dawnay, interview of 24.8.78.

[2] Ibid.

[3] Letter to Maj-General 'Simbo' Simpson, M539 of 25.12.44, Montgomery Papers.

Allied offensive to seize the Ruhr, could not be mounted; therefore Monty himself favoured the creation of a counter-stroke reserve from within the American First and Ninth Army. 'In order to accomplish this latter purpose, he was quite prepared to give up certain ground presently held by US Forces to the East, South East and South of AACHEN. All the same, Lt-General Dempsey was to be prepared to use 30 Brit Corps in a counter-offensive role as far South as Givet.'[1]

Monty's willingness to give up American-held ground was to prove one of the most controversial aspects of Monty's command of American forces in the Ardennes. Time and again American writers would attempt to portray Monty as defeatist or at least unwarrantably concerned with lines of withdrawal, in comparison with the swashbuckling George S. Patton, who was all for instant counter-attack. Such a response was unworthy and ungrateful—and was certainly not echoed by the Official US Historian of the Ardennes battle, Hugh M. Cole. General Crerar's notes on the 20 December conference at Monty's Tac HQ, before Monty left to meet his new American subordinates, demonstrate the confidence Monty felt in the positive outcome of the battle.

> The C-in-C opened his remarks by stating that from such information as was presently available to him, he thought it necessary to assume that 7, 28 and 106 US Divisions should be considered as 'written off'.
>
> On the other hand, he was inclined to take the view that First U.S Army had 'firmed up' fairly definitely, along the northern flank of the breakthrough . . .
>
> The C-in-C intimated that it was possible that the situation confronting the Allied armies would improve materially within the next few days. If such turned out to be the case and 30 British Corps was not required for counter-offensive purposes on the right flank, then it was quite probable that HQ 30 Corps and several Divisions would be returned to First Cdn Army, in order to proceed on Operation 'VERITABLE'. With that in view, the work of improving the communications in First Cdn Army area, leading to the NIJMEGEN salient [the launching terrain for Canadian Army's forthcoming Rhineland offensive], would vigorously proceed. . . .[2]

It is clear that, even before assuming command of his two American armies, Monty had decided that, if possible, it would be an all-American battle, and was reluctant to use British reserves unless it

[1] Diary of Lt-General Crerar, entry of 20.12.44 (CAB 106/1064), PRO.
[2] Ibid.

was deemed vital. To do so would be to acknowledge German strategic success in wresting the initiative from the Allies and 'spoiling' their plans for advance to the Rhine. In theory there were ample American troops to ensure an American defensive victory: they only needed to be 'sorted out' on an inter-army masterplan. 'While 30 Brit Corps must be prepared to take part in the counter-stroke by developing a thrust southwards of the R. MEUSE between NAMUR and LIEGE, it was the C-in-C's intention to organize, if at all possible, a strategic reserve for this purpose from US forces in First and Ninth US Armies,' Crerar noted.[1] Patton was supposed to be organising an American counter-attack south of Bastogne, with six divisions, kicking off on 23 December. What Monty could do in the north remained to be seen. 'The C-in-C was proceeding to a further conference with Generals Hodges and Simpson of First and Ninth US Armies, as soon as he had finished his discussion with General Dempsey and myself,' Crerar concluded. 'The conference ended at 12.05 hrs.'[2]

Immediately after the conference Monty set off for his first visit to Hodges and Simpson as their new commander. With the Union Jack flying on the bonnet and his cavalcade of outriders, he arrived at Hodges' headquarters at 1.30 p.m. in the words of one ADC, 'like Christ come to cleanse the Temple'. 'The American armies in the north, Ninth and First, were in a complete muddle,' Monty wrote a few days later to 'Simbo' Simpson; 'Bradley had not visited either Army since the attack began; there had been no grip, or tight control, of the battle; the Army Commanders did what they thought best.'[3]

General Simpson, commander of the Ninth US Army, had been asked to come to Hodges' headquarters. 'Neither army commander had seen BRADLEY or any of his staff since this battle began,' Monty cabled the CIGS that night. 'Ninth Army had three divisions and First Army fifteen divisions,' he recorded, 'and there were no reserves anywhere behind the front. Morale was very low. They seemed delighted to have someone to give them firm orders.'[4]

After the battle was over, Monty's lack of tact in his relations with Americans would be magnified and ridiculed; but what counted in the midst of the battle was leadership, and all evidence points to the fact that Hodges, Simpson and the American Corps commanders accepted Monty's 'take-over' with respect, gratitude and relief. Bradley had formulated, even after four days of battle, no plan of

[1] Ibid.
[2] Ibid.
[3] M539, Montgomery Papers.
[4] M383 of 2255 hrs, 20.12.44, Montgomery Papers.

manoeuvre on the northern flank of the penetration, and it is hard to see how he could have done so without personally conferring with both Simpson and Hodges. Shut up in his hotel, without a car or communications, without even showing insignia of rank for fear of recognition and assassination, this was something Bradley could not do.

Monty however, was in his element. He was now a past master at the art of assuming instant command, in battle or in preparation for battle. His conferences with Hodges and Simpson began at 2 p.m. Both Hodges and Simpson were asked to give the latest picture of the battle on their respective fronts; Monty thereupon announced the way he wished to redispose the armies. Simpson's Ninth Army would assume responsibility for the sector north of the German penetration north of Monschau, taking under command 'the divisions now in it' and inserting a new Corps headquarters (19 Corps). Next, as Hodges' ADC noted in his diary, Monty wanted to form a reserve Corps of at least three divisions to mount an eventual counter-attack; for this attack 'he told General Hodges he wanted the most aggressive fighting Corps Commander'[1]—namely General 'Lightning Joe' Collins. (Collins had captured Cherbourg under Monty's overall command three weeks after D-Day and was much admired by him.) Collins would be given the 84th Division from Simpson's Ninth Army, the newly arrived 75th Division, and 3rd Armoured Division; 'this Corps is to assemble in the general area about DURBUY and MARCHE and is not to be used offensively until it is all assembled and ready for battle,' Monty informed Eisenhower that night.[2]

In London, however, there had been no news from Eisenhower or SHAEF about the battle or about change in command. In answer to Monty's plea the night before, Brooke had asked the DMO to draft a reply to Monty saying 'why he was unable to do anything more at that time'.[3] Churchill meanwhile had seen a copy of Monty's signal of 19 December, and by the afternoon of 20 December, exhilarated by the news that Monty was assembling a British reserve Corps under General Horrocks, and his boozy luncheon, Churchill was all for its instantly plunging into battle, regardless of future plans, command sectors, fronts or lines of communication:

[1] Diary of William C. Sylvan, loc. cit.

[2] M384 of 2245 hrs, 20.12.44, Montgomery Papers. In fact, owing to enemy pressure on 18 US Corps front, 3rd US Armoured Division was tied to the west flank of 18 US Corps, to be replaced by 2nd US Armoured Division from Ninth Army: see cable to Eisenhower, M385 of 1645 hrs, 21.12.44, Montgomery Papers.

[3] General Sir Frank Simpson, Wason interview, loc. cit.

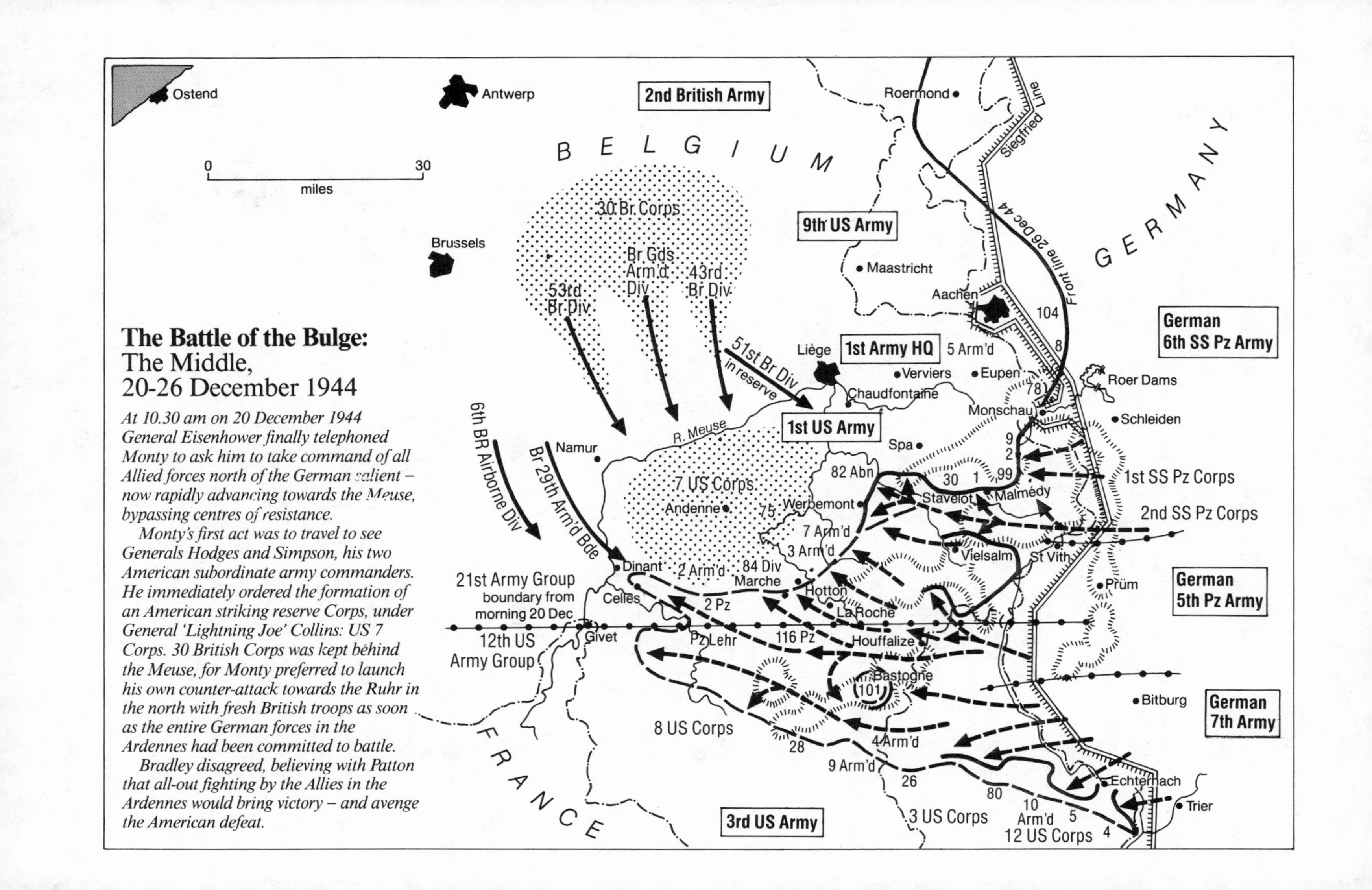

The Battle of the Bulge: The Middle, 20-26 December 1944

At 10.30 am on 20 December 1944 General Eisenhower finally telephoned Monty to ask him to take command of all Allied forces north of the German salient – now rapidly advancing towards the Meuse, bypassing centres of resistance.

Monty's first act was to travel to see Generals Hodges and Simpson, his two American subordinate army commanders. He immediately ordered the formation of an American striking reserve Corps, under General 'Lightning Joe' Collins: US 7 Corps. 30 British Corps was kept behind the Meuse, for Monty preferred to launch his own counter-attack towards the Ruhr in the north with fresh British troops as soon as the entire German forces in the Ardennes had been committed to battle.

Bradley disagreed, believing with Patton that all-out fighting by the Allies in the Ardennes would bring victory – and avenge the American defeat.

> On the same day the Prime Minister asked to see the CIGS before 4 p.m. By that time Winston had worked himself up into a considerable state of excitement and was preparing a telegraphic order to Monty instructing him to take action at once with 30 Corps on some thrust line or other,

'Simbo' Simpson recorded.

> In effect Winston was trying to get down to ordering formations, put under Monty. The CIGS was appalled at the possibility and pointed out to the Prime Minister that any order to Monty could only come from Ike; also it was quite impossible for anyone in London to say at that time how Monty should act seeing that circumstances on the spot were not known in London.[1]

In fact the only information that *was* known came from Monty, Brooke explained.

> The Prime Minister admitted the force of that argument very reluctantly and gave up the attempt to telegraph to Monty. He then asked the CIGS what he could do to help. The CIGS suggested that he should telephone to Ike, ask him about the situation, and then put the suggestion that the whole of the northern half of the front should be put under one general, preferably Monty. That call was put through at 5. p.m.[2]

It seems incredible today that the British Prime Minister/Minister of Defence should have been kept in ignorance of the decision to give Monty command of all the northern forces in the Ardennes for an entire day. How long Eisenhower intended to keep the decision secret is a moot question, but it well illustrates the state of Allied command and communications at this time.

[1] Ibid.

[2] Ibid. Brooke's diary entry of 20.12.44 recorded: 'I sent copy [of Monty's telegram] to P.M. who sent for me at 3.30 p.m. in Map Room. I found him very much the worse for wear having evidently consumed several glasses of sherry for lunch. It was not very easy to ensure that he was absorbing the seriousness of the situation. We had many references to Marlborough and other irrelevant matters! However I got him to telephone Ike to put the proposal to him that Monty should take over the whole of Northern wing while Bradley [word indecipherable] the south. He agreed and had apparently already issued orders to that effect': Alanbrooke Papers, LHCMA, King's College, London. 'I asked whether this [the Allied pincer attacks "upon the German offensive bulge"] would not be best effected by putting Montgomery in command of everything north of the German inroad and Omar Bradley of everything south, while he at Reims controlled the two battles. He [Eisenhower] replied that this was exactly what he had done': Churchill memo to War Cabinet, 20.12.44. Copy in Alanbrooke Papers (14/2), loc. cit. In fact Eisenhower remained incarcerated at the Trianon Palace Hotel for the next eight days of battle.

Eisenhower's secret news that he had already delegated to Monty command of all Allied troops to the north quietened Churchill; both Churchill and the CIGS now awaited Monty's nightly telegram for details of what he proposed to do. When Monty's telegram arrived, ending tongue in cheek, 'We can not come out by DUNKIRK this time as the Germans hold that place!!!'[1] Brooke had to censor it before passing it to Churchill. 'It was thought quite inadvisable to let the Prime Minister see this jocular remark of Monty's,' 'Simbo' Simpson recalled[2]—a remark which was calculated to raise a chuckle from the CIGS, who had been Monty's Corps commander at Dunkirk in 1940.

The tenor of Monty's telegram was, however, hopeful:

> I have every hope that the situation can be put right now that we have a properly organised set up for command and that a proper supervision and control can be kept over the battle. But it will take a day or two to get the American front reorganised and in better shape and we may have a few more shocks before that is completed,

Monty warned.[3] He saw no need to use his British 30 Corps—'I do NOT propose to use 30 Corps beyond the MEUSE if it can be avoided.'[4] By retaining 30 Corps out of the battle he would hold a *strategic* reserve, capable of decisive action lest the Germans break through across the Meuse; more importantly it would leave him an offensive reserve with which to mount his own British preparatory attack to the crossing of the Rhine *after* the Ardennes battle, in Operation 'Veritable'. By keeping 30 Corps north of the 'general line, LOUVAIN–TONGRE', moreover, Monty would ensure unhindered lines of communication to the American armies, 'as once it crossed this line it would cut across the line of supply of the American armies'.[5]

By and large Monty saw no problem in restoring the situation once the battlefield was 'tidied up'. Although some American units had cracked and some tens of thousands of American prisoners had been taken, the remaining US troops were fighting with singular tenacity and courage. 'I think I can deal with the situation south of the MEUSE with the American troops already there,' Monty thus

[1] M383, loc. cit.

[2] Wason interview, loc. cit. Monty himself annotated the copy of his Ardennes telegrams: 'When M383 was sent to him [the Prime Minister] the War Office cut out para. 7. They reckoned his sense of humour was not up to it!!' Montgomery Papers.

[3] M383, loc. cit.

[4] Ibid.

[5] Ibid.

remarked to Brooke. 'There are plenty of American troops available and they merely wanted sorting out.' Hodges' First US Army 'shoulder' ran from Elsenborn westwards through Malmedy, Stavelot and Durbuy and Hotton to Marche; it was from Marche southwards to Bastogne that the Allied line was broken—'there is a gap between MARCHE and BASTOGNE from which place the [Allied] line runs SE to ECHTERNACH'. Would the Germans reinforce their success by pushing westwards through this gap? 'All the bridges over the MEUSE from excl LIEGE to incl GIVET are now held by British garrisons,' Monty reassured the CIGS. 'In rear of this screen I shall have 30 Corps assembled and ready by tomorrow night 21 Dec.'[1]

Without further reference to Eisenhower—who was still officially commanding the Allied Land Forces—Monty had thus put the Allied house in order in the Ardennes, only hours after assuming command of First and Ninth US Armies. He held a firm northern shoulder parallel to the Meuse between Elsenborn and Marche; he was already organizing an American counter-attack Corps under General Collins; he held all the main crossings over the Meuse—Huy, Andennes, Namur, Dinant, and Givet—with British armoured garrisons; and west of the Meuse he had Horrocks' 30 Corps preparing to do battle should any Germans penetrate beyond the river. As he wrote a few days later to 'Simbo' Simpson: 'By 20 Dec I was sitting very pretty; I did not much mind what happened on my right so long as the Germans did not get over the MEUSE, and I was pretty certain I could stop that.'[2]

Monty's first biographer, Alan Moorehead, told the American Official Historian after the war that in his estimation this was Monty's 'finest hour' as a battlefield commander, eclipsing even his performance as Allied Land Forces C-in-C for D-Day and the invasion of Normandy.[3] But this time it was a battlefield performance unacceptable to punctured American amour-propre, and which would be made all the more unacceptable by Monty's own worst enemy: his boastful, cocksure, irrepressible self.

[1] Ibid.
[2] M539, loc. cit.
[3] Alan Moorehead, Pogue interview of 21.1.47, loc. cit.

CHAPTER FIVE

Tidying Up the Mess

'I WOULD LIKE TO give you a word of warning. Events and enemy action have forced on Eisenhower the setting up of a more satisfactory system of command,' the CIGS wrote to Monty on 21 December. 'I feel it is most important that you should not even in the slightest degree appear to rub this undoubted fact in to anyone at SHAEF or elsewhere. Any remarks you may make are bound to come to Eisenhower's ears sooner or later and that may make it more difficult to ensure that this new set-up for Command remains even after the present emergency has passed.'[1]

Brooke's warning was particularly prescient because, as 'Simbo' Simpson recalled, even on 21 December Eisenhower seemed to be going back on the decisions he had made the day before. He confirmed in a cable to the War Office that Monty had formally been given command of 'all units of Central Group of Armies north of the boundary ... Givet–St Vith–Cologne' but had reneged on the idea of the Western Front being divided into two, with General Bradley being given command of all forces south of the German penetration—i.e. the rump of 12th Army Group *and* 6th Army Group. 'Simbo' Simpson therefore wrote to Monty to enquire whether Monty knew what was happening:

> I asked, because we were not clear about it, whether General Bradley was in command of the whole of the southern half of the front, from Prum to the Swiss border. We had thought that he had been given all that, but then rereading all the directives that were coming out thick and fast from Supreme HQ we could not find that they established definitely that Bradley had been put in command of the 6th Army Group.[2]

This was ominous—for with an Army 'Group' containing merely one army (Patton's 3rd US Army now that Ninth and First US Armies had passed to Monty's command) Bradley would be bound to press for the eventual return of his American armies once Monty had restored the situation. Worse still, without command of the 6th

[1] 53641 cypher telegram of 1700 hrs, 21.12.44, Montgomery Papers.
[2] Wason interview, loc. cit.

Army Group, Bradley could not do what Monty was doing in the north: namely, thin out that part of the Allied line unaffected by the German attack and thus create reserves for use in counter-offensive operations. As the War Office feared, the Sixth Army Group Commander, General Devers, was reluctant to assist in the formation of fresh offensive forces for use in a different Army Group; Patton, who disliked Devers, was equally unwilling to surrender Third US Army territory to Devers since Patton still dreamed of completing his Saar offensive once the Ardennes business was over. Had Bradley been named the overall commander between the Ardennes and Switzerland, coherent military decisions could have been made. Instead Eisenhower seemed to be clinging to his policy of 'divide and rule'—though patently incapable of military rule himself, penned inside the Trianon Palace Hotel.

Monty had no time, however, to concern himself with this. Eisenhower had made no mention that Monty's command of First and Ninth US Armies was only temporary, either verbally or in his confirmatory directive; Monty therefore believed he would probably retain command *after* the Ardennes, as he had always argued should be the case if the Allies wished to capture their primary objective, the Ruhr. Brooke's warning did not therefore have the cautionary effect the CIGS had hoped for. From 10.30 a.m. on 20 December Monty considered himself effectively the Allied Land Forces C-in-C from Givet northwards, and all Monty's tactical decisions made in the ensuing days of the Battle of the Ardennes were made on the assumption that Eisenhower had 'seen the light', and that he, Field-Marshal Montgomery, would command the subsequent strategic Allied thrust to the Ruhr.

For this reason Monty refused to endorse Eisenhower's plan, given out at the Verdun conference of 19 December, of 'plugging the holes in the north',[1] or to be stampeded into costly, piecemeal counter-attacks. As his Liaison Officers returned to his Zonhoven headquarters on the evening of 21 December, Monty began to doubt the battle picture Hodges had given him at Verviers that day and the day before. At Verviers Monty had arranged that 51st Highland Division would be transferred to Simpson's Ninth US Army as a tactical reserve, thus releasing the 84th US Division for Collins' counter-thrust Corps—which Monty hoped to have ready by 23 December. Monty had also announced that Simpson's only armoured reserve division—2nd US Armoured Division—would be transferred to General Collins' counter-attack Corps. 'This head-

[1] SCAF 149: 'The general plan is to plug the holes in the North and launch co-ordinated attack from the south': in the Diary of Harry C. Butcher/desk diary of C-in-C, loc. cit.

quarters heartily approved,' Hodges' ADC noted in his diary.[1] When, at the end of the conference, Monty had asked Hodges whether things looked better, 'General Hodges replied in the affirmative.'[2]

But were they? Once again virtually no Allied aircraft had been able to operate owing to the weather—and in his diary Captain Sylvan confessed that things might not be as improved as Hodges had declared to Monty: 'It is impossible to tell where we stand at this point. One minute things look good and the next minute bad. On the ability of [General Collins'] VII Corps to assemble without being committed and then attack eastward will depend much. General Kean [Hodges' Chief of Staff] . . . now says that on Friday [22 December] we can tell whether we can hold or will have to further withdraw to a defense line such as the MEUSE.'[3]

Collins was all for instant counter-attack in the Patton style—'General Collins is full of his usual fighting Irish vigor. He is confident that with the 2nd and 3rd Armd Divs he can beat any collection that the Boche want to throw at him.'[4]

Monty applauded such 'vigour', but refused to surrender his nascent reserve Corps by impetuous counter-attack that would deprive him of the tactical initiative if—as he suspected from his Intelligence staff—the Germans were themselves keeping reserve formations in order to exploit whatever gaps they could engineer. Monty's Liaison Officers had after all reported a very different image from that given by Hodges' staff, as Monty cabled that night to Brooke:

> My personal LOs are now operating within the American armies and I am gradually building up a very different picture to that given me at Army HQ and this is complicating the problem somewhat. I shall have the final and true picture by tomorrow night and I think it may well prove to be somewhat better than that given me by the Army.[5]

All day General Ridgway, who now commanded 18 US Corps made up of 30th, 82nd and 7th US Armoured Divisions, had 'telephoned frequently . . . to say that he is being attacked in strength by an estimated two or three armoured divisions'. There were definitely Germans in Marche, but Hodges was unsure whether 7th Armoured Division still held St Vith or what was the true fate of the

[1] Diary of William C. Sylvan, loc. cit.
[2] Ibid.
[3] Ibid.
[4] Ibid.
[5] M387 of 2235 hrs, 21.12.44, Montgomery Papers.

106th US Infantry Division south of St Vith. 'It is impossible to tell where we stand at this point', Hodges' ADC recorded the First Army headquarters view on the evening of 21 December[1]—but Monty was determined to find out the true picture from his 'gallopers', as General Horrocks called them. 'This was a very confused battle and it was under these circumstances that Monty's liaison officers, or gallopers, really came into their own. They consisted of hand-picked, intelligent, tough young staff officers who lived at his tactical headquarters. Every day they were dispatched to the different formations fighting the battle. In the evening after dinner each in turn would report to Monty on what he had seen and heard. As a result of their reports Monty was probably the only man who had a completely up-to-date picture of the whole battle front. The only way I could keep touch with what was going on was to send my intelligence officer daily to study Monty's own operational map.'[2]

Monty himself summarized his approach: 'My policy in the north is to get the show tidied up and to ensure absolute security before passing over to offensive action'; moreover 'that action will be taken by 7 [US] Corps only when that Corps is fully assembled and ready to deal a hard blow.'[3] This he emphasized in his nightly telegram to Brooke, for his view of affairs beyond his southern boundary was far from sanguine. It was all very well Patton boasting that he would be launching his counter-attack 'with six divisions' in less than twenty-four hours; according to Monty's 'gallopers' the three divisions of General Middleton's 8 US Corps were in chaos: 'I sent an LO down that way yesterday and he returned tonight with a picture of a very disorganised front with divisions in bits and pieces all over the place.' Monty's forecast of the result of Patton's counter-thrust was therefore pessimistic. 'My information about the situation on the southern front about BASTOGNE is somewhat alarming and it looks to me as if the enemy columns are moving westwards having passed that place.'[4] Whatever Patton might proclaim, Monty was frankly doubtful that Patton's premature attack would do anything to halt the enemy's westward drive.

Not even SHAEF believed Patton in this respect—as Air Vice-Marshal Robb's diary entry of 21 December 1944 demonstrates:

[1] Diary of William C. Sylvan, loc. cit.
[2] B. G. Horrocks, *A Full Life*, London 1960.
[3] M387, loc. cit.
[4] Ibid.

> Concern was expressed [at Supreme Commander's morning conference] by the Deputy Supreme Commander and others that the counter attack being mounted by Bradley might be a piecemeal affair similar to the German counter-attacks in Normandy. This might happen if the two divisions that were on their way were put in without awaiting build-up of greater strength.[1]

Delay in the relief of Patton's erstwhile sector by Devers' 6th Army Group was not helping matters;[2] moreover Bastogne was untenable except by employing the two counter-attack divisions to relieve it. For all his bombastic assurances, Patton's reputation, after the enormous casualties suffered in his attacks on Metz, was not good—as Eisenhower confessed openly at the SHAEF meeting:

> The Supreme Commander mentioned that what he was afraid of was that the impetuous Patton would talk Bradley round into allowing him to attack at once with the object of going right through and not awaiting a fully coordinated counter-offensive.[3]

Bradley was thus ordered to relieve Bastogne, but not to let the attack 'spread' until a 'firm stepping off point' had been established, with sufficient reserves to sustain a genuine 'main counter-offensive'.[4]

Sadly, Eisenhower's worst fears were to be realized—as Monty reported to Brooke the following evening:

> 12 Army Group attack began today before it was really ready . . . From the limited information at my disposal I am not happy about the southern front and I have a definite feeling that Third U.S. Army will get involved with 7 German Army [the force protecting the southern flank of the German counter-offensive] and will be stopped from thrusting northwards to interfere with 5 Pz Army. I do not think Third U.S. Army will be strong enough to do what is needed. If my forecast proves true then I shall have to deal unaided with both 5 and 6 Panzer Armies,

Monty warned.

[1] Robb Papers, loc. cit. Admiral Ramsay, attending the daily SHAEF conference at 9 a.m. the following day, noted the same: 'Weather prevented air forces taking any part in the battle. Patton launching a counter attack on the southern flank with three divisions that seems to have made little progress. Monty having taken over the northern half of the battle gives one confidence that this part will soon be stabilized. I am less sure of the southern half': entry of 22.12.44, extracts from the Diary of Admiral Sir Bartram Ramsay, loc. cit.

[2] Ibid.

[3] Ibid.

[4] Ibid.

I think I can probably manage this but it will be a bit of a party.[1]

How Eisenhower imagined he could fight the Battle of the Ardennes by telephone from his locked and shuttered office room at Versailles must remain a mystery. Even his own staff admitted that, as the battle developed, information at SHAEF became both scarcer and more belated—sometimes thirty-six to forty-eight hours so. At the end of a telephone and cable cypher system Eisenhower could not really hope to dictate effective orders to Bradley or to Devers—as Monty was well aware in relation to the guarding of the Meuse bridges below his own boundary at Givet. 'I have rubbed in to SHAEF the vital importance of ensuring that all bridges over the MEUSE south of GIVET are well and truly held,' Monty explained to Brooke. 'My present information is that they are not and that 12 Army Group are not bothering about it as they consider the attack north of Third US Army is going to finish the Germans completely.'[2]

This was indeed the case. SHAEF had already cabled to Bradley during the night of 19/20 December concerning the bridges—but Bradley's Chief of Staff considered the message so unimportant he refused to wake Bradley and merely put the telephone message in Bradley's in-tray. 'A wire came in from Gen Ike at 2345 [hours] cautioning Bradley to make certain no Meuse River bridges fall to the enemy. I gave the wire to Allen,' Bradley's ADC noted in his diary that night, 'who said there was little likelihood of such a possibility—asked me to give it to the general on the following morning.'[3] Even days later Bradley had done nothing to protect the bridges; on 22 December, having been told that SHAEF, in response to Monty's signals, had itself ensured the guarding of the bridges, Bradley merely authorized a 12th Army Group staff officer to inspect the SHAEF garrisons—a full seven days after the German offensive began![4] Bradley's carelessness about the Meuse crossings and his failure either to visit his field commanders or to send staff officers to see them were indeed signs of bewildering complacency, based largely on ignorance of the true battle situation and the presence of the swashbuckling Patton, who had moved his headquarters into Luxembourg, alongside Bradley. 'Patton has been living with the general, scurrying quickly to his headquarters each morning. . . . He and Brad

[1] M388 of 2020 hrs, 22.12.44, Montgomery Papers.
[2] Ibid.
[3] Diary of Chester B. Hansen, loc. cit.
[4] 'Mines and demolitions have been prepared at all approaches to the Meuse river. This much we have been assured of. General Bradley afterwards directed that an officer from our headquarters get himself back there and see that it was done satisfactorily': diary of Chester B. Hansen, loc. cit.

get along famously with their 'Brad' and 'George' adlibbing. 'Don't come in George, if you're not bringing good news', and Brad would laugh.'[1] American newspapermen and even leading baseball players were touring the front, yet still Bradley remained in his office or hotel, his three stars concealed beneath white tape and changing his bedroom each night for fear of assassination. When confronted by the prospect of the Germans reaching the Meuse bridges a few days later, he declared that he had 'been expecting it for several days.' 'SHAEF is terribly worried about this,' he declared. 'I'm not. If they get up to the river, there aren't many bridges he can use.' 'The prospect that advance elements of the German penetration may soon reach the Meuse does not seem to worry him a bit,' his ADC recorded on 23 December.[2]

Confined in Luxembourg, however, Bradley was living in cloud-cuckoo land, determined to minimize the seriousness of the enemy penetration in order that his own mistaken dispositions, as 12th Army Group Commander, should be concealed as far as possible. On 24 December he gave a press briefing in which he announced that he had foreseen the possibility of the enemy's attack in the Ardennes six weeks before the battle, and that for this reason there were no American dumps of ammunition or petrol east of the Meuse.[3] This was blatantly untrue; the truth was that the whole area east of the Meuse around Liège was littered with American dumps. Had for instance the Germans broken through to Spa on the day that Hodges evacuated his headquarters, they would have captured no less than four million gallons of fuel, much of which had to be destroyed by the Americans lest it fall into German hands. It was nothing short of a miracle that the German onslaught had missed major American supply depots—as Bradley's staff privately confessed.[4]

Part of Bradley's optimism was based on the mistaken advice of his Chief of Intelligence, Brigadier-General Sibert, who on 22 December estimated that the bulk of the enemy's reserves had now been committed—an estimate he would rue in the days ahead, as he did his failure to foresee the offensive.[5] By 24 December Sibert was 're-

[1] Ibid.
[2] Ibid.
[3] Ibid.
[4] 'General Moses, our G-4, tells me the enemy could not have chosen a more fortunate route of advance as far as the movement of supplies is concerned': Diary of Chester B. Hansen, entry of 20.12.44, loc. cit.
[5] Sibert's G2 Summary No. 18, written out by the ex-journalist Ralph Ingersoll shortly before the German offensive, predicted that, notwithstanding the 125,000 American casualties already sustained by 12th US Army Group over the past four weeks, the Germans were suffering a 'deathly weakness' in infantry and 'the breaking point may develop suddenly and without warning' as long as the Allies kept up their

vising upwards' all his estimates of enemy strength, with some 25,000 extra enemy troops committed (totalling 335,000) and almost three times the number of Panzers (some 905 tanks now as opposed to the 345 he had originally ascribed)—news which, although it did not visibly upset General Bradley's demeanour, evidently affected his digestive system—'a light recurrent attack of those stomach troubles that aggravated his condition last week,' his ADC recorded.[1]

As Bradley's counter-offensive foundered in the fighting around Bastogne, both he and his staff became more and more critical of Monty's performance in the north—ridiculing Monty's concern for the security of the Meuse bridges and his 'characteristic caution' in 'building a conventional line of defence'.[2]

Whatever Bradley might think in the ivory tower of his closely guarded headquarters, however, reality was very different in the field. Bearing the brunt of the German offensive, Hodges had become increasingly anxious on 21 December that the Germans would make an all-out drive on Liège through Ridgway's 18 Corps sector at Malmédy; the following morning Collins became alarmed that the Germans would attempt to drive west through his 7 Corps assembly area and across the Meuse, and asked Hodges' Chief Engineer 'to find out what bridges in that area had been prepared for demolition. . . . There was, however, no need for him to worry about this,' Hodges' ADC noted in the evening of 22 December, 'as Monty arrived shortly after 1.45 and brought the General the good news that an Armoured Brigade with 50 tanks at NAMUR, 50 at GIVET and 50 at a point equi-distant between those two towns, had sent its reconnaissance elements forward to the VII assembly area and would methodically clean up any small pockets of Germans if such existed. . . . Monty was chipper and confident as usual. The employment of this Armoured Brigade to screen in back of VII Corps area lifted a tremendous load off the General's mind. Obviously we had no troops to do it,' Captain Sylvan candidly confessed.[3]

What Sylvan did not relate was a further 'load' Monty had taken off General Hodges' mind. Hodges was intending to move his headquarters again that day, this time west of the Meuse; he was not in touch with all his First US Army formations and units and had made no attempt to go forward to see them or give heart

---

pressure all along the line, 'in the south and north': C. B. Macdonald, *The Battle of the Bulge*, London 1984. Sibert's view was largely based on Maj-General Strong's belief that by force of attrition alone the Germans could be defeated.

[1] Ibid.

[2] Ibid.

[3] Diary of William C. Sylvan, loc. cit.

to their commanders. Disconcerted by the shortage of reserves, he had, despite his own movement rearwards, refused to authorize any withdrawals on the battle-front. When General Gerow, the experienced 5 US Corps commander, asked permission to pull back to a better defensive line from Monschau to Elsenborn, Hodges had only been willing to give unofficial approval, forcing Gerow to take formal responsibility for the retreat lest there be recriminations after the battle. Similarly, when Maj-General Hasbrouk requested permission to withdraw 7th US Armoured Division from the American salient at St Vith while there was still time, Hodges refused.

Monty had, since taking command of First US Army on 20 December, been determined to obtain a true picture of Hodges' front. As he reported to Brooke on the night of 22 December,

> my own personal team of LOs has now gained for me a very complete picture of the situation of First Army. Many stray combat teams were discovered in strange and unexpected places. As a result of this careful reconnaissance I am now satisfied that First Army line runs as follows. From MONSCHAU south to WIRTZFIELD thence westwards through WAIMES and MALMEDY and STAVELOT to TROIS PONTS thence south through VIELSALM to SALMCHATEAU thence west to cross roads in 5785 thence northwest to GRANDMENIL thence west to HOTTON thence S.W. to MARCHE.
>
> The most curious discovery was the situation S.E. of VIELSALM. 7 US Armd Div stretches in a sausage shape area from incl VIELSALM through PETIT THIER and POTEAU to ST VITH. Then in the general area NEUNDOR THOMMEN ALDRINGEN BOUIGNY are three combat teams one each of 28 DIV, 106 DIV, 9 ARMD DIV and two task forces of stragglers. The whole party to the S.E. of VIELSALM consisting of 7 Armd Div and other stray units was heavily attacked this morning by SS troops and was in grave danger of being done in. I was at HQ First US Army at the time and I gave orders at once that the whole party was to be withdrawn at once into reserve in the BRA area 5793 and this is being done. This reserve will be very useful in that area where before there was none.[1]

Monty's decisiveness was viewed with disbelief at Bradley's headquarters, where Bradley spent his time poring over paper maps but failing to ascertain the real picture on the battlefield. Bradley's paper plans, rehearsed on the floor of his office before his devoted ADC, Major Hansen, make sorry reading:

[1] M388, loc. cit.

I found the general on his knees before the map, peering through his bifocals at the road net in the Luxembourg area used by the Germans to support his effort. The general marked them in carefully with a brown crayon pencil. Figured that the XII Corps offensive [under Patton] would cut one, permit the other to be interdicted by art[iller]y fire. He figured similarly on road cuts and interdictions from the St Vith sector, turned about and pointed to the road—'if we cut this and cover this with arty fire,' he said, 'this fellow will begin to sweat.'[1]

Such paper courage bore no relation to the trials and tribulations of American troops in the field. Far from being in a position to make 'road cuts and interdictions' from the St Vith sector, the unhappy Maj-General Hasbrouk was aware, on 22 December, that his hours were numbered. Monty's LO arrived in the morning; having given the young captain a briefing on the situation in St Vith, Hasbrouk declared that he would fight on in his present positions if the stand was considered vital, but that he personally favoured withdrawal to a cohesive defensive line. By 11 a.m. he was predicting to General Ridgway, his 18 Corps commander, that he would be unable to 'prevent a complete breakthrough if another all-out attack comes tonight'; and in a postscript, as the next German attack by Fifth Panzer Army came, added: 'In my opinion if we don't get out of here and up north of the 82nd before night, we will not have a 7th Armoured Division left.'[2] As the American Official Historian remarked, Monty's decision to overrule Hodges and pull back Hasbrouk 'here showed the ability to honor the fighting man which had endeared him to the hearts of the Desert Rats in North Africa' ... 'They can come back with all honour. They come back to more secure positions. They put up a wonderful fight,' Monty declared. 'The First Army Commander, tired and worried from the strain under which he had lived since 16 December, agreed to the withdrawal.'[3]

Bradley and Patton meanwhile refused to think of anything but counter-attack, leading Eisenhower to underestimate, in Monty's view, the seriousness of the position. Monty's own appreciation was that both Fifth and Sixth Panzer Armies were by-passing Bastogne and sweeping westwards and northwards against First Army: '6th Pz Army is thrusting NW through MALMEDY and STAVELOT and aiming at the MEUSE between LIEGE and NAMUR. 5 Pz Army is

[1] Diary of Chester B. Hansen, loc. cit.

[2] H. M. Cole, *The Ardennes: The Battle of the Bulge*, Washington 1965.

[3] Ibid.

thrusting westwards, with its left on BASTOGNE and then seems to be swinging N.W. towards the MEUSE with its left about DINANT. 7 German Army is attacking S.W. towards ARLON with the intention of widening the gap and keeping Third US Army in the south away from 5 Pz Army.'[1] This pattern did not alarm Monty; but as a soldier and a general he took his hat off to the German C-in-C: 'RUNSTEDT is fighting a good battle,' he acknowledged in his nightly cable to Brooke.[2] He was quite confident he could handle von Rundstedt, however, now that he had 'tidied up the mess and have got the two American armies properly organised.'[3] Despite General Simpson's anxieties about a possible German attack against the Ninth US Army, Monty had ordered two divisions to be pulled out of line—one as a reserve for the Ninth Army, and one as a reserve division for Hodges' First US Army. Within First US Army Monty now had a reserve Corps of four divisions under General Collins: 'I have now managed to make 7 US Corps up to four divisions and these are 75 Div, 84 Div, 2 Armd Div, 3 Armd Div which will make a very powerful force.' With Patton failing—as Monty predicted—to 'interfere with 5 Pz Army', Collins' 7 US Corps would have to do so—'it will be a bit of a party. 5 Pz Army will have to deal with my 7 Corps positioned as in Para 4 [Barvaux–Marche–Nettenne–Terwagne area] and that Corps will not be easy to by pass or to shift.'[4]

Monty was thus fully convinced he could deal with the combined weight of the Fifth and Sixth German Panzer Armies. Where he 'saw rocks ahead' was in the 'optimism that IKE seems to feel' at SHAEF, for which Monty could see 'no ground'. For with the enemy fighting such a good battle, the Americans were in for considerable further casualties as well as much disappointment if they truly considered 'the attack north of Third US Army is going to finish the Germans completely'.[5]

[1] M388, loc. cit.
[2] Ibid.
[3] Ibid.
[4] Ibid.
[5] Ibid. Brooke was equally sceptical. In his diary for 22.12.44, he recorded, 'The German offensive appears to be held in the North but I am a little more doubtful in the South. Patton is reported to have put in a counter-attack. This could only have been a half-baked affair and I doubt its doing much good.' Alanbrooke Papers, loc. cit.

CHAPTER SIX

Stretching the Enemy

MONTY'S TELEGRAM ON the night of 22 December was judged so important by the War Office that it was 'sent over by messenger to the Prime Minister together with a map'. As the DMO, 'Simbo' Simpson, wrote to Monty the next day, 'it gave a very clear picture, including the Southern flank, and one which we have been quite unable to get from SHAEF. They seem very disinclined to tell us anything: I think it is because they don't know much themselves.'[1]

Eisenhower had directed that a Special Order of the Day be prepared—'and this was not to be a Backs to the Wall Order but, on the contrary, an order of encouragement and pointing out that this is the opportunity,' the Chief of Staff, Air Operations, at SHAEF recorded.[2] The Order, when drafted, ended with the stirring slogan: 'United in this determination and with unshakeable faith in the cause for which we fight, we will, with God's help, go forward to our greatest victory.'[3]

Such paper messages about great victories reinforced Monty's conviction that Eisenhower, like Bradley, was living still in cloud-cuckoo land—though Eisenhower was more anxious than Monty knew. His PA recorded frankly in her desk diary,

> Our attack [by Patton's 3 US Corps] got off. It now appears that the German Forces in the North are stronger than we had antisipated [sic], they are still attacking, the weather has been bad, for the last 3 days it has been impossible to use our air. Long sessions for E[isenhower]. with Strong, Bull [Chief of Operations]. Strong is uneasy regarding the Russians, we do not know what they are going to do, the German is withdrawing Divs from the R[ussian]. front. E. is going to send a cable to the CCS [Combined Chiefs of Staff] re the Russians. G_2 [Intelligence staff] have no new reports re E's life, the [assassination] 'party' is supposed to be in Paris.'[4]

By the following day, Mrs Summersby was recording: 'Patton is still

[1] Letter of 23.12.44 (DMO/113/M), loc. cit.
[2] Diary of Air Vice-Marshal J. M. Robb, Robb Papers, loc. cit.
[3] *The Papers of Dwight David Eisenhower*, op. cit.
[4] Diary of Mrs K. Summersby, loc. cit.

attacking, going is slow on account of demolitions, munes [sic] etc. . . . E. is still pinned up in the office.'[1]

Admiral Sir Bertram Ramsay, in his own diary, was less than charitable to Eisenhower, locked up in his office since 19 December while he, Ramsay, and seemingly every journalist in North-west Europe appeared at liberty to move where he wished. Nor did Ramsay have a great deal of faith in the much-vaunted Bradley–Patton counter-offensive, launched on 22 December: 'The centre of the breakthrough is still unsealed. Three divisions are on their way to close it, but two of these have never been in action before,' he remarked caustically.[2] The following day he was even more forthright:

> Very little news, gap still open. It is most disturbing that Supreme HQ should be without information later than about 36–48 hours. It is only too clear that there is no Supreme Operational Command in existence. No master-mind and therefore no staff of one.[3]

Much specious historiography would later emerge to extol Eisenhower's role in the battle of the Ardennes, designed to honour a great man, but concealing his lamentable inadequacy as Allied Land Force Commander—a command that he resolutely insisted on retaining.[4]

From now on, in fact, Churchill gave up relying on SHAEF for information; and on the basis of Monty's unexpurgated telegrams of 22, 23 and 24 December Churchill felt content to leave the Ardennes battle in Monty's hands, deciding to fly out instead to Greece to harden the British garrison in Athens.

Monty, commanding some four Allied Armies comprising eleven Allied Corps, was now by far and away the senior Allied Army Group Commander, with Bradley and Devers each commanding four Corps. General Collins, the 'piss and vinegar' commander chosen to command the northern counter-attack, later considered that 'Eisenhower was right in my judgement in placing Montgomery . . . in command of all troops on the north side. . . . A dangerous front had been opened, which would have made it difficult if not impossible for Bradley to have controlled operations north of the Bulge from his headquarters in Luxembourg. For the Army's part of this success [driving the enemy back to the west wall] Monty deserves much

[1] Ibid.

[2] Diary of Admiral Sir Bertram Ramsay, loc. cit.

[3] Ibid.

[4] S. E. Ambrose, op. cit.: 'Eisenhower's confidence in himself had grown tremendously during the crisis. . . . Whatever Brooke and Montgomery might say about his lack of experience, he had taken control of the battle and made it his.'

credit,' he felt—'though the same results could have been achieved sooner and with more devastating losses to the enemy if he [Montgomery] had acted boldly and with greater confidence in the ability of the American troops and their combat leaders.'[1]

Collins felt Monty ought to have instantly counter-attacked towards St Vith, so as to hit the enemy salient at its neck; Lt-General Horrocks, Collins' counterpart, commanding the British 30 Corps in reserve west of the Meuse, was equally convinced that Monty ought to have withheld all American counter-attacks and allowed the German Panzer Armies to penetrate as far west as Waterloo, thirty miles beyond Namur; whereupon he, Horrocks, would have seen to their destruction in tribute to Wellington.

Monty himself spurned both suggestions. Hitler was not to be given the honour of crossing the Meuse; equally, an offensive towards St Vith, where the Germans were strongest and nearest to their supplies, would entail senseless casualties. From the beginning he had chosen Bastogne as the target of his counter-attack; but even this axis was likely to be more difficult than Collins presumed, as Monty explained to Brooke on the evening of 23 December. Monty's answer was to let the combined Panzer offensive run on against his own reorganized defensive line, as at Alam Halfa and Medenine, forcing the enemy to lose heavy casualties by having to assault prepared defences. Then 'when the time comes to pass over to the offensive with [Collins's] 7 Corps my present idea is to direct it south-eastwards towards the road centre of HOUFFALIZE about eight miles north of BASTOGNE. I am not clear yet as to when I shall be able to begin this movement and hope to be able to let you know further on this point tomorrow night by which time the intention of 6 and 5 Panzer Armies may have become clearer.' At the moment, two enemy Panzer divisions from Fifth Panzer Army were 'tapping in against 7 US Corps and trying to overlap to the west', while Sixth Panzer Army, despairing of a breakthrough at the northern shoulder of the salient, seemed also to be moving west and 'may possibly try again in a north-westerly direction' on Ridgway's 18 Corps front.[2] This was all to the good; what caused Monty to question the likelihood of effective Allied counter-attack was the lack of infantry troops in the American divisions:

> A disturbing factor which is coming to light as I visit American formations is the weak state of most divisions. I visited HQ 5 Corps at EUPEN today and found that the four divisions of that

[1] J. Lawton Collins, *'Lightning' Joe*, Baton Rouge 1980.
[2] M391 of 2235 hrs, 23.12.44, Montgomery Papers.

> Corps in the line are together deficient of 7,000 men mostly infantry and that 5 Armd Div in reserve is only sixty per cent of its strength.[1]

One of his LOs, visiting 29th US Division, found it 2,000 men below strength, mainly in infantry. 'I fear it is much the same in all divisions and I am told that there are no replacements in sight in Europe. This shortage of manpower in American divisions is a new one on me,' Monty confessed—and it cast a deep shadow over Bradley's claims to have been inflicting, in his abortive November offensive and south of the Ardennes, unbearable losses upon the enemy. As was becoming clear, it was the Americans, not the Germans, who had failed to replace their losses.

Collins, eager to 'have a crack' at the Boche, was not interested in such minutiae. Indeed, all too often American commanders were indifferent to the welfare of their own men, as General Horrocks had discovered when having under command Collins' 84th US Division a few weeks prior to the Ardennes battle:

> The thing that worried me most was the initial failure of the Americans to get a hot meal through to their forward troops. This is where battle experience counts. It may be necessary to make the most elaborate plans many hours beforehand; but if troops are to go on fighting in winter, somehow or other they must get hot food. Every day my first question to the 84th was: 'How many units have had a hot meal during the night?'
>
> The first day the answer was—none. The second day—fifty per cent, and the third day—100 per cent. The great thing about the Americans was that they were very quick to learn.[2]

As Monty toured his northern flank, however, he was less and less convinced that the Americans had learned about soldier-welfare. Many troops had not had a hot meal since the beginning of the battle; and the chances of 'great victory' in such bitter December weather with divisions so short in infantry struck Monty as unlikely. He might be criticized behind his back for being over-cautious, but his loyalty was to the lives of the men fighting the German penetration, and such lives ought not, he felt, to be squandered in unco-ordinated and expensive counter-attacks against Germans in possession of ground of their own choosing. Bradley had expected Patton to relieve Bastogne in a matter of hours; as Bradley's ADC recorded in his diary, the failure of Patton's attack came as a grave

[1] Ibid.

[2] B. G. Horrocks, op. cit.

disappointment to Bradley's headquarters.[1] Patton's three divisions were attacking line abreast on a front of almost thirty miles. 'Third Army will without a doubt make a great effort to get to BASTOGNE and I hope it may do so,' Monty remarked to Brooke;[2] but he doubted that it would achieve this without heavy fighting, after which it would be unlikely to smash its way much further.

The following day, Christmas Eve, 1944, Monty reported of Patton's advance: 'My information from the southern flank is scanty and I am under the impression that no great progress has been made.'[3] On his own northern flank the enemy, unhindered by Patton, was 'now attacking 7 US Corps in the area about HOTTON and MARCHE and is overlapping the west flank of the corps in the CINEY area'. In fact 2nd Panzer Division was now within striking distance of the Meuse, leading to the first confrontation between German and British tanks in the battle of the Ardennes:

> Between CINEY and DINANT is a gap and 3 R Tanks from the DINANT bridgehead has been engaged with 2 Pz Div today in this gap and has destroyed four TIGER tanks without loss.[4]

Monty's plan was, if necessary, to lure the German spearhead northwards from the Marche area up to the Meuse between Namur and Huy. The spearhead would not be able to cross the Meuse, since the river was defended by the Guards Armoured Division; there it would be hammered on both sides—Horrocks' 30 British Corps attacking from the west, Collins' 7 US Corps from the east—as well as from the air, now the Allied air forces were once again in operation. For this reason Monty had given orders that Collins should not commit his reserve corps to battle yet, but swing back his right flank to the Meuse at Ardennes and Huy if attacked in strength. When Collins received the order, by telephone, he misunderstood it however; Hodges' Chief of Staff dared not spell out the names Ardennes and Huy, so referred to them as 'A' and 'H'. Collins, who already had his 2nd US Armoured Division positioned between the villages of Achêne and Houisse, was dumbfounded when, that evening, he was told by a special messenger from Hodges of the true meaning of the initials. To him, the idea of withdrawal was tinged

[1] 'Although the fourth armoured continues to attack fiercely against the ribbon of German strength separating it from the besieged 101st A/B [Airborne Division] they seem unable to get through. . . . Today we hoped for contact with the 101st but were unable to make it. We shall hope tomorrow': diary of Chester B. Hansen, entry of 24.12.44, loc. cit.

[2] M391, loc. cit.

[3] M393 of 2225 hrs, 24.12.44, Montgomery Papers.

[4] Ibid.

with defeatism, and by locking 2nd US Armoured Division in combat with 2nd Panzer Division he was able to get Hodges to rescind the order.

Monty was unperturbed by Collins' disobedience, since he admired Collins' aggressive spirit; nevertheless such premature combat weakened the potential effectiveness of the four-divisional corps offensive he had in mind, as he lamented to Brooke: 'I had hoped that 7 Corps would be able to remain concentrated and available for offensive action but it is now getting involved with 5 Panzer Army.'[1]

Similarly, Monty had given orders to pull Ridgway's 18 Corps back from the Vielsalm salient to the 'general line GRANDMENIL–TROIS PONTS. This will give it a shorter front and some useful reserves.'[2] Such orders, when heard at Bradley's headquarters, gave rise to rumours that Monty was being unnecessarily defeatist—ignoring the fact that, the previous day, Monty had ordered all demolition charges to be removed from the Meuse bridges, so confident did he now feel about being able to hold the line of the Meuse and to use it as a jumping-off point for co-ordinated counter-attack. By such tactics he had forced Rommel to maintain an over-extended front line at Himeimat, south of Alamein, prior to the great offensive battle, and again before the triumphant Eighth Army drive upon Tripoli. With Collins becoming involved, however, Monty's hopes of such an offensive by the American forces dwindled:

> I cannot pass over to any large offensive action just at present as I am very stretched and the American divisions are all weak and below establishment. I shall hold firm on my present line and I do not think the enemy will be able to break it or to get over the MEUSE at GIVET. I shall aim at getting the enemy very stretched and shall harry and jab him all the time,

Monty confided to Brooke.[3] 'The main offensive action just at present must be from the air and given a spell of fine weather we should make his life intolerable by air action. While this air action is going on I shall form another striking force.'[4]

As in Normandy, the effectiveness of Monty's strategy—however misunderstood then and later—was proved by the actions of the enemy. Field-Marshal Model, commanding the three German armies attacking the Ardennes, was unhappy about Patton's thrust to relieve Bastogne; but von Rundstedt, as the C-in-C in the west, overruled

[1] M393, loc. cit.
[2] Ibid.
[3] Ibid.
[4] Ibid.

him, arguing on 24 December that, from his Intelligence and Planning Staff, he was certain the Allies could not assemble a force strong enough to defend the Meuse before 30 December. The German Panzer armies thus had six days in which to reinforce their successful advance, now only six miles from the river. Apart from a combat group peeled from 15th Panzer Grenadier Division, *no* German forces were switched to the siege of Bastogne, and no further forces whatever assigned to meet Patton's thrust from the south. As Monty had predicted, he was having to deal with Fifth and Sixth Panzer Armies unaided. As in a game of chess, the Germans had ignored the threat on one side of the board in order to concentrate their offensive strength upon the primary objective: the Meuse.

With 30 British and 7 US Corps already assembled by 23 December, Monty had confounded German expectations by some seven days. General Collins' understandable desire to join battle meant, however, that a concentrated American counter-attack from the north would have now to be delayed—a fact which Bradley, not knowing the state of his troops on the northern flank, deplored. Already Bradley was formulating plans for an American 12th Army Group offensive through the Eifel area of the Ardennes once the current battle was over and Ninth and First US Armies were once again under his control—and was openly critical of Monty, claiming that Monty, not Collins, had 'dissipated the VII Corps by committing them on a defense line that runs west to Givet and the river'.[1] Despite the slow and costly advance made by Patton, Bradley considered that 'we have been making good progress from the south. He is anxious for a closing movement from the north,' Bradley's ADC recorded.[2]

Bradley's misreading of Monty's performance in the north was perhaps inevitable, given the setback he had suffered, his lack of communications and the loss of two-thirds of his Army Group. From now on his ADC's diary would become a repository of coloured facts, of snide references to Monty, even deprecating reassessments of Monty's previous war career, deriding Monty's 'stagnating conservatism of tactics', accusing him of becoming 'quite panicky initially', and remarking that 'Monty's contributions in the Sicilian campaign were negligible. His part in the battle of France and the Lowlands have always been subordinated to ours. . . .'[3] Since Major Hansen was later to ghost Bradley's memoirs[4] this was unfortunate;

[1] Diary of Chester B. Hansen, loc. cit.
[2] Ibid.
[3] Ibid.
[4] O. N. Bradley, *A Soldier's Story*, New York 1951.

but it confirms Monty's subsequent impression that whatever he said of the battle, he was bound to be misunderstood. The humiliation of the Ardennes had been too much; thereafter Monty would inevitably become the scapegoat of American shame at their misfortune.

In the meantime, on Christmas Day, 1944, Bradley finally ventured out from his headquarters at Luxembourg to meet the Field-Marshal who had taken command of two-thirds of his American troops. It was a meeting neither man would forget—and one which Bradley—essentially a simple, gentle, shy soul—would never forgive.

CHAPTER SEVEN

The Humiliation of Bradley

Tac Headquarters:
21 Army Group
Xmas Day 25-12-44

My dear Phyllis

My plans for coming home for a few days at Christmas did not mature; events, and the enemy, decreed otherwise. The Americans have taken a 1st Class bloody nose; I have taken over command of the First and Ninth American armies and all troops in the northern part of the front, and I am busy sorting out the mess. I hope you will all have a very happy time.

What a life!!

My love to you all.

Monty

Brooke had warned Monty not to 'rub in' the American catastrophe; but such cautioning from the paper world of London did not take sufficient account of Monty's natural sense of revenge. His demotion from Allied Land Force Command on 1 September 1944 and the American refusal to follow his strategy of concentration in the north thereafter had produced in Monty's somewhat schoolboy make-up a sense of outrage he had found difficult to control. Now, with the demise of Eisenhower's policy of separated thrusts and the humiliation of Bradley as 12th US Army Group Commander, Monty exulted. To Lord Louis Mountbatten, Supreme Allied Commander in South-east Asia, he wrote on the same day, in almost the same triumphant words, purportedly restraining himself, but more than making clear his feelings:

> I won't add my comments on the war. The Americans have taken the most awful 'bloody nose' and have been cut clean in half. I now once more find myself commander of two American armies, as well as 21 Army Group, and am trying to clean up the mess.
>
> Personally I always enjoy a good battle,

he remarked in a singularly revealing phrase.

> But this thing should never have happened; one ought really to burst into tears. It has prolonged the war by months.

Beyond exultation there was undoubtedly sincere anger at the unnecessary waste of time and of human life. To General Sir Oliver Leese, newly appointed as Land Force C-in-C to Mountbatten, Monty also wrote on Christmas Day, enclosing a copy of his most recent pamphlet (*The Armoured Division in Battle*) as well as a stifled exclamation of his disgust:

> I won't add my comment on the war. There is no ink that I know would stand up to what I would like to say.[1]

Bradley only arrived at Monty's headquarters at 3 p.m. Fearing German fighter interception, Bradley's Chief of Intelligence had insisted Bradley fly from Etain, almost fifty miles from Luxembourg; but when Bradley reached Etain it was to find that his air crew was still waiting for him at Luxembourg. By the time he had been given an aircraft with a makeshift crew and had had to line up with dozens of transport aircraft awaiting take-off at 1 p.m., Bradley became more and more impatient. 'Another 10 minutes and I would have called the damned thing off,' he told his ADC.[2]

Accompanied by an escort of fighters Bradley finally flew to St Trond. There, by the runway, he could see no car to greet him. 'If there's no transportation,' he said, 'we'll climb in the plane and go back.'[3]

Bradley had not seen Hodges since before the battle of the Ardennes had begun; Monty he had not seen since the Maastricht Conference on 7 December. His victory at Maastricht had turned unpleasantly sour, and half of him evidently had no wish to see Monty at all. Indeed, so distracted was he, that while riding to Monty's headquarters in the staff car provided by General Hodges, Bradley expressed astonishment at the way the people in the villages were wearing their Sunday clothes. He had then to be reminded it was Christmas Day.[4]

Dressed in a simple, loose-hanging arctic coat, his general's stars still concealed, Bradley entered Monty's headquarters with understandable apprehension.

> Hqs were located in a small house near the road front and the officers there had celebrated Christmas, smoked pipes over port in

[1] Letter communicated by Mrs Frances Denby.
[2] Diary of Chester B. Hansen, loc. cit.
[3] Ibid.
[4] Ibid.

> the lower room where all of Monty's Christmas cards were tacked to a wall in exhibition,

Bradley's ADC recorded in his diary.

> They came from everyone and from almost all of his regiments. Quite different from the Amerks where many of our people busily engaged in heavy fighting, neglected to send their cards this year.[1]

Bradley had only dared to walk from his headquarters to his hotel for the first time the previous day. For Christmas lunch he had munched an apple and a pear, given him by the Chief of US Supplies. 'I felt suddenly conscious for my old combat jacket and patched GI trousers,' Major Hansen confessed, as his revered general mounted the stairs alone with Monty 'for a conference'.[2]

According to Monty, the tête-à-tête lasted but half an hour. Major Hansen 'conjectured' in his diary that Bradley had come to 'press for counter attack forces readied to slam through on a pincer movement and cut off his [the enemy's] salient. We have been making good progress from the south. He [Bradley] is anxious for a closing movement from the north.'[3]

If Bradley really hoped for such a 'slamming' pincer movement, he was to be greatly disappointed; however, it is more likely that he said little or nothing at the conference. He commanded now only a single army; his much vaunted counter-attack in the south had not yet succeeded in relieving Bastogne, let alone deflect the advance of the two German Panzer Armies. Meanwhile he was visiting the Allied Army Group Commander responsible for some thirty-four Allied divisions on a front of almost three hundred miles. Given Monty's exultant anger expressed in his private correspondence that day, it is more likely that Monty did the talking—taking Bradley's silence as agreement.

In his letter to 'Simbo' Simpson later that day, Monty gave the background to his conference with Bradley:

> The German attack was launched on 17 [sic] Dec and by 18 Dec it was clear to me what was going to happen. The Americans were strung out all along the front; everyone had been attacking everywhere and every day; there were few reserves available.
>
> So I began, at once, to take the necessary steps to ensure that the British sector would be safe: whatever might happen on my right.

[1] Ibid.
[2] Ibid.
[3] Ibid.

By 20 Dec I was sitting pretty; I did not much mind what happened on my right so long as the Germans did not get over the MEUSE, and I was pretty certain I could stop that.

At 1030 hrs on 20 Dec Eisenhower got on to me by telephone from SHAEF. . . .

The rest you know.

The American armies in the north, Ninth and First, were in a complete muddle; Bradley had not visited either army since the attack began; there had been no grip, or tight control, of the battle; the Army Commanders did what they thought best.

For five days, 20 to 24 Dec, I spared no effort trying to sort the thing out, and get a properly organised show in the American zone, and get reserves formed and suitably positioned.

That has now been done, and today, Xmas Day, is the first day I have been in at my HQ.

There is no point now in examining the past,

he went on, though failing to hold back at least a spittleful of righteous indignation.

If I produced all the correspondence and telegrams that have passed between me and Eisenhower since 1st September last, it could be proved in any court of law that Eisenhower persisted in pursuing the course he took in direct defiance of all British advice; it was pointed out to him on paper that if he neglected to concentrate his main strength on his left and instead attempted to develop two thrusts, and if he refused to have a sound and simple set up for command, he would get no good results and would prolong the war. He refused to listen to my advice; he was quite unable to make up his mind himself as to what he *did* want to do; and now the blow has fallen and the war has been put back FOR MONTHS.[1]

It was Monty's virtue, tantamount in the fog of war to genius, to see things in simple, ruthlessly clear terms. His personal austerity was the matrix to his asperity—he did not eschew alcohol or cigarettes or rich food or late nights because he did not like them, but because they impeded him from bringing to bear the clarity of his mind; a mind that like an X-ray machine reduced each focused object to its bones. It was not Eisenhower the Supreme Commander he was criticizing; it was Eisenhower the Allied Land Force Commander. What Monty's X-ray eyes could *not* discern was that, in an alliance of democratic nations, bonded solely for the purpose and the duration of a specific war, muddle and misadventure were inevit-

[1] M539, loc. cit.

able, and not easily overcome. Time and again Monty had pointed to the triumph in Normandy as an example of Allied success when major operations were run upon a sound military set-up; but the battle of Normandy had seen, in fact, immense stresses and strains developing between the Allies—and Eisenhower's insistence on assuming overall land command was undoubtedly a bid to ensure, indeed to instil, a continued *Allied* prosecution of the war in Europe to its end. A better battlefield commander than Eisenhower might, as Monty claimed, have averted the Ardennes catastrophe ('If we had had a sound set-up for command even two months ago, the situation today could have been very different'); but for all his failings as a general, Eisenhower had ensured that the Allies fought together in a contiguous line from Holland to Switzerland, employing units from countries all over the world (Canada, Poland, Belgium, France, as well as Britain and the United States). American paratroopers had dropped behind enemy lines to secure the forward passage of British armoured divisions at Arnhem; British divisions were moving into the American line to release American divisions for counter-attack in the Ardennes. To have promoted and personified that degree of military interaction and goodwill was Eisenhower's true mark of greatness.

In moments of contemplation Monty did recognize this; indeed in his letter to Simpson he acknowledged that he 'did not know what may be passing on a high level in this matter [of command]. Nor is it my business. But certain things are very clear to me, and it may be as well to make certain you know these things. I therefore set out below the main points.' He then gave a strictly soldierly view of the battle of the Ardennes—the same résumé he had given Bradley.

'The enemy has the initiative,' it began ominously.

> He is using his left to hold off Bradley and with his right—two Panzer Armies—he is attacking me.
>
> I shall hold him.
>
> But the American divisions are all very weak, and any major offensive action from the north against the right flank of the enemy penetrations is definitely not possible at present. The 5 Panzer Army is now engaged with the garrison of the DINANT bridgehead.
>
> In the south, Bradley is trying hard to get to BASTOGNE to relieve 101 Airborne Div. He may possibly get that place, but he admits himself that he is not strong enough to get any further.
>
> The enemy is in such strength that, neither from the north nor from the south, can we develop offensive action in sufficient strength to cause him to react.

All we can do is to attack him ceaselessly from the air; for this we require good weather, which we have now had for two days.

The enemy will get very stretched and this, combined with our air attack, may cause him to wonder if he should not pull back a bit: having given us a real 'bloody nose'.

This is all we can hope for *as things are at present*. And we can hope for that much, only if we get good weather.

We are holding the two enemy Panzer Armies off from infiltrating the First US Army area only because for the last two days it has been good flying weather and we have been able to hit the enemy hard from the air. If the weather goes bad on us, then we may have difficulty in holding him. This is a very important point to bear in mind.[1]

Delusions would later be fostered that, if only Monty had been more aggressive, he and Patton could miraculously have cut off the German forces in the Ardennes salient, as at Falaise. But Monty visited, in the five days between 20 and 24 December, all the Corps Commanders in his two American armies, many divisional commanders, and a considerable number of American troops. He was not simply speaking for himself when he declared that no major American offensive was on the cards. At considerable risk (for there were reports of enemy troops massing at Monschau for renewed attacks on the Ninth/First US Army boundary) he had ordered General Simpson to thin out his Ninth US Army front in order to send reserves to First US Army; yet even on Christmas Day Hodges was appealing to Monty urgently for more troops and expressing grave anxieties about enemy infiltration on his 150-mile front, as his ADC's unpublished diary reveals.[2] So anxious had Hodges become that during 24 December he actually prepared 'plans for the movement to the rear of all heavy equipment of V Corps divisions [between Monschau and Malmédy], in order that, if it becomes necessary for these troops to withdraw, the roads would not be clogged with this heavy material and it would be necessary to hand it over to the enemy. . . . Despite the air's magnificent performance today things tonight look, if anything, worse than before. Indications from G_2 [Intelligence] are that the Boche will attempt to drive north with everything he possesses towards VERVIERS and LIEGE. . . . We are doing our best to organize a defence in depth and only time can make that possible.'[3] The following day Major Sylvan recorded:

[1] Ibid.

[2] Diary of William C. Sylvan, loc. cit.

[3] Ibid.

'This morning the situation looked bad; strong enemy pressure being directed due north from MANNAY and also in the CELLES area.' Several American units were overrun and 'forced to destroy their equipment'; in the evening a V1 rocket landed outside First US Army headquarters, injuring sixty-five men. 'Tonight it can be said that the enemy is temporarily at least halted,' Sylvan noted. 'No more gains were chalked up by him today. This does not mean, as both the General and General Kean realise, that he is going to stop attacking. . . . General Kean impressed most forcibly on Field Marshal Montgomery this afternoon, in a telephone conversation that he wished to obtain at once an infantry division preferably the 102nd which could be replaced by a British division. We have the 51st Highlanders backing up our line [the division had been moved south of the Meuse, southeast of Liège with 17,800 men on 24 December] but the general would prefer to stick in the 102nd to strengthen the front of the XVIII and VII Corps.' Hodges and his Chief of Staff Kean feared the 'infiltration, since the front is extremely wide, of small groups of Germans, which infiltration could become extremely serious. Field Marshal Montgomery said he would give an answer tomorrow.'[1]

Such diary entries were excluded from official and unofficial American narratives of the battle of the Ardennes since they did not accord with the 'blood and guts' idea of American military prowess. Bradley, made late by the mix-up over his aircraft at Luxembourg and Etain, did not even have time to see Hodges; his view of the battle, commanding only Patton's Third US Army in the south, was thus prejudiced not only by bitterness at his humiliating defeat, but upon ignorance of the true position on the American northern flank, never once meeting either Hodges or Simpson during the entire thirty-three-day battle. As will be seen, although Bradley would promote a view of Monty as super-cautious and unoffensive in the Ardennes battle, this caution partly emanated from the First US Army Commander himself, responsible for the American divisions in the field on the northern flank. Ignorant writers might condemn Monty for his failure to 'get on' with Americans, his allies; but at a professional, fighting level this was simply untrue. From the moment Monty was given command of First and Ninth US Armies in the Ardennes, he sought to restore confidence and morale among the American commanders by convincing them that this was *their* battle, and that in the end they would win it. By moving British divisions into reserve positions he enabled Hodges to fight his *own* battle without looking over his shoulder; and his daily visits to Hodges' headquarters were

[1] Ibid.

considered, at the time, to have saved Hodges from collapse. By his system of hand-picked Liaison Officers Monty was able to offset the alarming breakdown in Hodges' communications and restore order out of chaos. As one of these Liaison Officers later wrote:

> Hodges' trouble was that once he left Spa he had no communications and it was then that we L.O's were so useful. We were able to tell the Corps Commanders what Bill Williams thought of the 'I' side of it [Ultra, etc.], having been briefed by Joe Ewart [intelligence Colonel at Monty's Tac headquarters], and also tell them what were Monty's orders for them that day. These orders were given to Hodges about noon each day when Monty went to his H.Q. In other words the Corps Commanders were acting on these daily orders some 12 hours before Kean—Hodges' Chief of Staff—had got them to the Corps Commanders in writing. I believe this had a profound effect on the battle.[1]

Nor did Monty simply rely on his LOs. Travelling in his heated Rolls-Royce with outriders he personally visited not only Hodges' Corps and divisional commanders, but the US troops too—as Major Harden recalled.

> The 7th US Armoured Division was very shaken but only really because their commander was so shaken. I well remember taking Monty and Johnny Henderson [Monty's ADC] to see this Division in the Rolls and I must say the effect of his talk to all ranks had an electric effect. At least they knew what it was all about and that they were on the winning side and not the other.[2]

Not only had Bradley failed to visit Hodges or Simpson; Hodges himself had failed to go out and restore confidence in his subordinate commanders and men. That Monty, as Army Group Commander responsible for more than forty Allied divisions, should have gone out and addressed the men at the front was to Major Harden an indication of Monty's extraordinary leadership in time of crisis. 'Lesson for Hodges,' he summarized, 'was that when you move in a hurry and lose all your communications then get a set of able and young LOs who should be able to keep you in the picture and issue your orders and get about your troops *without a tin hat* so that they can see you and believe they have an able commander. In my opinion,' he concluded, 'Monty's greatest battle.'[3]

[1] Major R. Harden, letter to Lt-Colonel T. S. Bigland of 6.11. 1958, communicated to author by Colonel Bigland.
[2] Ibid.
[3] Ibid.

Even Major Bigland, who had a 'higher opinion of [Hodges'] H.Q. than most Americans' and was to some extent affected by the over-optimism prevalent at Bradley's headquarters, considered Monty's resurrection of Hodges to have been a remarkable feat:

> On the Monday morning, 18th December, I set out in my car . . . and in spite of the snow and ice we got from Luxembourg to Spa in time for lunch . . . the position was out of control. The Army HQ was ordering about even Regiments to stop gaps so that divisions were all split up and Corps had under their command bits of as many as nine divisions. The H.Q. themselves were not too happy about their own position and were certainly not planning far enough ahead to order the formation of a reserve Corps under General Collins.[1]

It was Monty who, on 20 December, immediately he assumed command of Ninth and First US Armies, had formed this reserve Corps—'when his Liaison Officers had reported to him at the First US Army H.Q. after visiting key points on the front.'[2] Unlike American LOs who were in essence merely messengers between commanders, Monty's team of young officers were trained to bring back their own reports on the battle situation—dispositions, morale and plans. With 'communications cut to First Army H.Q. [from Luxembourg] even by wireless because the relay station for direct transmission was overrun', and considering the fact that 'neither General Bradley nor any senior officer from his staff had visited the First Army' since the battle began, Lt-Colonel Bigland felt afterwards that there was no alternative to Monty being given command of First US Army[3]—command which Monty exercised with the same professionalism that had so impressed even anti-British American subordinate commanders and staff officers in Normandy. As Colonel 'Red' Akers, Hodges' Chief of Operations, had remarked to Bigland after Monty's first visit to First US Army in Normandy: 'It is going to work. He [Monty] did not tell us how to do things but just what he wanted.'[4]

Once again Monty was in command of First US Army—and in his element. His 'uniform' generally consisted of fur-lined boots, baggy corduroy trousers, a grey turtle-neck pullover and up to eight pullovers; but on Christmas Day, taking Bradley up to his study,

[1] Lt-Colonel T. S. Bigland, letter to Ralph Ingersoll of August 1946, communicated to author.
[2] Ibid.
[3] Ibid.
[4] Ibid.

Monty chose to wear regulation uniform, with a tailored battle-blouse coloured by his many rows of medal ribbons, knife-edged trousers, and shining leather shoes. Bradley, wrapped in his arctic coat, 'looked thin, and worn, and ill at ease,' Monty described. 'He was obviously tired. I explained my situation, and made certain he understood the points [re German initiative, firm defence, but lack of strength for immediate American counter-attack] above. He agreed with my summary of the situation. I then asked him what Eisenhower proposed to do.'[1]

This, perhaps more than any other feature of the Ardennes, was the most extraordinary. During the Normandy battle, as Supreme Commander, Eisenhower had constantly badgered Monty. Now ten days of battle had passed; apart from an indistinct phone call, prematurely cut off, the Allied Land Force C-in-C had not once spoken to or seen his senior Army Group Commander, in charge of countering the main offensive by two German Panzer Armies.

But Bradley himself had not seen Eisenhower, the supposed Land Forces Commander, for six days. It was an almost unbelievable situation that would be glossed over by four decades of less than frank historiography. 'He said he had not seen Eisenhower recently, and did not know [what Eisenhower proposed to do],' Monty recorded, almost in disbelief.[2]

Monty's answer was quite clear. The German onslaught should blunt itself against a firm Allied line, employing Corps artillery and Allied air attack. But as far as counter-offensive was concerned, Monty was now convinced that, without more troops, the Americans were unlikely to regain the initiative.

> I said it was quite clear that neither of us could do anything without more troops.
>
> We must shorten our front somewhere and thus save divisions; this can be done only by withdrawing back our right flank [between the Ardennes and Switzerland].
>
> I was absolutely frank with Bradley. I said the Germans had given us a real 'bloody nose'; it was useless trying to pretend that we were going to turn this quickly into a great victory; it was a proper defeat, and we had much better admit it, and it would take time to put right.
>
> I then said it was entirely our fault; we had gone much too far with our right; we had tried to develop two thrusts [north and

[1] M393, loc, cit.
[2] Ibid.

south of the Ardennes] at the same time, and neither had been strong enough to gain decisive results.

The enemy saw his chance and took it.

Now we were in a proper muddle. We must admit all this, and then someone must make a big decision as regards withdrawing on the right.

For the future we must at all costs hang on to our present bridgehead area beyond the MEUSE in the north; if we lost that then any advance against the RUHR would be off. The enemy knows this well.

Therefore there must be no withdrawal in the north; we might be driven back, but we must not withdraw.

But there is no objective in the south, and I have never understood what we were after down there.

A withdrawal to the line of the SAAR river, running south from SAARBRUCKEN and linking with the COLMAR pocket, would 'iron out' the STRASBOURG salient and save four divisions. A big withdrawal, back to the line of the MEUSE from CHARLEVILLE southwards to TOUL and thence down the MOSELLE, would save possibly 12 divisions.

We talk about passing over to the offensive, but it must be clearly understood that we had not now got the troops for the offensive.

We should never have gone so far with our right; we must now come back with our right and thus collect divisions for offensive action. I said I had always advised against the right going so far; I said I knew that he (Bradley) had advised in favour of it; Eisenhower had decided to take his (Bradley's) advice.

Bradley agreed entirely with all I said. Poor chap; he is such a decent fellow and the whole thing is a bitter pill for him. But he is man enough to admit it, and he did.[1]

But did Bradley admit his mistake? Bradley dictated no memorandum of the meeting; however it is improbable that he would have admitted to Monty that his whole tactical strategy since the autumn had been an error of military judgment. More likely he remained quiet during the half-hour interview, his silence being construed by Monty as agreement. A shy, reserved man, it would have been most unlike Bradley to 'confess'; whereas Monty's habit of nagging, if not downright bullying, went back to his days at Sandhurst. Domination was, in fact, an essential motivating force ingrained in Monty's character—a fact which in turn explained his dislike of conferences where

[1] Ibid.

he was unable to dictate policy or decisions. In the privacy of his study Monty had harangued not only subordinates and colleagues, but even his superiors, such as Alexander, Eisenhower, and even Churchill on the eve of D-Day. Worse still, it was Monty's wont to see life and personalities in broad strokes amounting almost to caricature. He despised politics for its fudged compromises, its absence of clear outline. War, by contrast, suited his pellucid mind, his desire to see clear answers given to clear questions, and his respect for simplistic issues: defeat or victory. In his clear-cut copybook, it was best to recognize defeat as a springboard to future victory; this he had done after Dunkirk, and it explained his predilection for using the term 'defeated' for the exhausted Eighth Army which he inherited in August 1942. Then and later there were fiery objections to this epithet. It is certainly unthinkable that Bradley would have admitted to having been 'defeated'. As Bradley wrote to General Marshall a few days afterwards, 'As a matter of fact, I do not blame my staff, my commanders, nor myself for the fact that the Germans were able to launch this attack against us and gain ground.'[1]

To Monty, such expostulations were 'fudging' the issue; far better, in his simplistic mind, to acknowledge the fact manfully, to pull oneself together and to seek diligently to reverse it.

Whatever was said during the interview with Monty, there can be little doubt that it was this personal humiliation, not the much-publicized press conference after the battle, that really turned Bradley's heart against Monty. He had been humbled, like a pupil before his headmaster, and the memory would rankle for the rest of his life. Far from encouraging Bradley to turn over a new leaf, Monty's 'lecture' only served to embitter Bradley and make him more obstinate than ever. Those who later claimed, as did Eisenhower's MA, Colonel Gault, that Bradley 'showed himself the big man he was'[2] in the Ardennes, were deliberately perpetuating a myth—for the evidence of all Bradley's private papers and the diary kept by his ADC demonstrate that Bradley failed to recognize or to respond to the severity of the German offensive, and afterwards poured scorn on Monty's performance in taking command of the broken American armies in the north. Far from showing how big a man he was, Bradley's response to the Ardennes was one of mortification, followed by distortion of the facts and vengefulness, however understandable. He consistently sought to misguide historians and chroniclers of the battle, including the American Official Historian in 1946. To the latter Bradley claimed that at Eisenhower's meeting

[1] Bradley Papers, loc. cit.

[2] Colonel James Gault, Pogue interview of 13.2 .47, loc. cit.

at Verdun on 19 December 'much of the later dispositions' of First and Ninth armies were made, and that Monty's subsequent 'selection' as commander of the two American armies therefore 'came as a surprise'. 'General Bradley said he knew of nothing particularly brilliant about Montgomery's tactics,' when asked; he claimed that Monty planned a withdrawal of American forces that 'was opposed by all American commanders'; and that he had been given charge of the two American armies not because of any break 'in communications between my Headquarters and the northern forces' but 'because it was the only way to get Monty to use British forces to help'.[1]

Such charges, given the true manner and circumstances in which Monty took command of the American armies in the Ardennes, were mean-minded and preposterous. Yet the fact remains that Monty himself incited such a response by his total lack of sensitivity towards a shamed colleague, a hitherto loyal and sincere ally. Monty's detractors would later consider this an example of Monty's failure to 'get on' with Americans; but Monty's relations with Hodges and Simpson and the American Corps and divisional commanders during the critical days of the German offensive belie this. Had Monty wished, he could have ensured Bradley's lasting loyalty and friendship by a display of gentle magnanimity, of understanding and sincere good will. Instead he humiliated the shyest and most professional of American generals in his hour of shame—not, it would seem, simply from spite but because he was at heart, as he had always been and would always be, a bully. And by bullying Bradley into a 'confession' of his errors since the autumn, Monty hoped to force Bradley into belated acceptance of the strategy Monty had proposed since the climax of the Normandy battle: the concentration of the main weight of Allied offensive effort upon the seizure of the Ruhr: the first stage of which would be the launching of Operation 'Veritable', from the Nijmegen island.

This meeting on Christmas Day 1944, largely ignored by subsequent writers, marked the nadir of Monty's relations with Bradley, cancelling in a brief half-hour one of the most distinguished feats of generalship in the Second World War. Whatever Monty said or did later to try and expunge his act of uncharitableness, it would never manage to eradicate the scars he inflicted in the quiet study of his Tactical Headquarters at Zonhoven that day. Far from returning to Luxembourg the repentant Christian, eager now to espouse Monty's gospel of war on the Western Front, Bradley returned to Luxembourg with a poisoned heart and an implacable determination to see that henceforth 'our own [American] interests come first.'[2]

[1] General Omar N. Bradley, Pogue interview of 14.10.46, loc. cit.

[2] Memorandum for Record of 23.1.45, Bradley Papers, loc. cit.

CHAPTER EIGHT

Eisenhower's Visit

EVERY DAY SINCE assuming command of the First and Ninth US Armies, Monty had despatched a telegram to Eisenhower reporting on events. Between December 21 and 26, however, Monty received only one communication in return, authorizing him on 22 December to recommend dismissal of Hodges or Simpson 'if any change needs to be made on United States side'.[1] Monty had considered removing Hodges[2] but decided against such action, which would inevitably be sensationalized in the American press and lead to bad inter-Allied feeling. 'Hodges was a bit shaken early on and needed moral support and was very tired,' he reported to Eisenhower. 'He is doing better now and I see him and SIMPSON every day.'[3] However the absence of any return word from Eisenhower irritated Monty—and when, by Boxing Day 1944, he had *still* heard nothing, he wrote in barely concealed anger to the DMO, 'Simbo' Simpson:

> An interesting feature of the present situation is that I have no idea where IKE is.
>
> I asked Bradley yesterday; he did not know.
>
> I told Freddie [de Guingand] to ask Bedell [Smith].
>
> Bedell's reply was that IKE is locked up—whatever that may mean.
>
> It may mean that they are frightened of his being shot up by enemy agents sent over here to kill him and me.
>
> Or it may mean that Bedell is fed up with the way IKE is quite unable to make up his mind about things, and he has persuaded him to stay at home and leave it to me and Bradley. Freddie

[1] Montgomery file, Eisenhower Papers, 1652 series, Eisenhower Library, Abilene, Kansas.

[2] Cf. Bedell Smith interview of 1947 with American Official Historian: 'When Monty took over First Army said might have to relieve Hodges. But said [inter-Allied] relations were such that he couldn't do it personally. Wanted Smith to handle. Smith said if were necessary SHAEF would do it. Monty said wait 24 hours. 24 hours later de Guingand called and said Monty said, "Hodges is not the man I would pick, but he is much better [now]"': Pogue interview of 8.5.47, loc. cit. Bedell Smith himself considered Hodges 'the weakest commander we had'. Ibid.

[3] M389 of 2155 hrs, 22.12.44, Montgomery Papers.

thinks this is it. Bedell I know is very fed up with the whole affair.[1]

Bedell Smith was certainly embarrassed by Eisenhower's self-imposed immurement in the Trianon Palace Hotel. 'E. is a bit low in his mind,' Mrs Summersby recorded in her diary on 25 December[2]—for with Monty's message decoded that morning, Eisenhower was near despair. Monty had already signalled to Eisenhower the deficiency of infantrymen in the American divisions, as well as his view that the two German Panzer Armies would ignore Patton's hastily-mounted counter-attack and continue to concentrate their assault upon First US Army; now Monty reported he 'could not at present pass over to offensive action'; nor could Bradley, once Bastogne had been relieved—'BRADLEY said he hoped to get BASTOGNE but doubted his ability to get any further without more troops.'[3]

Where were such troops to come from? Two divisions—6th British Airborne and 17th US Airborne Divisions—were on their way from England; 11th US Armoured Division was moving up from France. Beyond that the cupboard was bare, save for those forces that could be thinned out from Devers' 6th Army Group, as Monty had suggested six days before, and was requesting yet again: 'I consider if we are to wrest the initiative from the Germans we shall need more troops and we can get these only by withdrawing from salients and holding shorter fronts. I suggest that this aspect of the problem might be examined on the Southern front.'[4]

Eisenhower's heart must have sunk on receiving this cable. So preoccupied with the crisis had he and his staff been that Christmas Day had been forgotten entirely; he dreaded having to act decisively as Supreme Allied Commander, ordering Devers to shorten his front and provide reinforcements for counter-attack in the Ardennes; and in his anxiety he had unwisely sent a message direct to Stalin asking if a senior SHAEF officer might be allowed to fly to Moscow to discuss Russian offensive plans. As Maj-General Strong later wrote, this was bound to smack of supplication in the midst of the Ardennes battle. Nevertheless Stalin's positive reply arrived on 26 December, and Eisenhower ordered his Deputy, Air-Marshal Tedder, his Chief of Operations Staff, Maj-General Bull and a senior Intelligence officer to fly to Russia to find out more as soon as weather permitted.

To Monty it seemed extraordinary that Eisenhower could send his deputy and most senior staff halfway across the world to discuss operations and the future, but did not himself dare send them to see

[1] Montgomery Papers.

[2] Diary of Mrs K. Summersby. loc. cit.

[3] M396 of 2210 hrs, 25.12.44, Montgomery Papers.

[4] Ibid.

Monty, or move from his office and visit his own commanders himself in the field. Something of Monty's annoyance must have reached Eisenhower's ears, for on the night of 26 December Eisenhower ordered that a special train be got ready for a night journey to Brussels to see Monty. This train was caught in a German bombing raid, and it proved impossible for Eisenhower to travel by road or air on 27 December. Thus it was only on the morning of 28 December, *eight days* after appointing Monty commander of all Allied forces north of the Givet–Cologne line, that the two men finally met at Hasselt Station: a meeting that was to be as humiliating to Eisenhower as Bradley's had been three days before, and even more damaging to Allied solidarity in high command—driving Eisenhower to threaten to resign.

Monty himself seems to have been supremely unaware of the personal command crisis that was evolving. Eisenhower's memoirs, published in 1948, sought to give the impression that Eisenhower had been the unwavering, decisive mind directing the efforts of the Allied armies. His decision to appoint Montgomery to command all Allied forces north of Givet was described as though Eisenhower were an exemplary battlefield commander—'I telephoned Bradley to inform him of this decision and then called Field Marshal Montgomery and gave him his orders.'[1] To Monty the truth was very different; only after five days of battle had Eisenhower made up his mind—and since that brief and garbled telephone call Eisenhower had issued *no* orders whatsoever regarding the battle! To Monty, Eisenhower had proved a broken reed as supposed Land Force Commander—a veritable mockery of the role: a performance that surpassed in incompetence even that of Lord Gort as Commander of the ill-fated British Expeditionary Force before Dunkirk. With every day's silence, Monty's estimation of Eisenhower as a field general declined still further, until his contempt, like a sore, burst open.

Monty's scorn for Eisenhower was in stark contrast to his feelings for his American fighting subordinates. As Monty had written to Mountbatten, he enjoyed a 'good battle', for it enabled him to pit his wits against an enemy and to employ his not inconsiderable powers of military leadership: infectious self-confidence, mastery of the military 'machine', complete control of the situation, radiant simplicity and decisiveness. General Simpson, commanding Ninth US Army, recalled shortly after the battle to his English namesake 'Simbo' Simpson the impact Monty had made:

'You see from the very start when I was under the command of the

[1] Dwight D. Eisenhower, *Crusade in Europe*, New York 1948.

Marshal' (he always called him the Marshal) 'I got clear and definite orders what I had to do. From Bradley and my own people I never get any orders that make it clear to me what I have got to do.

'After the Ardennes break-through I was at my H.Q. with about a hundred different problems on my plate.

'While I was scratching my head the Marshal happened to be passing by and he came in and said, "Bill, how are things going with you?" I was not under his command then (though I was placed under his command the next day), and I told him all my problems.

'He [Monty] had a look through them and said, "There are only three of these problems that matter: this one, this one and this one. The answer to those three are: so and so, and so and so, and so and so." He said, "Let the others go to hell." I did what he told me and the others just disappeared.'[1]

As Maj-General 'Simbo' Simpson commented, 'Bill' Simpson had seen 'that Monty's supreme virtue in command was selecting the essentials, and like all problems in life, you concentrate on the essentials; the small stuff does not matter very much.'[2] But the Ninth US Army Commander was wrong in assuming that Monty just 'happened to be passing'. When later told this story, Monty remarked: 'Yes. It was not that I was just passing by. I knew Bill was in big trouble. My Liaison Officer had told me. I deliberately passed by. I went in, and what he described to you did happen.'[3]

It was Monty's *forte* to sense such emerging problems, and to be able to impart crystal clear orders and advice. That Monty acted as a powerful restorative to the exhausted Hodges is amply demonstrated by the diary kept each day by Hodges' ADC—and Bradley's contention, to the American Official Historian, that all the American commanders disagreed with Monty's tactics was ridiculous. General Collins, the US 7 Corps Commander, certainly hoped for a more aggressive stance—but Collins' somewhat myopic courage was not shared by his own American Army headquarters. On the day that Monty met Eisenhower, Collins submitted to Hodges 'three possible attack plans . . . two of which have BASTOGNE as the objective, one of which has ST VITH. They are broad and sweeping in their concept of offensive action and General Collins frankly admits in the papers submitted with them that they will require some strength because of the exposed flanks. General Hodges has had enough of exposed flanks for the last two weeks,' his ADC recorded caustically,

[1] General Sir Frank Simpson, Wason interview, loc. cit.
[2] Ibid.
[3] Ibid.

'and it is thought that the most conservative of the three plans will be the one finally adopted.'[1]

While Collins was urging a bold counter-attack with exposed flanks into the heart of a German salient held by two German Panzer armies, his neighbouring British Corps Commander, General Horrocks, was urging that Collins fall back and allow the Germans to cross the Meuse and to penetrate as far as Waterloo; General Ridgway, on Collins' left, was urging that *his* Corps meanwhile be allowed to counter-attack on its own.

It was Monty's task, therefore, having restored order out of chaos, to ensure that sensible decisions were made about Allied counter-attack. The Germans had prepared their offensive for *three months*; it was idle to imagine that Allied troops, hastily thrown into counter-attack at a few days notice, would achieve worthwhile results. With the existing shortage of infantrymen in the American divisions, costly counter-attacks mounted with blind courage but without real reconnaissance or carefully prepared artillery support would only serve to weaken those divisions still further, for little gain. Horrocks he sent straight back to England on enforced medical leave, just as he had sent Crerar in September. The DMO vividly recalled Monty's telephone call on 27 December 1944:

> Monty had ordered the Second Army to position 30 Corps behind the Meuse to hold the crossings, and it had got definite orders to prevent any German units crossing the Meuse. 30 Corps was commanded by General Horrocks, and Monty went to see him at his H.Q. to make certain Horrocks was clear about his orders. Horrocks was full of enthusiasm as always, but he had great ideas that he would let the Germans over the river and then win the final battle of the war on the field of Waterloo, which was not far away.
>
> Monty told Dempsey that on no account was Horrocks to let any Germans over the river. Monty rang me that afternoon and said: 'I am sending Horrocks back to England for a few days. He has gone mad. . . .' Those were his very words.[2]

The decision to send Horrocks home, however, was based upon more than Horrocks' wild proposal. 'Am sending Horrocks home on leave tomorrow,' Monty signalled on the morning of 27 December to the CIGS.

> During the past ten days he has been nervy and difficult with his

[1] Diary of William C. Sylvan, loc. cit.

[2] General Sir Frank Simpson, Wason interview, loc. cit.

staff and has attempted to act foolishly with his Corps. He is definitely in need of a rest and I want him to have 3 to 4 weeks quietly in UK. Grateful if you will see that he really does rest and is not asked to lecture at schools and colleges and so on. He is a valuable officer and I want him back. Have appointed THOMAS [Commander of 43rd Division] to act temporarily in command 30 Corps in his present rank. Have appointed RAWLINS CCRA Corps to act in command 43 Div in his present rank. It is a good opportunity to try out these two.[1]

That Monty was unworried by the prospect of the Germans now reaching the Meuse is demonstrated by the fact that he gave temporary command of 30 Corps to Maj-General Thomas, who had no Corps experience whatsoever. What Monty was adamant about, was that the battle of the Ardennes should not degenerate into a rag-bag of ideas promulgated by individual Corps commanders, each anxious to prove his abilities. Collins' decision to combat 2nd Panzer Division around Celles had forced Monty to commit his only American reserve Corps to battle, but he quickly accepted this and after pulling back Ridgway's more exposed 18 US Corps positions, felt confident he now had an excellent defensive line, upon which the Germans would only break themselves. As he signalled to Brooke on 25 December, he was giving Hodges the extra division he wished (though not the 102nd US Division; instead he had ordered 83rd US Division to move down from Simpson's Ninth Army front at Aachen, replacing it with 43rd British Division). 'I hope to be able to maintain this [new] line which will be far better than having to swing back the right flank to ANDENNE on the MEUSE east of NAMUR.'[2] On 26 December, as the British 6th Airborne Division began to arrive from England to cover the Meuse from Namur to Givet, he felt his line to be 'quite firm from MARCHE across to DINANT'.[3] This gave him a 'bridgehead' from Düren on the Roer down to Elsenborn, and then westwards to the Meuse. 'This bridgehead is important to us for the development of offensive action in the future,' he remarked.[4] Far from 'frigging about' at Waterloo, he planned to move 30 British Corps east of the Meuse to assume the front held by Collins which could then be launched into counter-attack. 'My present idea is that First US Army using 7 US Corps of four divisions will strike a hard blow SE to secure HOUFFALIZE

[1] M399 0820 hrs, 27.12.44, Montgomery Papers.
[2] M395 of 2205 hrs, 25.12.44, Montgomery Papers.
[3] M397 of 2200 hrs, 26.12.44, Montgomery Papers.
[4] Ibid.

and then operate eastwards to secure the road centres south and south east of VIELSAM. Reconnaissance and plans for this operation began today.'[1]

Monty's plan was to allow the German Panzer Armies to butt up against the Allied line; they would thus incur heavy casualties as well as use up their dwindling stocks of ammunition and petrol in the forward areas, Coningham's fighter-bombers ensuring that the roads behind were interdicted. Then, 'as soon as it is clear to me that there is no further danger from the enemy and he is definitely held,'[2] Monty planned to withdraw Collins's 7 US Corps and 'beef' it up for the drive to Houffalize. By Wednesday 27 December he had given orders that 30 Corps relieve 7 US Corps west of Hotton in two days' time, and waited all day ready to fly to Brussels to meet Eisenhower. At 10.30 p.m. he signalled to Brooke: 'EISENHOWER could not get here by air today and is coming up tonight by train.'[3]

That night there was a hard frost, and the roads by morning were dangerously icy. Nevertheless Hodges, Dempsey, Crerar and Simpson all managed to motor to Monty's Zonhoven headquarters for a crucial conference at 9.45 a.m.—for it was at Zonhoven that Monty made clear he had no intention of attacking the two German Panzer armies either immediately or with more than token British help. 'Ultra' Intelligence pointed to renewed German attempts to reach Liège. 'The C-in-C said that it was not his intention to strike with the 7 US Corps until the expected enemy Northward thrust on LIEGE had been launched, and failed,' Crerar noted. 'Then, he intended that 7 US Corps would strike South East on HOUFFALIZE and the greater the weight of 7 US Corps on its Eastern flank the better . . .' But Collins' attack ought not to raise any fantastical hopes, for Monty doubted whether, in the fearful winter terrain of the Ardennes, he could do more than force the Germans to withdraw from the salient they had created. Strategic victory was impossible in the Ardennes—which led nowhere save country even more inhospitable in winter. Monty's hope, therefore, was that Collins' attack would force the Germans to keep their main Panzer and infantry reserves committed in the Ardennes, while Monty struck at the true Allied strategic target, from the far north: the Ruhr.

> We were already well positioned and 7 US Corps, on right First US Army, was now getting organized for intended subsequent counter-offensive. This re-grouping had been accomplished without the actual intermingling of British and US formations

[1] Ibid.
[2] Ibid.
[3] M400 of 2200 hrs, 27.12.44, Montgomery Papers.

in the active operations—a situation he [Monty] was glad to have avoided for administrative reasons. *Also, from the point of view of the future mounting of Operation 'VERITABLE', by First Canadian Army, he wished to keep H.Q. 30 Brit Corps, Corps troops and several British Divisions, earmarked for that operation, uncommitted to any active, exhausting operations. 'VERITABLE' would be mounted just as soon as the Bosche became thoroughly involved in the counter-offensive which would shortly be launched by First US and Third US Armies.*[1]

This reason has been italicized, for it was to become a cardinal misunderstanding with Bradley, Eisenhower, the 'blood and guts' American Corps and divisional commanders, and the majority of American critics and later military historians who found it difficult to credit Monty's caution in the Ardennes. As Bradley later claimed, Monty had been put in command of all troops north of Givet in the hope that he would use his British reserves to good counter-offensive effect. But Monty believed he had been put in charge in order to iron-out the mess Bradley had made—not to mount a costly Allied counter-offensive in appalling winter conditions, without full air-support, training or preparation. He had moved 30 Corps from Canadian Army on 19 December to the Meuse: but he had never intended it should be wasted in local fighting unless there were an unexpected German breakthrough. The *real* role of 30 Corps was to be the backbone of Operation Veritable: a northern flank attack down the west bank of the Rhine under Canadian Army that would enable Dempsey's British Second Army subsequently to vault across the Rhine at Wesel—its abortive aim before the Arnhem landings. Hence Monty's willingness to send home the Commander of 30 Corps for a temporary rest. 'As soon, therefore, as 12 and 21 Army Groups' counter-offensives developed favourably,' Monty summarized, 'it was his [Monty's] intention to transfer 30 Brit Corps, and the several Brit formations previously planned to be under its command, to Cdn Army and launch Operation "VERITABLE" as speedily and forcefully as possible.' The role of 30 Corps on Collins' right flank was 'protective, rather than in an operational role' in order to retain as much strength as possible for its *real* offensive operations, which would be mounted roughly a fortnight after being released from the Ardennes.

General Hodges and Simpson understood this, as did Crerar and Dempsey. But there is much evidence that Eisenhower, when finally he met Monty at Hasselt station that afternoon (Monty had sent

[1] Entry of 28.12.44, Diary of General Crerar (CAB 106/1064), PRO; author's italics.

word that he could not be expected to drive to Brussels, the roads were so icy), did not.

It was early afternoon on Thursday 28 December when Eisenhower's train finally pulled into Hasselt station. According to Mrs Summersby's diary entry, written on Eisenhower's return, Eisenhower was peeved even before the meeting by virtue of the extended journey, just as Bradley three days before: 'E. and staff had a long and trying journey, delays on account of fog. On arrival in Bruxelles, E. found Monty was at Haselt [sic], had to proceed by train as the conditions on the roads made driving impossible.'[1] Eisenhower's security staff had insisted on sending a large squad of guards, which made the interminable journey tediously claustrophobic. 'At every stop—and these were frequent because of difficulties with ice and snowbanks—these men would jump out of the train and take up an alert position to protect us,' Eisenhower himself chronicled.[2]

Monty was therefore somewhat surprised by Eisenhower's royal arrival—as he told 'Simbo' Simpson when the latter flew over to Monty's headquarters the following day. 'He said it was most impressive. The train drew into the station and immediately teams of machine-gunners leapt out, placed their machine guns on both platforms at each end of the train, and guards leapt out and took up every possible vantage point. No question of letting any German assassination troops get at the Supreme Commander. Monty commented that he himself felt rather naked just arriving with an armoured car behind him, and he felt much safer with this enormous American guard before he met Ike.'[3] Eisenhower was, however, embarrassed and ashamed, instituting an official investigation after the battle to determine whether there had in fact been due cause for such exaggerated security measures.

Monty's own fearlessness was legendary. Standing on the beaches of Dunkirk he had berated his ADC for not wearing a helmet after a shell had landed almost beside them. 'But sir, nor are you,' the helpless young officer had complained.[4] Landing in Sicily, Monty had toured the bridge-head in a DUKW with Lord Louis Mountbatten, C-in-C Combined Operations. When a German aircraft screamed very low over their heads Mountbatten had wisely thrown himself to the floor of the vehicle. 'Get up, get up,' Monty had chided him impatiently.[5] Though he was conscious and careful of his health, with a near-

[1] Diary of Mrs K. Summersby, loc. cit.
[2] Dwight D. Eisenhower, op. cit.
[3] General Sir Frank Simpson, Wason interview, loc. cit.
[4] Lt-Colonel 'Kit' Dawnay, interview of 24.8.78.
[5] Lt-Colonel Trumbull Warren, interview of 9.11.81.

fetish for pullovers worn one on top of the other, he seemed to feel no fear of enemy sniper, artillery or aircraft fire. Indeed so oblivious did he seem to the danger of snipers in Normandy that the War Office had sent a special cable pleading with him to wear less conspicuous 'uniform', lest like Nelson he fall needless victim to an enemy sharp-shooter—a cable that amused Monty since it so patently ignored the dictates of great leadership in battle, that a commander must be seen by his men and recognized. Bradley's and Eisenhower's caution in view of the rumour of enemy assassination teams struck Monty as excessive—but though he went out of his way to be seen and recognized during the battle, Monty took no chances at night—as Simpson later recalled:

> There has been a feeling in London that Monty was not taking enough precautions for his own protection. He was inclined, openly at any rate, to treat over-protection with scorn, and one thing the CIGS particularly asked me to do . . . was to find out how Monty was being protected, particularly at night. We were not worried about what was happening during the day. Monty travelled with a small escort; nobody knew what roads he was to travel along, and it would have been next to impossible to prepare an ambush. But we thought it was quite possible that his Tac H.Q. position would be known to the enemy, and that some attempt might be made on him at night. . . .
>
> After he had gone to bed, which he always did by 10 o'clock at night, I went down to the front door with an ADC and asked to see what precautions were being taken outside. And I was immediately reassured. There was a tank right outside the front door, a couple of British soldiers looking out of the top of it. There were two armoured cars in bushes on either side, and there was similar protection at the back. It would have needed something that the Germans could not possibly have mounted to have raided that small villa, so I was able to tell the CIGS on my return that none of us need have any worry as to Monty's safety.[1]

Meanwhile, impressed by Eisenhower's safety precautions at Hasselt on 28 December, Monty had immediately asked to get down to business—in private. At Maastricht on 7 December Eisenhower had insisted that his Chief of Staff, Bedell Smith, be present. As a result, Monty felt, the American policy of dissipating Allied strength into two separate thrusts had prevailed, and he had lost the day. This time, the situation was different. Monty was now in command of four Allied armies. Eisenhower had been forced to appeal to

[1] General Sir Frank Simpson, Wason interview, loc. cit.

Monty to get him out of his 'mess' in the Ardennes. Bedell Smith had not this time accompanied him, and Monty refused to let his own Chief of Staff, de Guingand, be present. The two men thus moved into Eisenhower's study on the train, without witnesses, de Guingand and Monty's Intelligence Chief, Brigadier Williams, remaining in the unheated corridor.

Did Monty tell Eisenhower he would not be using his British 30 Corps in an offensive role in the Ardennes, and why he did not wish so to do? The previous day Eisenhower had heard from 21 Army Group that the northern counter-attack would, when assembled, comprise two Allied Corps (7 US and 30 British)—indeed so relieved was Eisenhower to hear this that he was heard to exclaim, at his daily conference in the Trianon Palace Hotel: 'Praise God from whom all blessings flow.'[1] With Bradley declaring that afternoon, on a personal visit to Versailles, that he had 'immediate plans for strengthening up the Southern flank of the salient and then attacking,' Eisenhower's main consideration in journeying to see Monty was: how soon would Monty counter-attack the northern face of the German salient? Monty's virtual refusal to discuss the timing of his own operations and his obvious lack of faith in the possibility or even advisability of all-out Allied offensive operations to achieve victory in the Ardennes, must have come—as it had to Bradley on Christmas Day—as a cruel blow to Eisenhower's hopes of expunging American defeat. It was clear that Monty, confident that he could handle the remainder of the Ardennes battle, was chiefly concerned with the Allied strategic offensive *after* the Ardennes—beginning with Operation 'Veritable' in the north, while the German Panzer divisions were still locked in combat in the Ardennes. To engineer this link between current battle plans and the resumption of the *real* Allied counter-offensive towards the Ruhr, Monty insisted that Allied operations north of the Moselle be handed over to one commander, as Monty related that evening (28 December) to the CIGS, on his return to Zonhoven from Hasselt:

> Personal for CIGS from Field Marshal Montgomery I met Eisenhower at 1430 hrs today at Hasselt in his train.
>
> He wanted to discuss first the details of the present tactical battle in the penetration area. I said that the forces engaged in eliminating the German penetration were coming in from all sides and that

[1] 'Meeting—Supreme Commander's Office,' Diary of Air Marshal Robb, entry of 27.12.44, Robb Papers (AC/71/9/26), RAF Museum, Hendon. Most American writers have used this as a further stick with which to beat the 'over-cautiousness' of Monty. Few, if any, have been prepared to analyse and investigate Monty's true motives and considerations in the battle.

> control of this battle should be vested in one man. He agreed and he accepted my views on the correct action to be taken by 12 Army Group and he sent an order to BRADLEY to take that action. This was just in time as BRADLEY was about to embark on another and somewhat unsound line.[1]

Monty then moved on to the Allied plan for invading Germany once the Ardennes battle was over: in Monty's view the assault upon the Ruhr.

> I then said it was vital to decide now on the master plan for the future conduct of the war so that all concerned could equate their present action with the future plan. In making this plan he [Eisenhower] must satisfy two basic conditions.
>
> First. All available offensive power must be allotted to the northern front.
>
> Second. One man must have powers of operational control and coordination of the whole northern thrust which would be from about PRUM northwards.
>
> I then said that he must clearly understand beyond any possibility of doubt what was my opinion on this matter of the master plan. My opinion was that if he did not comply with the two basic conditions in para 3 then he would fail.[2]

Air Vice-Marshal Robb's notes, made the following day upon Eisenhower's return to Versailles, bear out this account of the Hasselt meeting. 'Monty firmly believes that unless he has control up to the Moselle everything will fall flat,'[3] Robb chronicled Eisenhower's

[1] M401 of 1940 hrs, 28.12.44, Montgomery Papers. Bradley was intending to attack towards St Vith, whereas Monty felt both Allied offensives should aim at Houffalize, only ten miles north of Bastogne. Eisenhower agreed, and his cable to Bedell Smith was sent from Monty's Tactical Headquarters at 5 p.m.: 'Have had discussions with MONTGOMERY.... There are great possibilities in the BASTOGNE to HOUFFALIZE thrust which should be reinforced promptly and in strength.... With the area BASTOGNE to HOUFFALIZE firmly in our possession profitable operations can later be developed. Make this clear to BRADLEY at once': MA74 of 1705 hrs, 28.12.44, Montgomery Papers. Judging by the vocabulary it seems clear this message was drafted by Monty. With Ultra Intelligence pointing to a renewed German attack on Hodges's front, Monty was unwilling to initiate the Allied counter-offensive until Bradley had performed the task he had been attempting to achieve since 22 December: namely distracting Fifth and Sixth German Panzer Armies from their northward and eastward thrusts: 'I cannot launch this attack [towards Houffalize] against the weight of 5 and 6 Panzer Armies and must wait for the right moment. I hope Bradley will advance north from BASTOGNE towards HOUFFALIZE and if he can do this then I would loose my attack': cable to Brooke, M402 of 2200 hrs, 28.12.44, Montgomery Papers.

[2] Ibid.

[3] Diary of Air Vice-Marshal Robb, Robb Papers, loc. cit.

report to his staff. Robb added 'Monty considers that Bradley has made a mess of the situation'—a statement that made the American members of Eisenhower's staff and even his British subordinates bristle. Monty's cable to Brooke, however, described how Eisenhower had agreed with him.

> He agreed at once to the first condition and said he realised now that he had been wrong before. But BRADLEY and PATTON and DEVERS had all wanted the FRANKFURT thrust and he had given way to them.[1]

Eisenhower had in fact already undergone a change of heart concerning his overall Allied strategy. From Versailles the previous day he had despatched his Chief of Operations to see Devers, bearing an order that 6th Army Group was to withdraw to the Vosges and begin thinning out its line in order to provide vital SHAEF reserves. Tedder had objected, but Eisenhower—though not daring to speak to Devers himself—had been adamant: '"Pink, you'd better go and see Devers today. I think your best line is this." (S[upreme] A[llied] C[ommander] thereupon outlined his view on the map on the line down the Vosges to join up with the French forces north of Colmar).... "See Devers and give him this line." He then explained in further detail on it, finishing: "It will be a great disappointment giving up ground but this area is not where I told Devers to put his weight."'[2]

Eisenhower had thus already seen the light: that the Allies must cease attacking in different directions and form sufficient reserves to concentrate their major effort on one particular target. But what of the command aspect? Even Monty saw how difficult this would be for Eisenhower:

> He said there would be difficulties about the second condition [that one man must have operational control . . . of the whole northern thrust] and it would be particularly difficult to explain the situation to the American public. I said he would probably find it somewhat difficult to explain away the true reasons for the 'bloody nose' we had just received from the Germans but this would be as nothing compared to the difficulty he would have in explaining away another failure to reach the RHINE. I again gave it as my definite opinion that if he did not comply with the second

[1] M401, loc. cit. Eisenhower's knowledge of German geography was evidently vague, to say the least, for at one point Eisenhower emerged from his tête-à-tête with Monty shouting with exasperation: 'Where in God's name *is* Frankfurt?' and asking to be shown a map: Sir Edgar Williams, interview of 29.2.84.

[2] Diary of Air Vice-Marshal Robb, loc. cit.

condition he would fail. It was not enough to comply with only one of the basic conditions. He must comply with both or fail.[1]

To 'Simbo' Simpson, the next day, Monty gave a 'detailed account of the interview', which Simpson passed on to Brooke on his return to England:

> Montgomery said that he had considerable difficulty in making his point about having power of operational control and coordination of the whole northern thrust. General Eisenhower thought that it would be possible to devise a formula giving F.M. Montgomery power of co-ordinating where co-ordination is necessary. F.M. Montgomery was emphatic that this would not do and that it must be made quite clear in any order or directive which is issued that he himself—or anybody else who might be appointed to control the northern thrust—should have full operational direction, control and co-ordination of the operations, subject of course to any instructions that the Supreme Commander might issue from time to time. Eventually General Eisenhower agreed to do what F.M. Montgomery wanted.[2]

Monty did in fact again offer to serve under Bradley, if American amour-propre demanded this:

> F.M. Montgomery said that he had again expressed his willingness to serve under General Bradley, if it was thought necessary to appoint an American to command the northern thrust. General Eisenhower had replied that he had no intention of giving Bradley such a command, nor was there any likelihood of his changing his mind on this point.[3]

This was not what Eisenhower reported to his staff. Monty, meanwhile, was quite certain Eisenhower *had* agreed:

> He finally agreed to comply with both conditions and he gave me powers of operational control and coordination over the two Army Groups employed for the northern thrust.

But would Eisenhower stand by his word, once released into the 'outer world'?

> We have reached agreement on these matters before and then he has run out. But I have a feeling that this time he will stick to the agreement

[1] M401, loc. cit.

[2] Simpson memo to CIGS (DMO/BM/605) of 31.12.44, in 'Command Set-up December 44–January 45' file, Montgomery Papers.

[3] Ibid.

Monty cabled.

> He was very pleasant and the meeting was most friendly but he was definitely in a somewhat humble frame of mind and clearly realises that the present trouble would not have occurred if he had accepted British advice and not that of American generals. There will be no trouble over the first basic condition [concentration upon the major Allied offensive targeted on the Ruhr]. I am taking steps to ensure he does not run out over the second.[1]

The squad of guards with their machine guns had returned to the train, which had departed for Brussels and then Versailles. What steps Monty had in mind to stop Eisenhower reneging on his new agreement is unclear. Eisenhower, once surrounded by his loyal staff, was soon urged to disown any undertaking he might have made. As Mrs Summersby noted in her diary: 'E. and Monty had a long talk, Monty wouldn't let his C/S [Chief of Staff] be present. Monty still tries to convince E. that there should be one commander of the entire battle front, left no doubt as to who should be that commander. From all accounts he was not very co-operative. E. has a conference with his staff. They are all mad at Minty [sic], especially Whiteley.'[2]

Whether Eisenhower had or had not made an unwritten agreement with Monty, it was clear that he thought better of it once back at the Trianon Palace Hotel. Seeing the outraged reaction of his staff, the Supreme Commander/Land Force C-in-C realized that if he was to maintain credibility, he could not allow himself to be barracked and bullied by one of his subordinate commanders in this way.'E[s] one aim is to keep the staff together,' Mrs Summersby recorded. It was in this atmosphere, then, that Eisenhower decided he had lost control over Monty and, urged on by his nobles, prepared a cable to General Marshall and the Combined Chiefs of Staff stating that it was 'him or me'.

[1] Ibid. Brooke, however, hearing of Monty's interview from Monty, was perturbed. In his diary on 30.12.44 he noted: 'Monty has had another interview with Ike. I do not like the account of it. It looks to me as if Monty with his usual lack of tact has been rubbing into Ike the results of not having listened to Monty's advice!! Too much "I told you so" to assist in producing the required friendly relations between them. According to Monty, Ike argues that the front should now be divided into two, and that only one major offensive is possible. But I suspect that whoever meets Ike next may swing him to any point of view. He [Eisenhower] is a hopeless commander': Alanbrooke Papers, loc. cit.

[2] Diary of Mrs K. Summersby, entry of 29.12.44, loc. cit.

CHAPTER NINE

Monty's Letter

FEARING THAT EISENHOWER might 'welch' on his agreement once back in Versailles, Monty had rung de Guingand at Brussels on the evening of 28 December 'and told him to try and get asked to SHAEF and see Bedell-Smith, the intention being to work on Bedell-Smith as well on the same lines as the Field Marshal had worked on General Eisenhower'.[1]

De Guingand got his invitation—but it was too late to 'work on' Bedell Smith, for by the time de Guingand reached Versailles in appalling weather on 30 December, the senior SHAEF officers were up in arms against Monty.

Monty had known this—for on Friday night, 29 December, 'Whiteley rang de Guingand up to discuss one or two operational matters and said in the course of the conversation "I am afraid Ike is not going to be able to do quite all your C-in-C wants him to do as regards the set up for Command."'[2] As Simpson noted in reporting this to the CIGS, 'F.M. Montgomery thought this ominous as showing that General Eisenhower was likely to whittle down to some extent the agreement reached in the train on Thursday. In order to make quite certain that General Eisenhower grasped his point regarding operational control of the northern thrust,'[3] Monty now wrote a new letter to Eisenhower, which de Guingand took by hand to Versailles.

Monty's letter of 29 December begged Eisenhower, in drawing up his new directive, to be firm and unequivocal about command of the Allied Ruhr offensive—'I would say that your directive will assign tasks and objectives to the two Army Groups, allot boundaries, and so on. Thereafter preparations are made and battle is joined. It is then that one commander must have power to direct and control the operations; you cannot possibly do it yourself, and so you would have to nominate someone else.'[4]

That Monty proposed himself for this task has been the bane of

[1] Simpson memo to CIGS (DMO/BM/605) of 31.12.44, loc. cit.
[2] Ibid.
[3] Ibid.
[4] M540 of 29.12.44, Montgomery Papers.

his reputation in the North-west European campaign. Bradley thought such a proposal tactical nonsense, leading to 'an unsound command set-up' in which the object seemed 'in general, to increase British prestige in this campaign, out of all proportion to the effort they have in it,' rather than genuine tactical advantage, as he put it in a memorandum after the Ardennes battle.[1]

Certainly, to the casual observer, Monty's insistence on a single battlefield commander to undertake an operation such as the capture of the Ruhr appears in retrospect to have been obsessive—a trait which was in any event ingrained in his character. Yet the biographer must needs look further than the historical bystander. If Monty's 'campaign' to get a single battlefield commander for the Ruhr thrust was obsessive, it was not from excessive vanity, patriotism or personal ambition. The matter of single battlefield command permeated Monty's entire correspondence and also his diary (kept by Lt-Colonel Dawnay) after Normandy—but it was churlish of Bradley to see in this merely an attempt to 'increase British prestige'. Monty's obsessive interest was the professional conduct of battle. While he admired American speed and mobility, he abhorred the tendency to combat simultaneously on all fronts, hoping that somewhere a thrust would prosper. Under his supervision, Bradley had fought a magnificent battle in Normandy, cautious at first, but gaining in confidence as the battle reached its climax at Mortain and Falaise. Since then, unguided by Eisenhower, Bradley's performance as 12th US Group Commander had been a 'mess' in Monty's eyes, Bradley permitting his Army Commanders to 'bash on' and become tactically so unbalanced that the Germans cut clean through their centre. It was not therefore Monty's vanity that made him cry out for single battlefield command so much as professional frustration, even despair, at the consequences when this tactical imperative was ignored. Time and again he had offered, in the autumn, to serve *under* Bradley in a thrust to the Ruhr; Eisenhower had declined those offers. Now, with Bradley's credibility shaken by his defeat in the Ardennes, Monty *could* only seriously propose himself for the job, since it was abundantly clear that Eisenhower could not marry both Supreme Command *and* battlefield command. 'I put this matter up to you because I am so anxious not to have another failure,' Monty pleaded. 'I am absolutely convinced that the key to success lies in: (a) *all* available offensive power being assigned to the northern line of advance to the RUHR. (b) A sound set-up for command, and this implies one man directing and controlling the whole tactical battle on the northern thrust.'[2]

[1] Bradley, Memorandum for Record, 23.1.45, loc. cit.
[2] M540, loc. cit.

To the experienced, thinking soldier, the matter was as plain as a pikestaff. One junior British officer lamented the Allied débâcle in the Ardennes in a letter to his father on 14 January 1945: 'The vaunted American offensive all along the frontier was designed, I suppose, by attacking everywhere to stretch the German resources to the breaking point. It enabled him to conserve a striking force of 25 divisions,' he commented sardonically—not in nationalistic envy, but as an ally intimately involved. 'Again the need is for one man to exercise supreme and military command. Separate and equal commanders means separate and equal attacks. One man means concentration upon a simple vital objective, and that way lies success. End of tonight's War Commentary.'[1]

No more succinct précis could have been given, and as long as Eisenhower sat with Monty he *was* convinced. But once he had left Monty's unique aura of clarity and conviction, Eisenhower became a prey to other convictions—indeed, as General Sir Frank Simpson remarked, it was Eisenhower's very intelligence and openness of mind that led him to sympathise with other, alternative views—and these he met in abundance on his return to Versailles. Ashamed at the débâcle in the Ardennes, frustrated by their paper role at SHAEF, Eisenhower's courtiers were not interested in plans for attacking Germany *after* the Ardennes battle was over: they desired victory *now*, to avenge their humiliation. Patton and Bradley had voiced their opinions that victory could be won immediately by energetic counter-attack from the shoulders of the German salient, repeating the Allied victory at Falaise. Monty's view, expressed on 26 December, that 'First Army is very tired and when it has seen off their present attack it will be incapable of offensive action' was therefore galling to the paper-generals in the Trianon Palace Hotel. In the first days of the German attack General Whiteley had actually prepared plans for a massive Allied retreat in the north, as Maj-General McLean confided to the American Official Historian shortly after the war: 'We drew up a plan for withdrawal to protect Liège and Antwerp . . . Whiteley used me instead of [Maj-General] Nevins.'[2] McLean, no friend of Monty's, considered that 'Monty was right in holding his forces back and letting Germans come in. Patton got his whole force committed and couldn't move elsewhere.'[3] Even on 26 December Eisenhower was exasperated by Patton's failure to reach Bastogne, which Patton had boasted he would relieve within hours of his six-division attack on 22 December: 'I have just been set back

[1] I. J. Crossthwaite, letter communicated to author, 1.2.84.
[2] Maj-General Kenneth R. McLean, Pogue interview of 11/13.3.47, loc. cit.
[3] Ibid.

thoroughly on my heels by this failure of the attack from the south to join up with the 101st,' Eisenhower exclaimed at his Boxing Day morning conference.[1] On 28 December, as Eisenhower travelled to confer with Monty, Bedell Smith held his usual Chief of Staffs' conference in Versailles, at which Maj-General Strong, Chief of SHAEF Intelligence, demonstrated the extent to which the Germans still held the initiative: 'the enemy can hold us round Bastogne'; 'he [the enemy] can make his attack North against the First Army'; and finally 'if he [the enemy] wants to, he can get out of the salient'. Yet by the following day, when Eisenhower returned from Hasselt, the atmosphere at SHAEF had switched yet again from realism to fantasy. Monty's proposal that he should be given command of the next battle produced scorn among men whose eyes were locked upon the current battle—and the gratitude all had felt for Monty's prompt action in restoring order in the north now turned to derision:

> It was agreed that while Monty had quickly restored the situation in the US Army area on the north flank and got this army straightened out by bringing order out of disorder, when it came to the necessity for rapid offensive action he was far behind Bradley and that his inherent overcarefulness was going to cause us to miss the opportunity of inflicting a severe defeat on the enemy in the immediate future. The above view was stated by Bedell Smith and confirmed by the other three present [Eisenhower, Strong and Whiteley].[2]

Only days before, Whiteley had been preparing plans for American retreat to Liège and Antwerp; now he produced from his briefcase plans for not only severing the German salient across its middle, but for an immediate Allied drive eastwards along the very supply routes the Germans had used to build up their attack:

> Offensive measures were reviewed after which Eisenhower stated that *our one object must be to break through the enemy, get inside the salient and move East along the enemy's supply lines*—lines he obviously could not demolish or obstruct as he has done other roads. Also that when Patton's attack from the Bastogne area converged with Collins' attack from the northern part of the salient, then Bradley should resume command of the First Army.[3]

The same delusional insanity which had overcome Eisenhower

[1] Diary of Air Vice-Marshal Robb, loc. cit.
[2] Ibid.
[3] Ibid. (author's italics).

and his senior advisers in August and September 1943, after the secret Italian agreement to surrender, appears to have afflicted these same men on 29 December 1944. A short while previously, surprised and stunned by the severity of the German counter-attack, they had locked themselves up in their offices and left the battle to the soldiers at the front. Now, as the steam began to go from the giant German onrush, they spread their maps upon carpeted floors and planned counter-offensive operations as though playing with tin soldiers.

To Monty, schooled by a lifetime's experience and study of battlefield command, it was risible, if not contemptible: a wanton, criminally superficial foolery with brave American, and British, lives.

CHAPTER TEN

Humble Pie

How Eisenhower could have genuinely believed he could immediately penetrate to the centre of the salient held by two German Panzer Armies and appropriate the German supply routes in a great Allied drive through the Siegfried Line is difficult to credit, save in terms of his sheer amateurishness. Yet this was the situation relayed to Monty when, on 31 December, Monty's Chief of Staff returned from Versailles. De Guingand had, on 30 December, personally delivered Monty's letter to Eisenhower regarding post-Ardennes strategy and command—only to find Eisenhower much more anxious to launch an immediate and 'decisive' counter-attack.

De Guingand had ridiculed such exhortations for instant counter-offensive. The German attack had taken months to prepare; Hodges had borne the brunt of the combined Panzer armies, and could not be expected to mount a 'decisive' counter-attack at the drop of a hat. Such a premature counter-offensive would not only fail, but it would involve needless casualties. 'You cannot switch suddenly from defensive positions to the offensive without careful preparations,' de Guingand explained to the 'gang of four' at Versailles. Besides, the Allies now had the German salient ringed tight, a prey to air and artillery attack. 'In any case we had got the enemy on the run like a wet hen from one side of the salient to the other, that time was on our side and that we should let him [the enemy] exhaust himself and [then] come back with a riposte, and that there is nothing worse than laying on a half-baked attack. That the fire-plan for an attack must be worked out carefully and reserves collected and disposed.'[1]

De Guingand was not only speaking for Monty; he was voicing his own experience from Alamein to Tunisia, from Sicily to Italy, from the shores of Normandy to the frontiers of Germany. But neither Eisenhower nor Bedell Smith nor Strong had ever commanded troops in battle or even served on the staff of a commander in battle.[2] The Allied High Command in North-west Europe was in the hands of battlefield amateurs, and de Guingand's warnings fell

[1] Ibid.

[2] Maj-General Whiteley had served as BGS to Ritchie during Eighth Army's retreat from Gazala in 1942.

on deaf ears. Bedell Smith countered by declaring that Monty had promised Eisenhower he would counter-attack by the 1st January at the latest—in two days' time.

De Guingand shook his head, knowing that Monty would never commit himself to such an arbitrary date. Bedell Smith ordered a search of the files hoping to turn up a signal from Monty confirming the date, but de Guingand scoffed. 'De Guingand said, knowing Monty the last thing he would do is commit himself on paper . . . De Guingand pointed out the basic difference in offensive policy between 21 and 12th Army Groups is that normally *all* US divisions attacked, whereas in 21 Army Group the attack is on a narrow concentrated front.'[1]

De Guingand, in answer to Eisenhower's repeated assertion that Monty had promised to attack by 1 January 1945, said that he 'would not commit himself to any possible date for attack, but suggested it might possibly be mounted by Jan 2nd or 3rd'. The whole issue of Operation 'Veritable' and post-Ardennes offensive strategy, as well as command of Hodges' First US Army, was left unraised—the 'gang of four' seemingly besotted by the notion that they could reverse their humiliation since 16 December by a great Allied counter-stroke, mounted without preparation or forethought. There thus arose the spectre of SHAEF having authorized Bradley to begin an offensive from the south—albeit turned north towards Houffalize to meet Monty's eventual American thrust—but without Monty's thrust materializing.

'There appears to be a complete lack of coordination between 21 and 12 Army Groups,'

Air Vice-Marshal Robb noted after the meeting at Versailles.

> Bradley has in fact launched his attack from the Bastogne area on the full understanding that Monty was going to attack from the north on or before the 1st. What happened is that no German attack on the north [as predicted by Ultra intelligence, and for which Monty wished to wait before launching his own offensive] has taken place but that one of the Panzer Divs being held for this attack has been switched south to hold up Bradley. It appears that if Monty does not attack soon the enemy may be able to hold off Bradley and switch his strength back to the north—in effect retaining the initiative which he would lose at once if we put in a coordinated attack. Far from being on the run like a wet hen the enemy is making use of his interior lines on a small scale.[2]

[1] Diary of Air Vice-Marshal Robb, loc. cit.
[2] Ibid.

Robb, an airman totally unversed in matters military, was expressing the same anxieties and frustrations that had characterized SHAEF all through the Normandy campaign—when, instead of concentrating upon a clear Allied plan for the conduct of hostilities *after* the battle of Normandy, Eisenhower's headquarters became more and more myopic, hindering a battle they did not and could not, by reason of their battlefield ignorance, understand. As Monty had once confessed, to a group of Guards officers on the day his American break-out from St Lô kicked off, on 25 July 1944:

> 'You may wonder why I've got time to talk to you for two hours. Because I've just attacked with 1,000 bombers. I am putting in three U.S. Divisions on a front of three miles this morning and four more to go through this afternoon. We'll be in Paris in 17 days. There is nothing I can do except interfere so I'd much better talk to you. . . .
>
> 'No general can win battles after he's been sacked. I have to spend one third of my time making sure I'm not sacked, talking to the Press, and the Politicians, one third of my time driving round the troops seeing their morale is as high as I can make it. That leaves one third of my time to defeat the enemy.'[1]

In the same way that SHAEF had once considered, in July 1944, that the Allies had lost the initiative at the very moment when Monty was preparing his massive American breakout, so on 30 December Eisenhower and his advisers refused to accept Monty's view that the Allies had regained the initiative. Where Monty saw the Germans running 'like a wet hen' and out of time before the next Russian offensive began, bombarded by air and artillery, and counter-attacked in force where and when it suited the Allies—thus preserving Allied strength for the *real* Allied offensive to seize the Ruhr, beginning with Operation 'Veritable'—Eisenhower's staff dreamed, as they had each time during operations in Normandy, of instant and decisive 'breakthrough', attainable in their eyes only by speed and simultaneous, all-out combat on all fronts.

In Monty's and de Guingand's experience, such tactics had not worked in Tunisia, nor in Sicily, nor in Italy. Patton's great armoured break-out, Operation Lucky Strike, had first been planned at 21st Army Group Headquarters less than a fortnight after D-Day, on 14 June, but it had not been possible to mount it *until* the main German forces in Western France had been locked, as at Alamein, in annihilating battle and so weakened that the break-out prospered, more than a month later. Such a favourable situation, Monty and de

[1] I. R. Crossthwaite, loc. cit.

Guingand felt, had *not* been reached in the Ardennes—indeed without fair weather for flying it would be criminal to risk so many Allied soldiers' lives.[1]

It was in this 'stalemate' over the conduct of the battle of the Ardennes that Eisenhower now read Monty's latest letter, reminding him that unless operational control of the combined Allied thrust to seize the Ruhr was put into his, Monty's, hands, the Allies would fail.

What happened next is hard to reconstruct, since the versions of both historians and participants differ widely. De Guingand's recollection, published in 1960, was in many respects mistaken;[2] but interviews with Bedell Smith and with Eisenhower after the war confirm de Guingand's main memory: namely that Eisenhower drafted a cable to the Combined Chiefs of Staff saying that, with Monty predicting failure unless given command of the whole Allied thrust to the Ruhr, 'it was impossible for the two of them to carry on working together'. Bedell Smith certainly recalled de Guingand's visit and its sequel, as he reminded de Guingand in 1954: 'I have looked over my own records of the hectic days referred to in your letter of April 1. If I interpret you correctly, you have reference to the letter from Monty to General Eisenhower which you hand carried to our Headquarters and which said, in effect, that nothing had really gone well since Eisenhower took command; therefore a ground commander must be appointed; and General Eisenhower's reply thereto.'[3]

Eisenhower's biographer, Stephen Ambrose, claimed that de Guingand made two trips to Versailles and back to Monty, on 30 and 31 December;[4] but this construction is not supported by documentary evidence or even common sense. Atrocious weather on both 30 and 31 December precluded most flying, and it is inconceivable that de Guingand could thus have made four air trips in less than thirty-six hours. De Guingand's version, wherein he stayed the night of 30 December with Bedell Smith, seems inherently the more likely. Mrs Summersby's diary confirms that on 30 December:

[1] See 21st Army Group War Diaries (WO 205/8) PRO.

[2] F. de Guingand, *Generals at War*, London 1960. De Guingand claimed he flew to Versailles because he had heard an unhappy report from his Liaison Officer there. But Robb's diary notes on the conference belie this, indicating that de Guingand came on behalf of Monty. De Guingand recalled the presence at SHAEF of Air-Marshal Sir Arthur Tedder who 'sat near [Eisenhower] to the right of the desk, sucking away as ever at his pipe, apparently reading a document'. Tedder in fact had already left Versailles for Moscow, as Eisenhower's emissary to Stalin.

[3] Bedell Smith Papers, Eisenhower Library, Abilene, Kansas.

[4] S. Ambrose, op. cit.

'De Guingand and Bedell have a 3 hours session with E[isenhower]. E. is drafting a message to Monty, sending a copy to the C[ombined]. C[hiefs]. S[taff].'

It would seem, then, that on the afternoon of 30 December de Guingand arrived from Brussels bringing Monty's letter; that at a Chiefs of Staff Conference at Versailles the next day, 31 December, de Guingand gave the battle picture on the northern flank of the German salient and refused to commit Monty to an attack in strength until 2 January or 3rd as well as deploring the American approach to war; that Eisenhower then joined the conference, whereupon the discussion was repeated.[1] Monty's intransigence—his lack of faith in the prospect of a great Allied victory to be won in the Ardennes and his insistence that Eisenhower concentrate Allied reserves on the *real* strategic target—the Ruhr—under a single field commander—were difficult crosses for Eisenhower to bear, bringing him to the point of resignation. What tipped the scales, however, was a signal from Washington: for during the day a cable arrived from Marshall which put a very different complexion on the matter. Marshall had seen British press reports, which worried him. Eisenhower's staff 'may or may not have brought to your attention', Marshall telegraphed, 'articles in certain London papers proposing a British Deputy Commander for all your ground forces and implying that you have undertaken too much of a task yourself. My feeling is this: Under no circumstances make any concessions of any kind whatsoever. You not only have our complete confidence but there would be a terrific resentment in this country following such action. I am not assuming that you had in mind such a concession. I just wish to be certain of our attitude on this side. You are doing a grand job and go and give them hell.'[2]

Marshall's new telegram altered the whole balance of power in the echelons of Allied high command in North-west Europe. Monty's star, in the wake of the German offensive in the Ardennes, had risen, while those of Eisenhower and Bradley had plummeted. But now the Chairman of the Combined Chiefs of Staff had sent a vote of full confidence in Eisenhower, together with a veto on any plans he might have to give Monty ground command. If Eisenhower went ahead with his intention to make the issue of command a resignation issue, it was obvious to de Guingand who would have to go. De Guingand wisely begged Eisenhower not to send the drafted cable, but to wait until he, de Guingand, had a chance to speak to Monty in person.

[1] Diary of Air Vice-Marshal Robb, loc. cit.
[2] Diary of Harry C. Butcher/Desk Diary of C-in-C, loc. cit.

That day, 31 December, there was thick fog, and it was only at 3 p.m. that de Guingand reached Zonhoven, landing at an advanced airstrip nearby. Tea was being served in the mess, but 'before I had been there very long, he [Montgomery] realized that I had something on my mind and that something must be wrong. As he left the table, he said, "I'm going upstairs to my office, Freddie. Please come up when you have finished your tea."'[1]

In Monty's study de Guingand related what had happened in Versailles. At first Monty refused to believe the seriousness of the situation. Besides, even if it came to a showdown, why did de Guingand believe that Eisenhower would win? De Guingand thereupon instanced the ratio of war effort between Britain and the United States, which made it difficult if not impossible for Churchill to make the Americans do anything against their wish. Monty acknowledged the force of this argument. But if Eisenhower sacked him, who was there who would or could take Monty's place?

It was at this juncture that de Guingand mentioned Alexander—'as to a successor in 21st Army Group there was always Alexander, and during my interview with the Supreme Commander, he had actually hinted at this very solution. In fact I seem to recall that Alexander's name was mentioned in the [draft] signal [to Marshall].'[2]

Monty was, for once in his life, completely floored. He considered that he now held the tactical initiative on the northern flank, having moved 30 Corps into position in the Ardennes between Marche and Givet in order to enable Collins' neighbouring 7 US Corps to bring 'three complete divisions in reserve', as Monty had cabled the CIGS the night before;[3] Monty intended to sidestep 30 Corps still further eastwards, swelling Collins' counter-attack force into a reserve of four complete divisions, ready to strike southwards to Houffalize with its right flank on the Ourthe river and left flank on the Grandmenil–Hotton road. His target date was 4 January for this attack, 'but as to whether I shall actually launch it then will depend on general situation and particularly on what happens on southern front'.[4] If he was to keep 30 Corps fresh and at full strength for the forthcoming 'Veritable' operation, and extract the Corps intact while the German Panzer armies were held by Collins' 7 US Corps, it was vital to avoid entangling it with the American forces involved in the Ardennes—'if the British troops went into battle in any place

[1] F. de Guingand, op. cit.
[2] Ibid.
[3] M404 of 2010 hrs, 28.12.44, Montgomery Papers.
[4] Ibid.

other than the western flank the supply and administration problems would become hopelessly mixed up'.[1] So confident did Monty feel about the situation in the Ardennes that he had, already on 29 December, recommended that Bradley push hard from Bastogne, so that Collins' attack would then catch the Panzer Armies unbalanced as they moved south to try and remove the thorn in their side at Bastogne—'it is from the south that our offensive operations should now be developed in as great strength as possible and I have urged SHAEF to give Third Army [Patton] all the reserve divisions that can be made available.'[2]

Given such a transformation from defeat to tactical Allied initiative, it seemed inconceivable to Monty that he should now be sacked. On the contrary, knowing that Tedder was journeying to Moscow to find out future Russian plans, and that Eisenhower was currently collecting ideas for the resumption of the Allied offensive after the Ardennes, Monty felt that Brooke should put pressure on Churchill and Marshall to see that Eisenhower kept his promise about the main Allied offensive being mounted in the north, and on the matter of who should command it. As 'ammunition' Monty had given the DMO, 'Simbo' Simpson, a short paper to take back to the War Office that very morning, 31 December. Entitled 'The Three Failures', it adumbrated the sorry saga of the Allied campaign since Eisenhower took charge of the land battle on 1 September 1944: Eisenhower's first SHAEF directive on 4 September which gave the Ruhr *and* the Saar/Frankfurt as objectives; his second directive on 28 October which gave advance to the Rhine both in the north *and* in the south as the Allied tasks. Both plans, in Monty's view, had failed. Finally 'on 16 Dec the enemy struck a hard blow at the centre of the American front. The American armies were deployed in a long line; there were few reserves anywhere. We suffered a severe defeat.'[3]

Simpson had already departed with this document; the War Office was already preparing for a thunderous attack on American prosecution of the Allied campaign in North-west Europe.[4] De Guingand's presentation of the view from SHAEF was thus a bombshell. As de Guingand recorded: 'I felt terribly sorry for my Chief, for he now looked completely non-plussed—I don't think I had ever seen him so deflated. It was as if a cloak of loneliness had descended on him.'[5]

[1] Ibid.
[2] M403 of 2125 hrs, 29.12.44, Montgomery Papers.
[3] Montgomery Papers.
[4] 'Command Set-up in Europe December 44–January 45' file, Montgomery Papers.
[5] F. de Guingand, op. cit.

The thought of Alexander usurping his role in command of 21st Army Group was a factor Monty had never considered. In his diary twelve months before, he had written: 'ALEXANDER is a very great friend of mine, and I am very fond of him. But I am under no delusion whatsoever as to his ability to conduct large scale operations in the field; he knows nothing about it; he is not a strong commander and he is incapable of giving firm and clear decisions as to what he wants. In fact no one ever knows what he *does* want, least of all his own staff; in fact he does not know himself.'[1] Increasingly, in Tunisia, Sicily and Italy, Alexander's loose-reined, un-co-ordinated conduct of command had irritated and finally exasperated Monty. Though Churchill's ideal figure of a soldier—brave, charming, imperturbable—Monty felt Alexander would prove a disaster in Northwest Europe; and that the combination of Eisenhower, Bradley and Alexander combatting on all fronts and laying themselves open to the sort of defeat they had suffered in the Ardennes . . . it was too awful to contemplate. The German offensive had already put back the end of the war for many months; with Eisenhower and Alexander at the helm, it might be prolonged even further, as had happened in Tunisia and again in Italy.

It seemed unfair to Monty that his command should be offered to a general as ineffective as Alexander; moreover it was untrue that he himself was agitating for command of *all* ground forces in Northwest Europe—he merely wished to see the *thrust to seize the Ruhr* put under a single commander, a man who would relentlessly ensure that the operation succeed. Yet Marshall's telegram, with its categorical insistence that Eisenhower not give way over the command issue, left little doubt that Monty was on a 'bad wicket'.

It was Monty's ruthless adherence to his own principles of command that had made him the outstanding Allied battlefield general of the war. Yet such ruthlessness was founded upon profound military realism. Again and again, when his battles did not go according to his prescribed plan, he had turned tactical reverse to advantage by altering his battle scheme—as he had done when the 'Geordies' were thrown back at Mareth, or in Normandy when he opted for a pivot at Caen rather than Falaise. Such tactical flexibility permitted him to adhere to his larger tactical strategy, by which he ensured retention of the initiative. In writing to Eisenhower he had sought to 'thump the table' and dictate both the Allied strategic objective and the terms by which it should be achieved. But it was now clear that he had misjudged the moment—and no one would thank him for engineering such a crisis in Allied High Command.

[1] N. Hamilton, *Monty: Master of the Battlefield 1942–44*, London 1983.

'What shall I do, Freddie?' he asked de Guingand.[1]

From his battle-dress pocket de Guingand pulled a piece of paper—the draft of an apologetic message to Eisenhower. It seemed the only solution, and it is to Monty's great credit that for all his vanity and self-assurance he was able at this moment to swallow his pride and recant. Six days previously he had humiliated Bradley in his study; three days previously he had put the Supreme Commander in his place on board 'Alive', Eisenhower's train at Hasselt. Now it was Monty's turn to undergo humiliation.

> Dear IKE,
>
> Have seen Freddie and understand you are greatly worried by many considerations in these difficult days. I have given you my frank views because I have felt you like this. I am sure there are many factors which may have a bearing quite beyond anything I realize. Whatever your decision may be you can rely on me one hundred percent to make it work and I know BRAD will do the same. Very distressed that my letter may have upset you and I would ask you to tear it up.
>
> Your very devoted subordinate,
> MONTY[2]

The cable was encyphered at 3.55 p.m. This was not all. When Hodges arrived early that evening with his final plans for the First US Army offensive Monty advanced the timing by 24 hours. 'After consultation with HODGES I am putting forward the attack of VII Corps towards HOUFFALIZE by one day and it will now be launched at first light on 3 January,' with 30 Corps taking over the Allied front as far east as Hotton by 2 January, Monty signalled to Eisenhower.[3] De Guingand meanwhile returned to Brussels having asked for an urgent meeting of British war correspondents.

In Normandy Monty had fought the finest Western Allied offensive battle of the war; in the Ardennes the finest defensive battle. But from being the 'saviour' of the Allies in the Ardennes, able to thump the table, Monty was now back to square one.

[1] F. de Guingand, op. cit.
[2] M406 of 1555 hrs, 31.12.44, Montgomery Papers.
[3] M408 of 2135 hrs, 31.12.44, Montgomery Papers.

PART FIVE

Beyond the Bulge

CHAPTER ONE

Hard and Bitter Fighting

THE IRONY BEHIND Eisenhower's threat to ask for Alexander to replace Monty was that Eisenhower had in fact abandoned the idea of an American advance towards Frankfurt, and had accepted Monty's case for concentrated Allied effort, after the battle in the Ardennes was over, upon the Ruhr. In fact as de Guingand flew up to Zonhoven on the afternoon of New Year's Eve, Eisenhower drew up new orders. Ninth US Army would remain under Monty's command in 21 Army Group. '*The main effort*' was now to be '*north of the Ruhr*', while all forces south of the Moselle 'to be strictly defensive'.[1] Patton was to move up north of the Moselle, under Bradley; Patton and Hodges were then to fight their way around the south of the Ruhr on the line Prum–Bonn, while Monty's 21st Army Group—including Ninth US Army—first cleared the west bank of the Rhine (Operation 'Veritable') and then swung round the north face of the Ruhr. Bradley was to move his headquarters north to be nearer Montgomery, and 'from now on, any detailed or emergency coordination required along Army Group boundaries in the north will be effected by the two Army Group Commanders with power of decision vested in C[ommanding] G[eneral] 21st Army Group'.[2]

This was, short of actually giving Monty command of the whole Ruhr offensive, all that Monty had been asking for since the previous autumn—and Monty was delighted. 'You can rely on me and all under my command to go all out 100% to implement your plans,' Monty cabled back[3]—having assured Eisenhower in a New Year's message that he wished 'to assure you of the personal devotion and loyalty of myself and all those under my command. We will follow you anywhere.'[4]

Deluged by such professions of apology and loyalty, Eisenhower now assured Marshall that there was no need to worry. 'You need have no fear as to my contemplating the establishment of a ground

[1] Letter and outline plan of 31.12.44 in *The Papers of Dwight David Eisenhower*, ed. Alfred D. Chandler, *The War Years* Vol. III, Baltimore 1970. Originals in Montgomery Papers.
[2] Ibid.
[3] M414 of 0930 hrs, 2.1.45, Montgomery Papers.
[4] M409 of 0840 hrs, 1.1.45, Montgomery Papers.

deputy,' he cabled.[1] To Monty he signalled his thanks for 'your very fine telegram [of apology] . . . I truly appreciate the understanding attitude it indicates'; moreover he was grateful that Monty had 'found it possible to speed up your re-grouping arrangements' for the attack southwards to Houffalize.[2]

General Bradley, however, was less pleased. 'When General Eisenhower informed me that he was leaving the Ninth Army under command of the 21 Army Group, I protested and stated that if nothing else, all American forces should be returned to Twelfth Army Group even if it were only for a few days,' Bradley recorded in a Memorandum For Record several weeks later. 'In my opinion, the failure to return all American troops to the command of Twelfth Army Group might be interpreted as a lack of confidence in the American command.'[3]

Bradley's humiliating Christmas Day interview at Zonhoven with Monty and now Eisenhower's decision to adopt Monty's strategy in the Ardennes; to give Monty continued command of Ninth US Army; to compel Bradley to move his headquarters near to Monty; and to allow Monty 'power of decision' in coordinating the Ruhr offensive—these were all knocks that Bradley found hard to stomach, as did his staff, who were mortified.

> SHAEF has issued its new directive on the Army Group effort and it now appears that we are committed to a principal effort in the north after the bulge has been eliminated . . . I expressed some surprise and disappointment at this,

Bradley's ADC recorded on 2 January[4] as Bradley drove to Etain airfield to protest in person to Eisenhower.[5] Bradley had been preparing plans not only for Patton to thrust south-east to the Saar, but for a 'break through in the Eifel' by First and Ninth US Armies that would put both armies on the Rhine at Cologne.[6] Eisenhower, arriving in a C-47, attempted to sugar the pill by saying that Bradley's 'estimate was the only correct one he had of the situation on the breakthrough. His [Eisenhower's SHAEF] staff leaned first one way and then the other.'[7] Meanwhile Major Hansen also made Bradley

[1] Cable S73275 of 1.1.45, in *The Papers of Dwight David Eisenhower*, op. cit.

[2] Cable S73249 of 1.1.45, in *The Papers of Dwight David Eisenhower*, op. cit. Original in Montgomery Papers.

[3] Memorandum For Record of 23.1.45, Bradley Papers, MHI, Carlisle, Pennsylvania.

[4] Diary of Chester B. Hansen, MHI, Carlisle, Pennsylvania.

[5] Ibid.

[6] Ibid.

[7] Ibid.

feel better by telling him 'of the panic and hysteria that gripped 21 Group when they heard of it [the German breakthrough]'.[1]

Such nonsense[2] could not cocoon Bradley for ever, though. Eisenhower had cabled to Marshall that Bradley had 'been making only slow and laborious progress from the south',[3] and even Bradley had to admit that he had 'as yet been unable to punch a hole we can pour through quickly'.[4] Monty had warned Eisenhower on 2 January that 'tactical victory within the salient is going to take some little time to achieve and that there will be heavy fighting';[5] but both Patton and Bradley felt the time was propitious to give their own Press Conferences—Patton boasting to reporters on 1 January that he knew 'of no [feat] equal to it in military history'—the move of his three divisions from their sector on 22 December, and claiming 'we can lick the Germans any place . . . I don't care where he fights. We'll find him and kick his teeth in.' The defence of Bastogne was 'as important as the Battle of Gettysburg'.[6] Bradley gave his own conference three days later—but by then even he was beginning to realize that 'our operation in the closing of the gap was apt to be a long one',[7] as Patton's divisions began to tire and the true extent of American casualties became clear. Patton blamed Bradley for not permitting him to attack through the shoulder of the German salient. But behind Patton's bombast was a Third US Army racked with contradictions, misunderstandings, and incompetence—as the unpublished diary kept by Patton's Chief of Staff, General 'Hap' Gay, reveals. Monty would later be criticized for his unwillingness to launch Collins' 7 US Corps counter-attack while Ultra Intelligence indicated a renewed German Panzer offensive towards Liège—an attack which Monty (as was his habit) wished to meet on ground of his own choosing. Meanwhile General Middleton, charged by Patton with the main 8 US Corps offensive northwards from Bastogne, had

[1] Ibid.

[2] It is clear Hansen had heard from Major Bigland, the Liaison Officer between Monty and Bradley, that there had in the early days of the battle been considerable anxiety at 21st Army Group Main Headquarters in Brussels (particularly among Dutch and Belgian liaison officers) lest the German offensive sweep right through the American front in the Ardennes. This was hardly surprising, given the breakdown in American communications and the lack of information coming from Bradley's and Hodges' headquarters. (This did *not* hold true of Monty's own Tactical Headquarters, where the clearest picture of the entire battlefield existed): Lt-Colonel T. S. Bigland, interview of 29.2.84.

[3] Cable S73275 of 1.1.45, loc. cit.

[4] Entry of 30.12.44, diary of Chester B. Hansen, loc. cit.

[5] M414, loc. cit.

[6] *The Patton Papers*, ed. M. Blumenson, Boston 1982.

[7] Entry of 4.1.45, diary of Chester B. Hansen, loc. cit.

no faith in it, as General Gay's diary shows. On Friday 29 December Middleton begged 'that the Army Commander [Patton] come to see him. General Gay told him that the Army Commander was sick and could not go out on a long trip. General Middleton then . . . asked for permission to launch his attack to the left [of Bastogne, owing to congestion in the town]. General Gay stated that the Army Commander said he didn't care how General Middleton made the attack, but he must make it, and he must take the objective.'[1] When the next day Middleton launched the attack—which Patton, Bradley and Eisenhower all felt should be matched by a similar, unprepared, attack from Monty's northern flank—Gay recorded:

> While history may prove that the launching of an attack on this line was necessary, at present it indicates a complete misunderstanding of the problem involved, on the part of the Commanding General, VIII Corps.[2]

As Middleton's attack failed and American Eighth Air Force bombers bombed their own 4th Armoured and 4th Infantry Divisions and American AA gunners shot down American fighters, Gay lambasted the incompetence of inexperienced American divisions and General Middleton's lack of aggressiveness. Middleton had been ordered to capture Houffalize, while 3 US Corps 'killed or captured some 8,000 Germans'[3] that would be caught in a salient southwest of Bastogne. Instead, Middleton was himself attacked by German forces, while 17th Airborne Division failed to attack because the American Communications Zone failed to bring up the necessary lorries in time. Middleton wished to take up defensive positions; Patton overruled him.

> The Army Commander refused this request and directed that the VIII Corps launch its attack on the morning of 4 January. During the last two years this 'séance', so to speak, has repeated itself many times and in each and every case the Army Commander has been correct. He has continuously held that once an attack is set to be launched, it should be launched; that our main mission is to destroy the German Army, and we can do it better by attacking them than we can by waiting for them to attack.[4]

Here indeed the difference between Monty's and Patton's—between British and American—conceptions of battle were epitomized.

[1] *The Patton Papers*, op. cit.
[2] Diary of General 'Hap' Gay, MHI, Carlisle, Pennsylvania.
[3] Ibid.
[4] Ibid.

Bradley, dining with Patton that night, approved Patton's orders—and one regiment of 17th Airborne Division was wiped out the following day, as its commander described a few weeks later to an American combat historian. The 17th Airborne Division had first been ordered to defend the Meuse south of Givet, then peremptorily to take over the attack from the south where 11th US Armoured Division had failed to make headway:

> When we arrived at NEUFCHATEAU, our destination had been changed and we were told to go 9 miles farther along and relieve 11 A[rmoured Division] again. That division in the meantime had moved up and taken a crack at the line, but the fighting had been heavy and 11 A had failed to make any dent on the enemy. It was felt infantry was needed for this situation.
>
> We started our move on 2 January. On 3 January we were ordered to make a night relief of 11 A and to attack the next day at daylight. But we couldn't do it because we couldn't get up there in time. We were still having truck troubles. When daylight came only 50 per cent of 17th [Division] was closed on the line. The assignment—to relieve and then attack at once—was a large order for a new division. But the high command was insistent at this time that there was nothing in front of us. By high command, I mean that Third Army was presenting this view to VIII Corps. . . .[1]

Patton had claimed to the newspapermen that he wanted 'to catch as many Germans as possible, but he [the enemy] is pulling out'; moreover he had boasted that 'unless they have reproductive tanks' the Germans had 'damn little armor left'.[2] This was not what the virgin US paratroopers of 17th Airborne Division found on 4 January. Fighting in sub-zero temperature, charging with their bayonets 'they did one hell of a fine job'[3] in clearing the woods at Flamizoulle, their divisional commander recorded, but then met German armour coming down the St Hubert-Bastogne road. The same happened at Maude. Because of the fog there was no possibility of artillery observation, and within hours the men were back on

[1] '17th Airborne in the Bulge', interview with Maj-General Miley of 19.1.45, OCMH Collection, MHI, Carlisle, Pennsylvania.

[2] *The Patton Papers*, op. cit. In fact the Germans were feeding in further tanks and equipment, as Maj-General Strong, Eisenhower's Chief of Intelligence, acknowledged on 5 January 1945, pointing out that the 'failure of the Russian offensive to start . . . had enabled GERMANS to bring in replacements and equipment; that although 400 tanks had been knocked out more were coming in': Robb Papers (AC 71/9/26), RAF Museum, Hendon.

[3] '17th Airborne in the Bulge', loc. cit.

their start line. When the 87th Division attempted to attack to reach them, they were also counter-attacked by the Germans and made no headway. By 5 January, when Gay went forward in person to see Middleton, he realized that it was futile to pursue attack for attack's sake:

> The Commanding General of the VIII Corps was quite depressed and felt that he could not attack, and also questioned if he could hold against the enemy's attacks. General Gay, feeling that for him to attack in this mood would result in a half-hearted attack and would probably gain nothing, told him that he would take the responsibility for calling off the attack on that date.[1]

The offensive by 8 US Corps was thus shut down. Monty was unsurprised—indeed in his nightly cable of 1 January 1945 he had warned Brooke not to expect too much of the attacks in the north either. 'I do not think we must expect any spectacular results from this [Collins'] attack but it should certainly serve to relieve pressure on the southern front about BASTOGNE.'[2] The following day, on the eve of Collins' attack, Monty expanded on this—for he had heard that Brooke and Churchill were planning a visit to Eisenhower's headquarters. He had already informed Brooke of the momentous fracas over the command issue and its result ('I am now going to withdraw from the contest. It is clear to me that we have got all we can and that we shall get no more')[3]; now he gave his military opinion on the forthcoming operations in the Ardennes:

> It is gradually becoming clear to me that we may not have sufficient strength to push the Germans out of the penetration area and obtain what IKE calls 'tactical victory in the salient'. The Germans are in great strength. The American divisions are either weak or inexperienced and there has been a tendency in the south to throw them in piecemeal and on wide fronts as they become available.
>
> I believe the only sure way to deal with the Germans is by means of a really strong counter offensive from one flank or the other. I doubt if we shall do much good by relatively small scale attacks from both flanks.
>
> I do not know what total resources are available to the American forces in this theatre. From what information I have it does not look as if we shall have enough strength to stage a really full-blooded counter offensive.
>
> The general tendency at SHAEF and among the American high

[1] Diary of General 'Hap' Gay, loc. cit.
[2] M412 of 1945 hrs, 1.1.45, Montgomery Papers.
[3] M413 of 2215 hrs, 1.1.45, Montgomery Papers.

command is one of considerable optimism. It is considered that very shortly the First and Third Armies will join hands and that the Germans will then soon be pushed back to where they started from. I must confess I cannot share this optimism. I foresee a very great deal of hard and bitter fighting in the penetration area and I doubt if the Americans have the reserves to keep it up and I have given these views to SHAEF.[1]

In order to help Bradley and to show his willingness to co-operate with Eisenhower, Monty had agreed to accelerate Collins' attack—but he was under no illusions.[2] As he had cabled to Eisenhower right at the start of the battle, only by ruthlessly withdrawing their over-extended line south of the Moselle could the Allies hope to produce the reserves necessary if they genuinely wished to gain victory in counter-attack. Eisenhower had declared he would do this—but apart from verbal directives passed on by SHAEF staff officers[3] no action had been taken in almost two weeks.

[1] M417 of 2220 hrs, 2.1.45, Montgomery Papers. Monty's evening Sitrep had also related the latest Intelligence picture, pointing to great German strength still in the penetration area: 'The overall picture is of very considerable enemy strength in the penetration area and I shall have to conduct my offensive with great care . . . Yesterday I indicated a possible enemy withdrawal from the extreme southwest corner of his penetration, but these indications have not repeat NOT been confirmed and it now seems quite definite that the enemy intends to hold on to everything he has gained until he is pushed out': M416 of 1940 hrs, 2.1.45, Montgomery Papers.

[2] 'The general picture on the northern front seems to be that the enemy is regrouping and is holding his front with infantry divisions while pulling the Panzer and SS divisions into reserve. This would be a very natural thing for him to do and there is evidence of a strong concentration of SS divisions to the north and northwest of HOUFFALIZE. . . . The attack of 7 US Corps begins at 0830 hrs tomorrow 3 Jan and initially should make good progress. . . . We may then have to face up to heavy counter-attacks by the SS divisions in reserve north of HOUFFALIZE': M416, loc. cit. Collins later recorded how fierce the fighting against such SS divisions became: 'Under such conditions progress against the veteran SS divisions was slow and costly, especially on the front of the 2nd [US] Armoured Division, and for the first and only time I had to put some pressure on my great friend and good fighter, Ernie Harmon, to keep his "Hell on Wheels" division moving': J. Lawton Collins, *'Lightning' Joe*, Baton Rouge 1980.

[3] Eisenhower's biographer Stephen Ambrose extolled Eisenhower's supposed growth of authority and decisiveness as a field commander during the battle of the Ardennes, describing the new confidence with which Eisenhower gave out his orders: 'Now he was laying down the line, telling the boys how it should be done': Stephen Ambrose, *Eisenhower 1890–1952*, New York 1983. Sadly, this is pure invention. Not only did Eisenhower spend most of the battle of the Ardennes incarcerated in the Trianon Palace Hotel, but when the moment came to create SHAEF reserves by thinning his line in the southern, Sixth Army Group sector, Eisenhower could not bring himself to give Devers a direct order or see him in person, hoping that by delegating the matter to 'Pink' Bull, his Chief of Operations, he would avoid the confrontations inseparable from great leadership. Inevitably Devers failed to respond.

'I give you these ideas of mine before your visit to IKE,' Monty added on 2 January.

> I wonder if you could discreetly explore the situation in the light of the above ideas before you come on to me and possibly find out the form? At the back of my mind is the thought that it may be necessary to make a considerable withdrawal in the south and come on to a shorter line so as to produce troops to deal with the Germans in the penetration area. I put this to IKE in his train on 28 Dec but have not referred to the subject again as I am completely in the dark as to what total forces the Americans can produce.[1]

Throughout this period—from 19 December in fact—Monty had steadfastly refused to commit his British reserve, 30 Corps, to major offensive operations in the Ardennes, lest he lose his vital, veteran divisions required for the *real* Allied offensive after the Ardennes.

On the evening of 2 January, in his nightly situation report to the War Office, Monty commented on the way the Germans seemed to be withdrawing their Panzer and SS divisions *into reserve*, indicating that if anything the enemy was not—as Patton supposed—pulling out, but intended 'to hold on to everything he has gained until he is pushed out'.[2] Although Collins' initial attack might make initial progress against positional infantry, Collins was thus bound to be counter-attacked in strength 'by the SS divisions in reserve north of HOUFFALIZE'.[3]

On the evening of the first day of Collins' attack, Monty's predictions were confirmed, and 30 Corps was therefore ordered to advance on Collins' flank. 'I shall have to conduct my offensive with great care so as to ensure absolute security and complete balance during the thrust southwards,' he had stated.[4] By 4 January the snow was 'three feet deep and nowhere less than about six inches and visibility on the battlefront has been almost nil'.[5] 30 British Corps had pushed its left flank forward alongside Collins' Houffalize thrust; nearer the Meuse both 29th Armoured Brigade and 6th British Airborne Division were fiercely engaged with 2nd Panzer Division.

As Collins pushed southwards Monty ordered that 53rd British

[1] M417 of 2220 hrs, 2.1.45, Montgomery Papers. At a Chiefs of Staff meeting at SHAEF headquarters on 25.1.45, it was estimated that 450,000 Allied troops were in the 6th Army Group alone, facing '90,000 of the enemy': Diary of Air-Marshal Robb, entry of 25.1.45, Robb Papers (AC/71/9/26), RAF Museum, Hendon.

[2] M415 of 1940 hrs, 2.1.45, loc. cit.

[3] Ibid.

[4] Ibid.

[5] M420 of 2200 hrs, 4.1.45, Montgomery Papers.

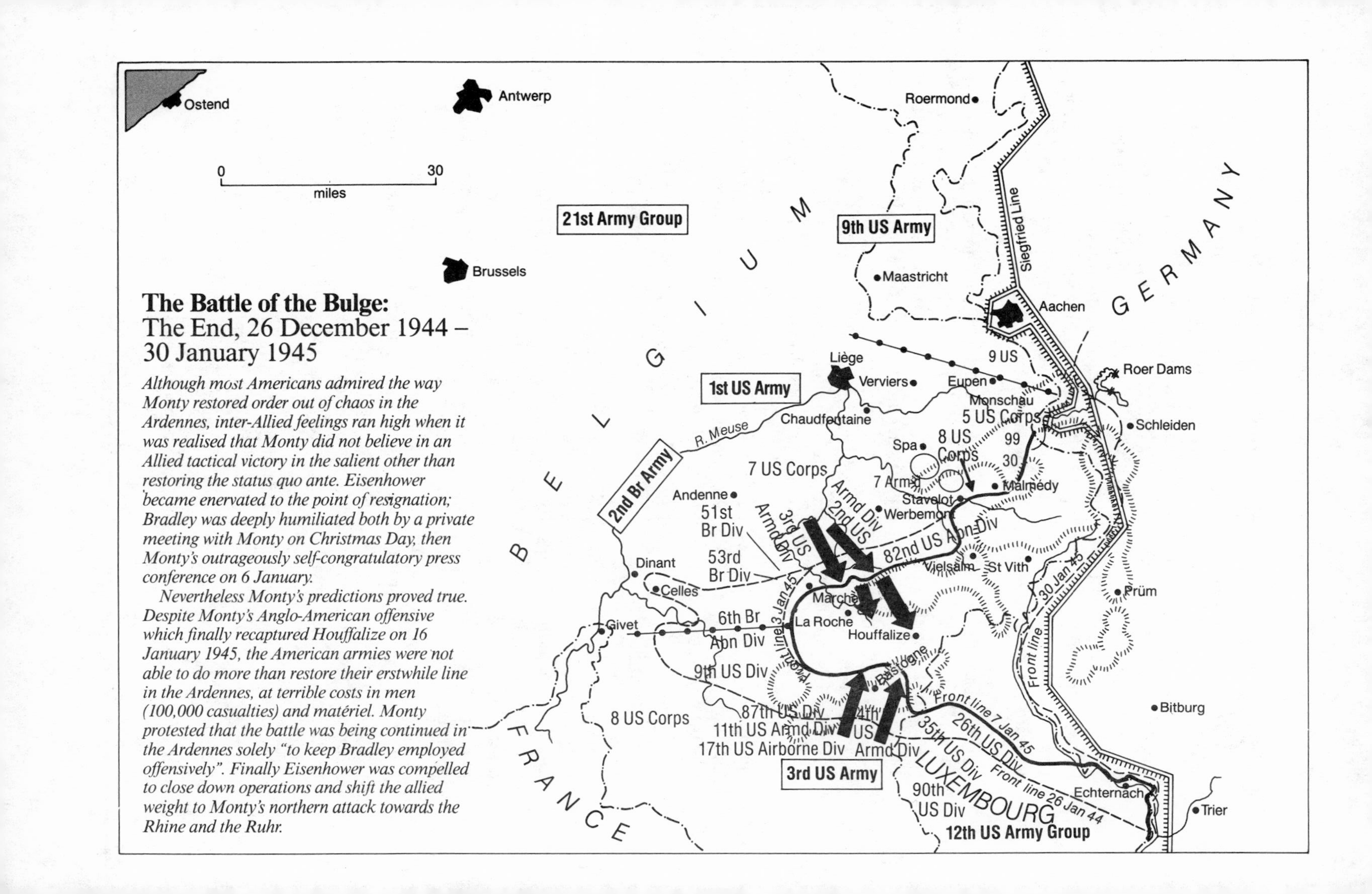

The Battle of the Bulge:
The End, 26 December 1944 – 30 January 1945

Although most Americans admired the way Monty restored order out of chaos in the Ardennes, inter-Allied feelings ran high when it was realised that Monty did not believe in an Allied tactical victory in the salient other than restoring the status quo ante. Eisenhower became enervated to the point of resignation; Bradley was deeply humiliated both by a private meeting with Monty on Christmas Day, then Monty's outrageously self-congratulatory press conference on 6 January.

Nevertheless Monty's predictions proved true. Despite Monty's Anglo-American offensive which finally recaptured Houffalize on 16 January 1945, the American armies were not able to do more than restore their erstwhile line in the Ardennes, at terrible costs in men (100,000 casualties) and matériel. Monty protested that the battle was being continued in the Ardennes solely "to keep Bradley employed offensively". Finally Eisenhower was compelled to close down operations and shift the allied weight to Monty's northern attack towards the Rhine and the Ruhr.

Division, adjoining Collins' right flank, 'be put into the battle to fight until it is exhausted when I will pull it out immediately and replace it by 51 [Highland] Div[ision] and thus keep up the tempo of the operation on the right flank of 7 US Corps' [1]—but he remained quite clear about the heavy fighting that lay ahead. 'From the operations today it would seem that the Germans at present have no intention of withdrawing from any part of their salient and as to whether they will decide later to do so this may well depend on the progress we can make in the north in the next few days,' he signalled on 5 January.

Even Eisenhower's headquarters acknowledged 'the fanaticism of the fighting'—though they ascribed this 'to the CASABLANCA declaration that unconditional surrender would be demanded. B[edell] S[mith] thought that this declaration by the President was to influence the JEWISH vote in his forthcoming election but he did not understand why the Prime Minister subscribed to it.' [2]

SHAEF's answer to this German fanaticism was one of utter frustration. Towards the end of December it had looked as though energetic Allied counter-attacks north and south of the German salient would miraculously restore Allied initiative. But with the fierceness of German resistance in the Ardennes, and the growing threat from German attacks in the south, Eisenhower and his staff became obsessed by their loss of initiative. 'We must seize the initiative,' Eisenhower's Chief of Staff felt—and Eisenhower agreed—'we must get the initiative quickly'.

As in Normandy, SHAEF headquarters was racked by its own impotence, by the seeming slowness of the Allied armies to gain ground and achieve 'concrete' results—at least results that would look good in communiqués. It was in this situation that Eisenhower, full of anxiety about Devers' performance in the south, returned to the agreement he had made with Monty at Hasselt on 28 December: that one man take over the northern sector and by co-ordinated offensive operations wrest back the Allied initiative; 'He considers it essential that operations', after the nose of the Ardennes salient had been cleared up, 'from then on be under the control of one man. S[upreme] A[llied] C[ommander]: "There is going to be a twilight period in there and I don't give a damn who is in command so long as it is under one man."' [3]

This was stated at the Supreme Commander's daily meeting on 8 January 1945. For a moment it seemed possible that Montgomery

[1] M423 of 2200 hrs, 5.1.45, Montgomery Papers.
[2] Ibid.
[3] Robb Diary, 8.1.45. Robb Papers (AC 71/9/26) RAF Museum, Hendon.

'We are off over the Rhine'
49 *below* Monty crosses the Rhine at Rees in late March 1945, and motors through shattered German towns (**50** *right*). Unwisely, Monty opposed Eisenhower's intention to send a second American army north of the Ruhr, necessitating the presence of General Bradley's 12 US Army Group headquarters.

Instead, at a conference on 25 March (**51** *bottom*), it was decided that Monty would advance north of the Ruhr, Bradley to the south – thus setting the stage for the final disaster of World War II in Europe: the Allied failure to seize Berlin.

On 28 March 1945 Monty received a bombshell from Eisenhower: an order to give back Ninth US Army – currently poised to advance on Berlin – to 12 US Army in the south, targeted on Dresden.

Monty, Brooke and Churchill protested – even Field-Marshal Wavell after a visit to Monty in the field (**52** *left*). At a conference with Monty, Dempsey and Simpson on 10 April (**53** *below*), Bradley refused to relent.

To Monty's chagrin were soon added the horrors of the discovery of Belsen (**54** *and* **55** *bottom left and right*).

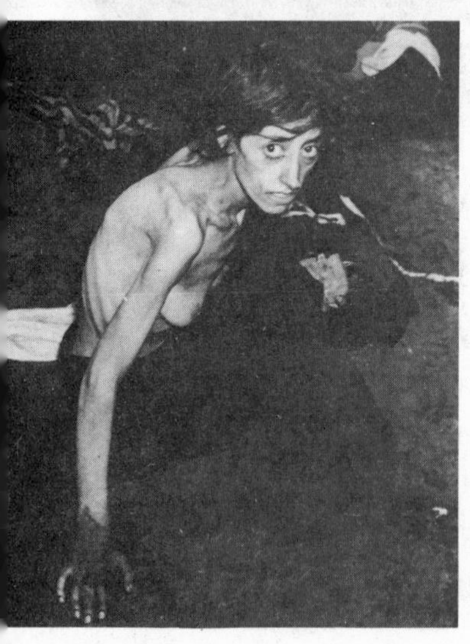

Monty's relentless 'grip' on his forces as an army group commander rested in part on his 'eyes and ears': a team of specially picked young Liaison Officers who toured the battlefront each day (**56** *top*). Denied the chance to seize Berlin and sickened by German atrocities at Belsen, Monty received a third shock when one of his Liaison Officers, John Poston, was 'murdered'. For a time Monty was distraught (**57** *above left*). He ordered Poston's body re-buried with full military honours (**58** *above right*) a stone's throw from his caravan (**59** *right*).

As troops of 21 Army Group began to tire, Monty kept up morale by personal visits and addresses to units (**60** *left*); he also found time to visit liberated British POWs in their camps (**61** *centre left*).

Meanwhile, belatedly recognizing he had overestimated the importance of the mythical Nazi 'Redoubt' in the south, Eisenhower became alarmed by Russian advances towards the Danish peninsula in the north. Almost a month after Monty's warning, Monty was finally given sufficient additional American troops to cross the Elbe (**62** *below*) and seize Wismar and Lübeck before the Russians.

63 *above* In his Miles Messenger aeroplane Monty reaches Lüneburg, site of his final Tactical Headquarters of the war. On 3 May 1945 the first German emissaries arrived by car (**64** *right*) sent on behalf of the new Führer, Grand Admiral Doenitz.

65 *below* The four German delegates line up beneath the Union Jack and salute as Monty emerges from his camouflaged caravan.

The German Surrender

66 *above left* On the afternoon of 4 May 1945, on a lonely forest road north of Hamburg, Monty's Canadian MA goes forward to meet the returning German emissaries, bringing with them Doenitz and Keitel's authority to surrender all German forces in Denmark, northern Germany and Holland.

Inside the specially erected marquee at 21 Army Group Tac HQ Monty reads out the terms of German surrender (**67** *centre left*). Before microphones and assembled war correspondents Monty ordered the chief of the German delegation, Admiral von Friedeburg, to sign first (**68** *below left*). After the remainder of the German delegation had signed, Monty himself added his name (**69** *below right*). 'His lips were firm, and as he finished he sighed faintly, sat back, and removed his tortoiseshell rims, relaxed. "That concludes the surrender," he said.'

70 *right* The original surrender document, misdated 5 May instead of 4 May 1945.

For British forces, this was the end of the war in Europe, after six long and arduous years (**71** *below*).

'It seems quite clear that DONITZ is prepared to surrender Norway and the forces under KESSELRING in the south and everything else', Monty signalled to the CIGS.

Eisenhower's refusal to meet in person the German emissaries resulted, however, in Doenitz being able to delay further German surrender for three more days.

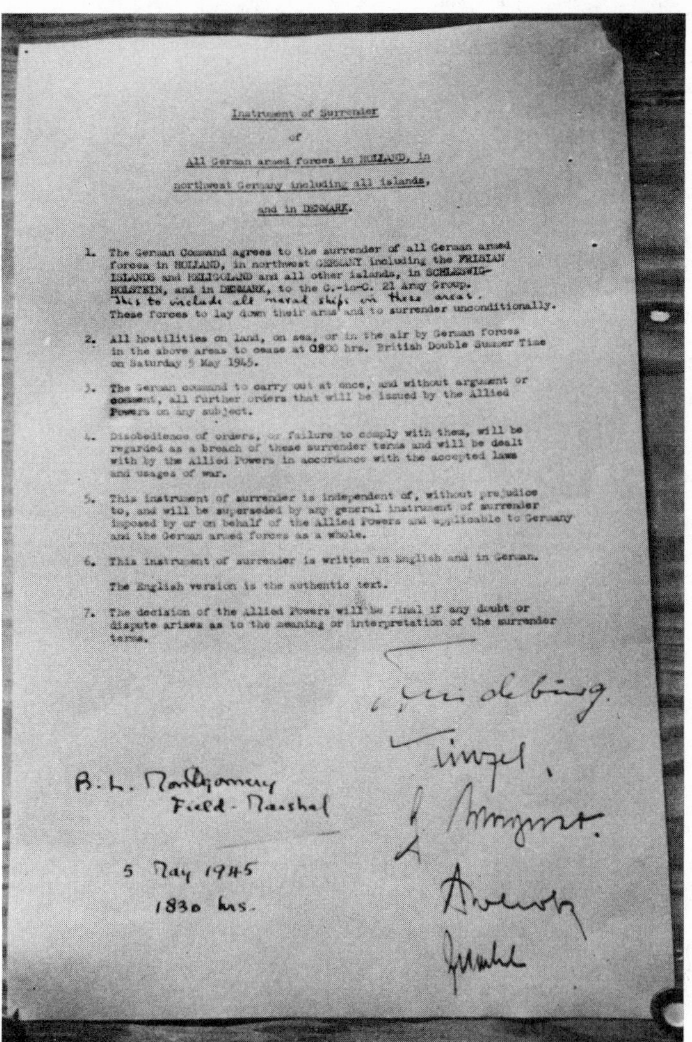

Instrument of Surrender

of

All German armed forces in HOLLAND, in

northwest Germany including all islands,

and in DENMARK.

1. The German Command agrees to the surrender of all German armed forces in HOLLAND, in northwest GERMANY including the FRISIAN ISLANDS and HELIGOLAND and all other islands, in SCHLESWIG-HOLSTEIN, and in DENMARK, to the C.-in-C. 21 Army Group. This to include all naval ships in these areas. These forces to lay down their arms and to surrender unconditionally.

2. All hostilities on land, on sea, or in the air by German forces in the above areas to cease at 0800 hrs. British Double Summer Time on Saturday 5 May 1945.

3. The German command to carry out at once, and without argument or comment, all further orders that will be issued by the Allied Powers on any subject.

4. Disobedience of orders, or failure to comply with them, will be regarded as a breach of these surrender terms and will be dealt with by the Allied Powers in accordance with the accepted laws and usages of war.

5. This instrument of surrender is independent of, without prejudice to, and will be superseded by any general instrument of surrender imposed by or on behalf of the Allied Powers and applicable to Germany and the German armed forces as a whole.

6. This instrument of surrender is written in English and in German.

The English version is the authentic text.

7. The decision of the Allied Powers will be final if any doubt or dispute arises as to the meaning or interpretation of the surrender terms.

B. L. Montgomery
Field-Marshal

5 May 1945
1830 hrs.

72 *above left* Paratroops of 6 British Airborne Division shake hands with the crew of a Russian T34 tank of the Russian Guards Division by the Baltic.

73 *above right* Some of the 2–million German prisoners taken.
74 *left* Monty thanks his Tac HQ staff at a special service of thanksgiving after the German surrender. In Copenhagen he is fêted by the people of Denmark he has liberated (**75** *below*).

would be given command; but in the wake of Monty's Press talk all such notions were sundered. Bradley, incensed by the press reports, refused point blank to serve under him.

CHAPTER TWO

Proposing a Press Talk

THE STORY BEHIND Monty's Press talk has never been properly told. For 'security' reasons it had been decided on 20 December that the press should not be allowed to print the true story of the change of command; in fact that there should be an almost complete news blackout until such time as the German threat was over. This decision stemmed primarily from Maj-General Strong's conviction that the Allies ought not to present the Germans with 'free' intelligence. Yet even Strong later acknowledged that this put a great strain on the Allied news services. By 5 January, anxious lest there be a leak after seventeen days of censorship, Monty's Chief of Staff, Freddie de Guingand, telephoned SHAEF to ask 'whether the press announcement could be made of the change in command, i.e. that "Monty" was now in command of the American First and Ninth Armies'.

Eisenhower refused to give permission. 'After discussion, the Supreme Commander decided that the present time was inopportune and that WHITELEY should inform DE GUINGAND that the announcement would be made when the situation in the salient was under full control and the two Armies [First and Third] were approaching each other. He [Eisenhower] also mentioned, of course, that there would be repercussions in AMERICA if such an announcement was made.'

Later that day, however, it was discovered that an American newspaper had already leaked the news—'the New York Times or Herald', as Eisenhower's Chief Air Staff Officer noted in his diary; as a result it was decided, after talking to the Director of Public Relations, that 'an announcement should be made from here', Air Marshal Robb recorded.[1]

In the meantime, however, Churchill had arrived at Eisenhower's headquarters on 3 January. Churchill had only just returned from Greece, where some 80,000 British troops were now involved in quelling the Communist *coup d'état*. Like Brooke, Monty felt the British intervention to be unpardonable at a time when the Allies ought to be concentrating their efforts on defeat of the Germans.

[1] Robb diary, Robb papers, loc. cit.

The Reynolds' own son 'may go to Greece', Monty had warned Phyllis Reynolds on New Year's Eve; 'part of his lot have gone already. We have made a sad mess of that show I fear and should have left it severely alone.'[1] In the midst of the Ardennes battle, moreover, with 18 US Airborne Corps, 7 US Corps and 30 British Corps all attacking, Monty had no wish to receive political leaders from home, particularly Churchill. However, the DMO had warned Monty of Churchill's intention, pointing out that Churchill still resented the way Monty had kept him largely out of the Normandy battle; thus Monty had been forced to invite the Prime Minister: 'Understand you may be coming over this way next week. I do hope you will come and see me. . . .'[2] 'This was received with great joy at Downing Street,' Sir Frank Simpson recalled forty years later.[3] Churchill proposed a two- or three-day visit. Eisenhower, knowing Monty's rule about visitors during a battle, offered to hold him back, but Monty felt the PM 'would be angry if we try and stop him', so suggested that Eisenhower authorize the visit, though surreptitiously curtailing it: 'I would be grateful if you could hang on to him your end so that he stays here only one night. I am sure you could do this without openly trying to ride him off.'[4]

On the night of 4 January Churchill thus set off from SHAEF for Monty's headquarters, travelling by train owing to the low visibility which precluded flying—using the same train ('Alive') which Eisenhower had used on his 28 December excursion. At Versailles Churchill had witnessed the showdown between Eisenhower and de Gaulle, wherein Eisenhower was forced to drop his plans to pull back to the Vosges on his southern front, and instead was compelled to help the French defend Strasbourg. There was thus little hope now of receiving the reinforcements necessary for a 'full-blooded' Allied counter-offensive in the Ardennes—indeed by 10 January Eisenhower would be ordering Patton to close down his southern attack towards Houffalize in order to provide reserves for the Alsace front. Monty was thus forced to persevere with what he had. Even before Churchill's arrival, on the morning of 5 January, Monty had assumed this would be the case, as he wrote to 'Simbo' Simpson:

> The party did not arrive last night; it was not flying weather. They come by train today and I am just off to meet them at Hasselt station.
>
> My reading of the situation is that the enemy is beginning to see the red light; if he loses the road centres of CHERAM and

[1] Letter to Phyllis Reynolds, 31.12.44, Montgomery Papers.
[2] M405 of 2000 hrs, 30.12.44, Montgomery Papers.
[3] General Sir Frank Simpson, Eugene Wason interview for Sir Denis Hamilton.
[4] M411 of 1810 hrs, 1.1.45, Montgomery Papers.

SAMREE he will find it very hard to supply his troops away to the west; and if he lost HOUFFALIZE as well, he would be done. I think he is therefore re-grouping, and is thinning out, so that if the need arises he can withdraw from the extreme west, and hold a line north and south through HOUFFALIZE—thence eastwards through VIELSALM, etc. etc.

I think we may get him back on to some such line, but thereafter it will not be so easy, and very considerable forces will be required for a large-scale counter offensive and I do not quite see where they are coming from.[1]

At Kermpt Station (near Zonhoven) Monty reiterated to Churchill this cautionary view—and described the sort of conditions in which his soldiers were now fighting. Only days before, Monty had harped on the 'bloody nose' the Americans had received; now, since the fracas with Eisenhower, he seemed a changed man. He had sent his American ADC back to Amesbury for a rest—and to spare him some of the ragging inevitable at Tac HQ. 'It is good of you to have him for so long,' he thanked Mrs Reynolds; 'he is a very decent chap and it is not always too easy for him in my mess—where he is the sole American in a very British mess; occasionally he hears things about the Americans' point of view which must upset him.'[2] To Churchill Monty now declared his allegiance to Eisenhower, despite the débâcle in the Ardennes. He was particularly touched that Eisenhower had instantly sent him a new C-47 when his own was destroyed in the brilliant German 'dawn raid' on British airfields at St Trond and Brussels;[3] conversely he had unilaterally ordered 200 new British tanks to be handed over to Hodges' First Army for the Houffalize thrust.[4] Three and a half British divisions were now fighting alongside American forces in the salient. The moral was clear: despite differences in tactical strategy the Allies' greatest strength lay in their unity.

That night Churchill prepared a cable to Roosevelt, expressing His Majesty's Government's 'complete confidence in General Eisenhower. . . . He and Montgomery are very closely knit, and also Bradley and Patton, and it would be disaster which broke up this

[1] Letter of 5.1.45, Montgomery Papers.

[2] Letter to Phyllis Reynolds, 4.1.45, Montgomery Papers.

[3] 'Have received the new C-47 you have so kindly lent me and I understand you have sent me one that was intended for yourself. Such spontaneous kindness touches me deeply and from my heart I send you my grateful thanks. If there is anything I can ever do for you to ease the tremendous burden that you bear you know you have only to command me. And I want you to know that I shall always stand firmly behind you in everything you do': M424, 6.1.45, Montgomery Papers.

[4] See H. M. Cole, *The Ardennes: the Battle of the Bulge*, Washington 1965.

combination, which has in 1944 yielded us results beyond the dreams of military avarice. Montgomery said to me to-day that the [German] break-through would have been most serious to the whole front but for the solidarity of the Anglo-American Army.' [1]

This was not mere Churchillian rhetoric. Monty had told him of the gallantry shown by American units when cut off in the early days of the German advance, and the punishing treatment meted out to 2nd Panzer Division by Collins at the extreme tip of the salient; this Churchill passed on to Roosevelt together with a plea for American infantry reinforcements—'I have not found a trace of discord at the British and American headquarters; but, Mr President, there is this brute fact: we need more fighting troops to make things move.' [2]

Whether Monty felt guilty at his recent disparagement of Eisenhower is difficult to determine. Within Monty the ruthlessly professional tactician and soldier existed a surprisingly emotional heart. Hearing Churchill's account of Eisenhower's difficulties with de Gaulle—whom Monty had had to expel from the Normandy beachhead in June—Monty was filled perhaps with an almost childlike desire to atone for his own misbehaviour. He thus implored Churchill to help counter the current British press campaign that was casting doubt on Eisenhower's fitness to command the Allied armies on the continent of Europe;[3] and in an excess of zeal asked Churchill if he, Monty, might set the matter straight in a frank talk to the Press.

It was thus on the next day, 6 January, as his Anglo-American forces conducted their northern offensive in the Ardennes in 'the most appalling mud and slush' [4] and snow, that Monty made arrangements for a Press conference. Both Patton and Bradley had already given their own; and on 5 January SHAEF had finally issued an official statement on the battle of the Ardennes, revealing for the first time that Field-Marshal Montgomery had been given command of all Allied troops north of the Givet-Prum line, the circumstances

[1] W. S. Churchill, *Triumph and Tragedy*, London 1954.

[2] Ibid. At a meeting in the Chief of Staffs' Office on 27 December 1944 General Bedell Smith had declared: 'Should we not go on record to our Masters in Washington that if they want us to win the war over here they must find us another ten (10) divisions. Look at BRITAIN, about to produce another 250,000 [infantry] men. If she can do that we should produce another 2,500,000': Diary of Air Marshal Robb, entry of 27.12.44, Robb Papers (AC 71/9/26), loc. cit.

[3] Cf. H. C. Butcher, *Three Years with Eisenhower*, New York 1948: diary entry of 1.1.45: 'The rumblings in the press, particularly in London, have now grown to a roar of demand that there be a British deputy commander for all of Ike's ground forces. The implication is clearly given that General Ike, greatly as he is respected, has undertaken too much of a task himself.'

[4] Letter to Phyllis Reynolds, 4.1.45, Montgomery Papers.

necessitating such a change in Allied command, and following it with a Press conference by Bedell Smith. Though Bradley would later exaggerate by claiming that Monty had refused to employ 'more than a *single* brigade of British troops against the Bulge offensive' and that 'Montgomery had not cleared his [Press] interview with Eisenhower',[1] the truth was in fact different. However unwilling Monty had been to employ divisions of his 30 British Corps in the battle lest they become inextricable in time for his 'Veritable' operation or worse still, weakened by heavy casualties, he had in fact used 53rd British Division, 51st Highland Division, 6th British Airborne Division and 29th Armoured Brigade in the northern counter-offensive both to help give flank protection to Collins' 7 US Corps and to show Allied solidarity towards Eisenhower: moreover Monty *had* cleared his press statement with Churchill, Brooke and Eisenhower before speaking—as the DMO at the War Office, Maj-General 'Simbo' Simpson, afterwards recalled:

> Monty felt that he had to get the British Prime Minister's approval for holding such a Press conference, which was a pretty sizeable one, so he sent a telegram direct and asked his [the Prime Minister's] approval, telling him what he intended to do, and Winston agreed to it. As I remember, the CIGS was all in favour of this too. It looked as if it was going to damp down the rather acrimonious slanging that had been going on between the British Press and the American Press.[2]

General Simpson's recollection was not mistaken—for in Monty's papers are copies both of Monty's signal to Churchill on 6 January at 9.13 a.m. and Churchill's reply. Monty's diarist, Lt-Colonel Dawnay, recorded that Monty had first suggested the Press conference on board Churchill's train at Kermpt during his 'three hour conference' with Churchill and Brooke on 5 January:

> Meanwhile the Field-Marshal pointed out that it was essential to preserve Allied solidarity, so as not to endanger the Allied team spirit which had been built up. Privately the Allies could be quite frank with each other; but articles in the press saying this or that was wrong, or that General Eisenhower or the Field-Marshal was no good, did much harm. He proposed to hold a Press Conference shortly, and to preach Allied solidarity.[3]

[1] O. N. Bradley, *A Soldier's Story*, New York 1951.
[2] General Sir Frank Simpson, Wason interview, loc. cit.
[3] 'Notes on the Campaign in North-Western Europe', Part VII, Montgomery Papers.

In his signal to Churchill the following morning, Monty reported to Churchill:

> In my talk tomorrow to British and American press correspondents I propose to deal with the following points:
> 1. The story of the battle which followed the German onslaught on First US Army, being careful not to compromise security.
> 2. I shall explain how the Germans were first 'headed off', then 'seen off', and are now being 'written off'.
> 3. I shall show how the whole Allied team rallied to the call and how national considerations were thrown overboard; team work saved a somewhat awkward situation.
> 4. I shall put in a strong plea for Allied solidarity. Nothing must be done by anyone that tends to break down the team spirit; it is team work that pulls you through dangerous times; it is team work that wins battles; it is victories in battle that wins wars. Anyone that tries to break up our team spirit is definitely helping the enemy.
>
> I shall stress the great friendship between myself and IKE and tell them that I myself have an American identity card and am identified in the Army of the United States, my finger prints being registered in the War Department at Washington.[1]

Churchill signalled by return: 'What you propose would be invaluable. I am not broadcasting till a few days later as the President himself will be putting out his message to Congress. Thank you very much.'[2]

But if Monty truly thought the existence of his fingerprints in Washington made him an American soldier in American eyes, he was much mistaken. To Bradley—who received a copy of Monty's statement brought by Major Bigland on 8 January—Monty's fingerprints were nothing less than hoofprints.

[1] Unnumbered signal dated 060913, Montgomery Papers.
[2] Montgomery Papers.

CHAPTER THREE

The Press Conference

FIRST REPORTS OF Monty's Press conference on 7 January 1945 were good—the American newspapers in particular quoting Monty's generous tribute to the fighting performance of US troops in the salient.[1] Such reporters had heard Patton's talk to the Press, Bradley's, and on 5 January Bedell Smith's. Monty's long prepared statement, charting the events leading up to his assumption of command of First and Ninth US Armies, and the battle since then, was sober, soldierly and a great deal less bombastic than Patton's: 'He clarified much that was obscure about this great conflict in the Ardennes, revealing how a broken line is mended bit by bit, stabilized and finally flung once more into offensive action,' the *New York Times* commented in a leader.[2] Thus when on 8 January Churchill received word from Eisenhower that Bradley had taken great umbrage at Monty's words, Churchill was puzzled.

Many chroniclers have assumed that Bradley's reaction stemmed from hearing a bastardization of Monty's talk broadcast by a local German radio station—'Mary of Arnhem'—purporting to be the BBC. But this was not the case. As his ADC's diary reveals, Bradley's distress went much deeper—and was first triggered by the official SHAEF statement on 5 January:

> The SHAEF announcement on January 5th that operational control of the First and Ninth Armies had passed to 21 Group of Field Marshal Montgomery has precipitated a crisis in our allied relationships,

Major Hansen noted already on 6 January, the day *before* Monty's Press conference.

> In the announcement it was explained that command of these armies passed from Bradley to Monty because communications had been cut between our headquarters and that of Hodges. For that reason it became necessary that the control revert as it did. However,

[1] E.g. the *New York Times*, 9.1.45: 'No handsomer tribute was ever paid to the American soldier than that of Field-Marshal Montgomery in the midst of combat.'
[2] Ibid.

Major Hansen remarked, 'the effect has been a cataclysmic Roman holiday in the British press which has exulted over the announcement, and hailed it as an increase in the Montgomery command.'[1]

For seventeen days of major battle, SHAEF had censored all mention of the shift of command. The secrecy now backfired; Patton and Bradley's January Press conferences had both given the impression that Bradley still commanded First Army; now newspaper editors discovered what they had long suspected—and the result, naturally, was offensive to Bradley and his staff. The Press reaction was 'intensely irritating', Major Hansen recorded.

> The First Army was always identified as First American Army and associated with the name of Hodges during the erratic days when the German launched his offensive and in that week before he was completely stopped. During the same period, the anti-American Daily Mail ran a picture of von Rundstedt and Bradley, called them the rivals in this great battle.

With the SHAEF announcement the Press learned that not Bradley but Montgomery had been in command since day four of the battle.

> Now the First Army of Hodges has suddenly lost its identity and Monty emerges as the commander. In all press releases the troops are referred to as 'Monty's' troops in a palavering gibberish that indicates a slavish hero devotion on the part of the British press.[2]

What rankled in the Luxembourg headquarters of General Bradley was the public revelation that Monty, not Bradley, had taken charge of the battle. But anger with SHAEF soon turned to personal mistrust of Monty.

'The issue, however, goes deeper than that,' Hansen went on.

> Monty is the symbol of the British effort on the Western front. He is regarded as such by the British press and by the quasi official BBC and London Times. . . . He is the symbol of success, the highly overrated and normally distorted picture of the British effort on our front.[3]

Monty could hardly be blamed for the 'slavish hero devotion' of a British press; but behind it all Hansen discerned 'a popular British campaign affot [sic] to have Monty named Eisenhower's field deputy and thereupon assume supreme command of all the ground forces while Ike devotes his time to policy matters. The implication in such

[1] Diary of Chester B. Hansen, loc. cit.
[2] Ibid.
[3] Ibid.

demands is simple. The German breakthrough would not have resulted had Monty been in command to prevent it.' Conversely, 'the current inference of all news stories now is that the German attack succeeded because of the negligence of the American commander—Bradley'.[1]

For this, Monty *could* in part be blamed. It is evident from Monty's own papers that he made no secret of his misgivings about Eisenhower attempting to combine the roles of Supreme Allied Commander and Allied Land Force Commander; moreover there is evidence that Monty actively encouraged journalists and influential friends—such as A. P. Herbert, MP—to do what they could back in England to press for a 'proper' military set-up in North-west Europe. In this most thinking men agreed, irrespective of their feelings about Monty. Both Brooke and Portal, the Army and Air Chiefs of Staff, thought Eisenhower's command set-up and tactical strategy mistaken, indeed bound to fail. Even Admiral Ramsey, Eisenhower's loyal Naval C-in-C who had mounted the D-Day landings and so successfully supplied the Allied armies across the Channel, foresaw a military setback unless something was done soon—writing to Monty only five days before the German counter-offensive:

> I was over in London all last week on business with the Admiralty . . . but I had time to go and have a long talk with the C.I.G.S., who told me of recent events of which you know and have been concerned in. It is annoying that what is the best and only solution cannot be made and that it seems we shall always accept an unsatisfactory compromise. However,

he added, echoing Brooke's prophecy,

> I am by no means so sure that events will not force an alternative which now seems quite unacceptable.[2]

The 'unacceptable' had, at least temporarily, been forced upon Eisenhower—and once the news finally became public on 5 January 1945, there was no real way in which Bradley could be shielded from opprobrium. Even the American newspaper *Stars and Stripes* added insult to injury on 6 January 'by describing the [American] troops as Monty's troops', Hansen lamented. 'Furthermore in their story they committed the grievous sin of speculating on Bradley's command and . . . said "it is presumed that Bradley continues to command the Twelfth Army Group which now consists of only the Third Army".

[1] Ibid.

[2] Letter of 11.12.44, 'Miscellaneous Correspondence file', Montgomery Papers.

This infuriated everyone. Bradley said Patton told him that he believes the Stars and Stripes has lengthened the war six months in its editorial policy and release of information to our units.'[1] 'If I become the [American] Theater Commander, the Stars and Stripes will undergo a major readjustment,' Bradley threatened in his ADC's hearing on 6 January.[2]

Bradley's distress was therefore plain *before* Monty spoke to the Press. In the circumstances, however, a Press interview by Monty was bound to exacerbate the wound—and it was in this respect that Monty was unwise to go ahead with it. Had de Guingand, for instance, spoken on Monty's behalf, the result might have been to calm rather than excite inter-Allied feeling. 'I ruffled people's feathers, Freddie smoothed them,' Monty once acknowledged of his Chief of Staff. But de Guingand was ill again,[3] and there was no one else, as before Arnhem, with sufficient 'sway' to convince Monty the conference was unwise. As Monty's Chief of Intelligence, Brigadier Williams, later recalled of the conference:

> I was there . . . It seemed to me, well, *disastrous*. I couldn't stop it.
>
> It was meant to be a tribute to the American troops, that is what he had meant it to be. The idea was okayed with Churchill. But when I read [the script] I tried to stop him doing it because it seemed to me that it was—he said of course that he wanted to pay a tribute to the American soldier and so on—but it came across as if he was, as if he had rescued the Americans—'of course they were jolly brave,' and so on and so forth, but he used that awful phrase 'a very interesting little battle', or words to that effect.
>
> I think Chester Wilmot was actually at that Press conference. Alan Moorehead certainly was because I remember him saying afterwards, 'Oh God, why didn't you stop him?' and I said, 'Look, I couldn't'; and he said, 'It was so awful.' Monty appeared in a new Airborne Corps beret with a double badge on it[4] and sort of said, 'How do you like my new hat?' so to speak—and the whole

[1] Diary of Chester B. Hansen, loc. cit.

[2] Ibid.

[3] 'I am afraid my Chief of Staff is not very well these days and the doctors tell me that he must go into the Cambridge Hospital for treatment and then really needs three or four weeks rest. I am acting on this advice and am sending him over to ENGLAND on Wednesday or Thursday this week': nightly signal to CIGS, M429, 7.1.45, Montgomery Papers.

[4] Monty had been appointed Colonel Commandant of the Parachute Regiment in December 1944.

sort of business of preening made one feel extremely uncomfortable.

Freddie was away. I remember going and spending some time with Monty, saying, 'Please don't give this conference.' And I think he said something about the CIGS. Now Brookie was our last card. When we couldn't stop anything we'd say, 'Have you cleared it with the CIGS?'—because the *one* person he was really afraid of or held in enormous respect was Brookie. If Brookie said it's all right, then what could a miserable BGS(I) do? And I can still remember this sort of feeling, as though hitting one's head against a rubber wall—'this is going to be awful'.

The text in a sense was innocuous; the presentation quite appalling.[1]

Bradley, smarting already from the general reaction to the SHAEF statement of 5 January, was now deluged by press cuttings. On 8 January 'we received our newspapers on the BBC announcement of the Shaef announcement that Montgomery had assumed command of the forces in the north,' Hansen recorded. 'The announcement created a storm of resentment which has had a widespread effect on the attitude of command, and we fear on the morale of troops subordinate in American command.'[2]

Monty's latest Press conference was, on top of this, the last straw. 'The British presentation on Montgomery's command whether deliberate or not would indicate that the Field Marshal was calling in preponderantly British strength in a desperate last ditch effort to retrieve from the chaos of American command some semblance of a better mind and stop a powerful moving offensive towards Antwerp and Paris. . . .'[3]

Bradley was tormented. Marrying the role of Allied Supreme Commander to that of American Theatre Commander, Eisenhower could not be expected to represent purely American considerations, Bradley felt. It was thus that Bradley now allowed himself to become the demi-official spokesman of such interests, egged on by his patriotic staff. 'We urged the General to remember that the US has no spokesman on the Western Front,' Hansen recorded candidly. 'Montgomery can speak as a Briton while Eisenhower must speak as an Allied Commander. . . . Because Eisenhower is, nevertheless, the senior American in this Theater, Bradley has consistently reiterated that he cannot speak for the American Command and has refused

[1] Brigadier Sir Edgar Williams, interview of 20.12.79.
[2] Diary of Chester B. Hansen, loc. cit.
[3] Ibid.

time and again to do so. This crisis, however, forces us to adopt such a change in policy and it now becomes unavoidably necessary that some spokesman present the American viewpoint of our co-ordinated Twelfth Army Group effort on this front.

'The General admitted this readily. We urged a release for publication of a statement of fact that would accurately state the issues involved in the transfer of command and correct such inaccuracies as were evident in the British newspapers and in the BBC broadcasts.'[1] Monty's Liaison Officer was temporarily banished from 12th Army Group Headquarters to spare his feelings; Hansen and Ingersoll thereupon spent the whole night of 8 January concocting a new unauthorized statement for Bradley to issue to the Press the next afternoon. At first Bradley had been reluctant—'I can't do it. The army is my life, Ingersoll,' he explained. 'A direct order [by SHAEF not to give a Press conference] is a direct order and I cannot break it.' At Ingersoll's repeated urging, Bradley had, however, consented. 'Tell Chet [Hansen] to get the press up here tomorrow morning—without informing Paris.'[2]

News of Bradley's reaction soon sped across the Channel, where it was greeted with disbelief, since the first American newspaper cuttings had given such a very favourable impression of Monty's conference. Soon, however, Churchill was having to send congratulatory signals to Bradley on his performance in the Ardennes, and Roosevelt to award Bradley the Bronze Star. Monty, hearing from his Liaison Officer how upset Bradley was, despatched his own congratulations upon the latter.[3]

The die, however, was cast. From now on the quiet, shy, reserved Bradley would have photographers escorting him everywhere as well as some fifteen 'resident' newspaper reporters at his Tactical Headquarters.[4]

But although Eisenhower loyally recommended that Bradley be promoted to full four-star General, Marshall refused.[5] Marshall was unhappy with Bradley's performance, and was not altogether convinced by his 'excuses', in particular that he had foreseen such a

[1] Ibid.

[2] R. Hoopes, *Ralph Ingersoll: A Biography*, New York 1985.

[3] 'I am so very glad to hear of the award to you of the BRONZE STAR and I send you hearty congratulations from us all. Divisions of First Army have fought a grand battle up here and it is a pleasure and an honour to command such fine troops': M433 of 2230 hrs, 9.1.45, Montgomery Papers.

[4] Diary of Chester B. Hansen, loc. cit.

[5] Message from Gen Marshall. 'He will not promote Bradely [sic] or Spaatz at this time. E. is sore at this': diary of Mrs Kay Summersby, entry of 19.1.45, Eisenhower Library, Abilene, Kansas.

German breakthrough and had taken a calculated risk. It was easy enough to blame Monty for the Press reactions to the battle; but the fact remained that America's much-vaunted armies in the West had been broken open, at least 80,000 American casualties had been suffered, a grave shortage of infantry had resulted; and, perhaps worst of all, the British had been given ammunition with which to criticize the American Chiefs of Staff—and to press yet harder for a Ground Forces Deputy to Eisenhower.

CHAPTER FOUR

The View from Luxembourg

'TRAGEDY—IT REALLY was a tragedy. I'd hoped, when General Bradley wrote his book he would be big enough to have forgotten it. But he wasn't!' the Liaison Officer between Monty and Bradley recalled many years later.[1]

Colonel Bigland's version of what went wrong in the Ardennes is important, for he alone travelled between the two Army Group Commanders, bearing their plans, noting their points of view, as well as the feeling in their respective headquarters.

Appointed by Monty as LO to Bradley's headquarters a week before D-Day, Bigland had witnessed the skill and dexterity with which Monty had handled the landings and the subsequent battle, surprising even those hostile to the British on Bradley's staff.

At first, in the Ardennes, Bigland was impressed by the clarity and grip which Monty imposed. Hodges, whom Bigland visited on 18 and 19 December, was 'a tired and old man—and I think a frightened man too. Red Akers ran his headquarters, make no mistake about it. Red Akers commanded that Army.'[2] Bradley's communications with Hodges were indisputably severed; meanwhile Bradley's 12th US Army Group team of Liaison Officers was incapable of substituting for telecommunications, since the officers had never been more than 'messengers'. 'You see, their system of liaison was carrying sealed envelopes at least twenty-four hours old.' With the danger of being captured by German advanced columns or paratroops, the American LO's were not permitted to carry information—hence 'their American system didn't work—they were entirely messengers'.[3] On 20 December Bigland managed by driving first south and then west to 'get round Americans. Make long report and long session with C-in-C [Monty]—fascinating. First and Ninth Armies come under Monty. Wonderful conception of the battle,' Bigland noted with admiration in his diary. 'Difficult now,' he added, 'I can carry *nothing* written.'[4]

Bigland's admiration for Monty's performance began to pall,

[1] Lt-Colonel T. S. Bigland, interview of 29.2.84.
[2] Ibid.
[3] Ibid.
[4] Diary of Lt-Colonel T. S. Bigland, communicated to author.

however, in the ensuing days, as Patton's 'first real counter-stroke' found no matrix in the north. What was holding Monty up? Bigland was asked with growing disquiet and frustration in Luxembourg. His explanations that Monty was 'reforming' and 're-grouping' began to ring very hollow in a headquarters that had, only days previously, been in a position to *order* Hodges to attack.

As the battle progressed, Bigland came to see that, for the first time in the war, a dangerous chasm was growing between the British and American commanders. With Patton's own attack starting on 22 December, Bradley ordered Bigland to convey Patton's plans to Monty and 'to take no risks as I must get through',[1] as Bigland noted in his diary. Bradley was hoping for news from Monty of a reciprocal attack from the north—and was desolated by Monty's negative response. On Christmas Day Bradley himself flew to Monty's headquarters—only to be humiliated for his 'tactical defeat'. By Boxing Day Bigland was frankly sceptical whether the Americans *could* carry out Monty's vision of a classic defensive battle as at Alam Halfa and Medenine: 'interesting time with Monty but don't think the Americans *can* do the withdrawal [in the south] and plan he wants'.[2] As Bigland afterwards explained, the Americans really had no idea how to fight a defensive battle, for which they had never been trained:

> Monty went up to General Simpson's Ninth US Army headquarters one day and said: 'General your troops are all going the wrong way—they're all b———g off to the West!'
>
> 'Oh, they always keep moving, Sir,' Simpson replied. 'This afternoon they'll be going the other way.'
>
> Apocryphal or not, it's true. . . . You see, I was at the American Staff College [1943–44]. They never taught defence! The only divisions they had which could defend were the airborne divisions. That is why Bastogne and St Vith . . . their ordinary troops wouldn't have held; the job of the airborne division is to land and defend—and they were marvellous at it. But the others didn't know anything about defence at all, and they b———d off and came back again![3]

In Bigland's view—reflecting the view of most Americans in Luxembourg—Monty did not understand this, or if he did, he failed to alter his own conception of Allied tactics to suit it. The drawn-back left flank at Alam Halfa had marked the demise of Rommel in the desert—like a matador dealing with a charging bull. The same

[1] Ibid.
[2] Ibid.
[3] Lt-Colonel T. S. Bigland, interview of 29.2.84.

had been true at Medenine—Rommel's last 'fling' in North Africa, and the death knell of the Afrika Korps. Thereafter, assiduously building up stocks of ammunition and petrol, Monty had refused to be hustled into premature offensive at Mareth, two weeks later. Monty was confident he would win, in his own time, by careful husbanding of his resources and the relentless application of superior strength and morale.

So, in the Ardennes, Monty had sought first to parry the German onslaught, then to corral it, aiming to inflict maximum destruction by air, artillery and co-ordinated infantry/tank assaults prior to the *real* resumption of offensive: Operation 'Veritable' and the seizure of the Ruhr, *north* of the Ardennes.

Such a conception, Bigland recognized, did *not* accord with American ideas on war. Monty's patient campaign in Normandy had succeeded because of the amazing grip Monty had imposed on the Allied armies before D-Day, and the loyalty of Monty's American subordinate commanders throughout the subsequent battle. But Normandy had been a carefully planned offensive battle—and even there frustrations had mounted at the slowness of the advance and the lack of 'gains'.

Granted that many American units had panicked and run away or surrendered in the early moments of the Ardennes battle, there was nevertheless, once order was restored, every expectation that 'in the afternoon they'll be going the other way'—an expectation to which Monty refused to conform. As Bigland noted in his diary on New Year's Eve, 1944, returning from Monty's tactical headquarters through snow and much ice: 'Difficult interview with Bradley' [1]—for Bradley's impatience regarding Monty's promised attack from the northern flank was becoming pronounced. 'It was absolutely intolerable,' Bigland later recalled, shaking his head. 'The time it took—they [Bradley's headquarters staff] were going mad! I was going absolutely hairless—it is difficult, unless you were there, to conceive the feeling.' [2]

Ultra Intelligence had indicated a renewed German drive to Liège—news which admirably suited Monty's defensive tactics and unwillingness to waste lives in attritional warfare unless based upon a well-conceived masterplan. Monty was thus disposed to give greater credence to such Intelligence reports than his own Chief of Intelligence, Brigadier Williams. Williams, who had been spectacularly wrong in his prediction of German offensive incapability in the Ardennes, was doubtless subdued. As he later remarked: 'Having

[1] Diary of Lt-Colonel T. S. Bigland, loc. cit.
[2] Lt-Colonel T. S. Bigland, interview of 29.2.84.

had so little before the battle we were inclined perhaps to overcherish the Ultra we did then get. Of course if you get Ultra that gives you the enemy's intentions, you've got to take it seriously—you'd be daft to discount it. But I remember thinking afterwards, well, this may be buying ahead because it [the Ultra] wasn't really corroborated on the ground. All through the desert, from Alamein onwards, we'd had "intentions" that were ignored by the Axis commanders in the field.'[1]

As the German intention to renew its attack towards Liège faded, Bradley's expectation rose that Monty would match Patton's offensive—making Bigland's position daily the more intolerable, caught between two profoundly professional soldiers, each with his own obstinate view of how to conduct the remainder of the battle. Monty's limited expectations of the Allied counter-offensive in the Ardennes sector were not only disappointing to Bradley, they were insulting. 'Awful drive with fog, ice and snow,' Bigland recorded in his diary the trip made from Luxembourg to Zonhoven on the day Collins' 7 US Corps attack finally kicked off on 3 January. 'Interesting [talk] with Monty but still two definite points of view.'[2] Elaborating on this some forty years later, Colonel Bigland sighed:

> They were poles apart! I couldn't get across to either of them the idea of the other.
>
> And as I was living probably more with the Americans I shared more of Bradley's and Patton's and his staff's opinion than probably I did Monty's. . . .
>
> By delaying we were allowing the Germans to form a defensive front—they were so very quick to put down minefields, etc. If Monty'd attacked earlier, the Germans wouldn't have had *time* to make a front.
>
> I was beginning to feel we [the British] were underestimating what the Americans could do—and that feeling has developed over the years since.
>
> I wouldn't dream of taking credit away from what Monty did. But by then the capability of the American Army compared to ours, the way we looked at war. . . . Ours was quite different from four years before. Over those four years we had got new weapons, artillery, tanks: we'd begun to find ways of staying alive, and we went more slowly. There is no doubt that we British were more cautious, more tired, we'd had many more people killed. We'd been fighting since 1940. The Americans were as we had been in

[1] Brigadier Sir Edgar Williams, interview of 29.2.84.
[2] Diary of Lt-Colonel T. S. Bigland, loc. cit.

the desert in 1940/1 when fighting the Italians—they [the Americans in the Ardennes, on the northern flank] could have counter-attacked within forty-eight hours and successfully.

After the war Chester Wilmot found documents showing that the German generals thought, at the time, that the Ardennes was their biggest mistake. So did Bradley—'it will shorten the war!' he said. And it should have done. It *cannot* take two weeks to reform and regroup . . . The time it took![1]

This then was the background to 12th US Army Group Headquarters' reaction to Monty's fateful Press conference, four days after the belated launching of Collins' attack. Bigland had set off for Monty's headquarters from Luxembourg in fog and snow on 7 January; he returned to Bradley's headquarters on the 9th to find uproar. 'Very bad feeling over Press reports of Monty's conference,' he recorded in his diary.[2] The next day he rang Monty's Intelligence officer at Zonhoven, Colonel Ewart, and tried 'to put right some of Press harm'.[3] But as he later commented, it was too late—the harm had been done.

Bigland had brought to Bradley's headquarters a copy of Monty's actual notes for the Press conference, with which he was able to disprove much of the British popular newspaper reports—'I took them for Bradley to look at. Thank God I had them, because the word that had gone round there was much worse than that [Monty's actual talk]. And that was bad enough!'[4]

Monty's statement was indeed insulting, given the sensitivity of Americans at Bradley's headquarters and their mounting conviction that Monty was failing to defeat a 'sitting duck'. Bigland remembered:

I rang Joe [Ewart]—I used the Phantom link—I'd never used the direct link until that time, since Normandy. And I said, 'Joe, I don't think you've got any *conception* of the bad feeling here. It's absolutely terrifying!' And Joe said: 'We're beginning to realize it and we *are* trying to put it right.' I nearly gave up. I was told by Joe that he'd got back to London [i.e. the War Office] and Churchill was trying to put it right too. And Churchill did a very good parliamentary speech. . . . But you can't put these things right.

Was Monty's conference a catalyst for existing feelings and resentments? Oh, very much so—you see, they were *seething* since

[1] Lt-Colonel T. S. Bigland, interview of 29.2.84.
[2] Diary of Lt-Colonel T. S. Bigland, loc. cit.
[3] Ibid.
[4] Lt-Colonel T. S. Bigland, interview of 29.2.84.

> the end of December. The feeling down in Luxembourg and with all Americans was getting absolutely hair-raising. I mean the *frustration* when you've all those troops and you're doing nothing—'regrouping'!
>
> I always maintain that Monty made an absolute balls-up by exaggerating—there never was a threat at all! That was the American view! It was the biggest mistake the Germans ever made—and Monty entirely failed to destroy the German armies.[1]

Against such a conviction, even Monty's actual text felt like acid thrown in his eyes when Bradley came to read Monty's 'Notes': patronizing, misleading (regarding the British effort), and so profoundly self-congratulatory:

'Rundstedt attacked on 16 Dec; he obtained tactical surprise,' Monty's account of the battle began.

> He drove a deep wedge into the centre of First US Army and split the American forces in two. . . . Then the situation began to deteriorate. But the whole Allied team rallied to meet the danger; national considerations were thrown overboard; General Eisenhower placed me in command of the whole Northern front. I employed the whole available power of the British Group of Armies; this power was brought into play very gradually and in such a way that it would not interfere with the American lines of communication. Finally it was put into battle with a bang and today British divisions are fighting hard on the right flank of First US Army.
>
> You thus have the picture of British troops fighting on both sides of American forces who have suffered a hard blow. This is a fine Allied picture.[2]

It was not—it was a catastrophic Allied picture that could not fail to upset American amour-propre. Monty had *not* employed 'the whole available power of the British Group of Armies'; he had massed a reserve British Corps behind the Meuse while only putting British divisions in or behind the American line to release *American* divisions for battle. He had appointed General Collins to command the main American counter-stroke Corps: and Horrocks' 30 Corps, far from being used to stiffen the Americans as Monty implied, had merely been put in—with some reluctance—to help advance Collins' right flank.

For reasons of security—the Ardennes battle had weeks still to

[1] Ibid.

[2] 'Tac HQ 21 Army Group. 7 JAN 45. Press Conference held by Field Marshal Montgomery', Montgomery Papers.

run—the precise details could not of course be proclaimed. Nor could be, of course, Monty's *real* reason for withholding British forces from the battle in order to have them available for the *next* battle—the battle for the Ruhr. Why then had Monty issued such a half-true proclamation at all? Why had he not simply made his appeal for Allied solidarity and a eulogy on the fighting valour of the American soldier without giving offence by a gross over-simplification of his battle orders?

Whether—given the tactical and nationalistic differences yawning between the Allies—a more tactful Press conference could have saved the day must remain a matter of conjecture. But nothing could have been worse. 'Bad reporting of this—particularly headlines—caused more bad feeling [among] the Americans than anything else in this war. Even the big efforts to put it right in the press failed,' Bigland later wrote in hand across his historic copy, returned to him by Bradley.[1]

[1] Communicated to author by Lt-Colonel T. S. Bigland.

CHAPTER FIVE

A Pretty Problem

BRADLEY'S OWN UNAUTHORIZED Press Conference on 9 January 1945 was ill-attended, went unreported in the next day's edition of *Stars and Stripes*, but caused a further furore in the British press. Monty, having innocently given rise to such inter-Allied feeling, tried hard to ignore it and to concentrate on the battle in hand. As he wrote to the Reynolds:

> There seems to have been a great 'flutter' in the press over my talk to war correspondents here on 7 Jan. And I see the Daily Mail of yesterday (12 Jan) has a leading article on the insult dealt out to me by Bradley!
>
> What fools people are; unless they will stop this 'slanging match' we shall cloud the main issue: which is to win the war.[1]

Night by night, after the CIGS's return to England, Monty had informed Brooke of the progress of the northern counter-attack towards Houffalize mounted by Collins' 7 US Corps, with divisions of 30 British Corps advancing on Collins' right flank. This was to be augmented on 13 January by an 18 US Corps attack towards St Vith in order to loosen resistance on Collins' left flank; but Monty was under no illusions about 'breakthroughs' or even swift progress in the appalling winter conditions. As he explained to the Reynolds:

> The cold here has been intense; heavy snowfalls in the Ardennes, intense frost at night and altogether very unpleasant. The Americans have suffered severely from frostbite; their man-management is not too good. . . .
>
> Life is very busy just at present as I have a very large parish to look after, with over two million men. . . .
>
> I long to get home for a day or two; I am getting rather exhausted and could do with a few days rest.[2]

Whatever others might say, Monty remained convinced, as he had signalled to Brooke on 2 January that 'relatively small scale attacks from both flanks' would not achieve the sort of victory which Eisen-

[1] Letter to Phyllis Reynolds, 13.1.45, Montgomery Papers.
[2] Ibid.

hower, Bradley and Patton were hoping for. 'All indications continue to point to the enemy holding on to everything he has gained,' Monty signalled on 6 January, having spent all day 'in the high ARDENNES where the conditions are most difficult with deep snow and icy roads and visibility less than 200 yards'—'appalling conditions' that made even limited advances 'a great achievement'.[1] Monty was therefore unsurprised by Patton's failure to thrust beyond Bastogne—particularly once Collins had severed the main German supply artery in the north: 'On the Bastogne front I understand there has been no progress today and this is understandable since the enemy must hold firm on the south if he is to get his troops out because he cannot now use Laroche and there are no bridges over the Ourthe between Laroche and Houffalize,' Monty signalled to Brooke on 8 January.[2]

Patton's response continued to be very different. He had authorized, on 5 January, the temporary cessation of Middleton's counter-attack, to be re-mounted on 9 January. But on 6 January Bradley had visited Patton's headquarters and had claimed he had Intelligence that the enemy was pulling out. 'Indications lead one to believe that this is true,' Patton's Chief of Staff recorded, referring to Ultra. Thus Patton ordered General Middleton, his 8 US Corps Commander, to launch 'one or two determined thrusts on a small front to see what they would run into'. 'I had to use the whip on both Middleton and Millikin [8 and 3 Corps Commanders] today,' Patton noted in his diary. 'They are too cautious. I know that their men are tired, but so are the Germans.'[3] Still the Germans kept attacking. On 7 January Bradley again spoke to Patton, this time by telephone, saying that the Germans were definitely withdrawing from their Bastogne 'pocket area'. The Intelligence officers of all Third US Army Corps and divisions were consulted; all denied that the Germans were pulling out[4]—in fact at the very moment Bradley called, the Germans were attacking 6th Armoured Division with 'a regiment of infantry, supported strongly by tanks and self-propelled guns'.[5] Nevertheless Middleton was coerced into bringing forward his attack, and the ill-fated 17th Airborne Division was ordered to push out its 507th Regiment. By 8 January the 513th Regiment had been overrun and thrown back by a new German attack 'by German tanks and

[1] M425 of 1950 hrs, 6.1.45, Montgomery Papers.
[2] M430 of 2000 hrs, 8.1.45, Montgomery Papers.
[3] *The Patton Papers*, ed. M. Blumenson, Boston 1982.
[4] 'The consensus of opinion of the aforementioned G-2s [Intelligence officers] was to the effect that there was no evidence to support the belief that the Germans were withdrawing from this area': Diary of General 'Hap' Gay, entry of 7.1.45, loc. cit.
[5] Ibid.

self-propelled guns'[1]—at a moment when Patton was boasting to newspaper reporters that the Germans had no more tanks. Poor General Middleton now telephoned Gay to say that his Corps attack, scheduled for 9 January, could not now be launched. Gay replied that 'during the months of battle which he, General Gay, had been associated with the Army Commander he had never known him [Patton] to change his orders reference making an attack. Therefore, General Middleton must be prepared to attack as ordered'. Patton later confirmed this—at which Middleton asked Gay to record that 'if disaster overtook them, in that they were cut off and another pocket was formed, that he [Middleton] had warned the Army of this possibility'.[2]

Such friction would later be hushed up in American official and unofficial accounts of the Ardennes battle since it would have disturbed the sedulous image of cavalry dash and aggressive self-confidence and harmony in the American Army—in contrast to the 'over-cautious', unaggressive Montgomery who had so singularly failed to exploit his great opportunity in the Ardennes.[3]

As Middleton thus prepared to launch an attack he did not himself believe in, he was yet again assaulted by German infantry and tanks—launched from a German armoured salient which according to Bradley and Patton no longer existed:

> The enemy was still out there in positions we had failed to take from him. The weather was as forbidding as ever. There was almost no visibility and no chance of air support. But [Third] Army was still insisting there was nothing in front of us. . . .
>
> And so we pushed,

the 17th Airborne Division's Commander related.[4] The cost was terrible. Flammierge was taken; but the Germans counter-attacked and annihilated the three battalions that had taken the village. The few that survived 'said that all of our men had fought to the last and that they had seen no prisoners taken'.[5]

Given the snow, fog and low cloud there could be no air support. Casualties were criminally high. The tank commander in 90th US Division's attack was killed almost immediately. Patton was contemptuous. The 11th US Armoured Division was 'very green and took

[1] Entry of 8.1.45. Ibid.
[2] Ibid.
[3] E.g. C. B. MacDonald, *The Battle of the Bulge*, London 1984; and interview of 18.6.84.
[4] '17th Airborne in the Bulge', interview with Maj-General Miley, loc. cit.
[5] Ibid.

unnecessary losses to no effect'; the 17th Airborne was being 'hysterical' in reporting its losses.[1] Against the advice of the Corps Commander, Patton kept attacking. Finally on 10 January Bradley telephoned to say the attack would have to be called off owing to the need to send reinforcements to Alsace, to meet the current German threat there. It was, far from being a demonstration of American offensive fighting ability, a shambles.

Monty, champion of balance, had used Ultra Intelligence to reinforce his own predilection for defence. Even in his talk to the Press in the midst of the battle, on 7 January, he had reminded reporters of the similarity with Alam Halfa. 'The battle has some similarity to the Battle that began on 31 August 1942 when Rommel made his last bid to capture Egypt and was "seen off" by the Eighth Army.' Bradley, by contrast, had seen in Ultra Intelligence the chance to avenge defeat by aggressive counter-attack—thus being deluded into believing the Germans were withdrawing at the very moment when green American troops were being overrun.

The two Allied Army Group Commanders were indeed 'poles apart'—and while Bradley and Patton fantasized about a breakthrough in the Ardennes, Monty gave daily encouragement to his American battle commanders in their limited offensive role—and began to fret about the future.

By 13 January Houffalize was in sight. 30 Corps was ordered to close down offensive operations on Collins' flank—'that ends the British part in this battle and I am halting 30 Corps in that [Warempage–Champlon] area,' he cabled to Brooke,[2] anxious that he keep enough fresh British troops to conduct both the 'Blackcock' operation on 15 January to clear the Heinsberg area for Ninth US Army and the major Anglo-Canadian attack to the Rhine, Operation 'Veritable', thereafter.

Eisenhower's Outline Plan of 31 December had formalized Monty's notion of a two-pronged assault upon the Ruhr. But with each day's fighting, and the evident Allied weakness in Alsace, Monty began to feel that it would be a mistake to launch both thrusts simultaneously. He therefore wrote on 13 January a long letter to the Director of Military Operations, Maj-General Simpson, which he wanted Simpson to show to Brooke.

My Dear Simbo,

Things are going well here in that the operations of Bradley from the south, and we from the north, have forced the Germans

[1] *The Patton Papers*, op. cit.
[2] M440 of 2000 hrs, 13.1.45, Montgomery Papers.

to pull out from the western end of the salient. That is all to the good.

I think the Germans will firm up and try and hold some sort of general line such as ST VITH–BOVIGNY–HOUFFALIZE–WILTZ, but may well be pushed further east than that. A good deal will depend on how he reacts to the ST VITH operation of 18 Corps.

The German offensive has done a great deal of damage to the Allied cause. I think we have got to admit that we have suffered a strategical and a tactical reverse; and we have been given a 'bloody nose'. Within the salient we have regained the tactical initiative, and I think we will be able to iron out the salient all right.

But I would say that we have for the present lost the strategical initiative; it has been wrested from us by Rundstedt.

The point now is, how can we regain it.

It is on that score that I am not so happy,

Monty confessed.[1] How would Rundstedt use this initiative?

Rundstedt must know that the Americans are very stretched; he must also know that the bulk of their available reserves are collected north of LUXEMBOURG trying to restore the situation created by the German offensive.

I suggest that he will work on this and will keep on prodding in tender spots, so as to keep the Americans running about from one spot to another and thus preventing them from concentrating to get on with the main business.

He has the RUHR and the SAAR both intact, and he will operate so as to keep them so. His next 'prod' will be in the south; that will draw in the SHAEF reserve, and has in fact already done so.

When he has withdrawn from the western portion of the salient he will be able to get one Panzer Army into reserve (probably 5 Panzer Army). And he has other forces on which he can draw.

To the east of the salient is the SIEGFRIED LINE, and country which is generally very good for defence.

As strong bastions in the SIEGFRIED LINE there are:

THE SCHWARZER MANN (east of Elsenborn)
THE SCHNEE EIFEL (north of Prum)
The high ground Pt 663 to the northeast of PRUM.

All these dominate the road PRUM–BONN, and they would have to be secured before we could use that road. . . .The whole thing is immensely strong, the country is very difficult, and it will be a very hard nut to crack.

[1] M541, 13.1.45, Montgomery Papers.

So from north to south he holds the MEUSE to ROERMOND—then the ROER through DUREN to SCHMIDT and MONSCHAU—then the SIEGFRIED LINE to KARLSRUHE—then the RHINE to the Swiss frontier.

It is a line which can be held defensively with few troops, thus freeing the maximum numbers for offensive action at selected places.

Altogether a very pretty problem for us, is it not!![1]

With von Rundstedt capitalizing on the chaotic French line in Alsace, 'considerable American strength will have to be kept down there', Monty concluded.

Will there then be enough strength available to launch a really strong offensive on the axis PRUM–BONN? That is my worry.

I am beginning to feel that the answer is 'No'. In fact I am pretty sure it must be 'No' so long as there are political objections to giving up ground in ALSACE.[2]

What then could be done to implement Eisenhower's plan of 31 December, which called for a double-pronged thrust to clear the west bank of the Rhine north of the Moselle and then encircle the Ruhr? 'First Army has been ordered by Bradley to be prepared to crack off towards BONN the moment the enemy has withdrawn from the salient and First Army returns to 12 Army Group,' Monty informed Simpson.

Third Army is to join in the hunt. All far too optimistic and unreal.

I know, and Army and Corps Commanders know, that neither First nor Third Army is in a fit state to embark on that sort of dogfight straight off: they require a rest, some training, and so on; all Divisions are tired and all are short of infantry.[3]

Both Collins and Ridgway then and later ridiculed Monty for his caution with American lives. 'Both General Ridgway and General Collins advocated bold and immediate attack policy,' Hodges's ADC had recorded on 9 January in relation to Ridgway's St Vith offensive. 'Gen Ridgway being convinced that no army in the world could push his Corps back off the high ground once it was reached. General Collins feels exactly the same way. . . .'[4] But with the weather too poor for Allied air support Monty felt it would be criminal to push

[1] Ibid.
[2] Ibid.
[3] Ibid.
[4] Diary of William C. Sylvan, MHI, Carlisle, Pennsylvania.

the men into premature, unrehearsed attack without even organized Corps artillery support or reconnaissance. Even then Monty knew the Germans would not surrender the high ground above such an important road easily. 'This may well upset the enemy a good bit,' he predicted in his letter to Simpson on 13 January, the day Ridgway kicked off. Success would help Collins, but 'I fancy the reactions will be such that we will not get to ST VITH: it is too important to the Germans.'[1]

To Ridgway's chagrin, Monty was proved right. When his 75th US Division failed to perform as he had boasted, Hodges was disappointed and Ridgway mortified—as Hodges' ADC noted on the night of 13 January.

> The attack of the XVIII Corps jumped off this morning at eight o'clock. The first news coming in was all to the good—the 120th, 119th, 424th and 517th Infs quickly reached lines two or three thousands yards from their departure. However, this is where they were at the end of the day and General Hodges is not pleased with the results.[2]

Ridgway's chief operations officer begged that 5 US Corps be thrown into the attack too in the traditional all-out combat philosophy pervading Bradley's erstwhile army, but Hodges refused. 'The General, however, turned this request promptly down saying that the 30th Div with attachments would have to reach its first phase line as previously directed before V Corps would put on any kind of show.'[3] The next day, as 7 US Corps neared Houffalize, Ridgway berated his men—'according to General Ridgway, resistance is nowhere near as stiff as the soldiers would have people believe. As his Aide remarked, he is accustomed to dealing with parachutists, the toughest breed of all, and is inclined to judge performance by their performance.'[4]

Whatever Ridgway and Collins might later say—Collins criticizing Monty for not acting more 'boldly', not committing Ridgway's Corps sooner, and not showing 'greater confidence in the ability of American troops and their combat leaders'[5]—it was Monty's profound military realism that spared Allied lives and limbs in the Ardennes by his calm judgment of what was possible and not possible to ask of his American troops. Bradley, Patton and Eisenhower might

[1] M541, loc. cit.
[2] Diary of William C. Sylvan, loc. cit.
[3] Ibid.
[4] Entry of 14.1.45. Ibid.
[5] J. Lawton Collins, *'Lightning' Joe*, Baton Rouge 1980.

fantasize about breakthroughs and Falaise-pincer tactics: but those Americans who fought in the Battle of the Bulge were painfully aware of the difference. Falaise had been the culmination of two months of Allied build-up and co-ordinated battle, ceaselessly pursuing an overall Allied master-plan; whereas the fight to regain the offensive in the Ardennes took place in appalling weather after a tactical Allied defeat and heavy casualties. Patton might brag about his ability to relieve the siege of Bastogne, fight eastwards to St Vith and break through the Schnee Eifel; but the tens of thousands of casualties suffered by his Third US Army—as much from frostbite as from enemy action—demonstrated the callousness of his claims. Third Army failed even to reach Houffalize, seven miles from Bastogne, before Collins' 7 US Corps—and Hodges felt as much or greater disdain for Patton's boasts as did Monty. As Hodges' ADC noted in his diary on 15 January while the Allied armies converged towards Houffalize, 'The Third Army made some advances during the day but they were not particularly noteworthy. Stars and Stripes tonight carried the story that they had accounted for some 80,000 Germans, which figure,' Major Sylvan remarked, 'is totalled in the usual Patton manner, of multiplying PWs captured by ten.' [1]

Whatever scorn Americans might later pour on Monty's lack of bravura in the Ardennes, it was Monty's patient professionalism and his unwillingness to risk unnecessary casualties that won the hearts of his men. Again and again since Patton's spectacular breakout in Normandy, Bradley had 'gone along' with Patton's assurances that great victory can result only from great willingness to take risks. The result had been a sad sacrifice of American life in futile battles around Metz and the Saarland—battles which not only involved high loss of life, but so stretched Bradley's front that the German counter-offensive was able to pierce its centre with frightening ease. None of Patton's much-vaunted, spur-of-the-moment counter-attacks in the Ardennes had succeeded in their larger aims—and had Monty not held the approaches to the Meuse with such firmness from 20 December onwards, von Rundstedt would not have bothered with Bastogne. It was the recognition that he would have to bring up greater strength to pierce Montgomery's Meuse defences that caused von Rundstedt to turn some of his Panzer strength southwards—running like a wet hen, as Monty remarked. As the German armour had grappled with Patton around Bastogne, Monty had launched his attack towards Houffalize—and the German game was up.

Such limited Allied tactics might be disappointing to military

[1] Diary of William C. Sylvan, loc. cit.

fantasists; but in appalling weather they capitalized on Allied artillery and tank strength, and ensured that the objective—Houffalize—was duly recaptured and the German salient bitten off. From the beginning of the battle Monty had marshalled and husbanded his reserves with great skill, recreating a coherent defensive line and minimizing American loss of life. It was for this he was admired [1]—and even those who abhorred his conceit and cocksure vanity adopted a different line when their own lives or the lives of their husbands, children or relatives were at stake. Few families in Britain did not have one relative at least under Monty's command—and from Yorkshire girl to millionaire mother they would write, as they had since Alamein, to thank Monty. Lady Astor's son Michael was one such ward of Monty's; and when Monty wrote to say he had inspected Michael's unit and had found him well, the Astors were overcome:

> I begged him, if ever he met you, to tell you that he was my son; but of course it was too much to ask of a young officer!

Nancy Astor wrote from Cliveden.

> I know you will realise what a word from you meant to both of us!
>
> It might interest you to know that Michael wrote me about you:—
>
> > 'I saw "Monty". He was absolutely charming and asked if we were alright and asked about our food, etc. and sent cigarettes, magazines and mittens the next day. He is an extraordinary man. . . . The most professional soldier in modern warfare, and as a tactician the master of any German (or American) in this war. His knowledge of the game, and clear thinking and decisiveness, inspires great confidence. . . .'

[1] 'He [Monty] conducted himself very well, I thought. He was cool and calm about the thing and very definite about what he wanted done [on 20 December 1944, on assuming command of First and Ninth US Armies]. What he did was a very good thing, I think. He took General Joe Collins . . . he (Montgomery) especially asked Hodges for Collins. He said, 'I would very much like to have him.' And then he took, let's see, the 2nd Armoured and a couple of my divisions and formed an army corps on the flank of this 'bulge' that was coming down there. . . . That was a splendid idea, I thought, that he form this corps on the flank, and eventually they stopped the [German] drive': General W. Simpson, Ninth US Army Commander, interview of 11.5.72, Eisenhower Library, Abilene, Kansas. 'Surely this was Monty's greatest military feat. . . . Not only were Monty's military decisions impeccable, but his handling of Hodges and Simpson was brilliant and compassionate . . . exercising his military charisma upon them, calming their fears, teaching them their business and obtaining a correct and immediate response. Surely this is greatness?' General Sir Charles Richardson (BGS Plans, 21st Army Group 1944–45), letter of 25.6.84 to author.

My prayers are with you all, day and night. Hurry up and end it and we know you are doing your best.[1]

Even the King's Private Secretary had relatives serving under Monty—as did the 'father' of the RAF, Lord Trenchard—on behalf of whom Monty was begged to remove the boy from the front line into a 'safe' job in the rear.[2] Such men might lament, in their clubs and their cups, Monty's schoolboy bumptiousness and vanity; but when the lives of their kith and kin were affected they sang to a very different tune.

Likewise, during the critical days of the German counter-offensive, few voices were raised against Monty's conduct as C-in-C of all Allied Ground forces north of Givet. Once the crisis was over, however, such goodwill began to run out—and Monty became the butt of much thankless criticism. After the war it would become fashionable to ignore the true background to Monty's assumption of command in the Ardennes, and to use his ill-advised Press conference as a way of tarring his contribution and performance in the battle.

Monty was soon aware of this trend, as his letter of 13 January to the Reynolds shows. To the DMO he also mentioned the row caused by his Press Conference: 'I am sorry this [Press talk] caused a flutter,' he apologized. 'The P.M. knew all about it and had agreed. I discussed it when he was here on 5 Jan. He asked me to let him know what I proposed to say so that he could refer to it when he broadcast. . . . Eisenhower knew about it, and had agreed. I may say that the Press here were all delighted, especially the American correspondents. It seems to have had a very favourable reception in America. Several American generals here have told me how much they liked it, and have sent me cuttings from American newspapers how well it went down in the States.'[3] As a result of the 'flutter' he had, however, deemed it politic to send Bradley a letter, congratulating First Army, and expressing his admiration for 'the operations that have been conducted on the southern side; if you had not held on firmly to BASTOGNE the whole situation might have become very awkward. My kind regards to you and to George Patton.'[4] Moreover Monty had, in the letter, assumed that once the battlefield was tidied up 'your armies will be returning to your operational command'—a way of saying that he had no permanent rights on either First or Ninth US Armies, command of which would depend on the next round of operations to be undertaken by the Allies.

[1] Letter of 3.1.45 'Personal letters Dec.44/Jan.45' file, Montgomery Papers.
[2] 'Correspondence with Secretary of State' file, Montgomery Papers.
[3] M541, 13.1.45, loc. cit.
[4] Letter of 12.1.45, Montgomery Papers.

It was in this latter respect that Monty's and Bradley's opinions again differed. It had been Monty's particular genius to look ahead always and to plan the next battle while, or even before, fighting the current one. In holding 30 Corps largely in reserve in the Ardennes he had given himself tactical security and ensured the integrity of the American lines of communication. But his deeper motive had been to withhold from the battle fresh and well-equipped troops with which to resume the *real* Allied offensive as he saw it, which was not the reduction of the Ardennes salient but the Allied attack upon the Ruhr which he had been planning before the German offensive. 'He is not a highly trained soldier and the wider fundamental issues are quite beyond his ken,' he remarked of one of his American staff officers, despite his fondness for the young officer; he did not therefore take too seriously the speculations of civilian journalists, nor the clamouring of certain American 'piss and vinegar' soldiers. Ever since the later stages of World War I he had tried to look beyond heroism. 'At plain straightforward fighting they are magnificent,' he had written of the Canadians to his mother after Passchendaele, 'but they are narrow-minded and lack soldierly instincts. . . . They forget that the whole art of war is to gain your objective with as little loss as possible.'[1]

What worried Monty, as Collins and Patton each drove their men towards Houffalize, was that Eisenhower, once again, was drifting into battle without a clear idea of what was possible and not possible. 'There is no point in saying I am 100 per cent happy about the war on the western front. I am definitely somewhat disturbed by it,' Monty complained to 'Simbo' Simpson. The plan envisaged by Eisenhower on 31 December had called for two converging thrusts towards the Ruhr, from north (Anglo-American) and south (American). 'We have reached the stage now where the very highest professional skill is required in the future planning and conduct of war; and I am afraid it is in the hands of amateurs.' Not only would Eisenhower have no real reserve to put behind this two-pronged thrust if, for political reasons, he had to fight hard in Alsace, but the Americans seemed not to realize their limitations in the wake of the Ardennes battle. 'The Americans are very stretched, far more so than people realize; they are very strung out and have great difficulty in collecting any fresh reserves for any purpose. The American armies, First and Third especially, are not in good shape. They have been fighting hard for many weeks and are tired; Divisions are low in strength and all their "teams" have been broken up; the Divisions require a period of rest and training. All the senior American

[1] Letter of 8.11.17, Montgomery Papers.

commanders are clear on this point.'[1] It was vital, therefore, that Eisenhower should not revert to his November tactics of separated, independent thrusts, none of which would be strong enough to succeed. Eisenhower's 'Outline Plan' of 31 December 1944 had given 'all priorities in building up strength of US Armies in personnel, material and units . . . to 12th Army Group' for the drive north-east of the Ardennes.[2] But with the current state of the First and Third Armies, and the forbidding weather and terrain in the Ardennes, Monty felt Eisenhower would be wiser to put his strength into 21st Army Group's thrust to the Rhine, north of Düsseldorf, beginning with the British 'Blackcock' operation to clear the Heinsberg area for Ninth US Army, then launching First Canadian and Ninth US Armies in a pincer attack to the Rhine, with Dempsey's Second British Army (reduced to two divisions, the rest being transferred to First Canadian Army) feinting in the centre:

> The British armies are in first class shape. Divisions are up to strength, except in regimental officers in the infantry; the average shortage per Bn. is about 6 subalterns.
>
> Morale is high.
>
> We are ready to start fighting hard; and in view of the knock that has been taken by the American armies, we must definitely take up the fight. We shall begin on 15 Jan.[3]

The next afternoon, 14 January, Monty signalled direct to Brooke. He had seen Eisenhower's British Operations officer, General Whiteley, and had 'got over to him the following plan':

> It is not possible that First and Third US Armies in their present condition could break through Siegfried Line on axis Prum to Bonn. But it is essential to wrest the initiative from the enemy as early as possible. We must therefore make a new plan and allot sufficient resources to the main effort to make absolutely certain of success. Elsewhere we must be defensive with ample reserves suitably positioned to give complete balance and security in all areas whatever the enemy may do.[4]

The 'main effort' was to be 21st Army Group's pincer-attack to the Rhine, north of the Ruhr. Ninth US Army would remain under Monty's command and be pumped up to some four Corps with

[1] M541, 13.1.45, loc. cit.

[2] Quoted in *The Papers of Dwight David Eisenhower*, op. cit. Original in Montgomery Papers.

[3] M541, 13.1.45, loc. cit.

[4] M542 of 1635 hrs, 14.1.45, Montgomery Papers.

thirteen divisions. A further US Corps would be inserted into Second Army, making 21st Army Group up to some thirty divisions. The two flanking armies (First Canadian and Ninth US) would smash their way in two giant pincers to the Rhine, trapping the enemy between and providing a springboard for a subsequent crossing of the Rhine, to be mounted by Second British Army, whose headquarters would be deliberately kept out of the Rhineland battle in order to prepare for the assault.

> I impressed on Whiteley the urgent need to ensure this time that really adequate strength was allotted for what we want to do. We have failed up to date by trying to do too many things and not giving enough resources to any one of them to ensure success. The above allotment of resources and grouping is minimum necessary to ensure success in my opinion. If it is cut down so will the prospect of success recede. As success is achieved so we must be prepared to put more weight into the blow and tired and battered divisions in 9th Army must be replaced by fresh divisions from a SHAEF reserve located in Namur area.
>
> Whiteley will put this outline plan to Eisenhower tonight,[1]

Monty concluded. 'He considers that Ike will accept it and that Bradley will agree.'

After the alarums and discord raised both by the battle and the various Press Conferences, this was a remarkably optimistic hope.

[1] Ibid.

CHAPTER SIX

Monty Versus Bradley

EISENHOWER'S FIRST REACTION to Monty's plan was encouraging. By 10.30 on the evening of 14 January Monty was excitedly signalling to Brooke: 'Whiteley has just telephoned to say he has put my plan across to Ike who is delighted with it and likes it very much.'[1]

But how would Bradley react? Bradley had objected to 'the tail wagging the dog' before the battle of the Ardennes; would he be any the more amenable to the main Allied initiative being placed under British command?

> The one snag is the old one as to whether the one main effort which contains a good many American divisions can be solely in the hands of a British commander. BRADLEY is being summoned to PARIS tomorrow for a conference and if that one point can be satisfied then WHITELEY considers the plan will be agreed. He says IKE would definitely like it as put forward by me but is nervous as to public opinion and so on and is thinking over how he can justify BRADLEY having a more or less defensive role.
>
> Meanwhile I am to go on working out the details on the assumption the plan will be agreed,

Monty informed Brooke.[2]

The next day, at the Chiefs of Staff and then Supreme Commander's daily meeting at SHAEF, Eisenhower's fears were borne out. Monty had refused to leave the battle area; Bradley found the weather too forbidding to travel. Whiteley outlined both Bradley's and Monty's different plans, Bradley preferring to attack immediately on the Prum–Euskirchen axis, Monty north of the Ruhr. As Air-Marshal Robb noted in his diary, 'the Monty plan' though avoiding the hazards of the Ardennes country or the mining area around Cologne, would 'put "Monty" in command of the major offensive'[3]—something which, in the aftermath of the ill-fated Press talk, would need steel nerves at

[1] M543 of 2230 hrs, 14.1.45, Montgomery Papers.

[2] Ibid.

[3] 'Meeting in Chiefs of Staffs' Office', 15.1.45, in the 'SHAEF Meetings' notes of Air-Marshal Sir James Robb (AC 71/9/26), Robb Papers, loc. cit.

SHAEF. A decision was thus postponed until Bradley could reach Versailles—which he did the following day, 16 January.

There can be no doubt that, in the days leading up to Bradley's arrival, Eisenhower and his staff had become steadily more concerned about the loss of Allied initiative. On 8 January Eisenhower had still favoured 'the possibility of striking N.E. on the PRUM/BONN axis', and stated that 'we would stick to the PRUM/BONN Plan and we must get the initiative quickly'. He had intended to 'hand back the command of the First Army to BRADLEY as soon as sufficient progress has been made to clear up the nose of the salient', giving 'the operations from then on' to a single commander.[1]

Monty's Press conference had ruled him out as this single commander; but would Bradley be able to conduct a successful offensive on the Prum–Bonn axis and regain the initiative? As the German attacks in the south necessitated more and more Allied divisions being sent to reinforce Devers, Eisenhower became less and less confident. 'It just shows what the power of initiative is in war,' he remarked on 10 January of the unholy mess produced by the German thrust towards Strasbourg[2] and on 12 January 'the Supreme Commander again emphasized the difficulties we were in through not having the initiative and STRONG stated that we must attack and keep on attacking if we were to regain this. It is hoped that BRADLEY's attack on the Southern shoulder of the salient, which is due in a day or two, would help us get the initiative back. S[upreme] A[llied] C[ommander] stated "You know, what gets me, I swear to God, is that the other fellow has only to keep moving one Division about to keep us guessing"—despite a "numerical superiority of about two to one" in the south.'[3]

Air-Marshal Robb, one of Eisenhower's most loyal staff officers, could not help questioning at this moment whether Eisenhower's method of command was really responsible for the loss of Allied initiative. Relations between SHAEF and both Bradley and Devers were such that SHAEF was now 'dealing in detail with the moves of individual Divisions inside an Army Group Commander's area, and in telling him in so many words how he should fight his battles', thus 'interfering with his prerogatives, and . . . the ultimate result will be that the Army Group Commander will not take any action or real responsibility without reference to SHAEF. The proper method would appear to be that the Army Group Commander should be given a directive and that his conduct of the battle should not be

[1] 'Meeting in Supreme Commander's Office', 8.1.45, Robb Papers, loc. cit.
[2] 'Meeting in Supreme Commander's Office', 10.1.45, Robb Papers, loc. cit.
[3] 'Meeting in Supreme Commander's Office', 12.1.45, Robb Papers, loc. cit.

interfered with unless it is seen that his actions are jeopardising his own or the adjoining armies.'[1] As Robb began to see, this meddling with Army Group prerogatives referred only to '12th and 6th Army Group Commanders. No calls are ever made to or from MONTGOMERY,'[2] who would never tolerate such interference. The inference was that Eisenhower and Bedell Smith, after the Ardennes, no longer trusted Bradley and Devers; in fact Eisenhower had spoken openly of dismissing Devers and replacing him by General Patch (commanding seventh US Army). Meanwhile Devers 'was always telling you of the mistakes BRADLEY has made', as Bedell Smith remarked with distaste.[3]

With Bradley making almost no progress on the southern flank of the German salient in the Ardennes, Monty's new plan did indeed arouse favourable initial reaction on 14 January; but once again the 'political' ramifications of putting 'Monty in command of the major offensive' were brought to bear. By the morning of 15 January, moreover, the Allied picture looked less bleak. Maj-General Strong reported the first real evidence that the Germans were withdrawing Fifth Panzer Army; a division from the Colmar pocket had left for Russia—where the Russian offensive had resumed on 12 January—and an idea could now be gleaned of German losses in the Ardennes—currently estimated at 500 tanks and 83,000 casualties. General Devers was 'now in favour of attacking all the way along the front'.[4] Bedell Smith, however, had been struck by the German bridgehead across the Rhine at Strasbourg, a model of pragmatic assault—pushing a motorized battalion across on barges and reinforcing it with a division before the Allies could properly react. Why could the Allies not take a leaf from the German book of warfare and 'if we find a weak spot in the Siegfried Line we might be able to drive a salient into the German Line,' as Mrs Summersby recorded his suggestion on 15 January. 'In other words adopt practically the same methods that the Germans employed against us.'[5]

The following day, however, Bedell Smith favoured a more studied attitude to strategy on the part of SHAEF—or at least a more decisive approach. 'We never do anything bold; there are always at least 17 people to be dealt with so we must compromise, and a compromise is never bold. How long is it going to take us to make up our minds to do anything?'[6]

[1] Ibid.
[2] Ibid.
[3] 'Meeting in Chiefs of Staffs' Office', 15.1.45, Robb Papers, loc. cit.
[4] Diary of Mrs K. Summersby, entry of 15.1.45, loc. cit.
[5] Ibid.
[6] 'Meeting in Chiefs of Staffs' Office', 16.1.45, Robb Papers, loc. cit.

But what could be done? Bedell Smith announced that he frankly had not 'much confidence in our friend Jakey [Devers]'.[1] Alsace would have to be tidied up before anything else was attempted. But then? Attack on 'Monty's proposed line N.E. towards DUSSELDORF for the initiative?'[2]

Eisenhower himself was unsure now; what he did feel was that it would be dangerous, in view of Bradley's and Devers' poor performances in defence, to go for a Rhine crossing in one place, such as the Ruhr, without first eliminating *all* German bridgeheads west of the Rhine. Not only was he afraid that the Germans might blunt such a concentrated attack as Monty proposed—as at Arnhem—but unless the German armies were brought to battle and defeated—or at least worn down—west of the Rhine, the Germans would retain the strategic initiative, able either to fire-fight with reserve Panzer armies or even launch counter-offensives—as they had in the Ardennes and in the south.

It was in this atmosphere of dissension that Bradley arrived in the late morning of 16 January, as First Army, still under Monty, recaptured Houffalize. Monty had already begun to grow pessimistic, for a phone call from Whiteley earlier that morning suggested that, although Eisenhower was likely to adopt his northern attack plan, he would put Simpson's Ninth Army under General Bradley:

> The tactical and administrative implications of the plan are such that if this is done I fear we shall not succeed.

Monty lamented.[3] He had heard via his Liaison Officer that Bradley was still intent on driving through the Ardennes to the Rhine—sure proof that even if Bradley was given command of Ninth US Army in Monty's thrust, he would not put his freshest divisions and main weight into Simpson's Ninth US Army attack. 'I am waiting on events and am keeping clear of the business as my views are well known and no good would be done by rubbing them in at this vital time,' Monty added.[4]

Meanwhile Bradley, 'plainly dressed, wearing only the Bronze Star which General Ike had given him several days before',[5] arrived at Versailles and was driven to the Trianon Palace Hotel to confer with Eisenhower.

Once in Eisenhower's office Bradley begged Eisenhower to let him

[1] Ibid.
[2] Ibid.
[3] Signal to CIGS, M544 of 0830 hrs, 16.1.45, Montgomery Papers.
[4] Ibid.
[5] Diary of Chester B. Hansen, entry of 16.1.45, loc. cit.

continue an offensive in the Ardennes with his two American armies as soon as Hodges' First US Army reverted, as agreed, to his command the following day. As Bradley afterwards confessed in an unpublished *aide-mémoire*: 'I had hoped that our attack would move so fast that we could drive right on to the Rhine through the Eiffel country,' since this could be done 'without any shifting of the axis of attack'.[1] Moreover he saw no reason why Simpson's Ninth US Army should not also revert to his command and assist by an attack south-eastwards towards Cologne, as had been the plan before the German offensive.

A few hours before, Eisenhower had been tempted at least to give Bradley command of Ninth US Army in Monty's pincer movement in the north. But looking into Bradley's tired face, exhausted by the dramas of the past weeks and his unbroken service in the field since D-Day, Eisenhower must have had second thoughts. It was obvious, as Monty had pointed out, that Bradley did not have his heart in a thrust to the north of the Ardennes; to give him command of Ninth US Army in Monty's impending operations might well lead to misunderstandings and ill-will. General 'Bill' Simpson, the Ninth US Army Commander, seemed quite happy to continue under Monty's command. Though approving Bradley's plans to attempt an immediate breakthrough in the Ardennes with his First and Third US Armies, Eisenhower thus declined to give Bradley Simpson's Army too. Bradley, though he stayed on to lunch in Eisenhower's private dining room 'in the modern French stucco house that houses him at Versailles',[2] was chagrined. Lunch was dour—Bradley looking 'a trifle constrained' as his ADC, who lunched with them, noted in his diary.[3] 'General Ike suggested to General Bradley that he might be getting tired and told him to find a little more diversion from his daily routine.'[4]

At Zonhoven, however, there was a profound sigh of relief. 'A meeting to discuss my proposed plan was held at SHAEF today,' Monty cabled to Brooke that night. 'It was a wholly American meeting except for Whiteley.' Apart from two changes—the scaling down of Ninth Army's proposed size and the involvement of First US Army to guard its flank—Monty's plan had been accepted. 'A further underlying object in these two changes was to get 12th Army Group in on the party in some small way. I was asked by telephone if I would accept these two modifications in the plan and given to

[1] Bradley ms., Bradley Papers, loc. cit.
[2] Entry of 16.1.45, diary of Chester B. Hansen, loc. cit.
[3] Ibid.
[4] Ibid.

understand by Whiteley that provided I did accept there would be no further trouble about command and that the 9th Army and the whole conduct of operations would be given to me. I said at once that I would accept modifications willingly.'[1]

As a result Monty had tentatively offered to start his offensive on 10 February in the 'Veritable' area, to be followed soon after by the American pincer—'Grenade'. 'Operations Veritable and Grenade will together be a terrific party and there will be little rest for most of us once we begin. The last few weeks have not been exactly in the nature of a rest cure and I shall try and get away for a short rest at Hindhead when our future plans are firm and preparations are going on smoothly.'[2]

[1] M545 of 2215 hrs, 16.1.45, Montgomery Papers.
[2] Ibid.

CHAPTER SEVEN

Keeping Bradley Employed Offensively

CONFIRMATION OF THE Supreme Commander's decision came on 17 January, Monty being 'told to go ahead' with the new plan. Bradley arranged to see Monty on 18 January, and details of which American divisions would be pumped into Ninth US Army were to be decided at a staff conference four days later.

Meanwhile the American commanders in Hodges' First US Army bade farewell to Monty. Hodges' ADC recorded on 16 January:

> This was our last day under command of Marshal Montgomery and he arrived at 2.30 this afternoon for a farewell chat with General Hodges. General Hodges told him what a great honour it had been to serve under the Marshal's command and what great assistance had been given by the cooperation of the British—in the way of tanks, in the way of movement of troops and tactical decisions. Bill later took up 5 lbs of coffee to the Marshal's headquarters at ZONHOVEN.[1]

Ridgway, commanding the 18 US Corps attack on St Vith, was equally deferential in his parting letter of 17 January:

> My dear Marshal Montgomery,
>
> It has been an honoured privilege and a very great personal pleasure to have served, even so briefly, under your distinguished leadership. To the gifted professional guidance you at once gave me, was added your own consummate courtesy and consideration.
>
> I am deeply grateful for both.
>
> My warm and sincere good wishes will follow you and with them the hope of again serving with you in the pursuit of a common goal.[2]

Even Eisenhower, in a letter the same day, thanked Monty repeatedly 'for the job you did. . . . Thank you again for the way you pitched in to help out during the German thrust. Some day I hope I can show my appreciation in a more lasting manner.'[3]

[1] Diary of William C. Sylvan, loc. cit.

[2] 'Miscellaneous Correspondence' file, Montgomery Papers.

[3] Quoted in *The Papers of Dwight David Eisenhower*, op. cit. Original in Montgomery Papers.

Eisenhower's letter was followed, on 18 January, by a new Supreme Commander's directive. In his letter, Eisenhower had stated that he liked 'the scheme for closing the Rhine, initially, north of Dusseldorf. Thereafter we can concentrate enough troops to let Bradley operate against the forces lying east of the Ardennes,' since it was important, Eisenhower underlined, '*to make certain he* [the enemy] *is not free, behind a strong defensive line, to organize sudden powerful thrusts into our lines of communication*'.[1] Eisenhower certainly seemed to have understood Monty's plan, and the need for Allied concentration in assault. 'We should not, of course, break ourselves to pieces against hedgehog types of defenses. . . . By concentrating on one job at a time we can use maximum forces.'[2]

All this boded well. And yet. . . . In one small sentence Monty detected the signs of Eisenhower's inability unequivocally to say no: 'All the time, of course, Bradley will continue following up and pushing the enemy forces in the present salient.'[3]

Monty's suspicions were duly borne out when, on 19 January, Eisenhower's new directive arrived. In a 'fine conference' with Bradley on 18 January at Hodges' headquarters, restored at Spa, Monty had outlined his 'Veritable' and 'Grenade' plans and Bradley had nominated two First US Army divisions to be transferred to Ninth US Army. But was Bradley 'coming clean' about his own plans for First US Army? Bradley was in conference with Hodges for some four hours, but not even Hodges' ADC knew what was discussed. 'What plans were announced for the First Army beyond the capture of St VITH are not yet known.'[4] Eisenhower's new directive gave, however, a clue:

> The [northern] offensive will be launched with the minimum delay if and when I decide NOT to continue with the offensive in the ARDENNES.[5]

Ominously, the 'rate of build-up' of Ninth US Army for 'Grenade' was to 'depend upon developments in the Ardennes'.[6] What then did Bradley and Eisenhower have in mind in the Ardennes? Monty's understanding had been that the Ardennes offensive would be closed down in order to concentrate on the northern attacks; now there seemed some doubt whether this was so. Summoning his mildest

[1] Ibid.
[2] Ibid.
[3] Ibid.
[4] Diary of William C. Sylvan, loc. cit.
[5] SCAF 176, in *The Papers of Dwight David Eisenhower*, op. cit.
[6] Ibid.

manner, Monty wrote on 19 January a 'sensible' letter to the Supreme Commander, quietly pointing out that he could not 'launch GRENADE until after you have closed down in the ARDENNES, as the necessary Divisions will not be available to Ninth Army until then. You may consider it desirable to close down in the Ardennes shortly, so that we can get on with preparations for GRENADE.'[1]

Eisenhower, however, did not find it desirable. To Monty it seemed pointless to expend further casualties in the Ardennes if, as was obvious to him, the Allies had not the strength to achieve decisive results there. The nature of the country, backed by the Siegfried Line, made it a very hard 'nut to crack' as Monty had remarked to 'Simbo' Simpson in his letter of 13 January.[2] What Monty could not appreciate, since he never journeyed to Versailles or saw any senior SHAEF officer save on occasion Whiteley, was that 'the running sore in the South' made Eisenhower deeply reluctant to push to the Rhine in the north and leave a sizeable enemy bridgehead in the Ardennes. 'What gets me, honest to God, is that when two of their Panzer divisions [10th and 11th] are loose we sit around and get scared,' Eisenhower lamented to his staff on 18 January.[3] As Air-Marshal Robb noted, the meeting had revealed 'a growing wonderment' at the ability of the Germans to mount effective attacks against a numerically superior foe;[4] whereas the Allies seemed unable, even with relatively large-scale attacks, to achieve comparable results. For Eisenhower, the virtue of allowing Bradley to continue his operations in the Ardennes was thus two-fold: that he should thereby clear up a potential German bridgehead from which German spoiling attacks, as in Colmar and Strasbourg, could be launched, and secondly the hope of perhaps, if lucky, retrieving the initiative.

As regards the latter, Robb was unconvinced by Bradley's promises of great gains. The Supreme Commander's directive, insisting 'there be no major diversion of forces to MONTGOMERY for his attack until BRADLEY has completed his work in the ARDENNES'[5] struck Robb as misguided, particularly since 'the Air was not consulted in the preparation of this Directive—nor even given a copy'.[6] But to Bradley, loth to see the major Allied offensive placed under British command, the American offensive in the

[1] M547, 19.1.45, Montgomery Papers.
[2] M541, loc. cit.
[3] 'Meeting in Supreme Commander's Office', 18.1.45, Robb Papers, loc. cit.
[4] Ibid.
[5] Ibid.
[6] Ibid.

Ardennes held out great promise. As he later wrote, the Ardennes battle had 'cost the Germans dearly in men and equipment. . . . They were therefore in no way prepared to meet our next attack. In addition to their losses in men and equipment their morale also suffered irreparably.'[1] In such circumstances Bradley hoped, by striking through the Ardennes, 'that our attack could move so fast that we could drive right on to the Rhine through the Eiffel country'.[2] Monty's proposal struck Bradley as misguided, as he noted on 23 January 1945 in a mood of intense frustration:

> Everything we do now is colored by our desire to keep operations tactically sound and at the same time to meet nationalistic requirements. There are many conflicts and, in my opinion, the command set up is definitely detrimental to efficiency.
>
> In view of the fact that we have 61 American divisions committed to this theater as compared to a total of 16 British and Dominion troops, including one Polish division, I see no reason why it should be necessary to accede so much to British demands. While we are fighting our own war, we are certainly helping the British very materially, and our own interests should come first.[3]

Moreover Bradley revealed, in this Memorandum for Record, that he had on 16 January protested to Eisenhower about the decision to put Ninth US Army under Monty: 'In my opinion the failure to return all American troops to the command of Twelfth Army Group might be interpreted as a lack of confidence in the American command.' What Bradley wanted was permission to continue his offensive in the Ardennes; if this failed, he wished authorization 'to shift' over to the Aachen sector with both First and Ninth Armies 'under my command'.[4] According to Bradley, Eisenhower reacted by stating 'that he had fought the propaganda to put Marshal Montgomery in command so long it was wearing him out; that we had all agreed[5] that eventually the Ninth Army should be under the 21 Army Group for the attack north of the Ruhr, and that by putting it under 21 Army Group at the present time, he might be able to shut up the element that was trying to put everything under Marshal Montgomery.'[6]

If this was what Eisenhower told Bradley—and Bradley repeated the assertion in 1948 in his memoirs—then Eisenhower was either

[1] Bradley ms., loc. cit.
[2] Ibid.
[3] 'Memorandum for Record', 23.1.45, Bradley Papers, loc. cit.
[4] Ibid.
[5] As in the 'Outline Plan' of 31.12.44, loc. cit.
[6] 'Memorandum for Record', 23.1.45, loc. cit.

revealing the true political and diplomatic motives behind his military decisions or—more likely—seeking to soothe Bradley's injured pride by making the decision palatable as a political rather than military necessity. Such diplomacy certainly worked in that Bradley accepted Eisenhower's decision regarding Ninth US Army; but it also deepened Bradley's bitterness by encouraging him to see Monty as a power-hungry Briton rather than a super-professional tactical commander fighting the Germans.

> In my opinion, the campaign to set up Monty and, in general, to increase British prestige in this campaign, out of all proportion to the effort they have in it, is definitely harmful to relations between the British and ourselves

Bradley noted in protest.[1]

Why did Eisenhower not remind Bradley that Monty's 'Veritable' and 'Grenade' plans were part of a *single* operation to bring to battle the German forces west of the Rhine between the Roer river and Arnhem—and that, regardless of Press or political considerations, it was militarily sound to put the planning and command under a single general?

Bradley, smarting and unhappy, was thus encouraged to try and compete with Monty by immediate all-out fighting in the Ardennes. Yet Eisenhower was well aware that, of all Bradley's premises for a breakthrough in the Eifel, none was in fact tenable. It was simply untrue that the 'Germans were in no way prepared to meet our next attack' in the Ardennes, because of their losses; in fact at the morning SHAEF conference on 19 January General Whiteley told Eisenhower the enemy would 'probably manage to withdraw the bulk of his formations' from the Ardennes salient;[2] moreover, far from having 'suffered irreparably' in morale, as Bradley claimed, General Strong announced that 'German morale is very high right now. It has been ever since the break through on Dec. 16. Previously they had suffered one defeat after another.'[3] Above all, neither the terrain nor the weather in the Ardennes favoured such an American offensive—as even Bradley came to confess:

> The country was so rough and the weather conditions so bad that our progress was slow. Many times our tanks would slide off on the icy roads. Vehicular movement across country was impossible except for short distances. Men would sometimes have to buck six

[1] Ibid.
[2] Diary of Mrs K. Summersby, entry of 19.1.45, loc. cit.
[3] Ibid.

foot snow drifts. All of this facilitated the Germans' ability to fight an efficient delaying action.[1]

Monty had predicted this—'I know, and Army and Corps Commanders know, that neither First nor Third Army is in a fit state to embark on that sort of dogfight straight off; they require a rest, some training and so on; Divisions are tired and all are short of infantry,' he had written to the DMO on 13 January, remarking of the likely German defensive line in the Ardennes: 'the whole thing is immensely strong, the country is very difficult and it will be a very hard nut to crack'.[2] Now, six days later, having secured—as he thought—agreement to a new Allied plan, Monty was tortured by the prospect of Eisenhower reverting to his policy of dispersed offensives: 'I see no chance of getting "decisive results" by going on in the Ardennes, and the present fighting is costing First Army some 800 casualties a day with very small gains of ground,' he lamented in a new letter to Simpson,[3] enclosing a copy of his letter to Eisenhower. To this, Eisenhower replied on 21 January, saying he was 'certain that we can determine the value of continuing to push through the Ardennes in plenty of time so that you may know the exact schedule of throwing more US Divisions into the area in which you are interested'.[4] To Brooke, Monty complained that night:

> Ike has replied to my M/547 saying he agrees with it. But it is clear from his letter that he is prepared to continue the Ardennes battle till the first week in Feb. This will mean that GRENADE could not be launched till 3rd week in Feb. If this is done I will have to postpone VERITABLE as I do not want too long between the operations.[5]

Originally Monty had said he would countenance a two-week interval between 'Veritable' and 'Grenade'; now he was claiming they must almost run in tandem in an effort to stop Bradley's Ardennes offensive—for every day's offensive fighting in the Ardennes meant less likelihood of fresh, battle-ready troops being transferred subsequently to the main Rhineland battle in the north, as Monty bewailed on 22 January:

[1] Bradley ms., loc. cit.
[2] M541, loc. cit.
[3] Letter of 20.1.45 (not numbered), 'North-West Europe 14 Jan 45–28 Feb 45' file, Montgomery Papers.
[4] Quoted in *The Papers of Dwight David Eisenhower*, op. cit. Original in Montgomery Papers.
[5] M456 of 1840 hrs, 21.1.45, Montgomery Papers.

> The prospect of getting by degrees sufficient numbers of really good fresh divs for GRENADE is fading away. I have urged continually that we should close down in Ardennes and come on to the defensive there as the Americans have not got enough fresh troops to operate offensively with success in more than one place. They do not understand that tired divs which have suffered severe casualties must have a period for rest and training before they can be used with success again.[1]

If SHAEF were able to provide reserve divisions from an Allied reserve, like the Germans, then this would not matter. But as Monty pointed out, 'SHAEF are very worried about situation in south about Colmar and Strasbourg. I understand the French divs are not fighting properly. I hear also that Devers is quite useless. Whiteley tells me that they may have to send considerable strength down there to get that area well in hand.[2] If this is done it will mean that GRENADE will be put back indefinitely.'[3] Such an open-ended interval between 'Veritable' and 'Grenade' Monty was unwilling to countenance, remembering the terrible British casualties he had taken at Caen to distract German armoured strength from Bradley's right wing. Day after day, when Operation 'Cobra' was cancelled, Dempsey had been forced to keep attacking—offensive operations whose casualties were worth sustaining if the second Allied punch was still forthcoming in overwhelming strength. But if 'Grenade' was watered down and postponed 'indefinitely', Monty refused to sacrifice British and Canadian lives. 'Veritable' would *also* have to be postponed indefinitely 'as the two operations are interdependent', he informed Brooke.[4] In fact in Monty's eyes, the situation was, once again, a shambles:

> So far as I can see the Ardennes battle is being continued for the sole reason of keeping Bradley employed offensively.[5]

If Devers was so useless—and Eisenhower acknowledged that same

[1] M550 of 1930 hrs, 22.1.45, Montgomery Papers.
[2] SHAEF planned on 23.1.45 to send five divisions to reinforce Devers. 'I swear to God I don't see the reason for moving 5 divisions; it's like using a sledgehammer to crack a nut,' Eisenhower protested when he heard of this. Whiteley then explained that '5 divisions was assuming the worst case, and that we had to relieve all the FRENCH in the COLMAR area. Supreme Allied Commander in discussing the FRENCH said "God! We have certainly been let down by the FRENCH"' 'Meeting in Supreme Commander's Office', 23.1.45, Robb Papers, loc. cit.
[3] M550, loc. cit.
[4] Ibid.
[5] Ibid.

day that this was so[1]—then why did Eisenhower not employ Bradley to take over Devers' front south of the Ardennes?

> We really have now two main problems i.e. one in the north and one in the south. It is a very great pity that Eisenhower was persuaded to take First Army away from me. The sound military course now would be to put 1st Army back under me and to put Bradley in command of whole of rest of front including Devers.[2]

In Bradley's view this was characteristic of but one thing: 'In considering any of Montgomery's plans,' he wrote after the war, 'it was necessary to consider how such plans affected Montgomery personally. His plans were most always designed to further his own aggrandizement.'[3]

As Brooke would find in the ensuing Anglo-American Chiefs of Staffs meetings in Malta and Yalta, American reaction to Monty was becoming increasingly personal and increasingly blind to the professionalism and military logic which motivated Monty's calls for a 'sound command set-up'. The lessons of North Africa, Sicily, Italy and the campaign from Normandy to the Siegfried Line had convinced Monty, however, that only by concentration of offensive effort and inter-relation of thrusts could the Allies prosper in battle against the Germans. Monty had been promised a decision regarding closure of the Ardennes front by 25 January; now, with anxiety over Devers' southern front, this was 'unlikely . . . I now fear that old snags of indecision and vacillation and refusal to consider the military problem fairly and squarely are coming to the front again. The old horses by names of "concentration" and "command set-up" are in the hunt again. The real trouble,' Monty wearily chronicled,

> is that there is no control and the three Army Groups are each intent on their own affairs. 12th Army Group are preparing to launch an offensive towards Euskirchen and Bonn in accordance with para 6 of SCAF 176 and Patton today issued a stirring order to 3rd Army saying that the next step would be Cologne. 12th Army Group takes no interest in GRENADE. A staff meeting

[1] 'E. told Whiteley to tell Devers in no uncertain language that he must get on with the kob [sic]. Devers has been a constant source of worry to E,' Eisenhower's P.A. Mrs Summersby noted in her diary, having been present at the morning SHAEF conference: Diary of Mrs K. Summersby, loc. cit.

[2] M550, loc. cit.

[3] Bradley ms, loc. cit.

> was held today at NAMUR . . . but little was achieved as 12th Army Group openly said they were off to Cologne and Bonn . . . One has to preserve a sense of humour these days otherwise one would go mad.[1]

To the King he wrote in similar vein: 'I very much regret that since 17 Jan we have lost all the ground we had gained; infirmity of purpose, indecision, and national pride are all becoming apparent; the agreed plan is fading into the distance; instead of regaining the strategical initiative it remains with the enemy on this front; and we are losing the opportunity created by the Russian offensive . . . It is a tragedy.'[2]

Towards Eisenhower Monty attempted to be as loyal and reasonable as he could; but in his private signals to Brooke he spoke from his military heart—as he did in his diary, kept by Colonel Dawnay. Far from having had a 'fine conference' with Bradley on 18 January 'it was clear that General Bradley proposed to continue with his operations in the ARDENNES with his objective COLOGNE, and that the divisions for Ninth US Army would not be forthcoming until General Eisenhower gave a direct order to General Bradley to close down his offensive operations'. Far from feeling a mild anxiety, as expressed in his letter to Eisenhower on receipt of the Supreme Commander's latest Directive, Monty was

> in truth greatly alarmed at the lack of decision and firm guidance shown in this directive; for as a result of it both General Bradley and the Field-Marshal were preparing independent thrusts and no proper concentration of effort was achieved. General Eisenhower's directive showed plainly that while he had accepted the Field-Marshal's plan to attack in the north, he had at the same time accepted General Bradley's plan to continue the attack in the centre; and meanwhile 6 US Army Group was gradually becoming seriously involved in the south at ALSACE. The Allied resources at this time were adequate only for one strong thrust, but this directive allowed each Army Group Commander to continue with his own offensive operations independently of each other.
>
> At a time when firm and clear guidance was most essential, this direction laid down no single clear objective, and made no attempt at a proper allocation of resources. It displayed infirmity of purpose and an attempt to compromise between two incompatible plans. It was accepted that the main effort was to be made in the

[1] M550, loc. cit.

[2] Letter to Sir Alan Lascelles, 24.1.45 (RA GVI/283), Royal Archives, Windsor.

> north, but the main strength was concentrated in the centre, and there was no firm intention to divert it from there. . . .
>
> The real reason for the offensive in the ARDENNES appeared to be to give General Bradley an offensive task, and not a purely defensive one. But the Allies had not sufficient resources to conduct a powerful offensive in more than one sector; it had to be either in the north, or in the centre, or in the south, but in only one sector and *not* in all three. General Eisenhower still could not see this.

As Dawnay remarked, 'this situation was very similar to that which existed in the Autumn of 1944 when it was agreed that the RUHR was the main objective, but the main resources were allotted to the attack against the SAAR.'[1]

There was, however, one crucial difference. In the autumn of 1944 Eisenhower's policy of independent, dispersed thrusts on a very wide front had given Hitler the opportunity both to build up and launch the most concentrated single offensive attack of the war. The blunting of that attack and the subsequent Russian offensive which opened on 12 January now made the chances of German exploitation of Allied 'infirmity of purpose' very slim. The danger was no longer German counter-attack, Monty felt. Rather it was the unnecessary prolongation of the war, with concomitant casualties—and the likelihood that in the end not the western Allies but the Russians would win.

[1] 'Notes on the Campaign in NW Europe', loc. cit.

CHAPTER EIGHT

A Stormy Conference

KEEPING HIS SANITY in the face of such vacillation was for Monty a harder task than commanding his armies. On 20 January he had written to the Reynolds to say he would be 'home' on 25 January—'I can see nothing to stop it . . . The cold spell has ceased here; it is now raining and thawing, and the mud and slush is indescribable. Two goldfish have died; over-eating I fear: my batman will give them too much food!!'[1]

With Eisenhower declining to close down the Ardennes, would Monty be able to come home, though? Monty was certain that his two Rhineland battles would, if properly mounted, presage the defeat of Germany and was thus loth to give up the prospect of 'a little rest before the further activities that lie ahead'. Telephone engineers were thus despatched to the Reynolds' school in Hindhead and 'scramblers' installed in order that he might speak in secret both to his staff at 21 Army Group and to SHAEF at Versailles.[2]

This was just as well—for the final week of January 1945 was to be, for Monty, one of the most tormenting of the war. On 21 January Monty had assembled his three Army Commanders and given out his orders for the forthcoming 'Veritable' and 'Grenade' operations—if they took place.[3] He had decided that Second British Army would hold in the centre, at Venlo, while First Canadian and Ninth US Armies struck out on either flank, drawing their pincers together along the west bank of the Rhine and trapping as many German troops as possible.

Eisenhower, not having seen Monty since December 1944, had meanwhile become more and more a prey to other voices at SHAEF. Bedell Smith still favoured a pragmatic approach, tapping all along the enemy line to discover his weakest point; General Juin, Commander-in-Chief of the French troops, declared on 23 January that, far from preparing an attack in the north, all Allied strength should now be concentrated on meeting the current German attacks in Alsace. 'The French are very tired, want more reinforcements,'

[1] Letter to Phyllis Reynolds, 20.1.45, Montgomery Papers.
[2] General Sir Frank Simpson, Wason interview, loc. cit.
[3] M548 Directive, 21.1.45, Montgomery Papers.

Eisenhower's PA recorded. 'He [Juin] accused the American G2 [Intelligence] of underestimating the strength of the Germans in the [Colmar] Pocket. The British idea of attacking in the North was wrong, he more or less intimated that we should fight a defensive battle, as we hadn't the strength to attack.'[1] Eisenhower, however, was aware of the impending summit meeting between Stalin, Roosevelt and Churchill—and as Tedder's Military Assistant confided to the DMO in London, 'Ike had informed Tedder that he (Ike) felt he must do something "big and spectacular" very soon in order to show the Russians that we too were out for a quick end to war.'[2] In a telephone conversation with Bradley on 23 January, Bradley had assured Eisenhower that the Ardennes offensive was going spectacularly well—'Our troops are on the outskirts of St Vith . . . 12th Corps picked up 1,000 prisoners. Air had a terrific day yesterday'[3]—and ought to be continued. Thus, as Monty prepared to leave Zonhoven for England, his hopes of a full-scale, concentrated Allied offensive in the north plummeted. As his diarist recorded:

> On the evening of 24th January, General Whiteley rang up the Field-Marshal from SHAEF, and informed him of the decision which General Eisenhower had taken on future operations. General Bradley had strongly recommended that the ARDENNES thrust should continue, as he was very confident that the First and Third US Armies could break through the SIEGFRIED LINE and could reach BONN and COLOGNE. Acting on this advice, General Eisenhower had decided that the ARDENNES thrust should continue, but that he would review the situation again about the 1st February. As a result of this decision, *no* American divisions would for the present be available to reinforce Ninth US Army, and operation 'GRENADE' could not be planned firmly. This would also prevent the launching of operation 'VERITABLE' unless the ARDENNES thrust achieved considerable success.[4]

Monty protested that 'the divisions attacking in the ARDENNES were weak and tired, the country was difficult and well suited to defence, and there were insufficient forces available to achieve decisive success';[5] but Eisenhower's decision had been made. As Monty signalled in despair to Brooke that night: 'I was given the information by Whiteley at 1700 hrs. I said that the decision of Supreme

[1] Diary of Mrs K. Summersby, loc. cit.
[2] General Sir Frank Simpson, loc. cit.
[3] Diary of Mrs K. Summersby, loc. cit.
[4] 'Notes on the Campaign in NW Europe', loc. cit.
[5] M551 (no time of origin), 24.1.45, Montgomery Papers.

Commander . . . was quite clear and that I would act accordingly.'[1] He had given Whiteley the reasons why he disagreed—'no decisive results are likely here as there is not sufficient power available. In my opinion they should close down in Ardennes and regroup and put on Veritable and Grenade as really powerful blows and they would achieve decisive results'—but Whiteley, while thanking Monty for his views, had said, 'Ike had decided to accept the advice of Bradley as he was so confident he could get to the Rhine.'[2]

Eisenhower, writing his war memoirs in 1948,[3] omitted to mention this development; Bradley, writing in 1951,[4] also ignored it. Even Monty, writing in 1958,[5] cast a complete veil of silence over the disagreement and its astonishing sequel. However, the unpublished records of all the participants demonstrate that, at the time, this was of seminal importance to all. The 'Battle of the Bulge' had, in a sense, distracted attention from the fundamental difference of opinion between Monty and Eisenhower. Now, in the final week of January, with the major Allied summit conference about to take place at Yalta,[6] this difference rose to a crescendo—with Monty and Eisenhower each flying to brief their bosses in preparation for the summit. Eisenhower flew first, having 'arranged to meet him [General Marshall] secretly at Marseille'[7] on 25 January.

According to Eisenhower, General Marshall was in 'full agreement' with Eisenhower's decisions—indeed was 'so impressed by the soundness of the whole plan that he suggested I send a chief of staff, General Smith, to Malta to participate in a Conference that was to take place there between the President, the Prime Minister, and their respective staffs before they went on to Yalta.'[8]

Brooke had in fact engineered the Malta meeting—and on 26 January (having been delayed a day by bad weather) Monty arrived in London to lunch with him and to see Churchill, 'as he is again very depressed with the American strategy and Eisenhower's inability to retain a definite policy without waffling about,' Brooke recorded in his diary.[9] At lunch on 26 January Brooke found 'the old trouble

[1] Ibid.
[2] Ibid.
[3] Dwight Eisenhower, *Crusade in Europe*, New York and London 1948.
[4] O. N. Bradley, *A Soldier's Story*, New York and London 1951.
[5] B. L. Montgomery, *Memoirs*, London 1958.
[6] Eisenhower had known of the impending conference for several weeks: 'In early January, I learned that the President, the Prime Minister and their staffs were again to meet with Generalissimo Stalin, this time at Yalta': Dwight D. Eisenhower, op. cit.
[7] Ibid.
[8] Ibid.
[9] Diary of Field-Marshal Sir Alan Brooke, Alanbrooke Papers, LHCMA, King's College, London.

keeps turning round and round in his [Monty's] head. Lack of organization of Command on the part of the Americans and their failure to concentrate their effort on the vital point.'[1]

Brooke, beset by a thousand problems in a global context, might have been forgiven for wishing he had a more complaisant C-in-C 21st Army Group. But Monty's distress mirrored his own. Far from proving a model of British determination to concentrate upon military essentials, Field-Marshal Alexander was turning out a broken reed as Supreme Commander in the Mediterranean—'he has now become completely lost in this damned Greek business and has forgotten the whole war on the strength of it. He [Alexander] relies on MacMillan [British political representative in the Mediterranean] as his confidential adviser on all matters including military ones and as a result loses all military perspective,' Brooke had noted on 12 January.[2] 'The more I see of him the more I marvel at the smallness of the man. I do not believe he has a single idea in his head of his own!'[3] By 18 January Brooke was despairing: 'It is too depressing to see how Alex's deficiency in brain allows him to be dominated by others!! He must have someone else to lean on! He has *no* personality of his own and lets anybody else climb into his skin!! In Africa, Sicily and South Italy he was carried by Montgomery. In central Italy by Oliver Leese and Harding & failed badly, & now he has selected MacMillan as his mount! His new charge may carry him over the political fences (perhaps) but will most certainly crash him over the military ones! My God how difficult war is to run owing to personalities. . . .'[4]

What made matters worse was that Churchill seemed oblivious to Alexander's failings—and having approved of the transfer of British and Canadian divisions from the Mediterranean to the western front to help Monty's effort, Churchill was now back-tracking. As Sir Frank Simpson later recalled: 'Churchill had agreed for divisions to be transferred from the Italian to the western front because the western front was badly in need of them and it had been decided not to go beyond the line of the southern Alps, but suddenly Winston reverted to his old idea of an advance on Vienna which, of course, was a very attractive proposition, and this drove the CIGS almost mad.'[5] This was no exaggeration, as Brooke's diary entry of 23 January reveals:

I don't feel that I can stand another day working with Winston. It

[1] Ibid.
[2] Ibid.
[3] Ibid.
[4] Ibid.
[5] General Sir Frank Simpson, loc. cit.

is quite hopeless. He is finished and gone, incapable of grasping any military situation & unable to give a decision. . . .[1]

What Brooke clearly recognized was that, given the growing preponderence of American divisions on the western front—now approaching sixty-one to fifteen—the British Chiefs of Staff *had* to transfer more divisions from the secondary Mediterranean theatre to the western front, not only to ensure success in the prime sector, but to avoid being elbowed off the military stage in the final act of a drama in which Britain had for six years provided—often alone—the primary resistance to Hitler's aims. It was England, not America, that was still, after five long years, being bombed, with tens of thousands of Londoners made homeless, living on meagre rations and fuel. . . . In Brooke's exhausted eyes, it was imperative to finish the war in Europe quickly; the timetable for the transfer of divisions from Italy had been agreed, and the Anglo-American talks in Malta were about to take place. Churchill's sudden reversion to opportunistic ambitions in the 'soft underbelly' of Europe struck Brooke as the height of inanity. According to 'Simbo' Simpson, Brooke 'came back to his office, put his head in his hands and said, as he had said several times before: "How much longer can I go on with this man?" He groaned several times and then he looked up and with a grin said: "Yes, but how are we going to get on without him?" '[2]

This was said not merely from personal loyalty. Churchill was, like Roosevelt, an ailing man—his Private Secretary told Lord Moran that Churchill's 'work has deteriorated a lot in the last few months; and that he has become very wordy, irritating his colleagues in the Cabinet by his verbosity'.[3] Nevertheless Churchill understood what so many of his colleagues ignored: that the Americans were naïve about Stalin's intentions in Europe and that any attempt to install Communist tyrannies by force and by terrorism in the aftermath of Hitler's conquests must be combatted forthrightly if the Allies were to revive the severed roots of democracy in Europe. Churchill was thus willing to fight almost single-handedly against the protests of his fellow MPs in Parliament, as well as the grave suspicions of Roosevelt and most Americans. Unfortunately this willingness to stand up and be counted in the face of American naïveté did not extend to the main military sphere—and when Monty arrived at 10 Downing Street to discuss the disastrous conduct of

[1] Diary of Field-Marshal Sir Alan Brooke, loc. cit.
[2] General Sir Frank Simpson loc. cit.
[3] Moran, *Winston Churchill: The Struggle for Survival*, London 1966; entry of 30.1.45.

command by Eisenhower on the Western Front, he received short shrift from the Prime Minister. Churchill berated Monty for his inability to 'get on' with the Americans, saying he had heard from Eisenhower that, thanks to Monty's 'cock-a-doodle' crowing after the Ardennes, the American generals had declared 'their troops would never again be put under an English general.'[1]

Churchill's instinct told him that he must accede to American strategy on the western front if he was to prevail upon Roosevelt over British strategy in the Mediterranean. Monty thus left the Prime Minister empty-handed—and Brooke's military prognosis was little better. The British Chiefs of Staff would try to put further pressure on their American counterparts—but it was known both from Eisenhower's 'Appreciation' of 20 January (which had not been shown to Monty) and subsequent private signals to Marshall (which British Intelligence had decrypted) that the American Chiefs of Staff approved of Eisenhower's handling of operations and tactical strategy, and it would be difficult, without Churchill's backing, to force them to rescind that approval.

Monty, smarting from Churchill's 'flea in the ear' and disappointed by Brooke's pessimistic response, retired to Hindhead to ponder his fate. Could he reasonably ask thousands of British, Canadian and Polish soldiers to sacrifice their lives in a 'half-baked' offensive which, without the full participation of the American pincer across the Roer, would be bound to fail? Moreover, Eisenhower's 'Appreciation' called for the Allies to close up to the Rhine 'in the north and in the south', even if or when Monty reached the Rhine—a cautiousness which Monty found fatuous. Both Bradley and Eisenhower considered that it would be dangerous to cross the Rhine before securing its entire length from Switzerland to the North Sea, since to advance into Germany without so doing would, in Bradley's words, 'give the Germans a chance to launch just such a counter-offensive as they did launch [in December 1944]. . . . My contention was that if you were going to advance into Germany on a narrow front, i.e. just north of the Ruhr, that you must have advanced to the Rhine all along the line so that you would have a strong defensive line which could be held with minimum troops without much danger of a major German attack.'[2] But with Konev's Russian forces having reached the Oder by 23 January, Monty felt such a cautious strategy to be utterly misguided.

Whether Brooke advised Monty to go ahead with 'Veritable' in

[1] Cf. Diary of Chester B. Hansen, entry of 5.2.45: 'It is reputed that the Field Marshal was severely redressed by the Prime Minister after the public bow on the Von Runstedt attack but he appears to continue bloody but unbowed.'

[2] Bradley MS., loc cit.

the hope of forcing Eisenhower's hand—since Eisenhower would not dare risk failure in the Ardennes *and* the Rhineland—is unknown. Possibly Brooke promised to try and 'square' the Americans; at all events General Marshall sensed trouble and advised Eisenhower, if he could not come himself, at least to send Bedell Smith to argue the American case at Malta. There would be no need for his strategy to be questioned at Malta, since military decisions as Supreme Commander 'fall within your sphere of responsibility. But your plan is so sound that I think it better for you to send General Smith to Malta so that he may explain these matters in detail. Their logic will be convincing.'[1]

Brooke reached the island on 29 January. Sensing his chance, he put Bedell Smith in the witness box at the Chiefs of Staff meeting at 2.30 p.m. the following day, 30 January—and under Brooke's relentless cross-examination the whole facile edifice of Eisenhower's 'strategy' came tumbling down—for what Bedell Smith said bore no relation to the plan Eisenhower was asking the Combined Chiefs of Staff to approve.

> As a result I said that we would probably be prepared to approve Bedell's statement and take down in the Minutes of the [Combined Chiefs of Staff] meeting that we could not approve the Appreciation by Eisenhower,

Brooke recorded in his diary.[2]

Eisenhower's 'Appreciation' had thus failed to get approval—and sparks soon began to fly. Bedell Smith cabled to Versailles with the alarming news, which filled Eisenhower with consternation. 'The British C.O.S. do not seem to share E's views,' Mrs Summersby noted in her diary.[3] Worse still, Bradley's offensive in the Ardennes was *not* bringing the German divisions to battle. Maj-General Strong had announced the previous day that the Sixth Panzer Army was being moved *away* from Bradley's target—Cologne—to the Eastern Front,[4] and by 30 January Eisenhower was having to acknowledge that 'we are not hurting the German very much. Although we are attacking in the Ardennes the German is moving troops away.'[5]

Eisenhower's attempt to regain the initiative was in tatters. In fact, unbeknown to Marshall or to Monty, there had been rising dissension *within* SHAEF about Bradley's operations. On 23 January

[1] Dwight Eisenhower, *Crusade in Europe*, op. cit.
[2] A. Bryant, *Triumph in the West*, London 1959.
[3] Diary of Mrs K. Summersby, entry of 30.1.45, loc. cit.
[4] Entry of 29.1.45. Ibid.
[5] Entry of 30.1.45. Ibid.

Eisenhower had phoned Bradley 'on the situation in the ARDENNES, and BRADLEY's reaction was that it would be a grave mistake to give up his offensive at the present. S[upreme] A[llied] C[ommander] seemed inclined to agree as this was the only part of the front on which we were taking positive action and getting results.'[1] But Eisenhower's Deputy, Air Chief Marshal Tedder, disagreed—'D/SAC, however, queried the long-term policy of this offensive—what is it going to achieve? He pointed out that although aimed at EUSKIRCHEN, even when through the SIEGFRIED LINE it still had a great deal of ARDENNES country to traverse, and there can be no rapid exploitation.'[2] General Spaatz, C-in-C of the American bomber forces, sided with Eisenhower, on the grounds that Bradley's offensive 'would at least have the advantage of having had the ground pretty well prepared by the bombing in the last month, a fact which BRADLEY had also mentioned.'[3] Air-Marshal Robb, no friend of Monty's (whose behaviour towards the Supreme Commander he could not forgive), found himself in uncommon agreement with the 21st Army Group Commander. 'To me it appears that we are ignoring the principles of war,' he added in a note beneath his record of the morning conference. 'We are attacking in the South, in the ARDENNES, and shortly expect to attack heavily in the North. We have reinforced DEVERS piecemeal . . . should we not give DEVERS a time limit of several days to produce positive results, and if he fails to do so, to call off his attacks and go on the defensive?'[4] Robb was similarly pessimistic about Bradley's chances of decisive success: 'The present ARDENNES attacks are attractive in producing something for the daily papers, but they obviously will not give us the major results we require. These should be called off and the large force that would then be available should be concentrated in the North to ensure, first of all, that VERITABLE and its following attack GRENADE are successful and have sufficient forces to exploit the success. These attacks take us to the RHINE in the area where we told the C[ombined] C.O.S. that we must reach to get suitable crossings for the further advance North of the RUHR.'[5]

The next day Robb noted that 'in view of the sweeping success of the RUSSIAN offensive' Eisenhower was 'reluctant' to stop Patton's attacks in the Ardennes;[6] and by the morning conference of 25

[1] 'Meeting in Supreme Commander's Office', 23.1.45, Robb Papers, loc. cit.
[2] Ibid.
[3] Ibid.
[4] Ibid.
[5] Ibid.
[6] 'Meeting in Supreme Commander's Office', 24.1.45, Robb Papers, loc. cit.

January Bradley was reported by General Bull as having 'reiterated his certainty that his attacks would go through the SIEGFRIED Line, and that they should not be stopped' [1]—whereas Tedder's view, and those of 'some others' was that 'nothing should be allowed to delay' Monty's Rhineland offensive, where fresh troops were required.[2] That night, at a dinner held for the President's adviser, Harry Hopkins, at Versailles, Hopkins assured Eisenhower that he 'had conducted the campaign beautifully, had the complete support of all people at home, official and unofficial'.[3] But Bedell Smith spoiled the cocoon by openly discussing, in front of Hopkins and the American Ambassador to France 'the differences between Monty and the Supreme Commander, Monty wanting two-thirds of the American troops under his direct command for an all out attack under his superior direction, whereas SHAEF's plan for the next offensive apparently is aimed toward Cologne [sic] under Bradley.' [4] As Eisenhower's naval aide-cum-PR officer understood Bedell Smith, 'Monty had made representations to the Supreme Commander that Bradley's attack was bound to fail and quite apparently had gone on record with this view. Ike had to settle the matter and of course had supported SHAEF's plan.' [5]

Tedder and his supporters at SHAEF were, however, not the only senior officers who doubted the wisdom of Eisenhower's Cologne-Bonn thrust. General Dempsey, visiting the Ninth US Army Commander at the latter's headquarters on 27 January, found that Simpson 'still has no news of any divisions joining his army'—as he noted in his diary that night. 'First and Third Armies are starting an attack tomorrow morning towards BONN. This will inevitably delay the build-up of Ninth Army and the start of their operation towards MUNCHEN-GLADBACH ["Grenade"].' [6] Though Bradley was still full of optimism, the senior staff at SHAEF were now divided. It had been obvious since the third week of January that the Germans planned to make a strategic withdrawal to the Siegfried Line; beyond following up this withdrawal there was no evidence that Bradley was about to break through.[7] On the contrary, it appeared that the

[1] 'Meeting in Chiefs of Staffs' Office', 25.1.45, Robb Papers, loc. cit.
[2] Ibid.
[3] H. C. Butcher, *Three Years with Eisenhower*, op. cit.
[4] 'Memorandum for Diary by Captain Butcher', 27.1.45, Desk Diary of C-in-C.
[5] Ibid.
[6] Diary of General Sir Miles Dempsey, entry of 27.1.45, PRO.
[7] Cf. Minutes of SHAEF and Air Commander's Conferences, 25.1.45, *re:* 'enemy's planned withdrawal in the Ardennes,' and the following day: '5th Panzer Army is now certainly withdrawing to the SIEGFRIED Line in the Ardennes sector' (AIR 37/1129), PRO.

Germans were actually thinning out their line, so confident were they of holding it. 'Although we are attacking in the Ardennes the German is moving troops away,' the Supreme Commander's morning meeting heard on 30 January. 'E[isenhower] says we are not hurting the German very much,' Mrs Summersby recorded ruefully.

Bradley had arranged to fly to Versailles on 30 January to present his 'case' for continued offensive in the Ardennes in person, but, symbolically, he was defeated by the weather and could not fly. Whiteley and Tedder, meanwhile, were more and more concerned to give Monty the green light, and to close down operations in the Ardennes—in fact a signal had been sent the night before ordering Monty to launch 'Veritable' on 8 February, but Monty had refused to undertake the operation without its matrix, Operation 'Grenade'.[1]

Thus when a signal was received from Bedell Smith in Malta on 30 January, notifying Eisenhower that his strategic 'Appreciation' had been rejected, Eisenhower—raised in the famous cowboy town of Abilene and an avid reader of Westerns—recognized that there would have to be a 'shoot out' with Bradley.

In a 'powerful resumption of the Allied offensive' Bradley had already launched, the previous day, his 18 Corps 'in waist deep snow against relatively light resistance in a re-opening of our drive on the Siegfried Line to Bonn and Koblenz.'[2] Patton's Third US Army was also attacking 'towards German objectives' further south towards the 'Silesian industrial area'[3] of the Saar, and Bradley wanted a 'comparatively small'[4] Ninth US Army to co-operate by covering 'the left flank of the First Army in the American drive towards the Rhine.'[5] But if Bradley went ahead, Monty's pincer-attack to close the Rhine and ultimately seize the Ruhr in the north was damned; moreover in two days' time the Combined Chiefs of Staff were scheduled to move on to meet the Russians at Yalta. The matter

[1] Secret signal (S-77053) sent at 1845 hrs on 29.1.45 to Montgomery instructing him to launch 'Operation "VERITABLE" with target date 8th Feb,' (SHAEF Directives File, Montgomery Papers); however Monty had already refused by telephone to do so without confirmation that 'Grenade' would be mounted in tandem—'Field Marshal Montgomery said that he had been talking with his own HQ and with SHAEF (General Whiteley) . . . Field-Marshal Montgomery had given orders for 'VERITABLE' to be got ready, but that it would not be launched until it had definitely been equated with 'GRENADE' or some similar operation': 'Note on telephone conversation between Field Marshal Montgomery (talking at Hindhead) and DDMO(A) at 1800 hrs on Monday, 29 January 1945', 'North-West Europe' file, Montgomery Papers.

[2] Diary of Chester B. Hansen, entry of 29.1.45, loc. cit.

[3] Ibid.

[4] Entry of 30.1.45. Ibid.

[5] Ibid.

must be ironed out, Eisenhower recognized—pronto. Bradley, delayed by the bad weather, was due to arrive at Versailles the following day. 31 January.[1] With a heavy heart, Eisenhower awaited his arrival.

Meanwhile at Amesbury School in Hindhead, Monty waited by the telephone. The day before, General Whiteley had phoned from SHAEF to say 'it was 10-1 on that a decision would be taken in favour of 'VERITABLE' and 'GRENADE' . . . General Bradley would be ordered to start transferring divisions for the 'GRENADE' build-up and to scale down the ARDENNES operations accordingly'; but Monty 'had had his hopes raised like this before' as he told Whiteley, and thus 'awaited the outcome of tomorrow's conference' having made 'quite clear to SHAEF' that he would *not* order Veritable *without* Grenade.[2]

With Bradley failing to fly to Versailles on 30 January, Monty was obliged to wait a further twenty-four hours.

It was now two weeks since Monty's signal to Brooke stating that it was not possible that First and Third US Armies could in their present condition break through the Siegfried Line on the axis Prum-Bonn. For two weeks Eisenhower had swung to and fro like a pendulum, unable to make a decisive commitment. It was not, Monty felt, a proper way to run a war. *Faute de mieux*, however, he must remain silent and, as in the days after the launching of the German offensive in the Ardennes, wait for the Allied High Command to come to its senses.

As the multitude of boys made their way between dormitory, refectory, playing field and classrooms, Monty thus waited upon events. At last, at lunchtime on 1 February, the telephone rang in Major Reynolds' study. It was a call from SHAEF. Pressing the scrambler button, Monty took the call from General Whiteley in Versailles. Whiteley had momentous news. For over twenty-four hours the 'Gunfight at the Trianon Palace Hotel' had raged, with conferences at 9 a.m. and 6.30 p.m. on 31 January, and 9.15 a.m. and noon the following day. None would reach the history books, for the level of personal and inter-Allied dissension was too scandalous to be revealed. Monty's diarist recorded:

> General Eisenhower summoned a conference . . . which took place on 31 January. This conference lasted about twenty-four hours

[1] 'Call from Bradley . . . He is coming to see E. tomorrow': entry of 30.12.44, Diary of Mrs Summersby, loc. cit.

[2] 'Notes on telephone conversation between Field-Marshal Montgomery (talking at Hindhead) and DDMO(A) at 1800 hrs on Monday, 29 January 1945', loc. cit.

and was of an extremely stormy nature. There was some very violent speaking on all sides, but luckily all the principal participants were American, and this prevented the quarrel developing into an international issue. It was in fact providential that the Field-Marshal was not in the theatre at this time, and so was not present.[1]

Providential, but not pleasing to Bradley who arrived at Versailles by car (the weather being still too poor to fly) on the afternoon of 31 January and had, in Monty's absence, to shoot at his shadow. According to Mrs Summersby Bradley began the evening conference by declaring that he was 'making good progress in the Ardennes,' and wished to continue there.[2] Eisenhower shook his head.

E. told Bradley that we must stop attacking in the Ardennes and attack North for the dams [controlling the Roer, where 'Grenade' would take place].[3]

Bradley was shaken.

Bradley is bitterly disappointed that he must stop attacking,

Mrs Summersby recorded.[4] Eisenhower, however was emphatic:

'Veritable' and 'Grenade' must go.[5]

The two Rhineland pincer attacks were vital. But, as Bradley pointed out, both would be 'commanded by Monty'.[6] To Bradley this was unacceptable.

Bradley pointed out to E. that there are 61 American Divs and equipment and that the American public is sore over Monty's continuous publicity in the press.[7]

Eisenhower reminded Bradley he had for months detailed Ninth US Army for Monty's operations north of the Ruhr—'21 Army Group had not the strength to attack without it.'[8] Bradley knew this, but, humiliated by having had two of his three armies withdrawn from his command, he had blocked Eisenhower's pre-Ardennes intentions from his mind and had laid great importance on the return of both US Armies after the end of the German offensive in the

[1] 'Notes on the Campaign in North-West Europe', loc. cit.
[2] Diary of Mrs K. Summersby, loc. cit.
[3] Ibid.
[4] Ibid.
[5] Ibid.
[6] Ibid.
[7] Ibid.
[8] Ibid.

Ardennes. Indeed Bradley's unauthorized press conference on 9 January had been a deliberate attempt to force Eisenhower's hand by whipping up a public expectation that Ninth US Army would return.[1]

Eisenhower's position was the more difficult since both he and Bradley were Americans.

'It is a most difficult problem for E.,' Mrs Summersby noted.

> Since the breakthrough on Dec 16 the 9th [Army] has been under Monty. Several weeks ago the 1st Army was returned to Bradley's command. Bradley tried his best to get the 9th Army back.[2]

Bradley's current objection was thus not so much tactical as personal, Eisenhower recognized. Still smarting from the disastrous effect of the Ardennes battle on his standing as a general—Marshall had on 16 January refused to award him his fourth star, so that he was still the same rank as he had been as a Corps Commander in Sicily—Bradley was deeply concerned by the likely press reactions to the news that his Ardennes offensive was to be closed down, and that Montgomery would be given command of the next major Allied offensive thrust.

'It was quite a stormy conference at moments,' Mrs Summersby recorded[3]—and revealed that Eisenhower, at its height, instructed General Whiteley to telephone Monty. 'Veritable' and 'Grenade' *would* go ahead but, he was told to warn Monty, if any member of 21 Army should talk to the press, 'Bradley will be given command of "Veritable and Grenade" . . . We finally quit at 8.30.'[4]

Bradley stayed the night with Eisenhower—and the next day, 1 February, begged Eisenhower to reconsider. But Eisenhower, aware of the Combined Chiefs of Staffs' veto of his 'Appreciation' and Bedell Smith's insistent telegrams urging revision of it, simply could not relent. Whiteley was instructed to telephone Monty again 'and tell him that "Veritable" must go Feb 8th'.[5] Meanwhile Bradley must close down his operations in the Ardennes and shift his strength north to capture the vital Roer dams, if 'Grenade' was to be launched

[1] 'It is possible that our use of the phrase 'Twelfth Army Group will resume command of all American Armies in this area' may force General Eisenhower to return to us the First and Ninth Armies, even though the Ninth assignment might only be temporary, to re-establish our prestige and repudiate any suggestion that the change in command to Montgomery was a result of the inefficiency of American command.'—Diary of Chester B. Hansen, entry of 9.1.45, loc. cit.

[2] Diary of Mrs K. Summersby, entry of 31.1.45, loc. cit.

[3] Ibid.

[4] Ibid.

[5] Entry of 1.2.45. Ibid.

in tandem with 'Veritable'—'Bradley must attack on the North edge of the Ardennes, south of Durren, and protect the dams. The above operation is vital to the success of the attack.'[1] Lending Bradley his personal aircraft, Eisenhower asked Bradley to return at once to his new headquarters and get working on the new plan. Bradley took off at 1.45, in high dudgeon.

> Bradley is badly upset over E.'s decision to leave 9th Army under Monty. He sees the logistics [sic] of E's decision, but the real trouble fates [sic] back to Dec and Jan. when Monty got so much publicity in the press. Of all E.'s Commanders, Monty is the one who has given him the greatest number of headaches. Monty has only come to Versailles twice for conferences. E. had always to send him a direct order [to come] otherwise he would send his C/S (Gen de Guingand) . . .
>
> Today has been a very ling [sic] and tiring day for E. How he keeps up the pressure I really do not know.[2]

Meanwhile at Malta, General Marshall was expressing 'his full dislike and antipathy for Monty', as Brooke recorded in his diary,[3] and was urging the Combined Chiefs of Staff to forbear issuing any directive to Eisenhower that might 'cramp his style', while in the meantime approving Eisenhower's original Appreciation. 'I refused to do this,' Brooke noted acidly.[4]

But at Amesbury, Monty was over the moon when he spoke, at 5.30 p.m., to the DMO at the War Office. 'General Eisenhower had had a conference with General Bradley during the past two days. General Bradley had again pressed for sufficient formations to remain available to him for purposes of developing his thrust from PRUM towards BONN. General Eisenhower has decided, however, that this thrust must now take second place to the making available of US formations for GRENADE,' Maj-General Simpson noted in a memorandum to be despatched by cypher to the CIGS in Malta.[5] Meanwhile Monty telephoned his headquarters and packed his bags. The next day he wrote from Claridge's in London to Phyllis Reynolds, on his return from Buckingham Palace:

> Thank you for a very pleasant holiday; a good deal of work was

[1] Ibid.
[2] Ibid.
[3] A. Bryant, op. cit.
[4] Ibid.
[5] 'Memorandum of a telephone conversation with Field-Marshal Montgomery at Hindhead, 5.30 p.m., 1.2.45' (file 14/6), Alanbrooke Papers, loc. cit.

involved at various moments, and if it had not been I could not have come at all: hence the telephone.

I had a very pleasant lunch with the King: just the two of us, alone. He was in very good form.

My love to you all

Yrs ever
Monty[1]

In the Field-Marshal's campaign diary, meanwhile, Monty's MA recorded his amazement at the 'frequent changes of plan':

> The situation had changed frequently between the 24th January and the 1st February. On the 24th it appeared that the Field-Marshal's plan had been accepted. By the 25th General Eisenhower had decided to let General Bradley continue with his thrust in the ARDENNES as he was so confident of success. Sometime between the 26th and the 29th General Marshall met General Eisenhower and told him he would have to agree to mount the Field-Marshal's plan, and at the stormy conference at General Bradley's headquarters on the 31st January and the 1st February Eisenhower at last insisted on this plan being put into effect.[2]

Dawnay was wrong about General Marshall who—like Roosevelt's adviser Harry Hopkins—thought Eisenhower was conducting the campaign splendidly. It was Brooke's refusal to approve Eisenhower's 'Appreciation', and the growing realization at SHAEF that the German army was *not* being brought to battle in the Ardennes, that had caused Eisenhower's volte-face.[3]

Ignorant of this but supremely confident that all would now be well, Monty flew back to his Main Headquarters in Brussels on 3 February. He had, *in absentia*, won the great gunfight at Versailles; now he had to prepare his three Allied armies for operations that were bound to involve severe casualties in the weeks ahead—but which might at last defeat the German forces west of the Rhine and offer the final springboard for the capture of the Ruhr.

[1] Letter to Phyllis Reynolds, 2.2.45, Montgomery Papers.

[2] 'Notes on the Campaign in NW Europe', loc. cit.

[3] At the SHAEF daily Chiefs of Staff conference on 1.2.45 the success of the German withdrawal in front of Bradley was finally acknowledged: 'By his decision to turn to the defensive and withdraw in the ARDENNES to the SIEGFRIED Line the enemy has succeeded in relieving from Front Line duty almost all his armour in the West': (AIR 37/1129), PRO.

PART SIX

Closing the Pincers

CHAPTER ONE

The American Approach to War

WITH THE FIRST concentrated Allied offensive of 1945 scheduled to start on 8 February, there was no time to lose. Bradley had reluctantly moved his headquarters nearer Monty, to Namur, and it was there on 5 February that a final conference was convened to make adjustments and decisions over reinforcing divisions. 'General Eisenhower will arrive at our headquarters, Sunday, for a meeting on Monday, February 5, with Montgomery and Bradley to seal the final planning for this hurry-up offensive,' Bradley's ADC recorded on 1 February.[1] 'No one looked forward with much eagerness to Montgomery's visit here,' he added. 'Since the von Runstedt attack he has grown in disfavour among command echelons where his refusal to compromise on decisions has made him a great numbers [sic] of enemies among the American commanders.'[2] According to Hansen, when it was suggested that Eisenhower's PA, Kay Summersby, should sit at lunch at Monty's table, 'she objected . . . assuring us she would, undoubtedly, become embroiled in a controversy if she did. Ably [sic] enough, this attitude concerning Montgomery prevails throughout the British elements of our high command where its tyrannical methods are generally abhorred.'[3]

Monty was certainly no more popular among certain senior British officers at SHAEF than among American. The American approach to war, with comfortable rear headquarters staffed by many thousands of officers (Hanson Baldwin, the American journalist, had recently created a storm over his assertion that Bradley's 12th US Army Group headquarters was the size of an entire American division—15,000 men; SHAEF headquarters was almost the size of an Army, numbering over 100,000) was indeed nearer to the British habits of World War I, and such officers certainly resented Montgomery's modern, crusading zeal. Such officers, hearing that Monty had 'got his way' over the forthcoming Rhineland battle, were thus the more incredulous when, on 3 February, Monty arrived in

[1] Diary of Chester B. Hansen, MHI, Carlisle, Pennsylvania. Bradley moved to the new headquarters on 28 January 1945.
[2] Entry of Sunday 4.2.45 (misdated: should be Monday 5.2.45).
[3] Ibid.

Brussels—and began to do battle on behalf of the Belgian workers! At 5 p.m. that day Monty's latest signal arrived at Versailles—and it was far from compromising:

> I consider that the level of subsistence of Belgian and Dutch civil population is too low and that there are signs of a disintegration of morale.
>
> There has already been sporadic strikes amongst ANTWERP dockers and coal miners. A strike of railway operatives would be most serious.
>
> The present ration for civilians amounts to about 1600 calories as compared with some 4500 for military personnel. It is obvious that this cannot be sufficient for labour doing hard physical work.
>
> I feel that the seriousness of the position may not be fully realized and would be grateful if you would personally intervene. . . .[1]

Eisenhower marked against the signal 'I agree'—and passed it to General Grasset, Chief Staff Officer for civil affairs, marked 'Personal—Action'.[2] Grasset did nothing, claiming that Belgian warehouses were full of rations which would ensure minimum calories per person. Two days later Monty was complaining:

> The plain facts are that we do not supply enough food and that what food we do supply is badly distributed by the Belgians. . . .
>
> In general it can be said that we want to give the Belgians less calories and more food,

Monty stated[3]—a quip that made the signal famous in 21st Army Group circles, as Brigadier Williams, Chief of Intelligence, later recalled:

> Grasset was the chap at Ike's headquarters who was sort of in charge of enemy territories and he—Monty felt the Belgians weren't getting enough to eat, and he sent a signal back to Ike. Grasset answered the signal by sending a signal saying how many calories they were getting a day, the Belgians, by their calculations at SHAEF.
>
> And Monty signalled back saying: I don't want calories, I want food!
>
> It's true—the famous signal about Calories and Food—you'll find it among the signals, I'll bet you.

[1] Signal (ref. 83 C-in-C) of 1530 hrs, 3.2.45, in 'Montgomery's Correspondence File', Eisenhower Papers, 1652 series, Eisenhower Library, Abilene, Kansas.

[2] Ibid.

[3] Ibid.

> It was very typical I think. You can just see him doing it—exasperating, but refusing to be driven off the vital point.[1]

If this was tyranny, there were many hundreds of thousands of Belgian workers whose welfare was at stake. Bedell Smith was finally sent to Brussels—and a week later Eisenhower was having to cable urgently to the Combined Chiefs of Staff for more provisions, as Monty had predicted.[2] To the Secretary of State for War, Sir James Grigg, Monty explained:

> I have had some anxious moments recently on the civil affairs side, and I took the matter up with Eisenhower and with SHAEF.[3]

With miners on strike and further sections of the working population threatening to join them Monty considered that

> the reason in all cases is: not enough to eat, no clothes to wear, and general discontent with our lack of provision for those we ask to do hard work.
>
> The plain truth is that Eisenhower is running round the front trying to run the battle and show that he is a great general, and he is neglecting his higher functions; he cannot do both jobs. Grasset is a charming person; I have known him for many years and he is an expert at free-wheeling down hill, and skating over thin ice, and avoiding all unpleasant problems; he is in fact quite useless, and is all bluff and eye-wash.[4]

Though he had 'shelled' SHAEF and ensured the shipping of almost 20,000 tons of grain, meat and egg powder, as well as 120,000 tons extra to create a reserve for Belgium and Holland, Monty was anxious that this should not become a foretaste of what was to follow on the cessation of hostilities.

> Appointments are now being made to the civil side of the set-up for Germany. . . . We must have good men and not second-raters. . . .

[1] Brigadier Sir Edgar Williams, interview of 20.12.79.

[2] 'I am very much concerned about the food situation in Belgium and Liberated Holland. . . . Unless this program is carried out as scheduled the civil population will gradually receive less and less food, and the result will be increasing unrest, civil disturbances, and disorders in the rear areas of 21st Army Group': cable S79113 of 14.2.45, in *The Papers of Dwight David Eisenhower*, ed. Alfred D. Chandler, *The War Years* Vol. III, Baltimore 1970.

[3] Letter of 11.2.45 (21 A Gp/1064/5/C-in-C), Montgomery Papers.

[4] Ibid.

On our own military side we have for some time used Civil Affairs as a dumping place for our duds: e.g.

Lt-Gen. Grasset.
Maj-Gen. West.
Brigadier Russell.

Morgan at SHAEF is also mixed up in it and he is, as you know, useless.

I think the time is approaching when we want to abandon this practice, and put into civil affairs officers who will face squarely up to practical facts and will not try and by-pass difficulties. Unless we do this we shall have great trouble later on.[1]

It is easy to see how Monty's insistence on 'proper chaps' aroused the ire and fear of 'second-raters'—as Monty himself was aware. 'It is quite normal for me to collect any mud that is being slung about!!' he remarked the following week to Grigg[2]—and, with the end of the war now in sight and with it the demise of SHAEF, Monty felt that SHAEF's incompetence would not matter as long as the British ensured that in their own zone of occupation in Germany a tough team of no-nonsense men ran the Civil Affairs side—headed by a 'first-class soldier. . . . The man I would like is Gerald TEMPLER.'[3] Templer had served under Monty in Home Forces in 1941/42 and had commanded with distinction a division in Italy. Under him, Monty was certain, there would be no duds.

Such no-nonsense generalship was applauded by those who had lived through the catastrophes from 1940 to 1942 and saw in Monty the new military messiah, the only Allied general to have the true measure of his German opponents, a soldier of awe-inspiring professionalism. To those who had not witnessed the nadir of British military performance in the years after Dunkirk, however, Monty's tyrannical bossiness was anathema—an ebullience of vanity and unyielding self-importance that daily inched towards megalomania. As Bradley's ADC noted, 'There is little doubt that occupying some diplomatic position in the British Government as he [Monty] does, that SHAEF has been compelled to relinquish an element of its control over 21 Army Group and cannot make freedom of movement it would deny any other commander on the Western Front.'[4] However ungrammatically expressed, there was no doubt that Major Hansen represented the views of many members of both Eisenhower's and Bradley's staffs, for whom Monty was manifestly too big for his

[1] Ibid.
[2] Letter of 20.2.45 (unnumbered), Montgomery Papers.
[3] Ibid.
[4] Diary of Chester B. Hansen, entry of Sunday 4.2.45, loc. cit.

boots—a response yet further aggravated by Monty's manner, his air of tension and his schoolboy sense of humour, delighting in caricature and in making people uncomfortable so that they should stand up for themselves. As long as Bradley, erstwhile Corps Commander, was serving under Monty's tutelage in Normandy, this manner had been accepted and forgiven in view of the amazing patience and leadership Monty displayed in the conduct of the campaign. But with Bradley now on a parallel footing with Monty, yet with the disaster in the Ardennes written like Calais across his heart, Bradley's entourage magnified and misunderstood every quirk of Monty's strange and discomfiting manner:

'Montgomery arrived shortly before eleven,' Hansen recorded on 5 February at 12th US Army Group's new Namur headquarters,[1]

> in a squared Rolls Royce driven by a British ensign. He was this time dressed in a battle jacket and made his customary slow, dramatic, deliberate, hawklike entrance. He commented casually on the grandeur of our provincial [governor's] offices and when ushered into General Bradley's office made much ado about the spaciousness of it. . . . Again at luncheon the same coolness was evident in the officers' treatment of Montgomery. His ego, however, remained impervious to it and he joked, talked and gesticulated. He prevailed constantly and talked too loudly throughout the meal.[2]

Monty was in fact being Monty—not realizing that Bradley had protested at having to move his headquarters north to Namur at all, and that Bradley's staff would be bound to be bitter at Eisenhower's decision to halt 12th US Army Group's offensive in the Ardennes. Churchill's 'wigging' had evidently done no good in this respect—for having, to his own surprise, won the argument over current Allied strategy, Monty's spirits were high. The conference had been convened to check up on Operations 'Veritable' and 'Grenade', but, filled with optimism at the likely outcome of the battle ('VERITABLE will be a really powerful operation supported by the fire of some 1800 guns and a great weight of air power and it should go well though possibly slowly because of the mud,' he had cabled to Brooke the night before[3]), Monty was intent on looking beyond the imminent battle to the next, perhaps decisive part of the campaign:

> EISENHOWER wanted my views on the problem of whether it

[1] Ibid.
[2] Ibid.
[3] M463 of 2200 hrs, 4.2.45, Montgomery Papers.

> was necessary to close up to the Rhine throughout its whole length before crossing it in strength in the north.

To Bradley's chagrin, Monty obliged:

> We must cross the RHINE in the north and isolate the RUHR from GERMANY as soon as we can. To do this we want to possess all territory west of the RHINE from about BONN northwards. Then we should go over the RHINE north of the RUHR and hold defensively everywhere else. All available resources must be put into this plan to capture the RUHR and we must have reserves of fresh divisions so that we can keep up the tempo of the operations at a high level.
>
> Initially the movement east of the RHINE would be limited to the requirements of capturing or isolating the RUHR . . .
>
> My views were opposed by BRADLEY who wanted to close up to the RHINE from BONN to SWITZERLAND at the same time as crossing it in the north. I said that we had not got the resources in divisions and ammunition to do both jobs at the same time. The really vital thing was to get over the RHINE in the north and to capture the RUHR and that all resources must be allotted to this object. If we attempted both tasks at the same time we would possibly be too weak to succeed in either. In the past we have never been strong enough anywhere to achieve decisive results because we had attempted too many things at the same time. This time we must concentrate on the vital job and do one thing at a time.[1]

It had been Eisenhower's fate to differ with Monty in regard to concentration and dispersal of effort since the spring of 1943—first over 'Husky', then over Salerno, then over 'Overlord'/'Anvil', then over exploitation of the great victory in Normandy, and only days before over continuation of operations after excision of the German salient of the Ardennes. This time, however, the situation was different, for by cross-examining Bedell Smith so ruthlessly at Malta, Field-Marshal Brooke had extracted from Eisenhower a formal amendment to his plan. 'You may assure the Combined Chiefs of Staff,' Eisenhower had cabled to Bedell Smith, 'that I will seize the Rhine crossings in the North immediately this is a feasible operation and without waiting to close the Rhine throughout its length.'[2] This had been placed on record in the Minutes of the Malta conference—and when the DMO heard that Eisenhower had raised the issue again at Namur, only a few days later, he was astonished. 'It is therefore a

[1] Signal to CIGS, M552 of 2245 hrs, 5.2.45, Montgomery Papers.
[2] Cable S77211 of 31.1.45, in *The Papers of Dwight David Eisenhower*, op. cit.

bit surprising to find Ike raising again, at a conference on 5 Feb, the question of whether it is necessary to close up to the Rhine throughout its whole length before crossing it in strength in the North,' Maj-General Simpson answered Monty's cabled report of the Namur conference.[1]

Eisenhower had stayed the night of 4/5 February with Bradley at Namur, and had undoubtedly been 'got at' by Bradley—who was still obsessed by the German ability to launch another offensive such as the Ardennes unless the Rhine was secured in its entire length—'all along the line'.[2] But it is doubtful if Eisenhower this time agreed with Bradley; more likely he left the matter in abeyance until the conference itself the following day, counting on Monty to present the case for immediate exploitation across the Rhine in the north with his customary clarity. Eisenhower could then in all justice act as chairman and make an 'impartial' decision that would avoid a personal confrontation with Bradley.

Whatever the truth, Eisenhower certainly adopted Monty's plan, as Monty signalled to the War Office that night with satisfaction:

> EISENHOWER accepted my conception of the problem . . . and gave orders that we would work to that general plan,

even agreeing to give Monty two American and one British airborne division from First Allied Airborne Army for the crossing of the Rhine.

> Altogether I am quite pleased with today's conference. It was quite clear that EISENHOWER was frightened of any scheme to advance east of the RHINE and deep into GERMANY while the Germans held a big bridgehead to the west of the RHINE in the south. But he was prepared to make a limited advance in the north, to secure the RUHR without first clearing the Germans from the west of the RHINE in the south and he accepted my proposals readily and agreed with my arguments.[3]

Given the American view that Monty had been over-cautious in

[1] Letter of 6.2.45 (DMO/125/M), Montgomery Papers.

[2] 'General Bradley has cautioned against any attempt to cross the Rhine until the entire effort in the Central and Southern Group of Armies is closed to the west bank of that river': Diary of Chester B. Hansen, entry of 3 [should be 4].2.45. 'My contention was that if you were going to advance into Germany on a narrow front i.e. just north of the Ruhr that you must have advanced to the Rhine all along the line so that you would have a strong defensive line which could be held with minimum troops without much danger of a major German attack. . . .': Bradley ms., Bradley Papers, MHI, Carlisle, Pennsylvania.

[3] M552, 5.2.45, loc. cit.

mounting the Allied counter-offensive in the Ardennes, there was some irony in the two most senior American generals in Europe begging Monty not to attempt more than a limited crossing of the Rhine to secure the Ruhr without first clearing up the entire length of the river from Switzerland to Holland. Thus, anxious lest the Russian offensive peter out once it closed on the fixed German defences of the Oder, it was Eisenhower and Bradley who were now deeply cautious in contemplating a future strike across the Rhine into Germany; whereas Monty, full of confidence that his forthcoming Rhineland battle would succeed in destroying the main enemy forces protecting the Ruhr, recommended boldness. Though Eisenhower would only agree to a limited Rhine crossing to seize the Ruhr, Monty was pleased. 'Now we are all right again,' he wrote to the King's Private Secretary. 'I think Eisenhower has had a bit of a dog fight and at the NAMUR Conference on 5 Feb he sided with me against Bradley: for the first time. We shall now have to see whether he can keep the ship on a steady course; he has lost his nerve several times before, and Bradley & Co will "get at" him in my absence.'[1]

[1] Letter to Sir Alan Lascelles, 8.2.45 (RA GVI/283), Royal Archives, Windsor.

CHAPTER TWO

The Rhineland Battle—A 21st Army Group Show

BRADLEY, UNDERSTANDABLY VEXED that he should, once again, have been overruled, rose from the lunch table early to take Eisenhower on a visit to Bastogne, where they met Patton—who in turn was mortified that his relief of Bastogne in January was now utterly forgotten, and was not even mentioned. Moreover, the proposal to take away forces from his Third US Army to put under Simpson's Ninth US Army command came as a terrible blow—so terrible that by the following day Patton was determined to repeat the Nelsonian tactic of deliberately underestimating enemy strength and attempting a breakthrough at Bitburg.[1] Of Bradley Patton was, in the privacy of his diary, shamefully contemptuous, referring to his Army Group Commander as 'the tent maker'. That Patton was able to launch a two-Corps attack in his sector without his commander, Bradley, even knowing was not only an illustration of Patton's impetuosity but also of Bradley's lack of control. 'His [Bradley's] success,' Patton sneered, 'is due to his lack of backbone and subservience to those above him. I will manage without him. In fact I always have; even in Sicily he had to be carried. Personally I fight every order that I do not like, which makes me unpopular but successful.'[2]

In truth Bradley had done his best to obtain an offensive role for Patton and Hodges, his two Army Commanders. But the price of having clung so long to his hopes of a breakthrough on their two fronts in the Ardennes was that Bradley had thereby neglected his original target, before the German attack in December: the Roer dams. For if the Germans opened the dam-gates, then Simpson's 'Grenade' attack would be stymied for as long as it took the resultant floods to subside—a prospect which SHAEF's Intelligence warned against repeatedly, Maj-General Strong even producing a

[1] 'I am trying to keep the impending Bitburg offensive secret so that the powers that be will not order it to be stopped': *The Patton Papers*, ed. M. Blumenson, Boston 1982; diary entry of 5.2.45.
[2] *The Patton Papers*, op. cit.; letter of 6.2.45.

captured German map of the likely flooding effects on 17 January.[1]

Belatedly, at Spa on the evening of 5 February, Bradley went over Hodges' plans to use his reserve Corps under General Collins to help take the vital Roer dams. But Collins' attack, scheduled for 10 February (the same date as 'Grenade'), was too late; the Germans were able to release the flood gates, jamming them half-open. Eisenhower was furious—'E. always [thought] this would happen.'[2] Combined with the great thaw that had already set in, the Roer now flooded to a level which made even an assault-boat crossing impossible.

Monty, far from showing disappointment or irritation at Bradley's belated and now failed attempt to seize the dams, was surprisingly unmoved. His 'rest' in England had restored his spirits and nothing could dampen his ardour as his great Rhineland battle began. The June storms in 1944 had altered the whole timing of his Normandy battle, forcing Bradley to delay the attack south on St Lô for a month and Dempsey thus to combat the main weight of Rommel's armour for that entire period; but such alterations had not radically undermined Monty's tactical strategy for the battle—rather, they had enabled him to inflict a more decisive defeat on the German armies than even Monty's impatient superiors had ever dreamed possible.

At Namur, however, in conversations with visiting dignitaries and journalists, Bradley's courtiers now began to broadcast the myth that the Normandy campaign had only been rescued from British stalemate by bold American opportunism;[3] in relation to the Ardennes, they now claimed that Bradley had foreseen the German intentions and given all the necessary corrective, verbal orders to forestall the German drive to the Meuse:

> At dinner he [Bradley] conversed freely. In recalling the staff organization during the Ardennes attack the General remembered that not a written order had been planned for the movement of troops. He stated that everything depended upon the essential movement of men and material to the Third and First Armies and

[1] 'Meeting in Chiefs of Staffs' Office', 17.1.45, Robb Papers (AC71/9/26), RAF Museum, Hendon.

[2] Diary of Mrs K. Summersby, entry of 10.2.45, loc. cit.

[3] The true story of Monty's patient tactical strategy in Normandy is told in Part Six, *Monty: Master of the Battlefield 1942–1944*, op. cit.; the full records of 21st Army Group planning, from 16 June 1944, for an American armoured break-out eastwards to Paris (Operation 'Lucky Strike') are to be found in 21st Army Group War Diaries (Chief of Staff's files, WO 205/8, and Operation 'Lucky Strike' file, 21 A Gp/20651/55/G (Plans) dated 16 June 1944, and subsequent refinements, (WO 205/668), PRO.

> they were tremendous. Bradley's decision to engage the forces immediately is probably his biggest and quickest of the war. Within five minutes after he ascertained the extent of the German drive, he had ordered armored divisions in the south to reinforce the Luxembourg front. It was this quick decision that permitted us to save the Duchy and at the same time provide the 101st with armored strength and permit them to hold Bastogne. General Bradley admits the decision was the quickest he had ever made—and incidentally one of the most crucial.[1]

By this time—6 February 1945—Bradley's original slowness to assess the strength of the German attack in the Ardennes had been expunged from memory; more and more the accent would be on opportunistic exploitation of circumstances rather than the hard, unromantic aspect of war: the business of planning, of detailed preparation and relentless will in execution of battle tactics against a professional German foe. This was sad, since it had been Bradley's quiet professionalism in command of 2 US Corps in Tunisia, in Sicily, and as Army Commander and Army Group Commander in Normandy that was his real talent—a soldier's soldier, intelligent, shy and undemonstrative. That he allowed his staff to concoct press statements and disseminate a misleading version of American tactics was unfortunate, since it did an injustice to his own profound professionalism as well as Monty's. Ingersoll even attempted, in the aftermath of the Ardennes, to 'plant' a rumour that Bradley had enticed the Germans to attack in the Ardennes in order deliberately to draw off German reserves from the eastern front prior to the Russian offensive![2] With such deliberate misrepresentation it is small wonder that American historiography has become so divorced from the reality of the campaign on the Western Front, and has been so unwilling to give Monty credit for his ruthless adherence to basic principles of modern warfare in fighting the Wehrmacht. As Bradley later remarked, the Rhineland battle 'was a 21 Army Group show'[3] and as such Bradley deemed it to be British—or, as General Hodges' ADC noted in his diary, a threat to the credit which would otherwise go to First US Army.[4]

[1] Diary of Chester B. Hansen, entry of 6.2.45, loc. cit.

[2] 'Ralph Ingersoll suggested that a rumour be planted to the effect that our ensnaring of German defences in the Battle of the Bulge, where they could not be released for commitment [sic] elsewhere, had enabled the Russians to attack with far greater numbers and more success than would otherwise have been possible': Diary of Chester B. Hansen, entry of 15.1.45, loc. cit.

[3] Bradley ms., loc. cit.

[4] 'The biggest and most unsatisfactory news of the day is that there will probably be

Given such inter-Allied rivalry and competition[1] it is scarcely suprising that hostility and resentment greeted Monty's '21 Army Group' show—and has characterized so much historical writing ever since. But for Monty himself and the troops of his British, Canadian and American armies, the Rhineland battle was, in its way, comparable to D-Day and the battle of Normandy. Once again a Canadian, a British and an American Army were in combat together, fighting a decisive battle whose outcome would determine the remaining duration of World War II. As Monty bet Bradley's Chief of Intelligence on 5 February, the war against Germany would either be over by 1 May or would go on until November; Bradley opted for a single conclusion in September.[2]

The early spring thaw, followed by the flooding of the Roer dams, did nothing to dampen Monty's spirits. As before D-Day, Monty was determined to visit as many of his commanders and men as possible before they went into battle and was well aware of the conditions in which they would have to fight. 'I visited the VERITABLE area today. The ground is very wet and roads and tracks are breaking up and these factors are likely to make progress somewhat slow after the operation is launched,' he warned the CIGS on 6 February, two days before 'Veritable' began.[3] 'I am visiting the GRENADE area tomorrow.' Simpson's 'Grenade' area was no better. 'The Roer River is very flooded,' Monty reported to the CIGS on 7 February. 'I met and talked to all the Corps and Divisional Commanders. All ten American Divisions are now assembled in 9th Army area and they are all in good shape and ready for battle. I have ordered that GRENADE will be launched on 10th Feb.'[4]

By the evening of 8 February Monty was immensely proud of the Canadian Army's achievement in launching 'Veritable' at all:

Operation VERITABLE was launched this morning according to

---

a general regrouping and shifting of forces in order that the British together with Ninth Army . . . may put on its long planned and long wanted "big show" across the ROER in the DUREN area. This news . . . is a blow to the General and to his key staff officers. . . . However it may still be possible for the XVIII Corps . . . to smash through the Siegfried Line and press onward, which will certainly take a good bit of ginger out of any credit which might go to the British or the Ninth Army': Diary of William C. Sylvan, MHI, Carlisle, Pennsylvania.

[1] When faced by the barrage of Press reports after Monty's talk of 7.1.45, Eisenhower was heard to say: 'For two and a half years I have been trying to get the press to talk of "ALLIED" operations, but look what has happened': 'Meeting in Supreme Commander's Office', 9.1.45, Robb Papers, loc. cit.

[2] Diary of Chester B. Hansen, entry of 7.2.45, loc. cit.

[3] M465 of 2200 hrs, 6.2.45, Montgomery Papers.

[4] M553 of 2245 hrs, 7.2.45, Montgomery Papers.

plan. The movement problem involved in getting formations and units in position for this very large scale attack has been a remarkable achievement in view of the very bad state of all the roads. Five infantry divs attacked at 1030 hrs under very heavy artillery support, the divs from south to north being 51 53 15 2 Cdn and 3 Cdn. Today's operations have been 98% successful. . . . We have captured today about 1000 prisoners. Our casualties have been light in all divisions engaged.[1]

To the Reynolds Monty wrote what was to be his last letter for a month, ending, 'I am beginning to be very busy here!!'[2] The days of Allied vacillation and indecision were over; the battle had begun. When Air-Marshal Tedder, the Deputy Supreme Commander, had visited Monty the day before, Monty had been very rude to him, as he admitted in a letter to the DMO:

Tedder came to see me; he made me very angry by trying to pretend that *he* had always been in complete agreement with the conception of one strong thrust on the left, as against two weak ones. I told him I was very well aware that he had always been a strong advocate of the Frankfurt thrust, and had sided with IKE against me several times, and that I had had to play a lone hand since September. Our meeting was not very cordial and I doubt if he will visit me again!!. . . .

VERITABLE is going very well.[3]

Monty was once again in his element. As in the Ardennes, he sent a detailed report of operations each evening, announcing that he was postponing 'Grenade' for twenty-four hours owing to the high level of the river on 9 February,[4] and once again on 10 February when news came through of the opening of the Roer dams:

The whole area north of this road [to Cleve] is under water and operations in it have to be conducted by means of ducks and buffaloes.[5] . . . There are a good many paratroops in the eastern part of the REICHSWALD forest. . . . The present plan is to continue to fight hard to secure CLEVE and GOCH and to clear the whole REICHSWALD forest and I think it will then be necessary to pause for a couple of days to get good communications through to these places after which we can crack off again.

[1] M470 of 2230 hrs, 8.2.45, Montgomery Papers.
[2] Letter to Phyllis Reynolds, 8.2.45, Montgomery Papers.
[3] Letter of 8.2.45 (unnumbered), Montgomery Papers.
[4] M471 of 2245 hrs, 9.2.45, Montgomery Papers.
[5] In other words, amphibious wheeled and tracked trucks.

> I had to postpone GRENADE for a further three days as the Germans have blown the dams and the ROER river is quite impassable. The earliest date for GRENADE is now 14 Feb and may well be 15 Feb.
>
> The enforced postponement of GRENADE is bound to have repercussions on VERITABLE but the more troops that VERITABLE draws up north the easier will go GRENADE.[1]

The parallel with Normandy was indeed remarkable; and the patience with which Monty had accepted both natural and local military setbacks in Normandy while waiting for First US Army to deliver its southern attack was now mirrored in the Rhineland, as Monty watched the German reaction to 'Veritable', and the necessary postponement of Ninth US Army's 'Grenade' attack. 'My dear Simbo,' Monty wrote on 11 February. 'I have had to postpone GRENADE for 3 days. The Germans monkeyed about with the dams and the water level in the ROER is now very high and the current is flowing over 7 miles an hour. Not even patrol boats can get over at present. The target date is now 14 Feb but it may well be 15 Feb. Meanwhile VERITABLE is going well. If only we had dry weather and hard ground we would sweep everything before us; as it is, the troops are operating in the most appalling conditions of mud and slush.'[2]

If 'Veritable' was to bring the enemy to all-out battle and to hold him day after day while 'Grenade' was postponed, Monty felt he must have further troops to keep 'Veritable' going—as he had for the British eastern flank at Caen. 'The postponement of GRENADE may be for longer than we think and this makes it very necessary for VERITABLE to be given all the strength that can be collected,' he explained in his nightly signal to Brooke.[3] The following day his fears were confirmed. Some 5000 prisoners had now been taken and the Reichswald Forest was in British hands, for a total of 1100 casualties; but during the day Monty had 'visited all the American divisions on the ROER front today in Ninth Army and examined the problem in that area. The conditions in the river valley are appalling and GRENADE is quite impossible for the present and it may well be one week or more before we can launch it. Meanwhile VERITABLE must carry on alone and it is therefore bound to go slowly unless it can be strengthened and this I propose to do . . . I shall in fact put all the strength I can into VERITABLE and will go on driving hard

[1] M473 of 2250 hrs, 10.2.45, Montgomery Papers.
[2] Letter of 11.2.45 (unnumbered), Montgomery Papers.
[3] M474 of 2240 hrs, 11.2.45, Montgomery Papers.

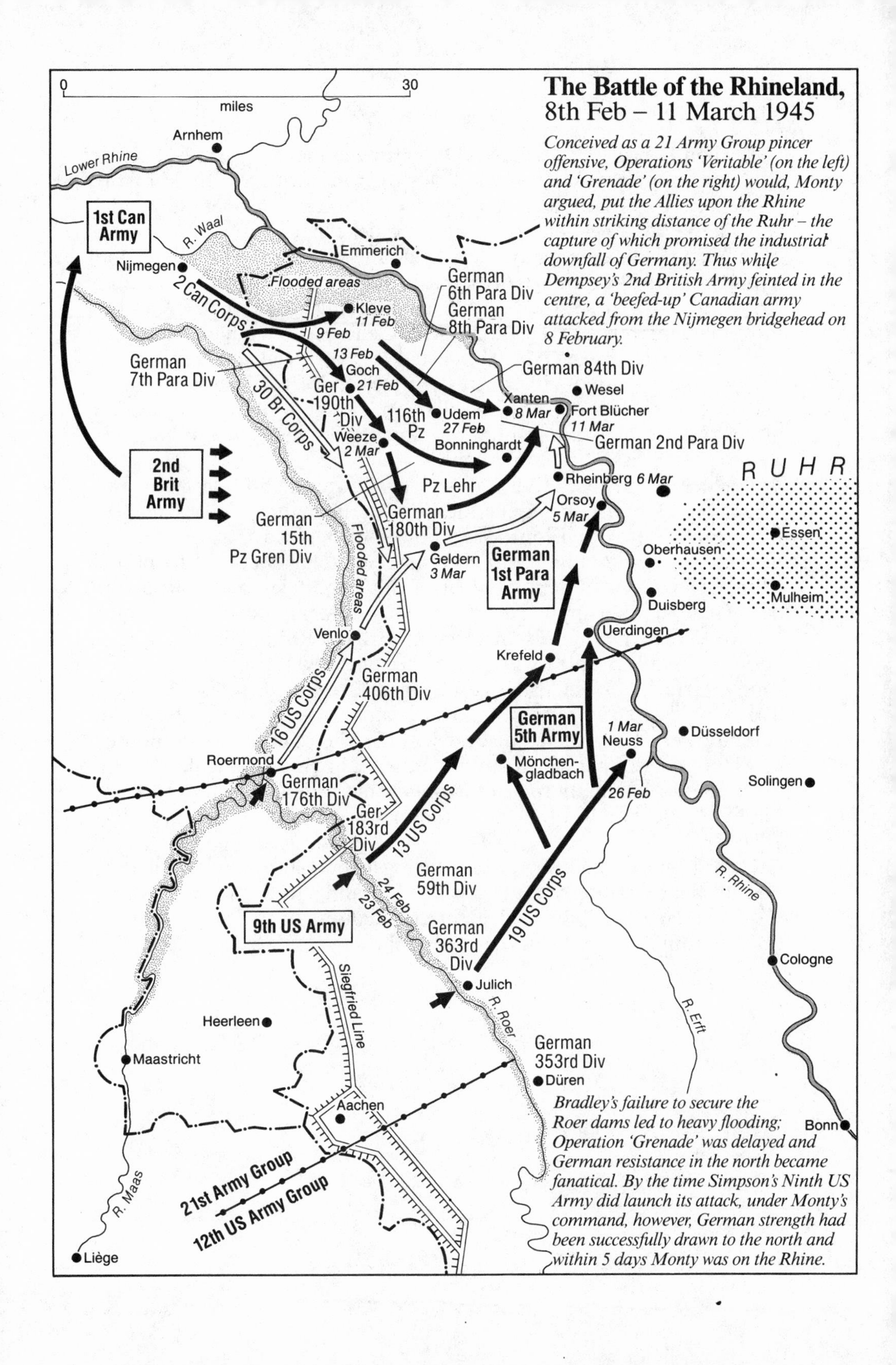
The Battle of the Rhineland,
8th Feb – 11 March 1945
Conceived as a 21 Army Group pincer offensive, Operations 'Veritable' (on the left) and 'Grenade' (on the right) would, Monty argued, put the Allies upon the Rhine within striking distance of the Ruhr – the capture of which promised the industrial downfall of Germany. Thus while Dempsey's 2nd British Army feinted in the centre, a 'beefed-up' Canadian army attacked from the Nijmegen bridgehead on 8 February.
Bradley's failure to secure the Roer dams led to heavy flooding; Operation 'Grenade' was delayed and German resistance in the north became fanatical. By the time Simpson's Ninth US Army did launch its attack, under Monty's command, however, German strength had been successfully drawn to the north and within 5 days Monty was on the Rhine.
0
30
miles
Arnhem
Lower Rhine
R. Waal
1st Can Army
Nijmegen
Emmerich
Flooded areas
2 Can Corps
Kleve
11 Feb
9 Feb
German 6th Para Div
German 8th Para Div
13 Feb
Goch
21 Feb
German 7th Para Div
German 84th Div
Wesel
Ger 190th Div
116th Pz
Udem
27 Feb
Xanten
8 Mar
Fort Blücher
11 Mar
30 Br Corps
Weeze
2 Mar
Bonninghardt
German 2nd Para Div
2nd Brit Army
RUHR
Rheinberg 6 Mar
Pz Lehr
Orsoy
5 Mar
German 15th Pz Gren Div
German 180th Div
Flooded areas
Geldern
3 Mar
German 1st Para Army
Essen
Oberhausen
Duisberg
Mulheim
Venlo
Uerdingen
Krefeld
German 406th Div
16 US Corps
German 5th Army
1 Mar
Neuss
Düsseldorf
Roermond
German 176th Div
Mönchen-gladbach
Solingen
26 Feb
Ger 183rd Div
13 US Corps
German 59th Div
24 Feb
23 Feb
R. Rhine
9th US Army
German 363rd Div
19 US Corps
Cologne
Julich
Siegfried Line
R. Roer
R. Erft
Heerleen
Maastricht
German 353rd Div
Düren
Aachen
Bonn
21st Army Group
12th US Army Group
R. Maas
Liège

to the south east until GRENADE can be launched.'[1] He was satisfied that the 'Veritable' 'operation is drawing up north most of the immediately available German reserves'—and when once 'Grenade' was finally launched 'should produce quicker results'.[2]

In Normandy such delays had gradually given rise to intrigue and a plot in rear headquarters to have Monty sacked; but this time SHAEF was well satisfied with the unfolding of the battle. At the morning conference at Versailles, Maj-General Strong had calculated that in four days some 22,000 casualties had been inflicted on the enemy, and declared—in contrast to his advice to Eisenhower ever since the previous November—that the 'Ruhr is the best place to attack'.[3] 'The question is how to launch "Grenade". Definitely not before the 18th and possibly later.'[4]

The consensus at SHAEF was now shifting behind Monty—and when, on 13 February, General Whiteley brought Monty's request for a further two divisions, Eisenhower recognized that once again he was in for a gunfight with Bradley. Whiteley was told to phone Monty. To Monty's deputy Chief of Staff Whiteley pointed out the repercussions: 'tells him that Monty must understand that if we give him the 2 divs, it will strip the present drive to Prum, which has been very successful. Bradley will be sore because it will probably stop the present attacks on the 3rd Army fronts. E. decides to visit Bradley. Takes off at 3.30 from field, accompanied by Whitely and John [Eisenhower]. E. wants to discuss with Bradley the following points. . . . The current operations and the attack North of the Ruhr. Before E. left he told Whitely to send Monty a message telling him to be at Namur [Bradley's headquarters] tomorrow evening at 11 for conference.'[5]

Operation 'Veritable' was producing over 1000 prisoners a day, despite the appalling weather. It was building to a crescendo—and 'Grenade' would, like 'Cobra' in Normandy, provide the *coup de grâce*, Monty was convinced—if Eisenhower would reinforce him.

[1] M475 of 2330 hrs, 12.2.45, Montgomery Papers.
[2] Ibid.
[3] Diary of Mrs K. Summersby, entry of 12.2.45, loc. cit.
[4] Ibid.
[5] Entry of 13.2.45. Ibid.

CHAPTER THREE

The Plot to Bring in Alexander

MONTY, WITH HIS troops fighting against fanatical resistance east of the Reichswald Forest, had arranged to visit his forward commanders on 14 February; rather than waste a day motoring to Bradley's headquarters at Namur, he therefore asked if Eisenhower could meet him halfway at his old Zonhoven command post. Not only did the appalling weather preclude flying, but the air above the Dutch–Belgian border was by no means safe—as two of Monty's Liaison Officers had found when flying up to Nijmegen on 9 February. Their experience had resulted in an extraordinary survival story:

> On the 9th Feb an Auster was carrying Dick Harden and Carol Mather up to the forward area and was attacked by a FW 190[1] over GRAVE. McQueen, the pilot, was killed at once. Carol received 4 bullets—arm, bottom, leg and kidney.
>
> Dick was sitting next to McQueen and he seized 'the stick' and managed in some amazing way to land the machine by crashing it into a field: where it came to rest in a ditch with very little damage. Dick cut his head open on landing and has 5 stitches in the forehead; he is a bit shaken.
>
> Carol has had an operation and one kidney has been removed. His left forearm is badly shattered and there is a possibility that some of the nerve has been shot away; if this proves to be so then he might not have the full use of his left arm. In any case he will be over 2 months in hospital, and then a long period of convalescence will follow,

Monty recounted to the DMO, 'Simbo' Simpson, on 11 February.[2] 'P.S. I have written full details to Mrs Mather.'

This was the human, compassionate side to Monty which few Americans were willing to see. Bradley's ADC was detailed to guide the Supreme Commander and General Bradley from Namur to Zonhoven after breakfast on 14 February. Convinced from rumours in the Operations Room at 12th US Army Group that Monty was

[1] The FW 190 was superior to the Spitfire—smaller, lighter, more manoeuvrable and yet with heavier armament.

[2] Letter, Simpson Papers, Imperial War Museum.

again angling to take ground command of *all* Allied troops from Eisenhower, Major Hansen was deeply suspicious of the British Field-Marshal:

> Yesterday afternoon Whitely [sic] called the Field Marshal to ask him to attend the meeting here but Montgomery offered regrets with the explanation that he had already made plans for a visit to his army on the north that day. The meeting was, therefore, arranged between the two at the former CP 21 Army Group near Schoonhoven [sic]. . . .
>
> It is evident that Field Marshal Montgomery has insisted from the outset that a senior field commander be named for the Western Front to establish headquarters between the Group and Shaef and conduct the technical coordination necessary on the front. . . .
>
> Montgomery had already arrived at the CP by the time we got there and he greeted General Eisenhower in his customary uniform, corduroys, turtle neck sweater, black-grey, reserving a thin smile for the rest of our entourage. . . .
>
> Our meeting was ended within the hour after some slight table thumping and General Eisenhower returned immediately to our headquarters for luncheon with General Bradley.[1]

The 'slight table thumping' concerned the two American infantry divisions Monty was demanding—and which Bradley was equally loth to surrender. 'I fear however that there is no love lost between Bradley and Monty,' Mrs Summersby recorded that evening on Eisenhower's return to Versailles. 'How E. keeps his disposition I really am at a loss to understand.'[2]

More and more since the Ardennes Eisenhower had had to become the broker between Monty and Bradley. Though ordered to move his headquarters from Luxembourg to Namur to be nearer Montgomery, Bradley later prided himself on the fact that he saw Monty but three times while there:

> Montgomery wanted me closer so I was moved, opening at Namur on Jan. 28th. I was in Namur about two months and during that time I think I saw Montgomery about three times. There was really no occasion for us to get together very often. We had our directives and the boundary between us. There was practically no coordinating for us to do along the boundaries under the tactical situations. That was done by adjoining divisions and Corps.[3]

[1] Diary of Chester B. Hansen, entry of 14.2.45, loc. cit.

[2] Diary of Mrs K. Summersby, entry of 14.2.45, loc. cit.

[3] Bradley ms., loc. cit.

If Eisenhower found such brokerage exhausting, there was a silver lining which even Major Hansen saw reflected in Eisenhower's 'exhuberant' mood on the way back. For Eisenhower had, in return for giving Monty all he wanted—American reinforcements for 'Veritable', an agreed plan for subsequent crossing of the Rhine between Rheinberg and Rees and at Arnhem, and command of 'Ninth US Army of twelve divisions for the rest of the war'[1]—obtained Monty's *imprimatur* for the continuation of the current command set-up. In his letter to the VCIGS that evening, Monty affected not to know what was at issue here: 'There is no doubt that he was worried about something when he arrived at ZONHOVEN, and appeared so during our talk. . . . I have even now no idea at what is at the bottom of his worry. But it was very obvious that as soon as I had said I was very well satisfied with the present situation about command, he became a different man; he drove away beaming all over his face.'[2]

Monty knew exactly what was in Eisenhower's mind: the latest proposal by the Prime Minister that Field-Marshal Alexander be brought into SHAEF as Deputy Supreme Commander instead of Tedder. Knowing that Brooke was also in favour of transferring Alex—both Brooke and Churchill had mooted the idea during their visit to Monty on 5 January at Hasselt—Monty had decided to play dumb.

In January Monty had—according to Brooke's diary[3]—expressed agreement with the proposal to bring Alex over to the Western Front. Now, as the battle for the Rhineland gathered pace and Eisenhower was at last backing Monty's proposals for crossing the Rhine in the north in contrast to Bradley's preference for closing the Rhine 'all along the line', Monty thought better of the Alexander idea. If Eisenhower would commit himself so-to-speak to a 'Monty-charter' for the prosecution of the campaign, Monty would in return back him as Supreme Commander/Ground Forces C-in-C without Alexander being called in. 'I gave him my views as follows,' Monty informed the VCIGS:

> a) I understood that he [Eisenhower] himself wished to handle the land operations and to command the three Army groups; he did not want a land force commander between him and the Army Groups.

[1] Letter to VCIGS, M556, 14.2.45, Montgomery Papers.
[2] Ibid.
[3] A. Bryant, *Triumph in the West*, London 1959; entry of 5.1.45.

b) He had now divided his theatre into 'fronts' which had a definite relation to strategical and geographical objectives; and he had allotted resources to each 'front' in accordance with the task.
c) My 'front' was to make the main effort. In order that one commander should command all the forces engaged in the main effort, he had placed an American Army of twelve divisions under my command. I also had an American Airborne Corps of two US Airborne divisions and one British airborne division.
d) Having in view (a) above, I therefore considered that the command set-up was now very satisfactory.
e) I then said that having arrived at the present command situation I hoped it would remain unchanged till the business was over.
Re-grouping might be necessary from time to time; resources would then be allotted to 'fronts' in accordance with their tasks. The great point was for one commander always to be responsible for all the forces engaged in the main effort; we should not depart from this principle.[1]

Monty was delighted with this charter. It guaranteed the primacy of Monty's northern front, it ensured adherence to the principle of unified command of all forces engaged in the major Allied battle, and it confirmed the concept of strategic tasks for each front rather than national considerations—'keeping Bradley employed'. Moreover it dealt a body-blow to Churchill's 'intrigue to get Field-Marshal Alexander appointed Deputy Supreme Commander to General Eisenhower', as Monty titled his account of the story in his diary.[2] For the more he thought about Alexander as his Allied Ground Force Commander, the more Monty gave way to a contempt for Alexander's inflated reputation as a soldier in the eyes of the Prime Minister:

> As a Commander-in-Chief in the field, the C.I.G.S. considered that Field-Marshal Alexander was not a success, and with this opinion most of the senior officers in the British Army agreed,

Monty's diarist claimed.

> This opinion was also shared by General Eisenhower and General Bedell Smith, but was not shared by the Prime Minister, who still considered him a highly successful commander. In the Middle East

[1] Letter to VCIGS, M556, loc. cit.
[2] 'Notes on the Campaign in North-Western Europe', Montgomery Papers.

> Field-Marshal Alexander had invariably left the conduct of operations to General Montgomery. Whenever he had attempted to mount an operation, it had failed. He had accepted the 'Husky' plan for the invasion of SICILY, which later had to be scrapped; and he had planned the SALERNO landing and the first CASSINO battle, both of which had failed. While he could not himself plan a large-scale operation, Field-Marshal Alexander was much liked by the Americans, with whom his personal charm and his tact were most valuable.
>
> For the above reasons the CIGS was keen to remove Field-Marshal Alexander from the Mediterranean theatre, where he filled a position which the C.I.G.S. considered was above the ceiling of his military capabilities. Therefore when the C.I.G.S. became convinced of the need for a new Deputy Supreme Commander, he suggested to the Prime Minister that Field-Marshal Alexander should be appointed.
>
> The Prime Minister also wished to move Field-Marshal Alexander from the Mediterranean theatre, because, with the transfer of a large number of troops from that theatre, he did not consider that there was any longer sufficient scope for Field-Marshal Alexander's military talents. He therefore agreed to the C.I.G.S.'s suggestion and he and the C.I.G.S. both set to work to secure the agreement of all concerned to this change.[1]

This was no less than the truth—for at Malta Churchill had raised the issue with President Roosevelt and obtained the latter's agreement. Marshall was furious, having just insisted, in his meeting with Eisenhower in Marseilles, that under no circumstances would the American Chiefs of Staff permit a British Ground Force Commander to be inserted between Eisenhower and Bradley—indeed Marshall would rather resign than permit this.[2] It was therefore agreed that the appointment would be postponed until after the Rhineland battle in approximately six weeks' time when the 'Ardennes operation' would have been 'more forgotten',[3] and Alexander was so informed.[4]

Monty's new declaration of satisfaction with the existing command set-up was the very ammunition Eisenhower needed if he was to

[1] Ibid.
[2] 'General Marshall will not agree to any proposal to set up a Ground Commander-in-Chief in this theatre. If this is done he will not remain as Chief of Staff': 'Notes on Conference with General G. C. Marshall', 28.1.45, Desk Diary of C-in-C, Eisenhower Papers, loc. cit.
[3] Quoted in A. Bryant, op. cit.; entry of 2.2.45.
[4] Entry of 9.2.45. Ibid.

scotch Churchill's scheme—and two days later the Supreme Commander wrote from Versailles a letter that was to rock not only Churchill's carefully laid plans for Alexander, but insult the Prime Minister in a way that no previous action or statement had ever done before.[1]

According to Monty's diary, he was well aware of this—'Field Marshal Montgomery was told of parts of these protracted negotiations in turn by the Prime Minister, by the C.I.G.S. and by General Eisenhower. He therefore obtained a much fuller account of the progress of the negotiations than was ever realised.'[2] But if Monty took a malicious delight in foiling Churchill's plan, and poisoning Alexander's promotion at its tap-root, his satisfaction was to be short-lived. The previous 'charter' he had obtained from Eisenhower was not set down in writing—and once safely across the Rhine without Bradley's fears of German counter-attack being realized, Eisenhower was to renege upon the agreement, even on his promise to keep Ninth US Army under Monty's command for the duration of the war. Without a British deputy to protest—for Tedder proved a complete cypher in this respect—Monty's charter was thrown to the four winds—and Churchill's vain prescience proved right. For Monty the soldier it was important to win the war as swiftly, with as few casualties and as decisively as possible. For Churchill, picturing the map of post-war Europe, knowing Stalin's aims in eastern Europe and Roosevelt's unwillingness to leave American troops for more than two years after the cessation of hostilities in Europe, it was vital to have at SHAEF a British deputy to Eisenhower who would represent the British view and be at Churchill's bidding. That man, as Churchill had found over Greece, was Alexander.[3] Eisenhower's letter, 'in which he proposes to employ Alex in the back areas if he comes to him as a Deputy!'—as Brooke noted in his diary[4]—was a great shock to Churchill, who refused to accept it. Summoning Brooke, Churchill suggested another visit to Versailles to put personal pressure on the hapless Supreme Commander—as well as a trip to Monty's headquarters to 'put the Field-Marshal in his place'.

[1] Letter to Sir Alan Brooke, 16.1.45, in *The Papers of Dwight David Eisenhower*, op. cit.

[2] 'Notes on the campaign in North-Western Europe', loc. cit.

[3] General Marshall was well aware of this. 'The man [Alexander] being who he is and our experience being what it has been, you would have great difficulty in offsetting the direct influence of the P.M.,' Marshall wrote (W 90175) to Eisenhower on 11.1.45. See *The Papers of Dwight David Eisenhower*, op. cit.

[4] A. Bryant, op. cit.; entry of 20.2.45.

CHAPTER FOUR

The Knock-out Blow

THOUGH HE WAS naïve in imagining he now had Eisenhower in his pocket, and though he underestimated the vital need for a British voice at SHAEF, Monty was nevertheless remarkably clear in his own mind how best to end the war and how best to govern Germany when it was over. The current War Office proposals he found cumbersome and bureaucratic, based on a belief that everything could be run from a vast central organization in Berlin. Monty's experience of SHAEF was that such blundering, centralized bureaucracies led to starvation, strikes and even rioting. Moreover, Berlin would be in a Russian zone of occupation. Edicts would thus have largely to be made by radio signal—a hopeless way of running a defeated nation. What was required, Monty felt, was a small central headquarters in Berlin to decide overall policy in co-operation with American and Russian Allies, and the rest to be decentralized as far as possible to suit local needs. Above all, the organization must at first be on a military basis—something all Germans would, after decades of militaristic indoctrination, accept. Gradually, within this military context, the Civil Affairs officers would seek to generate a new Germany, beginning at the roots. Monty's signal to the VCIGS, General Nye, on 13 February in the midst of the Rhineland battle, is an example of his transcending simplicity and directness in tackling a problem:

> Personal for VCIGS from Field Marshal Montgomery
> In my opinion there are four basic fundamentals which must form the framework of any plan which is to succeed.
>
> First we need the maximum decentralization if we are to get a move on and get quick results.
>
> Secondly we must work in all respects through our normal military chain of command and staff increments as may be necessary.
>
> Thirdly we require a small and very efficient central organization in Berlin which will decide the Allied policy and issue Directives in broad general terms.
>
> Fourthly in the British set-up there must be only one con-

trolling authority in administrative matters both British and German.[1]

The current War Office plan for the occupation of Germany met none of these requirements:

> My brief study of the proposed plan gives me the impression that these basic fundamental points get lost sight of as the plan develops. It seems to me that we are to work up gradually to the most clumsy and cumbersome organization that could possibly be devised.
>
> I note that the British set-up in Berlin forecasts one Lieut-General and thirteen Major-Generals. Is this high ranking outfit really necessary?[2]

The difficulty was that no Commander-in-Chief had been designated for the occupation of Germany. 'I see some of the newspapers are tipping the C.I.G.S. for the job but as far as I am aware there is not the remotest foundation for this rumour,' General Nye replied, noting that no War Office 'theoretical organization drawn up in London, however good it may be, can be expected to work without close liaison with the Commander who is required to work it'—and 'no decision had been made as to who is to be the Commander-in-Chief'.[3] Until Churchill made up his mind—something which Churchill was to refuse to do until well after the war had ended—all planning for the administration and organization of the occupation of Germany was to be hindered by this failure to appoint a C-in-C in good time. It was COSSAC all over again.

The Yalta conference early in February 1945 had, moreover, produced a further complication—for the Polish Government in exile in London refused to ratify the decisions made by the 'Big Three' at Yalta. Would the Polish armoured division under General Maczek continue to fight in 21st Army Group? To the VCIGS Monty thus wrote on 14 February:

> *The Polish Problem*
> I have received your telegrams about the Poles, and the decisions taken at the Crimea conference.
>
> I sent for Maczek to come and see me today, and I explained things to him as you suggested.
>
> He says the troops in his division quite understand the situation and there will be no trouble for the present; they will fight the Germans as before.

[1] M477 of 1545 hrs, 13.2.45, Montgomery Papers.
[2] Ibid.
[3] Signal 68303 of 1235 hrs, 14.2.45, Montgomery Papers.

He thinks there may well be trouble *after the elections*, especially if the Lublin party get returned to power and the present President of Poland in London is kicked out.

He says that there will be no free elections if it is left to the Russians to supervise.

The guts of his opinion is that they originally had two enemies who invaded Poland i.e. Germany and Russia. One enemy has now been driven out; but the other enemy (Russia) remains.

Of the two enemies, the Poles hate the Russians most!![1]

To Monty this was but one of the historical ironies of the past six years. Britain had gone to war to guarantee Poland's independence; the subsequent Russian pact with Hitler had enabled the Germans to overrun most of Western Europe with impunity. Then it had been Russia's turn to be attacked, just as Russia had herself attacked Finland and Poland in 1939, with the result that Hitler's eastern consort, a Communist tyranny, had become Britain's ally. Moreover, throughout this extraordinary development, America had refused to stand by the democratic nations of Europe; only when she herself had been attacked had the United States finally entered the war in December 1941, as Britain's ally, like the Russians.

Monty's awareness of this irony was quite open. Certainly he did not keep it from his troops. On the eve of 'Veritable' Monty had issued his by now traditional 'Personal Message from the C-in-C to be read out to all Troops':

The operations of the Allies on all fronts have now brought the German war to its final stage. There was a time, some years ago, when it did not seem possible that we *could* win this war; the present situation is that we cannot lose it; in fact the terrific successes of our Russian allies on the eastern front have brought victory in sight. . . .

The last round may be long and difficult, and the fighting hard; but we now fight on German soil; we have got our opponent where we want him; and he is going to receive the knock-out blow: a somewhat unusual one, delivered from more than one direction. . . .

And so we embark on the final round, in close cooperation with our American allies on our right and with complete confidence in the successful outcome of the onslaught being delivered by our Russian allies on the other side of the ring.

Somewhat curious rules you may say. But the whole match has been *most* curious; the Germans began this all-out contest and

[1] M556, 14.2.45, Montgomery Papers.

they must not complain when in the last round they are hit from several directions at the same time. . . .

Good luck to you all—and God bless you.[1]

Another 'unusual' blow referred to Operation 'Grenade', the second pincer of the Rhineland attack—which on Wednesday 14 February Monty still hoped to launch the following weekend, satisfied that, despite growing German resistance—there were now four German parachute divisions, two Panzer divisions and three infantry divisions opposing 'Veritable'—and British casualties, 'the conditions for GRENADE have been made excellent by this enemy concentration in the north'.[2]

The weather was not only to rule out any prospect of launching 'Grenade' that weekend (17/18 February), but even to preclude air support for the British and Canadian troops battling towards the Rhine. It was, as the 30 Corps Commander later described, 'the grimmest battle in which I took part during the last war'[3]—and the postponement of 'Grenade' made it one of the most costly in British and Canadian lives. 'At the start of our attack we had been faced by one division approximately. Now, nine divisions had been drawn into the battle against us and Operation "Veritable" developed into a slogging match under the worst possible conditions, when air support was rarely possible. It became a soldier's battle, and the men who really influenced it were the Battalion Commanders who, for twenty-eight horrible days, never gave up the struggle which continued by day and by night, against some of the best and most experienced German Panzer and Parachute troops,' Horrocks related.[4]

As in Normandy, Monty was intimately aware of the casualties being incurred in 'Veritable', tabulated each evening for his nightly signal to Brooke. But as long as Eisenhower did not—as in Normandy—become impatient and start 'rocking the boat' Monty was supremely confident that the German reaction would make 'Grenade' all the easier once it was launched. By 17 February he was signalling to Brooke that 'the prisoners are mounting and fresh [enemy] formations are appearing on this front and it looks as if VERITABLE is going to draw in all the available enemy reserves.'[5] He had fixed, with the Ninth US Army Commander General Simpson, the new target date for 'Grenade' as 23 February, and by 20 February he was grimly satisfied with the battle in the north. A further two German

[1] Montgomery Papers.
[2] M481 of 2200 hrs, 14.2.45, Montgomery Papers.
[3] B. G. Horrocks, *A Full Life*, London 1962.
[4] Ibid.
[5] M486 of 2240 hrs, 17.2.45, Montgomery Papers.

divisions had been sucked in, including the Panzer Lehr Armoured Division which was launching 'some very savage counter-attacks against 2 Canadian Div' near Calcar. 'In addition to the nine divisions mentioned in M481 of 14 Feb two more have now appeared. . . . All this is good and is sowing the seeds for a successful GRENADE.'[1]

This, and the 11,000 prisoners now taken in the battle, were reported by telephone to SHAEF, where at the morning conference on 20 February Monty's Chief of Staff had given a briefing on the battle. De Guingand was optimistic, repeating Monty's assurance that the more German divisions which were drawn into the battle, the more successful the 'Grenade' attack would become; moreover, in forcing the Germans to do battle west of the Rhine, the subsequent crossing of the river and entry into Germany proper would be made easier. But as Bradley's ADC noted in his diary several days later, 'at the start of that ["Veritable"] offensive, Montgomery with customary bravado, suggested that this was the start of the offensive to force a decision on the Western Front. The attack was heavily publicized in the press and may now be causing some chagrin because of its obvious exaggeration. . . . Two days ago [21 February] Montgomery again indicated to the press that the offensive of the Ninth Army . . . would decide the success of Allied Armies in the West.'[2] What if Monty's predictions proved, as Major Hansen believed, without substance? Eisenhower himself remained loyal to Monty's patient unfolding of the 'Veritable'–'Grenade' pincer battle, but his SHAEF staff—as in Normandy—began once again to voice doubts. Major Hansen was frankly defeatist: 'While the success of this effort ["Grenade"] will materially determine our future movements, it will not itself cause any severe breakdown of the enemy front. The Germans have bested themselves in recuperative efforts and may be expected to offer heavy resistance in defending the localities along the entire line.'[3] Worse still, Eisenhower's own Chief of Intelligence, Maj-General Strong, had on 20 February reversed his opinion that 'the Ruhr was the best place to attack'—and was now advocating transfer of Allied weight to the southern front, south of the Moselle![4]

Strong's volte-face was worrying, not only because it threatened to prejudice Eisenhower's view of operations, but because it reflected the almost incredible command set-up at Versailles where the Senior

[1] M493 of 2245 hrs, 20.2.45, Montgomery Papers.
[2] Diary of Chester B. Hansen, entry of 23.2.45, loc. cit.
[3] Ibid.
[4] Diary of Mrs K. Summersby, entry of 20.2.45, loc. cit.

Intelligence officer, without any experience of actual battle in his entire life, was allowed and encouraged to recommend *operational* plans. Strong's sudden loss of faith in Monty's Rhineland attack was reported back to the War Office by Lt-General Weeks, the Deputy CIGS. As Maj-General 'Simbo' Simpson, now promoted to Assistant CIGS, reported to Monty, Weeks 'said that Strong had held forth at a meeting about the necessity for throwing our main weight into a thrust *South* of the Moselle. Strong's arguments had been that the German opposition there was very light and that we would get the best dividend by putting our weight there instead of in the North.'[1] Fortunately Bedell Smith had squashed this by reminding Strong that the Supreme Commander wished not to run away from the enemy, but to *defeat* him as far as possible west of the Rhine—'DCIGS said Bedell had been quite firm and had refused to budge an inch from present plans: but it really is monstrous that the head "I" chap should be allowed to get up at all and express strong views as to what our own operational strategy ought to be. No harm has come of it yet, but I suggest we must all watch matters very closely.'[2]

Small wonder then that Monty was dubious about Eisenhower's latest directive to General Bradley of 20 February, outlining current and future Allied offensive plans. 'I regard with some suspicion sub-para (c) of Phase II and of Phase III,' Monty wrote to Simpson on 21 February, referring to Eisenhower's plan to capture the Saar—'great problems regarding the civil population will arise in Holland and in Germany, in the north, once we are over the Rhine. We shall need all the transport and maintenance resources possible if we are to solve all these problems; if resources are taken away for the SAAR venture we will be sunk in the north.'[3]

Brooke, however, was confident that, in accompanying Churchill in a renewed visit to SHAEF the following week, he could 'keep them in the satisfactory state of mind in which they are at present,'[4] and Monty was told, in effect, not to look over his shoulder.

Meanwhile, at a conference on the afternoon of 21 February at General Simpson's Ninth US Army headquarters, it was confirmed that Operation 'Grenade' would be launched before dawn on 23 February. 'The country is drying up nicely,' Monty signalled with satisfaction to Brooke. 'I am going forward tomorrow [22 Feb] to stay for two days at TAC HQ Canadian Army south of Nijmegen to

[1] Letter of 24.2.45 (ACIGS (o)/1/M), Montgomery Papers.
[2] Ibid.
[3] M557, 21.2.45, Montgomery Papers.
[4] Letter from Maj-General 'Simbo' Simpson of 24.2.45 (ACIGS (O)/1/M), loc. cit.

examine the battle in detail and will return to my TAC HQ on Saturday [24 Feb].'[1] The following night he confirmed that 'everything is all set for GRENADE. It has been another very fine day and the country is drying nicely'.[2]

Now, as at the end of July 1944, all Monty's patience and confidence were rewarded—and those who, like Major Hansen, had mocked Monty's bombastic predictions for 'Grenade' were confounded.

From the very start 'Grenade' went like clockwork. At Monty's request Eisenhower had issued a directive giving engineering priority, throughout the Allied sectors from Holland to Switzerland, to the bridging requirements of Ninth US Army. By the evening of 23 February it was evident that 'Grenade' had achieved almost total surprise. 'This operation was successfully launched at 0330 hrs today and Ninth Army has now 23 bridges across the ROER river with four class 40 bridges,' Monty reported delightedly to Brooke. '700 prisoners have been taken. Casualties to our troops have been light.'[3]

Eisenhower was visiting troops in the Cherbourg, Le Havre and Soissons areas, and thus missed the gathering excitement as 'Grenade' 'took off'.

'This operation continues to go well,' Monty cabled Brooke on 24 February.

> We now have a great many bridges over the river and troops and supplies of all sorts are moving forward. Ninth US Army has four complete divisions east of the ROER river and a fifth division is in process of moving over. The total prisoners taken yesterday were 1500 and the total casualties were 1000.
>
> I visited Ninth Army HQ today and ordered that the advance be pressed relentlessly and every legitimate risk to be taken to get forward.
>
> The weather is fine and the ground is drying up and the enemy has few reserves immediately to hand with which to stop an advance and it is therefore important to take full advantage of this situation.[4]

For the first time since Normandy the operations of three major Allied armies had been married to a single tactical purpose, under a single commander. The result was triumphant—yet even before this

[1] M498 of 2225 hrs, 21.2.45, Montgomery Papers.
[2] M499, 22.2.45, Montgomery Papers.
[3] M1000, 23.2.45, Montgomery Papers.
[4] M1001 of 2255 hrs, 24.2.45, Montgomery Papers.

became clear to SHAEF's renovated command post at Reims or to the world at large, Monty was thinking of the next battle; the crossing of the Rhine north of the Ruhr. 'My dear Simbo,' he wrote on 25 February, only two days after the launching of 'Grenade',

> Some pretty big stuff lies ahead. VERITABLE and GRENADE have to be joined up; then the crossing of the Rhine, with airborne divisions co-operating: target date 31 March, but we may not manage this.
>
> I shall have to keep a clear head, and also keep fit and well.[1]

So far only American infantry had crossed the Roer, with sappers and artillery; but that evening the first American armoured divisions began to cross—and the following day, as 'Veritable' burst into renewed flames with a full Corps attack by 2 Canadian Corps southwards and in parallel to the Rhine, Monty directed that Simpson's left Corps hold fast in the Mönchen gladbach area, while his right Corps swung forward in a wide pincer eastwards and then northwards along the Rhine to meet the Canadians—'I have directed Ninth Army to operate with 13 Corps on the west side of MUNCHEN-GLADBACH . . . and then to hold firm in that area. The main thrust is to be with 19 Corps on the right which will pass east of MUNCHEN-GLADBACH directed on the area NEUSS-KREFELD KEMPEN.'[2]

As in Normandy Monty hoped that the German predilection—stiffened by Hitler's orders—for do-or-die resistance would make them vulnerable to being surrounded. Thus, only three days after the launch of 'Grenade', he was confessing to Brooke the same hopes he had communicated before Falaise:

> I am very well satisfied with the operations so far. You will see that I am aiming at what the Prime Minister would call a quote 'COP' and if we can bring it off and write off or capture the bulk of the Germans west of the RHINE and cut off their escape there will be all the fewer Germans to oppose us on the east bank of the RHINE.
>
> But this converging operation with two large armies is a tricky business and I have got to keep a pretty tight grip on the battle to ensure it goes the way required.
>
> We are planning the maximum activity of air forces on the RHINE by day and night to make the enemy get-away as difficult as possible.'[3]

[1] Letter of 25.2.45, Montgomery Papers.

[2] Signal to CIGS, M1005 of 2310 hrs, 26.2.45, Montgomery Papers.

[3] Ibid.

What was difficult, however, was to get the Air Force to act. If vacillation, dissension and indecision had marred SHAEF's performance in the military sphere since the Ardennes, this was doubly true of air operations. Air support to the armies, when weather conditions permitted, had been of critical importance to the outcome of the Ardennes battle. The pilots of the four tactical air groups—83rd RAF, 84th RAF, 9th US and 29th US Tactical Air Commands—had operated with great valour, under determined leadership; indeed by 26 December General Hodges was being quoted as stating 'that he had only been able to meet the enemy threat against his 1st Army through the Air support he has been given. If he could not get this support, then—!'[1] By 30 December Air Marshal Robb was noting that 'the Air contribution to the blocking of the German offensive stands out more clearly each day'.[2] Even the Allied heavy bomber effort had been turned to the task of disrupting the flow of men and materials to the front—to the point where, on 17 January 1945, SHAEF was concerned lest the Germans learn to what extent their Ardennes gamble had paid off, both in wresting the strategic military initiative from the Allies, and the Air initiative: 'One thing that should not be revealed was the success of Runstedt in diverting strategic [Allied] bombers to the battle area and away from strategic targets.'[3]

With the gradual reduction of the German salient in the Ardennes, however, such unity of air effort in support of the army evaporated. Not since September 1944, after Leigh-Mallory's departure, had Eisenhower had a C-in-C Air Forces at SHAEF. Tedder refused to act as one, and Air Vice-Marshal Robb was of insufficient rank (as Chief Air Staff Officer) and personality to bend the wills of competing air barons. Thus for the second time since victory in Normandy, the high command of the Allied air forces deteriorated into a sanhedrin of discordant voices. On 11 January 'General Anderson [commanding 9th US Bomber Command] delivered a long and impassioned plea for replanning the strategic air offensive on the assumption of a longer duration of the war. The German success in the Ardennes had not only upset our plans for the ground offensive, but also our strategic air plans, and the whole strategic air situation would have to be reviewed'.[4] After seeing the Allied screw tightened on German U-boat, aircraft, oil and industrial production relentlessly

[1] Stated by Bedell Smith, 'Notes of Meeting held in Chief of Staff's Office', 26.12.45, Robb Papers, loc. cit.

[2] 'Notes of Meeting held in Chief of Staff's Office', 30.12.45, Robb Papers, loc. cit.

[3] 'Minutes of SHAEF Chiefs of Staff Conference', 17.1.45 (Air 37/1129), PRO.

[4] 'Minutes of Allied Air Commanders' Conference', 11.1.45 (AIR 37/1129), PRO.

since 1942, the winter months of 1944/5 had shown suddenly *increasing* German production. 'From the strategic point of view, the picture is very sad,' Anderson lamented. 'We were paying a tremendous price by concentrating on helping the ground forces.'[1]

After much discussion, the attention of the Allied strategic air forces began to shift inexorably back to strategic targets—the British concerned to 'blot out' some sixty German towns in an effort to stop the dispersal of German component manufacture, the Americans concentrating particularly on factories and oil installations. It was apparent that the bomber barons, despite the decisive unity of effort in the Ardennes, had lost faith in the army, and were working on the assumption that the war would go on for a long time. Thus when requests were made for the Rhine bridges to be bombed behind the German bridgeheads west of the river, beginning in January, they were met with indifference and refusal. The first official plan was considered by SHAEF on 13 January, but was quickly turned down. 'Air Marshal Robb said that the complete destruction of the RHINE bridges was an impossible task. It would take the whole visual effort of Eighth [US] Air Force for at least a month.'[2] Two days later, it was again raised—and refused as 'impossible. . . . General Schlatter [air staff, SHAEF] thought there was a danger of our being fooled by the glitter of the flexibility of air power.'[3] By 25 January, as the army began to press harder for such bombing, Air-Marshal Tedder decided to put his oar in—'Deputy Supreme Commander warned the [SHAEF] meeting against attacking bridges.'[4] It was time for the Allies to put their entire bomber effort into systematic destruction of cities such as Berlin, Tedder felt. Thus as planning for Monty's 'Veritable' and 'Grenade' effort accelerated with Eisenhower's belated go-ahead at the end of January, 21st Army Group's plea for interdiction of the German lines of reinforcement and retreat, across the Rhine bridges, was once again sabotaged by Tedder, a man too proud to surrender his title of Deputy Supreme Commander and take over command of the combined air force effort, yet too querulous to resist meddling in the matter of 21st Army Group's request. As in Normandy he had denied Monty the use of the heavy bomber forces, so again he put paid to 21st Army Group's request in the battle of the Rhineland, aided and abetted by Air-Marshal Sir Arthur Coningham, commanding 2nd Tactical

[1] Ibid.
[2] 'Minutes of Allied Air Commanders' Conference', 13.1.45 (AIR 37/1129), PRO.
[3] 'Minutes of Chief of Staff and Air Staff Meeting', 15.1.45 (AIR 37/1129), PRO.
[4] 'Minutes of Allied Air Commanders' Conference', 25.1.45 (AIR 37/1129), PRO.

Air Force, whose jealousy of his own two Tactical Group Commanders—Air Vice-Marshals Huddleston and Broadhurst—was such that Coningham declined even to discuss with them the possibility of medium-bomber interdiction of the bridges.[1] On 1 February, a bare week before 'Veritable' was due to begin, the matter was again raised:

> Lt-Gen. Spaatz then raised the specific point as to the wisdom of attacking bridges, and instanced the 21st Army Group's request for the destruction of the WESEL bridges.[2]

Spaatz was concerned at the large percentage of bombs that missed and would thereby be wasted, compared with industrial or city bombing. It was decided therefore that the 'bridges are not worth attacking unless the immediate decision demands it, in which case the job should be given to the Mediums'.[3] This Coningham flatly refused to undertake, claiming that the flak around the bridges was too heavy—something which the 8th Tactical Group Commander, Air Vice-Marshal Broadhurst, later bitterly denied.[4] The *coup de grâce*, however, was administered by Tedder, who now stated that the interdiction of the Seine bridges the previous summer had not prevented the escape of large numbers of the enemy, despite his almost total loss of heavy equipment west of the Seine—'in the course of this discussion on bridges, the Deputy Supreme Commander pointed out that the destruction of bridges did not isolate armies. The Germans were adept in crossing the Rhine in pontoons.'[5] In vain, as the Canadian Army launched its 'Veritable' attack on 8 February, 21st Army Group protested: 'the destruction of the RHINE bridges between WESEL and COLOGNE, though not essential for interdiction of supplies, would seriously hamper the withdrawal of the German Armies east of the Rhine. Air Chief Marshal Tedder pointed out that the Germans had managed to withdraw a good deal across the Seine in August 1944.'[6] The strategic air forces were thus ordered to concentrate on 'the big population centres of Germany such as Berlin, Leipzig and Dresden' as 'second priority after Oil'[7]—with bridges barely figuring at all. Dresden was reduced to a funeral pyre; but the German armies were permitted to retreat across the Rhine, as Tedder had failed to prevent the evacuation of the German garrison in Sicily eighteen months before.

[1] Air Chief Marshal Sir Harry Broadhurst, interview of 21.6.84.
[2] 'Minutes of Allied Air Commanders' Conference', 1.2.45 (AIR 37/1129), PRO.
[3] Ibid.
[4] Loc. cit.
[5] 'Minutes of Allied Air Commanders' Conference', 1.2.45, loc. cit.
[6] Ibid.
[7] Ibid.

On 27 February, General Whiteley presented a final plea from 21st Army Group 'for the destruction by air attack of all bridges north of Cologne. The object was to cut off the twelve to fifteen German divisions north of the American [Ninth US Army and 7 US Corps] break-through and make it difficult for them to withdraw their transport and heavy equipment to the east of the RHINE.'[1] But as Whiteley remarked, it was in a sense already too late: nine bridges remained intact between Cologne and Wesel and with the speed of Simpson's breakthrough this left the air forces little time to mount an operation they had consistently refused to contemplate since January. Brigadier Foord, General Strong's Intelligence deputy, had also been infected by Strong's operational lunacy: he thus announced that 'in view of the tottering condition of Germany as a whole, he doubted the value of diverting the air effort from the main strategic objectives'.[2] Tedder, yet again, concurred: 'agreed with Brig. Foord that it was more valuable to keep up the attack on the existing strategic targets—oil and population centres.'[3] Thus Monty's full 'cop' was denied him.

Brooke, veteran of Churchill's moods of depression and elation, had meanwhile decided to delete the sentence referring to a possible 'cop' from Monty's signal of 26 February when showing it to the Prime Minister—as 'Simbo' Simpson explained to Monty the next day:

> CIGS felt that it would be inadvisable to let the Prime Minister have this particular sentence as he might well take your 'cop' to be a certainty and start pestering both CIGS and yourself as to when it was going to come off! The 'cop' would be all the more gratefully appreciated by the PM when it takes place a little later on.[4]

Monty, as the soldier in the field, was excited by the prospect of a great victory in the Rhineland; Brooke, owlishly wise, wanted no crowing before victory was assured.

Bradley had meanwhile been watching from the sidelines—and flying to see Patton on 25 February, proposed to Eisenhower at Reims that all incoming reinforcements and new divisions now be put into Patton's 'developing offensive'[5] in the Moselle triangle. But when he returned, through thick fog, on 27 February, to Namur, Bradley found that the left-hand Corps of Hodges' First US Army,

[1] 'Minutes of Allied Air Staff Meeting, Tedder in Chair', 27.2.45 (AIR 37/1129), PRO.
[2] Ibid.
[3] Ibid.
[4] Letter of 27.2.45 (ACIGS (o)/2/M), Montgomery Papers.
[5] Diary of Chester B. Hansen, entry of 25.2.45, loc. cit.

fighting on the right flank of Simpson's 'Grenade' offensive, was now taking off. 'Simbo' Simpson had commented to Monty on 24 February that he was 'interested to see that Hodges is doing his stuff on your right flank. When you were here [in London] you feared that you would get no help there and that any of Bradley's operations would take place a good bit further south. I think myself that Bradley has realised now that his only chance of getting lined up on the RHINE anywhere is to hang on to one side of your own coat-tails as you go forward.' [1]

Bradley's discovery, on 27 February, that his 7 US Corps was racing for the Rhine, put a different complexion on the campaign. Far from Monty's prophecy of decisive victory seeming far-fetched, Bradley was suddenly confronted by a situation similar to that of Falaise. To his amazement there were reports that Collins' 7 US Corps, on Monty's flank, had taken eight *thousand* prisoners on 26 February alone, while Bradley was having oysters and champagne with Eisenhower at Reims—'one of our greatest bags since the march across France . . . General Bradley is highly optimistic over the progress made in the Seventh Corps sector and along the entire Ninth Army front.' [2] It was high time he paid a visit to Hodges, whom he had not seen for more than a week. On 27 February Bradley thus set off for Spa—and by the following evening was 'greatly encouraged over the progress we have made in this offensive and believes that it will carry us through ultimately to the Rhine. He ventured a guess this morning that the war would be over by September 1.' [3]

Bradley's cautious confidence was in marked contrast to the excitement at Monty's Tac HQ and in 21st Army Group on 28 February. Over the preceding days Monty had been feeding more American armoured divisions from the Roermond area into Simpson's 'right-hook'—and by 1 March the 'cop' was being fulfilled, as he cabled with delight to Brooke:

> GRENADE: The most sensational results have been achieved today. Our troops are now fighting in the outskirts of NEUSS and our line runs from there northwest . . . to VENLO. This line had been reached by 1600 hours and our troops are pressing on towards the bridges [across the Rhine] east of NEUSS and KREFELD and may well reach them by dawn tomorrow morning, one division going to each place while a third division will tomorrow be directed north of KREFELD towards the bridge at DUISBURG.

[1] Letter of 24.2.45 (ACIGS (o)/1/M), Montgomery Papers.
[2] Diary of Chester B. Hansen, entry of 27.2.45, loc. cit.
[3] Entry of 28.2.45. Ibid.

> By tomorrow night we shall have a bridge over the MEUSE at VENLO.

As in Patton's great armoured sweep in Normandy the year before, the Germans seemed helpless:

> The enemy seems to have lost all grip on the battle in this area and his command organisation seems to have broken down. We have captured static back area units who are quite unaware of the situation and in one area we captured a complete armoured column of tanks moving westwards from NEUSS towards MUNCHEN GLADBACH which was very astonished at being captured.
>
> I am unable to say how many prisoners have been captured today but the number is considerable and divisions are finding them an embarrassment in the fast moving battle.
>
> All headquarters are moving forward and the distances for liaison are becoming great and I shall be on the move myself very shortly and back to the caravan life in the fields.
>
> On my right flank 7 US Corps is having some difficulty in enlarging its bridgehead over the ERFT river and very little progress has been made today beyond the river. I am not letting that interfere with my northward progress and am holding a flank along the line of the ERFT river from NEUSS southwards to BEDBURG.
>
> I am planning to move my Tac HQ on about Monday to the woods just west of VENLO.[1]

Aware that the war was now 'hotting up', Eisenhower had to decide whether and how the Allies should carry out the second and third phases of his last directive. Driving to Bradley's headquarters on 28 February, Eisenhower found Bradley convinced still that the Allies should close up to the Rhine all along the front before crossing. What would Monty think? Together, Eisenhower and Bradley drove to Eindhoven on the morning of 1 March 1945. The sun was shining as they left Namur, driving at seventy miles an hour; but with strange symbolism 'the skies darkened and the weather thickened'[2] as they reached the Dutch border; and by the time they arrived at Monty's 'small Dutch house comfortably furnished'[3] north of Eindhoven, there was drizzling rain.

[1] M1009 of 2255 hrs, 1.3.45, Montgomery Papers.
[2] Diary of Chester B. Hansen, entry of 1.3.45, loc. cit.
[3] Ibid.

CHAPTER FIVE

The Domino Effect

AT EINDHOVEN ON 1 March 1945, Monty outlined to the Supreme Commander and to General Bradley the progress of operations 'Veritable' and 'Grenade': 21st Army Group would be on the Rhine that night and the two pincers of Monty's offensive would meet in the next few days. Prisoners were almost up to the 30,000 mark—equivalent to the numbers at El Alamein. Given the confusion and disorder evident in the north, Monty considered that it would be wrong now to disperse Allied strength by laboriously closing up to the Rhine throughout its length. It would take several weeks to prepare for a major assault crossing of the Rhine in the north. This crossing should be undertaken as soon as possible (Monty had already advanced the target date by a week, to 24 March), irrespective of whether the Rhine had meanwhile been closed throughout its length—for it was patently clear that although capable of desperate and fanatic resistance, as in the north, the Germans had not the reserves now to launch the counter-attack west of the Rhine which Bradley feared.

Bradley disagreed, but as further reports came in of the collapse of German resistance in front of Ninth US Army and 7 US Corps, Eisenhower sided with Monty. Now would be the wrong time to divert troops to the Saar; Patton must manage with what he had got, and Bradley use the magnificent achievement of 21st Army Group to get First Army up onto the Rhine alongside it, as far south as the Moselle. 'All up and down the Roer, where our divisions have forced their bridgeheads,' Bradley's ADC learned in the Operations Room of Monty's headquarters, 'the advances are progressing at a startling pace. This morning troops of the 29th Infantry Division entered and took Munchen Gladbach, a textile city of approximately 140,000. In many of the cities the civilian staffs were functioning totally oblivious to the impending advances of the American Armies.' The moment was similar to that when Patton's Third Army broke out from Avranches, as even Bradley acknowledged: 'General Bradley estimated that our troops would be on the Rhine this evening. . . . The general effect of this sledge hammer drive to the Rhine has been reflected in the crumbling resistance up and down the Rhineland.' [1]

[1] Ibid.

Monty's diary recorded his satisfaction with the results of the conference that day. 'On the 1st March General Eisenhower accompanied by General Bradley visited the Field-Marshal at his Tac Headquarters, and had a long conference with him about future operations. At this conference complete agreement was reached on all matters discussed, and General Eisenhower reaffirmed that he intended to concentrate all necessary resources in 21 Army Group in the north to enable 21 Army Group to isolate the RUHR from Germany.'[1]

Eisenhower, knowing that the Prime Minister and the CIGS would be visiting Monty the following day, had, however, a deeper motive in conferring with Monty. The 'plot' to bring Field-Marshal Alexander to SHAEF as Deputy Supreme Commander was once more on the boil, fanned by Alexander's unrepentant admirer Churchill. In return for agreeing to the priority of Monty's 21st Army Group operations north of the Ruhr, Eisenhower hoped to earn Monty's loyalty and then use him as a stick to beat down Churchill's fire.

Monty, essentially simple-minded when it came to politics, fell neatly into line, fearing that Alexander's introduction into the SHAEF hierarchy might arouse further resentment in the various American field headquarters and thus sunder his hard-won agreement with Eisenhower over a 21st Army Group strategy for bringing the campaign in the West to its conclusion, with 9th US Army under command. That Monty did in fact make such a renewed *quid pro quo* with Eisenhower is demonstrated by Monty's diary:

> After this conference [of 1 March] at which General Bradley was present, the Field Marshal had a talk alone with General Eisenhower, and asked him about the intrigue which was going on to get Field-Marshal Alexander appointed Deputy Supreme Commander. He told General Eisenhower what he had heard about this intrigue and General Eisenhower confirmed it all and asked the Field-Marshal for his views.[2]

These Monty gave. The Allies had been through a number of storms, he said; they were however now 'set with a fair wind to take them into port'. If Alexander was brought in there would be further inter-Allied feeling—'another great storm would arise and the old disagreements would be revived'. As a result 'the Field-Marshal therefore gave his very definite opinion that Field-Marshal Alexander

[1] 'Notes on the Campaign in North-West Europe', Montgomery Papers.
[2] Ibid.

should be left where he was, and that any further causes of friction should be avoided at all cost'.[1]

Churchill's lobbying was thus doomed to fail. As Monty recorded:

> On the 2nd March the Prime Minister accompanied by the C.I.G.S. and General Ismay arrived for a two day visit. . . . During their discussions the Field-Marshal raised with the Prime Minister the question of the appointment of Field-Marshal Alexander as Deputy Supreme Commander. He emphasized most strongly that a change of this nature would inevitably raise a great storm especially among the American generals, and that the bitterness and suspicions aroused would more than offset any good which the change might achieve. He therefore strongly recommended that no change be made.
>
> The Prime Minister was much upset by the Field-Marshal's frank expression of his opinion. In spite of this however he made it quite clear that he would not be deterred from the course of action on which he had decided, from fear of hurting the feelings of American generals. He left by train on the evening of 4th March to visit General Eisenhower.[2]

Before Churchill even rose from his bed on 4 March, however, Monty was signalling Eisenhower:

> The question of Alex was raised by my visitor. I have given him my very definite opinion that we should leave things as they are and that a change like this at this stage will merely raise a storm and will put everything back. I hope very much we shall stay as we are. I have no objection to your telling him that you know this is my opinion of the problem.[3]

Armed with Monty's telegram, Eisenhower met Churchill at Reims—and put the 'kibosh' on the Prime Minister's proposal. Brooke, watching from the sideline, was in two minds as he breakfasted with Eisenhower on 6 March:

> There is no doubt that he [Eisenhower] is a most attractive personality and, at the same time, a very, very limited brain from a strategic point of view. This comes out the whole time in conversation with him. His relations with Monty are quite insoluble; he only sees the worst side of Monty and cannot appreciate the better side,

[1] Ibid.
[2] Ibid.
[3] M1012 of 0810 hrs, 4.3.45, 'Montgomery' file, Eisenhower Papers, loc. cit.

Brooke noted that night in his diary.[1] Once again Brooke had watched with fascination how, at Geldrop, Monty ran his three armies—'after dinner we attended the interview which he holds every evening with his liaison officers. It was most interesting and most impressive. After completing this interview he dictated his daily wire to me based on his conception of the situation arrived at from the liaison officers' reports.'[2] The next day he had accompanied Monty to Simpson's Ninth US Army headquarters; Monty's 'grip', the relentless simplification of command and conduct of battle down to bare, military essentials was something Brooke had watched since Monty commanded a division under him in 1940, yet each time Brooke was awed, and found Eisenhower's failure to comprehend Monty's military (rather than personal) motives galling.

> Things are running smoothly for the present, but this cannot last, and I foresee trouble ahead before long,

Brooke recorded prophetically.

> For all that, to insert Alex now is only likely to lead to immediate trouble for all, I gather. The war may not last long and possibly matters may run smoothly till the end. Therefore, I feel that it is best to leave Alex where he is. I think that Winston is now of the same opinion.[3]

To Monty Brooke then explained the latest position:

> As regards the Alex business I think I have arranged matters so that he will remain where he is. But I can't swear for certain yet.

Churchill had, after seeing Eisenhower, relented: 'the PM told me afterwards that he had had doubts as to the wisdom of the change. I said that as things were running well now it might be better to leave matters alone. He said he would write to Alex to find out his reactions. I think that as a result Alex will say that he is content to stop where he is.' But would the matter rest there?

> So I hope this will do the trick as you wanted,

Brooke continued in his letter to Monty,

> and all may be well for the present. But I am not at all certain that you won't be shouting again before long that you are in trouble!

[1] A. Bryant, op. cit.
[2] Ibid.
[3] Ibid.

Brooke warned.

> For the present no doubt all goes as we want it, but the old sources of trouble and all the old causes still exist and will be liable to crop up. Let us hope the war may be over before they do![1]

A cable was meanwhile despatched to Alexander who with typical good grace consented to do as he was bidden.

To Brooke Monty replied several days later:

> My dear Brookie,
>
> Thank you for your letter. I am delighted that the Alexander business has been postponed: and I hope this will lead to a cancellation. The change would have upset matters, without any doubt. We are now on a very good wicket; Ike has learnt his lesson and he consults me before taking any action.[2]

The following day Monty heard direct from Churchill. Bluntly, Churchill informed him: 'Re Alex: I decided not to make the change. . . . The matter is therefore closed.'[3]

Meanwhile Eisenhower's new operational directive, dated 3 March, bore out his agreement with Monty. There would be no shift of Allied priority away from Monty's thrust in the north. While 21st Army Group prepared to cross the Rhine, however, 12th US Army Group was to exploit the enemy's weak points and his lack of reserves. 'Few or NO reserves of trained troops from outside the WEST are believed to be immediately available; reserves from within the WEST have virtually all been thrown in. The enemy must now be prepared, as and when pressure is exerted, to get back behind the RHINE, at least north of the MOSELLE. . . .'[4]

Hodges and Patton were licensed to go all out for the Rhine north of the Moselle, but using only the forces they had. The race to the Rhine in 12th Army Group was now on. Though Eisenhower refused to transfer forces back from Ninth US Army to help Bradley, Bradley had for weeks been receiving the benefit of stepped-up reinforcements and divisions entering the theatre from the United States.[5] Bradley travelled straight to Hodges' headquarters at Spa, where Bradley decided to emulate Monty's success in the north. Thus, as soon as

[1] Letter of 7.3.45 (file 14/8), Alanbrooke Papers, loc. cit.

[2] Letter of 10.3.45. Ibid.

[3] Letter from Churchill to Montgomery, 11.3.45. Ibid.

[4] FWD 17545 of 3.3.45, quoted in *The Papers of Dwight David Eisenhower*, op. cit.

[5] 'The reason for the initial directive from Gen. E. placing the Third army on the defensive, was the shortage of replacements. With the main attack ['Grenade'] delayed two weeks, our replacement situation permitted some action.' Bradley ms., loc. cit.

'the success of 21st Army Group's operation was assured . . . we then turned our efforts towards Cologne and the whole First Army was ready to strike east and south east,' Bradley later chronicled.[1] 'With its right Corps holding in place, the other two Corps struck south east towards Cologne and Bonn . . . I had asked Gen. Patton to keep up the pressure and to get a bridgehead across the Kyll River, the last stream of any size between the Siegfried Line and the Rhine, so that we might be able to time his thrust to the Rhine with Gen. Hodges' thrust up the Rhine from Cologne and thus bag several German divisions in front of the V and VIII Corps. Actually this worked better than any of us had dared to hope.'[2]

In subsequent days both of Bradley's two armies would achieve magnificent results—Hodges capturing a bridge across the Rhine at Remagen, Patton capturing the town of Trier and blazing a trail to the Rhine north of Coblenz, as the 'domino' effect of 21st Army Group's breakthrough in the north rippled southwards. Starved of praise or publicity since his January counter-attack at Bastogne, Patton would however give Monty no credit. As in Normandy, the myth that victory had been achieved by American opportunism was started by Americans very early on, for whom Monty's patient tactical conception of battle, involving in the Rhineland some twenty-four divisions, 'just don't mean a thing to me'. Thus while Monty signalled each night to Sir Alan Brooke the heavy casualties suffered by British and Canadian divisions in 'Veritable' while waiting for the necessarily belated 'Grenade' attack by Ninth US Army, this picture was unfortunately translated at Patton's and Bradley's headquarters as failure by the British. 'The Ninth Army seems to be doing all right, but the Second British has not done a thing, nor probably will it,' Patton noted obtusely in his diary on 24 February.[3] Patton was neither aware of the secret shift of British divisions from Second Army into First Canadian Army for 'Veritable'[4] nor of the 'Caen' tactics of drawing and retaining German strength in the northern sector to make Simpson's Ninth US Army attack progress the easier. 'Very hard and bitter fighting has taken place today in the VERITABLE area particularly about LABBECK and KIRVENHEIM and WEEZE,' Monty reported to the CIGS on 1 March.[5] 'The enemy up here seems to be quite unaware as to what is taking place behind him in the south and he is holding to his positions with great

[1] Ibid.
[2] Ibid.
[3] *The Patton Papers*, op. cit.
[4] In order to deceive the Germans and give tactical surprise to 'Veritable' almost all Dempsey's Second Army divisions had been transferred to Crerar's First Canadian Army for the operation. First Canadian Army thus comprised seven British divisions and two Canadian.
[5] M1009, loc. cit.

tenacity and is counterattacking savagely to stop our progress. As a result we have made little progress though we have killed a good many enemy.'[1] 'Veritable's' very fierceness had however given rise to the 'sensational results'[2] on the 'Grenade' front, and the next evening Monty was informing Brooke he would probably bring Ninth US Army up into the enemy's rear rather than observe the original targets for each army:

> More heavy fighting has taken place today in the HOCHWALD area . . . The general picture in the north is that the enemy is endeavouring to hold with his right in the HOCHWALD area while he pulls back his left and his object obviously is to hold a bridgehead covering XANTEN WESEL and RHEINBURG. We shall have to hustle him out of this bridgehead and this may well best be done by Ninth US Army from the south.[3]

Such tactical flexibility on the part of a commander controlling the operations of three armies was quite beyond Patton, whose genius lay in local exploitation of enemy weakness and mistakes, as did Rommel's. Neither Patton nor Rommel were mentally or psychologically equipped to command whole army groups, and Patton abhorred the concept of a master-plan, urging in his diary—widely published—that 'It may be of interest to future generals to realize that one makes plans to fit circumstances and does not try to create circumstances to fit plans. That way lies danger.'[4]

This jibe at Monty's insistence on a 'proper' SHAEF plan was understandable, coming from a general who had been ordered by SHAEF to close down his attack upon Trier unless it prospered by a certain date, had disobeyed, and had succeeded in the end in seizing the town. Patton's brilliance in exploiting enemy weakness was indeed phenomenal—but it was a brilliance that worked only when the enemy's attention was drawn towards other major Allied thrusts which *had* to be contained at all costs. Now, however, Patton's hour had come again. The Russian advances on the eastern front and Monty's great Rhineland battle in the north had denuded the enemy of vital reserves necessary to prevent a breakthrough. As in Sicily, Patton likened the campaign to a horse trial—'we are in a horse race with Courtney [Hodges],' he wrote to his wife on 5 March. 'If he beats me, I shall be ashamed.'[5]

The war was meanwhile reaching its final phase. By 3 March almost 40,000 prisoners had been taken in the 'Veritable'–'Grenade'

[1] Ibid.
[2] Ibid.
[3] M1010 of 2310 hrs, 2.3.45, Montgomery Papers.
[4] *The Patton Papers*, op. cit.; diary entry of 26.2.45.
[5] *The Patton Papers*, op. cit. Patton's contempt for Hodges was even greater than

operation, with a further 20,000 by 7 US Corps on Simpson's right flank. Together with the numbers of enemy killed and wounded, this suggested total enemy casualties exceeding 100,000—losses which Hitler could never replace. By 6 March Hitler was known to have given orders for evacuation of all German troops east of the Rhine, save for bridgeheads at Wesel, Mainz and Coblenz. It was therefore obvious from Ultra that Bradley should do everything in his power to push forward armoured columns and cut off remaining German divisions before they could cross. Poor flying weather and the failure of the heavy air forces to interdict the Rhine bridges meant that large numbers of Germans did escape—but many were cut off and, equally important, 12th Army Group secured a bridge across the Rhine at Remagen in 1st US Army's sector. Monty was delighted—'9 Armd Div of First US Army has reached the RHINE at REMAGEN and has secured intact the railway bridge over the river at that place,' he cabled excitedly to Brooke on 7 March.[1] 'It is reported that one company of infantry is over the river holding a very small company bridgehead. Further south 4 Armd Div of Third US Army has reached the RHINE just downstream from COBLENZ and I understand that this movement has greatly surprised the enemy and a very large number of prisoners has been captured.'[2] The next evening he informed Brooke:

> First US Army are up on the RHINE down to a point just north of BONN. BONN itself is held by the enemy and then First US Army are on the RHINE southwards to REMAGEN.
>
> A complete infantry division is now over the RHINE at REMAGEN and a pontoon bridge has been made. The plan is to extend this holding to a bridgehead from BONN to ANDERNACH which will be held by four divisions. I was consulted by EISENHOWER by telephone this morning as to my opinion on this matter and said I considered it to be an excellent move as it would be an unpleasant threat to the enemy and would undoubtedly draw enemy strength on to it and away from my business in the north.
>
> Troops of Third US Army have reached the RHINE at COBLENZ. This move was a very rapid thrust and there should

---

for Montgomery—with Patton threatening to refuse a fourth star (promotion to full General) if Hodges was promoted at the same time: letter to Beatrice Patton of 14.3.45. Ibid.

[1] M1020 of 2225 hrs, 7.3.45, Montgomery Papers.

[2] Ibid.

> be a good many Germans in the pocket which extends for 25 miles west of the RHINE between COBLENZ and REMAGEN.[1]

Far from discouraging such opportunism, as later writers have averred, Monty applauded it. Now was the moment to exploit German confusion—and commanders like 'Lightning Joe' Collins and George S. Patton were ideal in that role. The fighting in the north, however, was of a different order; Simpson's spectacular break-through was over, and it remained to extinguish the last German bridgehead in that area west of the Rhine before launching Operation 'Plunder'—the Allied crossing north of the Ruhr. 'It is tough going,' Monty commented in his cable of 8 March to Brooke, 'and many enemy paratroopers refuse to surrender even when they have run out of ammunition and have to be shot. . . . If we could get two days of good flying weather it would be a great help but we have not been able to operate the fighter bombers for several days.'[2] The British and Canadian troops had been fighting hard since 8 February, a whole month, in the most appalling conditions. If they were to cross the Rhine, encircle the Ruhr and finish the war in northern Germany it was imperative that as many divisions as possible be withdrawn from battle, rested, re-equipped, reinforcements introduced, and trained for the next battle, due to begin at the end of the month. In fact Monty had already begun to do this on 6 March—having asked his three Army Commanders to present their plans, as before the invasion of Normandy, at a special conference to be convened at his headquarters on 9 March. In some haste he had written to his son's guardians on 6 March:

> I have, I fear, not written for some days. I have had two very large battles on hand and have had no time for anything. But I have received all your letters; for which my grateful thanks. . . .
>
> The battle here has gone on well. My armies (First Canadian and Ninth American) have taken 45,000 prisoners since 8th Feb and we are now lined up on the Rhine from Dusseldorf northwards, except for a very small enemy pocket at XANTEN and WESEL.
>
> We have captured many very large German cities, all full of German civilians i.e. Krefeld, Munchen-Gladbach etc. The civil population is well fed and there is no lack of food supplies,

he commented, with surprise, as in Normandy;

[1] M1021, of 2235 hrs, 8.3.45, Montgomery Papers.

[2] Ibid.

> the idea that the Germans are starving seems to be a complete fable.
>
> The weather has not been too good, and we have had many days when air action has been quite impossible. The Germans have taken full advantage of this to get what he can away over the Rhine bridges: which he then blew up.
>
> The battle has gone very well and I am delighted with it.[1]

He had good cause to be. 'Veritable' and 'Grenade' had prised open the German defence line west of the Rhine. The enemy was, once again, in full retreat. It remained only for the Allies to cross the Rhine in strength, and German collapse seemed certain.

[1] Letter to Phyllis Reynolds, 6.3.45, Montgomery Papers.

PART SEVEN

The Defeat of Germany

CHAPTER ONE

North of the Ruhr

ON 9 MARCH 1945 Monty held his first full 'Plunder' Conference, at which his three Army Commanders from 21st Army Group gave a presentation of their respective plans for crossing the Rhine. Maj-General 'Simbo' Simpson, the new ACIGS (Operations), stayed with Monty the night of 8 March, and was thus present at the proceedings:

> It was a most informal little affair, held out in the open air, with just General Dempsey of the Second Army, General Crerar of the Canadian Army, and General Simpson of the Ninth US Army.
>
> Monty had given them the outline of his plans before, and he wanted them to say what they proposed to do. No staff officers were in attendance. Each of the generals had his own very clear plans which, subject to one or two quite minor amendments made by Monty, were completely accepted. The whole conference could have taken no longer than two hours.
>
> This really was to my mind an ideal way of arranging what was clearly going to be a most complex operation because in addition to the Rhine being historically symbolic as an obstacle, it was a very wide river indeed and on some parts of the British front it was 500 yards wide, which meant that the crossing operations and the eventual bridging operations were very considerable.
>
> I went back to London on March 10 with a very clear picture in my own mind as to what everyone was going to do and was able to put the CIGS fully in the picture.[1]

Monty was full of confidence. 'I am busy getting ready for the next battle. The Rhine is *some* river,' he remarked in a letter to the Reynolds on 10 March, 'but we shall get over it. I move out tomorrow into the fields, and from now on will have a caravan-tent life. It will be cold at first, after a house with central heating, but I vastly prefer it and will be glad to get back to my caravans again. I shall take great care not to get cold.'[2] By hand of Maj-General Simpson he was sending home photographs of himself, Press cuttings about

[1] General Sir Frank Simpson, Eugene Wason interview for Sir Denis Hamilton.
[2] Letter to Phyllis Reynolds, 10.3.45, Montgomery Papers.

himself, and 'some of my messages to the Parachute Regt which the boys [of Amesbury School] may care to have (selected for good work or deeds)'.[1] For his son David Monty was sending a wristwatch, cake from New Zealand—and more photographs of himself. A photograph of James Gunn's portrait, about to be hung in the Royal Academy summer exhibition, was also included.

These paraphernalia of Monty's vanity were taken with a pinch of salt by those who admired Monty; but they irritated intensely those who saw in them the signs of self-advertising megalomania. As in the finale to the battle of the Ardennes, Monty's image of himself, his overweening vanity as a victorious battlefield general, was bound to disturb the amour-propre of American *confrères* still striving to repair the humiliation of the German breakthrough.

The first rumblings of dissension came when Monty announced, early in the planning of 'Plunder', that General Dempsey's Second British Army would alone conduct the crossing. The Ninth US Army Commander, General 'Bill' Simpson, was asked to furnish Dempsey with an American Corps for the operation; Ninth Army itself would not participate in the initial assault.

For Monty, as in Sicily, it was axiomatic that major operations should be under single command. Dempsey had been given only a paper part to play in 'Veritable' and 'Grenade', thus freeing him to plan and eventually command the Rhine assault. Once Dempsey had crossed the Rhine, Crerar's Canadian and Simpson's American armies were to be funnelled through in exploitation.

Simpson, like Patton in Sicily, objected. He would provide the required Corps, but under Ninth US Army command—for there were other considerations than the purely military at stake. If this was to be the main Allied invasion of Germany across the Rhine, the world would be watching—and credit could not go to British Second Army alone. Monty, unwilling that Simpson refer the matter to Eisenhower, relented.

Simpson's objection was but the forerunner of an American wave that grew to tidal force as Hodges and Patton swept to the Rhine. Eisenhower's Chief of Operations Staff, Lt-General Bull, was at Bradley's headquarters on 7 March when news came through of the capture of the Remagen bridge. Bull was unenthusiastic, arguing that the terrain beyond Remagen did not favour large-scale offensive movement, such as was envisaged on the British front. 'Ike's heart is in your sector, Pinky explained, but his mind is made up on the north. I detected what I thought was the influence of SHAEF thinking,' Bradley's ADC recorded in his diary.

[1] Ibid.

They were trying to make a contest of this. We were trying to help . . . Bradley is afraid that if we going strickly [sic] according to plan on the north, our supply line will be able to maintain no more than forty or thirty-five divisions. This would leave the others idle without a mission. Let's develop our strategy so that we can employ them all, he [Bradley] urged. Pinky slumped wearily in his seat . . . then suggested that the wrong persons were simply on the wrong fronts at this stage. Perhaps Bradley should be in the north, ready to push his Third Army across the river to Berlin.[1]

Eisenhower's most recent directive had demarcated phases or stepping stones for the current campaign. In drawing it he had been anxious that Monty should not strike out 'towards Berlin' before the rest of the west bank of the Rhine had at least been reduced to manageable German pockets incapable of spoiling attacks into the Allied lines. Now, however, the whole complexion of the war was changing: 'The strong movement forward of the Grenade operation has, of course, weakened the entire enemy line,' Bradley's ADC acknowledged on 7 March. 'Tonight the war went to pieces. That is, the war we had planned.' Though the Remagen bridgehead led nowhere, in strategic terms, it was a ready-made crossing which must be exploited. 'However, there is evidence of an inability and inflexibility of higher headquarters to adjust themselves rapidly to changes resulting from exploitations not foreseen in their plans. This marks quite readily one of the primary differences between our army and the British. The latter are magnificent planners but because of their thorough planning they are unable to improvise and meet the situation as it develops. Accordingly they lack imagination, they lack the recklessness to follow closely on successes and make the most of them.'[2]

There was an undeniable truth in this. A bare two months before, Monty had written to the Secretary of State for War that 'the real trouble with the Yanks is that they are completely ignorant as to the rules of the game we are playing with the Germans. You play so much better when you know the rules.'[3] Now, however, the game had changed, and with it the rules. Once again, as after Normandy, the German armies in the West were in disarray. Demoralization had set in and whole units were willing to surrender. With Eisenhower's Rhine directive now virtually fulfilled, the question began

[1] Diary of Chester B. Hansen, entry of 7.3.45, MHI, Carlisle, Pennsylvania.
[2] Ibid.
[3] Letter of 6.1.45, P. J. Grigg Papers (9/9), Churchill College Archives, Cambridge.

to loom: where should the Allies attack in order to finish the war most expeditiously?

The parallel with Normandy was acute—the Americans for the main part anxious to exploit in every direction while the enemy was disorganized, Montgomery adamant that the thrusts in the southern sectors of the Allied line should not be allowed to draw Allied strength away from a concentrated punch across the Rhine north of the Ruhr, employing at least thirty-five divisions, much as the Germans for their part had done in the Ardennes.

As in Normandy, Eisenhower was torn between two contrasting strategies and two contrasting approaches to war. His SHAEF directive of 8 March, drawn up by General Bull, still conformed to Monty's strategy, though allowing Bradley and Devers to co-ordinate a pincer attack on German forces south of the Moselle, west of the Rhine. Thereafter, however, Eisenhower became a prey to ambivalence, on the one hand convinced by Monty's logic of a massive Allied thrust north of the Ruhr, on the other by the keenness of his American commanders to show their paces and assume a greater role. As General 'Pinky' Bull had told Bradley, the American misfortune was its 'Atlantic' position on the right of the Anglo-Canadian armies. This was a theme that would vex historians for decades thereafter, with many military writers convinced that if the American armies had landed on the left flank in Normandy, the European campaign could have been greatly accelerated by virtue of American mobility and manpower on the primary front. Logistical factors had determined otherwise, resulting in the British forces being given the critical roles—but without the necessary resources to carry them out speedily. Now the Allies were poised for the final act of the European war—and Montgomery, a Briton, was *still* holding the Allied military reins, as he had done on the day the campaign began the previous June in Normandy.

Nothing was said, openly, to Monty. But in the offices of SHAEF and 12th US Army Group at Namur there was great debate. Should Simpson's Ninth US Army be put back under Bradley's command so that Bradley would at least share equally the honour of crossing the Rhine in the north and advancing into Germany?

Bradley's dissatisfaction with his 12th US Army subsidiary role was made very clear to General Bull on 7 and 8 March; and by 12 March the Supreme Commander was writing to Marshall that he was getting 'tired of trying to arrange the blankets smoothly over several prima donnas in the same bed'.[1] The same day Eisenhower

[1] *The Papers of Dwight David Eisenhower*, ed. Alfred D. Chandler, *The War Years* Vol. III, Baltimore 1970.

was also cabling to Marshall a secret plan to drop an entire seven-to-ten division airborne army on the Kassel area (east of the Ruhr) in May or June, to link up with a future break-out by Bradley's forces from Remagen.[1] But the next day, 13 March, with the spectacular success of Patton's Third US Army in the south, he approved Bradley's plan to break out from the Remagen bridgehead south-*eastwards* down the autobahn to Frankfurt, thus outflanking the German forces facing Patton between Coblenz and Worms—target date 15 April, one month away. At the same time Bradley was to hold in readiness at least ten divisions of First Army in case it was decided to exploit Monty's future bridgehead *north* of the Ruhr.[2]

Eisenhower, aware that the German armies were collapsing and anxious to retain flexibility, was thus unwilling to put all his eggs in one basket—Monty's. Yet if Monty's crossing—planned for 23 March—proved the undoing of German resistance on the Western Front and left the road to Berlin open, Eisenhower did not wish to miss this opportunity. However, assuming that some ten American divisions from Hodges' First US Army were sent north to reinforce Monty's success, could Monty be left as overall Army Group Commander? Bradley was adamant that, with American divisions now outnumbering British almost four to one on the Western Front, it would be scandalous for Monty to have sole command. Monty's insistence on concentrating the Allied Rhine offensive at one point north of the Ruhr Bradley found both tactically misguided and deeply suspicious—as he wrote in a private memoir after the war:

> . . . I was told that I must have ten divisions available to send north to help Montgomery in addition to the Ninth Army which he already had. . . . [By March however] we had our bridgehead at Remagen, German opposition indicated an easy crossing near Frankffurt [sic]. We had largely destroyed the German forces, and Montgomery was still wanting to confine our crossing to north of the Ruhr . . . [although] we had so effectively destroyed the Germans' ability to resist. In considering any of Montgomery's plans or recommendations it was necessary to consider how such plans affected Montgomery personally. His plans were most always designed to further his own aggrandisement.[3]

Bradley's suspicions were becoming neurotic in relation to Monty. On the one hand Bradley felt the Allies should attack in strength across the Rhine at a number of different points; but on the other he

[1] Cable FWD 17807. Ibid.
[2] Cable FWD 17839. Ibid.
[3] Bradley ms., Bradley Papers, MHI, Carlisle, Pennsylvania.

felt it wrong for Monty to retain command of the American armies if in fact Monty was proved right and the northern passage deep into Germany proved decisive. Torn between these two possibilities Bradley began to put pressure on SHAEF to be given command of all American forces north of the Ruhr if two American armies were in fact required there. Eisenhower duly attempted to draw up a directive to cover this eventuality, as Maj-General Simpson, who happened to be visiting Reims at this time, vividly remembered:

> I had a short talk with Eisenhower himself. In that talk we did not touch on any controversial topic . . . he was very interesting in what he intended to do. It all seemed to be in line with what had been agreed, but my talks with Bedell Smith, Air Chief Marshal Tedder, General Morgan, General Whiteley and the like were full of controversial topics. . . .
>
> What all of them at SHAEF did put to me was the question of command of the Ninth Army, still under British command for the crossing of the Rhine. The Supreme Commander's latest directive had told the 12th Army Group under Bradley to be prepared to make the First Army available for employment in exploitation of Monty's bridgehead north of the Ruhr when that comes off, and it fixed for that the target date of April 15 [i.e. three weeks after Monty's Rhine crossing].
>
> What they did say was when that happened 12th Army Group would inevitably have to take command of both the First and the Ninth Army. I was asked what I thought Monty's reactions would be and what I thought Whitehall would say. I had replied that I had no idea what Monty's reactions would be. As regards Whitehall, I felt I could not give them what the views of the Chiefs-of-Staff were likely to be, but I myself would advise the CIGS that a change in command would be unfortunate. My own view was that one man ought to be in command of all operations north of the Ruhr.
>
> There had been considerable discussion on that. Their point of view was that a move of a First Army of ten divisions north of the Ruhr would put twenty-two American divisions in that sector, which would necessitate an American Army Group Commander to take command of them. I had said that while this was all right, possibly, *one* man ought to have operational control of both Army Groups.
>
> I also said I realized that while the majority of formations would be American, that one man might well have to be an American: i.e. General Bradley. Bedell Smith came back at me at once and

said that that would never do. The Supreme Commander could never face the howl there would be from the British Press if Bradley was put over Monty.

I said that that was nonsense. If the matter was put fairly to the British Press there would be no howl except perhaps from one or two yellow papers. Anyhow, I added, if that was their trouble, why not put Monty in command?

Bedell Smith then said that they could not then face the American press.[1]

Simpson's view was that 'the Supreme Commander ought to leave the Press out of consideration and to do what was tactically right'.[2]

A measure of Eisenhower's tortured inability to give clear military direction was the three-page letter he had drafted, telling Monty of his decision to put two Allied Army Groups north of the Ruhr if 'Plunder' prospered:

> Bedell Smith had then said that Ike had already taken the decision over the command and was busy drafting a letter trying to tell Monty so. Bedell asked if I would mind listening to the draft and saying whether it would do. He had then read out a long letter of some three sheets of foolscap which had been drafted by Eisenhower himself.
>
> I asked whether they wanted my frank comment. When they said they did, I said I thought Monty would have difficulty in finding out from so involved a letter what Eisenhower really did mean. If they had really made their minds up and were going to change the command regardless of what Monty's own views were, then they ought to tell Monty so quite shortly.
>
> Bedell entirely agreed and said that he himself would redraft the letter in a very short form. He said 'Ike always tries to sugar the pill and the result is that the issues become confused. Monty has several times given us his views on this subject and we can fairly say that we know them. But Monty himself knows our difficulties. I agree that we only need to tell him what the decision is. I will tackle Ike.'[3]

As a result, on 18 March, five days before Monty's crossing of the Rhine, Eisenhower gave his decision, in the form of a secret personal letter to Montgomery, Bradley and Devers. If Monty's attack north of the Ruhr proved successful, the thrust would be subdivided into

[1] General Sir Frank Simpson, loc. cit.

[2] Ibid.

[3] Ibid.

two Army Groups, operating alongside one another: 21st and 12th. General Devers would take command of the remainder of the Allied front, south of the Ruhr.[1]

Monty was aghast. 'For the present I am making no comment, and taking no action,' he wrote to the ACIGS; 'the letter does not call for any answer and I shall remain silent; this is no time to introduce worries about changes ahead.'[2] Yet the idea was, in Monty's relentlessly professional eyes, a notion of such amateurishness that he could not refrain from scorn for the naïveté of Eisenhower, and the men advising him at Reims—all so deeply engrossed in Anglo–American politics and rivalry that they could not perceive the military ramifications of their proposals. The assault across the Rhine was to take place through the sectors of two Corps; subsequent exploitation by the three armies in 21st Army Group would require the closest supervision and dexterity both to keep up the momentum of advance—by-passing centres of resistance—and pinching out pockets of enemy troops by converging actions:

> Actually of course the whole thing is complete nonsense; the employment of two Army Groups round the *north* of the RUHR is not only unsound tactically, it is quite impossible administratively.
>
> One man must be in general command north of the Ruhr.[3]

Had Eisenhower considered Bradley's employment north of the Ruhr to be essential, he ought in Monty's eyes to have appointed Bradley C-in-C of the northern thrust earlier, as Monty had repeatedly advised. Now, at this late date, with the assault planned and the orders given out, it seemed inconceivable to Monty that Eisenhower could seriously imagine Bradley side-stepping north, establishing his headquarters and necessary communications in the wake of the assault north of the Ruhr, and taking over the tactical running of the battle. Yet only if he was to take overall tactical command would Bradley's introduction serve any military purpose, since it was patently obvious that to put two Allied Army Group headquarters north of the Ruhr was pointless if one Group headquarters could perfectly well control the battle. Bradley would have no major role to play if 21st Army Group's crossing of the Rhine proved—as daily seemed more likely—a decisive success. There could certainly be no *military* objection to Monty's command of four Allied armies, since he had commanded all four of them only eight weeks previously, in the Ardennes. Once again, Eisenhower did not dare

[1] Letter no. GCT/370-62/Plans, Montgomery Papers.
[2] Letter of 20.3.45 (unnumbered), Montgomery Papers.
[3] Ibid.

stand up to 'public opinion' in America: the same argument Eisenhower had used when refusing to back Monty's proposals in August 1944.

Had Monty only remained as silent as he promised; had he only assumed a less strictly military stance and proved more willing to overlook the tactical and administrative problems of running two Army Group headquarters alongside one another in the narrow 'Plunder' corridor across the Rhine, then World War II in the West might have ended very differently. With Bradley in tactical command in the north, Berlin would almost certainly have been taken by the Allies, and the myth of the Southern Redoubt consigned to the waste paper basket.

Monty's Chief of Staff, Freddie de Guingand, certainly assumed that Eisenhower's decision would be enacted, as did Brooke, who had already discussed with de Guingand on 16 March the likelihood that 'probably an American Army Group Commander would accompany the American 1st Army on its move to the north of the Ruhr should this become necessary in mid-April.' Had Brooke only put pressure on Monty to accept the inevitable with good grace, Monty might well have done so. Given de Guingand's friendship with Bedell Smith and popularity with most Americans, moreover, the unlikely military tandem could have been made to work, as in Normandy, despite the tactical and administrative disadvantages. Above all, it would have kept Allied strength concentrated in the sort of forty-divisional thrust 'so strong that it need fear nothing', as Monty had hectored Eisenhower when suggesting it the previous August.

Instead, Monty bridled—with results that were to affect the whole military and political scenario of post-war Europe.

CHAPTER TWO

Across the Rhine

HAVING SENT OUT his letter to his three Army Group Commanders on 18 March, Eisenhower flew for a brief holiday to the Riviera with his PA, Mrs Summersby. On 20 March he was joined in Cannes by Bradley. Though the Mediterranean was too cold for swimming, the sun shone and for the first time 'E. was able to really relax and enjoy himself', Mrs Summersby recorded in her diary. In the evening, in the Villa 'Sous le vent' there were films 'for those that didn't play cards'.

Monty, meanwhile, had moved his Tac headquarters across the Maas into Germany, where the famous caravans and tents were set up 'in the grounds of a riding-school not far south of STRAELEN. This site in the pine woods, scored across by a great anti-tank ditch, was delightful during the perfect week's weather of the Battle of the Rhine,' the senior Operations Officer later recorded.[1] 'I am pretty busy just at present,' Monty himself wrote to the Reynolds: 'getting ready to cross the Rhine, so the papers tell me!!'[2] To Brooke he described his feelings, six years after they had both set forth with the British Expeditionary Force under Lord Gort:

> My dear Brookie,
> My HQ are now in Germany. I have waited a long time for this moment, and have travelled a long way before bringing it to pass.
> It is a great thrill.
> All goes well here. Given good weather, operation PLUNDER should be very successful. Looking forward to seeing you on the 23rd.
>
> Yrs ever
> Monty[3]

To the Reynolds Monty wrote in similar terms, adding, 'I have just spent two days visiting troops away in the Ypres area; the Belgian people gave me a great reception.' Together with caravan life

[1] 'A Tac Chronicle' by Major P. R. Odgers, communicated to author.
[2] Letter of 17.3.45, Montgomery Papers.
[3] Letter of 20.3.45 (file 14/7), Alanbrooke Papers, LHCMA, King's College, London.

there had been a resuscitation of the Tac Headquarters farmyard—'our present stock consists of one cow, four geese, 10 chickens. The geese have already laid many eggs: which we use in omelettes.'[1] All was set for the historic crossing and, as before the battles that had brought him such renown over the past years, Monty insisted on addressing the commanders who would be leading the men in the forthcoming operation. At two large gatherings on 21 and 22 March Monty thus assembled and addressed the senior officers from his three armies, summing up the enemy's strategic situation, and then outlining the main features of 'Plunder'. The Germans, Monty began, had made three great military blunders—accepting decisive battle south of the Seine in the summer of 1944, then launching their Ardennes offensive without adequate air support and reserves, and finally 'fighting it out' west of the Rhine—where some 200,000 German casualties had been suffered. The only strategic reserve, Sixth Panzer Army, had now been drawn off into combat on the eastern front in Hungary; the Ruhr had been paralyzed by Allied air interdiction, and the Saar and Palatinate industrial belts had been overrun. The speed of her collapse would depend on the ability of the Russians to attack in the east when the Allies attacked in the west. 'The capitulation of the German Army as a whole was unlikely, but large proportions were likely to be cut off, and large-scale local surrenders would probably take place,' Monty's diarist summarized.[2] Operation 'Plunder' was opposed only by five enemy divisions, with two in reserve. 'Thereafter apart from odd battle groups, the enemy had no further reserves capable of opposing our advance. By D + 4 we should have established twelve divisions east of the RHINE which would be opposed by eight German divisions. It was essential to go all out in the early stages and seize quickly a large bridgehead within which the enemy would be unable to pin us down.'[3]

Those who had attended Monty's great conferences the year before in St Paul's School before D-Day were aware of the same sense of historical moment. The weather was fine, the troops were confident. As in the Normandy landings, the airborne drop would help guarantee the waterborne assault, even if the latter met stiff opposition; thereafter it would be up to the armour to strike out, if necessary being re-supplied by air.

> The enemy has been driven into a corner

Monty declared in the last 'Personal Message from the C-in-C to

[1] Letter of 20.3.45, Montgomery Papers.
[2] 'Notes on the Campaign in North-West Europe', Montgomery Papers.
[3] Ibid.

be read out to all Troops' he would issue during World War II.

> Events are moving rapidly.
> The complete and decisive defeat of the Germans is certain; there is no possibility of doubt on this matter.
> 21 ARMY GROUP WILL NOW CROSS THE RHINE.
> The enemy thinks he is safe behind this great river obstacle . . . but we will show the enemy that he is far from safe behind it. . . .
> And having crossed the RHINE, we will crack about in the plains of Northern Germany, chasing the enemy from pillar to post. . . .
> Over the RHINE, then, let us go. And good hunting to you all on the other side.
> May the 'Lord Mighty in battle' give us the victory in this, our latest undertaking, as He has done in all our battles since we landed in Normandy.

Not all were so confident. The Commander of the famed 51st Highland Division had a premonition of death;[1] there were anxieties about the strength of German anti-aircraft fire in relation to the daylight airborne drop. General 'Bill' Simpson would have preferred an earlier, unplanned assault, as at Remagen. But Monty himself exuded optimism. It had been the most striking feature of his military campaigning since Alamein to face an enemy on the defensive, whether across minefields, wadis, mountains, seas or, as now, the greatest river in Europe, some 1500 feet wide. As Monty had found before Dunkirk and thereafter in Home Forces in England, no defensive line can be made safe against invasion, for the defender must needs spread his forces throughout the line. Given tactical surprise, great concentration of men and firepower, and a violent and relentless prosecution of the assault, success was assured; moreover, having drawn the enemy into all-out combat in a particular area, the Allies could exploit their advantages of superior air and artillery firepower to gain *decisive* victory, and open the way to the interior of Germany without fear of enemy counter-attack.

In the case of 'Plunder', Monty was more confident than he had ever been. The Germans did not have the mobile reserves to prevent a ruthlessly mounted breakthrough, and the plan for the assault, beginning at dusk on 23 March and rising to a crescendo the following morning as the two Allied airborne divisions were dropped, was in Monty's eyes so good that he was quite prepared to postpone the operation if bad weather prevented the airborne drop. Thus in the early afternoon of 23 March he wrote a final word 'in haste' to his son David's guardians:

[1] See B. G. Horrocks, *A Full Life*, London 1960.

The Occupation of Germany

76 *right* Beneath the Union Jack at his Tac Headquarters at Lüneburg Monty 'ticks off' Field-Marshal Busch, C-in-C of the surrendered German armies in the north, for failing to obey orders promptly: 'The German army had been utterly defeated in the field, and must now accept the consequences of defeat.'

77 *below* Monty tours Kiel harbour, part of his new 'see' as Military Governor of the British occupation zone of Germany.

Meeting Russian Allies
Monty's 'opposite number' in north-east Germany was Marshal Rokossovsky. To the Russians Monty was the outstanding Allied battlefield commander of the West, and the welcome given to him at Rokossovsky's headquarters was warm and genuine (**78** *above*), with a banquet beneath portraits of Stalin and Churchill (**79** *left*), and a parade of Cossack cavalry (**80** *below*).

81 *right* In the famous courtyard of the Invalides, General de Gaulle decorates Monty with the Grand Cordon de la Légion d'honneur, 25 May 1945. It was Monty's first visit to Paris since the war began – he had refused to appear in victory celebrations at the end of the battle of Normandy – and Parisians went wild (**82** *below*).

Military Governor
After a somewhat 'acrimonious exchange of telegrams' Churchill finally announced Monty's appointment as Military Governor and British Member of the Allied Control Council in Germany on 22 May 1945.

Monty insisted on keeping away from detailed administration by setting up a personal headquarters some distance from Main Headquarters. He chose a previous Tac HQ site, Schloss Ostenwalde, where he was photographed on Rommel's captured Arab stallion in July 1945 (**83** *above*).

Schloss Ostenwalde
Situated 15 miles from Main HQ at Bad Oynhausen, Monty's new residence (**84**, **85** and **86**) afforded him tranquillity and comfort after six years of campaigning. 'I live there alone, with my personal staff and my small set-up for command, e.g. signals, cypher, liaison, etc. . .

'I sit back, keep in personal touch with commanders, concentrate my attention on the larger issues on which everything depends, and avoid being cumbered with detail.'

Berlin, July 1945

On 3 and 4 July 1945 the first US and British contingents were permitted to enter and occupy their respective sectors of Berlin. On 12 July Field-Marshal Montgomery, as British Control Commissioner, decorated senior Russian generals – including Marshals Zhukov and Rokossovsky – at a special ceremony by the Brandenburg gate (**87** *above*), filmed by a Soviet camerawoman (**88** *centre left*).

Three days later Prime Minister Churchill arrived to attend the Potsdam Conference, greeted by Monty at the airfield (**89** *below left*). 'No one knows anything about the [Potsdam] problem; the P.M. has been electioneering for weeks and has read nothing; there is no agreed agenda.... The P.M. looks very old; I was shocked... he has put on 10 years since I last saw him,' Monty wrote. In fact Churchill was only eleven days from electoral defeat.

90 *top* Monty, Churchill, Alexander, Attlee and Eden on the saluting stand at the march-past of 7th Armoured Division, the 'desert Rats', 21 July 1945. At the 'Winston Club' Monty introduces the Prime Minister (**92** *below right*). Relations with Truman and Stalin were more strained (**91** *centre above*). Truman's failure to stand up for the independence and freedom of Poland 'struck a knell in my breast,' Churchill later wrote. The result of the British General Election was declared on 26 July, and on 28 July Clement Attlee returned to Potsdam as Prime Minister, Churchill declining to accompany him.

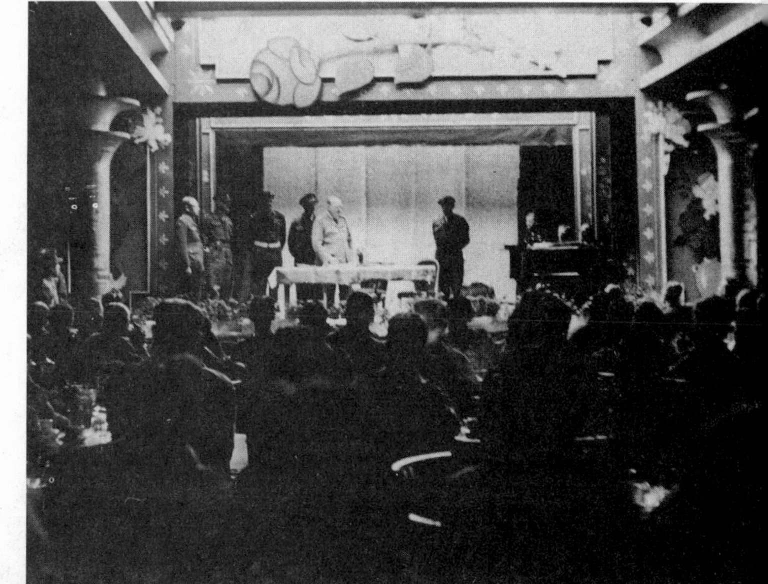

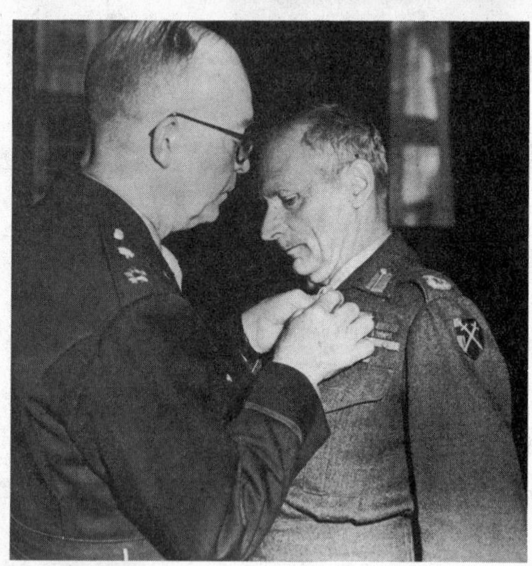

In the early days of occupation the British, US and USSR Military Governors got on surprisingly well. **93** *top left* Monty shares a joke with Marshal Zhukov, his Russian opposite number in Berlin. **94** *top right* Monty, Ike and Zhukov pose together and (**96** *centre right*) Eisenhower awards Monty the US Distinguished Service Medal in Frankfurt in recognition of his part in the defeat of Nazi Germany. **95** *centre left* Monty acknowledges the cheers of more than a quarter of a million grateful people in Brussels, as also in Amsterdam (**97** *below*).

My dear Phyllis,

We are off over the Rhine. I send you two copies of my message to the soldiers; give one to David. I also enclose a copy of my letter on Non-Fraternisation, a copy of which has been given to every man.

The weather is lovely, and if it keeps fine we should have a very good operation. The P.M. arrives this evening to stay the week-end. . . .

In haste

Yrs ever
Monty[1]

Monty had, as before D-Day, attempted to stop Churchill coming to view the operation. The Prime Minister's presence on the day could have no military value and would only distract the attention of the commanders at a moment when officers and men needed to concentrate one hundred per cent not on visiting dignitaries, but upon the battle.

As usual, it was Brooke who first perceived that Churchill would not be 'ridden off' his intention. Following their visit to Monty on 4 March Brooke had written to Monty 'telling him the P.M. would get into another of his rages if he felt that Monty was again trying to dictate to him, and stop him from coming out'.[2] On 10 March, therefore, Monty had been forced to invite Churchill to witness the historic assault. As he explained some days later to Sir James Grigg, the Secretary of State for War, 'I didn't want him but he was determined to come; so I have invited him in order to keep the peace.'[3] Monty had promised Grigg he would address personally every unit of every division that had been transferred from Italy, and on Saturday 17 March he set off on his 'tour', as before D-Day, standing on the bonnet of his jeep while parades of 5,000 men gathered around him. Meanwhile, given the possible postponement of the assault if bad weather made the landing of the two airborne divisions impossible, he begged Churchill 'not to leave England to come here until they hear that the operation *has actually been launched*': which could be anything 'up to 4 or 5 days, if we have bad weather'.[4]

Churchill refused to oblige. 'He will be difficult to manage and has no business to be going,' Brooke noted in his diary on 22 March. 'All he will do is to endanger life unnecessarily. However, nothing on

[1] Letter of 23.3.45, Montgomery Papers.
[2] Alanbrooke Diary, entry of 12.3.45, Alanbrooke Papers, loc. cit.
[3] Letter of 16.3.45, P. J. Grigg Papers, loc. cit.
[4] Letter to Maj-General 'Simbo' Simpson, 17.3.45, Montgomery Papers.

earth will stop him.'[1] The august party landed near Monty's new Straelen HQ at 5 p.m. on 23 March, and after tea Monty gave Brooke and Churchill a personal briefing in his map-lorry. 'The whole plan of our deployment and attack was easily comprehended,' Churchill later recalled with typically romantic grasp of the great drama to which he was privy. 'We were to force a passage over the river at ten points on a twenty-mile front from Rheinberg to Rees. All our resources were to be used. Eighty thousand men, the advance guard of armies a million strong, were to be hurled forward. Masses of boats and pontoons lay ready. On the far side stood the Germans, entrenched and organised in all the strength of modern fire power.'[2]

Monty retired punctually at 9.30 to his bed. But for Brooke it was a 'momentous moment', and one to be savoured. Churchill asked Brooke to walk outside in the moonlight. For all his austerity and reserve, Brooke was a sentimental man. Churchill's moonlight reminiscences, harking back to the desert days of August 1942 and the long but triumphant years since then, were especially moving for Brooke, since Churchill for the first time chose to thank his CIGS for his unfailingly wise counsel, his refusal to be intimidated, and his ability to choose good men and delegate responsibility. But when they returned to Churchill's 'wagon', the mood of quiet pride in their mutual achievement was disrupted by a new signal from Stalin, accusing Churchill of duplicity in trying to make a separate peace with the Germans, and once again Brooke witnessed the daily burden the Prime Minister carried. Brooke himself now began to consider the less romantic side of the imminent battle about to take place only fifteen miles away—the inevitable casualties in killed and wounded soldiers, despite the looming end to the war—and marvelled at Monty's sang-froid and brimming self-confidence.

Monty's own mask of optimism had concealed, however, days of anxiety about what was to happen *after* the Rhine crossing. 'One man must be in general command north of the Ruhr,' Monty had stated emphatically in his letter of 20 March to 'Simbo' Simpson. 'I shall be interested to see what comes next. Jock Whiteley is coming to stay here tomorrow night and he will get my view in no uncertain voice.' Far from remaining silent, Monty intended to shoot down the proposal for two Army Groups to operate north of the Ruhr; instead, he would propose that Bradley remain south of the Ruhr, breaking out of his Remagen bridgehead to encircle the Ruhr from the south, as Monty had originally counselled before the battle of the Ardennes: '12 Army Group should get a good large bridgehead

[1] A. Bryant, *Triumph in the West*, London 1959.
[2] W. S. Churchill, *Triumph and Tragedy*, London 1954.

from BONN to MAINZ and then strike north-east; joining me east of the RUHR.'[1]

This was the alternative plan which Monty had put to Whiteley on 21 March. In between their two Army Groups the nascent Fifteenth US Army headquarters under General Gerow could hold a defensive front across the west face of the Ruhr; Devers' 6th Army Group would be responsible for the front south of Mainz. Instead of Bradley holding ten divisions of First US Army in reserve lest they be required north of the Ruhr, these '10 to 12 American divs' should be held by SHAEF, ready to be fed into the battle wherever required.[2]

For two days Monty heard nothing. Eisenhower was on the Riviera, and no decision could be given in his absence. However, on 23 March, anxious like Churchill to witness the historic Rhine crossing north of the Ruhr, Eisenhower flew from Cannes to General Bill Simpson's Ninth US Army headquarters at Maastricht. There he received word from SHAEF's operations staff, who presented Monty's new plan as their own. Eisenhower telephoned Bradley, who was—so Monty was told—'very pleased with it'.[3] Instead of waiting until mid-April to take command of First and Ninth US Armies north of the Ruhr, Bradley could under the new plan push ahead into Germany south of the Ruhr with First and Third US Armies—of which the latter had, unknown to Monty, erected that morning a pontoon bridge across the Rhine, north of Worms. With General Marshall cabling that same day from Washington to complain about 'the overdose of Montgomery which is now coming into the country'[4] in the form of Press coverage of Monty's imminent assault, Eisenhower not only approved on the telephone the gist of Whiteley's new plan, but asked Bradley to throw an immediate Press conference that day to obtain better Press coverage in America of 12th US Army Group operations.

Monty heard the 'good' news about his plan shortly before Churchill arrived on 23 March. The next morning, as Churchill and Brooke set off with a hamper to watch the airborne operation from a nearby hill, Monty drove to his Ninth US Army Assault Corps headquarters at Rheinberg to see General Anderson, the Corps Commander, the Army Commander General Bill Simpson—and Eisenhower.

[1] Loc. cit.

[2] 'I put the problem clearly to him [Whiteley] and got his agreement to the following plan which he will now put up to Ike as the view of the operations staff at SHAEF': signal to CIGS, M560 of 2200 hrs, 21.3.45, Montgomery Papers.

[3] Signal to ACIGS(O), M1030 of 2205 hrs, 23.3.45, Montgomery Papers.

[4] Cable WX57751 of 23.3.45, in *The Papers of Dwight David Eisenhower*, op. cit.

Simpson reported that the Rhine crossing in his 16th US Corps sector was going excellently—some thirteen battalions of US infantry were across the river. But it was in a side office alone with Eisenhower that Monty formally 'fixed' the matter of strategy and command. Eisenhower confirmed that he was agreeable to the new plan for enveloping the Ruhr from north *and* south and it was arranged that a conference be held the next day at Simpson's headquarters attended by Eisenhower, Bradley and Monty to go over the details and boundaries.

Monty thus returned to Straelen well satisfied. With the Russians now on the Oder, only thirty-five miles from Berlin, speed was essential. SHAEF's notion of two Allied Army Groups operating north of the Ruhr had threatened to disrupt Monty's tidy picture of infantry and airborne assault, followed quickly by armoured exploitation in the 'plains of northern Germany'. Whether he realized the frustration and distrust he was engendering by yet again overturning Eisenhower's operational instructions is hard to say. As in Normandy, Monty was in the midst of what he considered decisive battle and thus insensitive to the feelings of staff officers in rear headquarters or Press opinion. With adequate forces he was certain he could now smash his way across northern Germany. It was the culmination of plans first composed in the autumn of 1944 when he attempted to vault the Rhine east of Arnhem and Nijmegen. 'Veritable' and 'Grenade'—postponed only by the American setback in the Ardennes—had been the overture to the great Rhine crossing; with the assault crossing now taking place successfully, and with his sights set upon Münster, Hanover, Magdeburg and the Elbe, his whole psyche was one of the hunter who, after patient tracking of his prey, moves in for the kill. The last thing Monty wanted was a complicated command re-organization that would distract from and perhaps slow down this kill—and seeing Monty's piercing blue eyes alight with victory, Eisenhower was loth to insist. Providing Bradley did not take exception to his new task south of the Ruhr, Monty's plan promised flexibility at a time when anything was possible—with secret surrender negotiations already being requested by Himmler, General Westphal (Chief of Staff to Rundstedt), Blaskowitz (Commanding German Army Group 'H') and von Zangen (commanding the German Fifteenth Army), Kesselring (C-in-C South) and Wolff (C-in-C in Italy).[1] Thus Eisenhower gave his personal blessing to Monty's proposal, flying that afternoon to Namur to discuss it with Bradley prior to the 'Big Three' conference the next day.

Bradley was still in two minds. On the one hand he was genuinely

[1] 'Notes on the Campaign in North-West Europe', Montgomery Papers.

pleased with the new strategy, mooted by 'phone the day before, for he had no real desire to move his headquarters north of the Ruhr and to relinquish Patton's Third US Army to Devers in the south. Moreover the idea of an envelopment of the Ruhr from north *and* south was a strategy he had himself come to espouse (with the idea of a third, Patton-led pincer driving north from Frankfurt) in November 1944. By launching both First and Third US Armies in a thrust eastwards towards Giessen he could surround those German troops east of the Rhine between Remagen and Worms; then direct both armies north to outflank the Ruhr. Thus 'we were delighted to get the "go-ahead" signal on our plans,' Bradley later chronicled, considering that this was in fact 'superior to Montgomery's [earlier] plan' of putting virtually the entire Allied weight into the thrust north of the Ruhr.[1] Monty's volte-face, however, filled him with suspicion; far from the plan being based on tactical or administrative reasoning, Bradley saw in it only Monty's absolute determination to cling to possession of Ninth US Army—'I got the very definite impression that Montgomery was more interested in commanding as many American troops as possible, than he was in having a large number of divisions attack north of the Ruhr.'[2] Nor was this merely Bradley's almost neurotic suspiciousness of Monty's motives after his humiliation in the Ardennes; hearing of the decision back at Reims, Eisenhower's own PA recorded the SHAEF feeling that Monty was interested only in feathering his own nest. Eisenhower, she noted, saw Monty 'who is very satisfied . . . the attack is going well. . . . He now says that he does not want any more American troops. Monty really wants to retain command of the 9th Army. He knows very well that if another American Army is committed in his area he will loose [sic] co[n]trol of the 9th. E. would be forced to put Bradley in comans [sic] of American troops.'[3]

If he was aware of such suspicions, Monty did not show it. That evening at his headquarters, with Churchill and Brooke in attendance, he listened to the reports of his Liaison Officers—and dictated his nightly telegram to the War Office:

> I can now say that the first day's operations in PLUNDER have been most successful. We have got six divisions over the RHINE including two airborne. We have captured 5,500 prisoners. Our total casualties are about 1200. . . .[4]

[1] Bradley ms., loc. cit.
[2] Ibid.
[3] Diary of Mrs K. Summersby, Eisenhower Library, Abilene, Kansas.
[4] M1035 of 2345 hrs, 24.3.45, Montgomery Papers.

Except in the 51st Highland Division sector (where the commanding general had been killed[1]) the enemy had either been overrun or was retreating—in fact 15th Scottish Division had already reached the airborne corps sector, thus cancelling the need for air re-supply. Bridging was going well, and the omens for a great Allied breakthrough seemed good. 'Looking on the day as a whole and the successes of the American forces in recent weeks south of the Moselle, I am quite certain that the end of the Germans is very near indeed,' Brooke wrote in his diary that night. Meanwhile Churchill was again mesmerized by Montgomery's 'methods of conducting a battle on this gigantic scale. For nearly two hours a succession of young officers, of about the rank of major, presented themselves. Each had come back from a different sector of the front. They were the direct personal representatives of the Commander-in-Chief, and could go anywhere and see anything and ask any questions they liked of any commander, whether at the divisional headquarters or with the forward troops. As in turn they made their reports and were searchingly questioned by their chief the whole story of the day's battle was unfolded. This gave Monty a complete account of what had happened by highly competent men whom he knew well and whose eyes he trusted. . . . I thought the system admirable, and indeed the only way in which a modern Commander-in-Chief could see as well as read what was going on in every part of the front. This process having finished, Montgomery gave a series of directions to de Guingand, which were turned into immediate action by the Staff machine. And so to bed.'[2]

There can be no doubt that Monty's grip on the day-to-day performance of such vast forces in the field was made possible by the courage and tenacity of his team of personal Liaison Officers. As Lt-Colonel Sanderson later recalled, the LOs travelled between 200 and 400 miles per day on their missions, using jeeps and Auster aircraft.[3] Joining Monty's team that spring as an LO after serving almost two years as MA to the CIGS in Whitehall, Major Earle noted in his diary:

[1] Maj-General T. G. Rennie had commanded 51st Highland Division since August 1944; under his leadership the division had quickly effaced its earlier showing in the Normandy battle. Its performance in the Rhine crossing was exemplary, as the ACIGS remarked to Monty on 26 March: '51 Div's battle for REES and beyond is a very fine show seeing that they had against them a P[anzer] G[renadier] Div. and parts of three para divs. In the circumstances, the completion of a Class 9 and a Class 12 bridge in that area is a magnificent effort': letter of ACIGS, Montgomery Papers.

[2] W. S. Churchill, op. cit.

[3] Lt-Colonel L. G. S. Sanderson, interview of 15.11.85.

> This is a mentally easy—providing one is not confused by detail—but physically exceptionally tiring job. Long drives in jeeps from dawn to dusk through battle areas, pitted and cratered roads, past dust and noise, belching guns and tanks. Getting entry to all commanders and getting a concise picture is also difficult; the long grind back not in the least knowing the way and no one except enemy to ask; the sudden limelight of the caravan with Monty as your audience—everything must be crystal clear by then.[1]

The difference between Alanbrooke and Monty came as a great shock to Earle. Even after 20 months as his Military Assistant, Brooke still addressed him by his surname; Monty, by contrast, called him by his first name on his first evening, in front of P. J. Grigg. Visiting Monty with Nye in Normandy the previous summer, Earle—an old Etonian with a passion for fast cars—had been repulsed by Monty's behaviour at table, his cocksure vanity, schoolboy jokes and bumptious bad taste:

> In his caravan Monty was at his best. Clear, simple, understanding, of single mind and purpose. Without the caravan at lunch he was terrible. Raucous, loud acting, public house jokes, bawdy . . . conversation. He is a very narrow minded man but more lenient and tolerant than a year ago. His greatness is his self confidence and absolute clarity and simplicity which he can impart to others. His downfall will be his acting which is bad and bad things never succeed.
>
> Archie Nye pulled his leg incessantly throughout lunch. Monty was talking throughout about himself. About the photograph that was taken of him with an umbrella talking to the Prime Minister. All rather disappointing. A very small man compared with Alex, Jumbo [General Wilson], Eik [Eisenhower] and minute compared with Brooke.[2]

The following Spring, working for Monty in the field of battle, Earle was astonished by Monty's thoughtfulness towards his staff, as well as his extraordinary brand of battlefield leadership: 'a bounder, a complete egoist, a very kind man, very thoughtful to his subordinates, a lucid tactician, a great commander,' he noted, perplexed, in his diary.

Meanwhile Churchill, pondering Monty's qualities as a commander, began to cast his mind back to Marlborough, whose life

[1] Diary of Colonel Peter Earle, communicated to author by Colonel Earle, 1985.
[2] Diary of Colonel Peter Earle, entry of 25.7.44, loc. cit.

and campaigns he had once studied in four volumes—which, bound in leather, he now presented to Monty.[1] On their way to meet Eisenhower—for Churchill had insisted on accompanying Monty—Churchill expounded the parallels between Monty's system of Liaison Officers and Marlborough's use of strategically stationed lieutenant-generals watching the battle. . . .

Monty listened, but his own mind was on the plains of northern Germany. 'His visit was very amusing,' Monty confided to the Reynolds; 'but it is difficult to attend properly to the battle while he is here.'[2] At Rheinberg Monty once again learned the latest 'score' on Ninth US Army's front, where German resistance was rapidly becoming a rout; however it was in a private tête-à-tête with Eisenhower and Bradley that the real meat of the campaign was to be decided. Though no record of the meeting was kept, it was one of enormous importance for the remaining prosecution of the war in Europe. According to Monty, the new strategy of enveloping the Ruhr from north and south was discussed so that Eisenhower might issue a formal Supreme Commander's directive; in doing so, over the map, Monty outlined his plan for racing on to the Elbe:

'I explained my plan of moving up to the ELBE line,' Monty recorded a fortnight later,

> and drew on the map the right boundary that I suggested for 21 Army Group i.e. between me and Bradley.
>
> The only comment made by IKE was that he thought MAGDEBURG (on the ELBE) should be inclusive to Bradley; it had drawn it [sic] as inclusive to me. I at once agreed, and Bradley agreed also. No other comment was made.[3]

Elated by 21st Army Group's 'blitzkrieg' success in crossing the Rhine, Monty's eyes were on the Elbe—and Berlin. The last thing Monty wanted now was a Stalingrad-like battle to mop up the Ruhr. Without reserves, fuel or air support, Field Marshal Model's Army Group 'B' could not do much offensive damage once surrounded in the Ruhr and would probably surrender in due course without heavy Allied casualties being incurred in house-to-house fighting. It was time, Monty felt, to cast caution aside and strike deep into Germany with Allied armour and close air support: and Eisenhower's lack of comment, save for the assignation of Magdeburg to Bradley, Monty construed as agreement.

[1] 'Winston gave me a very nicely bound copy of his book "Marlborough, His Life and Times", four volumes . . .': letter to Phyllis Reynolds, 29.3.45, Montgomery Papers.
[2] Ibid.
[3] Letter to Maj-General 'Simbo' Simpson, M569, 8.4.45, Montgomery Papers.

Had Monty only complied with Eisenhower's erstwhile notion of two Allied Army Groups operating north of the Ruhr, it is impossible to imagine that the Allied campaign could have deteriorated as it now did, in the very moment of its greatest success since Normandy. Armed with sufficient forces to flank the north face of the Ruhr, Bradley and Monty could without difficulty have swept on to seize the North Sea ports and have struck out for Berlin, before the Russians crossed the Oder. Instead, to Monty's chagrin the Allies threw away, in their hour of victory, the goal of their campaign since D-Day. Why?

CHAPTER THREE

Eisenhower's Carte Blanche

FAR FROM AGREEING with Monty over the race to the Elbe, Eisenhower had merely acknowledged Monty's general intentions. But with the spectacular domino effect of Monty's Rhineland victory further south, Eisenhower was under great pressure—as at the end of the battle of Normandy—to back American endeavour—and once again, Bradley disagreed with Monty's bold strategy of masking the Ruhr and sweeping on to the Elbe—and Berlin.

If Eisenhower was to back Bradley's alternative strategy, based on a 12th US Army Group push south of the Ruhr, he would have to seek permission from the Combined Chiefs of Staff, whose directive agreed at Malta had called for priority of Allied effort to be made *north* of the Ruhr. The presence of Churchill and Brooke at Rheinberg on 25 March was thus a godsend for Eisenhower—who promptly bearded Field-Marshal Brooke and requested release from his February undertaking, encapsulated at the 'gunfight at the Trianon Palace Hotel'. And Brooke, giant of British military strategy since 1941, the one man who could at this juncture have persuaded Eisenhower to abide by the Malta directive, gave way.

Despite his powerful and implacable military vision, there had always been a slight flaw in Brooke's nature, an occasional failure to stand by his profound insight and convictions. Thus in August 1942 he had seen with his own eyes that the Eighth Army Corps Commander, Lt-General Gott, was unfit to assume command of the desert army against Rommel—yet had bowed to Smuts' and Churchill's choice of Gott. He had bowed to Churchill's determination to allow Mountbatten, as Chief of Combined Operations, to sit in on the meetings of the Chiefs of Staff, and subsequently to promote Mountbatten to Supreme Commander in South-East Asia—something which not even Brooke's staunchest and most loyal colleague, the VCIGS, could understand.[1] Again, in December 1943 Brooke had proved willing to support Churchill's preference for

[1] 'The appointment of Mountbatten and the yielding to the Prime Minister's wearing down tactics in the Far East . . . are the only two major points on which VCIGS has disagreed with CIGS and has considered him weak in giving way':

Alexander as C-in-C Ground Forces for the D-Day invasion—something which Brooke himself found difficult to believe when re-reading his own diary after the war. Time and again when critical choices had to be made, Brooke had deferred to Churchill's romantic and unsoldierly judgement, to avoid further exhausting clashes—and as the war in Europe reached its final chapter, Brooke became even less willing to countenance abrasive confrontation, seeking solace and escape in his beloved hobby of ornithology, and attempting where possible to laugh at the Allied comedy of errors.

Eisenhower's performance as Supreme Commander on the western front was, to Brooke, not uniquely inadequate. Alexander's performance as Supreme Commander in the Mediterranean theatre had for months led Brooke to explosions of disappointment and anger, culminating in the 'intrigue' to get him removed and posted to SHAEF as Eisenhower's deputy. But even Alexander's conduct was laudable in comparison with the pantomime being performed at Admiral Mountbatten's South-East Asia Supreme Headquarters, which the VCIGS, Lt-General 'Archie' Nye, had just visited. Both Brooke and Nye felt that British strategy in the Far East was wholly misguided, forced upon them by Churchill largely in order to keep Mountbatten employed, as Brooke later confided.[1]

Nye's version of Mountbatten's morning conference in Kandy, two thousand miles from the front in Burma, was typical of Nye's spiced perceptions:

> That conference quite appalled me. It was held in a theatre-like building with a stage, a large audience, with black-coated professors all sitting in the front rows of the stalls. There was lovely scenery in the shape of highly coloured maps of all the various theatres of operations, which could be moved to and fro.
>
> It was really like a well-produced pantomime, and there the Principal Boy himself, dressed in immaculate white ducks, came onto the centre of the stage in the person of the Supreme Commander himself, looking quite gorgeous, and various fairies floated in from the wings, dressed in air-force coloured silk, signals in their hands for the Supreme Commander.
>
> The black-coated professors were appealed to, as the pantomime comedian usually appeals to the people in the stalls during some

Diary of MA to CIGS, Major P. Earle, entry of 21–28 August, communicated to author by Colonel Earle, 1985.

[1] 'I am certain that Winston ... was largely influenced by his desire to find employment for Dickie Mountbatten': letter of 29.1.59 from Lord Alanbrooke to Sir Arthur Bryant, Bryant Papers.

> part of the show, and it seemed to me that it was a wonderful piece of play-acting, but it was not anything in the shape of real war. In fact, the real war was the best part of 2,000 miles away in Burma. I was extremely depressed.[1]

Nye had then visited the Fourteenth Army Commander in Burma. There, in the jungle, Nye witnessed the Anglo-Indian Army at work—and was deeply impressed both by General Slim and by his Fourteenth Army. When Nye returned to London and read Mountbatten's references to 'his' plans for the land campaign in Burma, he recognized Slim's hand, and was reassured:

> I came to the conclusion that perhaps I need not have been depressed after my visit to Kandy. It was a very good arrangement really. Supreme HQ was there to be a buffer between the Chiefs-of-Staff in London and the troops fighting the battle on the ground. They received all the directives from London. They had their morning conferences with the black-coated professors, and left people in Burma fighting the battle to get on with the job.[2]

This view of Mountbatten's function was borne out by a letter received at this time from a former staff officer from the War Office, serving on Mountbatten's Secretariat. The letter, addressed to Maj-General 'Simbo' Simpson, gave a vivid and unforgettable inside picture of Mountbatten's headquarters.

'As a military HQ this outfit baffles and defeats my pen,' the officer—a colonel—reported.

> I never thought to see the day when so many senior officers would speak so much unco-ordinated piffle about so many unnecessary topics. . . . Everything lies dormant until it is raised at a meeting and then every Tom, Dick and Harry bandies his observations in bewildering rapidity and lack of purpose. The day goes to the most garrulous and the loudest mouth, and counsel of moderation is lost in the general fracas.
>
> Naturally, no one is briefed because no one under the rank of brigadier is allowed to know what is happening, and no one who has reached that exalted station can see any cause for going to the trouble of briefing himself in advance. There are so many ardent souls longing to solve his problems for him.
>
> These meetings happen perpetually. Each morning the Chief-of-Staff [Lt-General 'Boy' Browning] gathers round him some score

[1] Nye to Maj-General 'Simbo' Simpson, quoted in Wason interviews, loc. cit.
[2] Ibid.

or more, ranging from air marshals to camp commandants, and has a sort of canter over the course going through the various processes which I have always been trained to believe were the prerogative of majors and captains on the staff.

In the afternoon there are a variety of little generals.

At all these the wretched Secretariat, of which I am a member, sit with steaming pencils and reams of foolscap paper. It would not be so bad if only a few people would adhere, even loosely, to the agenda.

When you have to compete with a Supreme Commander who appears more interested in the 'footage of film expended during the week ending . . .' than in future operations, and a Chief of Staff who personally writes memoranda on the wearing of hats between offices—'because I am interested in that sort of thing'—I think you will agree that anything may happen, and anything does happen.[1]

This was the man Eisenhower had in 1942 recommended as Supreme Commander for the invasion of France.

He has infinite drive, infinite charm and a wonderful ability to create harmony

the colonel acknowledged of Lord Louis Mountbatten.

He is intensely interested in matters which in other places are regarded as essential trimmings—[news]papers, films, broadcasting and the like, and he brings the whole weight of his status and brain to bear on them. Consequently they are, I think, outstanding successes.

In other things, including strategy and the waging of war, he is impetuous and impulsive and vastly temperamental. His brain I would rate as no more than fair and he will always overcall his hand. It follows automatically that the troops worship him and the Chiefs-of-Staff are sceptical.

He is astonishingly jealous and will not have any decentralization; so much so that a draft telegram he has approved can not be sent off until he has personally signed the fair copy that goes in to the signal office. That is inherent in his character and has been humoured so long that high horses would not break it down.[2]

Mountbatten's actual methods of producing his Supreme Com-

[1] Ibid.

[2] Ibid.

mander's nightly cable to the Chiefs of Staff—concocted over the dinner table, often after copious amounts of wine—aroused the colonel's 'very strong revulsion'—indeed, when Sir Alan Brooke read the description he asked 'Simbo' Simpson if he might show it to his fellow Chiefs of Staff, since it at last explained the vague, plaintive, directionless and often less than sober cypher signals from Kandy. Later that day Brooke returned the letter:

> He gave me back the letter and said: 'You know, this has made a great deal of difference to the whole conduct of the Eastern War. I read it to the other two Chiefs-of-Staff. They laughed so much that we could hardly get on with our meeting because they too felt that the description fitted the pattern exactly of all the SEACOS telegrams that had come in.' And he added, 'You know, we all decided that we would not get cross any more. Every SEACOS telegram we would just have a good laugh over. We would do our best to meet whatever demands we were asked to meet, but it was no good getting cross.'[1]

Brooke even recommended the Secretariat colonel for an OBE for his contribution to the South-east Asia war effort. 'He deserves it more than most of your staff officers working in the War Office,' Brooke remarked to Simpson.[2]

Similarly, Eisenhower's frequent changes of mind no longer disturbed Brooke. For Brooke, exhausted by having to work with Supreme Commanders of great personal charm but devoid of strategic realism or the capacity to give clear, authoritative and consistent military leadership, had now taken the view that the war was almost won, and that it would not pay to get cross. As he had laughed over the description of the comic genesis of Mountbatten's fatuous telegrams, so Brooke refused to be upset by Eisenhower's fumblings for a formula by which Bradley could be made to feel he would be 'in' on the final Allied offensive into Germany—and hoped he could convince Monty not to take it seriously either. If the Americans wanted Bradley to command an Army Group north of the Ruhr—as de Guingand informed him on 16 March—then, however administratively unsound, so be it. When on 19 March de Guingand telephoned to say the idea was 'off', only to learn via 'Simbo' Simpson that it was 'on' according to Eisenhower's latest letter to Monty, Brooke 'laughed' and declined to fret. 'He did not feel the Operations Staff at SHAEF were being very firm in any

[1] Ibid.
[2] Ibid.

view of theirs,' Simpson informed Monty;[1] but did it matter at this stage of the war?

> CIGS said he hoped that you would not let any of this talk about the future disturb you at all: you had quite enough to do with your immediate problems. He said he will talk to you about it when he sees you tomorrow evening and would strongly advise not to start working against anything coming out of SHAEF, however futile their productions may seem.[2]

Provided Eisenhower did not actually withdraw forces from Monty's three armies in the north, Brooke agreed with Monty that events would dictate 'the tactical strategy to be employed.' Thus when he met Eisenhower at Rheinberg on 25 March, Brooke saw no danger in Eisenhower's new plan to surround the Ruhr from north *and* by a double envelopment in the south, as Brooke himself recorded in his diary that night:

> He [Eisenhower] also wanted to know whether I agreed with his present plan of pushing in the south for Frankfurt and Kassel. I told him that, with the Germans crumbling as they are, the whole situation is now altered from the lines of our previous discussions. Evidently the Boche is cracking and what we want now is to push him relentlessly, wherever we can, until he crumbles. In his present condition we certainly have the necessary strength for a double envelopment strategy, which I did not consider applicable when he [the enemy] was still in a position to resist seriously.[3]

In this way Field-Marshal Sir Alan Brooke came, unwittingly, to authorize Eisenhower to rewrite the Allied strategy for finishing off the war with Germany. For both Monty and Brooke completely underestimated the consequences of Eisenhower's new mood of elation. The brief holiday on the Riviera had restored his energies, and he had returned to the western front a new man, aware that the Allies were now on the threshold of final victory. The 'plot' to bring in Field-Marshal Alexander as his Ground Forces Deputy had been quashed (Churchill having formally withdrawn the proposal on 9 March) and he was thus in sole control of the Allied land forces. Better still, Brooke, on behalf of the British Chiefs of Staff, had now given him *carte blanche* in effecting the defeat of the collapsing German armies.

Eisenhower thus left the meeting at Simpson's Ninth US Army

[1] Letter of 22.3.45 (ACIGS(O)/7/M), Montgomery Papers.
[2] Ibid.
[3] Alanbrooke Diary, entry of 25.3.45, loc. cit.

headquarters a proud and confident man. For the first time in the entire campaign in North-west Europe he felt he had Churchill and Brooke wholeheartedly behind him. The failures that had beset the Allies since the moment he had authorized Bradley to attack the Saar while Monty attacked the Ruhr, culminating in the disaster in the Ardennes, were suddenly forgotten. As he telegraphed to his mentor, General Marshall: 'Naturally I am immensely pleased that the campaign west of the Rhine that Bradley and I planned last summer and insisted upon as a necessary preliminary to a deep penetration of the Rhine, has been carried out so closely in accordance with conception. You possibly know that at one time the C.I.G.S. thought I was wrong in what I was trying to do and argued heatedly upon the matter [on the eve of the Ardennes catastrophe]. Yesterday I saw him on the banks of the Rhine and he was gracious enough to say I was right, and that my current plan operations are well calculated to meet the current situation . . . I hope this does not sound boastful, but I must admit to a great satisfaction that the things that Bradley and I have believed in from the beginning and have carried out in the face of some opposition both from within and without, have matured so splendidly. . . .'[1]

Such self-congratulation and misrepresentation of what Brooke had said[2] indicated the rosy world Eisenhower now inhabited, having dismissed from memory his flabby conduct of field command and his endless changes of mind in the preceding seven months of the campaign.

Monty, witnessing Eisenhower's expansiveness now that victory was assured, was reminded of the change that had come over Eisenhower in August 1944 when he realized the true extent of Monty's Normandy victory—'Ike is apt to get very excited and talk wildly—at the top of his voice!!! . . . His ignorance as to how to run a war is absolute and complete; he has all the popular cries, but nothing else.'[3] Now, once again, Eisenhower was talking at the top of his voice. As Monty noted in his diary, Eisenhower still had no idea *how* such Allied victories had come about, since he had never commanded troops in battle and thus had only a paper notion of tactics and strategy. As long as victory emerged in the end—as it had in North Africa, Sicily and Normandy—Eisenhower simply forgot his own

[1] Letter of 26.3.45, in *The Papers of Dwight David Eisenhower*, op. cit.

[2] Eisenhower repeated this assertion in his memoirs of the campaign, *Crusade in Europe*, in 1948. Brooke was enraged, but waited some eleven years before authorizing Arthur Bryant to publish his diary entry, contradicting Eisenhower's account—adding 'I am quite certain that I never said to him "You were completely right", as I am still convinced that he was completely wrong!': A. Bryant, op. cit.

[3] Quoted in author's *Monty: Master of the Battlefield 1942–1944*, London 1983.

unsatisfactory conduct of high command, or the men who had by their professional mastery in battle saved Eisenhower's face and military fortune. Nor was such forgetfulness a wholly bad thing—for at least it restored amity between Allies and served to vaporize the more hurtful memories of altercation and even humiliation:

> The great successes all along the front, which followed as a natural result of the successful battle in the north, made everyone happy; all was well, the end of the war in Europe was clearly in sight, and success had united the Allied commanders in a way that nothing else could,

Monty's diarist summarized.[1]

Eisenhower and Bradley thus left Rheinberg convinced that their broad-front strategy was finally paying off; Monty and Brooke that their insistence upon concentrated effort to defeat the main German opposition was doing so.

[1] 'Notes on the Campaign in North-West Europe', Montgomery Papers.

CHAPTER FOUR

Berlin—The Biggest Shock of the War

EVEN CHURCHILL WAS surprised by Monty's wild good humour tantamount to recklessness, now it was clear that Operation 'Plunder' was successful. Expecting to be rebuffed, Churchill suggested going across the Rhine after Eisenhower's and Bradley's departure from Ninth US Army headquarters. 'Why not?' Monty replied.[1] To General 'Bill' Simpson's consternation the three most important British figures of the war—Brooke, Churchill and Montgomery—squeezed into a tank landing craft, crossed the Rhine, and walked for about half an hour on the east bank. Not content with this excursion into territory liberated a bare day and a half, Monty then asked the craft's captain to motor down-river to the town of Wesel. When the captain refused, owing to the danger of floating mines, Monty packed the august party into his Rolls and drove them to Wesel, where Churchill was soon scrambling across the twisted wreckage of the iron-girder railway bridge. General Simpson finally appealed to Churchill's good sense, as German shells began to land uncomfortably close to the bridge, raising great plumes of white spray from the dark river: 'Prime Minister, there are snipers in front of you; they are shelling both sides of the bridge and now they have started shelling the road behind you. I cannot accept the responsibility for your being here and must ask you to come away.' As Brooke noted in his diary, 'we decided it was time to remove the P.M., who was thrilled with the situation and very reluctant to leave!'[2]

That evening Monty's Liaison Officers reported on the latest situation. Though the airborne drop had resulted in considerably higher casualties than at first thought—'30% in personnel' in 6th British Airborne Division as Monty recorded with sadness in his nightly cable to the War Office—its effect had been to smash enemy morale. Thus on the front of 30 Corps on the left of the assault area where there had been no airborne drop, progress was still poor, with hand-to-hand fighting—whereas in front of 12 Corps and 16 US Corps resistance had melted. Simpson already had three Class 40 bridges across the Rhine in 16 US Corps area, and had taken 3,500 prisoners;

[1] W. S. Churchill, op. cit.
[2] A. Bryant, op. cit.

12 Corps had three bridges across. Prisoners already exceeded 10,500. The way to the plains of north Germany seemed at last unbarred: 'I shall exploit to the full the good progress made on the right flank by 16 US Corps and on 12 Corps front will drive eastwards toward BRUNEN and RAESFELD and northwards towards BOCHOLT,' Monty signalled to the War Office.[1]

So far the Rhine crossing had comprised airborne and infantry assaults; now, however, with six bridges erected and more being constructed each hour, the time was approaching when the Allied armoured divisions could be fed across the Rhine. By the following evening, 26 March, as Churchill and Brooke returned to England, Monty was convinced that he was 'approaching the stage when spectacular advances are quite possible on the right and in the centre . . . I think we are approaching a stage when we can get our armoured divisions into action. . . . The enemy is being fought to a standstill and on the right and in the centre he has nothing more to put into the battle. I am assembling Army Commanders at my Tac HQ tomorrow morning and will then issue orders regarding the more mobile phase of the battle which lies ahead and I will send you details of this plan tomorrow.'[2]

In fact Monty had already telephoned his three Army Commanders on the afternoon of 26 March to give them the 'gist' of his new plan—as he explained later in a letter to the ACIGS:

> My dear Simbo,
>
> I managed to get rid of the P.M. on Monday afternoon . . . it was difficult to get down to the battle properly till he had gone.
>
> It was then clear to me that there was not very much in front of me between DORSTEN and BOCHOLT, and I then decided to burst through between these two places and to repeat the PAS DE CALAIS tactics [i.e. masking centres of resistance while pushing ahead with armoured columns]: and to make for the ELBE. This was on the evening of 26 March.
>
> I ordered Army Commanders to come to my Tac HQ at 10 a.m. 27 March, and gave out my orders; I had given them the gist of my intentions on evening 26 March by telephone.[3]

Monty was quite aware that in ordering his Army Commanders to race straight to the Elbe, he was contravening Eisenhower's latest directive, issued after the Rheinberg Conference the day before, in which it was clearly laid down that the Ruhr was to be sur-

[1] M1036 of 2355 hours, 25.3.45, Montgomery Papers.
[2] M1039 of 2310 hours, 26.3.45, Montgomery Papers.
[3] Letter of 28.3.45, Montgomery Papers.

rounded and mopped up *before* an advance further east took place:

> You will note that I have ignored completely SCAF 247; there are moments in war when you take risks and act boldly; and use the doctrine of the 'blind optic'!![1]

he remarked. Monty felt 'certain that SHAEF will be delighted', and after meeting his Army Commanders the next morning sent the following signal to Eisenhower:

> Today I issued orders to Army Commanders for the operations eastwards which are now about to begin. My general plan is as outlined in following para.
>
> My intention is to drive hard for the line of the ELBE using Ninth Army and Second Army. The right of the Ninth Army will be directed on MAGDEBURG and the left of the Second Army on HAMBURG.
>
> Right boundary of Ninth Army will be the general line HAMM–PADERBORN–MAGDEBURG. Left boundary of Second Army will be the general line LINGEN–HASELUNNE–BREMEN–HAMBURG. Inter Army boundaries will be the general line all inclusive Ninth Army MUNSTER–HANNOVER–WITTENBERG inclusive on the ELBE.
>
> The operation will be similar in design to those when we crossed the SEINE and drove hard across the rear of the PAS DE CALAIS with Canadian Army mopping up the coastal belt of the PAS DE CALAIS later.
>
> I have ordered Ninth and Second Armies to move their armoured and mobile forces forward at once and to get through to the ELBE with the utmost speed and drive. The situation looks good and events should begin to move rapidly in a few days.[2]

Had this been all, it would have been enough. But in a last paragraph Monty added, with typical Monty-flourish:

> My Tactical Headquarters move to an area 1033 Northwest of BONNINGHARDT on Thursday 29th March. Thereafter the axis on which my Tactical Headquarters move will be WESSEL–MUNSTER–WIEDENBRUCK–HERFORD–HANNOVER—thence via the Autobahn to BERLIN I hope.

The signal was encyphered at 6.10 p.m. and received and decyphered two hours and fifteen minutes later, on the evening of 27

[1] Ibid.

[2] M562 of 1810 hours, 27.3.45, Montgomery Papers.

March.[1] An identical signal was sent to the CIGS, Sir Alan Brooke, who showed it to Churchill.[2] Eisenhower's headquarters acknowledged receipt, as requested, the following morning, 28 March, without comment.[3]

Monty had assumed that SHAEF would be delighted,[4] but he was wrong. His nagging insistence that Eisenhower adhere to his, Monty's, tactical strategy for winning the war had more than once brought Eisenhower to the brink of despair. Now, pepped up by his recent holiday and the spectacular Allied successes not only in the north but in First and Third US Army sectors also, Eisenhower had no longer any wish to be dictated to by a British field-marshal patently too big for his boots. From Rheinberg Eisenhower had travelled to Bradley's headquarters on 25 March; the following day he had crossed the Rhine at Remagen together with Generals Hodges, Patton and Bradley. He had visited no British formation or Army Commander for months, and the presence of the American Army Commanders on 26 March, each 'buttering him up', endowed him for the first time in the war with a real sense of being an American Caesar. From Remagen he returned to Reims on the morning of 27 March, and in the afternoon drove to Paris for a major press conference—a performance which his ADC-cum-PR officer, Captain Butcher, considered 'a peach'. Thereafter he watched a preview of a SHAEF D-Day film in the Champs-Elysées, and spent the night incognito at the Raphaël Hotel with his PA Mrs Summersby and Captain Butcher. It was thus on his return to Reims the next morning, 28 March, that he saw Monty's cable about advancing to the Elbe—and Berlin.

Only days before, in an official message to the Combined Chiefs

[1] Original decyphered signal in Eisenhower Papers, 1652 series, Eisenhower Library, Abilene, Kansas.

[2] M561 of 1520 hours, 27.3.45, Montgomery Papers. It was forwarded by the VCIGS on 31.3.45 (CIGS/PM/602), Montgomery Papers.

[3] FWD18255, Eisenhower Papers, loc. cit.

[4] The War Office had also assumed that Monty would race on to the Elbe rather than pausing for a slow mopping-up operation in the Ruhr. On 22.3.45 'Simbo' Simpson wrote to Monty that the CIGS was 'talking only yesterday of carrying mobile war against the Germans in the plain of North Germany. He felt that once you had burst properly through the defences facing you East of the Rhine you would be able to send a large armoured force cracking about in North Germany with tremendous effect' (ACIGS(O)/7/M). On 26.3.45 Simpson—having received news of Eisenhower's Ruhr directive (SCAF 247)—recorded his anxiety that Monty would be forced to move 'south-eastwards' instead of to the Elbe. The VCIGS, however, 'took the view that, if you saw an opportunity north-eastward, you would not feel obliged to take too much notice of SCAF 247!' (ACIGS(O)/8/M), Montgomery Papers.

of Staff, Eisenhower had declared: 'While we are continuing to plan for army to be ready to meet strong resistance, it is my personal belief that the enemy strength on the western front is becoming so stretched that penetrations and advances will soon be limited only by our own maintenance . . . I intend to reinforce every success with the utmost speed.' [1]

Why, then, did Eisenhower now decide, without reference to the Chiefs of Staff, to stop Monty and to rewrite the final act of the war? How did Eisenhower, apostle of territorial 'gains', believer in tactical flexibility rather than adherence to carefully prescribed plans, turn so suddenly restrictive: abandoning Berlin as the ultimate target of the Allied invasion of Germany and supplanting it by a wholly mythical notion of a Nazi Southern Redoubt?

No biographer or historian has ever adequately explained Eisenhower's strange and sudden metamorphosis in the last days of March, 1945. Certainly Monty never understood the decision to halt him in his tracks and up-end the logical conclusion of the campaign—though his shrewd suspicion was that Bradley had had a significant hand in what was to him SHAEF's 'skulduggery'.

Monty's first intimation that his advance to the Elbe and Berlin was unacceptable to Eisenhower came on the evening of 28 March. Encyphered at 7 o'clock in the evening Eisenhower's signal was prepared in Reims on his return from the Raphaël Hotel in Paris. For Monty it was perhaps the biggest shock of the war:

> For Field Marshal Montgomery's eyes only from Eisenhower. Top Secret.
>
> I agree in general with your plans up to the point of gaining contact with Bradley east of the Ruhr. However thereafter my present plans being coordinated with Stalin are as outlined in following paragraphs.

The mention of Stalin stunned Monty. He had spent three days in the company of Churchill, from 23 to 25 March, and no reference had ever been made to an arrangement with Stalin regarding co-ordination of the end of the war; nor had Eisenhower mentioned such a plan when conferring with Monty and Bradley at Rheinberg on 25 March. What then could such a plan possibly entail?

Eisenhower's signal spelled out the new strategy:

> As soon as you have joined hands with Bradley in the Kassel–Padderborn area Ninth United States Army will revert to Bradley's command.

[1] FWD 18141, 24.3.45, in *The Papers of Dwight David Eisenhower*, op. cit.

Bradley will be responsible for mopping up and occupying the Ruhr and with the minimum delay will deliver his main thrust on the axis Erfurt–Leipzig–Dresden to join hands with the Russians.

The mission of your army group will be to protect Bradley's northern flank. . . .[1]

Monty was aghast. Not only had Eisenhower abandoned Berlin as an Allied target, but only *after* Bradley had laboriously mopped up the Ruhr and prepared an advance to meet the Russians in south-east Germany would Monty be given any US forces with which to cross the Elbe and secure the Danish peninsula—if the Russians, currently preparing to cross the Oder at Stettin, did not get there first. As Monty wrote a few days later to Maj-General Simpson: 'On 27 March I sent . . . M562 to Ike. On 28 March I issued M563, my written directive [to Army Commanders]. On this same day I received the blow from IKE in which he disagrees with my plan and removes Ninth Army from me; a very good counter-attack!! All very dirty work, I fear.'[2] Monty even included a photograph taken of himself with Eisenhower and Bradley on 25 March, three days before the 'blow.' 'From the look on Bradley's face there is obviously trouble ahead!'[3] Looking back, Monty felt Eisenhower and Bradley had on 25 March known that they were going to revise the Allied plan, but had deliberately kept silent until Churchill and Brooke were out of the way. Apart from commenting that he thought Magdeburg should be inclusive to Bradley, Eisenhower had made no objection to Monty's explanation 'round the map' of his next moves to the Elbe—'no other comment was made. Yet on that day IKE must have known that he was going to take Ninth Army away from me, and that he intended the main thrust to be southeast towards DRESDEN so as to join up with the Russians in that area'[4]—for this would explain the two SHAEF directives despatched that evening, the first authorizing Bradley to disregard previous orders and cease holding a reserve of ten divisions in First US Army for possible exploitation of 21st Army Group's thrust north of the Ruhr; the second confining immediate Allied strategy to the isolation and mopping up of the Ruhr.[5]

Was Monty right? No record was kept by Eisenhower or Bradley

[1] Cable FWD 18272 of 28.3.45, in *The Papers of Dwight David Eisenhower*, op. cit.

[2] M569, 8.4.45, loc. cit.

[3] Ibid.

[4] Ibid.

[5] 'Having effected junction Northern and Central Groups of Armies will mop up and occupy the whole area east of the Rhine enclosed by their advances': SCAF 247 of 25.3.45, in *The Papers of Dwight David Eisenhower*, op. cit.

of the 25 March meeting, but it seems unlikely that the change of strategy was premeditated. As late as 29 March Bradley's own ADC, Major Hansen, assumed that the Allied target was Berlin.[1] It would appear much more likely that the change of strategy took place at SHAEF in the days *after* Monty's meeting with Eisenhower and Bradley at Rheinberg, and evolved from a number of factors. First among these was the matter of the hypothetical enemy stand to be made in the south German mountains, the so-called 'Southern Redoubt'. Intelligence information about such a stand had begun to circulate in the second week of March. Monty did not take the notion too seriously, as his letter a few weeks later to Churchill shows:

> I would say Germans have still got left considerable resisting power . . . but their army will gradually diminish in size and will lose cohesion as chunks of it are cut off and destroyed. Finally I suggest that a fanatical residue will retire to the BAVARIAN mountains not so much to fight on but as soon as possible to create the legend of an undefeated Germany.

Bradley's appreciation was very different. Far from mounting a token rearguard fight to maintain the honour of undefeated Nazi Germany, Bradley 'believes and is convinced that we shall have to fight the German in to the mountain fortresses of southern Germany and there destroy the core of his SS units which are determined to carry on the battle,' Bradley's ADC recorded on 9 March—a battle that might go on for a further *year*, Bradley cautioned. This concern with the Southern Redoubt seems to have grown like a cancer at SHAEF, fuelled by Eisenhower's Chief of Intelligence, Maj-General Strong. By 27 March, as both 21st Army Group and 12th Army Group began to cut great swathes into the German interior, Eisenhower was openly announcing at his Paris Press conference that 'the German would probably make a stand in the mountains'.[2] The next day, 28 March 1945, General Bradley arrived to lunch with Eisenhower at Reims. By this time Eisenhower, on his return from Paris, had seen Monty's cable about advancing to the Elbe—and Berlin. Bedell Smith was still ill—he had 'not been feeling too good these days and has had to spend several days in bed', Mrs Summersby noted—so that Eisenhower was having to make decisions without him, based on the advice of less senior staff officers such as Strong—and Bradley.

[1] 'In the Third Army sector the 4th Armoured Division is continuing its smashing penetrations eastward and is now being turned north toward Kassel to complete our first phase of the battle for Berlin': Diary of Chester B. Hansen, entry of 29.3.45, loc. cit.

[2] Diary of Mrs Kay Summersby, entry of 27.3.45, loc. cit.

Bradley's visit to Reims on 28 March may well have played a crucial part in Eisenhower's sudden change of strategy. It was shortly after Bradley left him that Eisenhower cabled to the Military Mission in Moscow for transmission to Stalin his decision not to go for Berlin:

> Personal Message to Marshal Stalin from General Eisenhower. My immediate operations are designed to encircle and destroy the enemy forces defending the Ruhr, and to isolate that area from the rest of Germany. This will be accomplished by developing offensives around the north of the Ruhr and from Frankfurt through Kassel, until the ring is closed. The enemy enclosed in this ring will then be mopped up.
> I estimate that this phase of operations will terminate in late April [i.e. in four weeks' time] or even earlier, and my next task will be to divide the enemy's remaining forces by joining hands with your forces.
> For my forces the best axis on which to effect this junction would be Erfurt–Leipzig–Dresden; moreover, I believe, this is the area to which the main German governmental departments are being moved. It is along this axis that I propose to place my main effort. In addition, as soon as the situation allows, a secondary advance will be made to effect a junction with your forces in the Regensburg–Linz area, thereby preventing the consolidation of German resistance in a redoubt in southern Germany.[1]

That he could have cabled to tell Stalin—unasked—of a new Allied plan he had neither placed before his own superiors (the Combined Chiefs of Staff), or his own Army Group Commanders save Bradley, was one of Eisenhower's most astonishing acts in World War II. Tedder, kept on as nominal Deputy Supreme Commander, was not present at Eisenhower's luncheon and was not consulted in the drafting of the new plan.[2]

Monty could scarcely believe his eyes when, early the following morning, he received Eisenhower's message. Not knowing what Eisenhower was transacting with Stalin he felt 'that complete silence is the best line of country at the moment', though convinced that Eisenhower's decision had nothing to do with military reality but was designed as a sop to Bradley, as he reported to the ACIGS:

> I hear privately that there has been great pressure from the staff at SHAEF, and from BRADLEY, to get Ninth Army back from 21

[1] Cable FWD 18264 of 28.3.45, in *The Papers of Dwight David Eisenhower*, op. cit.
[2] 'He [Eisenhower] therefore sent to Stalin on 28 March a personal message which was not shown to me before despatch': Tedder, *With Prejudice*, London 1966.

> Army Group.
> Ninth Army has done very well in 21 Army Group; the better it does, the greater is the pull to get it back: and BRADLEY shoves very hard at the back of the scrum. With victory in sight the violent pro-American element at SHAEF is pressing for a set-up which will clip the wings of the British Group of Armies, and relegate it to an unimportant role on the flank; the Americans then finish off the business alone.[1]

As a result Monty was refusing to alter his own instructions to his armies—'I am making no change in my plans and orders'[2]—in the hope that with Brooke's help he might get Eisenhower's order rescinded without having to close down his thrust to the Elbe. He had, after all, managed to get withdrawal of Eisenhower's plan for Bradley's Army Group to be moved north of the Ruhr only a few days previously. There was a strong chance that, if his two British and American armies looked like breaking out for the Elbe without hindrance, the very force of circumstance would suffice. To Eisenhower he therefore signalled a brief and poignant 'holding' plea:

> I note from FWD 18272 that you intend to change the command set-up. If you feel this is necessary I pray you not to do so until we reach the ELBE as such action would not help the great movement which is now beginning to develop.[3]

Copies of Monty's supplicatory telegram, together with Eisenhower's directives, were immediately forwarded by Brooke to the Prime Minister, but it was too late.

It was now that Monty's failure to treat Eisenhower as a professional equal, throughout all the months since their first meeting in the field exactly two years before in Tunisia, came home to roost. The previous day, 28 March 1945, before receiving Eisenhower's fateful signal, Monty had explained to the ACIGS, Maj-General 'Simbo' Simpson, the reason why he did not keep Eisenhower, the Allied Ground Force Commander, abreast of his operations as he did the War Office each night:

> I trust you will be careful not to send Jumbo Wilson [Britain's military representative to the American Chiefs of Staff in Washington] any 'hot news' you get from me. It would make things awkward for me if [General] Marshall receives from Jumbo—via

[1] Letter (confusingly numbered M562, the same number as Monty's signal to Eisenhower of 27.3.45) of 28.3.45, Montgomery Papers.
[2] Ibid.
[3] M562/1 of 1955 hours, 29.3.45, Montgomery Papers.

> the C.I.G.S.—better news than he gets from IKE. Actually you are far better informed, and in the picture, than is IKE.
>
> I do not send IKE a personal telegram; I used to do so [in Normandy], but then I found it was put across to him wrongly by his personal staff, and he didn't really understand it, as he never told his operations staff about it; and awful bellyaches used to result.[1]

All this was true. In fact Marshall heard of Eisenhower's decision to go for Dresden rather than Berlin from Field-Marshal Wilson instead of Eisenhower. Moreover, the diaries of Eisenhower's naval ADC and his PA in Normandy both amply demonstrate the way Monty's telegrams were misunderstood by Eisenhower's personal staff. Yet Monty's failure to keep Eisenhower *au fait* with his operations and operational thinking, as well as his refusal ever to visit Eisenhower at SHAEF unless ordered to appear, left the field free for Bradley to win Eisenhower's ear. Bradley had joined Eisenhower in the 'Sous le Vent' villa with Kay Summersby and two other Women's Army Corps girls for two days prior to Monty's crossing of the Rhine; Eisenhower had stayed the night at Bradley's Namur headquarters on 24 March; and Bradley had come to Reims for lunch on 28 March, the day of Eisenhower's fateful decision. During that period Eisenhower's signals to his American commanders, to Washington, and to his Public Relations executive—as well as his Press conference in Paris on 27 March—all testified to what Monty saw as a burgeoning American desire to clip his British wings and ring down an American curtain on the war. From Monty's point of view this was deplorable at a moment when he was poised to strike for the Elbe and Berlin; but from an American point of view there was no conspiracy, only—as after Monty's great victory in Normandy—the natural desire of proud Americans to seize their share of the credit before the war ended.[2] Bradley, not slated for transfer to the Pacific on the cessation of hostilities in Germany, was naturally concerned about his fourth star—indeed the subject loomed in his ADC's diary larger than any other. Patton was neurotically concerned to exceed the numbers of prisoners captured by Hodges' First

[1] Letter of 28.3.45, Montgomery Papers.

[2] 'I cannot quite understand why Montgomery should be getting a big play at this time in the States. It seems that even when operations carried out under his direction are of considerably less magnitude than those in other parts of the front, and even though large American forces co-operate, there is some influence at work that insists on giving Monty credit that belongs to other field commanders . . . I will continue to give my attention to this matter': personal cable from Eisenhower to Marshall, 24.3.45, in *The Papers of Dwight David Eisenhower*, op. cit.

US Army; and however well 'Bill' Simpson was doing under Monty's command, he too was concerned lest his great achievements be ignored or undervalued at home merely because he was in a British Army Group. . . .

All this might have been avoided if Monty had only encouraged Eisenhower's original intention to transfer Bradley's 12th Army Group north of the Ruhr instead of ridiculing the proposal. American honour would thereby have been preserved, the main Allied armies would have remained together and the road to Berlin secured—for there can be little doubt that it was Bradley's influence that persuaded Eisenhower at this cardinal moment of the war to drive on Dresden, not Berlin. Dresden lay due east of Bradley's pincer-thrust on Frankfurt, along the autobahn; in fact already by 26 March Bradley's ADC had been reconnoitring a new 12th US Army Headquarters in Luxembourg once more[1]—due west of Dresden.

Thus Monty reaped the harvest which he himself had seeded. The chance of a final combined Allied thrust to end the war was lost—and with it the prize of Berlin.

[1] 12th US Army Group Headquarters opened officially in Luxembourg—its final location in WWII—on 2 April 1945.

CHAPTER FIVE

A Terrible Mistake

MONTY WAS NOT alone in being shocked by Eisenhower's decision not to go for Berlin. Berlin had been, from the beginning of the campaign in North-west Europe, the goal of the Allied Expeditionary Force, and officially designated by SHAEF as such. 'Our main object must be the early capture of BERLIN, the most important objective in Germany,' its planning staff had laid down the previous September, as Monty battled for Arnhem. Although topographically there was 'little to choose between an advance from the RUHR or from the FRANKFURT area', SHAEF had opted for the Ruhr approach on military grounds:

> Logistically an advance from the RUHR could be supported more rapidly and in greater strength than from the FRANKFURT area, it is closer to the [North Sea] ports, ensuring a shorter L of C.[1]

SHAEF's planning staff therefore recommended that the Allied armies should 'carry out a main thrust from the RUHR on the axis HANOVER–BERLIN', with a *subsidiary* force covering the southern flank 'moving from FRANKFURT'. Only if the Allied advance was 'delayed', or 'if the Russians forestall us in Berlin' should the Allies alter their priority; in which case the area 'Kiel–Hamburg–Bremen' was the next most important priority, as well as inner industrial conurbations.[2]

The Russians had, however, *not* reached Berlin. They were stalled on the Oder; and the Leipzig–Dresden area, like the approaches to Berlin, was inside the area assigned for Russian occupation at the Yalta conference. Why then did Eisenhower suddenly wish to give it Allied priority over Berlin?

Churchill was the first to become suspicious; he had seen a copy of Monty's signal of 27 March heralding a great Anglo-American advance to the Elbe, and when a copy of Eisenhower's message to Stalin arrived in London on the evening of 28 March, concerning the 'main' Allied effort in the Leipzig–Dresden area—in fact not even

[1] Memorandum by Planning Staff, SHAEF G3 Fwd, 24.9.44, in 'Development of Operations After Occupation of the Ruhr' file (WO 705/682), PRO.
[2] Ibid.

mentioning northern Germany, the North Sea ports or Denmark—Churchill was nonplussed. 'This seems to differ from last night's Montgomery,' Churchill sent a note to General Ismay, his Military Secretary, 'who spoke of the Elbe. Please explain.'[1]

Ismay could not, for the British Chiefs of Staff were as puzzled as Churchill—though not, initially, as suspicious. 'In our innocence in the War Office, from CIGS downwards,' Maj-General Simpson wrote a few days later to Monty, 'we assumed that this was in no way whittling down the Northern thrust.'[2] The absence of any mention of the North Sea ports, however, alarmed Sir Andrew Cunningham, the First Sea Lord, and the sparks soon began to fly: 'the Navy got wind from someone that it might not be so. It did not take long for the three Chiefs of Staff to work themselves into a passion over it and to send a very stiff telegram to Washington.'[3]

Thus 'a fair gale' had started to blow by the morning of Thursday, 29 March. 'The PM also bridled quite independently,' Simpson related to Monty.[4] In fact the Prime Minister telephoned SHAEF on the 'scrambler' to protest to Eisenhower—'6.45 call from the P.M.,' Eisenhower's PA logged in her diary. 'He does not agree with E's future operational plans and wants our forces to turn *North* instead of *East*. In other words he wants to keep a large force under Monty.'[5]

Whatever operational reasons Eisenhower concocted in the days thereafter to excuse his sudden and unilateral rewriting of Allied strategy, there can be little doubt that the initial motivation for such a radical alteration was personal, as well as one of 'national' justice. Irrespective of the gloss sober historians might later apply to the decisions, the parties concerned were all infected by the sea change which American predominance in arms and soldiers had incurred. As Sir Ian Jacob, deputy to General Ismay, later recalled, the American piper had begun to play the tune already at the Tehran conference in November 1943; and with every month thereafter the American 'voice' in the Allied councils of state grew more strident. Indeed when Bedell Smith arrived in Malta at the end of January 1945, he 'announced that, if the British intended to insert a new Ground Force Commander under Eisenhower, then both Eisenhower and Bedell Smith would resign'. 'I remember it clearly,' Sir Ian Jacob recalled almost forty years later. 'I mean, it wasn't everybody who dared

[1] J. Ehrman, *Grand Strategy* Vol. VI, London 1956.
[2] Letter of 31.3.45 (ACIGS(o)/10/M), Montgomery Papers.
[3] Ibid.
[4] Ibid.
[5] Diary of Mrs K. Summersby, entry of 29.3.45, loc. cit.

stand up like that to Sir Alan Brooke—who was a very formidable character. But that's what Bedell Smith said—and he obviously meant it! Brooke was stunned. We could say nothing.'[1] Churchill in fact went over Eisenhower's and Marshall's heads by getting Roosevelt's personal approval for Alexander to replace Tedder; but as has been seen, Eisenhower had been able to disarm Churchill by his seemingly generous charter to Monty which promised to keep Ninth US Army under 21st Army Group for the remainder of the war.

Now Eisenhower was reneging on this charter—and though Monty, Churchill and the British Chiefs of Staff expostulated, there was nothing they could do. The war was all but won, and with Britain now only contributing a fraction of the Allied Expeditionary Force armies, the British could not hope to alter American war aims save by an appeal to better sense. Given a sick American President—Roosevelt was dying—and with Eisenhower determined to give Bradley the lion's share of the final battle, British protests could only serve to exacerbate ill-feeling between the Allies, without benefit, as Churchill quickly perceived. Rebuking the Chiefs of Staff for the tone and content of their signals to the American Chiefs of Staff, Churchill now demonstrated the genius of his political, diplomatic and military perception. He pointed out that Britain was only contributing a 'quarter of the forces invading Germany'; that, although it owed its *true* genesis to Monty's great battle in the Rhineland, the fact was that Eisenhower's policy of closing the Rhine throughout its whole length had been enacted, enabling the Allies to mount a double advance now, rather than the single one insisted upon by the British Chiefs of Staff at Malta. Eisenhower's 'stock' thus stood very high—and accusations that he was not considering 'issues which have a wider import than the destruction of the main enemy force in Germany'[2] sounded very odd coming from men who had for so long sought to teach the Americans to concentrate their forces on defeating the enemy rather than territorial or political gain. To argue that Montgomery ought to be given sufficient American strength to help clear up the North Sea ports, Denmark and the Baltic *before* Eisenhower had dealt with the 'main enemy forces' was inconsistent with previous British military policy; moreover the argument about U-boat bases was unsound, since the current U-boat menace was far less damaging than had been anticipated.

What Churchill perceived, after seeing a copy of Monty's signal to the CIGS about the imminent removal of Ninth US Army from 21st

[1] Lt-General Sir Ian Jacob, interview of 28.6.84.

[2] Phrase used by the British Chiefs of Staff in protesting to Washington. See J. Ehrman, op. cit.

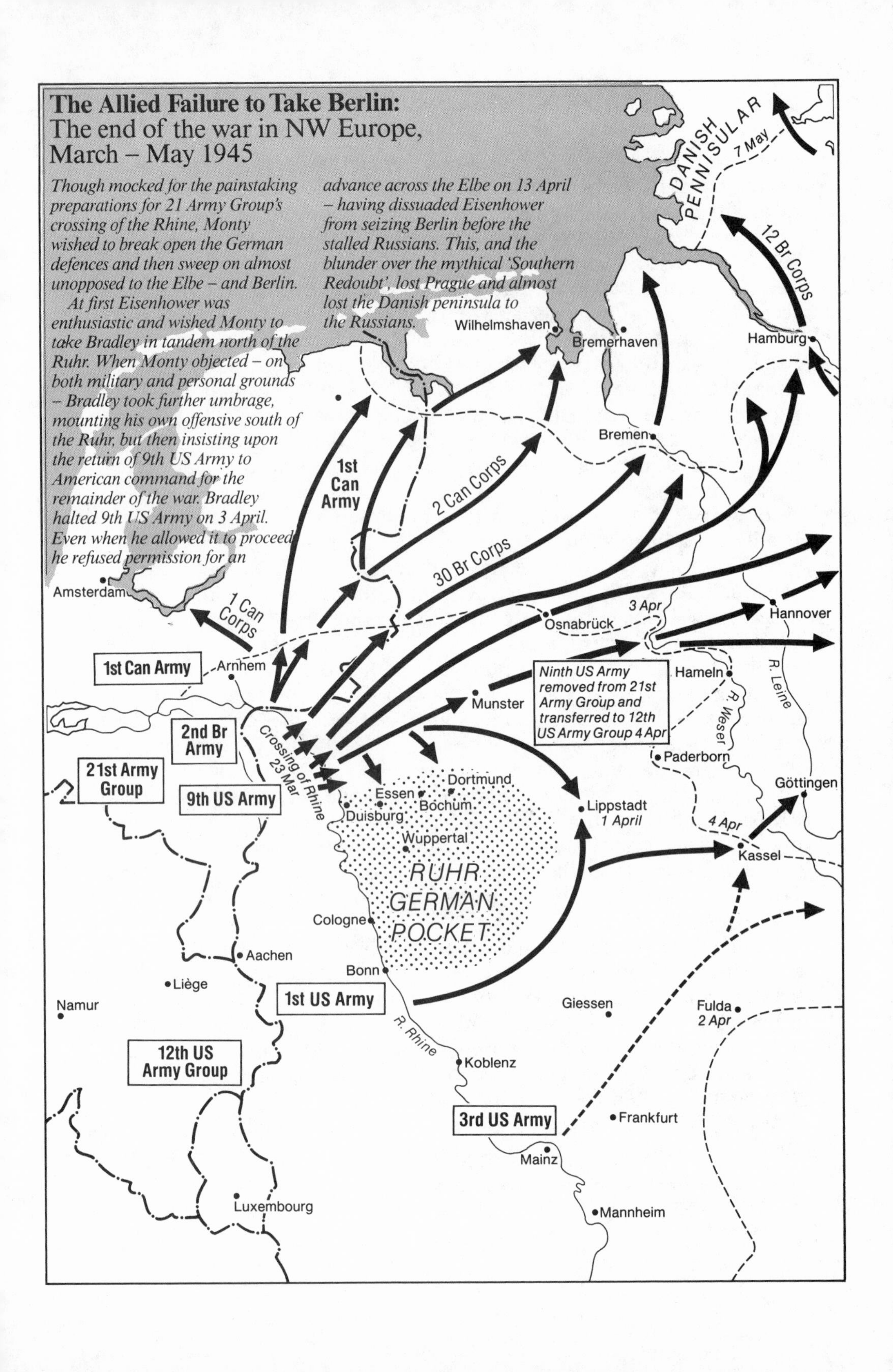

The Allied Failure to Take Berlin:
The end of the war in NW Europe, March – May 1945
Though mocked for the painstaking preparations for 21 Army Group's crossing of the Rhine, Monty wished to break open the German defences and then sweep on almost unopposed to the Elbe – and Berlin.
At first Eisenhower was enthusiastic and wished Monty to take Bradley in tandem north of the Ruhr. When Monty objected – on both military and personal grounds – Bradley took further umbrage, mounting his own offensive south of the Ruhr, but then insisting upon the return of 9th US Army to American command for the remainder of the war. Bradley halted 9th US Army on 3 April. Even when he allowed it to proceed he refused permission for an advance across the Elbe on 13 April – having dissuaded Eisenhower from seizing Berlin before the stalled Russians. This, and the blunder over the mythical 'Southern Redoubt', lost Prague and almost lost the Danish peninsula to the Russians.
DANISH PENINSULAR
7 May
12 Br Corps
Wilhelmshaven
Bremerhaven
Hamburg
Bremen
1st Can Army
2 Can Corps
30 Br Corps
Amsterdam
1 Can Corps
Osnabrück
3 Apr
Hannover
1st Can Army
Arnhem
Ninth US Army removed from 21st Army Group and transferred to 12th US Army Group 4 Apr
Hameln
Munster
R. Leine
R. Weser
2nd Br Army
Crossing of Rhine 23 Mar
Paderborn
21st Army Group
9th US Army
Dortmund
Essen
Bochum
Göttingen
Duisburg
Lippstadt
1 April
4 Apr
Wuppertal
Kassel
RUHR GERMAN POCKET
Cologne
Aachen
Bonn
Liège
1st US Army
Giessen
Fulda
2 Apr
Namur
R. Rhine
12th US Army Group
Koblenz
3rd US Army
Frankfurt
Mainz
Luxembourg
Mannheim

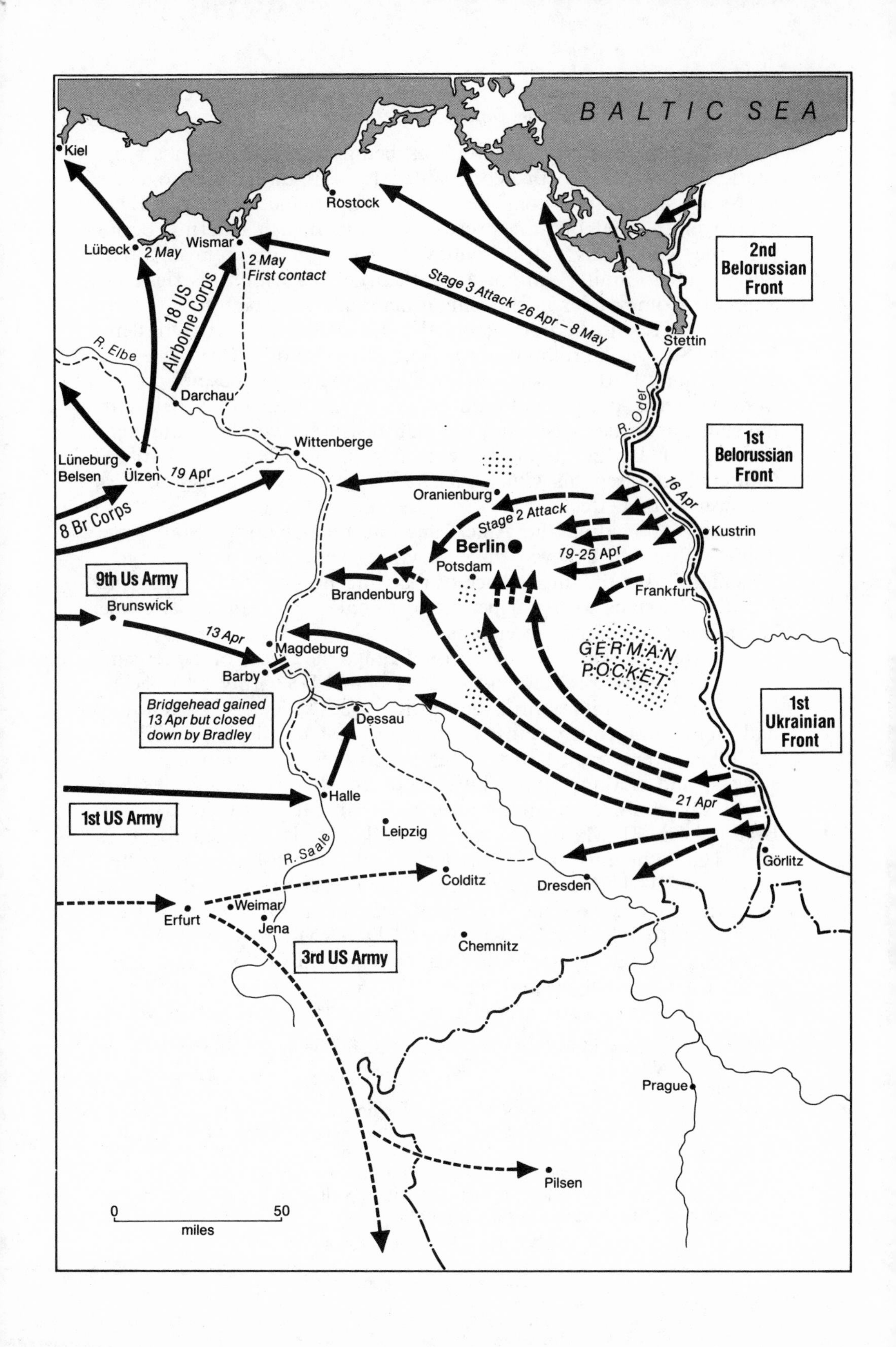
BALTIC SEA
Kiel
Lübeck
2 May
Wismar
2 May
First contact
Rostock
2nd Belorussian Front
Stage 3 Attack 26 Apr – 8 May
Stettin
18 US Airborne Corps
R. Elbe
Darchau
R. Oder
Wittenberge
Lüneburg
Belsen
Ülzen
19 Apr
8 Br Corps
1st Belorussian Front
16 Apr
Oranienburg
Stage 2 Attack
Kustrin
Berlin
19-25 Apr
Potsdam
Brandenburg
Frankfurt
9th US Army
Brunswick
13 Apr
Magdeburg
Barby
GERMAN POCKET
Bridgehead gained 13 Apr but closed down by Bradley
Dessau
1st Ukrainian Front
Halle
21 Apr
1st US Army
Leipzig
R. Saale
Görlitz
Colditz
Dresden
Erfurt
Weimar
Jena
Chemnitz
3rd US Army
Prague
Pilsen
0
50
miles

Army Group, was that Britain was being relegated to an almost 'static role in the North', condemned to wait until an 'altogether later stage in the operations' before it could advance across the Elbe. Moreover it ruled out the prospect of 'the British entering Berlin with the Americans'.[1] If Eisenhower was right in supposing that Berlin had no military importance, then he was within his rights as Supreme Commander in choosing a main axis of attack to sever the German forces in the north from those in the south—i.e. Dresden–Leipzig. But *was* he right about Berlin? 'The idea of neglecting Berlin and leaving it to the Russians to take at a later stage does not appear to me correct. As long as Berlin holds out and withstands a siege in the ruins, as it may easily do, German resistance will be stimulated. The fall of Berlin might cause nearly all Germans to despair,' Churchill minuted his Chiefs of Staff,[2] and sent a signal to Eisenhower to this effect.[3]

Instead of chiding the Americans—as the Chiefs of Staff were doing—Churchill believed that everything should be done to make Washington see the importance of reaching Berlin—and of ensuring that the Russians were not permitted to enter the Danish peninsula before the British and Americans.

Not even Churchill, however, could gauge the extent of 'American' feeling at Reims. Bradley had wanted Ninth US Army returned to him after the humiliation of the Battle of the Ardennes; Eisenhower had then courageously refused, irrespective of Bradley's pride. Now the tables were turned; the American armies were enjoying great success, and nothing that Churchill or the British Chiefs of Staff might say could alter Eisenhower's determination to do right by Bradley. On 31 March Eisenhower had already rejected Monty's plea. The Ruhr must first be 'brought under control'; thereafter 'the axis KASSEL–LEIPZIG' seemed to Eisenhower 'the most direct line of advance' to divide and destroy the German forces opposing the Allies and to join hands 'with the RED ARMY'. Beyond that he was unsure what he would do—either to go north 'to seize the important naval, political and shipping objectives across the ELBE or to the south to destroy any effective concentration of forces which

[1] Memo from Churchill to Ismay for Chiefs of Staff Committee, 31.3.45, in W. S. Churchill, op. cit.

[2] Minute of 31.3.45, loc. cit.

[3] 'I do not know why it would be an advantage not to cross the Elbe . . . I do not consider that Berlin has yet lost its military and political significance': signal of 31.3.45, in W. S. Churchill op. cit. Churchill was right: the move of 'German ministries' which Eisenhower was citing as his reason for discounting the importance of Berlin, was insignificant beside the fact that Hitler, Keitel, Jodl and the main Nazi barons remained in Berlin for a further month.

the enemy may succeed in creating. The course I shall adopt must depend upon the development of a very fluid situation,' Eisenhower wrote.[1] Either way, the encirclement of the Ruhr and its mopping-up was number one priority before even the thrust to Leipzig could be underaken—and this was a task for one commander: Bradley. With Bradley in charge of the Ruhr operation, Bradley would be 'in the position to judge' when was the best moment to strike east to Leipzig—with Ninth US Army under command. Later, if operations across the Elbe were required, 'an American formation' could be furnished to 21st Army Group. 'You will note that in none of this do I mention BERLIN. That place has become, so far as I am concerned, nothing but a geographical location, and I have never been interested in these,' Eisenhower added a trifle untruthfully. 'My purpose is to destroy the enemy's forces and his powers to resist.'[2]

Monty was beside himself with frustration waiting for this response to his plea of 29 March. He had told 'Simbo' Simpson that, in the meantime, he was not going to change his plans or orders.[3] It was futile to waste time mopping up the Ruhr when the 'main business' lay to the east and the north; it would be enough, he felt, to turn one corps of Ninth US Army around the north face of the Ruhr and direct the rest, alongside Dempsey's Second Army, to the Elbe. But with Eisenhower's new signal of 31 March, it was obvious that the advance to the Elbe would collapse: 'The gist of his [Eisenhower's] reply is that he intends halting the present movements whilst 12th Army Group cleans up the Ruhr. After that 12th Army Group will develop a thrust on Axis LEIPZIG–DRESDEN to join up with Red Army. For all these operations he intends that 9th Army will return to Bradley and he adheres to this decision and this alone is quite enough to halt the present movement . . . I consider we are about to make a terrible mistake. The great point now is speed of action so that we can finish off German war in shortest possible time. We must keep going and NOT give enemy time to recover and especially we must not let his troops in Holland and northern Germany get down to the south.'[4]

For the life of him Monty could not understand why Eisenhower wished to waste time first laboriously mopping up the Ruhr, then putting three entire American armies into a thrust to Leipzig—whose industrial capacity, like that of the Ruhr, was now paralyzed by Allied air interdiction and fuel shortage. Monty's recommendation,

[1] Cable FWD 18389, in *The Papers of Dwight David Eisenhower*, op. cit.
[2] Ibid.
[3] M562 to Simpson, loc. cit.
[4] Signal to CIGS, M564 of 1210 hours, 1.4.45, Montgomery Papers.

therefore, was that General Gerow's nascent Fifteenth US Army should 'clear up Ruhr pocket while other armies continue operations at present in progress'.[1] Ninth US Army should remain in 21st Army Group which should continue its breakout to the Elbe and, if Berlin was still 'off', to turn northwards to the Baltic coast. Meanwhile Bradley's 12th US Army Group, flanked on the right by Devers' Sixth Army Group, could move eastwards towards Leipzig if that was where it wished to meet the Red Army, peeling off a single corps, as would 21st Army Group, to help Fifteenth Army clean up the Ruhr.[2] 'It seems doctrine that public opinion wins wars is coming to the fore again,' Monty lamented, knowing that Bradley was behind the pull to get Ninth US Army transferred to the Ruhr-and-Leipzig strategy. 'I have many times told Ike that this is a dangerous doctrine and in my opinion it is victories in battle that win wars. The Germans have had a great defeat and are in a state when if we act correctly we can finish the business quickly.'[3]

In reporting this to the CIGS on 1 April Monty promised to 'maintain complete silence', merely sending home copies of Eisenhower's signals via Field-Marshal Wavell who was visiting him in the field. But Monty was never one to surrender without a fight, whatever Brooke's advice. Summoning his Chief of Staff, Freddie de Guingand, Monty urged him to put pressure on his friend Bedell Smith. This, according to Monty, de Guingand did—and Bedell Smith at first agreed with Monty's strategy, as Monty wrote to 'Simbo' Simpson on 2 April.

> I got Freddie to put over to Bedell the plan outlined in para 5 of M564 [the Ruhr to be flanked by 15 Army; 21st and 12th Army Groups to remain as constituted and to race on while the Germans were in disarray, 21st Army Group to the Elbe and the north coast, 12th Army Group to Leipzig]; this was done and Bedell agreed. Conference took place at SHAEF last night and this morning, to try and reach a sound decision.
>
> Now they have reached one. But what a one!![4]

Monty sighed—for by telephone that morning, 2 April 1945, he had been ordered to hand over Simpson's Ninth US Army at midnight on 3 April. As Monty pointed out, this meant that '12 Army Group

[1] Ibid.

[2] 'The inner corps of 21st Army Group and 12th Army Group to turn back against the RUHR and to clear up that area under 15th Army of 12th Army Group, which army is now holding the Rhine north of Bonn and has two corps of its own'—M564, loc. cit.

[3] Ibid.

[4] M566, 2.4.45, Montgomery Papers.

stands fast and cleans up the Ruhr pocket'; after which, with Ninth US Army under command, it would set off in 'a S.E. direction towards DRESDEN'. Meanwhile 21st Army Group would, with Canadian and British armies, be left to undertake its coastal tasks alone—just as Eisenhower had decided to denude 21st Army Group of American help in the final stages of the Normandy triumph the previous August. No 12th US Army Group forces would be available to support or even flank Dempsey beyond Hannover: '21 Army Group effort is secondary and it does what it can, looking after its own flanks; it is not visualized that it will go beyond the line BREMEN–HANNOVER.'[1] To SHAEF Monty had warned that the whole march of events in the north would now be slowed down. 'I was planning to turn some Ninth Army troops northwards to get in behind the enemy opposing Second Army; that is now "off"'.[2]

> I cannot now implement the plan in M 561 and M 563 [the race to the Elbe between Magdeburg and Hamburg], unless of course the Germans all run away.
>
> I shall go on to the WESER on the general line MINDEN–BREMEN [half-way to the Elbe] and there I may have to stop; even this may take some time,[3]

Monty remarked, for experience in the aftermath of Normandy had shown that both in Brittany and in the Pas de Calais it took far longer and far more troops to mask or reduce enemy-held ports than was anticipated. Yet the North Sea ports were vital not only to the effective overrunning of Germany but to its administration thereafter; and with Russian forces on the Oder, the Red Army had only half the distance to advance to reach the east bank of the Elbe—giving it free access to the Danish peninsula and Kiel canal: an alarming prospect.

'I have always fought for being strong on the left i.e. in the north,' Monty added, looking back over the campaign.

> From September 44 to January 45 we were never strong enough in the north to get decisive results.
>
> Then in February 45 I was given the Ninth Army and for the first time we were really strong in the north; the results were terrific and everything else was 'added unto us'.
>
> Now we are to be weak again in the north, and no good will come of it,

[1] Ibid. By cable Monty reported the same news to Brooke at 1346 hrs on 2.4.45. M565, Montgomery Papers.

[2] M566, loc. cit.

[3] Ibid.

he prophesied.

> A strong effort in north Germany is the correct strategy in this campaign; it is vital from the naval point of view.
>
> Nothing could have stopped us getting to the ELBE, and then we hamstring the whole enemy naval and submarine campaign.
>
> Now, it is not even contemplated that we should get there; the north is to play a secondary role while the main effort goes off to the S.E.
>
> I have a feeling that this new plan of IKE'S will prolong the war. I hope the P.M. understands this.

Meanwhile 'these alarms' had caused de Guingand to have another breakdown—'he is not sleeping and has to take drugs again; his brain races along and gets no rest. If he gets no better I shall send him home for a few days rest.'

> All work would be so much easier if the 'captain of the ship' would handle his ship properly; we spend so much time rushing from one side of the ship to the other side, trying to keep it on an even keel.[1]

De Guingand, sensitive, warm-hearted, and a champion of inter-Allied harmony, was indeed rendered sleepless and ill by the tensions and misunderstandings surfacing now, at the very moment when the war seemed won. Vainly he attempted to make SHAEF see that, without Ninth US Army, Monty could not be expected to liberate Holland, seize the north German sea-ports, cross the Elbe *and* forestall the Russians reaching the Kiel canal. However, at Supreme Headquarters in Reims, possession of the Ninth US Army had now become an emotive, indeed patriotic issue—as 'Simbo' Simpson also discovered on 2 April. Like Monty, Simpson had pleaded by telephone with 'Jock' Whiteley, Eisenhower's deputy chief of operations, as he reported to Monty:

> I told him [Whiteley] that the British COS were very unhappy over the question of the Ninth Army and that they had asked for it to be reconsidered. I said that the feeling here was that the removal of this Army would seriously affect your advance to the ELBE. . . . Jock said the change should not at all affect your advance. The Ninth Army would still be on the right flank of Second Army and the boundary between the two would be exactly where 21 Army Group had wanted it. I pointed out that the fact that the Ninth Army was no longer under your command would make all

[1] Ibid.

> the difference, as it could not help being sucked down to the LEIPZIG axis—or left to mop up the RUHR. Jock said this would not be so, but he sounded rather lame about it.
>
> I am very much afraid that this is a political decision made, as you say, to satisfy American public opinion. SHAEF cannot get away from their respect for public opinion. Feeling is not helped by [General 'Bill'] Simpson's obvious opinion that he is being far better commanded now than he ever has been before. I shudder to think of the way Bradley will treat him when he gets him under command again.
>
> CIGS is away today, but VCIGS read him your M564 [of 1 April] over the telephone this morning. CIGS said that he would send you a reply tomorrow, but I am afraid it will not hold out any great hope. I doubt whether we can get the US Chiefs of Staff to make IKE leave the Ninth Army with you if he is set on satisfying Bradley by removing it.[1]

That this was the case was demonstrated by a further phone call from Whiteley at 6 p.m., complaining about Monty's request to alter the boundary between Dempsey's and Simpson's armies.

> I returned to my point that all these difficulties would be avoided if Ike could meet the request made by the British COS to the U.S. COS for the Ninth Army to be left in 21 Army Group. Then you could adjust the boundary as you wanted without affecting SHAEF,

Simpson added in a postscript to his letter to Monty.

> I told Jock that he had more than once today informed me that Ninth Army was going to do exactly as you wanted even though it was moving to 12 Army Group; and that I could see no point in moving it in this case. Surely the operation could be better carried out by one man commanding the three Northern armies. I said I could only assume, in spite of all his assurances, the Ninth Army was *not* now going to fill the role you had planned for it.
>
> He repeated that it was going to do exactly what you wanted, but on further cross-examination it emerged that there was no guarantee that it would be where you wanted it *at the time you want it to be there*. Jock said 'Geographically it will be exactly where Monty wants it, but of course the timing may be somewhat different.'
>
> I frankly confessed to him that it certainly made a difference and would vitiate your whole plan. He clearly thought I was being

[1] Letter of 2.4.45 (ACIGS(O)/11/M), Montgomery Papers.

> obstinate, and repeated that it really made no difference to your plan.

Simpson's nagging, however, produced an insight into Eisenhower's thinking which now explained how Bedell Smith could first have welcomed Monty's proposal on 1 April only for the plan to be rejected the following day.

> I again rubbed in that I was this time giving not my own personal view but that of the British COS and there need be no secret about this. I still maintained that, if the Ninth Army's role remained unchanged in SHAEF's opinion, it was madness of them to take it away from you. I said, 'Can you not imagine Monty's feelings when he finds that his most promising plan has been whittled down. Have you had any communication with him and do you know whether he is happy about it?' Jock then made a most illuminating remark in reply: 'Oh! Simbo, do try and be fair. Bradley has feelings too; and he must be allowed to have the Ninth Army for a bit.'[1]

For Simpson this was 'the matter in a nutshell'. All historical evidence points to the same conclusion: namely, that it was Bradley's natural desire as the senior American battlefield commander to employ the full weight of the American armies at the conclusion of the European campaign and in so doing iron away the stains of the Ardennes disaster, which precluded Eisenhower from accepting Monty's logic. For this in the end, Monty had only himself to blame. Not only had he humiliated Bradley in the preceding months; he had himself rejected Eisenhower's proposal to insert Bradley's Army Group headquarters north of the Ruhr to ensure overwhelming Allied strength in the north—the very policy Monty now criticized Eisenhower for departing from.

As Brooke warned,[2] there was nothing to be done.

[1] Ibid.

[2] 'We have done our best but I doubt whether the Combined Chiefs of Staff will feel able to forbid Eisenhower to make the change if he is set on it. . . . I feel that as your views are already fully known to Eisenhower you should take no further action': CIGS to Monty, signal 81861 of 3.4.45, Montgomery Papers.

CHAPTER SIX

Making Do

'WHAT A TRAGEDY it all is, coming too just when both Ninth and Second Armies had got into top gear. It was not as if we had not had a previous lesson—we have had several of them now. We certainly can't help winning the war now, but it is maddening to think that the process may drag on longer than it might otherwise do,' Maj-General 'Simbo' Simpson wrote to Monty on 2 April. 'You must feel very disheartened over the whole affair.'[1]

Monty was—as were his Army Commanders. On 29 March Tac HQ of 21st Army Group had moved close to the Rhine at Bonninghardt, on 31 March it had moved across the river to Brunen, and by 2 April sappers were clearing a windswept site at Nutteln, outside Münster. Over 30,000 prisoners had been taken in the preceding week since crossing the Rhine, and already on 1 April Ninth US Army had made physical contact with Hodges' First US Army at Lippstadt—thus effecting the encirclement of the Ruhr.

On 2 April Monty gave General Simpson his final orders for Ninth US Army 'to seize the crossing over the WESER' due east of him 'by tomorrow night and I do not think that Army will go much further than that', he lamented in his nightly signal to Brooke. 'It passes from my command at midnight tomorrow night as you know. I shall try and get 12 US Army Group to advance the left of the Ninth Army up to HANNOVER and if they will do this I shall be able to get on myself up to the line of the ALLER river. But if the Ninth Army is not to go beyond HANNOVER it may not be possible for me to get to the ELBE at any rate until I can clear the coastal belt with Canadian Army and get that Army up to HAMBURG.'[2] His whole plan of campaign had been wrecked.

Dempsey, not normally other than factual in his diary, was desolated:

> *2 April 1945*
> 1200 hrs—Met C-in-C and Commander Ninth Army at HALTERN.

[1] Loc. cit.
[2] M1055 of 2310 hours, 2.4.45, Montgomery Papers.

> Ninth Army will pass to 12 Army Group at midnight 3/4 April. It is probable that the Supreme Commander will halt Ninth Army on the line of the R. WESER . . . and that no advance EAST of the river will take place until the RUHR has been cleared up. This seems a pity.
>
> Commander Ninth Army is confident that he will reach R. WESER soon as there is little opposition on his front—but if he halts there I cannot advance to the R. ELBE alone, and will have to stop on the line of R. WESER between MINDEN and BREMEN. It all depends upon the orders issued by Supreme Headquarters.[1]

Bradley was now hundreds of miles away, at Luxembourg, still not having crossed the Rhine, with the Supreme Commander another hundred miles behind him, in France. What was ironic was that at this final stage of the war, when exploitation ought to have been the order of the day, both Eisenhower and Bradley were excusing their tortoise-like tactical strategy by using 'Monty-concepts' of battle—concentration of Allied effort in a single decisive blow and adherence to the principle of defeating enemy forces rather than making territorial and place-name gains—concepts that were now, Monty knew, redundant. It was a mark of Monty's essential flexibility that once he saw the battle of the Rhine was won, he ordered immediate bypassing of all centres of resistance and all-out armoured exploitation to reach the key German ports and cities. Meanwhile Bradley, the champion of tactical flexibility and exploitation in the eyes of his courtiers, adopted in his hour of triumph, with no less than four American armies under his command, the most conservative tactics conceivable—halting the entire American effort of 12 US Army Group to 'clear up' the Ruhr, declining to advance on Berlin, and allowing himself to be infected by the American pre-occupation with numbers of prisoners—'bags'—like some proud participant in a Scottish shoot, while the vital importance of pushing ahead to preempt the Russians quite escaped him.

Once again it was left to Churchill to beg and cajole Eisenhower into a more realistic understanding of the historical moment:

> If the enemy's resistance should weaken, why should we not cross the Elbe and advance as far eastward as possible,

Churchill pleaded with Eisenhower in a letter which 'upset E. quite a lot', as Mrs Summersby recorded.[2]

> This has an important political bearing, as the Russian armies of

[1] Diary of General Sir Miles Dempsey (WO 285/11), PRO.

[2] Diary of Mrs K. Summersby, entry of 1.4.45, loc. cit.

the South seem certain to enter Vienna and Austria. If we deliberately leave Berlin to them, even if it should be in our grasp, the double event may strengthen their conviction, already apparent, that they have done everything.

Further, I do not consider myself that Berlin has yet lost its military and certainly not its political significance. The fall of Berlin would have a profound psychological effect on German resistance in every part of the Reich. While Berlin holds out great masses of Germans will feel it their duty to go down fighting. The idea that the capture of Dresden and junction with the Russians there would be a superior gain does not commend itself to me. . . . While Berlin remains under the German flag it cannot, in my opinion, fail to be the most decisive point in Germany.

Therefore I should greatly prefer persistence in the plan on which we crossed the Rhine, namely that the Ninth US Army should march with the Twenty-first Army Group to the Elbe, and beyond to Berlin.[1]

Churchill's signal was waiting at Reims on 1 April to greet Eisenhower on his return from Bradley's headquarters at Luxembourg—where Bradley had thrown a party and Eisenhower and Mrs Summersby had stayed the night. 'Message f[r]om the P.M. He does not agree with E's directive. He wants Monty to retain command of the 9th Army and march to Berlin. The P.M. points out the importance of the latter plan, he also emphasizes that the fall of Berlin would have a profound psychological effect and political effect on the German. He almost accuses E. of belittling the British forces. The P.M.'s message upset E. quite a bit. He is the only person in this whole campaign, irrespective of nationality, who is utterly selfless.'[2]

But was Eisenhower being utterly impartial? As Churchill pointed out, there was *no need* now to put so many American armies into a single thrust to Dresden—a town already reduced to a ghoulish skeleton by the RAF and of no importance to the Russians or the Western Allies. By simply allowing a single US Army to remain under Monty's command, where it had been since 20 December 1944, there was every indication that, given the current collapse of German resistance, *all* Allied tasks could be achieved: the Bremen, Hamburg and Kiel seaports would be seized, the Danish peninsula sealed, Berlin reached, if not actually captured, a meeting with the Red Army in the Silesian basin effected, and sufficient forces assembled to prevent concentration of a Final Redoubt in the south.

[1] Message of 31.3.45, in W. S. Churchill, op. cit.
[2] Loc. cit.

Eisenhower, however, could not bring himself to renege now on his promise to Bradley. Possession of Simpson's Ninth US Army had become a matter of personal honour—and in her diary on 2 April Mrs Summersby recorded: 'Conference . . . Bedell, Bull, Strong. Relative 9th Army reverting to Bradley's command. As usual Monty is making all sorts of petty difficulties.'[1] The mood at SHAEF was now of American triumph, with Eisenhower doing his best to see that the Press give due credit to the American commanders of the campaign, in particular the hitherto untrumpeted General Hodges—'the scintillating star' of the campaign as Eisenhower extolled him in a message to Marshall. 'Equally with Hodges the part that Bradley has played in this campaign should be painted in more brilliant colors,' Eisenhower also exhorted. 'Never once has he held back in attempting any maneuver, no matter how bold in conception and never once has he "paused to re-group"' as had his British counterpart Montgomery. 'His handling of his army commanders has been superb and his energy, common sense, tactical skill and complete loyalty have made him a great Lieutenant on whom I always rely with the greatest confidence.'[2]

Eisenhower himself was now slated—according to Mrs Summersby's diary record of a conversation with General Arnold, the American Chief of Air Staff—to succeed Marshall as Chief of Staff US Army 'after hostilities have ceased in Europe'.[3] Meanwhile Eisenhower's 'great lieutenant' was still not satisfied by Press coverage of his exploits—Bradley giving his publicity staff 'a difficult time of it . . . when they talked of the publicity efforts of the OWI [Office of War Information] in this theatre and although there is a remakrable [sic] amount of wordage going out over the wire we do not feel that enough attention is being given the American effort, that people are not being truthfully appraosed [sic] of the real extent of our participation as compared to that of the British.'[4]

For Bradley, command of Ninth US Army was vital not so much for military reasons as those of personal and national prestige. As his aide, Major Hansen, noted in his diary a few days later, 'In a recent interview with Charlie Wertenbacker, *Time* Magazine, General Ike told the latter that General Bradley was the greatest field commander of World War II. This opinion is substantiated by the current establishment in command to Bradley who now commands

[1] Entry of 2.4.45, loc. cit.
[2] Cable to Marshall, FWD 18341, 31.3.45, Montgomery Papers.
[3] Diary of Mrs K. Summersby, entry of 3.4.45, loc. cit.
[4] Diary of Chester B. Hansen, entry of 5.4.45, loc. cit.

all the Armies engaged in the direct assault eastward across Germany.'[1]

Such last-minute chauvinism was all too understandable after the humiliation of the Ardennes, and Monty's hitherto patronizing attitude. 'They still accept us only as country cousins,' Hansen complained—with entry after entry in his diary chipping at Monty's inflated reputation, particularly in the 'Battle of the Bulge'. When Hansen heard a rumour that Monty had 'proposed that our [American] defenses be withdrawn to the Meuse river and that we hold there on a defensive line for three months through the winter', he instantly believed it—and the heroic alternative proposed by Bradley and Patton:

> Bradley hotly contested [Monty's] view, called it tommy rot and announced that he would initiate an offensive on the southern front immediately to close the gap. Patton, supporting Bradley's view, is supposed to have spoken dramatically, 'The American army has never made a single American soldier incapable of offensive action at any time.'
>
> The implications of Monty's recommendation [for withdrawal to a three-month winter defensive line] are enormous. It becomes all the more damning when you recall that the British press colored him as the hero of the campaign.[2]

That Monty's generalship in the Ardennes should have so quickly become the target of American ire rather than gratitude was unfortunate. As in Normandy, his patient professional mastery was denigrated, to be painted over—at a moment when four American armies were poised, under Bradley's command, to finish off the war in Europe—by 'scintillating' American 'stars' with dash and offensive vigour. 'Our commanders now feel that the American army is the best in the world. We are experts on amphibious crossings of anything; we have made them when all others predicted that we would be unable to . . . Georgie continues to be the headline hunter while Bradley remains the genius behind our moves.'[3]

Given such determination to show their paces, though, with complete Allied victory in their grasp, why were the Americans now holding back? Monty asked. The Russians seemed stalled on the Oder by the unexpectedly early thaw; Germany was at the mercy of the Western Allies—and the Americans refused to move! Simpson's Ninth US Army had reached the Weser at Minden under 21st Army

[1] Entry of 6.4.45. Ibid.
[2] Entry of 14.4.45. Ibid.
[3] Ibid.

Group command on 3 April: there it sat under the aegis of 12th US Army Group for forty-eight hours as Monty protested to Brooke. Was this the genius behind American command? Eisenhower had fobbed off Churchill's signals by discounting the importance of Berlin and by claiming, belatedly, that the only difference between his own plans and those of Monty was in the matter of timing. As Supreme Commander he wished *first* to clear up the Ruhr, *then* to push three American armies in a single thrust to Dresden; only after all this was accomplished would he turn his attention to Monty's tasks to the north, and Devers in the south.

Churchill, unwilling to provoke an Anglo-American rift at this final moment of the war, climbed down; but Monty, although outwardly expressing his loyalty to the Supreme Commander, was filled with disbelief at the magnitude of the error Eisenhower was making. Not only did he feel the 'central drive' to Dresden was of less importance than Berlin, but he did not see the need for such a concentration of Allied strength to go to Dresden—a thrust in which, according to Eisenhower's directive of 2 April, 21st Army Group was to provide flank 'protection'![1] Why had Eisenhower rejected Monty's pleas for a single, concentrated Allied thrust into Germany after the victory in Normandy, only to insist upon it now, when the Germans were clearly beaten, and the country was at the Allies' feet? In addition, Eisenhower's excuses about timing struck Monty as militarily naïve. Why waste time mopping up the Ruhr when time was of the very essence—when it was possible still to forestall the Russians and overrun most of Germany, including Berlin, before the Russians could move?

Behind Eisenhower's new strategy and timing, however, was the 12th US Army Group Commander—and Bradley was adamant both that he command the major American thrust to Dresden, and that this thrust be postponed until *after* the Ruhr had been 'mopped up'— as he made clear to American Press correspondents on 6 April.

> There are now 57 American divisions on the Continent engaged in current operations against the enemy with the great bulk of these divisions concentrated in the 12th Army Group among the First, Third and Ninth Armies with a few of the newer divisions holding with the Fifteenth Army on the western bank of the Rhine opposite the Ruhr pocket. At this stage in our advances the impetus of our movement has been slowed while the First and Ninth Armies are turned rearwards with a portion of their forces to eliminate the pocket. . . .

[1] SCAF 247, in *The Papers of Dwight David Eisenhower*, op. cit.

> The General indicated that it will be necessary to eliminate or reduce the Ruhr pocket before pushing further east 'so we cannot', he said, 'push on until we have cleaned up these [elements of] 18 divisions in our rear. The pocket involves too many of our troops and we must release these additional units before pressing farther east.'[1]

Patton would not be given the go-ahead until all the three main American armies were free of the Ruhr commitment and lined up abreast of one another to strike on the 'Kassel–Leipzig axis. . . . The timing of this phase is being entirely left to Bradley, who now has the green light for the final assault that will join our armies with those of the Russians on the east. . . . Bradley estimates that he will presumably be ready to jump on about the 15th [April] although the armies assured him they can be ready earlier. . . . If the General is able to time his attack for the 15th [April], he may reach the Elbe on about the 25th [April] . . . He warned again, however, of too much optimism and told correspondents that only a short while ago he had predicted fighting "might continue until the summer of 1946."'[2]

Not only did the cautious Bradley now decline to push east until the Ruhr was mopped up, but he persisted with his belief in the Southern Redoubt, where the Germans would hold out with a force larger than that in the Ruhr. 'The General holds to the theory that the German, conforming to the Nazi intent to resist to the last man and the last village, will fall back into the Redoubt where with approximately twenty SS divisions supplied through a system of underground factories and supported by aircraft from underground hangars, he could presumably hold out for a year,' Hansen recorded.[3]

To Monty this was piffle. The Germans in the Ruhr pocket had neither the fuel nor the ammunition to break out, and Bradley's caution seemed to him utterly misguided at this junction of the campaign—lending further credence to his conviction that Bradley was 'useless' without firm guidance from above. In the Ardennes Bradley had persisted in the face of terrible casualties in his belief that decisive victory could be won by all-out, unplanned, penny-packet assault in adverse winter conditions; now, with the primary enemy forces completely surrounded in the Ruhr, Bradley refused to move across Germany until the pocket was cleaned up—and then only with three entire American armies 'abreast' on the Dresden

[1] Diary of Chester B. Hansen, entry of 7.4.45, loc. cit.
[2] Ibid.
[3] Ibid.

axis,[1] with a further two Army Groups, those of the North and South, providing additional flank 'protection'!

Though Monty remained silent towards Eisenhower, he made clear to General Whiteley his complete disagreement with the Eisenhower–Bradley strategy. Then, while Bradley briefed American war correspondents on the need to mark time for a further *ten* days, word reached Monty from Reims that Eisenhower himself was having second thoughts at least about waiting for the Ruhr to be mopped up. At 10 a.m. on 6 April Monty met Dempsey at the latter's headquarters near Emsdetten. Dempsey noted in his diary:

> Saw C-in-C at my Headquarters. The Supreme Commander is now coming round to the view that an advance to the R. ELBE, without waiting for the RUHR to be cleaned up, is correct. This is the British recommendation.[2]

Dempsey declared that he could push straight on for Hamburg and the Elbe without waiting for the Canadian Army, provided that Ninth US Army kept up with him on the right.

> C-in-C thinks that this plan will be put into effect, and it is possible that the American Army on the right of Second Army will be under his command.[3]

To press for this, Monty had agreed to meet Eisenhower and Tedder that afternoon at Mönchen-gladbach airfield. The weather, however, was too poor for flying and in the absence of de Guingand, Monty's young Chief of Operations Brigadier Belchem drove from 21st Army Group Main Headquarters in Brussels to deputize for Monty.

Given the current controversy over Allied strategy, this was yet another tragedy, for Belchem had neither the force of personality nor rank to impress Eisenhower or Tedder—whose snobbery regarding rank was notorious. Tedder was in a mean mood, furthermore, having just been 'hauled over the coals' in London by the British Chiefs of Staff—as 'Simbo' Simpson had informed Monty on 4 April:

> Tedder appeared before the British COS yesterday and had a pretty rough time. The secretaries were turned out of the room while they dealt with him! He was asked why Ike had sent a

[1] 'Before jumping off on the attack to the east, the General is desirous of lining his three armies abreast . . . and then concentrating his action generally on the Kassel–Leipzig axis': Ibid.

[2] Diary of General Sir Miles Dempsey, entry of 6.4.45, loc. cit.

[3] Ibid.

telegram to Stalin without warning to anyone else, and replied that they had to go at matters quickly as you were going off [to the Elbe] on the plans outlined in your M 262. Brooke's comment was, 'It is not very satisfactory when Ike has to appeal to Stalin to help him control Monty.'![1]

Knowing of Tedder's humiliation and his accompaniment of Eisenhower, Monty may have felt the moment was inopportune to raise, in person, the matter of command of Ninth US Army, and the question of Berlin. If so, it was idle to imagine that a young Brigadier from his Main Headquarters staff could do better—and in fact Belchem gave no more than the current operational picture and Army Group plans, as Monty informed 'Simbo' Simpson—

> I have maintained complete silence with IKE and have carried on quietly with my own affairs. He asked me to meet him at an airfield 100 miles back on Friday 6 April; I made all plans to go but bad weather stopped me and no flying was possible. David Belchem met and explained my intentions. . . . IKE then asked that I should send him a letter giving my views about the future development of the campaign.[2]

That the Allied Supreme Commander should be unable to meet his Northern Army Group Commander in person and was forced to ask for an appreciation of future campaign strategy by letter was a disastrous reflection upon Monty's prickly personality. Had Monty journeyed by car to Mönchen-gladbach, Eisenhower would undoubtedly have waited. Instead Monty squandered his last chance to convince Eisenhower in person of the stupidity of waiting for the Ruhr to be mopped up and of concentrating a surfeit of Allied forces for a consequent push to Dresden, at a time when Berlin was still accessible from the west and the vital north German sea-ports were uncaptured. Dempsey was under the impression that Eisenhower was 'coming round' to the British view; but with Monty's failure to meet Eisenhower in person, the British were forced to wait on tenterhooks for days on end while Eisenhower, studying Monty's appreciation and consulting his staff at Reims, made up his mind.

[1] Letter of 4.4.45 (ACIGS(O)/12/M), Montgomery Papers.
[2] Letter of 8.4.45, M569, Montgomery Papers.

CHAPTER SEVEN

If the American Public Only Knew the Truth

BRADLEY HAD NOT only wished to pause while mopping-up the Ruhr; he had even favoured delaying his American push to Dresden thereafter in order to wait for an equivalent Russian offensive from the east.[1] But as Maj-General 'Simbo' Simpson had informed Monty on 4 April, the British Chiefs of Staff had appealed to their colleagues in Washington to tell Eisenhower 'that the probable Russian delay in doing anything on the DRESDEN–LEIPZIG axis strengthens the case for maintaining the emphasis on the thrust in the North, particularly towards Berlin. Ike has told you that he is not interested in Berlin—I thought his wording of this very curious—and the Russians too now say that they also have no interest there. Yet none of us here put it past them trying to steal a march on Ike in that direction.'[2]

When Monty thus drew up for Eisenhower on 6 April his own appreciation of the tactical strategy the Allies should adopt, it was in the knowledge that the War Office was behind him. Monty now 'presumed' that Bradley would not wait for the Ruhr to be mopped up, but would be 'cracking off towards LEIPZIG in 3 or 4 days time'. Far from Monty having to 'protect' Bradley's Leipzig thrust, Monty also now understood from SHAEF that Bradley would 'establish the left flank of Ninth Army on the high ground west of HANOVER and will be able to come up to the ELBE line when I move forward'. If this was so, Monty suggested, would it not be sensible for 21st Army Group at least to have operational command of these forces, for 'only in this way will we get proper cohesion in the advance'. Only on the final page of his three-page letter did Monty address himself to the question of Allied strategy:

> I understand you want my views on the best course of action to be taken after we have got HAMBURG and the ELBE line.

[1] Diary of Chester B. Hansen, entries of 6.4.45 ('if the Russians will go when we go . . .') and again 13.4.45 ('Bradley envisions that he will be stopped on his present line while we wait for the Russians to get going on their offensive'), loc. cit.
[2] Letter of 4.4.45 (ACIGS(O)/12/M), loc. cit.

My view are are follows:

a) we should thrust northeast to LUBECK, cut off the SCHLESWIG peninsula, and operate northwards to clear the KIEL area and DENMARK.

b) we should thrust south-east to BERLIN, coming in to it from the northwest. This manoeuvre will be from an unexpected direction, and should be comparatively easy.

In Monty's view 21st Army Group 'could carry out the operation' but 'would require to be reinforced by about ten American divisions'. He went on:

> In your telegram to me of 31 March (FWD 18389) you give the impression that you are not interested in BERLIN and consider that it has no value as an objective.
>
> I would personally not agree with this; I consider that BERLIN has definite value as an objective and I have no doubt whatever that the Russians think the same; but they may well pretend that this is not the case!!

Monty's letter put Eisenhower in a renewed quandary. Censured for dealing direct with Stalin[1] and under pressure from London regarding the need to strike north and east as quickly as possible[2] Eisenhower was once again under pressure to alter his strategy. He had elected to give Bradley charge of the *coup de grâce* in Germany, mopping up the Ruhr, and striking south-east to Dresden, ignoring Berlin. Now Bradley was making heavy weather of the Ruhr operation, refusing to move east until the Ruhr was cleaned up and the Russians began their own advance into Silesia. For days General Simpson's Ninth US Army had been inactive, giving the Germans time to organize themselves after their rout upon the Rhine; and without Simpson's help, Dempsey could not be expected to reduce the German sea-ports of Bremen and Hamburg *and* cross the rivers Weser, Leine and Elbe, fighting eastwards across northern Germany to the Baltic, cutting off the Schleswig peninsula and securing the Kiel canal—all with three Corps. Eisenhower himself thought Bradley was exaggerating the danger of the surrounded Ruhr pocket,

[1] Cable from General Marshall to Eisenhower, W64244, received on 7.4.45, reporting Churchill's complaint to President Roosevelt 'that Eisenhower's telegram was sent to Stalin without anything being said to our Chiefs of Staff or to our deputy, Air Chief Marshal Tedder, or to our Commander-in-Chief, Field-Marshal Montgomery'. See *The Papers of Dwight David Eisenhower*, op. cit.

[2] Cable from General Marshall to Eisenhower, W 64349, also received on 7.4.45 regarding 'the desirability of maintaining momentum in the north, with a view to the capture of Berlin (before the Russians can get there)'. Ibid.

as he confessed to Marshall on 6 April: 'The enemy has been making efforts to break out of the area but our persistent policy of knocking out his communications to the eastward, and his lack of mobility within the pocket, both make it very difficult for him to launch a really concerted attack. I am confident that he can do nothing about it.'[1] Even so, he could not bring himself to overrule Bradley, and warned Marshall: 'You must expect, now, a period in which the lines on your map will not advance as rapidly as they did during the past several weeks because we must pause to digest the big mouthful that we have swallowed in the Ruhr area.'[2] The following morning, after again speaking to Bradley on the telephone, he affirmed that the 'substantial elimination of the enemy forces in the Ruhr' was 'a military necessity'[3]—and later in the day cabled Marshall to repeat his 'reluctance from the military viewpoint to lay down Berlin as a major objective of our operations', and his conviction that his main thrust 'should be in great strength to the area including Leipzig'—a thrust Stalin had 'agreed' to, even though it was 'deep into that part of Germany that the Russians are eventually to occupy'.[4]

Nevertheless it appeared that Eisenhower was wavering. He had already authorized the left Corps of Ninth US Army to co-operate with Dempsey in taking Hannover and even advancing to the Elbe at Wittenberge—as Monty excitedly signalled to Brooke. 'I heard tonight on the telephone from SHAEF that the first reactions to [my] letter are very favourable and that it is quite likely to be agreed generally though of course there may be certain modifications.'[5]

In fact, in his signal to Marshall, Eisenhower attempted to clear a path behind him ready for a personal *volte-face* should this prove necessary. Once Bradley's Leipzig thrust was 'assured, it seems obvious that we should get our left flank firmly established on the coast near Lübeck, which is not only on the boundary of the British occupational zone, but the holding of it would prevent Russian occupation of any part of the Danish peninsula. To this extent I thoroughly agree that the northern thrust is a most important one.' Moreover—responding to British pressure and Monty's letter—he even offered now to take Berlin; 'if the Combined Chiefs of Staff should decide that the Allied need to take Berlin outweighs purely military considerations in the theater, I would cheerfully adjust my plans and my thinking so as to carry out this operation.'[6]

[1] Letter of 6.4.45. Ibid.
[2] Ibid.
[3] Cable FWD 18697. Ibid.
[4] Cable FWD 18710. Ibid.
[5] M1068 of 2315 hrs, 7.4.45, Montgomery Papers.
[6] Cable FWD 18710 of 7.4.45, in *The Papers of Dwight David Eisenhower*, op. cit.

Unfortunately Eisenhower addressed no similar signal to the British Chiefs of Staff, and Marshall withheld Eisenhower's offer from them. In the meantime Eisenhower was stuck with Bradley's insistence on first mopping up the Ruhr, then advancing towards Leipzig–Dresden—a strategy which Eisenhower hoped would give him 'maximum flexibility', but which, if it took a further month—as Bradley predicted—threatened to paralyze the whole momentum of Allied advance. Loyally supporting his American 12th Army Group Commander, Eisenhower now warned in a new directive that Monty 'must not lose sight of the fact that during the advance to Leipzig you have the role of protecting Bradley's northern flank. It is not his role to protect your southern flank. My directive is quite clear on this point.' The timing of the thrust was put in Bradley's hands, though he hoped Bradley would attack eastwards before the Ruhr pocket was 'completely eliminated': 'The timing of the blow will have to be determined by Bradley, depending upon when he can reduce the Ruhr pocket to an area and strength that will not be too troublesome. . . . I am hopeful that Bradley can get started on his main thrust by the end of next week at the latest, that is, by the 14th [April].'[1]

Sent on 8 April 1945, this was fiddling while Rome burned—entailing a further week of senseless delay. Patton felt nothing but contempt: 'Whenever those two [Eisenhower and Bradley] get together, they get timid,' he noted in his diary, and could only explain the 'tentmaker's' caution, when there was so little opposition in front of them, as an attempt to ensure that 'no one gets undue credit'. Meanwhile Monty, waiting for Eisenhower's reaction to his letter on 7 April, entertained the Secretary of State for War, Sir James Grigg, and returned to his perennial outlet when tense or frustrated: epistles from afar concerning the proper care of his son David: 'I am not at all keen that David should go north to Scotland with Carol Mather. He will merely do too much and get knocked up before going back to Winchester; Carol is a nice lad, but he is not the companion I would choose for an adolescent boy for a holiday à deux. David is very likely to develop bad habits, and drink and smoke.'[2]

When Eisenhower's new directive finally arrived on 9 April ordering Monty to guard Bradley's left flank in the eventual drive to Dresden, still a further week away, Monty's worst fears were realized. As he wrote dejectedly to 'Simbo' Simpson that day, before receiving Eisenhower's directive, even the eventual move of Ninth US Army up to the Elbe at Wittenberge was of little consequence, since by telephone SHAEF had informed Monty that Ninth US Army's south-

[1] Letter of 8.4.45. Original in Montgomery Papers.

[2] Letter of 7.4.45, Montgomery Papers.

ern boundary would stretch more than a hundred miles south, down to Dessau. 'This gives Ninth Army a very wide front,' Monty lamented. It was obvious that the whole Lübeck/Berlin business was to be of secondary importance. 'I think it is IKE's intention that from the BREMEN–HANNOVER line onwards the main effort is to be by 12 Army Group. My role will be to protect Bradley's northern front; it will not be his role to protect my southern front. I think the above is the form. So I shall crack along with what I have got, and do the best I can. It will be a slow business I fear, but that cannot be helped and must be accepted as the natural repercussion of IKE's plan: and is his business and not mine.'[1] His bid for Berlin and Lübeck as two vital and immediate Allied objectives had been turned down, and the hope that Eisenhower might be changing his mind was seen to be illusory, vitiating the whole obedient and loyal tenor of Monty's letter to Eisenhower three days before. Had he fought harder and more uncompromisingly for these objectives, had he only met Eisenhower at Mönchen-gladbach by car and threatened catastrophe unless 21st Army Group was reinforced by Ninth US Army and permitted to drive for Lübeck. . . .

But the days when Monty could thump the table were over, as even Monty was now aware. As soon as he received Eisenhower's letter he cabled Rheims:

> Have received your letter dated 8 April. It is quite clear to me what you want. I will crack along on the northern flank 100 per cent and will do all I can to draw the enemy forces away from the main effort being made by Bradley.[2]

Bradley, hearing that his Ninth US Army Commander, 'Bill' Simpson, was due to attend a conference at Dempsey's Second Army headquarters the next day in Monty's presence, decided himself to attend. Monty's loyal promises to Eisenhower were all very well, but Bradley knew of the pressure still being applied by Churchill and the British Chiefs of Staff and was determined to make sure Ninth Army was not sucked north into Monty's orbit. In fact, to sidestep this danger, Bradley was prepared to ignore Eisenhower's edict on the need for Monty to protect 12th Army Group's left flank: without consulting the Supreme Commander Bradley assured Monty that the two Army Groups could now go separate ways. As Monty cabled to Brooke that evening, 10 April, 'Bradley came to see me today and we had a long talk and a very friendly one. As a result of our talk I have now been relieved of all responsibility for protecting the left

[1] Letter of 9.4.45, Montgomery Papers.
[2] M1070 of 0925 hrs, 9.4.45, Montgomery Papers.

flank of 12 Army Group. BRADLEY will look after his own northern flank as he moves forward. I will look after my own southern flank.'[1]

Bradley also announced that he had accepted the need to strike east without waiting to mop up the Ruhr, and had advanced the 'green light' to 11 April. But the command structure and grouping of American divisions in 12th Army Group made Monty wince, as he described in his signal to Brooke:

> The grouping and command situation in 12 Army Group is interesting.
>
> Ninth Army has only six divisions available for the eastward move as its other six divisions are fighting in the RUHR pocket about DORTMUND and SIMPSON is running both battles.
>
> First Army has six divisions for the eastward move and eight divisions in the RUHR pocket and HODGES is running both battles.
>
> PATTON is not involved in the RUHR and has eleven divisions available for his advance. . . .
>
> Fifteen Army is also engaged in the RUHR and there are thus three army commanders involved in that battle.
>
> 12 Army Group begins to move eastwards tomorrow and two of the Army Commanders will be looking and fighting in two directions, i.e. eastwards towards the ELBE and westwards towards the RUHR. . . .
>
> I have made no comments of any sort and shall do the best I can in the north while watching the whole thing very carefully.[2]

Why Bradley needed three armies abreast to reach Leipzig against nominal opposition, Monty never fathomed; indeed it was to take only a day to reach the outskirts—and only a few *hours* for Ninth US Army to reach the Elbe, which it did the next day, on 11 April. Yet there it was to all intents halted, since Bradley would furnish no further divisions to Simpson for an eastward thrust; indeed when Simpson 'phoned to say there was a possibility that the main bridge across the Elbe at Magdeburg might fall intact to Ninth Army, Bradley was far from pleased. 'I was afraid Ninth Army would get entangled in too large a bridgehead to the north,' Bradley explained a few days later to his ADC, Major Hansen. 'I almost hoped the other fellow would destroy it.' When Simpson's Operations Chief telephoned to say the Germans *had* destroyed the Magdeburg bridge,

[1] M570 of 1950 hrs, 10.4.45, Montgomery Papers.
[2] Ibid.

Bradley was profoundly relieved. 'Thank Gawd, there's no need to worry about a bridgehead there,' he exclaimed.[1]

But there was—for Ninth Army refused to be balked of the chance to reach Potsdam or Berlin (only sixty miles away) by lack of a bridge at Magdeburg. As General 'Bill' Simpson, the Ninth US Army Commander, later recalled, he had quickly established a new bridgehead south of Magdeburg:

> It was really a very rapid advance. So we got to the Elbe River and we got across the Elbe with a bridgehead about, I think April 11th or 12th. And that little bridgehead was knocked back; but the 83rd [US] Division came along, got a firm bridgehead on 13 April [at Barby, south of Magdeburg] which we enlarged to about thirty square miles, got a pontoon bridge across, and were planning to build another one that night.[2]

It was in this situation, on 13 April 1945, that Eisenhower was given a *third* opportunity to reach Berlin. Simpson's army was across the Elbe at Barby; Bradley's thrust to Leipzig was virtually over, making his massive south-eastern offensive redundant. Bradley himself was well aware of this. 'I shall have to get back quickly and get to work on a new set of plans,' he told his ADC that day. As Hansen commented in his diary, '[Bradley] is right; the others have suddenly become outdated,'[3] adding the following day, 'There is some question as to where we go now.'[4]

Eisenhower had hitherto refused to tackle Berlin, or to reinforce Monty's 21st Army Group, on the grounds that he wished first to separate German forces in the West by a strike from the Ruhr to Leipzig. The very speed with which the Allies had been able to achieve this objective surprised both Bradley and Eisenhower—yet *still* they remained adamant that Berlin was of no military importance and that Ninth Army must not be transferred to Monty's 21st Army Group. 'From a tactical point of view, it is highly inadvisable for the American Army to take Berlin, and he [Eisenhower] hoped political influence would not cause him to take the city,' Patton's Chief of Staff recorded the Supreme Commander's views on a visit to 12 Army Group on 12/13 April. Patton had protested vigorously: 'IKE, I don't see how you figure that one. We had better take Berlin and quick and [advance] on to the Oder.'[5] Even the American

[1] O. N. Bradley, *A Soldier's Story*, New York 1951. This reminiscence was based on Chester B. Hansen's diary entry of 19.4.45, recording the story, loc. cit.

[2] Interviews with Dr M. Burg of 5.11.72, Eisenhower Library, Abilene, Kansas.

[3] Diary of Chester B. Hansen, entry of 13.4.45, loc. cit.

[4] Entry of 14.4.45. Ibid.

[5] *The Patton Papers*, ed. M. Blumenson, Boston 1982.

Chiefs of Staff had begun to back-track on the issue, as 'Simbo' Simpson had reported to Monty from the War Office:

> I had hoped SHAEF had seen sense as regards plans. It really is frightful to think of all the lives being wasted to satisfy American public opinion. If the American public only knew the truth!

This truth was that, yet again, the British Chiefs of Staff had pleaded with their American counterparts to recognize the importance of reaching Berlin before, or at least simultaneously with, the Russians. But:

> The British Chiefs of Staff have not got very far with the U.S. COS. The U.S. COS felt that the capture of Berlin before the Russians 'should not override the imperative military consideration,' which in their opinion is the destruction and dismemberment of the German armed forces. But they point out something which is quite new to us, i.e. that 'Berlin as a matter of fact is within the centre of impact of the main thrust. Recent boundaries would indicate that it will probably be within the right of the Ninth Army sector or the left of Fifteenth Army.' We have not yet seen any plan with these boundaries and I wonder if you have. . . . It looks to me a little like IKE trying to save face on both sides.[1]

But with Eisenhower adamantly maintaining that Berlin was a purely political prize, the situation was now exacerbated by a sudden political vacuum in America. For after spending the evening of 12 April drinking champagne with four Red Cross girls, Eisenhower, Bradley and Patton had retired to bed. Switching on his radio, Patton had heard the announcement of the death of President Franklin D. Roosevelt.

> He went up to Brad's room, knocked at the door, walked in with his riding boots, the curt pink breeches and the glossy blouse he wears, announced, 'Better come in Ike's room; the President has died.' They went in and talked for a few minutes before returning again to bed. . . .

America, in its hour of victory, was leaderless. As Bradley's ADC recorded, 'we all wondered what the implications would be.'[2]

[1] Letter of 9.4.45 (ACIGS(o)/13/M) with handwritten postscript, Montgomery Papers.

[2] Diary of Chester B. Hansen, entry of 12.4.45, loc. cit.

CHAPTER EIGHT

The Death of John Poston

HAD EISENHOWER RECEIVED an order from the President, from General Marshall, or from the Combined Chiefs of Staff to seize Berlin, he would undoubtedly have obeyed. Indeed Bradley, 'hurrying back' from the front on 13 April, actually now ordered a plan to be 'readied . . . for the taking of Berlin from the west even though he believes it should be taken from the east'.[1]

But with Roosevelt's death no clear guidance came from Washington. Marshall was adamant that the Combined Chiefs of Staff should not interfere with Eisenhower's prerogatives as Supreme Commander and, as in the aftermath of the victory in Normandy, Eisenhower became a prey to pressure from every side. For a day—13 April 1945—he faltered; 'Ike is waiting on an order but until he gets one we have to make our [own] plans,' Hansen noted on the morning of 13 April.[2] The next day Eisenhower had 'hurried off quickly to the airfield' and flown to Reims.[3] There was still no message from Washington, however. Eisenhower was thus forced to formulate his own strategy beyond the Elbe, cabling Washington with an 'Appreciation' drawn up by his Operations Staff.[4] When no response to this was received from Washington (none was to come for a further four days in the wake of Roosevelt's death), Eisenhower sent out his new orders on 15 April to his Army Group Commanders.

Monty was shattered by the directive. Berlin, once again, was 'off': 'Present bridgeheads over the Elbe will be secured but offensive operations beyond the Elbe will be undertaken only on later orders,' Eisenhower stipulated.[5] Bradley's entire front from the Elbe at Darchau to the Mulde below Leipzig would become a holding front, while Bradley was to direct his offensive forces southwards now into the Danube valley to meet the Russians there—and cut off the supposed Southern Redoubt. Meanwhile, without major reinforce-

[1] Diary of Chester B. Hansen, entry of 14.4.45, loc. cit.
[2] Entry of 13.4.45. Ibid.
[3] Entry of 14.4.45. Ibid.
[4] Cable FWF 19190 of 14.4.45, in *The Papers of Dwight David Eisenhower*, op. cit.
[5] SCAF 281 of 15.4.45. Ibid.

ment, 21st Army Group was to operate alone across the Elbe, seize Hamburg and Kiel, cut off the Danish peninsula and 'be prepared to conduct operations to liberate Denmark'—as well as clearing 'western Holland, north-east Holland and the coastal belt and enemy naval bases and fortifications [Emden–Wilhelmshaven–Friesian Islands] which threaten the approaches to Hamburg.' [1]

Monty was dumbfounded. Already on 13 April he had got wind from SHAEF of such plans—as he had cabled to Brooke that night. 'I have even heard it stated that 21 Army Group may have to go up through DENMARK and via SWEDEN into NORWAY and clean up that country. I think it is necessary at this stage to be clear as to what IS and is NOT possible and what are the repercussions of the various courses of action proposed.' [2]

Eisenhower's orders on 15 April did nothing to dispel Monty's feeling that, as in Italy in 1943, Eisenhower was giving in to folly. The decision not to try at least to reach Berlin was to Monty misguided; but the decision to halt Ninth and Third US Armies in static 'defensive' positions and to attack a mythical Southern Redoubt, while fantasizing that Monty could clear Holland, North Germany, the Baltic, the Danish peninsula, Denmark and Norway with his two armies, unaided, seemed to Monty the height of inanity.

General 'Bill' Simpson, poised to break out from his Barby bridgehead towards Berlin, was equally disbelieving. 'Where did this [order] come from?' he demanded when, having flown up to Bradley's headquarters, he was told the news. Bradley passed the buck. 'Well, from General Eisenhower.' [3] As Simpson later lamented, it was galling. Berlin lay a bare sixty miles away:

> The north Corps [of Ninth Army] was about fifty-three miles from Berlin and was there at Magdeburg. It was about sixty miles—just about the way we had been going, about a day's march really. And this bridgehead was opposed by a kind of a crust of newly formed outfits that were putting up some opposition; but with another pontoon bridge and another division or two across, we could have broken through. I think we could have been in Berlin in twenty-four hours. . . . What was left of the German armies were over there against the Russians except this little crust that was around me, and a good part of that was pulled away about the time I was halted. And, I don't know, I have a feeling that may be the Germans might have welcomed us. . . . They were in terrible shape, you know.

[1] Ibid.
[2] M571 of 1600 hrs, 13.4.45, Montgomery Papers.
[3] Interview with Dr M. Burg of 5.11.72, loc. cit.

> I had six or seven divisions on the Elbe river there: the 2nd Armoured Division; the 30th; the 83rd had the bridgehead; and the 35th. I had two army corps there and was in very good shape to have gone on and made the advance. . . . Harry Hopkins made a statement [later] that we'd outrun our supplies and all that sort of thing. Well he didn't know what he was talking about because my army was in good shape, the supplies were in good shape, and we could have gone right on to Berlin and put up a darned good show. I had even rail roads coming down into my area, carrying supplies. And I had these 10-ton truck companies, hundreds of them. . . . We had a bridgehead across there with one pontoon bridge across and another one to be built that night and another corps up, oh, about twenty or thirty miles to the north getting ready to cross that same night with very little opposition up there. So I think we could have ploughed across there within twenty-four hours and been in Berlin in twenty-four to forty-eight hours easily.[1]

Bradley was embarrassed—according to Simpson, Bradley had never mentioned the possibility that Ninth Army would be halted on the Elbe.[2] Back at 12th US Army Group headquarters at Luxembourg, however, he seemed delighted by Eisenhower's decision. 'Our new direction of attack is to the south-east,' his ADC recorded on 16 April. 'Our Twelfth Army Group has now reached the limits of the advance prescribed for us and we have now presumably to await the arrival of the Russian armies, holding a static position.'[3]

To Monty this was almost criminal at a time when it was becoming increasingly obvious that, without Ninth Army's help, operations in the north could not suddenly be expected to accelerate overnight. On 14 April Monty had warned Brooke:

> The general picture in the BREMEN area and on the WESER front is of very determined resistance to keep us away from BREMEN and stop us crossing the WESER and ALLER.[4]

The following day the Canadian Corps reached the Zuiderzee, cutting off western Holland; but the bulk of the Canadian Army was needed to turn north-eastwards to seize northern Holland and the vital German naval bases at Emden and Wilhelmshaven. Meanwhile, with only three Corps to capture Bremen, Hamburg, Lübeck, the whole of Germany north of Hannover, as well as Kiel and the ter-

[1] Ibid.
[2] Ibid.
[3] Diary of Chester B. Hansen, entry of 16.4.45, loc. cit.
[4] M1083 of 2240 hrs, 14.4.45, Montgomery Papers.

ritory up to the Danish border, Dempsey's British Second Army was faced by a hard challenge. By-passing centres of resistance could speed up advance in the interior; but where ports were required for immediate use by the Allied navies, they could not be by-passed, they *had* to be taken—as well as all outlying peninsulas, islands and estuaries. Thus, although Monty foresaw no intrinsic problem regarding Dempsey's thrust to the Elbe, he was less certain about the ease with which Second Army could take Bremen itself, ordering the entire left Corps of Second Army—some four Infantry divisions—to concentrate upon the task. This left Dempsey with only three divisions to advance towards and across the Elbe. At a moment when 15th Scottish Division was exploiting a gap in the German line north of Celle, and when Simpson's Ninth US Army was reporting 'very little resistance from MAGDEBURG northwards to WITTENBERGE',[1] it seemed incredible for Eisenhower to concentrate so much Allied effort upon the mythical Southern Redoubt, leaving 21st Army Group to manage with what it had.

Bradley's initial plan was to *halt* both Simpson's and Patton's two armies while directing Hodges to swing right, through Patton's lines of communication, and make for the Danube basin and Southern Redoubt. 'If this is to be our last, I would like you to do the job,' Bradley had confided to Hodges, loth to allow Patton further glory. 'Here was Bradley, inconspicuous behind the facade of Eisenhower, working quietly and working all the time,' Major Hansen recorded proudly;[2] but with Eisenhower's green light to go for the Southern Redoubt, the administrative chaos that would be caused by such an ill-considered First US Army scheme became apparent even to Bradley, as his ADC recorded:

> With our line running to the south along the mountain line and stopping short of the Sczech border, our sector now resembles a giant bow bent into the heart of Germany. General Bradley can point an arrow in any direction and immediately follow it with the full force of the mightiest group of American armies ever to be put in the field. . . .
>
> Originally it had been Bradley's intention to turn the First Army down behind the Third to use that army in his drive to the south-

[1] 'On my right flank Ninth US Army is up on the ELBE from WITTENBERGE southwards through STENDAL and MAGDEBURG to AKEN. They report heavy resistance in the MAGDEBURG area but have got three battalions over the river just south of MAGDEBURG and gained a shallow bridgehead in that area': M1080 of 2230 hrs, 13.4.45, Montgomery Papers.

[2] Diary of Chester B. Hansen, entry of 13.4.45, loc. cit.

> east and turn the campaign over to the deliberate direction of Hodges. However, it is now apparent that the supply difficulties will prevent this. . . . Bradley, therefore, immediately decided to give the effort to Patton—with probable close supervision by him [Bradley] during the effort inasmuch as the remainder of his front will be holding in a static situation.[1]

That two-thirds of Bradley's attacking armies could be halted in a 'static situation' at this most critical juncture of the war was a sad reflection on Eisenhower's performance as Allied Land Force Commander—and Bradley's unfortunate influence upon him. Even Bradley was to confess after the war that he had been 'naïve' about the Russian menace and obsessed about the Southern Redoubt[2]—but at the time he seemed anxious only for the chance to end the war in command of American armies; and was frankly uninterested either in Berlin or the need to secure Denmark and Norway before the Russians—whose long-awaited offensive across the Oder was being launched that day.

> As we move forward our communications with SHAEF become more difficult, but we are thereby less subjected to supervision from that headquarters . . . Bradley sat alone in his trailer with Devers, Patton and Hodges, reversed on his chair with his long legs stretched to the sides, his chin in his hands, his combat jacket high up about his ears, lolling in the sunlight, talking easily, thinking brilliantly as he is wont to do before a map,

his ADC rhapsodized,[3] recounting several days later how Bradley 'feels quite exhuberant on the way plans are progressing for the development to the southeast', with Ninth and First US Armies still halted, and Bradley remarking how grateful he was that he had not been sucked into a campaign across the Elbe:

> We were not anxious to get another bridgehead across the Elbe. Bradley does not want to extend any further east than is necessary in order for him to concentrate the bulk of his effort in a drive to link up with the Russians [in the Danube basin] and thereby cut the escape route of the Germans in the north to the Redoubt in the south.[4]

[1] Diary of Chester B. Hansen, entry of 16.4.45, loc. cit.

[2] 'As soldiers we looked naïvely on this British inclination [regarding Berlin] to complicate the war with political foresight and nonmilitary objectives': O. Bradley, op. cit; 'it was this obsession with the Redoubt that accounted for my gloomy caution on the probable end of the war.' Ibid.

[3] Diary of Chester B. Hansen, entry of 16.4.45, loc. cit.

[4] Entry of 19.4.45. Ibid.

When, on 19 April, Bradley's headquarters learned from Eisenhower—who had flown to meet Bradley—that SHAEF was *again* having second thoughts and now wished Bradley to halt his south-eastern movement and help Monty to secure the Danish peninsula before the Russians reached it, there was consternation:

> He [Bradley] has disorganized the German to his front, destroyed what remained of his organized resistance and he is supremely anxious to exploit the opportunities, push quickly down to union with the Russians and seal the Germans off [from the Southern Redoubt].
>
> Ingersoll, however, is worried.
>
> He claims that Ike came to ask Bradley to put a stop line in the limit of our advance to the South-east. We are now ordered to assist the British in cutting off Denmark and ports on the north. Ralph: 'They regard ships as a helluva lot more imp[ortan]t than the war and they are anxious to prevent the Russians from getting to Denmark and thereby menace the British political situation or influence there.'
>
> Whatever the reason, this much is certain. Ike has apparently acceded to demands from the British that we support their effort to the north. They have fallen badly behind in their schedule and Monty is exasperated over the inability of his commanders to advance as quickly as our armies.[1]

Monty was exasperated—but it was not with his British troops or commanders. Given German reserve Panzer divisions now coming down from Denmark, SS training schools and several *million* German troops now crowding into northern Germany, it was amazing with what speed Dempsey's few divisions had progressed, by-passing wherever possible centres of resistance. Nevertheless as Monty had warned 'Simbo' Simpson on 16 April, the 'formations in 21 Army Group were nearly all of them getting very tired. They had been fighting continuously since 8th February and operations across the Elbe to the area LUBECK–KIEL would probably go very slowly.'[2] The Polish Armoured Division had now dropped out of the advance ('in north east Holland Polish Armd Div yesterday liberated a concentration camp of 1700 Polish women south of Winschoten and have made little progress since then'[3]) and on 15 April Monty had warned Brooke that with stiffening enemy resistance 'it may well be that we

[1] Ibid.

[2] Minute to CIGS by ACIGS(o) of 17.4.45, Alanbrooke Papers, LHCMA, King's College, London.

[3] M1083, loc. cit.

shall have difficulty between the Ems and Bremen'.[1] It was for this reason that Monty asked SHAEF for an American Corps to help exploit Dempsey's breakthrough around Uelzen by taking over Dempsey's right-hand boundary on the Elbe north of Darchau—but given Bradley's unwillingness to get involved in operations east of the Elbe, SHAEF refused to allow any American forces under Monty's command to operate across the Elbe. 'The stipulation was being made that this US Corps should not be employed East of the River Elbe.' To men like Ralph Ingersoll and Bradley's ADC, Major Hansen, Monty's performance was simply a mark of British cumbersomeness compared with American 'brilliance'. Despite the fact that Bradley had stopped his armies, first to mop up the Ruhr, then to wait for the Russians (it was not until 25 April that the Russians in fact made contact), such patriots were blind to all but their own virtues, Hansen recording on 19 April:

> Ralph Ingersoll claims the British are again astounded by it [American speed]. He [Monty] asked for a corps of American troops to assist his Canadians [in N.E. Holland]. We responded by taking over a greater portion of the British front [Wittenberge to Darchau, on the Elbe but only permitted to operate west of the river], allowing him to concentrate his forces. This was not sufficient, and it is now possible that we may accede to their request for a corps.
>
> It is believed that when the British received our order for the attack due to start tomorrow morning [south east to cut off the Southern Redoubt], they were astounded by the speed with which we have readied ourselves and by the rapidity of our staff work and troop movements. Monty may have seen his reputation again menaced by the brilliant tactics of General Bradley.[2]

It was not the 'brilliant tactics' of Bradley which worried Monty now: it was the failure of SHAEF to recognize the sheer magnitude of the problem facing a tired 21st Army Group in Holland and northern Germany, with the Russians racing across the Oder towards Rostock and the Elbe. Had Eisenhower only left Simpson's Ninth US Army under 21st Army Group command, the situation would have been quite the reverse; instead, the potential power of an American army operating on Dempsey's inland flank had been squandered. Berlin had not been taken or even reached by the Allies, the Elbe had not been crossed, and it now looked as though the Russians,

[1] M1084 of 2240 hrs, 15.4.45, Montgomery Papers.
[2] Diary of Chester B. Hansen, entry of 19.4.45, loc. cit.

stalled for so many weeks on the Oder, might actually reach the Danish peninsula and islands before the Allies. Major Hansen blamed 'political pressure' for Eisenhower's new doubts about the south-eastern American drive upon the Southern Redoubt; with almost paranoid suspicion he even wondered whether Eisenhower's 'stop-line' was to give Monty time to turn British troops southwards to participate in the reduction of the Southern Redoubt: 'to allow a large scale movement of British troops towards the redoubt'![1] Hansen feared that this would cause a delay that would inevitably give time for 'concentration of enemy along a battle line that will seriously hamper our ability to get going again. He [the enemy] is off balance now but it is possible that he may be able to muster some strength if we delay several weeks. Supply will not permit simultaneous development in every direction.'

Nor was this a mere personal opinion; according to Hansen it reflected the views of commanders and staff alike in 12th US Army Group, who were now obsessed by the notion of the Southern Redoubt—and adamant that the British should not be permitted to end the war in command of an American army:

> Brits are again pulling for the northern effort of the Ninth Army

Hansen went on.

> Bradley was supposed to have been considerably irritated by this change. Maddox, the G.3 in Patton's army was supposed to have cried in anger when he heard it. Patton is largely disgusted.[2]

The following day, 20 April, Eisenhower flew to Diepholz airfield to meet Monty. SHAEF had granted Monty's request for an American corps, promising that as soon as Bradley had dealt with the Southern Redoubt Monty should have Ridgway's 18 Airbone Corps, as for the crossing of the Rhine—'Corps going to the Brit is the XVIII of Ridgways [sic], Monty always picks his men and he usually picks about the best we have,' Hansen remarked grudgingly a few days later.[3] In a 'very friendly talk alone in his plane', Monty had outlined to Eisenhower the sequence of his 21st Army Group's current operations, as he had explained to the ACIGS, Maj-General 'Simbo' Simpson, the night before:

> Battle for BREMEN is to be fought by 30 Corps. 43, 51 and 3 British Divs will attack BREMEN South and West of R. WESER

[1] Ibid.
[2] Ibid.
[3] Diary of Chester B. Hansen, entry of 21.4.45, loc. cit.

> while 52 Div North of this River is to come in at BREMEN from the East. . . . Assault on BREMEN will be on either 23 or 24 April.
>
> Simultaneously with battle for BREMEN, or just after it, Canadian Army is to clear up the WILHELMSHAVEN–EMDEN peninsula. Canadian Army will probably leave only one division in EAST HOLLAND while this is going on.
>
> Meanwhile, Second Army will be closing up to R. ELBE.[1]

To vault the Elbe, the three divisions of 8 Corps had been ordered to establish crossings at or near Lauenburg 'as soon as possible'.

> If opposition is not severe, the crossing may take place on night 20/21 April. If, as seems likely, there is strong opposition and a staged assault has to take place, it will probably not be until about a week after assault on BREMEN.[2]

As Monty explained in his nightly signal to Brooke, this was not from lack of offensive fervour, but simply because, without Ninth US Army, Second Army did not possess sufficient engineers and specialist resources to conduct both the battle for a vital Allied seaport on the Atlantic seaboard *and* an assault crossing of a major river against determined opposition. 'If the situation allows of our crossing against little or no resistance then we shall get across tomorrow night,' he assured Brooke. 'If however it is found that the enemy intends seriously to dispute the crossing then a pause will be necessary. The reason is that all the resources necessary for the battle to force a crossing are employed in the BREMEN battle and I must first capture that place and then move the resources up to LAUENBURG.'[3]

The lesson of Antwerp had been taken truly to heart—and only the furnishing of an additional army could speed up Dempsey's advance across the Elbe to Lübeck. Had Simpson's Ninth US Army been allowed over the Elbe, American troops might well have been able to encircle the enemy from behind. Now, however, the whole Allied timetable for 'cracking about the plains of northern Germany' had been sundered, with Simpson's reserve Corps still back at Salzwedel, on the River Veetze south-east of Uelzen. If this reserve Corps could now fight its way north to Darchau, and if Ridgway's 18 US Corps could be quickly assembled and permitted to cross the

[1] 'Notes on Field-Marshal Montgomery's Future Plans (as given to ACIGS(O) on 19 April)', in 'North-West Europe From 1 March 45–6 May 1945' file (later annotated 'a very interesting file—very secret, M of A'), Montgomery Papers.
[2] Ibid.
[3] M1092 of 2300 hrs, 19.4.45, Montgomery Papers.

Elbe, driving from Darchau to the Baltic at Wismar, the Russian bid to reach the Danish peninsula before the Allies would at least be foiled[1]—with Dempsey's forces swinging left to seize Hamburg from the east and racing up to Kiel and the Danish border.

Such a plan, with an American Corps sealing off the Danish peninsula in front of the Russians, was hardly the British 'political' conspiracy so feared by Ingersoll and others at Bradley's headquarters. Moreover in asking for Simpson's Ninth US Army once more, Monty was not reacting in pique to the 'menace' of Bradley, the 'brilliant' tactician, but was simply attempting to ensure that sufficient troops were allotted to achieve vital Allied objectives irrespective of their nationality:

> I recommended [to Eisenhower] that the troops to go into DENMARK should be the ones which would go right on to SWEDEN and NORWAY,

Monty reported to Brooke of his meeting with Eisenhower.

> He [Eisenhower] should decide on this matter soon so that all concerned could study the problem. My recommendation was that the troops should be Ninth US Army with two Corps. One Corps to be four American divisions. One Corps to be one British division and one Canadian division.[2]

Did such a recommendation merit the 'considerable irritation' of Bradley and his staff? The tragedy, as Major Bigland perceived, was that American suspicion of British motives became impossible to allay in the wake of Bradley's Ardennes humiliation—with the whole struggle in North-west Europe coming more and more to appear—at 12th Army Group headquarters—as a struggle *between* Britons and Americans, rather than Allies working together in a common cause.

Eisenhower, listening to Monty's recommendation, affected surprise—'he had not considered that way of doing it and naturally wanted to think it over,' Monty recorded[3]—for yet again the problem was: how to get Bradley to agree to Ninth US Army coming under 21st Army Group command, as well as the political consequences of an American Corps operating east of the Elbe.

In the event, though Eisenhower duly authorized the use of 18 US

[1] 'Once a firm British and US bridgehead has been established N.E. of R. ELBE, 18 US Corps ['shortly concentrating in the HANNOVER area'] is to go for WISMAR and form an Eastern flank on the line WISMAR–SCHWERIN lake–DARCHAU, holding it against Germans, Russians or refugees': 'Notes on Field Marshal Montgomery's Future Plans', loc. cit.

[2] M573 of 1710 hrs, 20.4.45, Montgomery Papers.

[3] Ibid.

Corps in this way, he did not dare brook Bradley's reaction to the transfer of Ninth US Army—and SHAEF's controversial plans for the liberation of Denmark and Norway were simply shelved. Possibly Eisenhower hoped—as he had forecast in his 'Appreciation' of 14 April to the Combined Chiefs of Staff—that 'rapid elimination of the [southern] redoubt might reduce the effectiveness of the German defense of Denmark, or even bring about a surrender in those countries. The capability of enemy forces in the south to resist will be greatly reduced by a thrust to join the Russians in the Danube Valley. However, the national redoubt could even then remain in being, and it must be our aim to break into it rapidly before the enemy has an opportunity to man it and organize its defense fully.'[1] Certainly by 23 April Eisenhower was confident that German surrender was at hand. 'Expect German to surrender in the near future,' his PA wrote in her diary.[2] The Russians were now only hours away from meeting Bradley's forces in the south, still halted on the Mulde near Leipzig. '"The Russian approacheth," he [Bradley] said and he laughed,' Hansen noted of Bradley's equanimity[3]—and recorded Bradley's satisfaction, on 23 April, that his 'early campaign to the redoubt' would 'speed the victory' of the Allies. 'We could give 21 Group the strength to go almost anywhere they wanted to,' Hansen recorded Bradley's candid confession, 'but if we did we would allow the Germans to build a defense line in front of the Third Army and materially slow his progress [to the Redoubt].'[4]

At his new Tac headquarters near Soltau, however, Monty was once again oppressed by the failure of the Allies to decide quickly upon their priorities—and stick to them. The chance of a rapid crossing of the Elbe had been lost when Ninth US Army was removed from 21st Army Group Command and halted on 3 April, three weeks before; now, with German resistance firming up on the river and all British bridging and engineering equipment concentrated on the vital seizure of Bremen, the advance of Dempsey's right flank at Lauenburg was stalled. 'The Elbe is a big river similar to the RHINE and to cross it in the face of stiff opposition is a major operation,' Monty had warned Brooke on 21 April.[5] The next day Dempsey dolefully confirmed the strength of German opposition, as a consequence of which he would be unable to force a crossing at Lauenburg before 1 May, following the capture—he hoped—of Bremen.

[1] SCAF 260, in *The Papers of Dwight David Eisenhower*, op. cit.
[2] Diary of Mrs K. Summersby, entry of 23.4.45, loc. cit.
[3] Diary of Chester B. Hansen, entry of 21.4.45, loc. cit.
[4] Entry of 23.4.45. Ibid.
[5] M1097 of 2240 hrs, 21.4.45, Montgomery Papers.

Meanwhile to add to this bleak picture, two of Monty's Liaison Officers—John Poston and Peter Earle—had gone missing. 'I think it likely that they have been captured,' Monty cabled optimistically, for a large pocket of Germans, between Munster and Soltau, close by Tac Headquarters of 21st Army Group, was holding out in the woods; 'if so we shall recover them because they cannot be got away.'[1] Monty was, however, wrong.

Poston was the youngest of Monty's LOs, but had been the longest in his service—since Alamein in fact. He had already twice been awarded the Military Cross for gallantry. With 'steely blue eyes' and 'furious hawk-like face' Poston simply did not know the meaning of fear. Between Monty's Tac Headquarters and General Barker's 8 Corps Headquarters at Lüneburg there were known to be enemy troops. Some 2,000 prisoners were eventually taken, including SS, Marines and 10 tanks, but given the need for up-to-date information Major Earle, the LO detailed to drive up to see Barker on 21 April, determined to take the shortest, uncleared route north of Lüneburg Forest. As he later recorded:

> As I was about to leave John Poston, who had just finished digging his [captured German] caravan out of the lawn, came over to me and said that he had been told to go to 11 Armoured Division. We both considered this a complete waste of time as 11 Armoured Division was known to be resting, and as I was going to the Corps H.Q. I would discover more about the future plans for the Division than John would discover from the Divisional Commander.[2]

Nevertheless, Poston offered to accompany Earle, and Earle's driver was dismissed. The two men reached Barker's headquarters without mishap and obtained Barker's plan for crossing the Elbe with 53rd Division, but on the way back, travelling at 45 m.p.h. along a route that ran closer to the Lüneburg Forest than the one they had taken (it was 6 p.m. and the officers wished to report back by nightfall) they ran into a German ambush. Wounded in the arm and temple, their ammunition exhausted, Earle drove the jeep straight at the German machine-gunner in front of him, killing him. Poston and Earle were thrown from the vehicle and soon surrounded by German soldiers. As Earle attempted to wipe clean his chinagraph location map of 8 Corps dispositions he was shot again from the back, and fell to the ground. Poston, his sten gun empty, 'was lying some three yards on my right,' Earle recalled. 'I heard John cry out in an urgent and desperate voice, 'N—No—stop—stop.' These

[1] M1100 of 2220 hrs, 22.4.45, Montgomery Papers.
[2] Diary of Colonel Peter Earle, communicated by Colonel Earle to author, 1985.

were his last words and were spoken as a bayonet thrust above the heart killed him instantaneously. At the time he was lying on the ground, unarmed and with his hands above his head. He was [left on] the spot, having been stripped of his watch and other valuables. . . . He was the most determined character for his age [twenty-five] I have ever met and, I should say, knew no fear. He was simple, ruthless and absolutely self-contained, a greater lover of animals than of his fellow beings. He would certainly have sailed with Drake.'[1]

That night a further two Reconnaissance Corps officers were ambushed and killed, as well as a cartload of innocent Russian and Belgian refugees. Earle, left wounded with a nearby farmer, survived in a German field hospital to be recaptured on the evening of 22 April, and moved to 212 Field Ambulance Station whence he sent a signal to 'Kit' Dawnay:

> Regret to report JOHN POSTON killed at 1800 hrs Saturday 21 April . . .

With Poston's death the romance of the Eighth Army/21st Army Group march from El Alamein to the Elbe seemed to go sour. 'I regret that JOHN POSTON was killed and we have recovered his body,' Monty signalled sadly to Brooke on 23 April. 'I would be grateful if you would inform the Prime Minister about these casualties to my L.O.'s as he knew them all and takes a keen interest in their work.'[2] So personally fearless, Poston's death was like the death of a son—a boy who had joined Monty as a young ADC in Cairo and who, as intrepid Liaison Officer from Normandy onwards, had now given his life in the service of the uniquely well-informed nexus of operations at Monty's mobile headquarters. Poston was subsequently buried 'with full military honours in a meadow on the forest edge'; he had been, the senior Ops Room Officer recorded, 'the most vivid officer we ever had amongst us and his energy ran like a current through all our doings'.[3]

Monty, standing by the grave, wept openly.

[1] Ibid.

[2] M1103 of 2225 hrs, 23.4.45, Montgomery Papers. Churchill replied: 'I share your grief at the death of John Poston and the wounding of Peter Earle. Will you kindly convey to their gallant comrades the sympathy which I feel for them and you. This marvellous service of Liaison Officers, whose eyes you know and whose judgements you can exactly measure, will be one of the characteristic features of the manner in which you exercise your superb command of great Armies': cable of 27.4.45 in the diary of Colonel Peter Earle, communicated by Colonel Earle, 1985.

[3] 'A Tac Chronicle', loc. cit.

CHAPTER NINE

The Race to Lübeck

'THE FIELD-MARSHAL was deeply moved when he received the news about John,' Major Earle subsequently recorded in his diary. 'Tears came into his eyes and he remained alone in his caravan for a considerable time. Bob Hunter (the doctor) said that he [Monty] was most depressed for two days and would not see anyone from outside [Tac Headquarters].'[1]

Hunter himself recalled, forty years later:

The LOs were a wild bunch. John Poston was created or thrown up by the war. He'd been with Monty a long time, was devoted to him. And Monty had a sort of paternal affection . . . Poston was always 'up to' something, there were tens of occasions where Monty could or should have hauled him over the coals but didn't—though he knew very well what John was up to. Monty . . . it was as though John Poston represented something Monty couldn't himself be—because Monty was so disciplined and kept himself on such a tight rein.

When Earle reported John's death, Monty sent me to recover the body. It wasn't buried, I found it still lying in the ditch where he'd died. There was no mark on it save where a bayonet had been plunged through his chest.

And for the first time I was tempted to tell Monty a lie—to say he'd been killed by a bullet or something during the skirmish. I . . . I knew Monty would be upset.

When I told him, he just nodded, turned on his heel, and went into his caravan.

Joe Ewart said that for a day they could get nothing out of him at all.

For a few days he was like that—would see nobody. Then suddenly he seemed to snap out of it, after the funeral at Soltau when he and his chosen padre, a Scottish Presbyterian Minister called Tindale, buried Poston.[2]

As Monty wrote to Phyllis Reynolds on 28 April:

[1] Diary of Colonel Peter Earle, entry of 18.6.45, communicated by Colonel Earle to author, 1985.
[2] Lord Hunter of Newington, interview of 17.12.85.

> We have been rather sad here the last few days as a former A.D.C. (John Poston) was killed on 21st; he was one of my Liaison Officers. He had been with me for nearly 3 years, i.e. since Alamein, and I was devoted to him. . . . He was buried by the Germans, but we found the place, dug it up, and gave him a very moving funeral at my HQ here yesterday afternoon. . . .[1]

Poston's death was not the only blow Monty was to suffer. On 27 April a telephone call came through from SHAEF at Reims 'to say they hoped I realised the urgent need to get LUBECK before the Russians', Monty reported to the War Office.[2] 'This is adding insult to injury,' he expostulated, remembering Eisenhower's deaf ears to his entreaties for the past *month* regarding Ninth US Army. Barely controlling his spleen Monty had asked de Guingand

> to get on to Whiteley and inform him as follows:
> 1. I have always been very well aware of the urgent need to reach and cross the ELBE quickly. See M563 dated 28 March [i.e. some four *weeks* past].
> 2. It was SHAEF that prevented this plan being implemented. They removed the Ninth Army from me and left 21 Army Group so weak that the tempo of the operations became slowed down.
> 3. If the Russians should get to LUBECK, and on up to KIEL and DENMARK, before we can do so, I would suggest that SHAEF should accept the full blame.
>
> I trust I shall have no more enquiries on that line![3]

He did, however—for that evening a cable arrived from Eisenhower himself, reminding Monty of the importance of Lübeck and the Danish peninsula—and now promising Monty that 'this HQ will do anything at all that is possible to help you insure the speed and success of the operation'.[4]

At a moment when no less than '7 Allied armies are closing on Hitler's "last stand" redoubt in the mountains of Austria and Bavaria' as was being openly reported in the Press,[5] the assignment of only two Allied armies to clear Holland and North Germany and seal the Danish peninsula before the arrival of the Russians was very needling, indeed an insult. As Monty replied in scarcely concealed

[1] Montgomery Papers.
[2] Letter to ACIGS, 28.4.45, Montgomery Papers.
[3] Ibid.
[4] Cable, FWD 20042, of 1358 hrs, 27.4.45, in *The Papers of Dwight David Eisenhower*, op. cit.
[5] Viz. *Daily Mirror*, 28.4.45 inter alia.

irritation to Eisenhower: 'I have always realised the great importance of getting quickly up to the ELBE and crossing it without delay and it was for that purpose that I issued M563 dated 28 March. That plan could not be implemented quickly as you took the Ninth Army away from me on 3 April and left me very weak in the north. The whole tempo of operations in the north slowed down after that and I did the best I could with what I had left. We have had some very heavy fighting against fanatical resistance,' he pointed out—thinking particularly of the suicidal stand made even by boys of eight around Bremen. 'It is not easy to recover lost time,' he told the Supreme Commander—adding, however: 'You can rely on me and my troops to do everything that is possible to get to LUBECK as quickly as we can.'[1]

In fact the target date fixed for the crossing of the Elbe had already been brought forward *before* SHAEF's belated requests, Monty informed the CIGS on 26 April, as Bremen fell to 30 Corps:

> I have examined the situation of the ELBE front about LAUENBURG and it seems that the enemy is in some strength in that area. But the need for an early crossing is great and I have given orders to Second Army that we must not wait until 1 May. The assault crossing will now be made on night 28/29 April, i.e. Saturday night.[2]

By 28 April, therefore, swallowing Eisenhower's affront, Monty wrote to 'Simbo' Simpson, the ACIGS, that all was now ready for the assault:

> We go over the ELBE tonight; the technique is the same as in the Rhine crossing, and the Commando Bde crosses first (at 0200 hrs) and secures LAUENBURG. 15 Div then goes over. . . . After a spell of lovely weather, it is now cold and wet and altogether very unpleasant. I hope it will clear up before tonight.[3]

To Eisenhower's 'insult' there was added yet another cause of irritation, though—for despite the choice of Monty as Military Governor-elect of British-occupied Germany by the British Chiefs of Staff on 10 April,[4] and the subsequent approval of the War Cabinet to this choice, Churchill had refused to ratify the appointment. Sir

[1] M576 of 2015 hrs, 27.4.45, Montgomery Papers.
[2] M1108 of 2230 hrs, 26.4.45, Montgomery Papers.
[3] Letter of 28.4.45, Montgomery Papers.
[4] 'Another long and very "boring" agenda for COS. Amongst other items we appointed Monty as "Gauleiter" for the British Occupied Zone. May heaven help him with that job!!' Alanbrooke Diary, entry of 10.4.45, Alanbrooke Papers, loc. cit.

James Grigg, the Secretary of State, could not fathom Churchill's sudden reluctance, and asked Monty to send a signal describing the urgency of a decision, which Monty had despatched on 24 April:

> Meetings and conferences in connection with the Control Commission take place daily, and every day it becomes more apparent that we are trying to stage and mount an immense operation without a commander. Once we adopt the principle of the absentee commander we tread on dangerous ground as we know from bitter experience in this war. The responsible commander must be appointed at once and his methods must be got across and he must make the necessary appointments from those suitable to his methods and personality.[1]

Not even this could sway Churchill, despite a second telegram sent by Monty on 29 April, as the ACIGS sadly let Monty know. Churchill was now balking at the idea of a military man as Monty's No. 2—'he said that our affairs in Germany were largely civil rather than military and we ought to have a civilian element in the top region of the Control Commission. He said that of course you would be C-in-C—that is at any rate something, although he does not deal with the question of appointing you immediately and announcing the appointment. . . . I hope something will be decided in the next day or two as all this delay must be infuriating to you and doing a great deal of harm,' Maj-General Simpson reported.[2]

Fortunately there was no time now for Monty to fret further over the appointments—for on the night of 29 April the crossing of the Elbe at Lauenburg duly took place. Some two hundred men were killed or wounded in the operation, but the bridgehead was secured and pontoon bridges soon began to span the river in the wake of the commandos, in readiness for the race to the Baltic. By the morning of 29 April Monty was confident he could still outrun the Russians—

[1] M575 of 1850 hrs, 24.4.45, Montgomery Papers.

[2] Letter of 30.4.45 (ACIGS(o)/16/M), Montgomery Papers. Grigg, who was 'very het-up about all this', was disposed to see in Churchill's sudden delaying action an Anglo–American conspiracy, prompted by the recent visit of Eisenhower to London (17/18 April)—'some plot for British–American combined control [of Germany] for a long period': letter from Simpson to Montgomery of 1.5.45 (ACIGS(O)/17/M), Montgomery Papers. Whatever the underlying reason, Churchill was certainly unwilling to accept Monty's choice for Deputy Control Commissioner: the young and still relatively inexperienced Corps Commander, Maj-General Sidney Kirkman. As Simpson noted, 'He [Churchill] thought that a really high-grade civilian would do better "as a Corps Commander would not know what to do."' Rumour had it that Churchill wished to appoint Desmond Morton, who held an undefined role in the Cabinet Office. Monty, aware of the immense and immediate military task facing 21st Army Group in the occupation, insisted that his deputy be a soldier.

who were now beginning to break out of their own bridgehead across the Oder around Stettin—as Monty cabled to Brooke:

> I have just returned from 8 Corps HQ where I met DEMPSEY and BARKER and RIDGWAY commander 18 US Airborne Corps and examined the situation . . .
> I have now given orders as [follows]
> 18 US Corps make an assault crossing over the ELBE in the BLECKEDE area at 0300 hours tomorrow and this will be done with 82 [US] Airborne Div. A further crossing to be made in the DARCHAU area if this is found suitable and possible. 18 US Corps to then operate towards SCHWERIN and WISMAR and it will be joined by 6 British Airborne Div which will be passed over at LAUENBURG and thence eastwards over the bridge at 898350 which we have captured intact. 11 Armd Div of 8 Corps to be moved forward and to start crossing the ELBE at ARTLENBURG at 1200 hours tomorrow and this division to be directed straight to LUBECK.[1]

The 82nd Airborne Division's crossing at Bleckede, advanced to 1 a.m. 'took the Germans completely by surprise',[2] though the German artillery barrage was the greatest the division had ever faced,[3] as the Wehrmacht expended their last stocks of ammunition—including even magnetic sea mines.

By funnelling his armour and mobile troops through the two good bridgeheads over the Elbe in British and American Corps sectors, Monty felt sure he could reach Lübeck in good time: 'In the Lauenburg area all is ready for rapid exploitation northwards towards LUBECK by armoured columns and this begins tomorrow. I have every hope that we shall reach the LUBECK area in two days time.'[4]

While General 'Pip' Roberts' 11th Armoured Division raced north, Monty's own 'tribe' began its final move of the war, leaving behind

[1] M1112 of 1315 hers, 29.4.45, Montgomery Papers.

[2] J. Gavin, *On to Berlin,* New York 1978. Gavin's 82nd Airborne Division was being squandered in 'its occupation role along the Rhine River' when Monty's request for US support was finally granted. 'General Dempsey was anxious that the crossing be made as soon as possible in order to cut off the Russian advance toward Denmark. About twenty miles to our left the British had established a bridgehead over the Elbe, but if we used it, it would delay [owing to congestion] our meeting the Russians by another five or six days. . . . We had to make a hasty crossing and establish our own bridgehead at Bleckede.' Ibid.

[3] R. Weigley, *Eisenhower's Lieutenants,* London 1981.

[4] Cable to CIGS, M1114 of 2300 hrs, 30.4.45, Montgomery Papers.

the flower-decked grave of Major John Poston, MC, in the meadow at Soltau—and the nearby concentration camp at Belsen. Though Monty had the month before warned all troops of 21st Army Group, in a specially printed pocket-sized booklet, that fraternization would be 'bitterly resented by your own families, by millions of people who have suffered under the Gestapo . . . you will have to remember that these are the same Germans who, a short while ago, were drunk with victory, who were boasting what they as the Master Race would do to you as their slaves, who were applauding the utter disregard by their leaders of any form of decency or of honourable dealings: the same Germans whose brothers, sons and fathers were carrying out a system of mass murder and torture of defenceless civilians',[1] nothing could have prepared them for the sight that had met their eyes at Belsen. On 15 April Monty had informed the War Office that '11 Armd Div have reached HERMANAUGBURG and BONSTORF and BERGEN. During this movement they have captured two large camps one of 10,000 and one of 30,000 mostly political prisoners and in both camps were many cases of typhus.'[2] But by the following evening he had begun to gain a more disturbing picture. 'The camps of political prisoners referred to in yesterday's message consist of 25,000 women and 35,000 men and are in an appalling condition the prisoners being practically starving and they have not even troubled to bury the dead.'[3] When, from his headquarters at Soltau, he had gone to see Belsen, Monty had been sickened: 'The concentration camp at BELSEN is only a few miles from my present HQ,' he wrote to Phyllis Reynolds on 29 April. 'You have actually to see the camp to realise fully the things that went on; the photographs [enclosed] were all taken by a photographer from my HQ. . . . . The SS Commandant is a nice looking specimen!' he added sardonically.[4]

The following day Tac HQ of 21st Army Group moved camp, making its way through the empty forest and across the Panzer training grounds towards Lüneburg. 'And so we came to the LUNEBURG HEATH—on a windswept site on the bluff above the village of DEUTSCH EVERN with a great view across the barren heath to Southward,' wrote the Senior Operations Officer, Major Odgers.[5] The nomad-like caravan, which had started on

[1] 'Letter by the Commander-in-Chief on Non-Fraternization, to all officers and men of 21 Army Group', March 1945, Montgomery Papers.
[2] M1084 of 2240 hrs, 15.4.45, Montgomery Papers.
[3] M1087, 2255 hrs, 16.4.45, Montgomery Papers.
[4] Letter of 29.4.45, Montgomery Papers.
[5] 'A Tac Chronicle', loc. cit.

D-Day with twenty-seven officers and 150 men had now swollen almost to regimental size. 'By now the Headquarters numbered nearly 50 officers and 600 other ranks with over 200 vehicles, and had travelled over 1,000 miles from the NORMANDY beaches,' Odgers chronicled.[1] As the nerve centre of some four Allied armies in the Ardennes, and three Allied armies until the removal of Ninth US Army three weeks before, Tac Headquarters 21st Army Group had performed outstandingly. Because of the great distances to be covered by the Liaison Officers, suitable Auster-aircraft landing strips had become pre-requisite in choosing each new site—for the more fluid the battle became, the more Monty depended on his 'gallopers':

'This job is not unlike that of a fighter pilot,' one of Monty's LOs had noted in his journal in mid-April.

> Each day one goes out on a sortie—probably 200 miles in a jeep. This is quite a severe physical strain; forcing one's way through columns of tanks, driving on the pavements of towns, forcing the pace everywhere, heeding no signs from the Military Police or 'NO ENTRY' notices. In the battle areas experiences are exhausting. I was held up yesterday in a column of tanks near UELZEN. The woods were ablaze; the noise of tanks, the bark of A Tk guns, the sweet stench of dead cows and here and there a dead horse, swollen and bloated with its legs jutting stiffly into space like an overturned wooden horse; the air filled with smoke and impenetrable dust. All this is tiring; then nearer the battle: that special silence that means danger and the absence of vehicles; or perhaps tanks deployed along edges of woods and the savage clatter of gunfire; huddled corpses, shattered lorries and tanks with clothing and litter hanging on the trees as though a Christmas tree decorated with death. . . .
>
> Then home again black with dust. A wash outside one's tent in the field; very difficult to get clean, marking the Field-Marshal's map is the first priority and if there is time marking the 'ops' maps and dictating a 'log'. Dinner may be before or after seeing the C-in-C.
>
> In the peace of the caravan one relates to Monty . . . what one has done. For example:—'General Barker [8 Corps Commander] hopes to have UELZEN encircled this evening . . . 3 Para have passed through 6 AL Bde and have reached the line so and so. Prisoners taken this morning by 11 Armd say that they have received orders to evacuate UELZEN by any means . . . Gen

[1] Ibid.

Barker hopes to get 5 Div and put it in between 15 (S) Div and 6 Airborne to reach the Elbe near so and so. . . . The refugees are quite appalling in this area—like a herd of locusts cooking and eating the dead horses by the roadside pillaging and ransacking all German property. 15 (S) Division are a bit slow—General Barker thinks they are very tired. . . .'

Monty sits back in his chair facing the map on which you are demonstrating. He wears a grey zip jacket and a duffle coat. He emits little high pitched grunts. . . . At the end he says, 'Very good, very clear. I think I have got that quite clearly. I shall fly up to see General Barker tomorrow morning.'[1]

As the Liaison Officer afterwards reflected, Monty listened with an intentness and responsiveness extraordinary in such a senior commander. His experiences as a brigade-major and chief of staff in World War One had taught him the importance of battlefield commanders going forward each day to back up their officers in the field and to be seen by the men. By listening carefully each evening to his 'eyes and ears' Monty was able to decide where his presence was most needed, in terms of 'gingering up' lagging formations, assessing what was realistic to expect—or giving encouragement and support when casualties were heavy.[2] In all three respects, the information and insight provided by Monty's Liaison Officers were vital.

Equally, upon good communications depended Monty's ability both to conduct the battle and to maintain instant radio and telephone contact with other headquarters—and London. As the battlefront moved into the heart of Germany the 'tyrannous influence' of the Number 10 radio communications mast ruled the selection of Tac HQ sites, as Major Odgers chronicled, including its final choice above Deutsch Evern. One by one, on 1 May 1945, the vehicles of Monty's Tac HQ drew into the familiar laager-formation, with Monty's own vehicles at the centre, beneath a cluster of birch trees: his sleeping caravan, his office caravan, and his map lorry, all screened by a vast camouflage net stretched across the three of them. 'The maps were mounted on the inside walls of the van so that you could walk up and down and see every forward position and the location of every headquarters in his command,' Monty's Personal

[1] Diary of Colonel Peter Earle, communicated to author, 1985.

[2] 'I remember one occasion, having seen the C.O. of an Armoured Brigade which had taken a lot of casualties that day, I mentioned it to Monty in my evening report. However much he might strut and pose and act at table, it shows something of his professionalism and military responsiveness that he trusted implicitly my account and reacted immediately: "I shall see them tomorrow"': Colonel Peter Earle, interview of 13.12.85.

Assistant, the Canadian Lt-Colonel Trumbull Warren, later recalled.[1] 'These caravans were all closely put together and completely camouflaged. About 25 feet in front of the caravans was a small portable flag pole where the Union Jack was always flown.'[2]

> I think we are approaching the moment when the Germans will give up the unequal contest,

Monty had written to the Reynolds on 29 April.

> They are hard pressed; they keep on fighting only because every German soldier has taken a personal oath to Hitler and so long as he is alive they must keep on fighting. Once it is known that he is dead, or has cleared out, there will be a big scale collapse.[3]

The Russians were now in the suburbs of Berlin, and German formations were beginning to surrender to the Allies without further fighting. By 1 May Russian troops were only a few hundred yards from Hitler's bunker—whereupon, from his temporary headquarters in Lübeck, Admiral Dönitz announced the Führer's death and his own succession as head of the Third Reich, broadcast by Hamburg radio. That same evening 11th Armoured Division had reached the outskirts of Lübeck, with 6th British Airborne Division being fed across the Lauenburg bridges and into Ridgway's 18 Corps bridgehead north of Bleckede, ready for Ridgway's race to Wismar.

The Russians too were racing. By 1 May they had reached Rostock, a bare thrity-five miles from Wismar, and a further thirty to Lübeck. The following day, however, patrols of 6th Airborne Division entered Wismar—'our arrival at WISMAR was very unexpected and there were in the harbour nine destroyers and five submarines but our paratroops had no means of shooting up these vessels and they all escaped,' Monty cabled the CIGS.[4] Lübeck fell too, to 11th Armoured Division—forcing Dönitz to move to Plön and then Flensburg. As Monty reported to Brooke on the evening of 2 May:

> There is no doubt that the very rapid movement from the ELBE bridgeheads northwards to the BALTIC was a very fine performance on the part of the troops concerned. There is also no doubt that we only just beat the Russians by about 12 hours. Alls well that ends well and the whole of the SCHLESWIG peninsula and DENMARK is now effectively sealed off and we shall keep it so.

[1] 'The Surrender of the German Armed Forces' by Lt-Colonel Trumbull Warren, communicated to author.
[2] Ibid.
[3] Letter of 29.4.45, Montgomery Papers.
[4] M1116 of 2325 hrs, 2.5.45, Montgomery Papers.

> The flood of German troops and civilians fleeing from the approaching Russians is a spectacle that can seldom have been seen before and it will be interesting to see how it sorts itself out tomorrow,

he remarked[1]—for during the day there had been two indications that the Germans were now ready to surrender, at least in the north. The Commander of the German Twenty-first Army had come into Ridgway's 18 US Corps headquarters to offer the surrender of his army, facing the Russians. This had been refused. Meanwhile there were indications that General Blumentritt of the German Parachute Army, commanding 'the forces facing us between the BALTIC and the WESER river', was willing to throw in the towel. 'He is coming in tomorrow at 1100 hours to offer the surrender of his forces,' Monty explained to Brooke. 'It may well be that he is plenipotentiary for some bigger commander and we shall not know this until tomorrow.' As Monty headed his telegram, 'we have had a remarkable day today and tomorrow may be even more so.'[2]

[1] Ibid.
[2] Ibid.

CHAPTER TEN

The Plenipotentiaries Arrive

THE GERMAN DELEGATION did indeed represent bigger fish than the German Parachute Army—as Monty's Canadian PA, Lt-Colonel Warren, later recalled:

At 0800 hours on 3 May Colonel Dawnay, the M.A., received a 'phone call from Colonel Murphy, who was General Dempsey's Intelligence Officer, to say that he had received a delegation of four officers, and although General Dempsey had not spoken to them it was thought that they wanted to try and compromise a surrender if they could get certain terms for Germany. Dawnay went immediately to the C-in-C, whom we called the Chief, and reported this to him. He told Dawnay to have Dempsey send them to his Headquarters and when this was done to report back to him. He then pushed the buzzer in his caravan, sending for me. Very quickly he told both of us to get the Union Jack put up; that when they [the four German officers] arrived they were to be lined up under the Union Jack facing his office caravan; that we were to get everyone else out of sight; the two of us were to put on our side arms, stand at ease to the side about 25 feet between his caravan and the Union Jack, and under no circumstances were we to make a move until he told us; also to get Colonel Ewart, his Intelligence Officer and interpreter.

We expected them to arrive in about twenty minutes. In due course they arrived, escorted by military police, who were immediately dismissed. These four officers were lined up under the Union Jack and being proper officers they stood to attention; two were Navy and two were Army. The Navy officers were dressed in long black leather greatcoats and the Army wore grey greatcoats and the General had the most beautiful red lapels.

On the right of this little line was the Senior Officer, General Admiral von Friedeburg, Commander-in-Chief of the Fleet. Next was General Kinsel, Chief of Staff of the German Army, North. He was a magnificent looking officer about 6′ 5″, in his late 40's, complete with monocle—a real professional Prussian. Next was Rear Admiral Wagner, Flag Officer to the Admiral of the Fleet.

> Last was Major Friedl. This chap was really something! He was at least 6′ 2″ and had the cruellest face of any man I have ever seen—he was 28 years old. . . .
>
> They stood to attention under the Union Jack with great-coats on early in May and it was getting quite warm. They faced the three caravans with the doors all closed. How long they stood there I do not know but it seemed like ages—it was probably four or five minutes and they never moved.
>
> Quietly the door of the centre caravan opened and there stood a rather short Anglo-Irishman, wearing khaki trousers and battle dress, a black beret (which he was not entitled to wear) with two badges, one of the Royal Tank Regiment and the other a hat badge of a general; his hands behind his back.[1]

Monty, as so often in his dealings with dignitaries in the past, deliberately intended to humble the delegation.

> The minute they saw him, they saluted. It is interesting to know that in the German Army the saluting procedure is different. . . . In the German Army the Junior Officer's hand comes up and his arm remains there until the Senior Officer has completed his salute—and it just so happened that Montgomery took a hell of a long time to complete his salute. With his hands behind his back he walked very slowly down the five steps to the ground and then the 25 feet so that he was directly in front of the Germans and all the time they remained at the salute. He then very casually put his right hand to his beret in a most slovenly manner and they dropped their arms.
>
> He then looked at the first officer and in a very sharp, austere voice bellowed out: 'Who are you?'—and the answer came back, 'General Admiral von Friedeburg, Commander-in-Chief the German Navy, Sir.' As quick as a flash, and in a loud voice, Montgomery shouted back at him: 'I have never heard of you.' [Von Friedeburg had in fact only been appointed C-in-C of the Navy that day by the new Reichsführer, Dönitz.]
>
> He then turned to the next fellow and said: 'Who are you?' and the same procedure followed until the last officer, who announced that he was 'Major Friedl'. The Chief barked back, 'Major! How dare you bring a major into my Headquarters!'
>
> I whispered to Dawnay the Chief was putting on a pretty good act. Dawnay whispered back, 'Shut up, you S.O.B., he has been rehearsing this all his life.'[2]

[1] 'The Surrender of the German Armed Forces', loc. cit. After 1 September 1944 Monty in fact replaced the General's cap badge by that of a Field Marshal.
[2] Ibid.

And so it seemed. The long road from appeasement and disastrous Allied performance in war had led inexorably, under Monty's command, from the sands of Egypt, close by the pyramids that marked the boundaries of Napoleon's bid for military supremacy, to the windswept, sandy heath at Lüneburg—and Monty intended to savour the cup of victory to the fullest. Yet behind this exercise in personal triumph there was a deeper motive. The German officers had come to discuss peace; it was important that they be made to bow to Monty's personal authority—to credit the power of his command and his personal determination to go on prosecuting the war to its final, bitter end. Without further American troops Monty did not in fact possess the forces necessary to crush quickly the German armies now hemmed into the Danish peninsula if they resisted. It was important, therefore, to seize this moment, in the wake of Hitler's death and the fall of Berlin, to demand instant and unconditional surrender lest a new Nazi loyalty to Dönitz could be inculcated and a Northern Redoubt, complete with submarine and surface vessels, necessitate systematic and costly reduction.

'What do you want?' Monty now barked.

Von Friedeburg answered on behalf of the delegation, saying that they had come from Field-Marshal Busch, the C-in-C North, to offer the surrender of the German armies facing the Russians in Mecklenburg—'this party came to ask me to accept the surrender of the three German armies that were withdrawing in front of the Russians between ROSTOCK and BERLIN,' as Monty cabled Brooke.[1] Monty refused. 'Certainly not! The armies concerned are fighting the Russians. If they surrender to anybody it must be to the Russians. Nothing to do with me.'[2] Colonel Ewart translated. Then, to soften the blow, Monty added the rider that he would 'naturally take prisoner all German soldiers who came in to my area with their hands up'.[3]

Monty now put forward his own demand: that von Friedeburg and Busch 'surrender to me all German forces on my western and northern flanks. These to include the following. All forces in west HOLLAND. All forces in FRIESLAND including the FRISIAN ISLANDS and HELIGOLAND. All forces in SCHLESWIG HOLSTEIN. All forces in DENMARK.'[4]

The delegation 'refused to agree'. But they said they were anxious

[1] M577 of 1730 hrs, 3.5.45, Montgomery Papers.

[2] R. W. Thompson 'Despatch' of 5.5.45, in R. W. Thompson, *Montgomery, the Field Marshal*, London 1969.

[3] M577, loc. cit.

[4] Ibid.

about the civil population in those areas and wished to come to some agreement with me about looking after them. If I would agree to this, they would arrange some plan by which they withdrew their forces as my forces advanced.'

For Monty, this new-found concern with civilian life cut no ice—as Colonel Warren witnessed:

> Montgomery replied to this by saying: 'Do you remember a little town in England called Coventry, which six years ago was blown off the face of the earth by your bombers? The people who took the brunt of it were the women, children, and old men. Your women and children get no sympathy from me—you should have thought of all this six years ago.'[1]

Such new-found anxiety about their own women and children, moreover, seemed hard to understand after the horrors of camps like Belsen had been revealed:

> He [Montgomery] then proceded to tongue-lash them for some minutes, explaining in great detail some of the concentration camps he had seen and bringing home as best he could, and he was a master of it, the horrors of the war and suffering that they had caused.

Concluding his harangue, Monty rejected agreement with regard to civilians—and answered the delegation that unless they surrendered unconditionally, he would order the fighting and bombing to continue, with the inevitable loss of German civilian and soldiers' lives. 'By this time I reckoned that I would not have much difficulty in getting them to accept my demands,' Monty later chronicled. 'But I thought that an interval for lunch might be desirable so that they could reflect on what I had said.'[2]

The delegation saluted as Monty turned about and walked slowly over to Colonels Dawnay and Warren, out of German earshot. 'He told us to put the best possible luncheon on we could in the Visitors' Mess and to supply them with all the drink they wanted.

> Quickly we got hold of the Mess Sergeant and told him to shoot the works. He used bed-sheets for table cloths. The Officer in charge of the visitor's set-up could speak German and he was instructed to act as Mess Sergeant. Somebody produced, and I don't know where it came from, a white Mess Sergeant's tunic that fitted pretty well, after which we did a job with a number of

[1] 'The Surrender of the German Armed Forces', loc. cit.
[2] B. L. Montgomery, *Memoirs*, London 1958.

> safety pins. Half-way through their lunch, in which they were given really good food, a bottle of red wine and a bottle of Cognac with their coffee, the supposed Mess Sergeant went in and apologized for the poor meal and explained that the day's rations had not yet arrived. One of them said, 'We have not eaten food like this for months,' and the Mess Sergeant came back with the remark 'Our Private Soldiers won't touch this muck!'
>
> In our own mess at lunch, the Chief knew exactly what he was going to do and how he was going to do it. He told us to put our two Mess tables together, to cover them with army blankets and to put one chair that he would sit at at one end and four chairs as close as they could be put at the other end; to put two maps on the table, one marked in red, which was to be our front line, and one marked in blue, which was to be their front line. He told Dawnay and me to sit at a table to the side and that we should be armed but to be sure our revolvers were not noticeable; the interpreter [Colonel Ewart] was to stand behind him. The rest was to be left up to him.[1]

All Monty's most competitive, domineering qualities seemed to merge into an absolute clarity about the way he should conduct the meeting. It was certainly an act—but an act upon which, as the final hours of the war ticked away, the lives of many Allied soldiers, airmen and seamen depended. Having given Dawnay and Warren their instructions, Monty walked to his caravan.

> In due course, after the Germans had had a really good whack at their coffee and brandy, they were asked to come into the C-in-C's mess.

This time Monty did not keep them waiting.

> Immediately following them, the C-in-C came in, with his tunic on, showing his [Field-Marshal's] rank and decorations. He was abrupt, to the point, and very quick.[2]

Monty put three points before them.

> First. They must surrender to me unconditionally all forces as in para three,

Monty telegraphed to Brooke.[3]

[1] 'The Surrender of the German Armed Forces', loc. cit.
[2] Ibid.
[3] M577, loc. cit.

> Second. Once they did this I would discuss with them the best way of occupying the areas and dealing with civilians and so on.
> Third. If they refused to agree as above then I would go on fighting and a great many German soldiers and civilians would be killed. I then showed them a map of the situation of the western front.[1]

As Colonel Warren recalled:

> He told them to look at the maps that showed where we were and where they were. He told them that we had tremendous strength pouring into Germany on the ground and that we had sufficient aircraft for 10,000 bombers, day and night.[2]

In fact the Secretary of State, Sir James Grigg, had just announced to Monty's consternation the government's 'early release' or demobilization scheme for soldiers with more than seven years' service; units were being earmarked for transfer to the Far East, and *no* new formations were available to reinforce 21st Army Group. The threat of further devastation from the air, however, was real enough. Hamburg, obliterated by Allied bombers, was only a taste of the air weapon the Allies could now wield—and would wield unless the Germans surrendered. 'They had clearly lost the war and the only answer was unconditional surrender.'[3] 'They had no idea of this situation and when they saw the map they at once gave in,' Monty cabled to Brooke.[4]

Monty had won—as was clear from the faces of the delegation. But von Friedeburg and Kinsel still needed to obtain formal permission.

> They explained that they had no power to agree with my demands as they had come solely to get me to agree as in para two above,

Monty related in his cable to the CIGS.[5] When SHAEF was informed in a similar manner that afternoon, Maj-General Strong completely misunderstood, assuming that formal surrender would emerge through different channels.[6] But Strong was being obtuse—as both Monty and the War Office knew. For von Friedeburg, staring at the special maps displayed on the blanket-covered tables in

[1] Ibid.
[2] 'The Surrender of the German Armed Forces', loc. cit.
[3] B. L. Montgomery, op. cit.
[4] M577, loc. cit.
[5] Ibid.
[6] 'Strong mentioned that the question of complete surrender was raised, but the Germans had said they had no power to discuss this': letter from 'Simbo' Simpson to Montgomery (ACIGS(O)/18/M), Montgomery Papers.

Monty's mess-tent, had lost all hope of prolonging the struggle and was now prepared to recommend to Dönitz as well as to the Chief of Staff at OKW, Field-Marshal Keitel, that they offer unconditional surrender to Montgomery in the North to save further loss of life. As Monty reported to Brooke: 'They were now prepared to recommend to KEITEL that he should accept my first point [re unconditional surrender]. Von Friedeburg has gone back to see KEITEL and has taken FRIEDL with him. KINSEL and WAGNER are staying at my Tac HQ until they return.'[1] Von Friedeburg had asked for forty-eight hours; Monty had given him twenty-four, promising to unleash the bombers if no surrender was forthcoming. Von Friedeburg was also asked to question Keitel about 'the surrender of other areas e.g. NORWAY. If so I would send him on to SHAEF.'[2]

To conclude the discussion Monty had drawn up an account of their meeting which von Friedeburg signed, taking one copy with him to Keitel. 'There is no doubt that the party came in to study the form generally and to try and get some compromise plan out of me. I think they will agree to surrender unconditionally all forces,' Monty summarized in his signal to Brooke, 'as they are now quite clear as to the hopelessness of their situation.'[3]

To the Reynolds Monty wrote:

> I really do think the German war is drawing to a close. Now that Hitler is dead we shall have large scale surrenders—in Denmark, Norway, and in fact everywhere. We took one million prisoners in April, and the total since D day is over three million.
>
> My love to you both
>
> Yrs ever
> Monty[4]

'I shall hope for a few days' rest soon,' Monty added in a postscript at the bottom of the page.[5] He had not left his armies since launching the battle of the Rhineland early in February. Down at Wiesbaden, General Bradley was still obsessed by the Southern Redoubt—'we may be fighting one month from now and we may be fighting a year from now', Bradley's ADC quoted him on 24 April. 'He is convinced the German is fleeing to the redoubt area with what he can salvage

[1] M577, loc. cit.
[2] Ibid.
[3] Ibid.
[4] Letter of 3.5.45, Montgomery Papers.
[5] Ibid.

to carry the fight on from there.'[1] But for Monty the war was almost all over. 'Thank you very much for telephoning to me,' 'Simbo' Simpson wrote from the War Office. 'I know that S. of S., CIGS and VCIGS are all very grateful for your taking so much trouble, whenever anything big is going on, in letting us know what you think about it personally. I don't think we in the War Office have ever been so completely in the mind of a Commander-in-Chief in the field!

'These are great days to live in. You must have felt a very fine triumph when the Germans came to see you to-day. I wish I could have been present at the interview.'[2]

As the two German parleyers were escorted back through the front lines, Monty's staff began to prepare for the possible surrender on the morrow. A marquee was erected for the occasion, Allied war correspondents were summoned, including the BBC.

Meanwhile, in the quiet of his office caravan, Monty drafted the surrender document he would ask the delegation to sign, five years after the German invasions of Norway, Denmark, Holland, France, Belgium and Luxembourg. The document was brief and allowed of no misunderstanding. Monty handed it to his ADC for typing and retired to his sleeping caravan—the same one which, with its marble bath, Monty had claimed as the spoil of war when Eighth Army Commander in May, 1943. Punctually at 9.30 p.m. his light went out, as it had on the eve of his most decisive battles.

[1] Diary of Chester B. Hansen, loc. cit.
[2] ACIGS(O)/18/M, loc. cit.

CHAPTER ELEVEN

Surrender at Lüneburg

As MONTY SLEPT, the signals personnel of Tac HQ, 21st Army Group tapped out the C-in-C's nightly report to Field-Marshal Sir Alan Brooke. On the eastern flank, from the Elbe town of Domitz to Wismar in the north 'we are now in contact with the Russians and everything is very friendly and it has been agreed that we remain in the positions we now hold', Monty's message ran.[1] From Wismar his north-western flank ran across the Danish peninsula via Bad Segeberg down to Hamburg 'and I have given orders that there is to be no further advance beyond this line for the present. . . . We entered HAMBURG this afternoon and are now in full possession of the city with all the bridges intact between that place and HARBURG and in the city itself.

'Between the two flanks there is still much congestion and this will be fully realised when I tell you that the prisoners taken yesterday and today probably total half a million and most of them are still in this area wandering about by themselves.'[2]

But would von Friedeburg persuade Dönitz and Keitel to surrender unconditionally straight away? Monty's Canadian PA, Lt.-Col. Warren, had been detailed to accompany the German emissaries back to the German lines.

'We started out immediately,' Warren later recalled.

> We had their car, with their driver, and an orderly. In front of this I had my own jeep with my driver and two British Provosts. Behind their car I had another jeep with four British Provosts. We put a small flag pole on each windshield with a white bed sheet which would be visible for some miles and we set out. . . .
>
> We then drove through Hamburg. . . . There was hardly a building left standing. We had to go down back alleys and the like to get around the debris on the main streets and we were driving quite slowly hoping, of course, nobody would take a shot at us. It took us well over an hour to go through Hamburg and an hour to come back and in that whole period we never saw one living thing—not even a cat.

[1] M1117, of 2310 hrs, 3.5.45, Montgomery Papers.
[2] Ibid.

After we had gone about 12 miles North of Hamburg we turned a corner and drove right into the muzzles of two guns mounted on two German tanks. A young looking officer, with one arm, was standing by the side of the road in command of these tanks and when he saw the German vehicle he gave the Heil Hitler sign. Major Friedl got out, spoke to him in German, got in the car and left with great speed. I was left facing this officer and I said out loud to my men 'Get in your jeeps, turn around, and let's get the hell out of here as quickly as we can.' Before they left it had been arranged that I would pick them up at this spot at 1400 hours the next day and that I would wait there for two hours only.[1]

The next day, 4 May, Warren returned, together with Colonel Ewart who had been 'instructed by the C-in-C to try and find out on the drive back to Headquarters if they had been given authority to sign unconditional surrender'.[2]

The two hours elapsed, and there was no sign of the delegation. Warren told his men, however, to wait, for Monty was quite certain the Germans would sign, as he had explained to Brooke:

You will now have received my M 577 giving you details of the meeting at my Tac HQ today which is almost certain to lead to the surrender of all the remaining troops between West HOLLAND and DENMARK. General KINSEL who is at my Headquarters tonight has had talks with my Intelligence Staff Officer and he states that the forces to be surrendered will total over one million men. He also states that there are four hundred thousand Russian prisoners of war in SCHLESWIG-HOLSTEIN. He further states that there has been an influx of two million civilians into SCHLESWIG-HOLSTEIN which came from the eastern counties as the Russians advanced and that the food situation in the area is such that there will be nothing for them to eat in about ten days time. He added that it is almost certain that KEITEL will surrender tomorrow because it is not possible to get the German soldiers to fight any more and they cannot cope with the frightful civil problem.

You can well imagine from all this that there are some nice problems to solve. . . .[3]

At 4.30 p.m. there were signs of vehicles approaching Warren's party:

[1] 'The Surrender of the German Armed Forces', loc. cit.
[2] Ibid.
[3] M1117, loc. cit.

> About 1630 hours we saw the German vehicles coming down the road towards us. We got out to meet them and discovered that they had brought another officer with them—it turned out to be a Colonel Pollok.[1]

Pollok carried, in his briefcase, the German Army and Navy wireless codes, as well as locations of the naval minefields in the North Sea, Friesian Islands, Heligoland Bight, and the Baltic.

> We arrived back at our headquarters shortly after 1700 hours and were told to take the Germans to the Visitors' Mess where there was hot coffee and cognac available for them, and the two that were left behind met them there. This, then, gave them an opportunity to have a private meeting amongst themselves. While this was going on Ewart went straight to see the C-in-C, where he advised the Chief that they [the Germans] were authorized to sign.

This was the news that Monty needed. He was addressing the War Correspondents on the background to the surrender when Ewart appeared. 'The General-Admiral will be back about five. Ha! He *is* back! He was to come back with the doings. Now we shall see what the form is!'[2]

In Monty's caravan Ewart explained, while the correspondents gathered around the 'surrender tent'. The war reporter R. W. Thompson described the moment in his despatch:

> There was complete stillness. The dark woods . . . seemed to enclose a kind of vacuum in which we waited. The rain was driving in the wind and it was bitterly cold.
>
> Fighter planes roaring overhead emphasized the stark bluntness of the ultimatum, and the might of the Allies. . . .
>
> And then they came. Through the woodland, over the crisp brown heather, over the path we had traversed five minutes earlier, the delegates owning the utter defeat of Nazi Germany. . . .
>
> They came slowly, the Admirals in blackish-grey rain-coats, the soldiers in their long grey coats, tight-belted at the high waists, the skirts swinging round their black jack-boots. Only the bright scarlet of General Kinsel's lapels relieved the drabness of their appearance, this solitary little procession bringing with it the submission of a once mighty nation. So they walked, General Kinsel, thick-set, tall, monocled, and the shorter, more thick-set naval officers, to the steps of the Field-Marshal's caravan. General

[1] 'The Surrender of the German Armed Forces', loc. cit.
[2] R. W. Thompson, 'Despatch', in op. cit.

> Admiral von Friedeburg climbed the steps alone, and entered. The others waited, as we all waited. And above these four figures the Union Jack fluttered, the flap of its bunting almost the only sound in this quiet woodland setting.[1]

'I took von Friedeburg into my caravan, to see him alone,' Monty himself recorded later. 'I asked him if he would sign the full surrender terms as I had demanded; he said he would do so. He was very dejected and I told him to rejoin the others outside.'[2]

Monty now gave orders that the surrender would be signed immediately. 'The German delegation went across to the tent, watched by groups of soldiers, war correspondents, photographers, and others—all very excited. They knew it was the end of the war.

'I had the surrender document all ready. The arrangements in the tent were very simple—a trestle table covered with an army blanket, an inkpot, an ordinary army pen that you could buy in a shop for two pence. There were two BBC microphones on the table.'[3]

The business, as Colonel Warren recalled, was brisk and to the point. It was clear that Monty was no longer treating the Germans as emissaries, but as men defeated in battle.

> This time they saluted Montgomery and he returned the salute properly and quickly; in fact he was most regimental. The senior members of the Press were then allowed in and stood round the tent wall.[4]

Seated at the head of the table Monty then read out the 'Instrument of Surrender' he had prepared:

> The German Command agrees to the surrender of all German armed forces in HOLLAND, in Northwest GERMANY including the FRISIAN ISLANDS and HELIGOLAND and all other islands, in SCHLESWIG-HOLSTEIN, and in DENMARK, to the C-in-C. 21 Army Group. . . .[5]

It was thus a surrender *personally to Montgomery*—the climax of a career as an army officer begun so inauspiciously at Sandhurst almost forty years before. Yet as he read aloud the terms of the surrender, with his lisping 'R', the simple, tortoiseshell-rimmed reading spec-

[1] Ibid.
[2] B. L. Montgomery, op. cit.
[3] Ibid.
[4] 'The Surrender of the German Armed Forces', loc. cit.
[5] B. L. Montgomery, op. cit.

tacles set upon the sharp, foxish nose, with the five rows of decorations below his lapel, the small gold chain linking the breast-pockets of his battle-blouse, the bony, sinewy hands resting upon the table on either side of the document, seated with the representatives of a vanquished army, giving that characteristic occasional emphasis to a point—the slightly gnarled knuckles which the artist James Gunn had captured in Monty's tent the summer before—it was evident that the once reprobate cadet had become a master of his profession. At the Press conference at 5 p.m. he had displayed the schoolboyish bumptiousness that so surprised those who did not know him, at one moment relating matter-of-factly the events of the past twenty-four hours, at the next gloating. '"My intention is," he said, "that they shall sign a piece of paper I have prepared,"' R. W. Thompson reported him saying. '"No doubt that if the piece of paper is signed, forces to be surrendered total over a million chaps. Not so bad, a million chaps! Good egg!" . . .'[1] An hour later, before the microphones that would broadcast his voice across the Western world, a quite different Monty was in evidence—the ruthless Army Group Commander who brooked no disobedience or vagueness, whose life had been devoted to the study and practice of the art of war. Having read out the 'Instrument of Surrender', Monty announced that, unless the German delegation signed the document in front of him, he would order hostilities to resume immediately.

There was a pause, while Colonel Ewart translated the threat into German. The German delegates nodded their assent. Then, rising from his chair, Monty announced that the German officers would sign in order of seniority—and handed General-Admiral von Friedeburg the two-penny pen. Von Friedeburg dejectedly rose, took the pen, and signed. Then General Kinsel, Rear Admiral Wagner, Colonel Pollok, each one's signature beneath its predecessor. 'And Major Friedl will sign last,' Monty rasped. There was silence in the tent save for the clicking of cameras.

'Now I will sign on behalf of the Supreme Allied Commander, General Eisenhower,' Monty declared, signing and dating the 'Instrument' to the left of the German signatures, together with his rank: 'B. L. Montgomery, Field-Marshal.'

'His lips were firm, and as he finished signing he sighed faintly, sat back, and removed his tortoiseshell rims, relaxed. 'That concludes the surrender,' he said. The tent flaps were let down, and we walked away over the brown heather,' R. W. Thompson recorded.[2]

[1] R. W. Thompson, op. cit.

[2] Ibid.

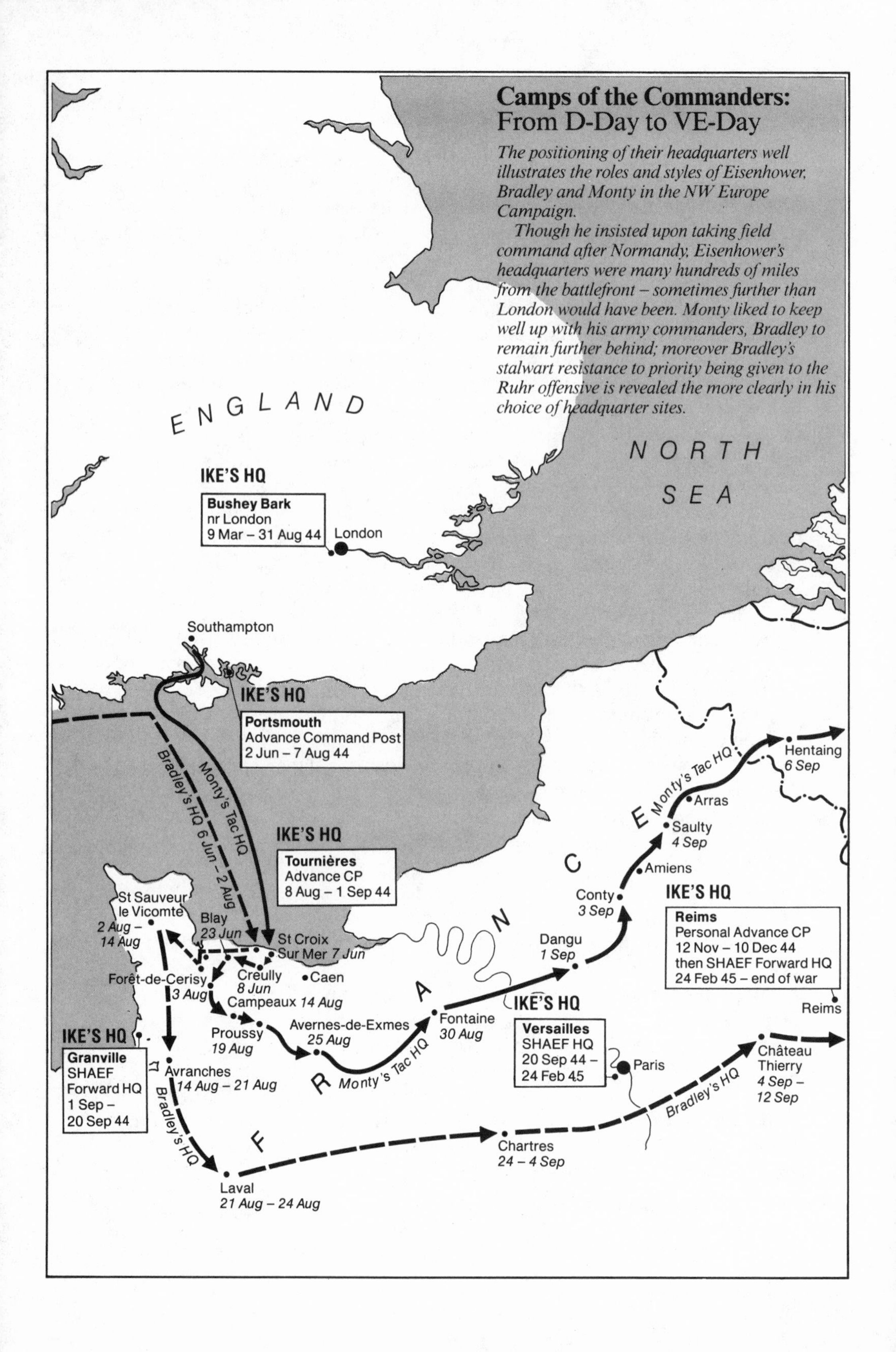
Camps of the Commanders:
From D-Day to VE-Day
The positioning of their headquarters well illustrates the roles and styles of Eisenhower, Bradley and Monty in the NW Europe Campaign.
Though he insisted upon taking field command after Normandy, Eisenhower's headquarters were many hundreds of miles from the battlefront – sometimes further than London would have been. Monty liked to keep well up with his army commanders, Bradley to remain further behind; moreover Bradley's stalwart resistance to priority being given to the Ruhr offensive is revealed the more clearly in his choice of headquarter sites.
ENGLAND
NORTH SEA
IKE'S HQ
Bushey Bark
nr London
9 Mar – 31 Aug 44
London
Southampton
IKE'S HQ
Portsmouth
Advance Command Post
2 Jun – 7 Aug 44
Monty's Tac HQ
Bradley's HQ 6 Jun – 2 Aug
IKE'S HQ
Tournières
Advance CP
8 Aug – 1 Sep 44
St Sauveur le Vicomte
2 Aug – 14 Aug
Blay
23 Jun
St Croix Sur Mer 7 Jun
Creully
8 Jun
Caen
Forêt-de-Cerisy
3 Aug
Campeaux 14 Aug
Proussy
19 Aug
Avernes-de-Exmes
25 Aug
Fontaine
30 Aug
Monty's Tac HQ
IKE'S HQ
Granville
SHAEF
Forward HQ
1 Sep –
20 Sep 44
Avranches
14 Aug – 21 Aug
Bradley's HQ
Laval
21 Aug – 24 Aug
Chartres
24 – 4 Sep
FRANCE
IKE'S HQ
Versailles
SHAEF HQ
20 Sep 44 –
24 Feb 45
Paris
Bradley's HQ
Château Thierry
4 Sep –
12 Sep
Dangu
1 Sep
Conty
3 Sep
Amiens
Saulty
4 Sep
Arras
Monty's Tac HQ
Hentaing
6 Sep
IKE'S HQ
Reims
Personal Advance CP
12 Nov – 10 Dec 44
then SHAEF Forward HQ
24 Feb 45 – end of war
Reims

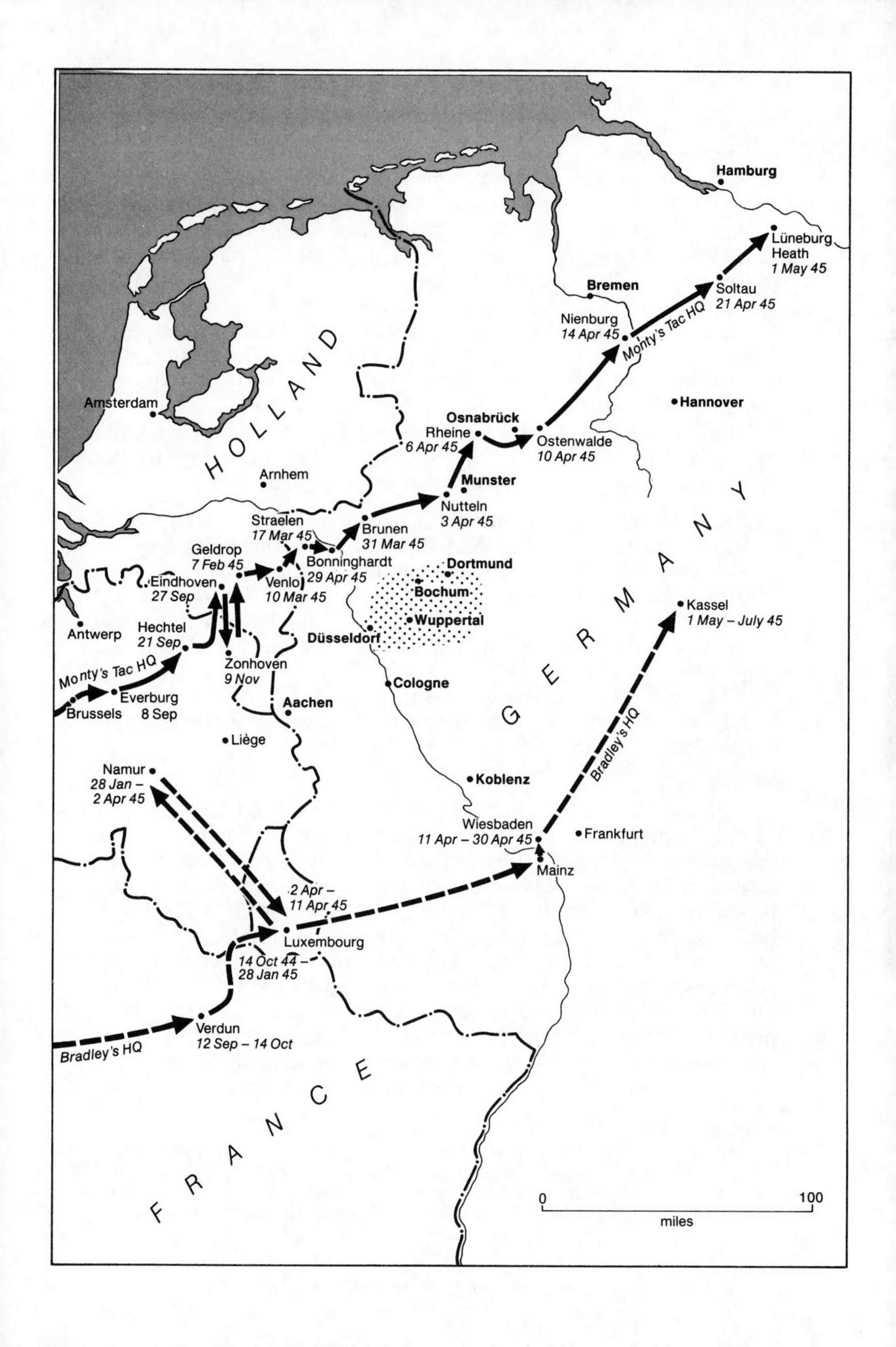

Hamburg
Lüneburg
Heath
1 May 45
Bremen
Soltau
21 Apr 45
Nienburg
14 Apr 45
Monty's Tac HQ
HOLLAND
Amsterdam
Hannover
Osnabrück
Rheine
6 Apr 45
Ostenwalde
10 Apr 45
Arnhem
Munster
Nutteln
3 Apr 45
GERMANY
Straelen
17 Mar 45
Brunen
31 Mar 45
Geldrop
7 Feb 45
Bonninghardt
29 Apr 45
Dortmund
Eindhoven
27 Sep
Venlo
10 Mar 45
Bochum
Kassel
1 May – July 45
Antwerp
Hechtel
21 Sep
Wuppertal
Düsseldorf
Monty's Tac HQ
Zonhoven
9 Nov
Cologne
Brussels
Everburg
8 Sep
Aachen
Liège
Bradley's HQ
Namur
28 Jan –
2 Apr 45
Koblenz
Wiesbaden
11 Apr – 30 Apr 45
Frankfurt
Mainz
2 Apr –
11 Apr 45
Luxembourg
14 Oct 44 –
28 Jan 45
Verdun
12 Sep – 14 Oct
Bradley's HQ
FRANCE
0
100
miles

The hour was 6.30 p.m. The time fixed for the formal cessation of hostilities was 8 a.m. the following morning, 5 May 1945. But as Monty cabled that night to Sir Alan Brooke, there was a further twist to the 'chief event of the day'—for in his talk with von Friedeburg, Monty had raised the question of Dunkirk, whose German garrison was still holding out. 'I raised the question of DUNKIRK but it could not be included in the terms that were signed tonight because von FRIEDEBURG had no powers to treat on that place. But a message has been sent to DONITZ asking for authority to surrender DUNKIRK also and a favourable reply is expected tonight.'[1]

Ironically Dönitz, the new Führer, and Field-Marshal Keitel, the head of OKW, were both in Flensburg, on the German-Dutch border and *inside* the area being surrendered to Montgomery:

> The German delegation raised the question of the status of OKW which is situated at FLENSBURG and from which HQ they are still conducting operations against the Americans and the Russians. I said that by the terms of the surrender OKW were my prisoners as from 0800 hours tomorrow and I could not allow them to conduct operations against the Russians and Americans after that time.
>
> This caused some consternation.
>
> I do not think the German delegation saw the humour of this situation,

Monty added.[2]

In fact it was more politic not to seize Dönitz and Keitel yet, as these men alone appeared to have the power, in the anarchic chaos descending on Germany after Hitler's death, to negotiate the sort of formal surrender of areas such as Norway that might otherwise pose formidable administrative and military problems for the Allies if they had physically to be liberated.[3] But all this was for Eisenhower to arrange. Lacking Monty's credibility as a ruthless field commander, Eisenhower and his staff would be deceived by Dönitz and Keitel into three further days of parleying before an end was put to such nonsense.[4] Monty, however, washed his hands of SHAEF'S inexpertise. For him and the men under his command, the war was

[1] M1118 of 2320 hrs, 4.5.45, Montgomery Papers.

[2] Ibid.

[3] In fact Keitel was not arrested until 13 May 1945.

[4] 'It was obvious to us that when the time came we would be asked to capitulate on the spot and without further ado: so it was a matter of expediting the transfer of what was still over three million troops from the eastern front to prevent them falling into Russian hands. This was also the object of the negotiations begun as

over. 'It seems quite clear that DONITZ is prepared to surrender Norway and the forces under KESSELRING in the south and everything else,' Monty considered in his cable to Brooke.

> I am sending von FRIEDEBURG by air to SHAEF tomorrow to go into these matters. I am keeping General KINSEL at my HQ and staff conferences begin tomorrow to work out all details of how we shall implement this very large scale surrender with all the problems involved in it. The HQ of BUSCH and OKW and most other people are at FLENSBURG and I am establishing tomorrow an LO service with my team of Liaison Officers between my HQ and that place.[1]

In fact, with his Number 10 radio communications set-up and the German army and naval cyphers, as well as his LO system, all Allied negotiations with Admiral Dönitz the Führer, and OKW had now to go through Monty's Tactical Headquarters at Lüneburg.

'Messages immediately went out to all our Naval, Land and Air Commands,' Lt-Colonel Warren afterwards recalled.

> At the same time, from our headquarters and with the codes that Colonel Pollok had brought in, similar messages went out to the German Fleet, Army and Air Forces. A message also went out to the German U-Boats in the North Atlantic to surface, remain in their present locations, and to wireless their headquarters at Flensburg their location. In due course they would be picked up by Royal Navy destroyers and escorted to port.[2]

As Major Odgers, the senior Ops officer, recorded, 'few who were there will forget the thrill when we heard the faint tapping which meant that the Germans were picking us up on the G.27 command link and would receive the armistice message from their delegation. . . .'[3]

It was the end of the war. 'I was persuaded to drink some champagne at dinner tonight,' Monty concluded his cable to Brooke. The signal, encyphered at 2320 hrs on 4 May, was numbered M1118.[4]

---

early as May 3rd on the Grand Admiral's initiative between Admiral von Friedeburg and the British Commander-in-Chief, Field Marshal Montgomery': *The Memoirs of Field-Marshal Keitel*, London 1965. As Keitel recorded, Montgomery 'refused to make special agreements with us', so General Jodl, the Chief of Operations Staff at OKW, was sent to SHAEF to gain time there.

[1] M1118, loc. cit.

[2] 'The Surrender of the German Armed Forces,' loc. cit.

[3] 'A Tac Chronicle', loc. cit.

[4] Loc. cit.

Congratulatory messages flooded in from across the Empire and the world throughout the night; in 'B' Mess the victory celebration continued. But Monty, aware of the 'nice problems' yet to solve, retired to his caravan. Leadership in peace, as well as war, would be required, and he did not propose to be found wanting. 'I think the solution will be in dealing with the matter through the Headquarters of Field-Marshal BUSCH which appears to be the only Headquarters still exercising control. But I have no doubt that the best way to tackle the problem will emerge as the days go by.'[1] Once again the C-in-C's light went out—this time for the last time in the campaign.

[1] Loc. cit.

PART EIGHT

Military Governor of Germany

CHAPTER ONE

Bungling VE-Day

WITH SURRENDER AT Lüneburg the 'British Empire Part of the German war in western Europe' was over, as Monty cabled to Brooke.[1] Or almost so: it remained to be seen whether fanatical Nazis in the surrendered territory would in fact lay down their arms. In certain pockets on the North Sea coast they refused, and desultory fighting went on for several days. But in Denmark, despite much anxiety shown in Whitehall and at SHAEF, the surrender worked better than could have been dreamed possible—Monty being certain that the quickest and safest way to effect the surrender was to work through Field-Marshal Busch. Thus the German commander in Denmark, General Lindemann, was placed at Monty's orders under command of Busch,[2] so that 21st Army Group did not need to send armoured forces into Denmark. Eisenhower had hitherto refused to give priority to the reinforcement of 21st Army Group for the liberation of Denmark and possibly Norway. With a million and a half armed prisoners in North Germany, as well as two million fleeing refugees, and over half a million displaced persons on top of the existing population, Dempsey could not be expected to furnish sufficient forces both to sort out the chaos in northern Germany *and* occupy Denmark, Monty felt. Instead it was decided that Lt-General Dewing would be flown with a small SHAEF mission by air to Copenhagen via Monty's Lüneburg headquarters—as Monty cabled the CIGS on 5 May:

> My general plan is to work through the German military machine and to make use of existing German HQ to get my orders conveyed to German formations and units. KINSEL and a very small staff will be at my Tac HQ. BUSCH with his Army Group Staff will sit in SCHLESWIG. We have at least got some people to whom we can give orders and we have the means for seeing that they are obeyed. When we have no further need of any of them they can be put inside as POW. . . .
>
> I sent DEWING today to COPENHAGEN with a strong company of paratroops from 6 Airborne Div and with signal

[1] Signal to CIGS, M1118 of 2320 hrs, 4.5.45, Montgomery Papers.
[2] Signal to CIGS, M578 of 2250 hrs, 5.5.45, Montgomery Papers.

communications. The party went in twelve DAKOTAS with strong fighter escort and arrived safely at 1700 hours and had a great reception. . . . I have sent forward no columns by land into DENMARK so far and will only do this if DEWING reports they are necessary.[1]

The following morning, after a worried cable from Whitehall ('The Prime Minister started belly-aching about DENMARK'[2]), Monty reassured the CIGS that all would be well.

I am convinced that it would be a grave error at this time to send strong armoured columns from my area northwards into DENMARK nor do I consider that it is necessary. . . . I have good communications with DEWING. I have this morning received a report from him that there is good order in COPENHAGEN, that German troops are keeping to barracks and that there are no disorders elsewhere in DENMARK. He reports no trouble from the resistance movement and has no confirmation of the presence of any Russians anywhere. I am sending him by air today one airborne battalion as a Reserve. I am also sending him one armoured car regiment as this unit has great mobility and good wireless communications and its patrols can circulate freely all over DENMARK and keep DEWING in touch with the overall situation. I had a long talk with DEWING before he left LUNEBURG for COPENHAGEN and we are both quite clear as to how we will deal with the problem.[3]

Monty's Tac HQ at Lüneburg was now the signals centre for the German *Götterdämmerung*. 'I am in very close touch with OKW and with Field Marshal BUSCH and am fully in the picture as to the military and civilian situation in the German areas where there is great confusion and much to be sorted out. Negotiations are still going on between DOENITZ and SHAEF and these pass through me,' Monty explained to Brooke.[4] For the operations and signals staff there was an air almost of unreality in these last days of the 'Thousand Year Reich', so pitifully short-lived yet with so many

[1] Ibid. In his personal diary Monty noted: 'Considerable excitement about some Russians who are reported to be trying to forestall us in DENMARK. I am sending a party of Para Troops with the Military Mission under General DEWING which goes there this afternoon. I saw Dewing and told him that I would supply any force he needed; I could fly in some troops of 1 Airborne Div from England; I could send him an armoured car regt., etc.': Montgomery Papers.

[2] Personal Diary, entry of 6.5.45, Montgomery Papers.

[3] Signal to CIGS, M579 of 1130 hrs, 6.5.45, Montgomery Papers.

[4] M579, loc. cit.

millions of deaths upon its head. Half a million soldiers had surrendered to 21st Army Group on 2 and 3 May; a further million and a half were rapidly being disarmed and herded into POW peninsulas. And still the new Reichsführer, Grand Admiral Dönitz, was playing for time in his negotiations with Eisenhower, eking out the final hours of the Third Reich in an attempt to save more Germans from the vengeance of a people and a territory they had mercilessly attacked and despoiled only four years before.

As Major Odgers recalled, the air of ethereality was compounded by the very nature of Tac HQ communications now—for 'without any physical lines to the rear . . . the Exchange vehicle on the heath was in touch with OSLO and RHEIMS, COPENHAGEN and LONDON. To the uninitiated it seemed a very high technical feat indeed. This was a time of remarkable achievements in the cipher world too. But all felt the pressure of great events and were working at full stretch now, from the clerks in the Ops branch to the General Duty men with Camp. . . .' [1] Liaison officers radiated in all directions, by jeep and light aircraft, both behind British and German lines, with one LO espying Himmler in a corridor at Flensburg, still alive but without portfolio in Dönitz's administration.

That men such as Himmler should have been able to imprint their names and the name of fear across the entire face of Europe reflected the tragic shortcomings of a nation as hard-working and disciplined as the Germans. Monty, in his Lüneburg lair, was undoubtedly amazed at what he saw, as his strange private epithet with its cryptic irony would demonstrate some days later in his diary. For Monty had, since the first intimations of his talent for training on a large scale in World War I, sought first to ensure a professional cadre of officers and NCOs in Britain's inter-war army; then, with the onset of war, to prepare and put into battle a largely civilian army: an army of stockbrokers, clerks, salesmen, farmers, factory workers and labourers; to gird a nation no longer martial for a test which no other major European nation had survived. And now, before him, surrendering in their millions were the men another leader had marshalled from the trades and industries that had made an already formidable economic power into a military state the like of which had not been seen since Roman days. Whatever crimes committed against humanity—particularly in the East—it was impossible for Monty not to feel a certain professional admiration for the organizational genius and level of obedience inculcated in the Wehrmacht. Small wonder the journey from Alamein had not been easy. However it was this respect which determined Monty that the swiftest way to

[1] 'A Tac Chronicle' by Major P. R. Odgers, communicated to author.

deal with the surrendered territories was to use the existing German military machine. Of Busch's Chief of Staff, for instance, he remarked on 5 May to Sir Alan Brooke: 'KINSEL is a very able and very highly trained staff officer and I shall keep him at my Tac HQ with a team of German liaison officers to work between myself and BUSCH.'[1] The rest of the German surrender delegation he despatched by air at 7.30 on the morning of 5 May, from Lüneburg to Eisenhower at Reims. As Monty's diarist noted:

> A very interesting situation now arose. . . . Before leaving for SHAEF, the German delegation let it be known privately to the Field-Marshal that, while the German High Command was prepared to surrender unconditionally, it was most anxious to make this surrender to the Western Allies and not to the Russians of whom all the Germans were profoundly afraid.
>
> The Field-Marshal at once informed General Eisenhower of the general intentions of the German delegation in order that he might have time to consider his own course of action prior to their arrival.[2]

Monty's warning was futile, however, since Eisenhower refused to meet von Friedeburg and his surrender-colleagues, leaving the negotiations to Maj-General Strong (who spoke fluent German) and Bedell Smith. This was counter-productive, since von Friedeburg quickly realized that neither Bedell Smith nor Strong were battlefield soldiers. Monty's threat to recommence both bombing and ground operations unless Keitel agreed to *immediate* unconditional surrender in the north had been a bluff von Friedeburg, confronted by Monty's grey-blue eyes and warrior-like intensity, dared not call. But at Reims von Friedeburg was faced by two overweight Allied staff officers, neither of whom had ever seen a dead man, neither of whom he had even heard of. In the circumstances he played for time, and drove the absentee Allied Supreme Commander, waiting in the next room, almost to distraction. As Eisenhower wrote to his wife the next morning: 'Last night I really expected some definite developments and went to bed early in anticipation of being waked up at 1, 2, 3, or 4 a.m. Nothing happened and as a result I was wide awake, very early—with nothing decent to read'—for the Westerns to which he was addicted were 'just now . . . terrible—I could write better ones, left-handed'.[3]

Frustrated and unable to sleep, Eisenhower was aware that the

[1] M578, loc. cit.

[2] 'Notes on the Campaign in North-West Europe', Montgomery Papers.

[3] Letter of 6.5.45, in D. D. Eisenhower, *Letters to Mamie*, New York 1978.

entire world was now waiting upon the outcome of these negotiations. But von Friedeburg claimed he had no permission to sign the tripartite surrender to Britain, the USA *and* Russia that was demanded of him; negotiations thus dragged on into the morning of 6 May without issue. Ironically Dönitz now turned to Monty—as Maj-General Simpson at the War Office learned that afternoon:

> Field Marshal Montgomery has just talked to me on the telephone (3.15 p.m.) to give me the latest information regarding surrender negotiations,

Simpson noted in a memorandum for the CIGS.

> He [Monty] sent a German-speaking Liaison Officer of his own to OKW this morning with General Kinsel (Chief of Staff to Field Marshal Busch). This Liaison Officer was sent for by Admiral Doenitz who stated that he was somewhat confused as to the action to be taken by him. He was being asked to surrender everything under his control to all three Allies, but there would be very great confusion if he ordered the Armies fighting the Russians to surrender to the Russians. These Armies were terrified that the Russians would immediately send them all to Siberia and they would therefore run away if ordered to surrender. Admiral Doenitz re-echoed what Kinsel had already said, i.e. that a surrender to the Russians was quite different to similar action in respect of the Western Allies. Kinsel had, however, informed Admiral Doenitz that it was quite useless his attempting to stand out against surrender to all the Allies and this attitude was supported by the Liaison Officer. Admiral Doenitz had therefore sent F.M. Jodl [Chief of Operations, OKW] back with the Liaison Officer to see F.M. Montgomery. Jodl was armed with full authority from Doenitz to surrender everything to everybody.

This was indeed an embarrassing situation, with the new Führer empowering Jodl to surrender to Montgomery rather than to the faceless Allied Supreme Commander—who insisted on staying in his room.

Jodl attempted to 'make his point about surrender to the Russians' to Monty, but Monty refused to listen, insisting that the surrender must be offered not to him, as 21st Army Group Commander, but to Eisenhower as the Supreme Allied Commander in Reims:

> F.M. Montgomery said that this was not a matter to be decided by him and he had sent Jodl straight on to SHAEF, where he should arrive at 5 p.m. today,

Maj-General 'Simbo' Simpson reported to the CIGS.[1] Monty had already telegraphed direct to Churchill at 11.30 a.m., who was busy preparing his broadcast to the nation, to be delivered upon the German surrender: 'My own personal opinion is that very shortly DOENITZ will agree to surrender everything to the Allies.'[2]

Jodl duly arrived at Reims. Once again, however, Eisenhower refused to show himself until a surrender document was signed. Seeing his chance to gain time for German troops to disengage on the eastern front, Jodl procrastinated, pretending that he also did not have authority to sign a tripartite surrender. Finally Eisenhower, aware that there might be political repercussions if he failed to secure a prompt capitulation more than two days and nights after the German surrender at Lüneburg, intervened. Unless the Germans signed, Bedell Smith conveyed Eisenhower's warning, the Allies would stop accepting individual German POWS coming into their lines from the east. *Still* Jodl played for more time—and wrought the concession that OKW might have forty-eight hours in which to pass the surrender orders to their units. Even after obtaining this concession Jodl declared he must first pass a message back to Flensburg to obtain Dönitz and Keitel's radio agreement. At last, at 9.30 p.m. on 6 May, Jodl's message was flashed to Monty's Tac HQ and from there was transmitted to Flensburg:

> To Grossadmiral Dönitz and General-Field Marshal Keitel. General Eisenhower insists we sign today otherwise Allied lines will be closed even to persons attempting to surrender individually and negotiations broken off. See no alternative other than chaos or signature. Request immediately you radio confirmation whether authorisation for signing capitulation can be put into effect. Hostilities will then cease on 9 May 0001 hours our time. Jodl, Colonel-General.[3]

As Monty's diarist chronicled, 'in view of the short time available for an answer to be received from the German High Command, all available wireless sets at the Field Marshal's Tactical Headquarters were put on a listening watch on the wavelength of the German High Command. Conditions for wireless reception during the night were very bad, and it was not until forty-five minutes after midnight that a comprehensible message was received.'[4]

Eisenhower's biographer later claimed that Keitel 'was enraged'

[1] Copy in Montgomery Papers.

[2] M579 of 1130 hrs, 6.5.45, Montgomery Papers.

[3] 'Notes on the Campaign in North-West Europe', loc. cit.

[4] Ibid.

by Eisenhower's ultimatum and characterized his demands as 'sheer extortion'.[1] This was nonsense; having surrendered to Monty in the North and to Alexander in Italy, Keitel's only concern, as Monty had well understood, was to delay the full Nazi surrender for as long as possible in order to save as many Germans as possible from the Russians. Far from being enraged, Keitel was *delighted* by SHAEF's fumblings—particularly when Jodl demanded, and was granted, forty-eight hours in which to broadcast the surrender to all subordinate formations. 'Although in guarded language,' Keitel recorded before his execution as a war criminal, Jodl's message from Reims 'left me in no doubt about the possibilities accorded by this two days grace'.[2] Far from ordering instant surrender Keitel now began to send messages to all his eastern units telling them to fight their way back into the Allied lines within the ensuing forty-eight hours.[3]

SHAEF's incompetence was meanwhile reaching its climax. When nothing was heard from Flensburg on the night of 6/7 May, 'there was great excitement [at Reims] . . .' Monty's diarist recorded. Jodl became worried he had taken his bluff too far, and suddenly announced that he *was* empowered to sign the surrender without radio confirmation. 'There was no need for this however' for just before 0200 hrs on 7 May, General Jodl received the message from Field-Marshal Keitel authorizing him to sign the unconditional surrender of the German armed forces to the three Allies:

> To Major Friedel for transmission to Colonel-General Jodl with Supreme Commander
> Full power to sign in accordance with conditions as given has been given by Grand Admiral Dönitz. Keitel.[4]

Thus 'at 0241 hours on the 7th May at RHEIMS, General Jodl signed the act of military surrender in the presence of American, Russian and French witnesses,' Monty's diarist concluded.[5] But if Eisenhower imagined his trials were over, he was mistaken.

Eisenhowever had intended that the signing should remain secret during the forty-eight-hour period of grace extended to Keitel, with Churchill and Roosevelt's successor, President Truman, broadcasting simultaneously a few hours before its expiry on the evening of 8 May.

[1] Stephen Ambrose, *Eisenhower 1890–1952*, New York 1983.
[2] *The Memoirs of Field-Marshal Keitel*, London 1965.
[3] 'I was able to signal the units on the eastern front . . . authorising their withdrawal westwards within . . . not more than 48 hours': Keitel, op. cit.
[4] 'Notes on the Campaign in North-West Europe', loc. cit.
[5] Ibid.

How SHAEF imagined it could keep the final surrender of the German armed forces a secret for two days, at the end of a seven-year struggle in which tens of millions had lost their lives, was a mystery only those who knew SHAEF could understand. Press leaks began almost immediately; then at 3 p.m. on 7 May, the German High Command *itself* announced that it had surrendered unconditionally. Very soon Eisenhower's plan was sundered, and both Churchill and Truman had to advance their broadcasts by twenty-four hours, intending to declare 8 May VE, or Victory in Europe, Day—despite the fact that hostilities were only formally to cease on 9 May.

But worse was to come. When Stalin received news from Eisenhower of Jodl's surrender, he refused to recognize it—causing Churchill and Truman to cancel their plans to broadcast to their nations yet again.

Such a comedy performance by SHAEF was nothing new in 21st Army Group eyes. Had not these same officers barricaded themselves in at Versailles during the German breakthrough in the Ardennes and sent missions to Moscow asking for relieving attacks by Stalin? Now they had failed to ensure that Jodl's surrender at Reims would be acceptable to Stalin—and Stalin was not slow to put Eisenhower in his place. Not all Eisenhower's desire over the past weeks to please Stalin with regard to Berlin, as well as the halting of American troops on the Elbe and Mulde and Patton short of Prague, could now rectify this affront to Russia's contribution in winning the war against Hitler.

> In their hurry to sign the act of surrender, SHAEF had not taken adequate steps to ensure that the Russians agreed to the terms of the capitulation or to the manner in which it would be signed,

Monty's diarist recorded with a certain *schadenfreude*.

> The document was, it is true, signed in the presence of a senior Russian General, but his mission was only connected with the repatriation of Prisoners of War and he was in no way empowered to accept the unconditional surrender of the German armed forces on behalf of the Russians.[1]
>
> General Eisenhower therefore had to agree to this Russian demand [that the surrender be repeated in Russian-occupied Berlin by Keitel himself, Friedeburg (for the German Navy) and Stumpf (for the German Air Force)].

[1] The Soviet High Command had in fact authorized General Susloparoff 'to take part in the surrender negotiations', though not to conclude any agreement without Soviet approval.

As a result of the delay by the Russians in accepting the German capitulation, the Prime Minister and President Truman agreed that they could not make any announcement to their respective nations until it was quite clear that the Russians were going to sign in BERLIN on the 8th May. The broadcasts which they had arranged to make on the 7th May were therefore called off at the last moment. VE day had however already been declared, and it was not possible to alter the arrangements for it which had been made; and in addition the leakage of information had made it quite clear to the public that victory in Europe had in fact been achieved.[1]

Churchill's broadcast was now scheduled for the afternoon of 8 May, which went ahead as VE-Day, irrespective of SHAEF's bungle. Churchill was furious; but in Monty's view SHAEF's muddling ineptitude was but a last comic insight into the amateurism of Eisenhower's headquarters ever since he landed in North Africa in 1942. As Monty wrote in a special note to be inserted at the end of his war diary:

And so the campaign in northwest Europe is finished.

I am glad; it has been a tough business.

When I review the campaign as a whole I am amazed at the mistakes we made.

The organisation for command was always faulty.

The Supreme Commander (Eisenhower) had no firm ideas as to how to conduct the war, and was 'blown about by the wind' all over the place; at *that particular business* [i.e. Land Force C-in-C] he was quite useless.

The Deputy Supreme Commander (Tedder) was completely ineffective; none of the Army Group Commanders would see him; and they growled at once if he ever appeared on the horizon.

The staff at SHAEF were completely out of their depth all the time.[2]

How differently he, Monty, would have conducted the Allied campaign beyond the Seine. With the entire weight of the Allied forces planted on the route to the Ruhr and to Berlin, Monty was quite certain the Germans could have been decisively beaten in 1944; instead, as in Italy, the campaign had disintegrated under prima-donna commanders, each pulling in different directions under an overall Ground Force Commander who—as Auchinleck had found in the Western Desert—could not be expected to marry both field

[1] 'Notes on the Campaign in North-West Europe', loc. cit.

[2] Ibid.

command and the loftier duties of a theatre commander-in-chief. In the circumstances it seemed incredible that the Allies had, after all, won the war only 11 months after the victorious D-Day landings.

> The point to understand is that if we had run the show properly the war could have been finished by Christmas 1944.
>
> The blame for this must rest with the Americans,

Monty concluded—though quickly adding the rider:

> To balance this it is merely necessary to say one thing i.e. if the Americans had not come along and lent a hand we would never have won the war at all.[1]

As the days went by, in May 1945, it would become apparent even to Monty that this American helping hand had not only been necessary to win Hitler's war; without it, the Allies were never going to win the peace. Moreover, at a time of inevitable nationalistic bigotry, as every conscript looked forward to his homegoing, his family and own way of life, there was really only one Allied soldier and leader who inspired a spirit of continuing Allied dignity and resolution. For all his ineptitude upon the battlefield and in negotiations with hardened professional German generals, that Allied leader was Eisenhower.

[1] Ibid.

CHAPTER TWO

Facing the Barbarians

EXCITEMENT AT THE final German surrender was tempered, at 21st Army Group Tac Headquarters at Lüneburg, by the natural psychological after-effect of the months of relentless overseas campaigning. 'It was perhaps inevitable that a reaction should set in at this Headquarters while all the Allied world was rejoicing,' Major Odgers chronicled. 'Now that it was all over many of us merely felt very tired and suddenly rather anxious for the future.'[1] And death was not confined to the battlefield. As Monty's other much-loved ADC turned Liaison Officer, the Irish boy who had once stood beside him on the beach at Dunkirk, was escorting a German admiral from Lüneburg to Flensburg in a jeep, there was an accident. Though pulled alive from the upturned vehicle, Major Sweeny was not expected to live. Informed of this, Sweeny's young wife—they had only just married—begged to be allowed to fly out to be at his bedside when he passed away. Remembering his own wife's death seven years before, Monty was torn between those two forces he had once so vividly described to Anthony Eden at the climax of the battle of Normandy: what you wanted to do and what you knew was your duty to do. To his PA, Trumbull Warren, Monty later remarked that 'it was one of the hardest decisions he made throughout the whole war; but if he let her come, where would he stop?'[2]

In a special obituary written after Sweeny's funeral on 13 May Monty recorded without shame the affection he had had for Sweeny:

> Charles was an orphan and possibly it was that fact which drew us close together; he knew the depth of my devotion to him because I had told him of it; he knew that he could call on me for anything he needed, as if I was his father.
>
> He was an Irish boy with a delightful brogue. There was nothing

[1] 'A Tac Chronicle', loc. cit.

[2] Lt-Colonel Trumbull Warren, interview of 9.11.81. Major Earle heard the news of Sweeny's death while recuperating in No 74 General Hospital at Lüneburg. 'He was the best of the L.O.'s, an excellent Regular soldier of great experience, resolution and common-sense': diary of Colonel Peter Earle, entry of 30.7.45, communicated by Colonel Earle to author, 1985. Colonel Ewart was also killed in a car crash, on 1.7.45.

he liked more than a good argument; he would 'trail his coat' with great skill and, when discussion was started, he would take whichever side was most likely to lead to the most heated argument; nothing would shake him from his adopted line of country.

He had a very strong character and was utterly incapable of any mean or underhand action; his sense of duty was highly developed, and his personal bravery very great. . . .

I loved this gallant Irish boy and his memory will remain with me for all time.[1]

Monty's loyalty to his personal staff was, writ large, his loyalty to all his troops. Other generals might be admired for their battle flair or, by their staffs, for their gentlemanly qualities. But Monty's appeal across the chasm between leader and those led rested in great measure on the trust he inspired: a trust that he had the ordinary soldier's well-being at heart, that he would not risk life unnecessarily but would wage war with a studied attention to casualties and the cost of victory.

Had Monty been made in a different mould he might have now relaxed. The war was over; his part in Allied victory of incalculable importance. Messages had poured in from across the world congratulating him—including, as he wrote to the Reynolds, a 'very nice personal message from the King; so personal that I cannot copy it but I will show it to you in due course'.[2]

King George VI had read each section of Monty's diary as it was typed and had therefore been privy to the secret machinations behind the direction of the Allied war effort. Like Monty, he warmed to Eisenhower as a man and an ally, but deplored the Supreme Commander's lack of military leadership. 'You have often told me your plans for defeating the Germans opposed to you. You have now done it, with a thoroughness which I hope satisfies you as fully as it does me,' the King signalled to Monty following the Lüneburg surrender. 'I send you my heartiest congratulations on your triumph over our enemies and over the many obstacles that you have had to surmount in a campaign that will always be historic.'[3] As the King's Private Secretary noted, in drafting the telegram, 'if any third party sees it, the "obstacles" are, of course,

[1] 'Major Charles Sweeny, MC', typescript in 'Personal Messages to Troops and other Services and Formations: And Obituary Notices' file, Montgomery Papers. The notice was published as a personal tribute by Field-Marshal Montgomery in the *Times*.

[2] Letter of 6.5.45, Montgomery Papers.

[3] Signal 2887 of 1335 hrs, 5.5.45, Montgomery Papers.

the rivers Rhine, Elbe, etc.; but Monty will understand that they include SHAEF!'[1]

Monty's pride in his achievement and disdain for SHAEF's failings were soon overshadowed by the enormity of the task facing 21st Army Group in Germany: a task which Monty now began to take as seriously as he had taken his duties as a 'peacetime' soldier in Ireland after World War I. Like his father before him, Monty was at heart a missionary; while Eisenhower dreamed of mountain fishing and retirement, Monty had for weeks before the cessation of hostilities been preparing himself for his duties as Military Governor of the British Zone—if Churchill would only ratify his appointment. Churchill, however, refused to be cajoled—leaving Monty in infuriated limbo. Congratulations from the Army Council and even from Churchill himself ('The fame of the [21st] Army Group like that of the Eighth Army will long shine in history, and other generations beside our own will honour their deeds and above all the character, profound strategy and untiring zeal of their Commander'[2]) would look well when framed in later years; but the challenge now was the administration of a defeated Germany—with no administrator yet appointed. On 8 May, as Tedder flew to Berlin for the full German surrender session with the Russians, Monty received a doleful letter from the ACIGS, Maj-General Simpson, regarding the question of Military Governor:

> I am sorry to say there has as yet been no progress in the matter of the Control Commission appointments. I have only just spoken (6 p.m.) to S. of S's Private Secretary, who says that S. of S. is almost in despair at not being able to get an answer from the P.M. The various minutes from S. of S., pleading for an early decision, are still in the P.M.'s pending tray. The P.M.'s various Private Secretaries, egged on from here, pick them out and put them on top from time to time during the day; but the old man completely ignores them. MacGregor (S. of S's private Secretary) is going to have another go this evening; but he says that there is so much excitement at No 10 today and tomorrow that he does not expect to be able to get anyone to pay attention to him until Thursday morning at the earliest![3]

Brooke was planning to take a few days' leave, as was Simpson himself—the latter remarking in a postscript to his letter to Monty:

[1] RA GVI PS/7479, Royal Archives, Windsor.

[2] Inscribed in Monty's autograph book, 24.5.45, privately published as *Ten Chapters 1942 to 1945*, July 1945.

[3] Letter of 8.5.45 (ACIGS (O)/19/M), Montgomery Papers.

> Talking of leave, is it not time you gave yourself another breather? You have such a colossal job before you in the government of Germany that I feel a week's rest would be the least you could do to give yourself a rest. The pressure during the last few months has been very heavy. No doubt you will soon be sent for to make a triumphal procession through London. But I feel a quiet week before that would be worth almost anything to you.[1]

Monty had come to think the same—and had earlier that afternoon signalled to Eisenhower to ask permission 'to go to ENGLAND on Monday 14th May for a short rest'.[2] 'Delighted,' Eisenhower signalled back. 'I hope you don't hear the word "war" while you are gone. Best of luck.'[3] But Monty's idea of a rest was very different from Eisenhower's. To Phyllis Reynolds Monty now wrote, informing her that he had 'given orders for the telephone to be put in working order in my bedroom, and I expect a Signals officer will arrive from my HQ and take up his abode at the Royal Huts. . . . I hope to be able to stay in England for 10 days. I am due in Paris on 25 May to open a big Military Exhibition.' And in a final postscript he added: 'Do not tell any of my family I am coming home!!'[4]

This latter injunction was, sadly, the start of a new Monty campaign, to exclude his family—particularly his aged mother in Ireland—from any part in his 'glory'. Now that he had become a world celebrity, the Montgomerys and Farrars would be bound to try and cash in on his fame, he feared; they must be kept strictly at arm's length and denied any reflected distinction—an attitude that was not confined to his family, either, as others were to find.

Before flying from Lüneburg to England, however, Monty felt he must leave a tidy house. Thus on 9 May he assembled his Army Commanders for a conference at which he gave out his orders for the treatment of POWs and German civilians, as well as the dispositions of 21st Army Group forces in the occupation. Two divisions and an armoured brigade would be sent home: the remainder would be split into four occupation areas (including Berlin), with one division in mobile reserve. The two and a quarter million German prisoners would be processed within the captivity peninsulas into which they had been herded; after documentation they would be released in civilian clothes to resume civilian life. 'The Field Marshal

[1] Ibid.
[2] M1135 of 1615 hrs, 8.5.45, Montgomery Papers.
[3] Signal FWD 20970 of 8.5.45, Montgomery Papers.
[4] Letter of 9.5.45, Montgomery Papers.

pointed out that the greatest problem was food, and much would depend on the coming harvest. Altogether tremendous problems would require to be solved, and it would be a race with the winter, as to whether these problems could be solved in time. If they were not solved before the winter, many Germans would die of starvation, of exposure, and of disease,' Monty's diarist chronicled.[1] Finally there was the question of looting. 'He said that in the heat of battle certain actions might be overlooked which under peace conditions constituted a very serious offence. In future therefore any case of looting, whatever the rank of the offender, would be tried by court-martial.' All looted cars were to be handed in 'to enable the Military Government of Germany to function efficiently'.[2]

The British occupation troops were to set an example of integrity and fairness; but what of the German troops? There was a danger, in using the German command system to help enact the surrender, that the Germans—especially senior officers—might begin to consider themselves 'almost tardy allies of ours against the Russians'.[3] Two days after addressing his Army Commanders, therefore, Monty decided to summon Field-Marshal von Busch and make clear that, whatever the future might hold with the Russians, the war that had just concluded after seven years of suffering was against Nazi, militarized Germany. This Germany had been defeated in battle, and would now be systematically demilitarized. Those responsible for war crimes would be punished. The remainder would be demobilized and put back to work as civilians to save Germany from starvation and disease. Busch's job had been to help speed up this process; but British orders were being queried and in some cases their implementation delayed. 'Busch must clearly understand his own position; the Field-Marshal proposed to make use of Busch and of his headquarters so long as the job of implementing the surrender could be more efficiently carried out by this method. If Busch did not carry out his orders promptly and efficiently, he would be removed from his command, and another senior German officer would be found to do his job; in the last resort the British army would do the job themselves, but this would result in delay, which delay would cause further hardship to the German civilian population. Busch had to remember that the German army had been utterly defeated in the field, and must now accept the consequences of its defeat.'[4]

[1] 'Notes on the Campaign in North-West Europe', loc. cit.
[2] Ibid.
[3] Ibid.
[4] Ibid. In his Personal Diary Monty remarked: '11 May. I sent for Field-Marshal

In fact the Germans in the British zone of occupation were lucky to be there, with the prospect of fair rule, a return to civilian life, and security. Beyond the boundary line at Wismar there were probably few females under seventy who had not been raped by Russian troops; POWs were promptly being shipped to Russia as forced labour. When Monty, who had lunched Marshal Rokossovsky, his opposite number, at Wismar on 7 May, paid a return visit to Rokossovsky on 10 May, he motored through half a million refugees within the British zone, whereas east of Wismar 'I motored for 20 miles into the Russian area and it is a dead area with not one single German civilian about. . . . There are some awkward problems ahead and I consider that it is essential to keep a very firm front facing east on the general line WISMAR–DONITZ,' Monty cabled to Eisenhower.[1] Whatever he might say to Busch, Monty was well aware of the Russian threat, and in fact he refused to release Ridgway's 18 US Airborne Corps.[2] Bradley had given orders to his formations that if the Russians insisted on US troops moving back to the agreed zonal boundaries, 12th US Army Group was to do so; but Monty did not trust his Eastern ally, and was privately shocked by the stories from his Liaison Officers regarding Russian behaviour. 'From their behaviour,' Monty's diarist concluded the Commander-in-Chief's War Diary, 'it was suddenly clear that the Russians, though a great fighting race, were savage barbarians who had never enjoyed a civilization comparable to that of the rest of Europe. Their approach to almost every problem was utterly different to the western approach, and their behaviour, especially in their treatment of women, was abhorrent to us. In certain sectors of the Russian zone, there were almost no Germans left, as they had all fled before the onrush of the barbarians; in the Allied zones the crowd of refugees was so great that the problems of food and housing were almost insoluble.

'Out of this impact of the Asiatic on the European culture a new Europe has been born. It is too early yet to say what shape it will take, one can only say that it will be wholly unlike the old Europe . . .

BUSCH and told him that his formations were not obeying my orders. I made it clear to him that the German Army had been defeated in battle and must now do what it is told. If my orders are not obeyed then I will remove him from his appointment': Montgomery Papers.

[1] M1145 of 1915 hrs, 10.5.45, Eisenhower Papers, Eisenhower Library, Abilene, Kansas.

[2] 'SHAEF asked if I could now release the American Corps of three divisions from Second Army. I said No': Personal Diary, Montgomery Papers.

its early years will be of supreme importance to the future of civilization.'[1]

Such sentiments were perhaps naïvely expressed; but they reflected the simple earnestness of an English warrior only a few days after the end of the Second World War in Europe, as British and American troops gazed with curiosity at their communist Russian allies. The tyranny of the Nazis had been crushed—to be replaced by the spectre of a Soviet empire reaching into Western Europe.

Thus Monty's wartime diary ended—supplemented by Monty's commentary on the amateurism of SHAEF. Victory had been won—but in the large part by the Russians. If the performance of the Western Allies was, behind the façade, so poor in war, it was alarming to think what it would be like in peace. The problems confronting the Allies in Germany—political, economic, social as well as inter-Allied—were frightening in their immensity. Firmness, clarity of approach and leadership were more vital now than ever before.

Beset by these anxieties and his profound irritation that Churchill would not announce his appointment as Military Governor, Monty flew back to England not to rest but to get action.

[1] 'Notes on the Campaign in North-West Europe', loc. cit.

CHAPTER THREE

A Colossal Task

'FIELD-MARSHAL MONTGOMERY was much worried about this lack of any proper organisation to govern Germany. . . . He therefore flew to London on the 14th May to impress on the Prime Minister and on the Secretary of State for War the importance of deciding and announcing who was to be the British member of the Allied Control Commission in Germany, and of allowing the man appointed to co-ordinate the planning by the Control Council [based in London] with the practical activities of Military Government [in Germany],' Monty's diarist recorded.[1]

The response was not negative but indifferent—for in the space of a few days, in the second week of May, all Churchill's anxious foreboding about the Russian menace switched to the matter of a General Election. Attlee and his colleagues in the coalition cabinet had expressed their willingness to serve under Churchill until the autumn. The Conservative Party managers favoured an immediate election. Churchill dithered, and Monty's arrival was seen as an irritant. As Monty's diarist was the first to acknowledge: 'the Field-Marshal arrived in England at a politically unfavourable moment. The Coalition Government was coming to its expected end, and the prospect of an early General Election discouraged Ministers from taking any but the most vital decisions.

'As a result the Field-Marshal had the greatest difficulty in getting the Prime Minister to consider the problems of Government in Germany as of such importance as to require an immediate decision. To persuade him of the urgency of the matter, the Field-Marshal dined with the Prime Minister [on 16 May] and discussed the problem with him and the C.I.G.S. until two o'clock in the morning.'[2]

Monty quickly discovered that Churchill's hesitation was not over his appointment, but over that of his deputy. Churchill disliked Monty's choice of the young Lt-General Kirkman, and before dinner Brooke warned Monty that Churchill would probably press for his own nominee—Lt-General 'Ronnie' Weeks, Deputy CIGS at the War Office. After dinner Brooke joined Churchill and Monty at 10

[1] 'Notes on the Occupation of Germany', Montgomery Papers.
[2] Ibid.

Downing Street. 'Blackmail!!' Brooke recorded with fury in his diary. 'Winston ready to announce Monty and Weeks tomorrow provided we accept Weeks, and that I agree!! I saw through the blackmail and said that I could not agree without his consulting P.J. [Grigg, Secretary of State for War].'[1]

Brooke was enraged at such private connivance, and therein lay an important and illustrative distinction between Brooke and Montgomery both as men and as leaders (a distinction that was of profound significance since Brooke was not expected to continue as CIGS beyond the end of the war with Japan or, at the latest, the end of 1945, leaving the question of his successor open). Brooke not only had a grasp of strategy far exceeding that of any other British general, airman or admiral of his generation; he also radiated a stern and implacable integrity of office. Though he might work subtly to get colleagues or political superiors to accept his views, he was wholly above intrigue and never stooped to short-circuit the established chain of command or proper protocol. In his diary he might express his frustration and personal dislike or disdain, but in office he was a man of towering self-discipline and firmness.

Not so his protégé of Dunkirk days. Though Monty amazed the Russian Field-Marshal Rokossovsky by his abstemiousness, nevertheless Monty's iron self-discipline rode in the strangest tandem with his inner self, producing surprising contradictions—at once vain and yet humble, dutiful and yet high-handed, emotional and yet often frosty, loyal and yet capable of adopting whatever means necessary to achieve his purpose. Thus, anxious to get the administration of a defeated Germany on to a proper footing, Monty was quite prepared to settle the matter privately with Churchill, irrespective of the Secretary of State or indeed the very War Office which he had, in messages after the surrender, extolled as having given the greatest support a general in the field had ever enjoyed. This capacity for arranging matters personally at the top may have had merit in war, since it often enabled Monty to cut or untangle Gordian knots that were defeating nobler but less decisive minds—as over the invasion of Sicily and the D-Day landings. But it was a dislikeable trait in peace-time, leaving even loyal colleagues—notably his great Chief of Staff de Guingand—concerned sometimes at the breathtaking lack of consideration towards others. Throughout the Allied campaign Monty had expressed his abhorrence for Eisenhower's methods of command—'he held conferences to collect ideas; I held them to give orders.'[2] But in the very different circum-

[1] Diary of Field-Marshal Viscount Alanbroke, entry of 16.5.45, LHCMA, King's College, London.
[2] Wilmot Papers, LHCMA, King's College, London.

stances of peace-time soldiering, Monty's dictatorial approach, often based on inadequate advice or hasty judgment, would be a distinct liability, casting an unfortunate shadow over a post-war career as dedicated to professionalism and high ideals as it had been during the long years between the two World Wars.

That Monty meant well, there can be no doubt. The same humanity that characterized his generalship in war, his concern with human life, did not desert him now that the war was over, as it did so many of his colleagues retiring to their estates or sinecures. Few envied him the job of governing a defeated Nazi Germany, with the multitude of concomitant problems; indeed it is altogether remarkable how, war-weary after four continuous years of high command in the field of battle, Monty was prepared to throw himself heart and soul into such an unenviable challenge. No other senior Allied battlefield commander did so. Generals Bradley and Devers soon returned to the USA; Patton, who had remained only an Army Commander, was soon dismissed from his command for his indiscretions. Alexander was appointed Governor-General of Canada in July 1945; the Eighth Army Commander, General McCreery, took over as Military Governor of Austria, but had only held Army command some six months. Only General Eisenhower remained in Germany (though reluctantly, and never having commanded on the battlefield or indeed lived in headquarters other than commandeered buildings in the rear). That Monty, with one lung permanently affected by his wounds in World War I, should have survived the rigours of life in the field of battle was a mark of his iron will—a will that refused to relent in the aftermath of war, motivated not by Patton-like dreams of glory but by a relentless inner energy. What linked him to Eisenhower was that both men possessed a simple, schoolboy willingness to serve, and both were at heart champions of a cause greater than their individual selves. Eisenhower's championship of Allied solidarity was not a myth: it was transparent and real, just as was Monty's championship of the ordinary soldier, and the latter's right to good generalship. No one can have had less love of Germans who had conducted two offensive wars of incalculable destruction outside their own borders; but from the start of his as yet unauthorized governorship Monty's concern for the proper rebuilding of Germany was emphatic, exhibiting that same paternalistic, pastoral concern that had distinguished his father's service as Bishop of Tasmania during Monty's childhood. Thus, though he intrigued with Churchill to get his appointment as Military Governor confirmed, it was not in any way from motives of personal ambition. The problem of Germany beckoned: and Monty the warrior expected and now *demanded* command of the relevant forces to tackle it. 'I have no fear that we shall make a mess of the British Zone [unless] Winston hurries up and does what he ought to have done long ago viz appoints you as C in C and [Control] Commissioner. Indeed I shall be quite confident that the best will be made of an extremely complicated and disagreeable job,' the Secretary of State, Sir James Grigg, had written on 10 May, before Monty left Lüneburg. 'As regards this last I am doing my best and really am being like the importunate widow but the PM has been entirely absorbed in basking in the VE sunshine.'[1]

Monty's dinner at Number 10 had at least elicited from Churchill the Prime Minister's intention to nominate him as British representative on the Allied Control Commission; but the plot to appoint General Weeks as his Deputy ran foul of Grigg. Grigg, as Secretary of State, was unwilling to release a man of Weeks' calibre, and a 'somewhat acrimonious exchange of telegrams' between Hindhead and Downing Street followed before the Prime Minister 'gave way and agreed to announce the appointment of the Field-Marshal as Commander-in-Chief British forces of occupation, and British Member of the Allied Control Council in Germany, and of Lt-General Weeks as his Deputy. This announcement was made on the 22nd May.'[2]

Having worked so assiduously to get this decision made during his stay in England, Monty lost no time summoning the heads of the British civil divisions of the Control Commission to a conference in London on 23 May, the day after Churchill's announcement. As Monty wrote afterwards, in thanking the Reynolds for their hospitality: 'With my present work and responsibilities it is not possible for me ever to get a complete rest; I get my rest by change: of people, of scenery, of food, of conversation, and so on.'[3] In London Monty had spoken to his new civil staff with the same directness and clarity that would mark all his post-war addresses. With its mixture of personal, almost evangelical appeal, total lucidity and yet distinct naïveté, it would become quintessential 'Monty'.

"Gentlemen,' he began, after his usual prohibition against smoking and coughing,

> I was anxious to take this opportunity of meeting together, and of getting to know each other. Between us we have to re-establish civil control, and to govern, a country which we have conquered and which has become sadly battered in the process.

[1] Montgomery Papers.

[2] 'Notes on the Occupation of Germany', loc. cit.

[3] Letter of 25.5.45, Montgomery Papers.

Monty's sympathy with the plight of Germany came as a shock to those in the auditorium who pictured him as a ruthless, Cromwellian commander, until two weeks ago waging implacable war upon the Nazis.

> It is a colossal task,

Monty continued, looking up from his notes;

> it will require all our combined brains and much sheer hard work. Without your help it could not be done. You gentlemen are vital to the work in hand.
>
> Having conquered the country, we imposed Military Government on it and that is going on now: through the Army. Our immediate object was twofold:
> a) to disarm and disband the German armed forces
> b) to re-establish civil control *sufficiently* to enable the [people] to live decently, and without disorder and disease.

With his appointment as Control Commissioner and C-in-C, British Zone, his terms of reference went far beyond mere military rule: 'We are all in this business together,' he declared—and proceeded to outline the problem and how he proposed to tackle it. Those who had never attended an address by Monty were now treated to a remarkably clear exposition of the 'set-up' in Germany, as well as the Chief-of-Staff system. It was a soldier's approach and therefore simplistic: but it demonstrated Monty's indefatigable determination to project himself to his subordinates from the start, so that his 'spirit' should work through these men, not as some dim and distant figure, but as someone real, identifiable, and even approachable. The Army was his main agent in ruling Germany at present.

> I have also the Navy and R.A.F., but they are not concerned so deeply in Military Government. 'Control' is now done by my Military Government Directorate (General Templer) which is part of my staff as C-in-C in the field, and comes under my Chief of Staff.
> I am dealing with the British Zone in this way. But eventually the Civil Divisions deal with the British Zone (through German channels). Therefore the short term planning of the Military Government regime must have a very definite relation to the long term planning of the Civil Divisions. Some, if not all, of your Deputies are over in Germany working with my Military Government staff, and I think you have some teams with us also.

All that is to the good.
We must now try and 'feed' the rest of the Civil Divisions over as soon as we can.
The basic aim therefore is to re-establish civil control as soon as we can, and to run the British Zone through German channels.
The great trouble will be to get hold of a German civil machine through which we can work.
But the problem is clear. It is to re-establish civil control in the British Zone and to co-ordinate our activities with those of the other Allies.

How to tackle it

5. I have been working on a limited object, vide para 2, because I had no civil machine to help me. Now that is different; we now have your help.
6. At present my HQ are in Germany; they move on 3 June to the general area HERFORD–BAD OEYNHAUSEN.
   You are here in London.
   I am convinced that we shall not begin to make real progress until we all get together.
   The Control Commission, including the Army Division, is supposed to go to Berlin: I do not see that happening at present as there is no adequate accommodation there; possibly the Secretariat may go later, and it should be held ready to do so.
   Therefore I consider we want to get you over to the BAD OEYNHAUSEN area, where we can all be together *in the British Zone* where the problem lies.
7. The American HQ are being set up at FRANKFURT.
   The French HQ will be somewhere in the French Zone.
   The Russian HQ will be, possibly, at BERLIN.
8. Co-ordination with the other Allies will be essential. This may not be too easy just yet with the Russians, though we must work for it, and try to get it.
   It will be *essential* with the other western Allies i.e. America and France. We must each have our Main HQ in our own Zone; but we must have liaison set-ups with each other, and I believe we should establish these with the American HQ at FRANKFURT.
   In our set-up at FRANKFURT would be 'cells' from each Civil Division; the size of each 'cell' will vary according to the problem, but initially I consider they must be very strong: especially in calibre and quality. Later, they can be scaled down.

My method of working in the Army.

10. I think I should explain to you my method of working.
11. I adopt the 'Chief of Staff' principle. I keep clear of all argument and discussion about details.
    I never attend a conference which is assembled to decide on what is to be done.
    If I assemble a conference, it is to give out orders.
    I sit back, keep in personal touch with commanders, concentrate my attention on the larger issues on which everything depends, and avoid being cumbered with detail.
    My Deputy, or Chief of Staff, has complete authority to give decisions on all matters of detail.

How we shall work now

12. I propose to work in the same general lines.
13. HQ 21 Army Group will co-ordinate all work in connection with the disarming and disbanding of the German armed forces. . .
14. General Weeks is my Deputy; in accordance with my method of working, he is also my Chief of Staff for my larger responsibilities. He will devise his own system for dealing with the Civil Divisions, and for issuing my orders and decisions.
    He has my complete confidence. He has my complete authority to issue orders and instructions on any matter. Any orders or instructions issued by him will be regarded as coming from me.
    I am always in very close touch with him; we consult daily, and he knows my views on all matters.
15. It is clear, from the above, that I deal with one man; my Deputy and Chief of Staff.
    He does the rest.
    But the head of any Service or Civil Division can see me at any time. It will be my custom to ask you to come and see me, and to tell me about your problems and work; by this way I shall always be in touch with your views. And this is vital; I must know first hand what you think about the big issues; without this knowledge I am sunk.
    The best way for these talks will be to get you to come and stay a night with me at my Tac, or personal, HQ.
16. My personal HQ is now on Lüneburg Heath; a historic site!! I move it on 3 June to OSTENWALDE SCHLOSS; this is east of OSNABRUCK, and about 15 miles from Main HQ 21 Army Group at BAD OEYNHAUSEN. I live there alone,

with my personal staff and my small set-up for command e.g. signals, cipher, liaison, etc. etc. The only other member of my personal HQ is my Deputy, or Chief of Staff, i.e. General Weeks. It is to this place that I shall ask you to come and see me.

There will be an airfield there for DAKOTAS about one mile away, and an airstrip for light aircraft within 300 yards of the SCHLOSS.

23 May 1945 B.L.M.[1]

This address is quoted at length because it must serve as an illustration of the many thousands of such addresses Monty was to give in the following decades—and which should not be forgotten when charting the less happy side of Monty's tenures of office, as his papal certainty in his own infallibility grew and his tolerance of dissenting voices diminished. Always the outward evangelist remained, transparently sincere in his call to duty, clear to the point of caricature in his picture of 'the problem' and the best means to tackle it. What he lacked was subtlety, grace, flexibility of mind. These—or virtues akin to them, namely cunning, charm and a willingness to learn the strengths and weaknesses of his foe—he had still possessed as an Army Commander in the desert, in 1942. There, fired by the camaraderie of a veteran if initially baffled army, he had been his own master, protected by the twin sheields of Sir Alan Brooke in London and the C-in-C Middle East, General Alexander, in Cairo. It is quite untrue, as the British military historian Michael Howard once claimed,[2] that Monty rose above his ceiling as Army Group Commander—for Monty's handling of D-Day and the Battle of Normandy, as well as the Ardennes and subsequent Rhine battles, revealed a quality of generalship in the field probably unmatched in modern history. Certainly the performance of other Army Group Commanders of the Second World War—Bradley, Devers, Alexander, Mark Clark—cannot really be considered in the same league. Yet if by ceiling is understood a mental or spiritual parameter, then there is much truth in the criticism. The exigencies of high command in war, fighting under and alongside amateurs or dullards when so many men's lives were at stake, wrought in Monty a transformation, often confused with the effects of fame. To be forced

[1] Filed in 'Notes on the Occupation of Germany', loc. cit.

[2] *Sunday Times*, 11.4.76. In an article in *The Times* the morning after Monty's death, Professor Howard claimed it 'doubtful whether he will be regarded by posterity as one of the great captains of history, or even as one of the truly outstanding figures of the Second World War': 'How will history judge Lord Montgomery's generalship?', *The Times*, 25.3.76.

to watch while the Allies repeated mistake after mistake upon the battlefield and abused the very term High Command, embittered Monty to a point where cunning, charm and openness became subsumed. What emerged was, increasingly, an overwrought, lonely tyrant without family or real friends, unable to *share* as once he had shared the fellowship of the desert warriors. Whether any other commander could have done as well, let alone better, in ruling Germany is doubtful; Monty had the prestige, the admiration of the enemy as well as his own troops, and the loyalty of his commanding officers—all of critical importance in the transition from military occupation to democratic genesis. Moreover the fact that he, the conqueror of Hitler's Third Reich, showed such an immediate and genuine determination to rebuild the 'sadly battered' state of Germany was—particularly when set against the pragmatic indifference of the Americans and the rabid fears of the French—a contribution to the post-war development of liberal Europe of considerable significance. To complain that he was not, at the same time, a great statesman or diplomat, that he did not rise to the stature, say, of MacArthur in Japan or even Eisenhower in Europe, is wilfully to overlook his achievement and belittle his profoundly Christian charity. Yet it cannot be denied that Monty's stature as man and statesman failed to grow in tandem with his high offices, leaving many scars and dented loyalties, as will be seen.

Monty was himself largely unaware of this. Just as Churchill misjudged the mood of the country and strutted like the emperor in new clothes, so too Monty completely misunderstood the nature of the peace-time challenge to his *own* persona: as a peace-time colleague now, rather than as a battlefield commander. Many of his actions after Dunkirk had suggested an unbalanced mind, a psyche fixated by a sense of destiny as his nation's deliverer; and in the unhappy years after World War II something of the same manic intensity swept him forwards, intent on serving the very highest ideals yet heedless of those he cut down and trampled. Like Nelson before Trafalgar, he had tasted greatness, a height of professional command where a whole navy thrilled to serve him; and as with Nelson, this sometimes induced a state of mind akin to madness. Fortunately, unlike Nelson he had no mistress to bequeath to a supposedly grateful nation; but many of Monty's actions in the coming months would proceed from the selfsame delusions of patriotic grandeur and self-importance, producing in the observer sheer astonishment. As the Queen remarked to her Private Secretary when stunned by Montgomery's gall the next year in claiming one of her prized war paintings: he was to tell the Field-Marshal that she acceded to his request for no other reason than that he had, quite simply, won the war. Otherwise she was 'not amused'.

The Occupation of Germany: May 1945 – May 1946

Soon after the war's end Monty was appointed C-in-C British forces and Military Governor of the British Zone of Occupied Germany, as well as British Control Commissioner in Berlin.

Separating himself from the detailed administration of his zone, Monty ruled autocratically from a rural Schloss near Osnabrück, issuing proclamations to the German people and deciding upon British policy at a time when the new Labour Government had few clear or constructive convictions. He reopened German schools and universities, encouraged free trade unions and youth groups, as well as political discussion: an approach not liked by the Americans at first.

Injured in an air crash, weakened by winter flu', and worried by signs of Russian determination to remain in east Germany, Monty was relieved to return to England in the early summer of 1946 to take up his post as CIGS, the head of the British Army. Germany had in fact been the last 'field' command Monty was ever to hold.

CHAPTER FOUR

Acting on His Own Initiative

'THANK YOU FOR a very pleasant visit home . . . I am having a terrific reception in Paris. Love to you all. Monty.'[1]

Monty's letter from the British Embassy on 24 May 1945 was no exaggeration. The *foule de Paris* had cheered Eisenhower on their liberation in August the year before, as well as de Gaulle. Now they paid belated homage to the man who, more than any other, had rid their country of the jackboot; and they went wild.

Monty's trip was ostensibly to open the British Military Exhibition in Paris and to be decorated by General de Gaulle with the Grande Croix of the Legion of Honour in the Invalides; but the day became a second victory celebration, with immense crowds assembling outside the Embassy in the evening, clamouring for Monty to appear. The same ecstatic welcome was given in Antwerp a fortnight later. Moreover, at the formal signing of the Allied declaration on the defeat of Germany in Berlin on 4 June, Marshal Zhukov announced that Stalin had awarded General Eisenhower and Field-Marshal Montgomery the highest Soviet order, the 'Order of Victory'.

Eisenhower and Monty were, now, the two 'big' men of the Allied occupying forces, standing alongside the very Russians Eisenhower had permitted to capture Berlin. But the ramifications of Eisenhower's decision were now apparent. Zhukov did not appear at Tempelhof airfield to greet the Allied visitors, no food was waiting at their villas, nor any programme for the signing of the declaration—in fact one was only drawn up when Monty threatened to fly home. At the signing itself, which constituted the first meeting of the Allied Control Commission in the occupation of Germany, Zhukov announced that there would be no Control Commission until the Allies withdrew within the areas allotted at Yalta. As the Western Allies held no territory worth keeping, Monty and Eisenhower had no option but to recommend to their governments that they agree.

[1] Letter to Phyllis Reynolds, 25.5.45, Montgomery Papers. The Ambassador's wife, Lady Diana Cooper, gave Monty a poodle: 'The Paris show was a terrific success and I hope has done some good to cement relations between our two countries. . . . Amongst other things I collected a black French poodle—4 months old: a very attractive puppy': letter to Phyllis Reynolds, 1.6.45. Ibid.

Though Monty was hailed as a conquering hero at home and in Northern Ireland (**98** *above left*) the strains of fame, battle and widowerhood soon began to tell. His possessive yet foreign attitude to his son David (**99** *above right*), his insulting rejection of his aged mother Maud (**100** *right*) and his platonic infatuation with a twelve-year-old Swiss boy Lucien Trueb (**101** *far right*) on a skiing holiday in Switzerland (**102** *below*) – all testified to the stunted emotions still warring inside the world-famous soldier.

Monty took his responsibility as Military Governor in Germany seriously. 'The Germans work best if they are given definite orders by some person whom they can identify,' he claimed, and soon adopted the tone of benevolent dictator in his proclamations and broadcasts (**103** *above left*). His Political Adviser, Sir William Strang (**104** *above right*), admired Monty's soldierly decisiveness – but felt his approach to war inappropriate to the dictates of peace. Americans in particular deplored Monty's positive attitude to freedom of the German Press, German Trade Unions, political organizations and youth work – even attempting to stop his Messages to the German people.

A near-fatal aircraft crash and hospitalization after contracting influenza in January 1946 led Monty to seek rest and relaxation in Switzerland in February that year (**105** *centre opposite*). Monty had been officially informed that he was, like Eisenhower, to be the next head of his country's army, and his last months in Germany were spent considering the future of western Germany – and the shake-up of the British Army he intended to enact once in Whitehall.

Monty's staff in Bad Oynhausen towed his car through the streets in a rousing send-off in April 1946 (**106** *bottom, opposite*), followed by a final Control Commission Conference in Berlin. On 2 May 1946 Monty left Gatow Airfield (**107** *above*), and after an air-tour of British military contingents in the Middle and Far East Monty became Chief of the Imperial General Staff (CIGS) in Whitehall on 26 June 1946 (**108** *right*).

At the War Office
Monty's ambition as CIGS was to create a 'New Model Army', this time professionally officered, well equipped and with a clear concept of its peacetime commitments and likely roles. Beneath portraits of his predecessors he lectured the press (**109** *right*), but was soon in trouble with the Cabinet and Labour Prime Minister at 10 Downing Street (**110** *below*), whose lack of strategic vision or backbone was anathema to Monty.

Unfortunately Monty's no-nonsense approach to the committee meetings of the three Air, Army and Naval Chiefs of Staff soon resulted in hostile relationships with Air Marshal Tedder and Admiral Sir John Cunningham (**111** *above left*).

Perhaps, in an age of post-war bankruptcy, Monty's greatest contribution to the Army as CIGS was his insistence on combined army-air exercises (**112** *above right*) and strategic and tactical discussions for senior officers from all three services at Camberley each year (**113** *below*).

Monty was, by his own admission, no diplomat. However his international fame as a soldier made him, inevitably, a world statesman while CIGS – a further cause for jealousy among his fellow Chiefs of Staff.

On his first ever visit to the USA, Monty was greeted by his opposite number General Eisenhower (**114** *above*) who warmly approved Monty's proposals for secret military talks between Canada, the USA and Britain: the germ-seed of the later North Atlantic Treaty Organization. President Truman (**116** *below*) approved such talks, which soon began on board SS *Sequoia*. Even Bradley cast aside his bitter memories of humiliation in the Ardennes to welcome Monty's call for Western strength through political and military alliances (**115** *centre*).

Stalin's invitation and welcome to Moscow in January 1947 (**118** *opposite top right*) showed that the Soviets were anxious also to woo Monty, even showing him around their military academies and tank schools (**117** *opposite top left*). In India Monty was a guest of the Viceroy Lord Mountbatten (**119** *opposite centre left*), met Indian leaders such as Jinnah and, **121** *opposite below left*, Jawaharlal Nehru. In Paris he was still considered the First Soldier of Europe (**120** *opposite centre right*). His faithful VCIGS, Lt-Gen. 'Simbo' Simpson (**122** *opposite below right*), admired Monty but was all too aware of the jealousy and discord Monty's manner engendered in Whitehall.

Monty's cool response in 1948 to the Berlin crisis (**123** *above*) was lauded by the Minister for War, Mr Shinwell (**124** *below*) – who openly proposed Monty as Supreme Commander charged with establishing a credible European defence.

After much argument, Monty was appointed first Chairman of the Committee of Commanders-in-Chief of Western Union (**125** *right*), comprising Britain, France, Belgium, Holland and Luxembourg in October 1948.

Monty's trip to Berlin made it quite clear to him that dealing with the Russians was going to be a nightmare—with the Russians able to do largely as they wished by refusing to operate the quadripartite Control Commission unless the Western Allies gave way.

On 10 June Monty visited Eisenhower's headquarters in Frankfurt, established in the untouched IG Farben building. This visit—during which Eisenhower conferred on Monty America's highest decoration for the soldier of another nation, the DSM—was also salutary. 'During the day one could not help but be impressed by the American organisation, and the lavishness of their welcome,' his diarist noted. 'It was a day which showed undeniably, for good or bad, the wealth and power of the United States.'[1]

This wealth and power, as untouched in the USA as the IG Farben building in Frankfurt, was well illustrated by President Truman who in mid-May suggested attending the forthcoming tripartite meeting with Stalin without first meeting Churchill, in order to avoid any Soviet suspicion of 'ganging up'. It required all Churchill's diplomatic skills to make Truman aware of the 'iron curtain' drawn down upon the Soviet front: that Stalin's *carte blanche* to do as he wished in Poland, Austria, the Balkans and Soviet-occupied Germany rested upon a prising apart of that very Atlantic solidarity which had enabled the western Allies to defeat Germany. The Yalta agreement about free elections in Poland was soon signed away by the President's adviser in Moscow—and the nation over whose independence Britain had gone to war in 1939 entered an era of even longer darkness. Since Yalta, as Churchill later observed, 'the Soviets had fought every inch of the road [to prevent free Polish elections]. They had gained their object by delay. During all this time the Lublin Administration, under Bierut, sustained by the might of the Russian armies, had given them a complete control of Poland, enforced by the usual deportations and liquidations. They had denied us all the access for our observers which they had promised. All the Polish parties, except their own Communist puppets, were in a hopeless minority in the newly recognized Polish Provisional Government. We were as far as ever from any real and fair attempt to obtain the will of the Polish nation by free elections. . . . So far only dust and ashes had been gathered, and these are all that remain to us today of Polish national freedom'—a lament penned in 1953[2] that would hold true for a further three decades and more.

What was clear to Churchill was that the Soviet time-scale was quite different from that of the Western Allies. Already American

[1] 'Notes on the Occupation of Germany', loc. cit.

[2] W. S. Churchill, *Triumph and Tragedy*, London 1954.

and British troops were being demobilized or transferred to the Pacific—whereas Russian forces, still not technically at war with Japan, were settling down in the Baltic States, in Poland, eastern Germany, Austria, Czechoslovakia, Roumania, Bulgaria and Hungary for a very long stay. 'Surely it is vital now to come to an understanding with Russia, or see where we are with her, before we weaken our armies mortally or retire to the zones of occupation,' Churchill begged Truman.[1] Without Berlin, however, the Allies had nothing to barter. Allied missions in Vienna were ordered out by Marshal Tolbukhin, and with the war in the Pacific reaching its climax, Truman quickly gave in to Stalin's demands regarding Poland. Churchill was abashed—'this struck a knell in my breast', he later chronicled[2]—for despite his inability to gauge the aspirations of ordinary people in Britain, he saw the political future of Europe with prophetic insight.

Monty, though he distrusted the Russians, wholly lacked Churchill's political perspicacity; he thus sided with Eisenhower and the Americans, innocently believing that a single German state would one day emerge from the chaos of Nazi defeat, and that the Allied Control Commission was the instrument that would give birth to this entity. For this Commission to function, the western Allies must withdraw to their agreed boundaries, for they did not have sufficient troops to oversee the Russian-intended areas, let alone defend them if the Russians moved in by force. Churchill had even ordered a stand-still on the destruction of German weapons and aircraft; this, too, Monty failed to appreciate; as he pointed out to Whitehall, guarding German munitions and weapon dumps required personnel at a time when, with more than twenty million Germans to 'rule', he was very short of men.

Churchill refused to relent, revealing why he had for so long barred Monty's appointment to the Control Commission or his choice of deputy. The very fate of Europe hung in the balance, and Churchill wanted in Germany a man who, if he did not foresee the political geography of the continent with Churchill's own depth of vision, would at least carry out the orders of the Prime Minister without 'belly-aching'.

But Churchill's days as Prime Minister were numbered. However deeply he might see into the geopolitical future, he was deaf to the immediate aspirations of his own countrymen, as well as physically and mentally broken by his titanic efforts during the war. The great tripartite Allied conference at Potsdam was scheduled to take place on

[1] Ibid.
[2] Ibid.

17 July 1945. On 16 July, having met Churchill at the airfield and seen the British delegation safely to its quarters, Monty wrote to 'Simbo' Simpson at the War Office:

> Very hot here in Berlin and we live in shirt sleeves. The atmosphere is amazing. No one knows anything about the problem; the P.M. has been electioneering for weeks and has read nothing; Eden has been sick; there is no agreed Agenda; everyone is reading Foreign Office briefs madly. A curious show!!! Pug Ismay is very depressed about the whole thing; but I have no doubt something will emerge: if we can keep their feet on the floor.
>
> The P.M. looks very old; I was shocked when I saw him; he has put on 10 years since I last saw him.[1]

On 25 July the Potsdam conference was adjourned while Churchill, Atlee and the British delegation flew home to hear the result of the General Election. It was a landslide victory for Clement Attlee and the Labour Party, resulting in a new British delegation returning to Potsdam.

Monty was favourably impressed by the new Labour team—particularly by the new Foreign Secretary, Ernest Bevin. As he wrote to Simpson on 1 August,

> I had a long talk in Berlin with Atlee [sic] and Bevin; I will tell you about it in due course. Atlee disclosed that the new S of S for War is to be Lawson, whom he said was a very good man. I was much impressed by Bevin; he will be the power behind the throne in the new set-up.[2]

Monty's admiration for the 'new set-up' increased when the conference agreed a directive to the Control Commission. 'From my point of view the Conference here is not going too badly; we have got the Big Three to O.K. a political directive to the Control Council,' Monty wrote to de Guingand on 20 July; 'if we can now get them to do the same with an economic directive, then I take no further interest. In other spheres the conference is not *at present* doing much good; but they may come on with a spurt at the end.'[3]

Neither Attlee nor Bevin, however, was prepared to do battle over the Poles. Thus, as Stalin had once seized a vast part of Finland to be incorporated in the USSR, so now he was permitted to annex a fifth of Poland—while encouraging the Poles to do likewise with the

[1] Letter of 16.7.46, Simpson Papers, Imperial War Museum. Churchill was in his seventy-first year.

[2] Letter of 1.8.46. Ibid.

[3] De Guingand Papers, IWM.

Germans! With Poland annexing East Prussia, however, the chances of Germany ever being able to feed its own population plummeted—the more so after Stalin had insisted that the Western Allies supply their own food to feed the three million Germans who would be living in the western sectors of Berlin. 'As BERLIN as a whole had normally drawn its food from the area within 50 miles of BERLIN, all of which was now occupied by the Russians, this seemed an unreasonable request,' Monty's diarist soon noted, 'and one suggesting that the Russians did not really wish to reconstitute Germany as one economic whole.'[1]

Here indeed was the crux of the German problem—and one to which there was no happy answer. The Western Allies had to govern a defeated Germany as if they were combined powers occupying a single state that would one day reassume its place among the independent nations of Europe. Yet these powers had refused to recognize the legality of Admiral Dönitz's government, receiving only the surrender of the German armed forces. What hope was there, in the light of events in Poland and Roumania, that a new government or indeed political system could ever be devised which was satisfactory to the Russians on the one hand and the Western Allies on the other? But if Germany was *not* reconstituted as a single state, how could it possibly feed itself?

Monty, charged with the rule of more than twenty million Germans and displaced persons, was as uncertain as the rest where the future might lead—having found, on his return to Germany in June 1945, that the Germans in the British Zone, both POWs and civilians, were understandably disquieted. He had therefore issued an immediate 'Message to the German Population', much as he had issued messages to the troops of Eighth Army and 21st Army Group:

> I have been appointed by the British Government to command and control the area occupied by the British Army.
>
> This area will be governed for the present by Military Government under my orders.
>
> My immediate object is to establish a simple and orderly life for the whole community.
>
> The first step will be to see that the population has:—
>
> a) food
> b) housing
> c) freedom from disease
>
> The harvest must be gathered in.
> The means of transportation must be re-established.

[1] 'Notes on the Occupation of Germany', loc. cit.

The postal services must be restarted.
Certain industries must be got going again.
All this will mean much hard work for everyone. . . .

Although this personal proclamation did not itself raise any political protest in England, it certainly raised suspicions in Whitehall that Monty was out to make himself a minor Führer in Germany—suspicions which were further inflamed when Monty was misreported in subsequent press briefings. 'I beseech you in the bowels of Christ to watch your step or at any rate your loudspeaker so long as SHAEF still exists. I have quite enough quarrels to cope with,'[1] the Secretary of State for War cabled Monty when Monty's 'Personal Message' caused rumblings in SHAEF—for the Americans wanted no Briton to steal a march on them. Conversely, when Monty suggested, at an investiture of American troops, that without American aid Britain could not have won the war, Churchill was infuriated. The Prime Minister wired to Ostenwalde, 'demanding to know what the Field-Marshal had said, and, if the Field-Marshal had been correctly reported, conveying his displeasure to him,' Monty's diarist recorded.[2] The Secretary of State for War again begged Monty to watch his words:

> Do for goodness sake stop making speeches for a bit. We are getting fuliginous minutes from the Prime Minister every day. The latest is contained in my immediate following [telegram].
>
> Anyway there are plenty of people about who will rejoice to see mischief between you and the Prime Minister and they aren't all Germans, Russians or Americans,

Sir James Grigg warned.

> There are, for example, an awful lot of near-Communists among the newspaper correspondents and there are certainly a lot of lice.[3]

Churchill's private Secretary, Flight-Lieutenant John Colville, witnessed many of the 'lice' berating Monty to the Prime Minister behind Monty's back. Such a mischief-maker was Air-Marshal Sir Arthur Coningham, who had done his best to sow discord ever since the first days in Normandy when he bore back to England tales of 'crisis' on the battle-front. Even on the eve of Monty's Rhine crossing and the breakout to the Elbe as Churchill returned from Monty's

[1] Signal of 31.5.45, Grigg Papers, Churchill College Archives.
[2] Loc. cit.
[3] Signal of 27.6.45, Grigg Papers, loc. cit.

Tac Headquarters, Coningham was in Brussels decrying the C-in-C of 21st Army Group—'the most egotistical man he had ever met', Coningham took pains to inform Churchill's Private Secretary. 'He was indiscriminate in his ruthlessness. . . . He aped the Americans who loathed him. Finally his handling of the recent operations, 'Veritable' and 'Grenade', to clear the west bank of the Rhine, had been slow and, considering the paucity of the opposition, very inadequately executed.'[1]

Those Canadians who survived the hand-to-hand fighting towards Cleve would have lynched the New Zealand airman for such rear-headquarters criticism of their efforts against the fanatical resistance of German parachute troops; Coningham seemed oblivious to the tactical effectiveness of the two related operations—or his own failure to undertake the destruction of the Rhine bridges in good time.

Monty was quite aware of the jealousy and ill-will he aroused in such men as Coningham. 'I went to Wiesbaden on 26 June to hold an investiture for American Officers and men,' he cabled back to Grigg. 'At the end of the investiture General Bradley asked me to say a few words to the assembled recipients. In my talk I made two points. Firstly I thanked the American Army for many kindnesses and great hospitality we had always received at their hands. Secondly I said that the turning point of the war came when Axis Powers committed their mistake in 1941 of attacking Russia and America. Up to that they [had] the British Empire just fighting alone against the combined might of the Axis Powers. The final defeat of Axis Powers was hastened when Russia and America had come in against them,' he reported somewhat lamely. 'I am pained and grieved that Prime Minister should have thought I would ever make the statement attributed to me.'[2]

Churchill thereupon let the matter drop. However one is entitled to speculate whether he would in fact have kept Monty for long as Control Commissioner and Military Governor in Germany had he survived the General Election. Though similar in certain respects—both men being bullies and unwilling for others to share their limelight—they were poles apart in their approach to life and to their work. Churchill smoked and drank heavily, rose late and retired late; he also liked to pick his way round a problem like an

[1] Diary of J. R. Colville, entry of 4.3.45, communicated to author by Sir John Colville.

[2] M1182, 27.6.45, Montgomery Papers. The attributed statement was 'that Britain was finished in 1941 and could not possibly have survived without American aid': second cable from Grigg of 27.6.45, Grigg Papers, loc. cit.

insect. Though he wanted immediate action when action was the thing, he had the statesman's feel for essentials and for timing. He would thus 'mull over' issues when all around him begged for a decision; then chide his acolytes for tardiness in executing it. His subordinates had to learn an obsequious tolerance, resigning themselves to unjust criticism and petty carping over details that had caught the 'Monster's' eye. When, for instance, Monty pressed Whitehall for relaxation of the Allied rule on non-fraternization, no response could be obtained; but when Churchill heard of a soldier being punished by fifty-six days in jail for contravening the rule on fraternization, he was incensed and asked Monty to lift the sentence. Such inconsistency was something Monty's superiors—Alexander, Eisenhower and Brooke—had for the most part parried on Monty's behalf; now there was no buffer, and without Churchill's sudden demise in the General Election of July 1945, the Monty–Churchill relationship would have become, without doubt, stormier and stormier. Monty's patience, it became clear, was a quality he reserved for battle; in peace-time it was anathema to him. His relentless 'Inspector-General's' energy drove him like a dynamo. Where Churchill stalked a problem, Monty faced it, analyzed it, and came to an immediate conclusion. This gift for simplification was his unique strength—perhaps the clearest military brain ever produced in the British Army. To those who yearned for clear guidance and rousing leadership, Monty was a commander without parallel. But in a post-war world with so many imponderables and uncertainties, his 'blitzkrieg' approach to problems had distinct disadvantages—the more so since Churchill, intent upon his Olympian performance at Potsdam, had left a disastrous vacuum in the corridors of Whitehall once the Labour Party withdrew from the coalition. As Monty's diarist plaintively summarized in July:

> Following his nomination as British Member of the Allied Control Council, the Field-Marshal received a wide and loosely worded directive to cover the course of action he was to pursue. This directive assumed that the Control Council would be functioning and would in fact by unanimous decision settle all problems which arose. The situation however was in fact quite other than that which the politicians had envisaged. The Russians were not prepared for the Control Council to commence to operate, and furthermore no central authority existed in Germany through which the Control Council could function. To meet this situation the Field-Marshal required further guidance from Whitehall on

the course of action which he should pursue. Eventually he received authority from the Secretary of State for War to act on his own initiative but to endeavour to work in line with the Americans as far as possible. He consequently issued a series of memoranda to his staff giving them his general policy for the government of the British zone of Germany.[1]

Political lack of direction thus forced Monty to become a sort of Cromwellian dictator in Germany—a fact much resented by those who disliked dictators, but hardly Monty's fault. With two and a half million German prisoners of war to discharge, over a million 'displaced persons' (Russians, Poles, Hungarians etc.) to resettle, as well as questions of food, housing, transportation, education, industry, health, and finance, this was a considerable challenge to face without a working Control Commission to agree common policy or an effective British policy from Whitehall to temporize. As Anthony Eden wrote to Monty the following year, it was a 'hard and thankless task'[2] and it is to Monty's credit that, for all his limitations as a statesman-like administrator, he tackled it so selflessly and conscientiously. If his rule smacked of the dictator, Monty was unabashed. As he noted on 14 July 1945, before Churchill began his negotiations with Truman and Stalin at Potsdam, his own task was to see that twenty million Germans, on the ground, were fed and governed:

> The Germans work best if they are given definite orders by some person whom they can identify.
> They will not respond in the same way to orders which come to them from 'Military Government', or from a 'Commission'.
> We must issue a series of Messages or Proclamations which will tell the Germans what we are going to do, and will demand their co-operation. These must be issued by 'The British C-in-C,' and must be signed by me. The German people understand this, and will do what they are told.[3]

For good or ill, then, Monty had embarked, even before the advent of a Labour government, on his dictatorship in Germany. If he lacked patience and saw issues in colours only of black and white, there were compensating advantages for the Germans within the British zone. As he had always sought to prepare himself for the next battle even while the current one was being fought, so as British

[1] 'Notes on the Occupation of Germany', loc. cit.
[2] Letter of 19.3.46, Montgomery Papers.
[3] 'British Zone: Notes on the Present Situation' of 14.7.45 in 'Notes on the Occupation of Germany', loc. cit.

Control Commissioner Monty's steel-blue eyes surveyed the calendar—and foresaw widescale disease and starvation that winter unless the British acted in good time.

CHAPTER FIVE

Not an 'Homme du Monde'

ONE OF THE reasons why Monty failed to grow in stature commensurate with his high office was time. Churchill, rejected at the General Election, retired to his estate at Chartwell to write his own version of the Second World War, leaving the Conservative opposition in Parliament largely to others. De Gaulle also retired from national office the following year. Both men were thus able to reflect on those events which had made them world figures, biding their time before their respective 'come-backs'. Field-Marshal Alexander gave up his post in the Mediterranean in 1945 to spend eight months without employment before assuming the post of Governor General of Canada and then Minister of Defence; Eisenhower also would retire from the army to assume the largely honorary post of President of Columbia University for three years before briefly resuming his military and then political career.

Monty, however, was denied such a period of reflection. After World War I Monty had attended the Staff College, served on the staff in a territorial division, returned to regimental soldiering and become a gifted teacher. Those were the years in which he had developed his ideas about command in modern warfare—as well as enjoying the only really sustained period of happiness in his life, married to Betty. After Lüneburg there was no such intellectual or emotional respite. Having secured his own appointment as Military Governor of the greater part of industrialized Germany from the Ruhr to the Baltic, Monty threw himself into his job with the same fervour that had marked his previous assumptions of command. In the two months alone from 19 May to 14 July he conferred with or dined with more than forty senior generals, admirals and air-marshals, including Crerar, Dempsey, de Guingand, Graham, Gammell, Dewing, Galloway, Brooke, Nye, Weeks, Simpson, Portal, Sholto Douglas, Koenig, Thomas, Templer, Hobart, Horrocks, Ritchie, Trenchard, Eisenhower, Kirkman, Crocker, Lyne, Whistler, Dennis, Barker, Groman, Burroughs, Bradley, Lethbridge, Lindsay, Slim, Feilden and Bishop, as well as padres, politicians, civil administrators and Russian dignitaries and generals. He attempted to visit every formation and unit of 21st Army Group slated for departure from

Germany and ordered a special printed record of personal thanks for every soldier leaving his command, as well as personally presenting many thousands of medal ribbons. Far more than revisionist historians would later credit, he believed in personal relationships and personal co-operation. He had a photographic memory for faces and names, and did not eschew the occasional sentimentality, such as visiting his old Warwickshire Regiment on occupational duty or writing touching letters to old colleagues, superiors or subordinates. He meant well, and kept a list of up-and-coming young officers whose careers he intended to further in future years. He even had his brother-in-law's son, a trooper, to stay at Tac Headquarters.

And yet, without Betty, there was a certain enervated sterility about such a life, a tension due to his relentless workload and his fundamental failure yet to come to terms with the fame and position he had achieved. Sometimes he would let the mask drop, and talk, for instance, to old soldiering subordinates with disarming friendliness and humour, as he did in private with his personal staff of young officers. But in public, increasingly, a sort of 'Monty' performance took over: 'Punch' in battledress, fiery and abrupt, standing no nonsense and seldom able to relax. As Sir William Strang later wrote:

> In June 1945 I was sent to Germany as Political Adviser to the British Commander-in-Chief, Field Marshal Montgomery. . . . This was not an appointment which I much welcomed. As an adviser, I had no responsibility for action. . . . What pleased me most was to renew my acquaintance with the army. In the First World War, I had seen it from within and from below. In the Second World War and after, I saw it from without and from above. It was natural to draw a comparison between the two armies. In the army of 1939–1945, the command and staff were undoubtedly superior. Appointments to higher commands were now made less on grounds of what may charitably be called professional prestige . . . than of sheer merit. This was true of the army as a whole, but especially true of the 21st Army Group under the Field Marshal. He was quite ruthless, in some cases perhaps unjustly so, in weeding out the less competent subordinates. For himself, he set a new standard. . . . For him, a Commander-in-Chief was not a remote and impersonal figure to his troops. He used modern scientific contrivances and the arts of propaganda to establish a direct contact between himself and every man of the rank and file under his command. On the strength of this and of certain deliberately cultivated personal idiosyncrasies he was able to make an impact

upon each individual. In a battle, he established what he called his tactical headquarters well forward, taking with him a small mobile staff and leaving the cumbrous impedimenta of a Main Headquarters in the rear. He gave his battle orders to Army Commanders by word of mouth, and supplemented the normal channels of communication and the established chain of command by having a group of young liaison officers under his personal orders who went out and brought him up-to-date and first-hand oral reports on the progress of the battle. All this made for intimacy of control and for flexibility in action.[1]

However Monty was no longer at war. As Strang also observed, there was a 'very natural' predilection in the profession of arms to 'take an immediate decision: act first and think afterwards. In politics—and the Control Commission's concern was politics—this is not usually the best course. In military operations immediate action, whatever it may be, may be better than delay. In politics there are few big problems that do not bear sleeping upon.'[2] Thus Monty, a professional soldier to his fingertips, now found himself with a persona and an 'approach to war' fundamentally unsuited to the dictates of peace. Delay made him irritable—yet delay, particularly with regard to the Russians on the Control Commission, was a part of peace. He had become a leopard *sans pareil*; he could not now change his spots and, to his own discredit, he did not try, solacing himself with expressions of unbecoming vanity rather than making an attempt to come to terms with a new and wholly different chapter in his life.

Nowhere was this better illustrated than in his relationship with his son David, a sixteen-year-old schoolboy at Winchester. Over the years since Tom and Phyllis Reynolds had been appointed guardians of David, Monty had not only begun to treat the Reynolds' house as his home, but their preparatory school as a sort of personal see, a private demesne in which he was treated as perhaps a Crusader knight might have been seven centuries before, returning from foreign fields. Even before 21st Army Group had mounted its crossing of the Elbe in April 1945 Monty had been writing to Phyllis Reynolds to say he had 'noted in my diary to be present at Amesbury at Sat 7 July—to judge the gym contest',[3] an intention repeated in his letter of 1 June. Judging boys' gymnastics, however, was not the only magisterial recreation he intended in England; for on a visit to David

[1] Strang, *Home and Abroad*, London 1956.
[2] Ibid.
[3] Letter of 20.4.45, Montgomery Papers.

at Winchester he had promised to attend the annual school cricket match between Winchester and Eton—and had promised the Winchester team captain a trip to Germany as the guest of the British Zone C-in-C if Winchester won. David, who scarcely knew the boy in question, was dumbfounded—and asked, pained to the quick, whether he, as Monty's son, would be invited too. 'Of course, of course,' Monty replied—but the sight of his own father 'lording it' over impressionable schoolboys, denying David any relaxed, personal attention after eight years of absence on duty, was a blow to David's emotional self-confidence that was hard to bear.[1]

Monty's gathering imperiousness, this insatiable need to impress even young schoolboys, was a disturbing reflection of his failure to re-examine and rediscover his true self after years of historic achievement. Tens of thousands of his own officers and men were beginning to return to civilian life, requiring them to adjust to estranged homes and mothballed suits. But for Monty there was no time nor reason for self-examination. In his letters to the Reynolds he recorded his personal spoils of war—the Order of the Grand Commander of the Bath awarded in the King's Birthday Honours List, the gold watches, silver swords, rubied medals and freedoms of cities that poured in. Perhaps in judging Amesbury School gym contests and attending Winchester College cricket matches Monty genuinely thought to preserve a lifeline with the young; yet the inference cannot be avoided that he wished also their adulation because it was innocent and unaffected—and so easily won. There was certainly something strange in an English Commander-in-Chief of occupation troops in Germany flying home in his Dakota, together with his personal staff, solely to witness a schoolboy cricket match. Yet this was what Monty did. 'I will be able to come only for the day,' he wrote to the Reynolds. 'I will fly direct to Winchester so as to reach the ground about 12 noon. Tom and you and David and myself, will all have a picnic lunch on the ground: in a quiet corner. I will bring the whole bunch from here, and the A.D.C.'s will get it ready in a corner: and we will go to it in the lunch interval. I shall have to leave about 5 p.m. to fly back here; I cannot stay the night. I enclose some photos [of myself].'[2] As the time drew near, the 'picnic lunch' became grander: 'we shall bring my Mess Sgt and a waiter, and a large lunch with plenty of bottles, and have a real show.'[3]

The showmanship that had given such personality to the campaign

[1] David, 2nd Viscount Montgomery of Alamein, interview of 11.5.84.
[2] Letter of 8.6.45, Montgomery Papers.
[3] Letter of 25.6.45, Montgomery Papers.

in North Africa and Europe now spilled over onto the school cricket ground at Winchester. For Monty's personal staff it was, of course, a bonus day in England, for David a day with his father, on the face of it something grand to swank about, just as the Reynolds could when driving Monty's Daimler left for their use at Amesbury. And yet there was something profoundly unbecoming about a world-historical figure—for such Monty had now become—swaggering before simple schoolboys. Possibly Monty was seeking to reverse the memory of his own boyhood, the ex-colonial of scant promise at St Paul's, the bully nearly expelled from Sandhurst. Flying from Germany with ADCs and waiters he could descend *deus ex machina*, dispensing bottled largesse and conferring distinction on all who were presented to him. In the event the Winchester team drew, favourably, and David was thus forced to spend his summer in Germany with a stranger—an older boy chosen to demonstrate his father's princely powers. Small wonder David was oppressed—as Monty's devoted ADCs could see but none put right.

De Guingand, Monty's faithful Chief of Staff from Alamein to Lüneburg, had been despatched on sick leave as soon as hostilities were over. Monty wrote a grateful letter to him on 31 May—'no commander can ever have had, or ever will have, a better Chief of Staff than you were; you never spared yourself, and in fact you wore yourself out completely for the good of the show. Together we achieved much; and together we saw the thing through to the end. You must now have a good rest. And then, later on, together we will conquer fresh fields.'[1] To this de Guingand replied with some emotion on 2 June:

> My dear Field-Marshal
>
> Thank you so very much for your charming letter. It has done a lot to help dispel a very natural feeling of melancholy and depression which has set in since leaving you. Parting from you and the Army Group was the most difficult thing that has happened to me since I joined the Army.
>
> It is no good my trying to say all I feel, or to thank you adequately for all you have done for me. Being Chief of Staff to you was not difficult for two main reasons. First, you gave us such clear direction, and secondly you showed me your confidence by letting me get on with the Business without petty interference. For these two Blessings I thank you most deeply.
>
> It has been a most wonderful experience for me. I was a very raw and untried Chief of Staff when you arrived to command 8th

[1] Letter of 31.5.45, de Guingand Papers, Imperial War Museum.

Army. But under you I have learnt a lot. I owe you a debt for this alone.

The past makes the future look pretty drab, and it will be hard for me to settle down. At the moment I feel rather like a deserter. But I hope that feeling will pass.

And so ends a colourful and unforgettable chapter in my life, which would never have been written without your confidence and your kindness. Perhaps there is another of a similar nature, just around the corner—who knows.

Yours ever
Freddie.[1]

However, there was not; on the contrary, de Guingand, for all his outward loyalty to Monty, came to feel more and more deeply distressed by the 'shabby' treatment Monty would now accord him. That Monty had failed to summon him to Tac Headquarters for the surrender at Lüneburg was the first sign that Monty was not going to allow his Chief of Staff to share the limelight of victory; then, with almost undue haste, Monty had insisted that de Guingand depart on sick leave, to be replaced as Chief of Staff by Maj-General Galloway who had been commanding 21st Army Group's lines of communication. Within weeks de Guingand heard that he was being demoted to his substantive rank of Colonel—despite having held a Lieutenant-General's post (albeit as a Maj-General) for nearly a year and a half of war. De Guingand appealed to Monty to get the decision reversed; Monty refused—and only when Eisenhower heard about the scandal and protested, in person, to Sir James Grigg was de Guingand's rank of Maj-General restored.

Worse was to follow. There can be no doubt that Monty had a great fondness for de Guingand, and that de Guingand did owe his 'elevation' to Monty, who had recognized in him a brilliant administrative talent. But Auchinleck had recognized this too, and had appointed de Guingand as Chief of the General Staff (though not full Chief of Staff) of Eighth Army several weeks before Monty's arrival in the desert. De Guingand's career in the Army would undoubtedly have prospered even without Monty's 'backing'. That Monty, as Allied Ground Force Commander for the D-Day invasion, chose to appoint de Guingand as his Chief of Staff and had subsequently asked the War Office to award an immediate knighthood to de Guingand once it was clear the Allies were successfully ashore, were testimonials of Monty's high regard. But thereafter, as Monty lived further and further from Main Headquarters and saw less and

[1] Letter of 2.6.45, Montgomery Papers.

less of de Guingand, their relationship faltered—particularly when de Guingand advised against Arnhem from his sick bed, and later warned Monty that he would be dismissed unless he obeyed the Supreme Commander. Monty consistently declined to promote de Guingand to Lieutenant-General; and later he refused to recommend him for an award at the end of the war, claiming that his knighthood at the age of forty-four had already been sufficient recompense.

While it is true that Monty abhorred the American system of over-promoting staff officers without insisting that they gain operational command experience, this cannot have been Monty's real reason for clipping de Guingand's wings—for within weeks, aware that he would probably succeed Brooke as CIGS at the end of the year, Monty was asking de Guingand if he would consent to become VCIGS—a lieutenant-general's job.

For the moment, Monty's jealous unwillingness to share his laurels with his most loyal and brilliant Chief of Staff was an ominous expression of his insecurity. It would be the same story with his family: with his mother, his brothers, and even his son. The moment someone now threatened to share or steal a portion of Monty's limelight, he acted at once to cut them down. Indeed had the newspaper cartoonists, who so often depicted him as the effortless conqueror of Rommel and von Rundstedt, known more about this side of Monty's character they might have pictured him as a famed survivor standing on a wooden raft while the ship of war sank in the distance—beating off those hands and arms now seeking to hold on to his fragile vessel.

That Monty could have achieved such undoubted greatness as military commander in war, yet failed to rise to an equivalent greatness of spirit or of stature in peace, was a strange paradox. Had he, like Nelson, fallen in his final battle, his reputation would certainly have been less vulnerable to the knives of subsequent British and American writers irritated or outraged by this lack of nobility. Greatness, however, may never be dealt as a full hand. It is perhaps as idle to expect great battlefield soldiers to be perfect gentlemen as to expect great writers to make good spouses. For all his grave failings of statesmanlike stature and his lapses of magnanimity, Monty's simple, soldier's heart remained bound to the Army and to his sense of duty. He might fly home to swagger on the games pitch of his son's school for an afternoon: but by the evening he was once more on his way to his Tactical Headquarters at Ostenwalde, charged with the welfare of an occupying army and the lives of twenty-three million defeated Germans and displaced persons: a task he carried out with the utmost conscientiousness. He did not drink or smoke or philander or eat rich food. He knew no relaxations; he was a widower, quite determined that he would never marry again. As the owner of the Château d'Everberg, Princesse de Mérode, recalled with a woman's perception, she admired Field-Marshal Montgomery as a military commander; but he was not what she understood as 'un homme du monde'.[1]

He was not. He conformed to no known mould either as gentleman or general. He was outrageous in his conceit, his egoism and self-righteousness. He liked to dominate rather than to share. These vices he had turned into qualities of greatness as a battlefield commander, imparting professional confidence and clarity of conviction unrivalled among Allied commanders. Yet with the war's end, he was faced by his own legacy, and could not find it in him, as he had before the war, to climb down and to *learn*. His need to 'put himself across' had become a veritable obsession, his desire to 'get on' with the job a liability in a fragmented post-war Europe. He had become accustomed to adulation too, and as so often with men or women who experience mass worship overnight, he began to use it as a mace against those who threatened his self-esteem or urged him to look into his own soul. The madness which subordinates like Goronwy Rees had noticed after Dunkirk remained with him, for the most part assuaged, as in the case of Patton, by the war. In peace, however, it stood out like a monstrous shackle, chained as he was to the stake of duty. Dimly he was aware of this. 'I am now busy getting down to the Government of my 25 million subjects! It is a terrific job and I shall probably go mad before long!!' he wrote on 1 June to Phyllis Reynolds.[2] It was a cross he tried to bear however unfitted for the role of pro-Consul. By September 1945 Patton, considered by most observers to be as mad as a March hare, as well as dangerously anti-semitic, was removed from his command of Third US Army. Within months he would be dead, as a result of an automobile accident, grateful to God for the release from a post-war life he could not face.

Given the enormous distances which senior wartime commanders had to travel, the chances of death in an air or car crash were considerable. Monty's wartime colleagues Admiral Sir Bertram Ramsay, Air-Marshal Sir Trafford Leigh-Mallory and Air-Marshal Sir Arthur Coningham all lost their lives in air crashes during or after the war.

For Monty also there seemed the prospect of such an accidental, perhaps merciful end when in late August 1945 his light aircraft suddenly developed engine failure. The propeller stopped and nothing the pilot tried could revive the motor as the aeroplane plummeted towards the ground.

[1] Letter from Henriette Claessens-Heuten to author, 6.8.84.
[2] Montgomery Papers.

CHAPTER SIX

Embarrassing the Americans

On the 22nd August [1945] the Field-Marshal flew to visit the 3rd Canadian Division. As he came in to land in his light aircraft, the Miles Messenger, the engine cut out, and his pilot, unable to make the airfield, crash-landed . . . [The] pilot and ADC, who were in the plane with [the Field-Marshal], were both uninjured, but the plane was written off. The Field-Marshal was much shaken and bruised, but after an X-ray examination he continued his full programme with the Division, carrying out an Investiture and making a speech.[1]

The Canadians attempted to persuade Monty to be driven back to Ostenwalde in an ambulance but Monty, in considerable pain, insisted on flying, claiming that never in flying history had a passenger crashed twice in a day. The consultant surgeon to 21st Army Group, Brigadier Porritt, had already been summoned from Brussels, and at Tactical Headquarters that evening Porritt examined both Monty and the X-rays, as he later recalled:

Yes, he was in pain, quite a lot of pain and I saw his X-rays. It was quite obvious what had happened. He hadn't broken his back, he'd broken a transverse process on one of his vertebrae.

It was typical of Monty that if you told him exactly in lay terms what was the matter he was a good patient. If you tried to camouflage anything he was querulous.

So I told him quite plainly what had happened and showed him the fracture. And he said, 'Well, what are we going to do?'

I said, 'Well, Sir, we can either treat it as a minor fracture, put you into plaster and you can get about tomorrow or as soon as you're comfortable; or we can treat it as a bad sprain in which case you'll have to go to bed for about ten days, and have physiotherapy (massage), and keep pretty quiet and have nursing care.'

'Nursing care?' he queried.

I said, 'Yes, because when I say quiet I *mean* quiet—no good if you're going to get up and move around. You've got to be in bed.'

[1] 'Notes on the Occupation of Germany', loc. cit.

But it was not the question of incarceration that concerned Monty, as Lord Porritt remembered with hilarity almost forty years later:

> He said, 'You know, Porritt, I've put up with a lot from you, but I'm not going to have any women in this headquarters!'[1]

He then dismissed Porritt, telling him to return the next morning.

Next day Porritt went in to see Monty, who was in bed. 'Ah, Porritt,' Monty said, as though discussing his condition with Porritt for the first time, 'You know I've got a bad sprain in my back . . .' It was typical of Monty that he, rather than the doctor, should make the decision. However, 'once he'd made up his mind he was a good patient,' Porritt recollected. 'He wouldn't have a nurse, but I got Hunter, his physician, back and he stayed with him, as well as a male nurse, and a physiotherapist. In ten days he was out of bed, and never went into plaster. Never worried him afterwards, the back.'[2] The Montgomerys of Donegal had always been long-lived, and Bernard Montgomery was to be no exception.

Meanwhile, on 25 August 1945 21st Army Group ceased to exist. No commander could have done more than Monty to make the men of 21st Army Group prouder of their achievement over the past year. Morale had remained high despite the inevitable psychological deflation, and the march-past of the 7th Armoured Division in Berlin on 21 July was a fitting swansong to the British Army's performance in North-west Europe—thenceforth to be known as the British Army of the Rhine, as after World War I.

SHAEF had also ceased to exist on 14 July, together with its 13,000-strong personnel—one of the largest and arguably least effective Allied Supreme Command headquarters ever assembled. Despite numerous exercises in whitewashing, its faults as a military command set-up were too obvious for anyone connected with it to be deceived, and it passed into history largely unmourned. Yet, like its predecessor in Algiers, SHAEF undoubtedly reflected a truly *Allied* commitment to the winning of World War II, and this 'tone' was undoubtedly the product of Eisenhower's personality and example. As Brigadier Sir Edgar Williams remarked several years later:

[1] Lord Porritt, interview of 8.11.84.

[2] Ibid. The physiotherapist was in fact a woman, Elspeth Hardie, who later recalled the warning given to her by Monty's physician Dr Robert (later Lord) Hunter. 'He told her that if Montgomery asked a question to which she did not know the answer to say so and not to try and make up some answer. During their first physiotherapy session, he [Montgomery] asked her what temperature his skin was under the heat lamp. She replied that she had no idea. They got on famously after that. . . . "He was a marvellous patient, very tough, would not go into plaster—he just had heat treatment and exercise," she recalled': Carol Thatcher, *Daily Telegraph*, 17.10.83.

> I suppose what is so remarkable about Eisenhower was that he wasn't so much himself one of the great captains, as a man to whom the great captains gladly paid allegiance—not so much a generalissimo as a military statesman, a man coming from a mixture of peoples which had become a nation, with much of the self-confidence of that nation and a knowledge learned in his homeland of how to get on with people.
>
> That was his great contribution—not as a general in the field, but as the 'architect' as he calls himself of the code of the Allies, and the man who forged that code because in his own generous personality, he himself represented it best—that friendly, confident, unselfish, quick-smiling willingness to accept responsibility but with no attempt to take the credit to himself—surely that was what made the Allies in the West a unity carrying all before it.[1]

Nor was Williams exaggerating. Even before the disbandment of SHAEF, Monty had written to Eisenhower to tell him something of his feelings for Ike as a Supreme Allied Commander. It was not sent by cable or as an official message, but was written in Monty's simple hand on 21st Army Group notepaper, dated 7.6.45:

> My dear Ike
>
> Now that we have all signed in Berlin I suppose we shall soon begin to run our own affairs.
>
> I would like, before this happens, to say what a privilege and an honour it has been to serve under you. I owe much to your wise guidance and kindly forbearance. I know my own faults very well and I do not suppose I am an easy subordinate; I like to go my own way.
>
> But you have kept me on the rails in difficult and stormy times, and have taught me much.
>
> For all this I am very grateful. And I thank you for all you have done for me.
>
> Your very devoted friend
> Monty[2]

Eisenhower was genuinely touched. It was 'one of the finest things I have ever received', he wrote back by return. 'In the aftermath of this Allied effort enduring friendships and feelings of mutual respect among higher commanders will have a most beneficial effect. The

[1] Transcript of BBC Radio discussion of Eisenhower's *Crusade in Europe*, in Wilmot Papers (LH/1515/133), loc. cit.

[2] Letter of 7.6.45, Eisenhower Papers, 1652 series, Eisenhower Library, Abilene, Kansas.

team must continue in spirit.'[1] But could it? 'It has been a great honour to have been a member of this historic force' Monty wrote again on SHAEF's official demise, 'and I have always been proud to serve under American command. We have achieved much in war; may we achieve even more in peace.'[2]

This was taking Allied piety too far: for with the demise of SHAEF, Eisenhower was reduced to command of the American contingent in Europe, presiding no longer over Allies but over tens of thousands of Americans on duty abroad, with conflicting notions of their role in Germany or indeed Europe. Thus from 14 July 1945 Monty's communications arrived no longer from a wayward but at heart devoted Allied subordinate, but from a 'Britisher'.

Nowhere was this turnabout from Allied to nationalistic imperative better illustrated than in the response to Monty's draft of a new message to the Germans in the British zone of occupation. Monty sent Eisenhower the draft on 15 July, shortly before attending the Allied summit meeting at Potsdam, assuring Eisenhower that he did not wish 'anything I do to be an embarrassment to you in the American Zone'.[3] 'Message No. 3' was typical Monty: direct, personal, simple and positive—the same voice as in a score of personal messages to his troops which lay filed among Eisenhower's war-time papers, but this time directed at improving the morale of Germans, not British or Allied troops:

> Two months have now passed since Germany surrendered and your country passed to the control of the Allied Nations.
> During this time the British Zone has been under Military Government.
> Members of the German armed forces have been sorted out by trades and occupations; many thousands have been discharged to work on the land and in other spheres, and this will continue.
> There is every prospect of a good harvest and you must see that it is gathered in.
> My officers have been active in their endeavours to arrange that the German population have adequate food and housing, and are kept free from disease.
> The first stage in the re-habilitation of Germany is under way.

There was certainly nothing to which Americans could object in this preamble. It was the next stage of rehabilitation that was the problem:

[1] Letter of 8.6.45. Copy in Eisenhower Papers, loc. cit.
[2] Signal of 14.7.45, Montgomery Papers.
[3] Handwritten original dated 15.7.45, Eisenhower Papers, loc. cit.

> I am now going to proceed with the second stage of the British policy.
> In this stage it is my intention that you shall have the freedom to get down to your own way of life: subject only to the provisions of military security.
> I will help you to eradicate the best Allies of Nazism, past and future: these are idleness, boredom, and fear of the future. Instead I want to give you 'hope'.

One by one Monty then outlined his intentions for the British zone:

> I will restore freedom of the Press; this will be done by stages.
> You may have Trades Unions.
> You may hold public meetings and discussions; I am anxious that you should talk over your problems among yourselves, and generally set on foot measures to help yourselves.
> Political activities will be allowed; the object of these, for the present, will be towards an orderly and well governed Zone.

Nor was this all. Voluntary juvenile organisations would be encouraged for the purpose of religious, cultural, health or recreational activities. Fraternization rules had already been relaxed. The main problem would be the winter.

> The coming winter may be a difficult time; there is much to mend and put right, and time is short. We are faced with the possibility of a shortage of food, a shortage of coal, insufficient accommodation, and inadequate services of transportation and distribution. It is well that you should realise this now.
> I will do all I can to get the population of the British Zone through the coming winter in good style. But you, the German people, must plan for these contingencies now; you must work to help yourselves.
> I will continue to see that you are all kept informed by radio, and by the newspapers, of how we are progressing; I will give you German news as well as foreign news,

Monty concluded.[1]

For days Eisenhower's Assistant Chief of Staff for Civil Affairs, General Adcock, mulled over Monty's proposed message. Then on 19 July he penned a blistering memorandum to Eisenhower. 'Field Marshal Montgomery's [covering] letter states that he does not want his acts to be an embarrassment in the US Zone,' Adcock began

[1] Original typescript draft, dated 15.7.45, Eisenhower Papers, loc. cit.

ominously. 'The adoption of the policy set forth in the Directive, and the issuance of the Message, would be an embarrassment in US Zone,' he stated—and gave his reasons.

a) The tone and underlying thought appear not that of a conqueror, but that of one competing for the good will of the Germans. Such competition must be avoided.
b) The detailed programme is inconsistent with current US policy in the following respects.
   (i) Freedom of the press, under present conditions of supply and control, is impossible.
   (ii) Neither our Public Safety or Political Advisers are yet prepared to authorize public meetings or political activities or organizations.
   (iii) Formation of youth organizations at this time and before the Hitler Youth is thoroughly eradicated, would be premature and dangerous.[1]

Adcock's recommendation was that Eisenhower advise Monty 'the adoption of the policy, and issuance of such a Message at this time, would be an embarrassment in the US Zone for the reasons stated'.[2]

Monty was amazed that such a simple, human document, designed to combat any resurgence of Nazi support and to avoid the lure of communism, could be so misinterpreted by his American Allies: as though he, Monty, was now 'competing' with the US Zone officials for German goodwill.

If Monty lacked Eisenhower's stature as statesman, he did at least attempt to 'think big' in terms of Western ideals. The reaction of men like General Adcock was small and restrictive—another example of why Monty had, as he had informed 'Simbo' Simpson in April, largely ceased to send Eisenhower informative signals after the battle of Normandy, as these were so rarely 'understood' by Eisenhower's low-calibre rear-headquarters staff. Now, faced with an American attitude that seemed to show no real awareness of the coming battle for the German mind,[3] both against Nazism and Communism,

[1] Memorandum of 19.7.45, in 'Montgomery' file, Eisenhower Papers, loc. cit.
[2] Ibid.
[3] Monty's 'Message No. 3' reflected not only his desire to offer conquered Germans hope for the future, but was also in line with current British Intelligence thinking. In a letter to a colleague Brigadier E. T. Williams had pointed out that: 'Non-fraternisation has now been dropped and I suppose in general the Germans never really understood what it all added up to (if indeed it really did add up to much) because by and large they have not betrayed many symptoms of individual guilt . . . Our job on the I side will be very much easier, and the C-in-C's desire to allow public meetings and the growth of Trade Unions will keep political developments above

Monty recognized for the first time Eisenhower's supra-national stature among soldiers. Indeed, surrounded by little men throughout the Mediterranean and European campaigns, it seemed the more remarkable that Eisenhower had given his field commanders such encouragement and support. Such 'have-a-go, Joe' methods of command had infuriated Monty when, against an enemy as professional as the Germans all-out concentration on priorities was required; but in retrospect it was Eisenhower's personal faith in and understanding of his disparate field commanders' personalities that Monty admired. Patton, raging at the short-sightedness of the new Headquarters, US Forces in Europe, would go to his grave denouncing Eisenhower for his obsequiousness to politicians and public opinion in America, considering that 'practically everyone but myself is a pusillanimous son of a bitch'.[1] 'The chief interest seems to center on doing nothing positive and never going counter to what the papers say,' Patton summarized American rule in Frankfurt[2]—the direct result of Eisenhower's military and political ambitions, Patton felt.

Monty, by contrast, began to see how *different* Eisenhower was from his advisers. Patton blamed Eisenhower for tolerating Civil Affairs officers as dim-witted as Adcock; Monty, however, began to realize that, given the small-minded, bigoted, and negative approach of so many American officers, Eisenhower was unique in his idealism and sensitivity to European ways of thinking: particularly his own. General Adcock had recommended blank rejection of Monty's proclamation; Eisenhower, sensing the importance of *positive* Allied steps to give hope to democratically-minded Germans, asked Monty merely to withhold the proclamation until the Americans could *themselves* draw up a similar document in line with Monty's, to be agreed between their deputies. This Monty willingly did—and the British and American zones thus marched in unison: a tribute to Monty's constructive idealism and to Eisenhower's statesmanship.

---

ground where we can watch and penetrate them instead of driving them into sullen disobedience in private: communicated to author.

[1] Letter of 18.10.45 to Colonel Codman, *The Patton Papers*, ed. M. Blumenson, New York 1982.

[2] Letter of 15.11.45 to Beatrice, *The Patton Papers*, op. cit.

CHAPTER SEVEN

The Rhineland Question

THE AMERICANS WERE not, unfortunately, the only ally involved in the occupation of Germany. Week by week Monty's hopes for a unified rehabilitation of the country proved more naïve. Negotiations with the Russians were fraught with difficulties—and the introduction of the French as a fourth occupying power proved the final straw.

The Russian approach to occupation was quite the opposite of that displayed in the Western Zones. Indeed it is one of the ironies of history that, even though Germans were still fleeing from the Russian Zone at up to 40,000 *a week* into the British Zone, communist propaganda in the Western Zones was considered potent and dangerous.

At first it seemed that Stalin's intention was to create in eastern Germany a desert, so that, once the occupying powers departed, Germany would never again present a threat to Russia. To Western onlookers this attitude seemed positively barbaric, following the sexual assault on almost the entire female population. The Russians removed all machinery and all stocks on which they could lay their hands. Moreover their occupying armies were told to live off the country, thus consuming all food supplies in their zone.

However shocking, this Russian approach was in essence the same as the American Morgenthau proposals for the de-industrialization of Germany, and the French desire to confiscate the German industrial regions of the Rhineland and Ruhr.

Monty, charged with his own quasi-messianic wish to give 'his' Germans in the north hope for the future, soon discovered that the international ramifications of Germany's future status were going to make his task as Military Governor virtually imposssible. When he greeted Churchill and Eden in Berlin in July for the Potsdam conference, he had still hoped the Allies could develop a common policy towards Germany, and that Germany itself would remain a single state. 'The main question was whether there was in future to be one Germany or two,' his diarist chronicled.[1] 'If Germany was to be treated as one administrative and economic whole,' Monty pointed

[1] 'Notes on the Occupation of Germany', loc. cit.

out to Churchill, then there would have to be a common policy towards the reconstruction of industry, wage rates, price controls, a central German administrative machine running transportation, communications and finance, free movement between zones, full exchange of resources such as food and goods between zones, and a method for raising funds to buy commodities from abroad.[1] In the context of the falling iron curtain and the fragmentation of the once-strong Western alliance, the prospects of this began to look bleak. Upon Attlee's supersession of Churchill, agreement had, it was true, been reached on the outlines of a future unified Germany, with freedom of speech, press and religion, free trades unions and a decentralized political structure until such time as a central German government be set up. This looked fine on paper, and Monty's Deputy, Lt-General Weeks, seemed to have obtained extraordinary results in establishing a co-ordinating committee of the Control Commission; but by the time the first regular meetings of the Control Council itself began in Berlin in August, the outlook began to deteriorate. Weeks himself was forced by ill-health to retire. The German harvest, which had looked so hopeful, was sundered by bad weather. Monty's air crash forced him to cancel his attendance at the Control Commission in Berlin on 30 August. Finally, after the Control Commission meeting in Berlin on 1 October, General Weeks' successor, Lt-General Sir Brian Robertson, reported disaster. It had been proposed to set up, as per the Potsdam agreement, a central German transport board, and a central German communications system. The British, Russians and Americans had agreed on the proposal; but the French, who had not been a party to the Potsdam conference, refused. General Robertson's report to Monty was despairing, for it was obvious that the Russian approach to commonality of occupation zones in a rehabilitated Germany was at best lukewarm; and the intransigence now of the French gave the Russians an excuse to drag their feet even more. 'The Russians are taking full advantage of the fact that they are no longer the only or even the chief obstruction to progress and agreement,' Robertson explained, warning that 'a continuation of this state of affairs will put a strain on this delicate machine from which it may never recover. . . [Lt-General] Clay, the US delegate, has made the following remark in conversation. "The French have taken the most direct step towards driving the Americans out of Europe. If central administrations are not set up quickly the clamour from America to withdraw from Europe will be insistent." '[2]

[1] Ibid.

[2] Quoted in 'Notes on the Occupation of Germany', loc. cit.

Monty took Robertson's warning extremely seriously. However professionally disdainful Monty might be about American generalship, he had since the invasion of Sicily learned the bitter truth that marked his epithet on the feeble conduct of Allied High Command: namely that without American help the British could not have won alone; and with the 'iron curtain' now stretching from Lübeck to Trieste, the very future of Liberal Europe depended on American willingness to stay. 'Americans are talking unofficially but openly about getting out of Germany as quickly as possible and are promising early release to their military personnel. If central administrations are established they will leave behind, it appears, sufficient personnel for control on a commission basis but if these administrations are not established they may become exasperated and withdraw altogether', Robertson prophesied. 'They are far less interested in the future of Germany from the point of view of security than the other three Powers. They are pursuing a short term policy and do not worry about rebuilding Germany on sound foundations for the future.'[1]

The Russians, Robertson considered, were at this stage still 'unreservedly in support of the establishment of central administration'. Robertson recognized that, in following the Potsdam agreement, the Russians might be seeking a greater say in the administration and politics of the western zones of occupied Germany without 'lifting the iron curtain over their zone'.[2] But this was a risk the Allies ought to take if they wanted America to maintain its commitment in Europe, and if Germany was to be re-established as a single state.

Robertson therefore recommended 'strong pressure' be put on the French to 'agree to the establishment of central administrations without prejudice to the ultimate settlement of the Rhineland question'[3]—for, just as at Versailles in 1919, it was French desire to put a buffer zone between themselves and the Rhine that was motivating French obstruction. This issue was further complicated by the calls for the Ruhr's de-industrialization as part of the Morgenthau proposals for a predominantly agricultural post-war economy in Germany.

At Potsdam in July the eastern borders of Germany had been settled; now the western borders were at issue, and Robertson was perhaps being naïve in imagining that a central administration of the country could be set up before the new borders of Germany were actually determined. Moreover, as the days went by, Robertson's

[1] Ibid.
[2] Ibid.
[3] Ibid.

assumption that the Russians were truly interested in a unified Germany seemed less and less convincing. On 11 September the second stage of the Potsdam conference had resumed in London, still without the French whom Stalin refused to admit. After three weeks of bitter wrangling the conference broke up without even a communiqué; and the vast public sympathy that had grown up during the war for the Russian people collapsed as Stalin's Foreign Minister, Molotov, made demand after demand while refusing to guarantee free elections in any of the 'Eastern bloc' countries, or even free reporting by Western correspondents.[1] 'After prolonged discussions, the LONDON Conference broke up in disagreement during the first days in October, without achieving much,' Monty's diarist recorded. 'International agreement on all levels was becoming very difficult.'[2] Monty, in England since 24 September, visited Prime Minister Attlee on 3 October, before returning to Germany, to report his growing pessimism. To Monty it did not now look as if the Russians were interested in returning their zone to a rehabilitated Germany, since they had 'altered the gauge of the German railways in their zone to the Russian gauge', he explained to Attlee. 'The only railway as yet unaltered was that leading from the Western zones to BERLIN.' Meanwhile the Americans 'in particular were becoming restless; they had tabled a motion that, when unanimous agreement in the Council was not possible, each zone could act as it thought best. This was the first rift in the lute,' Monty remarked. In fact, he now doubted 'whether Four Power Government in Germany . . . could be made to work'.[3]

If the Russians were set to stay in their zone, or at least treat it permanently as a puppet regime, were the Allies right in weakening Western Europe's industrial capacity by implementing the American proposals for de-industrialization of the Ruhr? 'It seemed to the Field-Marshal, as a soldier, that it was not really a practicable proposition to de-industrialise the RUHR, when Germany and all the Allied States on her frontiers were suffering great privations due to the destruction of industrial potential. Provided the industry of the RUHR was properly controlled it would fulfil a very useful function in supplying the needs of the western Allies.'[4] To this extent Monty favoured the French view—even to the point of re-drawing the western frontiers of Germany. If the borders of France, Belgium and Holland were advanced to the Rhine, the river could be made to

[1] Cf. A. Bullock, *Ernest Bevin, Foreign Secretary 1945–1951*, London 1983.
[2] 'Notes on the Occupation of Germany', loc. cit.
[3] 'Talk with the Prime Minister' in 'Notes on the Occupation of Germany', loc. cit.
[4] Ibid.

serve as a perfect barrier both against Russian expansion and any future German aggression. Indeed, if they did this, the Western Allies would not need to station occupying forces in Germany at all once a West German democratic government had been set up—'if this were done,' Monty pointed out to Attlee, 'we could withdraw our forces of occupation from Germany.'[1]

Attlee listened, but did not agree. As Sir George Mallaby, a Cabinet Secretary, later remarked, Attlee's robust method of conducting government business, however admirable, concealed a basic lack of political imagination:

> Cabinet Committee meetings were usually orderly and brisk. Attention was paid to the Agenda and to the order in which the items were to be discussed. The time-table was adhered to. The meetings ended on time. The business was concluded. But there was nothing very constructive about all this. The Prime Minister . . . listened, or appeared to listen, patiently and fairly attentively. . . . When the discussion was finished his summing-up was often blurred and incomplete and he rarely produced any constructive ideas of his own or seemed to give a powerful lead. His chairmanship was only a negative success. He was like a schoolmaster who kept order very well but did not really teach you very much.[2]

As Mallaby observed, Attlee remained leader of the Labour Party principally because he did not have as many enemies as Cripps, Bevin, Morrison or Bevan—and this lack of central, presiding vision mirrored the very absence of driving vision Monty had suffered under Eisenhower at AFHQ and SHAEF. Significantly, although Attlee—an erstwhile infantry major in World War I—admired Monty as a great battlefield commander, he admired Alexander even more as a 'great soldier statesman under whose aegis, and within the framework of whose guidance and control, Montgomery was allowed to conceive and execute [his] battle plans . . . Alexander and Slim [were] superior to Montgomery as all-round soldiers,' Attlee later reflected, since they understood the delicate balance of civil and military spheres—how to 'make do' with what you have got rather than cry loudly for more. 'Being able to do this is, of course, the test of the soldier-statesman as opposed to the commander in the field.'[3]

Doubtless there was much truth in this—and in Attlee's 'disappointment' with Monty's post-war performance, when Monty had to 'deal

[1] Ibid.
[2] G. Mallaby, *From My Level: Unwritten Minutes*, London 1965.
[3] Review of Montgomery's *Memoirs* in the *Observer*, 2.11.58.

with affairs which he did not properly grasp'.[1] Yet the result of Attlee's negative response was the casting away, in the autumn of 1945, of the only real chance the Allies had of resolving post-war security in Europe. By annulling German frontiers beyond the Oder-Neisse line, Stalin ensured that neither Russia nor Poland would ever again be vulnerable to attack from the west. As Stalin pointed out to Churchill at Potsdam, 'nothing definite' had been fixed at Yalta about the western frontiers of Germany.[2] Churchill had however balked at Stalin's inference that the Western Allies should now redraw Germany's western frontiers; the matter had thus been postponed for decision at the ultimate peace conference that was scheduled to take place.

Monty's proposal, had it been adopted, would have transformed the post-war development of Europe. Indeed it is not exaggerating to say that the rest of Monty's military career—a further thirteen years of high office—would be spent combatting the results of Allied trepidation in the autumn of 1945. The Americans were anxious to withdraw their forces from Europe; France was concerned for her future security, as was Belgium and also Holland. Had Britain taken the lead in re-drawing the western borders of Germany along the river Rhine, the unnatural fragmentation of Germany might well have been avoided. Like Austria and Finland, a disarmed Germany could then have become a 'buffer' state between communist and non-communist Europe. The creation of the demilitarized Rhineland in 1919, in the wake of World War I, had in fact represented an attempt to achieve this aim of security—though the Rhineland had remained German and in any case extended both east and west of the river. But it did fulfil its role: for a decade and a half, until Hitler's seizure in 1936, the demilitarized Rhineland had permitted the Western Allies to withdraw their forces of occupation. Given Stalin's logical—if ruthless—excision of German territory beyond the Oder, Germany now had a clear eastern frontier; advancement of the borders of Holland, Belgium and France would in 1945 have secured a similarly effective frontier. But it was not to be.

[1] Ibid.

[2] W. S. Churchill, *Triumph and Tragedy*, op. cit.

CHAPTER EIGHT

The Question of CIGS

ATTLEE'S REBUFF MEANWHILE made Monty's task in Germany doubly difficult. The Labour Government was committed to quick demobilization—but the task of ruling twenty-three million Germans without agreement on central German administration and with future Russian intentions uncertain, made a run-down of British occupation forces impossible, particularly with over a million and a half German troops still in camps in the British zone. These German soldiers could not all be released when there were no jobs for such a number to go to, and when there was still a danger of their spreading fascist disaffection. Yet the very presence of so many German POWs in the British Zone made the Russians suspicious—and their claims, in the Control Council, that Britain was deliberately harbouring a potentially anti-Russian German military machine distressed Monty since, for no fault of his own, it was potentially true.

To add to Monty's impossible burden, Eisenhower was now appointed, late in October 1945, to succeed General Marshall as Chief of Staff, US Army in Washington. Eisenhower left Europe on 11 November, his post in Germany taken by General McNarney—but within weeks, on vacation in the USA, he was hospitalized, suffering from bronchial pneumonia and exhaustion.

Monty himself was approaching fifty-eight. Like Eisenhower he had been told, on 6 August, he was probably to be his country's next Chief of Staff of the Army, or CIGS, in succession to Brooke. (Alexander had already been chosen to become the next Governor-General of Canada.[1]) At a Chief of Staff meeting on 23 August

[1] According to Field-Marshal Alexander, Brooke had definitely intended that Alexander should succeed him as CIGS: 'Soon after the German surrender I was told by Field-Marshal Lord Alanbrooke that he intended to retire shortly from the post of Chief of the Imperial General Staff and that I was to succeed him. . . . It was as CIGS-designate that I went to the Potsdam Conference in July 1945. During that period in Berlin I used to go to the Prime Minister's villa of an evening to discuss the events of the day with him. It was at one of these evening meetings that Winston Churchill said to me, "Let's take a stroll in the garden; there is something very important I want to talk to you about. . . ." He said, "Canada has asked for you to be its next Governor General. I know that Brookie wants you to succeed him as

'both Portal and Cunningham [were] strongly in favour of Monty,' Brooke noted in his diary. On 5 September, however, the new Secretary of State for War, Jack Lawson, begged Brooke to stay on 'for another year. He told me that Attlee had again tackled him about it and insisted that I should stop on to see them through their troubles.' Brooke weakly agreed, repenting bitterly back in his office. 'I feel I am cooked and played out,' he confessed in his diary that night,[1] and the next day wrote: 'I am still very worried as to whether I really ought to try and knock another 6 months work out of myself, and am very doubtful whether I can stick it. I should say the odds are definitely against me.'[2]

At the CIGS's Camberley conference of senior commanders Brooke looked worn out; whereas Monty, flying over from Germany, seemed to have fully recovered from his plane crash. Monty had already been considering the subject of Britain's post-war army since July 1945, writing to Brooke that 'the shape and fashion of the post-war army must now be considered, and this can be done properly only by those who have fought in command of units and formations in battle and who understand clearly what weapons and equipment are needed, and why: and how each article fits into the tactical picture. You will probably tell me to mind my own business, and get on with my job, and that it is nothing to do with me. But so long as you will read this letter, I do not mind.'[3]

Brooke was too big a man to take umbrage. He wrote to Monty a few months later: 'I knew well that you could always be trusted to carry out the military tasks given to you with maximum efficiency, but I also appreciated that some people would not understand you fully, that you might make some enemies, and would require guarding against all outside influences that might impede you from rendering your maximum output.'[4] Monty's somewhat arrogant assertions about war and the structure of Britain's post-war army Brooke accepted for what, behind the papal style, they were: namely the distillation of the ideas of a military *thinker* as well as battlefield general:

> It has emerged clearly from this war that, from a purely Army point of view, the following factors are vital for success in battle,

---

CIGS but this is a much more important post and I hope you will accept it" ': statement dictated by Field-Marshal Lord Alexander, 1962, for C. D. Hamilton, Papers of Sir Denis Hamilton.

[1] Alanbrooke Diary, Alanbrooke Papers, loc. cit.

[2] Entry of 6.9.45, loc. cit.

[3] Letter of 9.7.45, M588, Montgomery Papers.

[4] Letter of 6.2.46, Montgomery Papers.

Monty claimed:

> Leadership
> Organisation
> Equipment
> Training[1]

It was therefore vital, Monty felt, that the War Office directorates responsible for these areas be put under the overall charge of a 'Lt-Gen who has commanded a Corps or Army in the field'. Training was an area that must be 'fastened on to' immediately 'so as to ensure nothing is missed and that the true lessons of this war are incorporated in our tactical doctrine and training. A foremost lesson is the need for combination; every operation is now combined; no single service completely predominates. This implies a much stronger integration of training staffs in the training directorates of the Services. Training of officers each in their own watertight compartments leads to ignorance; education and training must be integrated throughout. It is not enough merely to combine Woolwich [Artillery and Engineering Cadet college] and Sandhurst; there must be further integration introducing the young officers of all three Services at the most suitable time: so that early in their Service career they begin to understand as much as possible of the other Services.'[2] The contribution of air power to ground operations had proved a battle-winning factor—but the old chasm that had existed between RAF and Army in England before D-Day was likely to re-emerge unless senior officers with practical battle experience were put into the key army-air positions at the War Office, Monty begged—and with Brooke's nod of assent the War Office took its cue, overlooking Monty's interference and seeking to incorporate his ideas as far as possible into War Office thinking. At Brooke's CIGS's conference at Camberley, therefore, Monty found no opposition—though whether he recognized the key role played by Brooke in ensuring such tolerance is doubtful. To 'Kit' Dawnay Monty boasted in a letter on 14 October 1945:

> All goes well here. The conference at Camberley went very well from my point of view. The most noteworthy feature was that there was practically no one there who had any qualification to speak on the subject of what sort of Army is needed in order to win battles; very few, incl. the Army Council, had ever seen a battle!! So I found it quite easy.[3]

[1] M588, loc. cit.
[2] Ibid.
[3] Papers of Lt-Colonel C. P. Dawnay.

Brooke had told Monty he would probably now remain as CIGS until the spring of 1946, at Attlee's request. Monty, loth to admit he was disappointed, pretended that this was in line with his, Monty's, own anxiousness not to leave Germany yet:

> I have told the Prime Minister and the C.I.G.S. that I consider it would be most unwise to move me from Germany until the Battle of the Winter has been won. This has been agreed,

he informed Dawnay.

> The C.I.G.S. will stay on till the Spring; it is his idea that I should succeed him, and he has told the Prime Minister this.[1]

Brooke could only recommend his successor, however, and for all his espousal of Monty's cause he was by no means certain that he would make an ideal CIGS. As had emerged at the August Chiefs of Staff meeting concerning successors, Monty was deemed 'very efficient from Army point of view but very unpopular with large proportion of the Army', Brooke had noted[2]—something of which, in his Ostenwalde lair, Monty seemed oblivious. Yet there were few if any alternatives. The VCIGS, Lt-General Nye, was the obvious contender—'very capable but after 7 years in War Office must have some outside experience', Brooke wrote.[3]

For the moment, however, Attlee would make no decision, and Monty was left to mark time in Germany.

[1] Ibid.
[2] Alanbrooke Diary, entry of 26.8.45, loc. cit.
[3] Ibid.

CHAPTER NINE

The Set-up at Ostenwalde

THOUGH HE PUT a brave face on Attlee's deferment of a decision, the uncertainty over his succession as CIGS stretched Monty's patience to breaking point. It seemed as if he was doomed to suffer the vacillation and procrastination of those in power, and there can be no doubt that, whatever he might write to Dawnay about the Battle of the Winter, he was, by the autumn of 1945, losing interest in Germany. 'I think you should not now stay on longer than you feel you want to,' he advised Dawnay, who was anxious to return to civilian life. Lt-Colonel Trumbull Warren's successor as Personal Assistant, Major Terry Coverdale, took Dawnay's post as Military Assistant, and another of Monty's Liaison Officers, Major Richard O'Brien, became PA. Despite their undoubted respect for Monty's leadership and professionalism,[1] both Coverdale and O'Brien came increasingly to question the 'set-up' at Ostenwalde. As Coverdale recalled:

> We lived an extraordinary life, there's no doubt about it. In the Schloss there was Monty, his MA and PA and the two ADCs, and then outside you had a security company, signals, a small Intelligence set-up, that sort of thing; but we were completely divorced from reality—completely divorced.[2]

O'Brien felt the same:

> It was a strange set-up really. Strange would be the word. He wanted to be kept away from the detail—and the starving Germans of course! The leafy lanes and prosperous countryside, even then, of the Hannoverian plain. It was so remote, and there we were, this privileged corps, playing tennis on a summer's afternoon, and calm reigned.
>
> Beyond was the Ruhr, or Berlin, or Düsseldorf. Don't get me wrong, it wasn't luxurious living. That was not his style. We lived in a modest Schloss, a perfectly decent place for him to live, not an enormously grand building, comfortable, but we ate very simple

[1] See 'A Good Listener' by Sir Richard O'Brien, in *Monty at Close Quarters*, ed. T. E. B. Howarth, London 1985.
[2] Major Terry Coverdale, interview of 19.3.78.

unpretentious army canteen-type meals. We weren't sloshing the wine about. It wasn't austere, either. You could never say Tac Headquarters was austere! This element of Monty's reputation derives from running-in-the-early-morning in 1940—all that sort of thing. That wasn't a feature of the scene at Ostenwalde at all.

We were remote. People came and went at Tac Headquarters. They were summoned to the 'presence'—it was almost like Berchtesgaden! I mean, you know, you were summoned to the presence, you rolled up and had a cup of tea and talked about old battles half the time and then you disappeared again. Ostenwalde was a long way from Bad Oynhausen itself. It was a kind of expedition to come there!

Whether it was appropriate for the developing administration of Germany? I doubt it.[1]

Coverdale, too, was astonished to see the way even Monty's most senior subordinates, even his Deputy Military Governor, had to wait to be summoned:

If Sandy Galloway, who became Chief of Staff to Monty, or Brian Robertson, or whoever [wanted to see Monty]: they had to come to us. Monty never went to 21st Army Group/BAOR—they had to come up, get in their cars and motor twenty miles and come up. They had to have an appointment and he gave them an hour or whatever it was, and then they went away.

We lived an extraordinary existence. No women were allowed, incidentally. I mean, if some chap rolled up with a female PA, we all dashed out and got hold of him—'I say, don't come here, clear off—out!' I mean the whole thing was ludicrous.

And he was surrounded only by young people, who clapped their hands to him and did everything for him. It was not good for him—it was not good for him,

Coverdale reflected.[2] As the months went by, Monty left more and more of the Control Commission business in Berlin to Brian Robertson—'Brian Robertson just came to him for a rubber stamp'[3]—while entrusting the administration of the British Zone to his subordinate commanders and his Civil Affairs officers.

You didn't get an impression of a kind of directing authority there, if you see what I mean,

recalled Sir Richard O'Brien forty years on:

[1] Sir Richard O'Brien, interview of 31.10.84.

[2] Loc. cit.

[3] Ibid.

> You would get particular problems dealt with: Strang would arrive on this, or Sholto Douglas [C-in-C, Air] would arrive on that. But Monty wasn't close to the Occupation, he didn't get himself close to that. He used us [Liaison Officers], he used to send us around—we covered the waterfront, the scene, very widely. So he had feelers out, but he wasn't interested, I would say.[1]

Coverdale sensed that, for all his outward show of energy and decisiveness, Monty was undergoing a painful metamorphosis:

> It was a very traumatic experience to find that suddenly your life's work was virtually done. The war had come to an end and what was he to do then?
>
> And he didn't like it. He didn't like Military Government—he didn't really like anything to do with it. Because he was geared to fighting battles—and he'd fought his last one. He was at sixes and sevens with himself. He wasn't all that fit then, because he'd had that air crash, and that knocked him up a bit.
>
> He was tired. He had a reaction—he had had this plane crash that didn't do him any good, and he disliked all the 'argy bargy' that one had to do at that time with the Control Council in Berlin, dealing with the Russians. It wasn't his scene. . . .
>
> I think, too—he *hoped* he was to be next CIGS, but I think this was worrying him, that he might not in fact become CIGS, and he was wondering what the future was going to hold.[2]

Discharged from hospital and working for the Political Intelligence Department of the Foreign Office, Lt-Colonel Peter Earle visited Monty at Ostenwalde in November. In April Earle had 'travelled through the most lovely undulating country almost like NORWAY. Great forests of fir trees, emerald green fields, prosperous, scrupulously tidy, red brick farms'[3] to reach Monty's new Tac Headquarters, established in the home of an old German baron, von Winterfeldt:

> a really lovely ancestral German home; fine pictures, vast and hideous furniture, delightful panelled drawing room. The inmates, ancient Hannoverian relations of our Royal family, were ordered out at 12 hours notice. . . . The prints in the house are nearly all English. Nelson, horse racing Newmarket; views of Germany, our Royal family etc.

[1] Loc. cit.
[2] Loc. cit.
[3] Diary of Colonel Peter Earle, entry of 10.4.45, communicated by Colonel Earle to author, 1985.

In the 'heavily crested' Visitors' Book, however, there had been evidence of a less anglophilic past—

> photos of German tanks killing British soldiers, and entries by German 8 Pz, whose HQ once was billeted here. The last entry is in German script. Monty has asked for it to be translated. He will write the next entry in the book! This is typical of the man. Dinner in the vast drawing room, with a bottle of Hock, was delightful. Following which I gave Monty the form [the latest information from General Ritchie, commanding 12 Corps south of Bremen] with great zeal.[1]

At that time, in April, Earle had been impressed by Monty's excellent health and good spirits, despite the years of campaigning from North Africa. On 12 April Monty had 'ordered' a photo of his HQ which he richly enjoyed.

> 'Now we will look at the camera,' he said, 'now we will look to the right,' and then: 'now we will look to the left.' Then the Liaison Officers went through to the other side of the house where his caravan stands and there we were photographed with him. He then demanded that we changed into our travelling clothes—'we are all too smart,' he said, 'take off your coat John—is that my coat by the way?' [addressing Poston].
>
> We changed and he changed into especially old clothes. 'And now I will be giving you the form,' he said 'and now I will point out the map, and now we will look at HANNOVER, you will be writing.' 'And now this will be for the Illustrated London News. I will be pointing at one of you—Dick [Harden] perhaps—yes—and you will be looking at me intelligently. I will have a map, which I understand I should have at my level.' And so it went on, Monty directing the whole affair.[2]

Now, in the same 'room that I had first entered in April as one of the first British officers to set foot there, I met Monty again,' Earle noted on 17 November.

> He looked older and greyer—like some tired old vulture. He wore a grey tweed golf jacket with a zip fastener, open to reveal a strawberry coloured tie with white stripes against his khaki shirt. He spoke of John's [Poston's] and Charles' [Sweeny's] graves and how they had been railed off by the Germans. He spoke of his apprehension at the increasing number of 'displaced persons'

[1] Ibid.

[2] Diary of Colonel Peter Earle, entry of 12.4.45, communicated to author 1985.

streaming into his Zone and the fear of flu or some disease gripping Germany and being passed to England.

Most of his time is spent in briefing Brian Robertson, the Chief of Staff, on whose level most of the important business is settled. He, himself, is seldom able to enter the arena. He neither likes nor understands the problems but has to shoulder the responsibility. His heart I think is in Army domestic affairs.

Archie [Nye] said when I met him . . . the other day that Monty would be invited to be C.I.G.S. although neither Chief of Staff, Army Council or Cabinet required [desired] him. There was no alternative if the Cabinet would not risk reducing the entire Army Council and Chief of Staff to the 50 age group instead of the 60. 'He will be C.I.G.S. I am afraid,' said Archie, 'and retire a tired, worn out and disillusioned old man.' All his Staff reckon on this—and their return in April.

I felt Monty had not all the drive and enthusiasm that he had had when I first met him in Winter 1944 in Brookie's office.[1]

There was little doubt that Monty was, despite his keenness to reform the post-war British army and absorb the lessons of war, a relatively exhausted man. Knowing that he would probably succeed Brooke as CIGS but not knowing for certain or even when, made Monty's condition no easier. It was in this limbo that Monty undoubtedly allowed fame to fan his ego, and far from becoming a mellower character in the wake of international recognition, his public persona became even more brittle, his egotism more pronounced—and the attitude towards those who stepped too close to his throne increasingly aggressive.

[1] Diary of Colonel Peter Earle, entry for 17.11.45, communicated to author 1985.

CHAPTER TEN

An Astonishing Display of Indignity

> I think he *was* becoming more egotistical. I really do,

Major Coverdale recalled, remembering life at Schloss Ostenwalde some thirty-five years later.

> He only admired one other commander in the whole of the British Army, and that was Brookie! Now he touched his hat to him—he didn't to anyone else.
>
> With all due respect to Monty, I never heard him say anything good about any other commander at his level. He would say about his Divisional Commanders or Corps Commanders—but he'd never say anything good about Alex or Anderson or 'Jumbo' Wilson or anyone on the same level as his.[1]

This arrogance disturbed his young staff, however surprised and flattered they were by his openness in discussion at the meal table. Sir Richard O'Brien recalled how, on his first summons to dine in the small, select mess of the C-in-C he had 'blotted his copybook' by giving rein to unrestricted criticism of the commanders in charge of the Italian campaign.

> I remember very clearly walking back across the courtyard aghast at what I'd done—I'd been led on in my stupidity. I had strong views about the conduct of the Italian campaign, where I'd been a regimental officer. I disagreed with the staff officers, I didn't think anything of the way it [the campaign] was run. I'd been in Eighth Army at Alamein, got wounded and then I'd been both in Anzio and also on the other [Adriatic] side.[2]

In fact O'Brien must have been the most decorated of all Monty's Liaison Officers, holding the DSO and two MCs.

> Anyway I was absolutely appalled; I thought what I'd said [at table, egged on by Monty] was singularly inappropriate. . . . I really thought that I would the next day get the most frightful ticking-off or perhaps worse. That was my mood as I went back to bed.

[1] Ibid.
[2] Loc. cit.

Not a bit of it! It turned out—had I wished it to be so—to be the cleverest thing I could have done, because he enjoyed all that sort of thing: criticizing others. He was very interested in going over battles conducted by others. Oh yes—and he loved gossip. He would be *keenly* interested.

But once you honed in on himself, once you got near himself, the climate changed. . . .

He couldn't *stand* criticism of his battles. I was once in the key position at Alamein—the leading officer in the army. There I was [at Ostenwalde] talking to the general conducting the damned battle—I thought this would be rather interesting to him, a few years later—dammit, he won the blasted thing!

And he was. . . . I had wanted to stage a conversation about the Battle of Alamein because I held strong views about the opportunities that seemed to me to arise at one point in the battle. There was I, in the gun line—I was with the New Zealand Division in the battle—and: not a bit of it. Absolutely no. He wanted no criticism.[1]

This brittleness whenever his own person was concerned was best illustrated at this time by Monty's incredible behaviour to his own mother.

On 25 September 1945 Monty left London by train, bound for Newport, where he was to receive the Freedom of the Town. A great banquet had been prepared, for the honour was not simply a tribute by the people of Newport or of Monmouthshire, but of all Wales to the man who had brought their sons safely home from the war. Monty had prepared his speech well in advance, extolling the part played in the defeat of Germany by 'your Welsh Division, the 53rd Division. Many of you no doubt have sons or husbands or relations in that Division, and you must know what a gallant part the Division played right the way through from Normandy to the Baltic. I would like to add my own word of praise and to tell you how magnificently they have fought, and how proud you may justly be of them,' Monty rehearsed his address in the train. 'We shall all long remember their contribution in the fight for the Liberation of Europe.'[2]

Copies of the speech had been run off for the Press who were expected to be in Newport in force. A limousine met the train, and at the Town Hall the Mayor of Newport announced to Monty that, in order to mark the auspicious occasion, the Council had invited the Field-Marshal's mother from Ireland to attend the

[1] Loc. cit.

[2] Notes for address in appendix to 'Notes on the Occupation of Germany', loc. cit.

banquet and ceremony. Monty turned white. 'What did you say?' he snapped at the Mayor. Then, shaking with anger, he added: 'I won't have her here. In fact if she comes, I go!'[1]

Monty's personal staff were chagrined—the more so as there were many journalists and Press photographers present. A compromise was arranged, in that 'Lady' Montgomery's place-name was removed from the top banqueting table and consigned to a far corner; Monty's ADC met her and kept her away from Monty, who refused to speak to her. It was to be the last time he saw her alive: a truly astonishing display of indignity.

Even those who did elicit Monty's affection found it hard to get to know him beyond a certain point or perimeter. As his ADC, Johnny Henderson, later recalled, having served with Monty from Alamein to the end of the war,

> He *never* let you get too close to him. I mean, this is the extraordinary thing, that you couldn't. As well as I got to know him at the end, you know, you never really got very close.[2]

Monty wanted no debts or obligations save those of his own choosing. He had trained himself through his adult life for high command; had seized his opportunity with both hands. Victory and fame had been the result—and he would surrender the metaphorical spoils to no one, least of all his mother. This self-isolation now gave him an increasingly maverick quality. He had, it is true, always been eccentric; but at heart he had always been a child of the British Army, anxious to serve rather than risk the wilderness. Whenever his career had been placed at risk he had climbed down, like a naughty child, to face his punishment rather than be cast outside. Now, however, he was becoming a parent of that Army, a Field-Marshal and a household name throughout the world. Climbing down became increasingly difficult from such a height, and, lacking a wife or close friends, he had no one with whom to discuss such problems. His relationship with his mother had become one of outright rejection—he would refuse to attend her funeral—and his relationship with his son David was, to say the least, kingly. As Johnny Henderson put it: 'Monty certainly didn't know how to deal with him, give him any fun. David . . . I think we were obviously closer to David than he ever was, at that time. There was no rapport. Oh, he was anxious at all times to do the right thing—but he just didn't know how to relax with him. He didn't know how to relax with David at all. I mean you couldn't have imagined David and him sharing a joke together,

[1] Major J. R. Henderson, interview of 13.8.81.
[2] Ibid.

or settling down and playing a game of cards or doing anything . . . I mean, the conversation was always rather false, and usually consisted of trying to impress David by making a crack at someone—he'd say, for instance: "Johnnie doesn't know what he's going to do in life—but of course he's useless"—you know, that sort of thing.'[1]

Monty's Chief of Intelligence, Brigadier Williams, was similarly mortified by Monty's excesses. 'Some things chilled the heart,' he confessed years later. 'I can remember things that were deeply embarrassing to the human race. But one sort of passed them by. . . .'[2] Williams had noticed how, as the war had gone on, Monty had used him less, partly because he had Williams' colleague Colonel 'Joe' Ewart permanently attached to his Tac Headquarters, but partly because Monty 'became less interested in the enemy *per se*'.[3] More and more Monty's struggle had become one of maintaining the morale of his own commanders and troops, while convincing his Allies of the need for concentration and clear priorities—a struggle which necessarily pivoted on Allied command arrangements rather than a deep continuing study of the enemy. This decreasing curiosity about the enemy went hand-in-hand with an increasingly papal certitude about his own infallibility. So de Guingand was sent home on sick leave not simply because the doctors insisted on it, but because Monty no longer saw the need for someone of de Guingand's calibre to advise him and to smooth down ruffled feathers. De Guingand's brilliant mind—'the best untrained brain I have ever encountered', Sir Edgar Williams later remarked of him[4]—and his flair for handling people were no longer advantages which Monty felt indispensable. 'I was surprised, quite honestly, about Freddie going back permanently to England in May 1945,' Johnnie Henderson later recalled.[5] De Guingand had been responsible, on top of his role as Chief of Staff in charge of 21st Army Group operations, for the administration of all rear areas in the liberated territory of France, Belgium and Holland. Yet Monty saw no need for de Guingand in Germany. 'No,' remarked Henderson, thinking of de Guingand's departure, 'Monty had got to the stage beyond wanting anyone's opinion except his own. I honestly feel that's true. At that stage he didn't—he didn't seem to ask people questions in the same way as if he wanted to know an answer. It was backing up his *own* convictions

[1] Ibid.
[2] Brigadier Sir Edgar Williams, interview of 28.1.83.
[3] Ibid.
[4] Brigadier Sir Edgar Williams, interview of 7.9.78.
[5] Loc. cit.

he wanted—I honestly think by that stage he didn't want an outsider muscling in on his act. . . .'[1]

He had elbowed his once 'darling mother' off the stage. Now, in December 1945, it was time to deal with his famous wartime Chief of Staff, Sir Francis de Guingand.

[1] Ibid.

CHAPTER ELEVEN

The Little Bastard Business

In July 1945 Monty asked me to come and see him in London. He told me that he had been appointed C.I.G.S. as from 1st January 1946. He had been asked who he would like to act as his V.C.I.G.S. and he had replied me—would I like to accept. I told Monty that I felt much better but was still not 100% fit. However he said it was important that I should join the War Office staff as soon as possible, so that I would be in a position to keep him all the more [informed] when he arrived. Brookie suggested that I should become DMI [Director of Military Intelligence] for 2–3 months. In the end I accepted the appointment and joined the War Office,

de Guingand recorded some years later.[1] By December 1945, however, Monty was having qualms about de Guingand as his possible VCIGS, and de Guingand was painfully aware of this:

My dear Field-Marshal,

It was good seeing you yesterday and I enjoyed the talk,

he wrote on 28 December.

In order to clarify the position regarding any possible future re-association between us, I would like to explain the position as best I can in a letter.

To start with you must know that I would love to find myself working directly under you once again. When we discussed the business in Germany and at Hindhead[2] there appeared to be two factors which looked as if they might become stumbling blocks:

a) my health

b) my marriage—i.e. my domestic life. . . .

As to my health—it is not easy to be very precise at the present moment. Since that bad patch a few weeks ago, I appear to have got steadily better. I am at this very moment taking a course of 'M & B' which might well clear up my tummy, and lead to much

[1] Memorandum by Sir Francis de Guingand, 'Monty and F. de G.', undated but presumably written in 1967, de Guingand Papers, loc. cit.

[2] According to Monty's diary, he saw de Guingand on 7.8.45 in London, again on 24.9.45 (possibly at Hindhead), and took him with him from Ostenwalde to Berlin on 9.11.45. In 'The Diary of Field-Marshal Montgomery's Movements' in 'Notes on the Occupation of Germany', loc. cit.

> better health in future. The doctors should have an idea about this in a week or so's time. In general I believe I am in better health than when you met me at the cross roads outside Alexandria and yet I managed since then to carry a pretty good load! Then again the more interesting the job, the easier it is to carry a load.[1]

De Guingand's wife was, however, an even more unpredictable factor than his health. De Guingand had met and married her (a war widow in 1942) in Egypt, with Monty's blessing and indeed connivance. She disliked living in England—though 'she feels much more reconciled to the prospect of being in England for another year or two' after de Guingand had promised to pay for a trip to Australia to see her parents. 'She also says that she knows I would be happier working for you than anyone else and therefore she feels that to favour the proposal might not be in the end the best from our particular "family" point of view.'

> So for my part, providing Arlie thinks she will be happy if we stay on in England, I feel that there is a good chance of my health standing the pace as long as I live a quiet life.
>
> All this of course apart from:
>
> a) Whether you want me
>
> b) Whether you think I am up to the job professionally.
>
> If you do in fact want me, I suggest when the time comes we get [Brigadier] Bulmer [de Guingand's physician] to come and examine me *with* the Millbank [Army Hospital] specialist, and see what opinion they arrive at.[2]

This was not the letter of a man to whom the post of VCIGS had been 'promised'; indeed it reflected, if anything, de Guingand's acute awareness of the factors mitigating *against* his selection, and his brave attempt to discount or overcome them. Monty's doubts can hardly have been erased by the letter. De Guingand had twice been hospitalized during the desert campaign, and twice again during the campaign in North-west Europe, as well as having to take sick leave on the conclusion. Even Sir Ronald Weeks, as Monty's deputy in Germany, had been forced to resign owing to overwork and ill-health; whether de Guingand could truly stand the strain as future VCIGS was deeply questionable. In replying, Monty certainly did not commit himself; he still had not officially been appointed CIGS-designate himself, nor had it been confirmed when the appointment would start, as he pointed out by return:

[1] Handwritten draft in de Guingand Papers, loc. cit.

[2] Ibid.

My dear Freddie

Thank you for your letter. The situation is now quite clear. The great point is for you to get Bulmer and the Millbank chap to agree.

For myself, we must wait on events. I have no idea what is intended by the great ones. But I am seeing Brookie on 1st Jan, and I am to address the Cabinet at 1100 hrs on 3 Jan. Possibly something may emerge: especially as I am going to say I want 6 weeks leave in the spring. And I will insist on it!!

Yrs ever

B. L. Montgomery[1]

Events moved quickly, however—for with Attlee's determination to rid Britain of her Indian commitment General Nye, the current VCIGS, had been selected as Military Governor of Madras. Brooke himself now needed a VCIGS—and it was this development which really led to the torpedoing of de Guingand's candidature, as Maj-General 'Simbo' Simpson recalled:

> In January 1946, the position was that Archie Nye was Vice-CIGS, but had just been selected to go as Governor of Madras. There was a Labour Government in power under Mr Attlee and they had definite ideas about handing over in India and they thought that Nye would make a very good governor in a transition period. . . . So Nye had to go, and a new Vice-CIGS had to be appointed to take over the duties pretty quickly.[2]

Monty, having spent Christmas at Hindhead, drove up to the War Office on New Year's Day, 1946. He had two interviews with Brooke, first on 1 Jan, and then again on 3 January 'concerning future appointments', as Brooke noted in his diary. 'He [Monty] is now taking an interest in these in view of his . . . succeeding me soon!'[3]

[1] Letter of 29.12.45, de Guingand Papers, loc. cit.

[2] General Sir Frank Simpson, Eugene Wason interview for Sir Denis Hamilton. Nye was offered, so he told Peter Earle in December 1945, any one of three governorships; 'he was offered also the Commander-in-Chief of Middle East, or Germany when Monty returns, or C.I.G.S. if he cared to command in the field first. He couldn't face Whitehall for a day longer than was vital nor the anti-climax of the other alternatives, so he decided to be a "monk" and clear right away to Madras. Thus the Army loses its most promising brain and most enlightened and energetic man, and probably its best advocate': diary of Colonel Peter Earle, communicated to author 1985. Nye subsequently became UK High Commissioner at Delhi in 1948 and High Commissioner to Canada from 1952 to 1956.

[3] Entry of 3.1.46, Alanbrooke Diary, loc. cit.

Monty asked Brooke who would succeed Nye as VCIGS. As Sir Frank Simpson later recalled:

> Alanbrooke [the title Brooke had chosen for his viscountcy conferred on 1 January] said he intended to get in General McCreery, who was commanding troops in Austria at the time.
>
> Monty replied that if McCreery, who he thought was 'mad', came in, McCreery would be out on his neck the moment Monty arrived at the War Office on July 1,

Simpson recounted.

> I personally do not think that that was fair comment on Monty's part, but he made it.[1]
>
> So Alanbrooke, slightly nettled, turned to Monty and said: 'Whom do you intend to get in?' and Monty said that he wanted de Guingand.
>
> Alanbrooke said: 'I won't have him. I don't trust him. He is an unbalanced chap now. I won't have him here as Vice-CIGS.'
>
> So presumably they passed other names under review, but the only one they could agree on as satisfactory to both parties was 'Simpson', and within half an hour of that conversation Monty arrived in my office to tell me exactly what had taken place during the conversation and that I was to be the new Vice-CIGS and how much he welcomed it.
>
> A few hours later that day, I went to see the CIGS on some operational matter, and he said: 'Have you been told that you are to be the new Vice-CIGS?' And I said, yes, I had just been told.
>
> He then told me of the conversation between the two Field-Marshals. It was pretty well the same story Monty had told me so I am pretty certain it was a true story.[2]

There can be little doubt that this was so. But instead of taking time to break the news gently to de Guingand Monty strode straight to de Guingand's office, called him into the corridor and dashed his hopes in the most astonishing display of rudeness towards a loyal friend and erstwhile Chief of Staff. As de Guingand recorded some years afterwards:

[1] McCreery, as a cavalry man and polo enthusiast, was not the deputy Monty wished in creating a new professional, meritocratic post-war British Army. After commanding Eighth Army with distinction in Italy in 1945 McCreery had become Military Governor of the British occupation zone in Austria.

[2] General Sir Frank Simpson, loc. cit.

One day in January 1946, Monty arrived at the War Office, flung the door of my [DMI's] office open. [General Sir] Bernard Freyberg was sitting with me. He called me outside and in great haste he said, 'Oh Freddie, I've decided not to have you as my Vice.'

I naturally asked 'Why not?'

His reply was, 'Because it wouldn't do me any good'! He then rushed off.

I entered my office again, feeling rather stunned and very hurt; Bernard Freyberg said, 'Did I hear correctly?' and I told him he had. He then said, 'The little bastard!' [1]

De Guingand, who retired from the Army some months after this interview, was understandably embittered by the experience, a memory which undoubtedly festered as the years went by. Told to others, the story assumed the status of a *cause célèbre* as demonstrating Monty's self-centredness and cruelty in 'dropping the pilot' shortly before assuming the throne of the British Army. By then, however, de Guingand's ill-health—first gall-stones and, towards the end of his life, a brain tumour—had distorted his memory, as his own papers reveal. For Monty had not guaranteed de Guingand the post of VCIGS; moreover Monty did in fact explain that it was *Brooke*'s decision, not his own, as de Guingand's draft letters written on the evening after the fateful interview, indicate:

I naturally accept the position and would hate it to be raised again,

de Guingand wrote.

I am sufficiently a realist to know that either age, seniority, efficiency, or health were factors which could have been put forward to support such a decision. I am however, to say the least of it, hurt at the particular reason given by the CIGS [Brooke], i.e. that such an appointment would be damaging to you personally.[2]

Brooke had evidently made the point that, in taking de Guingand as VCIGS, Monty might weaken his authority over Britain's post-war army by appearing only to promote and favour men who had already served under him. With an empire to police and gradually relinquish—Brooke had only just returned from a two-month transworld tour—it was in Brooke's eyes vital to retain the morale of senior officers in the Middle and Far East. Monty's abrupt, in-

[1] Memorandum by Sir Francis de Guingand, 'Monty and F. de G.' undated but presumably written in 1967, de Guingand Papers, loc. cit.

[2] Draft in de Guingand Papers, loc. cit.

sulting announcement of the decision had not, however, made this clear. To de Guingand's mind, Brooke's excuse seemed to suggest that de Guingand's installation as VCIGS would somehow reduce the esteem in which Monty was held:

> To start with, he might have thought of that before instead of, as you told me at Claridges in August, that he agreed with the proposal. It infers that our 3 years association in war was not a successful one, and/or that the army generally would be put out by such a natural re-union. It certainly suggests that your position and prestige are not very firm.[1]

This inference deeply disturbed de Guingand, who believed with ample reason that he had served both Monty and the whole Allied cause with complete selflessness, accepting rank far junior to that of his American opposite numbers as Chiefs of Staff to Army Group Commanders; the absence of any British decoration at the end of hostilities; and even an order from Monty that he was not to accept foreign decorations other than the Russian Order of Kutuzov First Class:

> I'm sure you will agree that I subordinated entirely my interests to yours, and never attempted to claim any kudos—and there were occasions when I might have done. This I know the army realise.
>
> When yesterday I said I saw the point—that was correct. But I did not agree with the argument used. So I wish some other reason had been given.

There were three drafts which de Guingand drew up for this letter, each one longer and more agonizing than the other. Ironically, had Monty simply told de Guingand that his candidature was 'off', de Guingand believed he could have faced up to this with equanimity. It was Brooke's point about the *damage* it would do to Monty that almost deranged de Guingand. 'In war one can and must subordinate all personal feelings,' he wrote, 'but in peace these to some extent must be taken into account.' His sense of hurt still howls from the pencilled foolscap sheets similar to those upon which he had for three crucial years translated Monty's battle decisions into orders. How *could* he be harmful to Monty's reputation, he who had always 'entirely subordinated my interest to yours'? 'Please don't think I am asking for the decision to be reversed—nothing could be further from my mind. I am merely getting something out of my system—something that has hurt me quite a lot,' de Guingand wrote with

[1] Ibid.

understatement. 'There comes a time when it is better to speak up rather than become a complete dogsbody or stooge.'[1]

The more de Guingand thought about the matter, the more he realized that his very subordination of his own interest had permitted Monty to take advantage of him: 'The trouble is that in looking back over a year or two several things have happened which I accepted at the time, but which in retrospect rightly or wrongly give me a sense of grievance.' There was Monty's failure to promote him to the rank of Lt-General when Chief of Staff of the Allied Land Forces before and after D-Day. There was Monty's failure to stop his demotion to colonel at the war's end. There was, too, the very manner in which Monty had treated him in front of others as the war drew to its close—'during the latter period of our association I was often treated in front of other people, not as a C[hief] of S[taff] but as a G3 [lowest grade of headquarters staff officer, usually ranked captain]. It could be said that I owe you a lot,' de Guingand concluded. 'I would never deny this, but on the other hand I may have helped you more than you really know, and certainly have not got much tangible advantage out of it all. I was C of S 8th Army *when* you arrived, and since that day I have completely subordinated myself to you and the common cause. And as far as I know I have never claimed any kudos—and on occasion I could quite honestly have done so.

'I may have a bit of Jays [simpleton] blood in me. But whatever it is I feel I have lost face. I feel there is a danger that if I carry on at the War Office I might not serve you loyally and so I feel there is no other course but to ask permission to resign from the Army. And this I propose to do.'[2]

In another draft of the letter, de Guingand proposed to 'put my case before him [the CIGS] and to ask his help';[3] but it was Brooke, not Monty, who had vetoed his selection as VCIGS, and this threat was soon dropped. Even the threat of resignation was shelved in the final letter, in which de Guingand merely protested against the implied insult in Brooke's statement, and declared that he would 'be only human if I found it difficult to serve you in a minor capacity at the War Office [i.e. as DMI] after our past association; particularly when the other plot [VCIGS] had been in the tapis . . . I hope therefore, if I stay in the Army that you will remember our talk in Germany as regards something *outside* the War Office.'[4]

[1] Ibid.
[2] Ibid.
[3] Ibid.
[4] Ibid.

Once again, by sending only a mild protest, de Guingand had subordinated his deeper feelings. But in doing so, he failed—as Bradley before him—to make clear to Monty how profoundly he had been injured by this, the final straw in a whole array of grievances. And Monty, preoccupied with the tasks still facing him as Military Governor of Germany and as probable CIGS-elect of the British Army, simply trampled over de Guingand's bruised pride.

CHAPTER TWELVE

Viscount Montgomery of Alamein

Tac Headquarters
British Army of the Rhine
7.1.46

My dear Freddie,

I have your letter of 4 Jan. I am quite unable to agree with the inferences you draw: i.e.

A. That our 3 years association in war was not a successful one

B. That my own position and prestige are not very firm,

Monty replied post haste.

As regards 'A'

Our association would be quoted for years to come as an example of complete trust and confidence. Of that there is no doubt.

As regards 'B'

I am not in the least interested in my own position. I have reached the top and can go no higher. I can at any time withdraw to the House of Lords and give tongue as I like!! I do not want to be C.I.G.S. and have told everyone so. Only a strong sense of duty makes me say that, if I am wanted for the job, then I will take it on.

I really want a good rest.

If I become C.I.G.S., my family will be the whole Army.

If I take you on as Vice, the Army will say that I am collecting in the old gang again and that no one will have any future unless he is one of my chaps. That would never do. I have already put in Kirkie [Kirkman] and Lyne, and all my old Corps Cdrs are now in the Home Commands. Future appointments will be watched, and criticized.

If it were War, I would not care what anyone said.

But it is Peace, and there is a herculean job ahead.

I can have only one yardstick: the best interests of the Army.

If I considered only my own interests, I would pull you straight in as Vice. But I have decided that I must not do so.

Do not make it any harder for me by 'bellyaching'.

No one has ever had, or will ever have, a more loyal and devoted Chief of Staff than you were. If we go to War again in my time, I would pull you straight in as Chief of Staff.

I hope above is clear.

Yours ever
B. L. Montgomery[1]

De Guingand duly piped down. But within a few weeks he had collapsed, his health broken by the war and domestic tribulations. He was sent on special War Office sick leave to Cannes, where he decided to submit his resignation. Thus was the British Army to lose its finest wartime Chief of Staff.

That he owed much to de Guingand, Monty knew. But it was an awareness that made him uneasy. As with his family, Monty wished to be beholden to no man; he thus let de Guingand resign from the Army without objection. In bowing to Brooke's wisdom over the post of VCIGS Monty had made a gesture of conciliation towards those who were not 'Monty men'; but in thereafter allowing de Guingand to resign from the Army, his adopted family, there can be no doubt that Monty cut a further chain anchoring him to worldly reality. With Brooke's imminent departure, Monty would lose the one man whose authority and judgment Monty bent to; in losing de Guingand, the one subordinate capable of providing a worthy foil to his dictatorial ways.

Meanwhile Maj-General Simpson went home delighted by the decision concerning the post of VCIGS—'there was general joy all round in the Simpson family,' he later recalled.[2] For Monty, unschooled in the procedures and bureaucracy of Whitehall, Simpson was to be a deputy of incalculable value. But Simpson's crystal-clear, procedural brain mirrored in many ways that of Monty himself. De Guingand's greatest contribution to Monty's wartime generalship had been the very *difference* between himself and Monty. *Bon viveur*, with wit and magnetic charm, de Guingand failed to impress the austere, puritan figure of Field-Marshal Brooke, but de Guingand was admired and liked—loved would not be too strong a word—by his staff and by Americans, for whom his warmth, intelligence, humour and frankness were considered almost unique in a senior British staff officer. In his way de Guingand resembled Eisenhower—the reason, perhaps, why de Guingand was later to declare his personal conviction that Eisenhower's broad-front strategy, in a war

[1] De Guingand Papers, loc. cit.
[2] General Sir Frank Simpson, loc. cit.

waged by disparate Allies, was both inevitable and in the end perfectly successful, as against Monty's 'Germanic' tactics of concentration and dictatorial command.

With de Guingand's loss, Monty's military life became the poorer. Brooke was not, as has been seen, infallible; and he completely underestimated the extent of de Guingand's contribution to Monty's wartime success. With de Guingand on his staff—even alongside Simpson—Monty might well have made a greater success of his appointment as CIGS.

Having made his decision, however, Monty was past caring. In the New Year's honours he had been made a Viscount, alongside Brooke and other wartime leaders. Congratulations poured in from six continents. 'Through press despatches I learned that His Majesty has additionally recognized your contribution to Allied victory by appointing you to the peerage stop please accept my enthusiastic and sincere congratulations stop signed Ike,' was one Monty prized.[1] However his staff in Germany had been expecting the honour, as the astute Brigadier Williams later recalled:

> When Monty returned to Germany after Christmas we congratulated him and asked him what title he was going to take.
>
> 'What do you think of "Montgomery of Alamein"?' he questioned us.
>
> Well we tried to look very surprised. 'Gosh, yes, hadn't ever thought of that . . .'—when of course we'd seen him practising his signature for weeks on the blotting pad![2]

Monty was certainly proud. He outranked his father (KCMG) and his grandfather Sir Robert Montgomery. The small boy within him thrilled at the 'rags-to-riches' romance of such elevation—he who had his life long been such a thorn in the side of superiors and establishment figures. 'My correct title address is now Field Marshal The Viscount Montgomery of Alamein G.C.B., D.S.O.,' he informed the Reynolds. 'My signature has become: Montgomery of Alamein, Field-Marshal,' he added proudly.[3]

Together with his viscountcy, Monty had at last been formally offered the post of CIGS. Brooke had written to Monty on 10

[1] Signal of 2.1.46, Eisenhower Papers, loc. cit.

[2] Sir Edgar Williams, interview of 7.9.78. Attlee's letter, offering him the viscountcy, had in fact been sent almost a month before. See letter dated 10.12.45 in Montgomery Papers. Williams also recalled how some of Monty's staff professed disappointment at his choice of title. 'Why, what's the matter with it?' Monty asked, defensively. 'Well . . . we rather hoped you might choose "The Lord Mighty in Battle" . . .!'—interview of 7.9.78.

[3] Undated letter, Montgomery Papers.

January to say he had 'discussed your taking over from me with S. of S. He is putting matter up to P.M. suggested date about middle or end of June. As soon as P.M. has agreed I think we might get a public announcement, shall let you know how things go.'[1] The announcement was duly made on 26 January 1946, to take effect five months thereafter, on 26 June 1946.

Once again Eisenhower, in Washington, was not slow to welcome the news. 'This high honour is a crowning recognition of the great leadership which you have displayed throughout the war in the Allied cause. I know that no gift in the power of your government to bestow could have brought deeper satisfaction. Your appointment is particularly gratifying to me because of our close association and friendship from the campaign in Tunisia to the final disintegration of the German enemy in the heart of his broken homeland. Best of luck!' Eisenhower generously cabled.[2]

Monty was now the most famous British warrior since the time of Nelson and Wellington. His presence attracted crowds larger than any film star's. In Northern Ireland in September 1945, 'the crowds in the street were so dense that all the windows of his car were broken,' his diarist recorded.[3] Not only was Monty now showered by honorary doctorates, freedom of cities and memberships of august societies, but he was asked to give speeches and lectures on every hand. Most of these were simple and soldierly, with Monty's characteristic mix of conceit and yet humbleness before the tasks which lay ahead of the free nations: 'winning the peace'. 'I have been making a number of speeches when receiving Freedoms, and have a good few more to make. I decided that I would get across certain things to the public: using the opportunity given to me,' he explained his 'policy' to the ousted Secretary of State for War, Sir James Grigg, and enclosed several copies of the speeches with his letter. 'You will notice the same theme in them all; I think in these cases that constant reiteration is the thing; in the end it will sink in.'[4]

But if Monty was concerned with winning the peace, there were a number of individuals who disliked the way he had won the war—or said he had.

[1] Letter of 10.1.46, Montgomery Papers.
[2] Letter of 2.2.46, Eisenhower papers, loc. cit.
[3] 'Notes on the Occupation of Germany', loc. cit.
[4] Letter of 6.9.45, Grigg Papers, loc. cit.

CHAPTER THIRTEEN

A Soldier's Vision

In October 1945 Monty had given a long and serious lecture to members of the Royal United Services Institution in Whitehall. He had submitted the draft of his lecture to the three Chiefs of Staff in September; all had approved the lecture which was titled '21st (British) Army Group in the Campaign in North-West Europe, 1944–1945', Brooke remarking that 'as far as I can see it seems all right, and I cannot see that you have said anything you should not have said or better said differently'.[1] Even the King's Private Secretary remarked, on behalf of King George VI: 'I can quite understand that you had to use a certain amount of discretion in lecturing on the details of the campaign!'[2]

American officers, however, felt differently. The lecture was soon printed as a thirty-four-page booklet and was considered so controversial when it reached US Forces in Europe Headquarters in Frankfurt that it was promptly made the subject of a special investigation at the request of General Bedell Smith. It was Monty's assertion that everything in Normandy had gone 'according to plan' which irritated Bedell Smith most. American D-Day planning documents were consulted. These and 'other documents fail to substantiate the accuracy of Field-Marshal Montgomery's claim that actual operations followed exactly the pattern of planned operations', as the US appreciation concluded.[3] To Monty this was quibbling: he had attempted to describe the campaign in bold strokes and was concerned to point out the reasons behind Allied success against the redoubted Wehrmacht rather than explore the minutiae of what went wrong. Though Bedell Smith was told to let the matter drop, it was clear that historical battle lines were now being drawn—and it was not long before Monty was under sustained attack by demobbed Americans from Bradley's and Eisenhower's erstwhile staff out for his blood. Thus Eisenhower, having telegraphed to congratulate Monty on his promotion to CIGS, was almost immediately having to apologize for his braying dogs—for on 28 January 1946 Monty

[1] Letter of 5.9.46, Montgomery Papers.
[2] Letter of 2.10.45 from Balmoral, Montgomery Papers.
[3] Appreciation dated 23.10.45, Eisenhower Papers, loc. cit.

had sent him a cutting from the *Sunday Despatch*, headlined: 'General's Aide says: EISENHOWER NEARLY SACKED MONTGOMERY.' It was a report of a serialized extract in the *Saturday Evening Post* from Harry C. Butcher's forthcoming book *My Three Years with Eisenhower*. As Monty lamented to Eisenhower:

> It seems to me a great pity that Butcher should go on writing these sort of things. And to bring Tedder's name into it.
>
> There is a lot of writing going on these days. American authors and writers have started to write you up; but they seem quite unable to do this without getting at me.
>
> This is a terrible pity. And the repercussion is bound to be that some British author will retaliate by getting at you,

Monty warned.

> I think Aides should be forbidden to write books about their Generals. I suppose there is nothing we can do to stop it all,

he concluded.[1] He had in fact made his own personal aides promise not to write anything after the war—much as the British Royal family demanded of their personal staff.

There can be little doubt, however, that Monty was pained by Butcher's 'rear-headquarters' account, and that, far from trying to 'stop it all', Monty now determined to see that British authors got the facts right. The Australian war correspondent Alan Moorehead was currently writing a biography of Monty. Monty had hitherto denied him access to his wartime papers, but after reading the extracts of Butcher's book, he authorized Moorehead to examine his files, as he did the British war correspondent Chester Wilmot, who began that spring a scholarly reconstruction of the North-West Europe campaign. Eisenhower himself claimed to be mortified by Butcher's account, remarking that although his mutual correspondence with Monty revealed 'certain differences of conviction', these were nevertheless 'honest and so far as I know have never been seen by anyone except myself and my own confidential secretaries (who I know have not revealed any secrets).'[2] This, and Eisenhower's claim to have 'repudiated any connection with the so-called [Butcher] "diary"',[3] were signs of wishful thinking. Eisenhower had *himself* ordered Butcher to keep such a diary from November 1942 onwards, and most of Monty's signals and correspondence were filed or copied into this diary, which Eisenhower

[1] Letter of 28.1.46, Eisenhower Papers, loc. cit.
[2] Letter of 12.2.46, loc. cit.
[3] Ibid.

regularly checked and added to with his own occasional memoranda (later published separately as *The Eisenhower Diaries*[1]). Moreover Eisenhower had not sought to impose any confidentiality on his staff—and Butcher's rear-headquarters revelations were soon followed by those of Eisenhower's chauffeur and later personal assistant, Kay Summersby.[2]

The strains of inter-Allied co-operation, so long subdued in common effort against a common enemy, were of course bound to surface in the aftermath of war—and Monty was being naïve in imagining that such expressions of partisanship could or should be muted. Moreover, in terms of geo-political post-war change, it was inevitable that American writers should reflect their nation's new status as superpower, just as jingoistic British writers had done during the heyday of British imperialism. In this respect Americans *had* to be given their head, regardless of the truth. It was something which, as a child of the fading British Empire, Monty was loth to accept, yet which, as British Military Governor of Germany and CIGS-elect, he understood very well. Thus Monty pointed out, in paper after paper for the War Office, the Foreign Office and leaders of the Commonwealth nations, that continued American military presence in Europe was *essential* to the peaceful revival of the non-Communist nations. To Eisenhower he signalled, thanking him for his congratulatory telegram, on 19 February 1946: 'There is no man from whom I would sooner have such warm congratulations than from yourself. I hope that you and I will have many opportunities of close co-operation in the future and indeed I feel that the whole future of the world may well depend on the closest co-operation between our two countries.'[3]

This was not mere rhetoric. If Monty was politically naïve and often blinkered in his approach to political problems, his soldier's vision was honest, direct and refreshingly clear. As his first deputy in Germany later remarked, Monty's clarity was an immense boon to his staff:

> In those early days, when we were struggling with the setting up of the Control Commission, and trying to make bricks without straw, I would take him [Monty] some complicated paper on finance or economics. Whilst he would profess ignorance on the question involved, he had the happy knack of reducing even these complicated subjects to a few paragraphs in his own handwriting, which

[1] Ed. R. Ferrell, New York 1981.

[2] K. Summersby, *Eisenhower Was My Boss*, London 1949.

[3] Eisenhower Papers, loc. cit.

were a godsend to his Chief of Staff, who, with his many activities, could not always see the wood for the trees.[1]

From the summer of 1945 Monty had seen the approaching 'drift' of America away from Europe, much as the USA had isolated itself after World War One—and whatever Monty's human and political limitations, his recognition of this danger and his work to counter it—particularly in the framework of his relationship with Eisenhower—were to be of incalculable historical importance. As had been the case during World War II, so thereafter Europe would remain the primary battleground of the world. If peace could be safeguarded in Europe, then the problems of the rest of the world could be tackled with confidence, however difficult they might prove—and on this basic premise Monty built the foundations of his post-war philosophy. At Brooke's CIGS's conference at Camberley on 8 October 1945 Monty had forecast a British Army of Occupation in Germany 'for at least 10, and possibly 20 years. The War Office must now plan the structure and organisation of the Army required. . . . The Field Army should normally be kept in and trained in Germany, where the cost would be borne by the Germans, and where training facilities were magnificent.'[2] Meanwhile German militarism must be smashed by breaking up the entire German military machine, and concentrating on re-educating the nation. Kiel, Hamburg and Göttingen universities had already been re-opened, as well as schools.[3] Elected local representative councils had been started, and

[1] Lord Weeks, BBC Home Service broadcast of 24.9.58, 'Montgomery of Alamein'.
[2] Accompanying letter to Sir Arthur Street, Permanent Secretary, Control Office, of 19.12.45, in appendix to 'Notes on the Occupation of Germany', loc. cit.
[3] As Sir Robert Birley, Educational Adviser to the British Military Governor of Germany, later recalled: 'I sometimes think that perhaps the most important step in the history of Education in the British Zone was Field-Marshal Montgomery's order, not long after the end of the war, that in future no schools were to be taken over by the Army or the Control Commission,' thus ensuring that German school and university education could be resumed without hindrance from British service units using educational premises for headquarters or barracks: R. Birley, 'British Policy in Retrospect' in *The British in Germany*, op. cit. In fact *all* German educational establishments in the British Zone re-opened in the autumn of 1945, following Monty's radio broadcast and printed 'Personal Message to the population of the British Zone in Germany' on 24 August 1945: 'Schools in some parts are already re-opening and more will re-open in the next month or so. By 1st October all available schools (except Nazi ones) should be functioning again. . . .

'My long-term aim is that, through a happy school life, German boys and girls should grow into worthy citizens of Germany and the world. Their independence of mind must make them secure against false doctrines of force and tyranny. . . . I shall impose on you no foreign principles of education nor methods of teaching. You will be free to experiment, to try out new ideas. My officers will help you. But I shall

German courts had begun to function again. Germany, at least in its Western mantle, was being reborn, beginning at the taproots, and though the credit for this must rightly go to the men 'on the ground' who inspired and executed such a unique historical refounding of a liberal nation, Monty's own role as the paternalistic leader ought not to be forgotten in chronicling West Germany's post-war resurrection.

Increasingly, however, Monty's eyes were turning towards his future role as CIGS. The 'Battle of the Winter' in Germany was, he felt, being won. At his insistence workers in vital sectors such as coal mining had been given increased rations (as in Belgium the winter before); production had soared; and though the problems remained frightening in their severity and complexity, there was growing confidence that the country *would* survive its hardships—lack of food, housing, fuel, the social problems of so many refugees and displaced persons—without falling prey to the evils of mythological saviours in the shape of Nazism or Communism. 'Self-help' had been instilled as the Allied order of the day—the occupying armies transforming themselves with responsibility and dexterity from conquerors into cousins.

Critics of Montgomery would later claim that he was a general who, by virtue of his prickly personality, could only perform in war. While it cannot be denied that Monty's generalship was uniquely suited to war, his military governorship of Germany was without doubt the least 'sung' and yet, in many ways, the most successful of all Monty's campaigns. Under his personal leadership, administering the most populous and industrialized zone of Germany, seeds were sown that later resulted in the world's most astonishing industrial revival within a free and liberal society. As he had before D-Day, Monty made it a feature of his generalship to tour his forces, both military and political, officers and other ranks. His austerity enabled him to concentrate upon his tasks, to preserve himself in good health, and above all to plan ahead. Far from abandoning his system of personal Liaison Officers, Monty used them now to continue to report on developments and morale throughout the British Zone, and to keep him informed of events and thinking in the French and American Zones. Though he was politically naïve with regard to

---

tolerate no return to Nazism, militarism, or aggression in any form.

'You German fathers and mothers must do your part to win back your children to a saner life. I shall help you. You must help me. That is my order': 'C-in-C's Message to the German People (No. 4)' of 21.8.45 (ISC/31899 in 'Messages to the Germans' file), Montgomery Papers.

what was possible or impossible for politicians to undertake, he sought the best advice from men of the highest calibre, but would never accept their views unless he saw in them common sense. When, for instance, his Control Commission staff produced a paper, beautifully set out, which damned French proposals for a French-controlled Rhineland and an internationalized Ruhr, Monty was quick to point out the fallacies in his *own* staff's thinking. Their proposal for an Army of Occupation in Germany for fifty years seemed, in the current political situation, unrealistic, since it was unlikely that all the Allied nations would be prepared to garrison Germany for 'so long a period'—a time span, which might, moreover, even be 'insufficient' if the Russians retained their Iron Curtain. By advancing the French, Belgian and Dutch borders to the Rhine, Monty countered (as he already had done in person to Attlee), there would be no need for garrison armies in Germany, since the Rhine river would provide the best defensive obstacle in Europe to halt either future German or Russian expansion: 'I therefore recommend that the RHINELAND should be handed over to FRANCE, BELGIUM and HOLLAND for permanent occupation and annexation . . . I do not, however, suggest that the RUHR should be detached from GERMANY politically or economically . . . I make my recommendations for the sake of military security in Western Europe. I recognize that there are many arguments valid on economical and political grounds, against my proposals. I am forwarding the attached paper [by British Control Commission staff] in order that these arguments may be before you,' Monty wrote to the Permanent Secretary of the Control Office in London, 'but I consider that, in the conclusions drawn from them, military security is sacrificed to obtain economic advantage. I should never agree to this.'[1]

In the light of history, with French, Dutch and Belgian occupying forces withdrawn but vast Anglo-American garrisons including strategic and tactical nuclear weapons having to be stationed in an indefensible West Germany, Monty's own view made simple, common sense. 'If the Germans in the annexed [Rhineland] territory were given freedom and prosperity,' Monty argued, there was 'no reason why they should be discontented.' It was a view the Labour Government under Clement Attlee and Ernest Bevin, the Foreign Secretary, declined to take seriously. Shrugging, Monty meanwhile prepared himself for his next challenge.

[1] Ibid.

CHAPTER FOURTEEN

A Peculiar Friendship

ON 11 JANUARY 1946, returning from a successful Control Commission meeting in Berlin—at which he had obtained agreement from Marshal Zhukov to a much higher German steel production capacity than Stalin had wished[1]—Monty fell ill. Though the King had ordered him to fly as Special Ambassador to Brazil for the inauguration of the new President, Monty was soon in hospital, and the trip was cancelled.

As in the aftermath of World War I, Asian 'flu had struck the European nations with particular severity, and Monty remained in hospital for eight days, his doctors anxious lest he contract pneumonia or complications of the right lung which had never fully recovered from his 1914 war wounds. Patton had died of a large pulmonary embolism, following a car crash on 21 December 1945, and the hospital staff were taking no chances.

On 2 February 1946, Monty left in his special train ('Lion') for a recuperative holiday in Switzerland, first at Saanen Moeser, then Gstaad, near the spot where he had holidayed before the war as an unknown British colonel. Now, by contrast, he travelled as the undisputed military hero of the Second World War, the British Military Governor of Germany, and the head of the British Army-elect. Newspapermen and photographers pursued him; the President of Switzerland invited him to dine in Berne; the Swiss Army carried out special mountain manoeuvres for him. Like an emperor, he had only to point to something—a Swiss watch, say—and it was presented to him. He admired the long white sheepskin coats worn by the Swiss mountain troops: one was immediately procured and despatched to him by the head of the Swiss Army. He was a celebrity, and like most celebrities, he basked contentedly in his fame—though occasionally allowing his stranger, maverick streak to prevail—as when he sent one of his Liaison Officers to Switzerland prior to his Swiss vacation:

[1] German steel capacity, though agreed at an actual output of 5.8 million tons before reparations, was given a ceiling of 7.5 million tons 'should that become necessary': letter to Sir Brian Robertson of 23.1.46, in appendix to 'Notes on the Occupation of Germany', loc. cit.

> What happened was: Monty saw in the Ski Club of Great Britain Journal

Carol Mather later recalled,

> a photograph of his ski boots in a glass cabinet in a hotel in Lenk, Switzerland. And there was a label beside them marked quite clearly: 'Colonel B. L. Montgomery.'
>
> 'Carol,' he said. 'My boots. I want you to go to Lenk and get them back.'![1]

The hotelier was shocked when a Liaison Officer arrived to reclaim Field-Marshal Montgomery's property after almost ten years' safe-keeping; but once Monty's mind was made up, Mather knew, nothing would dissuade him. The glass case was opened; the boots went back.

There were, indeed, many who thought Monty was becoming too big for such boots—that his succession of campaign histories and printed lectures on the war and on high command were marks of an excessive egoism, drawing to itself much of the praise rightly due to others. Even those, like King George VI and his Private Secretary Sir Alan Lascelles, who had the most intimate knowledge of Monty's thinking, were suspicious of Monty's world-wide popularity and the rough-shod way he hogged the limelight—as was demonstrated when he announced publicly that he had been invited to Canada in the spring of 1946. The King's Private Secretary was concerned—as he wrote to the CIGS:

> I should be very grateful for your help in the following matter, if you feel able to give it.
>
> As you know Alex goes to Canada in March to take up his duties as Governor General. Monty has announced in the newspapers that he proposes to visit Canada, presumably as a private individual, in the early summer. Whatever the character of his visit he will inevitably attract large crowds wherever he goes and will make a number of speeches to Canadian clubs, Universities, etc.
>
> It has been represented to me by several people who know Canada well, that such a visit from his brother Field-Marshal will be somewhat unfair to Alex, who will be barely settled in the saddle, and who will certainly not have had time to visit many parts of Canada outside Ottawa.
>
> I agree with this view. I dare say the visit would not do any serious damage, but, in this early stage of his career as G.G. it

[1] Carol Mather, interview of 14.11.84.

would be a bit of an embarrassment to Alex, and I think he ought to be protected from it.[1]

That men like Alexander needed 'protection' from Monty indicated the amazing difference in their public esteem, especially abroad. Brooke bided his time until he next saw Monty—on the day de Guingand was dropped as VCIGS-elect—noting in his diary:

> Monty came at 11 A.M. and I had a long talk with him, stopping him from going to Canada at same time as Alex takes over, drilling into him how he is to behave if he is to take over as C.I.G.S. etc.[2]

Thereafter Brooke wrote to Lascelles that Monty would now postpone his trip until the autumn. Monty himself was chagrined at the notion he had upset the King; he also wrote to Lascelles, insisting that 'the invitation to Canada came to me from the Canadian Government via [the Prime Minister] McKenzie King. They asked me to go in the Spring, in May. The Press got hold of it (as they do of everything!) and it appeared in the newspapers. I always thought it rather curious myself. But I have now written to McKenzie King and have said that it would be a bad thing to have two Field-Marshals gadding about at the same time and that I would prefer not to come until Alex was firmly in the saddle. I feel sure he will agree. I am delighted that you raised the question.'[3]

Monty was speaking the truth—for Mackenzie King's handwritten invitation is preserved among Monty's papers.[4] But Monty had failed to check with the Dominion Office whether the trip's timing was suitable, and had made no effort to conceal it from the Press. Certainly it caused others to question Monty's motives and character—the retiring Governor-General, Lord Athlone, writing to Lascelles to confirm that 'many here think it would be a mistake for Monty to come out so soon after the arrival of Alex so that no doubt your advice to him may meet with success. When he comes I wonder whether as Field Marshal he will receive 19 guns?' he added sarcastically.[5]

[1] Letter of 19.12.45, Alanbrooke Papers, loc. cit.
[2] Alanbrooke Diary, entry of 3.1.45, Alanbrooke Papers, loc. cit.
[3] Letter of 3.1.46 (RA GVI/PS 6988), Royal Archives, Windsor.
[4] 'I was glad, too, to have the opportunity to extending to you, in the presence of Mr and Mrs Salisbury, the invitation of my colleagues to you to visit Canada in the Spring—in May or June. . . . The Canadian people will look forward to this visit': letter of 28.10.45. 'We are all greatly looking forward to your visit to Canada in The New Year,' McKenzie King again signalled on Christmas Day 1945: 'Letters 1945–1946' file, Montgomery Papers.
[5] Letter of 9.1.46 (extract) (RA GVI/PS 6988), Royal Archives, Windsor.

Such doubts were understandable. Few if any British warriors since Nelson had aroused such intense adulation, both in England and abroad. Both men were marked by their supreme self-confidence and arrogance in war. It was Nelson who had ordered the signal 'Nelson expects that every man will do his duty' at the commencement of the Battle of Trafalgar—amended to 'England expects . . .'. Both men were also similarly naïve—Nelson expressing in his will the innocent hope that England would honour and reward his mistress! This view of his country's debt found a revealing parallel a century and a half later, for shortly after the defeat of Japan and the conclusion of World War II, the King's Private Secretary had written to Monty suggesting that this time there should be *no* state grants to the military leaders like those given after World War I. Monty had agreed. 'But there is one aspect of the matter which is worthy of consideration,' Monty had declared:

> I have always imagined that the reason for the grants of money was to ensure that those who deserved well of their country should have the means to live decently in their later years, and should not live in poverty. For this reason I think the capital was never handed over; the recipient had only the income.
>
> My own case is as follows:
>
> I am a poor man. I have no money of my own. All my belongings have been destroyed during this war by enemy bombing—i.e. my furniture, silver, plate, linen, china, glass, books, clothes, etc. etc. Every single thing I possess has gone; it was all stored in a big depository at Portsmouth and was lost in a bombing attack on that city in January 1941. I have no home; even if I had a house I have nothing to put in it. I have nowhere which my stepsons and my own boy can come to, and call 'home'. I make my temporary war home with friends, but that cannot go on for ever. I am now beginning to realise what I lack; it is a place I can call 'home'. I cannot afford to buy and equip a house; I am faced with living in hotels or with friends. I must honestly confess that I look forward to the future, and the 'evening of life', with some concern.
>
> If therefore I were asked if I would accept a large grant of money, I would say no. Instead I would say: 'Could you give me a small house and equip it with what is necessary so that I can have a home. Quite a small house; 7 or 8 bedrooms would be ample, and it need not be a gift, it could be only for my lifetime. I would not ask it as a gift which I could leave for my descendants.'[1]

Such humble supplication, with its schoolboy pathos, was extraordin-

[1] Letter of 12.9.45 (RA GVI 283), Royal Archives, Windsor.

ary coming from the undoubted 'hero' of the Second World War, at the very height of his fame. Monty was of course well aware that this fame would be a passport to riches if he consented, like Patton, Eisenhower and Bradley, to write his war memoirs, based on his diaries:

> Many people have said to me that I could easily make the money to buy what I want, by writing. That is very true; I have had many offers; the last one was from America and guaranteed me half a million dollars. But I could not do this; it would not be right. It would stir up too much 'mud'; my inside knowledge of the war must never be published.
>
> In any case I do not want to have to resort to that sort of thing.
>
> Nor do I want to go into the City and take up Directorships and so on.
>
> I feel I can continue to serve my country for some years yet; and after that I can lend a hand in many ways. I was very nearly 'written off' the other day in an air crash, but I managed to survive.
>
> But I do terribly want a home for my lifetime. I hope I have made myself clear.[1]

Lascelles responded frostily. The war had been won; no longer was the King soliciting invitations to Monty's Tactical Headquarters in the field, now that his Imperial throne had been made secure. By contrast, with the future of his empire and even the monarchy itself looking shaky, the palace was wary of being tainted by accusations of feudal patronage. Monty's request was refused. Churchill, Brooke and Montgomery would all have to obtain funds for their old age by the power of the pen.

Such ingratitude abashed Monty. It was, in a way, the story of his relationship with his mother Maud Montgomery all over again—years of neglect followed by reluctant general recognition; but never the personal acceptance he so craved.

Brooke, too, was chagrined by the failure of the government or monarchy to reward him for his services. The barony he was awarded in the victory awards of August 1945 disappointed him—'when you look at some of the other Barons and Viscounts etc. one wonders whether it really is such an honour and a distinction. . . . We [the Chiefs of Staff] then discussed the cost of becoming a Baron, apparently I can't get out of it under £200 which appals me,' he noted in his diary.[2] Forced to sell his lifetime's collection of ornithological

[1] Ibid.

[2] Alanbrooke Diary, entries of 14 and 28.8.45, Alanbrooke Papers, loc. cit.

books and to take city directorships to survive, Brooke was understandably bitter at the unfairness with which the state looked after its most deserving servants. The idle and charming Alexander had been given the Governorship of Canada which Brooke coveted, and had performed no duties between the summers of 1945 and 1946. On 19 March 1946 both men went to the Mansion House to receive the Freedom of the City of London, followed by a grand banquet. Though 'very interested in the whole ceremony', it was Brooke's companion-in-honour whom Brooke studied most closely:

> I went over in my mind the whole sequence of events in Alexander's career during the war,

he noted in his diary that night.

> His wonderful charm on the one side and his wonderful luck on the other.
>
> Could it all be luck? If not, where were the qualities of the real leader? I had never found them during the whole war,

Brooke remarked, puncturing the Alexander myth.

> A man with great personal courage, great confidence in himself and even greater lack of any power to fully appreciate or even understand a strategic problem!!
>
> I cannot help being fond of him and admiring him and fully realize that he possesses the most attractive qualities. That being said I consider that fortune has favoured him more, yes, far more than any other leader that I know.
>
> Bluntly and shortly a most attractive small and very ordinary man on whom fortune has thrown the mantle of a great man which he wears with some dignity and evidently complete ignorance of his lack of qualities to justify him to it,

he concluded.[1] Lest this damnation smack of sour grapes, Brooke asked himself, in his diary, if there was 'any jealousy in this appreciation of him? I do not think so,' he answered. 'I am too fond of him for that. He is,' Brooke summarized at his most scathing, 'a mirror, with a most attractive frame, reflecting other human beings, but "who" and "where" is Alex?'[2]

Homeless, widowed, charged with the thankless rôle of ruling a defeated German nation which had caused the deaths of countless millions of innocent people, Monty could never be said to have comported himself with 'dignity', as did the vacuous Alexander. As

[1] Alanbrooke Diary, entry of 19.3.46, loc. cit.

[2] Ibid.

the Princesse de Mérode had noted, he was not an *homme du monde*—indeed he was the most unlikely figure to excite so much adulation and to lead twentieth-century armies into battle. His simple heart had genuinely hoped his King might help. Rejected, Monty began to seek friendship and emotional outlet in the most unlikely places. Spurned by his King, paranoically suspicious of his own family—particularly his own mother—Monty sought now to create a mythical family out of the British Army—and to recreate a mythically affectionate childhood by forming romantic friendships with young boys.

The first of these friendships began in Saanen Moeser in February 1946. The boy was twelve-year-old Lucien Trueb, who was holidaying there with his parents and who engaged Monty's affectionate attention.[1] When he wrote to Monty, sending a box of Swiss chocolates, Monty responded with an invitation to Gstaad, where he had moved into a luxury private chalet;[2] and the strangest of platonic 'romances' began. In return for battle photographs of the victorious British commander 'taken in Germany before the war ended',[3] young Lucien sent photos of his father's château. 'Your house looks lovely,' Monty thanked him. 'I will gladly come and visit you there on my next visit to Switzerland. I cannot come this time as I leave in my train from Berne on the night of 23 Feb: for Germany. I hope you will write to me from time to time and tell me how you are getting on, and how your English is progressing. . . . If you can get to Berne on the afternoon of 23 Feb I shall be very glad to see you. I feel that we are now very good friends. With my love,' Monty signed himself, 'Yrs sincerely / Montgomery of Alamein / Field-Marshal.'[4]

Trueb came—and the following day Monty wrote from his headquarters with new photographs, taken in Berne and printed instantly. 'I did so enjoy seeing you at the British Legation in Berne yesterday. We had never actually met before. Now we have and have become real friends. My love to you my little friend'—and signed himself again 'Montgomery of Alamein/Field-Marshal'.[5]

[1] Trueb later recalled how, as an innocent admirer of the British Field-Marshal, he had approached him on skis and exchanged a few words. A Press photographer had seen the encounter and a picture of the British Field-Marshal with his 'young Swiss friend' was soon in the Swiss newspapers: '*Erinnerungen an* "Monty"', *Neue Zürcher Zeitung*, 10/11.4.76.

[2] 'On 7 Feb we moved into a chalet which has been lent me; it is complete with servants etc, and is the acme of comfort; the owners are very rich people': letter to Phyllis Reynolds, 10.2.46, Montgomery Papers.

[3] Letter of 14.2.46, Trueb Papers.

[4] Letter of 21.2.46, Trueb Papers.

[5] Letter of 24.2.46, loc. cit.

Anxious lest there be any misunderstanding with Trueb's parents, Monty wrote to Lucien's father a few days later:

> Dear Mr Trueb
>
> I feel I ought to write to you regarding the friendship that has grown up between Lucien and myself.
>
> I am devoted to children and Lucien reminds me of my favourite brother,

Monty explained:

> the youngest of our family, who died when 12 years old. The likeness is very remarkable; and when I met Lucien in Berne I saw at once the same delightful character.
>
> So Lucien and I have become great friends. I love the little chap and I have told him he must write to me every month and tell me all his news.
>
> I should much like to pay you a visit at Chateau d'Hauterive next time I come to Switzerland; this will be in January or February 1947, if I can manage it.
>
> And if there is anything I can do for Lucien [to] help him as he grows up, you must not hesitate to let me know.
>
> With kind regards.
> Yrs sincerely
> Montgomery of Alamein
> Field-Marshal[1]

For Monty there was nothing embarrassing or shameful in feeling a growing affection for the young Swiss boy. But to those who witnessed the romance, there was something pitiful about Monty's yearning to share feelings of affection with a twelve-year-old boy who could barely write English. Thus, from his isolated castle near Hanover, Monty commenced the strangest of correspondences.

'It must be difficult for you to write English,' Monty wrote a few weeks later,

> and it means you have to get someone to translate.
>
> I would like you to write to me in French; I can read French quite well, and you can write more naturally and say things in your own way.
>
> I had a good journey back to Berlin; I send you a photo taken in the train. I also send you some photos showing my schloss in Germany; it is a lovely house with a big park and we have swans on the lake. . . .

[1] Letter of 27.2.46, loc. cit.

I am making my plans to come to Switzerland in February next; I shall go to Gstaad.

I want you to come and stay with me there in the chalet for a week. Ask your parents if they will let you do this. It will be great fun and I shall love to have you with me.

I do not know how that will fit in with your school holidays; but perhaps you could get special leave. . . .

My very best love to you, my little friend.

Yours sincerely
Montgomery of Alamein
Field-Marshal[1]

As Lucien Trueb later remarked,[2] nothing improper was ever to take place. Yet there was little doubt—as his letters over the succeeding months demonstrated—that Monty was infatuated. He soon signed himself 'Your very loving big friend'[3]—adding 'Je vous aime beaucoup: tres beaucoup'.[4] This in turn became 'Yr very devoted Papa' as Monty played doting father to the thirteen-year-old. Switzerland was of course associated with the happiest romance of Monty's life, when courting his beloved Betty; in befriending a young Swiss boy, impressing him with bemedalled battle-blouse and war photos, Monty was giving rein to that same yearning for someone with whom he could share feelings of love. Lucien would love him as a substitute father, a figure of power and authority in the outside world but who bent down like Gulliver to pluck him from the crowd and confer favours upon him; he, on the other hand, would love Lucien as the image of his adored youngest brother, graced with beauty and innocence: an image of a 'beautiful' childhood that Monty had never enjoyed, having been cast as the awkward, unwanted, black sheep of his family. The years of dedication to soldiering had brought laurels such as Monty could scarcely have dreamed possible when a boy; but emotionally his had been an arid, stunted life with its one blade of genuine domestic happiness savagely cut down. Thus the two sides of Monty's strange personality—the cold, merciless pursuer of professional excellence and the simple, emotionally retarded adult—moved in tandem. Just as Monty's ancestor, the great Vicomte Montgomerie d'Exmes, had dispossessed his Norman rivals and yet ended his life in the rough habit of an

[1] Letter of 12.3.46, loc. cit.

[2] Letter to author of 16.1.84. See also 'Monty's Little Swiss Friend' by Dr Trueb in *Monty at Close Quarters*, ed. T. E. B. Howarth, London 1985.

[3] Letter of 4.8.46, Trueb Papers.

[4] Letter of 23.9.46, loc. cit.

English monk, so now Monty planned the greatest shake-up of the British Army since the time of Cromwell while writing simple love-letters to a Swiss 'son'.

> I like the photo very much, and it stands in my bedroom next to the clock,

Monty would write a few days after his enthronement as CIGS;

> I then see you when I wake up. . . .
>
> Goodbye my little friend. I think often of you and you have all my love.
>
> Montgomery of Alamein
> Votre grand ami.[1]

[1] Letter of 6.5.46. Ibid.

CHAPTER FIFTEEN

Leaving Ceremony

ALTHOUGH MONTY'S 'SUCCESSION' as CIGS was only to take effect at the end of June 1946, Monty had not been slow to throw his weight around. He had claimed that the Army was to be his family, to whom he owed his first loyalty; but this did not mean accepting the family as he found it.

The first warning shot Monty fired was an official letter to the War Office in which he made clear that all British officers who had not seen active service in World War II were, in his view, 'suspect'. Such officers—as well as those old enough to have seen service in World War I—ought, Monty felt, to be swept into retirement in order to promote talented younger officers. In proposing this, he wished to avoid the fatal block in promotion that had bedevilled the Allied armies after World War I; but such damocletian threats were bound to raise hackles in Whitehall—where almost the entire staff of the War Office would be 'suspect'.

Apart from the one act of dropping de Guingand as prospective VCIGS, Monty did nothing to allay fears in the War Office. Indeed, on 10 February 1946 he wrote to 'Kit' Dawnay that, unless the War Office found him a London 'Tactical Headquarters' home, there was going to be trouble:

> The housing problem is going to be awkward as C.I.G.S. I have told the War Office I want to have a C.I.G.S.'s Mess in London: which they must take, and get the Office of Works to furnish it. I am told that the first reactions in the War Office was that there was no precedent for it and it could'nt [sic] be done!!
>
> We shall see.[1]

More important than his own accommodation, however, was the state of the Army. As his diarist recorded, Monty had been 'chafing at the way in which pressure of events [foreign problems, demobilization and the recovery of industry] had forced delay in the preparation of the army of the future. . . .' He felt that changes at the top and the promulgation of a clear policy for the Army were six months overdue; it was therefore very important that he should formu-

[1] Papers of Lt-Colonel C. P. Dawnay.

late his policy and prepare the way so that no further time should be lost when he took up his office as CIGS. 'The Army must not, as after World War I, be allowed to drift aimlessly without a doctrine and without control.'[1]

Each further month waiting in the wings had sharpened Monty's determination to shake up the British Army. Both in 1914 and 1939 it had been unprepared for a major land campaign on the continent of Europe. This time there was to be no such lack of preparation for Britain's international role: for it was Monty's amibition to restore to a post-war British army the professionalism of Marlborough and Wellington—an army that could be sent overseas and confront any enemy, anywhere; a new 'Model Army' on the lines of Cromwell: efficient, compact, well-generalled, with dedicated professional officers and men. However dismally Monty might fail as CIGS, this vision of Britain's post-war Army, despite the problems of running down an empire and safeguarding the security of Europe, would gradually be achieved; and while British industry and commerce often failed to meet the challenges of the post-war world in competitiveness, marketing and productivity, Monty's 'Model Army' would in time emerge the most successful and professional army of any major liberal power. While the armed forces of France and America would both meet their nemesis in Vietnam, with the French Army subsequently racked by political revolt over Algeria and the US Army riddled by drug abuse and poor morale, Monty's 'New Model Army' would go on not only to police a shrinking empire, but to remain solidly apolitical and professionally competent, ensuring the successful British withdrawals from the Far East, India, Malaya, Singapore, Kenya, Uganda and the Middle East without loss of morale—as well as keeping a small but potent army in Germany, keeping order in strife-torn Northern Ireland and even mounting the recapture of the Falkland Islands 8,000 miles from Britain.

Maverick, at times almost childishly insecure and naïve, determined never again to marry and without a house to call his home, there was something pathetic, and yet noble, about Monty's self-isolation and high ideals. God had given him the gift of lucidity, the ability to assess any situation and instantly reduce it to its essentials. This talent he had nurtured and developed throughout the years from 1914, disciplining himself always to look forward, and by mental and physical rehearsal to be prepared for the exactions of the future: a future which now entailed command of his nation's Army.

Returning from Gstaad to his Tactical Headquarters on 24 Feb-

[1] Diary of F.M. The Viscount Montgomery of Alamein, 1.5.46–20.9.46, Montgomery Papers.

ruary 1946 Monty's eyes were no longer directed on his charges in Germany, but on the men he would be commanding from Whitehall. He had, symbolically, given away Rommel's white victory stallion which his troops had captured in Germany;[1] he had used the period of his convalescence to write a paper on the 'Problem in Germany' as it would affect his successor;[2] and he had, in an exchange of telegrams with the War Office, laid down the structure of command in Germany as he would like to see it under that successor.[3] But who should that successor be?

Here Monty gave way to a disturbing streak that would mar his remaining Army career: namely, an increasing vindictiveness towards those whom he did not respect, as well as a growing anxiousness not to share the stage, or even leave it to other actors who might, given good lines, detract from the impact Monty had just made. Thus, on hearing that Brooke wished to appoint Sir Richard McCreery as Monty's successor in Germany, Monty went all out to defeat the proposal, just as he had destroyed McCreery's chance of becoming VCIGS. McCreery was a cavalryman; he had, after Oliver Leese, inherited the mantle of Eighth Army Commander in Italy and had become British C-in-C in Austria; but he was known to be less than servile in his regard for Monty, and Monty disliked the idea of McCreery yet again stepping into his shoes—especially when, as British C-in-C and Control Commissioner in Germany, McCreery would be in overall command of the largest battle contingent of the British Army.

At Monty's insistence, therefore, an airman was thus appointed to succeed him: Air-Marshal Sir Sholto Douglas, who had already left Germany as C-in-C, Air, at the end of 1945. Douglas did not want the post, and twice refused it. Monty's will, however, prevailed. Typically, Monty telephoned to congratulate Douglas, and invited himself to Douglas's London flat the following morning. Douglas was an admirer of Monty and did not dare refuse, though he considered breakfast 'a time of day that I have never recognized as human':

[1] The stallion was given to King George VI, as a final tribute by the men of 21st Army Group (now the BAOR) to their monarch. When Churchill read in the *Illustrated London News* that the stallion was to be led through the streets of London in the Victory Parade of 1946, however, he objected to the King. 'Naturally I was rather upset by the idea of this poor creature being led in triumph through the streets': Letter of 6.6.46 (RA GVI/PS 6988), Royal Archives, Windsor. 'Rommel' did not take part in the parade.

[2] 'Memorandum by Field-Marshal Montgomery. The problem in Germany: February 1946', 10 pp., in appendix to 'Notes on the Occupation of Germany', loc. cit.

[3] Signal 1292 of 20.1.46, in appendix to 'Notes on the Occupation of Germany', loc. cit.

> My wife made preparations for it; but when Monty arrived he had already had breakfast, and he wanted to get down without further delay to a serious discussion.
>
> For an hour and a half, Montgomery lectured me in his high-spirited way about what I should do in the work that lay ahead for me. One of the biggest problems, he stressed, was still that of food, for the Germans were then receiving only one third of what we were having in Britain under our own rationing scheme, and that was not exactly plentiful. There were innumerable problems, and as Monty went on talking about them I was forced to accept a prospect that was even grimmer than I had anticipated,

Douglas later recollected.[1]

Leaving Sholto Douglas to mull over his 'formidable' forthcoming task, Monty meanwhile travelled in April to Belgium and Normandy, where—appropriate to the name of his special train—he was lionized. 'Whole villages turned out to welcome the Field-Marshal and the roads were lined with cheering crowds wherever he went,' his diarist recorded.[2] In England he again addressed the Cabinet on the situation in Germany, received the Freedom of Edinburgh, of Dover and of Hastings and finally, back at his headquarters in Germany on 27 April 1946, recorded his farewell broadcast to the British Army of the Rhine, which was to be transmitted on the day of his departure to England, 2 May 1946.

> 1. I am leaving Germany today,

it began,

> and I feel I would like to say a special word to the soldiers of the Rhine Army: with whom I have had such close connections in the past years. In fact there are many of you who were with me in the Eighth Army and then returned to England to join me in 21 Army Group.
>
> 2. At such a time as this I cannot fail to look back and feel proud to have commanded this great Army, the like of which our country can never before have put in the field. I shall never forget with what heroism it went ashore on the beaches of Normandy in June 1944, with what fortitude it fought its way out of the beachhead and up through France, Belgium and Holland, and with what determination it struggled through the winter months of 1944/45 until the final victory was won in May 1945. It was eleven months of triumphs and disappoint-

[1] Douglas of Kirtleside, *Years of Command*, London 1966.
[2] 'Notes on the Occupation of Germany', loc. cit.

ments, of sorrows and glorious deeds. Such experiences bound us together the more closely, and made us realise how dependent we all were on each other.

3. We then had to begin governing our zone in Germany through Military Government, in which the Army had a large part to play. It was no easy task to turn from the ravages of war to the problems of occupying the country of our enemy. But it was done in such a way that I can justly say the Army has been a fine example to the Germans of the ideals for which we fought. During this time I have not been able to see as much of you as I should have wished. I have had to spend much time on the innumerable problems which face the Control Commission; I have constantly had to visit Berlin and London; and in January last I got ill and had to take a rest.
4. And now, at this time when many of you are returning to your homes for which you have had to wait all too long, it is only natural that those left behind should begin to feel restless. Your job may seem unspectacular and dull, but I hope you realise its importance towards the future peace of the world. I know how anxious many of you are to have your families out here in Germany; I wish it could be done at once, but just at present the general situation is such that it cannot be managed.
5. And now I am leaving you to prepare myself for my next post, that of Chief of the Imperial General Staff. In that appointment it will be my job to watch over the interests of all soldiers. This I shall do to the best of my ability, and thereby I shall be able to keep in touch with you all. I feel I have a great debt towards all British soldiers and I shall take every opportunity of repaying it in any way I can.

   Good luck to you all in the years to come.[1]

There can be no doubt that Monty wrote this farewell address with his hand upon his heart. It was not always, as those close to him knew, an easy heart to fathom.

On 28 April Monty flew to Berlin to attend his last Allied Control Council meeting in Berlin. That night he gave a dinner party for the Leaders of the British Control Commission Divisions. The following day, 29 April, he lunched with Sir William Strang, his Political Adviser, before the Control Council meeting, and dined with Sir Brian Robertson, his Deputy.

All seemed full of bonhomie. Nevertheless, early the next morning,

[1] In appendix to 'Notes on the Occupation of Germany', loc. cit.

30 April 1946, Monty departed without waiting to hand over officially—or even privately—to his successor, Sir Sholto Douglas. To add injury to insult, Monty's 'Special Memorandum' on the German situation, drawn up the following day at Schloss Ostenwalde, was never shown to Sholto Douglas—who only learned of the document twelve years later when reading Monty's *Memoirs*![1] Shown only to Mr Attlee, the Prime Minister, and circulated to the Cabinet, the memorandum would, Douglas felt, 'have provided an excellent basis for a fuller briefing on the work that was expected of me. . . . After so many years, any comment that I might make must be much more in sorrow than in anger; but it does seem to me that it was an extraordinary state of affairs that such a vitally important document should have been handed around in London while the man who was most intimately concerned—the man who was literally on the spot in taking over from Montgomery—should have been left so much in the dark.'[2]

For Monty it was the first such handover since the night of 30 December 1943, when Sir Oliver Leese arrived to take command of Eighth Army in Italy. Then, too, Monty's eyes had been upon his future role, and his half-hour session with Leese of the most perfunctory kind. General Sir John Hackett, in his penetrating study of military history, *The Profession of Arms*, illustrated how, even in the autumn of 1943, Monty's eyes had been on command of the cross-Channel invasion, and how he had produced consternation when asked, in front of a group of Eighth Army soldiers in Italy, who would command Eighth Army after his departure: 'Eighth Army? Anyone can have Eighth Army.' 'Does this sound brutal?' Hackett asked. 'Perhaps it does, but it also illustrates a main characteristic of military leadership. I think of it as the principle of total engagement . . . when the time comes for him to leave [his command] he extracts himself completely—to engage himself totally in whatever he is put to next. People can be hurt here,' Hackett noted.[3] There can be no doubt that Monty's successor, Sholto Douglas, was one of them, and he was not alone.

Whatever Monty might say to de Guingand about his reluctance to go to the War Office, Monty '*wanted* to be CIGS,' Monty's MA Major Terry Coverdale recalled. 'That was the culmination after all, wasn't it? CIGS was the top military post—the pinnacle of the career—and if you are career-minded you don't want to stop short

[1] Douglas of Kirtleside, *Years of Command*, op. cit.

[2] In fact Monty's 'Notes' differed very little from Monty's Memorandum 'The Problem in Germany: February 1946' which was issued to all senior members of the Control Commission staff as well as the three Corps District Commanders.

[3] *The Profession of Arms*, London 1983.

of the pinnacle, do you? He'd never served in the War Office, he wasn't in touch with the sort of machinery that works in Whitehall, but that didn't matter to him.'[1] The son of David Montgomery's guardians, Major Tom Reynolds, also recalled Monty's sense of challenge in going to Whitehall: 'I remember him saying at dinner just before he became CIGS, he said, "We've won the war, but the biggest battle is going to be the winning of the peace. I hope to be able to use my influence at the War Office to get the Army organized so that we have a chance of winning that peace." '[2]

For about a year Monty had been considering the sort of 'shake-up' he wanted in the British army, as Coverdale explained.

> I could give you a paper that Monty wrote on the reorganisation of the Army that he intended to institute when he got to the War Office. He wrote this in Germany before he went there. And the whole reorganisation of the army was based on this paper that he produced *before* he went to the War Office. He had very clear-cut ideas.
>
> But then, of course, his ideas weren't acceptable in many cases to a Labour Government.[3]

Possibly it was Monty's awareness of the enormity of the challenge and of his own ambition to succeed where others had failed which made him insensitive to certain corns on which he now trod. Brooke, who had managed to control the worst of Churchill's excesses and ensure a coherent British strategy from November 1941, was certainly clear about the difficulties facing a post-war CIGS. 'It is high time I retired!' Brooke declared with exasperation in his diary on 24 April 1946. 'I no longer have any patience left in me to deal with Secretary of States who are totally unfit for the post they hold and Dominion Prime Ministers with mentalities limited to the normal horizon of a Whitehall charwoman.'[4] To Monty Brooke confessed, in a letter of 29 April, that he had 'seldom felt more cooked in all my life'; however he was sure that Monty would cope: 'Never once in the whole 6 years of this war did you give me the slightest occasion to doubt your ability to grapple with the task given to you. . . . You will I know find certain difficulties when you take on this job, but I have the same confidence that I have had on each occasion that you have been moved up to a new and more difficult appoint[ment].'[5]

[1] Major Terry Coverdale, interview of 19.3.78.
[2] Major Tom Reynolds, interview of 19.3.78.
[3] Major Terry Coverdale, loc. cit. Monty's 'Notes on the Post-War Army' were dated October 1945.
[4] Alanbrooke Diary, entry of 24.4.1946, loc. cit.
[5] Montgomery Papers.

Whether Monty would be able to master the military problems posed by the running-down of the largest empire in human history remained to be seen. He had triumphed as an Army Commander in the field, then as an Army Group Commander. As an Occupation Zone commander he had provided clear leadership to a brilliant team of administrators as well as loyal occupation forces. Even jealous minds at home were impressed by the clarity and grasp he evinced in addressing the Cabinet. But would his strange, quirky personality cope with the demands of the job of CIGS, after so many gruelling years of war at the top? Even those closest to him were unsure—among them his Military Assistant.

A regular soldier, Major Terence Coverdale had originally served under Monty as a subaltern, in 9th Infantry Brigade in Portsmouth before the war, then in 3rd (Iron) Division from 1939 to the evacuation from Dunkirk in 1940, and again in Home Forces. Like Dawnay before him, Coverdale had been devoted to his C-in-C—the 'Chief'—and had served on his staff in Germany since April 1945. Monty had in fact recommended that Sholto Douglas take on Coverdale as his own Military Assistant; Coverdale was thus to remain behind in Berlin when Monty left on the morning of 30 April 1946. As he later recalled:

> We were in Berlin and the rule was, Monty always sat in the back of the car by himself. He never had anyone in the back of the car, ever. This was the rule. He had an ADC in the front, and that was it.
>
> Our house was way outside the city, near Gatow airfield. Noël Chevasse was ADC at that time, and Noël said, 'Look, Terry, I'm not ordering another car from Berlin, it's only two miles down the road to Gatow. You sit in the back of the car with the Chief and I'll sit in the front and we'll put the luggage in the jeep.'
>
> I said, 'Sounds sensible,' and that's what we did.
>
> So I got in the car, in the back, and Monty said, 'What are you doing?'
>
> 'Oh,' I said, 'Sir, I didn't think it was necessary to order a car all the way from Berlin to come out here to take me to the airfield.'
>
> He said, 'You know my rules, don't you?'
>
> He never spoke to me again [during the car journey],

Coverdale recounted, his voice becoming dry and quiet.

> And he left Gatow. Never said goodbye, never thanked me.

That was it. And I never said another word to him till—I don't know when. I'd broken the rules. I knew damned well I'd broken the rules. And he didn't like it.

Most extraordinary. . . . He was a most extraordinary man.[1]

[1] Major Terry Coverdale, loc. cit.

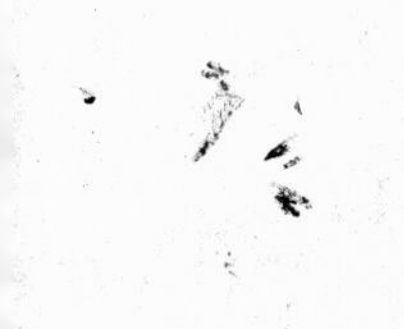

PART NINE

The New Model Army

CHAPTER ONE

Getting the Strategic Picture

Monty's original intention had been to spend two months resting before taking up his post as CIGS.

> My present idea is to leave Germany on 1st May and have all May and June in England: on leave and resting quietly at Hindhead. I feel that unless I have a quiet May and June before taking on the job of C.I.G.S., I shall probably go mad.[1]

As the time drew nearer, however, Monty grew anxious about Britain's overseas commitments. Hitherto he had seen himself as a sort of long-awaited Messiah, coming to cleanse the British military temple—indeed in April 1946 he had already submitted his twelve-page draft paper on the 'Problem of the Post-War Army' to the ex-Secretary of State for War, Sir James Grigg, for his comments. 'It gives a plan which we might try and achieve in say 10 years time,' he wrote in his covering letter, indicating the ambitiousness of his proposals. Conditions of service, morale, the structure of the army, promotion, training, formulation of tactical and inter-service doctrine—all were drawn together into Monty's prospective bible. 'Above all, we must all work to a definite plan which everyone understands,' Monty insisted.[2] That he saw himself in the same role as he had performed after Dunkirk, only writ large to include the entire British Army, was evident; but it was unfortunate that he brooked no one senior enough in his entourage to suggest that he was being too ambitious.

On 18 March 1946 he received a signal from the Chiefs of Staff in London informing him that 'drastic cuts below the figures on which we have been planning hitherto' had been ordered by the Labour government.[3] The effect of this on Britain's world-wide commitment was likely to be significant, Monty realized. He thus decided he would have to visit the Mediterranean and Middle East before taking up his mantle as CIGS. 'I want the tour to be really valuable and would like it to include Greece, Palestine, Egypt, Sudan and East Africa,'

[1] Letter to Phyllis Reynolds, 10.2.46, Montgomery Papers.

[2] Letter of 3.4.46, P. J. Grigg Papers, Churchill College Archives, Cambridge.

[3] Chiefs of Staff signal 092894 of 1640 hrs, 18.3.46, Montgomery Papers.

he cabled Brooke. 'I leave Germany on 3 May and must spend that month in England as I have some important engagements and also want a little leave.' He therefore suggested he start his overseas tour on 2 June and return by 20 June 'so as to have one free week before I come to the War Office on 26 June'.[1] This would necessitate his absence from the great Victory Parade planned for 8 June 1946, and Monty duly requested permission not to be present.[2] As in August 1944 when asked to accompany Eisenhower on his triumphal entry into Paris, Monty felt he had more important tasks in hand. Perhaps, too, he did not wish to have to share the limelight, preferring those occasions, such as the march-past of 7th Armoured Division in Tripoli in February 1943 and again in Berlin in July 1945: ceremonies where *his* troops marched, men of whom Monty was justly proud and whose very turnout testified to Monty's leadership. Brooke, however, refused the request, fearing that Monty's absence would make nonsense of the event—Monty being the man who, with Churchill, was most associated in the public mind with victory in World War II. Monty was thus forced to attend, though excusing himself from the fireworks display in the evening as he wished to retire early to bed, prior to his departure the following morning for the Mediterranean.

Brooke wept during the Parade. As he himself confessed, he was 'cooked', and had spent the whole month of May on leave, fishing in Scotland and birdwatching. For Monty there was no such rest. 'I had brought my caravans back from Germany,' he later recorded, 'and parked them in the grounds [of Amesbury School]. I was supposed to be on leave, but I soon realised that no rest was possible; there was too much to be done. I worked all day and every day, in my office caravan.'[3]

Tirelessly Monty sent out his preparatory missives: to the other two Chiefs of Staff (Air-Marshal Tedder and Admiral Sir John Cunningham) in order to get their approval for the text of his statement on Combined Service strategy and tactics in his 'Problem of the Post-War Army' draft; to the Secretary of State for permission to publish his 'Normandy to the Baltic' and 'Alamein to the Sangro' campaign narratives commercially in order to counter the spate of 'books and articles containing much indiscreet matter and much misinformed criticism';[4] to the Military Secretary on the continuing

[1] Signal M1321, 27.3.46, Montgomery Papers.

[2] Ibid.

[3] B. L. Montgomery, *Memoirs*, London 1958.

[4] Letter to Principal Under Secretary, War Office, M601, 6.5.46, Montgomery Papers.

failure of the War Office to get rid of 'dead wood' among senior officers. 'At present the Army is the wrong shape,' he declared with characteristic frankness. 'It should be a pyramid, properly proportioned, with good senior officers at the top and the base of the pyramid being all subalterns. But today it resembles a snake that has swallowed a sheep whole, and there is a great bulge about halfway down its stomach.'

This bulge was causing a shortage of younger officers, since 'they won't come forward to accept commissions, or take short service commissions, so long as the bulge remains undigested or until it is got rid of'. Without such junior officers, paradoxically, the Adjutant General's branch was forced to declare a shortage of officers, and the Army Council to state that 'no one can retire'.

> We are riding for a fall; we must get rid of the bulge; we must open the door wider for retirement,

he warned. 'Indifferent' officers 'should be got rid of'. Oliver Leese, commanding Eastern District, had given Monty the names of four sub-District Commanders (county or area commanders) who were 'quite useless. I am convinced the whole future of the Army depends on a happy and contented corps of officers. We will not have this until we get the pyramid the right shape: see para. 2.'[1]

Monty was nearing sixty. The missionary zeal, the concern with soldiers' welfare, the unremitting application of his logical and straightforward military brain, were the same as they had been since the end of World War I. Had Brooke only recognized this, and had he recommended to Attlee that Monty be appointed Commander-in-Chief of the British Army, reserving the post of CIGS for a man with greater experience of Whitehall—such as General Nye-then the sorrier side of Monty's stewardship of the British Army between 1946 and 1948 might well have been muted. Exhausted and depressed by the future—he was forced to sell his home to raise money for retirement—Brooke handed over everything to Monty: even his War Office flat in Westminster Gardens. And Monty, zealous, irrepressible and even dangerous in his innocence about politics and diplomacy, rushed foolishly in, determined to be the C-in-C towards whom all soldiers looked for leadership, as well as a Chief of Staff capable of clarifying and directing Britain's military strategy. Though his new diarist might extol his efforts on his tour of the Middle East—extended to cover India—as 'an enormous success', the journey resolved nothing. It merely deluded Monty into believing he was a latter-day Alexander the Great, able to step into any situation

[1] Ibid.

and impose order on chaos. Thus in Egypt he overrode General Paget's grave reservations about military withdrawal, believing innocently that British bases in Palestine and Libya would be sufficient to safeguard Western oil interests and provide a strategic springboard to the re-invasion of the Continent in the event of Russian advance. Such logic failed to take into account Attlee's fundamental wish to divest Britain as soon as possible of all overseas commitments, the better to concentrate on British welfare at home. Brooke had fought against such a sudden, myopic attitude, but it was a losing struggle and Monty wholly lacked Brooke's ability to weld the Chiefs of Staff Committee together in opposition to such abandonment of British bases.

Like Wavell and Mountbatten, Monty favoured self-determination and independence on the part of liberated colonies. At the same time he saw clearly the need to safeguard the world's maritime routes, and in particular the oil of the Middle East, upon which post-war European recovery depended. To do this, he argued, a British presence in the Eastern Mediterranean was essential. But where? Monty's choice of Palestine was, given the civil war now raging between Jews and Arabs, unwise, since the British Mandate was due to terminate in 1948. Within months, Monty would have cause to regret his rashness in assuring the Egyptian king that Britain was committed to immediate withdrawal—indeed as soon as his plane landed in Damascus Monty recognized the parlous state of Palestine, with a High Commissioner incapable of the moral and military firmness necessary to restore order in the country. Sir Alan Cunningham had been sacked by Auchinleck for his lack of determination in the field; and his performance as High Commissioner in Palestine revealed the same weakness. Monty was 'perturbed by what he heard and saw', as his diarist noted. 'He was firmly convinced that General Cunningham was not the man to be High Commissioner in these troublous times. He appeared to be quite unable to make up his mind what to do and was pathetically anxious to avoid a showdown. This indecision on the part of the High Commissioner had led to a state of affairs in which British rule existed only in name, the true rulers being the Jews whose unspoken slogan was "You dare not touch us".'

Monty's response was identical to that which he had himself carried out in 1938/9 as the divisional commander for Northern Palestine.

> The Field Marshal very clearly emphasized to Generals Paget and Barker [GOC Palestine] that they must set about indoctrinating

> the troops in Palestine with a proper understanding of the task that lay ahead of them. All ranks must understand that they were in for a very unpleasant job: the first task was a political one, namely to re-establish British authority; this would mean that the Army would have to strike a real blow against the Jews by arresting the heads of the illegal Jewish armed organisations and those members of the Jewish agency known to be collaborating with the Hagana; this would lead to war against the Jews: a war against a fanatical and cunning enemy who would use the weapons of kidnap, murder and sabotage: women would fight against us as well as men: no one would know who was friend and who was foe. All this demanded a drastic revision of the way of life of the serviceman in Palestine: social activities would have to cease; the fullest precautions would have to be taken and all ranks would have to be 100% prepared to enter into this unpleasant task with the fullest determination to finish it off with 100% success in the shortest possible time.[1]

Monty was not yet CIGS—he was in fact in the same limbo in which he had found himself on return from Palestine in 1939, and again before taking command of Eighth Army in August 1942. Neither then nor now did this worry Monty: there was no time to lose, and he ordered Paget and Barker to begin carrying out his policy as though he had already assumed Brooke's mantle. Though he subsequently bullied the Cabinet and Secretary of State for the Colonies into accepting his measures to restore order in Palestine, Monty failed to understand that in tackling the Jews he was declaring war on those Jewish Americans urging the President to increase Jewish admission to Palestine—particularly in the wake of the recent Anglo–American Committee Report which, to Brooke's chagrin, had recommended that a *further* 100,000 Jews be permitted entry into Palestine, with all the consequent Arab unrest this would entail.

Brooke himself had not been able to do more than stonewall in the face of American naïveté over Palestine—as over India, too. Liberal minds in the West were quick to see Britain as an imperial oppressor, stifling the legitimate national aspirations of local peoples: whereas both Brooke and Monty saw the problem as soldiers—keeping the peace, and safeguarding sufficient base installations to protect the world's highways in time of war or of threat to vital natural resources. Monty's first question to the President of the

[1] Diary of Field-Marshal The Viscount Montgomery of Alamein, Parts I and II (1.5–20.9.46), Montgomery Papers.

Indian Congress, when invited by Wavell to extend his trip as far as India, was 'whether he supported the popular demand for the withdrawal of British troops. Azad said that he did,' Monty's diarist recorded, 'at which the Field Marshal expressed his delight and, briefly referring to the other demands on British Army manpower, asked Azad if he would agree to their *immediate* withdrawal. Azad was horrified at this request and replied, "No, no. Not for a long time."'[1]

Though prospects of an all-India settlement looked, at that moment, relatively hopeful, Monty spent many hours with Wavell, the Viceroy, and in meetings with the various Indian leaders. Jinnah, the Muslim League chairman, told him that Hindu rule over Muslims would never be tolerated and that 'civil war was inevitable if British troops were withdrawn'. Though Auchinleck assured Monty, as C-in-C of the Indian Army, that he could count on the collective loyalty of Sikh, Muslim and Hindu troops, Monty was 'not easy in his mind', and decided to 'go for the appointment of a "Major-General, British Troops" at GHQ India as soon as the Indian Government came into power'.[2]

Wavell, beset by the interminable attempts to get Hindu and Muslim leaders to co-operate with one another in a provisional government at least, was impressed by Monty's appearance—'refreshingly vital, self-confident and shrewdly egotistical'.[3]

The meetings between Wavell and Monty were of considerable interest. Wavell had been Monty's commanding officer in 1937–38, and had held command in North Africa and the Mediterranean, until replaced by Auchinleck in 1941. A year later Auchinleck was replaced—both men being shunted to India—and both were still in command, as Viceroy and C-in-C, in 1946.

Auchinleck clearly resented Monty's appearance—as he had done in 1942: 'As C-in-C, India and War Member of the Viceroy's Council, he [Auchinleck] was in a position of tremendous power and authority. It was quite clear that he was very conscious of his position and was jealous of it, all of which was reflected in his attitude towards Field Marshal Montgomery during the discussions,' Monty's diarist described.[4] As a result, instead of asking Monty for more British troops in order to preserve order in India during the transition to Independence, Auchinleck refused to admit he had any need of Monty's help, save a brigade from Palestine to protect ports and

[1] Ibid.
[2] Ibid.
[3] Wavell, *The Viceroy's Journal*, ed. P. Moon, London 1973.
[4] Diary, Parts I and II, loc. cit.

base installations in the event of civil war.

Wavell, as Viceroy, could have overruled Auchinleck in this respect. He was a man Monty admired almost as much as he did Brooke: a man of granite-like integrity, a thinker and poet, the most intellectual of British generals, but chronically shy, a poor speaker and incapable of dominating his political masters. Instead, he retreated into himself when crossed by lesser men, contenting himself with diary-writing or like a lonely Moghul prince, with his beloved poetry, leaving Auchinleck to command the British and Indian troops, and the Indian leaders to play havoc with visiting British politicians. So British India lurched towards her nemesis.

Monty meanwhile flew back to England via Greece—where he knocked firmly on the head the current fear of imminent Russian-backed war. The British would withdraw before the end of the year; but no external aggression was likely as long as internal order was maintained. The Greek Army must therefore be trained and prepared for take-over 'in the shortest possible time'—with PT 'compulsory for the senior ranks', Monty joked at a dinner with the Greek C-in-C.[1]

In Italy there was the same local fear of Russian-backed *coup d'état* and possibly invasion; again Monty dismissed the idea, declaring that he 'did not believe that Tito would receive Russian backing to such an extent as to allow him to pull off or even attempt a coup in Venezia Giulia'; he was of the firm conviction that there was no 'danger of an outbreak of war at present'.[2] The Russians, he felt sure, would remain satisfied with a war of nerves, but as long as the British kept their nerve, despite the current abandonment of Europe by the Americans, all would be well.

Such strategic realism and infectious confidence were greatly to Monty's credit; but the 'success' of the tour, in which Monty had thrown a great deal of as yet unofficial weight around, sadly inflamed his burgeoning ambition to wield power in every direction—he who had always criticized Eisenhower for descending from his 'lofty perch' and attempting to combine Supreme Command with battlefield captaincy. Thus, even before assuming the post of CIGS, Monty had laid down the framework of the new British Army he wished to create, as well as giving orders for British military policy in the Mediterranean. There remained, on his return, the matter of the Chiefs of Staff Committee—the body which, under Brooke's great mantle, had turned defeat into victory in World War II. All his life Monty had distrusted and avoided

[1] Ibid.
[2] Ibid.

committees. It was not long before the sparks flew, and the unity of Britain's three services, so hard won during six years of struggle, was sundered.

CHAPTER TWO

Caught in a Spell of Hatred

MONTY WAS SO certain his first tour abroad had 'proved an enormous success' that he 'therefore decided that he will in future spend two months in his office followed by one month on tour'.[1] On this basis he planned visits to Canada and USA in September 1946, the Middle East, India and Singapore in December, the same again in March 1947, Australia and New Zealand in July 1947, West Africa and South Africa in November 1947.

This new ambition—to be a missionary CIGS as well as responsible for the shake-up of Whitehall and the Army at home—was viewed with much suspicion by politicians and civil servants (who foresaw Monty meddling in Foreign Office affairs) as well as by Monty's new colleagues on the Chiefs of Staff Committee, chaired by Air-Marshal Lord Tedder. Tedder and the First Sea Lord, Sir John Cunningham, however, had approved Monty's 'broad tactical doctrine' on which the post-war Army was to base its organization, training and operational approach. 'I have managed to get the Navy and RAF and Imperial Defence College to agree on the principles of war, strategy, and so on as set out by me in the [enclosed] book,' Monty wrote with satisfaction to the King's Private Secretary, Sir Alan Lascelles. 'Therefore there will be no argument about it; this book will be the Army teaching in broad outline. Within that framework we will argue and discuss tactical doctrines and will evolve in broad outline a tactical doctrine for the army as regards offence. . . . I remember so well in 1919 that this was never done; every commander evolved his own doctrine. When you changed your general you changed your doctrines; the result was chaos. I always determined in those days that we must do better next time. Hence the conference [for all generals of the British Army and the Chiefs of General Staff of all dominion countries] next month, dates 14–17 August.'[2]

Meanwhile, on 6 August 1946, Monty addressed all the main editors of the British Press[3]—as well as giving a series of widely-

[1] Diary, Parts I and II, loc. cit.

[2] Letter of 24.7.46, Royal Archives, Windsor.

[3] Monty had in fact cleared the notes for his meeting with the Prime Minister, but a letter was soon published in *The Times* questioning the 'constitutional propriety of the CIGS holding a Press Conference'.

reported speeches 'in praise of the British soldier' when receiving further Freedoms.

In theory no incoming CIGS could have done more to begin his reign with a clear concept of what he hoped to achieve, having taken great pains to prepare himself in advance, and with a concern to enlist the support of all. His popularity exceeded now even that of the ousted Churchill as the 'hero' of the war, and people still queued to catch sight of him. Sir Robert Bruce-Lockhart, ex-Director of the Political Warfare Executive, complained he had 'some difficulty in getting through the London crowd for Montgomery's Freedom of the City performance' on 18 July.[1] But when Monty made it increasingly plain that he wished not only to be a crusading CIGS on behalf of the Army, but wished also to usurp Tedder's role as Chairman of the Chiefs of Staff Committee (which met twice a week to review current British defence and inter-service problems), the inter-service harmony created by Brooke collapsed. Tedder in particular resented Monty's unilateral response, over the August Bank holiday, when both Tedder and Cunningham were out of London, to the matter of illegal Jewish refugees attempting to enter Palestine. 'The publicity given to the Press Conference held by CIGS on 6th August' fanned the first sparks of discord, and 'there was a flare up on 13th August', Monty's diarist acknowledged,[2] when Monty seemingly deliberately failed to attend a Chiefs of Staff meeting.

Monty had in fact intended to be present at the Chiefs of Staff conference that afternoon. Instead, he sent his VCIGS, General Simpson. 'When CIGS did not arrive at the meeting both CAS and First Sea Lord were hopping mad and were extremely hostile to VCIGS. The latter said that he had never attended such an unpleasant COS meeting.'[3]

Though peace was restored when Tedder and Cunningham attended Monty's Exercise 'Evolution' the following day at Camberley—and were invited to speak—the signs were ominous. 'Relations became for a time pretty severely strained,' Monty's diarist chronicled. 'On the surface harmony had now been restored, but it is doubtful if all jealousy has gone and CIGS will have to handle his colleagues (particularly CAS) with care and delicacy if he is to keep things running smoothly in the future.'[4]

Monty undoubtedly *meant* to be more careful: but his was not the sort of character capable of dissimulation or the monumental

[1] *The Diaries of Sir Robert Bruce-Lockhart*, entry of 18.7.46, London 1980.
[2] Diary, Parts I and II, loc. cit.
[3] Ibid.
[4] Ibid.

and austere patience of Brooke. Knowing that Tedder had intrigued to get him sacked in Normandy did not help. Furthermore, as the Director of Plans, Brigadier Poett, later observed:

> The other Chiefs of Staff, they resented Monty. That was part of the trouble, that they resented Monty very much indeed because Monty had been built up as a great national figure, whereas these other Chiefs of Staff. . . . Tedder, who'd been No. 2 at SHAEF, but was barely known outside the RAF—you asked most people who is the RAF Chief, they couldn't tell you; and John Cunningham nobody had ever heard of.
>
> Whereas Monty, not only was he, had he become a public figure but he damned well saw that he remained a public figure! There was no funny business about that! [1]

With such bubbling antipathy, Poett now found, the very protocol of the Chiefs of Staff meetings had to be altered.

> In the days when Brookie was in the chair, the Director of Plans went into every Chief of Staff meeting and stayed the whole way through.
>
> As soon as Brookie left, or fairly soon after, it became obvious to all the three Chiefs of Staff that it was not a good practical proposition—because the rows became so very considerable; because quite frankly they all three of them disliked each other very much indeed.
>
> Monty couldn't stand Tedder, had declared war on Tedder at an earlier stage. John Cunningham was very clever, and Monty didn't like his style of cleverness, didn't like him at all. John Cunningham didn't like Monty, Tedder didn't like Monty so it was not a very happy organization—with Cunningham and Tedder ganging up on Monty.
>
> I'm sure if it hadn't been for Simbo [Simpson], wheels wouldn't have gone around at all. The wheels went round in a rusty fashion with the Chiefs of Staff Committee, but never very smoothly, because Monty didn't agree with the whole thing anyway. He didn't agree that all these things should be decided by a meeting where everybody gives their views. He liked the command structure. He wanted a chap who'd say: This is how it's going to be!
>
> But that's not how the Chiefs of Staff Committee sought to work. They all wanted to give their views and generally wanted to win their point—because it was at a period when each service was still struggling for the goodies. And so you can imagine, the friction

[1] General Sir Nigel Poett, interview of 8.11.84.

was very great. And we were then not allowed in the Chiefs of Staff Committee, we sat in the ante-room, and only went in when called to give the Director of Plans' papers—but after that we were pushed back into the ante-room and there we waited, giving our views on what the Chiefs of Staff had said, and what we thought of them![1]

Not even Monty's most loyal subordinates were impressed by Monty's failure in this respect. General Kirkman, denied the post of Deputy Military Governor of Germany by Churchill at the end of the war, had moved to the War Office as DCIGS after commanding 1 British Corps in the Ruhr for eight months. Kirkman's recollection of Monty's performance in Whitehall was laconic:

Then Monty arrived.

Now Monty thought he was still Commander-in-Chief. Of course he wasn't. He did, to my mind, lots of foolish things. He would lay down a paper. This is how the Army of the future should be organised—not having taken political advice—just as if he was still commanding Germany. And he wasn't really terribly good as CIGS. That's what it comes to.[2]

General Dudley Ward, who became Monty's Director of Military Operations, felt the same:

Monty's great gift was his reasoning—that was the thing; a marvellous capacity, through the whole time I knew him, of penetrating straight through the fluff, seeing what were the essentials, and stating them: 'Therefore that is what we will do.'

And of course when he got into Whitehall, it isn't like that. It's a very foggy and confused area.

I would say that wasn't his great field. It wasn't—the very gift of simplification of all issues, which was the thing that had got him such marvellous unified support through enormous forces during the war—because everybody knew what they were up to, it being so clearly said—was and isn't an advantage when dealing with politicians![3]

Monty was certainly an oversimplifier, and disliked the fudged compromises of politics; but his failure in Whitehall was much more a failure to get on with his fellow Chiefs of Staff than with politicians. Even the owlish Brooke had failed to foresee this problem, which

[1] Ibid.
[2] General Sir Sidney Kirkman, interview of 16.4.80.
[3] General Sir Dudley Ward, interview of 22.7.78.

was primarily one of personality. 'He was not a negotiator really, it wasn't his strength,' General Sir Dudley Ward later remarked.[1] Monty had tried—as was frankly admitted in his own diary—to dominate the COS Committee from the start:

> Resulting from the first hand knowledge which he had acquired on this trip, the CIGS was able to speak with great authority on at least the most important problems of the day with which the Chiefs had to deal during this period. This personal knowledge and authority soon enabled the CIGS to impress his personality on the Committee as a whole and he began to emerge as the unofficial leader—the C.A.S. [Chief of Air Staff] being the Chairman and official head of the Committee. This leadership was also reflected in the Chiefs of Staff dealings with the Defence Committee and with the Cabinet.[2]

Monty was, however, deluding himself and his diarist. Far from accepting Monty's 'unofficial' leadership, Tedder and Cunningham were *incensed* at Monty's brazenness and egoism. Monty blamed Tedder for his spinelessness and quickly became converted to the idea of a single Chief of Staff of the Armed Services—whereas it was his own failure to see the need for a united and amicable Committee of the three Chiefs of Staff that was the problem, in an age of manpower rundown and a fragmenting post-war world. As Sir George Mallaby, Secretary of the Joint Planning Staff of the three services, and link-man between the JPS and COS Committee, later put it, there had been, despite the strong personalities of Brooke, Portal and Andrew Cunningham, 'a determination to achieve a unity of view' in the Chiefs of Staff Committee—if only successfully to counter the pressure of the Minister of Defence, Churchill. But 'when Monty succeeded Brooke as CIGS in 1946, the achievement of unified aims and harmonious co-operation became impossible; and the main reason for this was that Monty was not in the habit of listening to anybody except his own closest personal advisers. He was not interested in what Tedder thought and hardly disguised his contempt for the somewhat melancholy interventions of Cunningham. As for the Joint Planning Staff, they were just a pack of fools, whose reports should be completely ignored—a prejudiced opinion which did not, however, prevent him from occasionally announcing their conclusions as his own. That was just the trouble. It was he who must develop the arguments, he must reach the conclusions and make the decisions. He must have all the credit for himself and the power

[1] Ibid.

[2] Diary, Parts I and II, loc. cit.

and the glory were not to be shared with anybody else. He could not work in any other way. He knew instinctively that it was no good telling soldiers that he was transmitting to them decisions which had been reached in a committee, that the decisions had been agreed by other equal Powers; that was no good, that would lead to a loss of confidence. The soldiers had faith in him, because they thought he made the decisions and, if they had thought otherwise, their confidence would have waned and disappeared.'[1]

As Mallaby noted, 'in the conditions of war his attitude was unquestionably right, but in Whitehall in peacetime it was disastrous. I can see the ill-starred Chiefs of Staff Committee now, sitting in what had been the Prime Minister's map room just inside the Storey's Gate entrance to the then Ministry of Defence, Tedder in the Chair, Cunningham on his right and Monty on his left, all three of them caught in a sort of spell of hatred and spite which they could not break.'

Mallaby blamed Monty. 'It was Monty's doing, of course. He hated the whole machine. He detested committees and, as it happened, he detested Tedder, a feeling fully reciprocated. He did not want the machine to work.'[2]

Without doubt this was the case; however, such verdicts were reached many years afterwards, and tend to telescope events—particularly the breakdown of the Chiefs of Staff Committee. As the VCIGS, General Sir Frank Simpson, recalled, it was not simply Monty's manner to which the other Chiefs of Staff objected: it was, by virtue of his Mediterranean and Indian tour, Monty's undisguised command of the facts and situation which threw them.[3] Both Tedder and Cunningham saw themselves largely in a defensive role, batting against national and international pressures, as filtered through the Cabinet and Minister of Defence; whereas Monty, by contrast, arrived fit and healthy, and ready for a good innings with plenty of fours and sixes to be hit. Indeed, as Simpson recalled, Monty refused to appear at the Chiefs of Staff Committee meetings during his first week as CIGS, since he was exhausted from the punishing tour to India and back. When he did appear at his first meeting, on Monday 1 July 1946, he dealt with the issues of evacuation to the Nile Delta in Egypt, the run-down of Army personnel in Austria, and the problem of illegal immigration into Palestine (where Monty favoured deflection of the refugee boats to Cyprus) with considerable decisiveness. Two days later he dealt with the problem of possible riots

[1] G. Mallaby, *Each in His Office*, London 1972.
[2] Ibid.
[3] General Sir Frank Simpson, Eugene Wason interview for Sir Denis Hamilton.

in Germany over reduced rations with the same aplomb—having dictated the course of action to be taken in this event before leaving the British zone. When the First Sea Lord showed anxiety about the need to cut down Naval forces in the Indian Ocean where India wished to retain as many ships as possible against 'some imagined attack from some quarters', Monty pointed out that he had discussed this with Wavell and Auchinleck and there would be 'no difficulty whatever in the Navy making what cuts it needed'.[1] Finally, in a third meeting that week, the matter of the Persian oilfields was discussed. Monty, once again, told his collegues that the subject had already been dealt with—that he had arranged for an Indian brigade to be stationed in the Basra-Shiber area to watch the oilfields, while a brigade from Egypt was standing ready for air transport to the area in the meantime. 'Monty said that had all been arranged when he was in Egypt [i.e. before formally becoming CIGS],' Simpson recalled. 'That got the CAS on the raw at once, CAS said that while he agreed a brigade could be got ready in Egypt, he would not like to commit himself to finding the aircraft to fly it.' When Tedder looked into the matter, he found Monty was right: the local air commander had already been alerted to the possibility, and 'was quite prepared to do what the army wanted'.[2]

The problem, then, was not that Monty did not understand world strategy as Brooke had done, but that his quick grasp of essentials and decisiveness were anathema to his fellow Chiefs of Staff and, subsequently, to politicians and civil servants. He liked to foresee problems, and to act in good time to meet them: preventive medicine. Like the shake-up of the Army, he felt he was bringing a new broom into Whitehall and the *modus operandi* of the Chiefs of Staff. But the brush was too stiff, and the result was counter-productive. Instead of being welcomed as a breath of fresh air, very soon he found himself loathed. And the more he was right, the more loathed he became.

[1] Ibid.
[2] Ibid.

CHAPTER THREE

Spelling Out the Future

THROUGHOUT THE SPRING of 1946, Monty had corresponded with Eisenhower, the new American Chief of Staff of the Army, with regard to a trip to Washington. Although King George VI had successfully squashed Monty's plans to visit Canada in the spring or early summer in order to protect Alexander from Monty's limelight-seeking, Monty's *real* reason for wishing to accept Mackenzie King's invitation was the chance to visit the United States as well. As Monty cabled to Eisenhower in February: 'Hope that you and I will have many opportunities of close cooperation in the future and indeed I feel that the whole future of the world may well depend on the closest cooperation between our two countries. I have been invited by Mackenzie King to visit Canada next September and I think it would be very suitable if I could pay you a short visit in Washington on my way home. Such a visit to you would give me the very greatest pleasure and there are many things we could discuss.'[1]

This appeal was sent a fortnight after Winston Churchill's celebrated Fulton speech—a speech which, as British Foreign Secretary Bevin's biographer remarked, caused 'consternation in Whitehall'.[2] *Pravda* claimed that Churchill was calling for 'war against the Soviet Union' and resented his apt phrase regarding the 'Iron Curtain' that had fallen across Europe from Lübeck to the Middle East. Whatever Labour Party idealists might proclaim, the volte-face by the US Foreign Secretary that spring and the gathering realization in Washington that the United States had to be firmer in their attitude to the Russians, did result in a Russian climb-down. Russian mobilization on Iran's border was cancelled, Russian troops withdrew from the country, Russian claims on Azerbaijan were withdrawn, and Russia appeared at the Paris Peace Conference soft-pedalling its insistence the previous year on the exclusion of France. Trieste was made a ward of court under the United Nations, Russia dropped its claims on Cyrenaica, and in July 1946 the USSR was exposed by Bevin for its hypocrisy in calling for British withdrawal from Greece.

[1] Signal of 19.2.46, 'Montgomery' file, Eisenhower Papers, 1652 series, Eisenhower Library, Abilene, Kansas.

[2] A. Bullock, *Ernest Bevin, Foreign Secretary*, London 1983.

Allied innocence in the aftermath of Potsdam was being replaced by a gradual recognition that under the guise of anti-imperialism, Russia was intent on extending her sphere of military, political and economic influence in the most flagrantly imperial manner throughout Europe, into the Mediterranean and the Middle East. Britain could not hope to combat this development on her own—and Bevin soon became a reluctant disciple of Churchill, though pilloried by his own left wing in the Labour Party.

Monty was anxious to match Churchill's political initiative by a military one. Eisenhower responded with alacrity to Monty's cable with an invitation to Washington in September for a week. 'In September I go to Canada (two weeks) and the United States (one week). The latter is at IKE's special request,' Monty informed de Guingand[1]—as if to prove his relationship with Eisenhower was not one-sided.

Whether Eisenhower understood the reason for Monty's self-invitation, however, is another matter—for a few weeks later he was inviting Zhukov to Washington as well. To those who knew Eisenhower, it was clear that he still retained the very hopes of American-Russian accord which had led him to surrender the prize of Berlin the year before; and by promoting good-will visits between the military emissaries of the major powers, he hoped to promote peace.

Monty, too, was all for good will; but his motives in wishing to see Eisenhower went much deeper. Like Churchill, Monty felt the Russians would only respond to strength, and if the peace of the Western World was to be safeguarded in the difficult economic post-war conditions, there must not be a power-vacuum resulting from a helpless Britain, a still hapless France, a recalcitrant America—and a Russia intent on exploiting the weakness and unrest to its own advantage. His presence on the Control Commission meetings in Berlin until May 1946 had made it quite clear to him—as to General Clay, the Deputy US Control Commissioner—that the Russians would never agree to withdraw from East Germany, nor were they interested in a unified, independent Germany. Moreover, Monty's tour of the Mediterranean and Middle East, as well as his first months as CIGS in the COS Committee, the Defence Committee and at Cabinet meetings convinced him that, although Russia was not willing to risk outright war for her aims, she would take advantage of every rift and crack in relations between the Western Allies in order to further her cause. As a soldier he felt the only answer was to marshal one's strength and show unity of defensive purpose. He was therefore

[1] Letter of 14.4.46, de Guingand Papers, Imperial War Museum.

mortified by the divergence of opinion over approach and method in the British Cabinet and Defence Committee meetings—as his VCIGS later recalled:

> In those days the Chiefs of Staff used to go to most of the Cabinet meetings because topics concerning the armed services kept cropping up. . . .
>
> Monty did not like these Cabinet meetings at all. After he had been to a couple he came back to the War Office and said to me, 'This is the wrong way to run the country. Cabinet is nothing but a Committee and I know well that no committee ever takes a proper decision. They talk a lot and then leave the subject in the air. The Prime Minister ought to tell them firmly what to do and see that they do it.'
>
> I did my best to explain to him that we were a democracy and the thing had to be run in the way it was. . . .
>
> Monty did not approve of that way of doing it. He said it wasted a lot of time. He said, 'Winston would never have put up with it. He told people what to do.' I tried to explain that Winston was a wartime Prime Minister and had to take quick decisions. In fact, my impression was that Churchill was as great a dictator as any of the enemy head men such as Hitler or Mussolini, only Winston was very much more skilful in that he gave his orders behind a façade of parliamentary democracy and was careful to say, even if it was not always quite true, that his colleagues were in complete agreement with him. Often it was the case that the colleagues were far too frightened of him to disagree openly, however much they may have muttered behind his back.[1]

Attlee's open forum at Cabinet meetings was anathema to Monty; he was able to witness the divide between Prime Minister and Foreign Secretary in a way that Eisenhower, as Chief of Staff of the Army, never did in Washington. Indeed, as Monty was to discover, Eisenhower scarcely ever saw President Truman, with whom relations were cool; nor was Eisenhower's opinion or advice ever sought by Truman, and rarely by Byrnes, the US Foreign Secretary.

Attlee, for all his canniness at conducting committee meetings, differed profoundly from Bevin in his views on world strategy, having early on declared that he saw no way in which Britain could keep open the Mediterranean in time of war, or bolster the Mediterranean countries, Turkey or the Persian oilfields, against Russian encroachment. Attlee therefore favoured simply keeping open the Cape of Good Hope sea route to Australia and New Zealand, abandoning

[1] General Sir Frank Simpson, loc. cit.

all intermediate bases and spheres of influence. 'Attlee is fresh minded on Defence. . . . It was no good, he thought, pretending any more that we could keep open the Mediterranean in time of war. That meant we could pull troops out of Egypt and the rest of the Middle East as well as Greece. Nor could we hope, he thought, to defend Turkey, Iraq or Persia against a steady pressure of the Russian land masses,' the British Chancellor of the Exchequer, Hugh Dalton, wrote in his diary in February 1946[1]—a view that had been confirmed by the Prime Minister's paper on the world outlook circulated on 2 March.[2]

To Monty—who clashed with Attlee on 12 July at a special meeting of the Defence Committee on the issue—this was defeatism and a bankruptcy of will: the very feebleness of spirit he had sought almost single-handedly to reverse in Home Forces after Dunkirk and in Eighth Army. Thus, in August 1946, four years after his desert take-over, Monty set off for the first time in his life to the North American continent with an armament of rousing speeches to veterans and the relatives of those sons of Canada who had given their lives for freedom in Europe: as well as a personal mission to stop Russian expansionism and exploitation of western weakness.

It was in this latter respect that Tedder and Cunningham were uneasy, for as they were 'beginning to feel that Monty might well commit us to all sorts of things of which they did not approve', General Simpson later recalled. 'Monty was warned very strongly that he should on no account attempt to meet American politicians. Mr Attlee and the British Cabinet would not have liked that at all.' Monty merely nodded his head—having made up his mind that he was not going to refrain from accepting an invitation to meet any of the American politicians should the invitation come.'[3]

Another reason why Tedder and Cunningham distrusted Monty's departure for America was Monty's approach to Western strategy. Monty had felt it impossible for the War Office to decide on future weapons and Army organization unless it had a clear idea of what requirements must be met over the coming years. 'No policy had so far been laid down which could enable planning on any of these matters to have any target at which to aim,' his diarist recorded. 'On the equipment side this meant that the army was in danger once again of witnessing a never-ending tug of war between continuance of research and the need to go into production *at some date*: the drift was on towards obsolete weapons or flags representing the new

[1] H. Dalton, *High Tide and After*, London 1962.
[2] Cabinet Defence Committee papers (DO(46)27) (CAB 131/1), PRO.
[3] General Sir Frank Simpson, loc. cit.

production. CIGS decided that this state of affairs must not be allowed to continue. It was clearly useless to ask the politicians for guidance,' he noted with contempt.[1] As General Simpson recalled, Monty's view was that Britain had 'a very wet Government',[2] and Monty's answer was, unilaterally, to write his own scenario of the future. Throughout the inter-war years he had taken pains to base his exercises on possible or likely future military challenges, had done so with astonishing foresight in France before Dunkirk, in Home Forces thereafter, and with Eighth Army before Alamein as well as 21st Army Group before D-Day. This desire to look ahead, to plan and train with a clear mental outline of the future was the attribute which had raised Monty head and shoulders above any battlefield general on any side in World War II—and the habit refused to die. If Attlee and Bevin could not agree on Britain's future rôle and commitments, at least he, Monty, would attempt to fashion the British Army and its weapons on a likely configuration of world commitments over the next two decades. On 6 July 1946 he therefore laid down that

> a) The Regular Army must within *5 years* be adequately equipped to be able to handle any small troubles that might arise and that it must continue thereafter to be so ready.
> b) That the *Balanced Whole*, the Regular and Territorial Armies, must be *ready by 1960* as regards equipment, manpower, ammunition, reserves etc. to fight a major war.
> c) That thereafter the Balanced Whole must be kept so ready.
> This was to be the policy which would guide the War Office in all its organisational problems. Amongst other things it would ensure that the old research versus production problem could not become a Timeless Test.[3]

Monty duly informed his fellow Chiefs of Staff, the Secretary of State and the Prime Minister of this instruction to his own War Office directors of departments; but with Attlee's personal reluctance to agree on a British Mediterranean presence in the future, Monty felt the Chiefs of Staff should spell out the strategic future as they saw it to submit to the Prime Minister. This Tedder and Cunningham refused to do, pleading lack of time. Monty scoffed—and had a War Office paper produced in thirteen days, based on his own conviction that, to dissuade Russia from countenancing war:

[1] Diary, Parts I and II, loc. cit.
[2] General Sir Frank Simpson, loc. cit.
[3] Diary, Parts I and II, loc. cit.

a) We should attempt to build up the strength of our potential allies in Europe to establish a Western Bloc which, by holding the land armies in the West, would keep the war away from Britain.
b) We should fight for the North African coast line and thus enable our communications through the Mediterranean to be kept open.
c) We should fight for the Middle East, which with the UK would form the bases for the launching of such a tremendous air offensive against Russian resources as to make it impossible for her to carry on the war.[1]

Still the Chiefs of Staff refused to submit this to the Prime Minister—and were thus appalled at the prospect of Monty's forthcoming talks across the Atlantic.

For Monty, however, clarification of the strategic future gave him a sort of religious radiance—a sense of conviction which was conspicuously lacking in the offices of so many western officers and officials. As with his St Paul's School presentation of plans before D-Day, some disliked this obsession with forward planning and were only too pleased, afterwards, to point out the divergences between prediction and actual events. The American Official War Historian, Dr Forrest Pogue, for instance deliberately sought copies of Monty's notes for his two great St Paul's School presentations of 1944 from the British Cabinet Office, analyzed them, and took it upon himself to bring his findings to Eisenhower's personal attention, pointing out with relish that Monty's plan had assumed a deeper British penetration into Normandy than was achieved, with consequently a deeper inland hinge than Caen.[2] Such nit-picking, by men who had not even been present at Monty's briefings, completely overlooked the true historical impact on Allied morale and confidence created by Monty's uninhibited willingness to plan ahead. Compared with the fiasco a few months previously at Anzio, Monty's preparation of the Allied armies for D-Day had been triumphant, and without his mental rehearsal of tactical strategy in Normandy, it is doubtful if he could have held the Allied armies upon the course which ultimately became the decisive battle of World War II in the West.

The publication of Eisenhower's headquarters' diary, kept by Eisenhower's naval aide Harry C. Butcher, in May 1946 had par-

[1] Ibid.

[2] Letter of 15.5.47 from Forrest C. Pogue to Deputy Chief, US Historical Division, marked: 'Dr Pogue suggested that General Eisenhower might be interested in glancing over these': Montgomery file, Eisenhower Papers, loc. cit.

ticularly embittered Monty—knowing as he did how little grip Eisenhower had ever exercised on land operations in North Africa and Europe; but with the whole future of Anglo-American co-operation in the melting pot, he held his tongue and attempted to make Eisenhower understand he was not simply coming to the USA to visit war colleges and training establishments but to 'have talks with you and your staff on matters of mutual interest'.[1] Eisenhower suggested a day in Washington, followed by trips to the Armored Force School, the Staff School, the Air Tactical School, and the Infantry School. But the more difficulty Monty had in convincing Attlee and the British Chiefs of Staff about future strategy and co-operation, the more Monty was determined to drag Britain backwards into a transatlantic alliance by his own personal effort. 'I do not think one day in Washington will be enough,' he therefore cabled to Eisenhower on 1 August. 'There are many things I want to talk about with you and I shall also hope to have talks with the British Ambassador. I feel that my tour round training establishments should be cut down so as to give three full days in Washington without any social entanglements.'[2]

Monty's aspirations were well-timed, for his self-invitation came at a moment when many senior American officers and officials were themselves alarmed about a possible Russian 'surge westwards'. The US Control Commissioner in Germany asked Monty's successor, Air-Marshal Sholto Douglas, to 'agree joint Anglo/American planning to begin in Germany for the preparation of plans for a "sauve qui peut" exit from the Continent in the event of a Russian attack.' As Monty's diarist recorded, 'the COS bluntly ordered C-in-C BAOR to have nothing to do with such an approach. The danger of planning any joint action *in Germany* was far too great as it was a sure bet that the Russians would hear about it within a matter of days if not hours.'[3] However, American fears soon spread back to Washington. 'The next approach came on 1 August 46 when the American Planners handed to our Planners in Washington [part of the Combined Chiefs of Staff organization surviving from the war] a paper asking for an exchange of views on a war against Russia; but their accompanying questionnaire made it clear once again that they were thinking in terms of the outbreak of war in the immediate future arising out of tension in such danger spots as Trieste, Turkey or Persia. It was clearly of the greatest importance that we should not let slip this official overture with all its significance for the future.'[4]

[1] Signal of 3.7.46, 'Montgomery' file, Eisenhower Papers, loc. cit.
[2] Signal of 1.8.46, 'Montgomery' file, Eisenhower Papers, loc. cit.
[3] Diary, Parts I and II, Montgomery Papers.
[4] Ibid.

The Americans and Monty's colleagues on the British Chiefs of Staff Committee were thinking—and only willing to think—in terms of the 'immediate future'. What Monty wished to do was to seize the barely-lit torch and bear it around the chancelleries of the Western Allies—for it was Monty's firm conviction 'that war with Russia within the next five years' was out of the question; he also maintained that it was futile to consider operations in, say, Venezia Giulia or Germany 'except within the framework of our strategy for a World War'.[1] It was Monty's long-term foresight which now galvanized him into action across the Atlantic. Whatever idle reporters or jealous diplomats in the Governor-General's residence in Canada might make of the trip, the speechifying was not simply self-advertising of a popular British hero, enjoying the limelight. Behind the locked doors of the Canadian Prime Minister's office in Ottawa Monty unveiled his true mission—and the first seeds of what one day would be called NATO were sown.

[1] Ibid.

CHAPTER FOUR

Squaring the US President

'I LEAVE ENGLAND ON 19 August on another big tour. This time I am going to Canada and America, and I do not get back to England till 20 September. I am going to Canada by sea in the Mauretania, and will fly back from America in an aeroplane. I shall send you some photographs when I get back; I expect a good many will be taken,' Monty boasted to his little Swiss friend Lucien Trueb—and signed himself 'Your very loving big friend Montgomery of Alamein'.[1]

The press were indeed in constant attendance on the tour. Receiving honorary degrees at Dalhousie, McGill and Toronto Universities, Monty paid tribute to the Canadian soldier, and Canadian loyalty to Britain during the war; and spoke of the post-war future. Together with his visits to the Canadian Staff College, Halifax, Charlottetown, Fredericton, Quebec, Montreal, Vancouver, Calgary, Victoria, Edmonton, Winnipeg and Ottawa it was a triumphal progress, with a measure of popular acclaim that was 'moving and often almost embarrassing', his diarist recorded. 'All of this official public business went very well but it was of minor importance compared with the CIGS's activities which took place in conversations once he was free from the public eye and which, starting from small beginnings, led up to a great crescendo.'[2]

The more Monty spoke to senior Canadian officials and politicians, the more he felt the time ripe for a transatlantic military pact tough enough to halt the domino-effect of Russian Communism. Thus, in a deliberately provocative speech in Ottawa to 'test the reaction of all the leading Government officials', Monty defied the mood of Canadian demobilization and spelt out the necessary steps Canada must take 'to meet the possibility of a future war'.[3]

To postulate 'future war' was to think the unthinkable—and at first Monty's words were greeted with awed silence. But his prescription for Canada—good scientific research, dispersed industrial

[1] Letter of 4.8.46, Papers of Lord Montgomery of Alamein, communicated to author.

[2] Diary, Parts I and II, loc. cit.

[3] Ibid.

potential, small but well-equipped and well-balanced forces, allied to a purposeful national will and a determination to 'be prepared'—aroused a 'buzz of excitement'. Radio Moscow summarized the speech as 'a call for Canada to prepare for war in order to live in peace'.[1]

Apprehensive of Russian intentions in Europe as well as in the northern territories of Canada, Canadian politicians proved more responsive to Monty's proposed medicine than were his own colleagues at home; and by the time Monty met Mackenzie King, on the final evening of his Canadian tour, the Prime Minister, the Minister of National Defence and the Chief of the Canadian General Staff all accepted Monty's assessment of the long-term future, agreeing that talks should begin immediately between Britain, Canada and if possible the USA not only on standardization of weapons, 'but should cover the whole field of co-operation and combined action in the event of war with Russia'[2]—Mackenzie King authorizing Monty to speak on Canada's behalf as well as Britain's when he met President Truman in Washington on 10 September.

Thus, under cover of a North American good-will visit, Monty travelled as an Ambassador Extraordinary not of Attlee's Labour Government or even the British Chiefs of Staff, but of those Western minds anxious to translate Churchill's Fulton speech into action. Pursued by British Chiefs of Staff signals begging him 'to do nothing till he had discussed the situation with Field Marshal Wilson' (Britain's representative to the Combined Chiefs of Staff in Washington) and emphasizing 'that no Minister in England knew what was going on',[3] Monty made his way from West Point to Leavenworth to Maxwell Field, Alabama to Fort Benning to New York. Tedder meanwhile 'went further and strongly urged CIGS to confine his talks in Washington to the USA Chiefs of Staff and to make no reference to his plans to the President'[4]—but Monty was in his element and Tedder's cautiousness only made him more determined to succeed. Eisenhower, on Monty's first evening in the United States, had said 'he thought it was high time that the Heads of State were brought in; but he did not wish to approach the President himself and he urged the CIGS to do so when he went to see him next day'.[5] This Monty did in the White House, opening the conversation by telling the President that he and General Eisenhower considered the time had come to open discussions covering the whole

[1] Ibid.
[2] Ibid.
[3] Signal Salt 33 of 10.9.46, annex 29, Diary, Parts I and II, loc. cit.
[4] Signal Salt 34, Tedder to Montgomery, of 10.9.46, annex 30. Ibid.
[5] Ibid.

field of defence. Truman seemed responsive, so, casting Tedder's advice to the four winds, Monty explained Mackenzie King's attitude and remarked that, if the three Heads of State were all agreed, they should 'leave it to the Military Staff to get on with the job. The President answered at once "that is quite O.K. by me, go straight ahead".'[1] With Truman's approval, Eisenhower then organized a special meeting of the American Chiefs of Staff aboard the SS *Sequoia* for 16 September, to take place under the guise of a social gathering to cruise down the Potomac to see George Washington's house at Mount Vernon: 'to avoid suspicion and preserve secrecy', as Monty informed the VCIGS in London.

> The present situation therefore is as follows: The Heads of State of Canada and America have both expressed their wish that we should cease being merely on friendly terms, but should get down to full and frank discussions on all defence matters. The opportunity is there for us to grasp. No further comment from me is necessary,

Monty concluded—adding that he wished Simpson to 'take the necessary action in London with the Chiefs of Staff who will presumably decide on the best method of approach to the Prime Minister and how to get on with the business'.[2]

Here indeed was the rub, however. Attlee had authorized no such approach by Monty either to the Canadian or American heads of state; he had a Labour Party to carry with him, as well as his Cabinet. Entering into specific and secret negotiations with Canada and the United States regarding a future joint military alliance against Russia in the event of war was a red hot issue—and Monty's 'Red Pepper' telegrams from North America were aptly named.

Attlee, when finally informed of what was going on, was appalled. Any other officer of the Crown he would instantly have dismissed—but Monty out of office might well prove an even sharper thorn in the government's side, given his popularity. Moreover, Monty claimed to have got both the Prime Minister of Canada and the President of the United States to underwrite such an initiative, putting Attlee in a very difficult position if he now attempted to pull out. The Foreign Secretary, Ernest Bevin, was ill, and for the moment Attlee had to content himself with a warning shot across Monty's bows prior to the Potomac conference:

> The issues now raised are of the utmost importance and potential value, but any leakage would have the gravest consequences. . . . While there is no objection to further exchanges of in-

[1] Ibid.

[2] Signal Red Pepper 38 of 11.9.46. Ibid.

formation or even discussions of methods of procedure, you should be careful to avoid entering into any specific commitments.[1]

Such was the secrecy of the proposed joint planning that the American Chiefs of Staff—Eisenhower, Nimitz and Spaatz, together with Truman's Chief of Staff Admiral Leahy—insisted that the planning staff from Canada should not be drawn from the existing Joint Canadian/American Defence Board since this had political representatives whose integrity could not be guaranteed. Moreover when Monty asked 'what value, if any, they attached to the Middle East oil', the reply by the American Chiefs of Staff was 'immediate and unanimous: vital'.[2] The way towards a joint Anglo-American strategy for the Mediterranean and Middle East was thus paved—and Monty returned to England cock-a-hoop.

As in the days after the battle of the Ardennes, when Monty managed to swing Eisenhower—and even Tedder—into wholehearted concentration upon the break-in to the river Rhine north of the Ruhr ('Veritable' and 'Grenade'), Monty failed however to see how unpopular his very success made him among his peers. Reluctant to miss the opportunity, aware that internal French and British-Canadian rivalries made speed of decision essential before Anglo-Canadian wartime loyalties evaporated, Monty was all for action—but was viewed with great misgivings by Attlee and the other Chiefs of Staff, who had no wish to be stampeded into secret military talks at such a high level.

To Monty, such spinsterish response was missing the very magnitude of what had been achieved. 'The fact remains that within a matter of a few days CIGS managed to obtain the approval of the Heads of State and COS of America, Canada and Britain to the opening of military discussions on a very wide basis, which potentially could lead to the unity of the defence policy and plans of the British Commonwealth and the United States *before* another war was thrust upon them. Such unity might in fact even prevent the outbreak of just such a war,' his diarist claimed on Monty's behalf.[3]

The boast was not idle—as history would demonstrate. 'For the moment American isolationism is dead,' Monty's diary recorded proudly. Tedder and Cunningham, humiliated for their faint-heartedness, had now to deal with the ramifications of Monty's 'victory'. Though outwardly acknowledging the enormity of Monty's achievement they were inwardly consumed by vexation—and relations between them and Monty soon plummetted to a level never experienced before or since in the Chiefs of Staff Committee.

[1] Signal 3080 of 14.9.46, annex 33. Ibid.
[2] Ibid.
[3] Ibid.

CHAPTER FIVE

A Law Unto Himself

MONTY TOUCHED DOWN in England on 21 September 1946. It was not long before the recriminations began. Unlike Eisenhower, Monty was not by temperament or character fitted to sit easily on committees or excite colleagues to serve a common goal out of personal affection. His secret success in North America—as well as the massive personal Press coverage—merely made his COS colleagues more resentful: and from triumph Monty's progress as CIGS now entered a period of bleakness as Britain's economic and overseas problems reached crisis proportions. Britain's commitments abroad had not decreased. Troops were likely to be needed in Venezia Giulia and Greece for some time to come; 'Palestine was in a state of grave unrest and fully occupied the 2/3 Divisions stationed there: peace seemed remote; Egypt was on the boil over the delay in the Treaty negotiations; there was the threat of trouble in the Persian oilfields; internal troubles threatened in India,' Monty's diarist acknowledged.[1] Volunteer recruitment had fallen far below expectation and even the Government's amended demobilization release scheme promised to leave the Army almost 70,000 men short by the end of the year. For a country hoping to join Canada and the United States in a world-wide military shield to contain Russian Communism, this was not encouraging.

Instead of doing his utmost first to weld and then wield the strength of the Chiefs of Staff, however, Monty's autocratic approach was strengthened by his success in America. He thus attempted to cajole Tedder and Cunningham into an immediate 'showdown' with the government, demanding national conscription of at least one and a half years' duration, together with reserve liability in the Territorial (Reserve) Army for a further six years. Once again, Monty's response to the problem was astonishingly quick and, indeed, prophetic: but such percipience was squandered by his inability to convince or carry his Service colleagues, who refused to have anything to do with Monty's special commissioning of a manpower report. Monty, scorning their feebleness, went straight to Attlee and on 30 September

[1] Diary of Field Marshal The Viscount Montgomery of Alamein, Part III (21.9–22.11.46), Montgomery Papers.

succeeded in so frightening him that Attlee asked him to prepare a paper on the subject straight away. This, then, was the far from immaculate conception of Britain's post-war National Service Bill to succeed wartime conscription.

Once again the Air and Naval Chiefs of Staff had been outpaced. Monty's stock with Tedder and Cunningham sank yet lower—a tragic state of affairs when unity of the three Service Chiefs was essential if the whole Labour Government was to be convinced of the necessity for such measures. At the Defence Committee meeting on 16 and 17 October there was a 'long and sometimes stormy'[1] debate on the issue of post-war conscription, Ministers arguing that it would be immensely expensive and would remove vital manpower from industry, with consequent loss of production. When the Chancellor of the Exchequer, Hugh Dalton, attacked Monty for putting forward a 'sketchily thought-out plan', Monty erupted and savaged Dalton—who never forgave Monty. Attlee subsequently asked the Secretary of State for War to caution Monty against making enemies in this way, but Monty stood on his high horse, declaring he 'would say exactly what he thought to whoever might make the accusation. . . . If the Prime Minister did not like his methods he would be perfectly prepared to resign and to go and say what he had got to say in the House of Lords.'[2]

Such threats and high-handedness were now reaching manic proportions. As so often before, Monty was becoming a law unto himself—and the spectacle was not good. He was not alone—Churchill, for all his visionary eloquence alongside Truman at Fulton and again in Zurich in September 1946 ['we must build a kind of United States of Europe'], had indulged in 'accusations, imputations and even personal abuse against his wartime colleagues', as *The Times* obituarist later recalled, 'which shocked his hearers—even his friends—and embittered his opponents. . . . In the House of Commons . . . .his weekly brushes with the Leader of the House, Mr Herbert Morrison, came to be known as "Children's Hour" and saddened many of his admirers. In his criticisms of the Labour Government's social policies, he never seemed to strike the right note.'[3]

Like Churchill, Monty was tolerated and supported as leader of the Army because no other military figure could equal his public popularity, experience, or creative inspiration; but this did not mean his demeanour was condoned. Monty's enemies multiplied, with

[1] Ibid.
[2] Ibid.
[3] *The Times*, 25.1.65.

more and more criticism being voiced behind his back. The publication of Ralph Ingersoll's scurrilous mish-mash of fact and wartime misunderstanding, *Top Secret*, became the trigger for many a jealous denigration of Monty's wartime achievements. Maj-General Kenneth Strong, the new head of the Political Warfare Executive, had since the German surrender gone about declaring Monty 'a cad and a crook'—'a fanatical, if not an evil man'[1] who in Strong's view had done his best to sour relations with Britain's American Allies; and it was said the London clubs were full each evening with stories of Monty's latest misdoings.

Monty had never shirked opprobrium. As early as August 1945 he had announced at a staff conference in Germany: 'Our task is to rehabilitate this great nation (Germany). The people at home must be told the truth. Who is going to do it? I suppose I shall have to. The politicians will say that I am interfering in politics. But never mind. I'm used to that. The truth must be told.'[2] But he made little attempt to render the truth palatable and rode rough-shod towards his target without concern for feelings or harmony. The unity of Chiefs of Staff, in the aftermath of World War II, was as imperative as during the war itself; yet Monty imagined he would counter the dithering feebleness of the Committee by a display of virtuoso foresight and determination.

After almost two months' argument, Attlee's Cabinet gave way and Monty's proposals for one and a half years of compulsory National Service were announced in the King's Speech on the prorogation of Parliament on 6 November 1946. 'Thus, in a matter of 6 weeks, CIGS had by his determination forced an issue of a problem which has long been recognized as inevitable but which has equally been continually postponed as no-one wished to face up to it,' his diarist chronicled on his behalf[3]—but it had been a thankless victory won in a thankless manner that turned almost the entire senior membership of the Labour Government against Monty.

This disfavour was fortified when Monty now took it upon himself to protest against the appointment of Mr Bellenger as the new Secretary of State for War, in place of Jack Lawson who had resigned for reasons of ill-health. Such a protest confirmed the view in government and in Whitehall that Monty was too big for his boots and wished to be the Emperor before whom all bowed in deference. As if to cock a snook at Monty, therefore, Air-Marshal Tedder suddenly let it be known, in mid-November, that he was leaving Britain on a

[1] *The Diaries of Sir Robert Bruce-Lockhart*, op. cit.
[2] Entry of 23.8.45. Ibid.
[3] Diary, Part III, loc. cit.

two-month tour of Japan—at the very time Monty had proposed to set out on his own tour number two to the Middle East and India.

Monty protested, claiming that he had given out the dates of his No. 2 Tour 'as early as 5 July 46—barely 10 days after assuming office', and the Minister of Defence had given his blessing. Details of Monty's trip were even appended to the Minutes of the 150th meeting of the Chiefs of Staff Committee in October—over which Tedder had himself presided. General Ismay, the Secretary of the Defence Committee, was alerted and there were 'many telephone calls and much buzzing in the Cabinet'. It was no use: Tedder departed by air on 16 November 1946, arranging for official notification of his tour to be delivered that day to the War Office, *after* his flight had already gone.

Monty was outraged. 'In these circumstances CIGS felt that he would have to curtail his long-planned tour unless CAS decided to come back. VCIGS got on the telephone to VCAS, who sent off a signal to CAS urging him to come back. But again, it was of no avail.'[1]

This childish charade would have been comic had it not been so indicative of the widening rift between Monty and his Service colleagues. 'Monty was writing letters to all and sundry with loud complaints against Tedder, against the Air Ministry and against everybody else,' General Simpson, the VCIGS, later recalled.

> The Vice-Chief of Air Staff, Dickson, came over in a flurry to see me and he said there was going to be a rift between the Army and the Air Force which would take years to heal, and pleaded with me to do all I could to calm Monty down. He said that he would tell me in confidence that the real reason that Tedder had gone to Japan was that Lady Tedder had made up her mind that she would like to go there; so the CAS's aircraft had been alerted and off they had gone.[2]

This explanation mollified Monty, who disliked Lady Tedder more than he disliked Tedder; but it did not make it any the easier to swallow the Prime Minister's displeasure—for Attlee now wrote to Monty 'making known in very clear terms his wish that not more than one Chief of Staff should be absent from the UK at any one time'.[3]

Though Attlee relented to the extent of permitting Monty's Tour No. 2 to go ahead, Monty had already cancelled the Asian end of his

[1] Ibid.
[2] General Sir Frank Simpson, loc. cit.
[3] Ibid.

visit and in pique declined to reinstate it. 'CAS's behaviour in this matter was nothing short of lamentable,' Monty's diarist noted. 'It is difficult to believe that he did not realise the repercussions that would certainly ensue from the simultaneous absence both of himself and CIGS. It is even more difficult to understand why he did not table his intentions openly and in good time. It was quite clear however that he would not lift a finger to undo what he had done and that he was not prepared to show any sign of normal courtesy by apologising to CIGS for upsetting his arrangements.'[1]

Tedder had got his own back on Monty—subsequently breezing back to England two weeks early and without explanation! Perhaps his purpose had been, beyond pleasing Lady Tedder, to teach Monty a lesson about selfishness, but it was a silly gesture that did more harm than good. Indeed it marked the turning point, as far as Monty was concerned. Hitherto Monty had, for all his egoism and desire to shake up Britain's post-war attitude to defence, considered his fellow Chiefs of Staff as partners—however inferior—in a great and ambitious challenge. That Tedder could seek to prejudice Monty's deeply professional approach to his job as head of the British Army was what hurt Monty most deeply—and he found it difficult to forgive Tedder. To know that Tedder, living in luxury with Lady Tedder in London, had actively conspired towards his dismissal as Allied Land Force Commander in Normandy in the summer of 1944—a fact now made public by the publication of Butcher's book based on Eisenhower's headquarters diary—and to find him *still* seeking to prejudice Monty's conduct of high command by disrupting a military tour planned and announced months previously, served to embitter Monty to an irrevocable degree—and within months they would be at such loggerheads that if one were to be present at the Chiefs of Staff Conference, the other would deliberately stay away.

Had Tedder been a true knight of his own Service, Monty would have overlooked Tedder's mischievousness—for what Monty admired above all was professionalism. What aroused Monty's ire was Tedder's deliberate obstructiveness, based on devilry. Yet short of resignation there was nothing he could do save swallow his pride, and redouble his efforts to steer Britain's Army responsibly and with foresight in a post-war world. With the situation in Palestine deteriorating daily, this was an increasingly difficult task—and the 'flurry' with Tedder proved only a gust of wind compared with the storms ahead.

[1] Diary of Field-Marshal The Viscount Montgomery of Alamein, Part IV (23.11–10.12.46), Montgomery Papers.

Monty was under no illusions over Palestine. The Colonial Office was claiming that, despite the Anglo-American Report urging acceptance of a further 100,000 Jewish refugees, it had made no change in Palestine 'which would constitute a serious limitation of the activity of the armed forces in dealing with terrorism'. The British High Commissioner, when questioned about limitations, had replied 'none'—whereas the new C-in-C Middle East Land Forces, General Sir Miles Dempsey, replied, 'Yes—the army has lost the initiative.' Where the High Commissioner considered that any differences between civil and military authorities in Palestine had been 'resolved without difficulty', Dempsey reported that the military authorities 'consider that the Army is being wrongly used'. And while the High Commissioner considered that relations between the civil and military authorities in Palestine 'needed no improvement', Dempsey considered the 'actual arrangements for dealing with violence are totally inadequate'.[1]

Not unnaturally, Monty sided with Dempsey. Monty had met Alan Cunningham, the High Commissioner, on his Tour No. 1 in June 1946 and had considered him a broken reed. Now, with Britain rejecting the Anglo-American Report until such time as the underground Jewish army had been brought under control, the British Army was caught in a cleft stick. Alan Cunningham's temporizing prevented the Army from carrying out its task—enabling Attlee to protest to his Cabinet and Defence Committee that they were defying Truman's wishes over the Report while failing to put down the very Jewish terrorism delaying Britain's acceptance of the Report.[2]

Monty's arrival in Jerusalem on 29 November 1946 put him at the eye of the gathering storm—for on 3 October Truman had destroyed all chances of an Arab-Jewish agreement over gradual partition of Palestine in a blatant bid for Jewish votes in the mid-term congressional elections. Attlee complained that the President had deliberately and callously frustrated Britain's 'patient efforts to achieve a settlement' and thus incurred 'the loss of still more lives in Palestine'.[3]

Truman's intercession—calling for immediate partition and admittance of 100,000 Jews into Palestine—severed any prospect of Arab agreement at the London conference. As Monty minuted on 29 November, however, 'a political solution is required. If this solution is not forthcoming soon it will be necessary to take strong military action in Palestine. It must be clearly understood that at present strong military action is not being taken to maintain law and

[1] Diary, Part IV, loc. cit.
[2] A. Bullock, op. cit.
[3] Ibid.

order'[1]—for the High Commissioner had ruled that the Army was not permitted to disarm the population, was not permitted offensive action against illegal armed organizations except as a direct result of Intelligence information, that no offensive action was to be taken after an outrage unless a definite connection was established between the perpetrators and the locality concerned, that no offensive action was in fact to be undertaken without the express permission of the High Commissioner himself, and that the Army must consider its primary task to be defensive—i.e. guarding railways and installations!

Monty, who had virtually single-handedly put down the Arab revolt in Palestine in 1938/9, regarded the whole situation as a 'dog's breakfast'. In his diary he noted that 'the High Commissioner is definitely of the opinion that providing we take no offensive action against lawlessness, the Jewish agency and the Hagana will suppress it themselves and restore peace. He also thinks that we could not stop lawlessness by offensive action and that any such action on our part would merely make matters worse and would annoy the Jews. In other words, he admits that we can no longer govern Palestine except on sufferance of the Jews.'[2]

At this, Monty bridled both as a soldier and as a strategist. He had not suppressed organized Arab revolt in Palestine in 1938/9 merely to hand over the same land now to Jewish terrorists; moreover a 'Jewish solution' to the Palestine problem that did not have the backing of the Arabs—both in Palestine and outside—spelled discord in the Middle East for the rest of time. Hence Monty's question to Eisenhower and the US Chiefs of Staff regarding the importance they attached to Middle East oil.

Now Truman had squandered all hopes of a political settlement, while landing the 'country which has the actual responsibility for the government of Palestine' (in Attlee's words) with the unholy task of keeping the peace. As Monty cabled back to Whitehall:

> Every thinking British person in this country realises that the thing is being handled in a gutless and spineless manner and that the whole business is just nonsense. There will always be lawlessness in Palestine until the forces at the disposal of the government are organised properly and are used properly.[3]

The police force would 'never be any better than third class soldiers'. They wanted a new Inspector-General and a new mandate to

[1] Diary, Part IV, loc. cit.
[2] Ibid.
[3] Signal Bacon 21, annex 56, Diary, Part IV, loc. cit.

work in conjunction with the Army. 'I consider that the whole business of dealing with the illegal armed organizations in Palestine is being tackled in a way which is completely gutless,' Monty reiterated, 'and is thoroughly unsound and which will not repeat not produce any good results. It is most important that this point should be grasped because my impression is that the Colonial Secretary and the Cabinet think that all proper methods to suppress lawlessness are being taken. My view is that the lawless elements or terrorists or whatever one likes to call them have almost complete liberty to do what they like . . . I have told Cunningham that it is my opinion that his methods have failed to produce law and order in Palestine and that it is my opinion that he will have no success unless he organises his police force in a proper way and uses the police and army properly and adopts a more robust mentality in his methods to keep the King's peace.'[1]

As Monty had shown in 1939—and as Field Marshal Templer would show in Malaya—it was worth involving the Army only if the government was prepared to rule the country with full military force: anything less simply acted as a stimulant to the sores. With a heavy heart Monty arranged for immediate extra pay for the British soldiers, addressed a gathering of their senior officers, and made his way on to Greece, Italy and Austria. Not even the award of the Order of the Garter could quieten his despair over Palestine. He had warned King George VI before he left: 'The situation in Palestine is growing steadily worse. I am disturbed about it'—and his visit only confirmed his worst fears—fears that would, over the succeeding months, be tragically borne out.[2]

[1] Ibid.

[2] Letter of 21.11.46 to Sir Alan Lascelles (RA GVI/PS 6988), Royal Archives, Windsor.

CHAPTER SIX

Leader of a New Movement?

As the situation deteriorated in Palestine, so did Monty's relations with his fellow Chiefs of Staff. He had never curried their favour; increasingly they resented his constructive energy and treated every recommendation he made as a challenge. Thus when Monty cabled from Greece that the British Army should not become involved 'in the fighting against the bandits' but merely keep a token presence in the country while training and financially supporting an enlarged Greek army, the Greeks agreed but Tedder and Cunningham did not. 'The noses of 1st Sea Lord and VCAS [in Tedder's absence] were apparently knocked right out of joint and they objected to receiving what they represented as being orders from CIGS, whom they alleged was acting as a super Chief of Staff,' Monty's diarist recorded. Going back to an earlier COS report on the Greek situation, they pointed out that they had recommended a full British division should be maintained in Greece for another year. 'They maintained that the situation had not changed since this report was compiled, and that a change of front as now suggested by the CIGS [reduction of British troops to 4 battalions by April 1947] would tend to weaken the confidence of the Cabinet in Chiefs of Staffs reports.' [1]

Such obstructionism was galling to Monty, but he had no one to blame but himself. He arrived back in England—via Austria and Italy—only four days after despatching his signals from Athens. Had he chosen to wait and to broach the subject privately with Tedder and Cunningham, he might have got his way without difficulty. It was Monty's impatience to arrive at a decision and to see it implemented that worked against him in Whitehall—and demonstrated how important had been de Guingand's role during the war. Monty's assumption of command of Eighth Army in August 1942 and of 21st Army Group in January 1944 had shown Monty's miraculous ability to assess an unhopeful situation and to transform it by decisiveness [2]—but it demonstrated too the genius with which de

[1] Diary, Part IV, loc. cit.

[2] Even Mountbatten, who as Chief of Combined Operations had first selected Normandy as the proper invasion site for 'Overlord', was pessimistic about its feasi-

Guingand welded together a brilliant team of staff officers to serve Monty and oiled the machinery whereby Monty's edicts were translated into action. Without de Guingand, it may fairly be said, Monty could be likened to a bull in a china shop—and not all the Whitehall expertise of the VCIGS, General Simpson, could help him in this respect. For without de Guingand, Monty appeared to have no one to whom he could turn for advice, nor for solace. The need for limelight and the almost demonic energy that drove him gave him no rest. He was determined always to be in command of the situation: assessing, deciding, seeing that things were done, orders obeyed—and there was no respite, even at Amesbury School at Christmas, as the Reynolds' son Tom later recalled:

> I always remember when I came back from Italy, after the end of the war. It was just my luck that Monty arrived the night after I'd got back. After dinner we were all going to bed and Mother said to Monty, 'Well, Monty, would you like breakfast in bed or will you have it in the dining room?'
>
> 'No! I'll have it with the boys, as I always do.'
>
> Turning to me, my mother said: 'Thwake (my nickname), I presume you'll come down when you're ready and have it in the dining room, you'll tell the maid, probably at 10 or 11?'
>
> Monty was appalled. 'Young Tom will have breakfast with the boys or he has no breakfast at all! Shaved and properly dressed—eight o'clock in the morning!'
>
> My mother said: 'He's home on leave. He's our son. Surely he can do what he likes at home?'
>
> 'I give an order. If he's not down for breakfast, his place will be cleared away and he will have no breakfast.'

At half past nine the following morning, young Tom Reynolds descended for breakfast.

> The maid asked what he would like, when Monty walked in.
>
> 'I gave an order last night. He will have no breakfast! This will teach him to obey orders!' [1]

Such martinet behaviour—in someone else's house—did not endear Monty to those who fell foul of him. More than with most men, Monty's heart was a house divided: on the one hand cold, relentless, implacable, a bully, insensitive; on the other, child-like in his sentimentality and craving for loving relationships. His loyalty to

---

bility, writing on 29.3.44: 'Without resolute leadership its chances of success are not too good': 'Mountbatten correspondence' file, Eisenhower Papers, loc. cit.

[1] Major Tom Reynolds, interview of 19.3.78.

those he cherished or admired was absolute; his letters to his adopted Swiss child affectionate to the point of silliness. Throughout the winter of 1946 he looked forward to Lucien Trueb's company at Gstaad, where he proposed to spend three weeks in the Guinness family's chalet, and there is little doubt that focussing his affection on the innocent thirteen-year-old helped Monty to bear the intolerable burden of his responsibilities and ambition. He was at the pinnacle of his career; he had but a handful of years to fulfil his vision of high command in peace—certainly the most ambitious 'dream' of any CIGS in British annals. Work on his next great War Office exercise—'Spearhead'—had begun in the summer of 1946, but this was only one of the reformist acts he had in mind as CIGS. He had wished to be a father to the Army, as he had told de Guingand—but not necessarily a benevolent father, and in his radicalism he was prepared to do battle with any who opposed him—even with the sovereign.

The Brigade of Guards, in common with other Army formations, was to be cut substantially. General infantry regiments were to be run down by 31%, the Brigade of Guards—as élite infantry—by only 20%. However their Maj-General—a man Monty felt had 'failed in battle' at Dunkirk [1]—went to King George VI to complain, asserting that the Guards were being savaged even more severely than normal infantry regiments. Monty was summoned by the King to explain the threatened cut, with the Maj-General Brigade of Guards present. Briskly, Monty pointed out that two of the four Guards battalions being axed were not really regular battalions, but had been raised in 1938 as war became inevitable. 'At this meeting CIGS explained the War Office view and came away with the impression that H.M. was in agreement with it,' for it was characteristic of Monty to assume that silence when he made a statement indicated assent. 'Next day, however, Sir Alan Lascelles rang up to say that H.M. did not agree.' [2] This was, in Monty's view, 'ascribable to the machinations of General Loyd, who saw fit to act in the interests of the Brigade of Guards rather than in the interests of the Army as a whole', Monty's diarist noted mournfully. Monty wisely decided not to insist: 'The final upshot was that General Loyd's point of view was accepted and accordingly the Brigade of Guards are to remain at their pre-war strength of 10 battalions.' For once, discretion had preceded valour.

Monty did not often give in so easily, however. When he heard, in Switzerland, that the War Office was proposing to break up the Royal Tank Regiment into individual tank regiments, each with its

[1] Diary, Part IV, loc. cit.

[2] Ibid.

own colonel—no doubt to foster 'family' pride—he was horrified. The War Office report had been compiled by General 'Dick' McCreery, whom Monty considered a polo-playing cavalry man of the very type he wished to remove from a professional modern British Army. Referring to 'the breaking up' of the RTR—the one really professional tank arm of the Army—Monty wrote to the Quartermaster-General: '*I will never agree to this.* I have not seen the report before and so I do not know how far you have got in the matter, but so far as I am concerned the RTR will be split up into 8 separate regiments over my dead body. The RTR must remain a regiment similar to the Parachute Regiment, officers belonging to the Royal Tank Regiment; they will be posted to units (regiments of the RTR) from time to time in accordance with the needs of the RTR *as a whole*, up to the rank of Majors; they come on to one RAC [Royal Armoured Corps] list for 2 i/c and for command . . . I do not know how far this matter has got . . ., If action is in train to implement the report and to "bust up" the RTR, please stop it at once.' [1] Unit loyalty was one thing, Monty felt; exaggerated loyalty to one's individual regiment—as he had found in the desert at Alamein—can become insular and hidebound, however. He had been impressed in the United States by the American career-concept of the professionally-educated officer. 'The Americans have gone beyond us in planning the officer's career from the time he is commissioned to 20 years service by when he should, if he is destined for high places, have graduated at his own Arms School, the Army Tactical College, the Army Staff College, the Joint Services Staff College and the National War College (equivalent to our I.D.C.),' his diarist had noted;[2] this, as well as the American system of attaching expert professorial staff to the faculties' training instructors, merited in Monty's eyes 'closer investigation and, if facilities allow, imitation.' [3] Whatever barricades might be erected by the die-hard elements of the old British Army, Monty was determined to reform it according to modern lights, and his radical eye peered at every facet of the soldier's life and career, from army quarters to senior officers' education. Thanking General Kirkman, the QMG, for his paper on the 'Role of the Army', Monty wrote from Gstaad:

[1] Letter of 17.2.47, communicated by General Sir Sidney Kirkman to author. The move to 'bust up' the RTR by splitting it into old-style individual regiments, each of which could be 'picked off' in times of government cuts by virtue of their junior ranking in the Royal Armoured Corps hierarchy (which included cavalry regiments) was subsequently quashed.

[2] Diary, Parts I and II, loc. cit.

[3] Ibid.

I spend every morning on the veranda of the chalet in the sun, facing due south; I sit and think; and occasionally I just sit! it is very refreshing.[1]

This ability to create the conditions whereby he might 'sit and think', whatever the fury of the current battle being fought, was what had marked Monty out as a higher commander—and whatever 'mud' was thrown at him, Monty intended to remain true to this talent, so that he could never be accused of 'drifting aimlessly'. Great leadership involved great thought; and great forethought.

However, it was not enough, Monty felt, to reform and modernize Britain's peace-time army; he must try also to keep the peace. He had already set in motion the first secret talks leading to military alliance between Canada, the USA and Great Britain; equally, he was anxious lest such potential unity be used to further polarize Western and Russian Communist attitudes. Accordingly, on 6 January 1947 Monty had flown to Moscow to take up an invitation Stalin had extended to him at Potsdam.

Many were aghast at the prospect of Monty's 'goodwill' mission to Moscow, knowing his naïveté in diplomatic affairs; however, with Anglo-Russian relations at a new low, Attlee had written to approve the visit which 'might be able to do much to dissipate the cloud of suspicion with which the Russians were involved'.[2]

Monty failed, inasmuch as anti-British Soviet propaganda continued unabated. Yet Monty's trip was seminal in other respects. He saw Stalin, conversed with all the senior generals of the Russian Army, visited Russian military academies to judge their training and educational standards, was shown the latest Russian tanks, and observed enough of life in Moscow to make a shrewd assessment of the future on his return. He even paved the way for a possible military alliance between the two countries. Speaking to assembled officers at the War Office Monty predicted that Russia would be unable to fight a major world war for a further 20 years—but would then be in possession of 'a really high class professional fighting machine', able to 'thump' the international table and get what she wished. It followed then that Britain need not, in her foreign policy and military strategy, fear a Russian-inspired war or invasion on any serious scale for another generation. During that time Britain could modernize her Army, run down her empire, and ensure a Western alliance so firm it could meet the threat of a modernized Russian army, whether

[1] Letter of 16.2.47, communicated by General Sir Sidney Kirkman to author.

[2] Diary of Field Marshal The Viscount Montgomery of Alamein Part VI (visit to Moscow 6–11.1.47), Montgomery Papers.

in Europe or elsewhere. If a tripartite friendship could, however, be fostered 'that is the best guarantee for a lasting peace'.[1]

Copies of Monty's report on his visit were circulated, at Attlee's request, to all members of the Cabinet and the other Service Ministers. The Foreign Office, furious that a British general should have muscled in on their special game reserve, coined an epigram that 'Monty thought he had been given a sable coat' by the Russians, 'whereas in reality it was only squirrel'.[2] However the British Minister in Moscow felt that Monty's trip had been 'very successful' in terms of Anglo-Russian relations. He told Sir Robert Bruce-Lockhart privately that 'Monty had gone down well. The Russian marshals had accepted him as a real man,' and *Pravda* had even extolled his victory in the battle of Alamein.[3] The King's Private Secretary remarked, in submitting Monty's report to George VI, that it was 'an extremely interesting and amusing paper for which I have thanked Monty. I would much like to read it again when Yr Majesty has done with it. He seems to me to have done a very good job—and thoroughly enjoyed doing it!'[4]

Monty had; but the experience made him yet more suspect to his fellow Chiefs of Staff, over whom he had stolen yet another march. Moreover his success was undoubtedly fuelling an ego already dangerously inflated by fame and the whisperings of king-makers—particularly newspaper magnates. During the war Lord Beaverbrook had repeatedly referred to the important post-war role Monty was destined to play in his country's history. Now, on the eve of Monty's Moscow trip the owner of the *Sunday Times*, Lord Kemsley, came to see Monty at his flat in Westminster Gardens. 'The interview was short and to the point,' Monty's diarist recorded.

> Lord Kemsley said that there was a very large and rapidly growing political movement in the country, known as the 'Freedom Movement', whose aim was to get rid of the present Socialist Government and take its place. The Kemsley Press was receiving thousands of letters per day declaring support for such a movement: and the movement wanted CIGS as its leader.
>
> Lord Kemsley put a straight question to CIGS: would he accept the leadership of this movement and become Prime Minister—for with him at its head the new party would quickly get into power.[5]

[1] Address of 20.1.47, annex 82, Diary, Part VI, loc. cit.

[2] *The Diaries of Sir Robert Bruce-Lockhart*, entry of 15.1.47, op. cit.

[3] Entry of 22.1.47. Ibid. The British Minister was Mr (later Sir) Frank Roberts.

[4] Memorandum of 12.1.47 (RA GVI/283), Royal Archives, Windsor.

[5] Diary of Field-Marshal The Viscount Montgomery of Alamein, Part V (10.12.46–3.2.47), Montgomery Papers.

The phenomenon was not confined to Monty, or to Britain. Eisenhower was being pressed to seek Presidential nomination, as was General MacArthur; in fact President Truman indicated in the course of 1947 that he would serve as Vice-President under Eisenhower, if Eisenhower would accept the Democratic nomination![1] Monty, meanwhile, affected to be stunned by Kemsley's suggestions:

> CIGS replied that he would certainly not agree to becoming the leader of any such movement; it was a monstrous thing to ask a serving CIGS to organise or lead a movement directed against the Government of the day.
>
> Lord Kemsley replied that he was not asking CIGS to be disloyal to the Government; he was asking him to resign and then to take over leadership of the Freedom Movement.[2]

Monty asked what would then happen to the Army. 'Lord Kemsley replied that the country was more important than the army,' but Monty was not convinced. As CIGS he had every chance of reforming the British Army for decades to come; as leader of a mythical political party, without roots or existing framework, he might fail ever to achieve that. 'CIGS said that he had no more to say, whereupon Lord Kemsley, as a parting shot, said that CIGS had not heard the end of this and that he (Lord Kemsley) expected to hear favourably from CIGS about it in 2 or 3 weeks time.'[3]

Fearful that there be a leak, Monty went to Attlee to inform him of Kemsley's machinations, 'for which the Prime Minister was most grateful. Nothing more has happened,' Monty's diarist chronicled—adding his own view, however, that Lord Kemsley had 'hit the nail on the head when he asked CIGS to become the leader of a new movement. On all sides it is recognised that what the country needs is leadership. Not very many people want Mr Churchill back as Prime Minister, yet, with the possible exception of Mr Herbert Morrison, there is no one in the political field who has the personality and ability to lead the country in these very difficult and dangerous times. Outside the political field there is one outstanding leader: CIGS. The writer [Monty's MA, Lt-Colonel George Cole] and others have frequently, and particularly recently, heard people from all walks of life sigh for an end to party politics coupled with the wish that CIGS should take over the leadership of the country.'[4]

This last remark was written, no doubt, to encourage Monty (when

[1] Stephen Ambrose, *Eisenhower 1890–1952*, New York 1983.

[2] Diary, Part V, loc. cit.

[3] Ibid.

[4] Ibid.

reading it) in such designs. Despite the growing rift with his fellow Chiefs of Staff, Monty had however no desire to leave the Army just when his reforms looked like being passed. 'As regards the Army, I am quite happy,' he wrote from the Chalet Grifferhorn in Gstaad to his old Chief of Staff, Freddie de Guingand. 'I am getting what I want; I am shaping the final peace time Army to the shape I want, and am getting the T[erritorial] A[rmy] as I want it. I have introduced the Chief of Staff system into the whole Army, including Home Commands. I am ensuring that if we go to war again we will have a proper set-up for high command, with the necessary signals, etc. etc. All this have [sic] been a terrific fight, but it is O.K. now.'[1]

On the wider horizon, however, Monty began to see the gale that would topple him—for in the few brief weeks he spent in Switzerland he watched the pillars of Britain's whole post-war strategy begin to crumble. 'When I left UK on 4 Feb I thought I had left things in a safe state,' he lamented to de Guingand. 'Palestine and India have gone west since I have been here on leave . . . it is all very distressing.'[2]

[1] Letter of 21.2.47, de Guingand Papers, loc. cit.
[2] Ibid.

CHAPTER SEVEN

Abandoning the Imperial Ship

MONTY WAS NOT the only one to be taken aback by the speed of Attlee's abandonment of the Middle East and of India. 'While I recognise the desirability of supporting the democratic elements in S.E. Europe and while I am conscious of the strategic importance of oil, I have, as you know always considered that the strategic importance of communications is very much overrated by our military advisors,' Attlee had written to his Foreign Secretary, Mr Bevin, on 1 December 1946. 'I am beginning to doubt whether the Greek game is worth the candle. I do not think that the countries bordering on Soviet Russia's zone, viz Greece, Turkey, Iraq and Persia, can be made strong enough to form an effective barrier.'[1]

Bevin had been out of Britain for a month—as had Monty, on his Tour No. 2. 'I got the Government to agree that a firm hold on the Middle East area was an essential part of our defence problem; we must hold it in peace and fight for it in war,' Monty related in a letter to de Guingand,[2] recording his 'profound shock', on returning from Moscow in January 1947, to find that British policy in the Middle East was being challenged by none other than the Prime Minister himself. 'At the first Chiefs of Staff meeting which he attended after his return [from Moscow]', Monty's diarist had noted, 'he asked the other two Chiefs of Staff if they were prepared, with him, to resign rather than give way over the Middle East. He told them that he would do so with or without them, but this was unnecessary as they both agreed wholeheartedly with him. General Hollis [Secretary of the Chiefs of Staff Committee] was accordingly instructed to convey, by private methods, this information to the Prime Minister. The result was immediate and no reference to the subject was made when the Cabinet met on 15th January to approve the new directive to the High Commissioner [of Palestine].'[3]

Monty's view was clear. Without Egypt or Cyrenaica, Britain could only hope to retain her hold on the Middle East from bases in

[1] Quoted in A. Bullock, op. cit.

[2] Letter of 21.2.47, loc. cit.

[3] Diary, Part V, loc. cit.

'France must be the hard core, militarily, of the Western Union. But she is in a state of chaos; her army is torn with intrigue, and lacks leadership and confidence; she is in no condition to give any lead in the matter.'

Thus wrote Monty in September 1948, shortly before his appointment as Supremo. With Naval, Air and Land Force C-in-C's under him, he was given a headquarters at Fontainebleau (**126** *above*). The Land Forces C-in-C, General de Lattre de Tassigny, welcomed Monty (**127** *right*) but immediately began a campaign of jealous intrigue and non-cooperation.

Monty's hopes of welding the free nations of Europe into a powerful military alliance soon fell foul of political hesitancy and French leaderlessness.

Nevertheless as Western Union's figurehead the French wished to do Monty proud. He was given for his personal residence the Marquis de Ganay's Louis XIII Château de Courances, near Paris, where to de Lattre's chagrin Monty refused to drink (**128** *left*) or to entertain amidst the armorial tapestries and sumptuous testimonies to France's past (**129** *below*).

De Lattre's lack of cooperation led Monty to concentrate, from his Courances residence (**130** *above*, **131** *right* and **132** *below*), on the larger aspects of Western Union: strategic defence analysis, forward planning, exercises and rehearsals of command – as well as performing the role of Inspector General of Western Union's potential defence forces.

Monty's 'exile' as paper supremo in France meant that he became a comparative stranger in his own country, seen in public only at state funerals and services (**133** *opposite left* and **134** *opposite right*) and the popular annual Alamein Reunions (**136** *right*, **137** *centre right* and **138** *below*).

Monty's successor as CIGS, Field-Marshal Slim, continued Monty's annual combined senior command exercises at Camberley (**135** *opposite below*), but refused to support Monty in pressing the British government to honour its military commitment to Europe in the event of war – leading to increased French suspicions that they would be 'Dunkirked' in any emergency.

The Birth of NATO
With the 'little Britain' policy of Attlee's government and the failure of France to furnish forces and leaders capable of defending Europe, it became obvious that the USA would have to be brought in to Western European defence and German manpower utilised. Belatedly, de Lattre and Monty made peace (**139** *left*) and sufficient unity was displayed by the Western Union defence ministers (**140** *below*) to persuade President Truman – alarmed by the crisis in Korea – to set up an enlarged North Atlantic Treaty Organization defence headquarters, under General Dwight D. Eisenhower (**141** *bottom below*).

Eisenhower soon appointed Monty his Deputy Supreme Commander, charged with 'forging the weapon'. Eisenhower, often sick and beset by the need to report back to America, used Monty both to galvanize his staff and to act as his link with European military and political leaders (**142** *right* and **143** *below*). Monty's continued fame as Europe's first soldier was also an inestimable advantage in gaining immediate credibility for NATO (**144** *bottom below*).

Monty's position as Deputy Supreme Commander in Europe certainly fanned the flames of his vanity. At his son's wedding (**145** *above*) he insisted on wearing full dress uniform. He regularly visited the Pope (**146** *below left*) and though he quarrelled with Eisenhower's successor General Ridgway, even intriguing to get him removed, he got on famously with General 'Al' Gruenther, Ridgway's successor (**147** *below right*).

Palestine; ergo, Palestine had to be held firmly. Once again he had taken silence as agreement in terms of the Prime Minister's response. He was therefore stunned now to hear, while in Switzerland, that Attlee had persuaded—or ordered—Bevin to divest Britain of its Palestine commitment by referring the whole problem to the United Nations. 'The handling of the Palestine situation has been so weak and spineless that we may well lose our position there: if U.N.O. decides against us,' Monty wrote to de Guingand in the same letter. 'If we have to come out of Palestine we are done.'[1]

To make matters worse, Attlee had also announced in the House of Commons that Britain would withdraw from its responsibilities in India on or before 1 June 1948—a date which, given its proximity, was bound to smack of weakness in the aftermath of the failed attempts to set up an interim Indian government and the warnings of Hindu-Muslim civil strife. Egypt had already broken off negotiations regarding the withdrawal of British troops, and an announcement of British withdrawal from Ceylon and Burma was expected at any moment. 'Egypt, Palestine, India, Burma: the thing is frightful,' Monty remarked to de Guingand[2]—and blamed the Chiefs of Staff as much as the politicians:

> The Chiefs of Staff are a useless body. We never initiate anything; we meet and deal with whatever the Secretariat put on the agenda; we resemble a Board of Directors. I would say we are a completely spineless outfit. Tedder is utterly useless as Chairman; he sits on the fence and never gives a definite opinion on any matter.
>
> Before I came here on leave I told Hollis my views on the subject in no uncertain manner. The time is coming when the Chiefs of Staff must line up to the Government with an ultimatum. United in a firm body, we would be unbeatable. I got them to agree to do this once before [over British strategy in the Middle East], but the mere threat that this might happen was enough and I won my point.[3]

Now, on holiday in Switzerland, it was evident he had lost it. Monty's implacable attitude had been that the politicians must decide on Britain's world-wide strategy and commitments; the Service Chiefs would then tailor the armed services to these requirements. But with the British economy lurching rapidly towards ruin (power cuts had been imposed across the country owing to the shortage of coal and the severity of the 1946/7 winter, with unemployment rising to 2.4

[1] Letter of 21.2.47, loc. cit.
[2] Ibid.
[3] Ibid.

millions) the British could no longer act alone among the bankrupt nations of Europe as a world power, dominating the Middle East and the sea lanes of the globe. Thus, in the spring of 1947 even Lord Wavell, the man who had originally proposed 1948 as the 'get out by' date for India, was sacked in favour of a Viceroy able to liquidate Britain's Indian commitment even faster: Lord Mountbatten. Abandoning Greece, Turkey, the Middle East, India, Burma and Ceylon, Attlee flung Britain's post-war peace-keeping responsibilities to the four winds, and, anxious lest the Soviet Union reap advantage of such a sell-out, the 'Truman Doctrine' was born.

Thus, backed by his Secretary of State for Defence George C. Marshall, President Truman took hold of Britain's baton; but the suddenness of Britain's profession of bankruptcy, moral as well as economic, wrecked the whole platform on which Monty, as CIGS, had intended to do strategic business. Henceforth he was, like Bevin at the Foreign Office, an emperor without clothes, his vision of responsible military leadership politely listened to—and ignored. Like Bevin, he would go down in Whitehall history as a failure not so much because of intrinsic lack of competence for the post of CIGS, but because his vision and determination were fundamentally out of kilter with the dissolutionist times. It does not pay to be in high command on the outbreak of war, was Monty's maxim; he might well have added that it does not pay to be in high command *after* a great and debilitating war. Brooke's VCIGS, General Nye, had warned of this, as well as himself declining the possible future offer of the post of CIGS. General Sir Miles Dempsey, the C-in-C Middle East whom Monty had begun to groom as his eventual successor as CIGS, certainly decided not to covet the post—announcing early in 1947 that he would retire from the Army to take up an appointment with the Betting Control Board. Even Eisenhower had told Truman he would not serve as US Chief of Army Staff for more than two years: and already in June 1947 declared his intention to leave the Pentagon.

Had Monty resigned as CIGS in the spring of 1947 following Attlee's call to 'abandon ship', he might well have preserved his military reputation intact: a great battlefield general who had sown the seeds of Britain's professional post-war Army. Like Churchill, Eisenhower and de Gaulle, he could then have concentrated on winning the Second World War a second time, exchanging his sword for a pen. Certainly he was aware that he was at the height of his international celebrity. Congratulating de Guingand on his book *Operation Victory*, currently being serialized in *The Times*, Monty predicted 'a tremendous sale'. 'You are on a rising market,' he boasted, 'as just at present I seem to be what is called "news". The first edition of Moorehead's book [*Montgomery*] is sold out.'[1] Even the commercial re-publication of his *Normandy to the Baltic* campaign account, written for training purposes, was being snapped up by general readers—'the first edition of 30,000 was all taken up two weeks ago: so I was told by Hutchinson, the publisher.'[2]

Despite his vanity, however, Monty was not prepared to leave the Army he had ruled for less than a year. Besides, he had not even a home to which he could retire. His flat in Westminster Gardens was owned by the War Office; his caravans were parked at Amesbury School, but could not stay there forever. Indeed the Reynolds had decided to move the school. Once again Monty found himself begging the sovereign for help:

> My dear Lascelles
>
> This is on a private matter, and I merely want to consult you. My friends at Hindhead with whom I have made my home during the war years are moving. By next Easter I and my boy will be homeless. I must therefore now begin to look for a home for ourselves. As you know, everything that I possess was destroyed by enemy bombing during the war.
>
> Once in conversation you mentioned Walmer Castle. I suppose it is now at the disposition of Mr Winston Churchill [as Warden of the Cinque Ports]; he does not use it as a residence and as far as I know has never been there. As it is not required by the Lord Warden of the Cinq [sic] Ports, it is presumably unoccupied.
>
> Is there any possibility it might be allotted to me as a residence *now*, for my lifetime? I would live in it and keep it up: which would I imagine be good for it.[3]

The King's answer was, however, negative: 'the present Lord Warden has given no indication that he wishes to relinquish it. . . . The houses in the King's gift seem to be all bespoke.'[4]

Major and Mrs Reynolds, preparing for retirement, had meanwhile bought the Miller's House at Isington, near Alton. Monty therefore persuaded them to sell off the derelict mill beside it, with a view to its conversion as a house. Stiff government controls were however in operation, restricting post-war rebuilding to 'essential' property development. When Monty applied for permission to use scarce building materials—particularly wood—to rebuild the mill, the local council refused; and not even reference to the Minister of Housing

[1] Letter of 21.2.47, de Guingand Papers, loc. cit.
[2] Ibid.
[3] Letter of 16.5.47 (RA GVI/283), Royal Archives, Windsor.
[4] Letter of 19.5.47. Ibid.

could alter the decision. It looked as if the famous British field-marshal, victor of so many battles of World War II, would be forced once more to live in a caravan.

Such ingratitude and obstruction did not deter Monty, who on his next Australian tour was given by grateful Australian and New Zealand governments all the wood he would need for converting the mill into a residence; however, it certainly reminded him (as it did his successor) that, without the necessary capital to buy a proper house, it was unwise to resign as CIGS. There was no indication that any other senior Army officer could better fight the Army's battle in Whitehall against financial cuts and the government's reluctance to impose National Service than Monty; indeed the reverse was true since the government was, by and large, afraid of him. His enormous public popularity might incite jealousy and mistrust among some, but it was a powerful weapon in standing up for his vision of the 'New Model Army', as he increasingly called it. 'I had dinner the other night with the little man, who is in terrific heart,' Sir Brian Horrocks wrote to de Guingand in the spring of 1947. 'He is doing extremely well as C.I.G.S. and has an immense influence with the Government. As usual, he is being rather naughty about attending the Chiefs of Staff meetings and this at times causes a little friction. Simbo has to go and take his place, and sometimes I am afraid, has rather a "rough passage". There are, however, a certain number of young politicians who are undoubtedly "gunning" for Monty, and whenever one of his speeches has the slightest political tinge, there is an immediate outcry. He is still, however, very popular with the general public, and when he came up to Chester a few months ago, we had the most amazing scenes. He is coming again in the middle of this month, and I expect we shall fight the battle of Alamein again with the crowd on the Square of Chester.'[1]

Monty's reaction to Attlee's announcement over Palestine and India, therefore, was not resignation. Instead he wrote from Switzerland to instruct the VCIGS to draft a memorandum pointing out the inevitable results of the government's imperial retreat.

> What are the Chiefs of Staff doing about all this? I imagine that we are doing what we always do i.e. we comment on each individual monstrosity as it occurs and as it is placed on the agenda. But have we considered the *collective effect* of the last 6 months on our British strategy? Have we represented to the Government that the repercussions of what has been done, are, *collectively*, immense? Have we made it clear that in the event of war we shall be

[1] Letter of 27.3.47, de Guingand Papers, loc. cit.

in a frightful predicament? . . . My own course of action is quite clear. On my return I shall table at the Chiefs of Staff a memorandum which sets out the matter quite simply and which can leave no doubt in anyone's mind *that we are drifting towards disaster*. The memorandum must be short, concise, absolutely clear, and 'utterly convincing'.

It must bring out the collective effect of all that has been done by the Government policy. It must bring out that we must now re-orientate our strategy; the East African base will now be a vital priority; a close tie-up with S. Africa, Australia and N. Zealand, is vital now, and we cannot just go on relying on some vague friendly arrangements. And so on.

Your staff will have some ideas on the things we must now go for *to offset what we have lost*.

Military alliances are now essential e.g. Russia, America. . . .

Please put your staff to work on the memorandum at once.[1]

The memorandum was ready by the time Monty returned from Switzerland. But Tedder would not sign it, and Monty's prediction that the Chiefs of Staff would do nothing—thus entitling the government 'to take our silence as acquiescence'[2]—came true. As Monty's diarist commented in June 1947, 'the Americans refused to give us the "know-how" on the construction of the atom bomb as, on the one hand they viewed us as a second-class power and on the other they doubted our ability to hold the secret in the face of pressure by the U.S.S.R. At the time of writing most papers in the USA and many prominent senators and Congressmen are talking about the British Empire in the past tense.'[3]

Such a view was not in itself mistaken. In his address to his Army commanders at the beginning of 1947 Monty had assumed the gradual liquidation of Britain's overseas military commitments in India, Greece, Egypt, Austria, Italy and Burma. It was the acceleration with which the British Government wished to divest itself of such commitments that worried Monty—such as the 'black month' in February 1947 when 'in a dismal succession, the following decisions were proclaimed to the world:

a) We would cease our aid to Greece after 31 March 47, just at the moment when the Spring campaign against the bandits was due to begin.

[1] Letter of 22.2.47, annex 84, Diary of Field-Marshal The Viscount Montgomery of Alamein, Part VII (3.2–21.6.47), Montgomery Papers.
[2] Ibid.
[3] Diary, Part VII, loc. cit.

b) We were to give up any attempt to hold the situation in Palestine and place our case without any British recommendation to the Security Council of UNO.
c) We were to hand over power in India in June, 1948.

'These were devastating decisions,' Monty's diarist noted. 'Withdrawal of support from the Greek Government at such a critical time would have inevitable and very serious effects on the morale of the Greek Army and would indeed prejudice the policy of the Government to hold the country in the face of Communist aggression supported by foreign weapons and money. Greece would inevitably be lost to the Western Democracies. With the loss of Greece the position of Turkey would become, to say the least, most difficult and if the Russians managed to get a foothold in Palestine, then Turkey would inevitably succumb. This would soon lead to the loss of Persia and her all important oil.'[1]

To surrender, overnight, Britain's Middle East base and her communications with the Far East seemed to Monty the height of irresponsibility. As he pointed out in his address to the assembled British Commonwealth and American generals gathered at Camberley in May for his 'Spearhead' Exercise, there were only two potential enemies Britain might have to face—Russia and possibly one day a united Germany. In such a war, Britain could assume that it would have 'the active support of the nations of the British Commonwealth, and *eventually* of other major powers as allies.'[2] But how long would the USA take before it declared its support for Britain—and how long would it take for that support to become materially effective? In the late war America had refrained from involvement for almost three years before declaring war—and even then only when herself attacked in her Far Eastern base in the Philippines. A further year had elapsed before American troops were in combat in Europe—and throughout those years Britain had had to maintain her own sea and land communications with the Commonwealth, and with her sources of supply. Monty's view was that Britain *had* to safeguard a network of bases and communications long enough to hold out, in time of war, until the USA and other allies could decide whether to join Britain and then send forces.

Small wonder, then, that Monty urged his VCIGS to start studying the ramifications of Attlee's sell-out—in particular the subject of military alliances.

[1] Ibid.
[2] Opening address at Exercise 'Spearhead', 5.5.47, annex 107, Diary, Part VII, loc. cit.

In fact Britain's declaration of bankruptcy forced America to take at least a financial stake in the reconstruction of the Western European nations as a bulwark against the spread of Russian-backed Communism. Britain's financial support to Greece was taken over in May by Truman; Marshall Aid to Europe began in June; but for the moment no military commitments beyond the secret discussions between Whitehall and the Pentagon were made.

In this vacuum, with Stalin consolidating puppet regimes in Poland, Czechoslovakia, Hungary, Rumania and Bulgaria, there was a brief lull as Britain, watched with amazement by the rest of the world, abandoned the imperial ship regardless of consequences. Wavell handed over to Mountbatten—who unilaterally decided in June 1947 to sell out in ten weeks.

CHAPTER EIGHT

Seeing the Red Light

When Monty wrote to his erstwhile Chief of Staff, Freddie de Guingand, on 1 June 1947 he had been CIGS almost a year. 'It has been a very hard year, with many battles to fight,' he related; yet he was not without hope, at least with regard to the British Army. 'I have gained my way in all vital issues,' he claimed, 'and I reckon the post-war Army is now well launched: Regular and T.A.'[1] But he was crowing too soon.

Two days later, at a Press conference in Delhi, Mountbatten announced to the world that Britain would transfer power not in June 1948 or even in the autumn of 1947, but on 15 August—a bare two months away.

On top of Attlee's decision to hand over to the United Nations the British mandate in Palestine, the repercussions on British military strategy and planning were immense. Monty had already decided to make another world tour, to Palestine, Singapore, Australia, New Zealand and Japan, starting on 21 June. India was now added.

Tirelessly, like the commander of a besieged garrison, Monty toured his troops and commanders overseas. In Palestine there must be no talk of withdrawal yet to East Africa: Britain *must* safeguard her oil supplies by maintaining a presence there and commanders must *not* look over their shoulders. In India (which Monty visited from 23 to 25 June) Field-Marshal Auchinleck must give up his hopes of being made executive Supreme Commander of both Pakistan's and India's emerging armies: instead, he must as a matter of urgency help Nehru and Jinnah recognize the vacuum that would result at the end of British rule on 15 August and the need to prepare their respective armed forces for the very problems of internal communal violence that the British Army was facing, for instance, in Palestine.[2]

[1] Letter of 1.6.47, de Guingand Papers, IWM.

[2] 'CIGS prepared a memorandum on these lines [26 June 1947] which he tabled at a meeting with the Viceroy and Lord Ismay [Mountbatten's Chief of Staff]. This plan was completely different from that on which C-in-C, India [Auchinleck] had been working: he had assumed that he would continue to be C-in-C over both the Pakistan and Indian Union Armies. For the sake of the Indian Army and the good of India as a whole this might well be the best plan: but it was clearly unacceptable to Jinnah

Equally, Admiral Mountbatten, the new Viceroy, must understand that Jinnah would never accept him as Governor-General of Pakistan [1] and that the fruits of his accelerated rush into independence and partition were potentially catastrophic—'the division of India into Pakistan and the Indian Union at such speed raises terrific problems,' he noted—adding that, unless the two new states co-operated as Mountbatten assumed, 'there will be the most awful chaos and much bloodshed.' [2] In Australia British tri-service representation was expensive and in Monty's view fatuous; as was the so-called trinity of British Services in the Far East, with Naval Headquarters over a thousand miles from army and air force counterparts.

Signal after signal was beamed back to the War Office as Monty flew across the world. But Monty's fellow Chiefs of Staff were neither interested in India nor in Supreme Command in the Far East, and his suggestion that the Navy move its headquarters to Singapore aroused such bitter feeling that the VCIGS, General Simpson, was soon begging Monty to keep quiet lest he destroy even the little army-navy accord that still survived.

Monty was now driving himself harder than at any previous period in his life, directing his relentlessly clarifying brain on political, strategic, military and social matters at home and abroad, always concise, logical and to the point, but seemingly no longer in tune with the times or the people with whom he was dealing. In Australia and New Zealand there were scenes of almost hysterical hero-worship

---

and therefore could not be carried out': Diary, Part VII, loc. cit. By late August, as the massacres began, Mountbatten reluctantly began to see that 'separate forces might not enforce the peace with . . . impartiality, but at least they would know what they were doing and could be relied on to obey the orders of their officers.' (P. Ziegler, *Mountbatten*, London 1985). It was too late, however. Though the Punjab Boundary Force was ordered to be disbanded and reconstituted on national lines, the scale of inter-communal violence escalated beyond military control. 'I fear you are having a very trying time and I wish I could help you!' Monty lamented in a letter from London in mid-September. 'My suggestion would be that you should speed up in every possible way the reconstitution of the two armies, and should close down Supreme HQ at the earliest possible date.' (Letter of 17.9.47, Broadlands Archive). Had Mountbatten delayed partition until such reconstitution of forces, many of the estimated four million deaths resulting from the massacres might have been spared.

[1] Mountbatten's fantasy that he would be acceptable as dual Governor General of both India and Pakistan was first punctured by Jinnah on 1.7.47, six days after Monty's departure. By the time Mountbatten drew up his personal Report No. 11 for the British Government on 4.7.47 he was accusing Jinnah, who had robbed him of the crowning achievement of his Viceroyalty, of 'suffering from megalomania in its worst form'—P. Ziegler, op. cit.

[2] B.L. Montgomery, *Memoirs*, London 1958.

wherever he went; gifts were showered upon him, the press followed him everywhere. He had to give more speeches than any contemporary politician, he spoke as the First Soldier of Europe. Yet his impatient, decisive approach to problems and to people could not, in itself, reverse the tide of history. At Alamein his infectious self-confidence and mastery of his profession had transformed a defeated army into one that could not lose; but he had arrived in the desert at a time when fresh troops, better guns, more tanks and new allies were about to bolster Britain's military performance. Whereas now, in the summer of 1947, Britain's Army was first rocked by the government's premature abandonment of its overseas strategic bases, then by a gathering economic crisis at home that threatened Monty's whole vision of a modern, professional, post-war Army.

The economic problems faced by the Labour Government early in 1947 were shown now to be but the tip of an iceberg. Monty had hoped, by leadership and vision, to ensure that Britain did not 'drift aimlessly' into an emasculated post-war posture, unprepared for war, incapable of resisting rearmament and the military conquests of a dictator in Europe, as had happened after World War I. But, apart from Bevin, no member of Attlee's government shared Monty's fears. The Conservatives, under Churchill, were more concerned with seeking electoral support (appealing for instance for the abolition of National Service, or only a nominal six-month term) than encouraging Britons to face up to the responsibilities of the way of life they had fought for, both in work and in defence. As a result, fearful of left-wing, back-bench criticism, the Government was now forced to reduce the forthcoming National Service requirement from eighteen months to twelve.

Fearing the worst Monty decided not to go on to Japan.

> I cancelled my visit to Japan because I do not at all like the look of things at home. Ministers are desperate to make cuts and economies and are making rash decisions, in a panic, about the armed forces,

he wrote to Mountbatten from Karachi.

> I have agreed to certain cuts by telegram from Australia. I then saw the red light and said I would agree to no more until I had personally examined the situation in SEALF, in the Middle East, and in Germany. I am doing the two first named on my way home, and go to Germany next week.
>
> Quite apart from the armed forces, there are other things at

home which cause me alarm. I fear we may have some trouble. But we must try and keep the ship on an even keel somehow. I shall have a quiet talk with Herbert Morrison when I get back.[1]

Monty arrived back in London on 8 August 1947, and was soon doing battle in the Chiefs of Staff Committee. 'I am far from happy about things; we are drifting down stream, and unless we get the set-up right and have a firm grip from on top, we shall drift to disaster,' he had predicted in a letter to Mountbatten in May[2]—begging him to use his personal influence on Attlee to create a 'Chief of Staff, Armed Forces, who would be an independent Chairman of the Chiefs of Staff Committee'.[3] Lacking such an independent Chairman, and racked by their personal and strategic differences, with a 'mobile whisky and soda'[4] for a Minister, the consequences of British economic and imperial bankruptcy appeared bleak.

Had the British Chiefs of Staff been united in their stance, the outlook might have been less depressing. Monty's 'Spearhead' exercise had concerned the mounting of a Combined Operations assault landing. Provided that the three Services *did* combine to produce effective task forces capable of mounting co-ordinated operations overseas, then the effects of premature abandonment of Britain's overseas bases and command centres might be mitigated, particularly if military alliances, such as the Dunkirk treaty recently signed between Britain and France, were sought. To Monty's chagrin, however, it looked as if Britain's three Services were drifting further apart rather than combining, and instead of developing balanced defence forces, Britain's military house, in the wake of national economic crisis, was in disarray. By the autumn of 1947 he had lost all faith in the concept of a committee of Chiefs of Staff; at the Chiefs of Staff meeting on 2 September 1947, he openly read out a statement decrying the very concept of Joint Chiefs of Staff. It had failed, he declared.

[1] Letter of 5.8.47, Broadlands Archive.

[2] Letter of 22.5.47, Broadlands Archive.

[3] Ibid.

[4] In a letter in January 1949 to the historian Arthur Bryant, who wrote regularly for the *Illustrated London News*, Monty recalled: 'After nearly 2 years on the Chiefs of Staff Committee I came to the conclusion that we were making no progress towards the co-ordinated development of our Defence Services. The White Paper of October 1946 had not achieved its object: a unified defence policy. The real answer was to have a first class Minister of Defence; that we have not got; A. V. Alexander is merely a mobile whisky and soda. So I wrote the enclosed paper and forced it up to the Prime Minister. The decision was that no change was needed and we must carry on as we were! Hence the condition of the fighting Services today': letter of 18.1.49, Bryant Papers.

> We are quite unable to agree on basic fundamental issues; every recommendation we make is a compromise on essentials. As Chiefs of Staff we have failed to produce a balanced national Defence Force.
>
> We have shelved the fundamental questions of the roles of the three Services, of their inter-relationship, and finally of their size so as to produce a balanced Defence organization: because no Service will give way and we have no one to give a final decision.

By making financial cuts on a percentage budget basis for each Service, the larger picture of balanced national defence in a time of radically altered strategic considerations was ignored.

> A continuation of this casual treatment of Defence questions is utterly amateur; it is in fact a complete 'nonsense'.
>
> If we continue in this way we shall end in disaster.

The statement did no good, Tedder and Cunningham merely assuming that Monty wished to attack Tedder's chairmanship. But Monty's statement was not a personal attack; he had, since the previous autumn, increasingly considered the Joint Chiefs of Staff system to be an anachronism. In a modern world, as in modern war, there had to be a Supreme Commander. This man should be a Chief of Staff to the Minister of Defence, charged with recommending to the Cabinet a coherent Combined Service defence policy, including the allotted Army, Navy and Air Force functions in executing that policy. Such a Chief of Staff would ex officio preside over the Services Chiefs of Staff. Together with the enactment of effective military alliances to counter-balance Britain's abnegation of overseas responsibilities, these were to be the twin targets to which Monty devoted the remainder of his military career.

CHAPTER NINE

If the Thing Goes Sky-High

'IN BRITAIN WE are moving rapidly towards a crisis the potentialities of which we can but dimly discern,' Monty confided to de Guingand in October 1947. 'Europe is in deep distress. There is serious discord in Asia. People are restive and critical the world over. Dickie [Mountbatten] has led the British statesmen right down the garden path in India; what is going on there now surpasses in savage butchery anything that the Japanese ever did. And it has only begun; there is worse to follow.'[1] In Britain, industrial output was a prey to war-weariness, absenteeism and, with the introduction of rationing, demoralization. Within six months Monty foresaw a national crisis. 'I do not believe the measures that are being taken will solve the problem. We will win prosperity only by hard work; there are 168 hours in the week and we will do no good by working only 40. There has got to be a row with those people who are stopping a man doing a full day's work when he really wants to, and with those who put restrictive practices on output. No good will result until this row, or showdown, has taken place and has been won. The Govt. won't face it; they think they can get through without it; but they can't. If the thing goes sky-high,' he warned, 'I may have to play a part: and would do so.'[2]

Whether Monty contemplated a military take-over, or merely a government of national unity in which he would play an active role, was as yet unclear; what was evident was that Monty himself was working too hard, on too many fronts, and on his own: the very faults which had so often marred his performance as a higher commander during the war.

By January 1948 the Minister of Defence, in response to the Government's orders for further massive cuts in defence expenditure, circulated a paper arguing that the RAF possessed Britain's best weapon for deterrence: the bomber. The Navy was required to safeguard sea communications. The Army would have to manage on what could thereafter be spared.

[1] Letter of 4.10.47, de Guingand Papers, loc. cit. Over four million lives are reckoned to have been lost in the disturbances following accelerated partition.
[2] Ibid.

Monty, agog at such defeatism, protested. The Minister's paper was withdrawn—but the writing was on the wall. He who had spent a lifetime preparing for stewardship of the British Army, not only in war but in peace, would now have to preside over its virtual destruction, at least in the terms in which he had always envisaged it. There would not even be room, in the projected 1949 estimates, for a single fully equipped British armoured division; in fact there would be difficulty in providing for a fully equipped field fighting force of even one infantry division and two infantry and parachute brigades. The rest of Britain's Army would be training cadres. As a world power Britain was bankrupt.

Food rationing and petrol restriction were now followed by travel embargo. 'Mon Lucien, darling boy, I have some very sad news for you,' Monty wrote soon after New Year. 'I cannot come to Switzerland this year. The British Government have asked me not to go, because of the restrictions on foreign travel that are now in force in England. I cannot tell you what this means to me; I was so very anxious to see you again and give you a big hug. But it cannot be this year. You must be brave, my Lucien. It is a shattering blow. But we can write to each other. And we have our great love for each other; nothing can ever upset that. . . . Be brave my darling boy; we will have a great meeting as soon as the restrictions on travel and currency are removed. You have all my love, always. Yr very devoted "Papa".'[1]

Scarcely a week had passed in 1947 without Monty writing to his 'bien aimé', and sending gifts of stamps, photographs, even the money for a bicycle. The cancellation of his trip to Gstaad, planned for February 1948, came as an added disappointment to Monty on top of the collapse of his vision of Britain's post-war Army. On 14 January 1948 he heard that not only would the Army's budget be cut substantially, but that, in order to provide further manpower for industry, a further 40,000 soldiers must be shed by the Army, reducing its regular army to 185,000 men and women.

Given such disappointments it was small wonder that Monty should sometimes give way to nostalgia for the old days of comradeship and shared hopes. Each October, on the anniversary of the great desert battle, an Alamein Reunion had been held. In October 1947 some 7000 veterans had attended, at the Albert Hall; indeed so many were denied seats that the BBC broadcast the proceedings, including speeches by Monty and the guest of honour that year, the Foreign Secretary Mr Ernest Bevin. Though he knew it was a mistake to look backwards rather than forwards, Monty's loneliness would

[1] Letter of 6.1.48, Papers of Lord Montgomery of Alamein.

occasionally well up and get the better of him. Such an occurrence came now when, denied his holiday with Lucien in Switzerland, he begged the Queen to return 'his' picture of Tac Headquarters, Normandy, 1944.

'My dear Lascelles,' Monty wrote on 20 January 1948,

> I write on a very delicate matter and it may be that there is 'nothing doing'. If so, please say so at once and I will pipe down at once.
>
> After the Falaise battle James Gunn came to my HQ in the field at my request to paint some pictures. One of these was a conversation piece in my Mess tent, with my personal staff; there is a rabbit on the ground near me. This was shown in the Royal Academy. The painting was to come to me but the Queen saw it, liked it very much, and asked Gunn if she could have it. So I lost it.
>
> My whole soul yearns for this picture; it is a great reminder of those stirring times and it was painted for me. The point is this. Would the Queen let me have the picture? Alternatively, I could have it for my lifetime: the picture to be returned to the Royal Family on my death.
>
> Will you let me know if there is any possibility of my request being granted.
>
> Yours sincerely
> Montgomery of Alamein
>
> P.S. My son David has never seen the picture.[1]

Monty's letter was passed by Lascelles to the Queen's Private Secretary, who was appalled. The Queen explained that when she asked to buy the picture at the Royal Academy Exhibition 'Gunn had said . . . that he had asked M[ontgomery] who had said he didn't want it'.[2] This was not the case, as Monty's boastful letter to Lascelles in the autumn of 1944,[3] after seeing the finished painting, clearly proves. But whatever the truth, the Queen was irritated by Monty's presumptuousness. However, she was quite certain in her own mind that Britain owed its survival in the war to two men: Churchill and Montgomery. She therefore agreed that 'Monty should certainly have the picture for winning the war, but for no other reason'.[4]

[1] Letter of 20.1.48, (RA GVI/283) Royal Archives, Windsor.

[2] Memo of 21.1.48. Ibid.

[3] 'James Gunn is now back in London, with some quite 1st Class pictures he has painted here—a portrait of myself, and a conversation piece in my mess. He thinks the portrait is the best one he has ever done; it is definitely superb. They will be going to my house in Hindhead in a few days. . . . Possibly the King might like to see the conversation piece; he would know the characters well': letter of 20.9.44 (RA/GVI PS/7214), Royal Archives, Windsor.

[4] Memo of 21.1.48 (RA GVI/283) Royal Archives, Windsor.

The Queen's response was, in a nutshell, that of a host of those who, outraged at Monty's tactlessness and egocentricity, tolerated his personal shortcomings because of the debt the free world owed him. Monty subsequently arranged for Gunn to paint him a copy of the group portrait; but the damage had been done and the Queen's staff peered like liveried retainers down their noses at Monty's 'upstartish' antics. 'Since M has succeeded in greatly vexing Gunn and slightly annoying HM, this is not perhaps one of his most successful campaigns,' Lascelles remarked in a memo to the Queen's Private Secretary. 'The Queen bought it as an example of a war picture by a living artist, but I have no doubt that the CIGS would find it difficult to believe that she was not really attracted by the subject,' he added scorningly.[1]

Monty's life was indeed coming full circle: the square peg in the round hole, the boy fated to clash with his mother in a battle of wills, self-centred and unable to control his urge to take charge and to lead. Fame and historic victories had done nothing to assuage his need to dominate, or to make him less prickly.

This was perhaps the most unhappy period of Monty's career, at least since the death of his wife in 1937; and his unhappiness showed in his behaviour as CIGS. He began to refuse to attend meetings of the Chiefs of Staff when Tedder was expected to be present. He was not forgiven by Cunningham for, first, suggesting the scrapping of the building of obsolete battleships, then the move of Naval headquarters in the Far East. His speeches about the need for new social incentives for harder work and greater political leadership were ill-received by a Government struggling to survive the worst financial crisis in British history. And the succession of cuts and distasteful overseas tasks facing the Army meant dwindling morale, ever worsening recruitment figures and much blame laid at the door of the Army's chief.

Nor did the situation look like improving in 1948. To the East India was still racked by communal atrocities, and the prospects in Palestine were becoming daily bleaker. In the West the Russian stance over quadri-partite control of Germany was leading to increasing tension, centring on Berlin.

Although Monty cancelled all foreign tours outside Europe to be 'on hand' if 'the thing goes sky-high', his services as National Leader or even dictator were not to be required. Instead it would be he himself who would be driven into 'exile', in the wake of Churchill, de Gaulle, Benes and others. He had made too many enemies, spoken too openly of the failings both of the party in power, and the whole

[1] Memo of 14.4.48, Royal Archives, Windsor.

Whitehall system of defence. His friends, like Her Majesty the Queen, had admired him for his generalship in Britain's service in World War II, and still did;[1] but by his performance and behaviour thereafter they became increasingly embarrassed.

[1] The Queen had, on the day after the German surrender at Lüneburg, sent Monty a moving personal tribute in her own hand: 'To Field Marshal Montgomery, my deep admiration for your Genius in Command which led to the greatest Victory': 'Congratulatory Messages' file, Montgomery Papers.

CHAPTER TEN

Fiasco in Palestine

IN RETROSPECT IT is remarkable that Monty held on to his job as CIGS for so long. He disagreed with his fellow Chiefs of Staff on major issues; worse still, with the exception of the Foreign Secretary Mr Bevin, Monty disagreed with the Prime Minister and every member of his Government regarding British military and political strategy. But by early 1948 he was quarrelling even with Bevin, and Attlee was asking despairingly, 'What *is* the matter with the C.I.G.S.? Why *is* Monty so difficult?' [1]

The 'matter' was that Monty was quite unsuited to his job in a period of inevitable retrenchment. His victories in World War II had given him the illusion that, with moral courage and an aggressive spirit, the tide of war could be reversed. In the aftermath of World War II he had assumed a period of extended peace, during which the Western Nations could re-build their peacetime economies and quietly and professionally prepare their armed forces for a possible confrontation with the Russian 'Empire' when Russia recovered from the human and economic ravages of Hitler's war.

Instead, Monty found his own country bereft of leadership, depressed economically and obsessed with imperial retreat whatever the consequences. Such abdication of responsibility was bound to encourage disorder across the world, exposing the emerging nations to terrorism, division and Communism. For all its criticisms of the British Mandate in Palestine, America had no desire to replace British civil or military rule; Britain was thus left holding the baby while the world protested about her quality of infant care. It was in this situation that Bevin and Attlee decided simply to abandon Palestine as they had abandoned India in August, declaring on 16 October 1947 that they would surrender the mandate and withdraw all their troops by 1 August of the following year. This was later advanced to 15 May 1948 in recognition of the United Nations recommendation in favour of partition—which, for fear of upsetting the all-important Arab states in the Middle East, Britain refused to enforce. As the UN would not provide a military force to police partition, the fate

[1] Diary of Field-Marshal The Viscount Montgomery of Alamein, Part XI (16.2–29.5.48), Montgomery Papers.

of the Holy Land was abandoned to the gods. British civil servants and troops were to withdraw in four timed phases, leaving local Jews and Arabs to divide the spoils, Britain washing its hands of the consequent catastrophe.

Such moral cowardice had been unthinkable before Mountbatten's announcement, on 4 June 1947, that Britain would abandon India in less than three months' time. Now, it was considered the British 'norm'. Monty was doubly distressed. Abandonment of Palestine meant the surrender of Britain's primary military base in the Middle East; moreover, without an adequate political settlement of Palestine's future, current inter-racial violence under the British Mandate would inevitably get worse and the lot of the British troops charged with the evacuation would be made difficult, if not impossible. By late April 1948 Bevin was complaining that world opinion was outraged by the way British troops were failing to halt the massacre of Arabs in Haifa—and claimed the Army had 'let him down'. Incensed, Monty almost engendered a Cabinet crisis by demanding that Bevin withdraw the insult and apologize. The Minister of Defence told Monty not to worry as Bevin's remarks had not been made in public. Whereupon

> CIGS told him that the whole Army now knew about it, as did S. of S. for War. This shook A.V.A.[lexander, Minister of Defence], who said that it was quite unnecessary for CIGS to have passed it on. CIGS tartly told him that insults of this nature could not be kept private nor could they be accepted without protest by those responsible: who included the Minister of Defence. CIGS, now worked up, went on to tell the Minister that the Army had not forgotten Mr Bevin's previous statement that he staked his political reputation on a successful solution of the Palestine problem; he had consistently refused to listen to the Army's views, so often reiterated by CIGS, that it was fatal to be weak in our handling of the Jews; on the contrary, he, the Foreign Secretary, had accepted the advice given by the High Commissioner and the Colonial Secretary and as a result he had made a proper mess of the whole thing; now that he realised what he had done he was looking for a scapegoat and in a thoroughly cowardly way, was trying to make the Army into this scapegoat. He, CIGS, was not going to put up with this and he was determined to pursue the matter and get it settled one way or the other.[1]

It was clear that Monty was indeed worked up. With the Jews effectively seizing control of Haifa by 27 April 1948 and having

[1] Ibid.

declared they would set up an independent Jewish state no matter what the United Nations decided, Bevin's fear of anti-British feeling among the Arab states increased, for it looked as if, in the civil war that was engulfing Palestine, the Arabs would be denied any Mediterranean port at all. Monty's subsequent signal to the C-in-C Middle East on 29 April was not anti-Semitic: it was the expression of his profound frustration at the sorry train of events leading up to British termination of the Mandate. On his African tour before Christmas, he had decided in his own mind that the Jews in Palestine deserved their likely fate, writing in his memorandum of 19 December 1947:

> The fact must be faced that there will be a complete breakdown of civil government, and law and order, as we vacate the [phased withdrawal] areas in turn. On 15 May, when the Mandate is surrendered, King Abdullah [of Transjordan] will move into the key Arab areas of Nablus, Hebron and Gaza, and will begin his plans to absorb the Arab State into Transjordan; this is actually the best thing that could happen and will be welcomed by the Palestinian Arabs. Jewish minorities in the Arab State will then be persecuted and plundered. No Arab troops or police will enter the Jewish State; but Arab minorities, re-inforced by special gangsters sent in for the purpose, will begin a campaign of banditry and sabotage in the Jewish State. This will continue until the Jews give up the contest. All communications will be disrupted and it will be economically very difficult for the Jews to carry on. In other words the Arabs are likely to win. The Jews have made a great mistake and will probably 'get it in the neck'.[1]

This view was based on a report by the GOC in Palestine, General Macmillan, who felt the Jews 'did not like fighting for any length of time and he did not think that they would have much stomach for a prolonged struggle'. But Macmillan was spectacularly wrong in this judgment, as in his view that economic factors would lead 'to the complete collapse of the Jewish State'.[2] Thus Monty, who had hoped like Bevin that the British Army could maintain impartiality and by a policy of great firmness with the Jewish terrorists withdraw from Palestine with its reputation unsullied, was now forced to acknowledge that the Jews were coming off best from British withdrawal. 'The fighting in JAFFA is causing concern in Whitehall in that it would

[1] Memorandum, 'Tour in Africa in Nov/Dec 1947' of Field-Marshal The Viscount Montgomery of Alamein, annex 206, Diary Part I (3.11.47–15.2.48) Montgomery Papers.
[2] Ibid.

place us in a difficult situation if the Jews were to gain possession of the town. The argument is that JAFFA is the only Arab port in Palestine and it is up to us to see that it does not change hands before 15 May,' Monty cabled to General Crocker's Middle East headquarters.

> Please take all necessary steps to ensure that the Arabs remain in possession of JAFFA. The Jewish forces which are attacking JAFFA must be attacked heavily by us with all the military force that can be made available. Use aircraft and bomb the Jews and shoot them up. Use British troops even if this entails casualties to our forces. The more armed members of the IZL [the Irgun Zvei Leumi] and Stern gangs that you can kill the better,

he added, thinking of the King David Hotel outrage.

> You will be supported from here in any measures you take. The great point is that the Jews must not capture Jaffa. If they do capture the town it must be retaken by us and handed back to the Arabs.[1]

The IZL were driven off by Spitfires, tanks, Highlanders and other British infantry; but with most Arabs fleeing for their lives 'the problem here is likely to be difficulty of finding an Arab authority to hand over to when the time comes for withdrawal', General Crocker telegraphed back.[2] Far from getting it 'in the neck', the Jews were able to attain more than they had ever dreamed possible, with the British discredited by both sides for their callous abandonment of the region, and the Middle East de-stabilized for decades to come. For all his faults, Mountbatten had at least obtained the agreement of Jinnah, Nehru and the main Indian Princes to partition before evacuation, as well as dominion status within the Commonwealth; whereas the British legacy to the people of Palestine was unmitigated disaster—save for Zionist immigrants and those tormented survivors of the holocaust who, refused a home in the United States, found sanctuary in Israel.

Monty had prejudiced his relationship with Bevin over Palestine. With the Colonial Secretary, Arthur Creech-Jônes, he had also aroused the deepest ill-will, first by touring Africa in December 1947, then by announcing widely that Britain had no 'grand design and no master plan', as a result of which 'no real progress in development is

[1] Signal of 1500 hrs, 29.4.48, 'Palestine, November 1947 to May 1948' file, Montgomery Papers.
[2] Signal of 2.5.48, in 'Palestine, November 47 to May 48' file, Montgomery Papers.

being made'.[1] Creech-Jones reacted with extreme irritation, issuing a counter-memorandum designed to demonstrate that 'the imposition on the African Territories of a grand design or master plan by central control and direction from London would not be practical politics and would conflict with our declared policy of devolution in the process of building up self-government . . . such a course would not secure the co-operation of the local people, without which effectual development cannot take place'.[2]

It was clear that Monty was out of step with his time, that he held, at heart, a Victorian concept of empire and spheres of influence: a vision of Britain retaining its Great Power status by an economic and military network increasingly based on Africa, thus counter-balancing the inevitable crumbling position of Britain in the Far East and in Asia. In fact the more setbacks to British post-war pre-stige and economic recovery, the more Monty searched for a vision to restore a sense of purpose. What he said about Africa made considerable sense, and both Attlee and Bevin took Monty's words seriously, for as yet Africa had not been penetrated by either Russian or American influence. Building up a grand design for the economic union of British pan-Africa territories would doubtless benefit both the African states and Britain; it would also act as a bulwark against Russian Communism. But it was a vision for Britain in its industrial heyday, not in bankruptcy; moreover, it did not address the issues of local and tribal nationalism, of racial and cultural apartheid. Just as the Far Eastern colonies were rejecting European paternalism, so too, inevitably, would black Africa.

Increasingly, therefore, Monty found himself at odds with his peers. Yet it was not only patriotism which motivated such a search for ideals: it was the knowledge that, if Britain did not at least associate itself with such ideals, the tide of Communism would sweep across the free world as surely as Hitler had toppled the moribund democratic regimes of Europe. Since the autumn of 1947 Monty had become more concerned by the possibility of war in Europe, given the weakness of will and economic distress of the Western nations. This now came to a head with the Anglo-American proposals to study the evacuation problems from the Continent if the Russians were to attack.

Once again Monty smelled defeatism. While Monty had been in Africa, the Foreign Secretary, following the collapse of the London talks with Russia on the future of Germany, had begun negotiations with Bidault of France and Marshall of the USA on the matter of

[1] Diary, Part X, loc. cit.

[2] Memorandum by Secretary of State for Colonies, annex 212, Diary, Part X, loc. cit.

Western alliances. The French favoured a common approach to western European defence, and though Marshall was dubious whether Congress would permit cast-iron American guarantees of military commitment to Europe, he applauded Bevin's initiative, while assuring him that secret military talks between Britain and the USA would continue.

Bevin's plan was for an Anglo-French Treaty with Belgium, Holland and Luxembourg: the Western European Union. At a later date it was hoped to associate it with the remaining non-Communist states, 'most notably Scandinavia and Italy'. Bevin spoke to Monty on 23 December 1947, asking him to authorize secret military talks between the three Western C-in-Cs in Germany 'with a view to ensuring concerted action in the event of any attempt by the Russians to move into Western Europe'.[1] Monty was himself to initiate military staff talks with the French—a process which began when Monty met his French opposite number, General Revers, on 21 January 1948.

Revers welcomed Monty's lead—and within months Monty had become the virtual consultant-general to the French and Belgian armies. Building on his success in starting Western Union, Bevin formally suggested an Atlantic pact and, if possible, a Mediterranean pact. Marshall's response was now favourable—if American politicians could be convinced that such a military pact made military sense. It was here that Monty's problems began—for Tedder and Cunningham were convinced that the continent of Europe could not be held in the event of Russian attack. They thus dismissed any idea of a continental strategy when the matter was raised in the Chiefs of Staff meeting on 2 February 1948. Forcing a meeting with the Prime Minister, Foreign Secretary, Minister of Defence and Chiefs of Staff on 4 February, Monty emphasized 'that it would be mighty difficult to achieve any effective Western Union if we could not promise support on land in the event of war', as his diarist chronicled. 'The Prime Minister then weighed in very strongly against a commitment to send our Army to the Continent, but he was counter-attacked by the Foreign Secretary and Minister of Defence, both of whom in their own ways supported CIGS's views. The meeting finally agreed to consider the implications of the strategy which CIGS advocated and the COS were instructed to produce the necessary paper.'[2]

Thus began Monty's struggle to make Western Union and the Atlantic Pact a military reality. Tedder's attitude was to refer all such questions to planners and then consider their verdicts. To Monty this was as much a nonsense in peace as in war. Planners had

[1] Diary, Part X, loc. cit.

[2] Ibid.

to have guidance, otherwise their verdicts reflected the vacuum in which the reports were concocted. Militarily it was of course impossible to justify standing either on the line of the Elbe or even the Rhine in the event of full-scale war with Russia. Evacuation was therefore bound to be the recommendation of any board of planners—and indeed was the inevitable finale to Operation 'Doublequick', the secret Anglo-American plan for reaction to Russian advance.[1] However sensible from a purely theoretical viewpoint, to plan actively for such a contingency was to encourage defeatism—as Monty had found on arrival in Cairo and Alamein in the summer of 1942. Western Union was in the process of being born: it would very quickly die if the parents and godparents absconded. Monty's paper, rejected by the Chiefs of Staff Committee on 2 February 1948, was prophetic:

> France is the key-stone of the Western Union and she must be made to understand that her safety does *not* lie in dismembering Germany and carving that country up into small states; her safety lies rather in a contented German State, which is strong politically, which has a well-planned and flourishing peace economy, and which looks westwards.
>
> Therefore France *must* come into the German Government being set up at Frankfurt; this Government must embrace the three western zones and the resulting state should be called 'Germany'. . . .
>
> Clearly we cannot afford to neglect any area which could provide fighting manpower and industrial potential. In both these respects Germany would be an important asset.
>
> Britain should make a Treaty with Germany and bring her into the Western Union.
>
> The political difficulties of including any part of Germany in a combination of which France is a member will be very great. But we must persuade France that in her own interests she should make friends with her age-long enemy: because of the great advantages of a friendly Germany in a Western Union which is resolutely prepared to fight Communism.
>
> The political difficulties of forming the Western Union and ensuring that the countries concerned present a united front from the outset, will be considerable.

[1] 'The planners estimated that the probable scale of enemy attack in Europe was more than we could possibly hold in the period under discussion and that therefore both the British and American forces in Germany would have to be evacuated.' Ibid.

Our aim must be to build up a Union which has the necessary economic and military strength to stop Russia in the initial stage [i.e. before American help could be brought in].

There is only one hope of achieving this object. *We must agree that, if attacked, the nations of the Western Union will hold this attack as far East as possible e.g. on the Rhine.* We must make it very clear that Britain will play her full part in this strategy and will support the battle on the Rhine or elsewhere with the fullest possible weight of our land, air and naval power.

Unless this basic point in our strategy is agreed and is accepted whole-heartedly by Britain, the Western Union can have no hope of survival, and Britain would be in the gravest danger.[1]

Despite Tedder's and Cunningham's opposition, Monty now began a campaign to push and cajole Britain into this life-saving commitment to its Western Union infant. Both he and Bevin[2] now considered Tedder and Cunningham's attitude potentially so stifling that talks between the British, American and French C-in-Cs in Germany on plans to meet a Russian attack had to be conducted without Tedder and Cunningham's knowledge! Monty himself wrote to Eisenhower's successor as Army Chief of Staff in Washington, General Bradley, to beg his support for Western Union—and for the policy of holding the Russians on the Rhine. He enclosed his paper on the strategy of war with Russia, remarking that, since writing it, 'Czechoslovakia has gone; Finland is now being 'lined up' [for puppetization]. My view is that the time has come to marshal the forces of the West against the menace from the East; we must agree on our line of action; we must create an organization which will allow of the problem being studied, and which will ensure quick action when the time comes.'

Monty admitted 'that my two colleagues on the British Chiefs of Staff are not yet convinced that my views are right', but only if a specific commitment to hold the line of the Rhine were made, he felt, would the countries of Western Europe find the determination to work towards that target. 'It is not militarily possible to fight the defensive battle on the Rhine alignment until the countries of the Western Union have to some considerable extent recovered their

[1] 'The Problem of Future War and the Strategy of War with Russia', 30.1.48, Montgomery Papers.

[2] Bevin had adopted Tedder's stance in the autumn of 1947, refusing to countenance British commitment to a land campaign on the Continent of Europe—'we do not want any more Dunkirks'—but had been won over by Monty's insistent arguments and the deteriorating international situation in Europe.

moral and military strength,' he allowed. 'This is an immensely important point. I can see no other strategic aim which will induce them to put their military house in order. They obviously will not subscribe to any strategy which envisages their being overrun in the early stages of the war.' He himself would see that the armies of the Western Union were 'properly organised and equipped', and that the 'system of command in each country' was got right. 'I consider that between the lot, we want 45 to 50 divisions, *and I am going flat out to see that we have them.*' National Service should not be the means to establish such defences: rather, the period of National Service should be seen as a training for Territorial or Reserve service, and the small standing armies of each nation should have as their primary aim the training and command of such Reserve troops. 'Any question of the withdrawal of the existing United States and British forces through Ostend, or any other port in Europe, is out of the question.' The forces in Western Europe, furthermore, needed an American Supreme Commander. 'A long time ago, I personally told Ike that I would back you for the job,' he confided to Bradley. 'That was before you took up your present appointment.' Monty therefore suggested 'Lightning' Joe Collins. Though 'politically impossible to appoint a Supreme Commander at the present time', Monty considered the American Supremo 'should be selected and should come over here to study the problem of the defensive battle'.[1]

All this would, in time, come to pass: a tribute to Bevin's political courage (in defiance of a Little-Britain Prime Minister and Cabinet) and to Monty's outstanding vision. Sadly, having worked in the greatest harmony to establish the concept of the Western Union alliance, Bevin and Monty now crossed swords. The French had invited Monty to visit their Army on 22 March, with a view to discussing the organization and training of the French Army, but Bevin refused to sanction the trip, saying that the visit would be premature before 'further discussions had taken place at the political level'. The 'refusal caused, of course, a big stir in Paris and was indeed a most unfortunate business', Monty's diarist noted. 'No one connected with the matter in London believed for one moment that there was any substance in the political reasons given. . . . The writer's own opinion is that the real reason lay in the Foreign Secretary's anxiety to secure for himself all the kudos of establishing Western Union as all his own work. He was jealous lest CIGS's visits to Belgium and France should give rise to a widely held view that it was in fact CIGS who was using his personality to negotiate the Union rather than that he (Mr Bevin) was doing it himself. The writer also believes that the

[1] Letter of 9.3.48, annex 233, Diary, Part XI, loc. cit.

Minister of Defence [A. V. Alexander], in his usual petty way, realised that he was not putting up much of a show as the British Minister of Defence and that he might even have sown the seed of jealousy in Mr Bevin's mind.'[1]

Had Monty been of larger character he would have accepted this rebuff and worked on quietly to achieve his goal. But with the deteriorating situation in Palestine in April, the Russian closure of road access to Berlin, and the increasing signs that Russia would tolerate no independent thought or activities on the part of her satellites, Monty lost his cool, as has been seen, demanding before the Cabinet that Bevin apologize for his claim that the Army had let him down. In pique Bevin again refused to let Monty go to France, on the grounds now that an inter-Allied committee would in fact be the best way of establishing a military framework for the Western Alliance. Bevin therefore announced that instead of sending Monty to Paris to discuss the matter, 'joint staff machinery' would forthwith be 'set up through which detailed planning will operate', and gave support to Tedder's proposal for an inter-Allied Military Committee with three service representatives from each of the five powers—a committee of fifteen! 'How Tedder could imagine that a Committee of 15, which he advocated, could achieve anything at all heaven knows,' Monty's diarist expostulated. 'A committee of five is, in CIGS's opinion, far too many.'[2]

Meanwhile newspapers in France and Belgium had already been speculating 'with big headlines to the effect that CIGS was to be appointed Super Chief of Staff to the Western Union. . . . Naturally enough the English papers took up the story and featured it gleefully and, equally naturally, it was resented in a good many quarters in Whitehall.'[3]

The germ of Monty's future role was thus being publicly propagated in the spring of 1948; but the actual appointment was not to be made without wrangling and even greater hostility in Whitehall—for Monty abhorred indecisiveness, committees, and time-wasting. Like Churchill he wanted 'action this day'; but without Churchill's entourage of trusted high-calibre advisers, Monty found himself constantly fighting a lonely battle and could not understand why he aroused such jealousy and enmity. He towered above his colleagues in his clarity of strategic and moral vision; but in terms of human relations, of the interplay of personality, he fell far below par. His VCIGS, General Simpson, had gone to Western Command, replaced

[1] Diary, Part XI, loc. cit.
[2] Ibid.
[3] Ibid.

by the abrasive and brilliant mind of Lt-General Gerald Templer. For all his admiration of Monty as a Commander, Templer was shocked by what he found and made no bones about his view that Monty was 'the worst CIGS for 50 years',[1] neither willing nor able to co-operate with his fellow Chiefs of Staff.

At the meeting of Ministers of Defence and Chiefs of Staff on 30 April 1948, the terms of reference for the nascent Military Committee of Western Union were agreed. Monty, after two years of Tedder's negative chairmanship of the Chiefs of Staff Committee, was past caring. Aware that he was outnumbered, he did not speak, but soon made his opinion of the Western Union committee-system of command known:

> CIGS was, however, once more horrified by the gathering of worn out Ministers of Defence and moth-eaten 'Chiefs of the General Staff' whom he saw gathered round the table. He considered that we had linked ourselves to a 'military nonsense' and he set about at once to ensure that his views were clearly known in official quarters in Whitehall.[2]

On 6 May 1948 Monty met the newly appointed British representative (with ambassadorial rank) on the Permanent Commission of the Western Union. Monty already distrusted the Foreign Office's involvement, having in April seen the Minister of State at the Foreign Office, Hector McNeill. McNeill, questioned by Monty, discussed British policy in Europe as patiently working away 'in an attempt to win over the satellite powers'. To Monty this was ridiculous. His own visits to Germany had convinced him that 'there was no chance whatsoever of achieving this end'.[3] The Iron Curtain had come down and would, in the conceivable future, stay down. The Russians would *never* permit their satellites to alter course, and would use force if necessary to maintain their orbits. To counter this—particularly with a view to the future affiliation of Germany, the nations of Western Europe *must* combine and pursue a common goal. 'The first vital factor is to imbue the Western Union Powers with a new and more robust outlook and to inculcate a fighting spirit in them,' Monty hectored the British Representative, Gladwyn Jebb. Britain *must* make clear she was committed to fighting alongside her Allies. That current continental defences were a shambles did not in itself matter; 'as the years go by we will become better equipped and better organ-

[1] Field-Marshal Sir Gerald Templer, interview of 27.4.79.
[2] Diary, Part XI, loc. cit.
[3] Ibid.

ised to meet aggression: but only if we all become imbued *now* with the right spirit.'[1]

Gladwyn Jebb's response was cold. Any spirit must come from the Foreign Secretary, whose representative to Western Union he was, Jebb answered indifferently.

Monty, angered, considered the only spirit currently coming from Bevin was alcoholic. Looking around it seemed he was surrounded by perfidious Albions, as inward-looking as Senator Taft in America. He had hoped the Chiefs of Staff Committee could become an instrument of military progress 'instead of being merely a debating society', as he wrote to de Guingand. 'But this is I fear almost impossible. Tedder is utterly ineffective; Cunningham's mentality is of the Boer War; Hollis is generally ill or tight, and A. V. Alexander is utterly and completely useless as Minister of Defence. There is only one hope for us and that is to have a "Chief of Staff Armed Forces" who will be an independent chairman of the Chiefs of Staff Committee, and who will advise the Minister what to do and will make him give decisions.'[2]

Not for another ten years would this come to pass.[3] In the meantime, in the early summer of 1949, Monty still believed a crisis would develop—'whether it will be political or financial one cannot yet quite discern. I have decided to stay in the UK this year and not to travel further afield than Germany and Austria; I want to be handy if things come to a head; I may have a part to play. We badly need leadership.'[4]

Stamping his feet impatiently over the delays in setting up the military side of Western Union, Monty now awaited the inevitable crisis that would decide his—and Britain's—fate. It was not long coming.

[1] Diary, Part XI, loc. cit.

[2] Letter of 1.3.48, de Guingand Papers, loc. cit.

[3] The first such Chief of Staff of the Armed Forces, or Chief of the Defence Staff, was Air-Marshal Dickson, appointed in 1957.

[4] Letter of 1.3.48, loc. cit.

CHAPTER ELEVEN

The Berlin Crisis

OVER EASTER 1948, Monty spent his last days at Amesbury School, Hindhead.

'When I left today I felt rather sad,' Monty wrote to Phyllis Reynolds,

> but one could not say much with all the boys about. And anyhow there seems no need to say anything. You and Tom know very well my feelings about Amesbury and how much it has meant to David and myself during the war years: and since the war. The fact that we had a home at Amesbury was the chief factor in enabling me to do what I did towards winning the war. If I had had worries about David I could hardly have won my battles.
>
> And in many ways the post-war period has contained more seeds of worry than the war years: in trying to keep the ship of state on an even keel. We are still in very rough waters.
>
> So you and Tom have really played a major part in winning the late war: and in keeping our country on an even keel since the war ended.
>
> The Nation should thank you for that.
>
> For myself and David, no thanks could ever be adequate. All the same, I *do* say, 'Thank you' to both of you.
>
> Yrs ever and gratefully
> Monty[1]

Once again, as in certain of his letters to the King, Monty's tone—in its mix of sentimentality, of ego, arrogance and childlike humility—was strangely reminiscent of Nelson. That he *did* feel gratitude to the Reynolds was undisputed; yet it was not enough to stop him subsequently severing relations when Phyllis Reynolds entered his mill-house at Isington without authorization while he was abroad (to hang curtains that had been delivered). As his Canadian PA Lt-Colonel Warren recalled, 'You did not get personal with this guy.'[2] Woe betide anyone who took liberties. 'He could crush you quicker than anyone I've ever met in my life. It was . . . humiliating,' Warren

[1] Letter of 29.3.48, Montgomery Papers.
[2] Lt.-Colonel Trumbull Warren, interview of 9.11.81.

reflected.[1] In Monty's mansion there were rooms for each guest; but his own remained locked and inviolate. To his stepson, Dick Carver, contemplating remarriage after the death of his first wife, Monty was full of encouragement—but ruled out, categorically, any such possibility in his own case. Around himself he erected an almost insuperable stockade. He might 'yearn' for the memory of companionship such as the 'family' life of Tac HQ during his campaigns: but in fact he felt instantly threatened by any presumption on his affection or friendship—as even his adopted 'son' Lucien would soon find. Monty must at all times be 'in control' of the relationship, suspending or severing it straight away if it oppressed him. Though he knew most of the senior statesmen of the world and an astonishing number of officers and men in the British Army by name, he was virtually without close friends: a circumstance for which he had but himself to blame. The military historian Basil Liddell Hart, for instance, wrote to Monty in 1946 to extend the hand of erstwhile friendship—even enclosing a copy of a laudatory article he had penned, in which he had declared that despite the higher ability of commanders in World War II, 'Montgomery stood out above his fellows and subordinates like a great peak in a mountain range. . . . Monty carried the "infinite capacity for taking pains" to the point where it was really near the mark as a definition of genius.'[2] For Liddell Hart this was an uncommon display of magnanimity towards someone of whom he was intensely jealous and by whom he had been rebuffed during the war.

Once again, however, Monty turned down Liddell Hart's request for a meeting, saying he was 'much too busy at present to meet you for a talk'—and returning the proof of Liddell Hart's laudatory article together with 'a copy of a lecture [on leadership] I gave at St Andrews last year; this will show you the methods I have always tried to follow. I have come to realise in the last few years,' Monty added, 'that the way to fame is a hard one. You must suffer, and be the butt of jealousy and ill-informed criticisms; it is a lonely matter. One just has to go on doing what you think is right, and doing your duty: whatever others may say or think; and this is what I try to do!'[3]

Monty also enclosed inscribed copies of his two campaign histories as gifts; but Liddell Hart was insulted by the 'formal inscriptions' and the refusal to meet him. Moreover he found Monty's postscript

[1] Ibid.

[2] 'Monty' article written for *Strand Magazine*, April 1946, in 'Montgomery' file, Liddell Hart Papers, LHCMA, King's College, London.

[3] Letter of 14.5.46, in 'Montgomery' file, Liddell Hart Papers, loc. cit.

'pathetic' in its self-defensiveness. 'Very small-boyish—rather touching, yet hardly worthy of a man who has reached such eminence,' Liddell Hart noted. 'It looks as if his inability to find time for a meeting may be due to an underlying fear of facing questions which he feels he could not satisfactorily answer. . . . A curious psychological case!'[1] To Monty, however, Liddell Hart replied that he sympathized with his feelings of loneliness. 'But if you can take a criticism from someone who knew you, intermittently, in earlier years—and did something to help you at one or two crucial times in your career (of which you may be unaware)—your manner has always been your worst handicap. I was brought to realise that by finding, both before and during the war, how hard you had, unwittingly, trodden on other people's corns, and turned against you people who had begun by being favourably disposed. (The offhand note of your Jan. 1944 reply to me—in such contrast to the tone of earlier letters—might have had a similar effect on me if I hadn't been accustomed to keep my historical judgement separate from my personal feelings),' he admitted.[2]

Liddell Hart was himself a vain and difficult character; but his criticism of Monty was well merited. Monty's rough-shod manner *did* contribute to his own loneliness. Had his wife Betty lived, no doubt the situation would have been very different. Instead the lonely widower seemed unable to make new friends or to stop himself upsetting old ones—even long-standing admirers, such as the Queen—by his lack of judgment in personal matters.

There were exceptions, though—and those who managed to penetrate Monty's icy reserve and preoccupations as CIGS often found a surprising depth of kindness. The wife of Monty's new VCIGS, Peggy Templer, refused to be downtrodden.

> He used to say, 'Can I speak to General Templer?' on the telephone without identifying himself or anything, so one time I took a deep breath and said: 'What name shall I say?' Dammit, I thought, he must know it's me he's speaking to. And from then on, Monty and I were *much better* friends. He *liked* people to stand up to him. He used to come into our house in the evening on his way home.
>
> One day he said to me, 'You're looking tired.' And I said, 'I *am* tired.'
>
> He asked why, and I said, 'Because I've got too many children and too much to do and not enough help.' And he said, 'Write out for me what you do, what the servants do, and what the children need and I will tell you how to organize your house.'

[1] Notes on Montgomery's letter of 14.5.46, in 'Montgomery' file, Liddell Hart Papers, loc. cit.

[2] Letter of 19.5.46, 'Montgomery' file, Liddell Hart Papers, loc. cit.

I said, 'How terribly kind of you'—and thought no more about it, naturally.

Next morning an ADC arrived and asked, 'Where's that paper?'!

So with the ADC standing over me I sat down and wrote it out. Monty sent it back with everybody's work changed round. And of course my house was then much better run!

Now, you see, he took the trouble to do that—as CIGS! [1]

This 'infinite capacity for taking pains' was indeed something irrepressible, whether at a domestic level or in running the Army. Having been promised in Australia and New Zealand the necessary timber for conversion of his water mill, he attended to its rebuilding with customary zeal and attention to detail, both in relation to the house and its setting. 'A year ago I bought an old mill in the country, on a lovely river. My idea is to turn it into a residence for myself, and make the meadow in which it stands into a garden. It is a big task but gives me a great interest. I hope to have it finished by September next,' he wrote to Lucien Trueb in May 1948;[2] the work was indeed finished on time.

Exercise 'Bamboo', Monty's annual Camberley gathering of senior officers of the British Commonwealth, was planned with equal clarity and precision. Mounted in May 1948 in order to study the 'stage-management and conduct of mobile operations in an undeveloped country in a Far East theatre of war', it reflected Monty's determination to think ahead, and to rehearse senior officers for their likely future roles. Attended by all generals in the British Army, as well as representatives from all the Dominion countries and the USA, it was a salutary preparation for operations in Korea in ensuing years. Monty's opening address covered some fifteen printed pages. But on the second evening of the exercise Monty gave a further talk which was not printed.

I am going to talk to you tonight about the general situation throughout the world,

he began.

I shall not issue you with any written record of this address; the subject matter is too secret and too explosive. You should keep it stored in your own mind, for reference as and when required.

My problem tonight is to get over to you clearly, logically and succinctly the main features of the world situation so that you

[1] Lady Templer, interview of 7.11.84.

[2] Letter of 6.5.48, Trueb Correspondence Papers of Viscount Montgomery of Alamein, communicated to author.

> may carry away a compehensive view of the world canvas. As in every problem, one has to clear away the mass of unimportant factors and expose the pillars on which the whole matter is based.
>
> Therefore we must first ask ourselves the question:
>
> What is the trouble in the world today?
>
> The answer is: there are two troubles:—
>
> a) economic weakness and distress.
>
> b) an ideological clash between two conflicting elements.

In either one alone we have the seeds of war. The two together are a very great menace.

Monty did not himself believe that war was imminent, despite the current rumbles over Berlin, for his visit to Russia had convinced him the Russians would be unable to undertake an offensive campaign for many years. Nevertheless the destructive effects of the Second World War, the rise of America, the spread of Russian Communism, the decay of the old political and religious institutions, and the phenomenal advance of scientific discovery and technology made Monty

> believe that the world is going through one of its vast secular crises or revolutions, and this one may last a long time and lead to great changes unforeseen today. We are witnessing a switch-over in human affairs such as the world has not seen since Roman days.
>
> The elimination of Hitler was only an incident; other grave dangers lie ahead.
>
> This is a very testing time; we need clear thinking and we need quick decisions; it is necessary to be right on top of your job,

he exhorted.

> You and I are soldiers and we naturally look at the situation today through military eyes.
>
> My eyes are fixed on Germany,

he announced.

> As the ideological conflict grows and hardens it is becoming fundamentally a struggle for the possession of Germany.
>
> That struggle is between the East and the West; the East is represented by Russia and her satellites, all of whom used to be German satellites; the West is represented by the Western Allies of World War II. . . .
>
> This conflict as it grows and hardens contains the seeds of future war,

he warned.

> You may say that Germany is a poverty stricken liability to those who conquered her.
>
> But she is a valuable military assistant to any country that can enlist her aid. It is this role of a pawn, available to the highest bidder that constitutes Germany's greatest menace.

It was vital, in Monty's eyes, that Germany should 'line up' with the forces of the West:

> The time has come to marshal the forces of the West against the danger from the East. It is important that Germany should march with the West.
>
> When you read that I am travelling about in Western Europe from time to time, you will understand that I am taking steps to ensure that we win the next war!!
>
> Some people talk of war as if it were an act of God. But war is not an act of God. War grows directly out of things which individuals, statesmen, and nations *do* or fail to do. It is, in short, the consequences of national policies or lack of policies. And once the nation's destiny is submitted to the terrible decisions of war, victory or defeat likewise ensues from what we *do* or *fail to do*.
>
> It is my view that what is going on in the world today will not lead to war *in the near future*.
>
> But there are grave dangers; and if those dangers are not faced up to and held, *then* there will have to be a show down *eventually*. If we want peace, we must understand war. And we must understand that economic strength is a first requirement of safety.
>
> And that is where I am not very happy.

Western civilization was fighting 'for the old values against the flood of Communism from the East and from within'.

> The immediate problem is to prevent Western Europe from succumbing to Communism as a result of economic despair. The degree of success to be achieved by the Marshall plan is of great political significance.

Once again, the future hinged, Monty felt, on Germany, as much economically as militarily.

> Germany is the key to the problem. Without the products of the industrial areas of Western Germany, European recovery is impossible.
>
> Russia will do everything in her power to prevent recovery.

> Sabotage within the countries participating in the European Recovery Plan is insufficient if Western Germany can be set up as an active contributor.
>
> The nations of the West have decided to weld themselves into an effective Union, economically, and militarily, so as to resist the threat from the East. In other words we are now going to split Europe into two. Hence the Western Union.[1]

Though Monty's peroration went on to cover global economic, political and military problems, it was to Western Union he returned—for the duel between East and West would be decided in Europe and in Germany, he felt. For all the tendency to dogma and blanket statements, history would bear out this fundamental analysis—and Monty's prophecies. About Western Union Monty was uncompromisingly forthright:

> It must be clearly understood that in taking on the Western Union commitment we have linked ourselves irrevocably to a group of States who are *completely useless* from a fighting point of view. We are committed to go to their help if attacked. An urgent and priority need is to build up the armies of the Benelux Powers and of France; at the same time we must integrate these armies into an effective fighting machine. Unless this is done we shall become involved in the most appalling disasters when the storm breaks. A proper set-up for command is required at once. The present Military Staff Committee is quite useless for this purpose.[2]

Throughout the spring Monty had been arguing for a 'proper' command set-up for Europe. Most politicians in Whitehall shied away from the notion of a Supreme Commander (feeling it to be too warlike), and the First Sea Lord, together with Tedder, proposed instead a COSSAC-type organization of staff officers to prepare plans for a Supreme Commander, who would be appointed only when war began.

Monty, driven almost insane by the 'wetness' of his colleagues, was finally rescued by the crisis which now rocked Europe. On 24 June, a month after Monty's Camberley address, the Russians closed all access to Berlin by road, rail and water. The Berlin 'blockade' had begun; and almost overnight war fever descended upon the ministries of the Western Allies. So great was the nervousness in London that once again Monty was approached with a view to his possible rôle in

[1] 'The World Situation', address by CIGS at Exercise 'Bamboo', 25.5.48, annex 250, Diary, Part XI, loc. cit.
[2] Ibid.

a National Government. On 6 July the three Western Occupation Powers sent a note to the Russians demanding restoration of access to Berlin. 'The Note was very strongly worded and virtually left no loophole for either side to climb down without serious loss of face,' Monty's diarist recorded.[1] 'It was in this atmosphere that the COS were summoned to a discussion with the Minister of Defence on 7 July. Whilst CIGS was being briefed for this discussion he received an urgent note from S. of S. to go and see him before he went to the meeting. CIGS duly walked along the passage. S. of S. went straight to the point. Saying that he wished to talk as man to man and not as S. of S. to CIGS, Mr Shinwell said, in approximately these words:

> 'Now Monty, you have a very big following in the country and so have I, despite,' with a wave of his arm indicating Downing Street, 'despite what they may think over there. You could save this country and I could rouse the workers to follow me. Between us, you and I, we could do anything.'[2]

According to Monty's MA, 'CIGS was somewhat flabbergasted' by this declaration. 'He had gone to see S. of S. in the belief that he was to discuss the Berlin situation and he could not clearly see what S. of S. was driving at. Subsequently he learned through private staff channels that Mr Shinwell meant that he was very worried at the way that H.M.G. was handling the Berlin crisis; that he feared they were muddling the country into war; that CIGS and himself were the only two sane and clear thinking people left in Whitehall and it was up to them to see that Britain was not suddenly launched into World War III.'[3]

If this was Shinwell's point, then it had some measure of truth. The repercussions of Attlee's helter-skelter abandonment both of empire and of overseas strategic responsibilities had encouraged the Russians to test the nerve of the Allies over Berlin. Already on 7 April Monty had drawn up a 'Report or Memorandum' as a result of visits paid to the Belgian Army and to Germany, in which he had predicted that 'the battle for Berlin . . . is now about to begin, and it will go on for a long time. Our difficulty will be to wrest the initiative from the Russians. They could get us out of Berlin at any time by shooting us out. This would mean World War III, for which they are not ready. Therefore they will not adopt this method.'[4] Instead,

[1] Diary of Field-Marshal The Viscount Montgomery of Alamein, Part XII (30.5–1.9.48), Montgomery Papers.
[2] Ibid.
[3] Ibid.
[4] 'Report by CIGS' of 7.4.48, annex 235, Diary, Part XI, loc. cit.

Monty predicted, the Russians would adopt a policy of 'squeeze' over a prolonged period, to challenge the resolve of the Western Allies, but without going to war. Providing the Allies prepared themselves for a long battle or siege, Monty was confident the Allies would win—a victory that was of no immediate military consequence but of incalculable political significance, since the loss of Berlin would signify 'the first step towards the final triumph of the East over the West; the Germans would begin to look East. And so we must not leave Berlin,' Monty considered.[1]

In fact in Monty's eyes the greatest threat was the American Military Governor, General Lucius Clay, who was more dangerous than the Russians—'General Clay considers that World War III will begin in six months time [i.e. October 1948]; indeed he might well bring it on himself by shooting his way up the autobahn to Berlin if the Russians were difficult about things. He is a real "He-man" and hates the Russians with a deadly hatred; he will never bargain or give an inch if he can help it.'[2]

Monty's report had been circulated throughout the War Office and Whitehall—but was ignored by the Government until the Berlin blockade escalated to the brink of war. With some venom Monty thus faced the Minister of Defence on 7 July: 'Leaning across the table he then taxed the Minister with a direct and very blunt question: "Is the Government prepared to go to war for Berlin?" '[3]

A. V. Alexander, 'shattered', could not answer, and referred the question to the Prime Minister—who procrastinated. 'The plain fact is that when H.M.G. framed their Note, they simply did not consider what they would do if it was rejected,'[4] Monty's diarist concluded. Monty himself had no illusions—he had met his erstwhile opposite number, Marshal Sokolovsky in Berlin in April. Though the Russians would attempt to 'squeeze us out of Berlin', Sokolovsky had 'ridiculed the suggestion that the Russians want war',[5] and Monty found the notion equally ridiculous. What the Russian challenge *did* show up, however, was 'our total state of unpreparedness' to meet the Russian threat. 'One gained the impression that they [the Government] seemed to think that if the button was pressed the Anglo-American armies would resume the advance at the place where they left off in May 1945; and under the same command organisation.'[6]

[1] Ibid.
[2] Ibid.
[3] Diary, Part XII, loc. cit.
[4] Ibid.
[5] 'Report by CIGS' of 7.4.48, loc. cit.
[6] Diary, Part XII, loc. cit.

At a Defence Staff meeting with the Prime Minister on 15 July Monty made clear the situation: that the British Army was *not* geared for immediate war in Europe, and the armies of the Western Union 'must be regarded as useless'.[1] A report on emergency mobilization measures was instantly commissioned; Bevin was asked to reassure the French 'of our determination to fight alongside France on land if war broke out'.[2] A proper command system in Europe appeared vital now to concert Allied defences—and the question of a Supreme Commander became urgent.

Monty, who had been pressing for these things since the spring, was both relieved and scornful of his colleagues—particularly the Minister of Defence. Tedder and Cunningham agreed to lobby the Prime Minister to get A. V. Alexander removed; but when the time came to word their case, Tedder announced he had, together with Cunningham, decided to go back on his agreement. A. V. Alexander thus remained 'solidly and uselessly in his office', Monty's diarist recorded when the plot misfired—adding with intentional double-entendre: 'HE STILL SITS TIGHT.'[3]

With the exception of A. V. Alexander's continuation as Minister of Defence, Monty appeared to have got all he had fought for. But, enervated by the months of in-fighting, Monty now made a series of mistakes which, though they did not appear so at the time, were to have far-reaching consequences.

Contemptuous of the state of the armies in France and Belgium, and despairing of the Defence Minister and Chiefs of Staff Committee in Britain, Monty felt it imperative that he should himself take Supreme Command in Europe. When the Chiefs of Staff, alarmed over the Berlin crisis, finally agreed to such a command set-up but plumped for a 'Chairman' of a three-man committee of commanders-in-chief (of Land, Sea and Air Forces), Monty unwisely put his signature to the proposal. Within days, as the Berlin crisis deepened and Monty saw in France the magnitude of what needed to be done, he began to rue his decision—and signalled to the VCIGS and Minister of Defence from Paris to withdraw his approval, insisting instead on a full-blown Supreme Commander:

> I have now seen something of what is required to be done. The safety of the West is at stake and a Chairman repeat Chairman would be useless. Some very firm and definite orders will have to be issued and they will have to be obeyed quickly. If we mean

[1] 'Certain factors affecting the situation in the West', statement by CIGS at Prime Minister's Staff conference on 15.7.48, Diary, Part XII, loc. cit.

[2] Ibid.

[3] Diary, Part XII, loc. cit.

> business in the West a Supreme Commander with full powers is absolutely essential and he will have to smack it about in no uncertain manner. Any other solution would be useless.
>
> I therefore withdraw my agreement to a Chairman. I adhere to and repeat my previous recommendation that a Supreme Commander with full powers is required at once. Any compromise on this issue is out of the question.[1]

The next day Monty again signalled:

> Command set-up. This has already been sold by me to Wedemeyer [representing American Chiefs of Staff]. If opinion in Whitehall considers that we can drift into war with the preparations in charge of a Committee under a Chairman then we can get ready for very early disaster. On no repeat no account will I agree to the Chairman philosophy. . . .[2]

Meanwhile, throughout the early summer General Bradley had, in Washington, given considerable thought to the matter of command in Europe. If the countries of Western Union wished an American Supreme Commander, as Monty had intimated in his letter of March, they could have one, he declared. But they offered not General Collins as Monty had recommended, but General Lucius Clay, the American Zone Commander.[3]

Monty was appalled. Clay he considered more unstable than Patton: a disastrous leader in time of crisis or emergency. To soften the blow, in informing Bradley of his rejection, he claimed that Clay's post as C-in-C of the American Zone made it impossible for Clay to combine both jobs—whereupon Bradley withdrew the suggestion of an American candidate altogether.

For the post of Land Force C-in-C, General Koenig—Military Governor of the French Zone of Occupation in Germany—was put forward. Once again Monty reacted by peremptory rejection[4]—as he did when General Juin's name was suggested as Acting Supreme Commander by Bradley on 11 August. Bradley's 'tentative and personal solution was to establish an integrated HQ in France under a French general as Acting Supreme Commander; in due course when

[1] Diary, Part XII, loc. cit.

[2] Ibid.

[3] Letter of 10.4.48 (a month after receiving Monty's letter), annex 234, Diary, Part XI, loc. cit.

[4] 'On no account must name of Koenig be mentioned in any circles. He has not the qualities required for this sort of rough-house and would be useless. It must be a French General but definitely not repeat not Koenig': signal (undated) to VCIGS, in Diary, Part XII, loc. cit.

the build-up had developed an American Supreme Commander could be appointed and the French general could either become his deputy or C-in-C Land Forces'. It was felt 'the only adequate Frenchman they could think of at the moment was Juin'.[1]

As Monty's diarist recorded, 'This proposal put an end to any further beating about the bush.'[2]

If Monty wanted the job, he would have to make clear his candidature. The VCIGS, General Templer, thus despatched an immediate signal to Washington, ruling out the idea of a Frenchman as Supreme Commander. 'Its general argument was that:—

a) no Frenchman has sufficient prestige, nor political backing, to give him the power and drive required to set French and the Benelux countries militarily on their feet. Nor had any Frenchman the character to inspire the will to fight amongst the timid and hesitant countries of the Western Union.
b) The only three people who could fill the bill were Eisenhower, Bradley and CIGS.[3]

'As the US President would probably not agree as yet to . . . the appointment of Eisenhower or Bradley to the post for fear of escalating still further the crisis with the Russians, then obviously CIGS was the only remaining candidate.'[4]

For some days there was silence from Washington. Word then came from the British Representative to the Combined Chiefs of Staff, General Sir William Morgan, to the effect that Bradley had 'already made this suggestion to him' in the past and would probably back Monty for the post now if he wished it. With the situation in Berlin still tense and an Anglo-American airlift under way, the US Chiefs of Staff finally came through on 24 August 1948 recommending the 'immediate establishment of a Land and Air HQ' in Europe. They also signified their agreement to the establishment of an Allied Supreme HQ, and suggested that the Supreme Commander should be either Field Marshal Alexander, CIGS or General Juin.'[5]

Once again—as before 'Overlord' and over the appointment of Brooke's successor as CIGS—Monty and Alexander were both nominated as candidates for the same post. At a meeting of the five

[1] Bradley to General Morgan, who reported conversation to CIGS: Diary, Part XII, loc. cit.
[2] Diary, Part XII, loc. cit.
[3] Ibid.
[4] Ibid.
[5] Ibid.

delegated Western Union Chiefs of Staff that day, however, it was decided to defer the question of who should become the first Supreme Commander of Chairman. It was, in any case, an appointment the politicians would have to make; but with the fall of the French Government the next meeting of Foreign Ministers set for 1 September was postponed: and Monty became more and more impatient for a decision, predicting disaster indeed unless the decision was soon made.

The Minister of Defence was naturally reluctant to press the matter, given the political crisis in France. Meanwhile a defence crisis was brewing at home over the 'parlous state' of the British armed forces, and without increasing National Service from twelve months to two years, the Chiefs of Staff no longer saw how the British Government could match its commitments in the event of war. Relations between A. V. Alexander and the Chiefs of Staff sank to a new level, A. V. Alexander claiming that he had been 'stabbed in the back' at the COS meeting on 10 September.[1] Open insults were bandied during a 'first-class row'.[2] Monty accused A. V. Alexander of being too cowardly to admit in public the need for more recruitment of regulars, then claimed that in his entire experience the Services had never been reduced to such a sorry state. A. V. Alexander challenged Monty to repeat his statement in another place (i.e. before the Prime Minister and Cabinet); Monty replied 'that he would gladly do so in any place and in any society, in fact in the House of Lords if A.V.A. liked. This was magnificent,' Monty's diarist recorded. 'But it was too much for A.V.A. He said goodnight with a sickly smile and left the room.'[3]

At a COS meeting on 1 September Monty had declared that 'France must be the hard core, militarily, of the Western Union. But she is in a state of chaos; her Army is torn with intrigue, and lacks leadership and confidence; she is in no condition to give any lead in any matter.'[4] Whether matters were any better in Britain, at least with respect to relations between the Government and the Chiefs of Staff, was a moot question. A. V. Alexander was undoubtedly a weak and vacillating Minister of Defence, but he had been ill-served by a Chiefs of Staff Committee that was rarely in agreement. Moreover the 'parlous state' of the Army was in part the fault of the

[1] Diary of Field-Marshal The Viscount Montgomery of Alamein, Part XIII (1.9–30.9.48) Montgomery Papers.
[2] Ibid.
[3] Ibid.
[4] Statement by CIGS to Chiefs of Staff Committee, 1.9.48, annex 296, Diary, Part XIII, loc. cit.

CIGS himself, who had argued consistently in 1946 and 1947 that Britain need not fear a war on the continent of Europe for at least a decade. Indeed it was Monty who, in 1947, had permitted the Government to reduce the planned eighteen-month National Service to twelve months, if British military commitments in Greece, Austria, India and Palestine were ended by 1948—which, with the exception of Austria, they were.[1] Yet here, a bare year later, was a CIGS attacking the Government for the Army's lamentable lack of preparedness for immediate confrontation with the Russians in Europe, and calling for a National Service engagement of two years under the colours.

[1] In his biography of Lord Slim (*Slim, the Standard-bearer*, London 1976), Ronald Lewin gave a garbled account of Monty's role in the machinations over National Service in the autumn of 1948, confusing Monty's stance with that of the year before. Monty had assented to a reduction of National Service to twelve months in April 1947 only as a concession to the Government during a political and economic crisis, but had warned that 'under certain adverse conditions we might have to come back and ask for the period of 18 months to be reintroduced'. In fact on 9 April 1947 he had asked the Minister of Defence to place on record his proviso concerning adverse conditions (annex 88, Diary, Part VII, loc. cit.), minuting on 10 April 1947: 'If things "go bad on us" in any part of the world, or if it is obvious by early 1948 that recruiting for the Regular Army is not going to produce by January 1949 the numbers we must have, then we would have to ask that the period of service with the active Army be stepped-up again to 18 months. This might have to be done in 1948 so as to take effect in 1949' (annex 90, Diary, Part VII, loc. cit.). These conditions, Monty felt in the summer of 1948, had definitely arisen. 'To sum up briefly, we have demobilized too quickly in the light of events as they have turned out, until we have reached a situation so critical that on 29th July, the Chiefs of Staff informed the Prime Minister in writing that "the state of the Defence Services of Britain today gives cause for grave concern" ': 'State of the Army: September 1948', statement by CIGS at Chiefs of Staff Committee, 17.9.48, annex 304, Diary, Part XIII, loc. cit. On 19 October 1948 Monty called a meeting of the Military Members of the Army Council to get backing for his intention to treat the necessity of an extension of National Service to at least eighteen months 'as a resignation issue': Minutes of Meeting, annex 316, Diary of Field-Marshal The Viscount Montgomery of Alamein, Part XIV (1.10–31.10.48), Montgomery Papers. At a meeting with the Secretary of State for War on 19 October Monty declared that 'although he himself was going to another appointment on 1st November, had he stayed as CIGS he would have had no hesitation whatsoever in resigning with all the other Military Members of the Army Council if anything less than 18 months National Service was decided upon by the Government': Diary, Part XIV, loc. cit. Monty certainly felt he had done his best to force the issue, but his VCIGS, General Templer, evidently considered that Monty had 'passed the buck' by not ensuring the issue was settled before he retired as CIGS at the end of October, thus committing his successor to threaten to resign instead (R. Lewin, *Slim, the Standard-bearer*, op. cit). The real problem, as Monty explained to the Standing Committee of Service Ministers on 21 October 1948, was that 12-month National Service conscription due to start in 1949 was based on the idea of an up-to-strength Regular Army, with a brief National Service training to prepare soldiers for Territorial or Reserve Army status. Originally, the National Service Act had been intended to cater for a Territorial Army of well-trained re-

Attlee, tired of hearing of the strife and hostility on the Chiefs of Staff Committee, was losing patience. If he could persuade the French to accept Monty as the new Supreme Commander or Chairman of the Commanders-in-Chief Committee of Western Union, he would rid the British Government of a persistent thorn. At 12.45 on 20 September 1948 Monty was summoned by the Minister of Defence. It was assumed by Monty's entourage that A. V. Alexander was now boiling over at Monty's latest gauntlet: a paper produced by the CIGS to set out in writing the 'parlous condition of the Army today'.[1]

The assumption was however wrong—for it was at this meeting that A. V. Alexander offered Monty the post of Chairman of the Western Union Cs-in-C. He had consulted Attlee, Bevin, Dalton and Herbert Morrison: all supported Monty's candidature.

Seven days later, at the next meeting of the Defence Ministers of the five powers of Western Union, Monty's appointment to the post was formally agreed. Unfortunately General Juin would not accept the post of Commander-in-Chief Land Forces under Monty, so that no public announcement could be made. The press leaked the appointment on 29 September, and finally, on 3 October 1948, the British Government confirmed the news.

There was little sign of mourning at Monty's departure. The Army Council recorded its gratitude, but from the ranks of the Army he had intended should regard him as a father, both in Britain and abroad, came but a solitary cable of good wishes and gratitude from General Gale, GOC Troops in Egypt:

> On behalf of all ranks British troops in Egypt and Mediterranean Cmd I send you our respectful good wishes on the occasion of your departure from the War Office to assume the appointment of Chairman Western Union Commanders in Chief Committee.[2]

As Monty's MA chronicled in the Field-Marshal's diary, it was 'the only telegram or letter which was seen by the narrator to the CIGS in farewell'.[3]

---

servists. Now, however, the primary need for National Service men was to take the place of regulars in carrying out the continuing post-war tasks of the Army—for recruiting of regulars had, owing to the Government's cuts, fallen beyond all predictions. 'Until regular recruiting could be stimulated by extra inducements, National Service men would have to be used for this purpose': Diary, Part XIV, loc. cit.

[1] 'State of the Army', loc. cit.

[2] Diary, Part XIV, loc. cit.

[3] Ibid.

If Monty was hurt by this, he did not show it. Once more he was moving on to higher things, his head swollen with the magnitude of the challenge. He had been asked by Attlee to remain CIGS a further month as well as taking up the post of Chairman of the Western Union Commanders-in-Chief Committee.

'I hand over my job . . . on 1st Nov. The Royal Review of the TA on 31 October will be my last appearance as CIGS,' he wrote to the King. 'Until then I have to watch over both jobs: CIGS *and* Chairman of the Western Union set-up. . . . My new job will be a monumental and herculean task: to weld the forces of the West into an effective fighting machine. It will not be easy: in fact it will be extremely difficult. But I will do my best.'[1]

It was to be far more difficult than Monty, even in his blackest dreams, can have imagined. Meanwhile, at the War Office in Whitehall, there was a brief hiatus as Monty attempted to get the Chiefs of Staff to resign *en masse* over the issue of National Service. Then, relinquishing that 'baby' to his successor, he left, unmourned.

[1] Letter of 12.10.48, Royal Archives, Windsor.

PART TEN

Western Union

CHAPTER ONE

Slim as Successor

MONTY'S SELF-SELECTION as Chairman of Western Union's military command set-up was, by and large, accepted as reasonable. No other candidate possessed the prestige which Monty could bring to the appointment. Not all, however, were happy with Monty's choice of successor as CIGS at home.

Monty's preferred candidate—now that General Dempsey had retired from the Army—was General Sir John Crocker; indeed Monty had assured Crocker that, as the reigning CIGS's choice, Crocker was almost bound to get the appointment—and was much put out when the Prime Minister, Mr Attlee, disagreed. Attlee's preference was for General Sir William Slim, who had been for two years Commandant of the re-created Imperial Defence College in London, had then retired from the Indian Army, and was currently employed as Deputy Chairman of the Railway Executive, the Board of the recently nationalized British Railways. Monty admired 'Bill' Slim; indeed he had advised Mountbatten to replace Auchinleck with Slim in April 1947, and again in June. Mountbatten, as Viceroy, did in fact offer Slim Auchinleck's job as C-in-C Indian Army (an offer Slim declined), and later claimed that it was his influence which gave Attlee the requisite toughness to reject Monty's candidate and appoint Slim to the post of CIGS in October 1948. 'This is out of the question. I have already told Crocker that he is going to succeed me,' Monty protested to Attlee, according to Mountbatten's later account—whereupon Attlee uttered the immortal words: 'Well, untell him!' [1] Mountbatten, as his biographer Philip Ziegler acknowledged, had a somewhat 'cavalier indifference to the truth'; [2] nevertheless Monty certainly told Crocker that he was likely to get the job, as his signal to Crocker's headquarters in Cairo on 8 October 1948 demonstrated:

> For some days the Prime Minister has been considering the question of who is to succeed me as CIGS. I have all along strongly advised him that you are the man and so has the Secretary of

[1] Quoted in P. Ziegler, *Mountbatten*, London 1985.
[2] Ibid.

State [Shinwell]. The Prime Minister has however always been of the opinion that he wants SLIM and he has now finally decided that he will recommend SLIM to the King as my successor. I am personally very sorry indeed but we will have to accept this decision. The appointment is of course entirely in the hands of the Prime Minister.[1]

According to Sir Frank Simpson, Crocker 'did not show his disappointment to anyone, but in later life he told me that he had been deeply disappointed. Of course, the fault was really Monty's for saying anything to him.' Attlee, apparently, had countered Monty's hectoring campaign on behalf of Crocker by a wily refusal to answer Monty's telephone calls to 10 Downing Street. 'Monty described to me in great detail how he kept telephoning the Prime Minister's office for Crocker to be appointed and not Slim. He never succeeded in getting through. Of course Mr Attlee realized only too well what Monty was trying to put to him and he was determined he was not going to give Monty a hearing,' Simpson related. 'Slim was a surprise choice to everyone. He was Indian Army, and no Indian Army general had ever been CIGS. Also he had retired from the Army. . . . Nevertheless Mr Attlee had him restored to the active list and promised him early promotion to Field-Marshal. I think everyone will agree now that Slim was one of the best CIGSs that the Army has had for a long time. . . . I got to know in later life John Crocker very well indeed and I am quite certain that he would not have made a good CIGS.'[2]

Slim, legendary commander of the Fourteenth Army in Burma, was admired by everyone who worked with or under him. He had Wavell's power of intellect without Wavell's taciturnity. He inspired loyalty and was receptive to new ideas—as he had proved at the Imperial Defence College by challenging almost all conventionally held theories of strategy and defence. It was therefore assumed that Monty's attempted blackballing of Slim reflected his lifetime bias against the Indian Army—stemming from his own failure to get into the Indian Army from Sandhurst forty years in the past.[3] Others, like Monty's VCIGS, General Templer (himself a possible candidate for the post), felt that Monty was jealous of Slim's reputation and—in Lady Templer's later phrase—was 'unwilling to surrender the stage to another star'.[4]

[1] CIGS cable 1118 of 17.30 hrs, 8.10.48, annex 317, Diary, Part XIV (1.10–31.10.48), Montgomery Papers.
[2] General Sir Frank Simpson, Eugene Wason interviews for Sir Denis Hamilton.
[3] Cf. R. Lewin, *Slim, the Standard-bearer*, London 1976, and P. Ziegler, op. cit.
[4] Lady Templer, interview of 7.11.84.

As a mender of bridges, particularly between the three Services, Slim was to prove an outstanding CIGS; moreover, Monty's fear that Slim's Indian Army background precluded the British Army from feeling loyalty to him as CIGS proved to be spectacularly unfounded. Templer continued to serve Slim as VCIGS; he later compared the two:

> Slim was a good CIGS; Monty was a disaster. I mean, he [Monty] couldn't get on with others, the Chiefs of Staff I mean. We Vices had to ring each other up; if Tedder was going to be there, Monty wouldn't go; if Tedder wasn't, Monty *might*. An awful lot of Army Council meetings he didn't bother to attend.
>
> That's no way to run a railway!
>
> Now Slim *cared* about the army. Monty only cared about himself.

Templer had never met Slim until the day Slim arrived to take office. His first encounter was typical:

> Monty left the CIGS's office 3 or 4 days before Slim arrived. Simply left the office—and left me to resign on the new CIGS's behalf over the length of National Service!
>
> When I told Slim I'd resigned in his name, he said:
>
> 'Sit down. I'm used to these things. Now tell me all about it.'[1]

After consulting his new colleagues on the Chiefs of Staff Committee, Slim went to Attlee and offered his resignation over the issue. Attlee asked him to hold fire, and some days later the Government caved in, agreeing to extend National Service to eighteen months.

By such calm willingness to shoulder the responsibilities of being CIGS in a period of economic and political crisis, Slim won the admiration of his peers and his subordinates. Even 'Simbo' Simpson who, as Monty's VCIGS, had quarrelled ceaselessly with Slim at the IDC, was won over by the new CIGS's magnanimity. Simpson had taken over Western Command, based in Chester, and within a few weeks of the new CIGS's reign in Whitehall, Slim landed at the airfield just outside the town. 'I have since realized he did it deliberately,' Simpson later recalled.

> I went to meet him . . . and he said immediately: 'Simpson, you and I have never agreed on anything yet, have we?' I reluctantly had to agree that that was so. He then went on: 'Well, don't you worry. You will find now that I have much the same ideas that

[1] Field-Marshal Sir Gerald Templer, interview of 27.4.79.

you had when you used to argue with me. . . . You see, I now have the responsibility and have to speak to what is in effect a War Office brief.'

After that we always got on famously. I like to think that he was one of the greatest men I have known. It was very generous of a new CIGS to come and make that sort of statement to one of his army commanders. He had clearly made up his mind that he must come to visit me first in order to put me at my ease. I doubt if we ever had a disagreement after that.[1]

However reluctantly, Monty would have seconded this appraisal, for Slim soon became a tower of strength behind Monty in his tribulations at Western Union, as his diary proves. Yet in recommending Crocker as CIGS in October 1948 Monty was not simply giving rein to vindictive jealousy. Slim had visited Monty in Germany in 1945 and had attended Monty's Camberley exercises each year. They had met frequently when Slim was Commandant of the Imperial Defence College, for it was practice that the Commandant would seek a short session with the Chiefs of Staff every three or four months. Not only was Slim an Indian Army officer, knowing only a small number of regular officers in the British Army, but he had spent the entire Second World War in South-east Asia, whereas Crocker had served in North Africa and then under Monty from Normandy to the Baltic as a Corps Commander. Subsequently he had succeeded Dempsey as C-in-C, Middle East. He could be depended upon not only to pursue Monty's strategy of keeping the Russians out of the Middle East, but, more importantly in Monty's mind, could be counted upon to support Monty's determination to back Western Union by a commitment to meet Russian aggression on the Rhine. Nothing less than such a commitment, *in writing*, would allay French mistrust of Britain and ensure the growth of Western Union defence. Whether Slim would give such a commitment Monty doubted, fearing that Slim would bow to Tedder's 'Little Britain' defence strategy and leave Western Union in the lurch.

Sadly, this was precisely what happened. At a Prime Minister's special Staff conference in 15 July 1948, at the height of the Berlin crisis, Attlee had authorized the Foreign Secretary 'to reassure the Western Union Foreign Ministers of our determination to fight alongside France on land if war broke out'.[2] After his visit to France in July Monty had reported that

[1] General Sir Frank Simpson, loc. cit.

[2] Diary, Part XII (30.5–1.9.48), Montgomery Papers.

> the French have an unpleasant feeling in the pit of the stomach that we British do not mean business over the Battle of the Rhine; there is a very definite fear that they may be 'carted', and left in the lurch. We will never get the French morale right, until we make it clear that there are not the slightest grounds for these suspicions. The French are desperately anxious to fight on the Rhine and to save their homelands from being overrun again. I seized every opportunity to make it clear *beyond any possibility of doubt* that a British Army will fight side by side with them on the Rhine; I said that the holding of the Rhine was vital to the salvation of the West and not only to the salvation of France. My own view is that they will continue to have these fears until the matter is put over on a Governmental level.[1]

As the Berlin crisis abated, Attlee refused to confirm in writing his Foreign Minister's July assurance. Slim, the new CIGS, also followed Tedder's lead in reneging on the summer's undertaking over the matter. Thus the French, who had accepted Monty as the first Chairman of the Western C-in-C's Committee in the hope of committing the British to a continental strategy, found they had been sold a pass—making Monty's position intolerable.

If the years from 1946 to 1948 had been unhappy for Monty in a Whitehall set-up he never suited, beset by national economic problems which made a mockery of his 'New Model Army' vision, and serving on a Chiefs of Staff Committee with colleagues he detested and without a firm Minister of Defence, the years from November 1948 to the summer of 1951 were to be even more unhappy. Western Union, in its military guise (its political and economic form never in fact materialized, despite Bevin's crusading zeal) was largely the inspiration of one man; yet with Attlee and Slim's refusal to confirm a British commitment to help defend France on land, Monty felt that he was stabbed in the back just as he undertook his 'herculean task'—undoubtedly the greatest Allied challenge since the war. Worse still, by failing to get his own appointment to Western Union ratified as Supreme Commander, Monty soon found his worst fears confirmed; for as 'Chairman of the Commanders-in-Chief Committee' he was to find the set-up even more of a 'debating society' than the British Chiefs of Staff Committee he had left in Whitehall. Stabbed in the back by Attlee, Tedder and Slim, he was soon stabbed in the chest by the first Commander-in-Chief of the Western Union Land Forces: Général Jean de Lattre de Tassigny.

[1] 'Memorandum by CIGS, Visit to Paris', 10/11.7.48, annex 270, Diary, Part XII, loc. cit.

CHAPTER TWO

Bringing de Lattre de Tassigny to Heel

DE LATTRE DE TASSIGNY was virtually the same age as Monty. Like Monty he had been decorated for outstanding leadership and bravery in the first months of World War I, had been wounded in the lung (by a cavalry lance) and had almost died of his wounds. Like Monty he was a man of tremendous, even insatiable energy, had distinguished himself in command of a division before Dunkirk and later as commander of the First French Army from 1944–5. Finally, like Monty, de Lattre was widely respected as a general but widely resented as a man: vain, ambitious, theatrical, visionary and passionate in his likes and dislikes.

Monty, visiting France in July, had been impressed by de Lattre, the Inspector-General of the French Armed Forces—indeed it was Monty who had recommended to the Minister of the French Armed Forces that de Lattre be appointed Commander of the Western Union Land Forces. At a 'Defence discussion' between Monty and the French Chiefs of Staff on 9 July 1948, 'General de Lattre, with his strong personality, dominated the talks from the French side', the British Military Attaché in Paris recorded[1]—and Monty had no hesitation in recommending de Lattre as the new C-in-C Land Forces. In a speech to the French Staff College on 10 July Monty had called for loyalty to de Lattre as the most senior French soldier. 'If you want loyalty from those below you, you yourself must be loyal to those above you. . . . In the British Army the officers are loyal to me. In the French Army you must be loyal to General de Lattre.'[2] De Lattre was touched by Monty's support, for he was aware that in the French Army he had more enemies than friends, having a reputation for intrigue. However, once appointed to Western Union, this gratitude soon withered and antipathy to Monty grew. Within a fortnight of the first meeting of the Western Union Commanders-in-Chief Committee, de Lattre 'cleared the decks and

[1] 'Visit to Paris of Field-Marshal The Viscount Montgomery of Alamein, CIGS: Report by British Military Attaché, British Embassy, Paris', 16.7.48, annex 271, Diary, Part XII, loc. cit.

[2] 'Address by Field-Marshal Montgomery to the Ecole Supérieure de Guerre', 10.7.48, annex 270, Diary, Part XII, loc cit.

opened with a broadside' in a 'struggle for power that was obviously about to boil up', Monty's diarist recorded.

> He [de Lattre] said that he had been appointed as a Commander-in-Chief, Western Europe Land Forces, responsible to the Western Union Chiefs of Staff Committee; as such, he added, he was a member of the Western Europe Cs-in-C Committee of which the Field Marshal was the Chairman. He knew, he said, what the term C-in-C meant: he commanded. But a Chairman was only a co-ordinator of a Committee. It was hard on the Field-Marshal that he was only a Chairman and not a Commander and he had his (General de Lattre's) sympathy.
>
> Nevertheless, the Field-Marshal had to face facts, amongst them being the fact that he, de Lattre, a C-in-C, was not going to take orders from the Field-Marshal, a Chairman. . . .
>
> A head-on collision.[1]

This grotesque confrontation took place while Monty was still doubling as CIGS, barely three weeks after his appointment to Western Union. It augured ill for Monty's future as the father of Western Union's military genesis—and it is fair to say that the achievements of Western Union over the succeeding two and a half years could have been produced by Monty in two and a half weeks without the bitter intrigues and insubordination of de Lattre.

'The Field-Marshal was very angry,' Monty's diarist recorded the ominous events of 26 October 1948.

> He reminded de Lattre that his (de Lattre's) Directive also placed him under his (the Field-Marshal's) orders for preparation and planning. . . . General de Lattre had better think again. The latter steadfastly refused to agree.
>
> Lunch concluded, the Field-Marshal hurried back to Dover House [London echelon HQ of Western Union] to study the Directives and to decide on his plan of action. General de Lattre had challenged the Field-Marshal's authority: he must be brought to heel at once.[2]

Monty's directive was tantalizingly vague. It stipulated that, although no Supreme Commander had actually been appointed, 'you will prepare your plans on the assumption that, in war, you may be called upon to assume operational control of all forces allocated for the defence of the Western Union countries from the Russian armed

[1] Diary of Field-Marshal The Viscount Montgomery of Alamein, Part XV (1.10.48–31.1.49), Montgomery Papers.
[2] Ibid.

threat'. This was, in effect, little better than General Morgan's COSSAC brief in 1943. De Lattre's directive stipulated that, without any maybes, he would become C-in-C of the Land Forces in war, though in peace-time he was to 'come under his [Montgomery's] orders for preparation and planning' as but the C-in-C *designate* of the Land Forces.[1]

Monty, nevertheless, considered the phrase 'come under his orders' was enough. 'He telephoned asking him [de Lattre] to come to Dover House to discuss the matter further. A heated interview took place, with neither party yielding an inch.'[2]

As there was to be a meeting of the Western Union Chiefs of Staff [representing the armed forces of the five Western Union nations] the next day, Monty decided to raise the issue then. 'The smiles soon disappeared at this the first joint meeting of the W.U.C.O.S. and the W.U. Cs-in-C,' Monty's diarist chronicled.[3] Monty declared that it was 'essential to air and resolve a difference of opinion that had arisen between himself and General de Lattre. . . . It was necessary to state precisely on whom the responsibility lay for planning and for dealing with Russian attacks if they came.' De Lattre argued that 'while he was under the authority or orders—the exact word was not important—of the Field-Marshal for planning, he was himself responsible [as C-in-C Land Forces (Designate)] directly to the Ministers of Defence of Western Union for the command of the defensive screen' in Europe.[4] In other words, he considered Monty a *planner* who might be superseded by a Supreme Commander in time of war, whereas he, de Lattre, was directly responsible for the existing defence forces of the West.

The Chiefs of Staff—Air-Marshal Tedder and General Lechères, representing Britain and France respectively—asked the Cs-in-C to withdraw, while they deliberated on the problem. Their subsequent ruling laid down that 'Field Marshal Montgomery was to be regarded as Supreme Commander with the responsibility for ensuring the defence of Western Europe in the best possible way'.[5] 'Any ordinary person would have thought that that was the last we would hear of that particular squabble,' Monty's diarist believed.[6] But de Lattre was only bowed, not defeated. He refused to pay more than lip service to the WUCOS ruling. When Monty produced his first

[1] Ibid.
[2] Ibid.
[3] Ibid.
[4] Ibid.
[5] Ibid.
[6] Ibid.

Planning Directive in 3 November 1948, de Lattre instantly refused to accept it on the grounds that it had not been 'discussed' in their committee. Moreover, de Lattre insisted on immediately establishing an advance HQ in Luxembourg in order to take command of the land battle of Europe. Monty felt this to be premature; not only had they still to clear and renovate the old cavalry barracks at Fontainebleau as a Main Headquarters and consider what forces were available for coherent Allied defence, but with a 1000-mile front to defend and no real consideration yet having been given to the likely avenues of Russian invasion, the site of Luxembourg (tinged with memories of Bradley's disastrous loss of control in the Ardennes) seemed most unwise. Attempting to set this aside for later attention, Monty concentrated on trying to produce three battle plans: an emergency or short-term plan; a two-year plan; and a five-year plan. But the moment Monty committed anything to paper, de Lattre objected. Monty assumed, for example, that command of existing forces belonging to Western Union states would pass to the Western Union Commander-in-Chief from the moment 'the first shot was fired'. But de Lattre felt there were 'many ways in which a war could start' without shots being fired, and therefore refused to endorse Monty's *new* planning document, Planning Directive No. 2. He also objected to Monty's touring the Western Union nations without first clearing in their committee everything he proposed to say or discuss on his tour. As the British Ambassador wrote to the Foreign Office on 25 November 1948:

> I would draw your attention to the misunderstanding which seems to exist as to the exact nature of the Field-Marshal's conception that although not nominally Supreme Commander-in-Chief, he was in fact authorised to issue orders to de Lattre, [Air Marshal] Robb and [Admiral] Jaujard who were specifically placed under his orders [as Cs-in-C Land, Air and Sea]. De Lattre himself spoke to me after the dinner at his house and said that he had much regretted that there was this misunderstanding but that according to the directive as accepted by his Minister, Ramadier, the Commanders-in-Chief were not subordinated to the Field-Marshal's orders, but were to co-operate with him and he [Montgomery] would act simply as Chairman and arbitrator.[1]

That he should meet such deliberate obstructionism within weeks of taking over the defence of Europe came as a distinct shock to Monty. The 'herculean' nature of his task he had expected to be the

[1] Extract from a letter from Sir Oliver Harvey, British Ambassador in Paris, to Sir Ivone Kirkpatrick, Foreign Office, of 25.11.48, in Diary, Part XV, loc. cit.

unwillingness of member states of Western Union to gird up their military loins; he had not imagined—despite his cables from Paris in July about the need for a Supreme Commander, not a Chairman—that the opposition he would meet would come primarily from his own committee.

For the first time in his life Monty began to recognize the problems on the other side of the fence as a Supreme Commander—a realization made all the sharper when Eisenhower's war memoirs, *Crusade in Europe*, were published in the winter of 1948. Eisenhower had written to warn Monty of forthcoming publication in June 1948. 'Like many others, I have finally succumbed to the temptation to write a personal account of the war. I resisted for a long time, but finally came to the conclusion that my own sense of fairness and justice demanded that I attempt to prepare a story that would be as factual and disinterested as I could possible make it.'[1]

In fact money had been the triggering consideration—for one of the trustees of Columbia University, of which Eisenhower was now President, offered him just under half a million dollars (after tax) in a single lump payment.[2] Small wonder that Eisenhower, with numerous researchers, two editors and three secretaries finished the 1000-page manuscript in two and a half months, dictating sixteen hours a day.

The result appalled Monty, who had asked for an advance copy, along with Kay Summersby's memoir *Eisenhower Was My Boss*, on 14 October 1948:

> My dear Ike,
>
> Your late lady driver and secretary has written a book in the States. I am being asked questions about it. Can you send me a copy; it is not obtainable in this country.
>
> I believe your own book is coming out soon. Would you send me an early copy. I am bound to be asked questions about it by the Press here. . . .
>
> My new job will be a monumental and herculean task. I shall probably go mad before I have been long in the job!! I hope you and Mamie are well. My kind regards to you both.
>
> Yrs ever
> Monty[3]

[1] Letter of 6.6.48, 'Montgomery' file, Eisenhower Papers 1652 series, Eisenhower Library, Abilene, Kansas.

[2] S. Ambrose, *Eisenhower*, *1890–1952*, New York 1983.

[3] Letter of 14.10.48, 'Montgomery' file, Eisenhower Papers, loc. cit.

Only after three months did Eisenhower send a special edition of *Crusade in Europe*; Mrs Summersby's book he refused to send at all. 'So far as Mrs Summersby's book is concerned, I have not read it and do not know where it can be obtained. . . . I do not see why you should be called upon to answer inquiries arising from inconsequential personal accounts of anything that was as big as the war was,' he had written in November;[1] but if his own account was more consequential it was equally controversial, and the Press were soon hounding Monty for his reaction.

10 January, 1949

My dear Ike,

I received on 5 January the special edition of your book 'Crusade in Europe'. It has unloosed a spate of comment over here. As soon as I knew it was to be published serially in a Sunday paper in London, I realised there would be comment and it was clear my name would be the centre of argument. That is why I wrote to you in October and asked if I could have an early copy, and you replied on 3 November that you would send me one. Perhaps something went wrong with it. . . .

I am sorry that you felt it necessary to analyse the characters of some of your colleagues and subordinates, and to indulge in criticism of them. The British Army will take some time to get over your description of Alanbrooke as a person who 'lacked the ability to weigh calmly the conflicting factors in a problem and so reach a rocklike decision'. It is definitely not true.

For myself, of course, I am by now quite used to having my ideas, and methods of working, misrepresented and twisted to convey an untrue picture: and even described as 'fantastic'.

But I agree with de Guingand; I think it is a pity that you should have thought it necessary to criticize me and my ways, just at this time in the history of the Western Union, when things are not too easy for any of us.

I am also sorry that you should have opened up a number of very controversial issues, which were lying dormant. . . . Such action so soon after the war is bound to stir up comment and controversy, and has in fact done so.

I am sure you will not mind my writing to you and saying what I feel. However, we must not let it upset our friendship and so far as I am concerned it will not do so.

But you will surely understand that I feel sad when an officer whom I have tried to serve loyally criticises me publicly, both

[1] Letter of 3.11.48. Ibid.

actually and by inference, and thereby makes my name the centre of argument in the Press. And I, of course, am not at liberty just at present to give my own story of the matters concerned.

Yours ever,
Monty[1]

Such self-imposed silence did not prevent Monty from writing personally to all and sundry to condemn Eisenhower's account. To the editor of one Yorkshire newspaper he had commented, the day before protesting to Eisenhower: 'His book is a mistake and he should not have written it. It is a mediocre work and in fifty years time will be completely unreadable. In the long run the only reputation it will damage will be Eisenhower's own, for it shows clearly that, whatever else he may have been, he was'nt [sic] a great soldier; had he kept silence, he might, through other men's silence, have passed for one. His book shows all this clearly enough to anyone with a rudimentary knowledge or memory of the broad facts of the war. A man who can't control historical facts in narrative certainly could'nt [sic] control an army in battle.'[2] To the editor of the *Sunday Times* he wrote that 'General Eisenhower and myself are still the best of friends and will remain so as far as I am concerned. That is not to say however that one day I will not write my own personal story of the war and give my own account of certain matters.'[3] It was clear that Monty had been wounded more deeply than he cared to admit. To de Guingand he confessed:

> I get some very rough treatment in some passages. I cannot understand why he should have done this.
>
> The crux of the matter is that he is the first great war leader who has written a personal story, opening up controversial issues and giving his views on the characters of his subordinates. . . .
>
> Why then do it, *just now*?
>
> The book is, naturally, written for American consumption and has brought in to IKE a lot of money. Was that the object?
>
> I cannot believe it.[4]

It was, however, true. Without such personal judgments on wartime personalities, Eisenhower's dull recitation would have sold in small numbers. What irked Monty, however, was not simply Eisenhower's personal criticisms, but the fact that 'Ike's book con-

[1] Letter of 10.1.49, M28, annex 353, Diary, Part XV, loc. cit.
[2] Letter to Mr Andrews, 9.1.49, handwritten draft in Montgomery Papers.
[3] Draft of Letter of 4.1.49, in Papers of Sir Denis Hamilton.
[4] Letter of 12.12.48, de Guingand Papers, Imperial War Museum.

veys the impression that America won the war; all British ideas were "shot down" by Marshall [sic] and IKE. Why has he done this? It is not good taste.'[1]

To the historian Arthur Bryant, who had asked for Monty's help in writing an article in the *Illustrated London News* on the controversy, Monty wrote:

> As his [Eisenhower's] book is written for American consumption one could hardly expect him to say that Brookie was the foremost strategist of the war. But he might at least refrain from insults.[2]

In Monty's view, Eisenhower was personally responsible for the Allied failure to defeat Germany in 1944, as he had already made clear to Bryant:

> The war against Germany could have been won by Christmas 1944; not September. Germany could have lasted about 3 months after losing the Ruhr; no longer.
>
> It would have made our post-war problems in Germany so much easier, and would have saved all the terrific destruction that went on. It is a sad story. I will tell you the inside truth one day. I do not care to write it.[3]

Several months later Monty had repeated the claim:

> If we had done our stuff properly, we would have been in Berlin, Prague and Viena before the Russians. And if we had done this, all our troubles today would never have arisen.[4]

With the publication of *Crusade in Europe* and Eisenhower's criticism of British leaders such as Brooke, Monty's admiration for Eisenhower dipped:

> When I reflect over IKE and his book I come more and more to the conclusion that he is not a really great man. I never thought he was. I am now certain. He lacks the character. Americans are great materialists. In theory their Constitution is based on great principles; in practice they have a materialistic disregard for principles and they concentrate on organised materialism.

[1] Letter to de Guingand, 14.12.48, de Guingand Papers, loc. cit. Monty's detailed criticisms of the book, covering eight typescript pages, are in annex 354, Diary, Part XV, loc. cit.

[2] Letter of 19.12.48, Bryant Papers.

[3] Letter of 8.6.48, Bryant Papers.

[4] Letter of 4.8.48, Bryant Papers.

> But what we need today in world affairs is not more organisation but less organisation,

he declared, bitterly aware of Britain's bankruptcy and national decline in the wake of well-meaning but misguided corporate socialism.

> The creative capacities of individual personality must not be drowned in a sea of organisation and restrictions. As I travel about Europe on my present task, I realise more and more that what we want today is leaders who have that character which will inspire confidence. Nations generally, and America in particular, have lost sight of the fact that character is more important than knowledge. If you concentrate too deeply on materialism, then you lose dominion over the minds of those you want to influence. This is a vital lesson for political leaders. It is also a vital lesson for all those who have to deal with the training of young people.
>
> Eisenhower lacks character.
>
> He, and the American nation, do not understand that character is more important than knowledge. The British Government also does not understand this great principle.
>
> I believe the greatest stumbling block that exists to mutual understanding and collaboration between British and Americans is the idea that we are similar. Each group expects the other to be a near replica of itself, because we speak the same language.
>
> Actually we are totally different people; we behave differently, we think differently and we don't really speak the same language.
>
> If only we all realised this we would suffer less disillusionment when the expectation of similarity is proved to be false.[1]

There can be little doubt that it was the publication of Eisenhower's book at a time when Monty was suffering grave difficulties in starting the Western Union Commanders-in-Chief Committee which made Monty determined to 'pay out' Eisenhower one day, even if he had to wait a further ten years—as indeed it turned out. For not only did he feel frustrated at being publicly criticized at a time when he could not answer back, but he was outraged by what he considered the untruthfulness of the picture given in Eisenhower's book. Eisenhower, stung by Monty's letter of protest, retorted that 'I did not, by a single iota, deviate from the truth as I knew it'[2]; but Monty's objection was not to the facts as such, it was to Eisenhower's presentation. Anyone who had served in the Mediterranean or in North-west Europe knew that Eisenhower's greatest contribution

[1] Letter of 19.12.48, Bryant Papers.

[2] Letter of 17.1.49, annex 358, Diary, Part XV, loc. cit.

had been the unifying of Allied purpose. But his headquarters in Algiers and later London, Granville, Versailles and Reims were very far from being the directing vision responsible for the campaigns in the Mediterranean and North-west Europe, as he made out they were. As Brigadier Williams remarked in a radio discussion of the book as has been seen, Eisenhower did not really command from his headquarters: he operated 'on the "Have a go, Joe" policy. . . . I suppose what is so remarkable about Eisenhower was that he wasn't so much himself one of the great captains, as a man to whom the great captains gladly paid allegiance. . . . That was his great contribution—not as a general in the field, but as the "architect" as he calls himself of the code of the Allies.'[1] Like Monty, Williams felt that the book largely fudged the great command issues of the war and gave a mythological picture of Eisenhower's role. 'Not I think a great book. If we remember Caesar's Gallic wars, it's perhaps because Caesar wrote about them. I don't think we shall remember Eisenhower's campaigns in Gaul because of his account of them.'[2]

Churchill had even said to Monty he considered 'that IKE's book, *plus* the Summersby book, have finished IKE as far as the Presidency in concerned'.[3] But Churchill was wrong: the American public *did* consider *Crusade in Europe* on a par with Caesar's oeuvre and was avid for further denunciations of the British after Butcher and Ingersoll had prepared the ground. Kay Summersby's implied relationship with Eisenhower was considered of small significance beside her bitter personal disparagement of Monty—a disparagement now confirmed by Eisenhower's book: 'You can hardly wonder at my dislike of the whole matter when headlines such as the enclosed appear in the London papers. I fear you have lost many friends in England,' Monty wrote to Eisenhower on 28 January 1949, enclosing the latest headline in the *Sunday Dispatch*, serializing *Crusade in Europe*: 'HOW MONTGOMERY UPSET AMERICANS by General EISENHOWER.'[4] The headline at the end of the newspaper cutting ran: 'NEXT WEEK: BRITISH METHODS THAT ALWAYS SHOCKED ME.'[5]

Far from losing votes in America, Eisenhower's book gained him millions: for the United States was now flowering into the superpower of the Western world, and wanted a version of World War II that would reflect this ascendancy. Nothing Monty could do could alter

[1] Chester Wilmot Papers (LH 15/15/133), LHCMA, King's College, London.
[2] Ibid.
[3] Letter to de Guingand, 14.12.48, de Guingand Papers, loc. cit.
[4] Letter of 28.1.49, 'Montgomery' file, Eisenhower Papers, loc. cit.
[5] *Sunday Dispatch*, 23.1.49, enclosed with letter of 28.1.49, loc. cit.

this. If he kept silent, as he did for ten years, Eisenhower's version of the World War II campaigns in Europe as the product of an American mastermind would be accepted by the public as the truth; if Monty countered with his own version, he would conform to the very caricature of himself which, increasingly, Americans held. In February 1949 the periodical *Newsweek* gleefully quoted an anonymous critic, having noted Monty's absence from the Dorchester Hotel party to celebrate British publication of Eisenhower's war memoirs:

> A man of studied poses and tricks which are carefully and skillfully employed to get the common soldier to talk about him and create Montgomery myths. . . . As a soldier he is cautious and prefers to stick to the old ways which have succeeded, instead of new ways which have not been tested. . . .
>
> As CIGS, he was a complete failure. . . . When he vacated his appointment last year, he left the British Army in a state of rock-bottom paralysis. Never since 1870 has it been so incapable of going to war.[1]

Such a view, *Newsweek* declared, 'would doubtless find many anonymous endorsers'.[2] But *Newsweek*'s account of Monty's 'Uniforce' headquarters in Fontainebleau was even more scathing. Established in an 'old cavalry barracks facing the Henri IV Court and the Château of Fontainebleau' it could do little more in an emergency than telephone Washington and ask for the United States to take action under the newly signed Atlantic Security Pact. Given that American politicians had made clear 'no United States Government can give guarantees of automatic military assistance' by virtue of the US Constitution, *Newsweek* was far from optimistic. The British could not furnish even a single armoured division in emergency, the French had 'few trained divisions and fewer new weapons, and the Benelux states could probably not muster a single fully trained and equipped division' of any kind. It was, as *Newsweek* summarized, a 'bleak' prospect. 'Unilion' (Monty's new codename) was but a paper tiger. 'Looking like a self-satisfied falcon', without even a guard at the gate of his gabled suburban mansion on the rue Général Charles de Gaulle (his temporary headquarters), Montgomery flew between the capitals of Western Union to drum up support for a charade of European defence.[3]

However much Monty may have disliked the tone of *Newsweek*'s article, he had himself—as his diary and letters reveal—no illusions: Western Union in its military guise *was* a sham, with a committee of

[1] *Newsweek*, 28.2.49.
[2] Ibid.
[3] Ibid.

paper commanders as incapable of unified action as the one he had left in Whitehall. If his relationship with Tedder had been hostile, his relationship with de Lattre de Tassigny was one of almost open war.

CHAPTER THREE

Cause Célèbre

THE STORY OF Montgomery and de Lattre was to become one of the *causes célèbres* of its time: an antipathy so great that it poisoned virtually the entire time-span of Western Union. Moreover its ripples went on to poison the birth of NATO—and de Gaulle's later decision to remove France from NATO and exclude England from the EEC may be ascribed at least symbolically to the Franco/Anglo-Saxon sore that festered behind the façade of Western Union and found its most potent expression in the relationship between these two men.

Monty's position was unenviable. Where the Foreign Ministers and representative Chiefs of Staff of Western Union could paper over their differences in polite communiqués and depart to more pressing engagements, Monty was left holding Western Union's military baby. And beside him there was a haunting presence, a shadow that would never go away nor could ever be circumvented. Whatever Monty did or proposed to do, de Lattre objected to. There seemed no way in which he could shake off this mirror ego who hated yet clung to him. By March 1949 Monty had found there was simply no point in attempting to humour de Lattre or to tolerate his insubordination. 'Up till now the Field-Marshal had always been most accommodating, but his trust had invariably been abused,' Monty's diarist recorded as the Cs-in-C Committee met on 22 March 1949. 'There was to be no more of that. The meeting was an extremely frigid and terse affair.'[1] Though Monty's outline short-term plan and Short Term Plan were agreed without dissent, de Lattre produced a paper in which, in order to curb Monty's authoritarian attitude to Western Union command, he 'sought to deny the right to the Field-Marshal to express an opinion on any matter of a single service nature;'[2] in addition to which he continued to object to Monty's conception of his rôle as that of acting Supreme Commander, entitled to give orders.

General Huebner, attending the Western Union Cs-in-C Com-

[1] Diary of Field-Marshal The Viscount Montgomery of Alamein, Part XVI (1.2.49–30.4.49), Montgomery Papers.
[2] Ibid.

mittee as official US observer (for Bradley, the Chief of Staff US Army, had promised to put the American contingent in West Germany under overall Western Union command in the event of sudden war), stated on 25 March that 'the American view was that the Commanders-in-Chief should have a firm and business-like constitution. He said that the Americans would not accept anything else.'[1] Bradley himself told Sir William Morgan, the British Military Representative to the Combined Chiefs of Staff in Washington, that he was 'quite clear that the Land Forces Commander, and, of course, the Air and Naval Commanders, must be under the orders of the Supreme Commander. He considered that the French have no right to aspire to Supreme Command in any theatre unless and until they are providing the preponderance of the armed forces in that theatre. He also remarked that no serving Frenchman has any experience of High Command in war.'[2]

The irony of the situation, as de Lattre was keenly aware, was that Monty had himself been a thorn in the Supreme Commander's side in the campaigns of World War II. As Land Force Commander for D-Day Monty had 'run the show' with only scant reference to Eisenhower—and had jibbed violently when Eisenhower descended from his 'lofty perch' in September 1944. Indeed it was well known that Monty considered the war could have been won by Christmas 1944 if Eisenhower had not interfered with the Land Force C-in-C set-up. Now Monty was being hoisted by his own petard—and de Lattre was determined to play the role of 'super-Montgomery' to the would-be Eisenhower of Western Union. At a shoot-out on 21 April at 4.30 p.m. Monty openly confronted de Lattre—as Eisenhower had once exploded in front of de Guingand, during the battle of the Ardennes, on the issue of a new Ground Force Commander:

> The Field-Marshal opened the meeting with some very frank talking, accusing de Lattre openly of gross disloyalty and intrigue; he pointed out the impossibility of working in an atmosphere and against a background of intrigue and suspicion and said that it must end. . . .
>
> The Field-Marshal then proposed 4 rules to govern future working, namely:
>
> 1. We will cease to say unpleasant things about each other to *any third person*. If either of us wants to say anything unpleasant about the other, he will say it *directly to the other* and to no one else.

[1] Ibid.
[2] Ibid.

2. If either of us disagrees violently with the other on some point, or is angry or upset about any matter he will go and have it out with the other *face to face*.
   We will not discuss our disagreements with any persons outside the Cs-in-C organisation.
3. If after full and frank discussion together vide the second point, we still cannot reach agreement, then we will refer the matter to W.U.C.O.S. [Western Union Chiefs of Staff]. We will both accept the W.U.C.O.S. decision loyally.
4. The Chairman and Members of Cs-in-C Committee must be international. As regards myself, I resigned my national appointment at the British War Office when I took up my present appointment of Chairman of the Cs-in-C Committee. I gave my assurance that I had no British links and was now entirely international.[1]

This fourth point referred to de Lattre's continuing position as Inspector-General of the French Armed Services, and Vice President of the Conseil Supérieur de la Guerre: a fact which in Monty's view was bound to divide his loyalties.

De Lattre agreed to these four points, verbally and in writing. As Monty's MA noted, 'a surprising amount of paper work—i.e. planning—has been done in view of the background of suspicion and intrigue; the Western Union Chiefs of Staff and Ministers of Defence have approved the Short Term Plan, on which detailed practical planning is now taking place. Even more surprising is the fact that there has been no single sign of bad feeling nor difficulties between British and French on any level below the top, which is an indication of the fund of goodwill and singleness of purpose that animates, I wish one could say everyone, in the Western Union set-up. The sole exception is de Lattre, and, as far as he is concerned, one is left to wonder whether he is animated by tremendous vanity and ambition or whether he is quite simply mad. Whichever the answer may be, one hopes that the Field-Marshal's activities . . . will have put an end to intrigue and will have prepared the way for happier days in the future.'[2] The war, however, went on—the French newspapers supporting de Lattre's view of the Cs-in-C Committee as a 'collegiate' body, and de Lattre himself refusing to give up his national appointments. By June 1949 Monty was complaining to the CIGS, Field-Marshal Slim, that 'Ramadier had not the slightest intention of doing anything

[1] Ibid.
[2] Ibid.

in the matter . . . and de Lattre is urging him to stand fast in the matter. . . . The nett result is that doubt, discord and friction are on the increase.'[1]

Sir George Mallaby, the Secretary-General of the Military Chiefs of Staff Committee of Western Union, described the mutual animosity between Monty and de Lattre as 'venomous' but primarily personal. 'Had they both been English or both French it would have been just the same.'[2] This may have been so, but the fact that they were not of common nationality certainly served to aggravate their mutual dislike. Mallaby's retrospective portrait of the two men was telling:

> The Field-Marshal terse and trenchant, given to oversimplification, ignoring or despising tangential considerations, using straightforward language, unadorned except by idioms borrowed from the world of sport, jocular with a kind of puerile humour, practical, decisive, self-assured, uneasy in the realm of speculative ideas, unacquainted with art and literature, undemonstrative though not without affection for lesser beings, flinty and unyielding, careless of personal feelings, insensitive to them, single-minded, somewhat ascetic, precise and punctual.[3]

Monty's punctuality was in fact legendary, the two watches he wore on his wrist being almost as famous as his beret. By contrast de Lattre invariably arrived late:

> General de Lattre, delighting in words and figures, leaving the highway of his talk for intriguing by-paths, elaborating and refining his expressions, dwelling in irony and wit, amused with life and with people, alternating wildly between anger and compassion, rage giving place to tears, acting somewhat, enthusiastic for life and art, loving people, including those whom he most violently chastened, tender and sensitive and yet in many ways unpardonably inconsiderate and unreasonable, taking pleasure in the flesh-pots, good wine, good company, good talk, uncontrolled and hopelessly unpunctual.[4]

Aware that the signing of the North Atlantic Treaty on 4 April 1949 would mean the eventual absorption of Western Union into a larger organization from Scandinavia to the Mediterranean, Monty felt that a system of Supreme Command must be set up if there was

[1] Letter of 28.6.49, annex 401, Diary of Field-Marshal The Viscount Montgomery of Alamein, Part XVII (1.5.49–18.6.49), Montgomery Papers.
[2] G. Mallaby, *From my Level*, London 1965.
[3] Ibid.
[4] Ibid.

to be a worthwhile organization to hand over when the time came—an organization, moreover, rehearsed in its rôle by means of challenging communications, command and logistics exercises.

Putting pressure on Sir George Mallaby, Monty managed to get the French Minister of Defence to agree in July 1949 to a new Western Union Defence Committee ruling that 'the system of command in war will be a Supreme Commander with the three Commanders-in-Chief under his orders',[1] though this might be altered when the Atlantic Pact was ratified.

Armed with a copy of this ruling, Monty unwisely summoned de Lattre on 19 July to his new abode—a wing of the Château de Courances, owned by the Marquis de Ganay, which had been equipped and staffed since April as his official residence in France.

De Lattre, however, had not seen the new ruling—and claimed that Ramadier 'had said quite definitely that no decision had in fact been taken'. Monty waved his letter from Mallaby, asking whether or not de Lattre 'accepted that decision'.

> *General de Lattre* replied that he imagined that he had come to the Château de Courances for a frank and open discussion on the subject of Command and not to receive an ultimatum to give an answer 'yes' or 'no' to a decision of which he was ignorant, and which according to his information had never been made.
>
> *The Field-Marshal* then asked General de Lattre for his views on the subject of command.
>
> *General de Lattre* began by saying that the Field-Marshal's assertion that he (General de Lattre) had done everything in his power to block, or at least postpone a decision on this matter of High Command in War, was, in general, true. It was a matter which would obviously be a source of considerable friction and he had felt that no useful decision could be reached upon it, until the effects of the Atlantic Pact were clear. The Field-Marshal, however, had pressed him for his views, and he would give them as frankly as he could,

the record of the meeting ran.[2] First, however, de Lattre rejected everything agreed earlier that summer, claiming that Monty had no right to 'take decisions on matters which were the concern only of the Land Forces. . . . Matters of concern to one service only were the province of the individual C-in-C and not of the Field Marshal.'

[1] Letter from Sir George Mallaby, Secretary-General, Western Union Defence Organisation, of 15.7.49 (WU 296/49), in annex 412, Diary, Part XVII, loc. cit.

[2] Annex 413, Diary, Part XVII, loc. cit.

Moreover, in representing to their masters the views of his committee, Monty ought only to communicate 'on matters touching more than one service, i.e. truly "combined" matters'—whereas 'it was for each individual Commander-in-Chief to represent his views directly to the Military Committee on matters touching only his own service'.[1] If war broke out in the immediate future, de Lattre maintained, 'he [de Lattre] could not share the responsibility for the battle in France with anyone else'; and if war did *not* break out in the immediate future, he was equally opposed to Monty's views on high command. 'The system of Supreme Command, as advocated by the Field-Marshal [i.e. with Supreme Commander over three C-in-C's], had been seriously tried out in war . . . in 1939 and 1940 when General Gamelin was Supreme Commander and General Georges was Commander-in-Chief of the Land Forces. The results had been disastrous.'[2]

De Lattre's steam was up; he was now unstoppable. Monty's system was as potentially disastrous in peace as it was in war he claimed—'in peace time, the system advocated by the Field-Marshal had been tried out in Indo-China, in Madagascar and in French West Africa, in each case with most unsatisfactory results'. De Lattre even commented on the North-west Europe campaign: 'In the early days of "Overlord", the system had been tried for a short time, and nobody knew better than the Field Marshal how impossible it had been. It had lasted only so long as General Eisenhower was in England and had been abandoned the moment he set foot in France.'[3]

Monty could scarcely believe his ears. Under his leadership as C-in-C Land Forces from January to September 1944 the Allies had not only mounted the greatest assault landing in human history, but had won the decisive battle of World War II in the West: the battle of Normandy. Only when the Supreme Commander insisted on taking over the running of the land battle on top of his other duties had the Allied campaign disintegrated. Before Monty could interject, however, de Lattre held up his hand and released a further broadside at the way in which, as mere Chairman of the current Western Union Cs-in-C Committee, Monty was comporting himself:

> *General de Lattre* asked leave to make one more point before concluding. It was a delicate one, but he would make it frankly. On his various journeys, the Field Marshal was in the habit of making speeches and statements in the Press, in which he arrogated to himself the position of military command of Western Europe. He

[1] Ibid.
[2] Ibid.
[3] Ibid.

had no title to do this: still less had he any title to enter the domain of politics which could only make difficulties for the Commanders-in-Chief Organisation.

WUCOS had expressly laid it down that the Commanders-in-Chief Organisation was forbidden to make statements to the Press without their authority. General de Lattre was under constant pressure to make speeches and statements to the Press, but he had resisted such pressure and had loyally observed the orders given by WUCOS. He felt the Field Marshal's conduct was lacking in discretion and placed the Commanders-in-Chief in an extremely difficult position. He asked that, in future, speeches and statements made by the Field Marshal should first be approved by the Cs-in-C Committee.[1]

In conclusion de Lattre felt that, if 'useful work was to continue'

a) The Field-Marshal must not set himself up as a Supreme Commander until he was appointed as such. . . .
b) The Field Marshal must not trespass in fields which were the sole responsibility of the Land Forces Commander.
c) The Field Marshal must not make public statements in which he usurped the position of military leader of Europe. He must maintain the team spirit—the spirit of a team of which he was captain.[2]

Monty was made speechless by such arrogance. Small wonder the French had lost the battle of France in a matter of weeks in 1940, had been a constant anxiety to SHAEF in the winter of 1944/5 and were facing defeat in Indo-China: for their love of argument and definition overrode any concern to match a professional enemy.

Tersely, Monty asked de Lattre if he would put his views in writing; then read out to him Mallaby's report of the Defence Minister's ruling at Luxembourg on 15 July. Unabashed, de Lattre declared that this 'changed nothing' since 'no decision had been reached on what the Command organisation in war would actually be'; all it laid down was an 'assumption' for 'planning purposes'.[3]

Monty was exasperated—and said he doubted whether he could ever count on de Lattre's loyalty, 'since, from the outset, General de Lattre had worked against him' rather than for the cause—an accusation that only inflamed de Lattre yet more:

[1] Ibid.
[2] Ibid.
[3] Ibid.

> General de Lattre denied that he had worked against the Field Marshal. He held different views from the Field Marshal, but that was not the same as working against him. . . . In point of fact, the Field Marshal had worked against General de Lattre from the first moment that it became clear to him that he was not prepared to accept unreservedly and without question all the opinions expressed by the Field Marshal. He had, he said, come to the meeting expecting a frank exchange of views as between soldiers. He had not expected to take part in an exchange of rudeness and had no intention of doing so. While differing from the Field Marshal on certain matters, he nevertheless respected his great reputation and his great abilities. If it had been the policy to create Marshals of France, he himself might well have been one of them. He respected the Field Marshal and he asked the Field Marshal to respect his own considerable reputation and his position as a soldier of France.[1]

Monty had certainly met his match for conceit and egoism—in a man he himself had recommended for the post of Land Force C-in-C! Ruefully Monty concluded the meeting by saying that he *did* respect de Lattre's 'position as a soldier of France' and saw no reason why they could not work together effectively on the Cs-in-C Committee in peace-time 'but that there could never be any question of their working together in time of war. It would be impossible.'[2]

De Lattre 'then took his leave',[3] but his protestations of loyalty did not prevent him from immediately sowing new rumours, to the effect that Monty was no longer planning the defence of continental Europe, but only the evacuation of British and American formations in Germany and Austria. 'It is now clear beyond any doubt the source of the slander campaign against Britain is de Lattre,' Monty informed King George VI in August; 'the cumulative evidence proves this. He is violently anti-British. I forced him to issue the statement about myself and my wish to stage another Dunkirk. That was good as he had been sowing the rumours. He is definitely evil. It is now also quite clear that he knows I know what he is doing. So I have to go very carefully these days and consider every move with great care before I make it.'[4]

Incensed by de Lattre's intrigues, rumour-mongering and complaints above his head to the British Chiefs of Staff, Monty was unable however to 'go very carefully'. The relationship between the two men became one of battle, with de Lattre dividing the

[1] Ibid.
[2] Ibid.
[3] Diary, Part XVII, loc. cit.
[4] Letter to Sir Alan Lascelles, 16.8.49 (RA GVI/283), Royal Archives, Windsor.

Fontainebleau staff into his own supporters on the one hand, and '*hommes de Montgomery*' on the other. In an audience with King George VI, Monty poured out his troubles with de Lattre, as Sir Frank Simpson later recalled:

> Monty unburdened himself of all the difficulties he was having with de Lattre, using phrases like 'quite unsound', 'refuses to see all sides of the problem' and that sort of thing. Then having delivered himself of all this, he added: 'I think I can sum up, Sir, by describing him as the French equivalent of Dickie Mountbatten!'

The King did not look amused by this comparison.

> He [Monty] felt all of a sudden that he had gone too far—after all Louis Mountbatten was the King's cousin—so he decided that he had better take his leave as quickly as possible and asked permission to retire from the King's presence. The King had said nothing.
>
> When he got in to the ante-chamber, he said to the King's Private Secretary, who was then Sir Alan Lascelles, that he had dropped a tremendous brick by comparing de Lattre with Louis Mountbatten. Monty said that Lascelles roared with laughter and said: 'Don't you worry. The Monarch has no illusions whatever about dear cousin Dickie!'[1]

Few people, equally, had any illusions about de Lattre. General Marshall, who had brushed with de Lattre in the autumn of 1944, considered him a French fanatic whose insubordination could only be tolerated as long as the Allies were fighting on French soil. Bradley referred to him as 'a skunk at a kitten party'. Wherever he went, de Lattre aroused ill will. His unpunctuality reflected a vanity even more inflated than Monty's. He liked to keep people waiting as a mark of his rank, and to vex. Once arrived, however, he wanted star treatment. When visiting the British Army of the Rhine on manoeuvres in October 1949 'he succeeded in making himself as unpleasant as possible and in being as rude as possible to General Keightley within a very few minutes of arrival. The initial fuss arose from the fact that he had been placed in the fifth jeep in the convoy to leave the airfield. The first jeep was Military Police and the others the usual paraphernalia of an Army Commander's escort. Nevertheless de Lattre thought and said that it was a deliberate insult that he had not been placed in the leading jeep. He also appeared to think that there was another deliberate insult in that the salute had been taken by the British Secretary of State for War instead of by himself,' Monty's diarist recorded. Officers at Fontainebleau were quite used to such antics, 'but BAOR were not accustomed to such goings on and

[1] General Sir Frank Simpson, loc. cit.

immediately, and quite rightly, took great umbrage. In fact de Lattre succeeded in making himself an enemy in almost a record short space of time.'[1]

As the British Army of the Rhine would come under de Lattre's supposed command in time of war, the enmity he aroused was unfortunate. But it was by no means unusual. Even in France Monty found on a reconnaissance of the potential front line from Basle, 'de Lattre is hated by the French Army generally, except by his own hangers-on. The whole Army is praying for his departure to some other sphere of usefulness,' he wrote sarcastically to de Guingand.[2]

Such prayers were, however, not answered and the mutual torment of the two men escalated without respite. Monty's call for command and staff/signal exercises, especially, aroused de Lattre's anger, since it was only at such exercises, attended by the complete Western Union military staffs as well as American observers, that de Lattre's subordinate role to Montgomery could be publicly demonstrated. De Lattre resorted to every possible means to stop the exercises taking place, succeeding in getting the army/air exercise of 4 July 1949 postponed for some four months.[3]

By the autumn of 1949 Monty was rueing his erstwhile objection to General Koenig as Land Force C-in-C, and conspiring to get Koenig to replace de Lattre who, having grasped Monty's trouser leg in his Gallic jaws, refused either to resign or let go. Admiral Jaujard, as a Frenchman, felt disinclined to get embroiled in the dispute, even though he disliked de Lattre; Air Marshal Robb, as a sometime courtier at Eisenhower's headquarters, felt that there was much to support in de Lattre's view of a chairman's job. Indeed had Field-Marshal Alexander been brought back from Canada to assume the mantle of chairman, de Lattre's view would undoubtedly have prevailed, just as Eisenhower and Alexander had permitted Mark Clark and Monty to dictate strategy in Italy.

In this sense, therefore, Monty's appointment to Western Union was as much a mistake as his previous appointment as CIGS had

[1] 'General de Lattre at BAOR Manoeuvres', October 1949, Diary of Field-Marshal The Viscount Montgomery of Alamein, Part XVIII (19.6.49–2.12.49), Montgomery Papers.

[2] Letter of 2.9.49, de Guingard Papers, loc. cit.

[3] De Lattre forced the abandonment of the 4 July exercise by simply summoning his Chief of Staff, General Blanc, and Colonel Beaufre to his own headquarters. As they were essential to the exercise, the exercise had to be cancelled. Blanc, Beaufre, and General Navereau (Deputy Chief of Staff) all resigned on the spot. De Lattre insisted they tender written resignations to the Minister for War, but on their way to Paris the three officers became aware of the public scandal that would ensue, returned to Fontainebleau and withdrew their resignations. The exercise was finally mounted on 27/28.10.49, Monty delivering the opening address (annex 457, Diary, Part XVIII, loc. cit.).

proved to be. There was no gainsaying his strategic vision, his decisive and determined mind, his legendary professionalism. The man who had laid down the tasks of the Allied Armies for D-Day and mounted the great presentation of plans at St Paul's School prior to the Normandy invasion could legitimately claim a place alongside the great captains of war across the centuries. For professionalism at this higher level of war, Monty had had no peer among the Allies, the Axis powers, or in Russia. But the World War was over and in terms of peacetime soldiering Monty's very professionalism was a handicap. His style of leadership, his god-like belief in his mission, made him a man for the moment of crisis: for command of a frustrated army at Alamein, for vitalizing the D-Day assault, for restoring confidence and calm during the American débâcle in the Ardennes. But once the battles were won, his very brand of leadership—that cocksure self-righteousness transmitted to the very base echelons of his armies—was bound to raise hackles, as it had in Algiers, in Sicily, in Italy, after Normandy, and after the Battle of the Bulge. And this Monty would not, could not see. Diplomacy was beyond him. What he saw, he saw more clearly perhaps than any man of his time—but it was a soldier's tunnel-vision that made no allowance for political or even human weakness. Just as he pressed for a Chief of Staff, Armed Services in Britain, so he quickly perceived that in Western Union there ought to be a man responsible for seeing that the decisions of the constituent states, made by their Defence Ministers, were actually carried out: a Director-General. This he proposed in 1949, to the consternation of the Western Union governments who had no real desire to implement the idealistic posturing of their Foreign Ministers. Moreover, if Western Union defence was eventually to be absorbed into a larger organization, stretching from Scandinavia to the Mediterranean, Monty was determined to rehearse the problems of command and staff procedures in Western Union, whatever de Lattre's objections. Not only would such exercises illuminate the current weakness of Western defence, but they would give the five-nation staffs at Fontainebleau something towards which they could strive during the limbo before a new military organization was set up. Though de Lattre howled, Monty would not be dissuaded: and on 8 November 1949 Monty's first major Western Union exercise began, codenamed, with some irony, 'Harmonie'.

CHAPTER FOUR

Façade of Co-operation

Exercise 'Harmonie' was a study of Western Union logistics, held in London in the presence of the entire Chiefs of Staff of Western Union, the Army Commanders from the British and American Zones of occupation in Germany, American Air and Naval Commanders, and many of their staff officers. 'This was a very notable gathering in view of the opposition which de Lattre had at first put up against holding the presentation at this level,' Monty's diarist recorded.[1] But no exercise could really rehearse the operational or administrative aspects of a war in Europe without a clear acceptance of the system of command—and this de Lattre had not accorded, despite the new ruling laid down by the Ministers of Defence on 15 July 1949.

When Monty thus raised the problem of command in public at Exercise 'Harmonie', de Lattre was furious—the more so as the two men were at such loggerheads over the employment of armour and the design of modern tanks that de Lattre had taken the unusual step of forwarding a letter he had received from Monty to the British Chiefs of Staff as an example of Monty's treatment of his Land Force C-in-C.

When Monty met the British Chiefs of Staff on 9 November 1949 prior to leaving on a trip to America, de Lattre's forwarding of the rude letter was deemed of greater importance than the international issues Monty had hoped to discuss. 'It was agreed by everybody present, including the FM, that it was a very rude letter indeed,' Monty's diarist chronicled.[2] The FM pointed out that it was a personal and strictly private letter and that it had no right to be bandied about for a lot of other people to see. He then asked what line the British Chiefs of Staff proposed to take if the matter was raised with them officially, to which the First Sea Lord [Lord Fraser of North Cape] replied, 'We should have to tell you not to write this sort of letter.'[3]

Monty, who had hoped the British Chiefs of Staff would tell de

[1] Diary, Part XVIII, loc. cit.
[2] Ibid.
[3] Ibid.

Lattre that 'they were not prepared to discuss in open session strictly private and personal letters written between Commanders-in-Chief', was taken aback. 'And then I would have to tell you that I do not take orders from the British Chiefs of Staff!' he retorted.[1]

Slim calmed down the meeting, and it was agreed that in view of de Lattre's supposedly impending retirement 'it would be as well to try and avoid any further trouble with him for the next two months. Rather he should be kept sweet and the FM should refrain from writing to him at all.'[2]

What Monty had hoped to discuss with the British Chiefs of Staff, however, was his imminent meetings with the American Chiefs of Staff in Washington—and with Eisenhower. A year had passed since the setting up of Western Union's command committee. 'It is time to take stock of the situation,' he began his proposed Memorandum to be discussed on 9 November.

> One year should be sufficient time in which to:
> a) produce some practical results and achievements.
> b) show a definite development of the attitude of mind to Western Union defence which will augur well for the future.
> c) demonstrate the will and determination of the Western Union Powers rapidly to provide for the defence of their homelands.
> d) produce practical proof that we could make some attempt to handle a sudden emergency.[3]

But 'in actual fact the results we have to show for the year's work', Monty's document made clear, were pathetic. A paper plan had been produced, planning staffs had been built up and operational procedures (communications and protocol) standardized. Otherwise, however, the balance sheet was empty—'we have little to show for our labours. In fact the "sharp end" of Western Union is making no progress among the four Continental nations; indeed, it is at a standstill.[4]

'The situation today can be described as follows,' Monty continued his exposition:

> a) The French Army is in an appalling state; this is no exaggeration.
> The French are cutting down Western Union expenditure and 'stall' as soon as efforts are made to implement the practical requirements of the Cs-in-C War Organisation. . . .

[1] Ibid.
[2] Ibid.
[3] Annex 465, Diary, Part XVIII, loc. cit.
[4] Ibid.

b) The Belgian Army is making no progress. The Belgian Defence organisation flounders about in uncertainties.
c) The Dutch Army progress is practically NIL. . . .
d) Among the British personnel in Uniforce there is a growing feeling that British participation is not taken seriously in Whitehall. Officers have been heard to say that the British find Western Europe defence a useful 'cover plan'.
e) The Americans decline to use the great influence they could bring to bear to hasten practical progress.
If they were to insist on practical progress before they supplied money and equipment, electric results might follow.[1]

'The picture is most depressing,' Monty claimed. 'I must therefore ask myself the following questions':

a) Do the responsible National Authorities accept the present situation, and the present rate of progress . . .?
b) If the responsible National Authorities are NOT satisfied with the present situation, what steps do they propose to take to improve matters?
c) Do the British Authorities propose to discuss the matter frankly with the U.S. Authorities?
d) Would the British Authorities care to give me any advice as to what line I should adopt with American personalities when I am asked for my views on the present military organisation in Western Europe, and on my forecast of its future development and needs.
I would welcome such advice.[2]

Under the guise of a request Monty was in fact trying to tell the British Chiefs of Staff what they should do. First, they must force Attlee's government to authorize a British military commitment to fight on the Rhine in the event of war. Second, they must back him in getting the Americans to force the French to put their military house in order. Without proper French forces, Western Europe was indefensible.

The British Chiefs of Staff—Tedder, Slim and Sir John Cunningham's successor, Lord Fraser—refused to be drawn, however. They refused to alter their Little Britain 'Dunkirk' strategy, and they were deeply suspicious of Monty's imminent trip to the USA. If Monty saw the American Chiefs of Staff and candidly exposed the sham of British commitment to European continental defence and

[1] Ibid.
[2] Ibid.

the parlous state of the French Army, he might simply frighten the Americans into withdrawing aid and Atlantic Pact commitment to Europe altogether. The British Chiefs of Staff thus begged Monty *not* to meet the American Chiefs of Staff 'to discuss this or any other subject'—a plea which was soon followed by a personal letter from Tedder pointing out the current spate of Press articles, on both sides of the Atlantic, 'reporting differences of opinion and policy between the Brussels Treaty Powers. Discussing these this morning, we [the British Chiefs of Staff] all felt that these reinforced the paramount importance of your saying nothing during your visit to the United States, either publicly or privately, which might result in a diminution of confidence in you by any of the Five Governments in whose service you are now working. The French are clearly apprehensive of what may happen while you are in the United States, and we feel that you will agree that even in your private talks with General Bradley—the gist of which he is bound to pass on to his colleagues—you should be very sparing in your criticisms. We feel it hardly necessary in this connection to remind you of the unhappy frequency with which such confidences leak out.'[1]

Such a shot across the bows merely redoubled Monty's determination—as in 1946—to use his immense personal military standing to 'get the ball rolling'. The British representative (and chairman) on the Permanent Commission of Western Union, Sir Gladwyn Jebb, reiterated Tedder's warning the next day: 'it is thought such articles can only have the most unfortunate effect on American support for the efforts of the five powers to defend themselves'.[2] But Monty's blood was up. He was quite prepared to lie in public for the good of Western Union's cause, and in his Press conferences and speeches—particularly his broadcast address to the English Speaking Union—he did so:

> I would say that in the Commanders-in-Chief organisation there exists something never before achieved in peacetime . . . We have achieved results that fifteen or twenty years ago would have appeared impossible on this international basis. We have not always agreed immediately at the top level; we should hardly have been human if we had. But differences of opinion have been argued and considered from every angle and agreed decisions have been reached. Our integrated staffs have then worked out the details in the greatest harmony. You may have heard it said that there is discord within our staffs; that is utterly untrue.[3]

[1] Letter of 14.11.49, annex 461, Diary, Part XVIII, loc. cit.
[2] Letter of 15.11.49, annex 462, Diary, Part XVIII, loc. cit.
[3] Speech of 29.11.49, annex 466, Diary, Part XVIII, loc. cit.

But in his private talks with the American Chiefs of Staff Committee in Washington, and in personal talks with Bradley, Collins, Eisenhower, Bedell Smith and Johnson, the new Secretary for Defence, Monty was uncompromisingly frank. In an age of long-range bombers and atomic weapons, it made sense to keep the battle-front as far away as possible. Little-Britain or Little-America strategies made no sense, since by drawing in one's lines of defence, one merely exposed one's country to greater and more proximate danger. Every pound or dollar spent on halting a possible Russian offensive on the Rhine meant less destruction at home in time of war. As in World War II, American defence should be based on priorities—and fighting in Europe was the number one priority. If Western Europe was secure, the United States was safe; moreover, by committing itself to Western European defence, the United States would encourage the constituent nations of Western Union to defend themselves. Given the state of the French army and the myopia of Attlee's Little-Britain caucus, however, the lead *must* now come from America.

Whether the United States would have fostered the problem-child that was Western Union without Monty's intervention is mere speculation. The North Atlantic Treaty Organization had been formally set-up in April 1949, but how its existence would affect the command structure in Western Europe was still a subject of debate when Monty travelled to America. Although both Bradley (since August 1949 Chief of US Defence Staff) and Collins (Chief of Staff, US Army) assured Monty they agreed privately with his views on the priority of European defence, they both doubted whether Truman's administration would commit itself in this direction any more than Attlee was doing. Monty was then ushered into the new US Defence Secretary's office on 23 November—and to Mr Johnson Monty made it clear that without 'a firm British and American guarantee of help on land—we would never be able to build up sufficient strength to hold the West'. Moreover, without such strength the West Germans would begin to pose a dire problem. Was West Germany to be brought under the umbrella of Western Europe, or was it to grow as an independent entity 'up for grabs' by Russians anxious lest it re-arm as under Hitler?

To Monty it was self-evident that a rapidly re-emerging West Germany should march with the West—and that its vital potential military manpower, by being 'kept at a greatly lower level than that of the combined strength of the other Western Europe Powers', become part of, not a threat to, Western European unity.[1]

Johnson, stunned by Monty's clear-cut presentation, refused to

[1] Talks held on 23.11.49, Diary, Part XVIII, loc. cit.

commit the administration, but did promise to reassure the French verbally that America would reinforce its divisions in Germany in time of war, and would not make for the beaches.[1]

For Monty this was, if not victory, at least a promising result. 'My visit to the U.S.A. was an immense success from every angle: militarily and also from the angle of British/American relations,' he boasted in a letter to de Guingand on Christmas Eve.[2]

The effect of Johnson's pledge, given to the new French Minister of Defence, soon subsided however, and by February 1950 Monty was lamenting to de Guingand:

> In my own sphere affairs are not going well. Under a façade of co-operation the nations will not budge an inch. I think the situation today is full of danger due to two things: 1 – the rise of Germany in the West; 2 – the march of Communism in the East. There is no plan for dealing with either of these two dangers.[3]

There was a third problem, too. De Lattre had been slated to retire in February 1950. February came and went—but de Lattre would not and did not go; and the relationship between the two men, never cordial, sank to new and alarming depths, reaching its nadir at Monty's second great exercise at Fontainebleau in May 1950: Exercise 'Unity'.

[1] Ibid.
[2] Letter of 24.12.49, de Guingand Papers, loc. cit.
[3] Letter of 10.2.50, de Guingand Papers, loc. cit.

CHAPTER FIVE

Reconciliation with de Lattre

EXERCISE 'UNITY' DEALT with 'the machinery for implementing the Short Term [Western Union] Plan and the system of Command for the conduct of the battle in Western Europe'. As Sir George Mallaby later recalled:

> The exercise was organized and mounted by the Field-Marshal's own staff and was most inappropriately named 'Unity', for at this moment relations between him and General de Lattre could not have been more frigid and unfriendly. The Commanders-in-Chief and all their staffs attended this excercise, together with representatives of Western Union Chiefs of Staff and some of my own central secretariat. The exercise, which lasted two or three days, I think, was opened by the Field Marshal with his customary succinct and confident *exposé*. At the end of this he was prompted by General Belchem to ask if the Commanders-in-Chief would like to make any comments or ask any questions. I could see that he did not much relish this. It was his exercise and he wanted to get on with it, but accepted the advice as a necessary courtesy. Whereupon he turned towards de Lattre, who was sitting in the front row, and said in his most perfunctory and graceless manner, 'De Lattre, do you want to say anything?'[1]

De Lattre did not. 'I was not truly surprised that the General should resent this incivility,' Mallaby recorded, 'offered in the presence of perhaps 200 staff officers; and his uncompromising refusal to say anything but "No, I will wait to the end", spitting out his words with contempt and dislike, was all that could have been expected.'[2]

De Lattre's desire to wait till the end was not merely a response to Monty's incivility, however. De Lattre knew that the Foreign Ministers and Chiefs of Staff Committee of Western Union were looking to Monty's exercise to provide a ready-made solution to the command problem: the question of whether Monty should exercise decisive, overall command of the defence of Western Europe, or whether the land battle should be handed over to de Lattre as C-in-

[1] *From My Level*, op. cit.
[2] Ibid.

C of the Land Forces. When, finally, his turn to speak arrived, de Lattre did not mince his words. 'The solution presented in "Unity" had suggested that command would be exercised by a series of committees and conferences during which the Supreme Commander [i.e. Montgomery] or his nominees interfered in a totally unacceptable manner in the province which properly belonged to the Land Force Commander. The Principal Administrative Officer [Monty's Chief of Staff] appeared to be a complete autocrat and the Land Force Commander [i.e. de Lattre] was reduced to the level of a man who attends committee meetings and puts forward suggestions for the consideration of the Supreme Commander and his staff officers. He was certainly not a Commander in the French sense of the word.'[1]

The strain, as Monty's own diarist acknowledged, was reaching breaking point. Monty had, during the week of the exercise, 'excluded de Lattre from the series of dinner parties at which he entertained most of the senior officers attending the exercise. As a reprisal General de Lattre did not attend the Field-Marshal's evening reception and instructed his staff, General Navereau, General Cogny and Colonel Beaufre, to follow his example. This incident caused a good deal of comment among the officers of all nationalities attending the exercise and unfortunately had the effect of causing some French officers, who had no particular love for de Lattre, to take his side in the affair.'[2]

As the London *People* had headlined a recent article, 'A Private Feud Has Become a Public Menace'—for since December, having heard that de Lattre was attempting to 'suborn' his personal French ADC Lt-Colonel Costa de Beauregard, Monty had 'resolved never to entertain de Lattre in his house except in the strict course of duty'.[3] As his house was the beautiful Château de Courances, provided, maintained and, above all, provisioned by the French Government, Monty's rejection of his *bon viveur* Land Force C-in-C was galling to the latter. Even the very meetings of the Commanders-in-Chief Committee, held until then in the morning so that the Commanders-in-Chief could subsequently lunch together at Courances, were switched to the afternoon for the sole purpose of avoiding lunch—'so that it was only necessary for de Lattre to be entertained to tea', as Monty's diarist candidly confessed.

Such gastronomic frigidity had not helped, however. 'It had been hoped rather optimistically that General de Lattre would be removed

[1] Diary of Field-Marshal The Viscount Montgomery of Alamein, Part XIX (28.12.49–14.5.50), Montgomery Papers.
[2] Ibid.
[3] Ibid.

from his appointment as C-in-C Land Forces, Western Europe on 2 February 1950, when he reached the age of 61, the retiring age for full generals in the French Army. The question of de Lattre's removal had however become an international problem,' Monty's diarist acknowledged. 'If de Lattre had vacated the appointment while the Field-Marshal retained his, it would have been regarded both in France and in England (and to some extent in America) as a victory for Field-Marshal Montgomery and Merrie England. The French however had found a way out of the difficulty by striking de Lattre off the books of the French Army but keeping him on the active list for employment outside the French Army with Western Union. For this type of employment there was no retiring age.'[1]

The thought that he might thus be saddled with de Lattre for the rest of his career in Europe was a nightmare. Faced by this prospect, Monty responded not only by renouncing all correspondence with de Lattre, as recommended by the British Chiefs of Staff, but lowering the temperature of their unavoidable meetings to one of permafrost. 'They avoided shaking hands with each other on any pretext,' Monty's diarist chronicled,[2] and with de Lattre's bitter protest at Exercise 'Unity' relations sank to their lowest ebb—a public menace the more unfortunate since Monty agreed with many of de Lattre's specific remarks relating to Exercise 'Unity', in particular the lack of Western Union troops. As de Lattre put it, 'We were devoting a lot of time and effort to make a frame and it was high time we set about painting a picture to put in it.'[3]

Monty, in closing Exercise 'Unity', had asked all officers below the rank of Maj-General to leave the room after the first part of his address; he had then spoken his true mind on the situation in Western Europe. In a letter to de Guingand the previous month Monty had confessed 'my own business is a complete façade',[4] with the nations of Europe 'quite unable to co-operate effectively against a centrally directed (Russian) threat'.[5] To King George VI he had privately admitted the same, relating that he had told the American Ambassador in London that 'the Western Union Defence set-up is a complete façade and that as things stand at present the West is indefensible.'[6] Now, on 5 May 1950, almost ten years since Hitler's invasion of France and the Benelux countries, Monty felt he must

[1] Ibid.
[2] Ibid.
[3] Ibid.
[4] Letter of 6.4.50, de Guingand Papers, loc. cit.
[5] Letter of 10.2.50. Ibid.
[6] Letter to Sir Alan Lascelles of 11.4.50 (RA GVI/283), Royal Archives, Windsor.

take the senior officers responsible for the so-called defence of Europe into his confidence:

'I am going to discuss this subject with complete frankness,' he began.

> This means facing facts. Some of you may think I am treading on dangerous ground.
>
> Surely we, among ourselves, can do this. And for this reason I have limited the audience at this talk to those of major-general or equivalent rank. I have excluded the junior officers.
>
> It is vital for Western security that we should face the facts dispassionately.
>
> The true facts are not good. The Exercise we have just completed has brought them out very clearly.
>
> Briefly, the facts are that there is today no effective fighting force in Western Europe that could offer any effective resistance to Russian aggression.
>
> Nor is any effective fighting force in sight in any foreseeable future.
>
> If war should break out there would be scenes of unparalleled and unholy confusion in the military and civil spheres in the territories of the West.[1]

First, Monty declared, there were political facts to be faced. Did the Western nations accept the Iron Curtain dividing Europe? And if they did, did they accept that, as a result, 'Western Europe might have to remain on a more or less permanent war footing: since the threat [from the East] is constant'? If West Germany was included—as economically it must be—in Western Europe, did the Western nations accept that German 'help in some form or another' would be necessary in Western defence?[2]

These were political questions—'I consider that the time has come when we must demand clear answers to these questions from our political chiefs. The questions deal with matters that are basic and fundamental to all our work.'[3] The military balance in Europe raised equally fundamental questions, however. Possibly 175 line divisions were maintained by the Russians, a figure which could be brought up to 320 divisions in three months following mobilization. 5000 Soviet tanks and 6000 tactical Soviet craft could support the eighty-eight Russian divisions available for an attack on the west in Europe,

[1] 'Address by Field-Marshal Montgomery to the Senior Officers of the Brussels Treaty Powers,' Fontainebleau, 5.5.50, annex 513, Diary, Part XIX, loc. cit.

[2] Ibid.

[3] Ibid.

backed by strategic bombers and at sea some 270 submarines. Against this there were ten Allied divisions, all far below war establishment. Only 370 Allied aircraft were on tap. Moreover, of the twenty-two airfields required for the planned deployment of these aircraft, only nine were operational. There was no logistical organization to back the Allies, nor any integrated air defence organization in the home territories. Civil defence organizations did not exist:

> We have not yet, after 18 months of arguing, agreed what will be the system of command in Western Europe in the event of war!! And we have not yet got even the necessary signal communications for *any* system of command.
>
> There is the picture. We must not let it be known to the troops. But we senior officers must understand it. . . .
>
> Millions of trusting people think that because we have a Western Union Defence Organisation, and a plan that has been approved by Defence Ministers and ordered to be put into operation, that all is well.
>
> These people think we are building in Europe a bulwark against war.
>
> Far from erecting a bulwark, our extreme weakness will one day offer a terrible temptation to Russia to resort to war.[1]

In Monty's view the Allies needed at least eighteen divisions available on D-Day, sixteen further divisions available within three days [i.e. the time it would take the Russians to force the Rhine] and 1500 tactical or air defence aircraft ready on Day One. To provide them, the Allies required an urgent sense of purpose and a willingness to co-operate. Moreover, within the Western Union Defence organisation was wanted '*some one person* who is completely international, and who can give unbiased and international advice to the Ministers of Defence—who are all intensely National'—a Director-General of the Allied committees whose task would be to 'initiate, co-ordinate, to stimulate, to make recommendations to Ministers, to follow up agreed decisions of principle and ensure that they are translated into practical measures with the least possible delay'—a man who would 'put some reality and life into the general defensive structure of Western Europe'. After all, Monty argued, 'The common cause is a matter of life and death; it is a matter involving the survival of nations and of western civilisation.'[2]

This was a critical address, in both senses of the word. It was passed to Mr Attlee, the Prime Minister, and all Ministers of Defence of

[1] Ibid.
[2] Ibid.

the Western Union, as well as to Washington. In many ways it was the blueprint of what, the following year, would become known as NATO: a seminal, visionary speech 'which he had prepared with some care', his diarist noted.

What lingered in the minds of those who attended Exercise 'Unity' but were excluded from Monty's secret address, however, was the disastrous personal relationship between Monty and de Lattre. Quite who tackled Monty over this is unclear, for Monty was loth ever to ascribe to others his own changes of mind lest he appear capricious or inconsistent—cardinal sins in his mind. But someone must have spoken to Monty, for in the days after Exercise 'Unity', aware that it was now de Lattre's turn to mount his own exercise—an exercise which might well turn out a counter-blast to 'Unity'—Monty evidently decided that discretion was the better part of valour: 'something must be done to relieve the situation. Feeling that it was more easy for him than for de Lattre to extend the olive branch without loss of face, Monty wrote to him suggesting that they should talk over matters in a calm and sensible atmosphere.' De Lattre, not having enjoyed a meal at the Château de Courances for almost six months, was invited to dinner on 10 May 'to have a quiet talk about things'.

> The Field-Marshal's French ADC, Commandant Costa de Beauregard, who was to deliver the letter, was at the same time to deliver a verbal message from the Field-Marshal to General de Lattre. This message of the Field Marshal's referred to his closing address at Exercise 'Unity' which had brought out so clearly the enormous amount of work that had to be done if an effective joint defence of Western Europe was to be built up. This work could never be done if the Field-Marshal and General de Lattre remained on their present unfriendly terms. He invited General de Lattre to forget the differences of the past and make a fresh start.[1]

De Lattre's response to Monty's verbal message was explosive—with Monty's French ADC having to bear the brunt of de Lattre's invective, as Monty noted in a memorandum afterwards:

> De Lattre listened in silence while the message was being got over. He asked for certain parts to be repeated.
>
> He then let drive at my A.D.C. and gave him a first-class 'rocket'. He said he [Costa de Beauregard] had sold himself to the British and thereby disgraced his ancient French name: did he not understand that his allegiance was to France and the French Army?

[1] Diary, Part XIX, loc. cit.

> He continued in this style for about 20 minutes. He finally said that he would never employ my A.D.C. on his staff again. (Before coming to me he had been on de Lattre's staff.)[1]

Costa de Beauregard was then dismissed and told to return in three days' time for another interview, at which he received 'another "rocket" on the error of his ways'[2]—but also an envelope containing de Lattre's acceptance of Monty's invitation to dinner on 10 May.

Monty, returning from London to Fontainebleau on 9 May, was uncertain how, at the dinner, de Lattre would respond to his olive branch. In London Monty had tried to explain to the new Defence Minister, Mr Shinwell, the truth behind de Lattre's behaviour—that de Lattre was 'fundamentally, violent anti-British. There burns inside him a deep hatred and suspicion of the British'.

> In ordinary times this hatred is concealed under a veneer of friendliness and charm, and it is very well concealed. But when he gets angry and excited, it all comes out.[3]

In fact a recent book by a Frenchman had suggested that de Lattre was so anti-British that he had offered to serve in a Vichy-German invasion of Britain after Dunkirk.[4]

On the evening of 10 May 1950, de Lattre arrived at the Château de Courances. The meal was taken in icy silence. Then, after dinner, Monty got down to business.

> I referred to my final address to the senior officers at Fontainebleau on 5 May and said it showed very clearly how much there was to be done in order to build up effective joint defence in Western Europe.
>
> Great issues were involved and the safety of the West was at stake.
>
> He and I must sink our differences, forget the past, and work together as friends and comrades in the common task.
>
> Let us shake hands and get on with the job.

Monty's French A.D.C. translated.

'De Lattre received all this rather coldly,' Monty recorded.

> He then launched into a lengthy statement of my misdeeds during the past 18 months and said the fault was all mine; he had reviewed his own conduct and was satisfied he had always acted

[1] 'The friendly approach to General de Lattre', 5–10.5.50, annex 514, Diary, Part XIX, loc. cit.

[2] Ibid.

[3] Ibid.

[4] J. Tracou, *Le Maréchal aux Lilas*, Paris 1949.

correctly. He had a clear conscience and could not be reproached on any matter.[1]

Monty refrained from interjecting or 'entering into an argument on who was to blame, and listened to de Lattre's accusations in silence', Monty's diarist chronicled. 'At the end he said that if the fault was his, he was sorry and again invited General de Lattre to shake hands. General de Lattre melted and such was his emotion that the Field-Marshal was obliged to comfort him.'[2]

Weeping like a child, de Lattre broke down and Monty, who had sworn never to shake hands again with such an 'evil' man, could not hold back. Enfolding de Lattre with his arm, he offered his *mouchoir* and told him their squabble was over; henceforth they would be friends, and nothing and no one would stop them working together to raise the phoenix of Western defence from the ashes of post-war discord and economic distress.

[1] 'The friendly approach to de Lattre', loc. cit.
[2] Diary, Part XIX, loc. cit.

CHAPTER SIX

German Help

IN HIS MEMOIRS Monty devoted only five pages to the story of Western Union—and the name of de Lattre was not even mentioned. Possibly Monty wished thereby to expunge the memory of a man who had caused him so much trouble and bitterness. But the other reason was that the 'Great Reconciliation', as his diarist termed it, did not of itself improve the parlous state of Western Union. The French Minister of Defence, M. Pléven, attempted to pin the blame for Western Union's shortcomings on the internecine quarrels of the Commanders-in-Chief Committee; but with de Lattre 'firmly hitched to the Field-Marshal's chariot', the result was the same.[1] Without a *political* lead, Western Union's military defence remained a '*tromperie*', or even '*escroquerie*' as de Lattre termed it at a meeting on 20 June 1950.[2]

Throughout the remaining months of 1950 Monty badgered, threatened, cajoled, pleaded with the various Chiefs of Staff, Defence Ministers, Foreign Ministers and political leaders of Western Union to make a reality of it. Largely at Monty's insistence, Britain extended National Service to two years as an example to France and the Benelux countries, Attlee reluctantly giving Monty his promise even before the Cabinet had met to discuss the issue.[3] But without American involvement on the continent of Europe it became increasingly clear that Western defence was, as Monty put it, 'in the doldrums'. The North Atlantic Treaty Organization had set up a Committee of Deputies on 17 May 1950 to help prosper the cause of inter-Allied defence, but its powers were limited and its effect stultifyingly feeble. More and more Monty was driven into the rôle of counsel for the defence or prophet of doom, unless the Western nations could be made to act in unison and with realistic de-

[1] 'Exercise Solution', 20.7.50, Diary of Field-Marshal The Viscount Montgomery of Alamein, Part XX (5.5.50–13.6.50), Montgomery Papers.

[2] 'The Meeting with WUCOS', 20.6.50, Diary, Part XX, loc. cit.

[3] 'Meeting with the Prime Minister' at 10 Downing Street, 9.8.50. 'The Field-Marshal then asked whether he might tell Ministers and others on the Continent that it was certain that the United Kingdom would introduce two years conscription, and the Prime Minister, with some hesitation, agreed': Diary, Part XX, loc. cit.

termination. His life became one of constant travel between the citadels of Europe, his files bulged with the letters and memoranda he wrote in his attempt to get action. The quarrel with de Lattre faded into the past—so much so that the Air and Naval C-in-Cs became quite upset by their loss of intermediary rôle. 'I find that my real task is to try and hold the balance between two personalities (Montgomery and de Lattre), who, as you well know, could hardly be further apart,' Robb had written to Eisenhower in February 1949;[1] without that task he was at sea in Western Union—indeed when Monty asked his three C-in-Cs to mount their own exercises to follow 'Unity', he considered Robb, like Jaujard, incapable of such a project.[2] De Lattre only succeeded in putting on his Land Forces exercise, 'Triade', at the eleventh hour, preparing each day's presentation the night before. But with 'Triade' proving not to be a counter-blast to 'Unity' at all, but a detailed 'proof' of the Allied inability even to hold the Rhine in war given its current forces, Robb soon felt ostracized by the new Monty–de Lattre accord. Monty's diarist certainly felt no sympathy:

> When de Lattre was at daggers drawn with the Field-Marshal he had no hesitation in seeking to make allies of his two slightly colourless colleagues [Robb and Jaujard]. But since he has basked in the radiance of the Field-Marshal's approval, or at all events, his tolerance, he [de Lattre] has not attempted to conceal the fact that he has no further use for them.
>
> While the results of this division within the Commanders-in-Chief Committee may be unfortunate, Robb and Jaujard have only themselves to blame. Ever since the setting up of the Commanders-in-Chief Committee they have been mere passengers. They have contributed nothing and initiated nothing. During the long months when the Field Marshal and de Lattre were in conflict they sat firmly on the fence and refused to make any effort to break the deadlock. They were no help in the past and there are no grounds for supposing that they will be any help in the future.[3]

Monty's own view was that the Commanders-in-Chief Committee meetings were 'a waste of time'. His exercises had proved beyond doubt the need for Western Union Ministers to reconsider the whole concept of Allied defence in Europe. Without the sort of Director-General he proposed, Monty was himself having to use 'his international position as his authority to speak with brutal frankness to the head politicians and soldiers in all the Continental countries. No

[1] Letter of 9.2.49, 'Robb' file, Eisenhower Papers, loc. cit.
[2] Diary, Part XX, loc. cit.
[3] Diary, Part XX, loc. cit.

country likes washing its dirty linen in public,' Monty's diarist noted, 'and the Field Marshal had therefore taken it upon himself to do it for them.'[1] On 18 May 1950 Monty was asked by the British Chiefs of Staff to give his views on the reorganization of the Brussels and North Atlantic Treaty machinery for defence. He replied that, in addition to a Director-General of sufficient political clout to elicit and enforce decisions among the Allies, what was needed was, one, a European Chiefs of Staff Committee and, two, a Supreme Commander, Western-Europe, whose 'territory' would stretch 'from the North Sea to Italy'.[2]

With nothing done to implement Monty's proposals in 1950, Monty concentrated at Western Union on inter-Allied training between the Brussels-Pact nations—and turned his eyes towards America once more. As the Western European nations had been bucked into unexpected action by the Berlin crisis of 1948, so in 1950 the war in Korea now frightened the Americans into abandoning their faith in the Committee of Deputies of NATO. Monty himself, as his diarist noted, had quickly despaired of any help from that quarter:

> The setting up of this Committee attracted a great deal of publicity and it was hoped that it might do something to produce the action which had been so notably lacking since the signing of the North Atlantic Treaty.
>
> It was hoped first of all that the nations would be prepared to delegate some executive authority to this Committee and that members of the Committee would be men of experience and standing. . . . It was considered particularly important that the Chairman of this Committee should be a man of outstanding and world-wide repute. In the event, however, the nations appointed nothing but second-raters as their Deputies.[3]

Britain's man was 'a certain Sir Frederick Hoyer-Millar, an unknown and undistinguished diplomat. France appointed a M. Alphand, of whom nobody had ever heard, while the American representative, who was also Chairman of the Committee, was a Mr C. Spoffard.'[4]

Despite its complete ineffectiveness as a directing Committee, Monty decided to use the American member Spoffard as a link-man with Washington. As the Korean crisis deepened, so the Americans began to favour an American Supreme Commander in Europe.

[1] Ibid.
[2] Ibid. Full record in annex 518, Diary, Part XX, loc. cit.
[3] Diary, Part XX, loc. cit.
[4] Ibid.

Given the current state of Western Union's forces, however, the Americans were adamant that, if they were to reinforce Europe, the Europeans must accept German involvement in the set-up, to the tune of eight to ten divisions.

Monty, who had supplied Spoffard with the necessary 'ammunition' to damn current Western Union defence and, as a result, to predicate assistance upon certain European concessions, was horrified by this American blunder. On his trip in November 1949 Monty had himself pleaded with Eisenhower, Bradley, Collins and various political leaders to begin facing up to the need for German manpower to be employed in the defence of Western Europe—indeed a leak in the Press had produced headlines referring to Monty's 'call for German re-armament'. Monty's intention, however, had been to start discussion of the issue well in advance of any action. For American negotiators suddenly to announce, a year after Monty's warning, that without reference to their Allies or indeed to possible Russian response they favoured, nay demanded, the immediate creation of some eight to ten German divisions was bound both to alarm the French and worry the Russians—even, unintentionally, leading to a third world war if Stalin felt the revival of a West German army of such magnitude threatened the status quo in Europe.

The French refused to agree to the American proposal, countering with their own conception of German units, no larger than battalion-size, serving within 'Allied' formations—the 'Pléven' plan. Monty, as a professional soldier with experience of small units from foreign nations serving in his armies, knew the French suggestion was impractical.[1] At the same time he sympathized with the French fear of German military renascence. The answer, surely, was to tackle the issue, as he had recommended the year before, in stages. Encouraging the Germans to produce eight to ten divisions would necessitate a 'German War Ministry and the re-creation of the German General Staff', which in turn would 'in the end lead inevitably to World War III', Monty prophesied to the American Chairman of the Council of

[1] 'The plan was of course completely unworkable from any military point of view, operational or administrative, and furthermore had no possible chance of receiving German acceptance,' Monty's diarist noted. 'The Germans were beginning to stretch their wings, and it did not seem likely they would be prepared to accept an arrangement which would place them in an obvious position of inferiority,' even if the French accepted brigade-size formations. 'They were being asked in fact to raise mercenary troops and thereafter to place them unreservedly at the disposal of the Allies. Even if the German politicians would accept such a suggestion it would be difficult to convince the German people that they were not being used merely as cannon-fodder': Diary, Part XXI (28.7.50–24.1.51), Montgomery Papers.

NATO Deputies and to the British Prime Minister on 17 October 1950.[1] 'Quite apart from the fact that the creation of such an army might well lead the Russians to embark on a preventative war before its organisation was complete,' Monty pointed out to Mr Spoffard again a month later, 'the creation of such a [German] army would rekindle the latent German desire to regain the lost territories beyond the Oder. However much we might think that we were creating a German Army to defend the Rhine, or perhaps the Elbe, we should in fact be creating a German Army whose private aim would be to attack the Oder.'[2] Instead, Monty urged, the Western Allies should build up their *own* forces in Europe to ensure they outnumbered any German formations. The Germans should be allowed to build up a *gendarmerie* of, say, 100,000 men immediately; only when the Western Allies were fully organized in a defensive NATO shield against the Russians should German *divisions* be raised.

Monty's warnings were not heeded, and a typical political compromise was reached whereby the Americans would withdraw their insistence on the raising of German divisions if the French would agree to have German brigades. Monty shook his head in disbelief:

> Thus all that had been achieved after months of talk, negotiations and ill-feeling, was an indefinite agreement, in principle, to the raising at an unspecified date of an unspecified number of German formations larger than battalions but smaller than divisions. As far as we know, no one had the slightest idea of how these units or formations were to be raised, trained, equipped, commanded or employed. There was also the little formality of obtaining German approval to the project,

Monty's diarist added sarcastically.[3] As a preliminary to political negotiations, the three Allied High Commissioners were to meet two German generals nominated by the West German government. 'The Allied representatives were to base their approach on certain papers provided by NATO. These papers were vague and indefinite and provided no basis for negotiation and no basis for answering the numerous questions which the German generals would undoubtedly ask. The cart was firmly before the horse. Just as the Field-Marshal always feared we were beginning to talk before we had started to think.'[4] In October 1949, as the Western Allies set up a West German Federal State, Monty had written to de Guingand: 'Things

[1] 'German Re-armament', Diary, Part XXI, loc. cit.

[2] 'Interview with Mr Spoffard', 14.11.50, Diary, Part XXI, loc. cit.

[3] Diary, Part XXI, loc. cit.

[4] Ibid.

are moving exactly as I forecast, but more rapidly than I thought: and too rapidly for safety.'[1] He had discussed the matter with all the American military and political leaders, including Eisenhower, in November 1949, but as he wrote to the French Minister of Defence on 5 October 1950 'no one would listen; and now the need for a decision has become urgent'.[2] To the British High Commissioner's Chief of Staff Monty declared on 4 January 1951 'it was vital that the Western Powers should approach Germany with a clear-cut plan which had a reasonable chance of being accepted by the Germans. The present plan was neither clear-cut nor did it stand any chance of being accepted'[3]—for Monty had had a long talk with Dr Adenauer, the West German Chancellor, that morning. Adenauer had told Monty he was suspicious of French intentions—'there was a strong feeling in France . . . that it should be the aim of France, in conjunction with Russia, to keep Germany down. . . . As long as this attitude persisted it was difficult for Germans to understand that they must be prepared to fight alongside the Western Allies.' Furthermore, Adenauer had no idea 'what was required' of Germany, militarily, nor the 'present plans for the defence of the West. It was difficult for Germany to consider what contribution she should make until she had been told what was required, and what conditions on German rearmament were to be imposed.'[4]

The defence of the West was, in truth, once more in the melting pot. Were the Americans to reinforce and take over the defence of Western Europe? If so, what was to be the European contribution to that defence? And was Germany to be re-armed as the Americans insisted, or could they be wooed into providing cannon-fodder, as the French desired—furnishing the forward defence troops on the Elbe that would be overrun as the Russians raced for the Rhine?

In an uncompromising foreword to his 'Planning Progress Report' on 18 December 1950 Monty outlined the 'long story of indecision, procrastination and frustration' that had marked Western Union's brief defence of the West—'two years of hesitation, indecision, disagreement, lack of genuine and effective co-operation, lack of leadership and a complete failure to face up to practical realities'. In conclusion he listed five fundamental requirements 'which must be met if a sound defensive system was to be built up':

[1] Letter of 14.10.49 (misdated December), de Guingand Papers, loc. cit.

[2] Annex 549, Diary, Part XXI, loc. cit.

[3] Diary, Part XXI, loc. cit. (full record in annex 558).

[4] 'Résumé of a discussion between Field-Marshal Montgomery and Doctor Adenauer, Chancellor of Western Germany' at Bonn on 4.1.50, in annex 557, Diary, Part XXI, loc. cit.

1. Europe could not be defended without German help in some form or another.
2. Europe could not be defended without a strong and effective French contribution and this was impossible without two years conscription.
3. There would never be defensive strength in Europe until each nation organised its manpower structure on a sound basis which would allow effective reserve forces to be mobilised quickly.
4. Equally, the organisation controlling joint European defence must have a focal point of decision accepted and acknowledged by all the nations.
5. Effective strength was impossible without mutual confidence between nations and a willingness to make sacrifices for the common good.[1]

All five requirements were not being met; all required not so much military solution as *political.* Tired of his two-year sojourn in the wilderness, the Jeremiah of Western Union, Monty told de Lattre's deputy—standing in for de Lattre who had been temporarily posted, early in December 1950, to Indo-China as French Governor General and Commander-in-Chief—that, when the Americans took over the running of Western Europe defence, he (Monty) hoped to be made Commander-in-Chief of Europe's armies: a soldier's task again, leaving the politics of Western defence to the American Supreme Commander and others. But if Monty imagined that de Lattre's absence would make this possible, he was sadly mistaken. General Navereau politely but firmly pointed out on 5 January 1951 that Britain's contribution to Western European land defence was nominal, being limited to its undermanned divisions of the British Army of the Rhine and still no written guarantee of further land forces being committed to continental defence. The C-in-C Land Forces would, therefore, have to be a Frenchman.[2]

Thus, as Western Union approached its end early in 1951, Monty's own future hung in the balance. He was now sixty-four. Would an incoming American Supreme Commander want a man of his age? If not, was this the termination of Monty's military career?

Initially the Americans had proposed a COSSAC-type arrangement whereby a Chief of Staff to the Supreme Commander (Designate) would be sent to Europe to 'keep the seat warm' for whoever was eventually appointed. Monty and the British Chiefs of Staff had strenuously objected. What was wanted was a leader, and until a

[1] Annex 555, Diary, Part XXI, loc. cit.
[2] 'General Navereau's visit to Dover House', 5.1.51, Diary, Part XXI, loc. cit.

leader was appointed no Chief of Staff could be expected to carry the weight necessary to make decisions of any magnitude. Western European defence would drift still further into the doldrums.

According to Eisenhower's diary, President Truman had asked him to become Supreme Commander of NATO's forces in Europe over the weekend of 28 October 1950.[1] Eisenhower was the unanimous choice of the American and European Chiefs of Staff, Truman indicated, but the decision would have to be ratified by the Foreign Ministers of the component nations. Moreover the US administration wished to use Eisenhower's possible appointment as a lever, to get the European nations first to agree on a package of military requirements—the most important of which was the matter of West Germany's military inclusion. Though Eisenhower's probable appointment quickly leaked into the Press, there was thus for months no official confirmation. De Guingand, writing from southern Africa, was hopeful that he might be brought back—particularly if Bedell Smith was also transferred to Europe from his current post as head of the CIA. But with French intransigence over German rearmament, Eisenhower could promise nothing. As he wrote to De Guingand on 15 November 1950:

> No command has been offered me and so there is nothing definite to say in response to your nice, and most welcome, letter. I think that there is to be no command set-up in Europe until the needful political agreements have been reached. I am not even aware of the progress of these negotiations and so you can understand how truly impossible it is for me to guess what is to happen to me.[2]

The day before, Eisenhower had sent birthday wishes to Monty—'I hope this reaches you on Friday so that it will be on time to bring my heartiest congratulations. . . . May this occasion be a splendid one and the harbinger of good things in all the years ahead.'[3] To which Monty, touched, replied:

> My dear Ike,
>
> Thank you very much for your birthday greetings. It was most kind of you to have remembered the day.
>
> I hope very much we shall see you over this way in the not too distant future. We need you badly: to get the nations to co-operate genuinely, and to give firm decisions on which everyone will act.
>
> At present there is no genuine co-operation, and no decision.[4]

[1] *The Eisenhower Diaries*, ed. R. Ferrell, New York 1981.

[2] De Guingand Papers, loc. cit.

[3] Montgomery file, Eisenhower Papers, loc. cit.

[4] Ibid.

But did Eisenhower need Monty? In his diary memorandum, written on 28 October 1950, Eisenhower had assumed he would remain in the new post for perhaps six years—but considered 'it is bad practice to allow such developments to fall into the hands of older men. Particularly, I would not want to see the habit started of assigning successive commanders who had almost reached the end of their usefulness as soldiers.'[1]

Meanwhile the situation in Korea became critical. Having boasted on 25 November that he was launching an offensive that would end the war by Christmas, MacArthur was rocked back by a Red China counter-attack which split his UN–American army and within days caused MacArthur to request permission either to escalate the battle into a nuclear war, or evacuate the Korean mainland. The American Chiefs of Staff, informed by MacArthur that some twenty-six Red Chinese divisions were now in combat, approved evacuation in order to be able to defend Japan.

The moral for Europe was clear. The nuclear deterrent could *not* be counted upon to deter, since the President of the US would be unlikely to sanction its use unless the USA was itself directly threatened. Only if sufficient ground forces were marshalled could the Western Allies hope to contain a Russian offensive. Thus, as the American government declared a 'state of national emergency' (on 15 December 1950) and quadrupled its defence budget, the US Joint Chiefs of Staff prepared a new strategic war plan in which much greater stress was given to holding Western Europe with NATO forces, along the Rhine–Alps line Monty had laid down at Western Union. On 18 December the Atlantic Pact Foreign and Defence Ministers, meeting in Brussels, agreed that an American Supreme Commander should be appointed for the forces of the West—including West Germany—and formally proposed General Eisenhower for the post. The following day it was officially announced that General Dwight D. Eisenhower was to be the new NATO Supreme Commander.[2] So great was the haste that Monty, Chairman of NATO's central defence organization, the Western Union Commanders-in-Chief Committee, was not even informed in advance: 'The Field-Marshal read the announcement on the tape at the Atheneum and it is interesting to record that this was the Field-Marshal's first and only intimation that General Eisenhower had been appointed,' Monty's diarist chronicled with amazement.[3]

[1] *The Eisenhower Diaries*, op. cit.
[2] 'The Appointment of General Eisenhower', Diary, Part XXI, loc. cit.
[3] Ibid.

Monty punctiliously sent Eisenhower an immediate cable, none the less.

> Delighted to see that you have been appointed Supreme Commander in Europe. If you should wish to make use of my services in any way I will of course be delighted to serve under you in any capacity you like.[1]

Monty then prepared to leave for an evening at the circus, but a telephone call came in from General Gruenther, who was to be Eisenhower's new Chief of Staff. He requested Monty's permission 'to visit Fontainebleau and see the set-up there for himself'. He also said that he had been meeting the Belgian and Dutch Foreign Ministers 'who had spoken most warmly of the Field-Marshal' and 'hoped that any future reorganisation would not mean the disappearance of the Field-Marshal from the scene'.[2] As Monty had always—and particularly in recent months—been extremely outspoken in his discussions with these Ministers, Monty was unsure whether Gruenther was telling the truth.

The next day Gruenther visited Western Union headquarters—according to Monty's diarist, clearly 'ignorant of the fact that a headquarters really did exist in Fontainebleau' but subsequently 'promising to recommend' on his return to America that 'whatever the organisation was to be in Western Europe, the Fontainebleau set-up should not be destroyed'.[3] Once again, the very negative in the assertion almost suggested the opposite.

Throughout Western Union's history, Monty had insisted on US observers being in permanent attendance as transatlantic Liaison Officers. But the haste in which, during the Korean crisis, Eisenhower's appointment was announced allowed no time for Eisenhower or his staff to communicate with these observers. Monty himself was a seasoned 'take-over' general, having brought a new broom to Eighth Army in the desert, to 21st Army Group and the planning for the invasion of Normandy, as well as to the War Office as CIGS. Now, however, it was Eisenhower's turn—and the Christmas of 1950 Monty spent at his mill at Isington, wondering what the future might hold: whether Eisenhower's impending broom would sweep him in, or out.

[1] Signal of 19.12.1950, Diary, Part XXI, loc. cit.
[2] Diary, Part XXI, loc. cit.
[3] Ibid.

PART ELEVEN

NATO

CHAPTER ONE

Eisenhower Takes Over

EISENHOWER'S ORDERS WERE to take command of NATO defences from Norway to Italy, on behalf of twelve Allied nations.[1] 'You may have seen the news of my designation to command the new European organization,' he signalled to Monty on 22 December 1950. 'I hope to proceed to Europe on a trip around the first of the year but as you know it takes a little time to set up a new Headquarters and organization for command. I assume that you will carry on in your present regional [i.e. Western Union] organization, as you must know how dependent I will be upon you during the initial stages.'[2]

Would Eisenhower want Monty in subsequent stages, however? Monty dutifully repeated that he was 'at your service and would serve under your command in any capacity you wished'.[3] Eisenhower informed Monty he would arrive in Paris from Washington on Sunday 7 January 1951. As Monty had an appointment in London the following day, he suggested that Eisenhower and his Chief of Staff General Gruenther 'lunch with me on Tuesday [9 January] at Château de Courance near Fontainebleau. We can then have a good talk and can go into Fontainebleau after lunch' to see the Western Union headquarters and 'meet the chief people'.[4]

This message was extraordinarily ill-considered. Eisenhower had no wish to 'cool his heels' in Paris for *two days* before being allowed to visit the only extant command headquarters of his new NATO set-up. 'I had hoped, of course, that one of my first visits in Europe would be to your Headquarters in Fontainebleau. Unfortunately, I must depart for Brussels Tuesday afternoon. I will be back in Paris about two weeks later at which time I will try and see you,' Eisenhower responded testily.[5]

[1] USA, Canada, Great Britain, Holland, France, Denmark, Belgium, Norway, Luxembourg, Iceland, Portugal and Italy.
[2] Quoted in Diary, Part XXI (28.7.50–24.1.51), Montgomery Papers.
[3] Ibid.
[4] Signal of 3.1.51, Eisenhower Papers, 1652 series, Eisenhower Library, Abilene, Kansas. Monty habitually spelled Courances without an s.
[5] Signal of 4.1.51, quoted in Diary, Part XXI, loc. cit.

Monty was shocked. Not only did he feel Eisenhower must be properly 'briefed' before touring the capitals and defence ministries of Europe, but his own future was 'on the line'. Instantly he cabled from Germany, where he was meeting Adenauer:

> My dear Ike. I have your message giving your movements. I consider it to be important I should see you as early as possible after your arrival in Europe. I will fly to Paris on Sunday morning 7 Jan and will be available to see you on Sunday afternoon. . . . I suggest I should see you in Paris as there will be no one at Fontainebleau on a Sunday.[1]

Monty duly met Eisenhower at the Hotel Astoria early on the afternoon of 7 January 1951. Slim, the CIGS, had already written the previous day to warn Monty which way the wind was blowing over the command set-up in Europe:

> My dear Monty,
>
> There has been an exchange of messages between the [US] Chiefs of Staff and Tedder about the set-up that Eisenhower proposes for Europe. What it boils down to, as far as we have been able to discover, is that Eisenhower's mind is pretty open but that he, not unnaturally, rather inclines to something very much on the lines of his old SHAEF, i.e. several Army Groups each with its own Tactical Air Force, all directly under SHAPE [Supreme Headquarters Allied Powers in Europe].[2]

Tedder had served as Eisenhower's Deputy at SHAEF. On behalf of the British Chiefs of Staff, therefore, he recommended 'that the Supreme Commander should have three Deputy Commanders for Land, Sea and Air'. Land and Sea Deputies would be French, in view of their preponderant commitment to the defence of Western Europe; the Air Deputy should be British. 'Our idea of the Deputies to Eisenhower is that they would relieve him of a certain amount of the dealing with national forces, keep a general supervision over training, equipment, etc. and form the Joint Advisory Planning Body for the Supreme Commander on the Strategic Level.'[3]

Where would Monty's place be in such a scheme of things, however? The British Chiefs of Staff idea was that Monty should become Land Force Commander in the central or Western Europe region. The 'flanks' of NATO could then be considered as Task Forces

[1] Signal of 4.1.51, quoted in Diary, Part XXI, loc. cit.

[2] Letter of 6.1.51, annex 565, Diary of Field-Marshal The Viscount Montgomery of Alamein, Part XXII (23.2.51–8.5.51), Montgomery Papers.

[3] Ibid.

'under, respectively, a Norwegian or Danish Commander-in-Chief and an Italian Commander-in-Chief. This seems to us the most efficient and economic organisation that could be set up.' From Air-Marshal Eliot, Slim gathered that Monty would 'waive all question of precedence and seniority and accept such an organisation'—a set-up which 'would have the advantage at any rate of putting you, the person most suited to conduct it, in charge of the battle'.[1]

Monty may well have longed, after the bitter wrangles with de Lattre, for battlefield command again. But he was sixty-four years of age. Moreover, as Slim foresaw, the French were 'determined to have their place in the Sun, and the Sun to them is, of course, Western Europe'. The French would doubtless insist on the Land Forces C-in-C being a Frenchman, and would not accept an alternative—unless it was the sort of overall C-in-C Air, Sea and Land Forces which was Monty's current role at Western Union. 'Frankly, what I am anxious to achieve is that you should command the battle,' Slim concluded. 'You will be seeing Eisenhower within the next few days and I suggest that you discuss these and any other alternatives which may occur to him or to you.'[2]

Monty's meeting with Eisenhower on 7 January was thus a critical one in terms of the future command structure and effectiveness of NATO.

Eisenhower did not see it that way. A few days before he had remarked in his diary that the hoo-ha over command systems smacked of 'the Monty situation in 1944', when Monty drove him to distraction. The real 'substance of the problem', as Eisenhower saw it, was 'national attitudes, industrial capacities, military programs and present strength'.[3]

The two men, therefore, appeared to be on collision course: Eisenhower favouring a large Supreme Headquarters in the SHAEF tradition, Monty preferring the idea of a small Foch-like Supreme Headquarters to decide upon the higher aspects of Western defence, delegating detailed defence to subordinate commanders.

Their meeting on 7 January, however, decided nothing. Monty began by giving a 'State of the Union' account of current defence in Western Europe on the lines of his Foreword to the recent Western Union Planning Report, a copy of which he had already sent to Eisenhower. At its heart was the urgent need for the Allied nations to reorganize their manpower-contributions to NATO—in fact, he

[1] Ibid.
[2] Ibid.
[3] Memorandum dated 3.1.51, in *The Eisenhower Diaries*, ed. R. Ferrell, New York, 1981.

felt confident, if every nation committed itself to two years' military service, the security of Europe was assured.

Manpower commitment was, however, a political matter. On the purely military side there was the question of command. Asked for his views, Monty considered that 'the Supreme Commander must remain on a lofty perch, otherwise he would be sunk'—words ominously reminiscent of the autumn of 1944. 'The Supreme Commander should have a small, high-powered headquarters,' Monty went on, 'including a big sailor and a big airman and that under him should be three Commanders-in-Chief; one for the North, one for the Centre and one for the South.'[1]

By excluding a 'big soldier' at Supreme Headquarters, Monty had foreseen Eisenhower's possible objection to the British Chiefs of Staff proposal. Eisenhower duly affirmed that 'nothing would induce him to have three Deputies'. On the other hand he was, as Monty had calculated, not in any way anxious to take field command—'neither did he wish to retain overall command of the land battle in the Western Theatre', Monty's diarist noted.[2]

What did Eisenhower want therefore? To Monty's astonishment, Eisenhower declared he 'particularly wished to ensure that he had naval forces under his command, both in the North and in the South. He considered that the Commander-in-Chief in Northern Europe should be an admiral (at sea) with a soldier and an airman fighting the tactical battle on land. Equally, General Eisenhower was emphatic that the Commander-in-Chief in Southern Europe should be an admiral.' To Monty's further consternation, 'General Eisenhower mentioned the figure of 25 aircraft carriers that might be in the Mediterranean at any one time, being used as mobile airstrips in accordance with the needs of the situation on land.'[3]

Monty was astonished. It was clear that Eisenhower had not the remotest practical idea how the battle of Europe would be fought in the event of war, and that, in a command set-up such as Eisenhower envisaged, the 'flanks' of Europe would fall as certainly as they had in World War II, from Norway to the Mediterranean, with seaborne admirals incapable of directing NATO's land battle. If the Allied flanks were thus to become hostages to fortune under Eisenhower's scheme, what of the crucial 'central' sector—the area covered by Monty's current Western Union forces?

Here, Eisenhower declared 'he did not know a single Frenchman fit to fight the Land/Air Battle'. Did he therefore feel that Monty should become C-in-C of the central region, as Slim wished? 'It

[1] Diary, Part XXII, loc. cit.
[2] Ibid.
[3] Ibid.

appeared to the Field-Marshal that General Eisenhower wanted the Field-Marshal as Commander-in-Chief in the Central Sector, if it could be worked politically. However, at no time during the meeting did General Eisenhower definitely say so and in fact he never discussed the nationality or the personality of any of the Commanders under discussion,' Monty told his MA and diarist. [1]

It was clear that there would be much haggling yet, both political and military, before the new Allied set-up was agreed. Moreover Eisenhower had a tour of the NATO capitals to make, as well as a presentation to Congress in Washington. It would therefore be at least three months before he could actually take command in Europe, whatever command structure was agreed.

'I very much enjoyed our talk today,' Monty wrote to Eisenhower that evening. 'I am confident we can solve all our problems,' he added [2]—for even if Monty did not agree with Eisenhower's strategic vision, Eisenhower looked at least set to provide the unifying spur so desperately needed if the various NATO countries were to pay more than lip service to the concept of European defence. 'I have had a very long talk with Ike and have put him completely in the picture as regards Western Europe,' Monty wrote on 10 January 1951 to de Guingand. 'We have of course also discussed the shape of the Command Set-up but I cannot say anything about that yet. He [Eisenhower] wants me in the party, of course; and I have agreed to do whatever he wants.' [3]

Monty had made clear to Eisenhower that there was no immediate threat of war in Europe—'There will be no war in Western Europe in 1951,' he declared in his letter to de Guingand.[4] 'In my view the dangerous time will be 1952. During 1951 the Soviet block will pursue their policy in the East, where they have very good objectives and are doing well. They will look at the West in the summer of 1952. And if by then we have not built up reasonable military strength, they may well throw their weight about. So it all depends on whether we can gain strength through uniting in Western Europe by the summer or autumn of 1952. If *we can*, then we will have peace for a bit. Only unselfish solidarity can do the job,' he felt. 'we want strength for two reasons: (1) to prevent war and (2) to make certain we win if there *is* war.' [5]

Eisenhower was meanwhile committed to hearing the views of all the NATO nations and reporting these back to Washington in order

[1] Ibid.
[2] Letter of 7.1.51, Eisenhower Papers, op. cit.
[3] De Guingand Papers, Imperial War Museum.
[4] Ibid.
[5] Ibid.

to convince the President and the Pentagon 'that the nations in Western Europe were really determined to defend their freedom'[1]—a vital necessity if he was to help counter the growing isolationist movement in America.[2] In the circumstances, he told Monty, he 'would be lucky if he would be able to take over effective command before 1st April'.[3] Eisenhower thus charged Monty with continuing to run the Western Union Commanders-in-Chief Committee in the meantime. This Monty did, making clear to his staff that, until something else replaced it, this was the organization that would have to take command in war or emergency, and must concentrate on getting its new emergency war headquarters in Margival ready, even if the staff had to live in tents.[4]

While Eisenhower made his round of the NATO capitals and returned to Washington, Monty mulled over the command question. Eisenhower had still not offered him command of NATO's Land Forces in the central sector, and the more Monty considered the matter, the more it seemed to him that the French would never agree to such an appointment.

On 24 January 1951 Monty left for Gstaad for his annual winter skiing holiday. This time there were no plans to meet Lucien, his 'adopted son'. 'As I explained to you at Gstaad, and to your Father in a letter,' Monty had written to Lucien the previous March, 'the relationship between us cannot be the same as when you were a little boy. Now you are growing up and you have much to learn. You must learn from your Swiss friends,' he added darkly. 'There must now be a break in your visits. You visited me between the ages of 12 and 15. Now we need a gap, during which you will become a young man. You can visit me again when you are 18. That will make things easier for everyone and it is the only sensible plan.

'You can of course continue to write to me. But I think 3 times a year is enough now—Easter, Midsummer, and my birthday. I am sure that if you think over what I say, you will come to realise it is sound and sensible.'[5] He no longer signed himself 'Yr very devoted "Papa"', but reverted to the formal 'Montgomery of Alamein'. The writing had in fact been on the wall ever since the preceding September when, after meeting Lucien in the Alps, Monty wrote: 'You

[1] Eisenhower to Monty, verbally, recorded in Diary, Part XXII, loc. cit.

[2] Eisenhower had offered the arch-isolationist Senator Taft that he would remain in Europe and not offer himself for the next Presidency if Taft would publicly agree to reinforce NATO by a further four divisions. Taft refused—and thus wrecked his own career. See Stephen Ambrose, *Eisenhower 1890–1952*, New York 1983.

[3] Eisenhower to Monty, verbally, recorded in Diary, Part XXII, loc. cit.

[4] Diary, Part XVI, Montgomery Papers.

[5] Letter of 6.3.50, Trueb correspondence, communicated to author by 2nd Viscount Montgomery of Alamein.

are definitely growing up and are no longer a little boy: 16 next year. I often wish you were 12 again!'[1]

Nevertheless Lucien was stunned by Monty's sudden decision to terminate their quasi-familial, loving relationship, and naturally felt rejected. Could it have been merely the lessening resemblance to Monty's doomed younger brother Desmond that lay behind Monty's decision? Several months before his letter to Lucien Monty had received a touching cable from Eisenhower and his wife Mamie, who had just read of the death of Monty's mother in Northern Ireland. 'Mamie and I extend to you our heartfelt sympathy in your bereavement,' Eisenhower had signalled, 'even though we realize that no words of ours can approach the consolation rooted in your memory of a great and good mother.'[2] Monty had thanked them—but the message made no difference to his determination, to the consternation of the Montgomery family and many people in Londonderry, not to attend his mother's funeral. Equally, early in 1951, Monty rejected de Guingand's request for a job in NATO: 'In my view you should stay where you are and build up financial strength for your family. . . . I will rope you in quick enough if there is going to be any dirty work.'[3]

What lay behind such deliberate alienations can only be a matter of speculation. De Guingand had been investing large sums of money in South Africa for Monty since 1947 and had done extremely well for him—a fact which made Monty's new rejection all the more galling. It was as if, for all his affability, Monty was drawing down blinds of black, condemning himself to an ever more spartan and austere private life. As Dr Trueb recalled in later years, even a winter walk with Monty became a sort of military inspection of the *trottoir*, as Monty examined logs outside people's houses to see that they were properly stacked, laundry hung on washing lines, or mounds of cleared snow from paths. Everything was 'carefully examined and appraised. Dog shit and empty cigarette packets were swept aside by well-aimed blows of his walking stick. Monty had always felt best in an environment that was well-ordered and run on a regular, well-established pattern: this *déformation professionelle* became the more pronounced the older he grew.'[4]

Trueb's observation was unerringly true. There was no sign of mellowing, no relaxation of Monty's domestic discipline—on the

[1] Letter of 6.10.49. Ibid.
[2] Signal of 11.7.49, Eisenhower Papers, loc. cit.
[3] Letter of 10.1.51, de Guingand Papers, loc. cit.
[4] L. Trueb, '*Erinnerungen an "Monty"*' (Memories of Monty'), in *Neue Zürcher Zeitung*, 10.11.76.

contrary Monty denied himself even the affection and loyal service of those who loved and admired him, lest they come too close. He only rarely saw his son David, who had finished his National Service in Germany in 1948 and then gone straight to Cambridge. It was as though, entering the last phase of his professional career, Monty was discarding all personal ballast in order to reach what he saw as the final heights of his life's work: the creation of a sound Allied defence organization. Thus, alone this time in Switzerland in the spring of 1951, Monty reflected on a command structure that would, he believed, be acceptable to the NATO nations and make military sense—if Eisenhower could be persuaded to adopt it.

CHAPTER TWO

Deputy Supreme Commander

MONTY WAS WELL aware of his own isolation. 'Apart from the Chiefs of Staff of the Nations of the Western Union, with whom I have very friendly relations and every help, I live in a welter of disloyalty and intrigue and it requires an immense amount of buoyancy not to let it get me down,' he had written when at Western Union to Sir Gerald Templer, his old VCIGS. 'In such situations one values real friends very highly.'[1]

But Monty had no real friends, and his perfectionist attitude with regard to military organization made him an uneasy man to deal with. His manner, vanity and outspokenness lent him to caricature, but few if any dared be disrespectful to his face. Even Templer himself, one of the most direct and caustic of British generals ('Dickie, you're so crooked that if you swallowed a nail you'd shit a corkscrew,' he once rapped Mountbatten), never openly addressed Monty with anything but subordinate respect, as Lady Templer later recalled:

> Gerald would *never* have questioned anything that Monty did. He'd stand up to him on matters where he thought Monty was wrong, but he would never have questioned anything Monty did. If Monty had said Gerald, go and take the Governorship of St Helena, he'd have gone. He didn't submit his judgement to Monty. He always treated Monty as a senior officer.[2]

In part such subordination was a mark of respect for Monty's unforgettable contribution to Allied Victory in World War II; but it rested too on a certain compassion for Monty's '*deformation professionelle*'—as for a man grievously scarred in his country's cause. This ingredient of compassion Lady Templer also noted: 'I thought that rather touching,' she commented on her husband's deference to Monty. 'I think it was partly niceness on Gerald's part.'[3]

However sorry such people might feel for the lonely widower, there was too a quality of admiration that was sincere. Just as Churchill,

[1] Letter of 21.3.49, Templer Papers, National Army Museum, London.
[2] Lady Templer, interview of 7.11.84.
[3] Ibid.

despite his many failings, still aroused wonder at his range of rhetoric and the scope of his imagination, so Monty's crystal-clear military gaze, his ability to reduce problems to essentials, also elicited a degree of veneration. For all his egoism, he had retained his genius for simplification—a talent relentlessly refined since his service on the general staff in World War I, and around which he had arranged his life with monastic care, lest the gift become blunted or blurred. The routine of his day, the asceticism of his life: everything he did seemed to be in the service of a higher mental purity, much as a mystic or guru. Each day was regulated to permit Monty time for reflection—'oases of thought', as he termed them—and vacations were part of this self-appointed order. Thus, just as he had pondered the future of the British Army on holiday in Switzerland in 1947 as CIGS, so in February 1951 he returned from the Alps with a new idea for NATO.

Monty's solution was simple. Instead of having admirals to command the northern and southern flanks of NATO, each region—north, centre and south—would have Land Force Commanders working alongside Air Force Commanders. In this way Eisenhower could retain direct overall command of NATO's land forces—with a deputy, or second-in-command, to assist him.

Gruenther did not like Monty's proposition when he heard it after dinner at the Château de Courances on 20 February. Eisenhower was still in the United States, but Gruenther doubted if he would agree to a Deputy Supreme Commander; moreover, he knew Eisenhower's preference for sea-based admirals taking command of NATO's flanks. Nevertheless Monty 'shot down most of General Gruenther's arguments',[1] and Gruenther finally undertook to put Monty's plan to Eisenhower on his return.

Monty's solution guaranteed himself a job. But if Monty became the Deputy Supreme Commander, would the French accept a hierarchy in which their most senior participant would be but the Land Force C-in-C of the central region—without command even of the Air Forces in that sector? Equally, Monty knew from the Chief of the British Air Staff that the British would not subordinate their tactical air forces in mainland Europe to a French soldier. The matter was bound therefore to raise controversy: 'In his [Monty's] opinion it would be extremely difficult to get General Juin to accept the position of Army Commander-in-Chief in Western Europe. He would do his utmost to obtain the position of overall Commander of the Central European Theatre.'[2]

[1] Diary, Part XXII, loc. cit.
[2] Ibid.

As the days went by Monty received evidence that Eisenhower was moving towards Monty's concept—which had been distributed in diagrammatic form to the British Chiefs of Staff and others.[1] On 26 February the Chief of the British Air Staff, Sir John Slessor, wrote that he had had a four-hour discussion with Eisenhower, whose 'ideas are moving in the right direction', but that Eisenhower still had a bee in his bonnet about carrier forces and sea support. 'He talked a lot about the value of the battle-ships' support in "Overlord", and he left me with the uneasy feeling that his "Overlord" experience weighs unduly strong with him. After all, in June 1944 we had killed the U-boat menace to all intents and purposes and had virtually complete air superiority. And I am quite sure that these carrier forces will not last long in these close waters of the Adriatic and Southern North Sea. . . . I am sure he is in for trouble if he places as much reliance upon them as he now seems to do.'[2]

The next day Monty himself saw Eisenhower in Paris—and Eisenhower caved in. Monty had got his way. On 28 February he confided to his MA, 'General Eisenhower wished the Field-Marshal to be his Deputy or Second-in-Command.'[3] As with Monty's appointment as Chairman of the Western Union Cs-in-C Committee, however, the appointment would have to be kept secret until the other command posts had been filled.

Monty was delighted—and wisely decided to vacate the scene while the remaining NATO appointments were decided. In Cairo on 4 March he unveiled a memorial window in All Saints Cathedral; but when he arrived back in France 'the question of command in Western Europe was still not resolved apart from the appointment of the Field-Marshal as Deputy' and for some weeks 'manoeuvring for position continued in the [Hotel] Astoria'.[4] Finally at 1 p.m. GMT on 20 March 1951, almost *four months* after his appointment as Supreme Commander, Eisenhower was able to release the major command appointments.

Eisenhower's insistence on a Naval C-in-C in the north had stuck—though the command was given to a British admiral (Sir Patrick Brind), who was to be based ashore. In the south, no decision had been made, save that an Italian would command on land. But in

[1] FM37, dated 22.2.51, annexe 566, Diary, Part XXII, loc. cit. Monty's command table included an 'Overall Air C-in-C under Eisenhower to control and coordinate the three regional air commanders. The Northern and Southern Fleets were to be independent, under Eisenhower's command to cooperate on the two flanks "when the situation so demands".'

[2] Annex 567, Diary, Part XXII, loc. cit.

[3] Diary, Part XXII, loc. cit.

[4] Ibid.

the centre, Monty's set-up had been accepted, with General Juin commanding the Land Forces, General Norstad the Air Forces, and Admiral Jaujard its Naval Forces.

Monty's own appointment as Deputy Supreme Commander had been spelled out by Eisenhower in a formal letter on 12 March, written at Monty's request. This time Monty wanted no French cavilling over his rôle or authority; his task was to act 'during any temporary incapacity of mine as Supreme Allied Commander, Europe, under authority invested in me by the North Atlantic Council'. Monty's principal duty was to 'further the organisation, equipping, training, and readiness of National Forces contemplated for later allocation to this command, and through and in co-operation with subordinate commanders, to performing a similar function for troops already allocated to SHAPE'. To this end Monty was 'to make contact, in my name, with the several governments, military staffs and agencies of NATO nations'.[1] Lest there be any confusion between Supreme and Deputy Supreme Commander, any executive order Monty wished to give would have to be made through the Supreme Commander's staff, not Monty's own. In this way Eisenhower would avoid the inference that he was tacitly handing over to a British soldier.

For Monty it was the end of executive command; he would not command either the land battle in Europe or even the overall battle, unless by any chance the Supreme Commander was killed, wounded or went sick. What he was to do was to 'forge the weapon', as he afterwards put it.

Eisenhower had declared he would take over NATO command on 1 April 1951, on which day the old Western Union military set-up would become defunct. Where Eisenhower would set up his headquarters and what would happen to the old Western Union headquarters at Fontainebleau were matters yet to be decided. In the meantime the Hotel Astoria would do for SHAPE; so, in the spring of 1951, Europe's defences were run from a Supreme Headquarters established in a comfortable Paris hotel. It was a headquarters which aroused Monty's profound professional contempt. It was 'a state of complete chaos' in his eyes,[2] as bad as or worse than Lord Gort's British Expeditionary Force Headquarters at Arras in 1939: an invitation to disaster. Having successfully hammered out a job for himself, Monty now 'tackled this problem with all his energy'. 'NATO needs an eloquent and inspired Moses as much as it needs planes, tanks, guns and ships,' Eisenhower had declared in his

[1] Annex 568, Diary, Part XXII, loc. cit.

[2] Diary, Part XXII, loc. cit.

address to Congress.[1] Eisenhower evidently felt himself to be that Moses; but without the Ten Commandments his staff were bound to go round in circles. What was wanted was a plan for NATO—a statement of strategy that would give the organization a sense of direction and purpose. NATO must not be allowed to 'drift aimlessly'. With his customary messianic zeal Monty hoped that Moses would lay down the law. If he did not, Monty himself would have to do so.

[1] Quoted in Stephen Ambrose, op. cit.

CHAPTER THREE

Defining the Problem

MONTY'S CONCEPT OF running a headquarters and Eisenhower's were very different. Monty's whole military career had consisted of promotions or appointments into which he thrust himself heart and soul, instantly assessing the task and giving out orders as to how that task would be dealt with. Eisenhower preferred to work the other way round, first attempting to learn all the problems involved in a new appointment, then arriving at a consensus in handling or resolving them. In many ways Eisenhower's attitude was that of a politician—a designation he was soon to fulfil as President of the United States.

The disadvantage of Eisenhower's approach was that it could give rise to huge headquarters with vast numbers of officers and staffs detailed to 'look after' something. It also lent itself to lobbying, since subordinates quickly became aware that decisions were made only in response to pressure: pressure that had to be mounted like campaigns. Monty, despite the years he had spent fighting under Eisenhower's overall command in the Mediterranean and North-west Europe, had never served at SHAEF. It was therefore not surprising that Monty viewed the antics of the Hotel Astoria—in which he was soon given an office—with grave misgiving.

'The first thing which was necessary was clearly a firm directive from the top,' Monty felt.[1] His own responsibilities were for the organization, equipping, training and preparing of the Allied forces under SHAPE. But as the days went by it was clear that no strategic directive was in the offing from the Supreme Commander. 'General Eisenhower himself, and his staff, appeared to be completely overwhelmed by the problem of the controversy over the question of the command organization and also by the problem of the internal organization of the staff at SHAPE. No clear directive of policy or of requirements appeared from the office of the Supreme Commander.'[2] As Monty wrote to Arthur Bryant on 12 March:

> I am immersed in the intrigues of Western Defence. Eisenhower came over here thinking it would be a very simple matter getting

[1] Diary, Part XXII, loc. cit.

[2] Ibid.

Western Europe and Atlantic Pact affairs moving along smoothly. I told him it would be difficult and gave him all my experience. He is now learning his lesson!! It would not surprise me if he had a nervous breakdown before the year is over. What a life![1]

By late March Monty was becoming desperate and therefore called a meeting on 27 March, with General Gruenther, General Festing (the new Assistant Chief of Staff Organization and Training) and Air Vice-Marshal Huddleston (the new Deputy Chief of Staff Organization and Plans). Huddleston failed to appear, but to the others Monty handed a fourteen-page memorandum. As he explained when sending a further copy to the Ministry of Defence and British Chiefs of Staff, 'it has been clear to me for some time that what is needed at SHAPE is some clear and simple statement of our problem, so worded that it can be used as a common starting point for all branches of the staff: which would then be able to get down to their work'.

So far no one has defined the problem and the members of the staff do not know what to do. The whole show is in fact lacking a clear and firm lead.

I therefore wrote the attached paper, FM/38, and used it as the basis for discussion at my conference with General Gruenther on 27 March. . . .

FM/38 may not be generally agreed by everyone.

That does not matter for the moment.

What does matter is that SHAPE should cease going round in circles, wondering what to do; that is thoroughly bad and will merely bring discredit on everyone.[2]

SHAPE's new staff was understandably at sea. Monty had been assessing the European military situation for more than two years and he felt 'that the first thing to be done was to agree the answers to the following questions':

a) Where are we going to fight the all-out battle, e.g. on the Rhine or East of it?
b) What are the *total* forces in Divisions and tactical air formations that we require for our task?
c) Of this total, what is the quota that will be provided by each nation?
d) By what date must the national quotas be ready and available for battle?

[1] Bryant Papers.
[2] Diary, Part XXII, loc. cit.

e) Of the national quotas, what forces will be maintained in actual existence in peace time, and what forces will be in reserve formations to be mobilised on the outbreak of war?[1]

It was essential that 'General Eisenhower should issue his directive giving the answers to these problems with the very least possible delay', Monty felt. The organization of the national forces, everything, depended upon the answers to these questions and in the opinion of the Field-Marshal the answers could be given by General Eisenhower in a matter of a week or less. In fact, they should have been laid down at the very earliest possible moment.'[2]

Monty, with characteristic straightforwardness, answered the questions himself. Now that Western Union was being upgraded into NATO, the Allies should aim to fight the 'all-out battle' east of the Rhine, employing German manpower, he believed—a policy laid down by the North Atlantic Defence Ministers as the 'Medium Term Plan' in April 1950. Monty's staff had estimated that within one month of Russian attack some fifty-four Allied divisions and 6000 aircraft would be required to stem invasion—if it was intended that the Russians be halted on the Rhine. To stand on the Elbe, further East, would require substantially larger forces. NATO must determine how much would be needed, and what each constituent nation could and should provide in the battle of Western Europe—and by when. 'The Field-Marshal reduced the questions to their simplest form':

Where are we going to fight?
What forces do we want?
When do we want them?
Who will produce them?[3]

As Monty's diarist noted laconically: 'it was apparent during the meeting that General Gruenther had given no consideration to the problems which the Field-Marshal outlined. He undertook to give careful study to the Field-Marshal's paper.'[4] To General McLean at the Ministry of Defence in Whitehall and the British Chiefs of Staff Monty was less polite:

I therefore wrote the attached paper, FM/38, and used it as the basis for discussion at my conference with General Gruenther on 27 March. He accepted it and agreed it was what was needed. He

[1] Ibid.
[2] Ibid.
[3] Ibid.
[4] Ibid.

will show it to General Eisenhower and get his reactions. The latter has retired to bed: with some internal trouble. I am not surprised!! [1]

This was vintage Monty, with strong overtones of the planning for the invasion of Sicily in 1943, intent on clear objectives, firm leadership from the top: an irrepressible, energetic, analytical and domineering Monty not out to please but, like Churchill on the warpath, determined to see 'action this day'. Eisenhower might argue that until 1 April he was not actually in formal command of NATO's European forces, but it was typical of Monty to want the incoming Commander to have a plan, and to radiate purposefulness. In his war memoirs, *Crusade in Europe*, Eisenhower had given the impression he had done this before D-Day as Supreme Commander of 'Overlord'. Those present knew that this was not the case: that it was *Monty's* astonishing display of decisiveness in January 1944 which had transformed a baffled and sometimes defeatist staff into a headquarters certain of victory—and that Eisenhower had merely followed suit, keeping their political and military masters sweet, and ensuring the overall co-operation of air, naval and land forces in the venture.[2] So too in the creation of NATO's defence structure in 1951 it was Monty's rôle to bring order out of chaos, and to get the staff working to a clear plan—a fact so unpalatable to Eisenhower's later biographer, Stephen Ambrose, that Montgomery's name was excluded from his account of Eisenhower's term of office at NATO altogether.[3] Such an American attitude, after Montgomery's death, would not have surprised Monty; indeed, even as SHAPE became 'operational' in April 1951 Monty was being assailed by renewed newspaper headlines after serialization of Bradley's war memoirs in *Life* magazine. 'My dear Brad,' Monty wrote on 15 April 1951 to protest:

The English papers are carrying great headlines:

BRADLEY CRITICISES MONTY

etc. etc. etc.

I presume it refers to what you say about me in your book. All I have seen are certain extracts in the British press.

I often wonder if it is entirely suitable that officers who are still

[1] M/7A, March 1951, annex 573, Diary, Part XXII, loc. cit.

[2] Despite the tenor of his memoirs, Eisenhower was in private well aware of this, as the veteran war correspondent Drew Middleton later recalled, Eisenhower openly admitting to Middleton that without Montgomery it was doubtful if the Allies would have succeeded in 'Overlord'—'Montgomery, Hard to Like or Ignore', *New York Times*, 25.3.76.

[3] Op. cit.

serving on the active list should criticise the character and professional ability of those who were their comrades and Allies in the late war: who are *also* on the active list of their own armies.

The shadow of another war hangs over us; we are still comrades and Allies in peace and we may have to be so *again* in war. Such action cannot improve Anglo-American relations, or help what we are trying to do over here in Europe. However, perhaps it has to be. But it is a pity.

Whatever you may choose to say about me I must of course accept in silence; this is no time for making more trouble; I cannot reply. It will not alter my high regard for you; or, I hope, our friendship—which I value greatly. Meanwhile, could you send me by return a copy of the book. I am being bombarded with questions from the press and other people and I think I should know what it is all about.

It would have helped if I could have had a little notice of the criticisms. I had no idea I was to be criticised in this way and I suppose more is to come.[1]

Bradley replied from the Pentagon that he had had no control over serialization and that *Life* magazine had 'tried to pick the most sensational parts in order to make it more interesting to a large group'. He apologized for causing Monty 'to be asked too many questions' and promised to send a copy of the book.[2] This promise did not appease Monty, who had to contend with further sensations each week in *Life*. On 1 May Monty therefore wrote back, still not having received the book itself:

My Dear Brad

Thank you for your reply to my letter of 15 April.

I fear I cannot agree that the book will do no harm. What has appeared so far in the Press in England has done great harm. If we were both retired, and were not both serving in very responsible jobs, then I suppose we could say what we liked about each other and about our respective nations.

But we are both still serving.

As things stand today, unity is vital. Anyone who attempts to create discord is doing great harm.

I have just been reading headlines in the Press:

'BRADLEY REFUSES TO SERVE UNDER MONTY.'

[1] Annex 584, Diary, Part XXII, loc. cit. Bradley's book was published that year as *A Soldier's Story* both in the USA and Britain.

[2] Letter of 24.4.51, annex 585, Diary, Part XXII, loc. cit.

> You neglected to say that, more than once, I offered to serve under you with great willingness: and did so in writing to Ike.
>
> And I cannot see what good will be done to Anglo-American relations by quoting Patton on saying he would like to push the British into the sea (from Falaise) and give them another Dunkirk. Nor do I see how such a statement by Patton can help you in an objective analysis of the campaign in Normandy. The statement has merely irritated the British intensely: they gave the lives of their men on the eastern flank of the bridgehead in order to make possible the breakout by the Americans on the western flank [Operation 'Lucky Strike', the American break-out, being planned at Monty's 21st Army Group headquarters on 16 June 1944 as soon as the German intention to place their main armoured weight on the eastern flank had been assessed]. And if they had *not* done so,

Monty ended emphatically,

> the Americans would *not* have broken out.
>
> We certainly do live in a curious world.[1]

In fact Bradley's account of the Normandy battle was most fair and gave Monty due credit both for conceiving the overall master-plan of D-Day and his tactical decision to hold the Germans on the eastern flank thereafter in order to facilitate an eventual American break-out from the close-knit bocage countryside in the west. Bradley was right, too, to point to serialization as the culprit, since newspaper serializations were inevitably sensational in order to justify huge payments to the author. Eisenhower had become a half-millionaire, nett of tax, merely on the proceeds of a widely serialized book. But Eisenhower had at least retired as Chief of Staff, US Army, on publication of *Crusade in Europe*; Bradley, by contrast, was still serving not only as Chairman of the American Chiefs of Staff but also as Chairman of the Military Defence Committee in control of NATO. He was thus, on publication of his *Soldier's Story*, Monty's boss, and his decision not to delay publication until his retirement was one which caused even Eisenhower to frown. 'It was quite extraordinary that an officer in General Bradley's position should have committed such an act of folly,' Monty's diarist noted. 'When the Field-Marshal spoke to General Eisenhower about it, General Eisenhower's only explanation was that he thought that General Bradley "was a little bit touched in the head".'[2]

Bradley's small spoke in the wheel of Allied solidarity was, how-

[1] Annex 585A, Diary, Part XXII, loc. cit.

[2] Diary, Part XXII, loc. cit.

ever, something for which Monty was himself largely to blame—since the only passion in Bradley's otherwise common-sense account of operations in North Africa, Sicily and North-West Europe was directed in the later 1944/45 chapters against Montgomery. It was clear that the memory of the Ardennes and his humiliating interview with Monty on the afternoon of Christmas Eve 1944 was something Bradley would never overcome—and his whole account of operations after Normandy reflected the increasing bias of his ADC-diarist, Major Hansen, against both Monty and those British officers who treated their American counterparts as 'country cousins'.

Thus impaled on his own past behaviour, Monty protested, but was powerless to prevent publication. Once again, in Monty's eyes, history was being distorted to make money for senior American generals—and he bided his time until he himself could enter the fray.

In the meantime Monty badgered Eisenhower and his staff for an entire month in an attempt to get a strategic directive for the new NATO headquarters. On Eisenhower's behalf he visited Belgium, Holland, Denmark and Norway—explaining to the respective Chiefs of Staff of each country that the Supreme Commander had asked him to report if their existing forces were effective, if their reserve forces would be effective on mobilization, and to see how the forces could be welded 'into an integrated Allied fighting machine'. The fact that he was no longer the outspoken, eccentric British field-marshal running a paper-team in Fontainebleau, but was now the representative of the American Supreme Commander of NATO, gave Monty the imprimatur he needed. Tirelessly and relentlessly he sought to strip away the thin façades of the various nations' contributions to NATO defence. As was the case in southern England after Dunkirk, Monty's visitations were both frightening and a tonic—for here was an Inspector-General with the greatest battle experience in the Western world, a soldier with a ruthlessly discerning eye, quick to detect prevarication and capable instantly of putting his finger on what was amateur. His tour convinced him that the NATO nations *were* beginning to grasp the importance of professionalism and forward planning in their defence efforts. All the more reason, therefore, why NATO's Supreme Headquarters should now give the strategic guidance necessary to weld and wield the weapon.

To his chagrin, on arriving back in Paris on 12 April 1951, after a fortnight abroad, Monty found the situation in the Astoria Hotel unchanged. In his absence no one was even willing to consult his Chief of Staff or Principal Staff Officer, General Redman. Not only was NATO still without a clear strategic plan, but his own position in the hierarchy as Deputy Supreme Commander was being questioned.

At Monty's request, yet another conference was called by General Gruenther. At this Monty made clear his own position, and his responsibility for 'forging the weapon' under Eisenhower. He must have access, via General Redman, to 'everything that was going in SHAPE in the various branches of the staff'. But more importantly, SHAPE *must* pull itself together and decide on a 'clear-cut directive of policy, a scaffolding within which we could build our structure'. The questions he had posed in his FM/38 paper *had* to be answered so that planning for the future could start. In his view, he reiterated, there would be no war in Europe in 1951 or indeed before the winter months of 1952. Why not therefore start planning for a NATO programme of defence to be ready by 1 December 1952, relying on his existing Western Union short-term emergency defence plan in the meantime—a plan Monty had put to Eisenhower on 29 March,[1] and which Eisenhower had adopted as his first directive on assuming Supreme Command on 2 April. 'I agree wholeheartedly with your suggestion that the Short Term plan, worked out at Fontainebleau, should be used as a basis for operations,' Eisenhower had responded. 'A signal to this effect is being dispatched to all concerned. I feel, however,' he added, 'now that our forces are at last beginning to build-up, that SHAPE should produce as soon as possible an Emergency Plan of its own.'[2]

In Monty's eyes it was idle to spend time on formulating a detailed new Emergency Plan. If all were agreed that there was little chance of a Russian-inspired war in Europe for a further year and a half, why waste time re-phrasing existing emergency plans? Surely it was better to turn the full attention of Supreme Headquarters to the future: a 'Medium Term Plan', effective from 1 December 1952. Having made his point as emphatically as he dared, Monty left Gruenther at the Hotel Astoria for London 'and waited to see the reactions of General Eisenhower and the staff at SHAPE to the proposals he had made.'[3]

Returning to Paris on 18 April 1951 Monty lunched with Eisenhower. 'It was quite clear that when he got back nothing had been done towards laying down the strategic directive which the Field-Marshal considered the first essential,' Monty's diarist recorded. 'The Field-Marshal therefore set himself the task of giving the necessary impetus to the headquarters, which was quite clearly lacking that direction which it so badly needed. He therefore sent for various of the more intelligent and active of the staff officers at the headquarters

[1] M/28, 29.3.51 enclosing FM/38, annex 574, Diary, Part XXII, loc. cit.

[2] Letter of 2.11.51, annex 575, Diary, Part XXII, loc. cit.

[3] Diary, Part XXII, loc. cit.

and tried to get them to infuse the necessary life into the machine.' In particular he singled out the British Deputy Chief of Staff in charge of Plans—the linchpin in SHAPE's headquarters. 'He [Monty] told Air Vice-Marshal Huddleston that it was from him that the necessary drive should come and that he had failed to provide it'—an opinion with which, privately, General Gruenther agreed. 'The Field-Marshal continued to emphasize the need for strategic direction whenever the opportunity arose.' Finally, on 24 April 'a paper on this subject was produced for consideration by the staff', Monty's diarist chronicled. 'Production of this paper . . . was due entirely to the efforts of the Field-Marshal and represents a major triumph over the inertia and chaos of the Hotel Astoria.' [1]

Considering Monty's age—rising sixty-five—and his gruelling travel commitments, it was a major achievement for him to have cajoled a new and chaotic SHAPE staff into adopting first his own emergency plan and then issuing an overall strategic directive, preparatory to a medium-term plan, within three and a half weeks of operational life. In doing so, he had doubtless made himself unpopular, straining his already uneasy relationship with Eisenhower. Yet Eisenhower, strangely, did not resent this. He had always relied on the no-nonsense, desk-banging firmness of General Bedell Smith during the war. Moreover, Eisenhower's particular genius had never been one of innovation or direct command. Like Hindenberg, he was, by his integrity, a genuine figurehead under whom men forgot their differences and were content to serve.

To Eisenhower's Hindenburg, Monty now played Ludendorff—and, considering the unique problems of a twelve-nation team, the partnership prospered in a manner few could have predicted the year before, when de Lattre and Monty both struggled so strenuously for their places in the sun.

[1] Ibid. The SHAPE paper ended:
a) Exactly where do we want to fight the battle in the West should it develop?
b) What forces are necessary for the successful control of this battle?
c) What nations can best suitably provide these forces?
d) Progressively by when do we need them?
Our planning should therefore be conducted within the framework of these four points.
Paper of 24.4.51, annex 577, Diary, Part XXII, loc. cit.

CHAPTER FOUR

Giving the Lead

VISITING MONTY IN France in the spring of 1951 Sir Brian Horrocks was impressed by the parallel between D-Day and the new NATO command in Europe. 'The same two men are in control—Eisenhower with Montgomery as his deputy. The only real difference is that the shooting war in Normandy has been replaced by the cold war in the East.'

There was, once again, the *esprit de corps*—'that family feeling which Eisenhower always manages to inspire in his staff; there is already a genuine feeling of affection for "Ike" himself', Horrocks noted. As for Monty, Horrocks wrote, 'when Montgomery's appointment was first announced, there were many armchair critics who murmured about disagreements between these two during the last war, and who prophesied that there would be continual friction between them now. *Nothing could be farther from the truth.* I was immensely impressed with Montgomery's genuine affection for his chief, and his deep sense of loyalty to the Supreme Commander.... Monty insisted over and over again that his role is to take the load off "Ike's" shoulders and prevent him becoming involved in detail.'[1]

Whether Eisenhower was so anxious for Monty rather than his Chief of Staff, 'Al' Gruenther, to take the weight of detail off his shoulders is less certain. Though Monty had an office at his disposal at the Astoria Hotel, he disliked the atmosphere of 'chaos' there and stayed largely at his château at Courances, communicating with Eisenhower by letter or telephone. Given his poor health and the seemingly intractable problems of setting up the Supreme Command, Eisenhower was doubtless relieved that Monty was prepared to act as his ambassador to the NATO Chiefs of Staff. 'Hardly a week passes without his [Monty] visiting at least one country; in fact he spends most of his time flying over Europe. He has just returned from four days in Italy; next month he will visit Belgium and Holland, and will spend some time in the United Kingdom. In July he goes for nine days to Norway, and will pay a fleeting visit to those northern territories where the sun never sets; he then goes for a period

[1] Article in *Picture Post*, 9.6.51.

to Denmark, and so it goes on . . . few would in reality wish to change places with him if they realised how exhausting these journeys can be. There is no rest for Montgomery when he arrives in any country; he is faced with endless talks, when he is giving of himself the whole time—possibly trying to put over in the name of the Supreme Commander a line of action which that country may be reluctant to adopt,' Horrocks described.[1]

This was an understatement. Monty's military gaze had always been unsparingly direct; as mere chairman of a paper committee at Western Union he had barked, however, without teeth. Now, with Eisenhower's backing, he could thump the table on his travels—and did. If a certain constituent NATO country declined to put into the NATO effort the men and resources Monty felt to be fair and adequate, he was quick to strike it off his list as worth defending by the rest of NATO in the event of war. When M. Spaak of Belgium published an article criticizing the extension of Belgian National Service to two years, Monty quickly threatened to expose 'how you did nothing about Belgian defence when you were Prime Minister'.[2] Yet his method was not simply to threaten. He insisted, whenever possible, on visiting military academies, inspecting troops and watching manoeuvres, and was unstinting in his praise where earned. Europe could not currently be defended east of the Rhine. This meant that, should the Russians invade, the battle would be uncomfortably close to most European NATO nations within days of the outbreak of hostilities. It was thus in *everyone's* interest to provide the necessary forces for a NATO defence line on the Elbe, giving time for reserve troops to be mobilized and thus keeping down the cost of standing armies—a simple message which, coming from a renowned battlefield soldier, undoubtedly helped stir the NATO nations into action that would have been inconceivable in 1950 at the behest of a Council of NATO Deputies who rarely met and even more rarely made decisions.

This was a task which Monty undoubtedly relished. In Holland, the year before, he had been stoned by Communist students as a warmonger,[3] but there could be no question about Monty's commitment to peace. When questioned in the United States in the winter of 1949 about plans for a land campaign against Russia in the event of a third World War, Monty was quite candid, as his diarist

[1] Ibid.

[2] Diary, Part XXII, loc. cit.

[3] 'Communists today threw stones at Field Marshal Viscount Montgomery, Western Union Defence Chief, while he was making a tour of Amsterdam by barge. He was not hit. Communists then burned an effigy of him': *Daily Mail*, 14.1.50.

recorded: 'Assuming that Russia was held in Germany or even pushed back to her own territories, what would the FM do next? The FM replied that he did not know. He had never had time to study this problem and fortunately it was not his duty to do so. He asked the questioner [at the US National War College] whether he was satisfied with this answer, to which came the reply: "I am not at all satisfied with your answer, but it is the best one I have heard so far".'[1]

Whatever stones might be thrown by Communist students, Monty was more deeply committed to peace by well-organized defence than left-wing protesters realized. Moreover, his commitment to the welfare, concerns and open education of young people was equally profound. He had espoused the cause of St John's School, Leatherhead, which gave free or assisted education to the sons of indigent clergymen, and became chairman of the governing body in 1951 only to find it had run into serious financial difficulties. He immediately launched an appeal, wrote many hundreds of personal letters to solicit contributions, and arranged a dinner at the Mansion House to be given by the Lord Mayor of London to publicize the appeal. Although in his diary Sir Robert Bruce-Lockhart quoted General 'Q' Martel decrying Monty as a 'dishonest self-advertiser' and 'notoriously stingy',[2] this was a gross calumny. Monty had declined to send a personal contribution to the Royal Cancer Hospital of whose governors Martel was himself chairman. This was not from stinginess but was a matter of priorities. All Monty's charitable efforts were devoted to St John's School, and to the end of his life Monty donated virtually all his income from occasional journalism, book-reviewing and the writing of Forewords to St John's School. Not since Baden-Powell, indeed, had a British general shown the concern with the needs and problems of youth that Monty evinced—and not merely the youth of his own country. Such concern reflected in part the pedagogic energy of Monty's grandfather, Dean Farrar, as well as the missionary zeal of Monty's father, Bishop Montgomery. At all events it was something that was ingrained in Monty's character, and which would remain so for the rest of his life. When unveiling the Eighth Army Memorial Window in Cairo in March 1951 Monty had declared in his address that 'moral purpose is the most powerful single factor in war. You do not get the best from soldiers unless they have a clear conscience in what they do and are

[1] Address to National War College, 23.11.49, Diary, Part XVIII, Montgomery Papers.

[2] *The Diaries of Sir Robert Bruce-Lockhart, 1939–65*, ed. K. Young, London 1960.

confident that it is right. . . . The moral brief must come from the Church. The Church must tell the soldiers not what is, but what should be behind their going forth.'[1] Though he took his Eighth Army Chief Padre, Canon Hughes, with him to Cairo, and extolled the part played by chaplains in war ('For that reason I said in this Cathedral after Alamein "I would as soon think of going into battle without my artillery as without my Chaplains" ')[2], Monty was perhaps overlooking the impact of his *own* spiritual leadership, born of pedagogic father and grandfather. One unkind historian later likened Monty's morale-raising leadership in the desert to the croonings of a pop singer;[3] but this was written to denigrate rather than to understand. For Monty's belief in the importance of his padres stemmed from his belief in himself, and his own mission as a military preacher. As Major O'Brien, his MA in occupied Germany, had found, Monty would tolerate no criticism of the way he had fought his battles, estimating himself to be a master tactician—which was undoubtedly the case. Yet this jealous guarding of his own image as an infallible battlefield general drew attention away from the very factor which had raised Monty head and shoulders above any Axis or Allied battlefield commander in the twentieth century: namely an inspired, biblical, preacher-like approach to generalship: a desire to win the hearts and minds of his men that was—and is still—considered unmilitary. 'He was mocked and jeered in the clubs,' Field-Marshal Sir Gerald Templer later reflected of Monty's attempts to instil a new professionalism in the British Army after Dunkirk, 'but his methods were copied till they spread everywhere—even into the factories—and became doctrine. I once said to him: "You think you're going down in history as the victor of Alamein. But it will be for your re-raising of morale, together with Churchill, that you will be chiefly remembered—not Alamein." '[4]

Once again, under a Supreme Commander who wisely gave him his head, Monty became biblical preacher—and teacher. Far more than he himself recognized, he was however slipping into the mantled robes of a truth-sayer, a merchant of military dreams rather than a military commander. Slim had, only weeks before, indicated the desire of the British Chiefs of Staff that Monty be 'in charge of the battle' in the event of war. But as the months went by it became increasingly clear that Eisenhower did not want Monty within the executive command machinery of SHAPE, but was content to have

[1] Annex 586, Diary, Part XXII, loc. cit.
[2] Ibid.
[3] C. Barnett, *The Desert Generals*, London 1960, reissued 1983.
[4] Field-Marshal Sir Gerald Templer, interview of 27.4.79.

Increasingly, Monty adopted the role of prophet and critic in NATO, and by the time he finally retired in 1958 at the age of almost seventy-one, his departure (**149** *below*) was long overdue.

Nevertheless Monty's contributions to the success of the NATO alliance were immense. He paved the way for the entry of West Germany, and his annual CPX command exercises were more honest and controversial in their scenarios than any other military figure would have dared put forward. The French Government duly awarded him the Médaille Militaire (**148** *right*); the British Government nothing.

Monty in retirement
150 *opposite* In baggy corduroy trousers Monty strolls outside his converted mill at Isington in Hampshire. Curiously he had made no master plan for his retirement beyond publication of his *Memoirs* – the most controversial military autobiography of the century.

A series of BBC television broadcasts followed (**151** *right* and **152** *below*), putting Monty's simple, soldierly view of World War II across to millions – but wounding many an ego in the process.

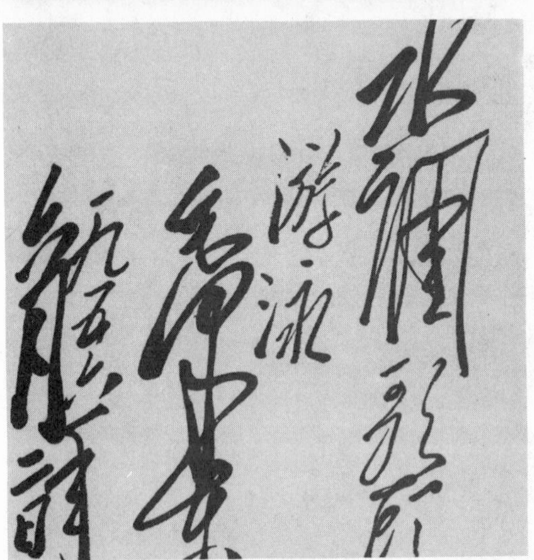

Once the storm over Monty's *Memoirs* had died down, Monty decided to devote the remainder of his life to two main tasks: the pursuit of peace in the world, and helping the young.

In 1959 he travelled to see Krushchev (**153** *above*) and to see Mao tse-Tung (**156** *below* and **154** *centre left*), touring a nation the U.S. still refused to recognize: Communist China (**155** *above*).

Monty's self-advertised friendship with Churchill (**157** *above left*) was in part lonely sentimentality, in part the genuine deference of a self-appointed statesman to a world-renowned practitioner.

At home Monty managed, with Mountbatten's help, to badger Macmillan into a reorganization of the British Chiefs of Staff upon American lines (**158** *above*) – as well as performing much charity work (**159** *left*).

Despite hiccups in their relationship, Monty remained firm friends with his old Chief of staff, Freddie de Guingand, and frequently visited him in South Africa (**161** *below right*), as well as reporting on apartheid (**160** *below left*).

Monty's stamina was astounding for a man of his age and wounds (**162** *above left*). He was hospitalized – but only for removal of a mole on his back (**163** *above right*). Otherwise he remained fit and active, travelling, lecturing, writing, working for charity, attending sports matches and the theatre. It was at the latter that Monty invited the entire cast of *Oliver!* to spend a day at his mill (**164** *below*).

165 *right* Monty shows the boys of *Oliver!* around his famous war-time caravans and **166** *below* gives them a beano tea in his wartime mess-tent.

Monty's fine photographs of the Alpine peaks were published in the *Illustrated London News*; but his portrait of Churchill in old age (**167** *above*) – reminiscent of Graham Sutherland's notorious oil painting – was not permitted to be reproduced.

him as his 'political' Vice-President—a co-figurehead, charged with the role of roving, ambassadorial deputy: inspecting, preaching, prophesying doom unless active and co-ordinated measures were taken; forecasting victory for peace if they were. As in Home Forces in 1940, there were some who mocked, who thought Monty's performance a sort of *opéra bouffe* considering the current military weakness of the Western Allies. But in doing so, they misunderstood the moral dimension of Monty's achievement, so clearly discerned by Templer and others. From now on, Monty's command-life was over, bar an accident that might render Eisenhower temporarily incapable. Like John the Baptist, he had prepared the West European nations for the coming of an American Supreme Commander; and under Eisenhower he loyally served, no longer as a battlefield commander, but as inspector and inspirer. In this respect he was, like his chaplains in Eighth Army, not concerned by 'what is, but what should be behind their going forth'—and his message was not one of matériel, but the necessity of clear-thinking and of moral and political courage in building up NATO.

'You ask about the form in Europe,' he responded to a letter from de Guingand in mid-May,1951. 'Actually it is not very good at the moment and the reason is two-fold':

> Firstly, lack of clear political guidance.
> Secondly, lack of unselfish solidarity among the nations concerned.

'You ask about my own position. I am nothing to do with the Land Forces. I have now taken up my residence at Supreme Headquarters where I am Deputy and Second-in-Command to Eisenhower. My special responsibility is to forge the weapon and be prepared to take over from him should he be absent or incapacitated. I have a very busy summer in front of me and one which involves a great deal of travelling.'[1]

Tirelessly Monty preached the new NATO gospel. Lethargy, weakness and deceit were scourges he was keen to clear; but always he retained a transcending simplicity of purpose. As he put this, in an address to all the senior staff officers of SHAPE the day after writing to de Guingand, the immediate task was:

a) To organise sufficient military power to offer effective resistance to aggression and thus to *deter* the Russian wish to strike in the West. In this way we gain time.
b) To create, within a definite period, a military force able, in the event of open war, to stop an onslaught by Russian forces until

[1] Letter of 17.5.51, de Guingand Papers, loc. cit.

further military forces can be mobilized and brought into battle.[1]

The Pope, when Monty had an audience with him early in May, had told Monty of certain Intelligence from Eastern Europe indicating that the Russians were preparing for possible war later that year;[2] but Monty discounted this, save as a useful stick to beat SHAPE into a more effective headquarters and the various political and military leaders in Europe into a more urgent commitment to agreed tasks and forces within NATO. His recommendation was that SHAPE would prepare a sound military plan for readiness three years ahead, in 1954, employing German troops—but allowing for the possibility, in December 1952, that the Russians might launch an Ardennes-type offensive to pre-empt West German rearmament.

As a result of Monty's conference on 18 May 1951, a new NATO 'Strategic Guidance Directive' was immediately issued, calling for the two plans Monty wished: a 'Defence Plan' for July 1954, and an 'Emergency Plan' for contingencies arising before then.[3] 'The Field-Marshal had, entirely by his own drive and initiative, given the lead to SHAPE,' his diarist chronicled. 'It was now to be seen whether the SHAPE staff and subordinate commands could keep up to the timetable.'[4]

[1] 'Staff Conference at SHAPE, 18 May 1951, Remarks by Field-Marshal Montgomery', FM/43, annex 591, Diary of Field-Marshal The Viscount Montgomery of Alamein, Part XXIII (9.5.51–14.6.51), Montgomery Papers.
[2] 'Visit to the Pope', 3.5.51, Diary, Part XXII, loc. cit.
[3] 'Strategic Guidance Directive', 19.5.51, annex 592, Diary, Part XXIII, loc. cit.
[4] Diary, Part XXIII, loc. cit.

CHAPTER FIVE

In the General Category of 'Great Men'

ONE OF THE qualities of a prophet or guru is the ability to see beyond everyday reality, undistracted by petty detail or minor setbacks.

Despite his lifetime's dedication to the art of battle, Monty's gradual concentration on the higher aspects of war, first as the head of his nation's army, then of Western Union's defence forces, and now Deputy Supremo of NATO's twelve-nation defences in Europe, gave him an increasingly oracular detachment, a Delphic removal from the day-to-day preoccupations of his staff. Perhaps this had always been so: a visionary, pedagogic quality masked only by the energy with which he threw himself into each new command in his career. Now, without an army or even a staff other than two ADCs, an MA and a Principal Staff Officer, he was once more the preacher which at heart he had always been, lending to his behaviour a quaint, sometimes comic, sometimes saintly air. Malcolm Muggeridge, visiting Monty at Western Union in 1949 had remarked on Monty's 'funny little wizened face . . . eyes are glazed over and mad-looking. In fact, his whole attitude suggested to me that the strain of his fame might have cracked his wits a bit.' Talking of the cold war and Communism, Monty spoke 'in the manner I remember so well from the war in which he used to analyze a military exercise or operation, pointing all the while with his hands as though to a huge map. . . . A clear case of advanced megalomania.'[1]

Sir George Mallaby, Secretary of the Military Committee of Western Union, had also observed the seemingly magalomaniacal manner of the Field-Marshal, the way in which he no longer seemed to inhabit the same reality as ordinary men. Taking Mallaby in his private aircraft to Paris, Monty was convinced that a throng of casual sightseers at Orly airport 'had all turned out to greet him. He walked across the tarmac to a large group of them, waving his hand in a jaunty fashion, and then shook hands with the few astonished Frenchmen who were not expecting to see him and therefore could form no clear conception of his identity. In a similar situation I should have felt embarrassed,' Mallaby remarked; 'not so, the Field-

[1] M. Muggeridge, *Like It Was*, London 1981.

Marshal, who walked quickly and smilingly on to his car and off we drove to Courances.'[1] At Courances much the same took place, for Monty was determined to show off his seventeenth-century palace with its elegant, double-curved stone staircase rising to the front doors, its formal gardens, waterworks and woods. 'When a young man he no doubt set his sights high and aimed at the greatest power and influence which the army could confer; but it can never have entered his young head that he would one day be the proprietor of a French château and the grand seigneur of the neighbouring village.' Touring the latter, on foot, Monty led Mallaby past 'the somewhat astonished villagers . . . and we entered various small shops and estaminets. At each port of call the Field Marshal, whose command of French at that time was little more than the rusty recollection of his lessons at St Paul's, would call out, in high good humour and without the least trace of self-consciousness, a series of direct questions—*"Ah, Madame, comment allez-vous? Combien d'enfants avez-vous?"* or to the men: *"Êtes-vous soldat? Moi je suis soldat. Beaucoup de médailles? Bon. Vous-êtes blessé? Ah, dans la grande guerre."* In some places which we visited our reception, I thought, was less than warm. In the first place nobody was expecting to see the Field Marshal and it took them a little time to realise who he was. In the second place it never became clear to most of them why he had come to see them.'[2]

Such puzzlement seemed to elude Monty—just as, at the still hugely popular Alamein Reunions each October, Monty preached his new gospel of the future and seemingly failed to take in what was transparently clear to newspaper reporters covering the occasion: namely that the four thousand veterans of the desert 'didn't really want to hear about the present or the future . . . for this one night they want to wallow in memories—to capture the atmosphere of sand and sun, of furtive "brews" and filthy cigarettes'.[3]

Whether Monty's failure to recognize the reality of the moment—that his audience might not even be an audience, might not know who he was, or might not be spellbound by his oratory as once they had listened—whether this blindness stemmed from advancing megalomania or from Monty's increasingly ascetic preoccupation is impossible to say. Tedder had drawn the attention of the First Sea Lord, Lord Fraser, to the way Monty was determined to enjoy his fame. 'He said once, "Watch when we leave Downing Street: you'll see that Monty'll either stop behind or go out first." And sure enough,

[1] G. Mallaby, *From My Level*, London 1965.
[2] Ibid.
[3] William Hickey column, *Daily Express*, 24.10.53.

we waited to look—and he lagged behind and waited until we'd all gone, and then came out and everybody cheered him.'[1] Malcolm Muggeridge, however, visiting Monty almost annually from 1949, certainly became more and more conscious of Monty's increasing dedication to matters of the spirit. In January 1950 Muggeridge logged in his diary the self-glorification in Monty's new home, the old miller's house at Isington. 'Fascinated by Monty's house which he has built and designed himself, very neat and clean . . . walls covered with huge oil paintings of himself, Freedom of the Cities, signed pictures of the King, Stalin, swords of honour, etc. etc.' And yet 'he is really rather charming in his odd way', Muggeridge allowed. 'Before we came [he] had been jotting down his ideas of what good generalship consists. Brought these notes away with me, real curiosity, written in his very immature hand. Reflected afterwards that all success in action pre-supposes great simplicity of character, and Monty in this document an excellent example.

'One cannot say that he is intelligent or even altogether "nice", and yet there is something quite remarkable about him, and one can see that, in his way, he fits into the general category of "great men", greatness being, I suspect, a kind of vitality and singleness of purpose more than anything else.'[2]

At Courances, two years later, Muggeridge was moved by Monty's simple and personal hospitality. 'Found Monty waiting up for me in his château near Fontainebleau with a large log fire burning—a draughty, majestic sort of place, very beautiful outside. . . . He took me up to my room, also vast, with canopied four-poster bed, and we sat talking by the fire. As I had no pyjamas he fetched a pair of his, thick, flannel, which he rather touched me by laying out in front of the fire to warm.'[3]

Muggeridge, pondering Monty's 'bizarre' character, was intrigued by Monty's increasing concern with 'essentials'—a concern which, when compared with the academic's love of detail, led Muggeridge to conclude that Monty was 'the precise converse of an intellectual'. Monty was—but Muggeridge's interpretation failed to identify the genesis. It was Monty's mastery of military detail which had marked him out as a first-class unflappable staff officer during the great battles on the Western Front in World War I—a grasp which he had never lost. His memory for names, faces and units remained phenomenal. Over the years, however, he had developed his mathematical gift for simplification, for the abstraction of essentials from a mass

[1] R. Humble, *Fraser of North Cape*, London 1983.
[2] M. Muggeridge, diary entry of 16.1.50, op. cit.
[3] Diary entry of 11.1.52. Ibid.

of detail, to the point of military genius. It was this gift of simplification which Monty now brought to bear at SHAPE. Eisenhower himself had little direct influence on the workings of the headquarters, leaving this almost entirely to his Chief of Staff, 'Al' Gruenther. Gruenther had never commanded troops in battle, any more than had Eisenhower—and was soon bogged down by the details of running a vast new headquarters. Monty's rôle, therefore, quickly became one of consultant surgeon to SHAPE—and it would be no exaggeration to say that in its first six months of life, SHAPE owed much of its success to Monty's guidance. He was personally responsible for laying down the NATO yardstick by which the effectiveness of national forces was assessed;[1] he had personally ensured that a SHAPE strategic war plan was produced and soon scotched SHAPE's first 'Tactical Directive' to write his own: 'Tactical Directive No. 1'.[2] As his diarist noted, the SHAPE planning staff's own effort 'reflected an entirely different approach' between the British and American outlook. 'The American procedure is for the commander to give detailed direction to his subordinates'—a policy which, after initial success, had gone disastrously wrong in Korea, with a Supreme Commander in Tokyo attempting to direct a land battle on the Asian mainland. The SHAPE draft tactical directive 'consisted of some 57 paragraphs of introduction, and then went into considerable detail as to the course of action to be pursued in each of the commands concerned. This was not what was wanted at all,' Monty felt. 'What was wanted was the necessary additional direction to the Commanders-in-Chief in order to get them to produce their *own* plans. The answer was not to produce a detailed plan for them; with which, in any case, they would probably not agree.'[3]

Monty's own draft directive, written on the evening of 25 June 1951, became SHAPE's first tactical orders. 'The Field-Marshal, speaking from his experience, both as a Commander, who had issued directives in war, and as one who had received them, was quite firm that what was needed was guidance on broad lines. It was a mistake to produce actual plans for the subordinate commanders and would only cause resentment.'[4]

[1] Monty's proposed measurement was, in particular, disliked by the French, since it threatened to give 'a realistic picture of their own contribution to European Defence. They did not like being shown up in a true light': Diary, Part XXIII, loc. cit. General Carpentier, the French Deputy Chief of Staff Administration at SHAPE resisted Monty's proposal for three months, but on 8.8.51 Eisenhower authorized official SHAPE promulgation of Monty's form of gauging in a SHAPE edict: 'Measurements for Effectiveness of Forces', 8.8.51, annex 599, Diary, Part XXIII, loc. cit.

[2] 'SHAPE Tactical Directive No. 1', 29.6.51, annex 601, Diary, Part XXIII, loc. cit.

[3] Diary, Part XXIII, loc. cit.

[4] Ibid.

Such advice undoubtedly helped set NATO on its effective path in the deterrence of war in Europe; but there was inevitably a certain amount of bruising—particularly among Americans—on the staff of SHAPE. Monty's eye let nothing pass that was unclear or wishful in its thinking. When, over lunch, General Gruenther declared that the aim of NATO was to prevent war, Monty corrected him. It was the aim of politicians to prevent war. It was the task of NATO to build up credible forces upon which politicians could base their efforts to deter aggression; and giving to the politicians pieces of paper representing fictional Allied forces in the event of war was not Monty's idea of responsible generalship. As Eisenhower prepared to deliver his first report to Congress and to the national leaders of NATO in August 1951, Monty thus unleashed a fierce broadside entitled 'The Great Illusion'.[1] 'He realised the difficulties which General Eisenhower faced in presenting a really true picture to the [NATO] Standing Group,' Monty's diarist noted. But Eisenhower *himself* should be under no illusion, Monty was adamant. Planned divisions might look very well on a paper balance-sheet of proposed armies—but paper divisions could not fight, and would not be able to do so 'until drastic action is taken by the [NATO] nations', Monty warned—instructing the SHAPE planning staff to produce an immediate secret paper on the subject for Eisenhower.

Monty's roving eye was not confined to Paris and Fontainebleau,[2] however: and within weeks of Eisenhower's Supreme Command in Europe Monty had been calling for NATO's first Exercise:

> The more the Field-Marshal saw of the Continental Armies, the more apparent it became to him that the standard of generalship was appallingly low. Most of the senior officers of the Continental Armies had taken very little part in the late war. . . . The Field-Marshal therefore suggested to General Eisenhower that a study period, on the lines of a Camberley Exercise, should be held at SHAPE in early April 1952. This exercise, to be called C.P.X. One, would be primarily directed towards the training of Divisional and higher Commanders of the Continental Armies. The exercise would be the forerunner of the actual manoeuvres which were to take place in 1952. General Eisenhower agreed . . . [and]

[1] Meeting of 13.8.51. Using the new SHAPE measurement 'it was, therefore, now possible to make a comparative study between fact and fiction. It would be illuminating': Diary, Part XXIII, loc. cit.

[2] It had been agreed, when Eisenhower took active command in Europe on 1 April 1951, that the existing Western Union headquarters at Fontainebleau should become the HQ Central Region of NATO's European forces.

asked the Field-Marshal to be responsible for the conduct of the exercise.[1]

As he had been doing since the 1920s, Monty himself wrote the scenario. 'The Field-Marshal himself drafted the initial strategic setting . . . based upon the situation which might occur in December 1952'[2]—and the groundwork for 'CPX One' began on 1 August 1951, handled by a special exercise staff formed for the purpose. Monty had, in the meantime, also proposed to Eisenhower that large-scale manoeuvres should take place in Germany under the direction of SHAPE in the autumn of 1952. 'Once again Eisenhower agreed and again asked the Field-Marshal to be responsible for the direction of these manoeuvres'[3]—with Monty's first instructions issued on 10 August 1951 to the Allied forces in Germany, as well as British, Danish and additional French and Belgian forces.

Even this was insufficient in Monty's own eyes. He arranged to be an observer at various manoeuvres currently being conducted by individual NATO countries—and was unsparing in the lessons he drew. For instance in Wales, after attending a Signals Exercise by 51st (Territorial) Division in July 1951, he wrote immediately to the CIGS, Field-Marshal Slim:

> I am disturbed at the low standard of tactical knowledge that was displayed. Many commanders did not understand the technique and procedure involved in tackling the problem. I met two Brigadiers who were in my opinion unfit to hold their jobs—one infantry and one armoured. Generally, training ability was lacking. I was left with the opinion that many senior officers did not know their stuff.
>
> All this was very alarming.
>
> It is clear to me that unless operational commanders are constantly exercised in carrying out their functions of command in their several grades . . . they quickly go down hill.[4]

To 'meddle' in the local prerogatives of national armies could easily be taken amiss, but Monty was speaking on behalf of the Supreme Allied Commander now, who would be relying on such troops in the event of war. There would simply not be time for mistakes or for learning by experience in battle in a modern war.

[1] Diary of Field-Marshal The Viscount Montgomery of Alamein, Part XXIV (15.6.51–24.1.52), Montgomery Papers.

[2] Ibid.

[3] Ibid.

[4] Signal exercise of 24/25.7.51, signal to CIGS, annex 605, Diary, Part XXII, loc. cit.

The only way in which NATO could provide effective defence on land was by accelerating the speed at which *Reserve* divisions could be mobilized and employed in battle. Britain's original intention was to provide Territorial (reserve) troops by D + 90; this had now to be condensed to one month. 'If the Divisions of the Territorial Army are to be fit for battle in one month after they begin to mobilize, some different and more energetic measures for their training will be necessary.'[1]

The professionalism which had once transformed the British Army in England after Dunkirk was now being applied by Monty to the twelve nations of NATO. He was as unsparing in his criticisms of the British Army as of those of the other European nations; but his keenest professional examination was reserved for the command situation in NATO's central sector, once the preserve of Western Union. Here, under the absentee lordship of General Juin (still commanding in Morocco), 'the whole organisation was slipping into a state of lethargy from which it would be difficult to arouse it when the time came. In fact, since the Field-Marshal had left Fontainebleau,' his MA recorded, 'little or nothing had been done.' The outline tactical plan produced by Juin's stand-in, General Guillaume, was scorned by Monty:

> This plan, if it may be called such, had been prepared entirely outside the headquarters [of NATO's Central European Command] at Fontainebleau. It consisted, in fact, of certain general views on strategy from General Guillaume's own head. This was not the way to conduct planning for the defence of Europe.[2]

General Norstad, the American Air C-in-C of the Central Command sector, had not even set up a headquarters in August, and in some perturbation Monty approached Eisenhower—who, according to Monty's MA, 'was in complete agreement with the Field-Marshal as to the necessity of getting the two Commanders-in-Chief for the Central sector into their jobs, and on the spot, with the minimum of delay.'[3]

Eisenhower's own performance in SHAPE's formative first year was greatly affected by the looming question of his candidature for the American Presidency—and his poor health. 'General Eisenhower was frequently unwell,' Monty's diarist noted. 'Eisenhower, for the procession through the streets of Paris, required a special bag suspended inside his trousers,' Monty later recalled of the state funeral

[1] Ibid.
[2] Ibid.
[3] Ibid.

of General de Lattre, at which Monty and Eisenhower were pall-bearers.[1]

By contrast Monty was brimming with good health, as General Horrocks noted when observing Monty's monastic existence:

> The Field-Marshal leads a very simple life, eats sparingly, drinks no alcohol, and never smokes. . . . During the war he lived in his caravan at an advanced HQ with a very small staff, and refused to be swamped by visitors.
>
> He lives exactly the same life now, eschewing society functions and spending every Saturday and Sunday quietly in the depths of the country, either at his mill house near Bentley in Hampshire, or at the lovely Louis XIII Château de Courances, belonging to the Marquis de Ganay, where he occupies a flat and lives in exclusion with two ADCs—one British and one French. He is the despair of the French society hostesses, who would give their eyes to get 'Monsieur le Maréchal' to come to their parties.[2]

Monty eschewed 'parties'. He still retired to bed at 9.30 p.m. to read, and by 10 p.m. his light would go out. But during his waking hours his keen, restless mind refused to flag. As one of the senior SHAPE staff officers notes, the job of Deputy Supreme Commander was really what Monty chose to make it; and the more ill Eisenhower became, the more Monty took on. At Monty's request, Juin had been ordered to submit an outline plan for NATO's central defence by the summer of 1951. No outline plan arrived; instead, Juin asked to see Eisenhower—to discuss withdrawal plans if the Rhine fell and the Allies were forced to retreat.

Monty was horrified. From his experience at Western Union he knew that 'this subject was dynamite. The Rhine line must be held and the necessary forces to do so must be developed. The nations could do so if they made sufficient effort. Anything else was unthinkable, and would only lead to "looking over the shoulder" '[3]—as the Eighth Army was doing when Monty arrived at Alamein in 1942.

Indefatigably Monty toured and re-toured the NATO nations to investigate defence positions, manpower figures, states of training, morale. When Denmark, for instance, showed little sign of producing sufficient trained troops and reservists, Monty 'spoke very bluntly to the Danish Foreign Minister and Minister of Defence. . . . At this

[1] A. Brett-James, *Conversations with Montgomery*, London 1984. De Lattre had returned from Indo-China in November 1951, suffering from cancer. His funeral took place on 16 January 1952.

[2] Article in *Picture Post*, 9.6.51.

[3] Diary, Part XXIII, loc. cit.

private session the Field-Marshal made it perfectly clear to the two Ministers that, unless action was taken which would produce a better mobilisation, Denmark could not be held against a major threat.'[1] At the Rome conference later that year, Monty made certain that the Danish failure to ensure sufficient reserves by introducing eighteen-month National Service was brought out. 'The danger that the Danes would leave the North Atlantic Treaty Organisation if driven too hard must be accepted. They were quite useless and even a liability at the moment,' his diarist chronicled;[2] but in a communication to Eisenhower Monty had been even more damning:

> The real trouble is that the [Danish] Government feels that if it makes too many demands on the people, the people will get fed up and the anti-Atlantic Pact movement will gain ground. The country is prosperous; there is a very high standard of living; everyone has plenty of money; the people want to be left in peace to enjoy themselves; they did not have a very bad time on the whole under the Germans, and they think it would be no worse under the Russians.[3]

This was a harsh indictment, but it well illustrated the difference between Monty's and Eisenhower's roles. Eisenhower took little interest in the running of SHAPE as an operational headquarters or indeed the operations of any of the subordinate command headquarters. Instead, he kept his finger on the pulse of political feeling both at home in America and in the NATO governments and parliaments, attempting to 'jolly along' the constituent countries; whereas Monty felt that the constituent nations would be willing each to contribute their fair share if they saw value for money: i.e. a NATO defence structure that *worked*. His own, self-appointed task under Eisenhower became, therefore, one of ensuring that SHAPE *did* work—and he was relentless in his inspections, examinations and scrutinies. In his quest for military efficiency he was ruthlessly international. He found, for instance, that the British Admiral Brind's Northern Command was poorly run owing to a 'useless' Naval officer as his Chief of Staff. Brind was ordered either to replace his Chief of Staff or accept an Army general on his staff who *did* understand the problems of land warfare and command. When Juin finally tendered his outline plan for central command, Monty rejected it as

[1] Ibid.
[2] Diary, Part XXIV, loc. cit.
[3] 'Note for General Eisenhower and Lt-General Gruenther on the headquarters situation in the Northern Europe Command', 14.7.51, annex 613, Diary, Part XXII, loc. cit.

unsatisfactory. When Gruenther seemed unable to cope with the amount of staff work in Paris, Monty proposed a Vice-Chief of Staff—offering his own Principal Staff Officer, General Redman. 'SHAPE was rapidly becoming a Super Ministry of Defence, clogged with matters of administration and political intrigue,' Monty's diarist summarized—and Monty did his best to unclog it. By hook or by crook he would ensure that NATO developed a credible defence plan, based on a defensive line it could hold and with adequate troops and reservists available in times of war, from Norway to the Mediterranean. Perhaps his most singular contribution was in August 1951 when he toured the Swiss defensive layout and persuaded the Swiss military authorities to realign it to the east to 'fit suitably into the grand tactical design in Europe'.

Such ceaseless advising and cajoling, moreover, did not stop at NATO defence. NATO's tasks ought to be seen as but part of a global strategy of the West, Monty felt—and his espousal of this supra-European view, driven by his own ebullient energy, now brought him within a hair's breadth of being sent, as de Lattre had been, to South-east Asia.

CHAPTER SIX

No to Malaya

CHURCHILL, HAVING WON the October 1951 election, was soon beset by the problem of Malaya, where the British High Commissioner had been assassinated by Communist insurgents. Asked by Churchill to give his views on British policy in Malaya, Monty considered, for a start, that the High Commissioner for South-east Asia should be sacked:

> Malcolm Macdonald is burnt out and is useless for the task. He must be removed at once. We want a ball of fire in Malaya and not a burnt out candle.

Monty recommended the appointment of a new 'Governor-General and Commander-in-Chief'—a soldier 'with fire in his belly'. Further detachments of British troops were not the answer, though, he warned:

> The cry for more and more troops in Malaya is wrong. . . . The ultimate aim must be for less and less soldiers. The Chinese must be brought in on the job, and the best type of Malayan. . . . Defeat or failure in that country would lead to a general lowering of morale in the Far East and to a great loss of confidence in the British; this would very quickly spread to Europe.[1]

Churchill offered Monty the job, as Monty confided to General Simpson, his erstwhile VCIGS. Monty, however, had 'no desire or intention to go to Malaya'. To Churchill Monty said, Simpson recalled, 'I understand Germans, and know how to deal with them. I would be no good whatsoever at dealing with scorpions and snakes!'[2]

Word soon leaked, however, that a soldier was to be sent to 'sort out' the situation in Malaya, and 'for six weeks before Christmas there were almost daily prophecies that the Field-Marshal would himself be going to Malaya as Supreme Commander,' Monty's diarist noted.[3]

Monty was not only concerned with snakes and scorpions, how-

[1] 'Policy in Malaya', 22.11.51, annex 669, Diary, Part XXIV, loc. cit.
[2] General Sir Frank Simpson, Eugene Wason interview for Sir Denis Hamilton.
[3] Diary, Part XXIV, loc. cit.

ever. It looked increasingly likely that Eisenhower would accept the next US Presidential nomination. As Monty wrote to Slim, the team of Eisenhower, Gruenther and Montgomery had been responsible for the current credibility of NATO defence in Europe; Greece and Turkey were about to join too. 'If one of the above team' were to go, no great harm would befall the infant organization. 'If *two* were to go, it would become very awkward and the machine would cease to work. . . . My overall opinion is that 1952 and 1953 are so important in the East/West struggle that those few of us who have knowledge, experience, and prestige must be prepared to serve on if we are needed by our political chiefs. If it was war time it would be different. . . . In peace, experience and wisdom are essential. At the present time, when confidence and civilian morale are so vital, we need in certain key jobs in 1952/1953 men of proved ability; the knowledge, name and prestige that goes with it.'[1]

In Monty's opinion, Slim should become Chief of Staff UK Armed Services or Defence Staff—'we need a General Bradley, so to speak'—when his tenure as CIGS ceased in 1952.[2] As his successor Monty considered General Harding to be the right choice, since General Robertson, the other prime contender for the post of CIGS, 'is not a high class soldier in the widest sense of the word. He is first class at administration and would make a good Q.M.G. or A.G. He is first class at diplomacy and political intrigue and is known in the Army as a political general. In my view he will never make a CIGS. Another point is that you cannot, in these days, have a CIGS who has never won a battle, even a Division or Brigade battle. Such a CIGS would cut no ice anywhere today. Robertson is not popular in the Army, and he commands no confidence.'[3]

Such a condemnation of the man who had been his superlative administrative chief in the desert and his Deputy Control Commissioner in the Occupation of Germany must have raised Slim's eyebrows, knowing as he did that Monty had bitterly opposed his own candidature as CIGS. As was his wont, Monty was exaggerating the importance of erstwhile battle command experience in peace-time rôles. Certainly Robertson was widely admired for the judicious and capable way he had governed Germany and was now commanding the Middle East. The C-in-C Suez Canal Zone, General Erskine, told General Simpson that Robertson 'is quite marvellous. He takes all the difficult decisions and then leaves me to get on with the job. He

[1] Letter to Field-Marshal Sir William Slim, 3.12.51, annex 672, Diary, Part XXIV, loc. cit.

[2] Ibid.

[3] Ibid.

does not worry me any more after he has given a decision. He has got the lightest touch of anyone under whom I have served.'[1]

Robertson's father had been CIGS; it was therefore natural that Robertson himself should covet the post. Thus when Churchill now offered the job of C-in-C Malaya to Robertson, the latter declined, pleading that he was 'worn out with all his responsibilities in the Middle East and too tired to take on a responsible job in Malaya'. When Simpson, the last senior general to visit Middle East Command, reported that Robertson was as fit as a fiddle and 'on top of everything'[2] Monty was furious. In his diary he claimed that 'Mr Churchill was extremely annoyed at General Robertson's attitude';[3] but it is more likely that Monty, feeling guilty at his own rejection of the post he had written up as the key British command in 1952, projected onto Robertson his own subconscious feelings. 'In his [Churchill's] opinion General Robertson had "had it" so far as his military career was concerned,' Monty's diarist continued. 'He had been asked to undertake one of the most important military missions, upon which the security of the British Empire depended. He had refused.'[4]

Robertson's refusal was perhaps unsoldierly, but it was soon echoed by Sir Miles Dempsey, currently director of a Reading brewery house. General Dempsey accepted only on condition that he was given command of Singapore Island as well as Malaya[5]—an offer Churchill and Lyttelton declined to make.

Monty, fearing that the ball might be thrown back into his own court, now produced another memorandum, 'Success in Malaya', on 2 January 1952. Time was pressing; Monty considered that whoever was appointed would have to be *ordered* to go. 'Any soldier who pleads he is tired and exhausted and therefore cannot face it, should be considered as unfit to hold his present job, and be relegated to retired pay. We are faced with a crisis and all must do their duty, or be discarded.'[6]

Monty's memorandum was forwarded with a covering letter to Churchill in America. This time Churchill acted vigorously. 'Monty, too, had sent a letter,' Lord Moran noted in his diary.[7] General Sir Gerald Templer was summoned to meet Churchill in Ottawa 'in order to be vetted for the command in Malaya', Moran recorded.[8] As Sir

[1] General Sir Frank Simpson, loc. cit.
[2] Ibid.
[3] Diary, Part XXIV, loc. cit.
[4] Ibid.
[5] General Sir Frank Simpson, loc. cit.
[6] 'Success in Malaya', M222, 2.1.52, annex 671, Diary, Part XXIV, loc. cit.
[7] Moran, *Churchill*, London 1966.
[8] Ibid.

Frank Simpson recalled—having been told the story by Templer—'Templer guessed what was in the wind but was supposed not to know. However he arrived at Ottawa and was put up very comfortably in an hotel; after which nobody seemed to take any interest in him at all, so he had a few drinks and went to bed, for he had just arrived from across the Atlantic.

'He was roused about 1 a.m. to be told that the Prime Minister wished to see him at once in some other hotel, so he dressed quickly and went across. Having arrived at the Prime Minister's hotel, he was shown in to the great man, who looked up and said something to the effect: "I must warn you that you have probably heard that Lord Acton said that absolute power corrupts absolutely. You will have absolute power in Malaya. See that you do not get corrupted by it. Good night."'[1]

In his second memorandum for Churchill Monty had declared:

> There is no alternative to success in Malaya.
> We know what is required to be done.
> We must now collect the men to do it.
> If we are not prepared to do this, we had better get ready to lose that part of the Colonial Empire and suffer all the repercussions that would follow: and will most certainly do so.[2]

But in his covering letter to Churchill, Monty had ruled himself out categorically, stating that 'continuity at SHAPE is vital' and how he had offered to serve under Gruenther if Gruenther was made Supreme Commander. 'It is very necessary that I should stay at SHAPE for the present and help to see all these things [CPX One, autumn 1952 manoeuvres, etc.] through, and forge the military weapon in Europe. I doubt if anyone else would pick up all the threads without a delay of many months. I do not think anyone else could handle our dealing with the Swiss; I have got them to re-deploy their Army to fit in with our defensive plans, and this is a great triumph. But I would not be accepted in Europe as Supreme Commander. The man to succeed Ike must be an American.'[3]

Monty thus scotched the possibility that Slim replace him as Deputy Supreme Commander in Europe, while he himself was sent out to Malaya. Churchill, tired of the business, brooked no refusal by Templer. As Templer told Simpson, 'he was never even offered the job. It was just assumed he had been appointed. He went off

[1] General Sir Frank Simpson, loc. cit.
[2] 'Success in Malaya', loc. cit.
[3] M100, 2.1.52, annex 673, Diary, Part XXIV, loc. cit.

almost immediately to Malaya and we all know what a success he made of the job.'[1]

The Tiger of Malaya had been loosed. Monty breathed a sigh of relief. But in hoping that General Gruenther would be appointed to succeed Eisenhower Monty was miscalculating American reaction. Instead of Gruenther, General Ridgway was brought back from Korea, where he had performed outstandingly in battle. Unfortunately Ridgway had no time for Monty's conception of the role of British Deputy Supreme Commander—and within months Monty must have wondered whether he would have preferred the snakes and scorpions of Malaya.

[1] General Sir Frank Simpson, loc. cit.

CHAPTER SEVEN

Fighting Ridgway

UNDER EISENHOWER, MONTY had enjoyed unique freedom as Deputy Supreme Commander, acting as his understudy across Europe and encouraged to criticize and even alter strategic and operational policies. Under Ridgway, who succeeded Eisenhower on 1 June 1952, the relationship between Supreme Commander and his Deputy was bound to be different—with Monty soon resenting the clipping of his wings by a man who had served under him as Divisional and Corps Commander in World War II.

Ridgway's first act on assuming Supreme NATO Command was to make clear to Monty that 'there was going to be but one commander—and when my decisions were announced, that was it. There wasn't to be any question about them.' Monty would be free to express his views: 'They would always be given attentive consideration.'[1] But Ridgway was to be the boss.

Friction was inevitable. Both were essentially battlefield commanders, both eager to make decisions rather than procrastinate. Ridgway genuinely admired Monty, but found it difficult to control a man who had already been responsible for European defence at Western Union and NATO for four years. Equally, Monty, having been midwife to NATO's birth, found it impossible to tame his tongue and accept a back-bench position now at SHAPE. His unflagging energy, his sharp inspecting eye, his trenchant military views—all conspired to make him feared and, in some quarters, thoroughly disliked. Moreover his reputation for iron, unalterable judgment was often, disconcertingly, found to be a myth. True, when Monty expressed himself on a certain subject, it was in crystal-clear, decisive and ringing tones. But he would never have achieved such success in his life without the capacity to adjust his views to changing circumstances—and had always been far more of a realist to those who knew him than his public persona allowed. He had, for instance, argued that SHAPE must put forward a strategic plan for the defence of Europe in a possible emergency in 1952, and for possible all-out war in 1954. But having got Eisenhower to issue such a directive in order to unite the staff and subordinate commanders of NATO in a

[1] M. Ridgway, *Soldier*, New York 1956.

common purpose, Monty soon began to change his mind. By the summer of 1952 Monty was quite certain there would be *no* 'hot war' in Europe. Despite the '*tromperie*'[1] of NATO's defences ('So long as France can produce only 12 Divisions after one month of war, it is pure moonshine to talk of a 50 Division NATO Army'[2]) which Monty openly revealed to all connected with NATO in the spring of 1952, his meetings with the politicians of Europe convinced him that NATO would *never* in fact be able to furnish the necessary resources to achieve the targets he and Eisenhower had set. Did they need to? As the spring of 1952 turned to summer Monty became certain that a turning-point had been reached in post-war history. He had never agreed with those—like the Pope and the French—who felt war in 1952 was likely, and for this reason had always argued that SHAPE should base its calculations on a possible war only from 1954 onwards. But current Intelligence suggested that the Russians were *not* intending aggression in 1952, or indeed in the ensuing years, as long as West German rearmament was played down. Did it therefore make sense still to attempt to procure ninety-seven Allied Divisions to be ready by D + 30 in the event of a war from July 1954 onwards? As Monty wrote to the new Supreme Commander, General Ridgway, on 18 July 1952:

> I know of no national plans for producing this number of Divisions. In my view it is impossible to produce an effective land force of this size, if we are to pay due attention to practical and economic possibilities.
>
> It is a matter for consideration as to whether this total of Divisions is, in fact, necessary. In my opinion the figures need re-examining. Having in view scientific progress and development in atomic air warfare, I consider we should be able to hold the West (excluding Greece and Turkey) with a lesser number of Divisions than 97: provided they were fully manned and equipped and were fit to fight by the times they were needed.
>
> I believe that a total of about 60 good Divisions, backed by powerful atomic warfare, would be found to be the sort of force with which we can achieve the object and ensure survival in the opening clashes.[3]

[1] 'The leader in today's *Times* entitled "The Phantom Army" is absolutely true. I might have written it myself! And many people have thought I did! The 50 Division NATO Army is not only a façade: it is a tromperie': letter to the Prime Minister, Winston Churchill, 26.2.52, annex 686, Diary of Field-Marshal The Viscount Montgomery of Alamein, Part XXV (1.2.52–30.5.52), Montgomery Papers.

[2] 'The French Army Situation: Feb. 1952', FM/60, annex 684, Diary, Part XXV, loc. cit.

[3] 'Note for General Ridgway', FM/67, 18.7.52, Annex 715, Diary, Part XXVI, Montgomery Papers.

Even in the desert, in the aftermath of Alamein, Monty had argued for small armies, well-trained and well-equipped, rather than larger, inchoate forces. Throughout his service as CIGS,. at Western Union and NATO, Monty had argued for small, regular armies backed by well-trained reservists as the only practical way in which the Western democracies could equate their military security with economic reality: a belief that went back to his own service as a Territorial or Reserve Division staff officer in 1923.

It was therefore 'the threat of a prolonged cold war' [1] which now exercised Monty's mind, and on 19 July 1952 Monty tackled Ridgway in person on the subject. 'It was quite clear that the Americans were still thinking only in terms of a hot war. They were against any reduction within our force requirements,' Monty's diarist noted. 'General Ridgway was naturally influenced by this thinking. There was no immediate move at SHAPE to set in motion the examination for which the Field-Marshal had asked.' [2] In vain Monty produced another memorandum on 13 August 1952:[3] 'SHAPE: Necessary background to our work.' 'Only *minimum* forces should be got ready to meet an emergency in Europe,' he argued, 'balanced with practical realities, economic possibilities, and scientific developments.' To support these minimum forces, the NATO countries should concentrate on the machinery for training and mobilizing reserves. Talk of hot war should cease. NATO's task should be to get 'an agreed Allied plan, and organisation, to handle and win the cold war'—as well as slotting NATO into the global strategy of the Western nations. 'If we win the cold war there might not be a hot war for a generation, or longer,' Monty prophesied.[4]

Ridgway was not convinced by this sudden volte-face. He was also hurt by the intemperate criticisms Monty had made of SHAPE and NATO at a lecture to the new NATO Defence College in June, during which Monty had declared: 'in the midst of all the wishful thinking, indecision, hesitation, etc. in the NATO nations, I consider that we at SHAPE are in very great danger of losing our clear and simple military purpose. The staff is immersed in details. The output of paper is enormous; I would say that half of it is not read and a good deal of it is not worth reading.' [5]

[1] 'The Need for a New Strategy', Diary, Part XXVI, Montgomery Papers.
[2] Ibid.
[3] FM/68, 13.8.52, annex 716, Diary of Field-Marshal The Viscount Montgomery of Alamein, Montgomery Papers.
[4] Ibid.
[5] 'Notes for NATO Defence College Address of 10.6.52', contained in letter to Ridgway of 18.6.52, annex 720, Diary, Part XXVI, loc. cit.

The American fear was that if SHAPE reduced its targets, the European nations would let up on their commitments to improve their armed forces, necessitating endless US provisions for an indefinite period of years. Moreover, Ridgway's attitude to command was one of hard-hitting combat generalship, firing grenades in war and subordinates in peace. Having just assumed Supreme Command in Europe, Ridgway had no wish to see NATO's planned forces diminished, or its part in global strategy downgraded.

If Monty's turncoat realism about NATO defence stunned Ridgway and the American staff at SHAPE, Monty's volte-face over the European Army surprised Churchill and his new Conservative government. Eisenhower had been the first to change his mind, reversing his erstwhile military objections to the practicality of a homogenous European army at the Rome Conference in November 1951. 'Although the Field Marshal did not say so in public, his feelings were that Eisenhower had made a very serious mistake in coming out so strongly in favour of the European Army,' Monty's diarist had then noted. 'If based on the premise of complete fusion, the European Army concept was bound to fail. General Eisenhower would only lose prestige for having backed a failure.'[1]

Although Monty had backed Eisenhower loyally in public discussion of the matter, in private he had done everything possible to abort the project, writing to Churchill on the eve of the new Prime Minister's journey to Washington in December 1951:

> I have been in the European Defence Organisation since October 1941 and I have seen it grow from nothing. It is my very definite opinion that the nations of Western Europe have not yet reached the stage when their armies can be fused into one.
>
> There are immense political decisions to be agreed before the nations can have a common army, a common budget, a common supranational authority to take vital decisions and give orders to Governments about their armed forces.
>
> The political association must be defined *first*; if we by-pass the political difficulties, and proceed to fuze the armies of Europe, we will get into an awful mess.
>
> That is my view, based on my experience in Europe over the past years. The time for fuzion is not yet.
>
> On the other hand, integration is quite possible: within a clearly defined, military and financial framework.
>
> As a first step in the European Army conception, nations could assign to it such forces as they wish, e.g., certain Divisions. Those

[1] Diary, Part XXIV, loc. cit.

> Divisions should retain their national identity; they would be integrated into a fighting machine under NATO command.
>
> Later, there may come a stage when national armies complete can be assigned to the European Army; but in my view they must always retain their national identity.
>
> Once we destroy national esprit and morale, we will never win battles.
>
> Fusion of national armies—No.
>
> Integration of national armies—Yes, provided the full implications are agreed first.[1]

This had been written on 10 December 1951. Exactly a year later, as Churchill set sail yet again for Washington—this time with Eisenhower President of the United States—Monty wrote both to Churchill and to Eisenhower declaring his change of heart:

> I have changed my mind during the past year about British participation in the European Defence Community and the European Army. A year ago I expressed the view to Mr Churchill, and to you, that the British should not participate until the Treaty had been ratified by all the original signatories and its full implications worked out in practice. Even then, it was my view that the British contribution should be by way of a British contingent to be integrated as an entity rather than fused with the Continental contingents. . . .
>
> I have now come to the conclusion that the French will never ratify unless the British are in the organisation from the start. The Germans might in the end ratify, though this is doubtful. . . . Even if by any chance both France and Germany ratify, it will be by very small minorities and the conception would break down in practice.
>
> So I have now changed my mind and have written to Churchill and to Eden to tell them so. I consider the British must now come into the European Army, and quickly, to save it from crashing on the rocks.[2]

'If the British Government does not join in,' Monty warned, 'then the European Army is dead. And with it will go all possibility of a German contribution to Western European Defence, for the French will never agree to a German participation in NATO.'[3]

This was the cause of Monty's change of mind. The French had

[1] Letter to the Prime Minister, 10.12.51, annex 646, Diary, Part XXIV, loc. cit.

[2] Letter to the Prime Minister, 10.12.52, annex 755, Diary of Field Marshal The Viscount Montgomery of Alamein, Part 27 (7.10.52–15.3.53), Montgomery Papers.

[3] Ibid.

failed to take the leadership of Europe by providing the vital reserve divisions needed to defend Europe in time of war. Therefore the Germans would have to defend Europe—and the only way in which the French would accept the rearmament of West Germany would be under the aegis of a European Army. Ergo, Britain must do everything in its power to encourage the European Army concept, in order to get West Germany to play the major part in the defence of Europe.

Churchill and Eden refused to have anything to do with the European Army concept—which inevitably collapsed. Once again the way had been opened for the French to blame the 'Dunkirk-minded' British for the failure of credible Allied defence in Europe—even though it was French determination to exclude Germany from NATO that was the point at issue.

Churchill, meanwhile, resented the way Monty had 'reversed props' and deliberately countered the British Government's view of the European Army. Summoning him to Chartwell, he remonstrated. He said that Monty 'had put him in a very embarrassing position by his 180° U-turn: that he'd totally reversed and was taking a completely different line from that of the British Government, and that he wasn't to do this again—it was a very bad thing.'

Monty, refusing to be browbeaten, protested that he was not a servant of the British Government but an 'international soldier—an international soldier'.

Churchill's eyes narrowed. 'Well, we pay you—and we can sack you!' he threatened.

Monty shrugged. 'If you sack me I shall write my memoirs—and I'll say a good deal about you!' he retorted.

Chester Wilmot, who heard the story from Field-Marshal Alexander, related that 'Winston grunted and said no more. But the moment Monty left, he rang Alex—then Minister of Defence—told him what had happened and said: "Which do you think would be worse? To leave Monty where he is, making nonsenses like this; or sack him and let him write his memoirs?" And Alex, without a moment's hesitation, said, "Far worse to sack him and let him write his memoirs!"' [1]

The reduction of NATO's planned forces, the shaking-up of SHAPE's paper-clogged bureaucracy and the machinations over the European Army/West German rearmament were not the only matters over which Monty and his new Supreme Commander were at loggerheads. With the accession of Greece and Turkey there were protracted arguments over command, defences, and groupings through-

[1] Chester Wilmot, as recalled by Field-Marshal Lord Carver, interview of 16.5.85.

out NATO. At Monty's insistence, Ridgway finally agreed that Admiral Brind's appointment as C-in-C North be terminated and a soldier, General Mansergh, appointed in his place. In the South a new fourth Command—Allied Mediterranean Command—was created under Admiral Mountbatten to incorporate Greece and Turkey, as Monty had been urging since June 1952. In the centre, Ridgway's approval of a new French plan whereby General Juin would set up a new headquarters as Central Region Supremo, with a C-in-C Land and C-in-C Air Forces each with separate headquarters under him, was quashed—as was planning for the possible Allied retreat and evacuation in the event of Russian attack. But the constant friction and disagreement undoubtedly wore down Monty's patience; more and more Ridgway attempted to ostracize Monty, causing Monty, in turn, to become more and more openly outspoken. 'One cannot go around these days trying to get people to agree with you,' Monty told one audience of American officers; 'you say what you think and then you pass on.'[1] But Ridgway protested that even this 'outsider' form of Deputy Supreme Commander was impermissible. 'It is not possible for a man of your world-wide reputation to deliver yourself of any off-the-cuff purely personal views. You are my Deputy. Whatever you say is going to be construed as an official SHAPE view despite your disclaimers,' Ridgway complained.[2]

Writing to de Guingand in the autumn of 1952, Monty had assumed he would retire after the Queen's Coronation the following summer, at the age of sixty-five and having served in Europe for five years.[3] Then, as the spring of 1953 approached, it became no longer a question of retirement, but of resignation. As Monty made clear to President Eisenhower, he was 'prepared to stay on at SHAPE as a member of any team which had a chance of making a success of the job; so long as he was needed. He was not prepared to stay on under the present regime: a regime which was heading for disaster.'[4] It had become a matter of Ridgway or Montgomery.

[1] Address to the National War College, Washington, 13.4.53, annex 718, Diary, Part 28 (13.3–21.7.53), Montgomery Papers.
[2] M. Ridgway, *Soldier*, op. cit.
[3] Letter of 30.9.52, de Guingand Papers, loc. cit.
[4] Diary, Part 28, loc. cit.

CHAPTER EIGHT

A Difficult Act to Compete With

MONTY'S TRIP TO the USA had begun in March 1953. In Washington, in discussions with Dulles, Bradley and Eisenhower, Monty spoke of 'world strategy' and the need for a declared and positive aim for the West, 'whether in the Far East, the Middle East or in Europe'. 'The main question, however,' his MA noted, 'was that of command.'

> In Europe there was a serious danger that we were going to fail. We had been building up strength with the idea that war was going to come at a particular date. We had not faced up to the fact that we were likely to be in for a period of continuous tension which might last for twenty to thirty years, or more.
>
> What we needed was that the nations should organise themselves so as to be able to cope with the problems. It needed a completely different outlook to that which we had at the moment. Unless we regeared ourselves to this concept, we were in danger of failing in the long term.[1]

The trouble, as Monty saw it, was that SHAPE and NATO were so immersed in details that the staff could not see the wood for the trees:

> The present NATO organisation was in need of complete reorganisation. It was too big, and incapable of giving any decisions. It was immersed in its own outpouring of paper.[2]

This bureaucratic debility could only be cured by high-class command. In this respect Monty felt Ridgway to have been a failure as Supreme Commander, as Monty's diarist noted:

> General Ridgway had proved himself, though no doubt an excellent commander in battle, to be quite incapable of fulfilling his present role. He lacked the touch, and had failed to understand the immensity of the problem which faced us. He was incapable of relating economic possibilities to military requirements. His con-

[1] Diary, Part 28, loc. cit.
[2] Ibid.

tinuous bleating for more and more forces, without any idea of how they were to be maintained over an indefinite period, was doing immense harm. He was unwilling to listen to advice.[1]

By this Monty meant, of course, his own. But according to Monty, Eisenhower agreed—'he had come to the same conclusion himself as to the unsuitability of General Ridgway in his present appointment'.[2]

Monty's solution was that Ridgway should be removed, General Gruenther should be promoted to Supreme Command of NATO, with Monty as his Deputy, and General Norstad as the chief NATO airman. 'This would make a good team, all of whom knew the business, and who could work together.'[3] Unfortunately Eisenhower currently had other plans for Gruenther—intending that he should return to America as Chief of Staff, US Army, with Norstad as Chief of Staff, US Air Force. Eisenhower was also worried that, in removing Ridgway from Europe, he might appear to be bowing to the pressure of press animosity to Ridgway, prevalent in Europe at the time. Monty therefore suggested that Ridgway be transferred to America as Chief of Staff, US Army. According to Monty's diarist, Eisenhower welcomed the idea—even offering to transfer Admiral Carney from NATO to Washington as Chairman of the US Joint Chiefs of Staff,[4] a move that would enable NATO to have a soldier commanding its Southern sector—for which Monty had argued since Eisenhower's first days at SHAPE.

Before Monty left Washington, he had a further after-dinner talk with President Eisenhower. 'At this talk they went through all the proposals which they had discussed. They were in complete agreement. The next morning the President sent for General Bradley and gave him his instructions.'[5] Bradley wrote to Ridgway, asking if he would accept the position of Chief of Staff, US Army in succession to Collins.[6] As Monty wrote with satisfaction to de Guingand, 'I stayed in the White House for a week with Ike and we discussed every problem at length. He is very well. We have got rid of Ridgway; he was a complete failure and had not the brains for the business. He never understood it. . . . Gruenther will be much better.'[7]

[1] Ibid.
[2] Ibid.
[3] Ibid.
[4] Carney became, in fact, Chief of Naval Operations in Washington.
[5] Diary, Part 28, loc. cit.
[6] M. Ridgway, op. cit.
[7] Letter of 2.8.53, de Guingand Papers, loc. cit.

If Monty's machinations to get rid of Ridgway smacked of intrigue, he could at least claim that he was conspiring for the good of NATO. With his visionary foresight, he had argued for almost a year that there would probably be no 'hot' war in Europe in the foreseeable future: and that NATO must start preparing itself for a generation of 'cold' war. The US Secretary of Defense's objection to Gruenther succeeding Ridgway was that 'he had no experience of command'. But Monty replied that NATO needed, in peacetime, brains not brawn: 'The Field-Marshal tried to set Mr Wilson's doubts aside by explaining that this was peace and that we were unlikely to have war in the immediate future. If war should come, changes could always be made.'[1]

Gruenther was, indeed, one of the finest senior staff officers ever produced by the American Army, on a par with and certainly cleverer than Bedell Smith. Monty was adamant that Gruenther was the man NATO needed to effect its transition from the old concept of military confrontation to modern contingency planning of a ruthlessly professional kind. If Gruenther lacked direct command experience,[2] Monty felt his own would make up for this; it was far more important to get NATO off to a new start. And Gruenther, he was certain, was the man to do this: likeable, immensely capable, experienced in dealing with Allies, and a human dynamo in his enthusiasm and determination to get things done.

Meanwhile, in his address to the National War College in Washington, Monty had poured scorn on a senator he had met who had asked if he could produce 'a military plan to finish the war in Korea':

> I said, 'No, of course we can't. And any person who tells you he can is talking nonsense.'
>
> He said, 'A lot of people have told me they can.'
>
> I said, 'They are talking nonsense because nobody can produce a military plan to end the war until you will first say what you want. Why don't you say what you want? Do you want the integrity of South Korea? Do you want to take North Korea and South Korea and weld them into one nation? Or do you want to take the boundary of South Korea and shift it northward to a better defensive line? If you will say what you want, the fighting men could then produce you a plan to achieve it and tell you how much it would cost in money and in blood. Until

[1] Diary, Part 28, loc. cit.

[2] Gruenther had been Chief of Staff to General Mark Clark from 1943 to 1945.

you say what you want, they can't. You have three nations [USA, Britain and France] fighting three wars in the Far East, and no agreed political aim in the Far East. It is absolutely nonsense.'[1]

Monty's realism, for an 'old soldier' on the seeming verge of retirement, was indeed remarkable. If his views on the future of NATO were anathema to General Ridgway, his views on the global future were equally disturbing to the assembled students and staff of the American War College. The West, Monty declared, began with major disadvantages in comparison with Communism—for the political tyrannies of the East enabled them to concentrate their military effort where they wished, irrespective of 'world opinion'; they could simply order increased production of whatever military weapons were needed, and finally could concentrate supreme power 'in the hands of one boss'. By contrast the West dissipated its strength across the globe, disagreed on world strategy, and had too many bosses to get decisions made. It was obvious, Monty felt, that the West must aim to separate Russia from China. 'I believe that eventually that will come. We have got to wait for it. I can't think that there is anything on an ideological basis to link the Chinese with the Russians. Chinese life and everything they do is based on family life, even to their ancestors. That is entirely against the Communist idea. I think the two peoples are not ideologically on the same wave length and eventually will split off.' For this reason Monty declared himself to be a 'non-Formosan'.[2]

Monty was not, however, responsible for the conduct of operations outside NATO—he could but look on and deplore the lack of unified purpose and practical realism. In Europe, however, he hoped he could still contribute. He had fought in North Africa and Europe in World War II and had been at the centre of the post-war defence of Europe since its inception. He knew West Germans, for the moment at least, still hoped for re-unification—Dr Adenauer having confessed to Monty that one day this would have to be achieved by war. 'I said, "Who will do the fighting?" He [Adenauer] said, "You will help." By "you" he meant the Western peoples. I think from that conversation you can see the germ of this matter,' Monty declared to his American audience. 'As a result the French are frightened that Germany will lead them eventually into another war to get this unity. That is what they are frightened about, and they are quite right,' Monty added—for a war in Europe over German re-unification

[1] Address to National War College, 13.4.53, loc. cit.
[2] Ibid.

would be a disaster. The West was therefore committed to maintaining a military shield in Europe against the East, while doing its best to 'win' the 'cold war'. 'We have everything to offer and the other side very little to offer a united Europe. Nothing should be done in developing policy which mitigates against it . . . all of the political measures and propaganda and forecasting should be devoted to trying to achieve that by peaceful means, trying to win them [East Germany, Austria, Yugoslavia, Czechoslovakia, Poland] over to our side.'[1]

If war did, however, take place, Monty's prescription was straightforward. The West could not currently afford to be strong in every department and in every region. Its war strategy must therefore be based on 'giving' in the centre, and maintaining iron flanks to the sides.

> I am quite convinced myself that the Russians would have as their first aim the cutting off of Europe from America. I am also quite convinced that if you cut Europe off from America, Europe will fall inevitably. Therefore it must not happen.
>
> Now, if you agree with that general approach, you find straightaway that it is essential in the beginning of a war to keep this chap's sea and air bases where they are now and in no wise let them come further westward. If you let them come further westward you would have a hell of a war at sea and I doubt if it could be handled. We *could* handle it, but while we were handling it, Europe might fall.[2]

In World War II, the only European nation supplied from across the Atlantic was Britain—and even that was achieved by a very narrow margin against the U-boat menace. To supply the 'whole of the NATO area' would be a nightmare—'the amount of shipping needed to do that will be terrific. . . . It is a nice question whether it can be handled. It can be handled eventually but in the first months it is a question whether Europe won't fall'—for Europe was a cupboard virtually bare in terms of ammunition.

> There is no ammunition made in Europe, no military equipment, nothing; it all comes from across the Atlantic. . . . There is only a three-day supply of 105 ammunition in Europe today. We shoot that off in three minutes these days.[3]

NATO's answer must therefore be to interdict the enemy's sea

[1] Ibid.
[2] Ibid.
[3] Ibid.

passages—'you must cork the Baltic and you must prevent the development of the maximum submarine effort around the North Cape. You must have the Scandinavian flank. You must hold Denmark, that is the key. And it is a devilish hard place to hold. Today there is nothing there—a few bands and boy scouts, that is all—and no Germans yet. . . . The Black Sea must be corked. . . . That means holding Thrace, and holding the Asiatic shore so that you can stop the stuff coming out.'[1]

If the flanks were thus held, 'I would be prepared myself to give a bit in the centre. And I think whether you are prepared to or not, you will have to. I believe that what you would lose in the middle if this flood came at you—I don't say when, I say "if"; it is a great mistake to say "when" we have a war, I say "if"—you could win back again provided you held the flanks. But if you lose the flanks and Italy goes too, it would be jolly difficult to get this back again. I doubt whether you could do it. So the flanks are extremely important in this European strategy which is based on sea power and air power and ringing him around with a chain of air bases all around and then bombing him.'[2] Owing to the vast number of forward enemy bases, it was no good hoping that air effort or atomic bombs would miraculously win the war for the West, however. Though the centre would have to give a little, there must be sufficient forces, sufficiently well stationed, to canalize the tide of the Eastern land forces—and in this balance between air, sea and land power lay the secret of NATO's future success.

Given without notes, this address was a tour de force, illustrating the range of Monty's strategic understanding alongside his legendary professionalism. Though the chorus of Press observers predicted his imminent departure, like Ridgway, from NATO, Monty had good reason to believe he was still an important voice in Paris and Fontainebleau.

What Monty could not see was that his own fame, calibre and experience made the position of an incoming American Supreme Commander of NATO extremely awkward, once Eisenhower left SHAPE. Alone at SHAPE Monty knew all the leading politicians and military personnel of the NATO nations; indeed, even non-NATO nations wished to consult him, such as Switzerland and Yugoslavia. Alone at SHAPE he had inspected not only the headquarters of the various NATO command sectors, but the entire 'battle-front' of what he called 'my parish'—stretching 'from Norway southwards across Europe to Italy and Sicily—thence eastwards to

[1] Ibid.
[2] Ibid.

the Caspian Sea, including Greece and Turkey. A truly gigantic area.'[1] Alone at NATO, Monty knew and vainly stressed the importance of centralized air power, urgently requiring a C-in-C Air at SHAPE. His CPX Exercises were NATO's only attempts to rehearse its higher command and communications in peace-time. It was a difficult act with which to compete, let alone to follow—and Ridgway's last months of office as Supreme Commander were, as will be seen, fraught with misunderstandings and disagreement.

[1] Letter to de Guingand, 31.3.53, de Guingand Papers, loc. cit.

CHAPTER NINE

The Story of the Ring

MEANWHILE, IF MONTY'S NATO act was a difficult one to follow, his parental act was even more difficult—as Monty's son David increasingly found.

After seeing David through National Service and University education at Trinity College, Cambridge, Monty learned with the greatest satisfaction that his son was courting the daughter of a Clydeside millionaire shipbuilder, Miss Mary Connell. For a 'people's general' Monty had, like Eisenhower, a surprising respect for millionaires. He declared the match an excellent one, and since David had become a management trainee with the firm of Shell in South-East Asia, he offered to 'take care' of the engagement ring in London—giving rise to what became known in the Montgomery family as the 'story of the ring'.

The Montgomerys were distinguished but relatively poor. Monty had no wish to be embarrassed. In his chauffeur-driven Rolls he therefore drove to a famous Hatton Garden jeweller's, having telephoned to warn of his arrival.

'My son is going to get married,' Monty began. 'He will not be back in this country until the wedding itself. He has therefore asked me to purchase an engagement ring for his bride. I want you to show me all your engagement rings—all your engagement rings.'

On the manager's instruction, trays of engagement rings were brought forth and set down before the Field-Marshal.

Monty surveyed them. 'Which ones are priced over £25?' he enquired. 'I want you to take them away.'

Ring by ring, the more expensive diamonds and precious stones were plucked from the trays and removed.

'Now,' said Monty, 'I want you to put all these'—indicating the remainder—onto two or three trays. I shall return on Thursday with my son's fiancée, Miss Connell. I shall ask to see all your engagement rings—all your engagement rings. You will say certainly, certainly—and bring out these trays,' he ordered, pointing to the rings under £25. 'Is that understood?'

Such guile, on his behalf, did not worry David at the time. On the contrary David was delighted that his father, despite his senior military role at NATO, had found time to help over the engagement ring. 'It was very kind, very helpful and I was very pleased. I thought that was all marvellous. I felt nothing but gratitude—for my father also sent an ADC up to the Connells to help organize the wedding.' At the wedding, in February 1953, Monty decided to wear uniform with decorations, an act considered *de trop* by some, but understandable in that Monty was there alone as David's father, while the church was filled by the bride's mother and father, relatives and friends.

It was only *after* the wedding that David began to be irritated by Monty's increasing habit of claiming authorship for lines he had not written. Because he had taken Mary to select the engagement ring and had offered assistance to the Connells over the wedding, Monty soon convinced himself that he had also been responsible for David meeting Mary in the first place—for the courtship and wedding in fact.

> He decided retrospectively that he'd introduced us, and he had invented the whole thing,

David later remarked with feeling—and wry laughter.

> Quite untrue—most monstrous falsification.[1]

No doubt Monty, in claiming authorship (he was an avid reader of romances, particularly by 'lady' novelists, and corresponded with authors he admired such as Daphne du Maurier) was merely purring at the fulfilment of his wishes that David marry well. At Paris and Fontainebleau he might exhort NATO to 'fit a new gearbox' and enter fully the new age of professionalism, with minimal troops in the field, atomic weapons and the right frame of mind to encompass the prospect of cold war in Europe for another thirty years; but at home he was the traditional distant Victorian father delighted by his son's scintillating marriage—and soon began to boast over the match and the way he personally had inspired and guided it, like his precious lovebirds in Sicily and Italy.

Had this been all, it could be forgiven on the part of a now ageing soldier, his mind undoubtedly beginning to show the marks of a lifetime's erosion in war and superhuman responsibility. But, as with Monty's rejection of his mother in her dotage, the relationship suggested a deeper, more malicious streak. David had chosen to work for an international company in the hope it would give him a chance to make his own way in life, independent of his father's fame. He had no inheritance and, having done well at school, university and

[1] 2nd Viscount Montgomery of Alamein, interview of 11.5.84.

National Service, wanted earlier responsibility than was usually given in England. Why then did Monty delight in telling strangers that, as with David's marriage, he, Monty, had 'engineered' David's job at Shell—and that without his influence, David's prospects were limited?

That Monty loved David and was intensely proud of him is beyond question. But the gremlin that had so often marred Monty's life, a malicious desire to deride, diminish, downgrade the achievements of others, now caused him to do the same with his own son, irritating David and leading inexorably to their 'family feud' some years later, as Monty cut David out of his will and they refused to speak to one another. The self-discipline Monty had exercised so implacably in mastering his profession and in devoting himself to it so wholly since the death of Betty was bound, perhaps, to have repercussions—as even Monty was at times aware. When staying with his erstwhile Personal Assistant, Trumbull Warren, in Canada on one occasion, Monty first encouraged, then resented Warren's attempt to celebrate his birthday by a children's party.

> 'Sir,' I said, 'the children know your birthday's coming, and it's the practice here: we have a cake, and then they have ice cream and so on. The children would like this—would you mind?'
>
> He said, 'No, not a bit—get a photographer.'
>
> So we had the local guy make us a big cake with soldiers on it and so on—Monty inspecting the Eighth Army. Pictures were taken, the children had their ice cream and eventually went back to their grandmother. Monty then went straight to his room—this was about five o'clock in the afternoon.
>
> We had dinner about 7.30. And the practice was, he'd come down fifteen to twenty minutes before dinner and have a tomato juice while Mary [my wife] and I had a drink.
>
> This time he came downstairs right on the dot, 7.30. We went in, had dinner. It was very quiet. Something was up, you could feel it. After dinner he went right upstairs.
>
> I said to Mary, 'There's something gone wrong. I can feel it—I know this guy so well. He's furious about something—something's happened.'
>
> Mary said, 'Well, what do we do?'

Warren had learned in the war that 'every once in a while the old man got bloody-minded—and then you got the hell away from him'. He instructed his wife:

> 'You just keep quiet, that's what you do. I'm going to get out of

here first thing in the morning and go to the office, early. I'll let you handle the guy.'

About 9.30 Mary phoned me at the office. She was in tears. 'My God,' I asked, 'what's happened?'

She said, 'He came downstairs this morning. I'm sitting at the end of the dining room table in my dressing gown and I've got my coffee there with the paper, and he came and put his arms around me and gave me a kiss and he said: "I want to apologize for my behaviour last night. It's the first birthday party I've had since my wife died and I couldn't handle it. . . ."'[1]

'Now there's the other side of the guy,' Warren reflected, shaking his head.

Lady Templer, wife of Sir Gerald Templer, also found out how, behind the austere and rigid façade, there often beat a heart of gold—as instanced by the way Monty first promised, then actually visited her eight-year-old son in his first term at boarding school in England while General Templer dealt with the insurgency in Malaya. 'My dear Peggy,' Monty wrote in October 1953:

> I am here [at Isington] for a couple of days and fitted in a visit to Miles at Sunningdale. I thought you would like a report early in the term.
>
> I found him in bed in the sick room with a feverish cold, nothing bad. There was one other boy with him also with a cold named Harrison—son of Rex Harrison the actor.
>
> Miles was in very good form and has quite settled down I would say. The other boys like him. I took him some Turkish Delight and some picture magazines; he got down to the Turkish Delight at once, and so did Harrison! . . .
>
> I also had a good talk with the Matron, *alone*. She is excellent and is good with the boys . . . I always reckon the Matron is one of the most important people at a prep school. . . .
>
> So altogether I reckon Miles is O.K. and is in a good place; he is quite happy and likes it. He was very lonely and upset the first day or two; that is natural; now he is geared to the new life, and accepts it and is happy. . . .
>
> The crux of the matter is that Miles is all right, is happy, accepts his new life, and is in good hands! You therefore need not worry.[2]

Monty telephoned the school before returning to NATO, and continued to visit Miles whenever in England—writing in the spring

[1] Lt-Colonel Trumbull Warren, interview of 9.11.81.
[2] Letter of 2.10.53, Templer Papers, National Army Museum.

of 1954: 'When I said goodbye to him I said, 'Will you give me a kiss before I go.' He flung his arms round my neck and kissed me. I should add that there was no one else in the room! He is a dear lad and I love him.'[1]

In the adult world, however, Monty's feelings remained quixotic. His insistence on being in command of a situation, of gaining and holding the initiative, meant that he did not always respond well to expectations or impositions of a personal nature—as the son of David's wartime guardian Phyllis Reynolds found when Phyllis died.

'I'd always thought that when my father died, Monty might marry my mother,' Tom Reynolds recalled in 1978.

> But then something happened, went wrong.
>
> Then later, my mother collapsed with a heart attack, after ghastly deep-ray treatment for a growth in her breast. I'd already informed Monty that I was going to see her. She seemed to be getting better; she said she would run me to the station in the car. I gave her a kiss—and she collapsed.
>
> I thought it would be right to ring Monty. Of course I had his ex-directory number.
>
> I rang him. I said, 'Is that Field-Marshal Montgomery?'
>
> He said, 'No, this is Field-Marshal the Viscount Montgomery of Alamein.'
>
> I said, 'It's Tom speaking.'
>
> 'Tom who?''
>
> I said, 'Tom Reynolds.'
>
> 'What do you want?'
>
> 'I thought, Field-Marshal——'
>
> He said, 'I'm Field-Marshal Montgomery!'
>
> I said, 'Field-Marshal, I thought you'd like to know my mother died half an hour ago.'
>
> 'Oh,' he said. There was a pause.
>
> 'I'll tell David when I next write to him.'
>
> And he hung up.
>
> He didn't send any flowers to the funeral. He wasn't represented.
>
> The tragedy was, David rang me up when he got back from abroad, a year later, and said, 'I've been ringing "Aunt" Phyllis and I'm getting no reply.'

There was a pause as Reynolds, deeply moved by the recollection, drew breath.

[1] Letter of 8.3.84, Templer Papers, National Army Museum.

Monty had not even told David.[1]

Such behaviour was inscrutable. As he turned against his own son David, so too would Monty feud with his brother Brian, with old colleagues, advisers, friends—often after some impetuous action which Monty was too proud to reconsider or apologize for. It seemed at times as though his deeper insecurity led him to commit follies almost calculated to produce such effects—just as, when a boy in Tasmania, he had thrown himself in the long grass of his parents' garden, knowing that he had done wrong and that retribution must come, whispering, 'What have I done? What have I done?'[2] Whether such impulsive actions stemmed from a desire to free himself of a restraint that irked him, or whether, child-like, he wished to 'test' the feelings of those around him, must remain a speculation. This self-destructive urge—at least destructive of Monty's better, socially acceptable self—continued to assail him, as will be seen, virtually to his dying day: a cruelty, almost, that he could not contain within himself: a Norman predilection that made him a formidable foe, but a tyrant-father—and NATO's most critical taskmaster.

[1] Major Tom Reynolds, interview of 19.3.78.
[2] A. Moorehead, *Montgomery*, London 1946.

CHAPTER TEN

The New Approach

THE FACT THAT General Ridgway was to be transferred to Washington in the summer of 1953 aroused no compassion in Monty; and until the day of Ridgway's departure the two men continued to clash. By August 1953 Monty was writing to de Guingand: 'Things are bad and NATO is moving to a crisis. Rearmament has reached its peak and there will now be a decline; Marshal [sic] aid will cease. There is no agreed political aim, or strategic aim, on a global scale. We are drifting towards chaos.'[1]

Ridgway's response was all wrong, Monty felt; and when Ridgway began to tamper with Monty's forthcoming CPX Three exercise, planned for November 1953, there were inevitable ructions. It was intended to be 'a gigantic exercise, on a scale which has probably never been attempted before anywhere in the world',[2] building on the lessons learned in Monty's CPX Two exercise, which concerned the use of tactical atomic weapons. Soon, however, there were protests at the scenario for CPX Three: namely, a Russian invasion in which Denmark was to be overrun before the exercise even began. Ridgway 'started to try and tinker with the strategic setting', Monty later chronicled in a history of his eight NATO CPX Exercises.[3] From America he wrote to his Principal Staff Officer that 'there are too many cooks and, between them, they will ruin what *could* be a good exercise'.[4] It was also a very expensive one, involving the move of Supreme Headquarters into the field for the first time since its inception in 1951, with full communications to subordinate commanders, also in the field, right across Europe. 'It may well be that the organisation [NATO] cannot digest such strong meat just at present; the conception is too vast for the nations to follow, and there are too many vested interests over the 4000 mile front.'[5] Monty

[1] Letter of 2.8.53, de Guingand Papers, loc. cit.

[2] Diary, Part 28, loc. cit.

[3] 'Summary of CPX's One–Eight', 1952–1958, Montgomery Papers. This was drawn up confidentially for Monty by his staff. An 'Official CPX Report' was subsequently produced for distribution at SHAPE, summarizing the summary.

[4] Letter to Maj-General Wansbrough-Jones, 7.4.53, annex 795, Diary, Part 28, loc. cit.

[5] Ibid.

therefore recommended cancellation, with an indoor exercise in its place like CPX Two. His opinion of—and relations with—Ridgway, however, deteriorated still further as a result—particularly when Monty's conception of CPX Four, planned for April 1954, was also compromised by Ridgway, who objected to the controversial scenario: a withdrawal by Allied troops to the Rhine, followed by a battle in which some penetrations across the river were made by the Russians, in order 'that SHAPE should be exercised'. This exercise was also therefore cancelled, to be replaced by an indoor exercise.

In Monty's view, Ridgway had interfered with his preserve. In retaliation, therefore, he openly disagreed with Ridgway's Supreme Commander's Annual Report to the NATO Standing Group, chaired by Bradley. When he saw it in draft Monty commented that the report was 'far too long and verbose', that it was 'wholly unsuitable for world-wide publication to the enemy about the effectiveness of the NATO forces'; that it 'should have emphasized the need for a long-term aim and not taken a somewhat short-sighted view of the problems to 1955 or 1956', and that it contained 'too much political matter'.[1] Ridgway, smarting at these criticisms, now objected to Monty travelling to Yugoslavia as the guest of Marshal Tito—'a dirty trick' as Monty's diarist remarked, since earlier in the year Ridgway had given his blessing to the visit.

The rift between the men was reaching an almost de Lattre-like level. In Monty's openly expressed opinion SHAPE was cumbersome, inefficient, and, for all its 'bleatings' about the need for more troops, incapable of mutating into a command headquarters in the event of war. It also had a faulty air command set-up. Monty's opinion of Ridgway was equally outspoken. In a conversation with Gruenther on 16 June 1953, Monty made clear his views:

> The affairs of the defence organisation of NATO are approaching a crisis. Ridgway has never had the wisdom or the vision to understand the problem, as is proved by his Annual Report just published—which is a frightful document. But as soon as he leaves, the new Boss must put the problem to the staff at SHAPE and work must begin on producing a simple and clear plan to solve it.
>
> The problem is this.
>
> Originally there was no military strength in the West and it was necessary to create quickly such forces as would provide a deterrent to war and give confidence to the nations of Western Europe. That was in fact the short term aim. The work on that

[1] Diary, Part 28, loc. cit.

aim has been proceeding for some years and we can now say that if the Russians attacked us today it would no longer be a walk-over; we could certainly hold them east of the Rhine for say two to three weeks, due chiefly to atomic air power and to the land forces we have created. . . .

But the economic ceilings are being reached and nations cannot carry much longer the enormous defence budgets of today. Indeed, next year we shall see certain nations having to reduce their armed forces that they keep in being in peace time.

Ridgway keeps on bleating for more 'active forces'. This is quite useless. He ignores the economic factor. Rearmament is near its peak and will soon level off.

Some other and more realistic approach is needed than merely trying to build up large 'active' forces—which it is not possible to do, and which could not be maintained over the years even if they *could* be produced.

Furthermore we have now got to build on a long term basis; it is not merely a matter of completing the short term aim; the two have got to be carefully woven together.

The new approach must have vision.[1]

'Nothing can, of course, be done till Ridgway goes,' Monty wrote in his record of the 'conversation' with Gruenther—a conversation in which only one party did the talking! Monty even expressed the hope, in a covering note, that when Ridgway left in July 1953, 'the *whole* of the Supreme Commander's personal staff will depart with him', since the 'attitude that is shown by the Supreme Commander's Office could hardly be worse'.[2]

That Monty, as Deputy Supreme Commander, was prepared to criticize his Supreme Commander was ungentlemanly; but for all its personal derision it was a statement of professional conviction, derived from Monty's desire always to look ahead, and to get things moving; to start the post-Ridgway era on a new footing. It was addressed to Gruenther for the reason that Gruenther was to be the new Supreme Commander in four weeks' time. Given the continuing political insecurity of NATO—politicians now responding to political pressures to reduce spending on NATO defence—Monty's attitude, moreover, was salutary. Just as he believed in economy of effort and

[1] 'Record of a conversation with General Gruenther on 16 June 1953', annex 783, Diary, Part 28, loc. cit.
[2] Ibid.

priorities in war, so too did he believe in these same virtues in peace. 'In the past the essential has always been to insist on large land armies as the first essential in our defence organisation. This attitude is not in keeping with modern times or with our particular problem,' he had lectured Gruenther.[1]

> Sea power and air power are the first two essentials. If we lose control of the seas, Europe falls. If we cannot hold our own in the air, Europe falls. We want to determine, then, the minimum land forces necessary to hold the situation until nations can spring to arms and get their reserves into action and their national war machines into full gear. . . .
>
> The problem is to find the right balance between active forces 'in being' in peace time, and reserve forces that can be mobilised quickly. . . . The system must be in full accord with practical realities and economic possibilities. . . .
>
> The whole object of the above outline philosophy is to get the national war machines so organised that nations can handle any emergency for 50 years ahead, without damaging their peace time economies. From the military angle this involves finding the correct balance between active and reserve forces, and also an organisation which will produce *effective and well trained* reserve formations quickly after mobilisation is ordered.[2]

'So far as I am concerned there is nothing new in the above philosophy,' Monty added. 'I have urged its adoption consistently to Ridgway; but he never understood it. We are now in grave danger of losing the cold war. Unless we take steps quickly to implement the above philosophy, we will be done.

'I proved this to Eisenhower in Washington in April and it is for this reason that Ridgway is being removed, as you know. You, Gruenther, must now succeed. We cannot afford to fail in Europe.'[3]

Such kingmaking—complete with the King's Speech to the Commons—might well have been resented by Gruenther. It was certainly resented by Ridgway, whose farewell ceremony at Orly airport Monty did not even attend, pleading a prior engagement. Fortunately Gruenther admired Monty and knew his heart was in the right place. NATO *was* in the 'doldrums', tied to an arms and troops race it could never win, with a top-heavy Supreme Headquarters incapable of taking effective field command, and with a faulty air command set-up.

[1] Ibid.
[2] Ibid.
[3] Ibid.

No sooner had Gruenther formally assumed command on 11 July 1953 than he instituted, at Monty's urging, a 'New Approach Group': in this way he was able to channel Monty's constant concern with the future and with NATO's mission and effectiveness into a constructive channel. Moreover, however rude Monty's critiques of NATO might be—and, spoken to large gatherings by a legendary British Field-Marshal they were often breath-takingly rude (such as when Monty circulated a note beginning: 'I have always considered that junior members of the staff at SHAPE do not understand the place of Austria in Western Defence. They fail to see the problem whole or to see it true. The first thing to understand is that the Austrians are useless when it comes to fighting. They are good waiters, singers and barbers; but they are useless at fighting.'[1] Or in an address, commenting on the SHAPE exercise 'Try-Out Two' on 20 July 1953: 'On no account must we become a mutual congratulation society: which we are inclined to be. . . . Do not let us try and hide things. Let us be honest; let us speak the truth. . . . The broad criticism we must accept is that our headquarters . . . is amateur. . . . There is no clear understanding among all the officers of the staff as to the function of SHAPE in war. . . . Air power is the dominant factor in modern war. . . . There must be an Air set-up at SHAPE [to wield centralised air control]. It does not exist. . . . The senior officers do too much work and have no time to think; the juniors have not enough to do, have plenty of time to think, but do not know what to think about'[2]—Monty never contented himself with criticism. His rudeness was always a technique to jerk people into constructive thought, just as his predictions of disaster, failure, grave danger, etc. were intended to concentrate the minds of his audience. Used constructively, Monty's energy, analytic ability and world renown were of immense potential advantage to NATO—and under Gruenther's leadership they were used to the full. As Field-Marshal Lord Carver later reflected:

> By this time Monty was perfectly clear in his mind that he really had no responsibility; he was excluded by the Americans from any real say as far as any executive action was concerned—which left him actually much freer to do what he wanted!
>
> And he pursued with great enjoyment this function of a gadfly. He would go round and be extremely rude to people like the Danes and the Portuguese. I mean, I went with him to Portugal—and

[1] 'Note on Austria', 23.11.53, in 'Some Correspondence with the PM, 1951 and 1953' file, Montgomery Papers.

[2] 'Comments by F M Montgomery at the Critique: Try Out Two, 20.7.53' file, Montgomery Papers.

really it was *embarrassing* the way he treated them there. It was very amusing—but very embarrassing. I mean, saying things like: 'You're all quite useless, you don't know what you're talking about; you should do this and that, and do away with this. And you should sack all officers over the age of 55.' Well, practically all their officers *were* over 55!

And then, having laid down the law, he'd go back to SHAPE—whereupon of course the Portuguese National Military Representative would go running along to the Chief of Staff and say what dreadful things Monty had said—and the official machine would have to calm things down.

Nevertheless it had served a purpose, for Monty was able to say to them things which the American Commander going round *couldn't* say because it would have been politically insensitive.

Everyone accepted that Monty behaved in a way that nobody else was allowed to behave.

He didn't like Ridgway. I think he tried to treat Ridgway in a way that he knew he couldn't have treated Ike—I think he told Ridgway what to do and bossed Ridgway around—that sort of thing. And Ridgway wasn't going to have that. Whereas Gruenther—between them Al Gruenther and Larry Norstad handled Monty to perfection. They had him absolutely taped. They buttered him up, flattered him like mad, told him they were consulting him—Gruenther was superbly good at it: had Monty eating out of his hand.[1]

Gruenther was adamant that ultimately NATO policy would be decided by the Americans—particularly in relation to nuclear weapons. Since Monty was prepared to act as NATO gadfly, an unimpeachable, roving Inspector-General, and to offer thoughtful views on strategy and organization without seeking to interfere with American decision-making it made sense to *use* Monty rather than to fight him—and it was both Gruenther's and Norstad's talent to recognize this and to harness Monty's unique experience, fame and pungent critical mind to the Supreme Commander's chariot. By humouring Monty, Gruenther humoured Great Britain, America's most important European ally—whereas Ridgway's unpopularity with the French, who deeply resented the way they were effectively excluded from all decision-making, certainly played a part in their ultimate secession.

Overnight, with Ridgway's departure and Gruenther's more flexible attitude, SHAPE buzzed with a new vocabulary: The 'New

[1] Field-Marshal Lord Carver, loc. cit.

Vision Group', the 'New Look' or 'New Approach' policy, the concept of the 'long haul'. In Monty's eyes the summer of 1953 marked the turning-point in NATO's fortunes. His file '1953—Present State of the game in NATO' contained 'possibly the most important papers I ever wrote during my time at SHAPE . . . written half-way through my 10 years in Western Defence.'[1] Morale at SHAPE soared, and sector commanders like Richard Gale, the C-in-C Northern Army Group, found Monty's 'new look' approach a great help in formulating their contingency battle plans. As Gale pointed out, 'I do not think we shall have sufficient land forces in peace at any time to justify our forcing a major conflict so far East [the line of the Elbe]. As you put it, we will be asking for defeat in detail.'[2] Better by far to recognize the economic realities of 'long haul' cold war, and to make paper plans that were realistic rather than idealistic—for Ridgway's artificial assumptions merely led commanders such as Juin to prepare secret plans for retreat into France and even North Africa,[3] since it was obvious the line of the Elbe could not be held without a German army (still politically unacceptable in Western as well as Eastern Europe) and a level of American and European rearmament over the next thirty years that would cripple the West.

Gruenther's succession and Monty's 'New Approach' swept away the assumptions and fetters of the past five years. From being on the brink of resignation/retirement, Monty was given a new lease of life at NATO, and may truly be said to have engineered its transformation in 1953. At Monty's insistent urging, General Norstad was moved from Juin's Central Sector Command to become the first Allied C-in-C Air alongside the Supreme Commander, and from then on Gruenther, Norstad and Monty ruled as a triumvirate—Monty begging Gruenther not to abandon NATO after a single year in the manner of his predecessors. 'In this team you as the Boss, and Norstad as your air adviser, are absolutely essential. You must both stay at SHAPE till the end of 1955; if either of you were to go before that date, we might well fail. I mention this because so far no Supreme Commander has remained at SHAPE more than one year.'

Given Monty's role in the removal of Ridgway after only one

[1] Annotation to '1953—Present State of the Game' file, Montgomery Papers.

[2] Letter of 19.6.53, 'Removal of Ridgway' file, Montgomery Papers.

[3] 'Once again the suggestion arose that a plan should be prepared for a withdrawal West of the Rhine. This time it came from Marshal Juin himself. This was not entirely unexpected as Marshal Juin had been saying for some time that such a plan should be prepared. . . . In the event of the worst happening he could now say that he had recommended such a study being made.' Ridgway authorized a 'staff study should be made behind locked doors'. Monty was 'quite adamant that it should not be studied at SHAPE': Diary, Part 28, loc. cit.

year, this was a bit steep. Monty himself was prepared to defer his retirement. 'I myself am prepared to stay here with you till the end of 1955: that is if you want me,' he added.[1]

In the circumstances, Gruenther had little choice.

[1] 'Note for Supreme Commander', 24.11.53, in '1953—SHAPE: What is to be done? Who is to do it?' file, Montgomery Papers. Writing to Arthur Bryant in the Spring of 1954 Monty considered he was 'likely to be in my present job till the end of 1955. I shall then retire from active work as I reckon I will by then have done my part in helping to get the Western nations properly geared; and by then any danger of a premeditated "hot" war will have receded into the background. In fact we can then look forward to 15 to 20 years of peace.

'I would like then to spend 1956 in writing my story of the business. The inside story of the war as seen by me, and what went on after the war was over—which is of enormous interest': letter of 16.3.54, Bryant Papers.

CHAPTER ELEVEN

NATO's Blacksmith

AS ARCHITECT OF the 'New Look', Monty was intimately involved in the New Approach Group, which produced a radically revised NATO defence programme for the North Atlantic Standing Group in July 1954. Not only did Monty brief and advise the New Approach Group, but he undertook to put across in person the new approach to all constituent NATO defence staffs and NATO commanders. He was featured in *Time* magazine in an article entitled 'The Blacksmith': forging the NATO weapon afresh. He insisted on a scientific adviser being appointed to SHAPE (an appointment Ridgway had resisted).[1] He also wanted World War III to be rewritten in his CPX exercises in the light of atomic weapons.

Such efforts would have a marked effect on NATO strategy and tactics; together with the likely contribution of West German troops, they would soon produce the possibility of fighting the Russians on the line of the Elbe rather than the Rhine—and Monty was adamant that the ramifications be studied well in advance, particularly the air aspects.

Monty was, in truth, the 'dynamo' behind NATO's new and confident rôle in the peace of Europe: responsible for drafting the 'Emergency Defence Plan' of October 1954 and for guiding the submission of Gruenther's new NATO proposals to the Standing Group in the summer of 1954. As 'Inspector-General' of NATO he sought to spread the new gospel from Norway to Portugal and to Turkey; but he abhorred complacency, and no senior officer within SHAPE could be more lacerating in his criticisms or more professional in his analysis.

As Field-Marshal Carver later recalled, Monty's annual CPX Exercise was 'one of the most valuable things' Monty contributed at SHAPE—valuable for NATO in that it was 'an opportunity to get

[1] Memorandum for the Supreme Commander, 17 August 1953, annex 811, Diary of Field Marshal The Viscount Montgomery of Alamein, Part 29 (22.7.53–23.10.53), Montgomery Papers. 'Military/Scientific Forward Planning, Memorandum for the Supreme Commander,' 22 January 1954, annex 833, Diary of Field Marshal The Viscount Montgomery of Alamein, Part 30 (23.10.53–27.1.54), Montgomery Papers.

together all those senior officers from the whole of NATO who didn't see each other otherwise at all' and also as a chance 'to look at NATO problems and discuss them'. In Lord Carver's view, CPX was 'very much a Monty do' not only because Monty was entirely responsible for its mounting, but because he was the only soldier at NATO with sufficient individuality and independence to organize such controversial, self-questioning discussions. 'Monty greatly *enjoyed* them,' Carver emphasized, 'because here he was at the centre of the stage in front of everybody else, running entirely his affair and nothing to do with the Supreme Commander.'[1]

This stage-aspect disturbed the French—'it was of course impossible to get the French to take part in the playlets, and only very reluctantly was an American officer persuaded'.[2] To the French, Monty's playlets were not taking war seriously enough; moreover the subsequent cloth-model symposia under Monty's headmastership aroused a mixture of resentment and envy. As always there was a ban on smoking; participants were summoned, at the end of the interval, by Monty himself ringing a bell or blowing a whistle. 'The last to come in were always Mountbatten and Juin,' Carver related. 'On one occasion Juin was dressed in a particularly World War I uniform: breeches with lots of bits of gold braid and oak leaves and things. Monty was standing on the huge model of the Mediterranean, having blown the whistle to get everybody back in their seats. And as Juin went past, out of the side of his mouth he said, in French: "What do you think you're doing there? There's only been one man who could walk upon the sea—and you're certainly not him!" '[3]

The culmination of each CPX was Monty's closing address, in which Monty gave out 'what would become the foundation of all his public speaking for the following year', Carver maintained.[4] Thus, at the conclusion of his CPX Four exercise, Monty sought to 'peer into the future': to 'look through a window at World War III'—a war in which the use of pilotless aircraft or missiles would gradually dominate the battlefield, imposing new tactical strategy on commanders. The NATO air forces were alive to this: not so the land forces, or political leaders responsible for commissioning the land forces. 'It is my view that if we went to war as things stand today, the land forces would fail us and would let the whole NATO team

[1] Field-Marshal Lord Carver, loc. cit.
[2] Ibid.
[3] Ibid.
[4] Ibid.

down very badly,' Monty declared—instancing the case of NATO reserve divisions.

> Does anyone in this room really consider that hastily mobilised reserve Divisions, which have been assembled for training only for a few days every second or third year, and in some cases not even *that* . . . does anyone here really consider that such Divisions are fit to take part in the early stages of mobile warfare in an atomic age? . . .
>
> Quite apart from all this, the tactical conceptions of our land forces are not such as are likely to give us victory in an atomic age; they are based on what we did in the late war, and to continue to organise and train our troops in the fashion of 1944/5 is folly. . . .
>
> Let us be honest and face facts, and give up living in a dream.[1]

It is easy to see how Monty's uncompromising professionalism and directness made him a prickly associate, and increasingly easy Press target. For security reasons no public account could be given of the workings of NATO or of Monty's actual contribution. Thus Americans soon appropriated the credit for the 'New Look'—the US Foreign Secretary remarking in December 1953 of his recent visit to NATO: 'We found the organisation in good shape. And it has adapted itself to a new concept which the United States brought to NATO at the meeting of last April.'[2] A leader in the *New York Herald Tribune* went further: 'If imitation is the sincerest form of flattery, then the designers of the American "new look" military policy must have felt sincerely flattered when the British Minister of Defence, Lord Alexander, gave a kind of preview, the other day, of the "new look" at which Britain, also, has been arriving.' As Monty's diarist noted tartly, 'these conceited and typical outbursts could not be a greater distortion of the facts.'[3]

In Paris, meanwhile, Monty had done his best to ensure the success of NATO's 'new approach' policy. Once Gruenther and the SHAPE staff had embraced it, Monty's thoughts began to pass again to the larger, global context of Western defence. With the British Press playing up the latest Woodford telegram story—the *Daily Express* running a headline across its entire front page: 'MONTY: I did get the order. New mystery after Winston apology'[4]—Monty's speech

[1] 'SHAPE CPX Four—Closing Address by DSACEUR', 30.4.54, annex 861, Diary of Field-Marshal The Viscount Montgomery of Alamein, Part 31 (28.1.54–30.4.54), Montgomery Papers.

[2] *New York Times*, reporting address by Mr Dulles to National Press Club, 22.12.53.

[3] Diary, Part 30, loc. cit.

[4] On 23.11.54 Churchill related in a speech at Woodford that he had ordered Monty

to the English-Speaking Union in New York was barely reported: 'At present we have only the North Atlantic Treaty Organisation. There is a small beginning in South-East Asia, as a treaty organisation has been signed in that region. We still lack, however, the global organisation, and we lack an agreed political aim on a global basis which is sufficiently clear to guide military strategy. . . . The Communist bloc is centrally directed from Moscow. The free nations have no such advantage.'

The tragedies of French Indo-China, of Vietnam, and Suez would all testify to Monty's sad prognosis: that by dissipating their national efforts locally across the globe, the free nations were risking defeat in detail. In vain Monty had begged Eden and Churchill, in the winter of 1953/54, to incorporate the defence of the Suez Canal into the NATO umbrella, rather than preserving it as a British problem. 'I intend to press upon Eisenhower the active and complete co-operation of Britain and the United States in winding up the Egyptian entanglement,' Churchill responded, minuting his Chiefs of Staff and Minister of Defence. Nothing however came of the idea: and the way for subsequent American abandonment of its Anglo-French allies in 1956 was opened.

---

in May 1945 to stack all captured German arms lest it prove necessary to re-arm the Germans in order to fight the Russians. Owing to the subsequent 'hoo-ha', Churchill retracted his claim. In fact he *did* send Monty such an order, on the Ultra link, which was afterwards destroyed (letter from Monty to Churchill, 6.12.54, Montgomery Papers). Monty in fact asked permission to destroy the weapons on 14.6.45 (M584) as they required so many troops to guard them. 'Things were pretty hectic in those [June 1945] days,' Monty later noted in an annotation to his files. 'The Coalition Government was coming to an end; a General Election was imminent; it was impossible to get a decision, a firm one on anything. I got no answer. I waited for one week. I then gave orders for all the personal weapons and equipment to be destroyed! . . . I never heard any more about it': 'The Telegram' file, Montgomery Papers.

CHAPTER TWELVE

Suez

For years, since the unhappy reign of General Ridgway, Monty had argued that a 'hot' war was unlikely in Europe in the coming years, and that NATO's role must be part of a global strategy agreed by the Western Allies. With the accession of West Germany in 1955,[1] the burden of NATO's defensive shield in central Europe ought now to be carried by the Germans, Monty argued—having decided to defer his retirement. As far as possible the remaining allied troops in the Central NATO Sector should withdraw to their own countries, leaving only Corps formations under eventual German Army command. This would be cheaper; it would be logistically more efficient; and above all it would permit the great nations of the West to concentrate their strength on those areas of the world where the Russians chose to challenge the Western democracies.

Having set out this personal view, Nasser's nationalization of the Suez Canal in July 1956 and his flirtation with the USSR (importing Russian arms and technicians) seemed to Monty the very challenge the Western Allies must confront if they were ever to maintain their credibility as guardians of the Middle East. Monty had not himself supported the Jewish conquest of all Palestine in 1948–9; however by the mid-1950s he had grown to accept the *de facto* position of Israel in the Middle East—indeed considered Israel to be one of the West's primary pillars against the spread of Russian-backed Communism in the area. Nasser's secret talks with other Arab states over the 'rubbing out' of Israel seemed to Monty, in conjunction with Nasser's Russian flirtation, too dangerous to condone. For this reason Monty urged the CIGS, and the new Minister of Defence, Brigadier Anthony Head (an old WWII associate) to be firm in handling

[1] Monty had done perhaps more than any other Allied soldier to bring Germany into NATO. When asked his reaction to those who feared a revival of German militarism, he replied 'with a trace of a smile: "Well, I have fought them twice in my life, but my answer is always the same; we have got to trust the Germans. And you must remember too that if we have them with us inside the NATO organisation it is just not going to be possible for any single nation to take independent action without being stopped. German forces, like anybody else's, would be under SHAPE. The old-fashioned sort of German nationalist militarism just isn't on" ': Gordon Young interview, *Daily Mail*, 8.9.54.

Nasser during the Suez crisis in the autumn of 1956. 'The part played by the Field-Marshal [Montgomery] during this time will probably never be generally realised and never officially recognized,' Monty's diarist remarked[1]—for Monty became the quasi-official medium by which the British Chiefs of Staff kept in touch with General Paul Ely, Chairman of the French Chiefs of Staff. As Monty's diarist put it: 'The Field Marshal also kept in close touch with the French through General Ely . . . not only ensuring that they should be fully conversant with the United Kingdom viewpoint on the turn of affairs but also giving General Ely great personal encouragement at a time when this was badly needed.'[2] In fact Monty had lunched with Ely on 3 September 1956—two months *before* the Anglo-French invasion of Egypt—to discuss 'the tie-in of French plans with British plans for the invasion of Egypt should the need for armed intervention arise'—in particular 'the shortage of suitable generals to lead the French contingent of an Egyptian Expedition'.[3] It was Monty who first raised at SHAPE, August 1956, the question of Admiral Grantham, C-in-C of NATO's forces in the Mediterranean, handing over his NATO responsibilities to Admiral Glover of the US Navy so that he could take command of the British invasion fleet.

Unlike the First Sea Lord, Lord Mountbatten (who wrote letters to the Prime Minister, Anthony Eden, deploring the impending invasion but did not send them[4]), Monty's commitment to Allied armed demonstration in the Middle East was total—and was undoubtedly the backbone behind General Ely's firmness in France as well as Templer's stand as CIGS in London. 'My dear Gerald,' Monty wrote to Templer on 1 November 1956, as the Speaker of the House of Commons was forced to suspend the sitting in uproar:

> I have just been listening [on the radio] to the Labour tirade in Parliament. *Don't weaken on any account*. Be brave and courageous, and all will be well. I will back you 100%—in American circles at SHAPE and elsewhere. Go in and win.[5]

Israel had attacked on 29 October, and at dawn on 5 November British and French parachute troops landed to pave the way for the short-lived Anglo-French assault on 6 November, which ended with a cease-fire at midnight that night.

[1] Diary of Field Marshal Viscount Montgomery of Alamein, Part 39 (1.8.56–4.3.57), Montgomery Papers.

[2] Ibid.

[3] Ibid.

[4] P. Ziegler, *Mountbatten*, London 1985.

[5] Templer Papers, loc. cit.

Monty was unabashed. He had supported Templer to the hilt and would continue to do so, as he assured the CIGS on 15 November:

> Many people in the NATO area in Europe did not understand the fundamental issues at stake in the Suez Canal problem. This was very much the case at SHAPE, where Gruenther and Norstad were initially inclined to be hostile.
>
> I have managed to stamp on all that, and these two now agree that what was done had to be done. I am continuing to sing the same song throughout the NATO countries, and next May I am going to stay with Ike, and will get him to play.
>
> You can rely on me to back you all one hundred per cent . . . in fact I am with you *to the end.*[1]

That Monty should have formed such a high opinion of someone like Tito—whom he defended before the Pope—and yet cared not a proverbial fig for the desert Colonel who had aroused such popular acclaim in Egypt, was strange—and would be altered when, in later years, Monty visited Egypt as Nasser's guest. But in the autumn of 1956, fixated by the fact that thermo-nuclear weapons made a 'hot' war in Europe unthinkable, Monty espoused his 'global view' of the West's responsibility with a dogmatism that brooked no alternative; and, in his treatment of certain personalities, was downright vindictive. As he wrote to Templer regarding the United Nations troops currently moving into Egypt. 'The great thing is to get them in quickly, even if they are armed only with walking sticks. And we must phase *out* as they phase *in*. Once Nasser refuses to play ball with this force, or tries to "jostle" them in any way, then we pounce on him quickly and settle him once and for all. We must all hope that Nasser will provide the opportunity for us to do this!!'[2]

Needless to say, Nasser did not. Monty, after noble attempts to procure a unified Allied global strategy that would encompass such problems as Suez and the Middle East, had discarded the realism for which he was renowned. Britain and France could not act without American support—and no amount of braveness or courage could help. As at Arnhem, Monty had miscalculated, leaving him bitter and frustrated—an attitude which, after a brilliant start, had also stolen over the manuscript Monty was secretly writing, telling the story of his life.

[1] Annex 1058, Diary, Part 39, loc. cit.
[2] Ibid.

CHAPTER THIRTEEN

Putting the Record Straight

TWO YEARS BEFORE, in the summer of 1954, Monty had made arrangements to become on his retirement 'military consultant' to Kemsley Newspapers. He would also 'write his memoirs (hereinafter called "The Memoirs")'[1] in which Kemsley Newspapers would acquire serial rights. His contract with Denis Hamilton, Editorial Director of Kemsley Newspapers, bound him to complete the writing of 'The Memoirs' within three years from the date of his retirement, which was called the 'starting date'.

It was Freddie de Guingand who, visiting Monty at SHAPE, in 1955, sensed Monty's growing frustration with the rôle of NATO prophet-cum-inspector, and persuaded the Field-Marshal to start writing his memoirs before retirement.[2] Early in 1955 Monty's château at Courances had been repossessed by the Marquis de Ganay. Monty had moved to Eisenhower's wartime HQ, the Trianon Palace Hotel at Versailles—'very comfortable quarters', Monty remarked to de Guingand[3]; and it was there, in the summer of 1955, that Monty had begun to write the story of his life.

At first Monty was avid for advice. 'The first thing is to discuss the problem and try and decide the best way to tackle the job,' he wrote to 'Bill' Williams in August—even offering to come to Oxford (where Williams was Warden of Rhodes House).[4] By mid August Monty was writing to Arthur Bryant:

> You will be interested to hear that I have begun work on the book. . . .
>
> My object is to get out of the way all the early part for which I have no diaries and no papers; everything I possessed was destroyed by enemy bombing in Jan 1941. . . .
>
> In the chapters dealing with my early life I have got to show how my early upbringing influenced my later life, and why it was that I was able to play my part when the opportunity came in 1942.

[1] Contract dated 13.9.54, Papers of Sir Denis Hamilton. A further contract ceding book publishing rights to William Collins was drawn up in November 1954.
[2] Diary, Part 36, loc. cit.
[3] Letter of 8.4.55, de Guingand Papers, loc. cit.
[4] Letter of 11.8.55, Papers of Sir Edgar Williams, IWM.

> Chapter I is headed
>
> 'Boyhood Days'
>
> and that will come to you later. This will be short but very important; it will aim to show what influence my unhappy childhood had on my character.[1]

Chapters 2 and 3 would take the reader up to the Second World War. 'Then will come the really exciting part, and I have not yet decided how to set that out. The whole may require two volumes. . . . The great point now is to get the first three chapters out of the way. One can then begin to think out the remainder of the book.'[2]

To set the scene of his autobiography Monty had already drafted an Introduction which he sent to Bryant—a document which, though later discarded, revealed much of the motivating and conflicting forces behind the venture:

> It is doubtful if the full truth can be told without causing offence in certain quarters, but one can try,

it began.

> It is my view that our troubles since the war ended have their basic origin in mistakes made during the latter part of the war itself, and the responsibility lies with the Allied statesmen who were responsible for the political direction of the contest. . . . Future generations must learn from our mistakes, and they will not be able to learn unless the story is told fearlessly and truthfully.
>
> I am conscious of the fact that I have enemies,

he went on, defensively,

> and many do not approve of my methods. Certain of these thought, and some hoped, that I would fail as the war proceeded.
>
> I know that I have always been a controversial figure, and have attracted trouble round me at every stage in my life. I have often been accused of being tactless, intolerant, vain, etc., etc. and in my younger days probably was. Possibly my accusers might agree that I have mellowed as the years went by but that is not for me to say. I have certainly always been intolerant about military inefficiency, and have been ruthless in dealing with it when men's lives were involved in war.[3]

[1] Letter of 12.8.55, Bryant Papers.
[2] Ibid.
[3] 'Draft Introduction' enclosed with letter of 12.8.55, Bryant Papers.

Having identified his autobiographical ambitions in his draft preface, Monty soon got down to work, and by September was reporting to de Guingand:

> I am progressing with the book.
>
> I am going to get it written up to the time I left England in 1942 for Africa—and to finish these chapters in the next few months. That will be a good thing to do, and will get that part out of the way. I shall call the chapters as follows:
>
> Chapter 1 Boyhood days
> 2 My early life in the Army
> 3 Between the wars
> 4 The outbreak of World War II and the Dunkirk Campaign
> 5 Soldiering in Britain after Dunkirk
> 6 The Eighth Army
>
> Bill [Williams] is coming to stay a night with me here on 8th October to discuss the whole affair. That was a good idea of yours.[1]

The early part of the book was certainly full of freshness, economy and vigour. In a letter to Billy Collins, publisher of Liddell Hart's edition of the *Rommel Papers* in 1953, Monty had deplored Liddell Hart's introduction. 'I would describe it as nauseating sentimentality,' he wrote.[2] Monty's own early chapters tingled with the opposite: a searing account of his unhappy childhood, told without coyness, shame, or artifice. By the time he left for his winter holiday in Gstaad, Monty had not only written the first six chapters, but reached the summer of 1944, as he boasted to de Guingand:

> The book proceeds well. I have now written it from my early boyhood days up to the moment when I leave Portsmouth in a destroyer for Normandy on the night of 6 June 1944. It has been pronounced 'very good' by Bill Williams, P. J. Grigg and Arthur Bryant—which ought to be enough!![3]

Once again awareness of his own ability inflated Monty's ego, already insufferable save to those who knew and revered him. He had begun the opus with humility, turning his mental searchlight on his early self, his struggle with his mother and with the Army in which he had hoped to shine. But the very voltage he generated gave

[1] Letter of 10.9.55, de Guingand Papers, loc. cit.
[2] Letter of 19.2.53. Copy in the Papers of Sir Denis Hamilton.
[3] Letter of 9.2.56, de Guingand Papers, loc. cit.

him a growing sensation of infallibility. Because the early chapters were so 'very good', he became convinced he could not fail in the further narration of his career. Though he still sought the opinion of his triumvirate of advisers—Williams, Grigg and Bryant—he grew less willing to accept their advice. Rather, as the spotlight of his memory approached the recent past, he became carried away by the chance to get back at those who had defied or defiled him. The irony and sense of humour which had informed the early chapters began to desert him, replaced by vanity of a titanic scale and cruel in its victimization of those with lesser brains or military ability than himself. Nothing his advisers said would now dissuade him, as his memorial to his own life and achievements grew. Sir Edgar Williams later considered that Monty 'genuinely enjoyed the production of it. He was interested in himself; he was his best subject, his own greatest admirer, and he was going to give himself a very good "chit"!'[1] Giving himself a good chit, however, often entailed giving others a bad one.

> I think he wanted to put the record right from his point of view. I would go down to the mill—he'd write saying 'I'm sending you this and I want it back tomorrow morning' sort of thing—as if I were not earning my living in an entirely different avocation but would meet him at 1100 hours at the Cenotaph! He was extremely amicable, though; we worked through the stuff in the evening; I was well fed and so on.
>
> Most of the time he was very amenable, but there were sticking points. He was curiously irrational about whether he'd take your advice or whether he didn't—he was extraordinary in that way. Sometimes, rather to one's surprise, he would say straight away, 'Well, if you don't think it's a good idea, yes, I'll drop it.' But certain things you couldn't get him to change because he was *determined* to say them.[2]

The matter of Alamein was, as Williams remembered, the 'nub' of the first part of the book—and nothing Williams could say would persuade Monty to alter his version of the 'take-over' in August 1942.

> I remember saying to Monty, 'Well I wasn't there [at the interview between Monty and Auchinleck in Cairo on 12 August 1942] when the Auk said this [that Eighth Army was to be kept in being and if necessary to retreat up the Nile], but can you show me any evidence?'

[1] Sir Edgar Williams, interview of 7.5.85.
[2] Ibid.

'Oh, well, I remember it.' And when I argued, he insisted: 'Well, it's going in! They're *my* Memoirs!'

I'd say, 'All right, they're your memoirs, but for goodness sake, as a historian I must challenge your sources.'

I don't think I thought about the repercussions. I thought only that I didn't think it was fair on the Auk in terms of my own memory. But he was so savagely determined that his version of that would go in. . . . Of course his contempt for the Auk was *very* extreme, because he'd always hated the time when he'd served under him at Southern Command.

I know he did feel very bitterly about it, because he didn't think the Auk was a good enough soldier in the strictest military sense—and he terribly underestimated the stature of the Auk as human being I think.[1]

Very soon Williams became torn between his duty as a professional historian and his loyalty to Monty 'as a friend and as an ex-employee as you might say'. 'They were so frank . . . one of the troubles about the memoirs is that they *are* in character. I'd say to myself: why should this silly little man not realise that saying this puts him in a very bad light? Should one rescue him from the bad light? It is a dilemma—I do remember this tension between the historian's desire to get the truth, and the desire to have a true account by a man.' As Williams was to reflect when writing Monty's obituary: 'You've got to say this chap was rather good at his stuff but that he wasn't a very nice man. But you don't win wars by having nice men—because that's the way to lose them!'[2]

Niceness, even fairness, to others was therefore an imperative Williams quickly discarded. 'My job was to stop him saying things that were positively untrue from the historian's point of view. I didn't try to reduce his opinions or subdue them in any way—only if they weren't provable could one challenge them. After all, they were *his* opinions and this was an autobiography.'[3]

What concerned Williams, more and more, was the difference between their respective retrospections. 'Evidence wasn't his "approach march",' Williams considered.[4] The trouble was, it was not in Monty's nature to admit he was ever wrong. Originally this had arisen from military necessity—the need 'to sustain the confidence of your soldiers. I mean I fully understand and appreciate that,' Wil-

[1] Ibid.
[2] Ibid.
[3] Ibid.
[4] Ibid.

liams allowed;[1] over the years, however, it had reached mythic dimensions—a legend of Monty's own infallibility that was impossible to sustain. Moreover, in becoming 'not only the author but the believer in his own legend of infallibility' Monty 'very much underestimated his own adaptable qualities and generalship—which in a sense reduced the praise owing to him: which he deserved'.[2] Thus, in his own account of the battle of Mareth, Monty's claim that the 'main feature of my plan' was an 'outflanking movement to the west of the Matmata hills: to be synchronised with a limited frontal attack',[3] was quite untrue. As Williams remarked, from a historian's point of view 'what was superb about the thing was the quick recovery from the mistake [to launch the main attack as a frontal assault] and to reinforce the left [originally a subsidiary effort]'.[4] Williams did, in fact, try to persuade Monty to tell the truth—'I tried to persuade him that there were sometimes examples where he was a better general than he was giving himself credit for, because of the successful adaptation—as at Mareth'. But Monty wouldn't play.

> He was tickled. But at the same time he had got it into his head this legend of infallibility.
>
> Everything, you see, had been tidied up—he hated untidiness. The fact that there was a compensation about 'second-tidiness' as distinct from the first untidiness. . . . He would have had to admit the first untidiness was of his own creation.[5]

Not even Arnhem would Monty see as a defeat, or at least as a mistake—a fact which increasingly jarred on his Oxford adviser.

> He was difficult to deal with, because they were his memoirs, not mine. I could check certain things and doubt certain things and ask for proof of certain things; but however many criticisms one might make, in the end if he wanted to say it that way, that was it—even though one thought: I don't think that is provable.[6]

Throughout 1956 Williams patiently read over the manuscript, querying statements of fact and attempting vainly to moderate the *gonflage*, as Monty's early reminiscences, often amusing and self-deprecating, gave way to his high-handed, hectoring self. 'I think

[1] Ibid.
[2] Ibid.
[3] B. L. Montgomery, *Memoirs*, London 1958.
[4] Sir Edgar Williams, loc. cit.
[5] Ibid.
[6] Ibid.

that at times you've made yourself less genial than you were, partly by an over-crisp vocabulary which tends to leave the smile out of the eyes and leaves only the glare,' he wrote in April 1956[1]—begging Monty not to lapse into long verbatim quotations from his wartime documents. 'This is autobiography not a military report: it should therefore be friendlier to the reader . . . at present we are liable to get the memoranda handed out of the caravan door. The reader wants access to the caravan.'[2] The post-war narrative worried Williams even more in its tone—'in general the whole batch of six chapters needs moderating', he wrote in November. 'A bit of understatement would not weaken the argument. . . . In short now that you've got this off your chest, it may be easier to consider reframing it. Some of the beans you spill in this draft could be used to hit you in the eye. There's not much "emotion recollected in tranquillity" here: rather it is emotion recollected in more emotion!'[3]

Though Monty assured Williams he was re-drafting the post-war chapters 'in the light of your comments',[4] he was approaching the end of the manuscript and had no real desire to 're-frame' it—and in fact finished the manuscript a few weeks later, in December 1956. 'The book is finished,' he wrote jubilantly to de Guingand on 9 January 1957.

> It has been read by Arthur Bryant and P. J. Grigg. Both were delighted by it. Bill Williams has read and commented on each chapter as it was written. You can take it that it will create quite a stir in Whitehall, and it may be that I will find it convenient to be out of England on the day it is published!![5]

As if to reinforce the point, Monty had entitled the manuscript 'The Sparks Fly Upward'—a quotation from Job.

Bryant, Grigg and Williams had been unable to prevail upon Monty to alter some of the more outspoken passages. When Monty showed the draft to his erstwhile Canadian PA Lt-Colonel 'Trum' Warren, Warren was shocked:

> One time he came to see us, he was writing his memoirs, and he gave me a chapter to read one night when I went to bed and he said, 'We'll discuss this at breakfast.'
>
> Well, it was a chapter that was not very complimentary about Eisenhower. At breakfast he asked, 'What do you think about that?'

[1] Letter of 24.4.56, Papers of Sir Edgar Williams, loc. cit.
[2] Letter of 16.7.56. Ibid.
[3] Letter of 20.11.56. Ibid.
[4] Letter of 25.11.56. Ibid.
[5] Letter of 9.1.57, de Guingand Papers, loc. cit.

I said, 'Sir, you can't publish this!'

'Why not? It's the truth!'

I said, 'It may be the truth, I'm not going to argue this with you, but if you publish that, Eisenhower will just hate you. You can do it after he dies—but you can't do it before he does.'

'But it's the truth! And I'm going to publish it.'

I said, 'Well, you'll be awfully unpopular with the Americans. He's the President of the United States.'

He said, 'I don't care who he is. . . .'

And he *did* publish it . . . he couldn't stop.[1]

The gremlin inside Monty was simply too bitter and determined to contain. The bile that had raged in him as a child, the 'black sheep' of the family, rose again as it had at certain moments throughout his life—in the desert, after Alamein when he became paranoid over the custodianship of his son David in England; in Wales after the war when confronted by the prospect of having to share the celebration of the award of the Freedom of Newport with his mother; his failure to attend her funeral. . . . In the summer of 1956, while writing the memoirs, Monty had written from Versailles to his stepson, John Carver:

> The Montgomery family seem to be assembling in England this summer: Harold from Kenya, and Donald from Canada. Una is trying to arrange family reunions. I am doing my best to avoid them; I dislike family reunions; they generally end in a row. I like to see my family one at a time and at long intervals—not more often than every 5 or 10 years.[2]

He saw 'no chance of coming your way this summer', he went on—adding a postscript, 'I go over to Isington Mill tomorrow to see the final of the singles at Wimbledon and stay with Winston at Chartwell.'[3]

This was Monty at his worst, gratuitously insulting, a law unto himself, gluing his name to the most powerful names of the world—Churchill, Eisenhower, Salazar, Tito, the Pope—in an effort to keep his own among lights. He was approaching his seventieth birthday and could not see that the trials and tribulations of his long life had taken their mental toll. He became obsessed by his physical health. Once, when mocking Templer's daughter for a bandage on her face to cover a recently-operated mole, he was told that unless removed, such warts could become malignant. Instantly Monty asked Lady Templer to telephone the Military Hospital at Millbank to book him

[1] Lt-Colonel Trumbull Warren, interview of 9.11.81.
[2] Letter of 5.7.56, communicated to author by Lt-Colonel John Carver.
[3] Ibid.

in for an operation to remove several such warts on his back and head.[1] Or in Canada, examined at Mrs Warren's suggestion by a doctor for a scalp disorder, he was advised to use a special ointment and shampoo. When Warren returned from his office in the evening, Monty asked him to come into the bathroom. 'Can you see anything wrong with my head? Damned women—get all upset about nothing!' he protested. But, as Warren recalled, 'If he took three showers he took five showers every day. He was terribly worried—but he wouldn't let on to me he was worried!'[2]

Monty would eye Churchill and Eisenhower with especial, almost morbid interest, assessing the extent of their physical frailty. To be ill meant surrendering control—and control over his own health, destiny or family was of paramount importance to the still tormented son of Maud Montgomery.

Despite a large entertainment allowance as Deputy Supreme Commander at SHAPE, Monty refused to entertain. He declined to resign from the colonelcy of the five British regiments of which he was honorary Colonel, forcing the Military Secretary at the War Office to extend his terms[3] and thus depriving many distinguished regimental soldiers from attaining what, in their eyes, was the most prestigious post of their lives. He even appropriated, at SHAPE, the right to be the British Army's main consultant and adviser on all British postings in NATO. This concession, wrung from Field-Marshal Slim before Slim's retirement, Monty then wielded in his typically autocratic and dogmatic fashion, blighting the potential careers of a number of senior British officers whom he considered to be 'above their ceiling' in the jobs proposed. When his own son David announced that Mary was expecting a child, Monty became almost deranged with impending pride—and prepared a telegram, as David recalled, to all the leaders of the world whom he knew to announce the birth of a grandson:

> The telegrams were all drafted, to send all over the world, and somebody said, 'But what if it's a girl?'
>
> He said, 'No question of such a thing!' He denied its possibility. It was going to be a boy. He was infallible.
>
> The irritating thing was that he was right![4]

[1] Lady Templer, loc. cit. The warts were later removed by Sir Arthur (later Lord) Porritt at King Edward VII Hospital.

[2] Lt-Colonel Trumbull Warren, loc. cit.

[3] Monty wrote to the Military Secretary in May 1955, and his colonelcies of the Royal Warwickshire Regiment, Parachute Regiment, Royal Tank Regiment, Army Physical Training Corps, and Royal Armoured Corps were duly extended until the end of 1956: Diary, Part 36 (1.8–28.11.55), Montgomery Papers.

[4] 2nd Viscount Montgomery of Alamein, interview of 11.5.84.

Monty had victoriously re-fought the battles of his life and of the Second World War in the manuscript of his autobiography; his dynasty was now assured by the birth of a grandson. All that remained was to give NATO a final crack of his whip—to go out not with a whimper, but with a bang. And this he intended to do in his April 1957 exercise: CPX Seven.

CHAPTER FOURTEEN

Lack of Good Taste

SO ENGROSSED DID Monty become by his forthcoming Exercise that he begged to be excused attending the Queen's State visit to France in the spring of 1957.

CPX Seven, attended by the entire NATO Council, marked a further turning point in the history of NATO. General Norstad had succeeded Gruenther as Supreme Commander on 20 November 1956.[1] Monty's 'New Approach' had been consolidated in NATO, the accent at SHAPE being on economy, scientific change, long-range planning, and re-organization where necessary. In this new atmosphere of positive self-analysis, Monty now 'stole the show' by calling yet again for a radical change of NATO strategy.

The accession of West Germany, the advent of satellite reconnaissance and the development of the nuclear deterrent now rendered NATO's current strategy an anachronism—a strategy of which he himself had been the original architect. With an effective nuclear shield it was time, Monty felt, to recast the role of NATO's ground forces. The days of the '*levée en masse*', of massive national reserve forces mobilized on the outbreak of war were over, he declared—for nuclear weaponry had reduced likely logistic mobility so significantly that there would be no prospect of effecting large-scale mobilization. 'It is time we learnt that the "levée en masse" philosophy is completely dead. If we continue with it, we can look forward only to disaster if we should ever be attacked.'[2] In Monty's eyes the ending of the *levée en masse* was no bad thing, since the economies of the West could ill afford the cost of large-scale land armies in uniform or in reserve. NATO should now seize the advantages offered by nuclear deterrence and abandon any

[1] Gruenther's forthcoming retirement was announced in April 1956. 'This gave rise to numerous rumours in the Press that the Field-Marshal would also be retiring. The Field-Marshal made it quite clear that this was not his intention. General Norstad had asked him to continue as DSACEUR and he had been delighted to agree to do so': Diary of Field Marshal Viscount Montgomery of Alamein, Part 38, (1.3.56–1.6.56), Montgomery Papers.

[2] 'CPX SEVEN: Final Address by D/SACEUR', 18.4.57, annex 1113, Diary of Field Marshal Viscount Montgomery of Alamein, Part 40 (4.6.57–2.10.57), Montgomery Papers.

intention of ever again indulging in large-scale land warfare in Europe.

> If I had to express in a very few words the root of the whole problem—the root from which everything else stems—I would say it all depends on the full acceptance of four words:
>
> 'Don't march on Moscow.'
>
> If these four words are written into all our thinking it will enable us to achieve an efficient defence posture within economic possibilities and practical realities. It will solve many of our logistic problems. . . . Our strategy must be based on putting our offensive punch into the air and missile arm—from air, sea and land. The land armies must adopt the strategical defensive initially; we must not give them the resources even to liberate the satellite countries. Only in this way will we be able to afford in peace time to provide the maximum weight for the offensive punch to be delivered by the air and missile arm.[1]

Or, as Monty put it in his subsequent press conference, the new purpose of NATO's land forces should be a highly professional shield which the Russians would not dare to challenge without provoking nuclear war. More likely, Monty considered, the Russians would limit their challenge to testing 'our firmness by seizing [without the use of nuclear weapons] a portion of territory of one nation in some isolated area, hoping that our unity would not be sufficient to launch combined NATO counter action.'[2] It was important, therefore, that NATO train fire-fighting forces to 'handle limited aggression in the NATO area [such as Turkey or Norway] without necessarily resorting to nuclear weapons, thus trying to isolate a limited attack before it could develop into an ugly situation which might lead to unlimited nuclear war.'[3] By providing adequate air transport, such forces could be held ready to move at a moment's notice, without the need for vast standing armies or reserve troops.

This brought Monty to the crux of the matter: namely, the way in which the 'balance of power' was now shifting back to the sea, with the advent of nuclear submarines both to police the sea routes and as mobile missile-launch-pads—and Monty's espousal of this renewed role of the Allied navies in global strategy earned him Mountbatten's 'most sincere congratulations and thanks. You certainly have put sea power on the map in the way no Admiral ever

[1] 'CPX SEVEN: Final Address by DSACEUR', loc. cit.
[2] Press conference of 18.4.57, in annex 1114, Diary, Part 40, loc. cit.
[3] Ibid.

could. . . . Each year after CPX I feel you have reached the high spot which it would be difficult to maintain and each year you not only maintain it but beat the previous year's efforts. I regard CPX 7 as an all-time high so far.'[1]

Monty did not confine himself to NATO strategy and forces; he questioned the whole existing NATO hierarchy, recommending the abolition of the Military Committee, the Standing Group and the Military Representatives Committee in Washington; the Supreme Commanders in Europe and the Atlantic would then become responsible to the NATO Council in Paris, who would be aided by Joint Service Advisers. 'The result would be a sound and simple organisation, streamlined and effective. Orders would then become the basis for action—instead of for argument (as they now are). There would be very great savings in staff officers and money.'[2]

The Commandant of the US Marine Corps wrote the same day: 'I am in full accord with your views and your strategy . . . I hope that the powers that be in SHAPE and in the NATO Council will listen very carefully to your recommendations. They warrant every consideration.'[3]

Soon, indeed, the Defence Ministries of every NATO nation were poring over Monty's remarks. Monty himself, however, was on his way to the United States, where, after delivering speeches in New York and Washington, he joined the President at his Gettysburg farm.

Monty's theme, in his new speeches, was that the very success of NATO, both currently and in the technological future, meant that Russia would intensify the cold war not in Europe, but elsewhere in the world—'fomenting and exploiting external and local issues everywhere in the world'—particularly in South-east Asia and the Middle East: the latter not only the source of the West's oil supplies, but the gateway to Africa.

> We have recently seen how the closing of a single waterway, the Suez Canal, can affect to a dangerous degree the economy and standard of living of a large group of nations. What happened was that while the Western world looked on, and did nothing to prevent it, a dictator in the Middle East worked himself into a position from which he could impose a stranglehold on the economies of many Western nations.
>
> The Middle East is one of the most important transit areas for nations which must import to be able to maintain their standard

[1] Letter of 23.4.57, annex 1115, Diary, Part 40, loc. cit.
[2] 'CPX SEVEN: Final Address by DSACEUR', loc. cit.
[3] Letter of 18.4.57, annex 1116, Diary, Part 40, loc. cit.

> of living at a reasonable level. Russia plans to destroy Western influence in that area and ultimately to bring the Arab States into the Soviet sphere of influence.
>
> Anyone who doubted the ruthlessness with which Russia would pursue her goals had only to look at the events of October and November 1956 in Hungary, where the West seemed incapable of acting forthrightly and in unison: her [Russia's] very clear subversive activities were based on making British/French co-operation with the United States difficult, by exploiting the differences between us. In pursuing this aim she has had a startling measure of success. The success of Russia will go much further unless the Western Alliance quickly comes to its senses—which it shows little sign of doing,[1]

Monty declared—a reference to Eisenhower's failure to endorse the Franco-British Suez invasion which was immediately reported throughout America, reaching Eisenhower's breakfast table at Gettysburg the next day.

Having invited Monty to stay from 10 to 14 May 1957, Eisenhower could not cancel his invitation without arousing a further furore in the press. Stoically, the President thus prepared himself for Monty's arrival; but even Eisenhower cannot have forecast Monty's tactlessness, indeed impertinence. On a private tour of the Gettysburg battlefield Monty and the President were pursued by journalists. Monty had always been fascinated by the American Civil War, and had read up some of the literature pertaining to the battle. Filled with conceit at the manner in which he had narrated his own battles in his manuscript memoirs, and basking in the passionate controversy his CPX Seven speech had aroused, Monty could not refrain from 'taking over' the Gettysburg battlefield tour. Though ostensibly speaking to Eisenhower, he would raise his voice so that the attendant newsmen could hear: a tactic Eisenhower so abhorred that he began to walk away from Monty, only to hear Monty remark: 'Both Lee and Meade should have been sacked!' As Eisenhower recalled, 'I think he added something about incompetence and then he called to me, "Don't you agree, Ike?" Frankly I was resentful of his obvious purpose and his lack of good taste in his public familiarity [the President of the USA always being addressed as "Mr President" by tradition], so I merely replied, "Listen, Monty, I live here. I have nothing to say about the matter. You have to make your own comment."'[2]

[1] Address to English-Speaking Union, Baltimore, 9.5.57, annex 1125, Diary, Part 40, loc. cit.

[2] Letter to L. T. Gerow, 15.11.58, quoted in Stephen Ambrose, *Eisenhower 1890–1952*, New York 1983.

Eisenhower's caution was well-warranted, for the next day the American Press burst into flames over Monty's remarks: a storm which soon penetrated the Pentagon, which Monty was due to visit on 14 May. As the Chief of Staff, US Army, General Maxwell Taylor, later related:

> I picked up the morning paper in the Pentagon and the headline said:
>
> MONTY CRITICIZES GETTYSBURG TACTICS!
>
> I read the report and went over and joined my colleagues at ten o'clock at the Joint Chiefs of Staff meeting. Now Monty was to come down and have lunch with us. Anyway all my colleagues were reacting in the same way. 'Look at this, look at this, have you seen what Monty says about Gettysburg and General Lee?'
>
> I said, 'I sure did.'
>
> Well, we laughed about it and somebody suggested, 'Look, when Monty comes, let's worry him a little bit. He doesn't know that he's made enemies of everybody south of the Pentagon and that he's in danger of his life!'
>
> So later, we all met together and Monty came in and we shook hands warmly, but with kind of peaky faces and we got around to it. We said, 'Monty, that's too bad about yesterday, isn't it.'
>
> 'Yesterday, yesterday? What about yesterday?'
>
> 'Well,' I said, 'your statement about the tactics of the battle of Gettysburg. The paper this morning says you claimed General Lee didn't know what he was doing or something like that.'
>
> 'Well,' he responded, 'I don't think he did, really! Look what he did, here and here and here. . . .'
>
> 'Yes, Monty,' we said, 'you may be right. Let's say you *are* right—but you're still in trouble.'
>
> 'Trouble? Trouble? What trouble?'

With a grave mien, Taylor warned that feeling in the South was running so high that Monty might well be lynched if he travelled there.

> 'We must warn you: don't go south of the Potomac, 'cos we can't guarantee your safety.'
>
> 'Oh,' Monty said, 'but I must go! I'm going south to visit the town named after me—Montgomery, Alabama.'
>
> 'You're joking, aren't you, Monty?'
>
> 'No indeed, no indeed.'
>
> 'Well, we'll double lay escort for you, but we think it's a very dangerous thing.'
>
> So Monty took off, went south. We didn't see him again.

I looked at the papers that night and the next day. No, Monty wasn't in.

So, a few days later, I called in this desk-colonel and said, 'What happened on the trip? Did the Press give Monty a bad time?'

'No,' he said, 'he gave the Press a bad time! He stepped off the plane at Atlanta, changing planes. He knew reporters were around and they assembled immediately around Monty. And one of them straightway asked, "We want to know why you think Lee's a bad general?"

'Monty said, "Who are you?"

'"My name's Smith," the man replied.

'"What's your newspaper?"

'"The *Montgomery Herald*."

'"I never heard of it—never heard of it."

'And he turned to another:

'"Where are you from?" Some reporter backed away.

'"I'm from the *Atlanta Constitution*."

'"I don't know that's a responsible paper. I'm not going to talk to you." Turned around and got on the plane. They never laid hands on him—got away scot-free!'

Whether he was a great general or not, Taylor added, chuckling,

it shows he knew how to face the Press—which can sometimes be more terrible than bayonets![1]

To Taylor, the episode had been a 'rather comical story'; but for President Eisenhower it was almost the last straw. For fifteen years, since the day he had first attended a Monty lecture in 1942 and been told not to smoke,[2] Eisenhower had exercised all the tolerance and understanding of which he was capable. In failing health, worn out by a lifetime's service to his country and the Western Allies, Eisenhower had lost patience with the impish British Field-Marshal who, as he later told Cornelius Ryan, suffered from an inferiority complex by virtue of not having gone to Eton or Harrow.[3]

But the last straw was yet to come.

[1] General Maxwell Taylor, interview of 17.10.81.

[2] M. Blumenson, *Mark Clark*, London 1985.

[3] The Papers of Cornelius Ryan, Ohio University Library.

CHAPTER FIFTEEN

Farewell to NATO

THE NEARER HIS retirement loomed, the more Monty's determination not to relinquish the limelight intensified. It was thought, for instance, that Monty might time his retirement to coincide with the end of Sir Richard Gale's tour of duty as C-in-C of NATO's Northern Army Group, Central Sector. Gale would then be able to succeed Monty as Deputy Supreme Commander. Instead, Monty extended his own term of office for yet another year, until 10 September 1958—which would make fifty years' uninterrupted active soldiering since he left Sandhurst in 1908.[1] Gale, whom Monty acknowledged to be by far the best commander in NATO, duly departed into obscurity in 1957—only to be brought back from retirement, to Monty's jealous irritation, by the British Chiefs of Staff in order to become Deputy Supreme Commander after all.

Monty's attitude towards his successor—as in the case of Slim in 1948—was indeed churlish and reflected Monty's still potent fear of being upstaged. It was an attitude mirrored in his relationship with his family and with his beloved Royal Warwickshire Regiment—the Colonelcy of which Monty refused to hand over to his logical successor, General Sir Geoffrey Evans (a distinguished veteran of Slim's Fourteenth Army), holding on to the post until Evans was ineligible, and insisting that his own protégé, Maj.-General R. C. Macdonald (son of Monty's predecessor as Deputy Colonel of the Royal Warwickshire Regiment), be appointed. Sir Geoffrey Evans was understandably so upset that he refused ever to attend a regimental function again.[2]

Equally, Monty's critical streak seemed to grow worse as his last months of service in NATO passed. Making preparations to mount his final triumphant CPX Eight exercise to be held in May 1958, Monty set off preliminary explosions both inside and outside the corridors of SHAPE concerning the need for a heavy dose of

[1] The official announcement of Monty's date of future resignation—20 September 1958—was made on 17 November 1957, though Monty's decision was made in the summer of 1957.

[2] Brian Montgomery, interview of 7.2.80.

weedkiller in NATO's vastly overgrown staff echelons;[1] ridiculed SHAPE's field headquarters in 'an old quarry near St Germain';[2] and put further pressure on Norstad to establish a multi-national air-transportable NATO fire-fighting division.[3]

Monty disliked *The Times* comment, in January 1958, that he was 'a kind of Old Testament prophet to NATO, pronouncing the military doom in store for us in five years' time if the West relaxes its grip',[4] for he felt, with some justice, that he was if anything a New Testament prophet trying to inculcate a higher, global awareness within NATO. Without this awareness, Monty considered, the NATO Supreme Commander was not justified in demanding control of the new intercontinental ballistic missiles planned for Europe, which should be controlled by a separate body—he therefore advised the British Chiefs of Staff and the Defence Minister, Duncan Sandys,

[1] Monty's war on waste began in August 1957 with a letter to the Chief of Staff deriding the SHAPE draft of a paper to the NATO Council: 'If we have a Prize List at SHAPE, I would give it 1st Prize, and an Olympic Gold Medal, for the maximum number of:

Platitudes
Clichés
Long-winded sentences
Unusual words, which many will not understand
Verboseness'

—Memorandum of 8.8.57, annex 1134, Diary, Part 41 (4.6.57–2.10.57), Montgomery Papers. It was followed by a second letter deploring the 'enormous headquarters we have in NATO . . . a highly complicated organisation, in which there is tremendous waste and duplication. It doesn't work well. It is very expensive. We could have an equally good defence for far less cost—in my opinion. . . . The real work at SHAPE is done by about fifty officers. The other four hundred are "passengers". Could we not discard half of the passengers?': letter of 11.8.57, annex 1133, Diary, Part 41, loc. cit.

[2] Monty visited the site during a twelve-hour exercise on 29.10.57. 'The Field-Marshal was not impressed and made it quite clear that he would never enter the place in time of war. The next day he saw General Norstad. . . . He felt that the Supreme Commander would be better off in a small caravan headquarters, which would be mobile and easily hidden. General Norstad said that he entirely agreed with the Field-Marshal, and that he would not be seen in the area either. . . . A more "open air" method of command was ordered to be investigated': Diary, Part 42 (3.10.57–28.2.57), Montgomery Papers.

[3] Monty's orginal suggestion for an air-transportable division was made at CPX Seven. As Monty informed the CIGS at Christmas 1957, beyond a short reference in a NATO study document 'nothing has been done. It is of course an essential part of the NATO military strength and I cannot understand why the Military Committee [supervising NATO] does not get on to it—and insist on it being formed': Diary, Part 42, loc. cit. The following April, despite the request of the Chairman of the British Chiefs of Staff, Norstad was still procrastinating: 'At this stage our thinking is not sufficiently well advanced to provide firm conclusions': letter to Sir William Dickson, 8.4.58, copy in annex 1240, Diary, Part 43 (1.3.58–7.6.58), Montgomery Papers.

[4] *The Times*, 29.1.58.

to withhold IBM control from the Supreme Commander [1]—a posture Norstad would have regarded as disloyal in any normal Deputy.

Monty was no normal deputy. By 1958, indeed, he had reserved the right to speak to whomsoever he wanted on whatever subject he wished. He appealed directly to Eisenhower to solve the Greek-Turkish dispute over Cyprus; he discussed NATO and world strategy openly with Tito; he predicted and then welcomed de Gaulle's return to power when the crisis in Algeria arose. His indiscretions were not mistakes. Deprived of any real power, they arose, more and more, from the need to needle, the urge to kindle controversy and fresh thought. When the Pope, commenting on the political situation in Italy, remarked that he applauded the Christian in the new Italian Government, but deplored the Democrat, Monty instantly stored the story for future fun. He had never been good at reserving judgment to himself in the manner of taciturn generals like Wavell; but as his retirement beckoned, so the prospect of freedom, of the chance to crow without even the vestiges of good judgment, seems to have taken over his personality—something of which he himself was sadly unaware. Indeed his hypocrisy became quite risible. 'Have you read "The Turn of the Tide" by Arthur Bryant,' he had written to de Guingand shortly after completing the first draft of his own memoirs.

> Bryant has created a man who never made a mistake, and whose diaries indicate that others made mistakes—but not he. We all make mistakes and it is far better to own up to them. I have made many and say so in my book.[2]

This was self-delusion of almost manic proportions—reflected in 1958 in a letter to his erstwhile subordinate, Lt-General Sir Brian Horrocks. 'My dear Jorrocks,' he wrote,

> I was somewhat disturbed at the announcement in the Sunday Times yesterday about articles you propose to write analysing the command and leadership qualities in the late war. Three of those commanders—Alanbrooke, Alexander, and myself are members of the House of Lords and also Knights of the Garter. I do suggest to you that it is hardly suitable for Black Rod [Horrocks' post in the House of Lords since his retirement from the Army] to bring these three into the public eye.

It was not the impropriety of Black Rod, servant of the House of Lords, criticizing his masters that irked Monty, however—it was the

[1] Cf. Diary, Part 42, loc. cit.
[2] Letter of 12.3.57, de Guingand Papers, loc. cit.

prospect that Horrocks' articles might 'compete' with his own forthcoming memoirs. Monty patronizingly suggested that Horrocks should concentrate upon the 'great commanders of the past and the battles in which they did their stuff, e.g. Wellington, Marlborough, Napoleon, Frederick the Great, Douglas Haig, French, and so on'—and threatened Horrocks if he did not: 'It would be a thousand pities if you were to become involved with personalities who are still living by writing about them in the Press—while holding your present office. You write so very attractively and interest so many people that to be told to shut down would be a tragedy.'

Knowing full well how controversial were his own impending criticisms of living personalities, this was monstrous, even deceitful. He had, after all, recently boasted in the spring of 1958 to de Guingand:

> Yes the book is finished and is handed over to the publishers. Serialisation begins in the Sunday Times on the 5th October and the book will be published by Collins on the 3rd November. I reckon it will create an immense sensation! Bill Williams has vetted it, and so have Arthur Bryant and P. J. Grigg. Bill was of the very greatest assistance, being a severe critic!! . . . I have my big SHAPE indoor exercise at the end of April, and on the 12th May I fly to Canada and then down to Washington to stay with Ike. I have to go round all the NATO governments to say goodbye, and start with Canada and the USA.[1]

It was in the USA, in fact, that Monty's hypocrisy reached its peak.

That Monty could have stayed at the White House with Eisenhower and his wife Mamie for three days in May 1958, knowing what he was shortly to publish about the US President, was something Monty would never have forgiven if done to him. Negotiations and meetings concerning the book dominated his US visit; from the White House Monty travelled to New York, where he conferred first with the senior editor of his American publishers (World Books) to discuss 'the publicity and publication arrangements for the Field-Marshal's forthcoming book',[2] then with the publisher of *Time-Life* which was to serialize the memoirs, and finally Ed Murrow who was to make a TV-broadcast relating to them.

[1] Letter of 5.3.58, de Guingand Papers, loc. cit.

[2] Monty was well aware how pained Eisenhower had been in 1957 by the publication of Arthur Bryant's edition of Alanbrooke's war diaries *The Turn of the Tide*. Writing to Bryant Monty had himself noted 'I have been in the USA during the whole of May [1957] and stayed with Ike for four days. He also is very angry about what Brookie says!!': letter of 6.6.57, Bryant Papers.

If Monty felt any pang of guilt towards the President, however, it was soon submerged in the gathering excitement of impending publication, as well as the farewell celebrations attending his departure from NATO. Though the British Government confined itself to a Government luncheon and an Army Council dinner, President de Gaulle announced the award to Monty of the Médaille Militaire, to be conferred in the Grande Cour of the Invalides, as a mark both of Monty's wartime Liberation of France, and his unceasing efforts to defend Western Europe since the war. Champagne lunches and dinners were given throughout the NATO countries and at SHAPE, but although there were some moving speeches and demonstrations of gratitude, there were few men left in office who really knew Monty's rôle in the post-war defence of Europe. Even those who did often found Monty's continual criticism too irritating to recognize his unique contribution. Rather, there was rejoicing that, at long last, the prickly prophet and inspector-general was going, never to return and cast his steel-blue eyes upon their institution or echelon.[1] Even at the supposedly uncontroversial farewell session of the NATO Council on 17 September Monty indulged less in praise than in criticism:

> NATO had stopped a war, and that was a tremendous achievement, and now the danger to Europe was least. But changes were necessary, and a complete overhaul should be undertaken. The NATO organisation was put together in a hurry when all-out war was a possibility. But it had grown to be cumbersome, complicated, wasteful, inefficient and grossly overstaffed. There were too many committees and too little decision,

his diarist recorded his harangue.[2] Not only was there no unity of political thinking among the fifteen NATO member-nations, but there was no attempt at a global strategy. The map that hung in the Council Room did not 'even show the Atlantic Ocean and America'.

Worse still was Monty's criticism of the NATO command set-up,

[1] At a dinner gathering of 'C' Division at the Staff College, Camberley, on 13 March 1958, for instance, Monty had been requested to give a talk and to answer subsequent questions. He did so—but posed so many pertinent questions himself in the course of the evening that he grew alarmed about the syllabus, the gross overstaffing, long hours of instruction and lack of historical command analysis. 'One member of the Directing Staff describing the impact of the Field-Marshal's [subsequent] letter [to the Commandant, with a copy to the CIGS] said that it caused a sort of 'thermo-nuclear explosion in the Commandant's Office' and added that certain parts of the building were still radio-active' months later, Monty's diarist recorded: Diary, Part 44 (8.6.58–25.9.58), Montgomery Papers.

[2] Ibid.

which was, in his opinion, both 'mad and crazy; it was highly unprofessional, it would break down if ever we had to fight, and it was the most complicated thing he had ever seen in his life'. What NATO needed was a single commander for all the NATO seas; a single directing and controlling brain for the global air space; a proper global early warning system; and centralized planning for global air defence. 'None of these vital needs exist. An overhaul was very urgently needed and there must be a re-allotment of functions.' Moreover the administration of NATO was 'ponderous and needed streamlining. . . . No business concern would tolerate the NATO system.' As he had pleaded almost a decade before, 'some sort of "general manager" was needed' by the NATO Council, a man 'who could get things done after the Council had taken the decision.'

M. Spaak, who had been one of Monty's political bosses from 1948, wound up the farewell meeting. 'He felt that the Field-Marshal's thoughts and opinions were ahead of his contemporaries'—particularly his point that big was not beautiful, but that small meant a corresponding simplicity and effectiveness in the organization for the command and control of such forces. Yet as Spaak explained, 'The difficulty of the NATO Council was that their members had first of all to convince their governments that a course of action was necessary, and then the governments had to convince the people of their separate countries. There was a difference between Army discipline and political discipline.' Nevertheless Spaak was 'sure that the Council Members would agree that in all his ideas the Field-Marshal was basically right. The meeting then ended.'[1]

Reports of Monty's address soon reached Versailles—'which upset the top officers not a little'.[2] As William Collins and Sons sent out the first printed copies of Monty's book to booksellers abroad and the *Sunday Times* began to set in type the first extract, Monty was determined to depart with a clash of memorable cymbals. Summoning the band of the Royal Warwickshire Regiment in his personal aeroplane, General Norstad appropriately provided them. There was a dinner for 300 officers at SHAPE—including General Gruenther who flew over from America. It was the fourteenth anniversary of the Arnhem landings. Telegrams from leaders all over the world were read. Eisenhower referred to 'your distinguished wartime record and your great contribution to the undertaking in which fifteen nations are now joined in a common effort toward peace and justice in the world. . . . Through the years it has been a

[1] Ibid.
[2] Ibid.

source of comfort and confidence to us all and to me personally to know that you were part of this endeavour.'[1] The next day, 18 September 1958, on the steps of the SHAPE building, Norstad bade Monty farewell to a final fanfare of trumpets. 'He may take great satisfaction from the fact that he has not only been a builder of essential military strength but that he has been one of the important designers of the people and the territories of NATO Europe.' A scroll, signed by Eisenhower, Ridgway, Gruenther and Norstad was presented. Monty replied, thanking the staff of SHAPE for having 'borne with me when I might have appeared to them to have said things rather strongly'. He thanked 'the people and Government of France for their ten years of hospitality, he urged the European Allies never to let Russia divide them from their alliance with the United States; and he urged the United States to provide leadership as well as dollars.'[2]

The Royal Warwickshire Regiment Band then played the 'Marseillaise'. There was a brief lunch, a walk to his car along a route lined by the NCOs and other ranks of SHAPE—who broke out of line and followed Monty, cheering 'in no known military formation'—a quick drive to Orly airport, inspection of the Guard of Honour of the Armée de l'Air, 'the briefest of Press conferences, then a series of handshakes',[3] and at 1450 hours, after ten years of 'exile', having flown almost half a million miles on behalf of Western Union and NATO, Monty took off for England and retirement.

General Norstad and his staff returned to their offices. But those who believed that Monty would lay down his arms quietly at the end of fifty years of active soldiering were to get a considerable shock. Monty had foretold the 'immense stir' his memoirs would cause. But not even he could foresee the scale of controversy—or the consequences.

[1] Letter of 15.9.58, annex 1337, Diary, Part 44, loc. cit.
[2] Diary, Part 44, loc. cit.
[3] Ibid.

PART TWELVE

The Evening of Life

CHAPTER ONE

The Sparks Fly Upward—
Monty's Memoirs

NOW IT'S TIME TO GO. . . .

MY JOB IS DONE SAYS MONTY AS HE FLIES IN FOR HIS LAST PARADE.

Field-Marshal Viscount Montgomery of Alamein, one of England's greatest soldiers since Wellington and the man who will be remembered as plain 'Monty', came back yesterday to retire.

His soldiering days will be over tomorrow and he will take off his uniform for the last time. . . . The uniform with ten rows of ribbons . . .

ran the *Daily Mail's* halfpage feature report by Arthur Crook on 19 September 1958.

His retirement will bring to an end what is probably the longest service of an active officer in the British Army.

For he was gazetted 50 years ago today. But it was a lively 70-year-old Monty with steel blue eyes as keen as ever who stepped from his private Dakota aircraft at Northolt last night.

With Marshal of the R.A.F. Sir William Dickson he inspected an R.A.F. guard of honour.

It was the same Monty wartime soldiers remembered who quipped at the photographers: 'Sounds like machine-guns.

'I'm a first-class photographer, you know, better than you chaps. Aim to do a lot of it now.'

BIG MOMENT

It was the same Monty who drew us together for a chat, as he did his staff officers and war correspondents in Normandy in 1944.

He talked of:

His greatest moment: 'When I was given the Eighth Army in the desert to do as I liked with, to put into practice all I had been [teaching] for years.'

His most difficult moment:

'When I ceased to fight the Germans and began to fight the politicians. When you fight the Germans you win or lose, and you know you have won or lost.

'When you fight the politicians you think you have won, but you find you have lost. . . .'

His NATO job: 'The object was to build up NATO so that no enemy would be able to attack us without being destroyed themselves.

'We have done that. I do not think Europe will ever be a battlefield again. Any future wars will be fought in Africa or Asia.'

The Battle of Arnhem: 'Arnhem was designed to get bridge-heads over the Rhine. We got them—over the Rhine and the Meuse. If Arnhem had not taken place it would have made the last fight harder and the casualties higher.

'I've always held the war should have been over by Christmas 1944.

'But we got into heavy winter fighting. The great thing is to win a war with the minimum loss of life.'

Asked if his reference to finishing the war amounted to a criticism of the American generals, he replied: 'I did not say so. It is all in my memoirs to be published in November.'

The future: 'I want a quiet life. I am a country lover. I don't think I want to do any more work.

'For a very long time I have led a very active life with no time to live in my own house and see my friends. Now I want to read and to think about the future of the world and generally not to be racketed about.'[1]

The racketing, however, was only about to begin. Monty had consistently refused to show the manuscript of his memoirs to the War Office, despite having signed the Official Secrets Act. Only at the eleventh hour was he persuaded to show it to the Secretary of State for War, Christopher Soames. 'My dear Christopher,' Monty wrote cheekily on 27 September 1958, a few days before the first serialized extract was due to appear in the *Sunday Times*:

> Here is a copy of the book. You will now be able to say that you received a copy before publication and had no comment to make.
>
> Publication date is 3rd November next.
>
> I hope you will enjoy it. I personally consider it is the cat's whiskers.[2]

Soames, after three weeks of perusal, duly furnished the War Office's *imprimatur* 'on military or security grounds', but begged Monty to delete the story of his long and acrimonious tussle with

[1] *Daily Mail*, 19.9.58.

[2] Letter of 27.9.58, Papers of Sir Denis Hamilton.

A. V. Alexander, the Minister of Defence when Monty was CIGS. 'I think that it clearly impairs the confidential relationships which subsist between Ministers and their advisers,' Soames considered; 'and it would certainly do no good to future relationships between the Chiefs of Staff and Members of the Labour Party.'[1] As the publication of Richard Crossman's diaries would later show, members of the Labour Party were no less constrained in the depiction of such relationships than Monty, who replied:

> As regards the passage about A. V. Alexander. My Memoirs are intended to tell the truth about what went on in military circles before the 1914/18 War, during that war, between the wars, during the 1939/45 war, and after that war. This I have done—only within my own knowledge, of course. To write a colourless book would be useless—it would not be 'me'.
>
> The troubles with A.V.A. were all part of the overall struggle to save the armed forces in general, and the Army in particular, from extinction. To leave out any part would destroy the whole; therefore I included the passage to which you take exception.
>
> You must admit that I have said very clearly that the troubles were my own fault.
>
> Even if I agreed to cut the passage out, which I do not, it would not now be possible to do so; it is too late. Some 150,000 copies have been printed; many of these are in the hands of booksellers throughout the Commonwealth, and with the reviewers, all ready for the publication date of 3rd November; in the United States many copies are already in circulation.[2]

Soames' response was the harbinger of many—and Monty's initial title *The Sparks Fly Upward* was no misnomer. As Monty had made history on the battlefield, so now he was making publishing history. Eisenhower and Bradley had both published their accounts in 1948 and 1951. Churchill had already penned his great *apologia pro vita sua*, culminating in his multi-volume history of his own rôle in the Second World War. The first volume of Alanbrooke's diaries, written up by Arthur Bryant, had appeared in 1957. The world, it seemed, was now avid for what the most controversial Allied general of World War II would have to say. As Sir Denis Hamilton later recalled:

> I was not shown the book until Monty handed over the complete manuscript, though he used to *talk* about it when my wife and I stayed with him each February in Gstaad.

[1] Letter of 17.10.58. Ibid.
[2] Papers of Sir Denis Hamilton.

I was slightly worried when I saw the typescript and I saw so much was on the post-war, frankly—quite a large slice of the book.

I said to him at the time, when he asked what did I think about it—he rang up the following *day* to see if I'd read it and what did I think of it—I said, I think it's marvellous for serialization, but you've certainly gone to town in the post-war. 'Well,' he said, 'I'm desperately anxious to get over the Western Union/NATO business, the importance of Western unity. What I want to get over while I have the chance, on the back of the campaign story, is the need for unity against the Russians, and secondly the need for unified defence at the Ministry of Defence. . . .'

It was important, very significant stuff and we printed several extracts from it.[1]

The meat of the book, however, as all who saw it before publication recognized, was the story of Monty's childhood—a series of battles with his mother which became a series of larger battles with his country's foes—and allies.

'I could see it was absolute dynamite,' Hamilton recalled.

But he'd made it perfectly clear to Collins and to me that not a word was going to be changed.

We did get him to change the title. The title was going to be *The Sparks Fly Upward*—that was the title on the folder of the typescript he delivered. But we both argued that for publicity and certainly for the cover of the book it had to be:

Field-Marshal Montgomery's Memoirs

He had told me he was refusing to submit it to the War Office. I think it was P. J. Grigg who advised him to send it, in the end, to Christopher Soames, which he did, but very much tongue-in-cheek. Technically he hid behind the fact that he was no longer a British soldier and didn't come under the War Office. There were a number of people at the War Office peeing in their bags at the likely repercussions; but it didn't worry me because I took the line, which I have always done, that I'd use my own judgement over what we serialized. In that respect Monty was a model author. I mean some authors like Arthur Bryant drove one silly—Arthur drove Leonard Russell [the Literary Editor of the *Sunday Times*] nearly into the grave by ringing up after press time wanting changes in serialization. Whereas Monty just said to me, 'Don't bother me—I don't want to see what you're serializing. You just get on with it. You know how to do these things. I trust you.'

[1] Sir Denis Hamilton, interview of 1.5.85.

Hamilton was well aware of the controversy it would cause across the Atlantic:

> I could see he was going to get into trouble with the Eisenhower stuff—but it suited me, as a [newspaper] publisher, to sell copies. Besides, I'd been through it all in reverse in 1948/9 when I reviewed Eisenhower's book. Monty was very cut up by that, and a lot of people were upset at what Eisenhower had said about the British Army, Alanbrooke and so forth.[1]

The Americans had got in first with Eisenhower's and Bradley's versions of the wartime campaigns, with anti-British critiques such as Ingersoll's *Top Secret*, with diaries such as Harry C. Butcher's *Three Years with Eisenhower*, and personal accounts such as Kay Summersby's *Eisenhower Was My Boss*. Hollywood had then capitalized on this all-American view of World War II.

'It wasn't only the books that were coming out in America, it was the films,' Hamilton reflected.

> The greatest joke of all time was Erroll Flynn having fought the battle of Burma single-handed! American movies were coming out on Europe and particularly the Pacific and Burma, but there was never . . . if there was anything British it was always that we were a lot of blimps. Even the film of Patton, later—it was all in a tradition that the British, once the war was won (movies during the war were scrupulously fair), had to be thumped, or ignored that they were there.[2]

Like many others, Hamilton (who had been a battalion commander in 21 Army Group from Normandy to the war's end) felt that the tide was now turning. Bryant's first volume of Alanbrooke's war diaries was aptly named, for not only did its title reflect the change in the flow of World War II, but of post-war historiography. Post-war austerity, the stiff British upper lip in the face of American derision or ignorance, was now giving way, under a confident Macmillan government, to a more assertive and investigative interest in the true history of the war. Tens of thousands of British and Commonwealth soldiers, sailors and airmen had died before the United States had even entered the fight, and America's first battle efforts such as Kasserine had, even after a year of hostilities, not shown its troops to be better than those of the European Allies at Dunkirk in 1940. Subsequent American grasp of strategy and tactical strategy, as evidenced at Salerno and Anzio, was rudimentary and

[1] Ibid.
[2] Ibid.

wasteful in human life—just as, after the war, Americans criticized the anachronism of British and European imperialism but had only a confused and muddling notion of their own responsibilities as a world power.

The time was thus ripe for a book such as Monty's: assertive, outspoken, trenchant, with no holds barred—a blow struck for Britain and a publishing phenomenon without parallel.

> It was one of the great milestones in the history of the *Sunday Times* in that it put on at least 100,000 copies, which stayed on as readers of the paper afterwards,

Hamilton recalled.

> It transformed the situation of the *Sunday Times* and the *Observer*, the battle between them, because the *Observer* had drawn, under David Astor, very close to the *Sunday Times* in sales in 1954/55, and then they fell back a bit over Suez. And then we started this feature serialization policy, the climax of which was Monty's *Memoirs*.
>
> It was the same in America—*Time-Life* were engaged in those days in a great competition with the *Saturday Evening Post* and *Look Magazine*. These were three highly competitive magazines, and they all wanted it.[1]

Rights were quickly sold all over the world—and as serialization commenced in October 1958 the sparks indeed began to fly. The Belgian government protested about Monty's description of their army in 1940, the Belgian Minister for Foreign Affairs summoning the British Ambassador in Brussels 'in a state of great agitation. . . . He wished me to know that this [the serialization of Monty's *Memoirs* in *Le Soir*] had caused consternation in certain quarters and, indeed, threatened to menace Anglo-Belgian relations,' the Ambassador signalled to London.[2] The Italians were also in uproar, as the British Ambassador in Rome soon reported to the Foreign Office.

> The whole [Italian] Press . . . reacted violently to that part of the memoirs in which the Field Marshal makes derogatory remarks about the morale and fighting ability of Italian soldiers and describes Italy's change of front as 'the greatest betrayal in history'.
>
> The Right Wing Independent *Il Tempo* urged Italian ex-servicemen and partisans to 'throw back into the Field-Marshal's

[1] Ibid.

[2] Signal from Sir G. Labouchère to Foreign Office and Whitehall, 11.10.58, Papers of Sir Denis Hamilton.

face any decorations which he might have given to them and which were evidently devoid of any value'.

The Social Democrat *Giustizia* and Socialist *Avanti* expressed the strongest indignation, while large headlines in the Communist *Unita* spoke of 'vile insults'.

The Independent Moderate *La Stampa* devoted half a page to an attack on Field Marshal Montgomery in which he is described as a 'fifteen-to-one General'. . . .

Il Popolo, hitherto silent, carries a long editorial note under the headline: 'An unmannerly and ungenerous General', listing some of the most offensive passages and observing that the author may be able to write memoirs but certainly not history. He is unmannerly 'because of his observations on Italian women, and ungenerous because he forgets the great difficulties in which the Italians found themselves, both before the armistice on the battlefield and after it in the course of the resistance and of open war.' *Il Popolo* concludes that whereas Italy's relations with other countries were once dependent on the outcome of battles and on the judgements of Marshal Montgomery, for the last ten years they have been entrusted to politicians who have made a point of recognizing each other's merits instead of exchanging insults because they are convinced of the 'beneficent results for both sides of "sincere and loyal cooperation".'[1]

A subsequent telegram indicated that the President of Italy had become involved, with talk of Italy's solidarity with NATO being affected, so that Sir Ashley Clarke, the British Ambassador, recommended a British Government statement repudiating Monty's private and in no way official views. Selwyn Lloyd, the Foreign Secretary, forwarding Clarke's telegrams to Monty, dolefully recounted the situation:

My dear Monty,

I am afraid, as you will see from the enclosed telegrams from Ashley Clarke in Rome, we have run into more trouble [after the Belgian protest] over your book.

I am bound to say that the Italians appear to be over-sensitive about your remarks on their wartime performance, but I suppose it is only natural that they should look at all this rather more from the standpoint of their membership of NATO today than in terms of allied strategy in 1943.[2]

[1] Signal from Sir Ashley Clarke to Foreign Office and Whitehall, 5.11.58, Papers of Sir Denis Hamilton.

[2] Letter of 6.11.58, Papers of Sir Denis Hamilton.

Selwyn Lloyd begged Monty—'without for a moment suggesting that you should retract what you have written'—to send Clarke a telegram of regret, which Monty did, adding generously:

> I am distressed that any words of mine should cause offence to a nation whose servant I have been for some years past. During those years I have watched the growth of the Italian Army; this gradual growth has resulted in a very high standard of training and discipline. Indeed, in my view the Italian Army is, today, as good as any army in NATO.[1]

A similar message was sent to the Belgian Foreign Minister.[2] But if NATO governments were thus appeased, individuals were not. One Italian even went so far as publicly to request a duel with Monty, as an ex-Guards officer wrote on 6 November:

> Guards Club,
> Berkeley Square, W.1
>
> Dear Field-Marshal,
>
> I see in to-night's paper that some Italian has challenged you to a duel in view of your quite justified remarks re the 'Wop' army's ability! How superb! If you need a fairly agile young ex-Serviceman as a Second I'm your man!
>
> I can't think why I'm wasting your time with this letter . . . but I'm getting great amusement from reading your book & thought I would like to tell you what a very pleasant change it is to the normal nonsense served up as a war book. And I was so delighted to see you draw blood in Italy![3]

The publication of Monty's *Memoirs* was thus the signal for some impassioned blood-letting. Those who admired Monty's candour congratulated him; those who deplored his simplistic and egotistical manner were outraged. Threats of writs and of libel action were soon flying with the sparks. 'I think it fair to warn you,' wrote one of the generals Monty sacked in the desert, 'that if you repeat your version of the action of 10 Armoured Division on Oct 25 1942, which you must, by now, be aware is quite untrue, I shall have to consider what action is open to me.'[4] Nor were writs confined to major-generals; Field-Marshal Sir Claude Auchinleck was soon drawn into the controversy over the state of the Eighth Army at Alamein when

[1] Letter of 9.11.58. Ibid.
[2] Letter of 21.10.58. Ibid.
[3] Letter of 6.11.58. Ibid.
[4] Letter from Maj-General A. Gatehouse, 5.12.58, 'Memoir Tributes' file, Montgomery Papers.

Monty assumed command in August 1942, and Auchinleck's plans for retreat:

> Auchinleck took me into his map-room [at GHQ, Cairo on 12 August 1942] and shut the door; we were alone. He asked me if I knew he was to go. I said that I did. He then explained to me his plan of operations; this was based on the fact that at all costs the Eighth Army was to be preserved 'in being' and must not be destroyed in battle. If Rommel attacked in strength, as was expected soon, the Eighth Army would fall back on the Delta; if Cairo and the Delta could not be held, the army would retreat southwards up the Nile, and another possibility was a withdrawal to Palestine. Plans were being made to move the Eighth Army HQ back up the Nile.[1]

This passage was to cause more upset in Britain than any other statement or story in the *Memoirs*. Auchinleck protested immediately to the Editor of the *Sunday Times*:

> Sir,
>
> I have read the extracts from Field Marshal Lord Montgomery's forthcoming book which appeared in *The Sunday Times* last Sunday.
>
> There is much in what the Field Marshal has written with which I disagree. Let me take one instance in which his memory has allowed him to make a statement which is not true. I refer to the account of his interview with me before he took over the command of the 8th Army in August 1942.
>
> It is incorrect and absurd to say that, at that time, I was contemplating a withdrawal from the Alamein position. Such a plan had ceased to be seriously considered since early in July 1942 when Rommel had been forced back on to the defensive and the 8th Army had regained the power of attack.[2]

As so often in Monty's life, battle lines were being drawn between 'les hommes de Montgomery' and opponents. Monty's post-bag bulged with letters from supporters, including those who had served in the desert and clearly recalled Auchinleck's orders for plans to be drawn up for retreat—plans which Monty had instantly ordered to be destroyed. Eighth Army's Deputy Adjutant and Quartermaster-General in the spring and summer of 1942, C. A. Roberts, wrote to:

> most heartily endorse everything you say in your book about the change of atmosphere when you took over at Alamein. Even

[1] B. L. Montgomery, *Memoirs*, London 1958.
[2] Papers of Sir Denis Hamilton.

to civilians in uniform like myself, it was obvious that the handling of the Army had been quite disastrous for at least a year, and that a retreat to the Delta so as to 'keep the 8th Army in being' would have led to its disintegration; and I shall never forget the feeling of relief with which I put away the plans for this operation in returning from your first talk to your staff.[1]

General Sir Miles Graham, an administrative colonel in Eighth Army's staff in 1942, had already recalled, in a BBC broadcast to commemorate Monty's fifty years of active soldiering, the moment Monty arrived at Eighth Army Headquarters on 13 August:

> I can remember so well, now, how he came to my tent—I didn't know who he was—I thought he was just another general, and he asked me what I was doing, and I was very tired and fed up, and I said, 'Well, I'm making plans to evacuate the 8th Army. I'm having different coloured flags put into the sand to take [guide] the various units out.[1]
>
> And he said, 'Flags put into the sand? Tear it up at once,' he said, 'tear it up. And if you ever mention it again you're sacked—sacked . . . is that clear?'[2]

Despite Monty's injunction 'to destroy' all plans for retreat, officers recalled them; moreover, in the formation War Diaries, to be kept secret (at that time) for fifty years, there was surviving written evidence of such plans still being drawn up in Eighth Army and at GHQ Cairo on the day Monty arrived in the desert. Auchinleck's assertion that by mid-August such plans had ceased was clearly untrue; and his claim that Rommel had been decisively halted and that Eighth Army was preparing a great counter-stroke rang very thin, given his chaotic orders for a mobile defensive battle to be fought later in August when Rommel was expected to attack again. Over the years Auchinleck's memory had become hazy, and he had allowed himself to become the figurehead of a caucus of sacked officers determined to subsume bitter memories of defeat and dismissal. 'I am not really concerned about myself. I did my best but I am determined to do all I can to remove the slur he has cast on many brave and able soldiers who served under me—I want no more and no less!' Auchinleck wrote to Freddie de Guingand[3]—having informed Monty by registered letter that he considered 'certain state-

[1] Letter from C. A. Roberts, 5.1.59, 'Memoir tributes' file, Montgomery Papers.
[2] General Sir Miles Graham, in BBC Radio broadcast 'Montgomery of Alamein', 24.9.58.
[3] Letter of 6.12.58, de Guingand Papers, Imperial War Museum.

ments, purporting to be extracts from your forthcoming book . . . to be untrue and defamatory of me as an officer of Her Majesty's Army and as a man' and stating that he would seek to 'prevent publication of your book' unless Monty made 'a public and immediate withdrawal of the statements already published'. Moreover, failing such a public retraction, Auchinleck threatened 'to place the whole matter in the hands of the Secretary of State for War'.[1]

As Auchinleck was adamant he could not accept Monty's slur, so Monty was adamant he would stand by what he had written—informing Colin Coote, the Editor of the *Telegraph* 'very privately, that Auchinleck has written me a letter demanding a public apology—failing which he will place the whole affair in the hands of the Secretary of State for War. Therefore, the sooner you can publish your notes [giving further details of the situation in the desert in August 1942] the better—particularly as the matter may be raised in Parliament.'[2]

Such a feud between two of Her Majesty's most distinguished field-marshals was undignified to say the least—yet Monty was determined to carry the feud onto the television screen, as Frank Gillard, who had arranged for the BBC to broadcast a series of live programmes based on Monty's career, recalled:

> The programmes were each sixty minutes long. First of all we'd decide what we would cover in each of the programmes, then draw up headings that he could memorize—and then we had to trust to him. I mean he really gave a Sandhurst lecture in each case, that's what it was, with maps, charts, and so forth. He and I used to discuss just privately beforehand what the actual content of each programme was going to be.
>
> I realised quite early on that the main trouble was going to be Auchinleck—that he was going to be defamatory about Auchinleck and that this was an absolute determination. Here was his great opportunity at last to tell the world what he thought of his predecessor in North Africa. And that Auchinleck had prepared these plans for a retreat down into the Delta and all the rest of it. I finally confronted him with this and said outright, 'Now is this really what you're proposing to say?'
>
> He said, 'Yes! That's exactly what I'm going to say.'
>
> I said, 'Well, I'm sorry, but I don't think you can do it.'
>
> 'Why not?'
>
> 'Well,' I said, 'I'm sure it's actionable. And we as publishers/

[1] Letter of 23.10.58, 'Auchinleck' file, Montgomery Papers.
[2] Letter of 27.10.58, 'Auchinleck' file, Montgomery Papers.

broadcasters would be as much involved in this as you would as the speaker.'

I was convinced I could persuade him to use a form of words that would get round this difficulty—would satisfy him to some extent and yet at the same time would not enrage Auchinleck so strongly that he would go for a legal action. And I only discovered forty-eight hours before transmission that I was not going to succeed—and that we were on the edge of quite a crisis.

I remember arguing with Monty through an afternoon and into an evening that he could not say this on the air. Without success.

I went home and I called Sir Ian Jacob who was the Director-General of the BBC. Jacob of course is the son of a Field-Marshal himself and therefore he was quite alarmed at the prospect of one field-marshal suing another field-marshal because of a BBC broadcast. 'When is all this going to be done?' he asked. And I said, 'Tomorrow, as ever is.'

'Right, right. I'll put everything aside and I'll catch the first train down to Bristol (where Monty would stay for three nights prior to each broadcast, at the Spa Hotel) and I'll be with you in the morning by 11 o'clock.'

He was. He, Monty and I sat in my office through the rest of the morning, right through the lunch period, just simply hammering away at what Monty was going to say about Auchinleck!

Finally it was Jacob rather than me who persuaded Monty to moderate what he was proposing to say. And once he'd given way to us, fair dos to him, he stuck by the obligation. He went on the air that same evening—and used the formula Jacob and I worked out with him.

But it was a very dicey business—he was quite determined about it, absolutely *determined* to speak his mind.[1]

Jacob's intervention had avoided the scandal of a libel suit with regard to the television series, but as tens of thousands of copies of the book were bought each week in the bookshops, the likelihood of a literary libel action against Monty and his publishers increased. Sir Edgar Williams later recalled how he too was called in as peacemaker. In a radio broadcast on 20 November, Williams had got Monty to temper his judgment of Auchinleck and the situation in the desert in August 1942. 'This gives me an opportunity to say some things which I should have put in the book,' Monty had said. 'I will always be grateful to Auchinleck for the

[1] Frank Gillard, interview of 21.5.85.

fact that when I succeeded him in command of the Eighth Army I took over a stabilized front: full credit must be given him for that and for certain other events before that time too. If he hadn't created that stabilized front, we couldn't have fought the battle of Alamein as, and when, we did.'[1]

Hearing the broadcast, Auchinleck's lawyer asked to see Williams. Williams, obliged to travel to London that day, called at the lawyer's office.

'And there, sitting in his office, was the Auk,' related Williams,

> which I hadn't been warned of! Of course I knew him and we gossiped for a bit, and then he suddenly said, 'You'd better explain.'
>
> The lawyer—who had served in 21st Army Group as a G2 Air, I think—said, 'We've consulted counsel and there is a cold hard libel suit against Field-Marshal Montgomery. But Field-Marshal Auchinleck doesn't want to bring it, because field-marshals don't do this sort of thing. So we'd like some sort of statement in future editions of the book and particularly the serialization in the *Sunday Times* to say this—and he put down a piece of paper.
>
> I read it. 'You couldn't begin to expect Field-Marshal Montgomery to sign this,' I said. It just stated 'I'm wrong', or words to that effect.

Instead, Williams went into another room and quietly drafted a statement he *did* think Monty might underwrite.

> It was then typed, the Auk read it through and he said, yes, that would suit him very well and he was grateful and all that.
>
> 'Well, I've got absolutely no status in this matter,' I warned. 'I'll first of all go to Collins, the publishers.'

At the publishers Williams was told there was no chance that Monty would consent to such a statement being published.

> 'There may not be any point, but have you any objection if I try?' I asked. 'I don't represent anybody, but I think it is frightfully important that everybody should behave rather better than they have done.'
>
> And I then went to the Savile and wrote this 'may be the end of a beautiful friendship' letter and enclosed the draft.[2]

Monty kept the letter, which ran:

> I have been approached to act as 'peacemaker'. I am sure that this

[1] BBC Radio discussion, Home Service, 20.11.58.
[2] Sir Edgar Williams, interview of 7.5.85.

is because Freddie [de Guingand] is not in England; otherwise the suggestion would not have come to anyone as junior as I am.

Briefly the idea is this: that your publishers should be allowed to insert a note in the front of your book to the effect of the typescript enclosed. This does not ask you personally to retract anything you have written. It allows your publishers to say that you have expanded on the book [in the radio discussion of 20 November] since it was published.

I know that you will think it impudence on my part to ask for this: and for that I am willing to take blame.

Yet I know (i.e. I'm not just guessing) that something of this sort would heal the breach and that if you would be good enough to agree, it would be a good thing all round.

Forgive my intrusion. You will know that I am trying to help. I am sure in my own mind that this is a sensible thing to agree to.

I don't know quite what else to say. So I'll end by begging you to agree. You may want to alter the wording. But please allow the idea to be carried out—as a healing formula: if only to oblige,

Yours ever,
Bill [1]

Monty had sworn he would never alter a word. He had proudly boasted to de Guingand a few days before:

The first edition was sold out the day after publication—the edition being 140,000. The second edition is now going out of print. A third edition is being rushed through. That brings the total to 200,000.[2]

The feud was, however, threatening to overshadow this extraordinary publishing phenomenon. Monty, sick of the endless phone calls and correspondence over what was a single paragraph in a 544-page book, gave in. 'I believe some step should be taken to heal the breach between myself and Auchinleck and soften his wounded feelings. I am not prepared to retract anything I have written. But I am informed that if you, my publishers,' he wrote to Billy Collins, 'will insert a note in the front of my Memoirs it will go a long way towards doing what I have in mind.'[3] The note was, word for word, that which Williams had had typed out for him—just as, on 30 December 1944, in the midst of the battle of the Ardennes, Monty had hearkened to de Guingand's plea that he signal his abject apologies to Eisenhower:

[1] 'Auchinleck' file, Montgomery Papers.
[2] Letter of 22.11.58, de Guingand Papers, loc. cit.
[3] Letter of 9.12.58, 'Auchinleck' file, Montgomery Papers.

> Since the publication of this book, the Author, in a broadcast in the BBC Home Service on Thursday, 20th November, 1958 stated that he was grateful to General (now Field Marshal) Sir Claude Auchinleck and the Eighth Army under his command for stabilising the British front on the El Alamein position, thereby enabling the Author to conduct his successful offensive, known to the world as the Battle of El Alamein, in October 1942. . . .

The note went on to declare that 'after General Auchinleck, commanding the Eighth Army, had successfully halted the enemy's attack in July, 1942, it was his intention to launch an offensive from the El Alamein position when his Army was rested and had been regrouped'.[1]

News of Monty's compromise produced newspaper headlines of relief on 15 December: 'Treaty ends battle', 'Magnanimity and Goodwill', 'A strategic retreat', 'End of the affair?' 'Monty–"Auk" Settlement', 'Montgomery Tribute to Auchinleck'. . . .

Honour was satisfied, and the two field-marshals retired to their corners of the ring. It was not long, however, before another bout was called: this time with the President of the United States.

[1] Ibid.

CHAPTER TWO

Eisenhower's Anger

THE TRAGEDY OF Monty's *Memoirs* was that he had started with so many advantages. He had a public of millions, the world over; he wrote with a freshness and clarity that amazed even professional authors. Daphne du Maurier wrote: 'They are the only military memoirs I have ever been able to read. They are so clear-cut and direct; and if I may be allowed to say so, extremely like yourself.' [1] As Monty the soldier had punctured the divide between leader and the led, so Monty the writer swept away the fustiness and cobwebs of most memoirists, addressing himself with frankness and honesty to each phase of his life. What he had failed to do was to summon compassion or understanding for the weaknesses and tribulations of others. Even his gesture towards Auchinleck was not wholly sincere—as de Guingand found when belatedly forwarding, from South Africa, his own peace formula: a draft letter to be published in the *Sunday Times* giving his own personal memory of Auchinleck's achievements in the Middle East in 1941 and 1942, Monty's 'almost magical transformation in outlook' thereafter—and his admiration for both men:

> I sincerely hope that this letter may help to prevent this regrettable controversy from deteriorating any further. Not unnaturally I have the highest regard and affection for my old Chief Montgomery, but I also admired and liked Auchinleck.
>
> When I visit England next year, I propose to invite both the Field Marshals to dinner. It should prove an entertaining evening. I hope they will both accept! [2]

In a covering letter to Monty, de Guingand quoted a recent private letter in which Auchinleck had said: 'Of course I have a high opinion of Monty—for his great achievement and great qualities.' [3]

Monty, however, had chewed enough on the bitter branch of peace. He had written his *Memoirs* with a directness and clarity

[1] Letter of 30.10.58, 'Memoir tributes' file, Montgomery Papers.
[2] Letter of 15.12.58, 'Auchinleck' file, Montgomery Papers.
[3] Letter from Field-Marshal Auchinleck to de Guingand, 6.12.58, de Guingand Papers, loc. cit.

unmatched perhaps by any other great general in history—a directness that found its power in the refusal to entertain ifs and buts, or the impedimenta of official versions. In his simple, Christian way he had sought to tell the ungarnished truth, however unpalatable. He had been wrong to claim that Auchinleck did not intend to defend the Alamein or Alam Halfa position if and when Rommel attacked in August 1942, or that Auchinleck did not intend, given time and new equipment, to remount a British offensive. Yet the truth, as he knew, was that Auchinleck's plans for a defensive battle at Alam Halfa were a licence for disaster; Eighth Army had lost coherence as a weapon of war, plans for retreat were still circulating in every headquarters, and even with the best equipment in the world, there was no hope of Auchinleck and Dorman-Smith, his deputy, ever restoring the sort of confidence and high morale needed for Eighth Army to halt a refuelled and re-equipped Rommel, let alone achieve offensive victory thereafter. Monty had swallowed his pride in deference to Williams's Oxford judgment; but his heart was filled with contempt for such 'bellyaching' and contorted truth. 'My dear Freddie,' Monty replied to de Guingand a few days before Christmas 1958:

> I am entirely opposed to your entering what people are pleased to call the Monty/Auk contest. It has now died down and the Press are on to other things. The notice in the Sunday Times of the 14th December has settled it so far as the Press are concerned. A letter like the one you suggest would cause the whole affair to flare up again and my telephone will then ring all day with the Press asking for my reactions. *Least said, soonest mended.* For God's sake leave it alone.
>
> And don't ask me to the dinner party you suggest in your last para. I would decline. The Press would be on to it at once.
>
> Your suggested letter will not 'kill the whole business'—as you say. It will cause the whole thing to flare up again. I would then have to say that I adhere to what I have written—which I do, and don't want to have to say.
>
> So pipe down—please.
>
> I note you say the Auk admires *me*. But I don't admire him—and never have from the day I first served under him in the Southern Command after Dunkirk. That experience was enough for me.
>
> Yrs ever
>
> Montgomery of Alamein[1]

Meanwhile serialization of the *Memoirs* had begun in *Life*

[1] Letter of 22.12.58, de Guingand Papers, loc. cit.

magazine on 10 November 1958. Eisenhower's biographer, Stephen Ambrose, described Eisenhower as 'absolutely incensed'.[1] Monty had sent proofs of the *Memoirs*, but the President was already so angered by reports of the *Life* magazine serialization that 'they convinced me that it was a waste of time to read it if I was looking for anything constructive', Eisenhower told his ex-Naval ADC, Harry Butcher—claiming that he had 'never even opened Monty's book.'[2]

That Eisenhower should have said this to a man who, ten years before, had published war diaries so scurrilous and controversial that Eisenhower had been forced to deny them did not lessen Eisenhower's sense of injustice. Butcher, after all, could be discounted; Monty could not. Ageing rapidly, unable to remember names, Eisenhower allowed himself to be distressed by Monty's criticisms in a way he had never done before in his life. 'No one had ever made him so furious—not de Gaulle, not McCarthy, not Krushchev . . . no one,' Ambrose recorded[3]—and already by 1 January 1959 Eisenhower was proposing a ten-day convention at Camp David of all his wartime colleagues and cronies to 'develop an agreed document' to rebut Monty's *Memoirs*. As Ambrose remarked, for a President of the USA to spend ten days away from the White House to mull over events decades in the past, simply in order to lash back at Monty, was an extraordinary spectacle—one which threatened, indeed, to affect US–British relations.[4]

Monty, having made in his *Memoirs* some very generous assessments of Eisenhower's character (as opposed to battlefield ability), was puzzled and could not at first credit reports of Eisenhower's anger. No Christmas card had come from the White House, no thanks or even acknowledgement of receipt of the inscribed copy of the *Memoirs* Monty had sent. Yet Monty was unrepentant, writing proudly to Trumbull Warren on 20 December, 1958:

> My information from USA is that the book is the talk of Washington. Apparently Ike has come to realise that he will not go down in history as a great President; he accepts that. But he reckoned his place in history as a 'Captain of War' was secure. My book has demolished that. It is considered in Washington as a damning indictment as a strategist.
>
> Ike considers that my book, and the *Life* serialisation, made a

[1] Stephen Ambrose, *Eisenhower 1890–1952*, New York 1983.
[2] Ibid.
[3] Ibid.
[4] Ibid.

definite contribution to the heavy defeat of the Republican Party in the Congressional Elections (in the November elections). I am told that Ike is more vehement about the book than anything else. It is all very curious. Ike seems to forget entirely that he was the first of us to write a book. He published his in November 1948 and said some very hurtful things about myself and Alanbrooke. As he employed a ghost writer and didn't write it himself, perhaps he didn't read it!![1]

Monty added sarcastically.

Two wrongs did not, however, make a right. Eisenhower's anger was for real—and when Monty's CBS interview with Ed Murrow and Charles Collingwood was broadcast across America in April 1959, he was further enraged. Monty had already criticized his performance as a general in his *Memoirs*; in Murrow's broadcast he declared to millions that 'one of the mysteries of the war' was why Eisenhower had failed to understand the battle plan in Normandy—and that by failing to concentrate the Allied armies thereafter, he had prolonged the war and invited the American débâcle in the Ardennes, in which 'eighty thousand American boys were killed or wounded'.[2]

Worse still, commenting on the political leadership of the United States, Monty remarked:

My observations would be that the leaders, your leaders over there, are people who are not awfully well. Foster Dulles . . . he's in hospital with cancer. Your President has had three very serious illnesses—very serious. A heart attack, this ileitis, and a stroke. The head of your State Department, today, walks about on two crutches. . . .[3]

'A Washington correspondent for the Scripps Howard chain of newspapers reported yesterday that Mr Eisenhower was "fed up to here" with Lord Montgomery's criticisms,' Reuter reported. 'The correspondent, in a despatch in New York World-Telegraph, quoted a White House Associate as saying: "Monty won't get invited up to Gettysburg again."'[4]

This was no exaggeration. 'The telecasting of an interview (which many of my friends saw but which I did not) has seemed to many people here as a deliberate affront,' Eisenhower wrote to de Guingand—rejecting any idea of a reconciliation if Monty visited

[1] Papers of Lt-Colonel Trumbull Warren.
[2] 'Montgomery speaks his mind', loc. cit.
[3] Ibid.
[4] Reuter report, 1.5.59.

the US on top of his intended trip to Canada—'it would likely be bad judgement, at this particular time, for Monty to make any attempt to visit me'. Such feelings, Eisenhower assured de Guingand, were 'not of rancor', merely 'disappointment'.[1] He still kept Monty's signed photograph in the White House—to Churchill's evident surprise—and 'felt little personal resentment toward Monty's publicity endeavours'.[2] Yet the matter rankled, for not even an apology by Monty, as in days gone by, could ever rescue their friendship now, he made clear to de Guingand:

> My feelings about any visit apply also to any explanatory statement Monty might conceivably make about the affair. He obviously cannot retreat from a public position that he has already made clear; consequently there would be no hope of such a statement making for better 'allied' feeling. Likewise, I think any correspondence between us could not be very helpful because of the reason that Monty, both by publications and broadcasts, has made the whole matter a public affair, not a private one.
>
> And this is, of course, negative. But I feel that if the matter is to be healed in any way, that *time* will have to be relied on as the healer.[3]

Save for a transatlantic TV discussion by satellite almost a decade later, Eisenhower never addressed another word to Monty for the rest of his life. Their relationship, never easy, was at an end, and once again Monty had no one to blame but himself.

[1] Letter of 29.6.59, de Guingand Papers, loc. cit.
[2] Ibid.
[3] Ibid.

CHAPTER THREE

Helping the Young

BY JANUARY 1959 Monty's *Memoirs* in its British edition alone had sold a quarter of a million copies. His BBC TV series, *Command in Battle*, had an audience, however, of ten millions. Those who worked alongside him, in the studio, found that his decisive, soldierly approach rubbed off even on the oldest hands. 'My wife tells me she can see the Monty influence on me,' Michael Bowen, the producer, told the *Daily Mail*. 'She says Monty is good for me. She says I talk like him and I go about making clear-cut decisions for the first time in my life. . . . Often, after being with Monty, I feel like ringing up some BBC department and ordering "I will have this by 1100 hours", and you can't do that sort of thing at the BBC!'[1]

For a man of Monty's age—seventy-two—to undertake an eight-part, live television series, each of sixty minutes' duration, at prime time, was itself a tribute to Monty's vitality and sheer mental powers, Gillard felt. Certainly it was inconceivable that any other major wartime commander—Alanbrooke, Alexander, Slim, Tedder—could have faced such a test.

> You must remember that Monty was totally inexperienced—I mean the whole environment of the television studio was something that was quite new to him and the business of having to keep rigidly to time and all those factors. I was amazed that he got away with it as well as he did. There was only one BBC channel in those days so he was exposed to a very large audience. One of the programmes actually went out on the evening of Boxing Day at prime time. I would have been at the receiving end of any public criticism—and there wasn't any. It was a very well-received series, even though Monty was anything but a polished performer,

Gillard recollected.[2] The television critic of the *Manchester Guardian* lauded 'just how much energy and cumulative force had gone into those carefully planned programmes. These had been like hammer blows; indeed during the series I used to think that whereas Sir

[1] 'With Monty in Studio A', Robert Muller interview in the *Daily Mail*, 8.12.58.
[2] Frank Gillard, loc. cit.

Brian Horrocks drew one into his battles on the screen, Lord Montgomery appeared to leap out of the screen into the room. He brought the battle to you.'[1]

It was Monty's talent to cut through the dross of war, imposing logic and clarity. Even the most hostile viewers melted before Monty's lucid narrative of the great desert battles of Alamein and Mareth. One female viewer wrote:

> I confess to having said, '*Oh* that man, I'd throw a brick at his head if I could get near enough, the conceited fool—he makes me sick. . . .'
>
> Against my will, I was overpersuaded to give half an hour of my time at Christmas to witness one of your talks. My *intention* was to remain five minutes and then quietly walk out!
>
> After the first two or three minutes I was completely 'held' and thrilled with interest, but, most of all, quite overcome with my own shame and appreciation of what you did. I have not missed another 'talk' although it has meant a long icy or wet walk to our nearest television neighbour![2]

Others, however, were left with a less appreciative impression—particularly over Monty's refusal to admit that any of his battles had gone wrong at any stage, and his failure to give credit to others, save the amorphous 'soldiery'. By and large the public were willing to forgive such egoism, partly out of wartime gratitude and partly because Monty's story brought pride to every Briton's heart just as did Churchill. In the clubs, however, military writers watched such self-exposure with distaste and bristled with professional revulsion at such over-simplification of history. Thus, at the very apogee of his media success, Monty was sowing the seeds of his own misfortune at the hands of jealous and outraged historians—a counter-culture which would, as wartime memory faded, grow each year until it infected even official and demi-official histories of the war. Stung by Monty's open criticisms, even Eisenhower denigrated Monty to others, deliberately devaluing his wartime rôle, accusing him of excessive slowness and caution, of having failed to break out on the eastern flank in Normandy, of a preposterous proposal to concentrate Allied strength on a drive on Berlin. . . .[3] Indeed, so dented was Eisenhower's own soldier's pride that he was led to make preposterous claims himself. Writing to Lord Ismay in January 1959 Eisenhower claimed that Monty would 'scarcely stand much chance

[1] *Manchester Guardian*, 26.1.59.
[2] Alice Gibbs, letter of 19.1.59, 'Memoir Tributes' file, Montgomery Papers.
[3] E.g. interview with Cornelius Ryan, Ohio State University Library.

of going down in history as one of the great British captains. [Field-Marshal] Alexander was much the abler.'[1] Lord Attlee, whose post-war government Monty had criticized, expressed the same preference, rating Alexander as 'superior to Montgomery'[2] as an all-round soldier who would have done equally well if not better than Monty in Normandy. That Alexander had proved one of the most ineffective British Ministers of Defence in twentieth-century history; had had his wartime despatches written by one of his Intelligence officers; and would have to have his own war memoirs ghosted by John North would not affect this wounded verdict. For Monty's sin was a fundamental lack of magnanimity. Churchill had perhaps the most caustic and maliciously wounding tongue of any British Prime Minister—but in his books he made sure that magnanimity and courteous rhetoric triumphed: whereas Monty, in order to lay to rest the myths and cobwebs relating to the Second World War, had spared no one. 'He was also modest,' Eisenhower added to his lauding of Field-Marshal Alexander[3]—an epitaph which could never be used on Montgomery.

Yet for all his self-trumpeting, Monty was not without his own brand of humility. He had promised that in retirement he would devote himself to two things: peace in the world and 'working for and helping youth. Not by prize-giving ceremonies—I have hundreds of invitations—but by spending a couple of nights at a school—or a gathering of apprentices, and debating with them the situation in the world and their chances,' as he told the *Sunday Times*'s Special Correspondent.[4]

He was as good as his word. His efforts on behalf of St John's School, Leatherhead, were unremitting as a Governor and Chairman of its Appeal Fund, both in soliciting donations to this establishment for the sons of the clergy, and in assigning all his fees for book reviews and newspaper articles to the school. He 'adopted' many pupils, giving financial support and watching their individual careers at school and beyond. For twenty years he was a Governor of his old school, St Paul's,[5] and though he upset many an *amour propre*, it was the welfare of the boys which motivated him. In 1952 he had demanded a 'Master Plan' for the renovation of St Paul's 'to be prepared before work begins; thereafter, continuity will be vital.'

[1] Letter of 14.1.59, quoted in S. Ambrose, op. cit.
[2] *The Observer*, 2.11.58.
[3] Letter of 14.1.59, loc. cit.
[4] 'Aftermath', Papers of Sir Denis Hamilton.
[5] Monty was on the Board of Governors of St Paul's School from 9.4.48 to 8.4.68.

It has always seemed to me that continuity is an important quality which is lacking in the handling of St Paul's School,

he declared in an 'official' letter.

The Master of the Mercers' Company [administering St Paul's School] is Chairman of the Governors for one year; he is then removed from the Governing Body and from all further contact with the affairs of the School.

I have never understood this curious procedure . . . it has always seemed to me to be lacking in sound common sense. When I have asked the reason, the one given to me is that this procedure has *always* been followed; if there is no better reason, it would appear to be sound policy to do something else, e.g. to adopt a more sensible procedure.[1]

Monty's 'more sensible' procedure—a Committee appointed to oversee for 10 years the rebuilding of the School—was duly adopted; but when Monty insisted on personal interviews with those involved in the refurbishments to ensure that there was neither delay nor lack of careful thought, there was consternation. As the Clerk to the Mercers' Company, Colonel Logsden, wrote to the High Master of the School on 12 December 1952:

I note that the Field-Marshal requires your 'plan' before Christmas . . . I feel that a firm line must be taken and that you must tell him, as tactfully as possible, that you are under the aegis of the Improvement Committee, who have notified you of their requirements and that you cannot serve two masters.

The Field-Marshal, as an ordinary Governor, will have every facility of knowing what the Committee is doing, when their reports are laid before the Governors at their meetings from time to time. . . . I feel that Mr Wathen [Chairman of the Committee] is going to have difficulty in distinguishing between the Field-Marshal's enthusiasms and his interference.[2]

Wathen was not alone in finding it difficult so to distinguish. When later his son Mark, an Eighth Army verteran, became Chairman of a small committee to find a new High Master for St Paul's, Monty 'had to be controlled a little', Wathen recalled with humour. 'A year or two after this he was at the Alamein Reunion at the Albert Hall with the Queen Mother. He spotted me standing in a corridor as he and the Queen Mother were leaving and said to her: "Oh, you must

[1] Letter of 23.6.52 to fellow Governors of Mercers' Company, Mercers' Company Archive, Mercers' Hall, London.
[2] Letter to R. L. James, Mercers' Company Archive, Mercer's Hall, London.

meet this man: he's one of the few people who has given me orders that I've had to obey." The Queen Mother came over and shook my hand with the words "You must be a very remarkable man."!!'[1] Though Monty was never relaxed in the normal sense of the word and used his fame to cast an aura of expectation around himself—visitations rather than visits—it was an aura he enjoyed puncturing by his own inimitable directness—and sincerity. For, like his distinguished grandfather Dean Farrar, Monty was at heart a teacher. If he failed in magnanimity or generosity towards the weakness of others in his service life and in his *Memoirs*, his very dedication to the job of teaching—begun as a teacher of reconnaissance 'scouts' in India in 1908 as a second lieutenant—was unmatched by any contemporary of his standing. Alanbrooke might have been the father of British military strategy in Word War II, but for all his tactlessness and *faux pas* Monty was, as an instructor, the senior master of the British Army, the greatest teacher it had ever known. Even in his eighties, the eyes of Field-Marshal Lord Harding would light up like those of a junior officer at the memory of Monty the Staff College lecturer. Training notes, instruction manuals, pamphlets on war; the little black book in which he noted the names of promising officers; the help and guidance given to them in their professional careers—these were not acts of selfishness, they sprang from a root of good will within him, a desire to teach and help others that did not diminish with age. Where most other great figures of his time retired into themselves, concentrating on bird-watching or painting, Monty's irrepressible need to tackle problems and to teach led him on an endless round of lecturing to adults, students, and pupils. In part this stemmed from an unacknowledged loneliness. When one newspaper alluded to this, Monty sent a batch of 'fan' letters he had received to Denis Hamilton as if such correspondence proved how sociable was his life—but his chauffeur and gardener, Staff Sergeant Parker, knew better:

> He spends a lot of time in the garden, in the house, its nice garden. But as far as what you and I would call a normal home life, it just doesn't exist, insofar as he's quite alone, there's no family. The Field Marshal, as regards family life, is quite alone in that big house of his.
>
> There won't be the military work, the important military and governmental figures won't go across the screen, as it were. And I would think that if he doesn't become involved, shall we say, with the normal life of the village and the country, I would think he's

[1] Letter to author, 29.10.85.

going to be very lonely. I can't think that he will ever, shall we say, come down from the heights . . .[1]

If Monty never really came down from the heights—his personality deformed by a lifetime's military service—he entertained the innocent hope that, in his lecturing and teaching, he could at least contribute to the education of the young. 'The modern boy particularly from the public and grammar schools is terrific but he needs help if he is not to be confused and frustrated by this changing world. This is perhaps the best thing I can do—getting a message across in this way.'[2]

Monty's first such 'message' was given to the students of Oxford in May 1959. 'The first Chichele lecture was given yesterday in the Sheldonian theatre; it was packed with an audience of 1400,' he boasted to 'Bill' Williams. 'How they got in I can't imagine!! It was received with very great enthusiasm. I spoke for one hour and you could have heard a pin drop.'[3]

Monty's conceit was too much a part of him to be discarded in old age. Nevertheless he could still penetrate to the heart of a subject and to the core of an audience, with the same extraordinary ability he had evinced in the war. As the Cheltenham College magazine noted in its summer issue in 1959:

> Big Classical could not have held another person—everyone was there—staff, the College ladies, and all College except for a few unfortunates unable to escape from their sickrooms. There was a great burst of applause when the Headmaster brought Lord Montgomery into Big Classical, and another, equally prolonged, when the Headmaster concluded his speech of welcome with the self explanatory phrase: 'Marlborough, Wellington, Nelson, Montgomery'. . . .
>
> Viscount Montgomery: 'Last December your Headmaster wrote to me and asked me if I would come down. He told me that he had written because you all wanted me to come. When I knew that, that finished it. If I hear the boys want to see me I do not mind where it is, I will go anywhere if I am invited. . . .
>
> 'I would like to give something to this school to commemorate this visit. I want to give you a book. . . . There are good books and bad books in this world; this is a good book. I should know because I wrote it! (laughter). If you want to find out what sort of

[1] Staff Sergeant Tom Parker in interview for 'Montgomery of Alamein', BBC Radio broadcast of 24.9.58.
[2] 'Aftermath', loc. cit.
[3] Letter of 16.5.59, Papers of Sir Edgar Williams.

a person you are, write a book. I described myself as an intolerable person—the critics seem to agree with me! (laughter). But I have been paid a few compliments. The best one was by my barber in London. He said "Sir, I am just an ordinary man in London who comes up by train from the suburbs each morning with my friends. During the past few weeks the main topic of our conversation has been your book. We have all read it. We did not entirely agree about it. None of us could put a finger on what was the real point of the book. And then an old man in one of the corner seats said,'It's the story of a little boy who was very unhappy, and had no influence, friends or money, he started right down there (pointing to the ground) and one day he had reached right up there (raising his arm to its full extent above him). How did he do it?—it's in the book!' " I thought that sums it up pretty well. . . .

'This book is really the story of my life.

'I would like to say that it has been a tremendous pleasure for me, visiting you, and I hope that it will not be the last time. I have to go away early tomorrow. I must leave at 8 o'clock, my son and his family are arriving home and I want to meet them and go with them to church for the morning service.

'But before leaving I would like to say this: I hope this great public school will continue to produce boys who will be of great service to the community, like my friend Field Marshal Sir John Dill. It is very important that a school should do this.

'I believe that the next five years will be the most important in History. The Western World has got to change, at least some of it has. . . . In recent past it has thought too much about the rights and not enough about its duties. We have duties and obligations and we've got to fulfil them. If we don't, then the West will disappear behind the Iron Curtain. It is up to us to prevent that. In the belief that this school will continue to turn out great men, men of value in the future, I leave you,' (sustained applause).[1]

In a perceptive commentary the author remarked that Monty's 'address captured everybody by storm and received the sincerest applause I have ever heard in Big Classical'. As in the war, it was not merely what he said, or how he said it, but the fact that he had *bothered* to come and say it, and was anxious to see a school he did not know, even to the point of staying the night. 'Quite apart from his qualities of simple sincerity, candour, mental aggressiveness and alertness and in spite of his foibles of outspoken overconfidence and brusqueries the most striking and permanent impression he left with

[1] Article by 'G.L.P.', *The Cheltonian*, summer issue 1959.

many of us was that he is so much more interested and appreciative of the doings and welfare of the young than the majority of his contemporaries, distinguished or otherwise, who persistently hark back to the prime of their own life.'[1]

On 17 November 1959, interviewed on his seventy-second birthday at his Isington Mill by the BBC, Monty declared:

> In my life I have seen a lot of fighting. I don't like it. I think fighting is unproductive. I would now like to make some contribution to a peaceful world. I want my children and my children's children to grow up to be good citizens in a peaceful world.[2]

By devoting his retirement to visiting and helping schools he could, he hoped, make a contribution towards the 'good citizens' of the future; but as for a peaceful world, Monty had already begun to entertain much grander ideas for the part he would play.

[1] Ibid.
[2] Reuter report, 17.11.59.

CHAPTER FOUR

One-Man Summit

As CIGS, CHAIRMAN of the Western Union Chiefs of Staff, and Deputy Supreme Commander of NATO, Monty had travelled the world, meeting most of its leaders from pope to presidents. 'I believe that the political leaders the world over haven't got time to think,' he announced. 'All action must be based on thinking and you must have time for it.' He himself now had ample time. 'My experience has been in this governmental business that the leaders never have some clear master plan, a grand design of what they want to achieve. I would like to have a master plan, a grand design, like we had in the last war.'[1]

Ironically, beyond the publication of his *Memoirs* and helping the young, Monty had no clear master-plan for his retirement. He had taken no City directorships, nor was he interested in daily attendance at the House of Lords. As Sgt Parker had put it, the Field-Marshal had been used to the heights—and without his NATO hat he was simply too active to content himself with his garden. Thus it was that in April 1959 Monty flew to Moscow on a private mission of peace.

Monty's previous trip to Russia had been twelve years before, in 1947. He wanted to get a more up-to-date impression of the way the Russians viewed the world and the future, particularly their attitude towards China and towards a unified Germany. Hinting that he would like to be invited, Monty soon received news from Krushchev that he would be an honoured visitor.

At the Foreign Office, officials shuddered at the thought of how the Russians might turn Monty's schoolboyish curiosity to their advantage, just as important high-level negotiations were about to begin in Geneva. Soon the London press was ablaze with indignation.

MONTY!
The Sketch says to an old and meddling soldier—
FADE AWAY

ran the front page headline in the *Daily Sketch* on 6 April.

[1] Reuter report of BBC broadcast, 17.11.59.

What on earth does Monty think he's up to? Inviting himself to Moscow for a one-man 'summit' must rate as the biggest clanger of his career.

And that's saying something.

For the truth is that every time Monty blunders into politics he makes an ass of himself. This time he can do untold damage to the West as well.

This is why we say:

STAY HOME MONTY
—AND FADE AWAY!

Following Mr Macmillan's visit to Moscow, the West has at last begun to shape a policy for Germany. Summit talks are in sight. But relations inside NATO are in a delicate state.

France and West Germany—which mean de Gaulle and Adenauer—are jealous of Macmillan's leadership.

They also resent his flexible attitude towards Russia. They are working hard to swing Ike back to his former anti-summit attitude.

At this highly sensitive moment, Monty decides to intervene. He is going to Moscow, he says with apparent innocence, because as a private citizen he is 'very interested in this conflict between East and West'. That's fine. So are we all.

But Krushchev won't welcome Monty because he's a distinguished private citizen. . . . K will put out the red carpet for Monty because this vain field marshal by his very presence will give the Russians a chance to try to split the West at a crucial time. . . .

WHAT DOES MONTY EXPECT TO BRING BACK THAT THE PRIME MINISTER DIDN'T—BURGESS AND MACLEAN?

We have a lot of respect for Monty the soldier. But we have precious little for Monty the political meddler.

Our message to Isington Mill, Hampshire this morning is short and sharp:

MONTY—FADE AWAY!

For good or ill, Monty had no intention, however, of fading away. He had flown almost half a million miles on NATO business; he was determined to travel now as an ambassador of peace. It was much easier to mock than to take action, and he was not cowed by criticism:

With hands dug deeply into shabby corduroy trousers and wearing two pullovers—blue over beige—under a well-worn tweed jacket, Lord Montgomery clipped off these quotes:

> 'I am going to see Kruschev personally. I want to learn his point of view.
>
> 'I'll be there from April 28 to May 1.
>
> 'I once spent a week with Stalin and I have met all the Russian generals. . . .
>
> 'It is too early to say much. I don't want to say anything that will upset a lot of people.
>
> 'Irritate them one at a time—that's my motto,'

he told newsmen at London airport with a grin.

> 'I am going as a private individual. I am an international person and I want to know about things over there.
>
> 'This East-West tension is just no good. I want to go to find out what causes it. I know the West's attitude. I have lived with it.
>
> 'But what I know about the East is only hearsay, so I am going to find out myself. . . .
>
> 'I am used to criticism. I am always being criticised. I should feel unhappy and that there was something wrong if I were not being attacked in some way.'[1]

Despite the attacks, Monty was seen by Krushchev on two consecutive days—'regarded here as virtually unprecedented', the *Daily Telegraph* Moscow correspondent reported on 29 April. 'Western observers, commenting on Mr Krushchev's willingness to see his visitor again tomorrow, said that they could not recall any previous example of a private citizen being received by the Soviet Prime Minister for long periods on two consecutive days.'

Monty's meeting was thus historic. Unfortunately his televised interview with Ed Murrow of CBS—'Montgomery Speaks His Mind'—was broadcast across America on the very day Monty reached Moscow. In this he criticized the 'suspect' American leadership of the world under President Eisenhower. If there should be war in Europe ever again, he maintained, 'the United States must be in it from the word go—not like what's happened in the past. In other words, American blood must be shed the first day. They've often said that to me and I said, 'Well, I quite agree, and I'll guarantee that. I'll shoot one myself—shoot one myself!'[2]

Such remarks were, understandably, resented in America—where, following his criticisms of Eisenhower as a wartime field commander, the City of Montgomery, Alabama, took the unique step of with-

[1] *Daily Sketch*, 6.4.59.
[2] 'Montgomery speaks his mind', loc. cit.

drawing the Freedom it had once conferred upon him. Once again, in order to give strident emphasis to a statement—as in his Press conference after the Ardennes—Monty had caused his real concern to be overlooked, for he did not in fact believe that Russia would ever resort to war in Europe—'I don't believe the Soviet Union would enter into an all-out nuclear war with the West, and be left devastated and prostrated, with a thousand million Chinese on her Eastern flank. Never!' Since the Western democracies also had no intention of launching a preventative war in Europe, it seemed to Monty quite absurd that NATO should field such heavy and expensive forces in the defence of Western Europe. He therefore favoured 'thinning out' the Western front, leaving West Germany to guard her own eastern border with tactical nuclear weapons, and allowing the Russian, American, British and French troops in the two Germanies gradually to pull back. This was the scheme he put to Mr Krushchev: a 'step-by-step' withdrawal on both sides from non-vital areas 'creating mutual confidence as we go'.[1]

That Monty, as a private citizen, could fly to Moscow and put his own plan to the political head of the most powerful Communist state in the world seemed extraordinary. Yet, as has been seen, he not only had long talks with Krushchev on the appointed day, but was invited to return the following day. Indeed the measure of agreement Monty wrought from Krushchev was remarkable, for having begun bombastically on the need for the West to recognize the existence of two Germanies, not one, Krushchev agreed to a series of proposals Monty put forward. First, Monty argued, the case of Berlin must be tidied up, lest it should ever lead to an unwanted 'hot' war; this could be simply done by employing United Nations forces, with United Nations guarantees of access. Once the Berlin problem was solved, Monty considered, the matter of peace treaties with the two Germanies would follow in due course. And with agreement over the two Germanies, the Russian and Allied armies could decamp from Germany. 'If it could be agreed that national forces should return to their own countries, then Russia would accept a very comprehensive plan of inspection and control of national territories,' Krushchev stated. 'But a truly comprehensive inspection system is not possible so long as the armed forces of the two blocs are facing each other in Europe, ready to be alerted for battle at short notice. To allow inspection of each other's forces and dispositions under such conditions would be absurd. But once all the forces had been withdrawn to their own countries, the proper con-

[1] 'My talks with Krushchev', *Sunday Times*, 10.5.59.

ditions for inspection would be created; the war situation would then be calmed down, and an inspection system would gradually remove mistrust and produce confidence.'[1]

How far Krushchev was being honest was, of course, questionable. Could Russia ever afford to remove its troops from Eastern Bloc countries whose commitment to Russian-style Communism—as shown in the Hungarian uprising three years before—was far from total? Nevertheless the absurdity of the current situation, in which millions of armed men faced each other across the Iron Curtain dividing Europe, each fearful of the other side attacking, was obvious. As Monty had concluded after his 1947 visit to Moscow, Russia had no intention of attacking the West in Europe:

> The plain truth is that neither side has any intention of attacking the other. I refer, of course, to an all-out shooting war, a nuclear war. And the amount of money each side spends on preparing to repel attack is stupendous. It would be interesting to know if such a situation has ever existed before in history. It is almost Gilbertian![2]

Monty's talks with Krushchev did not bear direct fruit; the Geneva talks duly broke down without agreement that summer, and the notion of Berlin under the aegis of the United Nations was never adopted. Russian forces remained in East Germany. The cost of European defence spending escalated mercilessly, as in the years before 1914, in preparation for a war which neither side wanted. Monty's recommendation—that the Western Allies drop the idea of reunification of Germany, separate the Berlin question from that of East Germany, and concentrate on better Anglo-Soviet trade 'in an atmosphere of "live and let live" '—was however the policy adopted by the West—a policy which was to see reduced tension in Europe and guarantee peace for a further twenty-five years.

Monty's talks with Krushchev—published in the *Sunday Times* and syndicated across the world—certainly gave Monty grounds for cautious optimism. But if Europe was not to be a battlefield, it was time, Monty felt, to renew his links with Africa and the Far East, as he had done on the eve of becoming CIGS in the summer of 1946. To general consternation—in particular of the Americans, who refused to recognize the existence of Communist China—Monty now announced he wished to travel to Peking.

[1] Ibid.
[2] Ibid.

CHAPTER FIVE

Freelance Observer

MONTY'S COMMITMENT TO peace, in a warrior of world standing, was a strange phenomenon. He, who had been stoned in the early days of Western Union as a war-monger, now aroused the ire and contempt of those he had once served. In China, which he visited in May 1960, he was an honoured personal guest of Mao-Tse-tung—the first Westerner of distinction to risk opprobrium and visit the country, twelve years after the establishment of the People's Republic. Western commentators jealously complained that the visit—repeated on an extended scale in 1961 at Mao-Tse-tung's request—was 'eye-wash'. *Time* magazine remarked that 'some of the worst nonsense ever spoken about Red China is being spread by a man who commands an audience because of his title and past record: Field-Marshal Viscount Montgomery of Alamein, 73. . . . In the face of overwhelming evidence to the contrary, Monty reported: "Talk of large-scale famine, of grim want, of apathy, of a restless nation, is nonsense, maybe even dangerous." '[1]

Years later, after China was admitted to the UN and President Nixon flew to Peking, *Time* magazine would have to eat its words. But Monty was undisturbed by such criticism. Though American writers liked to label him as over-cautious, those who knew Monty intimately generally found the opposite, even in his seventies: namely a relentlessly challenging and decisive mind which brooked no 'belly-aching'. As George Malcom Thomson observed in a newspaper review of the book recording Monty's travels, 'It is a book of assured impressions, of snap judgements, rather than studied reflections'—a book that bore 'all the marks of the Field-Marshal's vivid personality'.[2]

It was, in fact, Monty's restless energy and decisiveness that was the problem—as Sir Denis Hamilton later recalled.

> I wasn't alone in this—there were a number of us who were anxious, after Monty's retirement and the publication of his *Memoirs*, as to what the Field-Marshal would do.

[1] *Time*, 27.10.61.

[2] Review of *Three Continents*, for Express Newspapers, 1962.

It was for this reason I put up to him the idea of a book on leadership—the *Path to Leadership*, it was eventually called.[1]

Hamilton's concern was not that Monty would otherwise vegetate. On the contrary, what worried him was the very dynamo of Monty's mind; the fear that, without adequate challenges, Monty's urge to tackle problems would lead to his 'firing off' on matters about which he knew very little or which were unworthy of his attention. By paying for Monty's trips to Moscow, Peking, India and Africa, Hamilton assured the *Sunday Times* a series of major journalistic scoops. 'A man of strong views and few prejudices, a lively curiosity, an alert and sceptical mind; gifted with a bright, perceptive eye and simple standards of character and achievement—there could hardly be a better free-lance observer in the world today than Lord Montgomery!' George Malcolm Thomson considered.[2] Above all, however, the patronage of the *Sunday Times* enabled Monty to concentrate upon issues of world significance. Though members of the US Congress placed on Congressional Record their venom, there can be little doubt that Monty's trips achieved a great measure of good will in the countries he visited—particularly China—and of public understanding in the West. However caricatured at home, Monty's simple Christian faith, his mastery of the profession of soldiering and his clear-cut, no-nonsense character appealed instantly to men often consumed with distrust of the West. When photographed with Krushchev and Marshal Sokolovsky at the Kremlin, Monty had remarked aloud, 'Three Generals together'. 'No, only two professional generals,' Krushchev had quickly demurred. 'Three footballers, then,' retorted Monty, equally quickly—an epithet Krushchev laughingly accepted.[3]

Monty's sense of fun, his patent sincerity in the search for peace, his genuine curiosity about alternative political and social systems: to Krushchev, Mao, Chou-En-lai, Nehru, Tito and other leaders, these were marks of a most unusual general in retirement, and there was no mistaking the sincerity of their welcome. Mao-Tse-tung not only invited Monty to make a second visit in 1961, but swam with him in the Yangtse river, and even wrote for him a poem entitled 'Swimming'. There could be no doubt about Chinese respect for 'Monty'.

The *Sunday Times* was delighted; as an independent, investigative liberal newspaper Monty's cobweb-sweeping style was refreshingly

[1] Sir Denis Hamilton, loc. cit.

[2] Review of *Three Continents*, loc. cit.

[3] *Daily Telegraph* report by Norman Riley, 30.4.59.

open and unprejudiced—and Hamilton's skill in employing Monty's talents was one which aroused great admiration in Fleet Street—as well as jealousy.

No author, however, likes to be completely in the pocket of his publisher—and Monty was no exception. By contract Monty could write only for the *Sunday Times*, which held exclusive rights on his newspaper articles; moreover, in return for an annuity, he acted as military correspondent exclusively to the newspaper, thus binding him still further. All that Hamilton had encouraged Monty to tackle, from the serialization of the *Memoirs* to the Field-Marshal's visits to China, had turned to gold. Was it precisely this, a certain underlying resentment at Hamilton's journalistic intuition and good judgment, that caused Monty to bridle—just as, in the past, he had resented Freddie de Guingand's 'better' judgment on relations with his superiors and allies?

The irony was that de Guingand's judgment as a civilian was by no means as good as his judgment as a soldier. Fearing that his book *Operation Victory* would be a commercial flop in 1947, de Guingand had overridden all professional advice and sold his copyright in the work for a modest lump sum—only to be chagrined by the worldwide sales of the work, which went into many editions. Equally it was de Guingand who persuaded Monty to accept a secret consultancy with his parent company, Tube Investments, which had shareholdings in many firms in South Africa. At de Guingand's urging and in order partly to 'earn' his £2,000 p.a. consultancy fee with TI, Monty visited South Africa in the autumn of 1959—the first of a series of trips in which Monty openly identified with and lauded the aims of apartheid.

De Guingand, who had been trying to get Monty to visit South Africa for many years, was naturally excited. But for Denis Hamilton, charged with publishing Monty's articles in a liberal London newspaper, Monty's sympathy with the Verwoerd doctrine posed a severe problem. Monty's first article, 'A Plain View of Apartheid', was on the whole an objective assessment of the problem, published on 20 December 1959 with certain agreed editorial changes. But even these did not cure the public impression that Monty was supporting 'Dr Verwoerd's racial oppression in South Africa', as the *Daily Mail* remarked in a leader on 22 December, entitled 'COME OFF IT, MONTY!' 'The trouble with Monty's latest outpouring is not that anyone in Britain cares a brass cap-badge for what he says. *The trouble is that people OUTSIDE Britain may really think that Monty's opinion still carries weight in spheres he knows nothing about.* This would be a sad mistake. . . . Was the Editor of the *Sunday Times* wise to publish this schoolboy essay?'

Fortunately, Monty's articles on China the following year and again in 1961 served to draw attention away from the complex problem of South Africa. But in the early months of 1962, Monty once again travelled to South Africa—and thenceforth the sparks again began to fly. Hamilton had in the autumn of 1961 succeeded H. V. Hodson as Editor of the *Sunday Times*, in addition to his other responsibilities—and was soon bombarded by warning shots from Johannesburg:

11.2.62

My dear C.D.

The article for the Sunday Times is well on the way to completion. It is going to be a really good analysis of the racial problem in South Africa—based on a very strenuous tour of nearly four weeks. People who were born and bred here, and lived here all their lives, have told me they have never been to many of the places I went to—or spoken [to] all those I talked with. I have a final talk with Verwoerd on Friday next and then return here to complete the article. . . . Please publish it as received. Don't muck it up. It will split very nicely into two articles.[1]

Hamilton's fears were not allayed by a further letter a week later:

My dear C.D.

Here are the two articles. I have tried to write a balanced story, having seen *all* sides.

It is essential that they be published exactly as written; they must not be cut about, nor bits of one removed and put in anywhere else. The problem here is so difficult and so complex that nobody in your office who has not studied it on the spot in detail, as I have, could possibly handle any re-grouping of the subject matter.

If you don't want to publish them as they stand, just let me know. I will then publish them elsewhere. I am not prepared to let anybody destroy or mutilate such a balanced viewpoint. Let me know when you have read the articles.[2]

Hamilton did—and on 24 February 1962 Monty complained bitterly to de Guingand:

Hamilton is frightened of getting the Sunday Times involved in the South Africa problem in view of the present climate of opinion against that country in the U.K. and in U.N.O. It is typical of the Press; when one writes the truth, as I have, they won't publish it;

[1] Papers of Sir Denis Hamilton.

[2] Letter of 20.2.62, Papers of Sir Denis Hamilton.

> when one tells lies, they publish them. In fact, they won't try and educate public opinion to see the facts.
>
> I have now placed the matter in the hands of my literary agent. He is offer[ing] them to the Daily Telegraph; I have spoken on the telephone to Colin Coote, the Editor, and I think he will publish them.[1]

But Coote would not do so, any more than Hamilton would.

> The articles have been refused by the Telegraph. Colin Coote explained to me that they have just appointed a man to study the South African problem in the way I did, and to publish articles from so 'eminent' a person would steal his thunder—which is understandable. My agent is pursuing other papers, but I rather think I shall call him off.
> (Note: I *have* called him off).[2]

For once Monty had to admit defeat, at least for the moment. It was his own fault; he had gone out to South Africa not as a military defence analyst or even an impartial private citizen in search of the truth. He had gone with a mission. As he had boasted in a letter to de Guingand the previous August, 'The important point will be to have a good talk with the Prime Minister (Dr Verwoerd) before starting on tour, and another talk when the tour is over. I hope you can fix this. The tour will have very great propaganda benefits for his government.'

It was clear that Monty was *parti pris* long before his trip—and his newspaper articles, given the transparent frankness and directness with which he wrote, could not disguise this. His desire to help de Guingand, indeed a desire to show off to de Guingand his own powers in the field of South African propaganda despite his age, had rendered him—as so often in the war—careless of the views or sensibilities of others, even of the reality of the situation. Thus, just as he was once stunned by Attlee's refusal to appoint Crocker to succeed him as CIGS, so now he was amazed by Denis Hamilton's refusal to print his propaganda on behalf of Dr Verwoerd.

Sadly, such a hiatus need never have happened—for, without prejudice, Monty's account of his visits to the Transkei and his talks to the tribal chiefs and Luthuli were in themselves unique and worthy of publication. On 18 March 1962 the *Sunday Times* did in fact publish an edited version of Monty's trip—but Monty was too abashed by his editorial and political defeat to take pride or solace

[1] De Guingand Papers, loc. cit.
[2] Letter of 24.2.62, de Guingand Papers, loc. cit.

in this, for even the BBC had cancelled their promised 'T.V. discussion about South Africa', as Monty lamented to de Guingand.[1] He still hoped to print the articles as chapters of his new book about his travels,[2] but he was in his seventy-fifth year and riding for a fall. By July he had suffered a minor stroke and was hospitalized.

'I am in here for a medical overhaul and rest, having done too much,' he wrote to de Guingand from the King Edward VII Hospital in London.

> I have made a complete recovery and go back home on August 7. I have decided to give up going to Switzerland in the winter. St Moritz, 6000ft, is too high for walking and I get rather breathless. Instead I shall take sea voyages each winter,

he informed him.[3] These would be to Cape Town—but he was not contemplating any further 'politicking'; instead, while the ship sailed to Durban and back he proposed to stay with de Guingand's friend 'Slip' Menell in Cape Town. 'I shall go nowhere else; just be quiet, and read and rest and talk with people. Perhaps you could fly down to Cape Town [from Johannesburg] and have a talk.'[4]

On 7 August Monty duly left hospital, writing the next day to de Guingand, who had cabled his best wishes:

> The trouble was that I have been living in top gear too long, and often in 'overdrive'. This is because in general health I have always been very well, and still am today. Lord Evans, the Queen's doctor, said he had never examined anybody of my age who was so fit and well in general health. In the end nature rebelled and I got very tired.
>
> I shall now give up running round the world, and will live a quieter life.[5]

Whether he would or not remained to be seen.

[1] Letter of 17.3.63, de Guingand Papers, IWM.
[2] *Three Continents,* op. cit.
[3] Letter of 31.7.62, de Guingand Papers, IWM.
[4] Ibid.
[5] Letter of 8.8.62, de Guingand Papers, loc. cit.

CHAPTER SIX

Chipping Away the Marble

MONTY WAS NOW, as even he admitted, entering the 'evening of life'. He had spent a lifetime battling with his mother, his family, the Army, the enemy. Now he wished to retire from the fray and to enjoy the tranquillity of his Hampshire home, attended by his cook, his two Swiss 'au pair' maids, his gardener/chauffeur, and his gardener's boy: a 'soldier's retreat', as *Life* magazine had styled it, with intentional ambiguity.

Monty's attempts, since 1948, to get a genuinely unified Ministry of Defence had at last borne fruit. In July 1960 Monty had put renewed pressure on the Prime Minister, Harold Macmillan:

> You may recall that when you were Minister of Defence we had some talk about the need for a closer control over the fighting services at the top level. . . . I am more than ever convinced that our nation will not get the best defence for the most economical expenditure so long as we adhere to the present set-up—nor will we ever get it until the Service empires are broken down, and each Service chief ceases to fight for his own corner.

The creation of a Chief of Defence Staff was not enough, Monty argued:

> I reckon the whole problem needs to be examined by one, or at most two, very high level persons—who would report to you.[1]

Two and a half years later Macmillan began to push for the reforms Monty had suggested privately and subsequently published in *Three Continents* in October 1962. Sir Ian Jacob was accordingly appointed to examine the 'whole problem' and to report personally to Macmillan. Proposals for the assimilation of the separate Service ministries into a single Ministry of Defence were officially put forward as a Government White Paper in July 1963. By the following summer Monty, alarmed that Field-Marshal Hull, the CIGS—an avowed anti-integrationist—would probably succeed Mountbatten as Chief of the Defence Staff, wrote in desperation to Mountbatten to beg him to stay at his post until the reforms were pushed through.

[1] Letter of 2.7.60, Papers of Sir Denis Hamilton.

Failing this, he proposed that Mountbatten offer himself as Minister of Defence and bring Monty—now aged seventy-seven—back as Chief of the Defence Staff until the matter was settled. 'Dick Hull was bitterly opposed to the whole scheme [of integrating the three Services] and told me so in a conversation I had with him in Hong Kong when he was C-in-C Far East Land Forces. If he succeeds you, all further integration will be put back. If it is considered to be the soldiers' turn, you had better bring me back as CDS. The right answer would be for you to be Minister of Defence and for me to be CDS under you. Then we could really get things done.'[1] Mountbatten was amused, but would not be drawn.[2] By 1965 Monty was lamenting: 'the Government fumbled the issue and declined to say *it was only a first step*, and declined to state the ultimate aim. The ultimate aim must be a completely integrated, functionally organised, Ministry of Defence—with the three Services retaining their identity in units and formations while being fused together in their higher organisation. . . . What is needed is Continuity/Decision/Courage in pursuing the ultimate aim,' he wrote in July.[3]

Since retirement he had continued to lecture to military establishments, forecasting vertical take-off aircraft, sputniks and Star Wars.[4] But his mind was less and less on war and more and more on peace.

He felt, with some justification, that he had mastered the art of war; he wished to be a force for moderation—and his 'consorting' with Churchill in the latter's old age was in part the loyalty of an old campaigner for his 'chief', in part the soldier in Monty belatedly deferring to the world statesman in Churchill. 'Christmas week is hopeless for me,' he wrote, turning down an invitation from his old MA, 'Kit' Dawnay, in December 1963:

> I have to go to London from 24 to 27 [December] to look after Winston and Lady Churchill—who will be alone over Christmas. He is going downhill fast; she is very frail; if left alone with him, the strain would be too much, as it is quite an ordeal. The family

[1] Letter of 25.8.64, Broadlands Archives.

[2] 'What fun it would be if we could have worked in double harness—but you would have to be the Minister as I won't go into politics': letter of 3.9.64, Broadlands Archives.

[3] 'Central Organisation for Defence' paper of 10.7.65, Papers of Sir Denis Hamilton.

[4] In his annual RUSI lecture in October 1954 Monty had stressed the need for an aircraft with a vertical lift, requiring smaller airfields. The following year he had pointed out the uses of satellites. 'The R.U.S.I. four lectures pointed the way to many other things which are now being mentioned as new ideas!!': letter to Denis Hamilton of 22.12.58, Papers of Sir Denis Hamilton.

> are useless. Randolph is hopeless; Diana committed suicide; Sarah is always drunk; Mary has her own large family in Kent. So I have stepped into the breach.[1]

Whether Lady Churchill needed Monty 'to look after her' was another question. Though charmed that Monty's loyalty to her husband had not ceased with Churchill's retirement, and though she was undoubtedly fond of Monty, she was not always certain what lay behind his assiduous attentions. The year before, after visiting Churchill in the Middlesex Hospital, Monty had told Press reporters that Churchill was against Britain joining the Common Market—an indiscretion that outraged the Churchill family and made Lady Churchill 'feel quite sick'. Monty was soon abjectly apologizing—much as he had to do in the war with Eisenhower:

> My very dear Winson . . .
> I am most deeply distressed to have involved you in a public controversy.
>
> I hope it does not mean you will never speak to me again. My affection and regard for you, and for Clemmie also, is beyond my power to express adequately; but you would both have every right if you decided that was to be my punishment.
>
> Can you ever forgive me?
>
> Yours always
> Monty

'Of course I forgive you, dear Monty,' Churchill had replied. 'We hope we may see you a little later on.'[2]

They did—'ever the faithful friend in these latter days', Churchill's daughter Mary chronicled.[3] For all Monty's genuine affection for the Churchills, however, there was a sort of pauper's relish in thus allying himself to the rich and famous. Monty's Christmas cards reflected this pathetic urge all too evidently; without consulting Churchill he would now invariably send out cards with a photograph of himself and Churchill, accompanied by his own caption: 'Relaxing with Winston Churchill in the South of France' in 1963; 'I lunch with my old friend Winston Churchill at his London home on 1st July 1964 and after lunch we go together to the Houses of Parliament—he to the Commons and I to the Lords' in 1964—even repeating the same photograph in 1965.

The war, too, increasingly fell into this category of caption-

[1] Letter of 14.12.63, Papers of Lt-Colonel C. P. Dawnay.

[2] Lady Soames, 'A Family Friend', in *Monty at Close Quarters*, ed. T. E. B. Howarth, London 1985.

[3] Ibid.

writing—whereas, in reality, a wave of revisionism had begun, in which Monty's contribution was, partly in pique at his lack of gentlemanly dignity and humility, deliberately undervalued. The wave had commenced with the publication of Correlli Barnett's critical book *The Desert Generals* in 1960. Monty was privately shown a typescript copy. 'It is an amazing work. Most of the material has been obtained from generals who got removed from their appointments, e.g. Auchlinleck, Gatehouse, Dorman-Smith,' Monty wrote to Denis Hamilton. 'My recommendation is that you have nothing to do with the book, and do not buy it for any papers in the Kemsley Group. It will do the author no good.'[1]

Such injunctions could not, however, make the book go away. It caused a scandal when published, and was followed by many others intent on chipping away some of the polished marble of Monty's reputation. Though Monty sometimes privately protested—as when Alexander's memoirs were published with the assertion that Monty had 'accepted' Auchinleck's plan of defence at Alamein[2]—he was no longer really interested in entering the historical fray. Friends persuaded him to invite, for instance, Correlli Barnett to Isington Mill, lest Monty alienate such younger historians by his manner more than his deeds.[3] As Barnett recalled, Monty was hospitable—

[1] 'A great deal of it is not in accord with the facts. The truth is that Auchinleck didn't understand how to command. No one really knew who was responsible for what—with Dorman-Smith running all over the place. The last page of Appendix "C" [in which Barnett published a condemnation of the British Army for not recognizing the genius of Auchinleck's Chief of Staff, Dorman-Smith] interested me: "As the brigade moved into the front at Florence, [Brigadier] Dorman-Smith was suddenly removed and returned to England [in 1944]'. The reader assumes this was another injustice! The fact is that the three C.O.'s formed up to the Div. Comd. and said they refused to serve any longer under Dorman-Smith; if he was to remain in command of the Brigade, they asked that they themselves might be employed elsewhere. It was Dorman-Smith who went—and rightly': letter of 7.8.59, papers of Sir Denis Hamilton.

[2] Alexander of Tunis, *Memoirs* 1939–45, ed. John North, London 1962. 'I never understood [since the time of Alexander's despatches of 1947, written by David Hunt, one of Alexander's Intelligence officers] the words "General Montgomery accepted this plan in principle". What plan? Perhaps you can tell me? I would much like to meet the man who gave me any plan in Cairo on the 12th August 1942—except the one outlined to me by Auchinleck that the Eighth Army must be kept "in being", and that in danger of being overrun it must be withdrawn. . . . We made the battle plan at Eighth Army HQ . . . I then told Alexander what I proposed to do. He agreed. He himself at that time had not even seen the ground! . . . It is a thousand pities that Alexander brought all this up in his book': letter to Mr Profumo, Secretary of State at the War Office, 18.10.62, Papers of Sir Denis Hamilton.

[3] Monty's refusal to see Barnett or reply to his questionnaire in 1959 had heavily influenced Barnett's depiction of Monty in his book.

'charming, most easy . . . most amusing, full of anecdotes'—and even drove his young visitor personally back to Bentley station; but to Barnett's chagrin Monty made only the most perfunctory mention of his book[1] and was clearly not interested in a genuine discussion of the desert battles. 'There are quite enough problems in this distracted world which will face us in the next 20 years, without arguing about "who did what" 20 years after,' he wrote to John Profumo, the Secretary of State at the War Office in 1962—despite the fact that it was the publication of his own *Memoirs* four years previously which had ignited the very issue of who indeed had done what.[2]

[1] 'The thing that really did surprise me in a way—we never got around to discussing the desert war in a personal sense, or my book or his role in the desert. He would talk about it in general terms, about Rommel and things of this kind, and in the middle of this he suddenly shot a look sideways out of his very blue eyes and said, "Let's see now, you wrote a book about the desert once, didn't you?" And I said, "Yes, I did," and that was the only reference he ever made to it': BBC broadcast, 'A Tried and Valiant Soldier', Radio 4, 1.4.76.

[2] Letter of 18.10.62, loc. cit.

CHAPTER SEVEN

No Scandals in the Family

IN THE AUTUMN of 1964, after experiencing difficulty in passing water, Monty went into King Edward VII Hospital for a prostate operation. It was this operation more than anything which broke Monty's hitherto amazing health. That winter he sailed again to South Africa; it was in Cape Town that he heard the news of Churchill's death. He was asked to return to England to act as pallbearer at the state funeral, but he refused, pleading that he had not yet recovered fully from his operation—an excuse that was ill-received by the Churchills after his years of importuning and expressing his devotion both to Churchill and to 'Clemmie'.

Monty's response was indeed selfish and strange, given his boast that Winston Churchill was his dearest friend. Certainly his health would have withstood a flight back to England—he who had flown over 500,000 miles since the war.

The truth was that for all his fearlessness in battle and his lifetime's dedication to the art of war, Monty was, in the evening of his life, afraid of the business of death. Even in the war he had largely avoided visiting field hospitals lest it affect his nerve as a commander whose duty it was to send men daily into battle.[1] After the war he had refused to attend the funeral of his mother; indeed he sedulously avoided funerals whenever he could.[2] Like Churchill he clung to life—indeed he made it his ambition, his boast that he would live longer than Churchill's ninety years. He disliked expectations being imposed upon him by others, too: situations in which he was not master of events, where he surrendered the initiative to others. Thus he declined to join with other mourners in the national tribute to Churchill on his funeral day, confining himself to a written elegy on his return in February 1965—and a photograph of himself visiting Churchill's grave at Bladon, near Blenheim, on his next Christmas card.

[1] 'I didn't want to have my nerves shaken by seeing those poor men all wounded and mangled and it might have weakened my resolution for the battle': 'Small World' US television broadcast with General Mark Clark and Friedolin von Saenger, presented by Ed Murrow, 22.11.59.

[2] 'As long as I remember Bernard has always disliked attending funerals and has avoided doing so whenever possible': Brian Montgomery, *A Field Marshal in the Family*, London 1973.

More and more Monty was living in a fantasy world of his own invention, as elderly people do. Cumulatively, the effect of Churchill's death was to isolate him even further from reality. In a sense, most of his life had been lived out in a sort of self-spun cocoon, a world of his own mental making which he could then control and conquer. It was for this reason he had been considered, at the nadir of Britain's fortunes after Dunkirk, to be halfway mad. Yet it was this same personal conviction of invincibility which infected the demoralized troops of Eighth Army and led to their extraordinary desert renascence. Battles are won in the hearts of men, Monty was fond of maintaining; but his victories were in fact the triumph of mind over matter, the imposition of his own mental picture upon the chaos and intransigence of the battlefield. Monty was invincible because he created and nurtured a mental picture of reality which did not allow the possibility of defeat, until, in the wake of the surgeon's knife and the bell tolling for Churchill's death he saw across the Jordan and was frightened not only by his powerlessness to defeat the Reaper, but his impotence even to preserve the neat mental picture which guaranteed his confident mastery over everyday life: an impotence that was now underscored by the breakdown of his son David's marriage.

'I fear it is all too true,' he wrote to Field-Marshal Templer;

> David's marriage has broken down. . . . The tension began a year or two ago with constant rows between them. I was told last summer that they were to separate. David blames Mary of course. My own view is that he is really to blame. . . .
>
> What with my major operation, the break-up of David's marriage, and Winston's death I have had about as much as I can stand.[1]

Monty was not exaggerating. He began to brood on the destruction of David's marriage with a kind of sickly despair, determined to picture Mary, the mother of his adored grandchildren, as the innocent and wronged wife, his only son as the blackguard. 'If a woman leaves her husband it is more than likely to be his fault,' he wrote to Templer. 'He wasn't kind enough to her; he was too critical in front of other people.'[2] Coming from Monty this was ironic; yet he meant it. He had never truly outgrown his emotional bondage to his own mother, and still worshipped the image of Mary-and-child, just as he had worshipped his wife, the mother of his son. That David had been too young to marry, had his own traumas to

[1] Letter of 6.4.65, Templer Papers, National Army Museum, London.
[2] Letter of 14.7.65. Ibid.

overcome with regard to the early loss of his mother and his strange, orphaned upbringing, Monty found irrelevant. By separating from Mary, David had broken the sanctity of Monty's mother-fantasy and must be punished. Separation became divorce—and Monty, tortured by his own impotence, responded by cutting David, his own son, from his will. 'What has upset me more than anything else about the David/Mary trouble,' Monty lamented to Templer, was the matter of "adultery". That this admission was concocted as part of David's own decree nisi against Mary, in order to conform to Britain's archaic laws of divorce, did not concern Monty. David 'is the first member of the family to have committed adultery—certainly for 200 years, and maybe longer. His mother would turn in her grave; so would my father.

'I can no longer sustain what I wrote in the last sentence on page 18 of Chapter 1 of my Memoirs,' he mourned, referring to his assertion that 'there have been no scandals in the family; none of us have appeared in the police courts or gone to prison; none of us have been in the divorce courts.' And he added, in a note of almost risible self-pity, 'It is hard to bear—particularly for a Knight of the Garter.'[1]

The mirror Monty had so carefully gilded and set up around his life had now shattered. He blamed David—but ignored the wounds he had himself inflicted, such as when, invited by the *Sunday Times* in 1966 to revisit the battlefield of El Alamein for the 25th Anniversary of the battle, Monty declined to take de Guingand, his Chief of Staff during the battle, with him. De Guingand, who had done so much to arrange Monty's visits to South Africa each winter, was frankly disbelieving. Unrepentant, Monty replied from the Carlton Hotel, Bournemouth:

> 8.1.67
>
> My dear Freddie,
>
> Yes, you are quite right. I plan to visit the Alamein battlefield in May next. It is the 25th Anniversary of the battle, and it is my 80th year. . . .
>
> It is a very small party, and a very 'closed shop'. I shall have a talk with Nasser in Cairo; he has agreed to this. I am very fit. But do not seem to get any younger![2]

De Guingand was mortified. 'Concerning your failure to get an invitation to the Alamein party,' Eisenhower consoled him, 'I repeat my belief that more than a tinge of jealousy is at the bottom of it all.

[1] Letter of 21.12.66. Ibid.

[2] De Guingand Papers, loc. cit.

Most of us cannot understand such an attitude but it is something that is in character for that particular individual. I would not let it bother me in the slightest' [1]—but with all the attendant publicity to the trip, de Guingand could not ignore the slight. 'I share your sadness over the abominable treatment you have received from a man who has every reason to feel deeply obligated to you for long years of service,' Eisenhower wrote yet again. 'Indeed I have often wondered how you found it possible to be so tolerant toward the whole affair.' [2]

Was Eisenhower right? Monty admired, loved de Guingand even—it was hard to resist de Guingand's infectious sense of humour, his *joie de vivre*, his love of life and affability. But Monty's own health was fragile and there was a limit to what he would be able to undertake at Alamein. Inevitably, he feared, de Guingand would steal the show, giving rise to the impression that he had been the 'brains' behind the battle. Monty thus took along his erstwhile Eighth Army Chief of Operations, the deferential Brigadier Hugh Mainwaring, who had been captured immediately after the battle, as well as General Sir Oliver Leese, who could be counted upon to 'toe the line'. Monty thus remained the star—and thoroughly enjoyed the visit. Typically, once he had met Nasser the two men got on very well: so much so that Monty was soon offering to act as personal intermediary between the Israeli Prime Minister and President Nasser after the brief but disastrous Six Day War in June. Monty had warned both Nasser and the Egyptian generals whom he met in May to steer clear of actual hostilities with Israel. 'All the friends we made in Egypt seem to have been sacked,' Monty wrote to Denis Hamilton on 14 June 1967. 'The naval C-in-C at Alexandria was clearly useless, as was the Air C-in-C. I am sorry about Amer, and more so about Mortagi. I don't believe Mortagi wanted a war with Israel, and I told him in no uncertain voice that if they went to war with the Israelis they would be well beaten. Nor do I believe Nasser wanted it; but he was pushed into war by some extremists.' [3] Aware of Nasser's extreme distrust of British Foreign Office officials Monty thus proposed to act as intermediary. The offer was not, however, taken up and as attitudes hardened the Israelis finally decided 'that the present "would not be an opportune moment" for going to see Nasser' on their behalf. 'They reckon the chances of success would be very slender; also Nasser would use my visit for propaganda purposes. The Israeli government is watching the situation, and future developments, carefully, and will let me know if the visit would

[1] Letter of 21.2.67, de Guingand Papers, loc. cit.
[2] Letter of 5.7.67, de Guingand Papers, loc. cit.
[3] Papers of Sir Denis Hamilton.

hold out more promising results at a future date. I would say they are right,' he acknowledged to Hamilton. 'The time when a visit might have been of some use is past—so it seems to me.'[1]

Meanwhile de Guingand, proscribed from the Alamein party, tried not to be bitter—something which became harder still when he heard from other sources that, following his 'belly-aching' protest over the Alamein affair, Monty was not intending to include him in the list of guests to his 80th birthday dinner in London, to be given by 'Simbo' Simpson at the Royal Hospital. Only when Miles Dempsey and Oliver Leese, hearing of the intended omission, threatened to boycott the proceedings did Monty relent. Dempsey, disgusted by Monty's behaviour, was not mollified, however—and remained absent as a mark of contempt.[2]

Monty's mean-mindedness did him no good. During the night, while Monty stayed at the Royal Hospital as Simpson's guest, his home at Isington was burgled and many of his priceless trophies, including his field-marshal's baton, were stolen. If the business over de Guingand had not caused Monty more than passing embarrassment, the theft of his war trophies now took the wind from his sails. Monty was heard on national radio begging for the return of his mementoes—a pathetic, lonely old soldier.[3]

Gradually Monty recovered from the shock—his spirits revived by a remarkable 'team' effort to write his final book, *A History of Warfare*. Already in December 1966 Monty had boasted to de Guingand that, two years before intended publication, orders for a quarter of a million copies had been received from booksellers. 'As you know the Memoirs sold 1 million copies, and are still selling. I have come to the conclusion that writing books is far more lucrative than soldiering—but not so enjoyable!!'[4] Guided by Anthony Brett-James, a lecturer at Sandhurst, and with two young researchers[5] to do the 'donkey work', *A History of Warfare* was duly published in September 1968 to a fanfare of appreciative reviews and resounding commercial success. The strain on Monty's health, however, had been too much. 'I have not been too well lately,' he wrote to Trumbull Warren in August 1968. 'The doctor can find nothing wrong but I am nearly 81 and have not the same resistance to chills and other

[1] Letter of 1.12.67, Papers of Sir Denis Hamilton.

[2] General Sir Frank Simpson, Eugene Wason interview for Sir Denis Hamilton.

[3] None was ever returned.

[4] Letter of 21.7.68, de Guingand Papers, loc. cit.

[5] Alan Howarth (son of one of Monty's wartime Liaison Officers, Tom Howarth) and Anthony Wainwright, Cf. A. Brett-James, *Conversations with Montgomery*, London 1984, and A. Howarth 'Monty the Author', in *Monty at Close Quarters*, op. cit.

ailments as, say, in the 1960's. The truth is, I have been doing too much too long, and in top gear. I must reduce to a lower gear. It is clear that my travelling days are over. I shall now spend the evening of life quietly in England and in my own home.' [1]

Even Monty's winter holiday at Bournemouth he gave up after the death of Basil Liddell Hart in January 1970—ending a friendship resurrected very late in life when Monty joined the 'writing profession'. His intended trip to Australia and New Zealand was cancelled, and he never left the shores of England again.

[1] Letter of 26.8.68, Papers of Lt-Colonel Trumbull Warren.

The Evening of Life

In September 1945 Monty had appealed to the King for help in obtaining 'a home for my lifetime.... Quite a small house; 7 or 8 bedrooms would be ample, and it need not be a gift, it could be only for my lifetime.'

No home was found for him, nor was any grant made by the government, as after World War I. Monty therefore purchased, in 1947, a ruined watermill on the river Wey in Hampshire. This he converted, despite government restrictions, into a personal residence, using timber given to him by the grateful governments of Australia and New Zealand. Out of ancient watermeadows Monty created an immaculate garden and lawn (**168** *top*), with barns to house his wartime caravans and original Lüneberg surrender monument (**169** *centre right*). In the museum-like house (**170** *below*) Monty surrounded himself with trophies and mementoes. 'It was terribly tidy and the furniture was beautifully polished,' recorded a visitor. 'What I always noticed was that he never allowed any flowers in the house. He said they made a mess and he didn't like messes.'

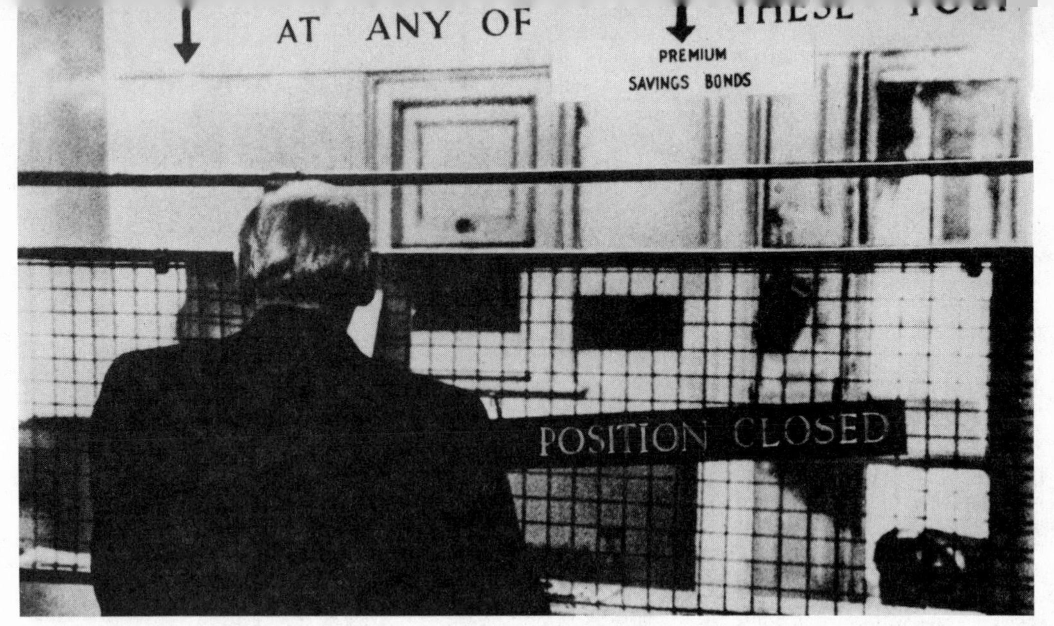

To the end of his life Monty insisted on drawing his old-age pension (**171** *above*), to the indignation of popular journalists. In fact he was not rich, and maintained his mill and personal staff largely by his writing. He continued to travel widely until a prostate operation in 1964 (**172** *below*) broke his amazing health. Recuperating in South Africa he refused to return to England for Churchill's funeral.

Despite his operation, Monty coveted the task of holding the Sword of State at the opening of Parliament each year (**173** *above*) – eventually collapsing in mid-ceremony in 1968. Nevertheless that year his final book *A History of Warfare*, delivered to the publishers in 1967 (**174** *right*), was published to a fanfare of appreciative reviews.

Monty's last trip abroad was to Egypt in 1967 for the 25th anniversary of the battle of Alamein. In specially mine-cleared areas he attempted to locate the site of his battle HQ (**176** *above*), explained the course of the battle to his hosts (**177** *right*) and visited the British and Commonwealth cemetery (**175** *top*).

On 17 November 1967 Monty celebrated his eightieth birthday in London. That night his home in Hampshire was burgled and many priceless trophies stolen. Vainly Monty called a press conference (**178** *above*) to appeal publicly for the return of his possessions.

'The doctor can find nothing wrong but I am nearly 81 and … have been doing too much too long, and in top gear,' he wrote in 1968. He still attended the annual Service of the Order of the Garter (**179** *below left*), as well as military parades (**180** *below right*), but it was evident the evening of life was turning into night.

181 *left* Monty, haggard and forced to remain seated, watches soldiers of his old regiment, now parading as the Royal Regiment of Fusiliers. Increasingly from 1970 Monty took to his bed, and by 1973 began to fade, lying like a small boy in the school sanatorium, looked after by his faithful housekeeper.

Monty died at his home in the early hours of 24 March 1976. His state funeral took place at Windsor a week later (**182** *below* and **184** *opposite below left*). He was buried in his local churchyard at Binsted in Hampshire, where a simple granite stone marks his grave (**183** *opposite above* and **185** *opposite below*).

BERNARD LAW
1ST VISCOUNT
MONTGOMERY OF ALAMEIN
K.G. G.C.B. D.S.O.
FIELD MARSHAL
17 NOVEMBER 1887
24 MARCH 1976

Although the British Government declined to decorate or reward Monty for his long service to NATO, nor would erect a statue in his memory, veterans of World War II and private individuals collected sufficient funds to commission Oscar Nemon to cast a bronze statue, unveiled in Whitehall on the thirty-sixth anniversary of D-Day by the Queen Mother (**186** *above*).

In Brussels, the city Monty had liberated in September 1944, a grateful people erected a similar statue in September 1980 (**187** *below*).

CHAPTER EIGHT

The Final Setting

INCREASINGLY, AS MONTY's health declined, his home at Isington became a sort of shrine, to which his many admirers came in order to show their respect. The immaculate garden, flanked on each side by the river Wey and the millstream, testified to the relentless Inspector-General in Monty, as he himself acknowledged. The mill had stood in 'a meadow overgrown with weeds and thistles' when he acquired it in 1947. 'Friends said I had better plough up the whole area and sow it with grass seed'—but Monty demurred.

> The turf of the meadow is probably a thousand years old. I decided not to plough it up, but to develop the old turf into a superb lawn,

he wrote in 1964. An army of local labourers was assigned to the task, pulling up every weed and thistle by hand; experts from the Sports Turf Research Institute had then been brought in.

> I have learnt that a good lawn costs money; it needs spring dressing, autumn dressing, de-worming, preventatives against disease, clover and moss—and all the rest. It is mown twice a week when the grass is growing strongly. . . . Care is needed in mowing. Once the grass has begun to grow strongly—in a normal year from early May onwards—the blades of my lawn mower are set fairly high. One does not want to shave a lawn; it is best to mow often, taking off a little grass each time and never allowing it to get long and coarse. The lawn is never rolled: the weight of the mower is enough.
>
> Worms are absolutely forbidden; you cannot have a good lawn if they are allowed to intrude from the orchard or beds. Moles are also forbidden; we have become expert at catching any which think they would like to hunt on my island; if there are no worms, there are no moles, since worms are their food.
>
> Also there is not one single weed in the 800 square yards of lawn; if one does appear it is immediately pulled out by hand. . . .
>
> One man alone could not cope with it all and keep the garden always neat and tidy; in the autumn the falling leaves have to be swept up daily. It needs two, a gardener and a garden boy. For

> myself, I plan and issue orders. My actual contribution to *work* is with a pair of secateurs, clipping and seeing the shrubs and plants get the light and plenty of sun, and do not overgrow each other.
>
> In a garden one must never let up; once you do, Nature takes over and then you are really in for trouble.[1]

The journalist and critic, Bernard Levin, was intrigued:

> He quite clearly kept the flower beds and lawns under the eye of some arboreal sergeant-major who had strict orders to put them in the guardhouse instantly if a weed should spring up in the wrong place or a leaf should fall where it's not supposed to be. . . . I've never seen anything done with such meticulousness and order as the garden.[2]

Or, as General Sir Charles Richardson recalled, 'we were taken round the garden, where I noticed that his "Rhus Cotinus" had been shorn "back and sides"; it was clear that discipline ruled in the garden as elsewhere.'[3]

Indoors, the story was the same: a museum-like interior, with his many battle honours and daily-dusted photographs of present royalty and past glory—pictures of Tac HQ, 21st Army Group, of Churchill, Stalin, Smuts, Tito, Mao Tse-tung. 'I must say I found it a little sad because what was missing from it, of course, was any kind of human warmth. This was a frame for him to live in, a setting for him to live in, but one never felt that he would re-arrange anything. One felt that that's the way it's been arranged and it had always been like that. Everything had been where it was and was dusted and put back exactly where it was and always would be,' Levin remarked.[4] Lady Liddell Hart felt the same: 'It was terribly tidy and the furniture was beautifully polished. What I always noticed was that he never allowed any flowers in the house. He said they made a mess and he didn't like messes.'[5]

Monty's daily routine was still as strict as ever—that obsession with tidiness which Lucien Trueb later characterized as *déformation professionelle*. Punctuality remained almost a fetish, as strict with regard to family as to strangers, Field-Marshals as to servants, sol-

[1] 'In My Garden' in 'Homes and Gardens' Magazine, November 1964.
[2] 'A Tried and Valiant Soldier', BBC broadcast compiled by Frank Gillard, Radio 4, 1.4.76.
[3] C. Richardson, *Flashback—A Soldier's Story*, London 1985.
[4] 'A Tried and Valiant Soldier', loc. cit.
[5] Ibid.

diers as to civilians. His young brother was enjoined to 'arrive here *as early as you like*; but not as late as you like. Lunch is at 1 p.m. It irritates my staff to put it back and me too.'[1] General Sir Oliver Leese's companion, Frances Denby, later recalled her astonishment at the way Leese deferred to this tyranny of time:

> We would arrive at the mill, having been invited for tea. Monty would be on the lawn, reading. We would sit in the car waiting for the hand of Oliver's wristwatch to reach 3.30 p.m. precisely. During these minutes Monty would continue reading as though our car had not entered his gates and was not standing by his main door, thirty yards away. Then, precisely at 3.30 p.m. Oliver would get out.
>
> 'Ah, Oliver,' Monty would get up to greet him . . .![2]

Such iron discipline was ingrained, the habits of a lifetime simply too encrusted to alter. His relentlessly critical eye had been trained over six decades to spot weakness, and he could still be cruel in his condemnation of it. When in Bournemouth one winter he was going down in the hotel lift to dinner, the doors suddenly opened at an intermediate floor. A man began to enter; recognizing Monty, he fell literally at his feet, sobbing, overcome by emotion at meeting in the flesh the Field-Marshal under whom he had served during the war, who had brought victory from defeat. . . .

'Get up! Get up!' Monty expostulated, pushing the man backwards out of the lift. 'And get your hair cut!'[3]

Yet, as the 'evening of life' grew darker, Monty *did* mellow slightly. 'When age and youth combine there are bound to be differences in points of view, and occasional clashes; indeed what surprises me is that we have had so few,' he wrote to Alan Howarth, his chief research assistant on *The History of Warfare*. 'You probably consider me to be very irritating at times. . . . Anyhow if I have hurt your feelings, of course I apologise; indeed that is the last thing I would ever want to do.'[4] 'Working with these boys is awfully good for me,' he told Anthony Brett-James. 'It keeps me young.'[5]

If the disciplined, fanatically tidied setting within which Monty lived was a sadly inhuman one, the sheer character of the man stood out all the more strongly. 'In his lonely years it was the company rather than the food that interested him,' Frank Gillard later

[1] B. Montgomery, op. cit.
[2] Frances Denby, interview with author.
[3] Mrs Sandra Hamilton, interview with author.
[4] 'Monty the Author', in *Monty at Close Quarters*, op. cit.
[5] A. Brett-James, op. cit.

related.[1] 'Monty had style. I learnt to know, and to admire, sometimes to be amused by, the grandness of the man,' Sir Solly Zuckerman recalled.[2] Bernard Levin, liberal, cultured and no respecter of establishment figures, was entranced:

> He was completely without pretentiousness or self-consciousness. . . . In the programme [one of a series of interviews with great men of the time] I asked him—after discussing his well founded reputation for never squandering a single life—to tell me how he felt about the fact that, when all the preparations for the battle had been made, and all the care and foresight expended, he nevertheless knew that within a few hours many men, perhaps thousands, would be dead. 'D'you know,' he said, 'I've never really thought about it like that,' and then and there, while the very cameras held their breath, he thought about it on-screen.[3]

Here was the other side of the cocksure, bombastic, self-serving image, the caricature purveyed by those who disliked him. '[He] then answered with a soldier's directness and simplicity that the important thing was to ensure that the troops knew that if they were killed their bodies would be "reverently collected and reverently buried".'[4]

'I know why I liked him,' Levin later recorded; 'it was because, so far from being the narrow Puritan of popular legend, I found him warm, touchingly innocent and vulnerable, full of a crisp, positively sly, humour, and quite extraordinarily thoughtful.'[5]

He was, to those whom he admired or was fond of. He stood godfather to the children of literally countless friends and erstwhile subordinates, and made an effort always to 'put himself across' to the young—and to hear from them their aspirations, difficulties and delights. His platonic befriending of young men and boys might arouse the cynical suspicions of some; but the sincerity of his interest, his valuation of the individuality and potential worth of those he aided would be attested by all—even members of his own family whom he slighted. As his brother Donald once wrote to Arthur Bryant: 'Bernard and I have kept in fairly close touch over the years and he has made several trips to Vancouver and I have visited him at Isington Mill. I know his eccentricities as well as anyone but I have always thought him a great man and am glad

[1] 'A Tried and Valiant Soldier', loc. cit.
[2] S. Zuckerman, *From Apes to Warlords*, London 1978.
[3] *The Times*, 31.3.76.
[4] Ibid.
[5] Ibid.

that he has your support. He has a most magnetic personality and power of expression, and when you are with him you believe everything he says must be true—whether or not you agree with what he writes. Certainly at our family gatherings here my two sons (who are pretty-hard-boiled) sat spell-bound. This is what Alexander means when he says on p. 16 of his memoirs "I always like him best when I am with him."'[1]

Certainly Monty's concern with the promise of youth had never wavered. 'We are living in very strange times, and they are going to get more strange before this year is out,' he had written before the Berlin crisis and airlift in 1948. 'The moral fibre of the nation wants a good spring cleaning, and we should begin on youth.'[2] 'I believe something must be done to improve the Youth Service in Britain; at present it is not right. We are not paying enough attention to character training,' he had remarked several months later.[3] His work for St John's School, Leatherhead and St Paul's, as well as his generosity towards and interest in individuals, had never ceased, even in his eighties.

But even Monty had to concede he was tiring, writing to Bryant in February 1970 when declining an invitation to a Foyle's literary luncheon:

> I am getting old (83 in November!) and large gatherings involve much talking; this is tiring and my main object now is to avoid tiredness and thus to keep well. So I lead a quiet life, and am very well. . . .
>
> Most of my old friends are dying, and all younger than me—Alex 5 years younger, Dempsey 10 years, and Bill Slim has had two strokes and is far from well. Liddell Hart was 8 years younger, and I had known him for over 50 years.
>
> I keep going, and intend to do so. But I reckon one would become a bit of a nuisance after about 90![4]

To his erstwhile Swiss protégé, Dr Lucien Trueb, he had written the previous November: 'You have indeed made a great success of your chosen career, and I am sure that further honours lie ahead for you. You have done it so far by hard work and concentration on the job in hand, and that is the right way.'[5]

[1] Letter from D. S. Montgomery, 18.12.63, Bryant Papers.
[2] Letter to Arthur Bryant, 20.6.48, Bryant Papers.
[3] Letter to Arthur Bryant, 10.10.48, Bryant Papers.
[4] Letter of 17.2.70, Bryant Papers.
[5] Letter of 25.11.69, Trueb Correspondence, Papers of 2nd Viscount Montgomery of Alamein.

In November 1970, thanking Lucien for his birthday greetings, Monty wrote:

> I was glad to hear from you and to learn the news. It always gives me great pleasure when boys I have known climb to great heights and succeed in life. This you have done and I congratulate you. You deserve success since you have worked hard. I hope you will climb higher. Good luck to you.
>
> Yrs sincerely
> Montgomery of Alamein [1]

It was the last letter Monty would write to his 'little Swiss friend'. 'Then it was silence; I kept writing faithfully, always [on Monty's birthday] in November, but there were no more answers.' [2]

The evening of life was turning into night.

[1] Letter of 20.11.70 in Lucien Trueb, 'Monty's Little Swiss Friend', in *Monty at Close Quarters*, op. cit.
[2] Ibid.

CHAPTER NINE

Monty is Dead

On 30 January 1970 Monty's son David re-married—this time choosing Tessa Browning, the beautiful daughter of Monty's Airborne Corps Commander, 'Boy' Browning, and of Daphne du Maurier, one of Monty's favourite novelists. 'I have always held that we humans should mate for life—like lions,' Monty lamented to Warren;[1] but at the urging of his brother Brian, Monty had at least patched up his quarrel with David, had reinstated him in his will, and was gracious to David's new wife. To the press, David announced his father had 'mellowed. . . . Having spent most of his life making his views felt, he now feels he has done his bit and is very peaceful and philosophical.'[2] In the latter years of his active life Monty had indeed delighted in 'making his views felt', delivering apocalyptic judgments on subjects as diverse as the Channel Tunnel, the folly of America's campaign in Vietnam and the Homosexual Reform Bill. 'I have a lot of friends, who come and see me; hardly a day passes without somebody calling,' he assured Trumbull Warren. 'I go to London for the Alamein Reunion and to Windsor Castle for the Garter Service in June. Occasionally I go up to the House of Lords and binge up the Noble Lords.'[3]

Even these forays now came to an end, however. His speeches in the Lords had always drawn a full House—'in his heyday he probably filled the Chamber more rapidly than any non-official speaker', the Earl of Longford later related.[4] At the state opening of Parliament in 1966, 1967 and 1968 Monty had borne the Sword of State[5]—but on the third occasion had wilted beneath the weight of his robes and the heavy sword, collapsing as the Queen read her speech. Though revived by champagne administered by a Labour

[1] Letter of 20.11.70, Papers of Lt-Colonel Trumbull Warren.
[2] *Daily Express*, 8.11.73.
[3] Letter of 20.11.70, loc. cit.
[4] Lord Longford, 'The CIGS', in *Monty at Close Quarters*, op. cit.
[5] 'It is a wonderful ceremony; it always reminds me of Gilbert and Sullivan! Iolanthe! You will see me carrying the Sword of State in front of the Queen. I did this when the Queen opened the new Parliament in April 1966. I doubt if it has ever been done before by the same peer twice running—but this I do not know. It will be the culmination of a wonderful year for me': letter to Sir Arthur Bryant, 2.10.67, Bryant Papers.

peer, Lady Summerskill, it was an indication that his years were numbered. Increasingly, from 1970 onwards, he took to his bed, rising only for visitors—and even this effort gradually became too much for him. When Anthony Brett-James visited him in June 1971, 'he was not sitting on the sofa as so often in the past. Instead the housekeeper showed me to his bedroom which opened off the long sitting-room. Monty lay in bed, propped up by pillows and reasonably perky. . . . A portrait of his father, the bishop, hung over the bed. Near the door was Eisenhower's painting of Monty wearing on his tunic the single ribbon of the American Legion of Merit.'[1]

Monty's memory, always so sharp and exact for names, faces and dates, began to fade after a bout of illness in 1972, and he tired quickly in conversation. The gardens, once so immaculately kept and weeded, began to fall into disorder without his watchful, supervising eye. The caravans in which he had lived and commanded from Alamein to Lüneburg lay locked in the barns. By the Spring of 1973 his once unshakeably clear, schoolboy handwriting had deteriorated into barely legible hieroglyphics. When signing a copy of one of his books for the Chinese Ambassador he could no longer recall the proper spelling of Alamein, his proud title. He had seemed determined to live to one hundred, not to surrender to death; now he appeared not to care, and was like a small boy, alone in the school sanatorium, looked after by his faithful housekeeper Miss Cox.

Those who had known Monty in his prime were disappointed at this seeming abdication of will. His whole career had been a triumph of the will to fight and to succeed. Field-Marshal Sir Gerald Templer, the 'Tiger of Malaya', penned in a note among his papers:

> On Tuesday 27th August, 1974 we went down to Isington Mill to see Monty. He has already been bedridden for well over a year and is now to all intends [sic] and purposes gaga.
>
> I think from time to time he recognized who we were for a few moments. At one stage in the proceedings he asked whether I was his grandson Henry.
>
> He takes not the slightest interest in anything, does not read though he can do so without using glasses, and will not see anybody. We were told to be there at 3.30 p.m., which we were punctually, and that we should go at 3.50 p.m.
>
> Actually he asked us to go as he felt tired at precisely 3.45 p.m. A terrible end of the life of a once great man.[2]

By the early months of 1976 it became obvious that Monty's days

[1] A. Brett-James, *Conversations with Montgomery*, op. cit.

[2] Templer Papers, loc. cit.

were numbered. 'Of course I have led a tough life, two great wars 1914–18 and 1939–45, and immense responsibilities in the Second,' he had written to Trumbull Warren in 1969.[1] 'And the Germans nearly killed me in October 1914. But I got my own back on them later on!' In retrospect it was amazing that Monty's frail frame had borne such wounds and such a relentlessly active life.

'There was an inevitable sadness about the final years as his powers waned,' his faithful wartime ADC Johnny Henderson recorded. 'The last time I went to see him, which can only have been a short time before he died, I had arrived after an hour and a half's drive. I went up to his bedroom and the first—and last—words he said were, "Johnny, I get very tired you know. I think you had better go." It was good to see that the authoritative command was still there,' Henderson commented. 'I turned on my heel and left.'[2]

The approach of death was not to be entirely peaceful, however. Late in February Sir Denis Hamilton was summoned by Miss Cox. The Field-Marshal, she explained, had had a very bad night. 'What is troubling you, Field-Marshal?' Hamilton asked.

> 'I couldn't sleep last night—I had great difficulty. I can't have very long to go now. I've got to go to meet God—and explain all those men I killed at Alamein—'

Hamilton had never seen Monty so agitated. 'It was quite uncharacteristic. And I stayed with him for about half an hour trying to pacify him.'[3]

'My soul wrestles with the future' had been one of Monty's favourite phrases. It was clear the end was near.

'We have certain characteristics which have caused us to clash in life,' Monty's son David had acknowledged the previous year in an interview. 'A tendency to be rather aggressive to each other. . . . As a parent, and someone with whom one communicates, his absolute need to hold the centre of the stage at all times and his refusal to allow other people to participate, and his overriding eccentricity—must be things which are a little frustrating, and detract from having any sort of intimate family relationship.' 'The clash of wills,' reminiscent of those between Monty and his mother Maud, 'has produced a sort of resentment between us, and therefore possibly not until latterly, when it's really too late, have we become closer together.'[4]

[1] Letter of 27.4.69, Papers of Lt-Colonel Trumbull Warren.
[2] J. R. Henderson, 'Morning, Noon and Night, the story of an ADC', in *Monty at Close Quarters*, op. cit.
[3] Sir Denis Hamilton, loc. cit.
[4] Contribution to 'A Tried and Valiant Soldier', loc. cit.

Late or not, Monty had at least become reconciled with David, his son. It was in the early hours of 24 March 1976, with David at his bedside, together with his loving brother Brian, that Monty's heart finally gave out and the news was flashed across the world: 'MONTY IS DEAD'.

CHAPTER TEN

The Funeral

TRIBUTES POURED IN from across the globe. The Russian Ministry of Defence issed a statement 'to the Ministry of Defence of Great Britain and to the bereaved relatives and friends. Field Marshal Montgomery is known to the Soviet Union as one of the prominent military leaders and active fighters of the anti-Hitlerite coalition during the Second World War. His military talent was especially evident in Africa and in the landing operations of the Allied forces in Normandy.' The acting Prime Minister of China, Hua Kuo-peng, cabled that 'on behalf of Chairman Mao Tse-tung and in my own name, I wish to express our deep condolences over the passing-away of Field Marshal Montgomery', the bravest of warriors in the fight against 'the fascist aggressors' of World War II. '*Victor of El Alamein who became a legend in his lifetime*,' *The Times* entitled its full-page obituary, which ended:

> In his mature years he was obsessively neat and punctual himself and deplored untidiness or unpunctuality in others. His unhappy childhood; his early lack of *rapport* with his mother; and the tragedy of his wife's death made him a difficult, lonely and complicated man. But he was, above everything a soldier. It was, in the mud, the snow or the sand, in the fear, the pain and the blood that he was at his greatest. He killed the enemy coldly and efficiently; but for the lives of his own soldiers he cared intensely. He was meticulous in preparation, in administration and in execution. He knew his dark trade better than anyone else in his time. Perhaps his greatest single virtue as a soldier was his sense of 'balance'. Like the great athlete he would have liked to be, he was always poised in battle, able to work out his plans however the enemy reacted; and if afterwards he was ready too often to say that everything had gone *exactly* as he had planned, there was more truth in the boast than literal minded critics have been ready to admit. The essence of his personal philosophy was that true freedom was having the liberty to do what you ought, not what you want. History will in time deliver its verdict on

Montgomery the soldier; until it does, he will be mourned not only as a national figure, but, even by those far removed in spirit or in sympathy from the profession of arms, as the last of the great battlefield commanders.[1]

'I wouldn't say they [his troops] loved him exactly, but he made them love themselves,' an obituarist in America remarked. 'I think of him mainly as an evangelist and faith-healer. There he was,' he recalled of Monty speechifying from his jeep in Italy, 1943, 'in his old sweater and corduroy pants, unsmiling and stern, telling these underpaid, underfed, ill-educated and somewhat bomb-happy wretches that they were good, that they could win and that they ought to be proud of themselves. And so they were.'[2]

Perhaps the finest tribute was one which had been paid almost two decades before, after the publication of Monty's *Memoirs*. Written by an Oxford historian, Dr Geoffrey Matthews, it drew attention to the parallel between Britain's most famous battle-commanders:

> These two men, Nelson on sea and Montgomery on land, are perhaps the greatest and most colourful battle-commanders Britain has ever produced. They were probably also our most single-minded and devoted students of war. Nelson died such a transcendent death that in the popular image he has almost the stature of an Homeric God of War: in the aura of glory surrounding him the mundane aspect of his ability is forgotten—how meticulous he was about the minutiae of naval training, how planned were all the great actions he fought. It is quite clear that his victories derived chiefly from a plan of battle which he had propounded to his captains and which they understood perfectly. There was nothing magical about Nelson's victories: they were gained by hard work and preparation long before the actual battles. In the same way Montgomery's success and the firmness of his grip upon war were based upon a 'master-plan' carefully devised beforehand and explained to his divisional generals. If genius is an infinite capacity for taking pains then Montgomery is a very superior kind of genius.
>
> The decisions made in war by these two men had a life or death value to those who served under them and both significantly were imbued with a profound religious feeling. Montgomery's orders are full of Biblical phrases and Nelson's prayer before Trafalgar (like Drake before meeting the Armada) is sublime in its way.

[1] *The Times*, 25.3.76.

[2] Tom Braden, 'Monty: This Chap was Different', *Los Angeles Times*, 1976.

Both were honestly convinced that they could do their job better than any other man alive, and far from offending their subordinates by this attitude they inspired a sense of complete devotion, almost of worship, in their men. Physically neither looked very military for they were smallish in stature, thin-faced and pale. Significantly enough both failed in politics, though of the two Nelson at the Court of Naples cut an even sorrier figure than Montgomery at Downing Street.

In his clinical exposition of war Clausewitz lists resolution and confidence in his own ability as the hallmarks of the great commander: both of these men possessed such qualities in supreme measure. Inevitably they were always disagreeing with their commanders since they imagined they could do the job better—and thus it invariably turned out. . . .

A battle, whether on land or sea, is essentially a contest of wills between the two rival commanders. The great commander shows his superiority by his moral ascendancy and his ability to dictate the course of the battle to his opponent. Nelson and Montgomery epitomize this facet of military genius.

I have said that both these great battle-commanders failed in politics. One might expect it, for the atmosphere of politics is far different from that of war. The soldier is trained to take direct action down certain well-defined lines and the military machine responds with speed and precision to the General's touch. But the political machine operates slowly, with many deviations, and the politician is trained in subtlety in debate, at gaining support by bargaining and, finally, in compromise. Little wonder then that Nelson and Montgomery found politics a shady and bewildering world. Both found two years of politics quite enough—Nelson at Naples from 1798 to 1800 and Montgomery at the War Office from 1946 to 1948—and were only too eager to return again to their military duties. This was natural since they had received no real political training. They simply specialized in war and although unskilled in other arts were, in this sphere, supreme. When in discussion with their respective political chiefs they no doubt appeared unsophisticated. But neither man cared at all about his limited range. They both lived in an age of war and they knew how to win battles: that was what counted: they knew it and so did the politicians.[1]

[1] 'Two Men of Battle' in the *Bullfrog*, Pembroke College, Oxford, Hilary Term, 1959. 'It is most interesting,' Monty had written to Arthur Bryant after reading it. 'I thought you might like to have a copy': letter of 10.3.59, Bryant Papers.

As a Knight of the Garter Monty was entitled to a State Funeral at St George's Chapel, Windsor. The Ministry of Defence, in cooperation with Monty's son David, had been making all the necessary arrangements for months past. De Guingand, suffering himself from a brain tumour and scarcely able to walk, was to fly from Cannes to lead the eight pallbearers—five Field-Marshals, an Admiral and an Air Marshal.

On 1 April 1976 the funeral duly took place. Veterans of El Alamein, of Mareth, Medenine, Wadi Akarit, Sicily, of the Sangro, Normandy, Arnhem and the bitter battles of the Reichswald gathered in their thousands along the route to St George's Chapel, Windsor, many weeping, some in wheelchairs, watching as the 'coffin, the wind grabbing at the Union Jack draped over it . . . was carried through the streets of Windsor on a gun carriage drawn by six black chargers of the Royal Horse Artillery. On top were laid 'Monty's' wartime black beret with its famous twin badges, his field marshal's baton and his sword. Surrounded by troops marching with precision, their black draped drums beating out a slow percussion, there were times when it seemed a very private, personal, military affair.'[1]

A troop of Royal Horse Artillery gunners fired a nineteen-gun salute as the procession made its way to St George's through the silent town. Outside the Chapel, more than eighty wreaths that were laid along the grassy banks 'lent a splash of colour to the grey morning. A wreath in the shape of a figure of eight came from Eighth Army veterans. But there was one from America too.' In a statement on the day of Monty's death, General Omar Bradley had declared: 'With the passing of Field Marshal Montgomery the world has lost a giant and I have lost a comrade in arms. Dear Monty liked to tweak our "Yankee noses", as he himself called it, but he was a fine wartime leader.' Drew Middleton, the veteran military correspondent of the *New York Times*, had remarked in an appraisal: 'He was everything the regular British officer disliked, pushing, innovative, lacking the social graces, unintentionally rude, iconoclastic. . . . Was he a good general? The Germans certainly thought so. Gerd von Rundstedt said he knew the Americans didn't like Montgomery, but that generals were like race horses. They were supposed to win and Montgomery won most of the time.' Eisenhower and Bedell Smith had, in private, once admitted to Middleton that 'no one else could have got us across the Channel and into Normandy'. 'Sure, Monty was a hard man to handle,' Bedell Smith had acknowledged; but, as Eisenhower confessed, 'I don't know if we could have done it without

[1] Henry Stanhope, report in *The Times*, 2.4.76.

Monty. It was his sort of battle. Whatever they say about him, he got us there.'[1]

Now, on the day of his funeral, Monty's erstwhile subordinate in the great Normandy landings marked with a wreath his gratitude: 'Dear Monty. Goodbye and thanks. Brad.'

Inside St George's, Monty's family, personal wartime staff, erstwhile colleagues, international representatives and dignitaries stood as the coffin, flanked by Freddie de Guingand and his fellow pallbearers, was lifted by the four pairs of uniformed Coldstream Guardsmen to the altar. The Dean of Windsor extolled the memory of Monty for his 'high sense of duty, for the courage and inspiration of his leadership in war and peace, for his ability to share his purpose with those who served under him.'

Frail and on her ninety-first birthday, Clementine, Lady Churchill sat in the chancel as the choir sang the hymn 'The Strife is O'er, the Battle Done'.

'The Military Knights of Windsor in their scarlet coats bore Lord Montgomery's Garter banner to the Dean who laid it on the altar, a bugler sounded the last post and reveille, and Lord Montgomery, lifted high by the eight guardsmen, left the chapel for the last time for the journey to Binsted by motor hearse.'[2]

It was not far from Isington, in the village churchyard of Holy Cross, Binsted, beneath a 250-year-old yew tree that Monty was to be buried. A guard of honour had been formed by twenty ten-year-old children from the local primary school as well as a party of boys from the Montgomery of Alamein Comprehensive School in Winchester.

Slowly, reverently, the guardsmen lowered the simple pine coffin into the grave. It weighed little, for the fighting bantam of World War I had grown tiny in his final years of life. Now he had 'passed over Jordan'.

The vicar, the Rev. David Dewing, spoke the last prayers. David Montgomery, now Second Viscount Montgomery of Alamein, scattered earth upon his father's remains.

It was the afternoon of Thursday, 1 April, 1976. The sky was still overcast. An anonymous wreath read, 'In grateful memory of all you did for England.'

[1] Drew Middleton, 'Montgomery, Hard to Like or Ignore', in *New York Times*, 25.3.76.

[2] Henry Stanhope, loc. cit.

Sources and Bibliography

The Montgomery Papers

As indicated in *Monty: Master of the Battlefield 1942–1944*, the Montgomery Papers have now been formally donated to the Imperial War Museum, London, where, following the publication of this final volume of the Montgomery biography, the Field-Marshal's papers will be open to students and researchers, covering Field-Marshal Montgomery's life up to the end of his term of office as CIGS in 1948. The Field-Marshal's Western Union and NATO papers from 1948 to 1958 form a separate collection and are not available to researchers.

Papers and documents assembled and collected during the writing of this Montgomery biography will be deposited in the Imperial War Museum and will be available to students at the discretion of the museum staff. An annotated set of the three *Monty* volumes will also be deposited at the Imperial War Museum, giving page references and further details of sources.

Further unpublished sources

Although the basis for this final volume has been the Private Papers of Field-Marshal Montgomery, I have been privileged, as before, to see and use many other collections of documents, private and public. Copyright in anything written by Field-Marshal Montgomery in such other collections remains, as noted before, with the present Viscount Montgomery of Alamein. Permission to see the material rests naturally with the respective owners, to whom I am most grateful.

The private collections I have used are as follows: The papers of Lt-Colonel C. P. ('Kit') Dawnay (Montgomery correspondence); the papers of General Sir Oliver Leese in the possession of Mrs Frances Denby (Montgomery-Leese correspondence); of Brigadier Sir Edgar Williams (Montgomery-Williams correspondence); Lt-Colonel Trumbull Warren (Montgomery correspondence); Lt-Colonel Tom Bigland (diaries and material relating to Montgomery and General Bradley); Viscount Montgomery of Alamein (Trueb correspondence); Lt-Colonel John Carver (Montgomery correspondence); Field-Marshal Lord Carver (Lecture to King's College, London); Major-General R. E. Urquhart (Arnhem/1st Airborne Division scrapbooks); Sir Arthur Bryant (Montgomery correspondence); Colonel Peter Earle; Sir John Ackroyd.

The institutional collections I have used are:

The Imperial War Museum, London: De Guingand Papers, Simpson Papers, Reynolds Correspondence, Bryant Papers.

The Public Record Office: Formation War Diaries, Cabinet Papers, Prime Minister's Papers, Foreign Office Papers, Dempsey Papers.

Royal Archives, Windsor: Montgomery Correspondence.

Liddell Hart Centre for Military Archives, King's College, London: Liddell-Hart–Montgomery Correspondence, Chester Wilmot Papers, Alanbrooke Papers.

RAF Museum, Hendon: Robb Papers.

Churchill College Archives, Cambridge: P. J. Grigg-Montgomery Correspondence and R. Lewin Papers.

Mercers' Company Archives, Mercers' Hall, London: Montgomery Correspondence and minutes of meetings of Governors of St Paul's School.

Military History Institute, Carlisle, Pennsylvania: OCMH Collections, Bradley Papers, Chester B. Hansen Papers, Gay Papers, Sylvan Papers, Ridgway Papers, Bull Papers.

Eisenhower Library, Abilene, Kansas: Eisenhower's Montgomery Correspondence file, also correspondence with other WWII figures; correspondence with de Guingand; Kay Summersby Diary; Diary of Harry C. Butcher/Desk Diary of C-in-C.

National Army Museum, London: Templer Papers.

Broadland Archives: Mountbatten-Montgomery Correspondence.

Royal United Services Institute, London: Arnhem Seminar Papers.

University of Ohio Library: Cornelius Ryan Papers.

To all of the above I am most grateful.

Published sources

ALEXANDER, H., *The Alexander Memoirs* (London 1962)

AMBROSE, S., *Eisenhower: Soldier, General of the Army, President Elect, 1890–1952* (New York 1983)

—*Eisenhower: The President* (New York 1984)

—*The Supreme Commander: The War Years of Dwight D. Eisenhower* (New York 1970)

ANDERSON, T. H., *The United States, Great Britain and the Cold War 1944–47* (Columbia, Missouri 1981)

ARGYLE, C., *Chronology of World War Two* (London 1980)

AVON, Earl of, *The Eden Memoirs—The Reckoning* (London 1962)

BACKER, J. H., *Wind of History* (*The German Years of Lucius Clay*) (New York 1983)

BALDWIN, H. W., *Battles Lost and Won* (New York 1966)

—*Great Mistakes of the War* (London 1950)

BALFOUR, M. AND MAIR, J., *Survey of International Affairs 1939–46* (London 1956)

BELCHEM, D., *All in the Day's March* (London 1978)

BENNETT, R., *Ultra in the West* (London 1979)

BERNARD, H., *Guerre Totale et Guerre Révolutionnaire*, Vol III (Brussels 1967)

BLAIR, C., *A General's Life* (New York 1983)

BLUMENSON, M., *Breakout and Pursuit* (Washington 1961)

—*Mark Clark* (London 1985)

—(ED) *The Patton Papers*, Vol II (Boston 1974)

BLUMENTRITT, G., *Von Rundstedt* (London 1952)

BOOTHBY, R., *Boothby, Recollections of a Rebel* (London 1978)

BRERETON, L. H., *The Brereton Diaries* (New York 1946)

BRETT-JAMES, A., *Conversations with Montgomery* (London 1984)

BRYANT, A., *Triumph in the West* (London 1959)

BULLOCK, A., *Ernest Bevin: Foreign Secretary 1945–51* (London 1983)

BUTCHER, H. C., *Three Years with Eisenhower* (London 1946)

CARVER, M., *The Seven Ages of the British Army* (London 1984)
—(ED) *The War Lords* (London 1976)
CHALFONT, A., *Montgomery of Alamein* (London 1976)
CHANDLER, A. D. (ED), *The Papers of Dwight David Eisenhower: The War Years*, Vols IV and V (Baltimore 1970)
CHURCHILL, W. S., *Triumph and Tragedy* (London 1954)
CLAY, L. D., *Decision in Germany* (London 1950)
CLOAKE, J., *Templer, Tiger of Malaya* (London 1985)
CODMAN, C. R., *Drive!* (Boston 1957)
COHEN, M. J., *Palestine and the Great Powers 1945–48* (New York 1982)
COLE, H. M., *The Ardennes: Battle of the Bulge* (Washington 1965)
COLLIER, R., *The War that Stalin Won* (London 1983)
COLLINS, J. L., *Lightning Joe* (Baton Rouge 1979)
COLVILLE, J., *The Churchillians* (London 1981)
—*The Fringes of Power* (London 1985)

DE GUINGAND, F. W., *From Brass Hat to Bowler Hat* (London 1979)
—*Generals at War* (London 1964)
—*Operation Victory* (London 1947)
DILKS, D. (ED), *Diaries of Sir Alexander Cadogan 1938–45* (London 1971)
DONNISON, F. S. V., *Civil Affairs and Military Government, North-West Europe 1944–1946* (London 1961)
DOVER, V., *The Sky Generals* (London 1981)

EHRMAN, J., *Grand Strategy*, Vol V (London 1956)
—*Grand Strategy*, Vol VI (London 1956)
ELLIS, L. F., *Victory in the West* Vol II, *The Defeat of Germany* (London 1968)
EISENHOWER, D. D., *At Ease* (New York 1967)
—*Crusade in Europe* (New York 1948)
—*Letters to Mamie* (New York 1978)
EISENHOWER, J. S. D., *The Bitter Woods* (New York 1969)
ENSER, A. G. S., *A Subject Bibliography of the Second World War* (London 1977)
ESSAME, H., *The Battle for Germany* (London 1969)
—*Patton the Commander* (London 1974)

FALLS, C., *The Second World War* (London 1948)
FARAGO, L., *Patton: Ordeal and Triumph* (New York 1948)
FERRELL, R. H. (ED), *The Eisenhower Diaries* (New York 1981)
FRASER, D., *Alanbrooke* (London 1982)
—*And we shall Shock Them* (London 1983)
FULLER, J. F. C., *The Decisive Battles of the Western World* (London 1956)
—*The Second World War* (London 1948)

GALE, R., *Call to Arms* (London 1968)
GAVIN, J. M., *On to Berlin* (New York 1978)
GOLDEN, L., *Echoes from Arnhem* (London 1984)
GOODENOUGH, S., *War Maps* (London 1982)
GORALSKI, R., *World War II Almanac 1931–1945* (London 1981)
GRIGG, P. J., *Prejudice and Judgment* (London 1948)

HACKETT, J. W., *I was a Stranger* (London 1977)
—*The Profession of Arms* (London 1983)
HARRIS, K., *Attlee* (London 1982)
HARRISON, D. I., *These Men are Dangerous* (London 1957)
HARVEY, O., *The War Diaries of Oliver Harvey 1941–45* (London 1978)
HASTINGS, M., *Victory in Europe* (London 1985)
HATHAWAY, R. M., *Ambiguous Partnership: Britain and America 1944–47* (New York 1981)
HEAPS, L., *The Grey Goose of Arnhem* (London 1976)
HEARNDEN, A., *Red Robert* (London 1984)
—(ED), *The British in Germany* (London 1978)
HIBBERT, C., *The Battle of Arnhem* (London 1962)
HOBBS, J. P., *Dear General* (Baltimore 1971)
HOOPES, R., *Ralph Ingersoll: A Biography* (New York 1985)
HORROCKS, B. G., *A Full Life* (London 1960)
——(and others), *Corps Commander* (London 1977)
HOWARTH, T. E. B. (ED), *Monty at Close Quarters* (London 1985)
HUMBLE, R., *Fraser of North Cape* (London 1983)

INGERSOLL, R., *Top Secret* (London 1946)
IRELAND, T. P., *Creating the Entangling Alliance: The Origins of the North Atlantic Treaty Organisation* (London 1981)
IRVING, D., *Hitler's War* (London 1977)
—*The War Between Generals* (London 1981)
ISMAY, H. L., *The Memoirs of Lord Ismay* (London 1960)
—*NATO 1949–54* (London 1955)

JACOBSEN, H. A. AND ROWHER, J., *Decisive Battles of World War II: The German View* (London 1965)
JEWELL, D. (ED), *Alamein and the Desert War* (London 1967)
JORDAN, R. S., *The NATO International Staff/Secretariat* (London 1967)

KEEGAN, J. (ED), *Encyclopaedia of World War II* (London 1977)
KEITEL, W., *Memoirs* (London 1965)
KENNEDY, J., *The Business of War* (London 1957)
KREIPE, F. (and others), *The Fatal Decisions* (London 1956)

LAMB, R., *Montgomery in Europe* (London 1983)
LEASOR, J., *War at the Top* (London 1959)
LEWIN, R., *Montgomery as Military Commander* (London 1971)
—*Slim: The Standardbearer* (London 1977)
LEWIN, R., *Ultra Goes to War* (London 1978)
LIDDELL HART, B. H., *History of the Second World War* (London 1970)
—*The Other Side of the Hill* (London 1970)
—*The Tanks* Vol II (London 1959)
LOUIS, W. R., *The British Empire in the Middle East 1945–1951* (London 1984)

MACDONALD, C. B., *The Battle of the Bulge* (London 1984)
MACMILLAN, H., *The Blast of War 1939–1945* (London 1967)

—*Tides of Fortune 1945–55* (London 1969)
MALLABY, G., *Each in his Office* (London 1972)
—*From my Level* (London 1965)
MALONE, R. S., *Missing from the Record* (Toronto 1946)
MASON, D., *Who's Who in World War II* (London 1978)
MEE, C. L., *Meeting at Potsdam* (New York 1975)
MELLENTHIN, W., *Panzer Battles 1939–45* (London 1955)
MERRIAM, R. E., *The Battle of the Ardennes* (London 1958)
MIDDLEMAS, K., *The Life and Times of George VI* (London 1974)
MONTGOMERY, B., *A Field-Marshal in the Family* (London 1973)
—*A Life in Pictures* (London 1985)
MONTGOMERY, B. L., *A History of Warfare* (London 1968)
—*Memoirs* (London 1958)
—*The Path to Leadership* (London 1961)
MOORE, R. J., *Escape from Empire: The Attlee Government and the Indian Problem* (Oxford 1983)
MOOREHEAD, A., *Montgomery* (London 1946)
MORAN, Lord, *Winston Churchill: The Struggle for Survival* (London 1966)
MORGAN, F. E., *Peace and War* (London 1961)
MORGAN, K. O., *Labour in Power, 1945–1951* (London 1984)
MOSLEY, L., *Marshall, Organizer of Victory* (London 1982)
MOULTON, J. L., *The Battle for Antwerp* (London 1978)
MUGGERIDGE, M., *Like it Was* (London 1981)

NICOLSON, N., *Alex* (London 1973)
NORTH, J., *North-West Europe 1944–5* (London 1953)
NORTON, C. G., *The Red Devils* (London 1971)

PATTON, G. S., *War as I Knew It* (Boston 1947)
PEACOCK, Lady, *Field-Marshal Viscount Montgomery, His Life* (London 1951)
PIEKALKIEWICZ, J., *Arnhem 1944* (London 1977)
PINKLEY, V., *Eisenhower Declassified* (Old Tappan, New Jersey 1979)
POGUE, F. C., *George C. Marshall, Organizer of Victory* (New York 1973)
—*The Supreme Command* (Washington 1954)
PYMAN, H., *Call to Arms* (London 1971)

REES, G., *A Bundle of Sensations* (London 1960)
REID, E., *Time of Fear and Hope: The Making of the North Atlantic Treaty 1947–49* (Toronto 1977)
RICHARDSON, C., *Flashback: A Soldier's Story* (London 1985)
RIDGWAY, M. B., *Soldier* (New York 1956)
ROTHWELL, V., *Britain and the Cold War 1941–1947* (London 1982)
RYAN, C., *A Bridge Too Far* (London 1974)
—*The Last Battle* (London 1966)

SAUNDERS, H. ST G., *The Red Beret* (London 1950)
SCHOENFELD, M. P., *The War Ministry of Winston Churchill* (Arnes, Iowa 1972)
SHERWOOD, R. E. (ED), *The White House Papers of Harry L. Hopkins* (London 1949)
SHULMAN, M., *Defeat in the West* (London 1947)

SIMONDS, P., *Maple Leaf Up, Maple Leaf Down* (New York 1946)
SIXSMITH, E. K. G., *British Generalship in the 20th Century* (London 1970)
—*Eisenhower* (London 1973)
SLESSOR, J. C., *The Central Blue* (London 1956)
SMITH, W. BEDELL, *Eisenhower's Six Great Decisions* (London 1956)
SMYTH, J., *Bolo Whistler* (London 1967)
SOAMES, M., *Clementine Churchill* (London 1979)
STACEY, C. P., *The Victory Campaign 1944–1945* (Ottawa 1960)
STRANG, W., *Home and Abroad* (London)
STRONG, K., *Intelligence at the Top* (London 1968)
—*Men of Intelligence* (London 1970)
SUMMERSBY, K., *Eisenhower Was My Boss* (London 1949)
SUMMERSBY MORGAN, K., *Past Forgetting* (London 1977)

TAYLOR, A. J. P., *English History* (London 1965)
—*How Wars End* (London 1985)
—*The Second World War* (London 1975)
TEDDER, A. W., *With Prejudice* (London 1966)
TERRAINE, J., *The Right of the Line* (London 1985)
THOMPSON, R. W., *The Eighty-five Days* (London 1957)
—*Montgomery the Field-Marshal* (London 1969)

WAVELL, Earl, *The Viceroy's Journal* (ED P. Moon) (London 1973)
WEIGLEY, R. F., *Eisenhower's Lieutenants* (New York 1981)
WESTPHAL, S., *The German Army in the West* (London 1951)
WHEELER-BENNETT, J. (ED), *Action This Day* (London 1969)
WILLIAMS, E. T. AND NICHOLLS, C. S. (ED), *The Dictionary of National Biography* (Oxford 1981)
WILMOT, C., *The Struggle for Europe* (London 1952)
WINTERBOTHAM, F. W., *The Ultra Secret* (London 1974)

YOUNG, K. (ED), *Diaries of Sir Robert Bruce-Lockhart 1939–1965* (London 1980)
YOUNG, P. (ED), *Decisive Battles of the Second World War* (London 1967)

ZIEGLER, P., *Mountbatten* (London 1985)
ZUCKERMAN, S., *From Apes to Warlords* (London 1978)

List of Abbreviations

ACIGS	Assistant Chief of the Imperial General Staff
ADC	Aide-de-Camp
AEAF	Allied Expeditionary Air Force
AG	Adjutant-General
AVM	Air Vice-Marshal
BAOR	British Army of the Rhine
BEF	British Expeditionary Force
BGS	Brigadier, General Staff
BGS(I)	Brigadier, General Staff (Intelligence)
CAB	Cabinet records
CAS	Chief of the Air Staff
CDS	Chief of the Defence Staff
CIGS	Chief of the Imperial General Staff
C-in-C	Commander-in-Chief
COS	Chief of Staff
COSSAC	Chief of Staff to the Supreme Allied Commander (Designate), i.e. senior staff officer at headquarters set up to plan cross-channel attack before Eisenhower was appointed Supreme Commander
CPX	Headquarters Command Exercise
DCIGS	Deputy Chief of the Imperial General Staff
DMI	Director of Military Intelligence
DMO	Director of Military Operations
DSM	Distinguished Service Medal
DSO	Distinguished Service Order
DUKW	Amphibious carrier
FWD	Supreme Commander's Forward Command Post or Headquarters
GCB	Knight, Grand Cross of the Bath
GG	Governor General
GOC	General Officer Commanding
IDC	Imperial Defence College
JPS	Joint Planning Staff
LHCMA	Liddell Hart Centre for Military Archives
LO	Liaison Officer
MA	Military Assistant
MC	Military Cross
MG	Machine gun/sports car marque
MHI	Military History Institute
MP	Member of Parliament/Military Police

NATO	North Atlantic Treaty Organisation
OBE	Order of the British Empire
OCMH	Office of the Chief of Military History
OKW	Oberkommando der Wehrmacht (German Armed Forces High Command)
PA	Personal Assistant
POW	Prisoner of War
PRO	Public Record Office
QMG	Quartermaster General
RAF	Royal Air Force
RTR	Royal Tank Regiment
RUSI	Royal United Services Institution
S of S	Secretary of State
SCAF	Supreme Commander Allied Forces
SEACOS	South East Asia Chief of Staff
SEALF	South East Asia Land Forces
SHAEF	Supreme Headquarters Allied Expeditionary Force
SHAPE	Supreme Headquarters Allied Powers in Europe
TA	Territorial Army
TI	Tube Investments
UK	United Kingdom
UNO	United Nations Organisation
VCIGS	Vice Chief of the Imperial General Staff
WO	War Office *also* Warrant Officer
W/T	Wireless Transmission
WU	Western Union
WUCOS	Western Union Chief of Staff

Index